Business in Ethical Focus

Business in Ethical Focus
An Anthology

EDITED BY

Fritz Allhoff and Anand J. Vaidya

broadview press

Library and Archives Canada Cataloguing in Publication
Business in ethical focus : an anthology / edited by Fritz Allhoff and Anand Vaidya.

Includes bibliographical references.
ISBN 978-1-55111-661-7

   1. Business ethics. I. Allhoff, Fritz II. Vaidya, Anand
HF5387.B883 2008   174'.4   C2008-902637-3

Broadview Press is an independent, international publishing house, incorporated in 1985. Broadview believes in shared ownership, both with its employees and with the general public; since the year 2000 Broadview shares have traded publicly on the Toronto Venture Exchange under the symbol BDP.

We welcome comments and suggestions regarding any aspect of our publications—please feel free to contact us at the addresses below or at broadview@broadviewpress.com.

North America   PO Box 1243, Peterborough, Ontario, Canada K9J 7H5
                        2215 Kenmore Ave., Buffalo, New York, USA 14207
                        Tel: (705) 743-8990; Fax: (705) 743-8353
                        email: customerservice@broadviewpress.com

UK, Ireland, and continental Europe   NBN International, Estover Road, Plymouth, UK PL6 7PY
                        Tel: 44 (0) 1752 202300; Fax: 44 (0) 1752 202330
                        email: enquiries@nbninternational.com

Australia and New Zealand   UNIREPS, University of New South Wales
                        Sydney, NSW, Australia 2052
                        Tel: 61 2 9664 0999; Fax: 61 2 9664 5420
                        email: info.press@unsw.edu.au

www.broadviewpress.com

Copy-edited by John Burbidge.

PRINTED IN CANADA

This book is printed on paper containing 100% post-consumer fibre.

CONTENTS

Unit 4   Distributive Justice

Unit 5   Advertising, Marketing, and the Consumer

Why Study Business Ethics?

ANAND VAIDYA and FRITZ ALLHOFF

Volume Introduction

The What and Why of Business Ethics

What is business ethics, and why study it? One good way to get an answer to this question is by taking note of what *business* is, what *ethics* is, and then tying the two together.

Business as will be understood here is the sum total of the relationships and activities that surround the trading of goods or services for profit. As a category, business includes everything from the selling of handmade products between two neighboring villages in India to large-scale multinational corporations like Nike and Microsoft engaged in global trade. Both the relationships between individuals involved in any aspect of business, such as production, distribution, marketing, and selling of goods and services; as well as the relationships between these groups is important to understanding business as a whole. Furthermore, business is, for most people, a central part of their life. It is so, largely, because most people are consumers of commercial goods, and for many it is where they seek employment. However, it is also a place where one has an identity and where creativity is expressed. And it is, ideally at least, an arena in which rewards are distributed on the basis of merit.

Ethics, in its broadest sense, is an investigation into how humans *should* live. This investigation is not reducible to the claim that any way of living that is legally permissible is a morally permissible way to live. From the perspective of ethics and morality, laws themselves are objects of criticism. Within the confines of a moral investigation, one can inquire as to whether a legal statute is consistent with morality. For example, slavery was once considered to be both morally permissible and legally permissible, later it

was legally permissible but not morally permissible, and now it is neither. In addition to thinking of moral inquiry as distinct from legal inquiry, ethicists divide their discipline into three "branches": meta-ethics, normative ethics, and applied ethics.

Meta-ethics explores conceptual and foundational questions in morality. Some of the questions are the following: Are there moral facts? Is morality objective? How do we come to know moral truths? Are moral claims the kinds of things that can be true or false, or are they simply expressions of emotion? What is the primary object of moral evaluation?

Normative ethics is the study of which principles determine the moral permissibility and impermissibility of an action, or, more simply, what constitutes right and wrong. One approach to this, deontology, holds that morality is constituted by rights and duties, and that those features take priority over the consequences of actions. An alternative approach, consequentialism, maintains that it is only the consequences of actions (often measured in terms of pleasure and pain) that determine the moral rightness of an action. Yet other theories, such as virtue theory, argue that actions are not the central objects of moral evaluation; rather, a person as a whole (and perhaps their character in particular) is the object of moral evaluation.

Applied ethics is the area in which normative ethical theories get applied to specific problems within sufficiently well-defined areas of inquiry in order to give answers to particular questions. In applied ethics, for example, one may ask, "Is it morally permissible to terminate the life of a fetus in the second trimester of pregnancy?" The answer to this question can be given by applying various normative theories to the question. Applied ethics includes such areas as biomedical ethics, computer ethics, and environmental ethics; and, of course, applied ethics is where business ethics is located. In applied ethics, one is concerned with the specific ethical issues that arise from the area being investigated. This does not rule out the possibility that there is overlap in applied ethics. Two areas of applied ethics, such as biomedical and business ethics, may share particular questions. In addition, ethicists recognize that often answers to questions within meta-ethics affect possible answers to questions in normative ethics, which subsequently either determine or delimit the possible answers one can have to an applied ethical question. In some sense there is a "top-down" relationship between meta-ethics and applied ethics. Nonetheless, most ethicists recognize that discussions of applied ethics are valuable independently of determining the answers to questions in meta-ethics and normative ethics.

Putting together this understanding of business and ethics we arrive at the following conception of business ethics. *Business ethics* is the area of inquiry in which normative ethical theories are applied to issues that arise out of the relationships and activities surrounding the production, distribution, marketing, and sale of goods and services. The issues that arise in business ethics can be further categorized by either being internal or external.

Internal ethical questions concern relations between those involved in a particular business entity. For example, taking a corporation as a basic kind of business entity, internal ethical questions pertain to the relations between members of the corporation, such as employees and upper management. External ethical questions pertain to the ethical questions arising out of the relationships between the corporation and other corporations or entities, such as local communities and consumers. On both the internal side and the external side, questions may arise that overlap with other areas of inquiry. Business is such a large enterprise that it is hard to think that there would be no questions that arise within it that would not be of substantial interest to other areas of applied ethics.

Some of the questions on the internal side revolve around the rights, responsibilities, and obligations that employees bear to each other and to their employers. Likewise there are questions about what rights, responsibilities, and obligations employers bear to employees. While employees want to sell their labor for a salary, they also expect that their employer will provide them with a safe work environment. However, we might ask: Is it the employer's obligation to provide an employee with a safe work environment? If so, what moral theory helps us understand why this is the case? Furthermore, in addition to the labor an employee owes their employer in return for the salary they are paid what obligations do they have to their fellow employees. Are they, for example, permitted to harass them, and to impede their ability to perform their work? If not, what moral theory helps us understand why this is the case? And what set of rights, in general, does an employee have when they sell their labor? Does an employer have, for example, a right to information about the employee that is irrelevant to job performance? If not, how is the concept of job relevance to be defined?

On the external side, the central debate has been over whether the sole responsibility of corporate executives, and of corporations in general, is to maximize profit for shareholders. On the external side, corporations bear relations both to the immediate physical and social environment that they are embedded in, and to the future physical and social environment they will create. As a consequence, there are a host of ethical questions about the permissibility of polluting in the physical environment, and promoting socially important causes in the social environment. Because corporations are such large entities capable of amassing large sums of wealth and yielding incredible power in influencing governments, straightforward ethical questions pertain to them.

In this volume, our goal has been to give as comprehensive as possible a survey of the breadth and depth of business ethics. In selecting essays, we have aimed at providing historically classic articles as well as contemporary work. The classical articles set up the core issues in each area. Given that so much of business is about innovation in technologies, it is impossible to give a comprehensive coverage of all the ethical issues that arise from emerging technologies. We feel that a good understanding of basic normative moral theory coupled with an understanding of the core issues in business ethics will prepare the reader for the study of business ethics beyond this anthology. We have provided theoretical work that is essential for understanding business ethics as an applied area of ethical inquiry. In addition, each unit in this volume contains case studies with study questions that can be used to generate fruitful discussion, as well as to inform the reader about events that have or could have happened in the business world.

Finally we are left with the following question: Why study business ethics? The simple answer is that, if you are like most people, you will at some point enter some sector of the business world. And, if you are like most people, you will discover very quickly that there are significant questions about right and wrong that arise in this walk of life. The issues that this volume discusses can at least provide you with the following: an understanding of the issues one faces in the business world; some theoretical and practical tools one can use for analyzing ethical issues; and a framework for helping one construct an overall moral point of view. It is the hope of the editors of this book that everyone who takes to a serious study of this volume will come away with an appreciation for role of morality within the world of business.

FOUNDATIONAL ISSUES

ANAND JAYPRAKASH VAIDYA

Ill-Founded Criticisms of Business Ethics

In the wake of corporate scandals, such as Enron, the average corporate executive today is a lot more knowledgeable about business ethics, and the consequences and penalties associated with corruption, than those of the past. However, one still finds a tendency amongst corporate executives to look at business ethics as not a serious area of inquiry, and not that relevant to doing good business. The default view is that business ethics is a laundry list of codes that one must obey in order to avoid penalties, and that to a certain degree can be broken if one is careful. As a challenge, ask the next Wall Street corporate employee you run into what he thinks of *business ethics* and you will probably find them making a cynical comment; and even if they do not say it—and only laugh—they probably think business ethics is an oxymoron. Something one only pays lip service to in the pursuit of profit.

The underlying assumption of this line of thought, both domestic and global, is that the concept of ethical conduct cannot be appropriately conjoined to the concept of business. Literally the concept of a business transaction and negotiation is in tension with the concept of ethical conduct. At root the idea may be as simple as the claim that ethics is about a concern for the other at a possible cost to oneself, while business transactions are about a concern for oneself at a cost to the other. Business, they say, involves wheeling, dealing, and getting the better of your opponent; and, so they continue, good wheeling and dealing leaves ethics at the door. Ideas like this are even found in business literature starting as far back as the 1950s.

For example, Albert Z. Carr's "Is Business Bluffing Ethical," argues that business is a lot like playing poker, and so one should adopt the ethics of poker, which is at odds with ethical codes prescribed by traditional religions, such as Christianity.

Others point out, behind closed doors, that even when they adopt the persona of the so-called "socially responsible company" they do so out of the profit motive. Being socially responsible is *profitable*; if it weren't companies could not afford to be socially responsible. In order to survive in the marketplace one needs to make a profit; if being socially responsible requires sacrificing profits, then one could expect that their competitors will eventually force them out of the marketplace. The logic of competition puts socially responsible companies at a disadvantage. Competitors who decided not to be socially responsible would be able to displace socially responsible ones forcing them to go under.

In order to clear the ground for the study of business ethics and to open the door to the fruits that may come from studying it, and actually employing an ethical perspective in business an end needs to be put to the idea that "business ethics" is an oxymoron, a somehow confused idea. In this essay I hope to rid/exonerate business ethics of a couple of different criticisms that go together with the claim that it is an oxymoron. These claims are in some sense the ill-founded ideas that motivate the view that business ethics is an oxymoron that is so common amongst those that have spent little time reflecting on how ethics and morality play a role in business. In section one, I will present the most common complaints about business ethics, and offer rebuttals. In section two, I will offer a diagnosis of the source of the view that business and ethics are incompatible, and show that it rests on a false understanding of what it takes for business to flourish.

I.

The three most common complaints about business ethics are that it is

- *Useless* because individuals upon reaching a certain age are incapable of changing the way in which they determine whether an action is morally permissible (i.e., good or bad).
- *Indeterminate* because ethicists disagree over normative principles (i.e., consequentialism, deontology, virtue ethics) rendering decisive answers impossible, which consequently takes the *value* out of business ethics.
- *Beside the point* because ethical *inquiry* is not what is needed, rather individuals *behaving* ethically is what is needed.

Each of these complaints serves as a reason for avoiding business ethics discussions in the corporate world. And each of these can easily be shown to be unfounded.

The claim that business ethics is *useless* because by the time people enter the business world, roughly in their mid 20s to late 20s, their moral character has been, for the most part, formed for bad or good, rests on bad psychology, as well as bad reasoning.

First, the psychology; in order for it to be true that studying business ethics is useless because a person's moral character is *already well formed* by the time they enter the workforce, it would additionally have to be true that a person's moral character is *static* rather than *revisable*. It may be true that it is harder for one to change how they morally evaluate a situation at an older age than at a younger age, because certain moral habits or evaluative behaviors are more ingrained. And, it is probably true that most of us enter the work force at an age at which we have lots of opinions about what is morally right and wrong. However, it is false to say that it is impossible for one to change their moral viewpoint. More importantly, the attitude expressed by the "useless" argument is exactly the attitude that bars one from really learning from and growing as a process of being part of community discussion about what is right and wrong.

The fact that we can change our moral point of view, and that by listening and discussing things with others we do change our moral point of view leads to the basic idea that business ethics is important because ethical discussion about business matters can help individuals decide what is the right thing to do by being responsive to the reasons considered in a community dialogue.

In addition, it is bad reasoning to think that if people's moral characters are well formed by the time they enter the workforce, then it is useless to engage in business ethics. For, even if it would be useless to force employees to take business ethics courses in order to change their moral character because they won't change anyway, we would only have a new problem on another plane.

If it turns out that people's moral characters are well formed by the time they enter the work force, and we can with a high degree of confidence determine which moral characters have a tendency to produce scandals, won't we now have to work out all the ethical problems that go along with whether or not we should hire people based on tests that determine their ethical character. If you thought drug-testing was a problem, won't moral-testing be a problem as well?

While some complain that business ethics is *useless*, others complain that the real problem is that business ethics is *indeterminate*, and therefore *valueless*. The position they offer is not without initial plausibility. Anyone who has taken a freshman level course in ethics is aware that there are at least three different schools of thought in ethics: consequentialism, deontology, and virtue ethics. Each of these major schools of thought has its own criterion as to what constitutes right action or right living (as in the case of virtue ethics).

One brand of consequentialism, act-utilitarianism, says that the right action is that action from the set of available actions that maximizes aggregate happiness. One brand of deontology, Kantianism, says that the right action is that action whose maxim can be universalized without contradiction. A businessman with some knowledge of these two schools can point out that, depending on which ethical school I subscribe to, I will get different answers as to the morality of any action I may have to take in the business world. He or she will continue, "What I wanted in the first place was to decide what to do based on what was morally permissible, but it is not possible for me to determine what is morally permissible until I know which school of moral thought is correct, and the ethicists have not settled that. Consequently, discussions of ethics in business will be indeterminate." And what is ultimately indeterminate, the critic of business ethics will argue is without value. In order to understand this argument and locate the weakness in it, consider it in the following formal presentation.

1. Business ethicists disagree over first principles.
2. If theorists in a field disagree over first principles, then determinate answers cannot be reached.
3. If determinate answers cannot be reached in a field of inquiry, then that field of inquiry is without value.
4. Therefore, business ethics is without value.

Interestingly enough, we can formulate the critic's argument with respect to any realm of inquiry where scholars of the discipline disagree over first principles and/or methodology. Consider the following argument about economics.

1. Economists disagree over first principles.
2. If theorists within a field of inquiry disagree over first principles, then determinate answers cannot be reached.
3. If determinate answers cannot be reached in a field of inquiry, then that field of inquiry is without value.
4. Therefore, economics is without value.

By looking at the mirror argument with respect to economics we can see the flaw in the critic's position. Before analyzing the premises we can note that while many in the business world feel comfortable offering the argument about business ethics, they would not feel as comfortable offering the corresponding argument for economics. Those that find themselves comfortable with the former argument, but not the latter put themselves in the following logical dilemma: accept the conclusion to both arguments, reject both arguments, or find the disanalogy between the two cases. The solution I find appealing is simply to reject both arguments as unsound because premises (2) and (3) are false.

First, regarding (2), it should be noted that the critic's use of "indeterminate" betrays an ambiguity. While it is true with respect to the whole discipline of economics that it is indeterminate whether some policy is the best policy to adopt, with respect to a certain first principle within economics it *may* not be indeterminate which policy is the best policy to adopt, additionally extraneous evidence may lead one to think that other principles are simply irrelevant. This holds in the case of ethics as well; one who adopts a consequentialist approach like act-utilitarianism, in a great many cases, will agree with one who adopts deontology in determining what the morally correct action is. Additionally, disagreements over first principles do not always make it the case that first principles do not converge in certain cases. While it is true that in letter and spirit consequentialism and deontology disagree, both agree about the moral permissibility of certain acts. Regarding (3), it is hard to maintain that the indeterminacy within a discipline over first principles and methodology renders the discipline *valueless*. The main reason why a field of inquiry is *not precluded* from being *valuable* in virtue of theoretical disagreements over first principles and methodology is due to the fact that *debates about principles and methodologies* are *themselves valuable* in so far as they can lead to clarification, resolution, and innovation.

Unlike the critic above that thinks that the indeterminacy of ethics renders it valueless, the frustrated critic of business ethics claims that the real problem is that business ethics is *beside the point* because we already know how people should act. The problem is getting them to act in that way. Knowledge and familiarity with moral reasoning is not to the point, rather getting people to *behave* morally is to the point. The members of Enron knew what they were doing was wrong, and they created a culture in which certain goals led to breaking the rules. What was needed was not more insight into what is wrong, but rather putting into play mechanisms that lead to people behaving morally.

While it is true that in general we would all benefit from everyone behaving morally, the criticism of business ethics as beside the point because we already, in general, know how to behave is just false. Ethics is an on-going project; as technology advances and business takes on a new face, new ethical questions arise; and the answers to an ethical dilemma presented by new technology and business practice are not always answered by just looking at what we said in the past in the most relevantly similar case.

But even if it were true that for the most part we know what the morally correct thing to do is in a given situation, it still would not be true that business ethics is beside the point. The underlying assumption required to make that inference is that *studying business ethics has no effect on our motivations.* What the frustrated business ethics critic wants is for the business community to focus on motivating people, and figuring out how to motivate people to act morally in their business dealings. And with respect to this project he/she sees studying business ethics as *beside the point*—because it focuses on what is the morally correct action, rather than how, once we have determined what the morally right action is, we are to motivate people.

However, studying business ethics is not necessarily motivationally inefficacious. What is import-

ant is how we unpack the idea of "studying." Sure if studying business ethics just amounts to memorizing a bunch of codes and passing an exam, it is fair to say that studying it can at best only provide one with knowledge of what codes and principles to obey. While this project is worthy in itself, it does not come close to motivating one to be ethical. But there is another way of understanding the idea of "studying" business ethics. Here the idea is closer to that of one that is involved in the discipline itself, and takes on the role of a contributor. For example, just as going to church can reinforce values, help provide a platform for discussion, and offer guidance, studying business ethics can do the same. In fact being part of a business community where one can openly discuss how business should be conducted, and where one's contributions are taken seriously and reflected upon by others can often open one's mind to the possibility of change in light of the criticism of others.

Those who find that the pressure of the real world corporate environment pushes them away from the moral principles they believed in prior to entering the corporate world may discover that reading about case histories and debating what to do in a particular and common situation extremely insightful. One of the best ways to learn about the consequences of cruelty is to read and discuss the great novels that portray it. Likewise, one of the best ways to understand why committing an immoral act in the business world is not a good idea is by reading about cases, in which individuals committed similar acts and suffered horrible consequences. Reading case histories and discussing them can reinforce values and bring clarity.

Secondly, ethics in general requires healthy debate and exchange of ideas. Moral discussions are intolerant to brute disagreement. When a person offers an ethical position on a topic, and another disagrees, both parties have a prima facie obligation to offer reasons and justifications for their positions. Unlike disputes about what is the best flavor of ice cream, where opponents may disagree with one another with no other reason than that they like the particular flavor that they do, the nature of moral discussion requires that reasons be offered. Moral discussions are often about the possibility of harm to others, and most people in most cultures see the actions which have potential to harm others as requiring reasons and justifications. Consequently, and as a result of moral engagement, individuals can come to be motivated to act one way rather than another by acquiring new desires and beliefs through moral debate. It is often times noted that one feels most comfortable with an action he/she is about to take when one feels confident in the reasons they have for taking that action. Moral discussions can provide reasons, and confidence in those reasons.

Third, all of us at one time were new to the corporate environment and the pressures that arise in it, and most of us looked for guidance, not just from our colleagues and our bosses, but also from something beyond them. One reason we searched for this was that we weren't always sure that our bosses and colleagues were doing the right thing, morally or economically, or, for that matter, that they were even concerned with the morally right thing to do. Clearly, business ethics can provide guidance here, and solace to the lost novice in attempting to weather the stormy oceans of the corporate world. The study of ethics can provide us with a firm grasp of principles that can be applied in new situations to help us determine for ourselves what the morally right action is. The ability to reason about ethics can provide us with that sense of independence in thought that allows us to judge for ourselves whether our actions are morally right, and to criticize others.

2.

Let's go back to the beginning. Where does the idea that business and ethics do not fit together come from? One promising place to look would be at the role of *self-interest* in economics. There is a famous passage quoted over and over from Adam Smith's 1778 *Wealth of Nations*:

> It is not from the benevolence of the butcher, the brewer, or the baker that we expect our dinner, but from their regard to their own interest. We address ourselves, not to their humanity but to their self-love ...

The standard story based on this passage is that the sellers want our money, we want their products, and the exchange benefits us all. As a result there doesn't seem to be any need for ethics in the exchange matrix. Rational individuals pursuing their own self-interest are all it takes to get the day-to-day business dealings off the ground. Any imposition of ethical principles would be redundant.

While it is true that Smith paid tribute to self-interest in the passage above, it is a misreading of the passage, pointed out by Amartya Sen, to suggest that it excludes ethics from the matrix of exchange. By locating the specific sense in which self-interest is being celebrated by Smith, Sen claims we can bring out the sense in which ethics is an essential component of a system of exchange. What Smith was saying in paying tribute to self-interest in the passage above is that our *motivation for exchange* is self-interest. We are motivated to come to the marketplace to exchange our goods, not out of love for the other, but in a quite Hobbesian spirit, out of the necessity of self-preservation. The butcher sells his meat, the brewer his beer, and the baker his bread out of the obvious desire to procure money in order to purchase the goods he desires. What Smith is not saying is that business can function without ethical principles to guide the exchange. By making a distinction between *the motivation for exchange* and *the features necessary for the flourishing of business* we can draw out the appropriate role of self-interest, ethics, and how business ethics makes sense.

Self-interest is, as already noted, our motivation for exchange. However, ethical principles and codes of conduct are what allow for a system of exchange to flourish over long periods of time. In order to see the necessity of ethical principles and codes of conduct in the marketplace it will be instructive to look at a point made by Socrates in Book 1 of *The Republic*.

In discussion with Thrasymachus, Socrates points out that if a group has a common goal and every member of the group acts unjustly, then the attainment of the common goal will be frustrated. His point is made in an attempt to praise justice against Thrasymachus' diatribe. Thrasymachus has praised the life of injustice and thievery because he understands justice to be a weakness, and injustice to be the power to take advantage of others with impunity. Socrates has pointed out that even though it is correct that thieves take advantage of others, and at times with impunity, it is not true that they live wholly unjust lives. In fact, Socrates points out, in their dealings with other thieves they obey rules, and have a code of conduct, that allows for their thievery in groups to prosper. Even in modern times Socrates' point is common knowledge. The mafia has their own code of conduct, and individuals within their circle obey a code of conduct out of fear of punishment. If you are convinced that "the ethics of the mafia" is not an oxymoron, then you should equally be convinced that "business ethics" is not an oxymoron.

Socrates' point connects well with the distinction between the motivation for exchange and those features of a system necessary for its flourishing. Codes of conduct, rules, and guidelines—ethical principles—are all required in order for business to flourish over time. We are motivated by self-interest and the necessity of self-preservation to exchange goods, and to set up a system of exchange. However, the process of setting up that system and ensuring that it flourishes over time requires a commitment to ethical investigation and rules. Without ethical principles and rules the common goal of business—the exchange of goods for the benefit of all—would be frustrated, and less successful.

So, business and ethics do go together; and business ethics is not *useless*, *valueless* because *indeterminate*, or *beside the point*. Rather, ethics and business are connected in a way that is essential for the very flourishing of business.

BIBLIOGRAPHY

Clarence C. Walton, "The State of Business Ethics," *Enriching Business Ethics* (New York: Plenum Press, 1990).

Plato, "Book 1," *Republic*, translated by G.M.A. Grube and revised by C.D.C. Reeve (Indianapolis, Indiana: Hackett Publishing Company, 1992).

Amartya Sen, "Does Business Ethics Make Economic Sense?" *Business Ethics Quarterly* 3.1 (January 1993). See below, 20–28.

Albert Z. Carr, "Is Business Bluffing Ethical?" *Harvard Business Review* (January/February 1968). See below, 400–08.

◆ ◆ ◆ ◆ ◆

AMARTYA SEN[1]

Does Business Ethics Make Economic Sense?

1. Introduction

I begin not with the need for business ethics, but at the other end—the idea that many people have that there is no need for such ethics. That conviction is quite widespread among practitioners of economics, though it is more often taken for granted implicitly rather than asserted explicitly. We have to understand better what that conviction rests on, to be able to see its inadequacies. Here, as in many other areas of knowledge, the importance of a claim depends to a great extent on what it denies.

How did this idea of the redundancy of ethics get launched in economics? The early authors on economic matters, from Aristotle and Kautilya (in ancient Greece and ancient India respectively—the two were contemporaries, as it happens) to medieval practitioners (including Aquinas, Ockham, Maimonides, and others), to the economists of the early modern age (William Petty, Gregory King, François Quesnay, and others) were all much concerned, in varying degrees, with ethical analysis. In one way or another, they saw economics as a branch of "practical reason," in which concepts of the good, the right and the obligatory were quite central.

What happened then? As the "official" story goes, all this changed with Adam Smith, who can certainly be described—rightly—as the father of modern economics. He made, so it is said, economics scientific and hard-headed, and the new economics that emerged, in the nineteenth and twentieth centuries, was all ready to do business, with no ethics to keep it tied to "morals and moralizing." That view of what happened—with Smith doing the decisive shooting of business and economic ethics—is not only reflected in volumes of professional economic writings, but has even reached the status of getting into the English literature via a limerick by Stephen Leacock, who was both a literary writer and an economist:

> Adam, Adam, Adam Smith
> Listen what I charge you with!
> Didn't you say
> In a class one day
> That selfishness was bound to pay?
> Of all doctrines that was the Pith.
> Wasn't it, wasn't it, wasn't it, Smith?[2]

The interest in going over this bit of history—or alleged history—does not lie, at least for this conference, in scholastic curiosity. I believe it is important to see how that ethics-less view of economics and business emerged in order to understand what it is that is being missed out. As it happens, that bit of potted history of "who killed business ethics" is al-together wrong, and it is particularly instructive to understand how that erroneous identification has come about.

2. Exchange, Production and Distribution

I get back, then, to Adam Smith. Indeed, he did try to make economics scientific, and to a great extent was successful in this task, within the limits of what was possible then. While that part of the alleged history is right (Smith certainly did much to enhance the scientific status of economics), what is altogether mistaken is the idea that Smith demonstrated—or believed that he had demonstrated—the redundancy of ethics in economic and business affairs. Indeed, quite the contrary. The Professor of Moral Philosophy at the University of Glasgow—for that is what Smith was—was as interested in the importance of ethics in behavior as anyone could have been. It is instructive to see how the odd reading of Smith—as a "no-nonsense" sceptic of economic and business ethics—has come about.

Perhaps the most widely quoted remark of Adam Smith is the one about the butcher, the brewer and the baker in *The Wealth of Nations*: "It is not from the benevolence of the butcher, the brewer, or the baker that we expect our dinner, but from their regard to their own interest. We address ourselves, not to their humanity but to their self-love...."[3] The butcher, the brewer and the baker want our money, and we want their products, and the exchange benefits us all. There would seem to be no need for any ethics—business or otherwise—in bringing about this betterment of all the parties involved. All that is needed is regard for our own respective interests, and the market is meant to do the rest in bringing about the mutually gainful exchanges.

In modern economics this Smithian tribute to self-interest is cited again and again—indeed with such exclusivity that one is inclined to wonder whether this is the only passage of Smith that is read these days. What did Smith really suggest? Smith did argue in this passage that the pursuit of self-interest would do fine to motivate the exchange of commodities. But that is a very limited claim, even though it is full of wonderful insights in explaining why it is that we seek exchange and how come exchange can be such a beneficial thing for all. But to understand the limits of what is being claimed here, we have to ask, first: Did Smith think that economic operations and business activities consist only of exchanges of this kind? Second, even in the context of exchange, we have to question: Did Smith think that the result would be just as good if the businesses involved, driven by self-interest, were to try to defraud the consumers, or the consumers in question were to attempt to swindle the sellers?

The answers to both these questions are clearly in the negative. The butcher-brewer-baker simplicity does not carry over to problems of production and distribution (and Smith never said that it did), nor to the problem as to how a system of exchange can flourish institutionally. This is exactly where we begin to see why Smith could have been right in his claim about *the motivation for exchange* without establishing or trying to establish *the redundancy of business or ethics* in general (or even in exchange). And this is central to the subject of this conference.

The importance of self-interest pursuit is a helpful part of understanding many practical problems, for example, the supply problems in the Soviet Union and East Europe. But it is quite unhelpful in explaining the success of, say, Japanese economic performance *vis-à-vis* West Europe or North America (since behavior modes in Japan are often deeply influenced by other conventions and pressures). Elsewhere in *The Wealth of Nations*, Adam Smith considers other problems which call for a more complex motivational structure. And in his *The Theory of Moral Sentiments*, Smith goes extensively into the need to go beyond profit maximization, arguing that "humanity, justice, generosity, and public spirit, are the qualities most useful to others."[4] Adam Smith

was very far from trying to deny the importance of ethics in behavior in general and business behavior in particular.[5]

Through overlooking everything else that Smith said in his wide-ranging writings and concentrating only on this one butcher-brewer-baker passage, the father of modern economics is too often made to look like an ideologue. He is transformed into a partisan exponent of an ethics-free view of life which would have horrified Smith. To adapt a Shakespearian aphorism, while some men are born small and some achieve smallness, the unfortunate Adam Smith has had much smallness thrust upon him.

It is important to see how Smith's wholeness tribute to self-interest as a motivation for exchange (best illustrated in the butcher-brewer-baker passage) can co-exist peacefully with Smith's advocacy of ethical behavior elsewhere. Smith's concern with ethics was, of course, extremely extensive and by no means confined to economic and business matters. But since this is not the occasion to review Smith's ethical beliefs, but only to get insights from his combination of economic and ethical expertise to understand better the exact role of business ethics, we have to point our inquiries in that particular direction.

The butcher-brewer-baker discussion is all about *motivation for exchange*, but Smith was—as any good economist should be—deeply concerned also with *production* as well as *distribution*. And to understand how exchange might itself actually work in practice, it is not adequate to concentrate only on the motivation that makes people *seek* exchange. It is necessary to look at the behavior patterns that could sustain a flourishing system of mutually profitable exchanges. The positive role of intelligent self-seeking in motivating exchange has to be supplemented by the motivational demands of production and distribution, and the systemic demands on the organization of the economy.

These issues are taken up now, linking the general discussion with practical problems faced in the contemporary world. In the next three sections I discuss in turn (1) the problem of organization (especially that of exchange), (2) the arrangement and performance of production, and (3) the challenge of distribution.

3. Organization and Exchange: Rules and Trust

I come back to the butcher-brewer-baker example. The concern of the different parties with their own interests certainly can adequately *motivate* all of them to take part in the exchange from which each benefits. But whether the exchange would operate well would depend also on organizational conditions. This requires institutional development which can take quite some time to work—a lesson that is currently being learned rather painfully in East Europe and the former Soviet Union. That point is now being recognized, even though it was comprehensively ignored in the first flush of enthusiasm in seeking the magic of allegedly automatic market processes.

But what must also be considered now is the extent to which the economic institutions operate on the basis of common behavior patterns, shared trusts, and a mutual confidence in the ethics of the different parties. When Adam Smith pointed to the motivational importance of "regard to their own interest," he did not suggest that this motivation is all that is needed to have a flourishing system of exchange. If he cannot trust the householder, the baker may have difficulty in proceeding to produce bread to meet orders, or in delivering bread without prepayment. And the householder may not be certain whether he would be sensible in relying on the delivery of the ordered bread if the baker is not always altogether reliable. These problems of mutual confidence—discussed in a very simple form here—can be incomparably more complex and more critical in extended and multifarious business arrangements.

Mutual confidence in certain rules of behavior is typically implicit rather than explicit—indeed so implicit that its importance can be easily overlooked in situations in which such confidence is unproblematic. But in the context of economic development, across the Third World, and also of institutional reform, now sweeping across what used to be the Second World, these issues of behavioral norms and ethics can be altogether central.

In the Third World there is often also a deep-rooted scepticism of the reliability and moral quality of business behavior. This can be directed both at local businessmen and the commercial people from abroad. The latter may sometimes be particularly galling to well established business firms including well-known multinationals. But the record of some multinationals and their unequal power in dealing with the more vulnerable countries have left grounds for much suspicion, even though such suspicion may be quite misplaced in many cases. Establishing high standards of business ethics is certainly one way of tackling this problem.

There is also, in many Third World countries, a traditional lack of confidence in the moral behavior of particular groups of traders, for example merchants of food grains. This is a subject on which—in the context of the-then Europe—Adam Smith himself commented substantially in *The Wealth of Nations*, though he thought these suspicions were by and large unjustified. In fact, the empirical record on this is quite diverse, and particular experiences of grain trade in conditions of scarcity and famine have left many questions to be answered.

This is an issue of extreme seriousness, since it is now becoming increasingly clear that typically the best way of organizing famine prevention and relief is to create additional incomes for the destitute (possibly through employment schemes) and then to rely on normal trade to meet (through standard arrangements of transport and sales) the resulting food demand.[6] The alternative of bureaucratic distribution of food in hastily organized relief camps is often much slower, more wasteful, seriously disruptive of family life and normal economic operations, and more conducive to the spread of epidemic diseases.

However, giving a crucial role to the grain traders at times of famine threats (as a complement to state-organized employment schemes to generate income) raises difficult issues of trust and trustworthiness, in particular, that the traders will not manipulate the precarious situation in search of unusual profit. The issue of business ethics, thus, becomes an altogether vital part of the arrangement of famine prevention and relief.

The problem can be, to some extent, dealt with by skillful use of the threat of government intervention in the market. But the credibility of that threat depends greatly on the size of grain reserves the government itself has. It can work well in some cases (generally it has in India), but not always. Ultimately, much depends on the extent to which the relevant business people can establish exacting standards of behavior, rather than fly off in search of unusual profits to be rapidly extracted from manipulated situations.

I have been discussing problems of organization in exchange, and it would seem to be right to conclude this particular discussion by noting that the need for business ethics is quite strong even in the field of exchange (despite the near-universal presence of the butcher-brewer-baker motivation of "regard to their own interest"). If we now move on from exchange to production and distribution, the need for business ethics becomes even more forceful and perspicuous. The issue of trust is central to all economic operations. But we now have to consider other problems of interrelation in the process of production and distribution.

4. Organization of Production: Firms and Public Goods

Capitalism has been successful enough in generating output and raising productivity. But the experiences of different countries are quite diverse. The recent experiences of East Asian economies—most notably Japan—raise deep questions about the modelling of capitalism in traditional economic theory. Japan is often seen—rightly in a particular sense—as a great example of successful capitalism, but it is clear that the motivation patterns that dominate Japanese business have much more content than would be provided by pure profit maximization.

Different commentators have emphasized distinct aspects of Japanese motivational features. Michio Morishima has outlined the special characteristics of "Japanese ethos" as emerging from its particular history of rule-based behavior pattern.[7] Ronald Dore has seen the influence of "Confucian ethics."[8] Recently, Eiko Ikegami has pointed to the importance of the traditional concern with "honor"—a kind of generalization of the Samurai code—as a crucial modifier of business and economic motivation.[9]

Indeed, there is some truth, oddly enough, even in the puzzlingly witty claim made by *The Wall Street Journal* that Japan is "the only communist nation that works" (30 January 1989, 1). It is, as one would expect, mainly a remark about the non-profit motivations underlying many economic and business activities in Japan. We have to understand and interpret the peculiar fact that the most successful capitalist nation in the world flourishes economically with a motivation structure that departs firmly—and often explicitly—from the pursuit of self-interest, which is meant to be the bedrock of capitalism.

In fact, Japan does not, by any means, provide the only example of a powerful role of business ethics in promoting capitalist success. The productive merits of selfless work and devotion to enterprise have been given much credit for economic achievements in many countries in the world. Indeed, the need of capitalism for a motivational structure more complex than pure profit maximization has been acknowledged in various forms, over a long time, by various social scientists (though typically not by many "mainstream" economists): I have in mind Marx, Weber, Tawney, and others.[10] The basic point about the observed success of non-profit motives is neither unusual nor new, even though that wealth of historical and conceptual insights is often thoroughly ignored in professional economics today.

It is useful to try to bring the discussion in line with Adam Smith's concerns, and also with the general analytical approaches successfully developed in modern microeconomic theory. In order to understand how motives other than self-seeking can have an important role, we have to see the limited reach of the butcher-brewer-baker argument, especially in dealing with what modern economists call "public good." This becomes particularly relevant because the overall success of a modern enterprise is, in a very real sense, a public good.

But what *is* a public good? That idea can be best understood by contrasting it with a "private good," such as a toothbrush or a shirt or an apple, which either you can use or I, but not both. Our respective uses would compete and be exclusive. This is not so with public goods, such as a livable environment or the absence of epidemics. All of us may benefit from breathing fresh air, living in an epidemic-free environment, and so on. When uses of commodities are non-competitive, as in the case of public goods, the rationale of the self-interest-based market mechanism comes under severe strain. The market system works by putting a price on a commodity and the allocation between consumers is done by the intensities of the respective willingness to buy it at the prevailing price. When "equilibrium prices" emerge, they balance demand with supply for each commodity. In contrast, in the case of public goods, the uses are—largely or entirely—non-competitive, and the system of giving a good to the highest bidder does not have much merit, since one person's consumption does not exclude that of another. Instead, optimum resource allocation would require that the *combined* benefits be compared with the costs of production, and here the market mechanism, based on profit maximization, functions badly.[11]

A related problem concerns the allocation of private goods involving strong "externalities," with interpersonal interdependences working outside the markets. If the smoke from a factory makes a neighbor's home dirty and unpleasant, without the neighbor being able to charge the factory owner for the loss she suffers, then that is an "external" relation. The market does not help in this case, since it is not there to allocate the effects—good or bad—that works outside the market.[12] Public goods and externalities are related phenomena, and they are both quite common in such fields as public health care, basic education, environmental protection, and so on.

There are two important issues to be addressed in this context, in analysing the organization and performance of production. First, there would tend to be some failure in resource allocation when the commodities produced are public goods or involve strong externalities. This can be taken either (1) as an argument for having *publicly owned enterprises*, which would be governed by principles other than profit maximization, or (2) as a case for *public regulations* governing private enterprise, or (3) as establishing a need for the use of non-profit values—particularly of *social concern*—in private decisions (perhaps because of the goodwill that it might generate). Since public enterprises have not exactly covered themselves with glory in the recent years, and public regulations—while useful—are sometimes quite hard to implement, the third option has become more important in public discussions. It is difficult, in this context, to escape the argument for encouraging business ethics, going well beyond the traditional values of honesty and reliability, and taking on social responsibility as well (for example, in matters of environmental degradation and pollution).

The second issue is more complex and less recognized in the literature, but also more interesting. Even in the production of private commodities, there can be an important "public good" aspect in the production process itself. This is because production itself is typically a joint activity, supervisions are costly and often unfeasible, and each participant contributes to the over-all success of the firm in a way that cannot be fully reflected in the private rewards that he or she gets.

The over-all success of the firm, thus, is really a public good, from which all benefit, to which all contribute, and which is not parcelled out in little boxes of person-specific rewards strictly linked with each person's *respective contribution*. And this is precisely where the motives other than narrow self-seeking becomes productively important. Even though I do not have the opportunity to pursue the point further here, I do believe that the successes of "Japanese ethos," "Confucian ethics," "Samurai codes of honor," etc., can be fruitfully linked to this aspect of the organization of production.

5. *The Challenge of Distribution: Values and Incentives*

I turn now to distribution. It is not hard to see that non-self-seeking motivations can be extremely important for *distributional* problems in general. In dividing a cake, one person's gain is another's loss. At a very obvious level, the contributions that can be made by ethics—business ethics and others—include the amelioration of misery through policies explicitly aimed at such a result. There is an extensive literature on donations, charity, and philanthropy in general, and also on the willingness to join in communal activities geared to social improvement. The connection with ethics is obvious enough in these cases.

What is perhaps more interesting to discuss is the fact that distributional and productional problems very often come mixed together, so that how the cake is divided influences the size of the cake itself. The so-called "incentive problem" is a part of this relationship. This too is a much discussed problem,[13] but it is important to clarify in the present context that the extent of the conflict between size and distribution depends crucially on the motivational and behavioral assumptions. The incentive problem is

not an immutable feature of production technology. For example, the more narrowly profit-oriented an enterprise is, the more it would, in general, tend to resist looking after the interests of others—workers, associates, consumers. This is an area in which ethics can make a big difference.

The relevance of all this to the question we have been asked to address ("Does business ethics make economic sense?") does, of course, depend on how "economic sense" is defined. If economic sense includes the achievement of a good society in which one lives, then the distributional improvements can be counted in as parts of sensible outcomes even for business. Visionary industrialists and businesspersons have tended to encourage this line of reasoning.

On the other hand, if "economic sense" is interpreted to mean nothing other than achievement of profits and business rewards, then the concerns for others and for distributional equity have to be judged entirely instrumentally—in terms of how they indirectly help to promote profits. That connection is not to be scoffed at, since firms that treat its workers well are often very richly rewarded for it. For one thing, the workers are then more reluctant to lose their jobs, since more would be sacrificed if dismissed from this (more lucrative) employment, compared with alternative opportunities. The contribution of goodwill to team spirit and thus to productivity can also be quite plentiful.

We have then an important contrast between two different ways in which good business behavior could make economic sense. One way is to see the improvement of the society in which one lives as a reward in itself; this works directly. The other is to use ultimately a business criterion for improvement, but to take note of the extent to which good business behavior could in its turn lead to favorable business performance; this enlightened self-interest involves an indirect reasoning.

It is often hard to disentangle the two features, but in understanding whether or how business ethics make economic sense, we have to take note of each feature. If, for example, a business firm pays inadequate attention to the safety of its workers, and this results accidentally in a disastrous tragedy, like the one that happened in Bhopal in India some years ago (though I am not commenting at present on the extent to which Union Carbide was in fact negligent there), that event would be harmful both for the firm's profits and for the general objectives of social well-being in which the firm may be expected to take an interest. The two effects are distinct and separable and should act cumulatively in an overall consequential analysis. Business ethics has to relate to both.

6. A Concluding Remark

I end with a brief recapitulation of some of the points discussed, even though I shall not attempt a real summary. First, the importance of business ethics is not contradicted in any way by Adam Smith's pointer to the fact that our "regards to our own interest" provide adequate motivation for exchange (section 2). Smith's butcher-brewer-baker argument is concerned (1) directly with *exchanges* only (not production or distribution), and (2) only with the *motivational aspect* of exchange (not its organizational and behavioral aspects).

Second, business ethics can be crucially important in economic organization in general and in exchange operations in particular. This relationship is extensive and fairly ubiquitous, but it is particularly important, at this time, for the development efforts of the Third World and the reorganizational attempts in what used to be the Second World (section 3).

Third, the importance of business ethics in the arrangement and performance of production can be illustrated by the contrasting experiences of different economies, e.g., Japan's unusual success. The advantages of going beyond the pure pursuit of profit can be understood in different ways. To some extent, this question relates to the failure of profit-based market allocation in dealing with "public goods." This is relevant in two different ways: (1) the presence of

public goods (and of the related phenomenon of externalities) in the commodities produced (e.g., environmental connections), and (2) the fact that the success of the firm can itself be fruitfully seen as a public good (section 4).

Finally, distributional problems—broadly defined—are particularly related to behavioral ethics. The connections can be both direct and valuational, and also indirect and instrumental. The interrelations between the size of the cake and its distribution increase the reach and relevance of ethical behavior, e.g., through the incentive problem (section 5).

NOTES

A paper presented at the International Conference on the Ethics of Business in a Global Economy, held in Columbus, Ohio, in March 1992.

1 Lamont University Professor, and Professor of Economics and Philosophy, at Harvard University.

2 Stephen Leacock, *Hellements of Hickonomics* (New York: Dodd, Mead & Co., 1936), p. 75.

3 Adam Smith, *An Inquiry into the Nature and Causes of the Wealth of Nations* (1776; republished, London: Dent, 1910), vol. I, p. 13.

4 Adam Smith, *The Theory of Moral Sentiments* (revised edition, 1790; reprinted, Oxford: Clarendon Press, 1976), p. 189.

5 On this and related matters, see my *On Ethics and Economics* (Oxford: Blackwell, 1987); Patricia H. Werhane, *Adam Smith and His Legacy for Modern Capitalism* (New York: Oxford University Press, 1991); Emma Rothschild, "Adam Smith and Conservative Economics," *Economic History Review*, 45 (1992).

6 On this see Jean Drèze and Amartya Sen, *Hunger and Public Action* (Oxford: Clarendon Press, 1989).

7 Michio Morishima, *Why Has Japan "Succeeded"? Western Technology and Japanese Ethos* (Cambridge: Cambridge University Press, 1982).

8 Ronald Dore, "Goodwill and the Spirit of Market Capitalism," *British Journal of Sociology*, 34 (1983), and *Taking Japan Seriously: A Confucian Perspective on Leading Economic Issues* (Stanford: Stanford University Press, 1987).

9 Eiko Ikegami, "The Logic of Cultural Change: Honor, State-Making, and the Samurai," mimeographed, Department of Sociology, Yale University, 1991.

10 Karl Marx (with F. Engels), *The German Ideology* (1845-46, English translation, New York: International Publishers, 1947); Richard Henry Tawney, *Religion and the Rise of Capitalism* (London: Murray, 1926); Max Weber, *The Protestant Ethic and the Spirit of Capitalism* (London: Allen & Unwin, 1930).

11 The classic treatment of public goods was provided by Paul A. Samuelson, "The Pure Theory of Public Expenditure," *Review of Economics and Statistics*, 35 (1954).

12 For a classic treatment of external effects, see A.C. Pigou, *The Economics of Welfare* (London: Macmillan, 1920). There are many different ways of defining "externalities," with rather disparate bearings on policy issues; on this see the wide-ranging critical work of Andreas Papandreou (*Jr.*, I should add to avoid an ambiguity, though I don't believe he uses that clarification), *Ideas of Externality*, to be published by Clarendon Press, Oxford, and Oxford University Press, New York.

13 A good general review of the literature can be found in A.B. Atkinson and J.E. Stiglitz, *Lectures on Public Economics* (New York: McGraw-Hill, 1980). On the conceptual and practical importance of the incentive problem and other sources of potential conflict between efficiency and equity, see my *Inequality Reexamined* (Cambridge, MA: Harvard University Press, 1992), Chapter 9.

SYSTEMS OF MORAL EVALUATION

HEATHER SALAZAR

Kantian Business Ethics

Imagine that you are the owner of a vitamin and supplement retail store. You must make many decisions regarding the purchasing of products that may be helpful, harmful, or ineffective practically-speaking. However, even ineffective and harmful supplements produce high profit-margins when they are in high-demand. For example, shark-cartilage has been touted as a cure for cancer due to the fact that sharks rarely contract cancer. Even though empirical studies on the impact of taking such supplements demonstrates no positive benefit apart from placebo effects, people who are in search for a cure for cancer often purchase large quantities of shark-cartilage, thus increasing the sales of vitamin and supplement retailers like you. The ethical question that you face is whether you should buy such products knowing that cancer patients are spending their money and hope for a lost cause as far as shark-cartilage goes.

An even more serious case arises in your ethical decisions regarding the purchasing of products that are actually harmful to people who take them. For example, Ephedra is an herbal weight-loss supplement that was banned in the US in Feb. 2004 due to a large number of potentially fatal side-effects associated with its misuse, including over 155 reported deaths. But it was re-released in April 2006 because there was no proof of its harmfulness when taken according to the instructions. You know that if you stock your shelves with Ephedra it will produce incredible profits since it was in extremely high-demand by the millions who are looking desperately for a solution to their obesity. Should you purchase such products and allow the consumer to determine for herself whether

the risk of taking these supplements is worth it? If you purchase the products are you allowing consumers their autonomy or are you using desperate people in order to make a profit for yourself? This is obviously a difficult question as are so many of the ethical dilemmas with which we are faced on a daily basis. Ethical theories help to guide people in their search for the correct decision in such complex cases.

The Kantian answer to whether you should purchase and sell ineffective and harmful supplements emphasizes, first, allowing and helping people to make rational decisions and, second, having a motivation that comes from what Kant calls the "good will," which means that your motivation is from duty and is not simply self-seeking. As the retailer, you can sell the supplements if you can do so while respecting people. One way you could respect people's autonomy and refrain from being paternalistic is by empowering people to make rational decisions about the supplements that they take. This would include making information available on the effectiveness and dangers of the supplements that you sell and helping people to use the resources that you provide. However, in order to be acting morally, in addition to providing such information, you must be motivated to do so because you know that this is the right thing to do, and not, for example, because you are afraid of creating a bad reputation for yourself. The Kantian principles will allow you to sell ineffective and harmful supplements if you are not deceiving or harming people, or otherwise using them for your own personal gain. When you help people to make the right decisions for themselves and others, by providing them with the best information that you have, you are respecting people and their ability to make good decisions.

The Kantian approach to business ethics, like Kantian ethics in general, emphasizes acting with respect toward all autonomous beings. It claims that we all have duties toward one another that depend on our relationships with one another, the most basic and all-pervasive relationship between persons being that of a fellow member of humanity. As members of humanity, we each have value that stems from our rational and moral capacities and we all ought to act in a way that shows appreciation for that value. It differs from the other standard approaches, most notably rights-based theories and utilitarianism, in various significant ways. Unlike utilitarianism, it does not ask us to maximize any particular value, it involves no complex calculations, and it does not treat groups of people as more or less valuable depending on the quantities of individuals or quality of experiences among them. Like rights-based approaches, it proposes constraints on actions, giving us rules upon which to act. Duties are unlike rights, however, since although every right possessed by a person creates a respective duty for others to respect that right, some duties on a duty-based approach do not have correlate rights. For example, I have a duty to love my sister, but she does not have a right to my love. I have a duty to protect my country, perhaps, but my country does not have the right to use my labor and life in defense of itself.[1] Whether one has a duty to someone else depends not on the other's rights, as it does on a rights-based theory, but on the rational assessment of what is the right thing to do based on the various types of relationship that you have with the person. Morality for Kantians is constituted by how we ought to treat each other as fellow members of humanity, although other duties can arise for other types of relationships. In addition to this, it differs from rights-based approaches and utilitarianism by claiming that it is not only what you do that matters morally, but with what motivation you do it.

The crux of Kant's ethics resides in his startling claim that the only thing that is intrinsically good, or good-in-itself, is the good will. He says that "There is no possibility for thinking of anything at all in the world, or even out of it, which can be regarded as good without qualification, except a *good will*" (MM 393). The will is the rational part of each person, and the good will is rationality which chooses to do what is right for the reason that it is good. This is why all members of humanity, or all rational beings, have value, and this is also the reason why these beings are the only thing of true value. The argument for the claim that the only thing that is good-in-itself is the good will relies on a further claim that it is the only thing that is truly under our control. Our external circumstances, like where, when and to whom we are born, is not under our control; so although it may be unfortunate that some, through no fault of their own, are living in absolute poverty with no hope of living happy or long lives, we cannot control these factors. Furthermore, although we can choose actions to better the situations of those who are less fortunate, the results of our actions are not fully under our control since they depend on external circumstances and other people. For example, I might donate money to UNICEF, but the money might never get to the destination to produce the help that is needed, if, for instance, there was a terrible hurricane that prevented the truck from delivering it or someone robbed it. The money might get to the needy families but it might not actually help them if they buy food with it and become ill due to contaminants in the food. These things are not under our control; the only thing that is truly under our control is our choices or our motivation with which we intend to act. Rationality enables me to reflect on the circumstances of others who are in need, and decide on a method of helping them. It allows me to intend to do what is good, but the results of my intentions and actions are not entirely up to me. So according to the Kantian, both the choice of what to do and the motivation are integral to the moral worth of the action. I have enumerated four simple steps for determining the moral worth of a choice below:

Determining the Right Action and Motivation:
1. Formulate a Maxim-for-Action.
2. Evaluate it as coming from the good will or not.

a. Ask whether it is the right action.
b. Ask whether in willing it, you have the right motivation.
3. If it comes from the good will, it is good, and you are good in doing it; it if doesn't, then see step (4).
4. If it doesn't come from the Good Will, but is *consistent* with it, then the action is good, but you are not doing it from the right motive and so you are not praiseworthy.

1. Maxims-for-Action

The first step in determining whether you should perform an action is to identify the action. Developing a statement of the action will allow you and others to analyze whether the action is correct or not. Such statements are called maxims-for-action and they involve asserting what you will do and for what purpose you will do it. For example: I will take philosophy courses in order to learn how to reason well.

2.1. The Good Will: Right Actions

The second step asks you to evaluate the maxim-for-action as coming from the good will or not. The good will is the part of you that is motivated to do what is good for the right reasons so it involves evaluating (a) whether the action is the right action and (b) whether the action is rightly motivated.

For Kant, the right actions to take are those that are rational. This is because the will is the rational part of each of us, and so, if the maxim is rational, it is fit to be willed. Kant thinks that there are various tests that will allow us to see whether a maxim is rational or not, which we can call the Categorical Imperative Tests. The Categorical Imperative is the law of rationality that does not depend on our desires, but depends only on pure rationality. When a maxim is tested by the Categorical Imperative, it tells us what maxims (and thus what actions) we can rationally take, those we cannot rationally take, and those that we rationally have to take. In other words, it determines permissible, impermissible, and required actions.

Kant has three formulations of the Categorical Imperative, or what he takes to be the supreme law of pure rationality. These are often called "The Formula of Universal Law," "The Formula of Humanity," and "The Formula of Autonomy." According to Kant, all three of these formulations have the same results. In this explanation, I will focus on the first two formulations.

2.1.1. The Formula of Universal Law

In order to be rational, one must also be logical, and the most primary logical rule that should be observed is to be consistent; anything that is inconsistent is illogical and thus irrational and immoral for Kant. Kant's first formulation, the Formula of Universal Law, uses the rule of consistency to eliminate those maxims that are internally inconsistent, or impossible to will if everyone willed them. It states that you ought to "Act only according to that maxim whereby you can at the same time will that it should become a universal law" (Kant, MM 421).

After you have created a maxim, you must universalize it, which means that you must make it a law that everyone act according to the maxim that you have developed for yourself. A universalized maxim involves transforming my maxim "I will use my company's funds in order to woo prospective clients and gain business for the company," to a universalized maxim which states "Everyone will use their company's funds in order to woo prospective clients and gain business for the company."

Once it is universalized, you must check for inconsistencies. Ask yourself whether it is possible for everyone to will the maxim and to achieve their goals. For example, is everyone doing the action consistent with your achieving the purpose of your original maxim? If everyone used their company's funds to gain new clients, then companies would be investing in and obtaining new business by exerting their own resources. It would be possible for all companies to invest and gain new clients, including you. Therefore, the maxim is fit to be willed and it is a permissible action for you to perform.

Some maxims are inconsistent when universalized and thus irrational and impermissible to act on. For example, take the maxim, "I will embezzle my company's funds in order to obtain extra money rather than invest extra resources into the company." Once universalized, everyone will be embezzling money from their companies and (1) the companies will not have enough money for people to embezzle and (2) the companies will know that everyone is embezzling money and they will stop people from embezzling money. If the companies do not have enough money for everyone to embezzle, then that defeats the purpose of your maxim, which is to gain money. It is therefore impermissible to act on that maxim. In addition, since the companies will know that you are trying to embezzle money, they will be able to stop you from doing so and punish you for it. This defeats the purpose of your maxim, as well, since they will stop you from embezzling the money. Since there is a contradiction in everyone willing this maxim, it is impermissible to act on it. Alternatively, it is required that you not act on it.

It is easy for people to misunderstand the Formula of Universal Law and think that the test requires that we see whether a good or a bad state of affairs *results* from the universalized version of the maxim. For example, someone might think that if the company knows that you are embezzling money you will be punished for it, and since you don't want to be punished, it is not a good maxim to act upon. Although it might be true that you should not act on maxims that will create bad outcomes, this is not what the Formula of Universal Law tests. It tests whether it is possible for everyone to will it and still achieve the purposes of the maxims.

By testing the universalizability of the maxim under scrutiny, the Formula of Universal Law prohibits people from making exceptions of themselves. It thus forbids, in general, all actions that rely on others not knowing what you are doing, which is a form of deceit. So stealing and lying are impermissible in any circumstance. And this has a tremendous impact on business as many of business's ethical issues concern just these sorts of problems. For example, fraud, stock-market schemes, piggyback trading, deception in advertising and accounting, honesty in contracting and in lawsuits, and various forms of the stealing of company resources, including taking extra time off, office supplies, extravagant spending, and the pumping of monies towards one's own investments.

2.1.2. The Formula of Humanity

The Formula of Humanity is a more intuitive version of the Categorical Imperative and it states to "Act in such a way that you treat humanity, whether in your own person or in the person of another, always at the same time as an end and never simply as a means" (Kant, MM 429). This statement, too, relies on the logical rule of consistency, but its focus is different. Humanity, which is the rational power within individuals, is valuable in-itself, and is the only thing, according to Kant, that is valuable in-itself. Because it is of value, and it is something that not only you possess, but all beings with rationality possess, everyone must respect each others' rationality. Respecting others' and your own rationality entails, according to this formulation, never treating it as mere means and always treating it as an end in itself. An end is something that is valuable in-itself and a means is something that is valuable only as a way to get what you want or to achieve an end. So we ought to always treat people's rationality as being valuable in-itself. Therefore, we should allow people to use their rationality and we should use our own rationality, and we should never circumvent the use of rationality in order to get something that we desire, even something that we think of as rational and good.

This formulation, like the Formula of Universal Law, eliminates lying and deceit of any kind. Furthermore, it eliminates using ourselves without the consent of our rationality and it prohibits our use of other people without the consent of their rationality. This is not the same thing as getting someone's consent, since a person can give his or her consent without giving her *rational* consent. Giving one's rational consent to something means reflecting on the action and its consequences, and examining whether it is a good thing for one to perform it. So someone might sign a contract for a credit card that charges an exorbitant amount of interest, but being charged this amount of interest is not what a rational person, under most circumstances, would choose. It is therefore impermissible and immoral for the person to sign the contract and it is impermissible and immoral for anyone to ask a person to sign such a contract.

In the Formula of Humanity it can also be seen quite clearly that people ought never to be unfair or treat people poorly. So issues in business that deal with inequities among the sexes, genders, races, and ages, and topics that concern the subjugation of individuals in unfair positions of bargaining power and sweatshop-like circumstances are also impermissible and immoral. All actions that are not impermissible, or do not involve the use of a person as a *mere* means, are permissible.

2.2. The Good Will: Right Motivations

After the maxim for action is evaluated as being permissible, impermissible, or required to act upon, and it passes the test, being either permissible or required to act upon, one must determine whether the motivation for acting on it is good. If the motivation is not good, then acting on it does not come from the Good Will. In order to distinguish the different kinds of motives that one may have in doing an action, let us first examine three different maxims and then the different motivations that accompany these maxims. Kant uses for this purpose an example that is relevant to businesses of a shopkeeper who treats his customers honestly for three distinct purposes.

Three Maxims in Kant's Shopkeeper:
1. I will be honest with my customers in order to gain their trust and get repeat-business.
2. I will be honest with my customers because I like them.

3. I will be honest with my customers because that's the right thing to do.

According to the Formula of Universal Law, it is permissible to treat one's customers honestly, no matter the purpose, because honesty never makes an exception of oneself. According to the Formula of Humanity, honesty is also good, because deceit involves using people by bypassing their rational consent. It may seem like the shopkeeper is using his customers in the first maxim that he devises since his purpose in being honest is to make money off of them, but this maxim is not eliminated by the Formula of Humanity as long as the shopkeeper respects the rationality of his customers while he intends to make a profit.

However, there is a moral difference in these three maxims even though each of them is permissible to act upon. These differences are revealed in the purposes within these maxims which correspond to three general types of motivation:

Three Types of Motivation:
A. Self-Interest (corresponding to (1))
B. Character or Sympathy (corresponding to (2))
C. The Moral Law or Duty (corresponding to (3))

Of these three kinds of motivation, Kant claims that the only good motivation is that which comes from the moral law or duty.

The reason why self-interest is eliminated as being a good motivation, where good is understood as "moral" or "praiseworthy" is fairly clear. Self-interested motivation is something that benefits the self by definition, and does not consider others, so it cannot be a moral motivation, or one which aims to benefit humanity in general. In fact, actions that are performed for a person's self-interest and moral actions are frequently seen as opposed to one another since people can maximize their self-interest by harming other people.

The second type of motivation, which comes from character or sympathy, on the other hand, is not so obviously lacking goodness. Good people have good characters. They are kind, honest, and charitable. A good person will do good things, so the shopkeeper, if he is good, will be honest because that is the kind of person he is. Isn't the fact that he is a good person of credit to him? And, furthermore, ought not we all to try to become good people such that we do good just because that is the way we are? Kant's answer to this is that our characters at birth and throughout our lives are not wholly under our control and so we ought not to be credited for doing actions that naturally arise from our constitutions. Some people are born irritable and have difficulties in their families and environments that exacerbate these genetic tendencies. It is not these people's fault that they were born with such disadvantages. Likewise, motivations that come from sympathy have no moral worth for Kant because whether we like or dislike someone can change from moment to moment, and morality has a more solid foundation than this; unshakeable by our fleeting feelings and desires. If the objection arises that a person with a good character will have sympathetic reactions to others reliably, then his objection to motivations arising from character will emerge again. Motivations from character and sympathy can help us to act in accordance with the moral law, if they come from a good character, but they are not good in-themselves. Kant concludes that the only motivation that is under our control (and thus capable of being morally praiseworthy) and that will provide an unshakeable ground for morality is that motivation issuing directly from the will to obey the moral law. If we are motivated to do the right thing *because it is the right thing*, then we are performing actions that are not merely in accordance with morality, but are in fact moral.

3. Conclusion

Kantian ethics does not prohibit individuals from seeking their own happiness, which includes prosperity in business. However, it identifies constraints on what we should do in the pursuit of our happiness or profits that gives equal respect to all rational individuals by requiring people to exercise their own rationality and allowing others to exercise their rationality, as well. Treating people as equal, autonomous agents with goals of their own and being honest and honoring the relationships that we have, will produce a community that in which we trust each other and are able to rely on and cooperate with each other more effectively. These results, being the foundations of a capitalistic economy, will enable businesses and individuals to prosper as well.

NOTE

1   It is unclear whether it even makes sense to ask whether ontological items that are constituted by groups of individuals with no independent existence (or at least no conscious existence) can possess rights.

FOR FURTHER READING

Guyer, Paul. (1997). *Kant's Groundwork on the Metaphysics of Morals: Critical Essays*. Lanham, MD: Rowman & Littlefield Publishers, Inc.

Guyer, Paul. (2007). *Kant's Groundwork for the Metaphysics of Morals: A Reader's Guide*. London: Continuum International Publishing Group.

Kant, Immanuel. (2008). *Groundwork of the Metaphysics of Morals*. Trans. Thomas Kingsmill Abbott. Radford, VA: Wilder Publications.

Sedgwick, Sally. (2008). *Kant's Groundwork of the Metaphysics of Morals: An Introduction*. Cambridge: Cambridge University Press.

Sullivan, Roger J. (1994). *An Introduction to Kant's Ethics*. Cambridge: Cambridge University Press.

Wood, Allen W. (2007). *Kantian Ethics*. Cambridge: Cambridge University Press.

◆ ◆ ◆ ◆ ◆

RITA C. MANNING

Caring as an Ethical Perspective

An ethic of care has emerged as a new way to conceptualize some deeply held moral intuitions. It provides an important tool for analyzing, discussing, and ultimately shaping moral practice. In what follows, I will briefly describe an ethic of care. I shall then have something to say about how this perspective emerged and about how it differs from other moral orientations.

Care for Others and Fostering Relationships

One characteristic of people with integrity is the ability to care for others and to foster good relationships. Caring for others is more than having sympathetic feelings for them; it requires that one take concrete action to look after the needs of others. Caring for others and fostering good relationships go together for two reasons. First, humans are essentially social creatures—we live and work in groups and most of us would be absolutely miserable if we didn't have meaningful relationships. So caring about persons means caring about their relationships. Second, we cannot accomplish many of the tasks we need to undertake unless we can foster good relationships. This includes the task of giving care to others.

Let's start with an example and see how caring works. Doug is concerned with trying to salvage an account and wants to send someone to visit the client. Kien is the most likely candidate since he has a good working relationship with the client, but he is scheduled to visit another client on a much bigger account. Susan has some experience with this client and has been known to save accounts in similar situations, so she is Doug's first choice. Carlos is a possibility, but he is not as familiar with the product as Susan. Doug recalls that Susan's father is in the last stages of his battle with congestive heart failure and he wonders whether it would be fair to ask her to go. He calls her into his office and Susan says that her father would probably want her to go. Satisfied, Doug sends Susan on the trip, but the account is lost anyway. Did Doug do the right thing? We can now answer this question by asking whether Doug was sufficiently caring.

Care

Though not all defenders of an ethic of care see care as a virtue, I think this is the most plausible way to understand it. Like other virtues, care is a general disposition to behave in a particular way. Unlike other virtues, care is what I call a meta-virtue—that is it provides an organizing principle for all the other virtues. If my overall orientation is to be a caring person, then I will be courageous when what I value is at risk; I will be honest because honesty is usually the best way to care for others; I will want to be prudent because I recognize that I must balance the needs of others and my own needs. So the traditional virtues of courage, honesty and prudence are organized under the meta-virtue of care.

When Carol Gilligan first described the care orientation, she described it as a typically female moral orientation. However, there is nothing gendered about caring; if it is more prevalent in women than in men, it is because women are socially conditioned to do much of society's caring work—they are more likely to be involved with caring for children and the sick, for example. Care is a basic human capacity and as such it is both possible and important for all of us to be caring persons. Developing one's capacity in giving care requires that we commit to this ideal and that we have practice exercising care. When we truly care about someone or something, we have certain emotions and motivations. If I see someone in dire need, for example, I will feel compassion and be motivated to do something to respond to the need. Finally, it is not enough to merely have the appropriate emotion and motivation; care involves an appropriate response.

Caring is a response to the variety of features of moral situations: need, harm, past promises, role relationships etc. In the case of need, our obligation to respond in an appropriately caring way arises when we are able to respond to need. We can roughly distinguish needs here from desires by describing needs as something that is basic to our survival and minimally decent life as opposed to something that we merely want. Humans need some things for their very survival: food, clothing, shelter, and health care are examples. There are also other things that we need for a minimally decent life: Aristotle cites friendship; Mill cites liberty and Rawls offers self-esteem as a need in this sense. Still, there is no universal, cross-cultural understanding of need. Rather, need is mediated by a number of factors including family, culture, economic class, gender and sexuality, disability and illness. Finally, as we respond to needs, we should recognize the vast differences in power that exist. Sometimes, people are unwilling to express their needs freely because they fear that their needs will not be met. They may even be in such a state of dependence or despair that they are no longer able to identify their needs.

Need is not the only feature of moral situations. Harm, for example, is an important one to consider. Most people understand that being the cause of harming someone else creates an obligation to respond. But causation is a complex idea. We can be part of the causal story even when we don't think of ourselves as the primary cause. Suppose, for example, that you see the person sitting next to you in an exam cheating. Suppose further that this is an exam that is designed to demonstrate competence in a skill crucial for a health care practitioner. Suppose that you simply look the other way and later find

out that a patient was seriously harmed because the practitioners really did not understand the procedure they should have followed, and that this procedure was the very one they were being tested on when you saw them cheating. Do you have a responsibility here? I would argue that you do, though it's not always clear what you can do after the fact. At the very least, you now know that you shouldn't look the other way when you see similar cheating in the future.

There are two other things that mark the moral dimension of a situation that are worth noting here—past promising and role responsibility. When we make a promise, we commit ourselves to a certain course of action. An ethic of care doesn't say that you are always committed to keeping a promise because sometimes doing so can be harmful to all concerned, but it does impose a moral obligation to respond. Similarly, being in a particular role, e.g., teacher, comes with a set of general obligations.

We've now looked at some of the features of situations that suggest that we have an obligation. In order to see what our obligations are in a particular situation, we need to look at the features of an ethic of care. There are four central ideas here: moral attention, sympathetic understanding, relationship awareness, and harmony and accommodation.

Moral Attention

Moral attention is the attention to the situation in all its complexity. When one is morally attentive, one wishes to become aware of all the details that will allow a sympathetic response to the situation. It is not enough to know that this is a case of a particular kind, say a case about lying or cruelty. In order to understand what our obligations are, we have to know all the details that might make a difference in our understanding and response to the particular situation at hand.

Sympathetic Understanding

When I sympathetically understand the situation, I am open to sympathizing and even identifying with the persons in the situation. I try to be aware of what the others in the situation would want me to do, what would most likely be in their best interests, and how they would like me to carry out their wishes and interests and meet their needs. I call this attention to the best interests of others maternalism. It is done in the context of a special sensitivity to the wishes of the other and with an understanding of the other's interest that is shaped by a deep sympathy and understanding. When it is hard to be sympathetic, one may try several strategies—perhaps imagining others as oneself in an earlier crisis. As one adopts this sympathetic attitude one often becomes aware of what others want and need. Finally, as we respond to others, we look to satisfy their needs in ways that will preserve their sense of competence and dignity while at the same time addressing their needs or even ameliorating their suffering.

Relationship Awareness

There is a special kind of relationship awareness that characterizes caring. A person recognizes that others are in a relationship with him. First there is the most basic relationship, that of fellow creatures. Second there is the immediate relationship of need and ability to fill the need. Finally, one may be in some role relationship with the other that calls for a particular response, such as teacher-student. One is aware of all these relationships as he surveys a situation from the perspective of care. But there is another kind of relationship awareness that is involved as well. One can be aware of the network of relationships that connect humans, and care about preserving and nurturing these relationships. As caring persons think about what to do, they try not to undermine these relationships but rather to nurture and extend the relationships that are supportive of human flourishing.

Accommodation and Harmony

Related to the notion of relationship awareness is accommodation. Often times there are many persons involved and how best to help is not obvious. The desire to nurture networks of care requires that one tries to accommodate the needs of all, including oneself. It is not always possible, or wise, to do what everyone thinks they need, but it is often important to do what you think is best while at the same time giving everyone concerned a sense of being involved and considered in the process. When we do this, we have a better chance of preserving harmony. If you do what you think is right without consulting anyone, you risk upsetting the harmony of the group. Of course not all harmony is worth preserving. The oppressive society may be pretty stable and harmonious, but at the price of those at the bottom. An ethic of care would be opposed to this type of superficial harmony since it is dependent on treating some as though they do not deserve the same care as others. Ideally, we should aim for the harmonious society in which all are treated with care.

Let's return to Doug and see how he might have thought about the situation if he'd been more skillful at caring. Doug did not really think about Susan's situation very carefully. He should have realized that she was very upset about her father's illness. Since we are all distracted when something this serious is going on in our lives, she was probably also worried that her concern might put her job performance in jeopardy. Doug should not have taken her words at face value because it's hard to believe that her father really wanted her to go. Perhaps he was just being a good father and trying to put Susan's needs above his own. Very likely, he was worried about how his illness was affecting her and might have told her to go to give her some time off or to protect her job. Doug also did not give much thought to how well Susan would be able to interact with the client while her father was dying miles away. The result of his action was a lost account and considerable discomfort for Susan. This lack of care on his part probably will affect his relationship with Susan and her effectiveness in future negotiations. Whenever she has to go visit a client, she will be reminded of that very precious time she lost with her father. Doug should have given more thought to finding other alternatives to sending Susan on the trip during this very trying time.

The Care Voice and the Justice Voice

Now that we've seen how the care perspective works, let's turn to a brief history. Carol Gilligan's pioneering work, *In a Different Voice*, was the first systematic attempt to describe the voice of care and to distinguish it from what she called the voice of justice (Gilligan, 1982). Since then, psychologists and philosophers have been busy elucidating the central concepts and testing for various aspects of the two voices.

Gilligan began by responding to the views of Lawrence Kohlberg, who developed a theory about how people reason and develop morally (Kohlberg, 1981). His theory of moral reasoning posited that people reason morally by applying principles to cases, thus yielding judgments about what they ought to do. Moral development, in Kohlberg's account, is cognitive and proceeds to progressively more general principles, with ideal moral development culminating in principles that are universal and binding on all persons.

Carol Gilligan noted that Kohlberg's subjects, though culturally diverse, were all male. She began to apply his tests to female subjects of various ages. Her conclusion was that some people, notably females, often used a different reasoning strategy than that described by Kohlberg and that they developed by moving through a different set of stages.

Gilligan theorized that some of her subjects appealed to an ethic of care. This involves a thorough understanding of the context, and a willingness to balance the needs of self and other in a way that preserves both. For Gilligan, moral development was both cognitive and emotional—the growth in the ability to see the situation from the perspective of self and other and to care about one's self as well as others.

She illustrated the differences in moral reasoning with two eleven year olds, Jake and Amy. Jake and Amy are both given Kohlberg's Heinz dilemma to solve. A druggist has invented a drug to combat cancer. Heinz's wife needs the drug but Heinz does not have the money to buy it and the druggist will not give it to him. The children are asked whether Heinz should steal the drug. Jake quickly answers affirmatively and defends his answer by appealing to the relative importance of life over property. Amy begins by saying that it depends. She points out that all the things that could go wrong if Heinz steals the drug—perhaps he will get caught and go to jail and his wife will be worse off. She suggests instead that Heinz and the druggist should sit down and work it out to everyone's satisfaction.

Jake fits easily into Kohlberg's schemata: he imagines himself in Heinz's position and applies a principle that quickly yields an answer. He does not need any more information about Heinz, the druggist, Heinz's wife, etc. Amy, on the other hand, is virtually impossible to analyze on Kohlberg's scale because she never states or even implies a principle that will yield an answer. Instead, as she imagines herself in Heinz's shoes, she sees the complexity of the situation and realizes that its solution requires that Heinz and the druggist and Heinz's wife recognize their involvement in a relationship and that they honor this awareness by working out a solution that will enable them all to survive and, if possible, flourish.

For Jake the solution is cognitive: he merely reasons about the situation and can take action on the basis of that reasoning. Amy sees a real solution as necessarily involving growth in moral sensitivity and commitment.

On the basis of such differences in her subjects' responses, Gilligan posited a moral orientation, which she calls the voice of care, in addition to the justice orientation of Kohlberg. I propose an additional way of assessing the usefulness of the two: How does each voice answer two questions: What are moral agents like? What is the moral standing of persons and communities?

The justice voice says that moral agents are or should be 1) isolated, abstract individuals who 2) follow abstract rules 3) in a cool and impartial manner. Moral agents are isolated in the sense that they are both independent of others and free to choose what relationship to have with others. The model of interaction is contractual—an individual as a moral agent chooses to whom s/he will be related and the conditions of the relationship. The individuals involved are abstract in the sense that their moral obligations are specified independently of any of the particular facts about them or about the situations they find themselves in. Their moral obligations are spelled out in abstract rules, rules that are general enough to bind similar cases. In following these general rules, individuals must be cool and impartial. This requires unemotionally applying the rules in the same fashion regardless of the ties of affection and/or enmity that might call on them to be partial.

The voice of care, on the other hand, understands moral agents as 1) embedded in particular social contexts, relationships and personal narratives, who 2) direct their moral attention to real others and 3) are open to sympathetic understanding and identification with those others.

In part because the justice voice conceives moral agency in the way it does, it gives the following answer to the question of the moral standing of persons and communities. 1) All persons are equally valuable—hence there are no special obligations to particular others. 2) Communities and relationships have no moral standing on their own account.

The care voice, on the other hand, agrees that 1) though all persons are valuable, there are special obligations: those imposed by actual and potential relationships and those imposed by roles. Since it understands communities as more than mere aggregates of individuals and relationships as more than properties of individual persons, it is committed to saying that communities and relationships have moral standing and that they need to be included in our thought and action.

Care, Justice and Self-Understanding

There is an additional way to sort out the differences between the care and justice voice and that is in terms of self-understanding. This was suggested by Nona Lyons, who argued that a particular self-understanding, a "distinct way of seeing and being in relation to others," explains the moral agent's preference for a particular moral voice (Lyons, 1983). Lyons identifies two different self-understandings: what she calls the separate/objective self and the connected self. Persons who fit the separate/objective self model describe themselves in terms of personal characteristics rather than connections to others. Connected selves, on the other hand, describe themselves in terms of connections to others: granddaughter of, friend of, etc. This suggests that the separate/objective self sees oneself as distinct from others in a more profound sense than does the connected self. The separate/objective self might, for example, see oneself as connected to others only through voluntary agreements. The separate/objective self might value autonomy more highly than good relationships with others.

Lyons describes further differences. Separate/objective selves recognize moral dilemmas as those that involve a conflict between their principles and someone else's desires, needs or demands. Connected selves, on the other hand, identify moral dilemmas as those that involve the breakdown of relationships with others.

Separate/objective selves fear connection and dependence, and hence value autonomy and independence. Connected selves fear separation and abandonment, and hence value connection and responsiveness.

We can see then how these self-understandings support different moral orientations. Separate selves understand themselves as distinct from others. They conceive moral dilemmas as arising from the conflict between their moral principles and the needs, demands, desires and principles of others. As such, they must mediate their interaction with others in the voice of justice—in terms of ground rules and procedures that can be accepted by all. This is the only foundation for interaction at all, since ties of affection are not seen as strong enough to provide a basis for interaction, especially in persons who fear connection and dependence. This fear of dependence and attachment also explains why they value the objectivity and impartiality that can stand between them and intimates. At the same time, separate/objective selves recognize that interaction with others plays a role in one's satisfaction, so they value community and relationship insofar as these play a role in individual satisfaction.

Connected selves see themselves in terms of others, so relationship is central to self-identity, rather than seen as voluntary and incidental. The problem of interaction is not then conceived of as how to get others to interact with oneself on terms that would be acceptable to all, but how to protect the ties of affection and connection that are central to one's very self-identity. Moral dilemmas arise over how to preserve these ties when they are threatened, and these dilemmas are mediated by the voice of care. Since the primary fear is of separation and abandonment, a strong value is placed on community and relationships.

Care and Other Moral Perspectives

At this point in the discussion of an ethic of care, I want to make a meta-ethical point. I am not convinced that in some ethically preferred world, everyone would adopt the same moral theory or the same way of dealing with the moral realities of life. I am certainly not convinced that in this world, everyone

can do so. Rather, I think that each moral theory has insight to offer and sheds light on a different aspect of our moral lives. I also think that each of us has a particular history and moral narrative that limits our ability to adopt new moral perspectives, regardless of how we may evaluate one moral theory against another. Finally, I think that when we try to make moral theories guides to action in the rough and tumble world of complex and difficult choices, we ought to take comfort where and when we can. If one particular moral theory sheds new light on a difficult and novel issue, then we should comb it for every bit of insight we find useful. It is for these reasons that I prefer to speak of moral perspectives rather than moral theories.

It is also important to distinguish between an ethic of care and an ethical approach to care giving. One need not subscribe to an ethic of care as a moral perspective to realize that there are special issues that arise for any of us in our various roles as caregivers. I think that an ethic of care will shed light on a range of issues, certainly including the ethics of care giving, but I am not committed to the view that moral perspectives are necessarily incompatible. They are often complementary. Care and Confucian ethics are similar in some important respects. Ideal Humanness (jen) and propriety (li) play a central role in Confucian ethics. Jen is analogous in some important respects to care, while li, like accommodation, reminds us that the good society must value harmony among its members.

I think that an ethic of care provides a corrective to some other ways of thinking about caring for patients. Kantian and utilitarian approaches are often seen as the gold standard in discussions of health care, but they are not quite up to every task. Patient autonomy and patient rights have a distinctly Kantian pedigree. We value patient autonomy because we see humans as rational moral agents who ought to be treated as ends in themselves and never merely as means. Patient rights provide the framework for our interactions with these autonomous persons. But if we rely exclusively on this perspective, we may lose sight of patients as needing care. When we are sick we may not be up to the task of asserting our rights, and while we may value our autonomy we also value being cared for. Utilitarianism is most useful at the macro-level in discussions of social issues, reminding us of problems of cost and allocation. Care reminds us never to lose sight of actual persons. An example of the preoccupation with the macro-level to the detriment of the person is the strategy for covering illness under Medicare in the US. Illnesses are grouped into diagnostically related groups and a reimbursement schedule is set for each group. Patients that do well get good care under this approach, while sicker patients are discharged before they are well enough. While it is important to control cost, care reminds us that we must treat each person and each illness individually.

There will be times when a care model appears to be in tension with a moral rights perspective. One obvious example comes from bioethics. The patients' rights conception of the autonomous, competent patient is quite remote from the care conception of patients as primarily persons in need of maternal assistance. Still these models can often work in tandem, and in my opinion ought to be so wedded. Care and rights should be fundamental values. I envision the marriage of justice and care in the following way. First, we must be sensitive to the self-understanding of those entrusted to our care. Second, respecting rights is a moral minimum below which we ought not to fall, but care is the moral ideal. Respecting rights, then, is a minimal moral requirement, but we have not completely discharged our responsibilities until we treat others in a genuinely caring way. There is a further amendment to the rights model that must be made to make this a successful marriage. We should no longer assume that everyone is always capable of asserting and defending their rights in an autonomous way. Rather, we should recognize that sometimes people might be in need of care while temporarily (and in some cases permanently) unable to assert and defend their rights. In this case, we care for them and see returning them to full autonomy as part of our obligation rather than as an assumption about their present status.

One helpful way to connect moral theories is to notice that they each focus primarily on a different component of our moral experience. Utilitarianism and other consequential views invite us to be sensitive to the consequences of our decisions and actions. Kant reminds us of two things. First, our motivation and not just the outcomes of our actions are morally significant. Second, persons have a special place in the moral hierarchy. Moral rights provide a way of understanding the implications of this special place in the moral hierarchy. Virtue theories focus not just on actions, but on the agents who are responsible for these actions. It directs our attention to the character traits that underlie our actions and our commitments. It also focuses our attention on how concepts of the good life both anchor our views about the good society and grow out of particular societies. An ethic of care adds yet another dimension. It reminds us of the importance of human relationships. It places moral value on communities as well as persons and asserts that our actions take place in the context of relationship: our decisions should consider existing relationships and are often carried out via social action. Doing the right thing and living the morally good life must be understood in the context of trust, reciprocity and concern for others.

Conclusion

An ethic of care is a moral orientation that is sorely needed in our increasingly fractured society. Whether we are managers or teachers or health care providers, an ethic of care provides guidance about how to live our lives. But it is not just a moral philosophy; it has a political dimension as well. If we are to meet our fellow creatures as caring individuals, we must rethink and, when necessary, restructure our institutions to make this possible.

NOTES

Gilligan, Carol. (1982). *In a Different Voice*. Cambridge, MA: Harvard University Press, 1982.

Kohlberg, Lawrence. (1981). *The Philosophy of Moral Development*. New York: Harper & Row.

Lyons, Nona. (1983). "Two Perspectives on Self, Relationship, and Morality," *Harvard Educational Review* 53 (1983): 125-45.

FOR FURTHER READING

Held, Virginia. (1993). *Feminist Morality*. Chicago: University of Chicago Press.

Holmes, Helen Bequaert, and Purdy, Laura (eds.). (1992). *Feminist Perspectives in Medical Ethics*. Bloomington and Indianapolis: Indiana University Press.

Kuhse, Helga. (1997). *Caring: Nurses, Women and Ethics*. Oxford: Blackwell Publishers Ltd.

Larrabee, Mary Jeanne (ed). (1993). *An Ethic of Care*. New York and London: Routledge Press.

Manning, Rita. (1992). *Speaking from the Heart: A Feminist Perspective on Ethics*. Lanham, MD: Rowman and Littlefield.

Murdoch, Iris. (1971). *The Sovereignty of Good*. New York: Schocken Books.

Noddings, Nel. (1984). *Caring: a Feminine Approach to Ethics and Moral Education*. Berkeley: University of California Press.

◆ ◆ ◆ ◆ ◆

KARIN BROWN

Buddhist Ethics

Buddhist philosophy originates with the teachings of the Buddha (566-486 BCE) which are framed by the goal of eliminating suffering. Buddhist ethics aims at providing the path to achieving this goal. The teachings of the Buddha were preserved as an oral tradition for 400 hundred years until compiled by monks in the Pali canon around the first century BCE. (There are many schools of Buddhist thought, but they share the same core teachings.) No separate discourse for Buddhist ethics exists in the ancient sources. Rather, a sophisticated and profound ethical theory is found throughout the canon and is inseparable from the rest of the philosophy. Works devoted explicitly to Buddhist ethics are recent, blending material from various sources into a more well-defined moral theory.

The Foundation of the Theory

Buddhist ethics is grounded in a theory of the nature of reality. It is logically embedded in Buddhist causality and the concomitant notion of non-substantiality. The presumption is that everything has a cause, that something cannot arise out of nothing, and that all phenomena thus fall under causal law. It follows that everything depends on something, indeed everything, else. This is known as the principle of dependent origination, and it lies at the heart of Buddhist philosophy.

On a physical level every object obviously depends on a variety of causes and conditions. For instance, a table is made of wood, which comes from trees, and trees depend on water, earth, and sunlight. The table comes into existence because of the carpenter, who also depends on food, air, water, etc. No element in nature can be conceived of as not connected to a myriad of others. We can also understand this principle conceptually. That is, this is a table by virtue of our definition of it; at other times the wood may be firewood, a chair, or a bat. No element or object possesses an intrinsic, independent identity.

The principle of interdependence naturally leads to the conclusion that there is no separate self or soul either. In addition, if everything is subject to causation, then everything is also constantly changing and is impermanent. According to Buddhist philosophy, a person is a combination of five fluctuating aggregates (body, sensation, perception, dispositions, and consciousness). We cannot claim that any of these constitutes an intransigent self.

The concept of dependency entails significant moral implications. From our dependency and interconnectedness with others, a sense of obligation and concern about the well-being of others follows. Since we are ultimately dependent on every aspect of the universe, ethical consequences follow regarding social philosophy, attitudes towards animals, and environmental ethics. Thus, understanding interdependence brings with it respect for nature and all living things.

Further moral implications ensue from the view of "no self." Without a permanent, fixed self-identity, one is not invested in one's own ego. Selflessness and other-directed actions follow. That is, without being preoccupied with oneself, a selfless concern for the well being of others becomes possible. Egoism is replaced by the idea that distinction between self and others is an illusion.

The most important manifestation of the Buddhist view of causality is the law of karma, which is a natural law. Karma, literally means actions. The principle that every effect has a cause means that actions have consequences for oneself and others. Karmic effects can be twofold, external and internal. One's actions affect others and accordingly accumulate merit or demerit. Immoral actions, such as killing, stealing, and lying, result in bad karma; good deeds result in good karma. Accepting a belief in reincarnation, people are reborn according to the moral ledger of their actions. The family one is born into, one's professional life, one's character, and even one's physical appearance may manifest past karma. The second aspect of karma is psychological, the way in which karma affects the agent. Here karma is a psychological law, the law of causation applied to mental events. Immoral actions have negative effects because they are embedded in states such as anger, resentment, and violence. Negative thoughts and emotions lead to anxiety, even depression, they cause internal turmoil, and they are in themselves forms of suffering. By harming others one harms oneself. Positive thoughts and emotions lead to calm and satisfaction. Belief in reincarnation is not necessary for appreciating the psychological aspect of karma.

Karma is also a moral law. Unlike the system of rewards and punishments in monotheistic religions, in Buddhism, without a god, responsibility for one's destiny lies within oneself. By understanding how character and events come about, we learn to re-direct the course of our lives, as the Buddha outlined in presenting his Four Noble Truths.

Four Noble Truths

The core of Buddhist teachings is expressed in the Buddha's Four Noble Truths, his first sermon. The Four Noble Truths sketch a moral path. The assumption is that all beings wish to avoid suffering and attain happiness. Buddhist ethics begins with the desire to end suffering, and Buddhist concepts of right and wrong follow. The Four Noble Truths provide an analysis of what causes suffering on the one hand and what brings peace and happiness on the other.

The first Noble Truth is the truth of suffering. The point is to identify the nature of suffering as a problem in order to eliminate suffering. The principle is that suffering pervades human existence. Buddhism identifies a broad spectrum of phenomena as suffering, and areas causing psychological and moral problems are broader than what we find in Western moral theories. Birth, sickness, old age, death, as well as pain, grief, and sorrow are all forms of suffering, but even pleasurable experiences cause suffering because of their transient nature. A new car, a new promotion, or a new relationship are only new for a short while. If our well-being depends on these highlights, we are subject to constant ups and downs. Not getting what one wants is suffering. Here the Buddha is referring to the idea that whenever there is a gap between what we have and what we want, or who we are and who we want to be, we will suffer. Expectations embedded in ignorance of the principle of dependent origination lead to suffering. Assuming a fixed, permanent self makes one a slave to the demands of the ego; one's social status and material possessions become central, and we try to satisfy aspects of an existence that cannot be satisfied because it does not exist *per se*.

The second Noble Truth identifies the origin of suffering. Desire and attachment cause suffering. Craving and attachment refer not only to pleasure and to material goods, but also to ideals, theories, and beliefs. Desires are viewed as insatiable, and thus in principle they cannot be satisfied. All forms of suffering, from personal problems to political struggles such as poverty and war, can be viewed as rooted in selfish cravings and desires and in attachment to material goods, ideologies, or religions.

The three roots of evil are greed, hatred, and delusion. Here the principle of causality and karma applies not only to action but also to intentions, thoughts, and feelings. Negative thoughts give rise to offensive speech and violent actions, just as sympathetic and compassionate thoughts give rise to kind words and actions. Thus, thoughts and feelings have karmic effects as well. Wishing someone ill is not morally neutral. In this sense, Buddhist philosophy offers a deeper analysis of morality by including human psychology as a cause of our behavior. This link between psychology and ethics is a central feature of Buddhism. The second Noble Truth shows that what causes psychological suffering also causes immorality. As the goal is to eliminate suffering, one must consider one's state of mind.

The third Noble Truth concerns the cessation of suffering and the possibility of attaining nirvana. Nirvana is mostly described in negative terms as it is impossible to convey this transcendent state rationally. Several Buddhist scholars refer to nirvana as a moral state because it includes the cessation of the causes of immorality, i.e., greed, hatred, delusion, desire, and attachment. Negative emotions or mental states are eradicated as well. The goal is to eliminate the cycle of birth and death, although, as mentioned previously, this point is not essential to the moral theory.

The Fourth Noble truth is the truth of the Eight-Fold Path. The Eight-Fold Path lies at the core of Buddhist practice. It embodies the main principles of Buddhism and represents the middle way prescribed by the Buddha between asceticism and self-indulgence. The path entails three aspects: wisdom, morality and meditation. Wisdom pertains to understanding the true nature of reality, that suffering is grounded in ignorance. Moral conduct is a way to purify one's actions, which also purifies one's motives. Meditation creates awareness and mental discipline. This path also embodies one of the main principles in Buddhist philosophy—non-violence.

The Eight-Fold Path entails the following: 1. Right view—that suffering originates in ignorance; hence understanding the true nature of reality is necessary for liberation. 2. Right resolve—after understanding the causes of suffering, one needs to intend to change them. 3. Right speech—one's words should be used only constructively, not destructively; one's speech should be honest and non-violent. 4. Right action—one should act in non-destructive, non-violent ways. 5. Right livelihood—one's livelihood should not involve harm to others, sentient beings, or the environment. 6. Right effort—the recognition that this path is not easy and requires work; one needs to replace negative emotions by positive ones, selfish motivations by selfless ones, unwholesome mental states by wholesome ones. 7. Right mindfulness—creates self-awareness essential for combating aggression and negative motivations. 8. Right concentration—meditation and stillness allow deeper insights. The Eight-Fold Path underscores how ethics are essential to eliminate suffering.

Virtue Ethics

In philosophy, virtue ethics concerns one's character. Beyond analyzing the causes of immorality,

Buddhist ethics proffers positive reasons to behave ethically and to resist unethical tendencies. There are four cardinal virtues: loving kindness, compassion, sympathetic joy, and equanimity. These are incompatible with their opposites and serve as antidotes to their negative counterparts. Loving kindness, the aspiration for another's well being, is incompatible with hatred for others. Compassion, the hope that others be free from suffering, is incompatible with cruelty. Sympathetic joy, the ability to truly rejoice in another's success, is incompatible with envy. Equanimity, being serene and of an even mind, helps dissolve desire and aversion. Cultivating these virtues, then, is an important part of Buddhist morality. Practicing virtues leads to thinking about others, identifying with others, and experiencing selflessness. Considering the positive effects of these virtues, we can see that by helping others one also helps oneself.

Ethical Precepts

Buddhist ethics also includes a normative component, and there are several sets of precepts governing action. Five basic precepts pertain to the lay person: no killing, no stealing, no lying, no sexual misconduct, and no intoxication. Additional sets of eight and ten precepts guide lay persons in deepening their practice. There are over two hundred precepts for monastic life.

Classification of Buddhist Ethics

Buddhist ethics is an ethics of enlightenment and compassion. As a non-authoritarian philosophy, clinging to scriptures or theory is viewed negatively. Truth can only be attained by one's own authority. Tolerance follows this anti-fundamentalist approach, with wisdom and compassion inseparably linked. By contrast, in Aristotle for instance, morality is a means to an end, to happiness. The Buddhist concept of nirvana as a moral state indicates that morality is not merely a means to enlightenment, but an end in itself as a feature of enlightenment.

Buddhist Economics

Economic teachings are scattered throughout Buddhist scriptures. "Right livelihood" is one of the requirements of the Eight-Fold Path. In applying the principles of non-violence and not harming others, right livelihood means that one should refrain from making one's living through any profession bringing harm to people, sentient beings, or the environment. Therefore the Buddha denounced professions that trade in weapons, drugs, or poisons, that violate human beings, or that kill animals. It follows that Buddhist economics cannot be a discipline separate from other aspects of life, notably from Buddhist ethics. Economics becomes a subset of morality and a normative social science with moral considerations providing the framework for economic thought. From this perspective, and given the principle of interdependence, economic decisions cannot be made without taking into consideration individuals, society, and the environment. One cannot consider costs alone. If economic decisions are made solely on the basis of profit and loss they are the source of social and environmental problems, rather than positive solutions.

Given the goal in Buddhist philosophy of liberation, well being cannot be defined by consumption or the accumulation of goods. Nevertheless, Buddhism is by no means adverse to wealth. On the contrary, wealth prevents poverty, about which the Buddha claims "Hunger is the greatest illness." The concept of the middle way rejects the extremes of poverty or seeking riches for their own sake. Moderation, simplicity, non-violence, and non-exploitation are watchwords for economic activity, and the accumulation of wealth must also be carried out without violating any of the Five Precepts against killing, stealing, lying, sexual misconduct, and taking intoxicants. Being born into wealth is considered a result of good karma, and wealth provides an opportunity to practice generosity. Sharing wealth supports individual well being and the community.

The goal of liberation implies that wealth is only a means to an end. If greed, craving, and attachment cause suffering and if one's attitude toward wealth includes these dispositions, wealth will bring suffering rather than enjoyment or solutions to the problem of suffering. In addition, economic activity motivated by greed will yield different results than when motivated by the desire for well being. Greed leads to over-consumption and needless accumulation of goods, whereas the desire for well being leads to moderation, balance, and sustainability. Distinctions between right and wrong consumption and use follow, given these attitudes towards wealth and its pursuit.

Buddhist philosophy consistently addresses the motivation behind human activity, and in the end the causes of suffering, unethical behavior, and immoral economic activity are the same. Thus ethics and economics are integrated through causal analysis and consequently provide guidelines that aim at both individual and social transformation.

FURTHER READING AND REFERENCES

Dharmasiri, Gunapala. (1989). *Fundamentals of Buddhist Ethics*. Antioch, California: Golden Leaves Publishing Company.

Harvey, Peter. (2000). *An Introduction to Buddhist Ethics*. Cambridge: Cambridge University Press.

The Journal of Buddhist Ethics, published online, <http://jbe.gold.au.uk>.

Keown, Damien. (2001). *The Nature of Buddhist Ethics* (2nd ed.). New York: Palgrave.

Nakasone, Ronald Y. (1990). *Ethics of Enlightenment: Essays and Sermons in Search of a Buddhist Ethics*. Fremont, California: Dharma Cloud Publishers.

Payutto, P.A. (1994). *Buddhist Economics: A Middle Way for the Market Place*. From <http://www.urbandharma.org/udharma2/becono.html/>.

Saddhatissa, Hammalawa. (1997). *Buddhist Ethics* (2nd ed.). Boston: Wisdom Publications.

Schumacher, E.F. (1973). Buddhist Economics. *Small Is Beautiful: Economics as if People Mattered*. New York, Hagerstown, San Francisco, London: Harper & Row Publishers.

◆ ◆ ◆ ◆ ◆

RICHARD M. GLATZ

Aristotelean Virtue Ethics and the Recommendations of Morality

Virtue theories of ethics—notably, theories like those advanced by Aristotle and a number of other ancient philosophers—are markedly different from other, more "traditional" theories of ethics. In the (translated) words of Socrates, "ethics is no smaller matter than how one ought to live." In the more traditional kinds of ethical theories—consequentialist theories like John Stuart Mill's utilitarianism and deontological theories like that advanced by Immanuel Kant—the question of how one ought to live is answered on a case-by-case basis. Such traditional theories of ethics focus on individual actions and (in light of various factors including the circumstances under which the action is to be performed and the intentions or motives of the agent who is to perform the action) classify given actions as *right, wrong, obligatory, permissible, impermissible*, and the like. In this way, the non-virtue based theories of ethics offer a (often) formulaic and typically straightforwardly applicable procedure for determining which of the courses of action available to us at a given time is the course of action we ought to pursue.

Virtue theories of ethics are not like this. Virtue theories of ethics supply neither a list of rules for conduct nor a procedure for picking the morally best course of action in a given situation. Virtue theories of ethics issue neither universal moral principles such as "it is wrong to lie" nor circumscribed moral judgments such as "it would be wrong for John to lie to his wife about the fact that he lost their mortgage payment last night betting against the Bears." Virtue theories of ethics instead issue moral judgments such as "honesty is a virtue" and "John is vicious (viceful)."

The primary reason that virtue theories of ethics differ in this way from other approaches to ethics is that virtue theories of ethics take *agents* and their *characters* to be the primary objects of moral scrutiny. Whereas consequentialists and deontologists develop theories for morally evaluating particular *actions* (as performed in particular circumstances and for particular reasons), virtue theorists develop theories for morally evaluating the *character traits* that underwrite agents' performances of those actions.

This aspect of the virtue theoretic approach to ethics is responsible not only for the fact that the judgments rendered by virtue theories differ so markedly from the judgments rendered by other kinds of theories of ethics; it is responsible also for a common objection to the virtue theoretic approach. It is thought by some that virtue ethics is unappealing because it does not provide action-guiding principles. Although it might be difficult to determine which action is the correct one on the basis of consequentialist or deontological principles, at least those principles provide some kind of basis for morally evaluating actions. Virtue theories of ethics, on the other hand, provide no basis for such an evaluation.

Even if this kind of objection does not show that virtue ethics is theoretically flawed, it does pose a particularly poignant problem for attempts (like those to be considered in this chapter) to employ a virtue theory of ethics to answer applied ethical questions. For this reason, the presentation of virtue ethics to follow is formulated with an eye on determining how virtue ethics can help us understand how to live

our lives—our personal, as well as our professional, lives—and how that kind of understanding can help us make decisions when confronted by morally difficult situations.

1. Aristotle's Virtue Ethics, In Sketch

It is fairly commonplace for us to think of ethics in terms of questions like "which actions are right and which are wrong?" and "which actions am I morally obligated to perform?" For Aristotle, however, the fundamental questions of ethics are instead questions like "what is a good *person*?" and "what is the best way *to live*?"

In pursuing answers to these questions Aristotle begins his principal ethical work—the *Nicomachean Ethics*—with a detailed discussion of "the good" for man. Through a variety of arguments that need not concern us here Aristotle reaches the conclusion that the highest good for man is *happiness*. Be warned, however, that the term Aristotle uses here, "*eudaimonea*," does not mean what we typically mean by "*happiness*." The English word "happiness" would be appropriate to describe the kind of *feeling* that I have when eating chocolate or the kind of *mood* into which most people are put by taking a walk on the beach with a lover. Aristotle's notion of *eudaimonea*, on the other hand, is meant to capture the kind of enduring *state* that one is in when, through *reasoned activity*, one has accomplished a life filled with all of the things that make a life wonderful and "choiceworthy." (It is often suggested that a more appropriate English translation of "*eudaimonea*" would be "(human) flourishing.")

The foregoing characterization of *eudaimonea* is by no means a definition. The important thing to remember is that, unlike John Stuart Mill's notion of happiness as pleasure, *eudaimonea* is neither a *feeling* nor a *mood*. Rather, it is a *state of being* for which any reasonable person would strive. As such, Aristotle claims that *eudaimonea* is the chief good for man and the end to which all of our actions ultimately aim. It is also important to notice the role that is here played by the notion of *reasoned activity*. *Eudaimonea* is a state that is only attainable for rational beings that use their reason to achieve ends. It is a kind of *psychological* happiness that cannot be attained by creatures that lack the kinds of mental lives required to engage in projects or plan their lives.

In part to determine how a person can achieve *eudaimonea* and in part to show that *eudaimonea* really is the chief good for man, Aristotle takes up the question of what a *good person* is. It is instructive to look at this part of his investigation as a particular instance of a general question form, namely:

(Q1)   What is a good *X*?

Aristotle takes it, perhaps mysteriously, that in order to answer an instance of (Q1) we must first find an answer to a subsidiary question of the following form:

(Q2)   What is the *characteristic function* of an *X*?

As an example to see what Aristotle has in mind here, consider an axe. On Aristotle's view in order to find out what a good axe is we must first understand what the function of an axe is. Of course, axes may be put to various different uses—we might use an axe to split firewood, chop down a tree, drive a nail, slice a loaf of bread, kill an enemy, or even direct traffic. Some of these uses we regard as deviant (whether morally or merely socially) while others we regard as perfectly normal. The reason for this, I shall hazard, is that we understand that the characteristic function or purpose of an axe is to chop.

When it comes to *artifacts*—objects that have been created for a particular purpose—it is to be expected that the function of an artifact is the purpose for which it has been made. Aristotle's notion of a function extends beyond this, however. Indeed, the fact that artifacts have been constructed for a particular purpose only makes it easier to see what function they have. For Aristotle, however, what the function of a thing is depends not upon how it is used or why it was made (if it was made) but on what activity that thing is best suited to do. Consider, for example, a person who has designed and uses a pair of tools—one for the slicing of bread and another for the chopping of firewood. Suppose that the tool created for the slicing of bread is exactly like what we call an "axe" and that the tool created for the chopping of firewood is exactly like what we call a "bread knife." When this artisan slices bread for his dinner he takes out his bread-slicing tool—a heavy, wedged blade attached to a meter long stick—and proceeds to hack at the loaf. The result is, of course, "slices" of bread that are mauled, flattened, and irregular. When the artisan chops wood for his fire, on the other hand, he takes out his wood-chopping tool—a lightweight, serrated blade attached to a hand-sized handle—and proceeds to saw, laboriously, at the logs. The process takes many hours and gives the artisan many splinters.

Holding aside judgment of the artisan regarding his rationality and intelligence, what is there to be said about his bread-slicer and wood-chopper? Although each has been made (and is used) for a particular purpose, it seems that the proper, characteristic *function* of the artisan's bread-slicer is to chop wood and that of the artisan's wood-chopper is to slice bread. I venture to say that if we approached the artisan as he swung his bread-slicer over his head, we would be correct to stop him, say "excuse me, but you are using that incorrectly," and hand him his wood-chopper. The reason for this is that the particular *qualities* of each tool make those tools especially suited for certain uses.

Let this serve, then, as a general approach for answering questions of the form (Q2) above. If a thing, *X*, has particular qualities that make it best suited for a certain activity, then that activity is (part of) the *function* of *X*. In light of this, what (if anything) might the function of a human be?[1]

Aristotle considers and rejects the suggestion that the function of a human is nourishment and growth. Given that these activities are common to plants, and given that Aristotle is looking for a function that is peculiar to humans, Aristotle concludes that nourishment and growth are not the function of humans. Aristotle also considers and rejects the suggestion that the function of a human is a life of perception or sensation as these are common to animals. Aristotle concludes that a life of *reasoned activity* is distinctively human and a kind of activity for which we are particularly well suited—indeed, it seems to be the activity that we are best at doing not only in the sense that we are best at doing *that activity* (from among activities that we do) but also in the sense that *we* (among beings who can engage in that activity) are the best at it. As a result, (if humans have a function, then) the function of a human is *to engage in reason-governed activity*—making plans, solving problems, communicating, interacting socially with other people, *et cetera*.

Let us assume that Aristotle is correct that humans have a function and that engaging in reason-governed activity is that function. We now have an answer to the question of form (Q2) above, but what of (Q1)?

Consider, again, an axe. What is a good axe? To answer this question we must first answer the subsidiary question "what is the *function* of an axe?" As discussed above, the function of an axe seems obviously to be *chopping*. What, then, is a good axe? An obvious and apparently trivial answer to this question is that a good axe is an axe that chops well. On Aristotle's view this is correct, but incomplete. In the direction of a complete answer, Aristotle would claim that a good axe is an axe that possesses the *excellences* of an axe, where the excellences of an axe are whatever *characteristics* an axe might have that contribute to the fulfillment or performance of the *function* of an axe. So the excellences of an axe are those characteristics that contribute to chopping—sharpness, weight (heavy but wieldable), balance (weighted near to head rather than the handle), sturdiness, *et cetera*. A good axe is one that possesses such characteristics.

As should be expected, Aristotle's answer to the question of what a good person is resembles this account of a good axe. A good person is a person who possesses the excellences of a person, where the excellences of a person are whatever characteristics a person might possess that contribute to the fulfillment of the human function—engaging in reason-governed activity. These characteristics or excellences are the *virtues*.

Aristotle distinguishes between two kinds of virtues—intellectual virtues and moral virtues. Intellectual virtues are characteristics like practical wisdom (wisdom with respect to making plans and achieving one's goals), philosophical wisdom, intuitive reason, *et cetera*. About these I will say no more than to note that lacking the intellectual virtues, one would face great difficulties in successfully engaging in the kind of life planning and social interaction that Aristotle understands by *reason-governed activity*.

Aristotle defines the moral virtues to be *traits of character* that consist in a *disposition to choose the mean*. In many circumstances—facing fear, managing money, pursuing pleasures, *et cetera*—there are two extremes, one of excess and the other of deficit. There are people who, in the face of frightful things, feel too much fear and are brought by their fear to flee from dangers that are minor or to "freeze up" and fail to accomplish important things. Such people are cowards and cowardice is their vice. On the other hand, there are people who, in the face of frightful things, feel too much confidence and are brought by their over-confidence to plunge into dangers that are beyond their abilities to handle. Such people are rash and rashness is their vice. A person is brave who, in the face of frightful things, feels the right amount of fear and the right amount of confidence and acts in accordance with these appropriate feelings.[2]

It is important to notice that Aristotle claims that it is virtuous to be disposed to choose the mean *relative to us*. What is excessive or deficient for one person might not be for another. A person trained in *khav magha* might exhibit bravery by facing a mugger with a knife while a wimpy philosopher such as myself would almost certainly be exhibiting rashness by doing the same thing. As Aristotle says, "... fear and confidence and appetite and anger and pity and in general pleasure and pain may be felt both too much and too little, and in both cases not well; but to feel them at the right times, with reference to the right objects, toward the right people, with the right motive, and in the right way, is what is both intermediate and best, and this is characteristic of virtue."[3] We must bear in mind, of course, that the right amount of an emotion to feel might depend upon the person who feels it.

According to Aristotle, then, possessing a virtue amounts to having the disposition to feel the right amount of a given emotion in the relevant circumstances and to act in accordance with that appropriately balanced emotion; possessing a vice amounts to having the disposition to feel either too much or too little of a given emotion in the relevant circumstances and to act in accordance with that inappropriately balanced emotion. Recall that Aristotle understands the virtues to be human excellences in the sense that they contribute to the well functioning of man—that is, to the successful engagement in reason-governed activity. When a person engages in reason-governed activity they are bound to be confronted by situations that evoke some kind of emotional response—fear, anger, sympathy, and the like. When a viceful person is confronted by such situations, their actions will be governed by inappropriate emotion responses—perhaps they will feel too much anger and behave wrathfully, or perhaps they will feel too little sympathy and behave callously. It is not Aristotle's position that their behavior then transgresses some kind of moral edict or law and is therefore wrong. Rather, their behavior fails to contribute to their success in whatever reason-governed activity in which they are engaged—be it business dealings, familial relations, or political decision-making. As the ultimate goal of all such activities is *eudaimonea*, the viceful person will not achieve true

happiness. Only by possessing and acting from the *virtues* can we succeed in our reason-governed lives and thereby achieve *eudaimonea*.

It is important to note here that Aristotle places primary moral significance on the character of an agent but places a kind of derivative or secondary moral significance on the actions that the agent performs. Although it is, for Aristotle, something of a misnomer to characterize a particular action as a brave one, such characterizations are commonplace for us and even present in Aristotle's writing. Strictly speaking it is the *agent* who is brave when performing a particular action, not the action itself. We might be tempted to think of a brave action simply as whatever action a brave person would do, it is very important for Aristotle that the action in question be performed *because* of the brave character of the agent. It is possible for an agent to exhibit cowardice when fleeing in the face of danger even if a brave agent would also flee in the same situation. If the agent in question flees as a result of overly pronounced fear, then the agent is not acting on the basis of feeling the right amount of fear given the situation. The fact that the situation calls for the agent to be afraid and flee does not change the fact that the agent in question actually did flee as a result of his cowardice.

There is another reason that actions themselves are morally significant on Aristotle's view. According to Aristotle, we develop and maintain the virtues through reflective training and habituation. Indeed, the root of the term "ethics" is "*ethos*," the Greek term for *habit*. People are neither virtuous nor vicious by nature. Rather, we become virtuous or vicious by repeatedly engaging in virtuous or vicious activity respectively. As a result, although virtue theories of ethics are not action-guiding in the same way that deontological and consequentialist theories are, virtue theories of ethics do call for us to routinely engage in the right kind of behavior. By engaging in viceful activity we damage our character and become vicious; only by engaging in virtuous activity do we develop and preserve a virtuous character and ensure that we will be neither overrun by our emotions nor emotionally detached in our dealings with others.[4]

2. *Toward Applied Virtue Ethics*

The foregoing sketch of Aristotle's theory is meant to show how Aristotle approaches what he takes to be the fundamental questions of ethics—"what is a good person?" and "how ought one to live?" According to Aristotle, we ought to live in accordance with the virtues. As humans our function is to engage in reason-governed activity. The virtues are human excellences in the sense that they contribute to fulfilling this function; the vices are human defects in the sense that they detract from fulfilling this function. Good people develop and maintain the virtues through reflective habituation and thereby enable themselves to achieve *eudaimonea*—the highest good for man, true happiness.

For many of us, our professional lives are lives of reasoned-activity. Business interactions—buying, selling, producing, serving—are social interactions. Social interactions generally require communication, trust, agreements, *et cetera*, all of which require engaging one another in a reasoned way. No doubt, then, we are required to conduct ourselves in our professional lives in accordance with the virtues. In this way, virtue ethics applies to our professional lives just as it applies to our personal lives. A truly virtuous person would not simply exhibit the virtues while dealing with family and friends and then go to work and deal with co-workers, suppliers, customers, and bosses in non-virtuous ways. If someone does exhibit this kind of moral two-facedness between their private and professional lives, then they really do not have the dispositions that embody the virtues—they are mere pretenders of virtue. Furthermore, if a truly virtuous person were to leave virtue aside in their professional dealings, then that person would eventually habituate themselves contrary to the virtues and would become vicious.

There is another way in which to apply a virtue theory of ethics to the applied moral issues that face professionals. In what follows I will develop a certain Aristotelian view of what is often termed "role-differentiated morality." Discussions of role-differentiated morality are attempts to understand apparently different moral requirements that we face as a result of occupying certain roles. With respect to the welfare of a child, parents have different moral responsibilities than do teachers who have still different moral responsibilities than neighbors or strangers. By pursuing a career in law enforcement or medicine one chooses to place one's self in a *role* that carries different moral responsibilities than other lines of work. Following Aristotle we may arrive at a certain understanding of the moral significance of different roles as they apply to businesspeople.

To begin with an example to illustrate how this is to work, consider what makes a computer a good one. The Aristotelian analysis would begin by identifying the *function* of a computer and then identifying as *excellences* for a computer those characteristics that a computer might possess that would contribute to its performing its functioning well. There are, however, many different kinds of computers with various different functions. My computer does little beyond word processing and spreadsheet managing. My parents recently bought a computer especially designed for managing the many pictures of grandchildren that they now have. So-called "gamers" have computers especially designed for playing video games, often networked for multi-player gaming. The computers in many business offices have specialized software for whatever kind of computing is required for a business of that sort.

What all of these different kinds of computers have in common, I suspect, is that they all serve the function of running software, taking input from a user, and displaying output to that user. Excellences for computers *considered simply as computers* would include characteristics that contribute to performing those functions well—fast, reliable processors, memory that can be written (and rewritten), user-friendly interfacing, *et cetera*. Such characteristics as these are analogous to the *human* virtues that Aristotle discusses—those being the excellences of a person *considered simply as a person*. Consider, however, a particular computer considered specifically as a *gaming* computer. The function of a gaming computer (beyond the basic function of a computer) is to allow the user to play games. To be a good gaming computer, then, a computer will need to have characteristics that contribute to that function—a high quality graphics card, suitable controller ports, hardware and software that enables fast, reliable networking, *et cetera*. While possessing such characteristics makes a gaming computer better, my glorified word-processor would not be improved by possessing those characteristics.

It is in this way that I suggest we handle the issue of role-differentiated morality from an Aristotelian perspective. Considering, for example, a corporate executive not simply as a person but *as a corporate executive* we might get some indication of how corporate executives ought to conduct themselves professionally. To do this, of course, we must first consider what the *function* of a corporate executive is.

This seems to be an easy question. The function of a corporate executive is to run a corporation or some aspect of its operation. Let us imagine, then, that we are dealing with Melissa, the CEO of some particular corporation—say, a pharmaceutical company. Melissa's function (considering her as the CEO of the pharmaceutical company) is to run that pharmaceutical company. To see how Melissa ought to conduct herself in the course of her job and to see what sorts of characteristics would contribute to Melissa's successful execution of her job we must first determine what successful running of the pharmaceutical company would amount to, and to determine this we must determine what the purpose of the pharmaceutical company is.

An overly cynical and simplistic answer that I would like to dismiss up front is that the purpose of the pharmaceutical company is to turn as large a profit as possible for the owners. Certainly part of the purpose or function of a corporation is to be profitable, but we must recognize that a pharmaceutical company is part of a wider social network that includes chemical companies (as suppliers), hospitals and private individuals (as customers), employees (as employees), and even other pharmaceutical companies (as competitors). I am not suggesting that it is the purpose of a company to operate for the advantage of each of these groups, but it must be understood how these groups socially interact with the company in question in determining how an executive ought to engage in the reason-governed activity that is her job.

This being said, I think that we should consider the purpose of a company like the pharmaceutical company imagined above in terms of the manufacture and distribution of pharmaceuticals. For a corporate executive like Melissa to fulfill her professional function well she must (at least) maintain trusting and mutually beneficial relationships among the parties involved in accomplishing these goals. In order to do this, I suggest, Melissa would be well served to think of suppliers, employees, customers, and others not simply as entities that satisfy some need of the company, but as entities whose interests actually matter. I suspect that such an attitude will be engendered by the general human virtues as discussed by Aristotle—for according to those we must choose the mean even in pursuing such things as profit. Even so, there might be room here for some distinctively corporate virtues. By following this kind of approach to role-differentiated morality we might be able to make some progress toward professional ethics in general and business ethics in particular.

NOTES

1 Aristotle offers no good argument for the conclusion that man has a function in the first place. However, he does think that man has a function and on the basis of the assumption

that that is so concludes as indicated in the text.

2 Aristotle develops similar analyses regarding money, pleasure, honor, anger, social intercourse, *et cetera*.

3 Aristotle, *Nicomachean Ethics*, II : 6, 18-23 (W.D. Ross, transl.); from McKeon, Richard (ed.) *Introduction to Aristotle*, Random House, Inc. (New York), 1947.

4 I have left out of this sketch of Aristotle's view the role that is played by *external goods*—wealth, health, good looks, pleasures, and other goods that Aristotle sees as necessary for *eudaimonea*. According to Aristotle, such external goods are achieved quite often by luck and, as a result, are seldom the sorts of things that we have much control over. What we do have control over is the state of our character—whether we habituate ourselves to have the virtues or whether we habituate ourselves to have the vices. It would be nice if we could achieve *eudaimonea* simply by attending to our characters in this way, but Aristotle thinks that virtue is insufficient for *eudaimonea*. To achieve *eudaimonea* we must not only have a good character, we must also have the good fortune to have a life filled with external goods.

◆ ◆ ◆ ◆ ◆

DAVID MEELER

Utilitarianism

In everyday life, we make a host of value judgments. Some of these have nothing to do with morality, such as which shoes are better for running or which restaurant has more tasty food. Other value judgments are obviously moral. For instance, many people think that murder is wrong or stealing violates basic human rights. Most of the ordinary claims we make can be tested for truth. If I say "The class average on the mid-term is 78," we can verify this. But how are we to test value claims? Suppose I say "Espresso is good." How can we determine if I am telling the truth? Maybe I just mean "I like espresso." Suppose instead that I say "Charity is good," or "Rape is wrong." Should the test be any different? Many people begin testing claims by checking for shared meaning of the terminology. If "espresso" is just my word for "mass murder" then we have a problem. Now, you and I probably won't have radical confusion between words like "espresso" and "mass murder," but terms like "good" and "bad" aren't always straightforward. So, one important way that many philosophers begin addressing issues in ethics is to investigate the *meaning* of our value terms. One of the factors differentiating utilitarians from other ethicists is their definition of value-terms, and this is where we'll start our look into utilitarianism.

To begin with, utilitarianism instructs us to do the greatest good we can for the greatest number of our ethical compatriots. Although some elements of utilitarian theory can be traced to Epicurus (341-270 BCE), its fullest form is that associated with Jeremy Bentham (1748-1832 CE) and John Stuart Mill (1806-73 CE). These two philosophers developed many of the principles and approaches still used by utilitarians today. Like many philosophical theories, it is easy to provide a quick statement of the key themes in utilitarianism, though it can be difficult to master the subtleties inherent in a richer understanding of the view. Let me start with a simplistic version.

In its most basic form, utilitarian thinking is associated with hedonism. Hedonism is the view that good and bad go along with pleasure and pain. Bentham's utilitarian foundations were hedonistic. When investigating the times we use the word "good," Bentham noticed that it's usually when we are talking about things that bring us pleasure (or at least diminish our pain); and those things we call "bad" are those that cause us pain (or take away our pleasure). For instance, I get pleasure from chocolate-chip cookies, while you may find apples to be a source of endless joy. Similarly, studying for math tests always brought me distress, while some people are perpetually vexed by writing philosophy papers. In terms of a utilitarian theory then, the hedonist version says we should generate the most pleasure (or diminish as much pain) as we can for the relevant moral parties. This aspect of hedonism only describes how people use the terms, and as a result this is referred to as "descriptive" hedonism. From this simple beginning based on the psychological preferences of people, Bentham goes on to suggest that we *ought* to promote pleasure and diminish pain in our daily choices and activities. Thus, Bentham shifts from speaking descriptively about the world to offering the guidance of a standard for behavior, which is called a "norm." As a result, we say that this version is "normative" hedonism.

This view sounds simple enough, but almost immediately an interesting question emerges. Is it the cookie that is good? Or the pleasure the cookie causes? For hedonists, it is really the pleasure or pain, and not the cookie itself that is the root of our value terms. Cookies are good because they *generate* pleasure; of course, too many cookies are bad because that produces displeasure. But the pleasure or pain we feel is an *effect* of some other cause. The general approach that focuses on effects, or outcomes, is called consequentialism because the value of an action, or a thing, is found in the consequences that result. Consequentialism, in general, has a strong foothold in common sense. Most of us believe that we should endeavor to improve the world. At the least, most people try to make things better for themselves and their families. When we strive to make the world a better place, we are trying to achieve certain outcomes, or consequences that we think are good; and we judge the value of our choices in part by the quality of the results. For example, we often trade today's struggle for tomorrow's gain, such as studying hard and making good grades in order to get better jobs that make it easier to provide well for our families. And when we assess our actions (as well as the actions of others) we generally look to see what good came from our choices, or whether any harm was done. The old adages "All's well that ends well" and "No harm; no foul" nicely sum up this intuition. Hedonism is merely one kind of utilitarian theory. We can say that utilitarianism is the most famous consequentialist theory.

While the basic idea of hedonism has some intuitive appeal, several aspects remain unaddressed. For example, critics say when we rest our morality on mere pleasure we debase humanity. Common sense tells us that consequences are important, but it also seems that not all consequences are equal. The distinction that arises here is between the mere *amount* of pleasure (quantitative consequentialism) and the *kind* of pleasure we get (qualitative consequentialism). Jeremy Bentham clearly seems to have advocated quantitative consequentialism, for he famously said that playing a simple board-game has as much value as reading fine poetry, so long as equal amounts of pleasure are created. After all, different people get pleasure from different activities. John Stuart Mill, on the other hand, favored qualitative consequentialism. Mill suggests that, like diamonds, pleasures can be divided into higher and lower grades. Higher pleasures include intellectual pleasures, such as working on mathematical proofs, while lower pleasures are more basic, like sensory experiences.

Having said that, Mill's choice of what kinds of activities we include in the higher and lower pleasures is not arbitrary. His strategy is quite interesting. Mill begins with the practical notion that we must ask people to judge whether pleasures of the intellect are qualitatively better than pleasures of the body. But there is a catch. We need only adhere to the opinions of *competent* judges. If someone can experience and appreciate both types of pleasure, then they are competent judges of the relative values. This also rests firmly on common sense. If you were going to ask someone whether reggae music is better than country music would you ask someone who only liked one and hated the other? Would you ask someone who hated both? No. Any time we make a comparative value judgment between things, Mill thinks it is important to first be capable of enjoying each. Only then will you be in a position to make the call. As it turns out, Mill says, all competent judges agree that intellectual pleasures are of a higher quality than physical pleasures. Mill's move from quantitative consequentialism to qualitative consequentialism is an important development in utilitarian ethical theories.

In addition to illustrating consequentialism, the example of pleasurable cookies highlights an important ethical distinction: that between intrinsic value and extrinsic value. Intrinsic value (which you can think of as "inside" value) is the value that a thing has in and of itself. Intrinsic value is also called "inherent" value. Extrinsic value (which you may think of as "outside" value) is when one thing is valuable because it leads to something else. Extrinsic value is also called "instrumental" value because one thing is valued as a tool, or an instrument, for getting something else. Money is often used as an example of something with only extrinsic value. When you think about it, money isn't really worth much in and of itself; the greatest value found in money is that other people are willing to trade things for it. So having at least average amounts of money usually brings pleasure to people because money is a general device that can be used to get the specific things that make us happy. As a result, money is valuable for what it can get you. But not all things are like this. If you are reading this book, it is highly probable that you are a university student. As such, you may have heard the saying "Education is its own reward." The meaning of this expression is built on the idea that education has intrinsic value. Of course, we all know education has extrinsic value as well. Studies indicate that college graduates have higher earning potential over the course of their lives. So your college education will likely lead to more money over the long term. Since education has both intrinsic and extrinsic value, ethicists say that education's value is "mixed." Many things in the world have mixed value because they are valued both intrinsically and extrinsically.

As well as making the switch from quantitative consequentialism to qualitative consequentialism, Mill made another important change to Bentham's basic utilitarian idea. Where Bentham focused his analysis of value terms on pleasure and pain, Mill's emphasis is on "happiness" more generally. Although Bentham speaks of happiness and Mill understood happiness (at least in part) as related to pleasure and pain, they each emphasized a different component. So Mill's idea represents a shift in utilitarian thinking. We can paraphrase Mill's understanding of utilitarianism as follows: produce the greatest balance of happiness over unhappiness for all members of our moral community. This focus on happiness rather than pleasure is one of the most fundamental changes Mill made to the utilitarian starting points elucidated by Bentham in part because it *includes* the shift to qualitative consequentialism.

Moreover, Mill thinks that happiness holds a special place in the world: it is the only thing that we value *only* inherently. Mill's argument for this claim has two primary points. First, Mill suggests that happiness is a universal goal; the greatest proof of the desirability of happiness is the simple fact that everyone desires to be happy. Obviously, we don't all desire the same things because different things make each of us happy. But in the end, every person wants to be happy. So, one aspect of Mill's argument for the inherent value of happiness is that happiness is the end result of our various chains of extrinsically valued achievements. Perhaps you get good grades to get into a good law-school to get a high-paying job to make enough money to buy a Ferrari to make you happy. In short, we might say that all of our value-roads lead to happiness. The second important feature of Mill's argument is that happiness just doesn't work like money; we don't want happiness *because of* other things that happiness can bring. Granted, it is probably true that if you are happy then you will have more positive relationships, or make more lucrative sales, etc. Mill's point is that this is not the *reason why* we value happiness. We value happiness purely for its own sake, and not for the other things it gets us. As a general rule, we don't seek to *use* our happiness to get something else more desirable. Even asking what we expect happiness to get us reveals a fundamental misunderstanding of the inherent value we place on happiness.

Another aspect of utilitarianism—or consequentialism more generally—that we haven't addressed centers on the recipient of the outcome. Up to now I have spoken of generating good consequences for our "ethical compatriots," "members of our moral community," and for "all relevant parties," but I have left these groups undefined. So we don't know who belongs to these groups. As a result, one might readily ask some important questions of utilitarians: Should I generate good consequences for myself or my family? Should I generate good consequences for my community or for everyone? In its weakest form, utilitarianism requires me to consider the impact of my actions on all those parties who are affected. But this apparently simple idea can quickly become complicated. First, it seems that many people can be affected by a single act. Imagine that I throw a glass bottle out of my car window, which breaks in the road. Another car drives over the glass and pops a tire. Changing the tire makes the driver late to get

home, which irritates his wife so much that she kicks the family dog, which then runs out of the house down to the park and bites a child. Does the child's dog-bite *count* as part of the consequence of my littering? It is difficult to specify exactly how many extended consequences I should be held accountable for. In general, utilitarians suggest that the consequences I am responsible for are those relatively close to the action itself, so the dog-bite would not count. For most utilitarians, the driver's upset wife would not count either since there is no way I could reasonably foresee those events. However, the driver getting a flat tire does count because it is to be expected when you throw glass onto the road.

Secondly, I am probably much *more interested* in the consequences for me than I am in the consequences for others, especially those who aren't significant to me. Nevertheless, utilitarian ideals forbid me from giving more importance to my consequences over others who are affected by my actions. Traditional utilitarians like Bentham and Mill believed in strict equality among those affected by an action. In other words, when you assess the value of your actions, you must be impartial as to who gets the good or bad consequences. Benefits or burdens that fall on one person are just as important as those befalling another; even when the person is you. So I can't count my pain as more important than your pain. In fact, this facet of neutrality in classical utilitarianism requires me to treat the consequences for you as equally important as I treat the consequences for myself. From an impartial point of view, one person's happiness is as valuable as another's; and utilitarians think ethics should be done from an impartial point of view. This impersonal accounting is meant to prevent personal bias from entering our value judgments.

Third, even if we settle how many links in the consequence-chain are relevant, and I give no special weight to my own consequences, we might wonder whether the consequences for dogs, cows, chickens or fish should ever count. If the chain of consequences I am responsible for stops at the dog, then it couldn't possibly include the child's bite. According to utilitarianism, the pleasure or suffering of animals *is relevant*. For hedonists like Bentham the connection is straightforward since they focus on pleasure and pain, and many animals obviously feel both. When qualitative consequentialism like Mill's is preferred, we give intellectual happiness more weight than bodily pleasures. However, we are still required to count physical pleasures and pains as comparable to other physical effects. Intellectual pleasures might outweigh some physical suffering, but we must treat like pains alike; and since animals can feel physical pain, we must emphasize it as much as we do our own physical pain. Impartiality and universality are important features of all utilitarian thinking because utilitarians adhere to strict equality when counting the various consequences of our actions for all those affected. So the members of our moral community include all creatures capable of experiencing any *kind* of pleasure, pain, happiness or unhappiness we think is morally relevant for normal humans; and we must assess those consequences for all those closely affected by our actions.

In its most concise expression, utilitarianism instructs us to generate the greatest good for the greatest number. Perhaps many of our actions directly impact only a small number of people. However, if you are in a special role the scope of your actions might be enormous. Consider a state legislator. If you are one of the state-senators for your county, then you must consider the impact proposed laws will have on a vast number of people. Similarly, if you are a judge then your decisions will carry the weight of precedent for court cases that follow. Clearly, legislators must be concerned with the general welfare of the populace, and utilitarians say they should base their decisions on whether more overall happiness (or less overall unhappiness) will result for the largest number of people. Politicians are just as constrained by the limits of strict equality as the rest of us, which means they cannot work for special interests, for the benefit of themselves, for the benefit of their own class, or their own race, gender, etc. Strict egalitarianism requires government representatives to always work towards the maximum happiness for everyone equally.

Impartially generating happiness for as many sentient beings as you can might be all a utilitarian would need if we only assessed the value of actions *after* they occurred and the consequences could be readily determined. But when it comes to ethics, we often seek *guidance* on how we ought to act *before* we decide what to do. Thus another important distinction in utilitarian thinking is that between whether we are to focus our ethical evaluations on actual consequences or merely foreseeable consequences. On first appearance, this hardly seems like a significant distinction. Wouldn't we just use foreseeable consequences when deciding what to do ahead of time and use actual consequences when evaluating what has already been done? This is a good question, and the guidelines it suggests seem to work reasonably well much of the time. However, problem cases might emerge. Imagine that someone wants to generate substantial happiness, thinks carefully and foresees positive results; but when the plan is put in place, disastrous results follow. The foreseeable consequences were good but the actual consequences were bad. How should we assess the merits of this person and the action? Even though the results were bad, should we soften our judgment because the intentions were good? Classical utilitarians would not favor such an approach. Bentham and Mill both advocated expected utility (which is a form of foreseeable consequences) when we make plans and choose actions; they advocated judging actions based only on actual consequences. Over time, we can be expected to get better at making more accurate predictions of expected utility.

One final aspect that bears consideration is *how* consequences are to be weighted. For both Bentham and Mill, we should assess the value of our actions by determining the best balance of utility over disutility, but even that is not obviously straightforward. For instance, should we balance the *total* amount of happiness over unhappiness, or should we balance the *average* amounts of happiness and unhappiness? Traditionally, utilitarians like Bentham and Mill based their moral assessments on total happiness, rather than average happiness. Classical utilitarians said we should determine all the morally-relevant parties to the foreseeable consequences of an act, total the amount of happiness (remember, happiness is "good") that each party should get, and subtract off the total amount of unhappiness (or "bad"), and we'll have the net happiness for each person. Then we total all the net results (gains and losses) for each morally-relevant person to get a total net happiness for a proposed action. We do this for every option we are faced with, and then compare the expected total net results. We should choose to do whichever option yields the best total net outcome, regardless of who gets what allotment of happiness in each.

Criticism of Utilitarianism

Traditionally, the philosophical criticism most often mounted against utilitarianism rests on the possibility that highly positive outcomes give good reasons for using horrendous measures to get them. The colloquial expression that captures this feature of utilitarian thinking is "the end justifies the means." Imagine the vast majority of the class decided that only one student will be responsible for doing all the assignments throughout the semester, for everyone; and they chose you. By heaping all the burdens on one person, everyone else benefits. Whenever those benefits outweigh the burdens, utilitarians say that nothing immoral has been done. On a larger scale, this means that some forms of slavery are permitted by utilitarian thinking. If enough happiness is generated for enough people to outweigh the unhappiness caused for the number of slaves, then the resulting happiness justifies the means of slavery. Critics point out that slavery is just plain wrong, re-

gardless of how much happiness results. The mere fact that we *use* one person to generate happiness for another violates basic principles of justice, which require us to respect the value of persons. Such criticisms are often associated with ideas from Immanuel Kant because they are based on the inherent value of human life. Recall that utilitarians think happiness itself is the only thing that has purely inherent value, so a person's life is valuable only inasmuch as it is a source of happiness. It is this very rejection of inherent value of human life that makes utilitarianism seem so cold. *You* are not important to a utilitarian; only the happiness you experience is significant.

Case Example

A careful look at the mission statement from almost any large corporation operating in the twenty-first century will reveal a common idea. By and large, all corporations claim they seek to serve the long-term interests of their stakeholders. Stakeholders, generally, are understood as parties with a significant "stake" in the company's survival; so stakeholders tend to include such groups as investors (stockholders), employees (management and labor), customers, suppliers, and financiers (banks or other loan organizations). Naturally, the interests of the various stakeholder groups are frequently at odds with one another. For example, local communities want people employed, business taxes paid and their environment unpolluted, customers want lower priced goods while employees want higher wages, all of which compete with each other as well as cut into the higher profits desired by stockholders. So managing the overall strategy of the company means finding the best way to balance all these competing interests. In short, it means maximizing the overall long-term benefit for all.

Perhaps an example will help to illustrate both the positive and negative aspects of utilitarian principles in action. Consider the impact the last decade has had on the textile industry in the United States.

Because textile plants historically relied on agricultural products, they are most often located in rural communities; and since these communities are generally small, the textile companies tend to be significant employers in these areas. Textile plants are also often primary employers of minorities and women in their communities, which has advanced social and economic justice in America. Textile workers tend to earn more in their communities, so the jobs are coveted by local workers. Around 1997, the dollar began rising in value as many currencies throughout Southeast Asia declined rapidly. As a result, it became more expensive to produce goods in America and less expensive to import goods from Asia. Since that time an increasing number of textile jobs have been lost in America while textile imports from Asia have increased dramatically. When major employers, like textile plants, close in small communities, the effects are far reaching. Local businesses cannot sell goods and services to people who no longer earn a living; burdens on local government support agencies increase; and contributions to charities and churches drop off precipitously.

Of course, we all exacerbate this situation on a daily basis because we usually look for low prices when we shop, and we rarely consider where goods are made. Stores even advertise, and position themselves, as "low price leaders." So consumers like you and me seem to prefer low prices and (perhaps inadvertently) choose to support the textile industries in other countries. Companies who supply goods to the retail market appreciate this, and therefore give us just what we demand: less expensive goods. So if manufacturers want to stay in business, they shift production to areas of the world where they can produce more goods at a lower cost. In short, our consumer demand for low-cost goods drives manufacturers to produce low-cost goods.

Naturally, corporate executives realize that individual people will lose their jobs during lay-offs or plant-closings; and they realize that in some cases entire communities will be very hard-hit. Of all the textile jobs lost in the US between 1997 and 2006, 88% were lost in North and South Carolina alone—where the bulk of the US textile manufacturing is located. But corporate executives are not trying to make decisions that destroy communities; rather they are trying to make decisions that ensure the long-term success of their companies as a whole, and this often means thinking about consequences on a global scale. Workers in the US may lose some jobs, while workers in another country gain jobs and a substantially improved lifestyle, and consumers in the US get cheaper goods, all while worldwide stockholder profits are maintained. Although one group's utility is decreased, many others are increased. Unsurprisingly, this probably does not comfort the worker who loses her job, but overall the benefits are substantial.

This style of utilitarian thinking is not confined to the overarching challenges of managing a global business. Most school children in the United States memorize the preamble to the Constitution which avows a deep concern to "promote the general welfare, and sustain the blessing of liberty" for all its citizens, now and in the future. Yet, this frequently means that government officials must balance a host of complex and competing interests in their pursuit of general welfare. For instance, after the Persian Gulf War in 1991, Turkey received a 50% increase in its textile importing quota from the US as a reward for its assistance during the war. Policy initiatives pursued by George W. Bush's administration in the years immediately following the terrorist attacks of September 11, 2001 were analogous. Subsequent to 9/11 the United States initiated a "free-trade" agreement with Jordan, the first ever for an Arab nation. Similarly, after Pakistan provided assistance in searching for Osama bin Laden and unseating the Taliban regime in Afghanistan, the Bush administration wanted to reward the Pakistani government. The most obvious way to do this was to soften the tariffs on Pakistani textiles. Textile manufacturing constitutes a significant portion of Pakistan's economy, and disenchanted, unemployed Pakistanis are ripe recruits for extremist Islamic terrorist organizations who attack Americans as well as seek to destabilize pro-American governments like the one in Pakistan. So, if we can assist Pakistan's economy, then more Pakistanis will have a decent job, which in turn means there will be fewer possible recruits for terrorist organizations. Moreover, the Bush administration reasoned that Pakistani citizens would see the increase in jobs as a direct result of US measures on their behalf, and therefore they would feel affinity towards America. (The specific Bush plan to offer economic assistance to Pakistan's textile industry was not approved by the US Congress.)

Thus, pursuing a solution to one set of economic or geo-political problems may create new troubles; but these too can be addressed with some utilitarian thinking. As a result of the devastating effects the shift in worldwide textile production has had on communities in the American South, a large amount of US tax-dollars are spent on support services and career retraining for displaced textile workers. Expenditures through the Worker Adjustment and Retraining Notification Act (WARN) and the Trade Adjustment Act (TAA) are the most notable. Spreading the costs out in this way prevents those citizens in one area from bearing a disproportionate burden to support our consumer desire for cheap goods and our political desires to prevent terrorism.

So the US textile industry was hit hard at the turn of the twenty-first century in part due to utilitarian thinking at three different levels. First, consumers generally try to get the most good they can while incurring the lowest burden possible, which means they usually satisfy their preference for lower-priced goods. This first level of utilitarian thinking was augmented when the relative values of global currencies shifted in a way that made production in Asia more cost-effective. Consequently, corporate managers made the second round of utilitarian-style decisions when they responded by shifting production to more cost-effective locales, thus securing more long-term benefit for their companies. Finally, political initiatives that comprise part of America's foreign policy sometimes sacrifice an impact at home for a benefit abroad. We can say that utilitarian thinking contributed to, if not generated, difficulties for the American textile industry at the turn of the twenty-first century. But it is also utilitarian-style thinking that offers a solution to those difficulties, and hope to those displaced workers here in America. Our government policy-makers realize that international gains must be paid for, but justice and impartiality demand that no one group bears a disproportionate share of the burden. So when one segment of our economy is hard-hit, all Americans contribute tax dollars to the support, retraining, and revitalization of our workforce.

Corporate Social Responsibility

ANAND VAIDYA

Corporate Social Responsibility

The central debate in business ethics concerns the nature of corporations. The central question can be put as follows: Are there any moral obligations that corporate executives/managers have other than to maximize profit for the stockholders? There are two standard responses to this question: stockholder theory and stakeholder theory.

Milton Friedman, a recently-deceased Nobel Laureate economist, famously argued that the sole moral responsibility of a corporate executive is to do whatever is permissible within the confines of the law and local ethical customs in order to maximize profits for the stockholders. Friedman saw this as the moral obligation of corporations in general, in so far as one could speak of corporations having moral obligations. As an employee of a corporation, it would be morally *impermissible* for an executive to use funds allocated for profit maximizing ventures for "socially responsible" activities, such as funding charities, environmental clean up, or the building of local schools. According to Friedman, social responsibility is a governmental function. The government is responsible for correcting acknowledged social ills by allotting funds and setting up institutions to deal with them. In addition, people are responsible for voting for the political leaders whose agenda includes the social ills they wish to be corrected.

On the stockholder analysis of the moral obligations of corporations, executives are employees of the stockholders and thus, as employees, are required to do what the board decides. Friedman holds that corporations are created for the purpose of making a profit, and thus since executives are the employees of the stockholders, their primary responsibility is to increase profits for the stockholders. Corporate executives are not to use funds for public works projects, since they are not employed to serve that function. Furthermore, if they were to take some of the stockholders' money and invest it in a specific public works project without the consent of the whole body of stockholders, they would be violating fiduciary obligations owed to the latter.

One critical response to Friedman's stockholder theory has been articulated by R. Edward Freeman and is known as stakeholder theory. Stakeholder theory maintains that stockholders are but one group *among others* that has a vested interest in a corporation's future. Freeman introduces the term "stakeholder" to stand for anyone who has a vested interest in the dealings of a corporation; that is anyone that has a stake in the future of the corporation. Under the narrow understanding of this term distributors, consumers, employees, manufacturers, and the local community in which the corporation is located are stakeholders because they have a vested interest in the corporation's survival and future well-being.

According to Freeman, stockholder theory is flawed because it does not accurately capture the fact that corporations are to be held accountable by interest groups that are not stockholders, such as environmental protection agencies and animal rights activist groups. Because corporations are held to be legally liable by groups extending outside of the sphere of stockholders, an accurate theory of corporations would model that by taking into consideration the real groups that an executive would have to take into consideration in making a decision for the future livelihood of the corporation. For example, employees depend on the corporations continued success and future growth for their job security. Local communities depend on the corporation for jobs, producers and distributors depend on the corporation for contracts, and stockholders depend on the corporation for profits. As a consequence of the kind of dependency relation each group bears to the corporation, those groups have a set of interests that are collectively in competition. A corporate executive must take into consideration these competing interests. Their decisions cannot be made solely in light of profit maximization. They must take into consideration that consumers want lower costs, local communities want more jobs, and employees want higher salaries and more time off. All of these competing interests must be weighed by executives in making decisions for the future sustainability of the corporation.

These two views present themselves as distinct accounts of what a corporation is and what its moral obligations are. According to stockholder theory, it appears as if it could never be the case that a corporate executive permissibly chooses a socially responsible action over pure profit maximization. For example, a corporate executive could not choose to spend some funds on building a school in the local community when that money could be used to fund research and development for a project that has a high probability of making profit for the stockholders. By contrast, it appears as if stakeholder theory allows for the possibility that a corporate executive may permissibly choose to fund the school project because his responsibility is not only to the stockholders, but also the local community. Although the two theories appear to be different, two things should be noted.

First, it is no strict part of stockholder theory that a corporate executive cannot allocate funds for social projects. The reason why is that the main claim of stockholder theory is that a corporate executive's sole responsibility is to the stockholders and not to any other group. However, in order for it to be the case that an executive cannot allocate funds for use in public works projects, it would additionally have to be true that stockholders always *want* their money spent on profit maximization. If the stockholders of a certain corporation *voted* to spend money on a public works project and not to pursue potential profits, then nothing in stockholder theory would block an executive from allocating funds and using them for that purpose. In essence, what stockholder theory holds is that corporate executives are employees of the stockholders and thus are at the mercy of their desires to the degree to which they conform to the law. The theory does not speak directly to the issue of whether a corporation may, after consulting with its stockholders, pursue the advancement of socially responsible projects at the cost of pure profit.

Second, on the plausible assumption that taking into consideration the interests of stakeholders is a good guide to maximizing profits for stockholders, stakeholder theory can be seen as a kind of special case of stockholder theory. In fact, the plausible assumption is more than that: failing to pay attention to stakeholder interests inevitably leads to poor long-term growth for a corporation. For example, closing down a car manufacturing facility in one town may, in the short term, increase profits by lowering costs; however it could lead to a loss in sales by boycotts prompted by the frustrated residents of the town. Overworking employees may lead to a strike. Failing to honor contracts with manufacturers and distributors because paying the cost of breaking the contract is less of a loss than living up to the contract may lead manufacturers and distributors to refrain from engaging in business with the corporation. Each of these considerations shows that recognizing and attempting to satisfy the interests of the various stakeholder groups may itself be a way of maximizing profit in the long term. Developing a more costly but environmentally sound product at a time where environmental soundness is in the eye of the consumer may actually lead consumers to buy the more expensive product over the less expensive and environmentally unsound product. The initial loss encumbered by research and development for the environmentally sound product is regained later by the future sustainability of the corporation as consumers' spending habits reflect concern for their environment.

In this unit, we have included the historically central essays by Friedman and Freeman. In addition, we have included a number of other essays that take the initial debate in various directions that concern the changing physical and social environments in which corporations exist. Both concerns about the environment and globalization have put corporate social responsibility back to the forefront of business ethics.

THE CENTRAL DEBATE

MILTON FRIEDMAN

The Social Responsibility of Business Is to Increase Its Profits

When I hear businessmen speak eloquently about the "social responsibilities of business in a free-enterprise system," I am reminded of the wonderful line about the Frenchman who discovered at the age of 70 that he had been speaking prose all his life. The businessmen believe that they are defending free enterprise when they declaim that business is not concerned "merely" with profit but also with promoting desirable "social" ends; that business has a "social conscience" and takes seriously its responsibilities for providing employment, eliminating discrimination, avoiding pollution and whatever else may be the catchwords of the contemporary crop of reformers. In fact they are—or would be if they or anyone else took them seriously—preaching pure and unadulterated socialism. Businessmen who talk this way are unwitting puppets of the intellectual forces that have been undermining the basis of a free society these past decades.

The discussions of the "social responsibilities of business" are notable for their analytical looseness and lack of rigor. What does it mean to say that "business" has responsibilities? Only people can have responsibilities. A corporation is an artificial person and in this sense may have artificial responsibilities, but "business" as a whole cannot be said to have responsibilities, even in this vague sense. The first step toward clarity in examining the doctrine of the social responsibility of business is to ask precisely what it implies for whom.

Presumably, the individuals who are to be responsible are businessmen, which means individual proprietors or corporate executives. Most of the discussion of social responsibility is directed at corporations, so in what follows I shall mostly neglect the individual proprietors and speak of corporate executives.

In a free-enterprise, private-property system, a corporate executive is an employee of the owners of the business. He has direct responsibility to his employers. That responsibility is to conduct the business in accordance with their desires, which generally will be to make as much money as possible while conforming to the basic rules of the society, both those embodied in law and those embodied in ethical custom. Of course, in some cases his employers may have a different objective. A group of persons might establish a corporation for an eleemosynary purpose—for example, a hospital or a school. The manager of such a corporation will not have money profit as his objective but the rendering of certain services.

In either case, the key point is that, in his capacity as a corporate executive, the manager is the agent of the individuals who own the corporation or establish the eleemosynary institution, and his primary responsibility is to them.

Needless to say, this does not mean that it is easy to judge how well he is performing his task. But at least the criterion of performance is straightforward, and the persons among whom a voluntary contractual arrangement exists are clearly defined.

Of course, the corporate executive is also a person in his own right. As a person, he may have many other responsibilities that he recognizes or assumes voluntarily—to his family, his conscience, his feelings of charity, his church, his clubs, his city, his country. He may feel impelled by these responsibilities to devote part of his income to causes he regards as worthy, to refuse to work for particular corporations, even to leave his job, for example, to join his country's armed forces. If we wish, we may refer to some of these responsibilities as "social responsibilities." But in these respects he is acting as a principal, not an agent; he is spending his own money or time or energy, not the money of his employers or the time or energy he has contracted to devote to their purposes. If these are "social responsibilities," they are the social responsibilities of individuals, not of business.

What does it mean to say that the corporate executive has a "social responsibility" in his capacity as businessman? If this statement is not pure rhetoric, it must mean that he is to act in some way that is not in the interest of his employers. For example, that he is to refrain from increasing the price of the product in order to contribute to the social objective of preventing inflation, even though a price increase would be in the best interests of the corporation. Or that he is to make expenditures on reducing pollution beyond the amount that is in the best interests of the corporation or that is required by law in order to contribute to the social objective of improving the environment. Or that, at the expense of corporate profits, he is to hire "hardcore" unemployed instead of better qualified available workmen to contribute to the social objective of reducing poverty.

In each of these cases, the corporate executive would be spending someone else's money for a general social interest. Insofar as his actions in accord with his "social responsibility" reduce returns to stockholders, he is spending their money. Insofar as his actions raise the price to customers, he is spending the customers' money. Insofar as his actions lower the wages of some employees, he is spending their money.

The stockholders or the customers or the employees could separately spend their own money on the particular action if they wished to do so. The executive is exercising a distinct "social responsibility," rather than serving as an agent of the stockholders or the customers or the employees, only if he spends the money in a different way than they would have spent it.

But if he does this, he is in effect imposing taxes, on the one hand, and deciding how the tax proceeds shall be spent, on the other.

This process raises political questions on two levels: principle and consequences. On the level of political principle, the imposition of taxes and the expenditure of tax proceeds are governmental functions. We have established elaborate constitutional, parliamentary, and judicial provisions to control these functions, to assure that taxes are imposed so far as possible in accordance with the preferences and desires of the public—after all, "taxation without representation" was one of the battle cries of the American Revolution. We have a system of checks and balances to separate the legislative function of imposing taxes and enacting expenditures from the executive function of collecting taxes and administering expenditure programs and from the judicial function of mediating disputes and interpreting the law.

Here the businessman—self-selected or appointed directly or indirectly by stockholders—is to be simultaneously legislator, executive, and jurist. He is to decide whom to tax by how much and for what purpose, and he is to spend the proceeds—all this guided only by general exhortations from on high to restrain inflation, improve the environment, fight poverty and so on and on.

The whole justification for permitting the corporate executive to be selected by the stockholders is that the executive is an agent sensing the interests of his principal. This justification disappears when the corporate executive imposes taxes and spends the proceeds for "social" purposes. He becomes in effect a public employee, a civil servant, even though he remains in name an employee of a private enterprise. On grounds of political principle, it is intolerable that such civil servants—insofar as their actions in the name of social responsibility are real and not just window-dressing—should be selected as they are now. If they are to be civil servants, then they must be elected through a political process. If they are to impose taxes and make expenditures to foster "social" objectives, then political machinery must be set up to make the assessment of taxes and to determine through a political process the objectives to be served.

This is the basic reason why the doctrine of "social responsibility" involves the acceptance of the socialist view that political mechanisms, not market mechanisms, are the appropriate way to determine the allocation of scarce resources to alternative uses.

On the grounds of consequences, can the corporate executive in fact discharge his alleged "social responsibilities?" On the other hand, suppose he could get away with spending the stockholders' or customers' or employees' money. How is he to know how to spend it? He is told that he must contribute to fighting inflation. How is he to know what action of his will contribute to that end? He is presumably an expert in running his company—in producing a product or selling it or financing it. But nothing about his selection makes him an expert on inflation. Will his holding down the price of his product reduce inflationary pressure? Or, by leaving more spending power in the hands of his customers, simply divert it elsewhere? Or, by forcing him to produce less because of the lower price, will it simply contribute to shortages? Even if he could answer these questions, how much cost is he justified in imposing on his stockholders, customers, and employees for this so-

cial purpose? What is his appropriate share and what is the appropriate share of others?

And, whether he wants to or not, can he get away with spending his stockholders', customers' or employees' money? Will not the stockholders fire him? (Either the present ones or those who take over when his actions in the name of social responsibility have reduced the corporation's profits and the price of its stock.) His customers and his employees can desert him for other producers and employers less scrupulous in exercising their social responsibilities.

This facet of "social responsibility" doctrine is brought into sharp relief when the doctrine is used to justify wage restraint by trade unions. The conflict of interest is naked and clear when union officials are asked to subordinate the interest of their members to some more general purpose. If the union officials try to enforce wage restraint, the consequence is likely to be wildcat strikes, rank-and-file revolts, and the emergence of strong competitors for their jobs. We thus have the ironic phenomenon that union leaders—at least in the US—have objected to Government interference with the market far more consistently and courageously than have business leaders.

The difficulty of exercising "social responsibility" illustrates, of course, the great virtue of private competitive enterprise—it forces people to be responsible for their own actions and makes it difficult for them to "exploit" other people for either selfish or unselfish purposes. They can do good—but only at their own expense.

Many a reader who has followed the argument this far may be tempted to remonstrate that it is all well and good to speak of Government's having the responsibility to impose taxes and determine expenditures for such "social" purposes as controlling pollution or training the hard-core unemployed, but that the problems are too urgent to wait on the slow course of political processes, that the exercise of social responsibility by businessmen is a quicker and surer way to solve pressing current problems.

Aside from the question of fact—I share Adam Smith's skepticism about the benefits that can be expected from "those who affected to trade for the public good"—this argument must be rejected on grounds of principle. What it amounts to is an assertion that those who favor the taxes and expenditures in question have failed to persuade a majority of their fellow citizens to be of like mind and that they are seeking to attain by undemocratic procedures what they cannot attain by democratic procedures. In a free society, it is hard for "evil" people to do "evil," especially since one man's good is another's evil.

I have, for simplicity, concentrated on the special case of the corporate executive, except only for the brief digression on trade unions. But precisely the same argument applies to the newer phenomenon of calling upon stockholders to require corporations to exercise social responsibility (the recent GM crusade for example). In most of these cases, what is in effect involved is some stockholders trying to get other stockholders (or customers or employees) to contribute against their will to "social" causes favored by the activists. Insofar as they succeed, they are again imposing taxes and spending the proceeds.

The situation of the individual proprietor is somewhat different. If he acts to reduce the returns of his enterprise in order to exercise his "social responsibility," he is spending his own money, not someone else's. If he wishes to spend his money on such purposes, that is his right, and I cannot see that there is any objection to his doing so. In the process, he, too, may impose costs on employees and customers. However, because he is far less likely than a large corporation or union to have monopolistic power, any such side effects will tend to be minor.

Of course, in practice, the doctrine of social responsibility is frequently a cloak for actions that are justified on other grounds rather than a reason for those actions.

To illustrate, it may well be in the long-run interest of a corporation that is a major employer in a small community to devote resources to providing amenities to that community or to improving its government. That may make it easier to attract desirable employees, it may reduce the wage bill or lessen losses from pilferage and sabotage or have other worthwhile effects. Or it may be that, given the laws about the deductibility of corporate charitable contributions, the stockholders can contribute more to charities they favor by having the corporation make the gift than by doing it themselves, since they can in that way contribute an amount that would otherwise have been paid as corporate taxes.

In each of these—and many similar—cases, there is a strong temptation to rationalize these actions as an exercise of "social responsibility." In the present climate of opinion, with its wide-spread aversion to "capitalism," "profits," the "soulless corporation," and so on, this is one way for a corporation to generate goodwill as a by-product of expenditures that are entirely justified in its own self-interest.

It would be inconsistent of me to call on corporate executives to refrain from this hypocritical window-dressing because it harms the foundations of a free society. That would be to call on them to exercise a "social responsibility"! If our institutions, and the attitudes of the public make it in their self-interest to cloak their actions in this way, I cannot summon much indignation to denounce them. At the same time, I can express admiration for those individual proprietors or owners of closely held corporations or stockholders of more broadly held corporations who disdain such tactics as approaching fraud.

Whether blameworthy or not, the use of the cloak of social responsibility, and the nonsense spoken in its name by influential and prestigious businessmen, does clearly harm the foundations of a free society. I have been impressed time and again by the schizophrenic character of many businessmen. They are capable of being extremely far-sighted and clear-headed in matters that are internal to their businesses. They are incredibly short-sighted and muddle-headed in matters that are outside their businesses but affect the possible survival of business in general. This shortsightedness is strikingly exemplified in the calls from many businessmen for wage and price guidelines or controls or income policies. There is nothing that could do more in a brief period to destroy a market system and replace it by a centrally controlled system than effective governmental control of prices and wages.

The shortsightedness is also exemplified in speeches by businessmen on social responsibility. This may gain them kudos in the short run. But it helps to strengthen the already too prevalent view that the pursuit of profits is wicked and immoral and must be curbed and controlled by external forces. Once this view is adopted, the external forces that curb the market will not be the social consciences, however highly developed, of the pontificating executives; it will be the iron fist of Government bureaucrats. Here, as with price and wage controls, businessmen seem to me to reveal a suicidal impulse.

The political principle that underlies the market mechanism is unanimity. In an ideal free market resting on private property, no individual can coerce any other, all cooperation is voluntary, all parties to such cooperation benefit or they need not participate. There are no values, no "social" responsibilities in any sense other than the shared values and responsibilities of individuals. Society is a collection of individuals and of the various groups they voluntarily form.

The political principle that underlies the political mechanism is conformity. The individual must serve a more general social interest—whether that be determined by a church or a dictator or a majority. The individual may have a vote and say in what is to be done, but if he is overruled, he must conform. It is appropriate for some to require others to contribute to a general social purpose whether they wish to or not.

Unfortunately, unanimity is not always feasible. There are some respects in which conformity appears unavoidable, so I do not see how one can avoid the use of the political mechanism altogether.

But the doctrine of "social responsibility" taken seriously would extend the scope of the apolitical mechanism to every human activity. It does not differ in philosophy from the most explicitly collectivist doctrine. It differs only by professing to believe that collectivist ends can be attained without collectivist means. That is why, in my book *Capitalism and Freedom*, I have called it a "fundamentally subversive doctrine" in a free society, and have said that in such a society, "there is one and only one social responsibility of business—to use its resources and engage in activities designed to increase its profits so long as it stays within the rules of the game, which is to say, engages in open and free competition without deception or fraud."

♦ ♦ ♦ ♦ ♦

R. EDWARD FREEMAN

A Stakeholder Theory of the Modern Corporation

Introduction

Corporations have ceased to be merely legal devices through which private business transactions of individuals may be carried on. Though still much used for this purpose, the corporate form has acquired a larger significance. The corporation has, in fact, become both a method of property tenure and a means of organizing economic life. Grown to tremendous proportions, there may be said to have evolved a "corporate system"—which has attracted to itself a combination of attributes and powers, and has attained a degree of prominence entitling it to be dealt with as a major social institution.[1]

Despite these prophetic words of Berle and Means (1932), scholars and managers alike continue to hold sacred the view that managers bear a special relationship to the stockholders in the firm. Since stockholders own shares in the firm, they have certain rights and privileges, which must be granted to them by management, as well as by others. Sanctions, in the form of "the law of corporations," and other protective mechanisms in the form of social custom, accepted management practice, myth, and ritual, are thought to reinforce the assumption of the primacy of the stockholder.

The purpose of this paper is to pose several challenges to this assumption, from within the framework of managerial capitalism, and to suggest the bare bones of an alternative theory, *a stakeholder theory of the modern corporation*. I do not seek the demise of the modern corporation, either intellectually or in fact. Rather, I seek its transformation. In the words of Neurath, we shall attempt to "rebuild the ship, plank by plank, while it remains afloat."[2]

My thesis is that I can revitalize the concept of managerial capitalism by replacing the notion that managers have a duty to stockholders with the concept that managers bear a fiduciary relationship to stakeholders. Stakeholders are those groups who have a stake in or claim on the firm. Specifically I include suppliers, customers, employees, stockholders, and the local community, as well as management in its role as agent for these groups. I argue that the legal, economic, political, and moral challenges to the currently received theory of the firm, as a nexus of contracts among the owners of the factors of production and customers, require us to revise this concept. That is, each of these stakeholder groups has a right not to be treated as a means to some end, and therefore must participate in determining the future direction of the firm in which they have a stake.

The crux of my argument is that we must reconceptualize the firm around the following question: For whose benefit and at whose expense should the firm be managed? I shall set forth such a reconceptualization in the form of a *stakeholder theory of the firm*. I shall then critically examine the stakeholder view and its implications for the future of the capitalist system.

The Attack on Managerial Capitalism

The Legal Argument

The basic idea of managerial capitalism is that in return for controlling the firm, management vigorously pursues the interests of stockholders. Central to the managerial view of the firm is the idea that management can pursue market transactions with suppliers and customers in an unconstrained manner.

The law of corporations gives a less clearcut answer to the question: in whose interest and for whose benefit should the modern corporation be governed? While it says that the corporations should be run primarily in the interests of the stockholders in the firm, it says further that the corporation exists "in contemplation of the law" and has personality as a "legal person," limited liability for its actions, and immortality, since its existence transcends that of its members. Therefore, directors and other officers of the firm have a fiduciary obligation to stockholders in the sense that the "affairs of the corporation" must be conducted in the interest of the stockholders. And stockholders can theoretically bring suit against those directors and managers for doing otherwise. But since the corporation is a legal person, existing in contemplation of the law, managers of the corporation are constrained by law.

Until recently, this was no constraint at all. In this century, however, the law has evolved to effectively constrain the pursuit of stockholder interests at the expense of other claimants on the firm. It has, in effect, required that the claims of customers, suppliers, local communities, and employees be taken into consideration, though in general they are subordinated to the claims of stockholders.

For instance, the doctrine of "privity of contract," as articulated in *Winterbottom v. Wright* in 1842, has been eroded by recent developments in products liability law. Indeed, *Greenman v. Yuba Power* gives the manufacturer strict liability for damage caused by its products, even though the seller has exercised all possible care in the preparation and sale of the product and the consumer has not bought the product from nor entered into any contractual arrangement with the manufacturer. Caveat emptor has been replaced, in large part, with caveat venditor.[3] The Consumer Product Safety Commission has the power to enact product recalls, and in 1980 one US automobile company recalled more cars than it built. Some industries are required to provide information to customers about a product's ingredients, whether or not the customers want and are willing to pay for this information.[4]

The same argument is applicable to management's dealings with employees. The National Labor Relations Act gave employees the right to unionize and to bargain in good faith. It set up the National Labor Relations board to enforce these rights with management. The Equal Pay Act of 1963 and Title VII of the Civil Rights Act of 1964 constrain management from discrimination in hiring practices; these have been followed with the Age Discrimination in Employment Act of 1967.[5] The emergence of a body of administrative case law arising from labor-management disputes and the historic settling of discrimination claims with large employers such as AT&T have caused the emergence of a body of practice in the corporation that is consistent with the legal guarantee of the rights of the employees. The law has protected the due process rights of those employees who enter into collective bargaining agreements with management. As of the present, however, only 30 per cent of the labor force are participating in such agreements; this has prompted one labor law scholar to propose a statutory law prohibiting dismissals of the 70 percent of the work force not protected.[6]

The law has also protected the interests of local communities. The Clean Air Act and Clean Water Act have constrained management from "spoiling the commons." In an historic case, *Marsh v. Alabama*, the Supreme Court ruled that a company owned town was subject to the provisions of the US Constitution, thereby guaranteeing the rights of local citizens and negating the "property rights" of the firm. Some states and municipalities have gone further and passed laws preventing firms from moving plants or limiting when and how plants can be closed. In sum, there is much current legal activity in this area to constrain management's pursuit of stockholders' interests at the expense of the local communities in which the firm operates.

I have argued that the result of such changes in the legal system can be viewed as giving some rights to those groups that have a claim on the firm, for example, customers, suppliers, employees, local communities, stockholders, and management. It raises the question, at the core of a theory of the firm: in whose interest and for whose benefit should the firm be managed? The answer proposed by managerial capitalism is clearly "the stockholders," but I have argued that the law has been progressively circumscribing this answer.

The Economic Argument

In its pure ideological form managerial capitalism seeks to maximize the interests of stockholders. In its perennial criticism of government regulation management espouses the "invisible hand" doctrine. It contends that it creates the greatest good for the greatest number, and therefore government need not intervene. However, we know that externalities, moral hazards, and monopoly power exist in fact, whether or not they exist in theory. Further, some of the legal apparatus mentioned above has evolved to deal with just these issues.

The problem of the "tragedy of the commons" or the free-rider problem pervades the concept of public goods such as water and air. No one has an incentive to incur the cost of clean-up or the cost of nonpollution, since the marginal gain of one firm's action is small. Every firm reasons this way, and the result is pollution of water and air. Since the industrial revolution, firms have sought to internalize the benefits and externalize the costs of their actions. The cost must be borne by all, through taxation and regulation; hence we have the emergence of the environmental regulations of the 1970s.

Similarly, moral hazards arise when the purchaser of a good or service can pass along the cost of that good. There is no incentive to economize, on the part of either the producer or the consumer, and there is excessive use of the resources involved. The institutionalized practice of third-party payment in health care is a prime example.

Finally, we see the avoidance of competitive behavior on the part of firms, each seeking to monopolize a small portion of the market and not compete with one another. In a number of industries, oligopolies have emerged, and while there is questionable evidence that oligopolies are not the most efficient corporate form in some industries, suffice it to say that the potential for abuse of market power has again led to regulation of managerial activity. In the classic case, AT&T, arguably one of the great technological and managerial achievements of the century, was broken up into eight separate companies to prevent its abuse of monopoly power.

Externalities, moral hazards, and monopoly power have led to more external control on managerial capitalism. There are de facto constraints, due to these economic facts of life, on the ability of management to act in the interests of stockholders.

A Stakeholder Theory of the Firm

The Stakeholder Concept

Corporations have stakeholders, that is, groups and individuals who benefit from or are harmed by, and whose rights are violated or respected by, corporate actions. The concept of stakeholders is a generalization of the notion of stockholders, who themselves have some special claim on the firm. Just as stockholders have a right to demand certain actions by management, so do other stakeholders have a right to make claims. The exact nature of these claims is a difficult question that I shall address, but the logic is identical to that of the stockholder theory. Stakes require action of a certain sort, and conflicting stakes require methods of resolution.

Freeman and Reed (1983)[7] distinguish two senses of *stakeholder*. The "narrow definition" includes those groups who are vital to the survival and success of the corporation. The "wide-definition" includes any group or individual who can affect or is affected by the corporation. I shall begin with a modest aim: to articulate a stakeholder theory using the narrow definition.

Stakeholders in the Modern Corporation

Figure 1 depicts the stakeholders in a typical large corporation. The stakes of each are reciprocal, since

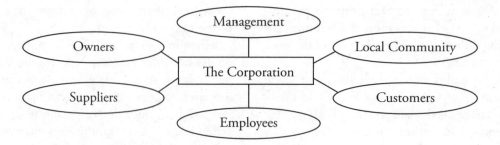

Figure 1. A Stakeholder Model of the Corporation

each can affect the other in terms of harms and benefits as well as rights and duties. The stakes of each are not univocal and would vary by particular corporation. I merely set forth some general notions that seem to be common to many large firms.

Owners have financial stake in the corporation in the form of stocks, bonds, and so on, and they expect some kind of financial return from them. Either they have given money directly to the firm, or they have some historical claim made through a series of morally justified exchanges. The firm affects their livelihood or, if a substantial portion of their retirement income is in stocks or bonds, their ability to care for themselves when they can no longer work. Of course, the stakes of owners will differ by type of owner, preferences for money, moral preferences, and so on, as well as by type of firm. The owners of AT&T are quite different from the owners of Ford Motor Company, with stock of the former company being widely dispersed among 3 million stockholders and that of the latter being held by a small family group as well as by a large group of public stockholders.

Employees have their jobs and usually their livelihood at stake; they often have specialized skills for which there is usually no perfectly elastic market. In return for their labor, they expect security, wages, benefits, and meaningful work. In return for their loyalty, the corporation is expected to provide for them and carry them through difficult times. Employees are expected to follow the instructions of management most of the time, to speak favorably about the company, and to be responsible citizens in the local communities in which the company operates. Where they are used as means to an end, they must participate in decisions affecting such use. The evidence that such policies and values as described here lead to productive company-employee relationships is compelling. It is equally compelling to realize that the opportunities for "bad faith" on the part of both management and employees are enormous. "Mock participation" in quality circles, singing the company song, and wearing the company uniform solely to please management all lead to distrust and unproductive work.

Suppliers, interpreted in a stakeholder sense, are vital to the success of the firm, for raw materials will determine the final product's quality and price. In turn the firm is a customer of the supplier and is therefore vital to the success and survival of the supplier. When the firm treats the supplier as a valued member of the stakeholder network, rather than simply as a source of materials, the supplier will respond when the firm is in need. Chrysler traditionally had very close ties to its suppliers, even to the extent that led some to suspect the transfer of illegal payments. And when Chrysler was on the brink of disaster, the suppliers responded with price cuts, accepting late payments, financing, and so on. Supplier and company can rise and fall together. Of course, again, the particular supplier relationships will depend on a number of variables such as the number of suppliers and whether the supplies are finished goods or raw materials.

Customers exchange resources for the products of the firm and in return receive the benefits of the products. Customers provide the lifeblood of the firm in the form of revenue. Given the level of reinvestment of earnings in large corporations, customers indirectly pay for the development of new products and services. Peters and Waterman (1982)[8] have argued that being close to the customer leads to success with other stakeholders and that a distinguishing characteristic of some companies that have performed well is their emphasis on the customer. By paying attention to customers' needs, management automatically addresses the needs of suppliers and owners. Moreover, it seems that the ethic of customer service carries over to the community. Almost without fail the "excellent companies" in Peters and Waterman's study have good reputations in the community. I would argue that Peters and Waterman have found multiple applications of Kant's dictum, "treat persons as ends unto themselves," and it should come as no surprise that persons respond to such respectful treatment, be they customers, suppliers, owners, employees, or members of the local community. The real surprise is the novelty of the application of Kant's rule in a theory of good management practice.

The local community grants the firm the right to build facilities and, in turn, it benefits from the tax base and economic and social contributions of the firm. In return for the provision of local services, the firm is expected to be a good citizen, as is any person, either "natural or artificial." The firm cannot expose the community to unreasonable hazards in the form of pollution, toxic waste, and so on. If for some reason the firm must leave a community, it is expected to work with local leaders to make the transition as smoothly as possible. Of course, the firm does not have perfect knowledge, but when it discovers some danger or runs afoul of new competition, it is expected to inform the local community and to work with the community to overcome any problem. When the firm mismanages its relationship with the local community, it is in the same position as a citizen who commits a crime. It has violated the implicit social contract with the community and should expect to be distrusted and ostracized. It should not be surprised when punitive measures are invoked.

I have not included "competitors" as stakeholders in the narrow sense, since strictly speaking they are not necessary for the survival and success of the firm; the stakeholder theory works equally well in monopoly contexts. However, competitors and government would be the first to be included in an extension of this basic theory. It is simply not true that the interests of competitors in an industry are always in conflict. There is no reason why trade associations and other multi-organizational groups cannot band together to solve common problems that have little to do with how to restrain trade. Implementation of stakeholder management principles, in the long run, mitigates the need for industrial policy and an increasing role for government intervention and regulation.

The Role of Management

Management plays a special role, for it too has a stake in the modern corporation. On the one hand, management's stake is like that of employees, with some kind of explicit or implicit employment contract. But, on the other hand, management has a duty of safeguarding the welfare of the abstract entity that is the corporation. In short, management, especially top management, must look after the health of the corporation, and this involves balancing the multiple claims of conflicting stakeholders. Owners want higher financial returns, while customers want more money spent on research and development. Employees want higher wages and better benefits, while the local community wants better parks and day-care facilities.

The task of management in today's corporation is akin to that of King Solomon. The stakeholder theory does not give primacy to one stakeholder group over another, though there will surely be times when one group will benefit at the expense of others. In general, however, management must keep the relationships among stakeholders in balance. When these relationships become imbalanced, the survival of the firm is in jeopardy.

When wages are too high and product quality is too low, customers leave, suppliers suffer, and owners sell their stocks and bonds, depressing the stock price and making it difficult to raise new capital at favorable rates. Note, however, that the reason for paying returns to owners is not that they "own" the firm, but that their support is necessary for the survival of the firm, and that they have a legitimate claim on the firm. Similar reasoning applies in turn to each stakeholder group.

A stakeholder theory of the firm must define the purpose of the firm. The stockholder theory claims that the purpose of the firm is to maximize the welfare of the stockholders, perhaps subject to some moral or social constraints, either because such maximization leads to the greatest good or because of property rights. The purpose of the firm is quite different in my view.

"The stakeholder theory" can be unpacked into a number of stakeholder theories, each of which has a "normative core," inextricably linked to the way that corporations should be governed and the way that managers should act. So, attempts to more fully define, or more carefully define, a stakeholder theory are misguided. Following Donaldson and Preston, I want to insist that the normative, descriptive, instrumental, and metaphorical (my addition to their framework) uses of "stakeholder" are tied together in particular political constructions to yield a number of possible "stakeholder theories." "Stakeholder theory" is thus a genre of stories about how we could live. Let me be more specific.

A "normative core" of a theory is a set of sentences that includes among others, sentences like:

(1) Corporations ought to be governed ...
(2) Managers ought to act to ...

where we need arguments or further narratives which include business and moral terms to fill in the blanks. This normative core is not always reducible to a fundamental ground like the theory of property, but certain normative cores are consistent with modern understandings of property. Certain elaborations of the theory of private property plus the other institutions of political liberalism give rise to particular normative cores. But there are other institutions, other political conceptions of how society ought to be structured, so that there are different possible normative cores.

So, one normative core of a stakeholder theory might be a feminist standpoint one, rethinking how we would restructure "value-creating activity" along principles of caring and connection.[9] Another would be an ecological (or several ecological) normative cores. Mark Starik has argued that the very idea of a stakeholder theory of the *firm* ignores certain ecological necessities.[10] Exhibit 1 is suggestive of how these theories could be developed.

In the next section I shall sketch the normative core based on pragmatic liberalism. But, any normative core must address the questions in columns A or B, or explain why these questions may be irrelevant,

Exhibit 1. A Reasonable Pluralism

	A. Corporations ought to be governed ...	B. Managers ought to act ...	C. The background disciplines of "value creation" are ...
Doctrine of ... Fair Contracts	in accordance with ... the six principles.	in the interests of stakeholders.	– business theories – theories that explain stakeholder behavior
Feminist Standpoint Theory	... in accordance with the principles of caring/connection and relationships.	... to maintain and care for relationships and networks of stakeholders.	– business theories – feminist theory – social science understanding of networks
Ecological Principles	... in accordance with the principle of caring for the earth.	... to care for the earth.	– business theories – ecology – other

as in the ecological view. In addition, each "theory," and I use the word hesitantly, must place the normative core within a more full-fledged account of how we could understand value-creating activity differently (column C). The only way to get on with this task is to see the stakeholder idea as a metaphor. The attempt to prescribe one and only one "normative core" and construct "a stakeholder theory" is at best a disguised attempt to smuggle a normative core past the unsophisticated noses of other unsuspecting academics who are just as happy to see the end of the stockholder orthodoxy.

If we begin with the view that we can understand value-creation activity as a contractual process among those parties affected, and if for simplicity's sake we initially designate those parties as financiers, customers, suppliers, employees, and communities, then we can construct a normative core that reflects the liberal notions of autonomy, solidarity, and fairness as articulated by John Rawls, Richard Rorty, and others.[11] Notice that building these moral notions into the foundations of how we understand value creation and contracting requires that we eschew separating the business part of the process from the "ethical" part, and that we start with the presumption of equality among the contractors, rather than the presumption in favor of financier rights.

The normative core for this redesigned contractual theory will capture the liberal idea of fairness if it ensures a basic equality among stakeholders in terms of their moral rights as these are realized in the firm, and if it recognizes that inequalities among stakeholders are justified if they raise the level of the least well-off stakeholder. The liberal ideal of autonomy is captured by the realization that each stakeholder must be free to enter agreements that create value for themselves and solidarity is realized by the recognition of the mutuality of stakeholder interests.

One way to understand fairness in this context is to claim à la Rawls that a contract is fair if parties to the contract would agree to it in ignorance of their actual stakes. Thus, a contract is like a fair bet, if each party is willing to turn the tables and accept the other side. What would a fair contract among corporate stakeholders look like? If we can articulate this ideal, a sort of corporate constitution, we could then ask whether actual corporations measure up to this standard, and we also begin to design corporate structures which are consistent with this Doctrine of Fair Contracts.

Imagine if you will, representative stakeholders trying to decide on "the rules of the game." Each is rational in a straightforward sense, looking out for its own self-interest. At least *ex ante*, stakeholders are the relevant parties since they will be materially affected. Stakeholders know how economic activity is organized and could be organized. They know general facts about the way the corporate world works. They know that in the real world there are or could be transaction costs, externalities, and positive costs of contracting. Suppose they are uncertain about what other social institutions exist, but they know the range of those institutions. They do not know if government exists to pick up the tab for any externalities, or if they will exist in the nightwatchman state of libertarian theory. They know success and failure stories of businesses around the world. In short, they are behind a Rawls-like veil of ignorance, and they do not know what stake each will have when the veil is lifted. What groundrules would they choose to guide them?

The first groundrule is "The Principle of Entry and Exit." Any contract that is the corporation must have clearly defined entry, exit, and renegotiation conditions, or at least it must have methods or processes for so defining these conditions. The logic is straightforward: each stakeholder must be able to determine when an agreement exists and has a chance of fulfillment. This is not to imply that contracts cannot contain contingent claims or other methods for resolving uncertainty, but rather that it must contain methods for determining whether or not it is valid.

The second groundrule I shall call "The Principle of Governance," and it says that the procedure for changing the rules of the game must be agreed upon by unanimous consent. Think about the consequences of a majority of stakeholders systematically "selling out" a minority. Each stakeholder, in ignorance of its actual role, would seek to avoid such a situation. In reality this principle translates into each stakeholder never giving up its right to participate in the governance of the corporation, or perhaps into the existence of stakeholder governing boards.

The third groundrule I shall call "The Principle of Externalities," and it says that if a contract between A and B imposes a cost on C, then C has the option to become a party to the contract, and the terms are renegotiated. Once again the rationality of this condition is clear. Each stakeholder will want insurance that it does not become C.

The fourth groundrule is "The Principle of Contracting Costs," and it says that all parties to the contract must share in the cost of contracting. Once again the logic is straightforward. Any one stakeholder can get stuck.

A fifth groundrule is "The Agency Principle" that says that any agent must serve the interests of all stakeholders. It must adjudicate conflicts within the bounds of the other principals. Once again the logic is clear. Agents for any one group would have a privileged place.

A sixth and final groundrule we might call, "The Principle of Limited Immortality." The corporation shall be managed as if it can continue to serve the interests of stakeholders through time. Stakeholders are uncertain about the future but, subject to exit conditions, they realize that the continued existence of the corporation is in their interest. Therefore, it would be rational to hire managers who are fiduciaries to their interest and the interest of the collective. If it turns out the collective interests is the empty set, then this principle simply collapses into the Agency Principle.

Thus, the Doctrine of Fair Contracts consists of these six groundrules or principles:

(1) The Principle of Entry and Exit
(2) The Principle of Governance
(3) The Principle of Externalities
(4) The Principle of Contracting Costs
(5) The Agency Principle
(6) The Principle of Limited Immortality

Think of these groundrules as a doctrine which would guide actual stakeholders in devising a corporate constitution or charter. Think of management as having the duty to act in accordance with some specific constitution or charter.

Obviously, if the Doctrine of Fair Contracts and its accompanying background narratives are to effect real change, there must be requisite changes in the enabling laws of the land. I propose the following three principles to serve as constitutive elements of attempts to reform the law of corporations.

The Stakeholder Enabling Principle

Corporations shall be managed in the interests of its stakeholders, defined as employees, financiers, customers, employees, and communities.

The Principle of Director Responsibility

Directors of the corporation shall have a duty of care to use reasonable judgment to define and direct the affairs of the corporation in accordance with the Stakeholder Enabling Principle.

The Principle of Stakeholder Recourse

Stakeholders may bring an action against the directors for failure to perform the required duty of care.

Obviously, there is more work to be done to spell out these principles in terms of model legislation. As they stand, they try to capture the intuitions that drive the liberal ideals. It is equally plain that corporate constitutions which meet a test like the doctrine of fair contracts are meant to enable directors and executives to manage the corporation in conjunction with these same liberal ideals.

NOTES

1 Cf. A. Berle and C. Means, *The Modern Corporation and Private Property* (New York: Commerce Clearing House, 1932), 1. For a re-assessment of Berle and Means' argument after 50 years, see *Journal of Law and Economics* 26 (June 1983), especially C. Stigler and C. Friedland, "The Literature of Economics: The Case of Berle and Means," 237-68; D. North, "Comment on Stigler and Friedland," 269-72; and C. Means, "Corporate Power in the Marketplace," 467-85.

2 The metaphor of rebuilding the ship while afloat is attributed to Neurath by W. Quine, *Word and Object* (Cambridge: Harvard University Press, 1960), and W. Quine and J. Ullian, *The Web of Belief* (New York: Random House, 1978). The point is that to keep the ship afloat during repairs we must replace a plank with one that will do a better job. Our argument is that stakeholder capitalism can so replace the current version of managerial capitalism.

3 See R. Charan and E. Freeman, "Planning for the Business Environment of the 1980s," *The Journal of Business Strategy* 1 (1980): 9-19, especially p. 15 for a brief account of the major developments in products liability law.

4 See S. Breyer, *Regulation and Its Reform* (Cambridge: Harvard University Press, 1983), 133, for an analysis of food additives.

5 See I. Millstein and S. Katsh, *The Limits of Corporate Power* (New York: Macmillan, 1981), Chapter 4.

6 Cf. C. Summers, "Protecting All Employees Against Unjust Dismissal," *Harvard Business Review* 58 (1980): 136, for a careful statement of the argument.

7 See E. Freeman and D. Reed, "Stockholders and Stakeholders: A New Perspective on Corporate Governance," in G. Huizinga, ed., *Corporate Governance: A Definitive Exploration of the Issues* (Los Angeles: UCLA Extension Press, 1983).

8 See T. Peters and R. Waterman, *In Search of Excellence* (New York: Harper and Row, 1982).

9 See, for instance, A. Wicks, D. Gilbert, and E. Freeman, "A Feminist Reinterpretation of the Stakeholder Concept," *Business Ethics Quarterly*, Vol. 4, No. 4, October 1994; and E. Freeman and J. Liedtka, "Corporate Social Responsibility: A Critical Approach," *Business Horizons* Vol. 34, No. 4, July-August 1991, 92-98.

10 At the Toronto workshop Mark Stark sketched how a theory would look if we took the environment to be a stakeholder. This fruitful line of work is one example of my main point about pluralism.

11 J. Rawls, *Political Liberalism* (New York: Columbia University Press, 1993); and R. Rorty, "The Priority of Democracy to Philosophy" in *Reading Rorty: Critical Responses to Philosophy and the Mirror of Nature (and Beyond)*, ed. Alan R. Malachowski (Cambridge, MA: Blackwell, 1990).

◆ ◆ ◆ ◆ ◆

JOHN HASNAS[1]

The Normative Theories of Business Ethics: A Guide for the Perplexed

I. Introduction

A charge that is frequently lodged against the practical utility of business ethics as a field of study concerns the apparent failure of communication between the theorist and the business practitioner.[2] Critics of the discipline often point out that business ethicists are usually academics, and worse, philosophers, who speak in the language of abstract ethical theory. Thus, they are accused of expressing their ideas in terms of "deontological requirements," "consequentialist considerations," "the categorical imperative," "rule utilitarianism," "the hedonistic calculus," "human flourishing" and other locutions that are essentially meaningless to the ordinary business person who possesses little or no philosophical training. Business people, it is pointed out, express themselves in ordinary language and tend to resist dealing in abstractions. What they want to know is how to resolve the specific problems that confront them.

To the extent that this criticism is justified, it places the business ethicist on the horns of a dilemma. Without the guidance of principles, ethical discussion is mere casuistry. Thus, general principles are necessary if business ethics is to constitute a substantive normative discipline. However, if the only principles available are expressed in language unfamiliar to those who must apply them, they can have no practical effect. This suggests that the task of the business ethicist is to produce a set of ethical principles that can be both expressed in language accessible to and conveniently applied by an ordinary business person who has no formal philosophical training.

The search for such principles has led to the development of several normative theories that have been specifically tailored to fit the business environment; theories that, for purposes of this article, I shall refer to as the normative theories of business ethics.[3] These theories attempt to derive what might be called "intermediate level" principles to mediate between the highly abstract principles of philosophical ethics and the concrete ethical dilemmas that arise in the business environment. Philosophical ethics must provide human beings with guidance in all aspects of their lives. A normative theory of business ethics is an attempt to focus this general theory exclusively upon those aspects of human life that involve business relationships. By thus limiting its range of application and translating the language of philosophical ethics into the everyday language of the business world, such a theory is specifically designed to provide human beings with ethical guidance while they are functioning in their capacity as business people.

Currently, the three leading normative theories of business ethics are the stockholder, stakeholder, and social contract theories. These theories present distinct and incompatible accounts of a business person's ethical obligations, and hence, at most one of them can be correct. The stockholder theory is the oldest of the three, and it would be fair to characterize it as out of favor with many contemporary business ethicists. To them, the stockholder theory represents a disreputable holdover from the bad old days of rampant capitalism. In contrast, the past decade and a half has seen the stakeholder theory gain such widespread adherence that it currently may be considered the conventionally-accepted position within the business ethics community.[4] In recent years, however, the social contract theory has been cited with considerable approbation and might accurately be characterized as challenging the stakeholder theory for preeminence among normative theorists.[5]

In this article, I propose to present a contrarian review of these theories. I will suggest that the stockholder theory is neither as outdated nor as unacceptable as it is often made to seem, and, further, that there are significant problems with both the stakeholder and the social contract theories. To do this, I propose to summarize each theory, analyze its supporting rationale, and canvass the chief objections against it. I will then draw a tentative conclusion regarding the adequacy of each theory. Finally, on the basis of these conclusions, I will attempt to suggest what the contours of a truly adequate normative theory of business ethics must be. Before turning to this, however, I feel compelled to say a word about the meaning of the phrase, "social responsibility."

In the business setting, "social responsibility" is often employed as a synonym for a business's or business person's ethical obligations. This is unfortunate because this loose, generic use of the phrase can often obscure or prejudice the issue of what a business's or business person's ethical obligations truly are. To see why, one must appreciate that the phrase is also used to contrast a business's or business person's "social" responsibilities with its or his or her ordinary ones. A business's or business person's ordinary responsibilities are to manage the business and expend business resources so as to accomplish the specific purposes for which the business was organized. Thus, in the case of a business organized for charitable or socially beneficial purposes (e.g., nonprofit corporations such as the Red Cross or the Nature Conservancy and for-profit corporations in which the stockholders pass resolutions compelling charitable contributions), it is a manager's ordinary responsibility to attempt to accomplish these goals. Even when a business is organized strictly for profit, it may be part of a manager's ordinary responsibilities to expend business resources for socially beneficial purposes when he or she believes that such expenditures will enhance the firm's long-term profitability (e.g., through the creation of customer goodwill). When the phrase "social responsibility" is used in contradistinction to this, the claim that businesses or business persons have social responsibilities indicates that they are obligated to expend business resources for socially beneficial purposes even when such expenditures are not designed to help the business achieve the ends for which it was organized.

When "social responsibility" in this narrow sense is conflated with "social responsibility" as a synonym for a business's or business person's ethical obligations in general, it groundlessly implies that businesses or business persons do, in fact, have ethical obligations to expend business resources in ways that do not promote the business's fundamental purposes. Since not all theorists agree that this is the case, a definition that carries such an implication should be scrupulously avoided. For this reason, I intend to employ "social responsibility" to refer exclusively to those ethical obligations, if any, that businesses or business persons have to expend business resources in ways that do not promote the specific purposes for which the business is organized. When the phrase is used in this way, it can make perfect sense to say that a business or business person has no social responsibilities. In fact, the first normative theory of business ethics that I will examine, the stockholder theory, makes precisely this claim.

II. The Stockholder Theory

The first normative theory of business ethics to be examined is the stockholder theory.[6] According to this theory, businesses are merely arrangements by which one group of people, the stockholders, advance capital to another group, the managers, to be used to realize specified ends and for which the stockholders receive an ownership interest in the venture.[7] Under this view, managers act as agents for the stockholders. They are empowered to manage the money advanced by the stockholders, but are bound by their agency relationship to do so exclusively for the purposes delineated by their stockholder principals.[8] The existence of this fiduciary relationship implies that managers cannot have an obligation to expend business resources in ways that have not been authorized by the stockholders regardless of any societal benefits that could be accrued by doing so. Of course, both stockholders and managers are free to spend their personal funds on any charitable or socially beneficial project they wish, but when functioning in their capacity as officers of the business, managers have a duty not to divert business resources away from the purposes expressly authorized by the stockholders. This implies that a business can have no social responsibilities.

Strictly speaking, the stockholder theory holds that managers are obligated to follow the (legal) directions of the stockholders, whatever these may be. Thus, if the stockholders vote that the business should not close a plant without giving its employees 90 days notice, should have no dealings with a country with a racist regime, or should endow a local public library, the management would be obligated to carry out such a directive regardless of its effect on the business's bottom line. In most cases, however, the stockholders issue no such explicit directives and purchase stock for the sole purpose of maximizing the return on their investment. When this is the purpose for which the stockholders have advanced their money, the managers' fiduciary obligation requires them to apply it to this end. For this reason, the stockholder theory is often imprecisely expressed as requiring managers to maximize the financial returns of the stockholders. The most famous statement of this shorthand description of the stockholder theory has been given by Milton Friedman who ironically refers to this as a "social responsibility." As he expresses it, "there is one and only one social responsibility of business—to use its resources and engage in activities designed to increase its profits so long as it stays within the rules of the game, which is to say, engages in open and free competition, without deception or fraud."[9]

It is important to note that even in this imprecise form, the stockholder theory does not instruct managers to do anything at all to increase the profitability of the business. It does not assert that managers have a moral blank check that allows them to ignore all ethical constraints in the pursuit of profits. Rather, it states that managers are obligated to pursue profit by all legal, nondeceptive means.[10] Far from asserting that there are no ethical constraints on a manager's obligation to increase profits, the stockholder theory contends that the ethical constraints society has embodied in its laws plus the general ethical tenet in favor of honest dealing constitute the ethical boundaries within which managers must pursue increased profitability.[11] A significant amount of the criticism that is directed against the stockholder theory results from overlooking these ethical limitations.[12]

For whatever reason, the stockholder theory has come to be associated with the type of utilitarian argument frequently advanced by free market economists.[13] Thus, supporting arguments often begin with the claim that when individual actors pursue private profit in a free market, they are led by Adam Smith's invisible hand to promote the general interest as well. It is then claimed that since, for each individual, "[b]y pursuing his own interest he frequently promotes that of the society more effectually than when he really intends to promote it,"[14] it is both unnecessary and counterproductive to exhort businesses or business persons to act directly to promote the common good. From this it is concluded that there is no justification for claiming that businesses or business persons have any social responsibilities other than to legally and honestly maximize the profits of the firm.

Although this consequentialist argument is the one most frequently cited in support of the stockholder theory, it must be noted that there is another, quite simple deontological argument for it as well. This argument is based on the observation that stockholders advance their money to business managers on the condition that it be used in accordance with their wishes. If the managers accept the money on this condition and then proceed to spend it to accomplish social goals not authorized by the stockholders, they would be violating their agreement and spending other people's money without their consent, which is wrong.[15]

The stockholder theory has been subjected to some harsh criticism by several of the leading business ethicists working today. It has been described as an outmoded relic of corporate law that even the law itself has evolved beyond,[16] as containing a "myopic view of corporate responsibility" that is unfortunately held by a significant number of business practitioners, and, more pointedly, as "corporate Neanderthalism ... with morally pernicious consequences,"[17] and as "not only foolish in theory, but cruel and dangerous in practice" and misguided "from its nonsensically one-sided assumption of responsibility to his pathetic understanding of stockholder personality as Homo economicus."[18] For a significant number of theorists, the stockholder theory is introduced into discussion not as a serious candidate for the proper ethical standard for the business environment, but merely as a foil for other, putatively more enlightened normative theories.

At least part of the explanation for this harsh treatment seems to be the stockholder theory's association with the utilitarian supporting argument described above. Few contemporary business ethicists have the kind of faith in the invisible hand of the market that neoclassical economists do. Most take for granted that a free market produces coercive monopolies, results in damaging externalities, and is beset by other instances of market failure such as the free rider and public goods problems, and thus cannot be relied upon to secure the common good.[19] Accordingly, to the extent that it is associated with this line of economic reasoning, the stockholder theory becomes tarred with the brush of these standard objections to laissez faire capitalism.

It should be pointed out, however, that it is not necessary to join the debate over the theoretical viability of laissez faire to demonstrate the vulnerability of the utilitarian defense of the stockholder theory.

This is because contemporary economic conditions are so far removed from those of a true free market as to render the point essentially moot. Regardless of the adequacy of the stockholder theory in a world of ideal markets, the world in which we currently reside is one where businesses may gain competitive advantages by obtaining government subsidies, tax breaks, protective tariffs, and state-conferred monopoly status (e.g., utilities, the Baby Bells, cable television franchises); having health, safety or environmental regulations written so as to burden small competitors; and otherwise purchasing governmental favor. In such a world, it is extremely unlikely that the pursuit of private profit will truly be productive of the public good. There is ample reason to be suspicious of such a claim in an environment in which 65 percent of the chief executive officers of the top 200 Fortune firms come to Washington, DC at least once every two weeks.[20]

It is important to note that the fact that the utilitarian argument for the stockholder theory may be seriously flawed does not mean that the theory is untenable. This is because the deontological argument for the theory, which has frequently been overlooked, is, in fact, the superior argument. To the extent that it has received serious consideration, the primary objection against it seems to consist in the contention that it is not wrong to spend other people's money without their consent as long as it is being done to promote the public interest.[21] This contention is usually bolstered by the observation that this is precisely what democratic governments do all the time (at least, in theory). Since such action is presumably justified in the political realm, so the objection goes, there is no reason to think that it is not equally justified in the business realm.

There are two serious problems with this objection, however. The first is that it misses the essential point of the argument. As stated above, this argument is deontological in character. It is based on an underlying assumption that there are certain principles of conduct that must be observed regardless of the generalized benefits that must be fore-gone by doing so. One of the most fundamental of these principles states that individuals must honor the commitments they voluntarily and knowingly undertake. Hence, the essence of the argument is the claim that it is morally wrong to violate one's freely-assumed agreement to use the stockholders' resources only as specified even though society could be made a somewhat better place by doing so. To assert that a manager may violate his or her agreement with the stockholders whenever doing so would promote the public interest is simply to deny this claim. It is to declare that one's duty to advance the common good overrides one's duty to honor one's agreements, and that the moral quality of one's actions must ultim-ately be judged according to a utilitarian standard. While some ethicists argue that the principle of util-ity is indeed the supreme ethical principle, this is far from obviously true, and any contention that merely assumes that it is cannot serve as a compelling objec-tion to a deontological argument.

The second problem is that the objection is based on a false analogy. The assumption that demo-cratic governments are morally justified in spending taxpayers' money without their consent to promote the general interest does not imply that businesses or business persons are justified in spending stock-holders' money without their consent for the same reason. Consider that once the citizens have made their required contribution to governmental efforts to benefit society, all should be equally entitled to the control of their remaining assets. Should a cit-izen elect to invest them in a savings account to pro-vide for his or her children's education or his or her old age, a banker who diverted some of these assets to other purposes, no matter how worthy, would clearly be guilty of embezzlement. For that matter, should the citizen elect to use his or her assets to purchase a new car, go on an extravagant vacation, or even take a course in business ethics, a car dealer, travel agent, or university that failed to deliver the bargained-for product in order to provide benefits to

others would be equally guilty. Why should it be any different if the citizen elects to invest in a business? At least superficially, it would appear that citizens have a right to control their after-tax assets that is not abrogated merely because they elect to purchase stock and that would be violated were business man-agers to use these assets in unauthorized ways. If this is not the case, some showing is required to demon-strate why not.

Of course, these comments in no way establish that the stockholder theory is correct. The most that they can demonstrate is that some of the objections that are frequently raised against it are ill-founded. Other, more serious objections remain to be consid-ered.[22] However, they do suggest that the cavalier dismissal the stockholder theory sometimes receives is unjustified, and that, at least at present, it should continue to be considered a serious candidate for the proper normative theory of business ethics.[23]

III. The Stakeholder Theory

The second of the leading normative theories of busi-ness ethics is the stakeholder theory. Unfortunately, "stakeholder theory" is somewhat of a troublesome label because it is used to refer to both an empirical theory of management and a normative theory of business ethics, often without clearly distinguishing between the two.[24] As an empirical theory of man-agement, the stakeholder theory holds that effective management requires the balanced consideration of and attention to the legitimate interests of all stake-holders,[25] defined as anyone who has "a stake in or claim on the firm."[26] This has been interpreted in both a wide sense that includes "any group or indi-vidual who can affect or is affected by the corpora-tion," and a more narrow sense that includes only "those groups who are vital to the survival and suc-cess of the corporation."[27] It is perhaps more familiar in its narrow sense in which the stakeholder groups are limited to stockholders, customers, employees, suppliers, management, and the local community.

Thus, as an empirical theory, the stakeholder theory asserts that a business's financial success can best be achieved by giving the interests of the business's stockholders, customers, employees, suppliers, management, and local community proper consideration and adopting policies which produce the optimal balance among them.[28]

When viewed as an empirical theory of management designed to prescribe a method for improving a business's performance, the stakeholder theory does not imply that businesses have any social responsibilities. In this sense, it is perfectly consistent with the normative stockholder theory since what is being asserted is the empirical claim that the best way to enhance the stockholders' return on their investment is to pay attention to the legitimate interests of all stakeholders. The essence of the stakeholder theory of management is that stakeholder management is required for managers to successfully meet their fiduciary obligation to the stockholders. For the purposes of this article, however, we are concerned with the stakeholder theory not as an empirical theory of management, but as a normative theory of business ethics.

When viewed as a normative theory, the stakeholder theory asserts that, regardless of whether stakeholder management leads to improved financial performance, managers should manage the business for the benefit of all stakeholders. It views the firm not as a mechanism for increasing the stockholders' financial returns, but as a vehicle for coordinating stakeholder interests and sees management as having a fiduciary relationship not only to the stockholders, but to all stakeholders. According to the normative stakeholder theory, management must give equal consideration to the interests of all stakeholders[29] and, when these interests conflict, manage the business so as to attain the optimal balance among them. This, of course, implies that there will be times when management is obligated to at least partially sacrifice the interests of the stockholders to those of other stakeholders. Hence, in its normative form, the stakeholder theory does imply that businesses have true social responsibilities.

The stakeholder theory holds that management's fundamental obligation is not to maximize the firm's financial success, but to ensure its survival by balancing the conflicting claims of multiple stakeholders. This obligation is to be met by acting in accordance with two principles of stakeholder management. The first, called the principle of corporate legitimacy, states that "the corporation should be managed for the benefit of its stakeholders: its customers, suppliers, owners, employees, and the local communities. The rights of these groups must be ensured and, further, the groups must participate, in some sense, in decisions that substantially affect their welfare."[30] The second, called the stakeholder fiduciary principle, states that "management bears a fiduciary relationship to stakeholders and to the corporation as an abstract entity. It must act in the interests of the stakeholders as their agent, and it must act in the interests of the corporation to ensure the survival of the firm, safeguarding the long-term stakes of each group."[31]

The stakeholder theory enjoys a considerable degree of approbation from both theorists and practitioners. In fact, it is probably fair to say that the stakeholder theory currently enjoys a breadth of acceptance equal to that the stockholder theory was said to have enjoyed in the past. To some extent, this may result from the fact that the theory seems to accord well with many people's moral intuitions, and, to some extent, it may simply be a spillover effect of the high regard in which the empirical version of the stakeholder theory is held as a theory of management. It is clear, however, that the normative theory's widespread acceptance does not derive from a careful examination of the arguments that have been offered in support of it. In fact, it is often remarked that the theory seems to lack a clear normative foundation.[32]

An argument that is frequently cited in support of the stakeholder theory is the one offered by Ed

Freeman and William Evan in their 1988 article.[33] That argument asserts that management's obligation to the stakeholders can be derived from Immanuel Kant's principle of respect for persons. This fundamental ethical principle holds that every human being is entitled to be treated not merely as a means to the achievement of the ends of others, but as a being valuable in his or her own right; that each person is entitled to be respected as an end in himself or herself. Since to respect someone as an end is to recognize that he or she is an autonomous moral agent, i.e., a being with desires of his or her own and the free will to act upon those desires, the principle of respect for persons requires respect for others' autonomy.

Freeman and Evan apply this principle to the world of business by claiming that businesses are bound to respect it as much as anyone else. Thus, businesses may not treat their stakeholders merely as means to the business's ends, but must recognize that as moral agents, all stakeholders are entitled "to agree to and hence participate (or choose not to participate) in the decisions to be used as such."[34] They then claim that it follows from this that all stakeholders are entitled to "participate in determining the future direction of the firm in which they have a stake."[35] However, because it is impossible to consult with all of a firm's stakeholders on every decision, this participation must be indirect. Therefore, the firm's management has an obligation to "represent" the interests of all stakeholders in the business's decision-making process. Accordingly, management is obligated to give equal consideration to the interests of all stakeholders in developing business policy and to manage the business so as to optimize the balance among these interests.

The main problem with this argument is that there is a gap in the reasoning that leads from the principle of respect for persons to the prescriptions of the stakeholder theory. It may readily be admitted that businesses are ethically bound to treat all persons, and hence all stakeholders, as entities worthy of respect as ends in themselves. It may further be admitted that this requires businesses to treat their stakeholders as autonomous moral agents, and hence, that stakeholders are indeed entitled "to agree to and hence participate (or choose not to participate) in the decisions to be used"[36] as means to business ends. The problem is that this implies only that no stakeholder may be forced to deal with the business without his or her consent, not that all stakeholders are entitled to a say in the business's decision-making process or that the business must be managed for their benefit.

It is certainly true that respect for the autonomy of others requires that one keep one's word. To deceive someone into doing something he or she would not otherwise agree to do would be to use him or her merely as a means to one's own ends. For this reason, the principle of respect for persons requires businesses to deal honestly with all of their stakeholders. This means that businesses must honor the contracts they enter into with their customers, employees, suppliers, managers, and stockholders and live up to any representations they freely make to the local community. However, it is simply incorrect to say that respect for another's autonomy requires that the other have a say in any decision that affects his or her interests. A student's interests may be crucially affected by what grade he or she receives in a course as may a Republican's by the decision of whom the Democrats nominate for President. But the autonomy of neither the student nor the Republican is violated when he or she is denied a say in these decisions.

An adherent of the stockholder theory could point out that employees (including managers), suppliers, and customers negotiate for and autonomously accept wage and benefit packages, purchasing arrangements, and sales contracts, respectively. It does not violate their autonomy or treat them with a lack of the respect they are due as persons to fail to provide them with benefits in excess of those they freely accept. However, if managers were to break their agreement with the stockholders to use business resources only as authorized in order to provide other stakeholders with such benefits, the managers would be violating the autonomy of the stockholders. Therefore, the stockholder theorist could contend that not only is the stakeholder theory not entailed by the principle of respect for persons, but to the extent that it instructs managers to use the stockholders' money in ways they have not approved, it is, in fact, violative of it.

Perhaps because of the problems with this argument, efforts have recently been made to provide a more adequate normative justification for the stakeholder theory. Indeed, Freeman and Evan have themselves offered an alternative argument that claims that changes in corporate law imply that businesses consist in sets of multilateral contracts among stakeholders that must be administered by managers.[37] Asserting that "all parties that are affected by a contract have a right to bargain about the distribution of those effects,"[38] they then apply a Rawlsian "veil of ignorance" decision procedure to deduce that "fair contracting" requires that all stakeholders be entitled to "participate in monitoring the actual effects of the firm on them,"[39] i.e., have a say in the business's decision-making process.

Unfortunately, this argument seems to have even more problems than the one it replaces. In the first place, Rawls' decision procedure was specifically designed to guide the construction of the basic structure of society and it is at least open to question whether it may be appropriately employed in the highly specific context of business governance issues. Further, deriving ethical conclusions from observations of the state of the law comes dangerously close to the classic fallacy of assuming that what is legally required must be ethically correct. More significantly, however, this new argument seems to suffer from the same defect as its predecessor since the assumption that all parties that are affected by a contract have a right to bargain about the distribution of those effects is virtually equivalent to the earlier

argument's problematic assumption that all parties affected by a business's actions have a right to participate in the business's decision-making process. As in the earlier argument, this is the assertion that must be established, not assumed.[40]

Another recent attempt at justification has been undertaken by Donaldson and Preston who claim to base the stakeholder theory on a theory of property. After asserting that the stockholder theory is "normatively unacceptable,"[41] they contend that because 1) property rights must be based on an underlying principle of distributive justice, 2) among theorists, "the trend is toward theories that are pluralistic, allowing more than one fundamental principle to play a role," and 3) "all critical characteristics underlying the classic theories of distributive justice are present among the stakeholders of a corporation," it follows that "the normative principles that underlie the contemporary theory of property rights also provide the foundation for the stakeholder theory as well."[42] However, because the authors have failed to provide any specification for what "the contemporary theory of property rights" is, this can be regarded as, at best, a preliminary sketch rather than a fully developed justificatory argument. Further, because premise 1 is open to serious question,[43] premise 2 seems to confuse academic opinion with evidence of truth, and premise 3 seems, at first glance, to be wholly unconnected to the conclusion, much work remains to be done before this argument can serve as an adequate basis for the stakeholder theory.

In sum, the lacunae in each of these supporting arguments suggest that, despite its widespread acceptance, the normative version of the stakeholder theory is simply not well-grounded. At this point, its adequacy as a normative theory of business ethics must be regarded as open to serious question.[44]

IV. The Social Contract Theory

The third normative theory of business ethics, the social contract theory, really comprises a family of closely related theories and, in some ways, is still in the process of formation.[45] However, in its most widely accepted form, the social contract theory asserts that all businesses are ethically obligated to enhance the welfare of society by satisfying consumer and employee interests without violating any of the general canons of justice.[46] Because the specific nature of this obligation can best be appreciated in the context of the theory's derivation, let us turn our attention immediately to the theory's supporting rationale.

The social contract theory is based on the traditional concept of a social contract, an implicit agreement between society and an artificial entity in which society recognizes the existence of the entity on the condition that it serves the interests of society in certain specified ways. As a normative theory of business ethics, the social contract theory is explicitly modeled on the political social contract theories of thinkers such as Thomas Hobbes, John Locke, and Jean-Jacques Rousseau. These political theorists each attempted to imagine what life would be like in the absence of a government, i.e., in the "state of nature," and asked what conditions would have to be met for citizens to agree to form one. The obligations of the government toward its citizens were then derived from the terms of this agreement.

The normative social contract theory of business ethics takes much the same approach toward deriving the social responsibilities of businesses. It begins by imagining a society in which there are no complex business organizations, i.e., a state of "individual production," and proceeds by asking what conditions would have to be met for the members of such a society to agree to allow businesses to be formed. The ethical obligations of businesses toward the individual members of society are then derived from the terms of this agreement. Thus, the social contract theory posits an implicit contract between the members of society and businesses in which the members of society grant businesses the right to exist in return for certain specified benefits.

In granting businesses the right to exist, the members of society give them legal recognition as single agents and authorize them to own and use land and natural resources and to hire the members of society as employees.[47] The question then becomes what the members of society would demand in return. The minimum would seem to be "that the benefits from authorizing the existence of productive organizations outweigh the detriments of doing so."[48] In general, this would mean that businesses would be required to "enhance the welfare of society ... in a way which relies on exploiting corporations' special advantages and minimizing disadvantages"[49] while remaining "within the bounds of the general canons of justice."[50]

This generalization may be thought of as giving rise to a social contract with two terms: the social welfare term and the justice term. The social welfare term recognizes that the members of society will be willing to authorize the existence of businesses only if they gain by doing so. Further, there are two distinct capacities in which the members of society stand to gain from businesses: as consumers and as employees. As consumers, people can benefit from the existence of businesses in at least three ways. First, businesses provide increased economic efficiency by maximizing the advantages of specialization, improving decisionmaking resources, and increasing the capacity to use and acquire expensive technology and resources. Second, businesses provide stable levels of output and channels of distribution. And third, they provide increased liability resources from which to compensate injured consumers. As employees, people can benefit from the existence of businesses by receiving increased income potential, diffused personal legal liability for harmful errors, and the ability to participate in "income-allocation schemes ... detached from the vicissitudes of [their] capacity to produce."[51] However, businesses can also have negative effects on consumers and employees. People's interests as consumers can be harmed when businesses pollute the environment and deplete natural resources, undermine the personal accountability of their constituent members, and misuse political power. People's interests as employees can be harmed when they are alienated from the product of their labor, suffer from lack of control over their working conditions, and are subjected to monotonous and dehumanizing working conditions. These, then, constitute the respective advantages and disadvantages that businesses can provide to and impose upon society. Therefore, when fully specified, the social welfare term of the social contract requires that businesses act so as to 1) benefit consumers by increasing economic efficiency, stabilizing levels of output and channels of distribution, and increasing liability resources; 2) benefit employees by increasing their income potential, diffusing their personal liability, and facilitating their income allocation; while 3) minimizing pollution and depletion of natural resources, the destruction of personal accountability, the misuse of political power, as well as worker alienation, lack of control over working conditions, and dehumanization.

The justice term recognizes that the members of society will be willing to authorize the existence of businesses only if businesses agree to remain within the bounds of the general canons of justice. Admittedly, precisely what these canons require is far from settled. However, since there seems to be general agreement that the least they require is that businesses "avoid fraud and deception, ... show respect for their workers as human beings, and ... avoid any practice that systematically worsens the situation of a given group in society,"[52] it is reasonable to read the justice term as requiring at least this much.

In general, then, the social contract theory holds that managers are ethically obligated to abide by both the social welfare and justice terms of the social contract. Clearly, when fully specified, these terms impose significant social responsibilities on the managers of business enterprises.

The social contract theory is often criticized on the ground that the "social contract" is not a contract at all. To appreciate the nature of this criticism, let us borrow some terminology from the legal realm. The law recognizes three types of contracts: express contracts, implied contracts, and quasi-contracts. An express contract consists in an explicit agreement made in speech or writing. In this case, there is a true meeting of the minds of the parties that is expressly memorialized through language. An implied contract consists in an agreement that is manifested in some other way. For example, continuing to deal with another party under the terms of an expired contract can imply an agreement to renew or, perhaps more familiarly, failing to return an invoice marked "cancel" following a trial membership can imply a contract to buy four books in the next twelve months. As with express contracts, in such cases, there is a true meeting of the minds. However, in implied contracts, that agreement is manifested through action rather than language. A quasi-contract, on the other hand, consists in the legal imposition of a contractual relationship where there has been no meeting of the minds because such is necessary to avoid injustice. For example, a doctor who expends resources aiding an unconscious patient in an emergency situation is said to have a quasi-contract for reasonable compensation even though there was no antecedent agreement between the parties. In quasi-contracts, the law acts as though there has been a meeting of the minds where none in fact exists in order to do justice.

Critics of the social contract theory point out that the social contract is neither an express nor an implied contract. This is because there has been no true meeting of the minds between those who decide to form businesses and the members of the society in which they do so. Most people who start businesses do so by simply following the steps prescribed by state law and would be quite surprised to learn that by doing so they had contractually agreed to serve society's interests in ways that were not specified in the law and that can significantly reduce the profitability of the newly formed firm.[53] To enter a contractual arrangement, whether expressly or by implication, one has to at least be aware that one is doing so. Thus, the critics maintain that the social contract must be a quasi-contract, which is merely a fiction rather than a true contract.

This objection is not very distressing to social contract theorists, however. They freely admit that the social contract is a fictional or hypothetical contract, but go on to claim that this is precisely what is required to identify managers' ethical obligations. As Thomas Donaldson has put it, "if the contract were something other than a 'fiction,' it would be inadequate for the purpose at hand: namely revealing the moral foundations of productive organizations."[54] What the social contract theorists are admitting here is that the moral force of the social contract is not derived from the consent of the parties. Rather, they are advancing a moral theory that holds that "[p]roductive organizations should behave as if they had struck a deal, the kind of deal that would be acceptable to free, informed parties acting from positions of equal moral authority ..."[55]

This seems perfectly adequate as a response to the objection. It does suggest, however, that much of the psychological appeal of the social contract theory is based on a confusion. This is because a great deal of the theory's appeal to ordinary (philosophically untrained) business practitioners derives from their natural, intuitive identification of contract terminology with consent. To the extent that the language of contract suggests that one has given consent, it has a strong emotive force. People generally accept consent as a source of moral obligation, and this is especially true of the business practitioner who makes contracts every day and whose success or failure often turns on his or her reputation for upholding them. Most people would agree that when one voluntarily gives one's word, one is ethically bound to keep it. Thus, business practitioners as well as people generally are psychologically more willing to accept obligations when they believe they have consented to them. By employing contract terminology when

consent plays no role in grounding the posited social responsibilities of business, the social contract theory inappropriately benefits from the positive psychological attitude that this terminology engenders. For this reason, it is not unreasonable to suggest that the social contract theory trades upon the layperson's favorable attitude toward consent with no intention of delivering the goods.

This, of course, casts no aspersions on the theory's philosophical adequacy. However, the admission that the social contract is actually a quasi-contract does provide good reason to believe that the social contract theory has not been adequately supported. Once consent has been abandoned as the basis for the posited social responsibilities, the acceptability of the social contract theory rests squarely on the adequacy of the moral theory that undergirds it. This theory asserts that justice requires businesses and business managers to behave as though they had struck a deal "that would be acceptable to free, informed parties acting from positions of equal moral authority."[56] This may be correct, but it is not patently so. It is far from obvious that justice demands that managers behave as if they had made an agreement with hypothetical people, especially when doing so would violate real-world agreements made with actual people (e.g., the company's stockholders). It seems equally reasonable to assert that justice demands only that managers abide by the will of the people as it has been expressed by their political representatives in the commercial law of the state, or perhaps merely that they deal honestly with all parties and refrain from taking any illegal or harmful actions. Until the theory of justice on which the social contract theory rests has been fully articulated and defended, there is simply no reason to prefer it to any other putative normative theory of business ethics.[57] At present, therefore, this version of the social contract theory cannot be regarded as established.

There is, however, another version of the social contract theory that is genuinely consent-based and thus cannot be criticized on this ground.[58] This version asserts that the business enterprise is characterized by a myriad of "extant social contracts," informal agreements that embody "actual behavioral norms which derive from shared goals, beliefs and attitudes of groups or communities of people."[59] These extant social contracts are not quasi-contracts, but true agreements which, although sometimes express, are usually "implied from [sic] certain characteristics, attitudes and patterns of the group"[60] and "represent the view of the community concerning what constitutes proper behavior within the confines of the community."[61] According to this version of the theory, whenever the extant social contracts pass a "filtering test," i.e., are found not to be violative of the tenets of general ethical theory, they give rise to "genuine ethical norms" that managers are ethically obligated to obey.

There is nothing patently objectionable about this version of the social contract theory. However, it is so underdeveloped that it is difficult to know what to make of it. For example, it is not clear whether the theory contains an implicit norm against entering into social contracts that give rise to incompatible obligations or are incompatible with obligations that arise from one's earlier voluntary agreements. If it does, the theory seems to collapse into the stockholder theory which instructs managers to deal honestly with others and honor all agreements that do not violate their antecedent voluntary agreement to use the stockholders' resources only as authorized. If it does not, it seems to prescribe a host of incompatible obligations.[62] Furthermore, because the filtering test has not been specified, this version of the social contract theory reduces to the claim that one is obligated to abide by the informal agreements one has entered into as long as doing so is ethically acceptable. Although this does not say nothing, it says very little. For example, if the filtering test places primacy on a deontological obligation to honor one's agreements, the theory becomes coextensive with the stockholder theory and implies that businesses have no social responsibilities. However, if it places

primacy on the principle of utility, the theory may produce a set of social responsibilities very much like that prescribed by the stakeholder theory. Finally, if it prescribes a general obligation to behave as though one had made an agreement with perfectly rational, self-interested, free and equal hypothetical people, the theory might produce a set of social responsibilities equivalent to those prescribed by the earlier version of the social contract theory. As this diversity of outcome suggests, in its present skeletal form, this version of the social contract theory is, at best, of limited usefulness.[63]

V. Conclusion

In this article, I have subjected each of the three leading normative theories of business ethics to critical examination. I have argued that the stockholder theory is not as obviously flawed as it is sometimes supposed to be and that several of the objections conventionally raised against it are misdirected. I have also suggested that the deontological argument in support of the stockholder theory is not obviously unsound, although I have admittedly not subjected this argument to the scrutiny that would be necessary to establish its soundness. Further, I have argued that the supporting arguments for the stakeholder theory are significantly flawed and that the social contract theory either has not been adequately supported or is too underdeveloped to be useful. Thus, I have suggested that the amount of confidence that is currently placed in the stakeholder theory and is coming to be placed in the social contract theory is not well founded.

Although it may appear surprising given these conclusions, I do not view this article as a brief for the stockholder theory. Rather, I view it as a compass that can point us in the direction of a truly adequate normative theory of business ethics. I should add, however, that I also believe it points to a serious difficulty that must be overcome in order to arrive at any such theory.

To see what I mean, I would ask you to consider that all three normative theories share a common feature; they all either explicitly or implicitly recognize the preeminent moral value of individual consent. The stockholder theory is explicitly based on consent. The ethical obligations it posits are claimed to derive directly from the voluntary agreement each business officer makes on accepting his or her position to use the stockholders' resources strictly in accordance with their wishes. Similarly, the stakeholder theory is at least implicitly based on consent. The ethical obligation it places on business officers to manage the firm in the interest of all stakeholders is supposed to derive from the claim that every stakeholder is entitled to a say in decisions that affect his or her interests, which itself contains the implicit recognition of each individual's right to control his or her own destiny.[64] Finally, consent resides at the heart of the social contract theory as well. This is clear with regard to the extant social contract variant of the theory in which the manager's ethical obligations are explicitly based on consent. However, even the hypothetical social contract variant indirectly recognizes the moral significance of consent. For although it derives managers' ethical obligations from a depersonalized, morally sanitized, hypothetical form of consent, there would be no reason to cast the theory in terms of a contract at all if consent were not recognized as a fundamental source of ethical obligation.

The fact that all three normative theories of business ethics rely on the moral force of individual consent should come as no surprise given a proper understanding of what a business is, i.e., "a voluntary association of individuals, united by a network of contracts"[65] organized to achieve a specified end.[66] Because businesses consist in nothing more than a multitude of voluntary agreements among individuals, it is entirely natural that the ethical obligations of the parties to these agreements, including those of the managers of the business, should derive from the individual consent of each. Clearly, any attempt to

provide a general account of the ethical obligations of businesses and business people must ultimately rely on the moral force of the individual's freely-given consent.[67]

Recognizing this tells us much about what an adequate normative theory of business ethics must look like. If businesses are merely voluntary associations of individuals, then the ethical obligations of business people will be the ethical obligations individuals incur by joining voluntary associations, i.e., the ordinary ethical obligations each has as a human being plus those each has voluntarily assumed by agreement. Just as individuals do not take on ethical obligations beyond those they agree to by joining a chess club, a political party, or a business school faculty, so too individuals do not become burdened with unagreed upon obligations by going into or joining a business. There is no point in time at which the collection of individuals that constitutes a business is magically transformed into a new, separate and distinct entity that is endowed with rights or laden with obligations not possessed by the individual human beings that comprise it.

This implies that an adequate normative theory of business ethics must capture the ethical obligations generated when an individual voluntarily enters the complex web of contractual agreements that constitutes a business. Of the three theories I have examined, the stockholder theory comes closest to achieving this because it focuses on the actual agreement that exists between the stockholders and managers. It is woefully incomplete, however, because it 1) does not adequately address the limits managers' ordinary ethical obligations as human beings place on the actions they may take in the business environment, and 2) entirely fails to address the managerial obligations that arise out of the actual agreements made with the non-stockholder participants in the business enterprise.[68] Of course, recognizing these deficiencies of the stockholder theory also highlights the essential difficulty in constructing a satisfactory normative theory of business ethics; the need to generalize across the myriad of individual contractual agreements that are the constituent elements of the business.

Can an adequate consent-based normative theory of business ethics be devised? Can the ethical obligations arising from the agreements that characterize the typical business as well as those that individuals carry with them when they enter the business venture be captured in a manageable set of principles expressed in language accessible to the ordinary business person? Considering the differing nature of the relationships and agreements involved in a business of any complexity, devising such a set of principles may appear to be a daunting, if not hopeless, task.[69] Nevertheless, I believe the present survey indicates that this is a challenge that must be undertaken if a supportable normative theory of business ethics is to be devised. Undertaking this challenge, however, must remain the project of another day.[70]

NOTES

1 J.D., Ph.D., Philosophy, Duke University, LL.M. Temple University School of Law. This paper has greatly benefitted from the thoughtful comments and suggestions of Thomas Donaldson, Dennis Quinn, and Tom Beauchamp of Georgetown University, Thomas Dunfee of the Wharton School, Thomas Jones of the University of Washington, Ian Maitland of the University of Minnesota, Jeff Nesteruk of Franklin & Marshall College, Douglas Den Uyl of Bellarmine College, Patricia Werhane of the Darden Graduate School of Business Administration, Ann C. Tunstall, and my anonymous reviewers. I am sincerely grateful to each of them for their assistance. An earlier version of this article was presented as part of the John F. Connelly Business Ethics Seminar Series at Georgetown University.

2 For a famous example of this, see Andrew Stark, "What's the Matter with Business Ethics?" *Harvard Business Review* Vol. 71 (1993): 38. See also Thomas Donaldson and Thomas W. Dunfee, "Integrative Social Contracts Theory: A Communitarian Conception of Business Ethics," *Economics and Philosophy* Vol. 11 (1995): 85, 87.

3 I am employing this phrase in an effort to avoid the confusion engendered by referring to strictly normative theories as "theories of corporate social responsibility." The latter phrase has been used to refer to not only normative theories, which attempt to identify the philosophically verifiable ethical obligations of businesses and business persons, but also to theories that are either purely or partially descriptive or instrumental in nature, such as those that focus on businesses' or business person's responsiveness to societal expectations or demands. Indeed, historically speaking, the concept of corporate social responsibility arose as a response to an increasing level of criticism of the business system in general and the power and privilege of large corporations in particular, see Thomas M. Jones. "Corporate Social Responsibility: Revisited, Redefined," *California Business Review* Vol. 22 (1980): 59, and, to some extent, as a reaction against the stockholder theory, one of the normative theories to be examined in the body of this article. As a result, the theories of corporate social responsibility should probably be seen as a genus of which what I am calling the normative theories of business ethics are a species.

4 Evidence for this may be found not only in the inordinately large percentage of business ethics journal articles that discuss the stakeholder theory favorably, but in the increasing number of textbooks that are being written from the stakeholder perspective. See, e.g., Ronald M. Green, *The Ethical Manager* (1994), Joseph W. Weiss, *Business Ethics: A Managerial, Stakeholder Approach* (1994), Archie B. Carroll, *Business*

and Society: Ethics and Stakeholder Management (1996).

5 Consider, for example, the recent special issue of *Business Ethics Quarterly* devoted to the social contract theory. *Business Ethics Quarterly* Vol. 5 (Thomas W. Dunfee, ed., 1995): 167.

6 In this article, I intentionally speak in terms of "the stockholder theory" rather than "agency theory" to emphasize that I am discussing a normative theory. "Agency theory" seems to be used ambiguously to refer to both the attempt to produce an empirical description of the relationship between managers and stockholders and the normative implications that would flow from such a relationship. See Norman E. Bowie and R. Edward Freeman, "Ethics and Agency Theory: An Introduction," in *Ethics and Agency Theory* (Norman E. Bowie and R. Edward Freeman, eds., 1992), 3-4. In order to avoid this ambiguity in the present context, I employ the label "stockholder theory" to indicate that I am referring strictly to a theory of how businesses or business people should behave.

7 Historically, the normative theories of business ethics grew out of the literature on corporate social responsibility. As a result, they are often expressed as though they apply only to corporations rather than to businesses generally. This is certainly the case with regard to the stockholder theory. To be adequate, however, a normative theory of business ethics should apply to businesses of all types.

   For ease of expression, I intend to follow the convention and employ the terminology of the corporate form in my representation of the theories. However, I will attempt to show how each of the theories may be generalized to apply to other forms of business as well. See infra notes 24, 45, 64.

8 I wish to emphasize again that the stockholder theory is a normative and not a descriptive theory. As such, it asserts not that managers are, in fact, the agents of the stockholders, but that they are ethically obligated to act as though they were.

9 Milton Friedman, *Capitalism and Freedom* (1962), 133. I should point out that Friedman does not always describe the constraints on the pursuit of profit this precisely. Often, he merely states that businesses should "make as much money as possible while conforming to the basic rules of society, both those embodied in law and those embodied in ethical custom." Milton Friedman, "The Social Responsibility of Business is to Increase Its Profits," *New York Times Magazine*, September 13, 1970 [above, pp. 65–68]. Of course, when stated this broadly, Friedman's injunction becomes a triviality asserting nothing more than that one should pursue profits ethically. Although this has been the source of much criticism of Friedman's particular expression of the stockholder theory, it need not concern us in the present context. The more specific statement given in the text does define a substantive position worthy of serious consideration, and so, that is the formulation that will be used in this article.

10 The additional restriction of Friedman's formulation that requires managers to engage solely in open and free competition is usually ignored. In today's regulatory environment, it is not regarded as unethical to lobby the government for favor. In many cases, such activities are necessary as a matter of corporate self-defense.

11 It may be accurate to characterize the stockholder theory as proposing an "ethical division of labor." According to the stockholder theory, the nature of the business environment itself imposes a basic duty of honest dealing on business people. However, the theory also claims that for there to be any more extensive restrictions on managers, it is the job of society as a whole to impose them through the legislative process.

It is, of course, true that this approach defines managers' ethical obligations partially in terms of their legal obligations and implies that their ethical obligations will change as the legislation that defines and regulates the business environment changes. This, in turn, implies that the stockholder theory is not self-sufficient, but is dependent upon the political theory (which delimits the scope of the state's power to legislate) within which it is embedded. This dependence does not render the theory unintelligible, however. At any particular point in time, the theory can be understood as asserting that a business or business person must refrain from engaging in deceptive practices and violating the laws of the land as they exist at that time.

12 It must be kept in mind at all times that the version of the stockholder theory that asserts that the manager is ethically obliged to increase the company's profits is true only for those for-profit companies in which it is reasonable to interpret the stockholders wishes as the maximization of profit. Whenever the stockholders have indicated that they wish their resources to be used for other purposes, the stockholder theory requires managers to attempt to fulfill those purposes, even if doing so comes at the expense of profits.

13 See, e.g., Dennis P. Quinn and Thomas M. Jones, "An Agent Morality View of Business Policy," *Academy of Management Review* Vol. 20 (1995): 22, 24; William M. Evan and R. Edward Freeman, "A Stakeholder Theory of the Modern Corporation: Kantian Capitalism," in *Ethical Theory and Business* (Tom L. Beauchamp and Norman E. Bowie, eds., 4th ed., 1993), 75, 77.

14 Adam Smith, *The Wealth of Nations*, bk. IV, ch. 2, para. 9.

15 This argument can be expressed in more philosophically sophisticated language by stating that one who breaches an agreement that in-

duced another to deal with him or her is treating the other merely as a means to his or her own ends, and is thus violating the Kantian principle of respect for persons.

It is useful to note that Friedman himself offers this deontological argument in support of the stockholder theory, not the utilitarian argument described previously. See Milton Friedman, "The Social Responsibility of Business is to Increase Its Profits," supra note 10. See also Friedman, *Capitalism and Freedom*, supra note 10, at 135.

16 See Evan and Freeman, supra note 14, at 76-77; Thomas Donaldson and Lee E. Preston, "The Stakeholder Theory of the Corporation: Concepts, Evidence, and Implications," *Academy of Management Review* Vol. 20 (1995): 65, 81-82.

17 Thomas Donaldson, *The Ethics of International Business* (1989), 45.

18 Robert C. Solomon, *Ethics and Excellence* (1992), 45.

19 Evan and Freeman, supra note 14, at 77-78.

20 See James D. Gwartney and Richard E. Wagner, "Public Choice and the Conduct of Representative Government," in *Public Choice and Constitutional Economics* (James D. Gwartney and Richard E. Wagner, eds., 1988), 3, 23.

21 This highly telescoped formulation of what is, in truth, a considerably more sophisticated consequentialist argument is employed strictly in the interest of conciseness. The fuller articulation it deserves must await a more detailed consideration of the stockholder theory than the present overview of the normative theories of business ethics permits.

22 For two examples, see infra p. 35.

23 As mentioned previously, see supra note 8, because of its historical association with debate over corporate social responsibility, the stockholder theory is expressed in language that suggests the corporate form, e.g., stock, stockholders. De-

spite this, the stockholder theory can be applied to all forms of business. In its generalized form, the theory would simply state that managers are ethically obligated to use business resources that have been advanced to them under condition that they be used for specified purposes to accomplish only those purposes. Thus, whether the managers are officers of a public corporation funded by stockholders, managing partners of a limited partnership funded by the limited partners, or sole proprietors funded by investors, they are obligated to use the business's resources in accordance with the agreements they entered into with the stockholders, limited partners, or investors.

24 Unlike "agency theory," however, the phrase "stakeholder theory" cannot be avoided.

Various attempts have been made to clarify the distinction between the normative and non-normative variants of the stakeholder theory. For example, Kenneth Goodpaster distinguishes non-normative "strategic stakeholder synthesis" from normative "multi-fiduciary stakeholder synthesis." Kenneth E. Goodpaster, "Business Ethics and Stakeholder Analysis," *Business Ethics Quarterly* Vol. 1 (1991): 53. Recently, Thomas Donaldson and Lee Preston have further clarified the situation by identifying and distinguishing three different "types" of stakeholder theory; descriptive/empirical, instrumental, and normative. See Donaldson and Preston, supra note 17, at 69-73.

For purposes of simplicity and because in this article I will not be commenting on the distinction between the descriptive/empirical and instrumental versions of the theory, I will employ the term "empirical" in a generic sense to refer to the non-normative versions of the stakeholder theory.

25 See R.E. Freeman, *Strategic Management: A Stakeholder Approach* (1984); Donaldson and Preston, supra note 17, at 71.

26 See Evan and Freeman, supra note 14, at 76.

27 Id. at 79. See also E. Freeman and D. Reed, "Stockholders and Stakeholders: A New Perspective on Corporate Governance," in *Corporate Governance: A Definitive Exploration of the Issues* (C. Huizinga, ed., 1983).

28 This corresponds to Goodpaster's strategic stakeholder synthesis and Donaldson and Preston's instrumental stakeholder theory. See supra note 25.

29 In stating that management must give equal consideration to the interests of all stakeholders, I am not ignoring the work being done to distinguish among different classes of stakeholders. See, e.g., Max B.E. Clarkson, "A Stakeholder Framework for Analyzing and Evaluating Corporate Social Performance," *Academy of Management Review* Vol. 20 (1995): 92, 105-08. On this point, it is essential to distinguish between the stakeholder theory as a normative theory of business ethics on the one hand and as either a theory of corporate social responsibility or a theory of management on the other. See supra note 4 and the material immediately preceding this note. For purposes of either evaluating a business's responsiveness to societal demands or describing effective management techniques, it can make perfect sense to distinguish among different classes of stakeholders. However, given the arguments that have been provided in support of the stakeholder theory as a normative theory of business ethics (to be discussed below), it can not. The logic of these arguments, whether Kantian, Rawlsian, or derived from property rights, makes no allowance for stakeholders of differing moral status. Each implies that all stakeholders are entitled to equal moral consideration. In my opinion, this represents a major difference between the normative and non-normative versions of the stakeholder theory, and one that is likely to generate confusion if not carefully attended to.

30 Evan and Freeman, supra note 14, at 82.

31 Id. Clearly, this is Goodpaster's multi-fiduciary stakeholder synthesis. See supra note 25.

This feature of the normative stakeholder theory immediately gives rise to the objection that it is based an oxymoron. Given the meaning of the word "fiduciary," it is impossible to have a fiduciary relationship to several parties who, like the stakeholders of a corporation, have potentially conflicting interests. Further, even if this did make sense, placing oneself in such a position would appear to be unethical. For example, an attorney who represented two parties with conflicting interests would clearly be guilty of a violation of the canon of ethics.

This objection clearly deserves a fuller treatment than it can be given in a footnote. However, because the purpose of the present work is limited to the critical examination of the arguments offered in support of the three main normative theories of business ethics, an attempt to fully evaluate the theories' adequacy would clearly be beyond its scope. Hence, a more detailed examination of this objection must be deferred until a later time.

32 See, e.g., Donaldson and Preston, supra note 17, at 72, who point out that in most of the stakeholder literature "the fundamental normative principles involved are often unexamined."

33 Evan and Freeman, supra note 14. This was not the earliest attempt to provide a normative grounding for the stakeholder theory. See, e.g., Thomas M. Jones and Leonard D. Goldberg, "Governing the Large Corporation: More Arguments for Public Directors," *Academy of Management Review* Vol. 7 (1982): 603. However, it does appear to be the first effort to derive the stakeholder theory directly from a widely accepted principle of philosophical ethics. This apparently accounts for the widespread attention it has commanded among the commentators.

34 Evan and Freeman, supra note 14.

35 Id. at 76.

36 Id. at 78.

37 R. Edward Freeman and William Evan, "Corporate Governance: A Stakeholder Interpretation," *Journal of Behavioral Economics* Vol. 19 (1990): 337.

38 Id. at 352.

39 Id. at 353.

40 The unsupported and counter-intuitive assumption that people are ethically entitled to a say in any decision which affects their interests appears to lie at the heart of most attempts to ground the stakeholder theory, and can be found even in those that predate the ones presently under consideration. For an early example of this, consider Jones and Goldberg's 1982 assertion that "if legitimacy centers on the consent of the governed, the legitimacy of corporate decisions made by managers would hinge on the willingness of people *affected* by these decisions to recognize the right of the managers to make them. Because several groups *are affected* by managerial decisions, legitimacy depends on acceptance of this authority by several types of 'stake holders.'" Jones and Goldberg, *supra* note 34, at 606 (emphasis added).

41 Donaldson and Preston, supra note 17, at 82. The rationale underlying this claim is, at best, somewhat murky. The sentence which immediately follows it is: "Changes in state incorporation laws to reflect a 'constituency' perspective have already been mentioned." Id. Professor Donaldson has assured me that this is not intended as an appeal to the ethical authority of the law, but rather to the normative reasons behind the change in the law as indicated by the article's next sentence: "The normative basis for these changes in current mainstream legal thinking is articulated in the recent American Law Institute report, *Principles of Corporate Governance* (1992)." Id. However, the sections

of the ALI report that the authors cite state nothing more than that corporate officials are legally permitted to take ethical considerations into account even where doing so would not enhance corporate profit or shareholder gain and that they are "subject to the same ethical considerations as other members of society." Id. This, however, is wholly consistent with the stockholder theory which asserts that corporate managers are not only legally permitted, but ethically required to restrict the means by which they seek to carry out the instructions of their stockholder principals to those which fall within the ethical boundaries set by the law and the principles of honest dealing and open and free competition. The ALI report is indeed inconsistent with the claim that corporate managers should pursue profit by any means without regard to legal or ethical constraints. It hardly needs repeating, however, that this is not the claim made by the stockholder theory, but that of the straw man the theory's opponents trot out to stand in its stead. At any rate, it is entirely unclear how the comments cited by Donaldson and Preston provide any support for the assertion that the stockholder theory is normatively unacceptable.

42 Donaldson and Preston, supra note 17, at 82-84.

43 Philosophers such as Robert Nozick would not accept this contention nor would anyone who argues from a classical liberal perspective. Further, as a matter of purely historical fact, the assertion is clearly false.

44 Like the other theories, the stakeholder theory is expressed in language suggesting the corporate form. However, the theory is clearly perfectly general. Whether the business concerned is a corporation, partnership, or sole proprietorship, the business's stakeholders, those who are vital to its survival and success, can be identified. The stakeholder theory requires the managers to manage the business for the benefit of these stakeholders, regardless of the business's form.

45 Professors Thomas Donaldson and Thomas Dunfee have recently introduced a complex and highly sophisticated version of social contract theory that they call Integrative Social Contracts Theory (ISCT). See Thomas Donaldson and Thomas W. Dunfee, "Toward a Unified Conception of Business Ethics: Integrative Social Contracts Theory," *Academy of Management Review* Vol. 19 (1994): 252. The authors are presently in the process of developing a book length exposition of this theory. Although this theory is beyond the scope of the present work and hence will not be directly addressed, it should be noted that ISCT constitutes an attempt to marry the individual social contract theories of Donaldson and Dunfee, both of which are addressed. Therefore, to some extent, the comments made in this article may be extrapolated to apply to ISCT as well.

46 See Thomas Donaldson, *Corporations and Morality*, ch. 2 (1982).

47 See Donaldson, *Corporations and Morality*, supra note 47, at 43. The specific description of the social contract theory that follows is taken from this source.

48 Id. at 44.

49 Id. at 54.

50 Id. at 53.

51 Id. at 48-49.

52 Id. at 53. This last requirement is apparently intended as an antidiscrimination provision.

53 Indeed, many entrepreneurs forum-shop, electing to go into business in the state whose legal regime appears least burdensome to them. Such individuals would clearly be shocked to be told that regardless of which state they chose, they had agreed to abide by the restrictions described by the social contract theory.

54 Thomas Donaldson, *The Ethics of International Business* (1989), 56.

55 Id. at 61.

56 Id.

57 Because this version of the social contract theory appears to be based on what is essentially a Rawlsian theory of justice, this task would indeed be a formidable one. It would require an examination not only of the relative merits of a Rawlsian conception of justice as opposed to Nozickian and other conceptions, but also of whether such a conception is appropriate in the present limited realm of application. However, once consent has been abandoned as the basis for the social contract, there seems to be no avoiding this. Currently, the best that can be said about this version of the social contract theory is that it is, at most, as well established as John Rawls' theory of justice.

58 See Thomas W. Dunfee, "Business Ethics and Extant Social Contracts," *Business Ethics Quarterly* Vol. 1 (1991): 23.

59 Id. at 32.

60 Id. In fact, there is some question whether all extant social contracts are true agreements since it is claimed that consent is implied by "merely enjoying the benefits of the community or even engaging in transactions within the realm of the community." Id. This raises the thorny problem of how one can be said to consent to an agreement without being aware one is doing so. However, because any attempt to resolve this point is beyond the scope of the current work, I will assume for purposes of the present discussion that all extant social contracts are true, consent-based agreements.

61 Id. at 33.

62 This may be an unfair characterization. The theory contemplates the possibility of one simultaneously belonging to several communities with incompatible social contracts and asserts that such conflicts must be resolved on the basis of an unspecified "priority rule." (It should be noted that, like the filtering test discussed below, as long as the priority rule remains unspecified, it is impossible to fully evaluate this theory.) However, the theory does not seem to address the situation in which one has entered into incompatible agreements within a single community. It is the latter point that I am presently addressing.

63 As was the case with the stakeholder theory, although the social contract theory is sometimes expressed in the language of the corporation, it clearly applies to businesses generally. Under a social contract approach, the members of society authorize the existence of not merely corporations, but businesses of any form. Thus, all businesses are bound by the terms of the social contract. As a matter of fact, Donaldson's early version of the theory was expressed in perfectly general terms, speaking not about corporations, but about "productive organizations."

64 I have argued in the body of this article that there is, in fact, no ethical entitlement to have a say in any decision that affects one's interests and that the attempts of stakeholder theorists to derive one from Kant's principle of respect for persons, Rawls' theory of justice, and a contemporary theory of property rights have been unsuccessful. However, assuming arguendo that the stakeholder theorists are correct and that such an entitlement does exist, it would certainly imply that individuals are ethically entitled to control their own lives.

65 Robert Hessen, "A New Concept of Corporations: A Contractual and Private Property Model," *Hastings Law Journal* Vol. 30 (1979): 1327, 1330.

66 This is as true of corporations as it is of any other type of business organization. The claim that a corporation is a "creature of the state," endowed by the government with special privileges not available to other freely-organized forms of business is asserted so frequently that it is typically regarded as a truism. That this is

not, in fact, the case, is amply demonstrated by Robert Hessen in the article cited in the immediately preceding note. I heartily recommend it to those unfamiliar with the history and law of corporations.

I should add that I am not claiming either that the idea of a business as a network of contracts is a new or original insight (its long lineage is indicated by the source I cite in support of it in the immediately preceding note) or that it commands universal acceptance. I am suggesting, however, that it is an accurate characterization of the ethical nature of business, and further, that support for it can be found in the centrality of consent to each of the three previously examined theories. I am also suggesting that it is an observation that deserves more consideration than it has yet received from those working on the normative theories of business ethics.

67   In this context, I am clearly referring to actual, as opposed to hypothetical or tacit, consent. Hypothetical or tacit consent is, in fact, not consent at all, but the presumption of consent where none has actually been given. It follows that in describing a business as a voluntary association of individuals united by a network of contracts, the contracts being referred to are actual interpersonal agreements, not hypothetical social contracts.

68   It may be more precise to say that the stockholder theory fails to address the obligations arising out of those agreements that are not inconsistent with the managers' antecedent agreement with the stockholders. However, it is at least arguable that what should be done when managers have made inconsistent commitments is itself an issue that would have to addressed by an adequate normative theory of business ethics.

69   This may well be an understatement. Given the wide variety of enterprises that are described by the word "business," from the smallest closely-held family business to the largest publicly-traded multinational conglomerate, and from the most mission-oriented nonprofit to the most bottom-line-oriented entrepreneurial venture, it is reasonable to doubt whether this term has a definite enough referent for the construction of a general normative theory of business ethics to even be possible. If it does not, we will simply have to content ourselves with the recognition that ethically proper behavior necessarily depends on the particular agreements the actor has entered into, and leave it at that.

70   Actually, some promising preliminary steps in meeting this challenge have already been taken by Professors Dennis Quinn and Thomas Jones in their article An Agent Morality View of Business Policy, supra note 14. This may serve as a useful starting point for those who believe that an adequate general normative theory of business ethics can, in fact, be formulated.

◆ ◆ ◆ ◆ ◆

GEORGE G. BRENKERT

Private Corporations and Public Welfare

I

The doctrine of corporate social responsibility comes in many varieties.[1] Its most developed version demands that corporations help alleviate "public welfare deficiencies," by which is understood problems of the inner city, drug problems, poverty, crime, illiteracy, lack of sufficient funding for educational institutions, inadequate health care delivery systems, chronic unemployment, etc.

In short, social responsibility, it is contended, requires that corporations assume part of the responsibility for the basic prerequisites of individual and social life within a community or society. Social responsibility demands this even though, it is claimed, corporations are not causally responsible for these conditions and doing so may not enhance their profits.

In response, corporations today provide job training for the hardcore unemployed, help renovate parks, sponsor clean-up programs, establish manufacturing plants in ghetto areas, offer seminars to high school students on how effectively to seek employment, support minority business adventures, provide educational films as well as additional instructors and tutors to public schools (i.e., "adopt" schools), etc.[2]

Such projects have, seemingly, met with a great deal of approval. Indeed, during a time when the welfare of many is deficient, one wonders how anyone could object to such activities. It might seem that any objections to such corporate behavior would stem not from their participating in these activities, but from their not participating even more.

Nevertheless, a number of objections to corporations engaging in such activities have been raised and are well-known. Many of these criticisms are not very good and will not be reviewed here. There is, however, one objection that is much more interesting, even if it is rarely developed. The essence of this objection is that corporate social responsibility to produce directly the public welfare involves the illegitimate encroachment of private organizations into the public realm. There is much greater merit to it than might appear at first glance.

II

This objection takes various forms, Theodore Levitt, for example, claims that the essence of free enterprise is the production of high-level profits. Private business corporations tend to impose this narrowly materialistic view on whatever they touch. Accordingly, corporate responsibility for welfare threatens to reduce pluralism and to create a monolithic society.[3] George C. Lodge similarly maintains that "the demand that business apply itself to problems which government is finding it increasingly difficult to comprehend or affect ... is ... absurd. Corporations, whatever else they may be, are not purveyors of social assistance."[4] Unelected businessmen, he claims, have "neither the right nor the competence" to define or establish the goals and the criteria by which society should repair or remake itself.[5] Finally, Richard DeGeorge claims that

there is great danger in expecting corporations to take upon themselves the production of public welfare, because they already have enormous power and are not answerable for its use to the general public. Politicians are elected by the public and are expected to have the common good as their end. We should not expect corporations to do what they are neither competent nor organized to do ...[6]

These criticisms question the right as well as the competence of corporations to contribute directly to the public welfare. Further, they challenge the influence which corporations in so acting may gain over society. Both increased corporate power and a decrease of social pluralism are feared results.[7]

Unfortunately, these criticisms are, more often than not, simply noted, rather than elaborated upon. In particular, the suggestion implicit within them that the provision of public welfare by private corporations runs afoul of an important distinction between what is public and what is private has not been discussed in recent literature. It is this point which requires greater attention.

The argument offered here is that corporate responsibility for public welfare threatens to reduce, transform, and in some cases eliminate important public dimensions of social life. For this reason we must be wary of it and reluctant to accept it in its present forms. Several characteristics of this argument should be noted at the outset. First, it does not pretend to show that all corporate measures that address public welfare deficiencies are (by themselves or individually) wrong, mischievous, or mistaken. Still, we must not be overly impressed by particular instances and thereby miss the systematic and general implications that are thereby promoted. It is not uncommon for individually rational actions to lead to collectively irrational or morally problematic results.

Second, this argument does not address corporate social responsibilities with regard to damages that corporations may themselves directly cause to the environment, employees, members of society, etc. For all these harms it is reasonable to believe that corporations do have responsibilities. The question this paper addresses concerns the implications of demanding that corporations go beyond correcting the damages they have brought about and assume responsibility for public welfare deficiencies for which they are not causally responsible.

Finally, if we could identify the harms that corporations directly *and* indirectly cause, then the arena of responsibilities that corporations have to society might significantly increase and the deficiencies in public welfare (assuming corporations fulfilled their responsibilities) might correspondingly decrease. This paper presupposes that, even in such a situation, there would remain public welfare deficiencies for which corporations are said to be socially responsible and for which they are neither directly nor indirectly causally responsible.[8]

The present argument has four parts. To begin with, it is important to highlight the different relation that exists between an individual (or group) who is aided by a private corporation, and the relation between such an individual (or group) and public attempts to aid their welfare. The differences in these relations will, in practice, often be insignificant—especially when things go well. However, when problems arise theoretical and practical differences can be important. Surely cases could be identified in which corporations have successfully enhanced the public welfare. However, it is not to be expected that corporations will always act so successfully or so clearly in accord with public needs.

The point here is not that corporations may act in misguided ways so much as what happens in those instances where there are problems. Obviously appeals and complaints can be made to the corporation. However, the fact remains that appeals to the corporation tend to be appeals from external constituencies. Inasmuch as those aided by the corporation are not members of the corporation, they have no standing, as it were, within the corporation other than the one the corporation decides to give them. They have no "constitutional" rights against corporations as they do against public endeavors. They are not "citizens" of the corporation. Thus, they have, in principle, no internal access to the corporation's decision-making processes. They are part of that process only if the corporation allows it. Those who make the decisions to undertake various programs cannot be voted out of office—there is no political, and little legal control, over them. Accordingly, to advocate corporate provision of, and responsibility for, public welfare is to advocate that the basic requisites for human well-being are to be provided by institutions whose deliberations, at least at present, do not in principle include representation of those whose interests are affected. Those deficient in welfare lack formal control or power over those agencies from whom they obtain their welfare. Further, since those deficient in welfare tend to be those who are (in general) powerless, the advocacy of corporate responsibility for welfare tends to continue their powerlessness. Corporate social responsibility, in excluding any formal relation between those who are recipients of corporate aid and the corporation, maintains a division between the powerless and the powerful. A democratic society, one would suppose, would seek to moderate, rather than increase, the inequality presupposed in this division.

This situation contrasts with the state or other public bodies which provide, as part of their nature, various forms of administrative, legal and political redress.[9] The state's activities on behalf of its citizenry are hemmed in (at least in principle) by safeguards and guarantees (voting, representation, public hearings, sunshine laws, etc.) which are not imposed on corporations. Indeed, such public forms of access and standing are generally said to be contrary to the corporation's private status. Accordingly, whenever people outside the private corporation are granted such access it is simply due to the benevolence of the corporation.

Now this different relation between individuals and the agencies (private or public) which provide support for them is particularly crucial when that support concerns their basic welfare, i.e., items to which one might reasonably claim a right: e.g., minimal health care, educational opportunities, physical security, shelter, and food. Surely various private institutions such as corporations, churches, etc. may appropriately give aid to those who are deficient in such welfare, when this occurs on an occasional or special basis. Accordingly, private institutions may aid the welfare of their members (those who have access and voice within the organization) as well as non-members (those who do not have such access and voice).

However, those who advocate that this become the normal situation are (implicitly at least) also advocating a condition that places the recipients in a tenuous position vis-à-vis the granting agencies. Though recipients may receive various goods and/ or services they need from private corporations, not only are such individuals dependent on those agencies for the aid they receive, but they also lose any formal or "constitutional" voice in the agency which purports to aid them. In effect, any right they have to such welfare is degraded to an act of benevolence on the part of the contributing organization. They can no longer insist or demand that they be treated in various ways, but must play the role of supplicants.

It is in this kind of situation that the view attributed to Andrew Carnegie can arise unchecked by formal mechanisms to control it: "In the exercise of his trust he was responsible only to his own conscience and judgment of what was best for the community."[10] Recipients of such aid lack means of redress which, in matters of basic importance such as welfare, are terribly significant.

Furthermore, when the institutions (i.e., large business corporations) involved in providing welfare are not themselves dedicated to the welfare of others but primarily focused on their own self-interested economic ends, and when these organizations are extremely large and powerful, then we must reflect on the implications of the lack of membership, and hence the lack of redress and voice, within those organizations. Specifically, we need to consider whether these needs ought not to be met by organizations which will grant those receiving such aid the voice and access which has traditionally protected people who are dependent upon others.

In short, when corporations are asked to undertake public welfare on an ongoing basis, the welfare they give is privatized in a manner that eliminates an important relation for those receiving such welfare. To the extent that it formalizes a relation between the powerful and the powerless, it exposes the recipients of such aid to abuses of power. At the same time, the equality that democracy implies is also jeopardized.[11]

Second, a variation on the preceding point concerns the standards by which decisions on the nature and means of implementing corporate welfare measures are made. Again, this might not appear to be a significant problem with regard to the construction or reconstruction of an inner-city park, a neighborhood clean-up campaign, or reading tutors in the schools.[12] Surely corporations will, by and large, consult with the people involved to get their ideas and approval. On other occasions, the people involved will seek out a corporation to aid them. But this does not lay the issue to rest since the standards the corporation seeks to follow may be primarily private in nature, rather than public or general.[13]

Suppose, for instance, that the welfare measures which the corporation seeks to provide (and to which their recipients agree) are of questionable constitutionality. They agree, perhaps, on educational films with a religious or a racist message for the public schools. Or, suppose they agree on an educational program but the corporation liberally sprinkles the presentation with its corporate logo, mascot, jingo, and the like. Suppose that in training of the hard-core unemployed they aim at white, rather than black or Hispanic, populations. The point at issue concerns the legitimacy of these decisions.

The standards according to which the public welfare is fulfilled must be a matter for the public (through its representatives) to determine, not the private corporation.[14] Two reasons lie behind this claim. Such welfare concerns what is common among the citizens, what holds the members of a society together, and what is the nature of their basic prerequisites. It constitutes a statement about how we, as a community or society, believe that we should live. Fulfillment of welfare deficiencies for some that manifests prejudice against other groups, or works to their disadvantage, requires special justification and close public scrutiny, if it is allowed to stand.

In addition, to the extent that corporate contributions to public welfare are tax deductible, the foregone tax revenues constitute a public contribution to itself, through the agency of the corporation. Since public monies are committed through such contributions, the public has a right to assure itself that the standards according to which such monies are expended meet its (minimal) standards.[15]

Accordingly, the legitimacy of the decisions the private corporation makes regarding public welfare cannot be judged simply according to its own private standards. Thus, if the corporation tries to impose its own view and standards, it is crossing an important line between the private and the public. It is naive, then, simply to argue that people's welfare

is the responsibility of corporations, without providing for social determination and direction of the activities which corporations undertake.[16]

In those instances in which corporate contributions are of a charitable (or prudential) nature *and* the objects of their actions are wholly private, it would seem that corporations might legitimately give to those individuals or organizations which promote their own values and ideas. In this way, their gifts may reflect their own idiosyncratic standards. Accordingly, some object to business giving to private universities whose faculty advocate ideas opposed to capitalism.[17] However, in contrast, the direction and satisfaction of public welfare according to private standards is not appropriate, since the public welfare is not to be determined simply by this or that individual corporation's ideas and values, but by a political process and, ideally a community dialogue, on what those values should be.[18]

Finally, if corporations are said to be responsible for remedying certain deficient levels of public welfare, but are not given control (both in terms of applicable standards and practical direction) over how such remedies are to be emplaced, then when these measures fail the corporation can hardly be held accountable. Nevertheless, since they will be associated with such efforts, they will often be faulted for their lack of success. Hence, if corporations are required to engage in social responsibility efforts, there will be an understandable tendency for them to seek control over the situations in which they participate. This means, however, supplanting (or reducing) public control and substituting their own judgments and standards for those of the public. Consequently, the demand for corporate social responsibility is a demand that encourages the substitution of private standards, authority and control for those of the public.

III

Third, the demand for corporate social responsibility arises, it has been assumed, due to deficient public welfare, which stems, at least in part, from inadequate public funding. Corporate opposition to higher taxes has played a contributing role to this situation, since taxes are viewed as coercive takings of corporate property.[19] The lower the taxes the greater the return on investment corporations make and the greater the flexibility corporations have to use their resources as they choose. Part of the appeal of corporate social responsibility for public welfare is that the aid that is given is voluntary. Provision of such aid heads off higher taxes, government regulation and hence coercion. In short, behind the demand for corporate social responsibility is a view that holds that the public realm and the state constitute a sphere of coercion, while the private realm and the actions it takes are voluntary.[20]

This is illustrated in Friedman's comment that "the political principle that underlies the political mechanism is conformity.... It is appropriate for some to require others to contribute to a general social purpose whether they wish to or not."[21] Corporate social responsibility, then, explicitly seeks to reduce the realm of the public, by reducing the area within which coercion and force might be used.

Now if the public were simply a realm of coercion, such a view would seem unexceptionable. On the contrary, however, such a view arguably distorts the realm of the public. Corporate social responsibility implies that the public is simply an area within which individual prudential interests are worked out and coercion imposed by the state. Both eliminate an important sense of the public.

The public is also the area within which general and common interests are articulated. It is what binds people together, in contrast to the private realm within which people are separated from each other and view each other as limitations upon their freedom.[22] Accordingly, it is the realm of the "we," rather than the "you" or "I." It is what is done in all our names, and not just yours or mine. It is the area, some have even held, within which freedom is only possible.[23] There is (or can be) a different sense

of accomplishment when the community builds or creates something rather than simply this or that private organization. Conversely, there is a different sense of loss when a public figure, a President or Prime Minister dies, rather than the head of a private corporation.

Now charity is an extension of the private into this public realm. It is personal, self-given, and can't be demanded in particular cases. It need not be based on political discussion or compromise so much as on one's own willingness to aid others. Those who receive do not have grounds upon which they can demand or negotiate beyond which the charitable organization allows. Charity does not necessarily involve any political or public process by which recipient and contributor are bound together. Thus, Hannah Arendt comments, "The bond of charity between people ... is incapable of founding a public realm of its own ..."[24] In short, charity cannot be the basis of a public or political dimension between people.

As such, corporate social responsibility drives out the political and the public. The appeal to corporate responsibility is a confession that the public or political realm has broken (or is breaking) down. It is an unwitting manifestation of liberal individualism extending the realm of the private to encompass the public.

Consequently, Friedman is quite wrong when he complains that the doctrine of social responsibility "taken serious would extend the scope of the political mechanism to every human activity."[25] This is plausible only in that case when the corporation and its executives both engage in social responsibility activities *and*, as a result, become subject to political election procedures since they are viewed as "civil servants."[26] On the other hand, if this does not happen (and there is little present evidence that it will), then the doctrine of social responsibility extends the nature of private activities to many activities in the public or political realm. In short, quite the opposite of what Friedman contends, it extends the scope of the private "to every human activity."

The problem with this approach is that it is implausible to treat society as simply an example of an ideal market situation. This is implied by the above comments on the nature of the public. Not all public (or private) values can be produced or sustained by market exchanges. Friedman slips from discussion of market activities to talk of society without argument. Thus, after he portrays the voluntary nature of the ideal free market, he immediately goes on (without argument) to equate such exchanges with society itself.[27] However, it does not follow (and it is not plausible) to think of society as itself simply an ideal free market. Once again, then, corporate social responsibility involves views and demands which question legitimate distinctions between the private and the public.

IV

Finally, though the relation of the public and the private is a shifting relation, we must guard against collapsing one—either one—term of this relation into the other. The view that the public is simply the arena in which individual actions affect others without their voluntary approval impoverishes the notion of the public.[28] As noted above, the public is more and different than this. The public is what binds a people together and relates them to each other.[29] It is what is done in their common name; it is what makes them a people, rather than simply a random collection of individuals. It embodies the values, norms and ideals we strive towards even if we fail fully to achieve them. It is the responsibility of public agencies (the state or its government) to foster (at least) the minimal conditions under which the public may exist. To be a citizen is to owe allegiance to the government as it works to realize these principles and values.

Now suppose that the government does not fulfill its responsibilities to individuals for basic welfare. The demand that private corporations—other than the government—dispense public welfare is a step in the privatization of the public realm. The benefits that individuals receive from the government have long been thought to play an important role in their obligations to the state and, hence, their citizenship within the state.[30] If these benefits come from private groups, rather than the state, then one would expect loyalties and obligations to be modified accordingly.

Consequently, if a corporation provides training for the hard-core unemployed, renovates the local park, or provides the house which shelters the sick, it is to the corporation that those aided will be grateful and indebted, not to the community or society of which they are members.[31] It is the corporation to which one's loyalties will be turned, and not to the city or state of which one is a citizen. Indeed, the very notion of citizenship thereby becomes impoverished. The grounds upon which the state has been said to acquire the obligations of its citizenry have been narrowed. In its place develop isolated (groups of) individuals beholden to private institutions of which they are not members (or citizens) and over which they have no formal control.

Surely in these days of popular advertising, the corporation may seem more personal, less abstract, than the community or the state. Through logos, jingoes and mascots corporations seek to get people to identify with them and their products. And through corporate measures to aid their welfare, individuals would have concrete reason to be indebted to them, even if not members or citizens of them. But to accept or promote this situation, and the view of the individual's relations to private and public institutions which it involves, merely reveals the state of poverty to which our notions of the public and citizenship have come. Such corporations encourage us to seek a common identity, rather than to foster our common (public) interests.[32] We are invited to replace the realm of the public which unavoidably involves impersonality with a personal and privatized realm. We transform a realm laden with political meanings into a private and psychologized realm.[33]

However, the danger here does not simply stem from the implications of the altered identifications and loyalties that characterize citizens. The increasing privatization of the public realm that we see in shopping malls, corporate housing developments, the suburban environment, and corporate attempts to establish their own identity and role models within the schools carry other consequences to which we must be keenly sensitive. For example, in private shopping malls people may be prevented from political speech; in corporate housing developments, they may be prohibited from having children and remaining in their home; and cultural exhibits may be skewed to suit corporate purposes.[34] Rights which all citizens share may be, wittingly or unwittingly, foregone through private efforts uninformed by public reflection and participation. In short, the public values and interests of a society can be threatened not simply by an authoritarian government but also by self-interested, though well-meaning, private groups and institutions which lack a sense of the significance of the public realm and the meaning of citizenship.

V

In conclusion, several comments are appropriate. First, it may be allowed that many objections which can be brought against corporate attempts to secure public welfare can also be brought against government or public attempts. Thus, both government and corporations may be inflexible, insensitive, impersonal, non-innovative, as well as hard to move or get through to. They may produce programs which are misconceived, uncoordinated, and/or precipitously stopped, leaving people in the lurch. The production of such programs may increase their power, size and influence; they may also deal paternalistically with those they seek to aid. One would be tempted to abandon all attempts to aid those deficient in welfare were it not for the fact that many people continue to suffer grievously from inadequate

welfare. Thus, the question is a complex and messy one. There is no easy and neat answer.

Second, large corporations, however, will continue to be part of our social and political landscape. Their significant economic and political power are obvious. In this situation, the thrust of the public/private argument is two-sided. It can be taken to urge the separation of private corporations and public institutions. This is fraught with all the problems of bureaucratization, distant government, powerful but indifferent corporations, and failed efforts to satisfy public welfare needs. This is not to say that these problems could not be overcome within a fairly strict separation of the private and the public.[35] Still, this would involve a recommitment (and rediscovery!) of the public realm that might be difficult in countries such as the US.

On the other hand, the above argument can also be taken to recommend that we require such large corporations be made more fully public, social organizations. Indeed, many argue that large corporations are no longer simply private organizations. George C. Lodge, for example, comments that "it is now obvious that our large public corporations are not private property at all ... The best we can say," he continues, "is that the corporation is a sort of collective, floating in philosophic limbo, dangerously vulnerable to the charge of illegitimacy and to the charge that it is not amenable to community control."[36] Thus, that corporations increasingly are called to participate in the production of public welfare is not so surprising given their present quasi-public nature. The further claim that has been made is that this quasi-public nature needs to be institutionalized so as to make it amenable to greater public control and direction. This direction, however, is one that others violently oppose.

Thus, we stand at a crossroads. This juncture is part and parcel of that "tension between self-reliant competitive enterprise and a sense of public solidarity espoused by civic republicans" that some have identified as "the most important unresolved problem in American history."[37] If one rejects the view that corporations must more fully take on the character of public institutions, then demands for corporate social responsibility for public welfare should be seriously curtailed.

The preceding arguments do not show conclusively that corporations ought never to aid public welfare. They are one set of considerations which might, in some circumstances, be overridden. However, they do indicate important reasons why we should be more reluctant to proceed down the path that many have been encouraging us to take. When we are repeatedly told that the sight of corporate social responsibility is so lovely, and that the prospects of corporate responsibility for public welfare are so rosy, one may rightfully come to suspect that we are being led down the garden path.[38]

NOTES

1 "Private corporation" will be used to refer exclusively to private corporations engaged in the production of goods and services for profit.

2 Sandra L. Holmes reports in a study of how executives perceive social responsibility that 78% of the executives surveyed either strongly agreed or agreed more than they disagreed with the statement that "Business possesses the ability and means to be a *major* force in the alleviation of social problems" (pp. 39-40). It is clear from the context that by "social problems" is meant the kinds of problems listed in the text under "public welfare." Cf. Sandra L. Holmes, "Executive Perceptions of Corporate Social Responsibility," *Business Horizons* (June, 1976).

3 Theodore Levitt, "The Dangers of Social Responsibility," *Harvard Business Review*, vol. 36 (September-October, 1958), pp. 44-41.

4 George C. Lodge, *The New American Ideology* (New York: Alfred A. Knopf, 1975), p. 189.

5 *Ibid.*, p. 190. Cf., also p. 218.

6 DeGeorge, *Business Ethics*, 3rd. ed. (New York: Macmillan publishing Co., 1986), p. 171.

7 Cf. Levitt, "The Dangers of Social Responsibility."

8 The importance of indirect causal factors and the resulting responsibility of corporations has been defended by Larry May in his comments, "Corporate Philanthropy and Social Responsibility," given on an earlier version of this paper, before the Society for Business Ethics meeting in Boston, MA, on December 28, 1990. How we might determine for which harms corporations are directly or indirectly causally responsible is not addressed in this paper. Both topics, but especially the latter, raise significant problems.

9 Even if this is not true in any particular case, it is still appropriate to demand such access and forms of redress of present (i.e., democratic or republican) forms of government.

10 Robert H. Bremner, *American Philanthropy*, 2nd ed. (Chicago: The University of Chicago Press, 1988), p. 101.

11 This argument allows that other private organizations, such as churches, etc., may legitimately contribute to individuals' welfare needs. The smaller the organization, the more individual the contribution, and the greater the identity of the organization is bound up with promoting the public good, the less there is a problem. On the other hand, some organizations, such as churches, run into problems (e.g., First Amendment issues and attempts to convert others rather than simply aid them) that other private groups do not.

12 Even the park example is not all that simple. There are questions that need to be asked before the park can be built or renovated: what will be the nature and form of the park? Who will maintain it (will anyone?)? Will trash containers be put out and regularly emptied (by whom?)? Is the construction of this park likely to require increased police patrols? Are additional burdens being placed on the city recrea-

tional department, trash department, police department? If so, who decides and upon what basis? Admittedly, these questions must be faced whether the city or a corporation builds the park. However, the important point is that when corporations aid public welfare many important questions remain to be answered. The city or the public is not suddenly let off the hook.

13 The problem is even more complex since those individuals the corporation addresses in the public forum may themselves primarily hold private values. That is, their vision of themselves and society may have lost any sense of the public. Bellah et al. document the degree to which "Americans ... are genuinely ambivalent about public life" (Bellah et al., *Habits of the Heart* [Berkeley: University of California Press, 1985], p. 250).

14 Similarly for a host of other projects there are questions which demand social or public decision, which only the public through the government can legitimately give. For example, it might be asked whether it is really so bad for corporations to provide tutors for secondary schools to help with basic reading skills. But are these tutors trained in teaching? Do they serve to justify inadequate teaching staffs? Do they undercut the demands of teachers for adequate social commitment for education? What programs are they trained to teach? Do they constitute an influx of business oriented courses rather than humanity courses, or science courses? These are serious issues which need to be addressed on the social and public level, not simply on the private corporation level.

Likewise, it might be asked whether it is wrong for corporations (e.g., McDonald's) to start drives for houses for relatives of the seriously ill to stay in while at the hospital. But again, supposing that the rest of the community contributes the preponderant amount, why should the community not get the credit for the house? Why doesn't the name of the house reflect public values or ideals?

We need not assume that public answers to all these questions may be easily arrived at. However, if corporations (or other private groups) simply operate on their own standards, the public discussion which may lead to public standards and agreement will be short-circuited. As a result, the public will be impoverished.

15 This claim applies to similar contributions that come from other private groups, e.g., churches, the Audubon Society, etc. When such contributions come from small and numerous groups, there is less reason for concern, since they may counterbalance each other. It is reasonable for a society to encourage such contributions. Nevertheless, society may legitimately review the nature of their contributions, given that their contributions are tax deductible and they enjoy (where applicable) tax-exempt status.

This issue is particularly of concern, however, when such contributions come from large corporations which can bring significant power and resources to bear. Similarly, when churches or other private groups become large and their powers significant, the consideration raised in the text applies as well. In short, when the contribution of private groups are supported by the public through tax deductions and when those contributions may in particular cases have a significant effect on the public, the public may legitimately review the standards according to which the contributions are made.

16 For example, Control Data's program, called "City Venture," which sought to write blueprints for economic rebirth of down-and-out city neighborhoods had to be withdrawn: "A bossy, 'we know what's best' attitude offended prickly independent community groups in Minneapolis and Miami, forcing City Venture to be withdrawn" (Neil R. Peirce, "To Corpor-

ate Social Involvement," *The Knoxville Journal*, 1982, p. A4).

17 Robert H. Malott, "Corporate Support of Education: Some Strings Attached," *Harvard Business Review*, vol. 56 (1978), pp. 133-38.

18 This is not to say that corporations, or anyone, must (or should) give to causes they believe to be wrongheaded. Rather, if corporations (or other organizations) are given responsibility for public welfare, they may not simply apply their own idiosyncratic standards. This allows, of course, that they could choose, from a range of public welfare needs, to support those compatible with their own views. Since the issue concerns basic deficiencies from which people suffer, this should not be impossible.

19 Similarly Levitt argues: "American capitalism also creates, fosters, and acquiesces in enormous social and economic cancers. Indeed, it fights against the achievement of certain forms of economic and social progress, pouring millions into campaigns against things which people have a right to expect from their government …" (Levitt, "The Dangers of Social Responsibility," p. 48).

20 Since corporate social responsibility is, usually, viewed either as charitable or as prudential in nature, corporations can make their own, voluntary choices as to when, what and how much they will do. The alternative is to have the public (the state or the government) take more from them in order to fulfill the public welfare needs. Because this restricts their choices—their freedom (as they would see it)—they argue against state action here. In short, corporate social responsibility is an expression of the liberal view of society. It is also an expression of an individualistic view: "utilitarian individualism" and "expressive individualism" (Bellah et al., *Habits of the Heart*, p. 27ff). These views contrast with what they call "civic republicanism."

21 Milton Friedman, "The Social Responsibility of Business is to Increase its Profits," in Milton Snoeyenbos, Robert Almeder, James Humber (eds.), *Business Ethics* (Buffalo, New York: Prometheus Books, 1983), p. 78.

22 *Ibid.*, pp. 245, 248.

23 Nancy L. Schwartz, "Distinction Between Public and Private Life," *Political Theory*, vol. 7 (1979), p. 245.

24 Hannah Arendt, *The Human Condition* (Chicago: The University of Chicago Press, 1958), p. 53.

25 Milton Friedman, "The Social Responsibility of Business is to Increase its Profits," in Milton Snoeyenbos, Robert Almeder, James Humber (eds.), *Business Ethics* (Buffalo, New York: Prometheus Books, 1983) p. 79.

26 Friedman, "The Social Responsibility of Business is to Increase its Profits," p. 75.

27 *Ibid.*

28 Cf. John Dewey, *The Public and its Problems* (Chicago: Gateway Books, 1946).

29 Cf. Hannah Arendt, "The Public Realm, as the Common World, Gathers Us Together and yet Prevents our Falling Over Each Other, So to Speak," *The Human Condition* (Chicago: The University of Chicago Press, 1958), p. 52.

30 Cf. A. John Simmons, *Moral Principles and Political Obligations* (Princeton: Princeton University Press, 1979), pp. 157-90.

31 The following comes from a letter to an editor from a mother of a child in a school adopted by IBM. She was responding to objections that others had raised because children in the school were preparing posters and having assemblies to thank IBM for adopting their school. She argues: "to say that this is taking away from the children's learning time is not true. What better learning experience is there than to teach our children what's going on in their schools and to have them have a special program to thank these companies? … I believe it is very import-

ant that these adopting companies realize, by way of parents and children, that we are honored and grateful that they are willing to help our children with their education" ("Letters to the Editor," *The Knoxville News-Sentinel*, November 28, 1986).

32 Cf. Richard Sennett who complains that as part of the end of public culture "the pursuit of common interests is destroyed in the search for a common identity" (p. 261); *The Fall of Public Man* (New York: Vintage Books, 1976).

33 Cf. Sennett, *Ibid.*

34 IBM, for example, "barred the display of computer-art works designed for the equipment of a major business competitor, Macintosh, in the company's heretofore prestigious IBM Gallery of Science and Art in midtown Manhattan"; Susan Davis, "IBM Nixes Macintosh," *Art in America*, vol. 76 (1990), p. 47. The works barred were part of a touring show organized by the Walker Art Center. IBM, which finances its namesake galleries, "bars its competition 'as a matter of policy'" (*Ibid.*, p. 47).

35 It would not, for example, prohibit linking education and business in various ways. Various courses of study in schools might be coordinated with job opportunities in private business, without corporations providing for those courses or other educational needs. Public and government welfare measures would have to be tied much more closely to local needs and allowed much greater flexibility in resolving those needs.

36 Lodge, *The New American Ideology*, p. 18.

37 Bellah et al., *Habits of the Heart*, p. 256.

38 I am indebted to John Hardwig, W. Michael Hoffman, Larry May, Richard Nunan, and an anonymous referee for their perceptive and helpful comments on earlier versions of this paper.

◆ ◆ ◆ ◆

JOSEPH HEATH

Business Ethics Without Stakeholders

Over the past two decades, the "stakeholder paradigm" has served as the basis for one of the most powerful currents of thinking in the field of business ethics. Of course, stakeholder vocabulary is used even more widely, in areas where it is not necessarily intended to have any moral implications (e.g., in strategic management).[1] In business ethics, however, the stakeholder approach is associated with a very characteristic style of normative analysis, viz. one that interprets ethical conduct in a business context in terms of a set of moral obligations toward stakeholder groups (or one that helps "to broaden management's vision of its roles and responsibilities to include interests and claims of non-stockholding groups"[2]). Seen in this light, the primary moral dilemmas that arise in a business context involve reconciling these obligations in cases where stakeholder interests conflict. Thus ethicists who are impressed by the stakeholder paradigm have become highly adept at translating any moral problem that arises in the workplace into the language of conflicting stakeholder claims.[3]

The question that I would like to pose in this paper is whether the stakeholder paradigm represents the most fruitful approach to the study of business ethics. The vocabulary of stakeholder obligations has become so ubiquitous that in many contexts it is simply taken for granted. Yet the stakeholder approach is one that comes freighted with very substantive—and controversial—normative assumptions. Naturally, there are many who have criticized the stakeholder paradigm as part of a broader skeptical critique of business ethics in general, one which denies that firms have any "social responsibilities" beyond the maximization of profit.[4] This is not my intention here. I will argue that firms do have important social responsibilities, ones that extend far beyond mere conformity to the law. The question is whether the stakeholder paradigm represents the best framework for articulating the logic and structure of these obligations.

In order to serve as a point of contrast, I would like to provide an outline of two other possible approaches to the study of business ethics: one, a more minimal conception, anchored in the notion of fiduciary obligations toward shareholders, and the other, a broader conception, focused on the regulatory environment in which firms operate.[5] I will then attempt to show that the latter, which I refer to as a "market failures" approach, offers a more satisfactory framework for the articulating the concerns that underlie traditional appeals for increased corporate social responsibility.

Business Ethics as Professional Ethics

There is one point that all three of the approaches that I will be presenting here have in common. All three conceive of business ethics as a species of professional ethics.[6] In the same way that medical ethics concerns, first and foremost, ethical questions that arise from the professional role of doctors, and legal ethics deals with questions that arise from the professional practice of lawyers, business ethics deals with questions that arise out of the professional role of managers. This is a narrower sense of the term "business ethics" than one sometimes encounters, but as we shall see, there are some advantages to be had from focusing on this somewhat constrained set of issues.

In each case, the assumption is that a professional role itself imposes its own set of obligations upon the person, which are not necessarily part of general morality (although they may be sanctioned by, or derived from, general morality). For example, both doctors and lawyers have a special obligation to protect client confidentiality, an obligation that arises out of their professional role. In other words, this obligation is one that is imposed upon each of them,

not *qua* individual, but *qua* doctor, or *qua* lawyer. According to this conception, business ethics is concerned with the special obligations that arise out of the managerial role, and which are imposed upon the manager *qua* manager.

The reason that it is helpful to conceive of business ethics as a set of moral obligations arising out of the professional role of the manager is that it serves to head off the commonly expressed accusation that business ethics is just blue sky dreaming, or a wish list of things that ethicists would like corporations to do, many of which will turn out to be unrealistic in practice. According to the "professional ethics" view, business ethics represents an attempt to articulate a code of conduct that is *already implicit* both in the structure of corporate law and in the best practices of working managers. This helps to allay the suspicion that business ethics is some alien code, which ethicists seek to impose upon corporations from the outside.

Not everyone accepts the "professional ethics" view. There is an influential strain of thinking in business ethics that treats moral obligations as perfectly invariant across persons. (This tendency is perhaps summed up best in the title of John C. Maxwell's recent book, *There is No Such Thing as "Business" Ethics: There's Only One Rule for Making Decisions*.[7]) Thus some theorists begin by specifying an undifferentiated moral code (whether it be Kantian, utilitarian, Christian, Aristotelian, or what have you); they then treat business ethics as a subject concerned primarily with reconciling pressures that arise in a business context with the obligations that are imposed by this general morality (e.g., the Bible says "thou shalt not bear false witness," so what do you do when the boss asks you to lie to a client?).[8] From this perspective, the managerial role shows up, not as a source of positive moral obligations, but primarily as a source of social pressures that may conflict with morality.

Absent from this perspective is any clear conception of the role that the professions play in a modern economic system (or of the way that a professional "ethos" can give rise to a system of distinctive moral constraints[9]). The primary difference between having a job and practicing a profession involves the element of trust and fiduciary responsibility associated with the latter. In some situations, it is possible for parties in an employment relation to specify all the terms of the contract, to monitor performance completely, and to institute a system of incentives that guarantees perfect compliance. Stacking boxes in a warehouse is an example of an employment relation of this type. These are jobs, and in them, employees are not usually thought to have any special responsibilities beyond those specified in the contract, i.e., the terms of employment. Employees in these sorts of jobs are normally paid by the hour, and have a fixed workday, in recognition of the market-like structure of the transaction.

Things become more complicated, however, when it is impossible to specify the terms of an employment contract completely, imperfect observability of effort makes monitoring difficult, or information asymmetries make the design of a perfect system of performance incentives impossible. In such cases it is impossible to eliminate moral hazard, and so the purchaser of labor services must rely in large measure upon the voluntary cooperation of the seller in order to secure adequate work effort.[10] Thus a certain amount of trust, or moral constraint, is required in these relationships. Contracts usually specify goals and obligations in very general terms, and the person supplying the services is expected to use his or her own judgment to decide how best these terms should be satisfied. The purchaser often lacks not only the information and skills to determine the best course on her own, but is often incapable of even verifying that the supplier has done so after the fact. This is the condition that Oliver Williamson refers to as "information impactedness," and it represents the primary force driving professionalization.[11]

In certain cases, reputation effects are enough to motivate good faith work effort for individuals in these roles. For example, most people have no ability to evaluate the claims and recommendations made by their auto mechanic, and the cost of getting a second opinion can be prohibitive (in both time and money). Thus they have no choice but to trust the mechanic. But as a result, reputation and "word-of-mouth" plays an important role in the market for automobile repairs. The market for contractors, plumbers, and hair stylists has a similar structure. These groups are not generally thought of as professionals, because the market still does a tolerable job of overcoming the important information asymmetries.

It is not an accident that these cases all involve purchases that consumers make frequently, where there is significant opportunity for repeat business. In markets where larger, more infrequent purchases are made, or where information asymmetries are even greater, it is much more difficult for purchasers of services to impose discipline upon suppliers through reputation mechanisms. As a result, suppliers who deploy highly specialized knowledge must work harder to secure the trust of potential clients, simply because the client may never have the opportunity to verify the quality or value of the services received. In some cases, the trust requirements are sufficiently high that these suppliers will form their own membership association, in order to impose an internal "code of conduct" more stringent than the requirements of general labor and contract law. The most well-known examples are the "bar" for lawyers, along with the various medical licensing boards for doctors. These sorts of associations are especially important in professions where the only people competent to evaluate a particular individual's performance are other members of that same profession.

Economists sometimes suggest that the function of these organizations is merely to cartelize a particular segment of the labor market. This is a good example of the "naïve cynicism" often exhibited in this field—where the automatic identification of pecuniary incentives as the dominant motive leads to sociologically naïve analyses of particular institutions. These associations also play an important socializing role, helping to instill genuine respect for a set of moral obligations that are often specific to the profession.[12] For example, many engineers in Canada wear an iron ring on their little finger, which is conferred during a ceremony called "The Ritual of the Calling of an Engineer" (developed in 1925 by Rudyard Kipling). The ring is a symbol of the Pont de Québec Bridge, which collapsed in 1907 as it was nearing completion, killing seventy-six people. A subsequent Royal Commission declared that errors committed by the bridge's principal engineers were the primary cause of the tragedy. Initially, the rings were said to have been made with iron from the collapsed bridge. In the present day, the rings are intended simply to serve as a reminder to working engineers that the lives of many people depend upon their efforts. Engineers have more than just an obligation to put in a day's work for a day's pay, they must also consider the impact that their actions will have upon the eventual users of the structures or products they design. Many engineering students describe the ceremony as genuinely moving, and find that the ring serves as a constant reminder of their professional ethical obligations.

The existence of a professional association, a certification system, a common body of accepted knowledge, and a shared ethics code, are sometimes treated as the distinguishing marks of a genuine profession.[13] This involves some confusion of cause and effect. What makes the complex body of knowledge important is that it generates an information asymmetry, which creates a moral hazard problem that threatens to undermine any market transaction involving such specialists. Thus specialists must work hard to cultivate trust among potential purchasers of their services. A certification system, along with a professional association that imposes a stringent code of conduct, is one way of achieving this objective. There may be cases, however, in which a certification system is difficult to devise, or a professional association difficult to organize. Such is the case, traditionally, with managers (especially during the era

when most were promoted up from the shop floor). Nevertheless, the *economic role* that managers occupy is a professional one, precisely because of the information impactedness in the domain of services they provide. The nature of the managerial role is such that they *need* to be both trusted and trustworthy. This is reflected in the fact that most systems of corporate law treat senior managers as fiduciaries of the firm.[14] Thus the mere fact that managers do not belong to professional associations does not mean that they are not professionals, or more importantly, that there is not a distinctive set of ethical obligations that arise out of their occupational role. The fact that they are in a position of trust is what matters.[15]

Thinking of business ethics in terms of "professional ethics for managers" is an attractive perspective, insofar as it offers some relatively clear criteria for the evaluation of different "theories" or "paradigms" within the field. Managers who take social responsibility seriously already have some very firm intuitions about what constitutes ethical and unethical conduct. The question is whether the vocabulary and the principles that business ethicists develop offer a more or less perspicuous and coherent articulation of these intuitions—whether their theories help us to achieve greater clarity, or whether they sow confusion. This is the standard that I shall be employing in this paper. Thus my criticism of the stakeholder approach to business ethics is not that it is false or incoherent. I shall merely try to show that the vocabulary, and the theory that underlies it, is *inherently misleading*, and thus does not promote useful ways of thinking about corporate social responsibility.[16]

The Shareholder Model

The managerial role arises as a consequence of the so-called separation of ownership and control in the modern corporation. In the early stages of development, most corporations are run by the founders, who are also generally the principal owners. At a later point, the owners may choose to employ managers to assist them in running the firm, or to take over that role entirely. In the same way that individuals employ lawyers in order to advance their interests in a legal context, owners hire managers in order to advance their interests in a business context. Of course, as the firm becomes more mature, this relationship becomes significantly more complex (leading many to argue that the shareholders in a publicly-traded corporation cannot be regarded as its "owners" in any coherent sense). Nevertheless, the fact that shareholders are residual claimants in a standard business corporation means that their interests are not protected by an explicit contract. As a result, there is a set of fiduciary principles governing the relationship between managers and shareholders.[17] Because the fiduciary relationship imposes upon managers a very broad "duty of loyalty" and "duty of care" toward shareholders—concepts with explicit moral overtones—this particular relationship might be thought to serve as a natural point of departure for the development of a theory of business ethics (in the same way that duties toward the patient form the core of professional ethics for doctors, duties toward the client the core of professional ethics for lawyers, etc.).

Yet despite the fact that moral obligations toward shareholders are such a striking feature of the managerial role, in the business ethics literature they are the subject of considerable controversy, and are often downplayed or dismissed. (Marjorie Kelly, the editor of *Business Ethics* magazine, set the tone for one end of this discussion with the title of her article, "Why All the Fuss About Stockholders?")[18] There are several reasons for this relative neglect of the shareholder, some worse than others. In popular debates, there is a tendency when talking about "the corporation" simply to conflate to the two groups (managers and owners), or to assume that there is a greater identity of interests between them than is usually the case. The standard microeconomics curriculum encourages this, by starting out with the assumption that individuals maximize utility, but then aggregating

consumers together into "households" and suppliers into "firms"—each of which is thought to maximize some joint utility function—without explaining the transition (this gets reserved for more advanced courses). Even though it is understood that "the firm" is something of a black box in this analysis, the result is still an unhelpful blurring of the distinction between the pursuit of self-interest on the part of individuals and the maximization of profit on the part of firms, and thus a tendency to overestimate the extent to which the latter flows naturally from the former. As a result, it is easy to underestimate the potential for moral hazard in the relationship between managers and shareholders.

The recent scandals at Enron, Parmalat, Tyco, WorldCom, Hollinger, and elsewhere, have shown that shareholders neglect these difficulties at their own peril. In each of the major scandals, managers were able to enrich themselves primarily at the expense of shareholders. (It may be helpful to recall that at its peak, Enron had 19,000 employees and a market capitalization of $77 billion. Thus for each employee who had to look for a new job as a result of the subsequent bankruptcy of the firm, shareholders lost at least $4 million.) The fact that most of these scandals involved illegal conduct should not distract us from the fact that each illegal act was surrounded by a very broad penumbral region of unethical conduct. For example, it was never decided specifically whether the $2.1 million dollar party thrown by Tyco CEO Dennis Kozlowski for his wife's birthday, half paid out of company funds, constituted fraud or theft, but it most certainly represented a violation of his moral obligation to shareholders.

It is a mistake to believe that self-interest alone, combined with a few performance incentives, is able to achieve a harmony of interest between managers and shareholders. In this respect, a lot of the work done by economists (and game theorists) on the "theory of the firm" has been quite misleading. The overriding objective of many economists has been to extend the methodological tools—and in particular, the action theory—used in the analysis of markets to model the internal structure of organizations.[19] Thus "principal-agent" theory has focused almost entirely upon the use of external incentives as a mechanism for overcoming collective action and control problems within the firm. In so doing, economists have dramatically underplayed the role that trust, values, social norms, and other aspects of "corporate culture" play in determining organizational behavior.[20] Thus they have wasted considerable time and energy devising increasingly baroque performance pay schemes, while neglecting more obvious managerial strategies, such as encouraging employee loyalty to the firm, or cultivating a direct concern for customer satisfaction.[21]

It is precisely because of the importance of these internal (i.e., moral) incentives, along with the enormous potential for abuse, that US corporate law essentially imposes a fiduciary relationship between senior managers and shareholders. It is helpful to recall, for example, the words of an influential US court judgment, concerning the obligations of managers:

> He who is in such a fiduciary position cannot serve himself and his cestius second. He cannot manipulate the affairs of his corporation to their detriment and in disregard of the standards of common decency and honesty. He cannot by the intervention of a corporate entity violate the ancient precept against serving two masters. He cannot by the use of the corporate device avail himself of privileges normally permitted outsiders in a race of creditors. He cannot utilize his inside information and his strategic position for his own preferment. He cannot violate rules of fair play by doing indirectly through the corporation what he could not do directly. He cannot use his power for his personal advantage and to the detriment of the stockholders and creditors, no matter how absolute in terms that power may be and no matter how meticulous he is to satisfy technical requirements, for that power is at all times subject to the equitable limitation that it may not be exercised for the aggrandizement, preference, or advantage of the fiduciary to the exclusion or detriment of the cestuis. Where there is a violation of those principles, equity will undo the wrong or intervene to prevent its consummation.[22]

The obligations enumerated here are sufficiently broad that one could only imagine legal prosecution in cases of the most egregious violation. Thus a very robust theory of business ethics could be developed based simply on the injunction to respect the spirit of this judgment, along with the fiduciary obligations that it outlines toward shareholders. Yet despite this fact, far too little has been said on this subject. The dominant assumption has been that shareholders are able to take care of themselves. Many introductory business ethics textbooks cover topics like whistle-blowing, truth in advertising, pollution, discrimination, and health and safety issues, yet neglect to discuss more common ethical challenges that employees encounter in their day-to-day affairs, such as the temptation to abuse expense accounts.[23] Strictly speaking, society should be no more willing to tolerate such abuses when carried out by business executives (wasting shareholders' money) than when carried out by politicians or civil servants (wasting taxpayers' money). The reality, needless to say, is quite different. Thus a simple duty of loyalty toward shareholders precludes a lot of the everyday immorality that goes on in firms (but which attracts attention only when it reaches spectacular proportions, as with the recent spate of corporate scandals).

Thus the tendency to overestimate the degree of alignment of managerial and shareholder interests leads to more general failure to appreciate the extent to which shareholders are *vulnerable* in their relations with managers (just as patients are vulnerable in their relations with doctors, or clients are vulnerable in their dealings with lawyers). There is, however, also a more principled reason that obligations toward shareholders tend to get downplayed. There is a widespread perception that the fiduciary relationship between the manager and the shareholder cannot serve as a source of genuine moral obligation. Even though I am morally obliged to keep my promises, if I promise my friend that I will rob a bank that does not mean that I am then morally obliged to rob a bank.[24] The same applies to fiduciary relations. Consider the following argument, due to Arthur Applbaum.[25] Imagine a Hobbesian state of nature, in which everyone treats everyone else abysmally. Such conduct is immoral. Now imagine that, in this state of nature, each person solemnly swears to stop pursing his own interests, and to begin pursuing the interests of the person next to him. What changes? From the moral point of view, nothing much. It is still the war of all against all, except that now it is being carried out by proxy. Certainly the mere fact that each person is acting "altruistically"—advancing the interests of her neighbor, rather than her own—is not enough to transform this into a morally acceptable state of affairs. If it could, then the simple act of promising would permit unlimited "laundering" of immoral acts into moral ones.

Thus the discussion of the fiduciary responsibilities of managers quickly turns into a discussion of the moral legitimacy of the goals being pursued by shareholders. This in turn must lead to a discussion of the moral status of *profit* (since this is the interest of shareholders that managers are generally understood to be advancing). It is here that the "ethical" status of business ethics begins to seem problematic. Indeed, Milton Friedman's well-known article "The Social Responsibility of Business Is to Increase its Profits," which presents the ethical obligation to maximize the returns of shareholders as the cornerstone of a conception of business ethics, usually shows up in business ethics textbooks, not as the point of departure for further development of the theory, but rather as an example of an instructively mistaken point of view.[26] The problem is that "profit" is associated, in many people's minds, with "self-interest."[27] "Ethics," on the other hand, is usually associated with behavior that is "altruistic," in some sense of the term. More precisely, morality can be understood as a "principled constraint on the pursuit of self-interest."[28] If this is the case, then substituting "profit" for "self-interest" yields the conclusion that business ethics must represent some sort of principled constraint on the pursuit of profit—not an injunction to maximize it.[29]

In the case of doctors, who must do everything in their power to promote the health of their patients, it is easy to see that health is a good thing, and so efforts to promote it in others must also be good. This is more difficult to see in the case of managers and wealth, especially in cases when increasing the wealth of shareholders can only be achieved at the expense of others. Yet managers who take their responsibilities toward shareholders seriously are often put in a situation where they must effect pure distributive transfers—often regressive ones between workers and shareholders. Here it becomes difficult to see what is so ethical about business ethics.

Thus in order to see managerial obligations toward shareholders as genuine moral obligations, one cannot merely point to their fiduciary status, one must also come up with some justification for the role that profit-taking plays in a capitalist economy. There are two general strategies for doing so. The first, which might be thought of as broadly Lockean, defends profits as the product of a legitimate exercise of the shareholder's property rights, under conditions of freedom of contract. According to this view, the shareholder is entitled to these profits for the same reason that the creditor is entitled to repayment with interest, or that the worker is entitled to her wages. This is not very compelling, however, because the Lockean theory is one that defines the individual's legal rights, but makes no pretence of accounting for her moral obligations. Thus, for example, the Lockean thinks that we have no legal obligation to give anything to charity, and our property rights protect us from any seizure of our assets for such purposes. But this does not mean that we have no moral obligation to give to charity. Ordinary morality tells us that wealth is not an overriding value, and so there would appear to be many cases where the profit motive is trumped by other considerations. This makes it unethical for shareholders to pursue profits in particular ways, and thus unethical for managers to assist them in carrying out such strategies.

The more promising defense of profit is the Paretian one, which points to the efficiency properties of the market economy as a way of justifying the profit orientation of firms. According to this view, the point of the market economy is not to respect individual property rights, but rather to ensure the smooth operation of the price system. The profit orientation is valued, not because individuals have a right to pursue certain interests, but rather because it generates the competition necessary to push prices toward the levels at which markets clear.[30] When markets clear, it means that all resources will have been put to their best use, by flowing to the individuals who derive the most relative satisfaction from their consumption. The spirit of the Paretian approach is best expressed in the "invisible hand" theorem of welfare economics, which shows that the equilibrium of a perfectly competitive market will be Pareto-optimal (i.e., it will be impossible to improve anyone's conditions without worsening someone else's).[31]

Yet this framework still seems to be, in many ways, not "ethical enough" to satisfy many people's intuitions.[32] It offers a seal of approval, for instance, to a wide range of so-called sharp practices in market transactions (which, despite being legal, nevertheless offend our intuitive moral sensibilities). And while it has been pointed out many times that firms seldom profit in the long run from abusing employees, cheating customers, or taking advantage of suppliers, it nevertheless remains true that *in certain cases* it can be profitable to do so. In other words, it is simply not the case that the interests of shareholders always line up with those of workers, customers, suppliers, and other groups with an interest in the firm's decisions. There are genuine conflicts that arise, and it is not obvious that the ethical course of action for managers in every instance is to take the side of shareholders, respecting no constraints beyond those imposed by law. But if this is so, the question becomes how far one should go, as a manager, in advancing the interests of the principal, and when one should start showing more concern for others who are affected by one's actions. Yet even to pose the question in this way is to reveal the limitations of any theoretical approach to business ethics that takes obligations to shareholders as the sole criterion of ethical conduct in business.

The Stakeholder Model

The shareholder approach to business ethics suffers, first and foremost, from the taint of moral laxity. It does not seem to impose *enough* obligations upon managers to satisfy the moral intuitions of many people. In particular, it suggests that, as R. Edward Freeman puts it, "management can pursue market transactions with suppliers and customers in an unconstrained manner."[33] Thus the suggestion has been made that managers have moral obligations, not just to shareholders, but to other groups as well. Freeman introduced the term "stakeholders" as a "generalization of the notion of stockholders," in order to refer to "groups and individuals who benefit from or are harmed by, and whose rights are violated or respected by, corporate actions."[34] He went on to make the suggestion that managers have *fiduciary* obligations toward multiple stakeholder groups.

This overall approach has proven to be remarkably influential, and it is not difficult to see why. After all, we understand quite clearly what it means for managers to have fiduciary obligations toward shareholders. By construing relations with "stakeholders" on analogy, Freeman provided an intuitively accessible framework for articulating the sorts of moral obligations that the shareholder model elides. (In the same way, the term "social capital" has become popular, precisely because people understand what capital is, and so construing social capital on analogy with real capital provides an intuitively accessible framework for thinking about collective action.)

Of course, the term "stakeholder" has been picked up and used quite widely, even by those who do not share Freeman's views on the structure of managerial obligations. For example, so-called strategic stakeholder theory argues that managers must exercise moral restraint in stakeholder relations *as a way of discharging their fiduciary obligations toward shareholders* (i.e., "ethics pays"). Freeman, on the other hand, claims that managers must exercise moral restraint in dealings with stakeholders *because managers have direct fiduciary obligations toward those stakeholders*. Shareholders, according to this view, are just one stakeholder group among many. Managers have fiduciary obligations toward shareholders only because shareholders are stakeholders, and managers have fiduciary obligations toward *all* stakeholders.[35]

Thus Kenneth Goodpaster identifies the key characteristic of Freeman's theory when he refers to it as the "multi-fiduciary stakeholder" theory.[36] What matters is the idea that managers have fiduciary obligations toward multiple groups—regardless of whether these groups are called stakeholders or something else. Thus the two components of the theory are separable—one need not conceive of stakeholder relations as fiduciary relations. Nevertheless, stakeholder vocabulary is often used as a way of expressing tacit commitment to the multi-fiduciary view. As a result, some of the obvious weaknesses of the position tend to be overlooked. As Goodpaster observes, the fact that managers have moral obligations with respect to customers, employees, and other groups, does not mean that these obligations must take a fiduciary form. There is some danger of being seduced by the metaphor, leading one to think that the status of stakeholders is much closer to that of shareholders than it in fact is. For example, the manager might have an obligation to respect certain

rights of customers, without also having a fiduciary duty to advance their *interests*.

If managers really are to be regarded as fiduciaries of stakeholder groups, it raises immediate difficulties with respect to questions of corporate governance. Freeman suggests that the manager must become like "King Solomon," adjudicating the rival claims of various stakeholder groups. Yet giving managers the legal freedom to balance these claims as they see fit would create extraordinary agency risks. On the one hand, managers would need to be protected from being fired by shareholders upset over the performance of their investments.[37] But even more significantly, it would become almost impossible for members of any stakeholder group to evaluate the performance of management. It is difficult enough for shareholders to determine whether managers are actually maximizing profits, given available resources. But when profits can be traded off against myriad other objectives, such as maintaining employment, sustaining supplier relationships, and protecting the environment, while managers have the discretion to balance these objectives as they see fit, then there is really no alternative but to trust the word of managers when they say that they are doing the best they can. The history of state-owned enterprises shows that the "multiple objectives" problem can completely undermine managerial discipline, and lead to firms behaving in a *less* socially responsible manner than those that are explicitly committed to maximizing shareholder value.[38]

Setting aside these practical difficulties, the plausibility of multi-fiduciary stakeholder theory also depends quite heavily upon how broadly the term "stakeholder" is understood. This so-called identification problem has attracted considerable attention.[39] Freeman distinguishes between a "narrow definition" of the term, which refers to groups that are "vital to the success and survival of the firm," and a "wide definition," which refers to any group "who can affect or is affected by the achievement of the organization's objectives."[40] The former includes employees, customers, suppliers, but also, in most formulations of the theory, the local community. The wide definition, on the other hand, is so wide that it becomes equivalent to "all of society." (For example, every pricing decision made by the firm contributes to the national inflation rate, which in turn affects every member of society. So if a stakeholder is anyone affected by the corporation, then everyone is a stakeholder in everything.) Yet the idea that managers are fiduciaries for "all of society" simply collapses business ethics into general ethics (i.e., general utilitarianism, Kantianism, Christian ethics, or what have you). Thus theorists who believe that the managerial role imposes special obligations upon the individual have tended to stick to the narrower definition of the stakeholder.

From the moral point of view, however, there seems to be no reason for the firm to pay special attention to stakeholders in the narrow sense of the term. There are plenty of good *strategic* reasons for managers to worry most about those whose contribution is vital to the success of the firm, but it is difficult to see what moral ones there could be. The groups that are conventionally classified as stakeholders in the narrow sense are not necessarily those with the most at stake in a particular decision, in terms of their potential welfare losses. In fact, if one looks at the standard list of stakeholder groups (customers, suppliers, employees and the local community), it tends rather to be those who are the best organized, or who have the most immediate relationship to the firm, or who are best positioned to make their voices heard. Thus stakeholder theory often has a "squeaky wheel" bias.[41] For example, when General Motors considers closing down a plant in Detroit and moving it to Mexico, a standard multi-fiduciary stakeholder theory would insist that managers take into account the impact of their decision, not just upon their workers in Detroit, but also upon other members of the community whose livelihood depends upon their wages. Thus the "local community" in Detroit where the plant is located would

normally be counted as a "stakeholder." But what about the "local community" in Mexico, where the plant *would* be located? And what about the people there who *would* be getting jobs?[42] Presumably they also have a lot at stake (possibly even more, in terms of welfare, given the relative poverty of the society in which they live). The fact that General Motors has built up a relationship over time with the people in Detroit may well count for something, but it cannot justify *ignoring* the interests of the people in Mexico. From the moral point of view, a potential relationship can be just as important as an actual one.[43] The only real difference between the groups is that potential employees do not know who they are, and so are unable to organize themselves to articulate their interests or express grievances. But it is difficult to see why—from a moral, rather than a strategic point of view—this should give managers the freedom to leave potential employees, or potential "local communities," off the list of groups that the firm has an obligation to.

Because stakeholder theory focuses on the relationship between the manager and different "groups" within society, it tends to privilege the interests of those who are well-organized over those who are poorly organized, simply because it is the former who are able to present themselves as a coherent body with a common set of interests. To see this bias in action, one need only look at the difference in the way that different stakeholder theorists conceive of "social responsibility" and the way that *governments* have traditionally approached it.[44] In this context, it is useful to recall that the widespread nationalization of industry that occurred in Western Europe after the Second World War was motivated, in large part, by the desire of democratic governments to make corporations behave in a more socially responsible manner. The thought was that corporations behaved irresponsibly because owners put their private interests ahead of the public good. By transferring ownership to the state, the people as a whole would become the owners, and so the corporation would no longer have an incentive to pursue anything other than the public good.

Needless to say, this initiative did not have precisely the results that were anticipated. The interesting point, however, lies in the agenda that various governments initially laid out for these firms. First and foremost, state-owned enterprises were expected to play an important role in assisting the state to implement macroeconomic stabilization policies: attenuating the business cycle by making countercyclical investments; maintaining excess employment during recessionary periods; and following self-imposed wage and price controls when necessary, in order to control inflation. Similarly, state-owned enterprises were expected to serve the national interest in various ways, either by providing goods at discounted prices when supplying domestic industry, serving as a guaranteed market for domestically produced goods, or by assisting in the "incubation" of industries intended to bolster international competitiveness. They were of course also expected to act as model employers with respect to their workers, to refrain from polluting, to promote regional development, and so forth. While there is significant overlap between the latter set of objectives and the traditional concerns of many stakeholder theorists, there are also some striking differences. In particular, one can search the stakeholder literature long and hard without finding any mention of the way that firms can contribute to macroeconomic stability. The reason, I would suggest, is that there are no organized or clearly identifiable "stakeholder" groups in this case. After all, how does one identify those who are harmed by inflation? It is, by and large, an extremely diffuse group of individuals. As a result, business ethicists working within the stakeholder paradigm have had a tendency simply to ignore them. For example, I am not aware of anyone having suggested that managers should refrain from granting inflationary wage increases to workers (i.e., increases that are not funded by productivity gains). Governments, on the other hand, have traditionally

been concerned with these questions, precisely because they do have a mandate to defend the welfare of all citizens, and to promote the public interest.

As a result, if one interprets the term "stakeholder" in the narrow sense, it introduces an unacceptable element of arbitrariness into business ethics. If one expands the definition, such that anyone affected by the firm's actions will be considered a stakeholder, multi-fiduciary stakeholder theory amounts to the claim that the manager should be motivated by general considerations of social justice. This risks rendering the stakeholder vocabulary nonsensical, since the concept of a "fiduciary" relation is inherently contrastive. Being a loyal fiduciary involves showing *partiality* toward the interests of one group, not an impartial concern for the interests of all. Furthermore, if the manager is obliged to show impartial concern, the question then becomes, is he or she the person best equipped, or best positioned, to be making these judgments? As Friedman pointed out long ago, normative issues at this level of generality seem to be a more appropriate topic for public policy and democratic deliberation.[45] It is simply not obvious that the *manager's* obligations should be determined by these concerns.

Part of the unwillingness to accept this line of reasoning stems from a rejection of the idea that there might be an institutional "division of moral labor," such that not everyone is morally responsible for everything at all times. Many of the most subtle and difficult questions in professional ethics involves dealing with the way that obligations are divided up and parceled out to different individuals occupying different institutional roles. This is especially tricky in cases where the institution has an adversarial structure.[46] For example, the role of a defense attorney in a criminal trial is to advance the interests of her client by mounting a vigorous defense. Naturally, the overall goal of the procedure is to see that "justice" is served. But that does not make the defense attorney *directly* accountable to what she thinks is "just" in any particular case. Her job is to defend her client (and in fact, mounting a less-than-vigorous defense, because she happens to believe that her client is guilty, constitutes a serious violation of professional ethics). The victim of the crime is no doubt a "stakeholder" in these proceedings, but that does not mean that the defense attorney has a fiduciary obligation toward this individual. Both as a human being and as an officer of the court, she no doubt has ethical obligations toward victims of crime. But *qua* defense attorney, her obligation in many cases will be to disregard this everyday moral constraint. Justice arises through the interaction of her role-specific obligations with those of the crown prosecutor (or district attorney) and the judge. Of course, this is not to say that defense attorneys should do *anything* to secure the acquittal of their clients, or should not respect certain constraints in dealing with victims. There are clearly ethical and unethical ways to proceed. The point is that the vocabulary of fiduciary obligation does not provide a useful way of formulating these constraints. Furthermore, the idea that attorneys should seek to promote justice by balancing the interests of all affected parties is in tension with the role-differentiation that is a central component of the adversarial trial procedure.

Turning to business ethics, the first thing to note is that market transactions also have an adversarial structure (insofar as prices are competitively determined). One can see the problems that this creates for multi-fiduciary stakeholder theory by considering the attempts that have been made to classify "competitors" amongst the relevant stakeholder groups (or more often, the way that "competitors" are tacitly excluded without discussion).47 After all, competitors are clearly affected by many of the decisions taken by the firm. Furthermore, since competitors have the power to drive the firm into bankruptcy, their behavior is often vital to its success or failure. Yet it seems obvious that managers do not have any fiduciary obligations toward rival corporations. After all, the price mechanism functions only because of an unresolved collective ac-

tion problem between firms. No company sets out with the intention of selling goods at a price that clears the market. Often no one even knows what that price is. It is only when firms compete with one another, undercutting each other's prices in order to increase their market share, that the selling price will be driven down to market-clearing levels. This is a classic form of non-cooperative behavior, since it is not normally profit-maximizing overall for firms to sell at this price level. They do it only because they are stuck in a collective action problem.

Thus there is a significant difference between market transactions and the administered transactions that occur within the organizational hierarchy of the firm. The former, because they are mediated through the price system, have an intrinsically adversarial element, since prices are supposed to be determined through competition (and considerable legal effort is invested in the task of keeping things that way). Since many of the socially desirable outcomes of the market economy are a consequence of the operation of the price mechanism, it is not clear that individual firms, much less managers, should be held directly accountable to them. Yet the possibility of such differentiated roles is tacitly denied by the wide version of stakeholder theory, which demands that the manager be ethically responsible for balancing the interests of everyone who is affected by the firm's actions, regardless of whether they are in a competitive or a cooperative relationship.

The Market Failures Model

Despite these difficulties, the stakeholder paradigm still exercises an extraordinary grip over the imagination of many business ethicists.48 It is all too often assumed that the stakeholder theory and the shareholder theory exhaust the logical space of alternatives. As a result, theorists like Marjorie Kelly and Max Clarkson have sought to defend stakeholder theory by mounting increasingly spirited attacks on the idea that managers have any particular obligations to shareholders. The cornerstone of this "nothing special about shareholders" defense is the claim that shareholders are not really "owners" of the firm in any meaningful sense.[49] Thus Clarkson cites with approval the fact that "serious questions are being raised about the belief, widely held in North America, that the purpose of the corporation in society is to maximize profits and financial value for the primary benefit of its shareholders, who are also assumed, mistakenly, to be the corporation's owners."[50]

It is perhaps worth noting that this particular strategy for defending the stakeholder paradigm has the unhelpful effect of making business ethics extremely unintuitive for those who actually work in a standard corporate environment, where the understanding that shareholders own the firm is still widespread. In particular, the downgrading of shareholder claims creates an enormous tension with corporate law, which remains very much committed to the idea that shareholders have a special status within the firm, and that managers owe them fiduciary duties.[51] Of course, it is always possible for the law to be unethical. Nevertheless, this problem is more serious than it would at first appear. If one could produce a sound argument for the conclusion that managers have fiduciary obligations toward various stakeholder groups, one would also have produced a strong *prima facie* argument for the legal enforcement of these obligations. Thus stakeholder theorists have invested some effort in attempting to show that corporate law has in fact been evolving in the direction of increased recognition of stakeholder claims.[52] And it is here, I think, that one can see where the most instructive misunderstanding arises.

There can be no doubt that the development of the welfare state in the twentieth century has coincided with increased regulation of the market. Health and safety in the workplace, the minimum wage, unionization procedures, product warranties, "truth in advertising" and product labeling, toxic emission controls, environmental impact studies, even the size and location of commercial signage—have all become subject to increasingly strict controls. Furthermore, it is clear that all of these regulations respond, in one way or another, to the type of issues that have traditionally been of concern to business ethicists. Each regulation amounts to a legal prohibition of a form of corporate conduct that was at one time merely unethical. The question is how we should understand these developments. Freeman argues that the growth in regulation *constitutes an increased legal recognition of stakeholder claims.*[53] This is, I will argue, a serious misunderstanding. The growth of regulation over the course of the twentieth century goes hand-in-hand with the increased positive economic role of the state in supplying public goods. Both represent strategies aimed at *correcting market failure*. As a result, I think that the concept of market failure provides a much more satisfactory framework for understanding the growth of regulation—and thus the increased legal entrenchment of the social responsibilities of business—than that of stakeholder claim recognition.

Setting aside Germany's "co-determination" arrangements, the closest one can find to an explicit recognition of stakeholder claims is the spread of statutes that allow boards of directors to consider the impact that a hostile takeover would have on non-shareholder groups in determining whether resistance to such takeovers would be "reasonable." These so-called other constituency statutes adopted in many US states (although not Delaware), typically permit (and occasionally require) "officers and directors to consider the impact of their decisions on constituencies besides shareholders."[54] Thomas Donaldson and Lee Preston describe this as a "trend toward stakeholder law."[55] It is significant, however, that these statutes do not impose fiduciary duties, and were largely motivated by a desire on the part of legislators to make hostile control transactions more difficult, based upon a perception that takeovers generate significant social costs. Thus "other constituency" statutes have a lot in common with enabling statutes for "poison pill" and "shark repellent" defenses. I would argue that they are therefore better understood as an attempt to curtail a (perceived) market failure in the stock market than as a legal recognition of stakeholder claims.

The politics of "other constituency" statutes is a complex issue, however, which I do not want to get into here. My primary concern is to illustrate the style of analysis suggested by the market failures perspective. A market failure represents a situation in which the competitive market fails to produce a Pareto-efficient outcome (or for our purposes, let us say, fails *egregiously* to produce an efficient outcome). There are two primary institutional responses to market failure. The first involves the creation of the corporation itself, which is based upon the substitution of an organizational hierarchy and a set of administered transactions for a competitive market. The central characteristic of the firm, as Ronald Coase observed in his classic work, is the internal elimination of market transactions and the "supersession of the price mechanism."[56] In more contemporary terms, we would say that the corporation substitutes a set of principal-agent relations for the non-cooperative relations of marketplace competition. However, because of the limitations of external incentive schemes, these agency relations can often be organized only through some combination of moral and prudential constraint.[57] Thus the central of focus of business ethics, in an *intrafirm* context, involves promoting cooperative behavior within these agency relationships (as Allen Buchanan has argued, in my view persuasively[58]). First and foremost among these obligations will be the fiduciary duty that managers have as the agents of shareholders. Thus when dealing with relationships or transactions "inside" the organizational hierarchy of the firm, the market failures approach to business ethics follows the shareholder-focused view quite closely. With respect to individuals who are "outside" the firm, on the other hand, it is quite different.

The second primary institutional response to market failure is less drastic than the first; it involves preservation of the market transaction, but subject to some more extensive set of legal, typically regulatory, constraints. To see the rationale for this strategy, it is helpful to recall that the point of permitting profit-maximizing behavior among firms in the first place is to promote price competition, along with all the beneficial "upstream" and "downstream" effects of such competition, such as technical innovation, quality improvement, etc. Under conditions of "perfect competition," lower price, improved quality and product innovation would be the *only* way that firms could compete with one another. We can refer to these as the set of *preferred* competitive strategies. Unfortunately, in the real world, the so-called Pareto conditions that specify the terms of perfect competition are never met. In order for competition to generate an efficient allocation of goods and services, there must be an absence of externalities (e.g., a complete set of property rights), symmetric information between buyers and sellers, a complete set of insurance markets, and rational, utility-maximizing agents with dynamically consistent preferences. Because of the practical impossibility of satisfying these constraints, firms are often able to make a profit using *non-preferred* competitive strategies, such as producing pollution, or selling products with hidden quality defects.[59] This is what generates market failure. The basic rules for marketplace competition laid down by the state—including the system of property rights—are designed to limit these possibilities, in order to bring real-world competition closer to the ideal (or to bring *outcomes* closer to those that would be achieved under the ideal, in cases where a functional competition cannot be organized). This is the motivation that underlies not only direct state provision of public goods, such as roads, but also state regulation of negative externalities, such as pollution.[60]

Unfortunately, the law is a somewhat blunt instrument. In many cases, the state simply lacks the information needed to implement the measures needed to improve upon a marketplace outcome (sometimes because the information does not exist, but often because the state has no way of extracting it truthfully from the relevant parties). Even when the information can be obtained, there are significant administrative costs associated with record-keeping and compliance monitoring, not to mention the costs incurred by firms in an effort to evade compliance. Thus the deadweight losses imposed through use of the legal mechanism can easily outweigh whatever efficiency gains might have been achieved through the intervention. This often makes legal regulation unfeasible or unwise.

It is at this point that ethical constraints become germane. As we have seen, profit is not intrinsically good. The profit-seeking orientation of the private firm is valued only because of the role that it plays in sustaining the price system, and thus the contribution that it makes to the efficiency properties of the market economy as a whole. Ideally, the only way that a firm could make a profit would be by employing one of the preferred strategies. However, for strictly practical reasons, it is often impossible to create a system of laws that prohibits the non-preferred ones. Thus according to the market failures perspective, specifically ethical conduct in an *extrafirm* business context (i.e., when dealing with external parties) consists in refraining from using non-preferred strategies to maximize profit, even when doing so would be legally permissible. Put more simply, the ethical firm does not seek to profit from market failure. In many cases, doing so will be illegal—precisely because the state has tried, through increased regulation, to eliminate the use of non-preferred competitive strategies. Ethical constraint becomes relevant in the rather large penumbral region of strategies that are not illegal, and yet at the same time are not among the preferred.

Corporations, for instance, are often in a position where they can produce advertising that will be quite likely to mislead the consumer, but which stops short of outright falsity. In a perfect world, advertising would provide nothing more than truthful information about the qualities and prices of goods.

However, the vagaries of interpretation make it impossible to prohibit anything but the most flagrant forms of misinformation. Thus misleading advertising stands to false advertising as deception does to fraud. It is something that would be illegal, were it not for practical limitations on the scope of the legal mechanism. Profiting from such actions is therefore morally objectionable, not because it violates some duty of loyalty to the customer (as stakeholder theory would have it), but because it undermines the social benefits that justify the profit orientation in the first place. (In a sense, the invisible hand no longer works to transform private vice into public virtue in this case, and so we are left merely with vice.)

In this respect, the market failures approach to business ethics is a version of what Bruce Langtry calls "tinged stockholder theory," which holds that "firms ought to be run to maximize the interests of stockholders, subject not only to legal constraints but also to moral or social obligations."[61] Indeed, it has been well understood for a long time that a shareholder-focused model with a set of deontic constraints (or "side constraints") on the set of permissible profit-maximizing strategies represents a plausible alternative to the stakeholder model.[62] What distinguishes the market failures approach from other such proposals is the specific account of how these constraints should be derived. Rather than trying to derive them from general morality (as Langtry does by focusing on the "moral rights" of individuals affected by the firm, or as Goodpaster does even more explicitly through appeal to the "moral obligations owed by any member of society to others"), the market failures approach takes its guidance from the policy objectives that underlie the regulatory environment in which firms compete, and more generally, from the conditions that must be satisfied in order for the market economy as a whole to achieve efficiency in the production and allocation of goods and services. Furthermore, by focusing on the distinction between administered transactions and market transactions, it is able to offer a principled basis for the difference in structure between the intrafirm obligations owed to shareholders and the extrafirm obligations owed to other groups affected by the actions of the corporation.

When one adopts this market failures perspective, there is no reason to think that a conception of business ethics that continues to place primary emphasis upon the fiduciary responsibility toward shareholders cannot deal with the ethical obligations that have traditionally been described under the heading of "corporate social responsibility." What so often upsets people about corporate behavior—and what gives profit-seeking a bad name—is the exploitation of one or another form of market imperfection. People generally have no problem with companies that make money by providing good service, quality goods, low prices, and so forth. For example, if all companies fully internalized all costs, and charged consumers the full price that the production of their goods imposed upon society, I believe it would be impossible to make the case for any further "social responsibility" with respect to the environment. Thus the market failures approach to business ethics is able to retain the intuitively familiar idea that managers have fiduciary duties toward shareholders, and that the primary goal of corporations is to make a profit. Yet it is able to avoid the charge of moral laxity often leveled against the shareholder model of business ethics, because it imposes strict moral constraints on the range of permissible profit-maximization strategies.

There is a close analogy, from this perspective, between "corporate social responsibility" and the concept of "good sportsmanship" in competitive team sports. In the case of sports, the goal is clearly to win—but not by any means available. Every sport has an official set of rules, which constrain the set of admissible strategies. Yet it will generally be impossible to exclude strategies that respect the letter of the law, while nevertheless violating its spirit (e.g., taking performance-enhancing drugs that have other legitimate uses, and therefore have not been

banned). "Good sportsmanship" consists in a willingness to refrain from exploiting these loopholes, while nevertheless retaining an adversarial orientation. In other words, the obligation is to be a team player and to compete fairly, but not necessarily to let the other side win. The fundamental problem with stakeholder theory is that it tries to eliminate the adversarialism of the managerial role, rather than merely imposing constraints upon it.

Conclusion

One of the charges that hostile critics frequently make against business ethicists is that they are implicitly, if not explicitly, anti-capitalist. Insofar as one equates business ethics with the stakeholder paradigm, there is more than a grain of truth in this accusation. Goodpaster was certainly not wrong to observe that the multi-fiduciary stakeholder theory "blurs traditional goals in terms of entrepreneurial risk-taking, pushes decision-making towards paralysis because of the dilemmas posed by divided loyalties and, in the final analysis, represents nothing less than the conversion of the modern private corporation into a public institution and probably calls for a corresponding restructuring of corporate governance (e.g., representatives of each stakeholder group on the board of directors)."[63] There is, of course, nothing wrong in principle with arguing for institutional reforms of this sort. But a theory that has this as its consequence is unlikely to provide much guidance when it comes to dealing with the ethical challenges that arise in the day-to-day operations of firms in an unreformed capitalist economy.

One of the central advantages of the market failures approach to business ethics is that, far from being antithetical to the spirit of capitalism, it can plausibly claim to be providing a more rigorous articulation of the central principles that structure the capitalist economy. If firms were to behave more ethically, according to this conception, the result would be an enhancement of the benefits that the market provides to society, and the elimination of many of its persistent weaknesses. It would help to perfect the private enterprise system, rather than destroy it.

Of course, none of this is intended to show that one *cannot* continue to talk about corporate social responsibility in terms of stakeholder interests. The question is simply whether this vocabulary encourages a more or less perspicuous articulation of the important moral issues. In this respect, it is important to remember that the term stakeholder was coined precisely in order to suggest an *analogy* between the relationship that managers have with shareholders and the relationship that they have with other interested parties. But as we have seen, the *moral* obligations that managers have toward these disparate groups are not analogous; in fact they are quite dissimilar. So while the term "stakeholder" may remain a useful piece of shop-talk in strategic management circles, as a piece of ethical vocabulary, for use in a theory that tries to articulate the central moral obligations of managers, it is inherently misleading. It creates considerable mischief in business ethics, while offering no real conceptual gain.

NOTES

The author would like to thank Wayne Norman and Alexei Marcoux for their input and advice with the writing of this paper.

1 For a discussion of the scope and impact of stakeholder theory, see Thomas Donaldson and Lee E. Preston, "The Stakeholder Theory of the Corporation: Concepts, Evidence and Implications," *Academy of Management Review* Vol. 20 (1995): 65-91. For an overview, see Jeffrey S. Harrison and R. Edward Freeman, "Stakeholders, Social Responsibility and Performance: Empirical Evidence and Theoretical Perspectives," *Academy of Management Journal* Vol. 42 (1999): 479-85.

2 Ronald K. Mitchell, Bradley R. Agle, and Donna J. Wood, "Toward a Theory of Stakeholder Identification and Salience," *Academy of Management Review* Vol. 22 (1997): 853-86, at 855.

3 See, for example, Joseph R. DesJardins and John J. McCall, *Contemporary Issues in Business Ethics*, 5th ed. (Belmont, CA: Wadsworth, 2005). In Robert C. Solomon and Clancy Martin, *Above the Bottom Line*, 3rd ed. (Belmont, CA: Wadsworth, 2004), the authors go so far as to introduce the environment as "the silent stakeholder," 310.

4 For a recent, high-profile example, see "Survey: Corporate Social Responsibility," *The Economist* (Jan. 20, 2005).

5 The first two correspond well to the typology introduced by John Hasnas, "The Normative Theories of Business Ethics: A Guide to the Perplexed," *Business Ethics Quarterly* 8:1 (1998): 19-42. On the third, my "market failures" model differs from the "social contract model," in that it provides more explicit recognition of the adversarial structure of market transactions.

6 Thus, for example, Milton Friedman, the most influential proponent of the shareholder-focused view, criticizes the loose talk about "business" having social responsibility, and argues that these responsibilities, should there be any, must fall upon the shoulders of managers. "The Social Responsibility of Business Is to Increase Its Profits," *New York Times Magazine* (Sept. 13, 1970). Similarly, R. Edward Freeman, in his classic work on stakeholder theory, *Strategic Management: A Stakeholder Approach* (Boston: Pitman, 1984), identifies it quite explicitly as a set of obligations that fall upon managers, as part of their professional role.

7 John C. Maxwell, *There's No Such Thing as "Business" Ethics: There's Only One Rule for Making Decision* (New York: First Warner, 2003). One can find a considerably more sophisticated, but essentially similar, version of this idea in Norman Bowie, *Business Ethics: A Kantian Perspective* (Oxford: Blackwell, 1995).

8 This is the framework that is implicitly assumed by Andrew Stark, in his widely discussed paper, "What's the Matter with Business Ethics?" *Harvard Business Review* (May/June 1993).

9 The *locus classicus* is Emile Durkheim, *Professional Ethics and Civic Morals*, trans. Cornelia Brookfield (Glencoe: Free Press, 1958).

10 For an overview of moral hazard in this context, see Paul Milgrom and John Roberts, *Economics, Organization and Management* (Upper Saddle River, NJ: Prentice Hall, 1992), 167-97.

11 Oliver Williamson, "Markets and Hierarchies: Some Elementary Considerations," *American Economic Review* Vol. 63 (1973): 316-25, at 318.

12 This is why, as R.M. MacIver emphasizes, "Each profession tends to leave its distinctive stamp upon a man, so that it is easier in general to distinguish, say the doctor and the priest, the teacher and the judge, the writer and the man of science than it is to discern, outside their work, the electrician from the railwayman or the plumber from the machinist." "The Social Significance of Professional Ethics," *Annals of the American Academy of Political and Social Science* Vol. 101 (1922): 5-11, at 11.

13 See, for example, Rakesh Khurana, Nitin Nohria, and Daniel Penrice, "Management as a Profession" in *Restoring Trust in American Business*, ed. Jay W. Lorsch, Leslie Berlowizt, and Andy Zelleke (Cambridge, MA: MIT Press, 2005).

14 Robert C. Clark, "Agency Costs vs. Fiduciary Duties," in John W. Pratt and Richard J. Zeckhauser, *Principals and Agents: The Structure of Business* (Cambridge, MA: Harvard Business School Press, 1985).

15 It is worth noting that there have been some moves afoot among business schools to start offering students some of the trappings of a professional association. One school in Canada, for instance, has begun offering a ring ceremony modeled on that of engineers, where students "make a public oath to behave honorably and, in return, receive an inscribed silver ring to wear as a reminder." Jane Gadd, "Is Ethics the New Bottom Line?" *The Globe and Mail* (March 8, 2005), E6. It seems to me that the question of whether we want to describe management as a profession should not depend upon the success or failure of such efforts.

16 There are parallels between this aspect of my argument and that of Wayne Norman and Chris MacDonald, who argue that so-called 3BL accounting is also "inherently misleading." See "Getting to the Bottom of the 'Triple Bottom Line,'" *Business Ethics Quarterly* Vol. 14 (2004): 243-62, at 254.

17 This should be interpreted as a positive (i.e., factual) claim about the structure of corporate law. See Frank H. Easterbrook and Daniel R. Fischel, *The Economic Structure of Corporate Law* (Cambridge, MA: Harvard University Press, 1991), 90-91. Whether managers should be fiduciaries of shareholders, or just shareholders, is of course the subject of considerable controversy among business ethicists. For a defense of the claim that they should be, see Alexei M. Marcoux, "A Fiduciary Argument Against Stakeholder Theory," *Business Ethics Quarterly* 13:1 (2003): 1-25.

18 Marjorie Kelly, "Why all the Fuss about Stockholders?" reprinted in her *The Divine Right of Capital* (San Francisco: Berrett-Koehler, 2001).

19 The paper that really set economists off in the wrong direction was Armen A. Alcian and Harold Demsetz's "Production, Information Costs, and Economic Organization," *American Economic Review* Vol. 63 (1972): 777-95, with their suggestion that the firm is really just a "privately owned market," 795. It should be noted, however, that subsequent work by incentive theorists has been considerably less san-

guine about the efficiency properties of such "markets."

20 For a critique of these and other "framing assumptions" in agency theory, see J. Gregory Dees, "Principals, Agents and Ethics," in *Ethics and Agency Theory*, ed. Norman E. Bowie and R. Edward Freeman (New York: Oxford University Press, 1992), 35; also John Boatright, *Ethics in Finance* (Oxford: Blackwell, 1999), 49.

21 For example, the chapter in Milgrom and Roberts, *Economics, Organization and Management*, on moral hazard has a section entitled "Controlling Moral Hazard" (185-92), which discusses, among other things, employee monitoring, supervision, incentive contracts, performance pay, bonding, and ownership changes as managerial strategies for preventing shirking. At no point is it mentioned that employees may respond to changes in "internal" motives (such as whether they love or hate the company they work for). It also exhibits a lack of concern for the fact that external performance incentives, such as pecuniary compensation, have the potential to "crowd out" moral incentives, and thus in some cases *generate* collective action problems rather than resolve them. See Bruno S. Frey, Felix Oberholzer-Gee, and Reiner Eichenberger, "The Old Lady Visits Your Backyard: A Tale of Morals and Markets," *Journal of Political Economy* Vol. 104 (1996): 1297-1313.

22 *Pepper v. Litton* 308 U.S. 295 (1939) at 311. Cited in Robert C. Clark, "Agency Costs versus Fiduciary Duties," 76. As Clark observes, the use of moral rhetoric in cases involving breach of managerial duty is highly significant, because as a general rule "our society is reluctant to allow or encourage organs of the state to try to instill moral feelings about commercial relationships in its citizens," 75.

23 Although admittedly an unscientific survey, I have in my office fifteen different introductory business ethics textbooks, many of which discuss insider trading, but only one of which (John E. Richardson, *Business Ethics*, 16th ed. [Dubuque: McGraw-Hill, 2004]) makes any mention of the issue of employee expense account abuse or employee theft. Even then, the discussion focuses upon falsification of expenses, and does not mention the issue of mere profligacy.

24 See Alex C. Michalos's critique of "the loyal agent's argument," in *A Pragmatic Approach to Business Ethics* (Thousand Oaks, CA: Sage, 1995), 50-52. Also Richard T. DeGeorge, "Agency Theory and the Ethics of Agency," in *Ethics and Agency Theory*, 65-66.

25 Arthur Isak Applbaum, *Ethics for Adversaries* (Princeton, NJ: Princeton University Press, 2000).

26 For example, see Tom L. Beauchamp and Norman E. Bowie, *Ethical Theory and Business*, 6th ed. (Upper Saddle River, NJ: Prentice Hall, 2001); Deborah C. Poff, *Business Ethics in Canada*, 4th ed. (Scarborough: Prentice Hall, 2005); and Thomas White, *Business Ethics: A Philosophical Reader* (New York: Macmillan Publishing, 1993).

27 Khurana, Nohria, and Penrice, for example, in "Management as a Profession," argue that a *bona fide* profession requires of its members "a renunciation of the profit motive." They then blame "the doctrine of shareholder primacy" for recent corporate ethics scandals, on the grounds that it "has legitimized the idea that the benefits of managerial expertise may be offered for purely private gain." This "led directly to many of the worst profit-maximizing abuses unmasked in the recent wave of corporate scandals." Such an analysis is almost exactly backwards. The problems at Enron (for example) were not due to managers maximizing profits; they were due to managers *failing* to maximize profits, then creating special-purpose entities to keep more than $26 billion worth of debt off

the balance sheet, precisely to generate the *illusion* of profitability. The fact that they were able to line their own pockets in the process demonstrates the extent to which the goal of maximizing one's own personal earnings and maximizing the profits of a firm can diverge. Professional conduct requires setting aside the goal of maximizing one's own earnings, but that does not preclude one from earning money *for others*. Divorce lawyers seek to secure the largest settlement *for their clients*, without that compromising their status as professionals.

28 David Gauthier, *Morals by Agreement* (Oxford: Clarendon Press, 1986).

29 For an especially clear example of confusion on this score, see Duska, "Why Be a Loyal Agent? A Systemic Ethical Analysis," 157-59. He talks about the "self-interested pursuit of profit," and argues that in order to diminish the level of self-interested behavior on the part of individuals within a firm it will be necessary to challenge the orientation toward profit-making on the part of the business as a whole.

30 John Kay, *The Truth About Markets* (London: Penguin, 2003), writes "it is not true that profit is the purpose of the market economy, and the production of goods and services the means to it: the purpose is the production of goods and services, profit the means," 351.

31 See Nicholas Barr, *The Economics of the Welfare State*, 3rd ed. (Stanford, CA: Stanford University Press, 1998), 70-85.

32 Kenneth Goodpaster, "Business Ethics and Stakeholder Analysis," *Business Ethics Quarterly* 1:1 (1991): 53-73, at 60.

33 R. Edward Freeman, "A Stakeholder Theory of the Modern Corporation," in *The Corporation and its Stakeholders*, ed. Max B.E. Clarkson (Toronto: University of Toronto Press, 1998), 126.

34 Freeman, "A Stakeholder Theory of the Modern Corporation," 129.

35 Ibid., 132. For an example of this view, further developed, see the list of "Principles of an Ethical Firm," in Norman Bowie *Business Ethics: A Kantian Perspective*, 90.

36 Goodpaster, "Business Ethics and Stakeholder Analysis," 61-62.

37 Some US states have been moving in this direction, see n. 54 below.

38 Joseph Heath and Wayne Norman, "Stakeholder Theory, Corporate Governance and Public Management," *Journal of Business Ethics* Vol. 53 (2004): 247-65.

39 For a survey of attempts to define the term, see Mitchell, Agle, and Wood, "Toward a Theory of Stakeholder Identification and Salience," 856-58.

40 The narrow definition is from Freeman, "A Stakeholder Theory of the Modern Corporation," 129; the wide is from Freeman, *Strategic Management*, 46.

41 Mitchell, Agle, and Wood, "Toward a Theory of Stakeholder Identification and Salience," propose a very nuanced analysis of stakeholder groups, classifying them in a way that reflects their relative "salience" to managers. They go on to observe that, "if the stakeholder is particularly clever, for example, at coalition-building, political action, or social construction of reality, that stakeholder can move into the 'definitive stakeholder' category (characterized by high salience to managers)," 879. This sort of observation shows how stakeholder analysis may be useful for strategic management, but when employed without further ado as the normative foundation of business ethics tends to favor the squeaky wheel.

42 See Bruce Langtry, "Stakeholders and the Moral Responsibility of Business," *Business Ethics Quarterly* Vol. 4 (1994): 431-43, at 432.

43 Mitchell, Agle, and Wood, "Toward a Theory of Stakeholder Identification and Salience," 859.

44 Heath and Norman, "Stakeholder Theory, Corporate Governance and Public Management," 255-56.

45 Milton Friedman, "The Social Responsibility of Business Is to Increase its Profits," 34.

46 Applbaum, *Ethics for Adversaries*.

47 For an example of the former, see Freeman, "A Stakeholder Theory of the Modern Corporation," 132; for an example of the latter, see Mitchell, Agle, and Wood, "Toward a Theory of Stakeholder Identification and Salience."

48 See Rogene A. Buchholz and Sandra B. Rosenthal, "Toward a Contemporary Conceptual Framework for Stakeholder Theory," *Journal of Business Ethics* Vol. 58 (2005): 137-48.

49 Kelly, "Why All the Fuss About Stockholders?" Also Max Clarkson's introduction to *The Corporation and its Stakeholders* (Toronto: University of Toronto Press, 1998). Bowie offers an approving survey of such strategies in *Business Ethics: A Kantian Perspective*, 144-45.

50 Clarkson, *The Corporation and its Stakeholders*, 1. For a clear antidote to these sorts of views, see Henry Hansmann, *The Ownership of Enterprise* (Cambridge, MA: Harvard University Press, 1992).

51 See Frank H. Easterbrook and Daniel R. Fischel, *The Economic Structure of Corporate Law* (Cambridge, MA: Harvard University Press 1991), 90-91.

52 See, for example, E.W. Orts, "Beyond Shareholders: Interpreting Corporate Constituency Statutes," *George Washington Law Review* Vol. 61 (1992): 14-135; also Donaldson and Preston, "The Stakeholder Theory of the Corporation," 75-76.

53 Freeman, "A Stakeholder Theory of the Modern Corporation," 128.

54 John Boatright, "Fiduciary Duties and the Shareholder Managements Relation: or, What's So Special about Shareholders?" *Business Ethics Quarterly* Vol. 4 (1994): 393-407, at 402. See also James J. Hanks, Jr., "Playing With Fire: Nonshareholder Constituency Statutes in the 1990s," *Stetson Law Review* Vol. 21 (1991): 97-120.

55 Donaldson and Preston, "The Stakeholder Theory of the Corporation," 76.

56 Ronald Coase, "The Nature of the Firm," *Economica* Vol. 4 (1937): 386-405, at 389. See also Williamson, "Markets and Hierarchies," 316.

57 Eric Noreen, "The Economics of Ethics: A New Perspective on Agency Theory," *Accounting Organizations and Society* Vol. 13 (1988): 359-69.

58 Allen Buchanan, "Toward a Theory of the Ethics of Bureaucratic Organizations," *Business Ethics Quarterly* Vol. 6 (1996): 419-40.

59 Kenneth Arrow, in "Social Responsibility and Economic Efficiency," *Public Policy* Vol. 21 (1973): 303-17, puts particular emphasis on the consequences of firms maximizing profits in cases where there are pollution externalities and information asymmetries that favor the firm. "The classical efficiency arguments for profit maximization do not apply here," he writes, "and it is wrong to obfuscate the issue by invoking them," 308.

60 For more extensive discussion, see Joseph Heath, *The Efficient Society* (Toronto: Penguin, 2001).

61 Langtry, "Stakeholders and the Moral Responsibility of Business," 434-35.

62 Goodpaster, for example, moots such a proposal in "Business Ethics and Stakeholder Analysis," 67-68. The term "side constraint" is from Robert Nozick, *Anarchy, State, and Utopia* (New York: Basic Books, 1974), 28-32, whose discussion of the issue is also quite helpful.

63 Goodpaster, "Business Ethics and Stakeholder Analysis," 66.

GLOBALIZATION AND ITS ETHICAL SIGNIFICANCE

THOMAS DONALDSON

The Ethics of Risk in the Global Economy

In India, The Philippines, Nigeria, and elsewhere, technology is spread thin on ancient cultures. In 1984, in Bhopal, India, the devastating potential of technology's hazards in a non-technological culture was brought home with awesome pain—over 2,000 dead and 200,000 injured. My aim here is to inquire about the justice of practices, like those in Bhopal, that subject foreign citizens to technological risks higher than those faced by either home country citizens or more favored foreign citizens. The object of exploration, hence, is the justice of the distribution of technological risks in and among nation states. What moral obligations underlie, what extra-national responsibilities should inform, the behavior of global actors such as Union Carbide and the United States? The question not only intrigues us, it demands answers on behalf of those who have been harmed or who have been harmed or who are presently at risk. Yet it appears disturbingly clear that the question as framed eludes answers because we possess no viable interpretive scheme for applying traditional moral precepts to the moral twilight created by the juxtaposition of differing legal and cultural traditions.

The key issue to address is obligation. In particular, what are the obligations of macro-agents or macro-organizations to third or fourth parties who are denied membership in those macro-organizations? The terms "macro-agents" or "macro-organizations" will be used interchangeably. They refer to key organizational actors in the international economy, and especially nation states and multi-national corporations. By "third party victims" I mean persons who are put at risk by a given macro-organization who are not themselves members of that organization, for example, innocent bystanders or citizens of another country; by "fourth party victims" I mean fetuses and future generations. In general, third and fourth party victims do not make policy decisions that affect the level or distribution of risk, and when harmed are entirely innocent. Both categories are to be contrasted to first-party victims such as corporate managers or government leaders, and second-party victims such as rank and file employees or national citizens.[1] These latter categories of persons, when harmed, may or not be innocent.

The point about non-membership is important. We expect corporations to honor certain responsibilities toward their employees (no matter how frequently some may violate them), and when they fail to do so, we are able to appeal to accepted moral principles in criticizing their behavior. Similarly, we expect nation states to exercise special care over their citizens, and doing so is regarded as a *sine qua non* of a national legal system. Hence when states fail in this regard, we know what to say. But we do not know, or know as well, what to say about the responsibilities of the United States government to the citizens of Bangladesh, or of Dow Chemical to the man or woman in the street in Cubatao, Brazil.

Let us begin by sketching key elements of the disaster in Bhopal, India. Bhopal is by no means unique in the history of chemical catastrophes,[2] but it is striking for the enormity of its scale and, more importantly, the lesson it teaches.[3]

Although the entire story remains to be told, blame for the disaster is likely to be spread through a complex constellation of persons and acts. Cost cutting measures in the year prior severely weakened safety control. The refrigeration unit designed to cool the methyl isocyanate had been broken for some time, and more than a score of crucial safety devices specified in the safety handbook prepared by Union Carbide in the United States were conspicuously absent. The training, habits, and attitudes of Indian employees were lax and naive. Safety procedures specified in the book were routinely circumvented by technicians who, lacking adequate training, went on with their work blissfully ignorant of the dangers lurking behind their daily routines. In responding to the disaster, employees showed bad judgement and bad training: upon learning of the initial leak, the officer in charge opted to think about it over tea. Outside the plant, government regulatory authorities and city officials were entirely at a loss either to inspect and regulate the plant on an ongoing basis, or to respond appropriately to a disaster once it occurred.

Finally, Union Carbide itself, despite holding a majority of its subsidiary's stock and accepting responsibility for all major economic and safety decisions, failed to maintain an adequate system of safety accountability, and consequently, to exercise appropriate control over its subsidiary.

Yet Bhopal was not only a story about tragedy and human frailty, it is also a story about injustice. For the people who died and suffered were not citizens of the nation whose corporation held responsibility. To make matters worse, the people who suffered the most were slum dwellers, the poorest of the Indian poor, who had pitched their tents literally next to the walls of the Carbide plant.

Cultural variables muddy moral analysis. Whereas in the context of our own culture we can estimate with some assurance the value of goods sacrificed or put at risk by undertaking a given act or policy, in a foreign one our intuitions are opaque. Our extra-cultural vision may be sufficiently clear to allow us to understand a tradeoff between risk and pro-

ductivity, between the dollar value of an increased gross national product on the one hand, and the higher dollar cost of the medical care necessary to accommodate higher levels of risk; but our vision is blurred by more ethnocentric tradeoffs. In many less developed countries a higher gross national product is only one of a handful of crucial goals informed by cultural tradition and experience.

This consideration highlights the second and more disruptive of two cultural variables that can sidetrack international risk analysis. The first is the level of gross marginal improvement in health or economic well-being, as statistically measurable by universally accepted norms of health and economic welfare. Let us call this marginal improvement in health or economic well-being, as statistically measurable by universally accepted norms of health and economic welfare. Let us call this marginal value that of "statistical welfare." Since, as suggested above, the analyst is free to factor cultural values into the determination of extra-national responsibilities, he is free to integrate the concept of "statistical welfare" into overall risk analysis, and estimate tradeoffs from the standpoint of the foreign country. Furthermore, since the concept is by definition compatible with the objective, quantitative methods of analysis, the task is manageable. Armed with an appropriate statistical method, he may well conclude that the marginal welfare resulting from the use of a hazardous drug or piece of technology is positive in the United States, while negative in another country, or vice versa. The notion of marginal statistical welfare thus aids in sidestepping one version of cultural myopia and in weighting the effect local conditions can have on the character of tradeoffs between risks and benefits.

The second variable is that of marginal cultural welfare. In contrast to marginal statistical welfare, it cannot be interpreted through standard norms of health or economic well-being. A citizen of Zimbabwe, Africa, may be willing to trade off a few marginal dollars in per capita gross national product for the unquantifiable improvement in her nation's economic independence from earlier colonial powers. For the same improvement, she may even be willing to trade off a fraction of a percentage point in the nation's infant mortality rate. Similarly, a citizen of Pakistan may be more eager to preserve her country's Muslim heritage, a heritage with strict sexual differentiation in the division of labor, than to increase the country's economic welfare through integrating women into the work place.

My point is simply that in instances where the tradeoffs involve marginal cultural welfare it is doubtful how accurately a cultural stranger can estimate the value that a citizen of another culture places on key goods involved in social tradeoffs. Hence, short of abdicating risk analysis entirely to the other culture (a move I will show later to be unwise), no decisive or even objective decision-making mechanism appears to exist for assessing risk tradeoffs.

Still further, cultural variables can aggravate weaknesses of traditional methods of risk analysis. This is especially true of most methods' tendency to focus on dollars and bodies at the expense of social and cultural criteria, a tendency which, while faulted in domestic contexts, becomes pernicious when the difference between two countries' social and cultural habits are marked.

Consider the twin issues of distributing risk and pricing risk. It is well known that the techniques of cost-benefit analysis are often mute regarding issues of distributive justice. That is, they tend to bypass questions of the fairness of a practice from the perspective of its relative impact on social subclasses, such as the poor, the infirm, or the members of a minority ethnic group. Such silence is less neglectful in the context of a national legal system whose rules have as a central function the protection of individual rights.[4] But in the context of international transactions, where the legal strictures affecting a macro agent's domestic activities do not (and in an important sense *can* not) regulate its activities in a separate legal jurisdiction, the silence is morally corrupting. Clearly pesticide risks to field workers must be weighed against the crying need of a poor country for greater food production; but when that development is carried entirely on the backs of the poor, when the life expectancy of the field worker is cut by a decade or more while the life expectancy of the urban elite *increases* by a decade, then distributive moral factors should trump consequential cost benefit considerations offered in the name of overall welfare.

The common and sometimes criticized distinction in risk analysis between voluntary assumptions of risks is of little help. If we are uneasy over the assumption that the decision of a lower class worker in the US to take a high risk job is "voluntary," despite that worker's limited technological sophistication and pressing financial needs, then surely we must reject the label of "voluntary" when applied to the starving, shoeless laborer in Bangladesh, who agrees to work in a pesticide infected field.

Finally, the tendency in cost-benefit analysis to tie costs to the market prices can distort risk tradeoffs in less developed countries. The dominant assumption of most risk analysis—and of cost-benefit analysis in particular—that risks must be balanced against costs, means that in the instance of life-threatening risks human life must be assigned a price. Despite the apparent barbarity of the very concept, defenders point out that most of us are willing to assume non-zero risks to our life for the sake of reducing cost and frequently do so when we, say, buy a smaller car or accept a higher paying, but riskier job.[5] But while assigning a price to human life may have beneficial consequences against the backdrop of a single, developed country, i.e., it may help policy makers better allocate scarce safety-promoting resources, in the Third World it can unfairly relativize human worth. Since the market price of a life is tied to the capacity of a person to generate income, and since in most parts of the Third World the absence of a capital infrastructure limits the average individual's productive capacity, it follows that in the Third World a human life will be given a lower price.

If cultural variables confound risk analysis, then how can such analysis address international problems? One tempting solution must be abandoned, namely, reliance on international market pressures for acceptable risk distribution. What the market does unsuccessfully in a national context, it fails utterly to do in an international context. As Charles Perrow has pointed out, even in the developed countries "there is no impersonal fair market that rewards those that risk their lives with higher wages."[6] The "jumpers" or "glow boys" in the nuclear industry, temporary workers "who dash into a radioactive area to make repairs, will be hired for two or three weeks' work, at only six dollars an hour ... Textile workers are not compensated for brown lung disease, nor are chemical plant workers compensated for cancer showing up ten or twenty years after exposure."[7]

The average level of unemployment in the Third World today exceeds forty percent, a figure that has frustrated the application of neo-classical economic principles to the international economy on a score of issues. With full employment, market forces will *ceteris paribus* encourage workers to make tradeoffs between job opportunities using safety as a variable. But with massive unemployment, market forces in Third World countries drive the unemployed to the jobs they are lucky enough to land, regardless of safety.

Does some criterion exist, itself not bound by culture or nation, that can give objectivity to intercultural assessments of risk distribution? At first glance nothing seems appropriate. The recent and monumental analysis of distributive justice undertaken by John Rawls[8] explicitly exempts international considerations from the reach of his two famous principles, i.e., that everyone is entitled to maximal liberty, and that inequalities in the distribution of primary goods are unjust unless everyone, including the average person in the worst affected group, stands to benefit. Rawls' reasons for nationalizing distributive justice are tied to his belief that distributive claims can be evaluated meaningfully only against a background scheme of cooperation that yields goods subject to distribution. Since nation states are customarily the agents which provide the mechanisms necessary for facilitating cooperative arrangements and for pooling and distributing the fruits of such arrangements, and since such mechanisms are conspicuously not provided on the international scale, it seems both idealistic and implausible to speak seriously of distributive justice on an international scale.

Yet, even if Rawls is correct in limiting the application of the two principles, it is noteworthy that many problems of risk assessment in a global context do not depend on *inter*-national distributive comparisons (distributions *among* nations) but on *intra*-national comparisons (distributions *within* a nation). Hence Rawls' principles have important application, even when *inter*-national distributive comparisons are excluded. For example, in assessing the fairness of exposing a disproportionate number of poor Indians to the risks of chemical accidents, Union Carbide need not enter into the moral calculus of distributing risk between Indians and US citizens; it need only calculate the fairness of risk distribution among Indians. Insofar as it is unfair to distribute risks disproportionately among US citizens without corresponding benefits for those at greatest risk (and sometimes not even fair when there are corresponding benefits), it is also unfair for an official of Union Carbide, or of the US Government, to undertake activities in India that unfairly distribute risks among Indian citizens.[9] Hence Rawls' second principle need only be modified for application to problems of risk distribution within Third World countries. At a minimum the principle must be adjusted to include freedom from risk as one member of the bundle of primary goods normally covered by the second principle. It may also be argued that modification is needed to Rawls' condition of moderate scarcity, insofar as some Third World countries may manifest poverty sufficiently harsh that "fruitful ventures must inevitably break down."[10] Whether the application of the second principle in risk contexts must be limited to societies fulfilling the moderate scarcity proviso, or whether it need not be so limited—at least *vis à vis* the risk issue—is a question I wish to sidestep at this point. My suspicion is either the application need not be limited in the standard Rawlsian way for risk contexts, or that if it must be limited, the effects are negligible since no matter how poor by European or US standards, most Third World countries are not at the point where "fruitful ventures must inevitably breakdown."

Turning next to *inter*-national issues, it is worth noting the possibility that for all his moral acumen Rawls is wrong about the scope of his own theory. As Brian Barry often notes, no scheme of cooperation need exist in order to demonstrate the unjustness of allowing toxic air pollution, generated in one country for the benefit of that country, to waft over into the unpolluted atmosphere of a second country.[11] And in Charles Beitz's influential book *Political Theory and International Relations*, Beitz points out that Rawls' argument for the inapplicability of his scheme seems not only to presuppose the *present* absence of such features as community and enforcement, but their *future* impossibility as well. What makes assertions of distributive justice and injustice meaningful, according to Beitz, are the shared features of agents to whom such assertions apply, such as rationality and purposiveness. To put it another way, what makes it wrong for me to refuse to spend $10 in order to save the life of a starving Ethiopian is our shared humanity, a humanity that may someday prompt international enforcement mechanisms.[12]

A distributive criterion for risks, then, may be appropriate for evaluating the actions of macro agents in international affairs, although the nature of that criterion remains unspecified. Giving precision to it is no easy matter, since Rawls' second principle of justice, even if applicable, must be weakened in the international context. It must be weakened because it is generally assumed that one has greater

duties to one's fellow citizens than to strangers. For example, people may have a duty to help the homeless in America, but the duty no doubt stops short of providing them with special attention and love, as one is bound to do in the case of one's own children. And similarly, one may have a duty to aid the starving poor in Africa, but it does not extend to providing them social security benefits in old age, as it may be the case of one's fellow citizens. For this and other reasons, I shall not attempt here the complex task of shaping Rawls' principle to fit problems of international risk distribution (despite my belief that such a project is promising). Instead, I will show that, while not reducible to a single principle, a set of moral parameters exists that governs issues from the perspective of international distributive fairness. I plan to show how these parameters are confirmed in the context of an analysis of two pivotal moral considerations: namely, universalization under conditions of relevant similarity, and the distinction between, value-intrinsic and value-extrinsic associations.

It will help to provide concrete contexts for the problem. Consider two incidents, the first involving selling banned goods abroad.

> *Case #1*   Morally speaking, selling banned goods abroad seems a clear example of double standards.[13] Nonetheless, developing countries sometimes argue that a given banned product is essential to meeting their standards.[14]

The US Congress in 1979 passed legislation amending the Export Administration Act which gave the President broad powers to control exports.[15] But just thirty-six days after the signing of the order, on February 17, 1981, newly elected President Reagan revoked the order.[16] In a further move, President Reagan called for a repeal on the export restrictions affecting unapproved drugs and pharmaceutical products. (Banned pharmaceuticals, in contrast to other banned goods, have been subject to export restrictions for over forty years.) In defense of the Reagan initiative, drug manufacturers in the United States argued by appealing to differing cultural variables. For example, a spokesman for the American Ciba-Geigy Pharmaceuticals justified relaxing restrictions on the sale of its Entero-Vioform, a drug he agrees has been associated with blindness and paralysis, on the basis of culture-specific, cost-benefit analysis. "The government of India," he pointed out, has requested Ciba-Geigy to continue producing the drug because it treats a dysentery problem that can be life-threatening.[17]

Before continuing, let us consider a second instance of international risk distribution, this time involving the world's worst pollution.

Case #2 A small triangle of land near Sao Paulo, Brazil, known as Cubatao, has more reported cases of cancer, stillbirths, and deformed babies than anywhere else in Brazil.[18] Factories, and especially petrochemical plants, dominate the landscape, where about 100,000 live and work. Cubatao has air considered unfit on a record number of days and has the highest level of pollutants in the rainfall recorded anywhere. In 1983, one hundred slum dwellers living alongside a gasoline duct were killed when the duct caught fire. The town was constructed during the heyday of the so-called "Brazilian miracle," a time when right-wing military rulers maintained pro-business labor laws, stable political conditions, and some of the highest profit margins in the world, conditions that allowed enormous influx of foreign investment. Even today, with the Brazilian miracle in disrepute, substantial foreign investment remains: Cubatao's 111

plants are owned by twenty-three foreign and Brazilian companies.

According to Marlise Simons of the *New York Times*, "Squatters have built rows of shacks above a vast underground grid of ducts and pipes that carry flammable, corrosive and explosive materials. Trucks lumber alongside loaded with poison, which has spilled in past accidents ... 'But we need the work,' one man said. 'We have nowhere else to go.'"[19]

The neglected responsibilities of importing countries to police more effectively incoming goods and of less developed countries in particular, such as Brazil, to improve pollution controls, are no doubt awesome. But while not forgetting these responsibilities I want for the moment to expand on the responsibilities of the exporting nations, and in particular of the developed nations. Now to hold the view that the former responsibilities preclude the latter amounts to adopting what I call the "sociocentric" view. This view holds that all nations, including Third World ones, have moral duties to tighten the inflow of dangerous goods and to insure an acceptable level of industrial risks. Government and corporate officials have fiduciary duties to their fellow citizens either through the fact of mutual citizenship, or, as in the case of the government official, because of a public trust. So far so good. But according to the sociocentric view, responsibilities for the citizens of other countries are exclusively of the officials and citizens of *those* countries.

The sociocentric view shares a packet of muddled assumptions with a sister theory, the doctrine of political realism, which is popular among international theorists perhaps because it accepts the convenient definition of statecraft as nothing more than maximizing the interests of one's nation. Both these views utilize a vague premise to draw a false conclusion. The premise is that we have stronger duties to friends than to strangers; the conclusion is that our *moral* responsibilities to citizens in other countries—responsibilities other than, of course, those defined by explicit covenants—are either negligible or nonexistent. The premise is vague because it says nothing about the relative weight of duties to friends and strangers, nor about possible distinctions among kinds of friends, i.e., family members, next-door neighbors, or fellow citizens, and kinds of strangers, i.e., non-family members, passing acquaintances, citizens of foreign countries, and so on. While it may be true that a father is morally permitted to spend a dollar to repair his own child's bike instead of sending it to a starving child abroad, or a congresswoman to spend millions on national park improvement instead of sending it to Afghan rebels, this in itself cannot be extended to an unlimited endorsement of *national* favoritism.

Let us back up. Good reasons do exist for limited favoritism. The first is that social arrangements which define memberships in associations as well as the specific fiduciary duties of members, often turn out to be *efficient* means of maximizing shared values. For example, the institution of the family is a remarkably efficient way of raising the young. It is simply more efficient for a single person, or a small group of persons (as in a Kibbutz) to specialize in caring for a particular child or group of children, than it is for people in general to diffuse love and attention broadly. Nation states, too, are efficient means of organizing judicial arbitration, military defense, and resource control.

The efficiency gained from organizing society in a manner where emotional and geographical realities are recognized through associations and where "each takes care of his own," recommends the creation and development of *permanent* associations, i.e., ones whose habits and rules cannot be changed at whim. Hence when a family or nation finds itself in the happy position of possessing a relative abundance of goods or a comparative international advantage, it is not necessarily true that the surplus should be shared equally with other nations or families. To do

so would necessitate the undoing of the very institutions and habits that benefit all persons in the long run.

A second reason sometimes offered for favoritism fails to justify state favoritism. The reason concerns what I have elsewhere called "value-intrinsic" associations, i.e., ones whose ends are by definition logically unobtainable without the existence of the associations themselves.[20] Such associations would no doubt include the family (in some version or other, although not necessarily in its present form) since part of the value of parenting—at least from the standpoint of the parent—appears to require the existence of the family for its realization. Hence, *ceteris paribus*, a certain amount of favoritism finds justification in associations, e.g., of family and friendship, where the favoritism seems essential for securing the value intrinsic to the association.

But the associations of family and friendship are to be contrasted with nation states, whose ends of providing judicial arbitration, military defense, and resource control could conceivably be met by other social arrangements (though perhaps not met as well). Hence, while it may be said that efficiency speaks not only on behalf of the existence of the nation state, but on behalf of a certain amount of state favoritism, additional state favoritism will be precluded insofar as the state is a value-extrinsic, not a value-intrinsic association.[21] Nation states or multinational corporations are unable to make appeals in the name of intrinsic value, for although patriotism and national pride may embody slight vestiges of our natural status as political animals, they are valued primarily for their instrumental value, that is, for their ability to secure collective goals such as self-defense, personal security, efficient legislation, and the protection of natural rights.

We may conclude that the amount of permissible favoritism by nation states or multinational corporations towards their own members in questions of international risk distribution is only the amount that can be justified in the name of efficiency. To put the matter in rule-consequential terms, a corporation or nation state is justified in adopting policies exhibiting favoritism to the extent that the favoritism itself is a non-eliminable aspect of policies which, if adopted by other relevantly similar states, would increase efficiency and thus maximize overall welfare.

The point is that precious little risk favoritism can be justified in this manner. I would stretch moral credibility, for example, to suppose that the toleration of frighteningly high levels of toxic pollution in Cubatao, Brazil, or of the export to Third World countries of most banned products—acts which tend to distribute risk to the favor of multinational corporations and First World citizens—could be justified in the name of rule-consequential sanctioned efficiency. It seems highly unlikely that these are non-eliminable aspects of policies that will maximize global welfare; rather the policies seem quite eliminable and of the sort which, if eliminated, would result in greater overall happiness. Hence, it is safe to conclude that the penchant for national egoism and for the favoring of fellow citizens over foreigners, or for favoring fellow employees and stockholders in the instance of the corporation, provides no justification for gross inequities in risk distribution.

But appeals to efficiency or to the duty to favor friends over strangers are not the only way to attempt to justify international risk inequities. A different, and in many respects more successful way, is through appeal to a nation's special needs, e.g., for economic development or the elimination of a particular problem. Lower safety, pollution, and import standards are explicitly maintained by some countries in order to achieve special ends. In Brazil, for example, lax standards of pollution enforcement are justified in the name of Brazil's desperate need for greater productivity, and the claim has a persuasive edge in a country where malnutrition is sufficiently widespread that by some estimates one in every five Brazilian children will suffer permanent brain damage.[22] In India, as mentioned earlier, special dysentery problems have prompted the government to encourage the import of drugs which, without such problems, would be considered unacceptably risky.[23] It seems morally arrogant to suppose that acts that encourage or tolerate lower standards abroad undertaken by the macro-agents of developed societies are impermissible simply for that reason. On the other hand, the convenient relativism of some corporate and government officials which excuses anything in the name of socio-centrism seems equally suspect.

Elsewhere I have argued for the need to distinguish cases of conflicting norms where the norms accepted by citizens of a host country appear inferior to those of the home country.[24] There I argued that a key distinction should be drawn between those instances in which from the standpoint of the foreign country (a) the reason for tolerating the "lower" norms refers to the country's relative level of economic development, and (b) the reason for tolerating them is related to inherent cultural beliefs, e.g., in religion or tradition. When an instance falls under the former (a) classification, a different moral analysis is required than when it falls under the latter. Here it makes sense to do what for cultural reasons cannot be done in the later instance (where inherent cultural beliefs intrude), namely, put ourselves in the shoes of the foreigner. To be more specific, it makes sense to consider ourselves and our own culture at a level of economic development relevantly similar to that of the other country. And, if, having done this, we find that *under such hypothetically altered social circumstances* we ourselves would accept the lower standards, then it is permissible to adopt the standards that appear inferior.

What lies behind the thought experiment is an age-old philosophical insight, namely, that when considering the universality of moral principles like must be compared to like, and cases must be evaluated in terms of morally relevant similarities. Hence, when considering the acceptability of practices abroad, the moralist must not err by applying wholesale, principles relevant to her own nation, but instead must ask herself what those principles would imply under the relevantly altered circumstances of the foreign nation.

Now as a practical matter of moral psychology, some acts of rational empathy are easier than others. This is reflected in the distinction between lower standards justified in terms of relative economic development and those that are not. It is relatively easy for us to empathize with the need for economic development in a poor nation, since economic well-being is an almost universally shared value, than to empathize with the need for a purer form of Muslim government, or for a more African, less European, social system. Indeed, the general principle governing the psychological possibility of rational empathy seems to be one restricting empathy to situations wherein the fundamental values motivating the decision-making of our object of empathy, are values that we share.

Let us be more specific. We can "test" the practices of shipping banned products abroad, and operating multinational branch facilities in Cubatao, by a thought experiment wherein we ask whether our own moral intuitions would find such practices acceptable were we in a state of social development relevantly similar to the countries in question. This test works in such cases because the values that presumably prompt the lower standards in foreign countries are ones we share, i.e., economic and medical well-being. For example, it makes sense to ask whether we in the United States would find levels of pollution equal to those in Cubatao justified here for the sake of economic progress, were we at Brazil's present level of economic development. If we answer yes, then we may conclude that it is permissible for US multinationals to adopt the lower standards existing in Cubatao. If not, then the practice is not permissible. (I suspect, by the way, that we would *not* find Cubatao's pollution permissible.)

The same test is appropriate in the case of banned products. Were we at a hypothetically lowered state of economic development similar to Ghana or Columbia, would we allow Tris-Treated Sleepwear (sleepwear treated with a fire retardant known to be highly carcinogenic and hence banned from the United States market) to be bought and sold? Probably not. Yet, lest one think that the test always returns negative results, consider the case of India's special request for the drug, Entero-Vioform. Dysentery, a widespread and virulent health problem, is often associated with undeveloped societies because of their lack of modern systems of food handling and sanitation. It may well be that as we imagine ourselves in a relevantly similar social situation, the tradeoffs between the risks to minority sufferers and the widespread dysentery that would occur without the drug, would favor Entero-Vioform, despite its properly being banned in developed countries.

In instances where we fail to share the moral values that prompt lower safety standards, the test of rational empathy is inappropriate for reasons already stated. Here the final appeal can only be to a floor of universal rights, with the presumption in favor of permitting the lower standards unless doing so violates a basic right or conflicts with standards of *intra*-national risk distribution mentioned earlier.[25] Unable to make appeal to the values that must ultimately underlie social-welfare tradeoffs, we must presume the validity of the foreign culture's stance except in the instance where a universal human right is at stake, or where we doubt the actual acceptance of the lower norms by rank and file citizens. Appealing to rights here has special validity because rights are, by definition, moral concepts that specify moral minimums and prescribe, as it were, the lowest common denominator of permissibility.[26]

The preceding analysis has shown, then, that there are firm limits to the extent to which macro-actors can impose risks on third and fourth parties in foreign countries, even when such risks fall within existing moral and legal guiding principles already operative in the foreign country. Hence, risk socio-centrism must be abandoned. Although reached by a different route, it is noteworthy how similar in tone this conclusion is to Rawls' second principle of justice, wherein, it is necessary to demonstrate universal benefit to justify a systematic inequality.

The only remaining appeal possible for risk sociocentrism is to moral and social autonomy. The argument runs something like this: in individual affairs the value of freedom often overrides even that of moral propriety. Even if we suppose it morally wrong for a person to risk his health by drinking excessively at home, we do not want the law to restrict his activity. Hence, if the Third World countries wish to expose themselves to unreasonable risks it is not our business.

This argument will not wash. In its present form it falls prey to the obvious objection that coercion of others is not directly at issue here (as it is in the instance of law proscribing home drinking). Were multinational corporations and First World nations to restrict voluntarily their risk-imposing activities, they would be exercising *self-control*, not coercion; and while certainly affecting the actions of others, their decision not to refuse to distribute risk in certain ways would merely limit the range of options available to others (e.g., they would no longer be able to purchase certain banned goods). The actions would be what Mill thought of as "primarily self-regarding," not "primarily other regarding."27

Even if reformulated to refer to actions that may *discourage* (rather than coercively restrict) unreasonable risks, however, the argument fails. This is not only because in morality, as in law abiding or abetting an irresponsible action is itself colored by the shadow of the action's irresponsibility. It is also because in the instance of most Third World countries the agents who assume risks are surrogate ones, which is to say that they act on behalf of third parties to whom they are presumably responsible. Surrogate agency would be less damning were it true that both democracy and informed public opinion lay behind such agency. But in most Third World countries this is seldom the case. Most are far from democratic in the sense of democracy to which we are accustomed, and even when democratic, possess a level of techno-

logical sophistication sufficiently low to rule out the possibility of rational risk assessment. In Bhopal, India, (which happens to be a good sized city), only one in a thousand households owns a telephone. It is arrogant self-delusion for us to imagine that such people make rational decisions about exposing themselves to the risks of methyl isocyanate.

The idea of a culture "choosing" to undertake risks when that culture lacks a sufficient political and technological infrastructure lies at the root of much unwitting technological imperialism. Again, consider Bhopal. Even the Indian employees of Union Carbide were unaware of methyl isocyanate's toxicity; most thought it was chiefly a skin-eye irritant, and almost none thought it could kill outright.

Outside the plant, the Indian regulatory apparatus was woefully unequal to its task. A few weeks before the disaster, the Union Carbide Plant had been granted an "environmental clearance certificate."28 Enforcement was left not to the national government, but to the separate states. In Madhya Pradesh, the state in which Bhopal lies, fifteen factory inspectors were given the task of regulating 8,000 plants, while the inspectors themselves, sometimes lacking even typewriters and telephones, were forced to use public trains and buses to get from factory to factory. The inspectors responsible for the Bhopal area held degrees only in mechanical engineering, and knew little about chemical risks.29 It should be added that India is considerably *more* advanced technologically, with a better technological infrastructure, than most of its Third World counterparts.

Bhopal offers many lessons about what Third World countries must do to reduce irrational technological risks, among which are the need for suitable zoning ordinances, better inspection and regulation of hazardous factories, and the acceptance of only those technologies that the local technological infrastructure is capable of handling. Similarly, there is little doubt that these same countries have unfulfilled responsibilities in other areas, including policies affecting the importation of banned products. Nicholas Ashford, for example, has offered a tidy list of recommendations that such countries coordinate industrial development policy with environmental policy (frequently the Ministry of Industry does not talk to the Ministry of the Environment); that they develop a data base for the assessment of effects on productivity and safety of imported products; and, finally, that they maintain a centralized purchasing control mechanism for choosing products or technology that will enter the country.[30]

But realism demands that we recognize the unlikelihood of such reforms in the near future. We cannot justify our own irresponsibility by thrusting the moral burden on the shoulders of societies still adolescent in the age of technology.

To conclude, let me summarize the moral limitations shown to affect the distribution of risk in the global economy. Both market-dominated risk distribution and cultural relativism were rejected as solutions. We found each to be excessively permissive. Next, the issues of *intra*-national and *inter*-national risk distribution were separated. For *intra*-national issues, no convincing reason exists for deviating from traditional canons of distributive justice, for example, a modified version of Rawls' second principle. *Inter*-national issues, on the other hand, are more recalcitrant. Sociocentrism, however tempting, is wrongheaded. Claims for state favoritism, while sometimes defensible, were shown to be limited to those justifiable in the name of institutional efficiency. A thought-experiment relying on the principle of adjusting empathy to conditions of relevant similarity may be used to assess risk tradeoffs justified by appeal to marginal welfare, but the experiment succeeds only in instances where the values motivating decisions are shared by the macro-agent and the foreign culture. Otherwise, the empathy necessary for the thought experiment is lacking, and risk decisions must be cashed in terms of basic rights. Finally, existing facts about surrogate agency and technological infra-structure in Third World countries refute attempts to reintroduce sociocentrism into the ethics of risk assessment through appeal to national autonomy and freedom.

NOTES

1 I have adopted this set of distinctions between first, second, third, and fourth party victims, from a somewhat different set appearing in Charles Perrow's book, *Normal Accidents* (New York: Basic Books, 1984), 67.

2 In 1972 anywhere from 400 to 5,000 Iraqis were killed as a result of eating unlabeled, mercury-treated grain from the United States. In 1979 workers and livestock were poisoned in Egypt by the pesticide leptophos; and, more recently, hundreds died and were injured in Mexico City as a result of a liquefied natural gas explosion. Nicholas A. Ashford, "Control the Transfer of Technology," in the *New York Times*, Sunday, December 9, 1984, 2.

3 The information used to construct the following description comes largely from an extended series of four articles appearing in the *New York Times* on December 9, 1984, shortly after the disaster, written by Stuart Diamond. Mr. Diamond's account comes largely from interviews with workers, including Mr. Suman Dey, who was the senior officer on duty.

4 The view that the fundamental function of a legal system is the protection of rights is articulated systematically by Ronald Dworkin in *Taking Rights Seriously* (Cambridge, MA: Harvard University Press, 1978).

5 For an insightful account of the moral assumptions involved in risk analysis see Kristin S. Shrader-Frechette, *Risk Analysis and Scientific Method: Methodological and Ethical Problems with Evaluating Societal Hazards* (Hingham, MA: D. Reidel Publishing, 1985).

6 Perrow, *Normal Accidents*, 68.

7 Perrow, *Normal Accidents*, 68.

8 John Rawls, *A Theory of Justice* (Cambridge, Mass.: Harvard University Press, 1971).

9 Here I don't mean to assert the unquestionable applicability of Rawls' principle to *intranational* risk assessment since to do so would necessarily involve a comparative assessment of Rawls' distributive approach in contrast to his competitors'. I want to claim only that *if* one accepts Rawls' principle as applying to analysis of one's own society, then one should also accept it in application to other societies. My own sympathies are Rawlsian, but I shall not presume their accuracy here.

10 Rawls' specific characterization of the "moderate scarcity" proviso (which he borrows from Hume) is that "natural and other resources are not so abundant that schemes of cooperation become superfluous, nor are conditions so harsh that fruitful ventures must inevitable breakdown." See John Rawls' *A Theory of Justice* (Cambridge, MA: Belknap Press of Harvard University Press, 1971), 127-28.

11 Brian Barry, "The Case for a New International Economic Order," *Ethics, Economics, and Law: Nomos Vol. XXIV*, ed. J. Roland Pennock and John W. Chapman (New York: New York University Press, 1982).

12 Beitz also notes that a common error prompting the denial of international distributive justice is the assumption that international mechanisms of community and enforcement must exactly resemble existing ones at the national level. Other arrangements, while different from those associated with nation states, would be capable of giving substance to distributive claims. Charles Beitz, *Political Theory and International Relations* (Princeton, NJ: University Press, 1979), parts II and III, and "Cosmopolitan Ideals and National Sentiment," *The Journal of Philosophy*, Vol. LXXX, No. 10, October 1983, 591-600.

13 A 1979 United Nations resolution stressed the need to "exchange information on hazardous chemicals and unsafe pharmaceutical products that have been banned in their territories and to discourage, in consultation with importing countries, the exportation of such products." Quoted in "Products Unsafe at Home Are Still Unloaded Abroad," in *The New York Times*, Sunday, August 22, 1982, 22.

14 The problem, by the way, is not limited to the United States, since Europe exports even more hazardous products to developing countries than does the US. See "Control the Transfer of Technology," by Nicholas Ashford in the *New York Times*, Sunday, December 9, 1984, 2F.

15 With this as a basis, President Carter issued on January 15, 1981, an executive order that asked for a comprehensive approach to hazardous exports. The complex notification schemes for alerting foreign countries about hazards were to be coordinated and streamlined. An annual list of all products banned in the US was to be compiled and made available, and government officials were empowered to seek international agreements on hazardous exports. Finally, the order required the creation of export controls on those "extremely hazardous substances" that constituted a "substantial threat to human health or safety or the environment." See "Control the Transfer of Technology," 2F.

16 Industry opposition, described as "massive" by Edward B. Cohen, executive director of the Carter Administration's Task Force on Hazardous Exports Policy, probably was what killed the Carter plan. See "Products Unsafe at Home," 22.

17 Quoted in "Products Unsafe at Home," 22.

18 Most of the information about Cubatao described here is from Marlise Simons, "Some Smell a Disaster in Brazil Industry Zone," *The New York Times*, May 18, 1985, 4.

19 Simons, "Some Smell a Disaster," 4.

20 In February, 1985, I presented a paper, as yet unpublished, to the Great Expectations Philosophy Forum at Great Expectations Bookstore,

Evanston, Illinois. This paper will eventually constitute Chapter 4 of a book I am finishing entitled *Ethics in the International Order.*

21 "Duties to Strangers," especially 20-26.

22 See "Controlling Interest," a film produced and distributed by California Newsreel (California, 1977).

23 "Products Unsafe at Home," 4.

24 See "Multinational Decision-Making: Recycling International Norms," *Journal of Business Ethics* (Summer, 1985).

25 In this paper I am able only to sketch what is worked out more fully in "Multinational Decision-Making: Reconciling International Norms" (cited above) regarding the thought-experiment of rational empathy and the use of basic rights in contexts where host country norms appear substandard from the perspective of the host country. Anyone interested in the fuller account should refer to that paper.

26 In attempting to isolate the list of rights with true claim to cultural universality, we might, for example, consult international documents such as the UN Declaration.

27 See John Stuart Mill, *On Liberty.*

28 Surprisingly, the Union Carbide plant in Bhopal was considered almost a model for other plants. In contrast to a steel plant in the same state that had 25 fatalities in the past year, Union Carbide had in recent years only a single fatal accident.

29 Robbert Reinhold, "Disaster in Bhopal: Where Does Blame Lie?" *The New York Times*, January 31, 1985, 1.

30 Ashford, "Control the Transfer of Technology," 2F.

◆ ◆ ◆ ◆ ◆

MANUEL VELASQUEZ

International Business, Morality, and the Common Good

During the last few years an increasing number of voices have urged that we pay more attention to ethics in international business, on the grounds that not only are all large corporations now internationally structured and thus engaging in international transactions, but that even the smallest domestic firm is increasingly buffeted by the pressures of international competition.[1] This call for increased attention to international business ethics has been answered by a slowly growing collection of ethicists who have begun to address issues in this field. The most comprehensive work on this subject to date is the recent book *The Ethics of International Business* by Thomas Donaldson.[2]

I want in this article to discuss certain realist objections to bringing ethics to bear on international transactions, an issue that, I believe, has not yet been either sufficiently acknowledged nor adequately addressed but that must be resolved if the topic of international business ethics is to proceed on solid foundations. Even so careful a writer as Thomas Donaldson fails to address this issue in its proper complexity. Oddly enough, in the first chapter where one would expect him to argue that, in spite of realist objections, *businesses* have international moral obligations, Donaldson argues only for the less pertinent claim that, in spite of realist objections, *states* have international moral obligations.[3] But international business organizations, I will argue, have special features that render realist objections quite compelling. The question I want to address, here, then, is a particular aspect of the question Donaldson and others have ignored: Can we say that businesses operating in a competitive international environment have any moral obligations to contribute to the international common good, particularly in light of realist objections? Unfortunately, my answer to this question will be in the negative.

My subject, then, is international business and the common good. What I will do is the following. I will begin by explaining what I mean by the common good, and what I mean by international business. Then I will turn directly to the question whether the views of the realist allow us to claim that international businesses have a moral obligation to contribute to the common good. I will first lay out the traditional realist treatment of this question and then revise the traditional realist view so that it can deal with certain shortcomings embedded in the traditional version of realism. I will then bring these revisions to bear on the question of whether international businesses have any obligations toward the common good, a question that I will answer in the negative. My hope is that I have identified some extremely problematic issues that are both critical and disturbing and that, I believe, need to be more widely discussed than they have been because they challenge our easy attribution of moral obligation to international business organizations.

I should note that what follows is quite tentative. I am attempting to work out the implications of certain arguments that have reappeared recently in the literature on morality in international affairs. I am not entirely convinced of the correctness of my conclusions, and offer them here as a way of trying to get clearer about their status. I should also note that although I have elsewhere argued that it is improper to attribute *moral responsibility* to corporate entities, I here set these arguments aside in order to show that even if we ignore the issue of moral responsibility, it is still questionable whether international businesses have obligations toward the common good.

I. The Common Good

Let me begin by distinguishing a weak from a strong conception of the common good, so that I might clarify what I have in mind when I refer to the common good.

What I have in mind by a weak conception of the common good is essentially the utilitarian notion of the common good. It is a notion that is quite clearly stated by Jeremy Bentham:

> The interest of the community then is— what? The sum of the interests of the several members who compose it.... It is vain to talk of the interest of the community, without understanding what is the interest of the individual. A thing is said to promote the interest or to be for the interest of an individual, when it tends to add to the sum total of his pleasure; or what comes to the same thing, to diminish the sum total of his pains.4

On the utilitarian notion of the common good, the common good is nothing more than the sum of the utilities of each individual. The reason why I call this the "weak" conception of the common good will become clear, I believe, once it is contrasted with another, quite different notion of the common good.

Let me describe, therefore, what I will call a strong conception of the common good, the conception on which I want to focus in this essay. It is a conception that has been elaborated in the Catholic tradition, and so I will refer to it as the Catholic conception of the common good. Here is how one writer, William A. Wallace, O.P., characterizes the conception:

> A common good is clearly distinct from a *private* good, the latter being the good of one person only, to the exclusion of its being possessed by any other. A common good is distinct also from a *collective* good,

which, though possessed by all of a group, is not really participated in by the members of the group; divided up, a collective good becomes respectively the private goods of the members. A true *common* good is universal, not singular or collective, and is distributive in character, being communicable to many without becoming anyone's private good. Moreover, each person participates in the whole common good, not merely in a part of it, nor can any one person possess it wholly.[5]

In the terms used by Wallace, the utilitarian conception of the common good is actually a "collective" good. That is, it is an aggregate of the private goods (the utilities) of the members of a society. The common good in the utilitarian conception is divisible in the sense that the aggregate consists of distinct parts and each part is enjoyable by only one individual. Moreover, the common good in the utilitarian conception is not universal in the sense that not all members of society can enjoy all of the aggregate; instead, each member enjoys only a portion of the aggregate.

By contrast, in the Catholic conception that Wallace is attempting to characterize, the common good consists of those goods that (1) benefit all the members of a society in the sense that all the members of the society have access to each of these goods, and (2) are not divisible in the sense that none of these goods can be divided up and allocated among individuals in such a way that others can be excluded from enjoying what another individual enjoys. The example that Wallace gives of one common good is the "good of peace and order."[6] Other examples are national security, a clean natural environment, public health and safety, a productive economic system to whose benefits all have access, a just legal and political system, and a system of natural and artificial associations in which persons can achieve their personal fulfillment.

It is this strong notion of the common good that the Catholic tradition has had in mind when it has defined the common good as "the sum total of those conditions of social living whereby men are enabled more fully and more readily to achieve their own perfection."[7] It is also the conception that John Rawls has in mind when he writes that "Government is assumed to aim at the common good, that is, at maintaining conditions and achieving objectives that are similarly to everyone's advantage," and "the common good I think of as certain general conditions that are in an appropriate sense equally to everyone's advantage."[8]

The Catholic conception of the common good is the conception that I have in mind in what follows. It is clear from the characterization of the common good laid out above that we can think of the common good on two different levels. We can think of the common good on a national and on an international level. On a national level, the common good is that set of conditions within a certain nation that are necessary for the citizens of that nation to achieve their individual fulfillment and so in which all of the citizens have an interest.

On an international level, we can speak of the global common good as that set of conditions that are necessary for the citizens of all or of most nations to achieve their individual fulfillment, and so those goods in which all the peoples of the world have an interest. In what follows, I will be speaking primarily about the global common good.

Now it is obvious that identifying the global common good is extremely difficult because cultures differ on their views of what conditions are necessary for humans to flourish. These differences are particularly acute between the cultures of the lesser developed third world nations who have demanded a "new economic order," and the cultures of the wealthier first world nations who have resisted this demand. Nevertheless, we can identify at least some elements of the global common good. Maintaining a congenial global climate, for example is certainly part of the global common good. Maintaining safe transportation routes for the international flow of goods is also part of the global common good. Maintaining clean oceans is another aspect of the global common good, as is the avoidance of a global nuclear war. In spite of the difficulties involved in trying to compile a list of the goods that qualify as part of the global common good, then, it is nevertheless possible to identify at least some of the items that belong on the list.

II. International Business

Now let me turn to the other term in my title: international business. When speaking of international business, I have in mind a particular kind of organization: the multinational corporation. Multinational corporations have a number of well known features, but let me briefly summarize a few of them. First, multinational corporations are businesses and as such they are organized primarily to increase their profits within a competitive environment. Virtually all of the activities of a multinational corporation can be explained as more or less rational attempts to achieve this dominant end. Secondly, multinational corporations are bureaucratic organizations. The implication of this is that the identity, the fundamental structure, and the dominant objectives of the corporation endure while the many individual human beings who fill the various offices and positions within the corporation come and go. As a consequence, the particular values and aspirations of individual members of the corporation have a relatively minimal and transitory impact on the organization as a whole. Thirdly, and most characteristically, multinational corporations operate in several nations. This has several implications. First, because the multinational is not confined to a single nation, it can easily escape the reach of the laws of any particular nation by simply moving its resources or operations out of one nation and transferring them to another nation. Second, because the multinational is not confined

to a single nation, its interests are not aligned with the interests of any single nation. The ability of the multinational to achieve its profit objectives does not depend upon the ability of any particular nation to achieve its own domestic objectives.

In saying that I want to discuss international business and the common good, I am saying that I want to discuss the relationship between the global common good and multinational corporations, that is, organizations that have the features I have just identified.

The general question I want to discuss is straightforward: I want to ask whether it is possible for us to say that multinational corporations with the features I have just described have an obligation to contribute toward the global common good. But I want to discuss only one particular aspect of this general question. I want to discuss this question in light of the realist objection.

III. The Traditional Realist Objection in Hobbes

The realist objection, of course, is the standard objection to the view that agents—whether corporations, governments, or individuals—have moral obligations on the international level. Generally, the realist holds that it is a mistake to apply moral concepts to international activities: morality has no place in international affairs. The classical statement of this view, which I am calling the "traditional" version of realism, is generally attributed to Thomas Hobbes. I will assume that this customary attribution is correct; my aim is to identify some of the implications of this traditional version of realism even if it is not quite historically accurate to attribute it to Hobbes.

In its Hobbesian form, as traditionally interpreted, the realist objection holds that moral concepts have no meaning in the absence of an agency powerful enough to guarantee that other agents generally adhere to the tenets of morality. Hobbes held, first, that in the absence of a sovereign power capable of forcing men to behave civilly with each other, men are in "the state of nature," a state he characterizes as a "war ... of every man, against every man."9 Secondly, Hobbes claimed, in such a state of war, moral concepts have no meaning:

> To this war of every man against every man, this also is consequent; that nothing can be unjust. The notions of right and wrong, justice and injustice have there no place. Where there is no common power, there is no law: where no law, no injustice.10

Moral concepts are meaningless, then, when applied to state of nature situations. And, Hobbes held, the international arena is a state of nature, since there is no international sovereign that can force agents to adhere to the tenets of morality.11

The Hobbesian objection to talking about morality in international affairs, then, is based on two premises: (1) an ethical premise about the applicability of moral terms and (2) an apparently empirical premise about how agents behave under certain conditions. The ethical premise, at least in its Hobbesian form, holds that there is a connection between the meaningfulness of moral terms and the extent to which agents adhere to the tenets of morality: If in a given situation agents do not adhere to the tenets of morality, then in that situation moral terms have no meaning. The apparently empirical premise holds that in the absence of a sovereign, agents will not adhere to the tenets of morality: they will be in a state of war. This appears to be an empirical generalization about the extent to which agents adhere to the tenets of morality in the absence of a third-party enforcer. Taken together, the two premises imply that in situations that lack a sovereign authority, such as one finds in many international exchanges, moral terms have no meaning and so moral obligations are nonexistent.

However, there are a number of reasons for thinking that the two Hobbesian premises are deficient as they stand. I want next, therefore, to examine each of these premises more closely and to determine the extent to which they need revision.

IV. Revising the Realist Objection: The First Premise

The ethical premise concerning the meaning of moral terms, is, in its original Hobbesian form, extremely difficult to defend. If one is in a situation in which others do not adhere to any moral restraints, it simply does not logically follow that in that situation one's actions are no longer subject to moral evaluation. At most what follows is that since such an extreme situation is different from the more normal situations in which we usually act, the moral requirements placed on us in such extreme situations are different from the moral requirements that obtain in more normal circumstances. For example, morality requires that in normal circumstances I am not to attack or kill my fellow citizens. But when one of those citizens is attacking me in a dark alley, morality allows me to defend myself by counterattacking or even killing that citizen. It is a truism that what moral principles require in one set of circumstances is different from what they require in other circumstances. And in extreme circumstances, the requirements of morality may become correspondingly extreme. But there is no reason to think that they vanish altogether.

Nevertheless, the realist can relinquish the Hobbesian premise about the meaning of moral terms, replace it with a weaker and more plausible premise, and still retain much of Hobbes' conclusion. The realist or neo-Hobbesian can claim that although moral concepts can be meaningfully applied to situations in which agents do not adhere to the tenets of morality, nevertheless it is not morally wrong for agents in such situations to also fail to adhere to those tenets of morality, particularly when doing so puts one at a significant competitive disadvantage.

The neo-Hobbesian or realist, then, might want to propose this premise: When one is in a situation in which others do not adhere to certain tenets of morality, and when adhering to those tenets of morality will put one at a significant competitive disadvantage, then it is not immoral for one to likewise fail to adhere to them. The realist might want to argue for this claim, first, by pointing out that in a world in which all are competing to secure significant benefits and avoid significant costs, and in which others do not adhere to the ordinary tenets of morality, one risks significant harm to one's interests if one continues to adhere to those tenets of morality. But no one can be morally required to take on major risks of harm to oneself. Consequently, in a competitive world in which others disregard moral constraints and take any means to advance their self-interests, no one can be morally required to take on major risks of injury by adopting the restraints of ordinary morality.

A second argument the realist might want to advance would go as follows. When one is in a situation in which others do not adhere to the ordinary tenets of morality, one is under heavy competitive pressures to do the same. And, when one is under such pressures, one cannot be blamed—i.e., one is excused—for also failing to adhere to the ordinary tenets of morality. One is excused because heavy pressures take away one's ability to control oneself, and thereby diminish one's moral culpability.

Yet a third argument advanced by the realist might go as follows. When one is in a situation in which others do not adhere to the ordinary tenets of morality it is not fair to require one to continue to adhere to those tenets, especially if doing so puts one at a significant competitive disadvantage. It is not fair because then one is laying a burden on one party that the other parties refuse to carry.

Thus, there are a number of arguments that can be given in defense of the revised Hobbesian ethical premise that when others do not adhere to the tenets of morality, it is not immoral for one to do likewise. The ethical premise of the Hobbesian or realist argument, then, can be restated as follows:

In situations in which other agents do not adhere to certain tenets of morality, it is not immoral for one to do likewise when one would otherwise be putting oneself at a significant competitive disadvantage.

In what follows, I will refer to this restatement as the ethical premise of the argument. I am not altogether convinced that this premise is correct. But it appears to me to have a great deal of plausibility, and it is, I believe, a premise that underlies the feelings of many that in a competitive international environment where others do not embrace the restraints of morality, one is under no obligation to be moral.

V. Revising the Realist Objection: The Second Premise

Let us turn, then, to the other premise in the Hobbesian argument, the assertion that in the absence of a sovereign, agents will be in a state of war. As I mentioned, this is an apparently empirical claim about the extent to which agents will adhere to the tenets of morality in the absence of a third-party enforcer.

Hobbes gives a little bit of empirical evidence for this claim. He cites several examples of situations in which there is no third party to enforce civility and where, as a result, individuals are in a "state of war."[12] Generalizing from these few examples, he reaches the conclusion that in the absence of a third-party enforcer, agents will always be in a "condition of war." But the meager evidence Hobbes provides is surely too thin to support his rather large empirical generalization. Numerous empirical counterexamples can be cited of people living in peace in the absence of a third-party enforcer, so it is difficult to accept Hobbes' claim as an empirical generalization.

Recently, the Hobbesian claim, however, has been defended on the basis of some of the theoretical claims of game theory, particularly of the prisoner's dilemma. Hobbes' state of nature, the defense goes, is an instance of a Prisoner's Dilemma, and *rational* agents in a Prisoner's Dilemma necessarily would choose not to adhere to a set of moral norms. Rationality is here construed in the sense that is standard in social theory: having a coherent set of preferences among the objects of choice, and selecting the one(s) that has the greatest probability of satisfying more of one's preferences rather than fewer.[13] Or, more simply, always choosing so as to maximize one's interests.

A Prisoner's Dilemma is a situation involving at least two individuals. Each individual is faced with two choices: he can cooperate with the other individual or he can choose not to cooperate. If he cooperates and the other individual also cooperates, then he gets a certain payoff. If, however, he chooses not to cooperate, while the other individual trustingly cooperates, the noncooperator gets a larger payoff while the cooperator suffers a loss. And if both choose not to cooperate, then both get nothing.

It is a commonplace now that in a Prisoner's Dilemma situation, the most rational strategy for a participant is to choose not to cooperate. For the other party will either cooperate or not cooperate. If the other party cooperates, then it is better for one not to cooperate and thereby get the larger payoff. On the other hand, if the other party does not cooperate, then it is also better for one not to cooperate and thereby avoid a loss. In either case, it is better for one to not cooperate.

Now Hobbes' state of nature, the neo-Hobbesian realist can argue, is in fact a Prisoner's Dilemma situation. In Hobbes' state of nature each individual must choose either to cooperate with others by adhering to the rules of morality (like the rule against theft), or to not cooperate by disregarding the rules of morality and attempting to take advantage of those who are adhering to the rules (e.g., by stealing from them). In such a situation it is more rational (in the sense defined above) to choose not to cooperate. For the other party will either cooperate or not cooperate. If the other party does not cooperate, then one puts oneself at a competitive disadvantage if one adheres to morality while the other party does not. On the other hand, if the other party chooses to cooperate, then one can take advantage of the other party by breaking the rules of morality at his expense. In either case, it is more rational to not cooperate.

Thus, the realist can argue that in a state of nature, where there is no one to enforce compliance with the rules of morality, it is more rational from the individual's point of view to choose not to comply with morality than to choose to comply. Assuming—and this is obviously a critical assumption—that agents behave rationally, then we can conclude that agents in a state of nature will choose not to comply with the tenets of ordinary morality. The second premise of the realist argument, then, can, tentatively, be put as follows:

> In the absence of an international sovereign, all rational agents will chose not to comply with the tenets of ordinary morality, when doing so will put one at a serious competitive disadvantage.

This is a striking, and ultimately revealing, defense of the Hobbesian claim that in the absence of a third-party enforcer, individuals will choose not to adhere to the tenets of morality in their relations with each other. It is striking because it correctly identifies, I think, the underlying reason for the Hobbesian claim. The Hobbesian claim is not an empirical claim about how most humans actually behave when they are put at a competitive disadvantage. It is a claim about whether agents that are *rational* (in the sense defined earlier) will adopt certain behaviors when doing otherwise would put them at a serious competitive disadvantage. For our purposes, this is significant since, as I claimed above, all, most, or at least a significant number of multinationals are rational agents in the required sense: all or most of their activities are rational means for achieving the dominant end of increasing profits. Multinationals, therefore, are precisely the kind of rational agents envisaged by the realist.

But this reading of the realist claim is also significant, I think, because it reveals certain limits inherent in the Hobbesian claim, and requires revising the claim so as to take these limits into account.

As more than one person has pointed out, moral interactions among agents are often quite unlike Prisoner's Dilemmas situations.[14] The most important difference is that a Prisoner's Dilemma is a single meeting between agents who do not meet again, whereas human persons in the real world tend to have repeated dealings with each other. If two people meet each other in a Prisoner's Dilemma situation, and never have anything to do with each other again, then it is rational (in the sense under discussion) from each individual's point of view to choose not to cooperate. However, if individuals meet each other in repeated Prisoner's Dilemma situations, then they are able to punish each other for failures to cooperate, and the cumulative costs of noncooperation can make cooperation the more rational strategy.[15] One can therefore expect that when rational agents know they will have repeated interactions with each other for an indefinite future, they will start to cooperate with each other even in the absence of a third party enforcer. The two cooperating parties in effect are the mutual enforcers of their own cooperative agreements.

The implication is that the realist is wrong in believing that in the absence of a third-party enforcer, rational individuals will always fail to adhere to the tenets of morality, presumably even when doing so would result in serious competitive disadvantage. On the contrary, we can expect that if agents know that they will interact with each other repeatedly in the indefinite future, it is rational for them to behave morally toward each other. In the international arena, then, we can expect that when persons know that they will have repeated interactions with each other, they will tend to adhere to ordinary tenets of morality with each other, assuming that they tend to behave rationally, even when doing so threatens to put them at a competitive disadvantage.

There is a second important way in which the Prisoner's Dilemma is defective as a characterization of real world interactions. Not only do agents repeatedly interact with each other, but, as Robert Frank has recently pointed out, human agents signal to each other the extent to which they can be relied on to behave morally in future interactions.[16] We humans can determine more often than not whether another person can be relied on to be moral by observing the natural visual cues of facial expression and the auditory cues of tone of voice that tend to give us away; by relying on our experience of past dealings with the person; and by relying on the reports of others who have had past dealings with the person. Moreover, based on these appraisals of each other's reliability, we then choose to interact with those who are reliable and choose not to interact with those who are not reliable. That is, we choose to enter Prisoner's Dilemmas situations with those who are reliable, and choose to avoid entering such situations with those who are not reliable. As Robert Frank has shown, given such conditions it is, under quite ordinary circumstances, rational to habitually be reliable since reliable persons tend to have mutually beneficial interactions with other reliable persons, while unreliable persons will tend to have mutually destructive interactions with other unreliable persons.

The implication again is that since signaling makes it rational to habitually cooperate in the rules of morality, even in the absence of a third-party enforcer, we can expect that rational humans, who can send and receive fairly reliable signals between each other, will tend to behave morally even, presumably, when doing so raises the prospect of competitive disadvantage.

These considerations should lead the realist to revise the tentative statement of the second premise of his argument that we laid out above. In its revised form, the second premise would have to read as follows:

> In the absence of an international sovereign, all rational agents will chose not to comply with the tenets of ordinary morality, when doing so will put one at a serious competitive disadvantage, provided that interactions are not repeated and that agents are not able to signal their reliability to each other.

This, I believe, is a persuasive and defensible version of the second premise in the Hobbesian argument. It is the one I will exploit in what follows.

VI. Revised Realism, Multinationals, and the Common Good

Now how does this apply to multinationals and the common good? Can we claim that it is clear that multinationals have a moral obligation to pursue the global common good in spite of the objections of the realist?

I do not believe that this claim can be made. We can conclude from the discussion of the realist objection that the Hobbesian claim about the pervasiveness of amorality in the international sphere is false when (1) interactions among international agents are repetitive in such a way that agents can retaliate against those who fail to cooperate, and (2) agents can determine the trustworthiness of other international agents.

But unfortunately, multinational activities often take place in a highly competitive arena in which these two conditions do not obtain. Moreover, these conditions are noticeably absent in the arena of activities that concern the global common good.

First, as I have noted, the common good consists of goods that are indivisible and accessible to all. This means that such goods are susceptible to the free rider problem. Everyone has access to such goods whether or not they do their part in maintaining such goods, so everyone is tempted to free ride on the generosity of others. Now governments can force domestic companies to do their part to maintain the national common good. Indeed, it is one of the functions of government to solve the free rider problem by forcing all to contribute to the domestic common good to which all have access. Moreover, all companies have to interact repeatedly with their host governments, and this leads them to adopt a cooperative stance toward their host government's objective of achieving the domestic common good.

But it is not clear that governments can or will do anything effective to force multinationals to do their part to maintain the global common good. For the governments of individual nations can themselves be free riders, and can join forces with willing multinationals seeking competitive advantages over others. Let me suggest an example. It is clear that a livable global environment is part of the global common good, and it is clear that the manufacture and use of chloroflurocarbons is destroying that good. Some nations have responded by requiring their domestic companies to cease manufacturing or using chloroflurocarbons. But other nations have refused to do the same, since they will share in any benefits that accrue from the restraint others practice, and they can also reap the benefits of continuing to manufacture and use chloroflurocarbons. Less developed nations, in particular, have advanced the position that since their development depends heavily on exploiting the industrial benefits of chloroflurocarbons, they cannot afford to curtail their use of these substances. Given this situation, it is open to multinationals to shift their operations to those countries that continue to allow the manufacture and use of chloroflurocarbons. For multinationals, too, will reason that they will share in any benefits that accrue from the restraint others practice, and that they can meanwhile reap the profits of continuing to manufacture and use chloroflurocarbons in a world where other companies are forced to use more expensive technologies. Moreover, those nations that practice restraint cannot force all such multinationals to discontinue the manufacture or use of chlorofluro-carbons because many multinationals can escape the reach of their laws. An exactly parallel, but perhaps even more compelling, set of considerations can be advanced to show that at least some multinationals will join forces with some developing countries to circumvent any global efforts made to control the global warming trends (the so-called "greenhouse effect") caused by the heavy use of fossil fuels.

The realist will conclude, of course, that in such situations, at least some multinationals will seek to gain competitive advantages by failing to contribute to the global common good (such as the good of a hospitable global environment). For multinationals are rational agents, i.e., agents bureaucratically structured to take rational means toward achieving their dominant end of increasing their profits. And in a competitive environment, contributing to the common good while others do not, will fail to achieve this dominant end. Joining this conclusion to the ethical premise that when others do not adhere to the requirements of morality it is not immoral for one to do likewise, the realist can conclude that multinationals are not morally obligated to contribute to such global common goods (such as environmental goods).

Moreover, global common goods often create interactions that are not iterated. This is particularly the case where the global environment is concerned. As I have already noted, preservation of a favorable global climate is clearly part of the global common good. Now the failure of the global climate will be a one-time affair. The breakdown of the ozone layer, for example, will happen once, with catastrophic consequences for us all; and the heating up of the global climate as a result of the infusion of carbon dioxide will happen once, with catastrophic consequences for us all. Because these environmental disasters are a one-time affair, they represent a non-iterated Prisoner's Dilemma for multinationals. It is irrational from an individual point of view for a multinational to choose to refrain from polluting the environment in such cases. Either others will refrain, and then one can enjoy the benefits of their refraining; or others will not refrain, and then it will be better to have also not refrained since refraining would have made little difference and would have entailed heavy losses.

Finally, we must also note that although natural persons may signal their reliability to other natural persons, it is not at all obvious that multinationals can do the same. As noted above, multinationals are bureaucratic organizations whose members are continually changing and shifting. The natural persons who make up an organization can signal their reliability to others, but such persons are soon replaced by others, and they in turn are replaced by others. What endures is each organization's single-minded pursuit of increasing its profits in a competitive environment. And an enduring commitment to the pursuit of profit in a competitive environment is not a signal of an enduring commitment to morality.

VII. Conclusions

The upshot of these considerations is that it is not obvious that we can say that multinationals have an obligation to contribute to the global common good in a competitive environment in the absence of an international authority that can force all agents to contribute to the global common good. Where other rational agents can be expected to shirk the burden of contributing to the common good and where carrying such a burden will put one at a serious competitive disadvantage, the realist argument that it is not immoral for one to also fail to contribute is a powerful argument.

I have not argued, of course, nor do I find it persuasive to claim that competitive pressures automatically relieve agents of their moral obligations, although my arguments here may be wrongly misinterpreted as making that claim. All that I have tried to do is to lay out a justification for the very narrow claim that *certain very special kinds of agents, under certain very limited and very special conditions, seem to have no obligations with respect to certain very special kinds of goods.*

This is not an argument, however, for complete despair. What the argument points to is the need to establish an effective international authority capable of forcing all agents to contribute their part toward the global common good. Perhaps several of the more powerful autonomous governments of the world, for example, will be prompted to establish such an international agency by relinquishing their autonomy and joining together into a coherently unified group that can exert consistent economic, political, or military pressures on any companies or smaller countries that do not contribute to the global common good. Such an international police group, of course, would transform the present world order, and would be much different from present world organizations such as the United Nations. Once such an international force exists, of course, then both Hobbes and the neo-realist would say that moral obligations can legitimately be attributed to all affected international organizations.

Of course, it is remotely possible but highly unlikely that multinationals themselves will be the source of such promptings for a transformed world order. For whereas governments are concerned with the well being of their citizens, multinationals are bureaucratically structured for the rational pursuit of profit in a competitive environment, not the pursuit of citizen well-being. Here and there we occasionally may see one or even several multinationals whose current cadre of leadership is enlightened enough to regularly steer the organization toward the global common good. But given time, that cadre will be replaced and profit objectives will reassert themselves as the enduring end built into the on-going structure of the multinational corporation.

NOTES

1 See, for example, the articles collected in W. Michael Hoffman, Ann E. Lange, and David A. Fedo, eds., *Ethics and the Multinational Enterprise* (New York: University Press of America, 1986).

2 Thomas Donaldson, *The Ethics of International Business* (New York: Oxford University Press, 1989).

3 Donaldson discusses the question whether *states* have moral obligations to each other in *op. cit.*, 10-29. The critical question, however, is whether *multinationals*, i.e., profit-driven types of international organizations, have moral obligations. Although Donaldson is able to point out without a great deal of trouble that the realist arguments against morality among nations are mistaken (see 20-23, where Donaldson points out that if the realist were correct, then there would be no cooperation among nations; but since there is cooperation, the realist must be wrong), his points leave untouched the arguments I discuss below which acknowledge that while much cooperation among nations is possible, nevertheless certain crucial forms of cooperation will not obtain among multinationals with respect to the global common good.

4 J. Bentham, *Principles of Morals and Legislation*, 1.4-5.

5 William A. Wallace, O.P., *The Elements of Philosophy, A Compendium for Philosophers and Theologians* (New York: Alba House, 1977), 166-67.

6 *Ibid.*, 167.

7 "Common Good," *The New Catholic Encyclopedia*.

8 John Rawls, *A Theory of Justice* (Cambridge, MA: Harvard University Press, 1971), 233 and 246.

9 Thomas Hobbes, *Leviathan, Parts I and II* [1651] (New York: The Bobbs-Merrill, 1958), 108.

10 *Ibid.* As noted earlier, I am simply assuming what I take to be the popular interpretation of

Hobbes' view on the state of nature. As Professor Philip Kain has pointed out to me, there is some controversy among Hobbes scholars about whether or not Hobbes actually held that moral obligation exists in the state of nature. Among those who hold that moral obligation does not exist in Hobbes' state of nature is M. Oakeshott in "The Moral Life in the Writings of Thomas Hobbes" in his *Hobbes on Civil Association* (Berkeley-Los Angeles: University of California Press, 1975), 95-113; among those who hold that moral obligation does exist in Hobbes' state of nature is A.E. Taylor in "The Ethical Doctrine of Hobbes" in *Hobbes Studies*, ed. K.C. Brown (Cambridge: Harvard, 1965), 41ff. Kain suggests that Hobbes simply contradicts himself—holding in some passages that moral obligation does exist in the state of nature and holding in others that it does not—because of his need to use the concept of the state of nature to achieve purposes that required incompatible conceptions of the state of nature; see his "Hobbes, Revolution and the Philosophy of History," in *"Hobbes's 'Science of Natural Justice,'"* ed. C. Walton and P.J. Johnson (Boston: Martinus Nijhoff, 1987), 203-18. In the present essay I am simply assuming without argument the traditional view that Hobbes made the claim that moral obligation does not exist in the state of nature; my aim is to pursue certain implications of this claim even if I am wrong in assuming that is Hobbes'.

11 See *ibid.*, where Hobbes writes that "yet in all times kings and persons of sovereign authority, because of their independency" are in this state of war.

12 *Ibid.*, 107-08.

13 See Amartya K. Sen, *Collective Choice and Social Welfare* (San Francisco: Holden-Day, 1970), 2-5.

14 See, for example, Gregory Kavka, "Hobbes' War of All Against All," *Ethics*, 93 (January,

1983), 291-310; a somewhat different approach is that of David Gauthier, *Morals By Agreement* (Oxford: Clarendon Press, 1986) and Russell Hardin, *Morality Within the Limits of Reason* (Chicago: University of Chicago Press, 1988).

15 See Robert Axelrod, *The Evolution of Cooperation* (New York: Basic Books, 1984), 27-69.

16 Robert Frank, *Passions Within Reason* (New York: W.W. Norton & Company, 1988).

◆ ◆ ◆ ◆ ◆

IAN MAITLAND

The Great Non-Debate Over International Sweatshops

Recent years have seen a dramatic growth in the contracting out of production by companies in the industrialized countries to suppliers in developing countries. This globalization of production has led to an emerging international division of labor in footwear and apparel in which companies like Nike and Reebok concentrate on product design and marketing but rely on a network of contractors in Asia and Central America, etc., to build shoes or sew shirts according to exact specifications and deliver a high quality good according to precise delivery schedules. These contracting arrangements have drawn intense fire from labor and human rights activists who charge that the companies are (by proxy) exploiting foreign workers. The companies stand accused of chasing cheap labor around the globe, failing to pay their workers living wages, using child labor, turning a blind eye to abuses of human rights, and being complicit with repressive regimes in denying workers the right to join unions and failing to enforce minimum labor standards in the workplace, and so on. Many companies have tried to address these concerns by developing codes of conduct for their overseas suppliers. This workshop will examine the desirability and pitfalls of such codes of conduct.

The campaign against international sweatshops has largely unfolded on television and, to a lesser extent, in the print media. What seems like no more than a handful of critics has mounted an aggressive, media-savvy campaign which has put the publicity-shy retail giants on the defensive. The critics have orchestrated a series of sensational "disclosures" on prime time television exposing the terrible pay and working conditions in factories making jeans for Levi's or sneakers for Nike or Pocahontas shirts for Disney. One of the principal scourges of the companies has been Charles Kernaghan who runs the National Labor Coalition (NLC), a labor human rights group involving 25 unions. It was Kernaghan who, in 1996, broke the news before a Congressional committee that Kathie Lee Gifford's clothing line was being made by 13- and 14-year olds working 20-hour days in factories in Honduras.[1] Kernaghan also arranged for teenage workers from sweatshops in Central America to testify before Congressional committees about abusive labor practices. At one of these hearings, one of the workers held up a Liz Claiborne cotton sweater identical to ones she had sewn since she was a 13-year old working 12 hour days. According to a news report, "[t]his image, accusations of oppressive conditions at the factory and the Claiborne logo played well on that evening's network news."[2] The result has been a circus-like atmosphere—as in Roman circus where Christians were thrown to lions.

Kernaghan has shrewdly targeted the companies' carefully cultivated public images. He has explained: "Their image is everything. They live and die by their image. That gives you a certain power over them." As a result, he says, "these companies are sitting ducks. They have no leg to stand on. That's why it's possible for a tiny group like us to take on a giant like Wal-Mart. You can't defend paying someone 31 cents an hour in Honduras...."[3] Apparently most of the companies agree with Ker-

naghan. Not a single company has tried to mount a serious defense of its contracting practices. They have judged that they cannot win a war of sound bites with the critics. Instead of making a fight of it, the companies have sued for peace in order to protect their principal asset—their image.

Major US retailers have responded by adopting codes of conduct on human and labor rights in their international operations. Levi-Strauss, Nike, Sears, JCPenney, Wal-Mart, Home Depot, Philips Van-Heusen now have such codes. As Lance Compa notes, such codes are the result of a blend of humanitarian and pragmatic impulses: "Often the altruistic motive coincides with 'bottom line' considerations related to brand name, company image, and other intangibles that make for core value to the firm."[4] Peter Jacobi, President of Global Sourcing for Levi-Strauss has advised: "If your company owns a popular brand, protect this priceless asset at all costs. Highly visible companies have any number of reasons to conduct their business not just responsibly but also in ways that cannot be portrayed as unfair, illegal, or unethical. This sets an extremely high standard since it must be applied to both company-owned businesses and contractors...."[5] And according to another Levi-Strauss spokesman, "In many respects, we're protecting our single largest asset: our brand image and corporate reputation."[6] Nike recently published the results of a generally favorable review of its international operations conducted by former American UN Ambassador Andrew Young.

Recently a truce of sorts between the critics and the companies was announced on the White House lawn with President Clinton and Kathie Lee Gifford in attendance. A presidential task force, including representatives of labor unions, human rights groups and apparel companies like L.L. Bean and Nike, has come up with a set of voluntary standards which, it hopes, will be embraced by the entire industry.[7] Companies that comply with the code will be entitled to use a "No Sweat" label.

Objective of This Paper

In this confrontation between the companies and their critics, neither side seems to have judged it to be in its interest to seriously engage the issue at the heart of this controversy, namely: What are appropriate wages and labor standards in international sweatshops? As we have seen, the companies have treated the charges about sweatshops as a public relations problem to be managed so as to minimize harm to their public images. The critics have apparently judged that the best way to keep public indignation at boiling point is to oversimplify the issue and treat it as a morality play featuring heartless exploiters and victimized third world workers. The result has been a great non-debate over international sweatshops. Paradoxically, if peace breaks out between the two sides, the chances that the debate will be seriously joined may recede still further. Indeed, there exists a real risk (I will argue) that any such truce may be collusive one that will come at the expense of the very third world workers it is supposed to help.

This paper takes up the issue of what are appropriate wages and labor standards in international sweatshops. Critics charge that the present arrangements are exploitative. I proceed by examining the specific charges of exploitation from the standpoints of both (a) their factual[8] and (b) their ethical sufficiency. However, in the absence of any well-established consensus among business ethicists (or other thoughtful observers), I simultaneously use the investigation of sweatshops as a setting for trying to adjudicate between competing views about what those standards should be. My examination will pay particular attention to (but will not be limited to) labor conditions at the plants of Nike's suppliers in Indonesia. I have not personally visited any international sweatshops, and so my conclusions are based entirely on secondary analysis of the voluminous published record on the topic.

What are Ethically Appropriate Labor Standards in International Sweatshops?

What are ethically acceptable or appropriate levels of wages and labor standards in international sweatshops? The following four possibilities just about run the gamut of standards or principles that have been seriously proposed to regulate such policies.

(1) *Home-country standards*: It might be argued (and in rare cases has been[9]) that international corporations have an ethical duty to pay the same wages and provide the same labor standards regardless of where they operate.[10] However, the view that home-country standards should apply in host-countries is rejected by most business ethicists and (officially at least) by the critics of international sweatshops. Thus Thomas Donaldson argues that "[b]y arbitrarily establishing US wage levels as the bench mark for fairness one eliminates the role of the international market in establishing salary levels, and this in turn eliminates the incentive US corporations have to hire foreign workers."[11] Richard DeGeorge makes much the same argument: If there were a rule that said that "that American MNCs [multinational corporations] that wish to be ethical must pay the same wages abroad as they do at home, ... [then] MNCs would have little incentive to move their manufacturing abroad; and if they did move abroad they would disrupt the local labor market with artificially high wages that bore no relation to the local standard or cost of living."[12]

(2) *"Living wage" standard*: It has been proposed that an international corporation should, at a minimum, pay a "living wage." Thus DeGeorge says that corporations should pay a living wage "even when this is not paid by local firms."[13] However, it is hard to pin down what this means operationally. According to DeGeorge, a living wage should "allow the worker to live in dignity as a human being." In order to

respect the human rights of its workers, he says, a corporation must pay "at least subsistence wages and as much above that as workers and their dependents need to live with reasonable dignity, given the general state of development of the society."[14] As we shall see, the living wage standard has become a rallying cry of the critics of international sweatshops. Apparently, DeGeorge believes that it is preferable for a corporation to provide no job at all than to offer one that pays less than a living wage.

(3) *Donaldson's test*: Thomas Donaldson believes that "it is irrelevant whether the standards of the host country comply or fail to comply with home country standards; what is relevant is whether they meet a universal, objective minimum."[15] He tries to specify "a moral minimum for the behavior of all international economic agents."[16] However, he concedes that this "leaves obscure not only the issue of less extreme threats but of harms other than physical injury. The language of rights and harm is sufficiently vague so as to leave shrouded in uncertainty a formidable list of issues crucial to multinationals."[17] He accepts that "many rights ... are dependent for their specification on the level of economic development of the country in question."[18] Accordingly, he proposes a test to determine when deviations from home-country standards are unethical. That test provides as follows: "The practice is permissible if and only if the members of the home country would, under conditions of economic development relevantly similar to those of the host country, regard the practice as permissible."[19] Donaldson's test is vulnerable to Bernard Shaw's objection to the Golden Rule, namely that we should not do unto others as we would they do unto us, because their tastes may be different. The test also complicates matters by introducing counterfactuals and hypotheticals (if I were in their place [which I'm not] what would I want?). This indeterminacy is a serious weakness in an ethical code: It is likely to confuse managers who want to act ethically and to provide loopholes for those don't.[20]

(4) *Classical liberal standard*: Finally there is what I will call the classical liberal standard. According to this standard a practice (wage or labor practice) is ethically acceptable if it is freely chosen by informed workers. For example, in a recent report the World Bank invoked this standard in connection with workplace safety. It said: "The appropriate level is therefore that at which the costs are commensurate with the value that informed workers place on improved working conditions and reduced risk."[21] Most business ethicists reject this standard on the grounds that there is some sort of market failure or the "background conditions" are lacking for markets to work effectively. Thus for Donaldson full (or near-full) employment is a prerequisite if workers are to make sound choices regarding workplace safety: "The average level of unemployment in the developing countries today exceeds 40 per cent, a figure that has frustrated the application of neoclassical economic principles to the international economy on a score of issues. With full employment, and all other things being equal, market forces will encourage workers to make trade-offs between job opportunities using safety as a variable. But with massive unemployment, market forces in developing countries drive the unemployed to the jobs they are lucky enough to land, regardless of the safety."[22] Apparently there are other forces, like Islamic fundamentalism and the global debt "bomb," that rule out reliance on market solutions, but Donaldson does not explain their relevance.[23] DeGeorge, too, believes that the necessary conditions are lacking for market forces to operate benignly. Without what he calls "background institutions" to protect the workers and the resources of the developing country (e.g., enforceable minimum wages) and/or greater equality of bargaining power exploitation is the most likely result.[24] "If American MNCs pay workers very low wages ... they clearly have the opportunity to make significant profits."[25] DeGeorge goes on to make the interesting observation that "competition has developed among multinationals themselves, so that the profit margin has

been driven down" and developing countries "can play one company against another."[26] But apparently that is not enough to rehabilitate market forces in his eyes.

The Case Against International Sweatshops

To many of their critics, international sweatshops exemplify the way in which the greater openness of the world economy is hurting workers. According to one critic, "as it is now constituted, the world trading system discriminates against workers, especially those in the Third World."[27] Globalization means a transition from (more or less) regulated domestic economies to an unregulated world economy. The superior mobility of capital, and the essentially fixed, immobile nature of world labor, means a fundamental shift in bargaining power in favor of large international corporations. Their global reach permits them to shift production almost costlessly from one location to another. As a consequence, instead of being able to exercise some degree of control over companies operating within their borders, governments are now locked in a bidding war with one another to attract and retain the business of large multinational companies.

The critics allege that international companies are using the threat of withdrawal or withholding of investment to pressure governments and workers to grant concessions. "Today [multinational companies] choose between workers in developing countries that compete against each other to depress wages to attract foreign investment."[28] The result is a race for the bottom—a "destructive downward bidding spiral of the labor conditions and wages of workers throughout the world...."[29] Kernaghan claims that "It is a race to the bottom over who will accept the lowest wages and the most miserable working conditions."[30] Thus, critics charge that in Indonesia wages are deliberately held below the poverty level or subsistence in order to make the country a desirable lo-

cation. The results of this competitive dismantling of worker protections, living standards and worker rights are predictable: deteriorating work conditions, declining real incomes for workers, and a widening gap between rich and poor in developing countries. I turn next to the specific charges made by the critics of international sweatshops.

Unconscionable wages: Critics charge that the companies, by their proxies, are paying "starvation wages"[31] and "slave wages."[32] They are far from clear about what wage level they consider to be appropriate. But they generally demand that companies pay a "living wage." Kernaghan has said that workers should be paid enough to support their families[33] and they should get a "living wage" and "be treated like human beings."[34] Jay Mazur of the textile employees union (UNITE) says "On the question of wages, generally, of course workers should be paid enough to meet their basic needs—and then some."[35] According to Tim Smith, wage levels should be "fair, decent or a living wage for an employee and his or her family." He has said that wages in the maquiladoras of Mexico averaged $35 to $55 a week (in or near 1993) which he calls a "shockingly substandard wage," apparently on the grounds that it "clearly does not allow an employee to feed and care for a family adequately."[36] In 1992, Nike came in for harsh criticism when a magazine published the pay stub of a worker at one of its Indonesian suppliers. It showed that the worker was paid at the rate of $1.03 per day which was reportedly less than the Indonesian government's figure for "minimum physical need."[37]

Immiserization thesis: Former Labor Secretary Robert Reich has proposed as a test of the fairness of development policies that "Low-wage workers should become better off, not worse off, as trade and investment boost national income." He has written that "[i]f a country pursues policies that ... limit to a narrow elite the benefits of trade, the promise of open commerce is perverted and drained of its rationale."[38] A key claim of the activists is that companies actually impoverish or immiserize developing country workers. They experience an absolute decline in living standards. This thesis follows from the claim that the bidding war among developing countries is depressing wages. Critics deride the claim that sweatshops are benefiting the poor by means of a global version of "trickle down" economics.[39] They reject as flawed "claims that US [free trade] policies are leading to the growth of huge middle classes—in such countries as China, India and Indonesia—that will drive the world economy in the twenty-first century."[40] This picture, they say, is belied by the fact that "Most of the 'global South'—some 45 per cent of humanity who reside mainly in the 140 poorest countries of the Third World—is locked in poverty and left behind as the richer strata grow...."[41]

Widening gap between rich and poor: A related charge is that international sweatshops are contributing to the increasing gap between rich and poor. Not only are the poor being absolutely impoverished, but trade is generating greater inequality within developing countries. Another test that Reich has proposed to establish the fairness of international trade is that "the gap between rich and poor should tend to narrow with development, not widen."[42] Critics charge that international sweatshops flunk that test. They say that the increasing GNPs of some developing countries simply mask a widening gap between rich and poor. "Across the world, both local and foreign elites are getting richer from the exploitation of the most vulnerable."[43] And, "The major adverse consequence of quickening global economic integration has been widening income disparity within almost all nations...."[44] There appears to be a tacit alliance between the elites of both first and third worlds to exploit the most vulnerable, to regiment and control and conscript them so that they can create the material conditions for the elites' extravagant lifestyles.

Collusion with repressive regimes: Critics charge that, in their zeal to make their countries safe for foreign investment, Third World regimes, notably China and Indonesia, have stepped up their repression. Not only have these countries have failed to enforce even the minimal labor rules on the books, but they have also used their military and police to break strikes and repress independent unions. They have stifled political dissent, both to retain their hold on political power and to avoid any instability that might scare off foreign investors. Consequently, critics charge, companies like Nike are profiting from political repression. "As unions spread in [Korea and Taiwan], Nike shifted its suppliers primarily to Indonesia, China and Thailand, where they could depend on governments to suppress independent union-organizing efforts."[45]

Evaluation of the Charges Against International Sweatshops

The critics' charges are undoubtedly accurate on a number of points: (1) There is no doubt that international companies are chasing cheap labor.[46] (2) The wages paid by the international sweatshops are—by American standards—shockingly low. (3) Some developing country governments have tightly controlled or repressed organized labor in order to prevent it from disturbing the flow of foreign investment. Thus, in Indonesia, independent unions have been suppressed.[47] (4) It is not unusual in developing countries for minimum wage levels to be lower than the official poverty level. (5) Developing country governments have winked at violations of minimum wage laws and labor rules. However, most jobs are in the informal sector and so largely outside the scope of government supervision.[48] (6) Some suppliers have employed children or have subcontracted work to other producers who have done so. (7) Some developing country governments deny their people basic political rights. China is the obvious example; Indonesia's record is pretty horrible but had shown steady improvement until the last two years. But on many of the other counts, the critics' charges appear to be seriously inaccurate. And, even where the charges are accurate, it is not self-evident that the practices in question are improper or unethical, as we see next.

Wages and conditions: Even the critics of international sweatshops do not dispute that the wages they pay are generally higher than—or at least equal to—comparable wages in the labor markets where they operate. According to the International Labor Organization (ILO), multinational companies often apply standards relating to wages, benefits, conditions of work, and occupational safety and health, which both exceed statutory requirements and those practised by local firms.[49] The ILO also says that wages and working conditions in so-called Export Processing Zones (EPZs) are often equal to or higher than jobs outside.[50] The World Bank says that the poorest workers in developing countries work in the informal sector where they often earn less than half what a formal sector employee earns. Moreover, "informal and rural workers often must work under more hazardous and insecure conditions than their formal sector counterparts."[51]

The same appears to hold true for the international sweatshops. In 1996, young women working in the plant of a Nike supplier in Serang, Indonesia were earning the Indonesian legal minimum wage of 5,200 rupiahs or about $2.28 each day. As a report in the *Washington Post* pointed out, just earning the minimum wage put these workers among higher-paid Indonesians: "In Indonesia, less than half the working population earns the minimum wage, since about half of all adults here are in farming, and the typical farmer would make only about 2,000 rupiahs each day."[52] The workers in the Serang plant reported that they save about three-quarters of their pay. A 17 year-old woman said: "I came here one year ago from central Java. I'm making more money than my father makes." This woman also said that she sent

about 75 per cent of her earnings back to her family on the farm.[53] Also in 1996, a Nike spokeswoman estimated that an entry-level factory worker in the plant of a Nike supplier made five times what a farmer makes.[54] Nike's chairman, Phil Knight, likes to teasingly remind critics that the average worker in one of Nike's Chinese factories is paid more than a professor at Beijing University.[55] There is also plentiful anecdotal evidence from non-Nike sources. A worker at the Taiwanese-owned King Star Garment Assembly plant in Honduras told a reporter that he was earning seven times what he earned in the countryside.[56] In Bangladesh, the country's fledgling garment industry was paying women who had never worked before between $40 and $55 a month in 1991. That compared with a national per capita income of about $200 and the approximately $1 a day earned by many of these women's husbands as day laborers or rickshaw drivers.[57]

The same news reports also shed some light on the working conditions in sweatshops. According to the *Washington Post*, in 1994 the Indonesian office of the international accounting firm Ernst & Young surveyed Nike workers concerning worker pay, safety conditions and attitudes toward the job. The auditors pulled workers off the assembly line at random and asked them questions that the workers answered anonymously. The survey of 25 workers at Nike's Serang plant found that 23 thought the hours and overtime worked were fair, and two thought the overtime hours too high. None of the workers reported that they had been discriminated against. Thirteen said the working environment was the key reason they worked at the Serang plant while eight cited salary and benefits.[58] The *Post* report also noted that the Serang plant closes for about ten days each year for Muslim holidays. It quoted Nike officials and the plant's Taiwanese owners as saying that 94 per cent of the workers had returned to the plant following the most recent break.

The *New York Times*'s Larry Rohter went to Honduras where he interviewed more than 75 apparel workers and union leaders and made visits to half a dozen plants, including the one that made clothes for the Gifford line. Workers and employers told Rohter that managers at some companies verbally abused their workers on a regular basis, but at other plants they treated their employees well. "What residents of a rich country see as exploitation," Rohter reported, "can seem a rare opportunity to residents of a poor country like Honduras, where the per capita income is $600 a year and unemployment is 40 per cent."[59]

There is also the mute testimony of the lines of job applicants outside the sweatshops in Guatemala and Honduras. According to Lucy Martinez-Mont, in Guatemala the sweatshops are conspicuous for the long lines of young people waiting to be interviewed for a job.[60] Outside the gates of the industrial park in Honduras that Rohter visited "anxious onlookers are always waiting, hoping for a chance at least to fill out a job application [for employment at one of the apparel plants]."[61]

The critics of sweatshops acknowledge that workers have voluntarily taken their jobs, consider themselves lucky to have them, and want to keep them. Thus Barnet and Cavanagh quote a worker as saying, "I am happy working here. I can make money and I can make friends."[62] But they go on to discount the workers' views as the product of confusion or ignorance, and/or they just argue that the workers' views are beside the point. Thus, while "it is undoubtedly true" that Nike has given jobs to thousands of people who wouldn't be working otherwise, they say that "neatly skirts the fundamental human-rights issue raised by these production arrangements that are now spreading all across the world."[63] Similarly the NLC's Kernaghan says that "[w]hether workers think they are better off in the assembly plants than elsewhere is not the real issue."[64] Kernaghan, and Jeff Ballinger of the AFL-CIO, concede that the workers desperately need these jobs. But "[t]hey say they're not asking that US companies stop operating in these countries. They're asking that workers be paid a living wage and treated like human beings."[65] Apparently these workers are victims of what Marx called false consciousness, or else they would grasp that they are being exploited. According to Barnet and Cavanagh, "For many workers ... exploitation is not a concept easily comprehended because the alternative prospects for earning a living are so bleak."[66]

Immiserization and inequality: The critics' claim that the countries that host international sweatshops are marked by growing poverty and inequality is flatly contradicted by the record. In fact, many of those countries have experienced sharp increases in living standards—for all strata of society. In trying to attract investment in simple manufacturing, Malaysia and Indonesia and, now, Vietnam and China, are retracing the industrialization path already successfully taken by East Asian countries like Taiwan, Korea, Singapore and Hong Kong. These four countries got their start by producing labor-intensive manufactured goods (often electrical and electronic components, shoes, and garments) for export markets. Over time they graduated to the export of higher value-added items that are skill-intensive and require a relatively developed industrial base.[67]

As is well known, these East Asian countries achieved growth rates exceeding eight per cent for a quarter century.[68] As Gary Fields says, the workers in these economies were not impoverished by growth. The benefits of growth were widely diffused: These economies achieved essentially full employment in the 1960s. Real wages rose by as much as a factor of four. Absolute poverty fell. And income inequality remained at low to moderate levels.[69] It is true that in the initial stages the rapid growth generated only moderate increases in wages. But once essentially-full employment was reached, and what economists call the Fei-Ranis turning point was reached, the increased demand for labor resulted in the bidding up of wages as firms competed for a scarce labor supply.[70]

Interestingly, given its historic mission as a watch-dog for international labor standards,[71] the ILO has embraced this development model. It recently noted that the most successful developing economies, in terms of output and employment growth, have been "those who best exploited emerging opportunities in the global economy."[72] An "export-oriented policy is vital in countries that are starting on the industrialization path and have large surpluses of cheap labour."[73] Countries which have succeeded in attracting foreign direct investment (FDI) have experienced rapid growth in manufacturing output and exports.[74] The successful attraction of foreign investment in plant and equipment "can be a powerful spur to rapid industrialization and employment creation."[75] "At low levels of industrialization, FDI in garments and shoes and some types of consumer electronics can be very useful for creating employment and opening the economy to international markets; there may be some entrepreneurial skills created in simple activities like garments (as has happened in Bangladesh). Moreover, in some cases, such as Malaysia, the investors may strike deeper roots and invest in more capital-intensive technologies as wages rise."[76]

According to the World Bank, the rapidly growing Asian economies (including Indonesia) "have also been unusually successful at sharing the fruits of their growth."[77] In fact, while inequality in the West has been growing, it has been shrinking in the Asian economies. They are the only economies in the world to have experienced high growth *and* declining inequality, and they also show shrinking gender gaps in education.[78]

This development strategy is working for Indonesia. According to a recent survey in the *Economist*, "Indonesia is now well and truly launched on the path of export-led growth already trodden by countries such as Malaysia, Thailand and South Korea."[79] "In 1967, when the president, Suharto, first took that job, Indonesia's GNP of $70 per person meant that it was twice as poor as India and Bangladesh.

Since then Indonesia's economy has grown at a rate of almost 7 per cent a year in real terms.... By the early 1990s, average annual incomes had spurted to $650 a person—twice what they had been a decade earlier—as gross national product had expanded at an average clip of 6.8 per cent."[80] Indonesia has spent significant sums on health, education and the advancement of women and the provision of credit to low income families and small-scale entrepreneurs.[81] It has also spread its wealth to the rural areas. Rural electrification and road construction have made rapid strides. By 1993, about half of the Indonesian countryside was expected to have electricity, up from 35 per cent the previous year. Largely because of improvements in rural medical facilities and sanitation, the infant mortality rate has fallen by nearly 60 per cent since the early 1970s.[82] These facts are reviewed here because they are so starkly different from the much darker picture painted by the critics of international sweatshops.

Profiting from repression?: What about the charge that international sweatshops are profiting from repression? It is undeniable that there is repression in many of the countries where sweatshops are located. But economic development appears to be relaxing that repression rather than strengthening its grip.[83] The companies are supposed to benefit from government policies (e.g., repression of unions) that hold down labor costs. However, as we have seen, the wages paid by the international sweatshops already match or exceed the prevailing local wages. Not only that, but incomes in the East Asian economies, and in Indonesia, have risen rapidly. Moreover, even the sweatshops' critics admit that the main factor restraining wages in countries like Indonesia is the state of the labor market. "Why is Indonesia the bargain basement of world labor?" ask Richard Barnet and John Cavanagh of the Institute for Policy Studies. Their principal explanation is that "[t]he reserve army of the unemployed is vast; 2.5 million people enter the job market every year."[84] The high rate of unemployment and underemployment acts as a brake on wages: Only about 55 per cent of the Indonesian labor force can find more than 35 hours of work each week, and about 2 million workers are unemployed.[85]

The critics, however, are right in saying that the Indonesian government has opposed independent unions in the sweatshops out of fear they would lead to higher wages and labor unrest. But the government's fear clearly is that unions might drive wages in the modern industrial sector *above* market-clearing levels—or, more exactly, further above market. It is ironic that critics like Barnet and Cavanagh would use the Marxian term "reserve army of the unemployed." According to Marx, capitalists deliberately maintain high levels of unemployment in order to control the working class. But the Indonesian government's policies (e.g., suppression of unions, resistance to a higher minimum wage and lax enforcement of labor rules) have been directed at achieving exactly the opposite result. The government appears to have calculated that high unemployment is a greater threat to its hold on power. I think we can safely take at face value its claims that its policies are genuinely intended to help the economy create jobs to absorb the massive numbers of unemployed and underemployed.[86]

Labor Standards in International Sweatshops: Painful Trade-offs

Who but the grinch could grudge paying a few additional pennies to some of the world's poorest workers? There is no doubt that the rhetorical force of the critics' case against international sweatshops rests on this apparently self-evident proposition. However, higher wages and improved labor standards are not free. After all, the critics themselves attack companies for chasing cheap labor. It follows that, if labor in developing countries is made more expensive (say, as the result of pressure by the critics), then those countries will receive less foreign investment, and fewer jobs will be created there. Imposing higher wages may deprive these countries of the one comparative advantage they enjoy, namely low-cost labor.

We have seen that workers in most "international sweatshops" are already relatively well paid. Workers in the urban, formal sectors of developing countries commonly earn more than twice what informal and rural workers get.[87] Simply earning the minimum wage put the young women making Nike shoes in Serang in the top half of the income distribution in Indonesia. Accordingly, the critics are in effect calling for a *widening* of the economic disparity that already greatly favors sweatshop workers.

By itself that may or may not be ethically objectionable. But these higher wages come at the expense of the incomes and the job opportunities of much poorer workers. As economists explain, higher wages in the formal sector reduce employment there and (by increasing the supply of labor) depress incomes in the informal sector. The case against requiring above-market wages for international sweatshop workers is essentially the same as the case against other measures that artificially raise labor costs, like the minimum wage. In Jagdish Bhagwati's words: "Requiring a minimum wage in an overpopulated, developing country, as is done in a developed country, may actually be morally wicked. A minimum wage might help the unionized, industrial proletariat, while limiting the ability to save and invest rapidly which is necessary to draw more of the unemployed and nonunionized rural poor into gainful employment and income."[88] The World Bank makes the same point: "Minimum wages may help the most poverty-stricken workers in industrial countries, but they clearly do not in developing nations.... The workers whom minimum wage legislation tries to protect—urban formal workers—already earn much more than the less favored majority.... And inasmuch as minimum wage and other regulations discourage formal employment by increasing wage and nonwage costs, they hurt the poor who aspire to formal employment."[89]

The story is no different when it comes to labor standards other than wages. If standards are set too high they will hurt investment and employment. The World Bank report points out that "[r]educing hazards in the workplace is costly, and typically the greater the reduction the more it costs. Moreover, the costs of compliance often fall largely on employees through lower wages or reduced employment. As a result, setting standards too high can actually lower workers' welfare...."[90] Perversely, if the higher standards advocated by critics retard the growth of formal sector jobs, then that will trap more informal and rural workers in jobs which are far more hazardous and insecure than those of their formal sector counterparts.[91]

The critics consistently advocate policies that will benefit better-off workers at the expense of worse-off ones. If it were within their power, it appears that they would re-invent the labor markets of much of Latin America. Alejandro Portes' description seems to be on the mark: "In Mexico, Brazil, Peru, and other Third World countries, [unlike East Asia], there are powerful independent unions representing the protected sector of the working class. Although there rhetoric is populist and even radical, the fact is that they tend to represent the better-paid and more stable fraction of the working class. Alongside, there toils a vast, unprotected proletariat, employed by informal enterprises and linked, in ways hidden from public view, with modern sector firms."[92]

Moreover the critics are embracing a development strategy—one that improves formal sector workers' wages and conditions by fiat—that has been tried and failed. It is in the process of being abandoned by Third World countries around the globe. Portes, who is no advocate of unfettered markets,[93] has warned against the overregulation of labor markets in developing countries. He says: "For those who advocate a full set of advanced regulations to be implemented in all countries, I offer the example of those less developed nations which attempted to do so and failed. More often than not, their sophisticated legal codes did not so much reflect labor market realities as the influence and prestige of things foreign. The common end-result was an acute labor market dualism which protected a privileged segment of the labor force at the expense of the majority."[94] It is precisely to escape the web of overregulation of their own making that developing countries have established so-called "special production zones" (SPZs). The governments of "heavily regulated countries attempting to break into export markets have adopted the strategy of establishing [SPZs] in remote areas away from the centers of union strength. What is 'special' about these zones is precisely that provisions of the existing tax and labor codes do not apply to them and that they are generally 'union-free.'"[95]

Of course it might be objected that trading off workers' rights for more jobs is unethical. But, so far as I can determine, the critics have not made this argument. Although they sometimes implicitly accept the existence of the trade-off (we saw that they attack Nike for chasing cheap labor), their public statements are silent on the lost or forgone jobs from higher wages and better labor standards. At other times, they imply or claim that improvements in workers' wages and conditions are essentially free: According to Kernaghan, "Companies could easily double their employees' wages, and it would be nothing."[96]

In summary, the result of the ostensibly humanitarian changes urged by critics are likely to be (1) reduced employment in the formal or modern sector of the economy, (2) lower incomes in the informal sector, (3) less investment and so slower economic growth, (4) reduced exports, (5) greater inequality and poverty.[97] As Fields says, "The poor workers of the world cannot afford this."[98]

Conclusion: The Case for not Exceeding Market Standards

It is part of the job description of business ethicists to exhort companies to treat their workers better (otherwise what purpose do they serve?). So it will have come as no surprise that both the business ethicists whose views I summarized at the beginning of this paper—Thomas Donaldson and Richard DeGeorge—objected to letting the market alone determine wages and labor standards in multinational companies. Both of them proposed criteria for setting wages that might occasionally "improve" on the outcomes of the market.

Their reasons for rejecting market determination of wages were similar. They both cited conditions that allegedly prevent international markets from generating ethically acceptable results. Donaldson argued that neoclassical economic principles are not applicable to international business because of high unemployment rates in developing countries. And DeGeorge argued that, in an unregulated international market, the gross inequality of bargaining power between workers and companies would lead to exploitation.

But this paper has shown that attempts to improve on market outcomes may have unforeseen tragic consequences. We saw how raising the wages of workers in international sweatshops might wind up penalizing the most vulnerable workers (those in the informal sectors of developing countries) by depressing their wages and reducing their job opportunities in the formal sector. Donaldson and DeGeorge cited high unemployment and unequal bargaining power as conditions that made it necessary to bypass or override the market determination of wages. However, in both cases, bypassing the market in order to prevent exploitation may aggravate these conditions. As we have seen, above-market wages paid to sweatshop workers may discourage further investment and so perpetuate high unemployment. In turn, the higher unemployment may weaken the bargaining power of workers vis-à-vis employers. Thus such market imperfections seem to call for more reliance on market forces rather than less.

Likewise, the experience of the newly industrialized East Asian economies suggests that the best cure for the ills of sweatshops is more sweatshops. But most of the well-intentioned policies that improve on market outcomes are likely to have the opposite effect.

Where does this leave the international manager? If the preceding analysis is correct, then it follows that it is ethically acceptable to pay market wage rates in developing countries (and to provide employment conditions appropriate for the level of development). That holds true even if the wages pay less than so-called living wages or subsistence or even (conceivably) the local minimum wage. The appropriate test is not whether the wage reaches some predetermined standard but whether it is freely accepted by (reasonably) informed workers. The workers themselves are in the best position to judge whether the wages offered are superior to their next-best alternatives. (The same logic applies *mutatis mutandis* to workplace labor standards.)

Indeed, not only is it ethically acceptable for a company to pay market wages, but it may be ethically unacceptable for it to pay wages that exceed market levels. That will be the case if the company's above-market wages set precedents for other international companies which raise labor costs to the point of discouraging foreign investment. Furthermore, companies may have a social responsibility to transcend their own narrow preoccupation with protecting their brand image and to publicly defend a system which has greatly improved the lot of millions of workers in developing countries.

NOTES

1 Stephanie Strom, "From Sweetheart to Scapegoat," *New York Times*, June 27, 1996. According to Strom, "Shortly after [Kernaghan] effectively charged Mrs. Gifford with exploiting children in the pursuit of profit, news broke of a factory in New York's garment district where workers making blouses for the Kathie Lee Gifford line had not been paid. Mrs. Gifford dissolved into tears on her talk show, while her husband, Frank, the football player and broad-

caster, hurried to the factory, Seo Fashions, and doled out three $100 bills to each of the workers.... [Kernaghan] recently apologized saying he and his organization 'never intended to hurt anyone personally and are truly sorry for any pain caused to Kathie Lee Gifford ...'"

2 Joanna Ramey and Joyce Barrett, "Apparel's Ethical Dilemma," *Women's Wear Daily*, March 18, 1996.

3 Steven Greenhouse, "A Crusader Makes Celebrities Tremble," *New York Times*, June 18, 1996, B4.

4 Lance A. Compa and Tashia Hinchliffe Darricarrere, "Enforcement Through Corporate Codes of Conduct," in Compa and Stephen F. Diamond, *Human Rights, Labor Rights, and International Trade* (Philadelphia: University of Pennsylvania Press, 1996) 193.

5 Peter Jacobi in Martha Nichols, "Third-World Families at Work: Child Labor or Child Care," *Harvard Business Review*, Jan.-Feb. 1993.

6 David Sampson in Robin G. Givhan, "A Stain on Fashion; The Garment Industry Profits from Cheap Labor," *Washington Post*, September 12, 1995, B1. According to the *Wall Street Journal's* G. Pascal Zachary, "Ethics aside, Levi's was frankly concerned with its image among hip customers." Zachary quotes Robert Dunn, who helped design Levi's code of conduct, as saying, "Anyone seeking to protect their brand and company reputation will realize these policies make business sense. The alternative is to put ourselves at risk." "Exporting Rights: Levi Tries to Make Sure Contract Plants in Asia Treat Workers Well," *Wall Street Journal*, July 28, 1994.

7 Steven Greenhouse, "Voluntary Rules on Apparel Labor Proving Elusive," *New York Times*, February 1, 1997.

8 As Thomas Donaldson rightly says, "In general, the solution to most difficult international problems requires a detailed understanding not

only of moral precepts, but of particular facts." *The Ethics of International Business* (New York: Oxford University Press, 1989) 90. This case is especially fact-intensive.

9 Arnold Berleant has proposed that the principle of equal treatment endorsed by most Americans requires that US corporations pay workers in developing countries exactly the same wages paid to US workers in comparable jobs. See Donaldson, *Ethics of International Business*, 97-98.

10 Formally, of course, workers at Nike's suppliers are not Nike employees. But critics say this is a distinction without a difference, and I will not distinguish the two cases in this paper.

11 Donaldson, 98.

12 Richard DeGeorge, *Competing with Integrity in International Business* (New York: Oxford University Press, 1993) 79.

13 DeGeorge, *Competing with Integrity*, 356-57.

14 *Id.*, 78.

15 Thomas Donaldson, *The Ethics of International Business* (New York: Oxford University Press, 1989), 100.

16 Donaldson, *Ethics of International Business*, 145.

17 *Id.*, 100.

18 *Id.*, 101.

19 *Id.*, 103.

20 Donaldson rather loftily dismisses the objection that his "algorithm" makes excessive demands on the sophistication and "ethical sensitivity" of managers. "[F]rom a theoretical perspective the problem is a contingent and practical one. It is no more a theoretical flaw of the proposed algorithm that it may be misunderstood or misapplied by a given multinational, than it is of Rawls's theory of justice that it may be conveniently misunderstood by a trickle-down Libertarian." *Ethics of International Business*, 108. That seems to be equivalent to saying that the operation

was a success but the patient died. Surely ethical guidelines for multinational managers are practical or they are irrelevant.

21 World Bank, *World Development Report 1995, "Workers in an Integrating World Economy"* (Oxford University Press, 1995) 77.

22 Donaldson, *Ethics of International Business*, 115.

23 *Id.*, 150.

24 DeGeorge, *Competing with Integrity*, 48.

25 *Id.*, 358.

26 *Id.*

27 Kenneth P. Hutchinson, "Third World Growth," *Harvard Business Review*, Nov.-Dec. 1994. (In 1994, Hutchinson was executive director of the Asian-American Free Labor Institute in Washington, DC, an affiliate of the AFL-CIO.)

28 Terry Collingsworth, J. William Goold, Pharis J. Harvey, "Time for a Global New Deal," *Foreign Affairs*, Jan.-Feb. 1994, 8.

29 Collingsworth et al., 8.

30 David Holmstrom, "One Man's Fight Against Sweatshops," *Christian Science Monitor*, July 3, 1996.

31 *Nightline* (ABC), June 13, 1996.

32 Kernaghan cited in Larry Rohter, "To US Critics, a Sweatshop; for Hondurans, a Better Life," *New York Times*, July 18, 1996.

33 Greenhouse, "A Crusader Makes Celebrities Tremble."

34 William B. Falk, "Dirty Little Secrets," *Newsday*, June 16, 1996.

35 Greenhouse, "Voluntary Rules."

36 Tim Smith, "The Power of Business for Human Rights," *Business & Society Review*, January 1994, 36.

37 Jeffrey Ballinger, "The New Free Trade Heel," *Harper's Magazine*, August 1992, 46-47. "As in many developing countries, Indonesia's minimum wage, ... is less than poverty level." Nina Baker, "The Hidden Hands of Nike," *Oregonian*, August 9, 1992.

38 Robert B. Reich, "Escape from the Global Sweatshop; Capitalism's Stake in Uniting the Workers of the World," *Washington Post*, May 22, 1994. Reich's test is intended to apply in developing countries "where democratic institutions are weak or absent."

39 Collingsworth et al., 8.

40 Robin Broad and John Cavanaugh, "Don't Neglect the Impoverished South," *Foreign Affairs*, December 22, 1995, 18. See also the typical muckraking piece by Merrill Goozner: "As the global economy pushes ever deeper into the poorest precincts of the developing world, its benefits aren't trickling down.... There is mounting evidence that the rising tide of rapid development is not lifting all boats, especially in China and Indonesia, the first and fourth most populous countries on earth." Goozner, "Asian Labor: Wages of Shame; Western Firms Help to Exploit Brutal Conditions," *Chicago Tribune*, Nov. 6, 1994, 1.

41 Broad and Cavanagh, "Don't Neglect the Impoverished South."

42 Reich, "Escape from the Global Sweatshop."

43 Hutchinson, "Third World Growth."

44 Broad and Cavanagh, "Don't Neglect the Impoverished South." See also Goozner, "Wages of Shame."

45 John Cavanagh and Robin Broad, "Global Reach; Workers Fight the Multinationals," *The Nation*, March 18, 1996, 21. See also Bob Herbert, "Nike's Bad Neighborhood," *New York Times*, June 14, 1996.

46 For example, see *Economist*, "Wealth in its Grasp, A Survey of Indonesia," April 17, 1993 (By Gideon Rachman).

47 Adam Schwartz, "Pressures of Work," *Far Eastern Economic Review*, June 20, 1991, 14.

48 Schwartz, "Pressures."

49 International Labor Organization, *World Employment 1995* (Geneva: ILO, 1995) 73.

50 ILO, 73.

51 World Bank, *Workers in an Integrating World Economy*, 5.

52 Keith B. Richburg, Anne Swardson, "US industry Overseas: Sweatshop or Job Source?: Indonesians Praise Work at Nike Factory," *Washington Post*, July 28, 1996.

53 Richburg and Swardson, "Sweatshop or Job Source?" The 17 year-old was interviewed in the presence of managers. For other reports that workers remit home large parts of their earnings see Seth Mydans, "Tangerang Journal; For Indonesian Workers at Nike Plant: Just Do It," *New York Times*, August 9, 1996, and Nina Baker, "The Hidden Hands of Nike."

54 Donna Gibbs, Nike spokeswoman on ABC's *World News Tonight*, June 6, 1996.

55 Mark Clifford, "Trading in Social Issues; Labor Policy and International Trade Regulation," *World Press Review*, June 1994, 36.

56 Larry Rohter, "To US Critics, a Sweatshop; for Hondurans, a Better Life," *New York Times*, July 18, 1996.

57 Marcus Brauchli, "Garment Industry Booms in Bangladesh," *Wall Street Journal*, August 6, 1991.

58 Richburg and Swardson, "Sweatshop or Job Source?"

59 See also Henry Tricks, "Salvador Textile Workers Face Bad Times," Reuters, March 8, 1996; Freddy Cuevas, "Sweatshop, or a Boon?," *St. Paul Pioneer Press*, July 17, 1996; and Seth Mydans, "Tangerang Journal."

60 Lucy Martinez-Mont, "Sweatshops are Better Than No Shops," *Wall Street Journal*, June 25, 1996.

61 Rohter, "To US Critics a Sweatshop."

62 Barnet and Cavanagh, *Global Dreams* (New York: Simon and Schuster, 1994) 327. Similarly, Nina Baker reported that "Tri Mugiyanti and her coworkers [at the Hasi plant in Indonesia] think they are lucky to get jobs at factories such as Hasi." Baker, "The Hidden Hands of Nike."

63 Barnet and Cavanagh, *Global Dreams*, 326.

64 Rohter, "To US Critics a Sweatshop."

65 William B. Falk, "Dirty Little Secrets," *Newsday*, June 16, 1996.

66 Barnet and Cavanagh, "Just Undo It: Nike's Exploited Workers," *New York Times*, February 13, 1994.

67 Sarosh Kuruvilla, "Linkages Between Industrialization Strategies and Industrial Relations/ Human Resources Policies: Singapore, Malaysia, The Philippines, and India," *Industrial & Labor Relations Review*, July 1996, 637.

68 Gary S. Fields, "Labor Standards, Economic Development, and International Trade," in Stephen Herzenberg and Jorge Perez-Lopez (eds.), *Labor Standards and the Development of the Global Economy* (Washington, DC: US Department of Labor, Bureau of International Affairs, 1990), 23.

69 Fields, 25.

70 Fields, 25.

71 The ILO's Constitution (of 1919) mentions that: "... the failure of any nation to adopt humane conditions of labour is an obstacle in the way of other nations which desire to improve the conditions in their own countries." ILO, *World Employment 1995*, 74.

72 ILO, 75.

73 *Id.*, 76.

74 *Id.*, 77.

75 *Id.*, 78.

76 *Id.*, 79.

77 World Bank, *The East Asian Miracle* (New York: Oxford University Press, 1993) 2.

78 World Bank, *East Asian Miracle*, 2-4, 47.

79 *Economist*, "Wealth in its Grasp."

80 Marcus W. Brauchli, "Indonesia is Striving to Prosper in Freedom but is Still Repressive," *Wall Street Journal*, October 11, 1994.

81 Barbara Crossette, "UN Survey Finds World Rich-Poor Gap Widening," *New York Times*, July 15, 1996, citing *UN Human Development*

Report 1996 (New York: Oxford University Press, 1996).

82 Philip Shenon, "Hidden Giant—A Special Report; Indonesia Improves Life for Many but the Political Shadows Remain," *New York Times*, August 27, 1993, 1.

83 See, for example, Brauchli, "Indonesia is Striving to Prosper."

84 Barnet and Cavanagh, "Just Undo It: Nike's Exploited Workers."

85 Schwartz, "Pressures of Work."

86 *Economist*, "Wealth in its Grasp," 14-15.

87 World Bank, *Workers in an Integrating World Economy*, 5.

88 Jagdish Bhagwati and Robert E. Hudec, eds. *Fair Trade and Harmonization* (Cambridge: MIT Press, 1996), vol. 1, 2.

89 World Bank, *Workers in an Integrating World Economy*, 75.

90 *Id.*, 77. As I have noted, the report proposes that the "appropriate level is therefore that at which the costs are commensurate with the value that informed workers place on improved working conditions and reduced risk...." (77).

91 World Bank, *Workers in an Integrating World Economy*, 5.

92 Compare the World Bank's analysis: "But unions can also have negative economic effects. In some countries they behave like monopolists, protecting a minority group of relatively well-off unionized workers at the expense of the unemployed and those in rural and informal markets, whose formal sector employment opportunities are correspondingly reduced." World Bank, *Workers in an Integrating World Economy*, 80. For estimates of the size of the "union wage effect"—the difference in compensation between otherwise similar workers that is that is attributed to union membership—in different countries, see sources cited in *id.*, 81.

93 Portes does not advocate "a removal of all state regulation in order to let popular entrepreneur-ial energies flourish" but believes that "[t]here is no alternative to state intervention in the labor market.... [B]asic rights which have become consensually accepted throughout the civilized world ..." Alejandro Portes, "When More Can Be Less; Labor Standards, Development, and the Informal Economy," in Herzenberg and Perez-Lopez, *Labor Standards and the Development of the Global Economy*, 234.

94 Portes, "When More Can Be Less," 234.

95 *Id.*, 228-29.

96 Rohter, "To US Critics a Sweatshop." The focus on labor conditions in the export sectors of developing economies, when conditions are worse elsewhere, has attracted charges of "protectionism in the guise of humanitarian concern." Paul Krugman, "Does Third World Growth Hurt First World Prosperity?," *Harvard Business Review*, July-Aug. 1994, 113. Critics are accused of advocating increased labor rights in third world export industries in order to reduce the competitive threat to first world jobs. Prime Minister Mahathir of Malaysia is outspoken on this point: Western pressure, he says, "is intended to stop multinationals from manufacturing in developing markets." "Striking a Balance; Pressured by Workers and the West, Asia Fights to Stay Competitive," *Asiaweek*, October 26, 1994. According to Krugman, "Developing countries are already warning, however, that such standards are simply an effort to deny them access to world markets by preventing them from making use of the only competitive advantage they have: abundant labor. The developing countries are right." Paul Krugman is right.

97 Gary S. Fields, "Employment, Income Distribution and Economic Growth in Seven Small Open Economies," *The Economic Journal*, 94 (March 1984), 81.

98 Fields, "Labor Standards," 21.

◆ ◆ ◆ ◆ ◆

THOMAS DONALDSON

Values in Tension: Ethics Away from Home

World View

When is different just different, and when is different wrong?

When we leave home and cross our nation's boundaries, moral clarity often blurs. Without a backdrop of shared attitudes, and without familiar laws and judicial procedures that define standards of ethical conduct, certainty is elusive. Should a company invest in a foreign country where civil and political rights are violated? Should a company go along with a host country's discriminatory employment practices? If companies in developed countries shift facilities to developing nations that lack strict environmental and health regulations, or if those companies choose to fill management and other top-level positions in a host nation with people from the home country, whose standards should prevail?

Even the best-informed, best-intentioned executives must rethink their assumptions about business practice in foreign settings. What works in a company's home country can fail in a country with different standards of ethical conduct. Such difficulties are unavoidable for businesspeople who live and work abroad.

But how can managers resolve the problems? What are the principles that can help them work through the maze of cultural differences and establish codes of conduct for globally ethical business practice? How can companies answer the toughest question in global business ethics: What happens when a host country's ethical standards seem lower than the home country's?

Competing Answers

One answer is as old as philosophical discourse. According to cultural relativism, no culture's ethics are better than any other's; therefore there are no international rights and wrongs. If the people of Indonesia tolerate the bribery of their public officials, so what? Their attitude is no better or worse than that of people in Denmark or Singapore who refuse to offer or accept bribes. Likewise, if Belgians fail to find insider trading morally repugnant, who cares? Not enforcing insider-trading laws is no more or less ethical than enforcing such laws.

The cultural relativist's creed—When in Rome, do as the Romans do—is tempting, especially when failing to do as the locals do means forfeiting business opportunities. The inadequacy of cultural relativism, however, becomes apparent when the practices in question are more damaging than petty bribery or insider trading.

In the late 1980s, some European tanneries and pharmaceutical companies were looking for cheap waste-dumping sites. They approached virtually every country on Africa's west coast from Morocco to the Congo. Nigeria agreed to take highly toxic polychlorinated biphenyls. Unprotected local workers, wearing thongs and shorts, unloaded barrels of PCBs and placed them near a residential area. Neither the residents nor the workers knew that the barrels contained toxic waste.

We may denounce governments that permit such abuses, but many countries are unable to police transnational corporations adequately even if they want to. And in many countries, the combination of ineffective enforcement and inadequate regulations leads to behavior by unscrupulous companies that is clearly wrong. A few years ago, for example, a group of investors became interested in restoring the SS *United States*, once a luxurious ocean liner. Before the actual restoration could begin, the ship had to be stripped of its asbestos lining. A bid from a US company, based on US standards for asbestos removal, priced the job at more than $100 million. A company in the Ukrainian city of Sevastopol offered to do the work for less than $2 million. In October 1993, the ship was towed to Sevastopol.

A cultural relativist would have no problem with that outcome, but I do. A country has the right to establish its own health and safety regulations, but in the case described above, the standards and the terms of the contract could not possibly have protected workers in Sevastopol from known health risks. Even if the contract met Ukrainian standards, ethical businesspeople must object. Cultural relativism is morally blind. There are fundamental values that cross cultures, and companies must uphold them. (For an economic argument against cultural relativism, see the insert "The Culture and Ethics of Software Piracy.")

At the other end of the spectrum from cultural relativism is ethical imperialism, which directs people to do everywhere exactly as they do at home. Again, an understandably appealing approach but one that is clearly inadequate. Consider the large US computer-products company that in 1993 introduced a course on sexual harassment in its Saudi Arabian facility. Under the banner of global consistency, instructors used the same approach to train Saudi Arabian managers that they had used with US managers: the participants were asked to discuss a case in which a manager makes sexually explicit remarks to a new female employee over drinks in a bar. The instructors failed to consider how the exercise would work in a culture with strict conventions governing relationships between men and women. As a result, the training sessions were ludicrous. They baffled and offended the Saudi participants, and the message to avoid coercion and sexual discrimination was lost.

The theory behind ethical imperialism is absolutism, which is based on three problematic principles. Absolutists believe that there is a single list of truths, that they can be expressed only with one set of concepts, and that they call for exactly the same behavior around the world.

The first claim clashes with many people's belief that different cultural traditions must be respected. In some cultures, loyalty to a community—family, organization, or society—is the foundation of all ethical behavior. The Japanese, for example, define business ethics in terms of loyalty to their companies, their business networks, and their nation. Americans place a higher value on liberty than on loyalty; the US tradition of rights emphasizes equality, fairness, and individual freedom. It is hard to conclude that truth lies on one side or the other, but an absolutist would have us select just one.

The second problem with absolutism is the presumption that people must express moral truth using only one set of concepts. For instance, some absolutists insist that the language of basic rights provide the framework for any discussion of ethics. That means, though, that entire cultural traditions must be ignored. The notion of a right evolved with the rise of democracy in post-Renaissance Europe and the United States, but the term is not found in either Confucian or Buddhist traditions. We all learn ethics in the context of our particular cultures, and the power in the principles is deeply tied to the way in which they are expressed. Internationally accepted lists of moral principles, such as the United Nations' Universal Declaration of Human Rights, draw on many cultural and religious traditions. As philosopher Michael Walzer has noted, "There is no Esperanto of global ethics."

The third problem with absolutism is the belief in a global standard of ethical behavior. Context must shape ethical practice. Very low wages, for example, may be considered unethical in rich, advanced countries, but developing nations may be acting ethically if they encourage investment and improve living standards by accepting low wages. Likewise, when people are malnourished or starving, a government may be wise to use more fertilizer in order to improve crop yields, even though that means settling for relatively high levels of thermal water pollution.

When cultures have different standards of ethical behavior—and different ways of handling unethical behavior—a company that takes an absolutist approach may find itself making a disastrous mistake. When a manager at a large US specialty-products company in China caught an employee stealing, she followed the company's practice and turned the employee over to the provincial authorities, who executed him. Managers cannot operate in another culture without being aware of that culture's attitudes toward ethics.

If companies can neither adopt a host country's ethics nor extend the home country's standards, what is the answer? Even the traditional litmus test—What would people think of your actions if they were written up on the front page of the newspaper?—is an unreliable guide, for there is no international consensus on standards of business conduct.

Balancing the Extremes: Three Guiding Principles

Companies must help managers distinguish between practices that are merely different and those that are wrong. For relativists, nothing is sacred and nothing is wrong. For absolutists, many things that are differ-

---

The Culture and Ethics of Software Piracy

Before jumping on the cultural relativism bandwagon, stop and consider the potential economic consequences of a when-in-Rome attitude toward business ethics. Take a look at the current statistics on software piracy: In the United States, pirated software is estimated to be 35 per cent of the total software market, and industry losses are estimated at $2.3 billion per year. The piracy rate is 57 per cent in Germany and 80 per cent in Italy and Japan; the rates in most Asian countries are estimated to be nearly 100 per cent.

There are similar laws against software piracy in those countries. What, then, accounts for the differences? Although a country's level of economic development plays a large part, culture, including ethical attitudes, may be a more crucial factor. The 1995 annual report of the Software Publishers Association connects software piracy directly to culture and attitude. It describes Italy and Hong Kong as having "'first world' per capita incomes, along with 'third world' rates of piracy." When asked whether one should use software without paying for it, most people, including people in Italy and Hong Kong, say no. But people in some countries regard the practice as *less* unethical than people in other countries do. Confucian culture, for example, stresses that individuals should share what they create with society. That may be, in part, what prompts the Chinese and other Asians to view the concept of intellectual property as a means for the West to monopolize its technological superiority.

What happens if ethical attitudes around the world permit large-scale software piracy? Software companies won't want to invest as much in developing new products, because they cannot expect any return on their investment in certain parts of the world. When ethics fail to support technological creativity, there are consequences that go beyond statistics—jobs are lost and livelihoods jeopardized.

Companies must do more than lobby foreign governments for tougher enforcement of piracy laws. They must cooperate with other companies and with local organizations to help citizens understand the consequences of piracy and to encourage the evolution of a different ethic toward the practice.

ent are wrong. Neither extreme illuminates the real world of business decision making. The answer lies somewhere in between.

When it comes to shaping ethical behavior, companies must be guided by three principles.

- Respect for core human values, which determine the absolute moral threshold for all business activities.
- Respect for local traditions.
- The belief that context matters when deciding what is right and what is wrong.

Consider those principles in action. In Japan, people doing business together often exchange gifts—sometimes expensive ones—in keeping with long-standing Japanese tradition. When US and European companies started doing a lot of business in Japan, many Western businesspeople thought that the practice of gift giving might be wrong rather than simply different. To them, accepting a gift felt like accepting a bribe. As Western companies have become more familiar with Japanese traditions, however, most have come to tolerate the practice and to set different limits on gift giving in Japan than they do elsewhere.

Respecting differences is a crucial ethical practice. Research shows that management ethics differ among cultures; respecting those differences means recognizing that some cultures have obvious weaknesses—as well as hidden strengths. Managers in Hong Kong, for example, have a higher tolerance for some forms of bribery than their Western counterparts, but they have a much lower tolerance for the failure to acknowledge a subordinate's work. In some parts of the Far East, stealing credit from a subordinate is nearly an unpardonable sin.

People often equate respect for local traditions with cultural relativism. That is incorrect. Some practices are clearly wrong. Union Carbide's tragic experience in Bhopal, India, provides one example. The company's executives seriously underestimated how much on-site management involvement was needed at the Bhopal plant to compensate for the country's poor infrastructure and regulatory capabilities. In the aftermath of the disastrous gas leak, the lesson is clear: companies using sophisticated technology in a developing country must evaluate that country's ability to oversee its safe use. Since the incident at Bhopal, Union Carbide has become a leader in advising companies on using hazardous technologies safely in developing countries.

Some activities are wrong no matter where they take place. But some practices that are unethical in one setting may be acceptable in another. For instance, the chemical EDB, a soil fungicide, is banned for use in the United States. In hot climates, however, it quickly becomes harmless through exposure to intense solar radiation and high soil temperatures. As long as the chemical is monitored, companies may be able to use EDB ethically in certain parts of the world.

Defining the Ethical Threshold: Core Values

Few ethical questions are easy for managers to answer. But there are some hard truths that must guide managers' actions, a set of what I call *core human values*, which define minimum ethical standards for all companies.[1] The right to good health and the right to economic advancement and an improved standard of living are two core human values. Another is what Westerners call the Golden Rule, which is recognizable in every major religious and ethical tradition around the world. In Book 15 of his *Analects*, for instance, Confucius counsels people to maintain reciprocity, or not to do to others what they do not want done to themselves.

Although no single list would satisfy every scholar, I believe it is possible to articulate three core values that incorporate the work of scores of theologians and philosophers around the world. To be broadly relevant, these values must include elements found in both Western and non-Western cultural and religious traditions. Consider the examples of values in the insert "What Do These Values Have in Common?"

At first glance, the values expressed in the two lists seem quite different. Nonetheless, in the spirit of what philosopher John Rawls calls *overlapping consensus*, one can see that the seemingly divergent values converge at key points. Despite important differences between Western and non-Western cultural and religious traditions, both express shared attitudes about what it means to be human. First, individuals must not treat others simply as tools; in other words, they must recognize a person's value as a human being. Next, individuals and communities must treat people in ways that respect people's basic rights. Finally, members of a community must work together to support and improve the institutions on which the community depends. I call those three values *respect for human dignity*, *respect for basic rights*, and *good citizenship*.

Those values must be the starting point for all companies as they formulate and evaluate standards of ethical conduct at home and abroad. But they are only a starting point. Companies need much more specific guidelines, and the first step to developing those is to translate the core human values into core values for business. What does it mean, for example, for a company to respect human dignity? How can a company be a good citizen?

I believe that companies can respect human dignity by creating and sustaining a corporate culture in which employees, customers, and suppliers are treated not as means to an end but as people whose intrinsic value must be acknowledged, and by producing safe products and services in a safe workplace. Companies can respect basic rights by acting in ways that support and protect the individual rights of employees, customers, and surrounding communities, and by avoiding relationships that violate human beings' rights to health, education, safety, and an adequate standard of living. And companies can be good citizens by supporting essential social institutions, such as the economic system and the education system, and by working with host governments and other organizations to protect the environment.

The core values establish a moral compass for business practice. They can help companies identify practices that are acceptable and those that are intolerable—even if the practices are compatible with a host country's norms and laws. Dumping pollutants near people's homes and accepting inadequate

---

What Do These Values Have in Common?

Non-Western	Western
Kyosei (Japanese): Living and working together for the common good.	Individual liberty
Dharma (Hindu): The fulfillment of inherited duty.	Egalitarianism
Santutthi (Buddhist): The importance of limited desires.	Political participation
Zakat (Muslim): The duty to give alms to the Muslim poor.	Human rights

standards for handling hazardous materials are two examples of actions that violate core values.

Similarly, if employing children prevents them from receiving a basic education, the practice is intolerable. Lying about product specifications in the act of selling may not affect human lives directly, but it too is intolerable because it violates the trust that is needed to sustain a corporate culture in which customers are respected.

Many companies don't do anything with their codes of conduct; they simply paste them on the wall.

Sometimes it is not a company's actions but those of a supplier or customer that pose problems. Take the case of the Tan family, a large supplier for Levi Strauss. The Tans were allegedly forcing 1,200 Chinese and Filipino women to work 74 hours per week in guarded compounds on the Mariana Islands. In 1992, after repeated warnings to the Tans, Levi Strauss broke off business relations with them.

Creating an Ethical Corporate Culture

The core values for business that I have enumerated can help companies begin to exercise ethical judgment and think about how to operate ethically in foreign cultures, but they are not specific enough to guide managers through actual ethical dilemmas. Levi Strauss relied on a written code of conduct when figuring out how to deal with the Tan family. The company's Global Sourcing and Operating Guidelines, formerly called the Business Partner Terms of Engagement, state that Levi Strauss will "seek to identify and utilize business partners who aspire as individuals and in the conduct of all their businesses to a set of ethical standards not incompatible with our own." Whenever intolerable business situations arise, managers should be guided by precise statements that spell out the behavior and operating practices that the company demands.

Ninety per cent of all *Fortune* 500 companies have codes of conduct, and 70 per cent have statements of vision and values. In Europe and the Far East, the percentages are lower but are increasing rapidly. Does that mean that most companies have what they need? Hardly. Even though most large US companies have both statements of values and codes of conduct, many might be better off if they didn't. Too many companies don't do anything with the documents; they simply paste them on the wall to impress employees, customers, suppliers, and the public. As a result, the senior managers who drafted the statements lose credibility by proclaiming values and not living up to them. Companies such as Johnson & Johnson, Levi Strauss, Motorola, Texas Instruments, and Lockheed Martin, however, do a great deal to make the words meaningful. Johnson & Johnson, for example, has become well known for its Credo Challenge sessions, in which managers discuss ethics in the context of their current business problems and are invited to criticize the company's credo and make suggestions for changes. The participants' ideas are passed on to the company's senior managers. Lockheed Martin has created an innovative site on the World Wide Web and on its local network that gives employees, customers, and suppliers access to the company's ethical code and the chance to voice complaints.

Many activities are neither good nor bad but exist in *moral free space*.

Codes of conduct must provide clear direction about ethical behavior when the temptation to behave unethically is strongest. The pronouncement in a code of conduct that bribery is unacceptable is useless unless accompanied by guidelines for gift giving, payments to get goods through customs, and "requests" from intermediaries who are hired to ask for bribes.

Motorola's values are stated very simply as "How we will always act: [with] constant respect for people [and] uncompromising integrity." The company's code of conduct, however, is explicit about actual business practice. With respect to bribery, for example, the code states that the "funds and assets of Motorola shall not be used, directly or indirectly, for illegal payments of any kind." It is unambiguous about what sort of payment is illegal: "the payment of a bribe to a public official or the kickback of funds to an employee of a customer...." The code goes on to prescribe specific procedures for handling commissions to intermediaries, issuing sales invoices, and disclosing confidential information in a sales transaction—all situations in which employees might have an opportunity to accept or offer bribes.

Codes of conduct must be explicit to be useful, but they must also leave room for a manager to use his or her judgment in situations requiring cultural sensitivity. Host-country employees shouldn't be forced to adopt all home-country values and renounce their own. Again, Motorola's code is exemplary. First, it gives clear direction: "Employees of Motorola will respect the laws, customs, and traditions of each country in which they operate, but will, at the same time, engage in no course of conduct which, even if legal, customary, and accepted in any such country, could be deemed to be in violation of the accepted business ethics of Motorola or the laws of the United States relating to business ethics." After laying down such absolutes, Motorola's code then makes clear when individual judgment will be necessary. For example, employees may sometimes accept certain kinds of small gifts "in rare circumstances, where the refusal to accept a gift" would injure Motorola's "legitimate business interests." Under certain circumstances, such gifts "may be accepted so long as the gift inures to the benefit of Motorola" and not "to the benefit of the Motorola employee."

Striking the appropriate balance between providing clear direction and leaving room for individual judgment makes crafting corporate values statements and ethics codes one of the hardest tasks that executives confront. The words are only a start. A company's leaders need to refer often to their organization's credo and code and must themselves be credible, committed, and consistent. If senior managers act as though ethics don't matter, the rest of the company's employees won't think they do, either.

Conflicts of Development and Conflicts of Tradition

Managers living and working abroad who are not prepared to grapple with moral ambiguity and tension should pack their bags and come home. The view that all business practices can be categorized as either ethical or unethical is too simple. As Einstein is reported to have said, "Things should be as simple as possible—but no simpler." Many business practices that are considered unethical in one setting may be ethical in another. Such activities are neither black nor white but exist in what Thomas Dunfee and I have called *moral free space*.[2] In this gray zone, there are no tight prescriptions for a company's behavior. Managers must chart their own courses—as long as they do not violate core human values.

Consider the following example. Some successful Indian companies offer employees the opportunity for one of their children to gain a job with the company once the child has completed a certain level in school. The companies honor this commitment even when other applicants are more qualified than an employee's child. The perk is extremely valuable in a country where jobs are hard to find, and it reflects the Indian culture's belief that the West has gone too far in allowing economic opportunities to break up families. Not surprisingly, the perk is among the most cherished by employees, but in most Western countries, it would be branded unacceptable nepotism. In the United States, for example, the ethical principle of equal opportunity holds that jobs should go to the applicants with the best qualifications. If a US company made such promises to its employees, it would violate regulations established by the Equal Employment Opportunity Commission. Given this difference in ethical attitudes, how should US managers react to Indian nepotism? Should they condemn the Indian companies, refusing to accept them as partners or suppliers until they agree to clean up their act?

Despite the obvious tension between nepotism and principles of equal opportunity, I cannot condemn the practice for Indians. In a country, such as India, that emphasizes clan and family relationships and has catastrophic levels of unemployment, the practice must be viewed in moral free space. The decision to allow a special perk for employees and their children is not necessarily wrong—at least for members of that country.

The Problem with Bribery

Bribery is widespread and insidious. Managers in transnational companies routinely confront bribery even though most countries have laws against it. The fact is that officials in many developing countries wink at the practice, and the salaries of local bureaucrats are so low that many consider bribes a form of remuneration. The US Foreign Corrupt Practices Act defines allowable limits on petty bribery in the form of routine payments required to move goods through customs. But demands for bribes often exceed those limits, and there is seldom a good solution.

Bribery disrupts distribution channels when goods languish on docks until local handlers are paid off, and it destroys incentives to compete on quality and cost when purchasing decisions are based on who pays what under the table. Refusing to acquiesce is often tantamount to giving business to unscrupulous companies.

I believe that even routine bribery is intolerable. Bribery undermines market efficiency and predictability, thus ultimately denying people their right to a minimal standard of living. Some degree of ethical commitment—some sense that everyone will play by the rules—is necessary for a sound economy. Without an ability to predict outcomes, who would be willing to invest?

There was a US company whose shipping crates were regularly pilfered by handlers on the docks of Rio de Janeiro. The handlers would take about 10 per cent of the contents of the crates, but the company was never sure which 10 per cent it would be. In a partial solution, the company began sending two crates—the first with 90 per cent of the merchandise, the second with 10 per cent. The handlers learned to take the second crate and leave the first untouched. From the company's perspective, at least knowing which goods it would lose was an improvement.

Bribery does more than destroy predictability; it undermines essential social and economic systems. That truth is not lost on businesspeople in countries where the practice is woven into the social fabric. CEOs in India admit that their companies engage constantly in bribery, and they say that they have considerable disgust for the practice. They blame government policies in part, but Indian executives also know that their country's business practices perpetuate corrupt behavior. Anyone walking the streets of Calcutta, where it is clear that even a dramatic redistribution of wealth would still leave most of India's inhabitants in dire poverty, comes face-to-face with the devastating effects of corruption.

How can managers discover the limits of moral free space? That is, how can they learn to distinguish a value in tension with their own from one that is intolerable? Helping managers develop good ethical judgment requires companies to be clear about their core values and codes of conduct. But even the most explicit set of guidelines cannot always provide answers. That is especially true in the thorniest ethical dilemmas in which the host country's ethical standards not only are different but also seem lower than the home country's. Managers must recognize that when countries have different ethical standards, there are two types of conflict that commonly arise. Each type requires its own line of reasoning.

If a company declared all gift giving unethical, it wouldn't be able to do business in Japan.

In the first type of conflict, which I call a *conflict of relative development*, ethical standards conflict because of the countries' different levels of economic development. As mentioned before, developing countries may accept wage rates that seem inhumane to more advanced countries in order to attract investment. As economic conditions in a developing country improve, the incidence of that sort of conflict usually decreases. The second type of conflict is a *conflict of cultural tradition*. For example, Saudi Arabia, unlike most other countries, does not allow women to serve as corporate managers. Instead, women may work in only a few professions, such as education and health care. The prohibition stems from strongly held religious and cultural beliefs; any increase in the country's level of economic development, which is already quite high, is not likely to change the rules.

To resolve a conflict of relative development, a manager must ask the following question: Would the practice be acceptable at home if my country were in a similar stage of economic development?

Consider the difference between wage and safety standards in the United States and in Angola, where citizens accept lower standards on both counts. If a US oil company is hiring Angolans to work on an offshore Angolan oil rig, can the company pay them lower wages than it pays US workers in the Gulf of Mexico? Reasonable people have to answer yes if the alternative for Angola is the loss of both the foreign investment and the jobs.

Consider, too, differences in regulatory environments. In the 1980s, the government of India fought hard to be able to import Ciba-Geigy's Entero Vioform, a drug known to be enormously effective in fighting dysentery but one that had been banned in the United States because some users experienced side effects. Although dysentery was not a big problem in the United States, in India, poor public sanitation was contributing to epidemic levels of the disease. Was it unethical to make the drug available in India after it had been banned in the United States? On the contrary, rational people should consider it unethical not to do so. Apply our test: Would the United States, at an earlier stage of development, have used this drug despite its side effects? The answer is clearly yes.

But there are many instances when the answer to similar questions is no. Sometimes a host country's standards are inadequate at any level of economic development. If a country's pollution standards are so low that working on an oil rig would considerably increase a person's risk of developing cancer, foreign oil companies must refuse to do business there. Likewise, if the dangerous side effects of a drug treatment outweigh its benefits, managers should not accept health standards that ignore the risks.

When relative economic conditions do not drive tensions, there is a more objective test for resolving ethical problems. Managers should deem a practice permissible only if they can answer no to both of the following questions: Is it possible to conduct business successfully in the host country without undertaking the practice? and Is the practice a violation of a core human value? Japanese gift giving is a perfect example of a conflict of cultural tradition. Most experienced businesspeople, Japanese and non-Japanese alike, would agree that doing business in Japan would be virtually impossible without adopting the practice. Does gift giving violate a core human value? I cannot identify one that it violates. As a result, gift giving may be permissible for foreign companies in Japan even if it conflicts with ethical attitudes at home. In fact, that conclusion is widely accepted, even by companies such as Texas Instruments and IBM, which are outspoken against bribery.

Does it follow that all nonmonetary gifts are acceptable or that bribes are generally acceptable in countries where they are common? Not at all. (See the insert "The Problem with Bribery.") What makes the routine practice of gift giving acceptable in Japan are the limits in its scope and intention. When gift giving moves outside those limits, it soon collides with core human values. For example, when Carl Kotchian, president of Lockheed in the 1970s, carried suitcases full of cash to Japanese politicians, he went beyond the norms established by Japanese tradition. That incident galvanized opinion in the United States Congress and helped lead to passage of the Foreign Corrupt Practices Act. Likewise, Roh Tae Woo went beyond the norms established by Korean cultural tradition when he accepted $635.4 million in bribes as president of the Republic of Korea between 1988 and 1993.

Guidelines for Ethical Leadership

Learning to spot intolerable practices and to exercise good judgment when ethical conflicts arise requires practice. Creating a company culture that rewards ethical behavior is essential. The following guidelines for developing a global ethical perspective among managers can help.

Treat corporate values and formal standards of conduct as absolutes. Whatever ethical standards a company chooses, it cannot waver on its principles either at home or abroad. Consider what has become part of company lore at Motorola. Around 1950, a senior executive was negotiating with officials of a South American government on a $10 million sale that would have increased the company's annual net profits by nearly 25 per cent. As the negotiations neared completion, however, the executive walked away from the deal because the officials were asking for $1 million for "fees." CEO Robert Galvin not only supported the executive's decision but also made it clear that Motorola would neither accept the sale on any terms nor do business with those government officials again. Retold over the decades, this story demonstrating Galvin's resolve has helped cement a culture of ethics for thousands of employees at Motorola.

Design and implement conditions of engagement for suppliers and customers. Will your company do business with any customer or supplier? What if a customer or supplier uses child labor? What if it has strong links with organized crime? What if it pressures your company to break a host country's laws? Such issues are best not left for spur-of-the-moment decisions. Some companies have realized that. Sears, for instance, has developed a policy of not contracting production to companies that use prison labor or infringe on workers' rights to health and safety. And BankAmerica has specified as a condition for many of its loans to developing countries that environmental standards and human rights must be observed.

Allow foreign business units to help formulate ethical standards and interpret ethical issues. The French pharmaceutical company Rhône-Poulenc Rorer has allowed foreign subsidiaries to augment lists of corporate ethical principles with their own suggestions. Texas Instruments has paid special attention to issues of international business ethics by creating the Global Business Practices Council, which is made up of managers from countries in which the company operates. With the overarching intent to create a "global ethics strategy, locally deployed," the council's mandate is to provide ethics education and create local processes that will help managers in the company's foreign business units resolve ethical conflicts.

In host countries, support efforts to decrease institutional corruption. Individual managers will not be able to wipe out corruption in a host country, no matter how many bribes they turn down. When a host country's tax system, import and export procedures, and procurement practices favor unethical players, companies must take action.

Many companies have begun to participate in reforming host-country institutions. General Electric, for example, has taken a strong stand in India, using the media to make repeated condemnations of bribery in business and government. General Electric and others have found, however, that a single company usually cannot drive out entrenched corruption. Transparency International, an organization based in Germany, has been effective in helping coalitions of companies, government officials, and others work to reform bribery-ridden bureaucracies in Russia, Bangladesh, and elsewhere.

Exercise moral imagination. Using moral imagination means resolving tensions responsibly and creatively. Coca-Cola, for instance, has consistently turned down requests for bribes from Egyptian officials but has managed to gain political support and public trust by sponsoring a project to plant fruit trees. And take the example of Levi Strauss, which discovered in the early 1990s that two of its suppliers in Bangladesh were employing children under the age of 14—a practice that violated the company's principles but was tolerated in Bangladesh. Forcing the suppliers to fire the children would not have ensured that the children received an education, and it would have caused serious hardship for the families depending on the children's wages. In a creative arrangement, the suppliers agreed to pay the children's regular wages while they attended school and to offer each child a job at age 14. Levi Strauss, in turn, agreed to pay the children's tuition and provide books and uniforms. That arrangement allowed Levi Strauss to uphold its principles and provide long-term benefits to its host country.

Many people think of values as soft; to some they are usually unspoken. A South Seas island society uses the word *mokita*, which means, "the truth that everybody knows but nobody speaks." However difficult they are to articulate, values affect how we all behave. In a global business environment, values in tension are the rule rather than the exception. Without a company's commitment, statements of values and codes of ethics end up as empty platitudes that provide managers with no foundation for behaving ethically. Employees need and deserve more, and responsible members of the global business community can set examples for others to follow. The dark consequences of incidents such as Union Carbide's disaster in Bhopal remind us how high the stakes can be.

NOTES

1 In other writings, Thomas W. Dunfee and I have used the term *hypernorm* instead of *core human value*.

2 Thomas Donaldson and Thomas W. Dunfee, "Toward a Unified Conception of Business Ethics: Integrative Social Contracts Theory," *Academy of Management Review*, April 1994; and "Integrative Social Contracts Theory: A Communitarian Conception of Economic Ethics," *Economics and Philosophy*, Spring 1995.

◆ ◆ ◆ ◆ ◆

DON MAYER AND ANITA CAVA

Ethics and the Gender Equality Dilemma for US Multinationals

We hold these truths to be self-evident: that all men are created equal, and endowed by their creator with certain rights—life, liberty, and the pursuit of happiness.

—US Declaration of
Independence, 1776

All human beings are born free and equal in dignity and rights.

—United Nations Universal Declaration of Human Rights, 1948

Judging from the US Declaration of Independence, gender equality was not self-evident in 1776. By 1948, however, the Universal Declaration of Human Rights took care not to exclude women from the ambit of declared rights. Since then, while gender equality has come a long way in the United States, many difficult and divisive issues remain unresolved. After completing a global inventory of attitudes on gender equality, Rhoodie (1989) concluded that many nations give only "lip service" to the goals of gender equality articulated in international conventions and declarations such as the UN Declaration of Human Rights (1948). Given the uneven progress of gender and racial equality in the world, it is inevitable that multinational enterprises (MNEs) encounter uneven ethical terrain.

Recently, the US Congress and the Supreme Court have differed markedly over how the principles of non-discrimination in Title VII of the Civil Rights Act of 1964 (Title VII) should be applied by US MNEs in their overseas activities. Both Congress and the Court recognized that US non-discrimina-tion laws may create difficulties for US companies doing business in host countries where racial and/or gender discrimination is a way of life. But Congress, having the last word, decided in the Civil Rights Act of 1991 that Title VII protects US citizens from employment discrimination by US MNEs in their overseas operations.[1]

In so doing, Congress effectively reversed the Supreme Court, which only a few months earlier had decided that Title VII did not apply "extraterritorially" (E.E.O.C. v. Aramco, 1991).[2] According to the Court, to apply US laws abroad might cause "unintended clashes between our laws and those of other nations which could result in international discord." The majority of the Court wanted Congress to be entirely clear about its intent before imposing the ethical values inherent in Title VII on the activities of a US company in a foreign country.

This reluctance is understandable. It seems logical to assume that companies would prefer not to have two personnel policies, one for US citizens and one for host country nationals and others. Human resource directors indicate a preference for following the laws and customs of the host country while doing business there, but a concern for furthering human rights values of the US.[3] Such a preference corresponds to other observed realities, since the recent history of law and business ethics shows that a number of US MNEs would engage in bribery in foreign countries, if that should be the custom, in order to remain "competitive." Similarly, many US MNEs were willing to acquiesce to *apartheid* in South Africa, despite the fact that such behavior would not be tolerated in the United States.

The multinational that adopts such a policy of moral neutrality follows what Bowie (1977) has identified as moral relativism. The approach of a moral relativism is characterized as—"When in Rome, do as the Romans do." This prescription has its arresting aspects. If Rome existed today as a commercial power, would US corporate executives entertain one another by watching slaves battle to the death, attending Bacchanalian orgies, or cheering while faithful but hapless Christians were being mauled by lions? While such practices do not have overt current counterparts, there are nonetheless substantial differences among cultures in matters of gender equality (Rhoodie, 1989).

How does the MNE deal ethically with such contrasts? Bowie suggests that while ethical relativism cannot support business ethics in the global economy, neither can we afford to be "ethnocentric" and assume that "our" way is the one "right way." Bowie uses the term "ethnocentric" to describe a view that "when in Rome, or anywhere else, do as you would at home" (Bowie, 1988; Wicks, 1990). Essentially, it was this concern that animated the Supreme Court's decision in *Aramco*, which explicitly worried about "unintended clashes" between US law and Saudi Arabian law. Further, it is this concern about "ethnocentrism" that fuels speculation that applying Title VII's equal opportunity provisions in countries like Japan is a recipe for corporate non-competitiveness and perhaps even a form of cultural imperialism.

This article explores some of the difficulties faced by US multinationals in complying with Title VII as applied abroad and examines the ethical arguments surrounding achieving the goal of gender equality. Part I discusses the current dilemma for international human resource managers and their employees, as well as for citizens of host countries. We focus on Japan as a model of a country in transition and consider the extreme situation of the Islamic countries as a counterpoint in the analysis. The emphasis is on practical and legal considerations. Part II returns to the issues of ethical relativism and cultural imperialism, and suggests that US multinationals should not opt for moral relativism by deferring entirely to cultural traditions in countries such as Japan, traditions that may be contrary to declared international standards for gender and racial equality and contrary to apparent global trends.

I. Perspectives on the Current Dilemma

Human resource managers, employees, and host country nationals will have varying perspectives on the application of US civil rights statutes for the promotion of gender equality in the foreign workplace. Each merits consideration in order to understand the framework within which an ethical analysis can be applied.

A. The MNE Managerial Perspective

For a MNE whose operations cover the US, Europe, Asia, and the Middle East, the differing cultural norms with respect to equal opportunity in the workplace are a bit unreal. Despite strong movements for gender equality in the Scandinavian countries and, to a lesser extent, in the US and Europe, the basic condition of women worldwide is largely "poor, pregnant, and powerless" (Rhoodie, 1989). The differences among various nations span a continuum from cultures with a strong commitment to gender equality in the workplace to those with strong commitments to keeping women out of the workplace entirely (Mayer, 1991).

For the MNE trying to "do the right thing," the situation suggests a kind of ethical surrealism, where reality retreats before an unreal mix of elements— social, cultural, legal, and philosophical. It seems natural that companies doing business abroad would want to follow host country laws and customs. Obviously, following US law only for US employees poses a dual dilemma. First, assuming that gender discrimination is culturally accepted and legally tolerated in many foreign countries, what should be the MNE personnel policy? The MNE has the option of designing a single non-discriminatory policy for all workers or creating a two-track system, protecting the legal rights of US nationals while accommodating the host country's norms for their nationals and others. Second, where the MNE has adopted a Code of Ethics for global application and the Code specifically refers to equal opportunity, can the MNE honor its commitment in a principled way?

Strict compliance with an ethical position would suggest a simple solution to this conundrum: Adopt an equal opportunity program, educate all employees, and enforce it consistent with Title VII's mandates across the board. Admittedly, however, following US law worldwide, for all employees, is surely "ethnocentric" and may also be unworkable. In some host countries, such as Saudi Arabia, the legal conflicts may be pronounced. In others, such as Japan, the cultural conflicts may undermine consistent enforcement of Title VII-oriented policies throughout the workforce.

Taking Japan as an example, the US MNE doing business in Tokyo is confronted with a patriarchal society in which women are expected to manage household work while men dominate the other forms of work (Lebra, 1984). Although men and women receive comparable educations through the high school level, women are expected to marry by age 25. Employment after that age is generally discouraged (Prater, 1981). There is seldom, if ever, a managerial track for Japanese women: if employed by a major Japanese company, they are often given positions largely designed to make the office environment more comfortable (such as by serving tea and appearing "decorative"), and are not taken seriously as career office workers (Seymour, 1991).

For a US MNE to announce a policy of equal opportunity for Japanese operations, tie that policy to Title VII enforcement, and expect no negative results would require a supposition that the overwhelmingly male population of Japanese customers, suppliers, and government officials would treat US women and Japanese women equally. But, in fact, the sensitivity of Japanese males to sexual harassment issues is only dawning (Ford, 1992; Lan, 1991), and some other forms of overt discrimination are likely. Assuming, as seems warranted, that the MNEs female employees will be adversely affected to some degree by prevailing male attitudes in Japan, how would the company find that balanced approach that yields the least friction and the best results?

Such a question suggests that a utilitarian analysis, or some pragmatism, may be entirely appropriate here. It is well beyond the scope of this paper to suggest how absolute adherence to Title VII and equal opportunity principles should be tempered to achieve greater harmony with the host country culture, but a few observations are in order. First, Title VII's dictates may need to be culturally adjusted. An "appropriate" response to repeated incidents of Japanese males looking up female employees' skirts may be more educational than admonitory, at least for the first transgressions. Second, companies should be wary of any utilitarian or pragmatic approaches that predict a "non-competitive" result unless business hews to some perceived cultural norms. This point needs further elaboration.

In a country such as Saudi Arabia, the cultural norms and the sacred law, or *Shari'a*, are fairly congruent. The winds of change are not, seemingly, as strong as in other parts of the world. Japan, on the other hand, has demonstrated its willingness to adopt some "Western ways" in order to be part of the global economy, and there is considerable evidence that Japanese pragmatism has already created some new opportunities for women in the workplace (Prater, 1991). Moreover, legislation exists which purports to promote gender equality in the workplace, though some critics have questioned its efficacy (Edwards, 1988). In short, the "downside" of promoting equal opportunity in Japan because of cultural norms may easily be overstated; while Japanese males are not as sensitive to sexual harassment issues, for example, there are signs that they are becoming so (Lan, 1991).

For a host country culture that is less in flux, and whose culture and laws present a unified force against social change, the ethical issues change somewhat. This is because Title VII expressly allows discrimination in certain instances through the *bona fide* occupational qualification (BFOQ)[4] exception. The BFOQ exception provides that it will *not* be illegal to discriminate "on the basis of ... religion, sex, or national origin in those certain instances where religion, sex, or national origin is a *bona fide* occupational qualification reasonably necessary to the normal operation of that particular business or enterprise."

In *Kern v. Dynalectron*,[5] for example, a company in the business of flying planes into the holy city of Mecca advised potential employees that Saudi Arabian law prohibited the entry of non-Muslims into the holy area under penalty of death. One pilot took instruction in the Muslim religion, but was Baptist at heart, and rescinded his "conversion." Returning to the US, he sued under Title VII for employment discrimination based on religion. The federal appeals court ultimately determined that Title VII applied but that being Muslim was, in this situation, a "*bona fide* occupational qualification" and nor discriminatory.

It remains to be seen how gender qualifications may be raised and litigated for alleged discrimination overseas. But if those qualifications have the force of law, and are not the result of cultural preferences only, the most serious ethical dilemma is whether or not to do business in that country at all. To take an example based on racial classification, if South African law prohibited blacks from being hired by MNEs, the MNEs' only ethical choices would be to (1) do business in South Africa and comply with the law, (2) refuse to do business in South Africa, or (3) do business there and hire blacks anyway.

How are these three options analyzed from a perspective of ethics and the law? Option (3) may certainly be seen as an ethical policy, though probably of the "ethnocentric" variety, yet few ethicists and even fewer business executives would counsel such a course. Option (1) is well within the mainstream of ethical relativism, and, we would argue, is less ethical than choosing option (2). But again, *cultural* conflicts do not create such choices; legal mandates

do. And countries whose cultural values are colliding with the values of "outsiders" may choose, at least temporarily, to preserve their culture through legal mandates. Saudi Arabia has laws which prohibit women from travelling alone, working with men, working with non-Muslim foreigners, and these laws apply to foreign women as well as host country women (Moghadam, 1988).

Even without such explicit laws of prohibition, MNEs and their human resource managers may hesitate to violate unwritten or cultural laws, and taking moral relativism's approach to the problem of gender equality in other countries may seem prudent. But such an approach seems to depend on a rather sketchy kind of utilitarian analysis: Engaging in overt equal opportunity policies will result in cultural condemnation, loss of customer and client contacts, and eventual unprofitability of the entire overseas enterprise. But in host countries whose culture is tied to the mainstream of world business, long-held attitudes will be difficult to maintain, and the negative impact of "doing things differently" should not be overestimated, nor should the definite benefits and opportunities of pursuing gender quality be overlooked (Lansing and Ready, 1988).

In this context, a comment about the employee's perspective seems appropriate. It might be difficult to generalize here because individual perspective often differs, depending upon personal ideology, situation, and career opportunities. However, from the viewpoint of a female manager in a US MNE, we will assume that the greatest good would be a business world safe for gender equality and supportive of same. Adler and others have noted the difficulty of persuading MNEs that women managers can succeed in many countries whose cultures actively promote gender inequality (Adler, 1984). Certainly, a US female manager's inability to obtain firsthand experience in dealing with Japanese businesses comes close to being a career handicap, and for Japanese women, the existence of opportunities outside the home may safely be regarded as benefits.

Ultimately, most American citizen employees of MNEs will test any policy by asking whether or not they are personally adversely affected. Companies that take care to structure career advancement opportunities such that experience in countries hostile to a protected class may find themselves with few employee complaints. However, MNEs not able to finesse the mandate of Title VII and the reality of certain foreign cultures will find themselves facing a similar set of choices described above with respect to apartheid. Now, however, a decision to accommodate host country norms must be accompanied by a fund out of which to pay judgments in Title VII litigation.

B. The Host Country's Perspective

From the overall Japanese societal perspective, the changes contemplated by a mandate of gender equality may indeed be troubling. The social structure that has built up over centuries, which has "worked" to achieve stability and a degree of consensus and comfort, could crumble if more and more women leave household work to obtain work in the "business world." Who will do the careful packing of lunches, the guidance for "cram courses" after school, tending to the children and dinner and bedtime while spouse is engaged in the obligatory socializing with office mates after hours? While Japanese men may now be undertaking more domestic duties, the differences are still staggering. One recent estimate suggested that Japanese women put in four to five hours of domestic work daily, while their husbands put in eight minutes (Watanabe, 1992).

Any change in the prescribed social order is bound to seem disruptive, and, therefore, negative. As one Islamic man declared to a National Public Radio correspondent during the Persian Gulf war, if women are allowed in the workplace, the forces of social decay would soon send the divorce and crime rates skyrocketing. This argument, a kind of utilitarian "parade of horribles,"[6] overtly trades on fear of

change, is not empirically rigorous, and assumes that changes in the US over a fifty year period represent the ultimate result of mindless social tampering. For the Islamic, this particular proponent of gender inequality in the workplace has a back-up argument, the *Qur'an*.

By appeal to divine, or infinite wisdom, we find an argument more akin to natural law or universalism. The argument may even suppose that not only Islamic society, but all other societies, would be well advised to follow this divinely decreed social ordering. What is manifest to the Islamic mind is contrary, it would seem, to "Western" notions of gender equality. This conflict pits two "objective" or "universal" truths against one another: the "truth" of the *Qur'an* and the "truth" of the Universal Declaration of Human Rights. Is the moral relativist right, after all?

II. Ethical Relativism and Ethical Ethnocentrism: A Synthesis for Overseas Gender Discrimination Issues

In general terms, the theory of moral relativism holds that different moral standards are "equally valid or equally invalid," and there are no "objective standards of right and wrong or good and evil that transcend the opinions of different individuals or different societies."[7] At the opposite extreme of the continuum is the objective approach, which is premised on the notion that there are "transcultural" norms that are universally valid.

Bowie (1988) suggests that the proper view is a point closer to the latter position. Although he stops short of embracing universalism, Bowie believes there are minimum ethical principles that are universally evident such as "do not commit murder" and "do not torture." These principles, clearly, can be enforced without imposing ethnocentric (or imperialistic) views upon a host country. To these minimum universal principles, Bowie adds the "morals of the marketplace," which are required to support transactions in the business world. These include honesty and trust. The combination of these two strands of quasi-universalism is as far as Bowie will go in staking his claim on the continuum.

Consider again the dilemmas faced by a US MNE doing business in Japan, trying to integrate a tradition and practice of equal opportunity into a tradition and practice of unequal opportunity. One strategy for "blending in" with the Japanese market might be to adopt a thoroughly Japanese outlook and approach. That would include differing pay scales for men and women, actively discouraging women past the age of 25 from working with the company, and pointedly not inviting women employees to the after-five work/social functions that seem to play such an important part in an employee's successful corporate bonding.

Other than outright moral relativism, the social contract approach would appear to be the most likely proponent of such assimilation. Social contract theory examines the ethical foundations of societies by the relationships that exist within and between people, organizations, and groups. In an article on "extant social contracts," Dunfee (1991) explains and defends this communitarian approach to ethics, which appears grounded in relativism, but he also appears to offer an escape clause by way of a "filtering" device using utilitarian or deontological approaches. Dunfee would apparently recognize that racial discrimination is more widely condemned, and that gender discrimination is more widely tolerated, and conclude that perpetuating gender discrimination is less unethical than perpetuating racial discrimination. In a subsequent article, Dunfee and Donaldson (1991) retreat somewhat from the relativism approach and appear to suggest some dimensions of gender equality qualify as a "hypernorm," that is, a norm "recognized as core or foundational by most humans, regardless of culture." The example they give, however, is that of Saudi Arabia prohibiting women from driving, a rule that violates

hypernorms of freedom of movement and rights of self-realization. Obviously, this issue does not approach the complexity posed by the international application of gender equality in the workplace.

In essence, what seems problematic for social contract theory is the substantial variance between the almost universally professed ideals of gender equality and the globally pervasive policies of gender inequality. If one looks to social practice for guidance as to what is ethical, gender inequality becomes relatively more ethical; yet if one looks to professed ideals and principles of equality, many existing forms of gender inequality (dowry deaths, female infanticide, widow-burning, and abortion based on male preference) (Howe, 1991) seem inexcusable. Ethical guidelines, apart from legal obligations, seem to require more explicit direction.

Bowie rejects relativism and argues for recognition of minimum universal principles and morals of the marketplace, an essentially deontological approach. He suggests that the latter may even control over the former where completely foreign agents meet to do business. Bowie draws upon democratic theory, torture and genocide, and examples based on bribery, apartheid, and political-economic values to make his point. He is, however, silent on gender discrimination. One wonders whether Bowie would view this issue as primarily social or as a political-economic priority on a plane with his other examples.

We take the position that neither relativism nor extant social contract theory are much help to MNEs in a host country whose values run counter to the company's ethical code or the laws and traditions of its country of origin. Instead, the concepts of minimum universal principles and morals of the marketplace legitimately can be broadened to embrace gender equality. Support for this position is evident in the increasingly international consensus on this point.

For example, as Frederick (1991) has pointed out, the United Nations Universal Declaration of Human Rights, the OECD Guidelines for Multinational Enterprises, and the International Labor Office Tripartite Declaration all give support to "nondiscriminatory employment policies" and the concept of "equal pay for equal work." Note that neither of these policies is widespread in Japan. In The United Nations Convention on the Elimination of All Forms of Discrimination Against Women (1979) was ratified by a large number of nations, both industrialized and developing. The European Community has passed a number of Council directives aimed at promoting gender equality in employment (Weiner, 1990).

We believe that by following policies which generally promote gender equality, without slavish adherence to all US judicial opinions on Title VII and with good faith adjustments where cultural conditions require, a US MNE in Japan can maintain its own code of ethics without the "inevitable" loss of "competitiveness." Moreover, it can do so without being "ethnocentric" or "imperialist," and by doing so it can avoid a kind of ethical balkanization that adherence to moral relativism would require. After all, a dozen different cultural traditions might require a dozen different HRM policies, each geared to the host country's dominant yet often changing traditions.

This does not mean that resort to more universal declarations of principle are based on a need for Wicks' "metaphysical comfort." We agree with Wicks that our grasp of certain principles in some sense depends on our own experience and what "works." Did the social movement toward greater gender and racial equality in the United States come about because of *a priori* arguments on the ethical treatment of women and blacks, or because there was already equality in some areas and a perception that things "were not working"? There is no way to know with certainty, but there need be no need to identify either "ideal principles" or "real experience" as the mother lode for ethical discoveries.

Values, to be shared, must be mutually discovered. Universal standards, such as those proposed by the United Nations, come out of experience, and do not just emerge *a priori* (Frederick, 1991). Even without "metaphysical comfort," a MNE can be satisfied that there is an emerging consensus on gender equality. In going to a traditional culture where gender inequality is the norm, the MNE must be aware that there is another community emerging, one whose shape is as yet dimly perceived, but a community where goods, services, and information are traded with ever-increasing speed. Included in the information exchange in the communication of different values, and while these values are not being passed along in traditional ways, their transmission is inevitable. In this exchange of values and ideas, the ideals of equality are manifest in many ways. Any MNE, whatever the cultural norms it confronts in a particular country, would be wise to pay attention.

NOTES

1 Civil Rights Restoration Act of 1991, P. L. 102-166, Nov. 21, 1991, 105 Stat. 1071. For the purposes of this discussion, a US MNE is an enterprise with operations in one or more foreign countries.

2 *E.E.O.C. v. Aramco, Boureslan v. Aramco*, 111 S. Ct. 1227 (1991).

3 The authors mailed a survey entitled "Use of US Employment Discrimination Law Abroad" to human resource directors of 120 companies identified as multinational enterprises. In part, the questionnaire solicited information about whether or no the company felt it wise to apply Title VII abroad. The eight responses that were received provide anecdotal, as opposed to statistically significant, information. Six respondents indicated it would be "unwise" to attempt to apply Title VII to US citizens working abroad. The reasons given appear predictable: it would be "difficult"; it is the "local manager's responsibility"; we "do not attempt" to impose our norms on others. Two respondents believed

it would be wise to implement such a policy despite the obstacles discussed in this paper. Nonetheless, all respondents indicated that the policy is appropriately enforced in the US and two believed it would be wise to do so abroad as well.

4 42 U.S.C. §2000e-l (1988).

5 577 F. Supp. 1196, *affirmed* 746 F.2d 810 (1984).

6 George Christie, of Duke University Law School, coined this phrase in reference to attorneys, who learn to see the dark possibilities issuing from any proposed action and are prone to recite a "parade of horribles" to their clients.

7 Van Wyk, *Introduction to Ethics*, St. Martin's Press, New York (1990), 15.

REFERENCES

Adachi, K. 1989, "Problems and Prospects of Management Development of Female Employees in Japan," *Journal of Management Development* 8(4), 32-40.

Alder, N. 1984, "Women in International Management: Where are They?," *California Management Review* 26, 78-89.

Bassiry, G.R. 1990, "Business Ethics and the United Nations: A Code of Conduct," *SAM Advanced Management Journal* (Autumn), 38-41.

Bellace, J. 1991, "The International Dimension of Title VII," *Cornell International Law Journal* 24, 1-24.

Bowie, N. 1988, "The Moral Obligations of Multinational Corporations," in Luper-Fay (ed.), *Problems of International Justice* (New York: Westview Press), 97-113.

Bowie, N. 1977, "A Taxonomy for Discussing the Conflicting Responsibilities of a Multinational Corporation," in *Responsibilities of Multinational Corporations to Society* (Arlington, VA: Council of Better Business Bureau), 21-43.

Carney, L. and O'Kelly. 1987, "Barriers and Constraints to the Recruitment and Mobility of Female Managers in the Japanese Labor Force," *Human Resource Management* 26(2), 193-216.

Daimon, S. 1991, "'Karoshi' Phenomenon Spreading to Female Workforce," *Japan Times Weekly* (Intl. Ed.), Sept. 30-Oct. 6, 7.

Donaldson, T. and T. Dunfee. 1991, "Social Contracts in Economic Life: A Theory," No. 91-156 (revised) Working Paper Series, Department of Legal Studies, The Wharton School, University of Pennsylvania, 27-32.

Dunfee, T. 1991, "Extant Social Contracts," *Business Ethics Quarterly* 1, 22-37.

Edwards, L. 1988, "Equal Employment Opportunity in Japan: A View from the West," *Industrial and Labor Relations Review* 41(2), 240-50.

Ford, J. 1992, "Sexual Harassment Taken for Granted," *Japan Times Weekly* (Intl. Ed.), Feb. 10-16, 4.

Frederick, W. 1991, "The Moral Authority of Transnational Corporate Codes," *Journal of Business Ethics* 10, 165-77.

Gundling, F. 1991, "Ethics and Working with the Japanese: The Entrepreneur and the Elite Coursel," *California Management Review* 33(3), 25-39.

Howe M. 1991, "Sex Discrimination Persists, According to a UN Study," *New York Times* June 16, A4, col. 1.

Lan, S. 1991, "Japanese Businessman Produces Video to Prevent Lawsuits," *Japan Times Weekly* (Intl. Ed.), Nov. 11-17, 8.

Lansing, P. and K. Ready. 1988, "Hiring Women Managers in Japan: An Alternative for Foreign Employers," *California Management Review* 30(3), 112-21.

Lebra, D. 1984, *Japanese Women: Constraint and Fulfillment* (Honolulu: University of Hawaii Press).

Mayer, D. 1991, "Sex Discrimination Policies for US Companies Abroad," in Sanders, W. (ed.), *Proceedings of the Council on Employee Responsibilities and Rights*.

Moghadam, V. 1988, "Women, Work, and Ideology in the Islamic Republic," *International Journal of Middle East Studies* 20, 221-43.

Neff, R. 1991, "When in Japan, Recruit as the Japanese Do—Aggressively," *Business Week* June 24, 58.

Prater, C. 1991, "Women Try on New Roles; But Hopes Can Still Collide With Tradition," *Detroit Free Press* November 27, 1 (5th in a series, later published in the *New York Times*).

Rhoodie, E. 1989, *Discrimination Against Women: A Global Survey of the Economic, Educational, Social and Political Status of Women* (London, UK: McFarland and Company).

Seymour, C. 1991, "The Ad-business: Talented Women Need Not Apply," *Japan Times Weekly* (Intl. Ed.), Dec. 9-15, 7.

Simon, H. and F. Brown, 1990/91, "International Enforcement of Title VII: A Small World After All?," *Employee Relations Law Journal* 16(3), 281-300.

United Nations. 1979, *Convention of the Elimination of All Forms of Discrimination Against Women*, UN Doc. A/34/36 (Dec. 18, 1979).

Watanabe, T. 1992, "In Japan, a 'Goat Man' or No Man; Women are Gaining More Clout in Relationships," *Los Angeles Times* Jan. 6, A1, Col. 1.

Weiner, M. 1990, "Fundamental Misconceptions About Fundamental Rights: The Changing Nature of Women's Rights in the EEC and Their Application in the United Kingdom," *Harvard International Law Journal* 31(2), 565-74.

Wicks, A. 1990, "Norman Bowie and Richard Rorty on Multinationals: Does Business Ethics Need 'Metaphysical Comfort'?," *Journal of Business Ethics* 9, 191-200.

ENVIRONMENTAL RESPONSIBILITY

MARK SAGOFF

At the Monument to General Meade, *or* On the Difference Between Beliefs and Benefits

When you visit Gettysburg National Military Park, you can take a tour that follows the course of the three-day battle. The route ends at the National Cemetery, where, four months after the fighting, Abraham Lincoln gave the 270-word speech that marked the emergence of the United States as one nation.[1] The tour will not cover all of the battlefield, however, because much of it lies outside the park. Various retail outlets and restaurants, including a Hardee's and a Howard Johnson's, stand where General Pickett, at two o'clock on a July afternoon in 1863, marched 15,000 Confederate soldiers to their deaths. The Peach Orchard and Wheatfield, where General Longstreet attacked, became the site of a Stuckey's family restaurant.[2] The Cavalry Heights Trailer Park graces fields where General George Custer turned back the final charge of the Confederate cavalry.[3] Over his restaurant, Colonel Sanders, purveyor of fried chicken, smiles with neon jowls upon the monument to George Meade, the victorious Union general.[4] Above this historic servicescape looms a 310-foot commercial observation tower many Civil War buffs consider to be "a wicked blight on the battlefield vista."[5]

One spring day, on my way to give a seminar on "economics and the environment" at Gettysburg College, I drove quickly past the battlefield where

23,000 Union and 28,000 Confederate soldiers fell in three days. I felt guilty speeding by the somber fields, but I had to teach at two o'clock. I checked my watch. I did not want to be late. How do you keep your appointments and still find time to pay homage to history?

My ruminations were soon relieved by a strip of tawdry motels, restaurants, amusement arcades, and gift shops touting plastic soldiers and "original bullets! $6.95 each." At the battlefield entrance, I caught sight of the famous golden arches of the battlefield McDonald's where, on a previous occasion, my then eight-year-old son enjoyed a Happy Meal combo called the "burger and cannon." Nearby, a sign for General Pickett's All-You-Can-Eat Buffet beckoned me to a restaurant that marks the spot where rifle and artillery fire had torn apart Pickett's underfed troops. If you have young children, you understand the deep and abiding significance of fast food and convenient restrooms in historic and scenic areas. You may ask yourself, though, how you can have comfort, convenience, and commerce and at the same time respect "hallowed ground."

I. Are Battlefields Scarce Resources?

I began the seminar at Gettysburg College by describing a Park Service plan, then under discussion, to build new facilities to absorb the tide of visitors—an increase of 400,000 to 1.7 million annually—that welled up in response to "Gettysburg," a 1993 movie based on Michael Shaara's blockbuster novel, *The Killer Angels*.[6] Working with a private developer, the Park Service proposed to construct a new $40 million visitor center, including a 500-seat family food court, a 450-seat theater, and a 150-seat "upscale casual" restaurant with "white tablecloth" service, gift shops, parking lots, and a bus terminal not far from the place where Lincoln delivered the Gettysburg Address.[7] Several senators, including Senate Majority Leader Trent Lott (R-Miss.), objected that

the project "commercializes the very ground and principle we strive to preserve."[8]

It is one thing to commercialize the *ground*; it is another to commercialize the *principle* we strive to preserve. Tour buses, fast food, and trinket shops, although they commercialize the ground, express a local entrepreneurial spirit consistent with the freedom, vitality, and mystery of the place. The soldiers probably would have liked such haunts as the National Wax Museum, the Colt Firearms Museum, and the Hall of Presidents. They certainly would have appreciated General Lee's Family Restaurant, which serves great hamburgers practically at the site of Lee's headquarters. Homespun businesses try to tell the story and perpetuate the glory of Gettysburg—and even when they succeed only absurdly, they do so with an innocence and ineptitude that does not intrude on the dignity and drama of the park.

In contrast, the upscale tourist mall envisioned by the initial Park Service plan seemed, at least to Senator Lott, to elevate commercialism into a principle for managing Gettysburg. Rather than stand by the principle of commercialism or consumer sovereignty, however, the Park Service scaled back its plan.[9] In its defense, the Service pointed out that Ziegler's Grove, where its Visitor Center and Cyclorama now stand, overlooks the main battle lines. The revised proposal, which received Interior Department approval in November 1999, calls for razing these facilities and for returning Ziegler's Grove to its 1863 appearance, in order, as one official said, "to honor the valor and sacrifices of those men who fought and died on that ground for their beliefs."[10]

Since the seminar took place in mid-afternoon—siesta time in civilized societies—I had to engage the students. I did so by proposing a thesis so outrageous and appalling that the students would attack me and it. I told the class that the value of any environment—or of any of its uses—depends on what people now and in the future are willing to pay for it. Accordingly, the Park Service should have stuck with its original plan or, even better, it should have auctioned the battlefield to the highest bidder, for example, to Disney Enterprises.[11]

I asked the students to bear with me long enough to consider my proposal in relation to the subject of the seminar, the theory of environmental economics. This theory defends consumer sovereignty as a principle for environmental policy. More specifically, this theory asserts that the goal of environmental policy is to maximize social welfare at least when equity issues—matters involving the distribution of benefits among individuals—are not pressing.[12] Welfare, in turn, is defined and measured by consumer willingness to pay ("WTP") for goods and services. According to this theory, environmental policy should allocate goods and services efficiently, that is, to those willing to pay the most for them and who, in that sense, will benefit from their enjoyment, possession, or use.

In the United States, unlike Europe, I explained, battlefields are scarce resources which, like any scarce environmental asset, should be allocated efficiently. To be sure, the Park Service tries to accommodate tourists. The problem, though, is that the Park Service does not exploit heritage values as efficiently as a competitive market would. At present, Gettysburg is woefully underutilized, or so I argued. Even Dollywood, Dolly Parton's theme park in rural east Tennessee, attracts more visitors every year.[13] The Park Service does not even try to allocate the resources efficiently. It pursues goals that are not economic but ethical; it seeks to educate the public and honor "the valor and sacrifices of those men who fought and died on that ground for their beliefs."[14]

A young lady in the class blurted out, "But that's what the Park Service should do." She acknowledged that the Park Service has to provide visitor services. It should do so, she said, only to the extent that it will not "detract from what they did here," to paraphrase President Lincoln.[15] This young lady thought that the history of the place, rather than what people are willing to pay for alternative uses of it, determined its value. She understood the significance of "what

they did here" in moral and historical rather than in economic terms. The value of hallowed ground or of any object with intrinsic value has nothing to do with market behavior or with WTP, she said.

I explicated her concern the following way. A private developer, I explained, might not realize in gate receipts at Gettysburg the WTP of those individuals, like herself, who wished to protect an area for ethical or aesthetic reasons. I promised to describe to the class the contingent valuation ("CV") method economists have developed to determine how much individuals are willing to pay for policies consistent with their disinterested moral beliefs.[16] Using this method, the Park Service could take her preference and therefore her welfare into account. It could then identify the policy that maximizes benefits over costs for all concerned, whether that concern is based on consumer desire or on ethical commitment.

This reply, I am afraid, did little more than taunt the student. In stating her opinion, she said, she implied nothing about her own well-being. She described what she thought society ought to do, not what would make her better off. The student did not see how scientific management, by measuring costs and benefits, served democracy. The Park Service, she added, had no responsibility, legal or moral, to maximize "satisfactions," including hers. Rather, it had an obligation keep faith with those who died on that ground for their beliefs. No CV survey, no amount of WTP, she said, could add to or detract from the value of Gettysburg. No action we take could alter, though it may honor or dishonor, what the soldiers did there; no cost-benefit study, however scientific, could change our obligation to those who gave their lives that this nation might live.

II. Conservation Revisited

To prepare for the seminar, I had asked the students to read *Conservation Reconsidered*,[17] an essay economist John V. Krutilla published in 1967 in response to neoclassical economists, who studied the effects of technological advance on economic growth. Neo-classical macroeconomists like James Tobin,[18] Robert Solow, and William Nordhaus[19] argued that techno-logical progress would always make more abundant materials do the work of less abundant ones—for example, the way kerosene substituted for whale oil in providing household illumination.[20] Solow, a Nobel laureate in economics, wrote that "[h]igher and ris-ing prices of exhaustible resources lead competing producers to substitute other materials that are more plentiful and therefore cheaper."[21] These economists adopted a model of economic growth that contained two factors: capital (including technology) and the labor to apply it.[22] This model differed from that of classical economists, such as Ricardo and Malthus, because "resources, the third member of the classical triad, have generally been dropped."[23]

In the essay the class read, Krutilla cited studies to show that advancing technology has "compensat-ed quite adequately for the depletion of the higher quality natural resource stocks."[24] He observed that "the traditional concerns of conservation econom-ics—the husbanding of natural resource stocks for the use of future generations—may now be out-moded by advances in technology."[25] Krutilla, along with other environmental economists in the 1970s, rejected the view that the resource base imposes lim-its on growth.[26] Had they accepted the Malthusian position, they would have risked losing credibility both with their mainstream colleagues and with foundations and institutions, such as the World Bank, that supported their work.[27]

The neoclassical model of growth, insofar as it takes natural resources for granted, did not sit well with environmentalists, many of whom rejected neo-classical thinking and joined the maverick discipline of ecological economics, which emphasizes tradition-al Malthusian concerns about resource depletion.[28] The neoclassical theory of perpetual resource abun-dance, moreover, left environmental economists no obvious scarcities to study. It suggested that econo-mists could do little more than to advise society to privatize resources, enforce contracts, and otherwise not to worry but just leave markets alone.

Krutilla and other mainstream environmental economists, to find fertile fields for research, moved the focus of their science from macroeconomic to microeconomic analysis.[29] Microeconomists study the behavior of individuals and firms as they trade in competitive markets. When markets fail properly to bring buyers together with sellers, prices at which goods and services change hands may fail to reflect the full WTP for them and the full costs involved in producing them. Microeconomists identify ways to correct market failure and to make prices better reflect marginal supply and demand.[30]

Pollution is the standard example. If the produc-tion of a good, say, an automobile, imposes costs, for example, dirty air, on members of society for which they are not compensated, these individuals unwill-ingly subsidize the production or consumption of that item. This subsidy distorts markets because it encourages the overproduction of some things (e.g., cars) and the underproduction of other things (e.g., clean air) relative to what people want to buy. The production and use of cars imposes social costs, costs on society, that are not reflected in the private costs, prices people pay, to own and drive those cars. This gap between social and private costs, economists rea-son, justifies regulation.

As early as 1920, welfare economist A.C. Pigou had distinguished between "private" and "social" costs and had characterized pollution as an unpriced "externality" or social cost of production.[31] Pigou had also proposed the solution: to tax the difference between private costs, those reflected in prices, and social costs, those people bear without compensa-tion, so that the prices charged for polluting goods would reflect the full costs, including the pollution costs, that go into providing them.[32]

By the 1960s and 1970s, economists had fully characterized Pigou's argument as what one called "the economic common sense of pollution."[33] After 1970, little new could be said or has been said on this subject. The microeconomic analysis of pollution in terms of a divergence between private and social costs, however, has had little if any effect on public policy. Pollution control law relies for its justification on common law principles of nuisance, not on a Pigouvian concept of market failure. Public law regulates pollution, in other words, not as an "externality" to be controlled to the extent that the benefits outweigh the costs, but as an invasion, trespass, or tort.[34]

Krutilla and colleagues saw a way, however, to apply the Pigouvian analysis of market failure far, far beyond the problems of pollution. These economists knew that people often make sacrifices, e.g., by paying dues, to support causes and to vindicate convictions concerning the natural world. These beliefs or commitments surely involve values; values, in the context of economic theory, suggest costs or benefits and, therefore WTP, that market prices may not fully capture.[35] This WTP, if entered into a social cost-benefit analysis, could serve environmentalism by justifying regulation.

The young lady in my seminar, for example, thought the Park Service should restore rather than commercialize the battlefield. If policy went her way, arguably, she would experience a benefit, if not, a cost. This example and many others like it suggest that markets may fail whenever people support principles or judgments they cannot easily vindicate through private exchange. Experts might correct market allocations by measuring WTP for outcomes consistent with political beliefs and moral commitments. This possibility opened a new vista to environmental economics.

III. Moral Commitment as Market Demand

At about the time neoclassical economics removed resource scarcity as a cause for concern, citizens across the country swelled the rolls of organizations such as the Sierra Club, which sought to preserve pristine places, endangered species, wild rivers, and other natural objects. These environmentalists, Krutilla pointed out, contributed to organizations such as the World Wildlife Fund "in an effort to save exotic species in remote areas of the world which few subscribers to the Fund ever hope to see."[36] Krutilla noted that people "place a value on the mere existence" of resources, such as species, even though they do not intend to consume or own them, as they would ordinary resources.[37]

Krutilla argued that if people value natural objects because they are natural, then technological advance cannot provide substitutes for them.[38] Among the permanently scarce phenomena of nature, Krutilla cited familiar examples including "the Grand Canyon, a threatened species, or an entire ecosystem or biotic community essential to the survival of the threatened species."[39] On this basis, Krutilla and many colleagues reinvented environmental economics as a "new conservation"[40] that addresses the failure of markets to respond to the "existence" or "non-use" value of natural objects people want to preserve but may not intend to experience, much less use or consume.

Krutilla was correct, of course, in observing that people often are willing to pay to preserve natural objects such as endangered species. Among them, for example, is Tom Finger, a Mennonite, who said, "we're eliminating God's creatures. All these non-human creatures ... have a certain intrinsic worth because they are part of God's creation."[41] People who believe species have an intrinsic worth may be willing to pay to protect them. Does this suggest that endangered species are scarce resources? Do those who believe extinction is wrong suffer a loss, a kind of social cost, when species vanish? Does endangered species habitat have an economic value market prices fail to reflect?

Krutilla thought so. He reasoned that those who wished to protect natural objects or environments find it difficult to communicate their WTP to those who own those resources. Given this practical difficulty, "the private resource owner would not be able to appropriate in gate receipts the entire social value of the resources when used in a manner compatible with preserving the natural state."[42] Accordingly, Krutilla proposed that the analysis Pigou had offered to justify the regulation of pollution might also serve to justify governmental action to protect species, wilderness, and other natural objects. He wrote, "private and social returns ... are likely to diverge significantly."[43]

Krutilla's analysis suggests an argument to show that a private firm should manage Dollywood but not Gettysburg, even if the principle of consumer sovereignty applies equally to both. At Dollywood, the owners can capture in gate and table receipts total WTP for the goods and services the resort provides. Owners who respond to market signals supply just those goods and services the public most wants to buy. The managers of Dollywood, moreover, cover all the costs in labor, materials, etc., of their business. The prices they charge, then, will reflect the full social costs involved in producing what they sell.

At Gettysburg, it is different. Patriotic Americans, many of whom may never visit the area, may be willing to pay to restore the battlefield or to save it from commercial exploitation. Private, for-profit owners of Gettysburg would have no incentive to take this WTP into account, however, because they cannot capture it in gate and table receipts. The prices managers charge for attractions, then, will not reflect the full social costs of providing them—particularly the costs to patriotic Americans who would suffer if the battlefield is desecrated. Because price signals distort true WTP for preservation, the government, rather than a for-profit firm, should manage or at least regulate Gettysburg. Thus, a Pigouvian argument may provide an economic and, in that sense, scientific rationale for the belief that society should restore Gettysburg to its 1863 condition rather than sell the area to Disney Enterprises to run as a theme park.

This kind of economic argument may appeal to environmentalists because it opposes the privatization of places, such as Gettysburg, that possess intrinsic value. This argument seems especially appealing because it rejects privatization for economic reasons—the very sorts of reasons that might be thought to justify it. Since this Pigouvian analysis leads to comfortable conclusions, environmentalists might embrace it. Why not agree with economic theory that the goal of social policy is to maximize net benefits with respect to all environmental assets, whether in places like Dollywood or in places like Gettysburg? After all, the cost-benefit analysis, once it factors in the WTP of environmentalists, surely will come out in favor of protecting the environment.

The problem is this: to buy into this argument, one must accept the idea that the same goal or principle—net benefits maximization—applies to both Dollywood and Gettysburg.[44] Critics of economic theory may contend, however, that the approach to valuation appropriate at Daydream Ridge in Dollywood is not appropriate at Cemetery Ridge in Gettysburg. At Daydream Ridge, the goal is to satisfy consumer demand. At Cemetery Ridge, the goal is to pay homage to those who died that this nation might live.

To say that the nation has a duty to pay homage to those from whom it received the last full measure of devotion is to state a moral fact. You can find other moral facts stated, for example, in the Ten Commandments. The imperative "Thou shalt not murder" should not be understood as a policy preference for which Moses and other like-minded reformers were willing to pay. Rather, like every statement of moral fact, it presents a hypothesis about what we stand for—what we maintain as true and expect others to believe—insofar as we identify ourselves as a moral and rational community.

Our Constitution puts certain questions, for example, religious belief, beyond the reach of democracy. Other moral questions, over military intervention in conflicts abroad, for example, invite reasoned deliberation in appropriate legislative councils. Environmental controversies, once the issues of resource scarcity are removed from the agenda, turn on the discovery and acceptance of moral and aesthetic judgments as facts. The belief that society should respect the sanctity of Cemetery Ridge states a moral fact so uncontroversial nobody would doubt it. This tells us nothing, however, about a scarcity of battlefields, an inelasticity of hallowed ground, market failure, or the divergence of social and private costs. It suggests only that the principle of consumer sovereignty that economists apply to evaluate management decisions at Dollywood do not apply at Gettysburg or, indeed, wherever the intrinsic value of an environment is at stake.[45]

IV. Are Beliefs Benefits?

By construing intrinsic or existence value as a kind of demand market prices fail to reflect, Krutilla and other environmental economists envisioned a brilliant strategy to respond to the quandary in which neoclassical economic theory had placed them.[46] They kept their credentials as mainstream economists by accepting the neoclassical macroeconomic model with respect to resources the economy uses. Yet they also "greened" their science by attributing a general scarcity to "non-use" resources such as wilderness, species, scenic rivers, historical landmarks, and so on, that people believe society has a duty to preserve. Indeed, by applying the divergence-of-private-and-social-cost argument not just to pollution but also to every plant, animal, or place that anyone may care about for ethical or cultural reasons, economic theory performed a great service to environmentalists. Environmentalists now could represent their moral, religious, or cultural beliefs as WTP market prices failed to reflect.[47] At last, they could claim that economic science was on their side.[48]

By transforming moral or cultural judgments about the environment into preferences for which people are willing to pay, Krutilla and his colleagues in the early 1970s achieved a great deal. First, they created a complex research agenda centering on the measurement of benefits associated with non-use or existence value.[49] Since 1970, indeed, research in environmental economics, both theoretical and empirical, has been preoccupied with measuring the economic benefits people are supposed to enjoy as a result of environmental policies consistent with their moral and religious beliefs.[50]

Second, Krutilla and colleagues created a division of labor between policy scientists and policy consumers.[51] As policy scientists, economists lay down the goals and principles of environmental policy—indeed of all social policy—on the basis of their own theory and without any political deliberation, consultation, or process.[52] Economists Edith Stokey and Richard Zeckhauser, for example, assert that "public policy should promote the welfare of society."[53] A. Myrick Freeman III explains, "The basic premises of welfare economics are that the purpose of economic activity is to increase the well-being of the individuals who make up the society."[54] In a widely used textbook, Eban Goodstein states, "Economic analysts are concerned with human welfare or well-being. From the economic perspective, the environment should be protected for the material benefit of humanity and not for strictly moral or ethical reasons."[55]

As policy consumers, citizens make judgments about what is good for them.[56] Economists reiterate that "each individual is the best judge of how well off he or she is in a given situation."[57] Henry Ford is reputed to have said that people could have automobiles "in any color so long as it's black."[58] From the standpoint of economic theory, individuals can make any social judgment they wish, as long as it concerns the extent to which policy outcomes harm or benefit them.[59]

Economists may offer a ceremonial bow in the direction of markets, but this is quickly followed by a story of market failure followed by a call for centralized management based on cost-benefit analysis.[60] Experts, i.e., economists themselves, must teach society how to allocate resources scientifically, since markets cannot cope with environmental public goods. In markets, individuals make choices and thus function as agents of change. In microeconomic theory, in contrast, individuals function not as agents but primarily as sites or locations where WTP may be found.

Third, as the methodology for benefits estimation developed, it typically assigned very high shadow prices to existence values, and this appealed to environmentalists. An endangered butterfly, for example, may be worth millions if every American is willing to pay a dime for its survival. Public interest groups, who associated economists with the enemy, now saw that economic science could be their friend.[61] Environmentalists, who might have complained that industry groups had "numbers," could now come up with numbers, too.[62] And since WTP adds up quickly when aggregated over all members of society, environmentalists could be sure that the numbers would come out "right."

V. Is Existence Value a Kind of Economic Value?

To establish a connection between existence value and economic value, economists have to explain in what sense people benefit from the existence of goods they may neither experience nor use. To be sure, individuals are willing to pay to protect endangered species, rain forests, and other wonders of nature they may never expect to see. That they are willing to pay for them, however, does not show that they expect to benefit from them. Generally speaking, just because a person's preferences are all his own, it does not follow that the satisfaction of all or any of those preferences necessarily improves his welfare or well-being. The students in my class were quite willing to contribute to a fund to protect hallowed ground at Gettysburg. They did so, however, largely from

a sense of moral obligation and not in any way or manner because they thought they would be better off personally if the battlefield were preserved.

I wrote the following syllogism on the blackboard.

Major premise: The terms "economic value" and "welfare change" are equivalent.

Minor premise: Existence value has no clear relation to welfare change.

Conclusion: Therefore, existence value has no clear relation to economic value.

I defended the major premise by quoting leading environmental economists. According to Freeman, "[T]he terms 'economic value' and 'welfare change' can be used interchangeably."[63] He adds that "[s]ociety should make changes in environmental and resource allocations only if the results are worth more in terms of individuals' welfare than what is given up by diverting resources and inputs from other uses."[64] Economists Robert D. Rowe and Lauraine G. Chestnut observe that "[e]conomists define value as the well-being, or utility, derived from the consumption of a good or service."[65]

The major premise, which equates economic value with welfare, explains the sense in which economic value is valuable. Unless "economic value" referred to some intrinsic good, such as felt happiness or satisfaction, one would be hard-pressed to explain the sense in which environmental economics can be a normative science.[66]

To establish the minor premise, I argued that the statement "society ought to do x and I will contribute to its cost" does not entail "I shall benefit from x." When behavior is motivated by ethical concerns rather than by self-interest, it lacks a meaningful connection with well-being or welfare. Accordingly, economist Paul Milgrom concedes that for existence value to be considered a kind of economic value, "it would be necessary for people's individual existence values to reflect only their own personal economic motives and not altruistic motives, or sense of duty, or moral obligation."[67]

To escape the conclusion that existence value has no relation to economic value, an economist may challenge either the major or minor premise. The major premise seems to be indispensable, however, if economics is to rest on a consequentialist moral theory such as utilitarianism. The reference to welfare explains why the benefits with which economists are concerned are benefits. The minor premise may be more vulnerable. This premise would be falsified if individuals made choices only in response to their beliefs about what will benefit them. Why not suppose, then, that people (other than economists) judge policy outcomes only on the basis of personal self interest? This assumption would connect preference with well-being for the ordinary citizen.

The students pointed out to me that Krutilla adopts this very position. In the essay the class read, he proposed that individuals who wish to protect the wonders of nature do so for self-seeking reasons, for example, to increase their own psychological satisfaction.[68] Krutilla wrote that

> These would be the spiritual descendants of John Muir, the present members of the Sierra Club, the Wilderness Society, National Wildlife Federation, Audubon Society and others to whom the loss of a species or the disfigurement of a scenic area causes acute distress and a sense of genuine relative impoverishment.[69]

The reference to "distress and a sense of genuine relative impoverishment" is crucial, of course, because these factors link existence value with economic value by connecting them with expected changes in welfare. Krutilla continued, "There are many persons who obtain satisfaction from mere knowledge that part of wilderness North America remains even though they would be appalled by the prospect of being exposed to it."[70] The reference to "satisfaction"

connects the "is" of WTP to the "ought" of economic value and valuation.[71]

VI. Contingent Valuation

During the past thirty years, economists have worked hard to develop a method, known as contingent valuation ("CV"), to assess the "existence" or "non-use" values of natural phenomena.[72] The CV method, as one authority writes, "is based on asking an individual to state his or her willingness to pay to bring about an environmental improvement, such as improved visibility from lessened air pollution, the protection of an endangered species, or the preservation of a wilderness area."[73] The authors of a textbook write that the CV method "asks people what they are willing to pay for an environmental benefit...."[74] They see this method as "uniquely suited to address non-use values."[75]

Contrary to what this textbook asserts, the CV questionnaire never asks people what they are willing to pay for an environmental benefit. It asks respondents to state their WTP for a particular policy outcome, for example, the protection of a rare butterfly. Economists interpret the stated WTP for the environmental improvement as if it were WTP for a personal benefit the respondent expects it to afford her or him. Yet a person who believes that society ought to protect a species of butterfly may have no expectation at all that he or she will benefit as a result. Indeed, as Tom Tietenberg observes, people who do not expect to benefit in any way from an environmental good may still be committed to its preservation.[76] He notes that "people reveal strong support for environmental resources even when those resources provide no direct or even indirect benefit."[77]

Empirical research shows that responses to CV questionnaires reflect moral commitments rather than concerns about personal welfare. In one example, a careful study showed that ethical considerations dominate economic ones in responses to CV surveys.[78] "Our results provide an assessment of the frequency and seriousness of these considerations in our sample: they are frequent and they are significant determinants of WTP responses."[79] In another study, researchers found that existence value "is almost entirely driven by ethical considerations precisely because it is disinterested value."[80]

Some observers acknowledge that "existence value has been argued to involve a moral 'commitment' which is not in any way at all self-interested."[81] They explain that: "Commitment can be defined in terms of a person choosing an act that he believes will yield a lower level of personal welfare to him than an alternative that is also available to him."[82] If the satisfaction of "existence" value lowers welfare, then on which side of the cost-benefit equation should it be entered? The individual does not want less welfare per se, but "adherence to one's moral commitments will be as important as personal economic welfare maximization and may conflict with it."[83]

However they can, respondents to CV questions express disinterested views about policy rather than judgments about what will benefit them. Reviewing several CV protocols, economists concluded that "responses to CV questions concerning environmental preservation are dominated by citizen judgments concerning desirable social goals rather than by consumer preferences."[84] Two commentators noted that the CV method asks people to "comment, without very much opportunity for thought, on a hard issue of public policy. In short, they most likely are exhibiting offhand opinions on the same policy issue to which the cost-benefit analyst purports to give his own answer, not private preferences that might be reflected in their own market transactions."[85]

We should not confuse WTP to protect a battlefield, species, or wilderness with WTP for some sort of benefit. Battlefields and benefits constitute different goods which can be provided and should be measured separately. If economists cared to measure the economic value, i.e., the benefits, of alterna-

tive outcomes, the CV questionnaire should ask respondents to state their WTP for the welfare change they associate an environmental policy. Here is an imaginary protocol I suggested to the class:

> Many people believe society should respect the "hallowed ground" at Gettysburg for moral, cultural, or other disinterested reasons. This questionnaire asks you to set aside all such disinterested values; it asks you not to consider what is right or wrong or good or bad from a social point of view. In responding to this survey, consider only the benefit you believe you will experience, i.e., the personal satisfaction, if the battlefield is preserved. Please state your WTP simply for the welfare change you expect, not your WTP for the protection of the battlefield itself.

Since CV questionnaires in fact ask nothing about benefits, responses to them tell us nothing relevant to economic valuation. Yet CV methodology, which economists have been developing for decades, has become the principal technique policymakers use to measure "nonmarket benefits based primarily on existence value" of assets such as old growth forests and endangered species.

As philosopher Ronald Dworkin points out, many of us recognize an obligation to places and objects that reflects a moral judgment about what society should do, not a subjective expectation about what may benefit us.[86] He writes that many of us seek to protect objects or events—which could include endangered species, for example—for reasons that have nothing to do with our well-being. Many of us "think we should admire and protect them because they are important in themselves, and not just if or because we or others want or enjoy them."[87] The idea of intrinsic worth depends on deeply held moral convictions and religious beliefs that underlie social policies for the environment, education, public health, and so on. Dworkin observes:

Much of what we think about knowledge, experience, art, and nature, for example, presupposes that in different ways these are valuable in themselves and not just for their utility or for the pleasure or satisfaction they bring us. The idea of intrinsic value is commonplace, and it has a central place in our shared scheme of values and opinions.[88]

Beliefs are not benefits. If economists believe that society should allocate resources to maximize welfare, they do not necessarily think this because they will be better off as a result. They are not simply trying to increase demand for their services. Similarly, as the evidence cited above suggests, people who believe that society should protect endangered species, old-growth forests, and other places with intrinsic value do not necessarily think that this will improve their well-being.[89] A person who wants the Park Service to respect hallowed ground may consider that policy justified by the historical qualities of the battlefield and not by the welfare consequences for her or him. It is hard to understand, then, how CV measures the non-market benefits of environmental goods.[90] If responses to CV surveys are based on moral beliefs or commitments, there would seem to be no relevant benefits to measure.

VII. Does WTP Measure Welfare?

A young man in the class referred back to the syllogism that remained on the blackboard. He asked whether the syllogism still would be sound if the term "existence value" were replaced by "willingness to pay." He reasoned that if existence value, when based on moral commitment rather than self interest, has no necessary relation to welfare, this would be true of WTP as well. He asked what WTP measures and how that relates to well-being and thus to economic value.

To answer this question, I reminded the class of what economic value consists in, namely, something

akin to human happiness. As R. Kerry Turner explains, "Positive economic value—a benefit—arises when people feel better off, and negative economic value—a cost—arises when they feel worse off."[91] As Goodstein points out, the "moral foundation underlying economic analysis, which has as its goal human happiness or utility, is known as utilitarianism."[92] Happiness, contentment, and feelings of satisfaction are psychological states which, arguably, have intrinsic value.[93] Insofar as economic value is 'valuable,' its value lies in or refers to subjective well-being or happiness.

Does WTP measure, correlate with, or have anything to do with happiness, well-being, or contentment? We can answer this question empirically by using income as a surrogate measure for WTP; after all, people with more money can obtain more of the things they want to buy. We can use perceived happiness or subjective well-being to measure how well off people are. To determine whether WTP relates to well-being, we can find out whether people who have more money are happier than those who have less. On this empirical question, a great deal of evidence exists.

Empirical research overwhelmingly shows that after basic needs are met, no correlation whatsoever holds between rising income and perceived happiness.[94] Researchers consistently find there is very little difference in the levels of reported happiness found in rich and very poor countries.[95] Although the buying power of Americans has doubled since the 1950s, reported happiness has remained almost unchanged.[96] Absolute levels of income seem not to affect happiness, although relative levels do. People may be less happy if they earn less than their peers.[97]

The literature contains studies in which people report they become less happy as their income and purchasing power increases.[98] Studies relating wealth to perceived happiness find that "rising prosperity in the USA since 1957 has been accompanied by a falling level of satisfaction. Studies of satisfaction and changing economic conditions have found overall no stable relationship at all."⁹⁹ One major survey states, "None of the respondents believed that money is a major source of happiness."¹⁰⁰ That money does not buy happiness may be one of the best established findings of social science research.¹⁰¹

A great many reasons explain why no empirical relation holds between what people are willing to pay for something and the happiness they derive or expect to derive from it. Happiness seems to depend on the things money cannot buy, e.g., love, friendship, and faith, not on the extent of one's possessions.¹⁰² Fred Hirsch, among others, argued persuasively that happiness correlates with status more than with wealth.¹⁰³ Even those who succeed at their "games" seem to be dissatisfied as their expectations climb. Michael Jordan has been quoted as saying, "I wish I came in first more often."¹⁰⁴

Although economists invoke utilitarianism as a moral foundation, WTP and therefore economic value has no clear relation to happiness and, therefore, no basis in utilitarianism. As Richard Posner wrote, the "most important thing to bear in mind about the concept of value [in the economist's sense] is that it is based on what people are willing to pay for something rather than the happiness they would derive from having it."¹⁰⁵ If economic value is a function of what people are willing to pay for something rather than the happiness they would derive from having it, it is unsurprising that those willing to pay the most for goods derive the most economic value from them. The term "economic value" simply coincides with "WTP" and has no connection to anything else.

I asked the class how we get from "people are willing to pay more for *A* than *B*" to "*A* is better than *B*"? To answer this question, I referred to the syllogism on the board, which now read:

Major premise: The terms "economic value" and "welfare change" are equivalent.

Minor premise: WTP has no clear relation to welfare change.

Conclusion: Therefore, WTP value has no clear relation to economic value.

Environmental economists escape this syllogism, I proposed, by ingeniously defining "welfare change" or "benefit" in terms of willingness to pay. Freeman describes this crucial step. He explains that economic theory defines "the benefit of an environmental improvement as the sum of the monetary values assigned to these effects by all individuals directly or indirectly affected by that action."¹⁰⁶ Tietenberg analyzes the connection between WTP and benefits in the same way. "Total willingness to pay is the concept we shall use to define total benefits," he explains.¹⁰⁷ Economic theory uses WTP to measure net benefits or welfare change because it defines "benefit" and "welfare change" in terms of willingness to pay. The statement that WTP measures or correlates with well-being means no more than the empty identity, "A is equivalent to A."

The central argument of environmental economics, then, comes to this—An allocation of resources to those willing to pay the most for them maximizes net benefits; net benefits, in turn, are measured in terms of the amount people are willing to pay for those resources. The central contention of environmental economics is logically equivalent to the claim that resources should go to those willing to pay the most for them, because they are willing to pay the most for those resources. In this tautology, the terms "welfare" or "well-being" simply drop out. These terms function only as stand-ins or as proxies for WTP and cannot logically be distinguished from it. The measuring rod of money—or WTP—correlates with or measures nothing but itself.

Environmental economics fails as a normative science because it cannot tell us why or in what sense an efficient allocation is better than a less efficient one. Lacking all normative content, terms like "utility," "well-being," or "welfare" fail to move environmental economics from the "is" of WTP to the "ought" of value or valuation.

VIII. Naked Preferences

A young man in the class wondered aloud if this critique of environmental economics had gone too far. The CV method, after all, attributes enormous economic value to so-called "useless" species and to remote places that few people may visit. Instead of rejecting this technique, he suggested, we should be grateful for it. "To the extent that people are willing to pay for existence value—whether the protection of species and habitats, the functioning of ecosystems, or the dignity of Gettysburg—these intangibles are appropriately included in the overall calculus of benefit," he said. He added that the CV method, because it aggregates WTP for policy preferences, provides valuable information to policymakers. This is true whether preferences reflect judgments about personal benefit or judgments about the goals or values of society.

The student suggested, then, that even if WTP and economic value are logically equivalent, environmental economics retains its usefulness as a policy science. He conceded that references to "welfare" or "well-being" could be dismissed as window-dressing. All that matters is WTP itself as an expression of preference. Preferences still matter whether or not they are based on self-interest or on moral or political judgment.

This view expresses what many economists believe. "The modern theory of social choice," writes W. Michael Hanemann, "considers it immaterial whether preferences reflect selfish interest or moral judgment."[108] This view goes back at least to Kenneth Arrow's observation: "It is not assumed here that an individual's attitude toward different social states is determined exclusively by commodity bundles which accrue to his lot under each.... [T]he individual orders all social states by whatever standards he deems relevant."[109]

Let us drop the reference to welfare or well-being, then, from the fundamental thesis of environmental economics. We are left, then, with the idea that preferences, as weighed or ranked by WTP, should be satisfied insofar as the resource base allows. "In this framework, preferences are treated as data of the most fundamental kind," writes economist Alan Randall.[110] "Value, in the economic sense, is ultimately derived from individual preferences."[111]

What sort of value can be derived from preferences? If we no longer refer to welfare or well-being, it is hard to understand why the satisfaction of preferences, weighed by WTP, matters. Plainly, individuals should have the greatest freedom possible, consistent with the like freedom of others, to try to satisfy their preferences, promote their beliefs, and vindicate their values both in markets and through democratic political processes. The statement that people should be free to pursue their own goals through social institutions that are equitable and open expresses a piety nobody denies.[112]

The thesis that social policy should aim at satisfying people's preferences, in contrast, expresses a dogma of welfare economics for which no good argument can be given. Having a preference may give the individual a reason to try to satisfy it, and he or she should have the greatest freedom to do so consistent with the like freedom of others. Absent a reference to a meaningful social goal such as welfare or well-being, however, what reason has society to try to satisfy that preference?

The idea that preferences should be satisfied just because or insofar as people are willing to pay to satisfy them[113] creates two problems for economists. First, they must explain why their own policy preferences, e.g., for efficient outcomes, should not be assessed or evaluated on the same WTP basis as the judgments or beliefs of others. Economists would also have to show why the satisfaction of preferences, even those preferences having no relation to well-being, is a good thing. Why should preferences count on a WTP basis rather than, say, in relation to the reasons or purposes that underlie them or in relation to the consequences, e.g., for welfare, of their satisfaction?

Consider, first, the way society evaluates policy proposals put forward by economists. Economists expect public officials to consider these proposals on their merits. Why should these officials, however, treat the views economists defend any differently from those put forward by other citizens? If society uses WTP to evaluate the views or judgments of some citizens, it should apply the same measure to all. A CV study of economist WTP for efficiency in the allocation of resources might be needed to assess the validity of this proposal on the same basis as that of any other policy preference.

Consider, second, the idea that it is a good thing that people's preferences be satisfied on a WTP basis, no matter how they are formed or what is gained by satisfying them. To test this theory, let us suppose that a visitor to Gettysburg suggests that the Park Service rebuild the Stuckey's Restaurant with its parking lots in the middle of the area where Longstreet attacked. This citizen might argue that since Longstreet himself may have dined there, the restaurant should be restored as part of the original battlefield.

Odd notions of this sort are not uncommon. One visitor to Gettysburg expressed amazement "that so many important battles had occurred on Park Service land. Another visitor expressed skepticism about a guide's description of the fierce fighting because there are no bullet marks on the monuments."[114] Silly ideas may lead people to propose silly policies. If the satisfaction of preference ranked by WTP is all that matters, then these proposals would be just as valid as those offered by Civil War historians. The WTP of those ignorant of history would be every bit as good as, possibly greater than, the WTP of those steeped in the lore of Gettysburg.

The idea that society use WTP as the standard by which to judge the merit of policy proposals defies common sense. We do not measure the worthiness of political candidates and their positions by toting up the campaign contributions they attract. On the contrary, those candidates able to raise the most money appear to be the most beholden to special interests. A recent survey revealed that about "half of young adults believe that separation of races is acceptable...."[115] That individuals are willing to pay to segregate schools by race or to exclude non-Christians from office, however, would not make those policies any better. It would only make those individuals worse.

Democracy relies on deliberative discourse in public to evaluate policy options. The point of political deliberation in a democracy is to separate, on the basis of argument and evidence, more reasonable from less reasonable policy proposals. The Park Service held public meetings (but did not commission CV studies) to reevaluate its plan for Gettysburg. It sought out the opinions of those who knew the history of the place. As a result, it located the new facility in an area where no soldier had fallen.[116] The outcome of political and moral deliberation depends less on the addition of individual utilities than on the force of the better argument about the public interest.[117]

IX. Designing for Dilemmas

The students who attended the seminar cared about the environment. One student opined that society has an obligation to save old growth forests, which he thought intrinsically valuable. Another mentioned pollution in the Grand Canyon. She said we have a responsibility to keep the area pristine no matter who benefits from it. Another argued that even if a species had no economic use, it is wrong to cause its extinction. Another student proposed that the government should promote prosperity and try to give everyone an opportunity to share in a booming economy. She understood the importance of macroeconomic goals but saw no reason to apply microeconomic theory to social policy.

I framed this thought for the students in the following way. If an environmental agency tries to pursue an ethical goal, for example, to minimize pollution as a moral trespass, it may have to design for a particular kind of dilemma. It must pursue its moral mission only in ways that allow the economy to prosper.[118] The agency would have to accommodate macroeconomic indicators of economic growth such as levels of employment. Full employment, unlike the microeconomic efficiencies about which environmental economists theorize, does affect human welfare and happiness.[119]

How might an agency balance its zeal to control pollution with its need to accommodate economic activity? To suggest an answer, I drew a graph in which the x-axis represented incremental pollution reduction and the y-axis represented the "misery index," i.e., the sum of the current unemployment and inflation rates. One may argue that statutes like the Clean Air Act mandate pollution control to the "knee of the curve."[120] This is the area where the curve begins to go asymptotic because further reductions in pollution cause rapidly increasing increases in unemployment and inflation.[121]

The authors of the Clean Air Act may have hoped that technological innovation would continually push the "knee of the curve" farther out along the pollution-control axis.[122] On this reading, the statute requires the EPA to minimize pollution (as a form of coercion), rather than to optimize it (as an external cost). The EPA may adopt the "knee of the curve" as a moral principle to balance two intrinsically valuable but competing goals. One is to make the environment cleaner; the other is to allow the economy to expand.[123]

Environmental agencies can pursue their moral missions without invoking the tautologies of welfare economics. The Park Service, for example, did not commission a cost-benefit analysis to plan for Gettysburg. It assumed it had a duty to design the Visitor Center in a way that respects hallowed ground; within that mandate, it also has to provide for the education and basic needs of visitors. Similarly, the Fish and Wildlife Service has to collaborate with landowners to design Habitat Conservation Plans that protect species while allowing economic development to take place.[124] Sometimes, a collaborative group can find an inexpensive technical "fix," for example, by relocating the endangered creature to another habitat where it can live in peace.[125] A deliberative body representing "stakeholders" can often deal with a particular problem better than a governmental agency located in Washington.[126] The Clinton Administration has called for initiatives to "reinvent regulation" by devolving decisionmaking to such groups.[127]

Environmental agencies may find it difficult, however, to embrace an approach to regulation that relies on collaboration and deliberation rather than centralized science-based decisionmaking. The statutes under which these agencies operate, such as the Clean Air Act, tend to be so vague, so aspirational, and so precatory that they offer little or no guidance to an agency that has to answer the hard questions, such as how safe or clean or natural is enough.[128] The agency, in the absence of a meaningful political mandate, has to find some way to give its decisions legitimacy. It therefore cloaks its ethical determinations in the language of science. Environmental professionals, in their eagerness to speak truth to power, may encourage this reliance on their disciplines.

The problem, however, is that science has no moral truth to speak; it cannot say how safe, clean, or natural is safe, clean, or natural enough. Nevertheless, agencies defend moral and political decisions with arguments to the effect that, "The science made me do it."[129] Environmental agencies, though they must adopt regulations that are ethical at bottom, rarely, if ever, offer a moral argument or principle for Congress to review and citizens to consider and debate. Instead, agencies tend to use the best available science to answer moral and political questions it cannot possibly answer. And the environmental sciences—strained in this way well beyond their limits—lose credibility as a result.[130]

X. Retreat from Gettysburg

After the seminar, I chose a route out of Gettysburg that avoided the battlefield and, with it, the ghosts of the past. But my path was full of portents of the future. At a 110-acre site southeast of the battleground, which had served as a staging area for Union troops, I saw equipment gathered to construct the massive mall the Park Service had decided not to build. The developer, the Boyle Group of Malvern, Pennsylvania, according to its promotional literature, promises to erect an "authentic village" containing seventy outlet stores, an eighty-room country inn, and a large restaurant. According to the flyer, visitors to Gettysburg will find the village a refuge from the drudgery of touring the battlefield and learning its history. "History is about the only thing these millions of tourists take home," the promo states. "That's because there is no serious shopping in Gettysburg."[131]

Society can count on firms such as the Boyle Group to provide shopping as serious as anyone could want at Gettysburg and everywhere else. The nation does not have to elevate shopping and, with it, the allocation of goods and services to those willing to pay the most for them, to the status of legislation. Environmental laws state general moral principles or set overall goals that reflect choices we have made together. These principles and goals do not include the empty and futile redundancy of environmental economics—the rule that society should allocate resources to those willing to pay the most for them because they are willing to pay the most for those resources.

An agency, such as the Park Service, may engage in public deliberation to determine which rule to apply in the circumstances. The principle economists tout, net benefits maximization, is rarely if ever relevant or appropriate. At Gettysburg, the principle speaks for itself. "What gives meaning to the place is the land on which the battle was fought and the men who died there," as longtime Gettysburg preservationist Robert Moore has said. "Keeping the place the same holy place, that's what's important."[132]

NOTES

1 Abraham Lincoln, *The Gettysburg Address* (1863), reprinted in *Lincoln on Democracy* (Mario M. Cuomo and Harold Holzer eds., 1990), 307.

2 See George Will, "A Conflict over Hallowed Ground," *New Orleans Times-Picayune*, June 11, 1998, B7. For a brief description of the events, see Lisa Reuter, "Gettysburg: The World Did Long Remember," *Columbus Dispatch*, Dec. 5, 1999, 1G ("At the wheat field alone, 6000 men fell in 2½ hours. One soldier would later write, 'Men were falling like leaves in autumn; my teeth chatter now when I think of it.' So many bodies covered the field, remembered another, that a person could walk across it without touching the ground.").

3 See Rupert Cornwell, "Out of the West; Developers March on Killing Fields," *Independent* (London), Dec. 18, 1991, 10 (43,000 deaths in total).

4 The Kentucky Fried Chicken restaurant has long occupied the area near the monument and by now may have its own authenticity. Kentucky nominally never left the Union.

5 Will, *supra* note 2, B7.

6 See Michael Shaara, *The Killer Angels: A Novel* (1974). For details about the effect on the visitor load, see Will, *supra* note 2, B7.

7 For a description of the Park Service plan and its history, see Edward T. Pound, "The Battle over Gettysburg," *USA Today*, Sept. 26, 1997, 4A.

8 Stephen Barr, "Hill General Retreats on Gettysburg Plan," *Wash. Post*, Oct. 2, 1998, A25. See also Ben White, "Lawmaker Criticizes Plan for Gettysburg," *Wash. Post*, Feb. 12, 1999, A33.

9 See Brett Lieberman, "Park Service Unveils Revised Gettysburg Plan," *Plains Dealer* (Cleveland), June 19, 1999, 14A.

10 APCWS "Position on Proposed Gettysburg Development Plan" (statement by Denis P. Gal-

vin, Deputy Director, National Park Service, Feb. 24, 1998) (visited Mar. 26, 2000) <http://users.erols.com/va-udc/nps.html> [hereinafter Proposed Development Plan].

11 In fact, such a proposal is not as far-fetched as it sounds. See Heather Dewar, "Corporate Cash Eyed for Parks, Bill Puts Sponsorships at $10 Million Apiece," *Denver Post*, June 8, 1996, A1; "Parks May Get 'Official' Sponsors, Senate Measure Would Lure Corporate Bucks," *St. Louis Post-Dispatch*, June 9, 1996, 1A. This plan was much derided. See, e.g., Joshua Reichert, "Commercializing Our National Parks A Bad Joke," *Houston Chron.*, Sept. 23, 1996, 19.

12 From the perspective of welfare economics, a regulation is rational—it promotes the welfare of society—only if it confers on members of society benefits in excess of costs. Since the benefits and costs may well accrue to different individuals, welfare economists recognize two fundamental values in terms of which regulatory policy may be justified. The first is economic *efficiency*, which is to say, the extent to which total benefits of the policy exceed total costs. The second goal is *equity*, which is to say, the extent to which the distribution of costs and benefits is equitable or fair. For a presentation of this view, see generally Arthur M. Okun, *Equality and Efficiency: The Big Tradeoff* (1975). He writes, "This concept of efficiency implies that more is better, insofar as the 'more' consists in items people want to buy." *Ibid.*, 2.

13 Dollywood attracts about 2 million patrons annually and is open only during the warmer months. See *Dollywood* (visited Mar. 26, 2000) <http://company.monster.com/dolly/>.

14 "Proposed Development Plan," *supra* note 10.

15 See Lincoln, *supra* note 1.

16 See discussion *infra* Part VI.

17 John V. Krutilla, "Conservation Reconsidered," *Am. Econ. Rev.* Vol. 57 (1967): 777.

18 See, e.g., William D. Nordhaus and James Tobin, "Is Economic Growth Obsolete?" *Econ. Growth* Vol. 5 (1972): 1.

19 See generally William D. Nordhaus, *Invention, Growth, and Welfare: A Theoretical treatment of Technological Change* (1969).

20 See Daniel Yergin, *The Prize: The Epic Quest for Oil, Money, and Power* (1992), 22.

21 Robert M. Solow, "Is the End of the World at Hand?" in *The Economic Growth Controversy* (Andrew Weintraub et al. eds., 1973), 39, 53 [herinafter Solow, "End of the World"]. Solow sought to establish that technological change, rather than the resource base, is essential to economic production. See, e.g., Robert M. Solow, "A Contribution to the Theory of Economic Growth," *Q.J. Econ* Vol. 70 (1956): 65; Robert M. Solow, "Technical Change and the Aggregate Production Function," *Rev. Econ. & Stat.* Vol. 39 (1957): 312.

22 Solow argued that if the future is like the past, raw materials will continually become more plentiful. See Solow, "End of the World," *supra* note 21, 49.

23 Nordhaus and Tobin, *supra* note 18, 14. Many mainstream economists accept Solow's argument. As analyst Peter Drucker has written, "[w]here there is effective management, that is, application of knowledge to knowledge, we can always obtain the other resources." Peter Drucker, *Post Capitalist Society* (1993), 45. Others have argued that our technical ability to substitute resources for one another is so great that "the particular resources with which one starts increasingly become a matter of indifference. The reservation of particular resources for later use, therefore, may contribute little to the welfare of future generations." Harold J. Barnett and Chandler Morse, *Scarcity and Growth: The Economics of Natural Resource Availability* (1963), 11.

24 Krutilla, *supra* note 17, 777.

25 *Ibid.*, 778.

26 See Krutilla, *supra* note 17, 784. See also, e.g., V. Kerry Smith, "The Effect of Technological Change on Different Uses of Environmental Resources," *Natural Environments: Studies in Theoretical and Applied Analysis* (John V. Krutilla ed., 1972), 54, 54-87. Smith wrote, "advances in scientific knowledge and a mastery of techniques have been sufficiently pervasive and rapid to allow for an ever expanding supply of natural resource commodities at constant or falling supply prices." *Ibid.*, 54.

27 See World Bank, *World Development Report: 1992* (1992). This document contains a sustained argument against the views of ecological economics and defends the neoclassical assumption that, with technological advance and good government, resources do not limit growth.

28 See, e.g., Robert Costanza et al., "Goals, Agenda, and Policy Recommendations for Ecological Economics," *Ecological Economics: The Science and Management of Sustainability* (Robert Costanza ed., 1991), 1, 8 (arguing that we have "entered a new era" in which "the limiting factor in development is no longer manmade capital but remaining natural capital").

29 See, e.g., Edwin Mansfield, *Microeconomics: Theory and Applications* (2nd ed. 1976). Mansfield writes that economics is divided "into two parts: microeconomics and macroeconomics. Microeconomics deals with the economic behavior of individual units like consumers, firms, and resource owners; while macroeconomics deals with the behavior of economic aggregates like gross national product and the level of unemployment." *Ibid.*, 2.

30 See generally *The Theory of Market Failure: A Critical Examination* (Tyler Cowen, ed., 1988).

31 See A.C. Pigou, *The Economics of Welfare* (4th ed. 1932), 172-203.

32 See *ibid.*

33 Larry E. Ruff, "The Economic Common Sense of Pollution," *Pub. Interest* (Spring 1970): 69.

34 Since pollution is clearly a form of coercion rather than of exchange, to ask how much pollution society should permit is to ask how far one individual may use the person or property of another without his or her consent. Nothing in our law, shared ethical intuitions, or cultural history supports or even tolerates the utilitarian principle that one person can trespass upon another—indeed, should do so—whenever the benefits to society exceed the costs. See, e.g., United States v. Kin-Buc, Inc., 532 F. Supp. 699, 702-03 (D.N.J. 1982) (holding that the Clean Air Act preempts federal common law claims of nuisance for air pollution). See also William C. Porter, "The Role of Private Nuisance Law in the Control of Air Pollution," *Ariz. L. Rev.* Vol. 10 (1968): 107, 108-17.

The non-utilitarian basis of pollution control law is so obvious that, as Maureen Cropper and Wallace Oates observe, "the cornerstones of federal environmental policy in the United States," such as the Clean Air and Clean Water Acts, "*explicitly* prohibited the weighing of benefits against costs in the setting of environmental standards." Maureen L. Cropper and Wallace E. Oates, "Environmental Economics: A Survey," *J. Econ. Lit.* Vol. 30 (1992): 675.

35 For an illustrative example of this sort of reasoning, see E.B. Barbier et al., "Economic Value of Biodiversity," *Global Biodiversity Assessment* (V.H. Heywood ed., 1995), 823, 829 ("Moral or ethical concerns, like tastes and preferences, can be translated into a willingness to commit resources to conserve biodiversity.").

36 Krutilla, *supra* note 17, 781.

37 *Ibid.*

38 *See ibid.*, 783 (arguing that "while the supply of fabricated goods and commercial services may be capable of continuous expansion

from a given resource base by reason of scientific discovery and mastery of technique, the supply of natural phenomena is virtually inelastic"). Krutilla had to show, however, that technology cannot provide substitutes for natural phenomena (such as the Grand Canyon) as it can for natural resources. Krutilla apparently infers from the inelasticity of the supply of natural phenomena that technology cannot offer substitutes for them. This is obviously a non-sequitor. Technology can provide amusements—for example, IMAX® theater presentations of the Grand Canyon followed by a great party where one can meet celebrities—for which people may be willing to pay as much as to go to the Canyon itself. It is not clear, then, that inelasticities of supply bear on the question of whether technology can provide economic substitutes for intrinsically valuable objects of nature. Technology may provide goods and services for which people are willing to pay the same amount.

39 *Ibid.*, 778.

40 *Ibid.*, 783.

41 Carlyle Murphy, "A Spiritual Lens on the Environment; Increasingly, Caring for Creation Is Viewed as a Religious Mandate," *Wash. Post*, Feb. 3, 1998, A1.

42 Krutilla, *supra* note 17, 779.

43 *Ibid.*

44 "Market-determined prices," some economists claim, "are the only reliable, legally significant measures of value.... [T]he value of a natural resource is the sum of the value of all of its associated marketable commodities, such as timber, minerals, animals, and recreational use fees." Daniel S. Levy and David Friedman, "The Revenge of the Redwoods? Reconsidering Property Rights and the Economic Allocation of Natural Resources," *U. Chi. L. Rev.* Vol. 61 (1994): 493, 500-01 (discussing the possibility of WTP estimates for existence values).

45 Gettysburg here serves as an example of any moral decision that confronts society. Economists have applied the WTP criterion to adjudicate the most important moral decisions that confront society. For example, economists have argued that the decision to wage war in Vietnam represented not a moral failure or political failure, but a market failure. The decision to carry on the war failed to reflect the WTP demonstrators revealed, for example, in the travel costs they paid to protest against it. See generally Charles J. Cicchetti et al., "On the Economics of Mass Demonstrations: A Case Study of the November 1969 March on Washington," *Am. Econ. Rev.* Vol. 61 (1971): 179 .

Whatever the question, from segregation in housing to certain kinds of slavery, practices people oppose for moral reasons may also be characterized as objectionable for economic reasons, once the WTP of those opponents is factored into the cost-benefit analysis. See generally Duncan Kennedy, "Cost-Benefit Analysis of Entitlement Problems: A Critique," *Stan. L. Rev.* Vol. 33 (1981): 387.

Microeconomists sometimes seem to hold that WTP can adjudicate all questions of truth, beauty, and justice. The use of WTP or utility "to measure preferences can be applied quite generally," three economists explain. "Utility or preference exists for any activity in which choice is involved, although the choices may themselves involve truth, justice, or beauty, just as easily as the consumption of goods and services." Jonathan A. Lesser et al., *Environmental Economics and Policy* (1997), 42.

46 That is, the quandary involved in finding a subject matter for environmental economics to study when mainstream economics had determined that natural resources could be taken for granted.

47 The high-water mark of this approach to environmental evaluation may be found in Rob-

ert Costanza et al., "The Value of the World's Ecosystem Services and Natural Capital," *Nature* Vol. 387 (1997): 253 (estimating the economic benefits of the world's ecosystem services and natural capital at $33 trillion per year).

48 See, e.g., Pete Morton, "The Economic Benefits of Wilderness: Theory and Practice," *Denv. U. L. Rev.* Vol. 76 (1999): 465. ("While steadfastly acknowledging that the economic benefits of wilderness will never be fully quantified, without at least qualitatively describing and understanding these benefits, politicians and public land managers will continue to make policy decisions that shortchange wilderness in public land management decisions.") Some environmentalists question the use of contingent valuation largely for technical reasons. See, e.g., Kristin M. Jakobsson and Andrew K. Dragun, *Contingent Valuation and Endangered Species* (1996), 78-82.

49 For examples of this research agenda, see *Valuing Natural Assets: The Economics of Natural Resource Damage Assessments* (Raymond J. Kopp and V. Kerry Smith eds., 1993).

50 For a good review of the literature, see generally A. Myrick Freeman III, *The Benefits of Environmental Improvement: Theory and Practice* (1979).

51 See Krutilla, *supra* note 17, 779 n.7 (describing environmentalists as having subjective reactions to, rather than objective opinions about, the loss of a species or the disfiguring of an environment).

52 For a general statement and defense of the position of welfare economics in environmental policy, see Daniel C. Esty, "Toward Optimal Environmental Governance," *N.Y.U. L. Rev.* Vol. 74 (1999): 1495. See also Louis Kaplow and Steven Shavell, "Property Rules Versus Liability Rules: An Economic Analysis," *Harv. L. Rev.* Vol. 109 (1996): 715, 725 (taking the cost-benefit balance to define ideal regulation).

53 Edith Stokey and Richard Zeckhauser, *A Primer for Policy Analysis* (1978), 277.

54 A. Myrick Freeman III, *The Measurement of Environmental Resource Values* (1993), 6.

55 Eban S. Goodstein, *Economics and the Environment* (2nd ed. 1999), 24.

56 Commentators generally refer to this idea as the principle of consumer sovereignty. For a general statement of how this principle fits within the foundations of economic theory, see Martha Nussbaum, "Flawed Foundations: The Philosophical Critique of (a Particular Type of) Economics," *U. Chi. L. Rev.* Vol. 64 (1997): 1197, 1197-98.

57 Freeman, *supra* note 54, 6.

58 For a discussion of Ford's beliefs, see Roland Marchand, *Advertising the American Dream: Making Way for Modernity, 1920-1940,* (1985), 118, 156-58.

59 Following social choice theory, economists apply the principle of consumer sovereignty to all views but their own—in other words, they regard everyone else as having wants rather than ideas. For the classic statement of this position, see Joseph Schumpeter, "On the Concept of Social Value," *Q.J. Econ.* Vol. 23 (1909): 213, 214-17.

60 See, e.g., Allen V. Kneese and Blair T. Bower, "Introduction," *Environmental Quality Analysis: Theory and Method in the Social Sciences* (Allen V. Kneese and Blair T. Bower eds., 1972), 3-4.

61 See Kennedy, *supra* note 45, 401-21.

62 Critics of Krutilla's approach charged that it came primarily "from economists desperately eager to play a more significant role in environmental policy and environmental groups seeking to gain the support of conservatives." Fred L. Smith, Jr., "A Free-Market Environmental Program," *Cato J.* Vol. 11 (1992): 457, 468 n. 15.

63 Freeman, *supra* note 54, 7.

64 *Ibid.*

65 Robert D. Rowe and Lauraine G. Chestnut, *The Value of Visibility: Theory and Application* (1982), 9. Economists often use consumer surplus as the appropriate measure of economic value in calculating the benefits associated with environmental improvements. See, e.g., Richard E. Just et al., *Applied Welfare Economics and Public Policy* (1982), 69-83; John R. Stoll et al., "A Framework for Identifying Economic Benefits and Beneficiaries of Outdoor Recreation," *Pol'y Stud. Rev.* Vol. 7 (1987): 443, 445-48.

66 Environmental economists typically ground economic valuation in the moral theory or utilitarianism according to which happiness has intrinsic value. As Goodstein points out, the "moral foundation underlying economic analysis, which has as its goal human happiness or utility, is known as utilitarianism." Goodstein, *supra* note 55, 24.

67 Paul Milgrom, "Is Sympathy an Economic Value? Philosophy, Economics, and the Contingent Valuation Method," *Contingent Valuation: A Critical Assessment* (J.A. Hausman ed., 1993), 417, 431.

68 Even if Krutilla were correct about what people want, namely a sense of satisfaction, this would not serve to justify the CV approach. One would then need to distinguish between the value of the policy option (which CV is supposed to measure) and the value of the expected moral satisfaction (which people are supposed to want). For further discussion of the possibility that WTP estimates in contingent valuation studies refer to the value not of a policy but of a state of moral satisfaction, see Daniel Kahneman and Jack L. Knetsch, "Valuing Public Goods: The Purchase of Moral Satisfaction," *J. Envtl. Econ. & Mgmt.* Vol. 22 (1992): 57, 57-70.

69 Krutilla, *supra* note 17, 779.

70 *Ibid.*, 781.

71 One can understand this argument in terms of an ambiguity between two senses—one logical, the other psychological—in the term "satisfaction." To satisfy a preference in the logical sense is to meet or fulfill it; this is the sense in which equations and conditions are satisfied. To satisfy a person in the psychological sense is to cause contentment or a feeling of well-being. Krutilla seems to have assumed that to satisfy a preference in the logical sense is to cause a psychological sense of satisfaction. Nothing justifies this inference.

72 For commentaries, see generally John F. Daum, "Some Legal and Regulatory Aspects of Contingent Valuation," *Contingent Valuation: A Critical Assessment, supra* note 67, 389; William H. Desvousges et al., "Measuring Natural Resource Damages with Contingent Valuation: Tests of Validity and Reliability," *Contingent Valuation: A Critical Assessment, supra* note 67, 91.

73 James R. Kahn, *The Economic Approach to Environmental and Natural Resources* (2nd ed. 1998), 102.

74 Lesser et al., *supra* note 45, 282.

75 *Ibid.*

76 Tom Tietenberg, *Environmental and Natural Resource Economics* (5th ed. 2000), 37.

77 Tom Tietenberg, *Environmental Economics and Policy* (1994), 62-63.

78 D.A. Schkade and J.W. Payne, "How People Respond to Contingent Valuation Questions: A Verbal Protocol Analysis of Willingness to Pay for an Environmental Regulation," *J. Envtl. Econ. & Mgmt.* Vol. 26 (1994): 88, 89.

79 *Ibid.*

80 Barbier et al., *supra* note 35, 836.

81 *Ibid.*, 836 (citing Amartya Sen, "Rational Fools: A Critique of the Behavior Foundations of Economic Theory," *Phil. & Pub. Aff.* Vol. 16 (1977): 317.

82 *Ibid.*

83 *Ibid.* The authors nicely summarize the question as follows: "Indeed, the debate over environmental values often turns on whether

values are considered as ethical judgements or equivalence measures, i.e. whether environmental values are statements of principle or a reflection of social costs." *Ibid.*, 829. This question should be asked of the value assumptions of economic theory, e.g., that society should maximize net benefits. Is this a statement of principle or a reflection of social costs? If the former, why is this not true of every other opinion as well?

84 R. Blamey et al., "Respondents to Contingent Valuation Surveys: Consumers or Citizens?," *Australian J. Agric. Econ.* Vol. 39 (1995): 263, 285.

85 Daniel A. Farber and Paul A. Hemmersbaugh, "The Shadow of the Future: Discount Rates, Later Generations, and the Environment," *Vand. L. Rev.* Vol. 46 (1993): 267, 301.

86 See Ronald Dworkin, *Life's Dominion: An Argument About Abortion, Euthanasia, and Individual Freedom* (1993), 69-77.

87 *Ibid.*, 71-72. See also *ibid.*, 75-77 (discussing the preservation of animal species).

88 *Ibid.*, 69-70.

89 Experiments show again and again that responses to CV questionnaires express what the individual believes to be good in general or good for society and not—as the CV methods seek to determine—what individuals believe is good for *them*. See, e.g., Thomas H. Stevens et al., "Measuring the Existence Value of Wildlife: What Do CVM Estimates Really Show?," *Land Econ.* Vol. 67 (1991): 390; Thomas H. Stevens et al., "Measuring the Existence Value of Wildlife: Reply," *Land Econ.* Vol. 69 (1993): 309.

90 Some economists agree and write: "[I]t may be inappropriate to use the [contingent valuation methodology] as an input to [benefit cost analysis] studies, unless means can be found to extract information on consumer preferences from data predominantly generated by citizen judgments." Blamey et al., *supra* note 85, 285.

91 Kerry Turner et al., *Environmental Economics: An Elementary Introduction* (1993), 38.

92 Goodstein, *supra* note 55, 24.

93 In fact, these states per se lack intrinsic value. Their value inheres in their appropriateness to the circumstances in which they arise. The joy sadists take in the pain of others, for example, has no positive value, intrinsic or otherwise; it is bad, not good. The sadness one feels in sympathy with others, in contrast, although a pain, possesses intrinsic value. Pleasure and pain have value insofar as they function cognitively, that is, as ways of knowing the moral qualities of the world. Pleasure and pain are both valuable, then, insofar as ways of knowing—knowledge being the ultimate intrinsic good.

94 See Ed Diener et al., "The Relationship Between Income and Subjective Well-Being: Relative or Absolute?," *Soc. Indicators Res.* Vol. 28 (1992): 253, 253-81 (finding that that people whose incomes went up, down, or stayed about the same over a 10-year period had approximately the same levels of subjective well being). See also Ruut Veenhoven, "Is Happiness Relative?," *Soc. Indicators Res.* Vol. 24 (1991): 1, 1-32.

95 See Michael Argyle, *The Psychology of Happiness* (1987), 102-06; Richard A. Easterlin, "Does Economic Growth Improve the Human Lot? Some Empirical Evidence," *Nations and Households in Economic Growth: Essays in Honor of Moses Abramovitz* (Paul A. David and Melvin W. Reder eds., 1974), 89, 106. See also generally F.E. Trainer, *Abandon Affluence* (1985); Paul Wachtel, *The Poverty of Affluence* (1989).

96 See David G. Myers, *Exploring Psychology* (3rd ed. 1996), 346-50. For all kinds of citations and charts, see "The Study of Happiness" (visited Mar. 26, 2000) <http://www.hope.edu/academic/psychology/myerstxt/happy/happy2.html/>.

97 See Michael Argyle and Maryanne Martin, "The Psychological Causes of Happiness," *Sub-*

jective Well-Being: An Interdisciplinary Perspective (Fritz Strack et al. eds., 1989), 77; Paul Krugman, "A Good Reason Growth Doesn't Necessarily Make Us Happier," *Ariz. Daily Star*, Apr. 2, 2000, F2.

98 See generally P.D. Rickman et al., "Lottery Winners and Accident Victims: Is Happiness Relative?," *J. Personality & Soc. Psych.* Vol. 36 (1978): 917; Mary Jordan, "Millions Don't Turn Everything To Gold: Many Lottery Winners Keep Same Jobs, Cars," *Wash. Post*, July 21, 1991, A1.

99 Argyle, *supra* note 95, 144.

100 Ed Diener et al., "Happiness of the Very Wealthy," *Soc. Indicators Res.* Vol. 16 (1985): 263, 263.

101 See Krugman, *supra* note 97, F2; Robert E. Lane, "Does Money Buy Happiness?," *Pub. Interest*, Fall 1993, 56-65.

102 For a general discussion, see Jonathan Freedman, *Happy People: What Happiness Is, Who Has It, and Why* (1978).

103 See Fred Hirsch, *Social Limits to Growth* (1976). See also generally Tibor Scitovsky, *The Joyless Economy* (1976); Robert H. Frank, "Frames of Reference and the Quality of Life," *Am. Econ. Rev.* Vol. 79 (1989): 80.

104 "Hey, I'm Terrific," *Newsweek*, Feb. 17, 1992, 46.

105 Richard Posner, *The Economics of Justice* (1981), 60.

106 Freeman, *supra* note 50, 3.

107 Tietenberg, *supra* note 76, 20.

108 W. Michael Hanemann, "Contingent Valuation and Economics," *Environmental Valuation: New Perspectives* (K.G. Willis and J.T. Corkindale eds., 1995), 79, 105.

109 Kenneth J. Arrow, *Social Choice and Individual Values* (2nd ed. 1963), 17.

110 Alan Randall, *Resource Economics: An Economic Approach to Natural Resource and Environmental Policy* (1981), 156.

111 *Ibid.*

112 Notice that in denying that society should adopt preference-satisfaction as a goal of social policy, one implies nothing whatever about paternalism. A paternalistic policy would prevent individuals from making certain choices, e.g., with respect to the consumption of drugs. The argument offered here is consistent with the largest libertarian tolerance for this sort of choice. It extends only to social policy, to the goals the government pursues, not to anything the individual might do in his or her private life.

113 For discussion of this concept in the larger context of political theory, see generally Cass R. Sunstein, "Naked Preferences and the Constitution," *Colum. L. Rev.* Vol. 84 (1984): 1689.

114 Will, *supra* note 2, B7.

115 J. Balz, "Separation of Races Found OK by Many Young People," *L.A. Times*, Aug. 17, 1999, A10.

116 See Elizabeth Stead Kaszubski, Letter to the Editor, "Park Plan Honors 'Hallowed Ground,'" *USA Today*, June 24, 1999, 14A (describing the events that transpired at the spot where the Park Service proposed to build its new Visitors' Center).

117 See generally Jürgen Habermas, *Justification and Application: Remarks on Discourse Ethics* (Ciaran Cronin trans., 1993).

118 A regulatory agency can take important macroeconomic indicators of prosperity into account while paying no attention to the concepts of microeconomics, such as marginal benefits and costs. The microeconomic concepts central to environmental economics—such as allocatory efficiency, net benefits, utility, and externality—have no clear relation, empirical or conceptual, to macroeconomic goals such as prosperity, full employment, and low inflation. Microeconomic efficiency has little or nothing to do with macroeconomic performance. See

generally *Microeconomic Efficiency and Macro-economic Performance* (David Shepherd et al. eds., 1983).

119 According to research summarized at the Mining Company's Economics web site, people's reported happiness, as measured by the annual United States General Social Survey, correlates negatively with the misery index, the sum of inflation and unemployment rates. See "Economics and Happiness" (visited Mar. 26, 2000) <http://economics.tqn.com/finance/economics/library/weekly/aa051498.htm>.

120 Interpreted in this light, technology-forcing statutes, such as the Clean Air Act, attempt to achieve as much environmental improvement as possible without hobbling the performance of the economy. The EPA, since it has to defend its policies politically, must take costs into account, where "costs" are understood in macroeconomic terms, e.g., terms of inflation and unemployment. The agency would not consider "costs" in the microeconomic sense of changes in net welfare or utility. Plainly, people consider the performance of the economy, i.e., prosperity, important enough that agencies that threaten to undermine it are unlikely to succeed politically. This presents no reason, however, for an agency to bother with cost-benefit analysis. Microeconomic efficiency, which cost-benefit analysis measures, has never been shown to have any relation to macroeconomic performance. See Sidney A. Shapiro and Thomas O. McGarity, "Not So Paradoxical: The Rationale for Technology-Based Regulation," *Duke L. J.* (1991): 729, 741-42 (arguing that the "willingness to pay" criterion does not provide the context for understanding the economic rationality of health-based environmental standards).

121 For a macroeconomic approach to assessing costs of environmental regulation, see Paul R. Portney, "Economics and the Clean Air Act," reprinted in *Cong. Rec.* Vol. 136 *H12911.01*, *H12916* (Oct. 26, 1990).

122 See Nicholas A. Ashford, "Understanding Technological Responses of Industrial Firms to Environmental Problems: Implications for Government Policy," *Environmental Strategies for Industry* (Kurt Fischer and Johan Schot eds., 1993), 282.

123 See American Trucking Ass'n v. EPA, 175 F.3d 1027, 1035-39, 1051-53 (D.C. Cir. 1999), modified on reh'g, 195 F.3d 4 (D.C. Cir. 1999), petition for cert. filed, Feb. 28, 2000 (No. 99-1442).

124 See generally A. Dan Tarlock, "The Creation of New Risk Sharing Water Entitlement Regimes: The Case of the Truckee-Carson Settlement," *Ecology L.Q.* Vol. 25 (1999): 674 (1999) (discussing collateral habitat conservation plans); A. Dan Tarlock, "Biodiversity Federalism," *Md. L. Rev.* Vol. 54 (1995): 1315 (surveying place-based environmental decision making).

Courts have required that agencies open decision-making processes to public participation. See, e.g., Scenic Hudson Preservation Conference v. Federal Power Comm'n, 354 F.2d 608, 616 (2d Cir. 1965) (stating that the Federal Power Commission should solicit public comment on aesthetic, conservation, and recreational interests). For a critical view of participatory initiatives, see Jim Rossi, "Participation Run Amok: The Costs of Mass Participation for Deliberative Agency Decisionmaking," *Nw. U. L. Rev.* Vol. 92 (1997): 173 (citing the vast literature on public participation in the regulatory process).

125 See, e.g., Les Line, "Microcosmic Captive Breeding Project Offers New Hope for Beleaguered Beetle," *Orange County Reg.*, Sept. 28, 1996, A14 (reporting that it cost less than $10,000 to protect and restore the beetle).

126 For an excellent introduction, see generally Jody Freeman, "Collaborative Governance in

the Administrative State," *UCLA L. Rev.* Vol. 45 (1997): 1. See also generally Richard H. Pildes and Cass R. Sunstein, "Reinventing the Regulatory State," *U. Chi. L. Rev.* Vol. 62 (1995): 1; Lawrence E. Susskind and Joshua Secunda, "The Risks and the Advantages of Agency Discretion: Evidence from EPA's Project XL," *UCLA J. Envtl. L. & Pol'y* Vol. 17 (1998-99): 67. For theoretical commentary on collaborative rule-making, see Daniel Fiorino, "Toward a New System of Environmental Regulation: The Case for an Industry Sector Approach," *Envtl. L.* Vol. 26 (1996): 457; Douglas Michael, "Cooperative Implementation of Federal Regulations," *Yale J. on Reg.* Vol. 13 (1996): 535, 574-89. For criticism, see Rena I. Steinzor, "Regulatory Reinvention and Project XL: Does the Emperor Have Any Clothes?," *Envtl. L. Rptr.* Vol. 26 (1996): 10527.

127 See, e.g., William J. Clinton, "Memorandum, Regulatory Reinvention Initiative, Mar. 4, 1995," (visited Jan. 27, 1999) <http://www.pub.whitehouse.gov/urires/I2R?urn:pdi://oma.eop.gov.us/1995/3/6/2.text.1>. See also "EPA Emphasis on Stakeholder Process Exasperates Risk Experts," *Risk Policy Rep.*, Oct. 16, 1998, 6-7; John S. Applegate, "Beyond the Usual Suspects: The Use of Citizen Advisory Boards in Environmental Decisionmaking," *Indiana L.J.* Vol. 73 (1998): 901, 901-57.

128 Chief Justice William Rehnquist, reviewing the Occupational Safety and Health Act, described the phrase "to the extent feasible" as one of many examples of "Congress simply avoiding a choice which was both fundamental for purposes of the statute and yet politically so divisive that the necessary decision or compromise was difficult, if not impossible, to hammer out in the legislative forge." Industrial Union Dep't, AFL-CIO v. American Petroleum Inst., 448 U.S. 607, 687 (1980) (Rehnquist, C.J., concurring). He implored the Court to invali-

date the vague and precatory laws which support today's regulatory state. These statutes, he said, "violate the doctrine against uncanalized delegations of legislative power." *Ibid.*, 675. For discussion of the penchant of Congress to delegate hard choices to others, see for example John P. Dwyer, "The Pathology of Symbolic Legislation," *Ecology L.Q.* Vol. 17 (1990): 233.

129 As Judge Williams remarked in "American Trucking," "[I]t seems bizarre that a statute intended to improve human health would, as EPA claimed at argument, lock the agency into looking at only one half of a substance's health effects in determining the maximum level for that substance." American Trucking Ass'n v. EPA, 175 F.3d 1027, 1052 (D.C. Cir. 1999), modified on reh'g, 195 F.3d 4 (D.C. Cir. 1999), petition for cert. filed, Feb. 28, 2000 (No. 99-1442). The point here is that the EPA, by citing the "knee-of-the-curve" or any other moral basis for its decision, could meet the requirements that Judge Williams and democratic theory impose on them. Utterly mired in the progressive tradition, however, the EPA will not concede that it makes moral or political judgments but will hide these judgments behind a smokescreen of environmental science. Even the threat by the D.C. Circuit panel—that the EPA's interpretation of the statute might be voided for overdelegation unless the agency acknowledges the ethical judgments it makes and must make—is unlikely to dislodge the agency from its scientism.

130 For commentary, see Sheila Jasanoff, *The Fifth Branch* (1990), 1 (arguing that appeals to science should not "take the politics out of policymaking"); Bruce Bimber and David H. Guston, "Politics by the Same Means: Government and Science in the United States," *Handbook of Science and Technology Studies* (Sheila Jasanoff et al. eds., 1995), 554, 559; Sheila Jasanoff, "Research Subpoenas and the Sociology of

Knowledge," *Law & Contemp. Probs.* (Summer 1996): 95, 98-100 (describing the deleterious effect of the expectations of law on the community of scientists).

131 Pound, *supra* note 7, 4A.

132 *Ibid.* (quoting Robert Moore).

◆ ◆ ◆ ◆ ◆

KRISTIN SHRADER-FRECHETTE

A Defense of Risk-Cost-Benefit Analysis

Environmentalists often criticize science. They frequently argue for a more romantic, sensitive, holistic, or profound view of the world than science provides. William Bees, for example, criticizes economics on the grounds that it falls victim to scientific materialism; in his article in this volume, he says we need a new paradigm, other than economics, for achieving sustainable development. Similarly, Mark Sagoff, also writing in this text, criticizes the economic model of benefit-cost analysis and argues that it is not always the proper method for making environmental decisions. In particular, he criticizes benefit-cost analysis as utilitarian.

This essay argues that environmentalists' criticisms of science often are misguided. The criticisms err mainly because they ignore the fact that good science can help environmental causes as well as hinder them. Economic methods, for example, can show that nuclear power is not cost effective,[1] that it makes little economic sense to bury long-lived hazardous wastes,[2] and that biological conservation is extraordinarily cost effective.[3] One reason some environmentalists are antiscience or antieconomics—and ignore the way science can help environmentalism—is that they misunderstand science. They attribute flaws to science when the errors are the result

of how people use, interpret, or apply science, not the result of science itself. Rees, for example, criticizes economics as guilty of scientific materialism, yet this essay will show that economics (benefit-cost analysis) can be interpreted in terms of many frameworks, not just scientific materialism. Similarly, Sagoff criticizes benefit-cost analysis as utilitarian, yet this essay will show that the technique is neither *purely* utilitarian, nor utilitarian in a flawed way, because those who use benefit-cost analysis can interpret it in terms of Kantian values, not just utilitarian ones. If this essay is right, then the ethical problems with economics are not with the science itself but with us, humans who interpret and use it in biased ways. In other words, the real problems of economics are the political and ethical biases of its users, not the science itself. To paraphrase Shakespeare: The fault, dear readers, is not with the science but with ourselves, that we are underlings who use it badly.

Consider the case of risk-cost-benefit analysis and attacks on it. Risk-cost benefit analysis (RCBA), the target of many philosophers' and environmentalists' criticisms, is very likely the single, most used economic method, at least in the United States, for evaluating the desirability of a variety of technological actions—from building a liquefied natural gas facility to adding yellow dye number 2 to margarine. The 1969 National Environmental Policy Act requires that some form of RCBA be used to evaluate all federal environment-related projects.[4] Also, all US regulatory agencies—with the exception perhaps of only the Occupational Health and Safety Administration (OSHA)—routinely use RCBA to help determine their policies.[5]

Basically, RCBA consists of three main steps. These are (1) identifying all the risks, costs, and benefits associated with a particular policy action; (2) converting those risk, cost, and benefit values into dollar figures; and (3) then adding them to determine whether benefits outweigh the risks and costs. Consider the proposed policy action of coating fresh vegetables with a waxy carcinogenic chemical to allow them to be stored for longer periods of time. Associated with such a policy would be items such as the risk of worker carcinogenesis or the cost of labor and materials for coating the vegetables. The relevant benefits would include factors such as increased market value of the vegetables since the preservative coating would reduce spoilage and losses in storage.

Those who favor RCBA argue that this technique—for identifying, quantifying, comparing, and adding all factors relevant to an economic decision—ought to be one of the major considerations that any rational person takes into account in developing social policy. To my knowledge, no economist or policymaker ever has argued that RCBA ought to be the sole basis on which any social or environmental choice is made. Despite the fact that RCBA, an application of welfare economics, dominates US decision making regarding environmental and technological issues, it continues to draw much criticism. Economists, industrial representatives, and governmental spokespersons tend to support use of RCBA, but philosophers, environmentalists, and consumer activists tend to criticize its employment.

This essay (1) summarizes the three main lines of criticism of RCBA, (2) outlines arguments for objections to RCBA, (3) shows that the allegedly most devastating criticisms of RCBA are at best misguided and at worst incorrect, and (4) reveals the real source of the alleged deficiencies of RCBA. Let us begin with the three main criticisms of RCBA. These are objections to RCBA (1) as a formal method, (2) as an economic method, and (3) as an ethical method.

Objection 1: RCBA as a Formal Method

The most strident criticisms of RCBA (as a *formal* method for making social decisions) come from phenomenologically oriented scholars, such as Hubert and Stuart Dreyfus at Berkeley. They argue that, because it is a rigid, formal method, RCBA cannot

model all instances of "human situational understanding."[6] For example, say Stuart Dreyfus, Lawrence Tribe, and Robert Socolow, whenever someone makes a decision, whether about playing chess or driving an automobile, he or she uses intuition and not some analytic, economic "point count."[7] They claim that formal models like RCBA fail to capture the essence of human decision making. The models are too narrow and oversimplified in focusing on allegedly transparent rationality and scientific know-how. Rather, say Dreyfus and others, human decision making is mysterious, unformalizable, and intuitive, something close to wisdom.[8] This is because the performance of human decision making requires expertise and human skill acquisition that cannot be taught by means of any algorithm or formal method like RCBA.[9]

Moreover, say Robert Coburn, Amory Lovins, Alasdair MacIntyre, and Peter Self, humans not only do not go through any formal routine like RCBA, but they could not, even if they wanted to. Why not? Humans, they say, often can't distinguish costs from benefits. For example, generating increased amounts of electricity represents a cost for most environmentalists, but a benefit for most economists. Lovins and his colleagues also claim that people don't know either the probability of certain events, such as energy-related accidents, or the consequences likely to follow from them; they don't know because humans are not like calculating machines; they cannot put a number on what they value.[10]

Although these criticisms of RCBA are thought provoking, they need not be evaluated in full here, in part because they are analyzed elsewhere.[11] Instead, it might be good merely to sketch the sorts of arguments that, when developed, are capable of answering these objections to the use of RCBA. There are at least six such arguments.

The first is that, since Dreyfus and others merely point to deficiencies in RCBA without arguing that there is some less deficient decision method superior to RCBA, they provide only necessary but not sufficient grounds for rejecting RCBA. A judgment about sufficient grounds for rejecting RCBA ought to be based on a relative evaluation of all methodologic alternatives because reasonable people only reject a method if they have a better alternative to it. Showing deficiencies in RCBA does not establish that a better method is available.

A second argument is that Dreyfus, Tribe, Socolow, and others have "proved too much." If human decision making is unavoidably intuitive and its benefits are indistinguishable from costs, as they say, then no rational, debatable, nonarbitrary form of technologic policymaking is possible. This is because rational policymaking presupposes at least that persons can distinguish what is undesirable from what is desirable, costs from benefits. If they cannot, then this problem does not count against only RCBA but against any method. Moreover, Dreyfus and others ignore the fact that no policymaking methods, including RCBA, are perfect. And if not, then no theory should be merely criticized separately, since such criticisms say nothing about which theory is the least desirable of all.

Another argument, especially relevant to Dreyfus's claims that RCBA is not useful for individual tasks, such as the decision making involved in driving a car, is that many of the objections to RCBA focus on a point not at issue. That RCBA is not amenable to individual decision making is not at issue. The real issue is how to take into account millions of individual opinions, to make societal decisions. This is because societal decision making presupposes some unifying perspective or method of aggregating preferences of many people, a problem not faced by the individual making choices. Of course, accomplishing RCBA is not like individual decision making, and that is precisely why social choices require some formal analytic tool like RCBA.

Criticisms of RCBA as a formal method are also questionable because Dreyfus and others provide an incomplete analysis of societal decision making in making appeals to wisdom and intuition. They fail to specify, in a political and practical context, whose wisdom and intuitions ought to be followed and what criteria ought to be used when the wisdom and intuitions of different persons conflict in an environmental controversy. RCBA answers these questions in a methodical way.

A final argument against criticisms of RCBA, as a formal method, is that Dreyfus and others are incomplete in using policy arguments that ignore the real-world importance of making decisions among finite alternatives and with finite resources. Wisdom may tell us that human life has an infinite value, but the scientific and economic reality is that attaining a zero-risk society is impossible and that there are not enough resources for saving all lives. In dismissing RCBA, Dreyfus and others fail to give their answers to the tough question of what criterion to use in distributing environmental health and safety.[12] If we do not use RCBA, what informal method is a bigger help? That realistic question they do not answer. If not, RCBA may be the best method among many bad methods.

Objection 2: RCBA as an Economic Method

Although these six argument-sketches are too brief to be conclusive in answering objections to RCBA as a formal method, let us move on to the second type of criticism so that we can get to the main focus of this essay. Philosophers of science and those who are critical of mainstream economics, like Kenneth Boulding, most often criticize RCBA as a deficient economic method. Perhaps the most powerful methodologic attack on RCBA deficiencies focuses on its central methodologic assumption: Societal welfare can be measured as the algebraic sum of compensating variations (CVs). By analytically unpacking the concept of compensating variation, one can bring many RCBA deficiencies to light.

According to RCBA theory, each individual has a CV that measures the change in his or her welfare as a consequence of a proposed policy action. For example, suppose a university was considering raising the price of student parking permits from $200 per year to $400 per year and using the additional money to build a parking garage on campus. Suppose also that the university would decide whether this act or policy was desirable on the basis of the way it affected all the students. Raising the parking fees and building a garage would affect the welfare of each student differently, depending on her (or his) circumstances. According to economic theory, the CV of each student would measure her particular change in welfare. To find exactly how each student would measure her CV, her change in welfare because of the changed parking fees, we would ask her to estimate it. For example, suppose Susan drives to campus each day and has a part-time job off campus, so she cannot carpool or ride a bus because she needs her car to move efficiently between campus and work. Susan wants to have the parking garage, however, because she has to look nice in her part-time job. If the university builds the parking garage, she will not get wet and muddy walking to her car and will not have to spend 20 minutes searching for a parking place. If someone asked Susan to put a monetary value on paying $200 more per year for parking in a garage, she might say this change was worth an additional $100, and that, even if the fees increased by $300, would rather have the parking garage. That is, Susan would say her CV was +$100 because she would gain from the new plan. However, suppose Sally also drives to campus each day and suppose her welfare is affected negatively by the increase in parking fees and the proposed parking garage. Because Sally lives at an inconvenient location two hours away, she must drive to campus and park her car every day. But because she lives so far away, has no part-time job, and is going to school with savings, Sally wants to pay as little as possible for parking and prefers the existing muddy, uncovered parking lots. If someone asks Sally to put a monetary value on paying $200 more per year

for parking in a garage, she might say this change harmed her by $200. That is, Sally would say her CV was -$200. Economists who use RCBA believe that, in order to determine the desirability of building the parking garage and charging $200 more per year, they should add all the CVs of gainers (like Susan) and losers (like Sally) and see whether the gains of the action outweigh the losses.

Or consider the case of using CVs to measure the effects of building a dam. The CVs of some persons will be positive, and those of others will be negative. Those in the tourism industry might be affected positively, whereas those interested in wilderness experiences might be affected negatively. The theory is that the proposed dam is cost-beneficial if the sum of the CVs of the gainers can outweigh the sum of the CVs of the losers. In more technical language, according to economist Ezra Mishan, a CV is the sum of money that, if received or paid after the economic (or technologic) change in question, would make the individual no better or worse off than before the change. If, for example, the price of a bread loaf falls by 10 cents, the CV is the maximum sum a man would pay to be allowed to buy bread at this lower price. Per contra, if the loaf rises by 10 cents, the CV is the minimum sum the man must receive if he is to continue to feel as well off as he was before the rise in price.[13] Implied in the notion of a CV are three basic presuppositions, all noted in standard texts on welfare economics and cost-benefit analysis: (1) the compensating variation is a measure of how gains can be so distributed to make everyone in the community better off;[14] (2) the criterion for whether one is better off is how well off feels subjectively;[15] and (3) one's feelings of being well off or better off are measured by a sum of money judged by the individual and calculated at the given set of prices on the market.[16]

According to the critics of RCBA, each of the three presuppositions buys into the concept of a CV contains controversial assumptions.[17] The first presupposition, that CVs provide a measure of how to make everyone better off, is built on at least two questionable assumptions: Gains and losses, costs and benefits, for every individual in every situation can be computed numerically.[18] A second questionable assumption built into this presupposition is that employing an economic change to improve the community welfare is acceptable, even though distributional effects of this change are ignored. Many people have argued that the effect of this assumption is merely to make economic changes that let the rich get richer and the poor get poorer, thus reflecting the dominant ideologies of the power groups dominating society.

The second presupposition built into the notion of CV, that the criterion for whether one is better off is how one feels subjectively, as measured in quantitative terms, also embodies a number of doubtful assumptions. Some of these are that, as Kenneth Arrow admits, individual welfare is defined in terms of egoistic hedonism;[19] that the individual is the best judge of his welfare, that is, that preferences reveal welfare, despite the fact that utility is often different from morality;[20] that summed preferences of *individual* members of a group reveal *group* welfare;[21] and that wealthy and poor persons are equally able to judge their well-being. This last assumption has been widely criticized since willingness to pay is a function of the marginal utility of one's income. That is, rich people are more easily able to pay for improvements to their welfare than poor people are. As a consequence, poor persons obviously cannot afford to pay as much as rich persons in order to avoid the risks and other disamenities of technology-related environmental pollution.[22] That is why poor people are often forced to live in areas of high pollution, while wealthy people can afford to live in cleaner environments.

Continuing the analysis of CV, critics of RCBA point out that the third presupposition built into the notion of CV also involves a number of questionable assumptions. The presupposition that one's feelings of being better off are measured by money,

and calculated in terms of market prices, includes at least one highly criticized assumption—that prices measure values. This assumption is controversial on a number of grounds. For one thing, it begs the difference between wants and morally good wants. It also ignores economic effects that distort prices. Some of these distorting effects include monopolies, externalities, speculative instabilities, and "free goods," such as clean air.[23]

Because methodologic criticisms such as these have been a major focus of much contemporary writing in philosophy of economics and in sociopolitical philosophy, discussion of them is extremely important. However, economists generally *admit* most of the preceding points but claim that they have no better alternative method to use than RCBA. If their claim is at least partially correct, as I suspect it is (see the previous section of this essay), then many of the preceding criticisms of RCBA are beside the point. Also, both economists and philosophers have devised ways of avoiding most of the troublesome presuppositions and consequences of the assumptions built into the notion of compensating variation. Chief among these ways of improving RCBA are use of alternative weighting schemes and employment of various ways to make the controversial aspects of RCBA explicit and open to evaluation. Use of a weighting scheme for RCBA would enable one, for example, to "cost" inequitably distributed risks more than equitably distributed ones. Also, if one desired, it would be possible to employ Rawlsian weighting schemes for promoting the welfare of the least-well-off persons. One of the chief reforms, important for addressing the economic deficiencies of RCBA, would be to employ a form of adversary assessment in which alternative RCBA studies would be performed by groups sharing different ethical and methodologic presuppositions. Such adversary assessment has already been accomplished, with success, in Ann Arbor, Michigan, and in Cambridge, Massachusetts.[24] Hence, at least in theory, there are ways to avoid the major economic deficiencies inherent in RCBA.

Objection 3: RCBA as an Ethical Method

The most potentially condemning criticisms of RCBA come from the ranks of moral philosophers. Most of those who criticize RCBA on ethical grounds, as one might suspect, are deontologists who employ standard complaints against utilitarians. Philosophers, such as Alasdair MacIntyre and Douglas MacLean, claim that some things are priceless and not amenable to risk-benefit costing. Alan Gewirth argues that certain commitments—for example, the right not to be caused to contract cancer—cannot be traded off (via RCBA) for some utilitarian benefit.[25] In sum, the claim of these ethicist critics of RCBA is that moral commitments, rights, and basic goods are inviolable and incommensurable and hence cannot be "bargained away" in a utilitarian scheme like RCBA, which is unable to take adequate account of them and of values like distributive justice.

Of course, the linchpin assumption of the arguments of Gewirth, MacLean, and others is that RCBA is indeed utilitarian. If this assumption can be proved wrong, then (whatever else is wrong with RCBA) it cannot be attacked on the grounds that it is utilitarian.

Misguided Ethical Criticism of RCBA

RCBA is not essentially utilitarian in some damaging sense for a number of reasons. First of all, let's admit that RCBA is indeed utilitarian in one crucial respect: The optimal choice is always determined by some function of the utilities attached to the consequences of all the options considered. Hence reasoning in RCBA is unavoidably consequentialist.

Because it is unavoidably consequentialist, however, means neither that RCBA is consequentialist in some *disparaging* sense, nor that it is only consequentialist, both points that are generally begged by deontological critics of RCBA. Of course, RCBA is necessarily consequentialist, but so what? Anyone who follows some deontological theory and ignores consequences altogether is just as simplistic as anyone who focuses merely on consequences and ignores deontological elements. This is exactly the point recognized by Amartya Sen when he notes that Jeremy Bentham and John Rawls capture two different but equally important aspects of interpersonal welfare considerations.[26] Both provide necessary conditions for ethical judgments, but neither is sufficient.

Although RCBA is necessarily consequentialist, there are at least four reasons that it is not only consequentialist in some extremist or disparaging sense. *First*, any application of RCBA principles presupposes that we make some value judgments that cannot be justified by utilitarian standards alone.[27] For example, suppose we are considering which of a variety of possible actions (e.g., building a nuclear plant, a coal plant, or a solar facility) ought to be evaluated in terms of RCBA. A utilitarian value judgment would not suffice for reducing the set of options. It would not suffice for deciding which of many available chemicals to use in preserving foods in a given situation, for example, because we would not have performed the utility weighting yet. Usually we use deontological grounds for rejecting some option. For instance, we might reject chemical X as a food preservative because it is a powerful carcinogen and use of it would threaten consumers' rights to life.

Second, RCBA also presupposes another type of nonutilitarian value judgment by virtue of the fact that it would be impossible to know the utilities attached to an infinity of options because they are infinite. To reduce these options, one would have to make some nonutilitarian value judgments about which options not to consider. For example, suppose chemical Z (considered for preserving food) were known to cause death to persons with certain allergy sensitivities or to persons with diabetes. On grounds of preventing a violation of a legal right to equal protection, analysts using RCBA could simply exclude chemical Z from consideration, much as they exclude technically or economically infeasible options for consideration.

Also, in the course of carrying out RCBA calculations—one is required to make a number of nonutilitarian value judgments. Some of these are: (1) There is a cardinal or ordinal scale in terms of which the consequences may be assigned some number, (2) a particular discount rate ought to be used, (3) or certain values ought to be assigned to certain consequences. For example, if policymakers subscribed to the deontological, evaluative judgment that future generations have rights equal to our own, then they could employ a zero discount rate. Nothing in the theory underlying RCBA would prevent them from doing so and from recognizing this deontological value.

Third, one could weight the RCBA parameters to reflect whatever value system society wishes. As Ralph Keeney has noted, one could always assign the value of negative infinity to consequences alleged to be the result of an action that violated some deontological principle.[28] Thus, if one wanted to avoid any technology likely to result in violation of people's rights not to be caused to contract cancer, one could easily do so.

Fourth, RCBA is not necessarily utilitarian, as Patrick Suppes points out, because the theory could, in principle, be adopted (without change) to represent a "calculus of obligation and a theory of expected obligation"; in other words, RCBA is materially indifferent, a purely formal calculus with an incomplete theory of rationality.[29] This being so, one need not interpret only market parameters as costs. Indeed, economists have already shown that one can interpret RCBA to accommodate egalitarianism and intuitionism as well as utilitarianism.[30] More generally, Kenneth Boulding has eloquently demonstrated that economic supply-demand curves can be easily interpreted to fit even a benevolent or an altruistic ethical framework, not merely a utilitarian ethical framework.[31]

The Real Source of RCBA Problems

If these four arguments, from experts such as Suppes and Keeney, are correct, then much of the criticism of RCBA, at least for its alleged ethical deficiencies, has been misguided. It has been directed at the formal, economic, and ethical *theory* underlying RCBA, when apparently something else is the culprit. This final section will argue that there are at least two sources of the problems that have made RCBA so notorious. One is the dominant political ideology in terms of which RCBA has been interpreted, applied, and used. The second source of the difficulties associated with RCBA has been the tendency of both theorists and practitioners—economists and philosophers alike—to claim more objectivity for the conclusions of RCBA than the evidence warrants. Let's investigate both of these problem areas.

Perhaps the major reason that people often think, erroneously, that RCBA is utilitarian is that capitalist utilitarians first used the techniques. Yet, to believe that the logical and ethical presuppositions built into economic methods can be identified with the logical and ethical beliefs of those who originate or use the methods is to commit the genetic fallacy.[32] *Origins* do not necessarily determine *content*. And, if not, then RCBA has no built-in ties to utilitarianism.[33] What has happened is that, in practice, one *interpretation* of RCBA has been dominant. This interpretation, in terms of capitalist utilitarianism, is what is incompatible with nonutilitarian values. But this means that the problem associated with the dominant political ideology, in terms of which RCBA is interpreted, has been confused with RCBA problems. Were the methods interpreted according to a different ideology, it would be just as wrong to equate RCBA with that ideology.

Confusion about the real source of the problems with RCBA has arisen because of the difficulty of determining causality. The cause of the apparent utilitarian biases in RCBA is the dominant *ideology* in terms of which people interpret it. The cause is not the method itself. This is like the familiar point, which often needs reiteration, that humans, not computers, cause computer errors. Given this explanation, it is easy to see why C.B. MacPherson argues that there is no necessary incompatibility between maximizing utilities and maximizing some nonutilitarian value. The alleged incompatibility arises only after one interprets the nonutilitarian value. In this case, the alleged incompatibility arises only when one interprets utilities in terms of unlimited individual appropriations and market incentives.[34]

If the preceding view of RCBA is correct and if people have erroneously identified one—of many possible—interpretations of RCBA with the method, then obviously they have forgotten that RCBA is a formal calculus to be used with a variety of interpretations. But if they have forgotten that RCBA is open to many different interpretations, then they have identified one dominant political interpretation with RCBA itself, then they have forgotten that because of this dominant interpretation, RCBA is politically loaded. And if they have forgotten that they are employing a utilitarian *interpretation* that is politically loaded, then they probably have assumed that RCBA is objective by virtue of its being part of science.

Utilitarian philosophers and welfare economists have been particularly prone to the errors of believing that utilitarian interpretations of decision making are objective and value-free. Utilitarian R.M. Hare argues in his book, for example, that moral philosophy can be done without ontology;[35] he also argues that moral philosophy can be done objectively and with certainty, that there are no irresolvable moral conflicts;[36] and that objective moral philosophy is utilitarian in character.[37] Hare even goes so far as to argue that a hypothetical-deductive method can be used to obtain moral evaluations and to test them.[38] Hare, one of the best moral philosophers of the century, equates utilitarian tenets with value-free, certain conclusions obtained by the scientific method of hypothesis-deduction. His error here means that we ought not to be surprised that lesser minds

also have failed to recognize the evaluative and interpretational component in utilitarianism and in the utilitarian interpretations of RCBA. Numerous well-known practitioners of RCBA have argued that the technique is objective, and they have failed to recognize its value component.[39] Milton Friedman calls economics "objective,"[40] and Chauncey Starr, Chris Whipple, David Okrent, and other practitioners of RCBA use the same terminology; they even claim that those who do not accept their value-laden interpretations of RCBA are following merely "subjective" interpretations.[41]

Given that both moral philosophers and practitioners of RCBA claim that their utilitarian analyses are objective, they create an intellectual climate in which RCBA is presumed to be more objective, value-free, and final than it really is. Hence, one of the major problems with RCBA is not that it is inherently utilitarian but that its users erroneously assume it has a finality that it does not possess. It is one of many possible techniques, and it has many interpretations. Were this recognized, then people would not oppose it so vehemently.

Summary and Conclusions

RCBA has many problems. As a formal method, it suggests that life is more exact and precise than it really is. As an economic method, it suggests that people make decisions on the basis of hedonism and egoism. As an ethical method, people have interpreted it in utilitarian ways, in ways that serve the majority of people, but not always the minority.

Despite all these criticisms, RCBA is often better than most environmentalists believe. It is better because criticisms of RCBA often miss the point in two important ways. First, the criticisms miss the point that society needs some methodical way to tally costs and benefits associated with its activities. While it is true that RCBA has problems because of its being a formal, economic method, this criticism of it misses the point. The point is that we humans need some clear, analytic way to help us with environmental decision making. Most people would not write a blank check in some area of personal life, and no one ought to write a blank check for solving societal problems. Not using some technique like RCBA means that we would be writing a blank check, making decisions and commitments without being aware of their costs, benefits, and consequences. All that RCBA asks of us is that we add up all the risks, benefits, and costs of our actions. It asks that we not make decisions without considering all the risks, costs, and benefits. The point is that RCBA does not need to be perfect to be useful in societal and environmental decision making; it needs only to be useful, helpful, and better than other available methods for making societal decisions.

Second, criticisms of RCBA miss the point because they blame RCBA for a variety of ethical problems, mainly problems associated with utilitarianism. RCBA, however, is merely a formal calculus for problem solving. The users of RCBA are responsible for the capitalistic, utilitarian interpretation of it. If so, then what needs to be done is neither to abandon RCBA, nor to condemn it as utilitarian, but to give some philosophical lessons in the value ladenness of its interpretations. We need more ethical and epistemological sensitivity among those who interpret RCBA, and we need to recognize practical, political problems for what they are. The problem is with us, with our values, with our politics. The problem is not with RCBA methods that merely reflect our values and politics.

NOTES

1 K.S. Shrader-Frechette, *Nuclear Power and Public Policy* (Boston: Kluwer, 1983), 54-60.

2 K.S. Shrader-Frechette, *Burying Uncertainty* (Berkeley: University of California Press, 1993), 239-41.

3 K.S. Shrader-Frechette and E. McCoy, *Method in Ecology* (New York: Cambridge University Press, 1993), 175-85.

4 See Ian G. Barbour, *Technology, Environment, and Human Values* (New York: Praeger, 1980), 163-64.

5 Luther J. Carter, "Dispute over Cancer Risk Quantification," *Science* 203, no. 4387 (1979): 1324-25.

6 Stuart E. Dreyfus, "Formal Models vs. Human Situational Understanding: Inherent Limitations on the Modeling of Business Expertise," *Technology and People* Vol. 1 (1982): 133-65. See also S. Dreyfus, "The Risks! and Benefits? of Risk-Benefit Analysis," unpublished paper presented on March 24, 1983, in Berkeley, California, at the Western Division meeting of the American Philosophical Association. Stuart Dreyfus and his brother Hubert Dreyfus share the beliefs attributed to Stuart in these and other publications. They often coauthor publications. See, for example, S. Dreyfus and H. Dreyfus, "The Scope, Limits, and Training Implications of Three Models of.... Behavior," ORC 79-2 (Berkeley: Operations Research Center, University of California, February 1979).

7 S. Dreyfus, "Formal Models," op. cit., note 6, 161. See also Lawrence H. Tribe, "Technology Assessment and the Fourth Discontinuity," *Southern California Law Review* Vol. 46, no. 3 (June 1973): 659; and Robert Socolow, "Failures of Discourse," in D. Scherer and T. Attig, eds., *Ethics and the Environment* (Englewood Cliffs, NJ: Prentice Hall, 1983), 152-66.

8 S. Dreyfus, "Formal Models," op. cit., note 6, 161-63; and Douglas MacLean, "Understanding the Nuclear Power Controversy," in A.L. Caplan and H. Englehard, eds., *Scientific Controversies* (Cambridge: Cambridge University Press, 1983), Part 5.

9 S. Dreyfus, "The Risks! and Benefits?" op. cit., note 6, 2.

10 Peter Self, *Econocrats and the Polity Process: The Politics and Philosophy of Cost-Benefit Analy-*

sis (London: Macmillan, 1975), 70; Alasdair MacIntyre, "Utilitarians and Cost-Benefit Analysis," in D. Scherer and T. Attig, eds., *Ethics and the Environment*, op. cit., note 7, 143-45; and Amory Lovins, "Cost-Risk-Benefit Assessment in Energy Policy," *George Washington Law Review* Vol. 45, no. 5 (August 1977): 913-16, 925-26. See also Robert Coburn, "Technology Assessment, Human Good, and Freedom," in K.E. Goodpaster and K.M. Sayer, eds., *Ethics and Problems of the 21st Century* (Notre Dame: University of Notre Dame Press, 1979), 108; E. J. Mishan, *Cost-Benefit Analysis* (New York: Praeger, 1976), 160-61; Gunnar Myrdal, *The Political Element in the Development of Economic Theory*, Paul Steeten, trans. (Cambridge: Harvard University Press, 1955), 89; and A. Radomysler, "Welfare Economics and Economic Policy," in K. Arrow and T. Scitovsky, eds., *Readings in Welfare Economics* (Homewood, IL: Irwin, 1969), 89.

11 See K.S. Shrader-Frechette, *Science, Policy, Ethics, and Economic Methodology* (Boston: Reidel, 1985), 38-54. See also K.S. Shrader-Frechette, *Risk and Rationality* (Berkeley: University of California Press, 1991), 169-96.

12 Shrader-Frechette, *Science Policy*, op. cit., note 11, 36-54; K.S. Shrader-Frechette, *Risk and Rationality*, op. cit., note 11, 169-83.

13 Mishan, *Cost-Benefit Analysis*, op. cit., note 10, 391.

14 Ibid., 390.

15 Ibid., 309.

16 E.J. Mishan, *Welfare Economics* (New York: Random House, 1969), 113; see also 107-13.

17 For a more complete analysis of these points, see K.S. Shrader-Frechette, "Technology Assessment as Applied Philosophy of Science," *Science, Technology, and Human Values* Vol. 6, no. 33 (Fall 1980), 33-50.

18 M.W. Jones-Lee, *The Value of Life* (Chicago: University of Chicago Press, 1976), 3; and R. Coburn, "Technology Assessment," in K.E. Goodpaster and K.M. Sayer, eds., *Ethics and Problems of the 21st Century*, op. cit., note 10, 109. See also Oskar Morgenstern, *On the Accuracy of Economic Observations* (Princeton, NJ: Princeton University Press, 1963), 100-01.

19 Cited in V.C. Walsh, "Axiomatic Choice Theory and Values," in Sidney Hook, ed., *Human Values and Economic Policy* (New York: New York University Press, 1967), 197.

20 See R. Coburn, "Technology Assessment," in K.E. Goodpaster and K.M. Sayer, eds., *Ethics and Problems of the 21st Century*, op. cit., note 10, 109-10; Gail Kennedy, "Social Choice and Policy Formation," in S. Hook, ed., *Human Values and Economic Policy*, op. cit., note 19, 142; and John Ladd, "The Use of Mechanical Models for the Solution of Ethical Problems," in S. Hook, ed., *Human Values and Economic Policy*, op. cit., 167-68. See also Mark Lutz and Kenneth Lux, *The Challenge of Humanistic Economics* (London: Benjamin/Cummings, 1979). Finally, see Richard Brandt, "Personal Values and the Justification of Institutions," in S. Hook, ed., *Human Values and Economic Policy*, op. cit., note 19, 37; and John Ladd, "Models," in S. Hook, ed., *Human Values and Economic Policy*, op. cit., note 19, 159-68.

21 G. Kennedy, "Social Choice," S. Hook, ed., *Human Values and Economic Policy*, op. cit., note 20, 148, makes the same point.

22 Peter S. Albin, "Economic Values and the Values of Human Life," in S. Hook, ed., *Human Values and Economic Policy*, op. cit., note 19, 97; and M.W. Jones-Lee, *Value of Life*, op. cit., note 18, 20-55.

23 See J.A. Hobson, *Confessions of an Economic Heretic* (Sussex, England: Harvester Press, 1976), 39-40; and Benjamin M. Anderson, *Social Value* (New York: A.M. Kelley, 1966), 24, 26, 31, 162. See also Kenneth Boulding, "The Basis of Value Judgments in Economics," in S.

Hook, ed., *Human Values and Economic Policy*, op. cit., note 19, 67-79; and O. Morgenstern, *Accuracy of Economic Observations*, op. cit., note 18, 19. Finally, see E.J. Mishan, *Cost-Benefit Analysis*, op. cit., note 10, 393-94; and E.F. Schumacher, *Small is Beautiful* (New York: Harper, 1973), 38-49; as well as N. Georgescu Roegen, *Energy and Economic Myths* (New York: Pergamon, 1976), x, 10-14.

24 See Shrader-Frechette, *Science Policy*, op. cit., note 11, Chapters 8-9; Shrader-Frechette, *Risk and Rationality*, op. cit., note 11; and B.A. Weisbrod, "Income Redistribution Effects and Benefit-Cost Analysis," in S. Chase, ed., *Problems in Public Expenditure Analysis* (Washington, DC: Brookings, 1972), 177-208. See also P. Dasgupta, S. Marglin, and A. Sen, *Guidelines of Project Evaluation* (New York: UNIDO, 1972); and A.V. Kneese, S. Ben-David, and W. Schulze, "The Ethical Foundations of Benefit-Cost Analysis," in D. MacLean and P. Brown, eds., "A Study of the Ethical Foundations of Benefit-Cost Techniques," unpublished report done with funding from the National Science Foundation, Program in Ethics and Values in Science and Technology, August 1979.

25 Lovins, "Cost-Risk-Benefit Assessment," op. cit., note 10, 929-30; Douglas MacLean, "Qualified Risk Assessment and the Quality of Life," in D. Zinberg, ed., *Uncertain Power* (New York: Pergamon, 1983), Part V; and Alan Gewirth, "Human Rights and the Prevention of Cancer," in D. Scherer and T. Attig, eds., *Ethics and the Environment*, op. cit., note 7, 177.

26 Amartya K. Sen, "Rawls Versus Bentham," in N. Daniels, ed., *Reading Rawls* (New York: Basic Books, 1981), 283-92.

27 Ronald Giere, "Technological Decision Making," in M. Bradie and K. Sayre, eds., *Reason and Decision* (Bowling Green, OH: Bowling Green State University Press, 1981), Part 3, makes a similar argument.

28 Ralph G. Keeney mentioned this to me in a private conversation at Berkeley in January 1983.

29 Patrick Suppes, "Decision Theory," in P. Edwards, ed., *Encyclopedia of Philosophy*, Vol. 1 and 2 (New York: Collier-Macmillan, 1967), 311.

30 P.S. Dasgupta and G.M. Heal, *Economic Theory and Exhaustible Resources* (Cambridge: Cambridge University Press, 1979), 269-81.

31 K. Boulding, "Value Judgments," in S. Hook, ed., *Human Values and Economic Policy*, op. cit., note 23, 67ff.

32 Alexander Rosenberg makes this point in *Macroeconomic Laws* (Pittsburgh: University of Pittsburgh Press, 1976), 203.

33 Tribe, "Technology Assessment," op. cit., note 7, 628-29; MacLean, "Qualified Risk Assessment," op. cit., note 25, Parts 5 and 6; MacIntyre, "Utilitarian and Cost-Benefit Analysis," op. cit., note 10, 139-42; Gewirth, "Human Rights," op. cit., note 25, 177; and C.B. MacPherson, "Democratic Theory: Ontology an Technology," in C. Mitcham and R. Mackey, eds., *Philosophy and Technology* (New York: Free Press, 1972), 167-68.

34 See note 33.

35 R.M. Hare, *Moral Thinking* (Oxford: Clarendon Press, 1981), 6 (see also 210-11).

36 Ibid., 26.

37 Ibid., 4.

38 Ibid., 12-14.

39 See, for example, Chauncey Starr, "Benefit-Cost Studies in Sociotechnical Systems," in Committee on Engineering Policy, *Perspectives on Benefit-Risk Decision Making* (Washington, DC: National Academy of Engineering, 1972), 26ff.; Chauncey Starr and Chris Whipple, "Risks of Risk Decisions," *Science* Vol. 208, no. 4448 (1980), 1116-17; and D. Okrent and C. Whipple, *Approach to Societal Risk Acceptance Criteria and Risk Management*, Report no.

PB-271264 (Washington, DC: Department of Commerce, 1977), 10.

40 Milton Friedman, "Value Judgments in Economics," in S. Hook, ed., *Human Values and Economic Policy*, op. cit., note 19, 85-88.

41 See also note 39; K.S. Shrader-Frechette, *Risk Analysis and Scientific Method* (Boston: Reidel, 1985), especially 176-89; and Shrader-Frechette, *Risk and Rationality*, op. cit., note 11, 169-96.

◆ ◆ ◆ ◆ ◆

DEBORAH C. POFF

Reconciling the Irreconcilable: The Global Economy and the Environment

For the past decade, we have been listening to a number of inconsistent and irreconcilable recommendations for solving the serious economic and environmental problems in both domestic and international economies. Our current language with respect to the significant sea changes we have witnessed in the global economy over the past decade is filled with, to use that most appropriate euphemism of the 1980s, disinformation.

This discussion will focus on how the relationship among structural adjustment policies and practices, the business activities of transnational corporations and what Robert Reich has called "the coming irrelevance of corporate nationality" makes environmental sustainability impossible. To begin, a brief discussion of the global economy and its relation to the diminishing significance of national boundaries will set the context.

The Global Economy and the Erosion of Statehood

In their 1989 book, *For the Common Good*, Daly and Cobb argued that if Adam Smith were alive today, he would probably not be preaching free trade. Their argument is based on what they believe to have been a necessary commitment of the 18th century capitalist to a sense of community and to an identification with his own nationhood. On this point, Smith is perhaps most universally known. He states, "By preferring the support of domestic to that of foreign industry, he (i.e., the capitalist) intends only his own security; and by directing that industry in such a manner as its produce may be of the greatest value, he intends only his own gain, and he is in this, as in many other cases, led by an invisible hand to promote an end which was no part of his intention" (Smith, 1776, 423). Daly and Cobb argue that the cornerstone of the free trade argument, capital immobility, that factored so strongly into Smith's belief that the capitalist was committed to investing in his or her own domestic economy has been eroded by

> A world of cosmopolitan money managers and transnational corporations which, in addition to having limited liability and immortality conferred on them by national governments, have now transcended those very governments and no longer see the national community as their residence. They may speak grandly of the "world community" as their residence, but in fact, since no world community exists, they have escaped from community into the gap between communities where individualism has a free reign. (Daly and Cobb, 215)

These capitalists, as Daly and Cobb rightly note, have no disinclination to move their capital abroad for the slightest favourable preferential rate of return. The concern which Daly and Cobb articulate here is frequently posed as a question or series of questions.

For example, "with the globalization of the economy are we living in a world system in which national economies are merely vestigial remnants of modernity or the earlier industrial period?," or, "are nations as political and social regulatory systems necessary agents for global economic negotiation and cooperation?" And what we've had as answers to these questions is essentially political positioning in two oppositional camps. As MacEwan and Tabb (1989) summarize this debate,

> The extreme globalist position often carries the implication that no change is possible except on the international level, and since there is no political mechanism for such change—aside from that of formal relations among governments—oppositional political activity is easily seen as useless. On the other extreme, those who view the national economic system as a viable unit are led to formulate programs that ignore the importance of economic forces which transcend national boundaries. Such an outlook can lead to both unrealistic programs which fail because of capital's international flexibility and implicit alliances with reactionary nationalist groups to advocate, for example, increased "competitiveness." (24)

Now while I will later argue that both of these alternatives are inadequate. I'd like first to spend some time discussing how we've gotten into our current economic crisis and that means a brief sojourn into the world of structural adjustment, the world we have essentially been living in for much of the past decade.

Structural Adjustment

I am going to address structural adjustment only as a consequence of the debt crisis and the stagnation and economic insecurity of the 1980s. Those familiar with the literature on the current economic crisis

know that a complete picture starts with the Bretton Woods conference of 1944 which set guidelines for what was to become the International Monetary Fund and the International Bank for Reconstruction and Development (the World Bank as it is now known). Bretton Woods also guaranteed the dominance of the United States in the world economy. As Jamie Swift notes, "the US dollar, linked to gold, would be the world's most important reserve currency and the United States effectively became banker to the Western world, with the right to print and spend the principal currency" (82). What ensued in the next forty plus years is too complex to examine here. It is sufficient to note that during that time, Japan and Germany rebuilt, the United States faced with a growing trade deficit and budget deficits abandoned the gold standard, and an unprecedented exchange of world currency as commodities ensued. This was followed by extensive loans to third world countries. And with those loans went conditionality, that conditionality being structural adjustment.

Structural adjustment as the salvation from national and international economic insecurity was a natural by-product of the Reagan-Thatcher-Mulroney era posited as it is on an idealized nineteenth-century laissez-faire. It comes from, as Foster (1989) notes, a "renewed faith in the rationalizing effect of market forces in the face of economic stagnation" (281).

Structural adjustment involves, in fact, a number of complementary actions, all mutually targeted to producing on a global scale, a so-called level playing field. These actions include privatization, deregulation and liberalization of national economies. Much of this is familiar to Canadians for this is precisely what the Canadian government has been pursuing in concert with the Canadian-American Free Trade agreement and with the North American Free Trade Agreement. The impact of structural adjustment it is assumed will remove the supposed artificial obstacles and allow for the rational correction of the current crisis by removing the obstructions to natural market forces. Part of adjusting to create a level playing field, however, means, to quote Rosenberg (1986) "a weakened, restructured labour force with lowered expectations" (as quoted in Foster, 281). Thus, part of the restructuring for global competitiveness has meant deregulating or decertifying unions in the United Kingdom, New Zealand and elsewhere in the developed world. In the developing world, it has meant devalued domestic currencies, high unemployment, increased poverty and starvation, inflation of the cost of living and, as a strategy for global competitiveness, the establishment of free trade zones within a number of these countries.

Furthermore, within the developing nations all of these factors have lead to disproportionately increased poverty among women. This appears somewhat paradoxical given that much of this increase in poverty happened during the second half of the United Nations Decade for Women. However, since women are the poorest and most politically and economically vulnerable members of the global community (the UN 1980 data argued that women do two-thirds of the world's labour, earn one-tenth of the world's income and own one-one hundredth of the world's property), they also represent the largest so called surplus labour force. Hence we have the incongruity that while both nationally and internationally, more equity legislation was introduced into charters and constitutions and international agreements than ever before in recorded history, at the same time, the transnational corporations of advanced economies were utilizing the world's poor women as an avenue out of the stagnation of their own domestic economies by moving some of their operations to free trade zones. As Beneria (1989) states,

> The existence of a large pool of female labour at a world scale is being used to deal with the pressures of international competition, profitability crises, and economic restructuring that characterize the current reorganization of production. The availability of cheap female labour has also been an instrumental factor in the export-led policies of their world countries shifting from previous import-substitution strategies. (250)

The United Nations World Survey on Women (1989) concludes that "[t]he bottom line shows that, … economic progress for women has virtually stopped, social progress has slowed, social well-being in many cases has deteriorated and, because of the importance of women's social and economic role, the aspirations for them in current development strategies will not be met" (xiv).

Environmental Sustainability

Having briefly outlined the parameters of structural adjustment, we can now ask: "What does it mean for environmental sustainability?" Well, if it is not already evident, any attempt to repay debts and remain competitive in such a global market under such conditions is almost impossible for a third world country and increasingly difficult for developed nations like Canada. To look first at the seemingly more favourable conditions in Canada, consider that environmental protection in developed nations like our own is only a relatively recent phenomenon. Snider (1993) argues that even within the boundaries of a nation state, where a conflict arises between business interests and environmental protection, business wins. Thus, she states that both in Canada and the United States "environmental protection varies from poor to nonexistent, basically … because of the power of business" (194). When we add to this the power of transnational corporations which take on supernumerary roles, traversing the globe and engaging in negotiations that change the quality of life and laws in various domestic economies, we begin to realize the resistance which any attempt to protect the environment meets. To again quote Snider with respect to the situation in Canada,

> As with occupational health and protection laws, provinces and countries fear they will be at a competitive disadvantage if they strengthen environmental regulations unilaterally. Industries have always tried to minimize the costs of operation by moving to the cheapest locations they can find. Free trade between Canada and the United States has often resulted in industries from Canada and northern US states relocating to the less regulated south ... With an extension of the free trade agreement to Mexico, many can be expected to join the already extensive migration, ... taking advantage of cheap labour and lax environmental regulations there. (194)

In developing countries, the situation is exacerbated by the very nature of their so-called competitive edge as outlined by Snider (i.e., cheap labour, lax environmental regulations). The result of a heavy debt load, structural adjustment, and a radical change in the basis of domestic economies in third world nations guarantees that such nations cannot put the environment before economic survival. As Swift (1991) summarizes the problem,

> It is simply not possible to push the idea of sustainable development while insisting also on debt repayment, favourable access to minerals and agricultural resources for transnational corporations, and cuts in the public sector and lower levels of social spending by Third World governments. Such an economic model is bound to focus not on environmental safeguards but on achieving a better trade and payments balance—the kind of policy package known as "structural adjustment." The notion that the same ideologies of industrial growth that created the environmental crisis can bring about

"sustainable growth" is, in the end, not only puzzling but also dangerous. (215-16)

The perversity of food-aid distribution over the past decade to countries where predictably famine follows deforestation and desertification and developed nation dogooders attempt to teach starving people in the third world modern farming methods to previously agrarian peoples who destroyed their environment cash-cropping for markets in the developed world, is sufficiently mind-boggling as to make us search for alternative, more coherent explanations to the problem. Essentially, we have here three cycles of activity. The first is the externally imposed requirement within a third world country to move from traditionally agrarian subsistence farming to large-scale cash crop farming. This results in a cycle of famine. And this, in turn, results in foreign food-aid and the attempt by non-profit organizations from industrialized countries to bring modern agricultural farming methods to the famine-stricken area along with the food-aid as a means of eliminating starvation. The latter cycle is initially done in relative ignorance by well-intentioned individuals who are unaware that the cycle of famine was predictable engineered by previous development strategies. Rather, it assumed that there is an inability among poor nations to deal with what are believed to be natural disasters like famine in Ethiopia or flooding in Bangladesh. However, as Berlan (1989) notes these disasters are not caused by whims of nature. Nor are they caused by the ignorance of peoples who merely need instruction in ecological conservation. Rather, "Third World countries are caught up in a desperate and vicious process of destroying their natural resources simply to service debt and allow short-term survival" (222). And they are doing so because they have lost control of their domestic economy and of national self-governance. The environmental damage seems reminiscent and evocative. It brings to mind images of the pollution and environmental degradation which was endemic to the Industrial Revolution. The difference here is that the negotiations and damages incurred by development have been transnational in nature and have seemingly gone beyond the capacity of nation-states to effectively control. This is not just a difference in scale but a difference in kind. As Berlan summarizes the problem,

> Transnational companies are involved in all manner of hazardous ventures in Third World countries. They are building nuclear power plants, constructing massive dam projects, undertaking large mining and mineral-processing ventures, and investing in manufacturing that uses dangerous chemicals and produces hazardous wastes. In most Third World countries health and safety regulations inside plants are either non-existent or weak. Environmental standards to govern industry are just starting to be taken seriously. Most Third World governments are so desperate to attract investment that companies are in a good position to reduce their costs by saving on expensive pollution controls and health and safety equipment for workers. (221-22)

Such radical shifts in power from national economies to transnational corporations and supranational monetary funds has led some intellectuals to embrace a new political cynicism and existential ennui captured by the general heading, post-modernism. David Harvey summarizes this state as a loss of faith in progress, science and technology and a total agnosticism with respect to any political or collective solutions. At least psychologically, if not epistemologically, this is similar to the political inertia noted at the beginning of this paper, the position of the extreme globalist which "carries the implication that no change is possible except on the international level, and since there is no political mechanism for such change—aside from that of formal relations among governments—oppositional political activity is easily seen as useless" (x).

The Remnant State?

This brings us to the final questions; "Do we have both conceptually and factually or descriptively an erosion of nationhood or statehood?" And, if so, "What does this mean for such global problems as environmental sustainability?"

Robert Reich (1991) argues that it is no longer meaningful to speak of nations in terms of national economies because the emerging global economy has rendered those economies irrelevant. He states,

> As almost every factor of production— money, technology, factories, and equipment—moves effortlessly across borders, the very idea of an American economy is becoming meaningless, as are the notions of an American corporation, American capital, American products, and American technology. A similar transformation is affecting every other nation, some faster and more profoundly than others. (8)

This perspective is echoed in the discussion of national governance in the UN World Investment Report (1991). The report notes,

> One of the trends highlighted in the present volume is the growing regionalization of the world economy. National economies are becoming increasingly linked in regional groupings, whether through initiatives at the political level, as in the case of the integration of the European Community, or through activities at the private-sector level ... As described in this report, regionalization is one of the important factors behind the recent growth of foreign direct investment and its growing role in the world economies. (40)

For those concerned with Canada's involvement in free trade agreements and the protection of Canada's natural resources in those agreements, the question of Canadian sovereignty is central. As Bienefeld (1991) notes with respect to financial deregulation, "the political content of financial regulation is usually entirely neglected when the multilateral agencies stress the importance of international regulation while advocating national deregulation even though this means giving up a large degree of autonomy in domestic ... policy" (50). To this, Easter (1992) adds "In Canada, our true sovereignty as a nation is being lost as we replace political debate and decision-making for community goals, with the absolute rule of the market ... Almost all ... [good policies] ... are now being lost or rendered useless under the 'competitiveness' and 'open borders'" (93).

But there is something to remain cognizant of when we look at the literature on the loss of national economic autonomy and sovereignty and that is that it is nations that are the key agents in negotiating deregulation, privatization and free trade deals. In the worst literature on the globalization of the economy it is as if Adam Smith's invisible hand had been replaced by the invisible man for all we hear about are global economic forces that require structural adjustments.

Nation states which, in liberal democracies, we view as protectors of basic rights, both positive and negative, and basic civil liberties are, in fact, involved in global negotiations which may erode the very principles on which they are based. And this not only affects rights meant to ensure the quality of life, including the right to live in a clean and sustainable environment, within given nations but also diminishes the possibility for the growth of democracy and democratic rights on a global scale. As Foster points out, "as each state makes its economy leaner and meaner to enlarge its own internally generated profits and export the crisis to others, the stress on the world economy intensifies, and international cooperation—always a dim possibility—becomes more remote" (294). Interestingly, as regional deprivation within developed economies more and more mirrors the economies in developing nations, we witness what we previously only saw in countries, like India, where prior to Bhopal, the prime minister of the country was willing to put jobs at any cost before anything else; safety, environment, quality of work life, etc. As we add the nations of the former Soviet Union to this mix, we observe with seeming fatalism the bottom-rung position which both environmental protection and quality of life issues take in the turmoil of establishing political and economic security.

Not only, however, do forward-looking principles of rights and benefits get undermined as nation after nation positions for a competitive advantage that results in levelling to the lowest common denominator, but global negotiation coupled with financial deregulation and the development of information technology has resulted in unbridled corruption and crime. As chief financial officer of the Bank of Montreal noted,

> I can hide money in the twinkling of an eye from all of the bloodhounds that could be put on the case, and I would be so far ahead of them that there would never be a hope of unravelling the trail ... Technology today means that that sort of thing can be done through electronic means. (quoted in Naylor, 1987, 12)

In a related argument, Thomas (1989) claims that "the contradictory development of bureaucracy in the face of ideological assaults on the state ... includes a burgeoning growth of corruption, which has reached such staggering proportions that some social scientists see it as an 'independent productive factor'" (337).

With respect to the environment, this level of corruption coupled with desperation has been evidenced in the third world as nations vie for position to accept toxic waste from developed countries in contravention to international law.

So, does all of this mean that indeed the notion of statehood has shifted, diminished or been eroded? I would say unequivocally not. What has been eroded here is not statehood but democracy and the ability for citizens within democratic states to exercise democratic rights. Democracy has been undermined or subverted and people have been disempowered, but states have not. And this is not only true with respect to developed countries which have some type of democratic governance but it also bodes ominously for the establishment of new fledgling democracies. Not only is Canada less democratic to the extent that deregulation, privatization and economic liberalization has been accomplished, but to the extent that nations are willing to use such factors as economic bargaining chips, so is the possibility for democracy in other nations. With deregulation, privatization and economic liberalization, environmental sustainability becomes one more barrier to competitiveness, as do social programs and other quality of life indicators.

Assuming as I do that democracy is a good thing, what should be done about this? At the beginning of this paper, I pointed out what I thought were false alternatives, on the one hand extreme globalism that accepts the world defeat of nationhood and, on the other, naive nationalism which we encounter frequently in Canada these days as Canadians try to claw back Canada's social democracy from its recent demise. So, what's my solution? Well, it is not a new idea. Essentially all nations need to negotiate internationally from a position where they can set their own national priorities with respect to the social, political and economic needs of their citizens. This is something that increasingly has been given up even in nations like Canada where there is still the possibility of exercising collective political will. All nations have to negotiate from a position of national self-sufficiency. Transnational corporations have a political and undemocratic message that citizens in all nations have to be more competitive and that that is to be accomplished by dismantling national institutions, social programs and environmental protections. The fact that competitiveness without the protection of our natural resources, our infrastruc-

ture and social programs amounts to mass suicide is rarely considered. And what I am going to conclude with here may sound reminiscent of the cultural imperalism of a former era but it behooves those of us with the privilege to still resist global degradation and the erosion of basic rights and freedoms to do so and not allow our nations to bargain away the world. As Keynes noted in 1933,

> The divorce between ownership and the real responsibility of management is serious within a country when, as a result of joint-stock enterprise, ownership is broken up between innumerable individuals who buy their interest today and sell it tomorrow and lack altogether both knowledge and responsibility towards what they monetarily own. But when this same principle is applied internationally, it is, in times of stress, intolerable—I am irresponsible towards what I own and those who operate what I own are irresponsible towards me. (193)

And the solution to the problem of divorce here is reconciliation rather than resignation and resistance to the false and alarming rhetoric of global greed that has benumbed our better sensibilities.

REFERENCES

Berlan, J.P. 1989, "Capital Accumulation, Transformation of Agriculture, and the Agricultural Crisis: A Long-Term Perspective," in *Instability and Change in the World Economy*.

Bienefeld, M. 1992, "Financial Deregulation: Disarming the Nation State," *Studies in Political Economy* 37, 31-58.

Daly, H. and J. Cobb. 1989, *For the Common Good: Redirecting the Economy Toward Community, the Environment and a Sustainable Future* (Boston: Beacon Press).

Easeer, W. 1992, "How Much Lower is Low Enough?" in J. Sinclair (ed.), *Crossing the Line* (Vancouver: New Star Books).

Foster, J.B. 1989, "The Age of Restructuring," in *Instability and Change in the World Economy*.

Keynes, J.M. 1933, "National Self-Sufficiency," in D. Moggeridge (ed.), *The Collected Writings of John Maynard Keynes*, Vol. 21 (London: Cambridge University Press).

MacEwan, A. and W. Tabb (eds.). 1989, *Instability and Change in the World Economy* (New York: Monthly Review Press).

Naylor, R. 1987, *Hot Money and the Politics of Debt* (Toronto: McClelland and Stewart).

Reich, R. 1991, *The Work of Nations: Preparing Ourselves for 21st Century Capitalism* (New York: Alfred Knopf).

Snider, L. 1993, *Bad Business: Corporate Crime in Canada* (Toronto: Nelson).

Swift, J. and the Ecumenical Coalition for Economic Justice. 1991, "The Debt Crisis: A Case of Global Usury," in J. Swift and B. Tomlinson (eds.), *Conflicts of Interest: Canada and the Third World* (Toronto: Between the Lines).

Swift, L. 1991, "The Environmental Challenge: Towards a Survival Economy," in *Conflicts of Interest: Canada and the Third World*.

Thomas, C. 1989, "Restructuring of the World Economy and its Political Implications for the Third World," in A. MacEwan and W. Tabb (eds.), *Instability and Change in the World Economy* (New York: Monthly Review Press).

United Nations. 1989, *1989 World Survey on the Role of Women in Development* (New York: United Nations).

United Nations. 1991, *World Investment Report: The Triad in Foreign Direct Investment* (New York: United Nations).

Wood, R. 1989, "The International Monetary Fund and the World Bank in a Changing World Economy," in *Instability and Change in the World Economy*.

◆ ◆ ◆ ◆ ◆

TIBOR R. MACHAN

Environmentalism Humanized

Introduction

I want to argue here the case of a certain type of anthropocentrism, the view that human beings are more important or valuable[1] than other aspects of nature, including plants and animals. I begin with some clarifications of terms I plan to use and then explore whether anything in my anthropocentric position contradicts the tenets of evolutionary biology. I also consider whether the ascription of a moral nature to human beings makes sense and how it squares with certain objections from those who would take animals, for example, to have nearly equal moral status to human beings. I consider, next, some political implications of what I have discussed, specifically as they bear on environmental public policy.

First, by anthropocentrism is not meant that human beings—as a collectivity—are the *telos* of existence, the ultimate aim or end or the central fact of the universe. All that is meant is that human beings are of the highest value in the known universe.

To construe human beings as the highest value in the known universe, they are identified thus as individuals of a given kind. There is no concrete universal "human being," only individual human beings.[2] The conception of humanity as a kind of collective whole entity derives, in the main, from the legacy of Platonic metaphysics that regarded general abstract ideas or universals, at least in its standard rendition, as concrete albeit intellectual or spiritual beings is not metaphysically sound. On the other hand, neither are individuals entirely unique. They are of a specific kind—e.g., human, feline, male, apple, etc. For anthropocentrism to be metaphysically cogent, *individual human beings* would have to be the most valuable entities in nature.

This point about the sort of individualist anthropocentrism to be discussed serves to preempt any objections that may be grounded on the philosophical and moral weaknesses of *radical* individualism, the sort derived from Hobbes and carried to its logical implications by the nineteenth-century German social thinker Max Stirner. The individualism or egoism discussed here—dubbed "classical," so as to distinguish it from the "atomic" or "radical" variety commonly criticized by those who wish to call attention to the social nature of human beings—recognizes that the human individual is so classified for good reasons, based on the rational recognition of kinds of beings in nature. This then renders justified not only personal but several social virtues—generosity, charity, compassion.[3] It is also recognized in this view that a virtue must be practiced by choice and cannot be coerced.

All in all, the position here considered is still a *bona fide* individualism since it identifies human nature as essentially individual, in contrast to, for example, Karl Marx who states that "The human essence is the true collectivity of man" or August Comte who argues that

> [The] social point of view ... cannot tolerate the notion of rights, for such notion rests on individualism. We are born under a load of obligations of every kind, to our predecessors, to our successors, to our contemporaries. After our birth these obligations increase or accumulate, for it is some time before we can return any service.... This ["to live for others"], the definitive formula of human morality, gives a direct sanction exclusively to our instincts of benevolence, the common source of happiness and duty. [Man must serve] Humanity, whose we are entirely.[4]

If this argument is sound, it will establish in large measure that in discussing environmental ethics—whether at the level of principles or applied morality—the highest value must be attributed to measures that enhance the lives of individual human beings on earth. There will be no reliance here on supernaturalism to advance the argument. The aim is to defend the anthropocentric position from within a naturalistic framework—that is, by sticking to considerations based on our understanding of the natural world, including the nature of living beings such as plants, animals and human beings.[5]

However, neither is it the position here that human beings are "uniquely important [or valuable]," a view avidly ridiculed by Stephen R.L. Clark, who claims that "there seems no decent ground in reason or revelation to suppose that man is uniquely important or significant."[6] If human beings were *uniquely* important, that would imply that one had no basis for assigning any value to plants or non-human animals apart from their relationship to human beings. That is not the position to be defended. What will be argued, instead, is that there is a scale of values in nature and among all the various kinds of beings, human beings are the most valuable—even while it is true that some members of the human species may indeed prove themselves to be the most vile and worthless, as well. This is all that anthropocentrism requires.

The Importance of Being Human

How do we establish that something is most valuable? First we must consider whether the idea of lesser or greater value in nature makes clear sense and we must apply these considerations to an understanding of whether human beings or other animals are the most valuable. If it turns out that ranking things in nature as more or less valuable makes sense, and if we qualify as more valuable than other animals, there is at least the beginning of a reason why we may make use of other animals for our purposes.

Let me make clear that even if it were not the case that human beings are more valuable than other aspects of nature, it is doubtful that any conclusions could follow from this warranting policies that favor these other aspects. It would seem that only if it can be shown that beings other than humans qualify as being of supreme importance, based on arguments that do not draw on esoteric knowledge or intuition but on commonly accessible evidence and sound theories, would we have to yield our policies focusing on our welfare in favor of some alternative objective.

Quite independently of the implicit acknowledgment even by many environmentalists of the qualitatively hierarchical structure of nature, there is evidence through the natural world of the existence of beings of greater complexity as well as of higher value. For example, while it makes no sense to evaluate as good or bad such things as planets or rocks or pebbles—except as they may relate to goals or purposes of living things—when it comes to plants and animals the process of evaluation commences very naturally indeed. We can and most of us tend to speak of better or worse trees, oaks, redwoods, or zebras, foxes or chimps. Clearly, if we could not do this rationally, there would be little point to environmental ethics in the first place, a field that presupposes value differentiation through and through.

Now, while at this stage we confine our evaluations to the condition or behavior of living beings without any intimation of their responsibility for being better or worse, when we start discussing human beings our evaluation takes on an additional, namely, moral component. Indeed, none are more ready to testify to this than environmental ethicists who, after all, do not demand any change of behavior on the part of non-human beings but insist that human beings conform to certain moral edicts as a matter of their own choice, as what ought or oughtn't be done but might not or might be done. This means that environmental ethicists admit outright that to the best of our knowledge it is with human beings that the idea of at least active moral goodness and active moral responsibility arises in the universe. Human moral goodness depends on individual human initiative.

Does this show a hierarchical structure in nature? What we may note is that some things do not invite evaluations at all—it is a matter of no significance or of indifference whether some beings are or are not or what they are or how they behave. Some beings invite evaluation but without implying any active moral standing with reference to whether they do well or badly. And some things—namely, human beings or their conduct—invite moral evaluation.

Why is a being that invites moral ranking more valuable in nature than one that invites mere ranking? Why would the addition of the moral component—one that involves the choosing capacity of the agent—elevate the being with such a component in the scale of values in nature?

When evaluation—or value—involves beings that are not self-determined, the capacity to contribute creatively to the values in nature is lacking. What human beings have the capacity to do is to create value,[7] not just exhibit it. They can produce a culture of science, art, athletics, etc., the diverse features of which can themselves all exhibit value. So while nature's non-human living beings can have value, human beings can create value as a matter of their own initiative. This would enable human beings, for example, to replace some lost values in nature, if that turned out to be the right course for them to take. So the addition of choice—the moral component—to value clear makes a valuable difference.

At this point one might object that simply because human beings are capable of moral responsibility, it does not follow that they are the only beings of moral worth. But we need to keep in mind that "moral worth" comes to. To ascribe moral worth or merit to something, or to deny that it has such worth or merit, amounts to relating it to human action from the start. A wonderful sunny day has no moral worth, an destructive earthquake does not lack it. Morality involves beings with the capacity to make choices. So something can have moral worth or lack it only if some human (or other rational choosing) agent produced or destroyed it. Thus the success of a symphony can have moral worth, just as the failure of a saving and loan association may lack it (or even have moral disvalue), because human agency was involved in making it happen.

Accordingly, the agents of moral worth can also have moral worth—thus we consider men and women who produce morally good actions and results as morally worthwhile. But we do not consider horses or tidal waves either morally good or evil. It all has to do with the fact that the concept "moral" or "ethical" arises from circumstances where actions and results come about through the initiative of the agent.

Does this show a hierarchical structure in nature? What we may note is that some things do not invite evaluations at all—it is a matter of no significance or of indifference whether some beings are or are not or what they are or how they behave. Some beings invite evaluation but without implying any active moral standing with reference to whether they do well or badly. And some things—namely, human beings or their conduct—invite moral evaluation.

It might now be argued, in opposition to the above, that the fact that human beings have the capacity to create value on grounds that they create science, art, etc., all of which have value. Does creating what has value come to the same thing as creating value? It would seem that this is the only sense we can make of "creating value"—since value is inherently relational (meaning value is the abstract category of the relationship of being of value to something). It is not confounding value with having value to say this, since value and having value differ only from the point of view of greater and lesser generality. X's having value is, more broadly characterized, the phenomena of value in nature. Nothing else works—things are not just values, all alone, without making contributions to something, being pleasing to or enhancing for or supportive of something.

After this brief defense of the superior value of human life, we may note, also, that the level or degree of value moves from the inanimate to the animate world, culminating, as far as we now know, with human life. Normal human life involves moral and creative tasks, and that is why we are, as a species, more valuable than other beings in nature—we are subject to moral appraisal regarding all our creative activities; it is a matter of our doing whether we succeed or fail in our lives.[8]

Now when it comes to our moral task, namely, to succeed as human beings, we are dependent upon reaching justified conclusions about what we should do and summoning the will to do it. What we will do, in turn, often involves the transformation and utilization of the natural world of which we are a part. We have the moral responsibility to engage in the needed transformation and utilization in a morally responsible fashion. We can fail to do this and do so too often. But we can also succeed. That, indeed, is once again implicit in the field of environmental ethics.

The process that leads to our success involves learning what nature contains with which we may achieve our highly varied tasks in life, tasks that share the one common feature to make us good at living our lives as our nature, including our individuality, requires. Among these highly varied tasks could be some that makes judicious use of nature's varied living beings, such as plants, animals, even others people (under certain conditions)—for example, to discover whether some medicine may cure us of some illness, is safe for our use, we might wish to use animals and plants.

Why would it be morally proper for us to make such use of nature? Because we are unique in having to make choices for purposes of doing well at living. We know from our study of the rest of the living world that doing well at living is what it means, at least predominantly, to be good. Our evaluations in zoology, botany, biology, and medicine makes this clear—the good is what is conducive and the bad is what is destructive of living, mostly of the individual living being, even if at times only in a complex fashion that may make it appear that individuals as such do not count for much.⁹ So when we come to human life, the same general standard remains in force, namely, pro-life versus anti-life; only given the specifics of human nature, this will involve now a moral dimension and whatever is requisite for that, including certain sociopolitical principles. There are those, of course, who claim that much if not all of what human beings invent so as to enhance their existence is a kind of intrusion or trampling upon nature—unnatural or artificial, in fact. But there is no good reason to suppose this. Human beings emerged in reality alongside all other living things, and their activities—such as playing football, bowl-ing, holding philosophy conferences in pleasant sur-roundings, driving cars from the airport to these surroundings, building tunnels, burning fossil fuels, cutting down trees, etc.—could be just as natural as it is for the bee to make honey, the swallow to fly south in winter time, or the beaver to dam up creeks. Human life is a form of natural life. Whatever de-rives from its consistent development or realization will be in accordance with nature, whatever subverts or corrupts it will not.

The major difference is, of course, something already mentioned, namely, that human beings can mismanage their lives, can (choose to) subvert their nature. But what would amount to a subversion of human nature? It would be to conduct oneself ir-rationally, thoughtlessly, imprudently, and by evad-ing what is most healthy and productive for one's life. That is what amounts to living a vicious rath-er than virtuous life. It is to fail to exercising one's unique capacity for coping with one's life, a capacity that in the case of human beings must be exercised by choice. Thinking is not automatic—and, in-deed, environmental ethicists appear to assume this, implicitly, when they criticize failed thinking and the resulting conduct in various areas of private be-havior and public policy. Indeed, ethics itself rests on the view that human beings can choose—"ought implies can" embodies this point.

Within the parameters of these broad standards, a great deal of the diverse things that human beings do can be perfectly natural, even when it is destruc-tive or—or rather transforms and utilizes—certain other aspects of nature. (Notice that the frequently used phrase "domination of nature" has something suspiciously pejorative about it—it suggests hostility and cruelty toward the rest of nature. Transforma-tion and use do not have to involve dominance.)

The rational thing for us to do is to make the best use of nature for our success in living our lives. That does not mean there need be no guidelines in-volved in how we might make use of plants, animals, etc.—any more than there need be no guidelines in-volved in how we make use of objects of art, technol-ogy, etc. But it can easily involve managing nature so as to serve our own goals and aspirations, to make ourselves happy.

Why Individual Human Rights?

At this point we need to make an excursion into the realm of politics and law. As already hinted, the pe-culiar value dimension of human life, involving as it does moral choices all individuals will need to make so as to succeed in living well, has socio-economic-political implications. This involves the emergence of a normative realm known as the domain of indi-vidual human rights.

Why do individual *human* rights come into this picture? The rights being talked of in connection with human beings have as their conceptual source the human capacity to make moral choices. For in-stance, if (as has been argued in other forums¹⁰), each of us has the right to life, liberty and prop-erty—as well as more specialized rights connected with politics, the press, religion—we do so because we have as our central task in life to act morally and this task needs to be shielded against intrusive ac-tions from other moral agents. In order to be able to engage in responsible and sound moral judgment and conduct throughout the scope of our lives, we require a reasonably clear sphere of personal juris-diction—a dominion where we are sovereign and can either succeed or fail to live well, to do right, to act properly.

If we did not have rights, we would not have such a sphere of personal jurisdiction and there could be no clear idea as to whether we are acting on our own behalf or those of other persons. A kind of *moral tragedy of the commons* would ensue, with an indeterminate measure of *moral dumping and sharing* without responsibility being assignable to any-one for either.[11] No one could be blamed or praised for we would not know clearly enough whether what the person is doing is in his or her authority to do or in someone else's. This is precisely the problem that arises in communal living and, especially, in to-talitarian countries where everything is under forced collective governance. The reason moral distinctions are still possible to make under such circumstances is that in fact—as distinct from law—there is always some sphere of personal jurisdiction wherein people may exhibit courage, prudence, justice, honesty, and other virtues. But where collectivism has been suc-cessfully enforced, there is no individual responsibil-ity at play and people's morality and immorality is submerged within the group.

Indeed the main reason for governments has for some time been recognized to be nothing other than that our individual human rights should be protected. In the past—and in many places even to-day—it was thought that government (or the State) has some kind of leadership role in human com-munities. This belief followed the view that human beings differ amongst themselves radically, some be-ing lower, some higher class, some possessing divine rights, others lacking them, some having a personal communion with God, others lacking this special advantage. With such views in place, it made clear enough sense to argue that government should have a patriarchal role in human communities—the view against which John Locke argued his theory of nat-ural individual human rights.[12]

Is There Room for Non-human Rights?

A crucial implication of a non-anthropocentric en-vironmental ethics is the view that at least animals, if not plants, are as valuable as human beings, possibly even to the extent that the law should acknowledge animal rights and the legal standing of plants.[13] There may be other grounds for rejecting anthropo-centrism but this one is certainly a significant aspect of the anti-anthropocentrist position or ethos.

We have seen that the most sensible and influen-tial doctrine of human rights rests on the purport-ed fact that human beings are indeed members of a discernibly different species. Central to what distin-guishes human beings from other animals is that they are moral agents and thus have as their central objective in life to live morally well, to uphold prin-ciples of right and wrong for them in their personal lives and in communities.

Quite uncontroversially, there is no valid intel-lectual place for rights in the non-human world, the world in which moral responsibility is for all prac-tical purposes absent. Some would want to argue that some measure of morality can be found with-in the world of at least higher animals—e.g., dogs. For example, Bernard Rollin holds that "In actual fact, some animals even seem to exhibit behavior that bespeaks something like moral agency or moral agreement."[14]

Rollin maintains that it is impossible to clearly distinguish between human and non-human ani-mals, including on the grounds of the former's char-acteristic as a moral agent. Yet what they do to defend this point is to invoke borderline cases, imaginary hypotheses, and anecdotes. While such arguments are suggestive, they are bested by others defending the opposite viewpoint.

Perhaps the central point in support of animal rights is the view that no fundamental differences may be identified between human beings and other animals. Yet, this is a mistake. Human individuals are indeed members of a distinct species of animals.

Their *human* nature is a fact, not merely a nominal category.[15]

No doubt many environmental ethicists sincerely believe that they have found a justification for opposing anthropocentrism. They seem to hold that anthropocentrism means human beings exercising random, capricious control over the rest of nature—trampling on the rest of the world as they desire. Yet many environmentalist might change their perspective if they became convinced that anthropocentrism does not endorse rapaciousness and is by no means in any inherent conflict with the rational management of the environment.

Not only does a perspective that favors human life above all appear to be better justified, as indicated in this discussion; as it happens it also generates the most environmentally sound public policy. Let's turn to this in the final section of this discussion.

Environmentalism and Politics

Of late no one can deny that collectivist political economies have fallen into some disrepute. Theoretically there were hints of this as far back as the 4th century BC when in the *Politics* Aristotle observed that private ownership of property encourages responsible human behavior more readily than does collectivism as spelled out in Plato's *Republic*. Aristotle said, "That all persons call the same thing mine in the sense in which each does so may be a fine thing, but it is impracticable; or if the words are taken in the other sense, such a unity in no way conduces to harmony. And there is another objection to the proposal. For that which is common to the greatest number has the least care bestowed upon it. Everyone thinks chiefly of his own, hardly at all of the common interest; and only when he is himself concerned as an individual. For besides other considerations, everybody is more inclined to neglect the duty which he expects another to fulfill; as in families many attendants are often less useful than a few."[16]

In our time the same general observation was advanced in more technical and rigorous terms by Ludwig von Mises, in his 1922 (German edition) book *Socialism*,[17] although he was mainly concerned with economic problems of production and allocation of resources for satisfying individual preferences. More recently, however, Garrett Hardin argued[18] that the difficulties first noticed by Aristotle plague us in the context of our concerns with the quintessentially public realm, namely, the ecological environment.

These various indictments[19] of collectivism, coupled with the few moral arguments against it, didn't manage to dissuade many intellectuals from the task of attempting to implement the system. Our own century is filled with enthusiastic, stubborn, visionary, opportunistic but almost always bloody efforts to implement the collectivist dream. Not until the crumpling of the Soviet attempt, in the form of its Marxist-Leninist internationalist socialist revolution, did it dawn on most people that collectivism is simply not going to do the job of enabling people to live a decent human social life. Although most admit that in small units—convents, kibbutzes, the family—a limited, temporary collectivist arrangement may be feasible, they no longer look with much hope toward transforming entire societies into collectivist human organizations.

The most recent admission of the failure of economic collectivism—in the wake of the collapse of the Soviet bloc economy (something most enthusiasts would not expect based on the kind of predictions advanced by Mises and F.A. Hayek)—comes from Professor Robert Heilbroner, one of socialism's most intelligent and loyal champions for the last several decades. As he puts it in his recent essay, "After Communism": "... Ludwig von Mises ... had written of the 'impossibility' of socialism, arguing that no Central Planning Board could ever gather the enormous amount of information needed to create a workable economic system.... It turns out, of course, that Mises was right...."[20]

But, not unlike previous thinkers who have seen various examples of the failure of some kind of perfectionist, idealist normative moral or political scheme, Heilbroner cannot quite say good bye to his utopia. He notes that there are two ways it may remain something of a handy concept. First, it may leave us piecemeal social objectives to strive for—but these have always come in the context of essentially capitalist economics systems. Secondly, it may reemerge as the adjunct of the ecological movement. As Heilbroner puts it,

> [If] there is any single problem that will have to be faced by any socioeconomic order over the coming decades it is the problem of making our economic peace with the demands of the environment. Making that peace means insuring that the vital processes of material provisioning do not contaminate the green-blue film on which life itself depends. This imperative need not affect all social formations, but none so profoundly as capitalism.[21]

What is one to say about this new fear, a new problem allegedly too complicated for free men and women to handle? Has Heilbroner not heard of the "tragedy of the commons" so that he could imagine the environmental difficulties that face the collectivist social systems? Here is how Heilbroner issues the "new" warning:

> It is, perhaps, possible that some of the institutions of capitalism—markets, dual realms of power, even private ownership of some kind of production—may be adapted to that new state of ecological vigilance, but, if so, they must be monitored, regulated, and contained to such a degree that it would be difficult to call the final social order capitalism.[22]

This somewhat novel but essentially old fashioned skepticism about free market capitalism needs to be addressed.

My first response is that there is no justification for any of this distrust of "the market," as opposed to trusting some scientific bureaucracy that is to do the monitoring, regulating, and containing Heilbroner and so many other champions of regimentation are calling for. Such distrust tends to arise from comparing the market system to some ideal and static construct developed in the mind of a theorist. But since human community life is dynamic, the most we can hope for in improving it is the establishment of certain basic principles of law, or a constitution, that will keep the dynamics of the community within certain bounds.[23]

Accordingly, put plainly, if men and women acting in the market place, guided by the rule of law based on their natural individual rights to life, liberty and property, were incapable of standing up to the ecological challenges Heilbroner and many others in the environmentalist movement have in mind, there is no reasonable doubt that those could not be met better by some new statist means.[24] Why should ecologically minded bureaucrats be better motivated, more competent, and more virtuous than those motivated by a concern for the hungry, the unjustly treated, the poor, the artistically deprived, the uneducated masses or the workers of the world? There is no reason to attribute to the members of any ecological politburo or central committee more noble characteristics than to the rest of those individuals who have made a try at coercing people into good behavior throughout human history.

As already suggested, lamentations about capitalism tend to rest on a kind of idealism that is ill suited to the formation of public policy for a dynamic human community. One might be able to imagine—in a Platonic sort of fashion, vis-à-vis the ideal state—a perfectly functioning ecological order. It is doubtful that even this much is possible. It is another thing entirely to attempt to implement policies that will produce such an idealized order in the actual world. What we actually face in our various human communities is a choice between what we may call live options, e.g., capitalism, socialism, the welfare state, fascism, etc. No ideal system is a contender and it is folly to compare any of the live options to such an ideal. In the actual contest, in turn, it seems the capitalist alternative is superior for reasons already alluded to and discussed elsewhere.[25] Yet it will help to sketch some central aspects of that alternative.

In the first place, if human beings have the right to private property, not to mention their lives and liberty, a just legal system would prohibit any kind of dumping by one person on another, including all environmental assaults such as transmitting toxic substances unto unsuspecting victims, polluting public realms, seepage, etc. Beyond a harmless level of waste disposal, no pollution would be legal, no matter whether jobs or the achievement of any other laudable purpose depended on it. Just as slavery may not be practiced regardless of how it might facilitate certain valued objectives, just as rape is impermissible no matter how desperate one may be, so too may pollution and other forms of environmental offenses not be carried out regardless of the various possible valued objectives the pursuit of which would generate it. To put the matter into the language of the economists, if one cannot internalize the negative externalities associated with some production or transportation process, one will simply have to stop it.

There are, of course, technical problems associated with measuring how much waste disposal constitutes reaching the threshold. But this is in principle no different from determining how much of some food substance or medicine constitutes poison. Just as the criminal law employs forensic science to determine who is guilty of what degree of homicide, so various branches of environmental science would be utilized so as to establish culpability in environmental crime.

The worry that industrial civilization would be slowed to a dead halt by the above approach is unfounded. Alternative technologies to those that involve environmental assault will certainly emerge and are already on the way. Past errors, of course,

cannot be fully remedied, yet some of what has been wrought upon us by way of the highly subsidized internal combustion engine could be mitigated by imposing full cost on transportation, not permitting owners of vehicles to dump on those whose permission they do not have or cannot obtain.

In general, then, clearly the anthropocentric—i.e., individual rights—oriented environmental ethics and law is more radical and just than anything offered within standard environmental ethics literature.

If free men and women will not manage the environment, nor will anyone else. In any case, more optimism about the capacity of free citizens to deal with this issue is warranted when we examine just what are the sources of our ecological troubles. Given, especially, the fact of collectivism's far greater mismanagement of the environment than that of the mixed economies we loosely label capitalist, there is already some suggestion implicit here about what the problem comes to, namely, too little free market capitalism. Given the comparatively worse environmental situation evident in political economies that rely on collective ownership and management, and given the natural individualism of human life, free markets appear to be more suited to solving the tragedy of the commons. What Heilbroner and friends fail to realize is that the environmental problems most people are concerned about are due to the tragedy of the commons, not due to the privatization of resources and the implementation of the principles that prohibit dumping and other kinds of trespassing. With more attention to protecting individual rights to life, liberty and property, solutions to our problems are more likely, period.

The best defense of the free market approach to environmentalism in matters of public policy begins with the realization that it is the nature of human beings to be essentially individual. This can be put alternatively by saying that the individual rights approach is most natural—it most readily accommodates nature and, therefore, the ecology.

If there is a crisis here, it amounts to the history of human action that has been out of line with ecological well being, health, flourishing. But how do we know what kinds of human action might have been more or less conducive to ecological well-being? It will not do to speculate on some ideal configuration of the living world, apart from considering what is best for human individuals. There simply is no standard of a right pattern to which the world should be made to conform—it is a dynamic system of living entities, with no final pattern discernible in it to which the current configuration should be adjusted. Indeed, if there is something we have learned about environmental wisdom, it is that the environment's health, so to speak, emerges spontaneously, reflecting something of a chaotic development, one that is not predictable.[26]

We need first of all to know about human nature—what it is that human beings are and what this implies for their conduct within the natural world. If, as the natural rights (classical liberal) tradition invoked here would have it, human beings are individuals with basic rights to life, liberty and property, that also implies, very generally at first, that this is how they are best fitted within the natural world, within the rest of nature. Environmentalism is most effectively promoted if we trust free men and women with the task of choosing the best policies bearing on the same, not relying on governments to determine the most suitable relationship various individuals and organizations should cultivate with the rest of nature. Not that this will serve to avoid all failings vis-à-vis this area of human concern—anymore than leaving human beings free to choose in other spheres creates utopia. Nevertheless, when we consider that governments are administered by persons with no greater claim to virtue and wisdom than others can make, and if we also consider that officials of the government make their mistakes, when they do, without the chance of full accountability and with the benefit of the legal use of force, it is not at all unreasonable to suppose that when problems need solutions, governments are not going to be the most useful for this purpose unless their particular means of dealing with persons, force, is required.

Last Reflections

The fact is that with human nature a problem arose in nature that had not been there before—basic choices had to be confronted, which other animals do not have to confront. The question "How should I live?" faces each human being but not other living things, not to mention inanimate nature. And that is what makes it unavoidable for human beings to dwell on moral issues as well as to see other human beings as having the same problem to solve, the same question to dwell on. For this reason we are very different from other living beings, plants and animals—we also do terrible, horrible, awful things to each other as well as to the rest of nature, but we can also do much, much better and achieve incredible feats nothing else in nature can come close to.

Yet, merely because we do have a moral dimension in our lives, it does not follow that we must agonize about everything in nature, as if we had the moral capacity to remake the entire universe.

Indeed, then, the moral life is the exclusive province of human beings, so far as we can tell for now. Other, lower—i.e., less important or valuable—animals simply cannot be accorded—because they have no requirement for—the kind of treatment that such a moral life demands, namely, respect for and protection of basic rights.

As such it is to human life we must, rationally considered, attribute the greatest value in the universe. And since human life is essentially individual, not collective—which does not preclude its vital social yet largely voluntary dimension—the individual rights approach, that protects each person as a moral agent and provides for him or her a sphere of privacy or exclusive jurisdiction, is the most sensible environmentalist public policy.

NOTES

1 In this paper no distinction will be made between "important" and "valuable." In some other context the difference between the meanings of these two terms may be significant but it is not for present purposes. Both terms are used to mean making a positive or advantageous difference to something or someone—e.g., the sun is important for the plant or the house is one of John's valuable possessions.

2 "Individual" does not have to translate to "atomistic, isolated, anti-social, asocial." Such a translation begs the question as to what kind of individual we are faced with. For a detailed discussion of the type of individual a human being is, see Tibor R. Machan, *Capitalism and Individualism, Reframing the Argument for the Free Society* (New York: St. Martin's Press, 1990).

   A different sort of defense of anthropocentrism is advanced in Thomas Palmer, "The Case for Human Beings," *The Atlantic*, 269 (January 1992): 83-88. Palmer notes that "in fact Homo sapiens is the crown of creation, if by creation we mean the explosion of earthly vitality and particularity long ago ignited by a weak solution of amino acids mixing in sunlit waters" (88). Unfortunately, Palmer does not emphasize enough this feature of particularity in his defense and, thus, ignores the bulk of the important political and policy issues that arise in environmentalism.

3 Here a point needs to be raised concerning the perfectly sensible Aristotelian understanding of human beings as essentially social animals. Ecologists tend to stress this point often when individualism is presented to them as a sociopolitical alternative to their widely embraced collectivism (whether in a socialist, welfare statist, or communitarian version).

   Being essentially an individual does not preclude having also an essential social dimension to one's life. Briefly, although one makes for oneself a given, particular but human life, given that such a life has much to benefit from social involvement, it could well be "in one's nature" to be social as well as a matter of one's individual decision to embark on a rich social, community and political life. It may well be one's moral responsibility as an individual to connect with other human beings—unless, of course, the available others are real dangers to one's life, which in the case of human beings is a clear possibility.

4 The source of this remark has eluded me since originally located in one of Comte's works.

5 There are many who believe that when one construes human beings as essentially individual, this means that they are "individual through and through." Yet something that is essentially individual—that is, the nature of which is such that its individuality cannot be omitted from understanding it—can also be elaborately involved with community, society, family, and other groups of individuals. It is, furthermore, an exaggeration indeed to say that, to cite an anonymous commentator on an earlier version of this paper, "life as studied by the life sciences is thoroughly social in nature with individual organisms embedded in interconnected supporting webs on which they are entirely dependent." Apart from the fact that being dependent on "supporting webs" does not render some being "thoroughly social"—so that, for example, the mere dependence of a Rembrandt, Liszt, Chekhov or Keats on innumerable social webs (economic, manufacturing, political, familiar, artistic, etc.) by no means deprives him of the capacity to inject into his art a decisive individuality. See, for more on this, Conway Zirkle, "Some Biological Aspects of Individualism," in F. Morley, ed., *Essays on Individualism* (Indianapolis, IN: Liberty Press, 1977), 53-86. See, also, Theodosus Dobzhansky, *The Biological Basis of Human Freedom* (New York: Col-

umbia University Press, 1956). If, as has been argued by Roger W. Sperry, *Science and Moral Priority* (New York: Columbia University Press, 1983), human beings have a naturally grounded capacity for self-determination—i.e., free will—it makes eminently good sense that they should become individuated depending on the extent and intensity of their choice to exercise their will. Their choices are then indeed their own, sovereign choices, not explainable without remainder by other aspects of their nature, including their social entanglements.

6   Stephen R.L. Clark, *The Moral Status of Animals* (Oxford, England: Clarendon Press, 1977), 13. "Uniquely important" means that the being in question is unique in its being important, whereas saying "most important or valuable" does not preclude the value of other beings not just in their relationship to what is uniquely important—i.e., derivatively—but to themselves, in terms of their own nature.

7   It might be argued that this point assumes anthropocentrism but it does not—we are not just talking about human beings creating values for themselves but values as such. For example, human beings breed animals and plants, they create provisions for the same, they protect or enhance the lives of non-human beings. They create values more abundantly than does anything else, although, of course, they also destroy values aplenty.

8   It might be objected here that this line of argumentation assumes away the troublesome "is/ought" gap, moving illegitimately from fact to value, etc. It isn't possible to deal with the matter here but see Tibor R. Machan, *Individuals and their Rights* (LaSalle, IL: Open Court Publ., Co., Inc., 1989), Chapter 2. The central point is that value is a type of fact attending to living beings for whom the alternative between flourishing and perishing is natural. What is value contributes to flourishing and what is of disvalue contributes to perishing, to put it into very general terms. I draw here on an idea developed in Ayn Rand, "The Objectivist Ethics," *The Virtue of Selfishness, A New Concept of Egoism* (New York: New American Library, 1961). See, also, Karl Popper, *Unending Quest* (Glasgow: Fontana/Collins, 1974), 194: "I think that values enter the world with life; and if there is life without consciousness (as I think there may well be, even in animals and man, for there appears to be such a thing as dreamless sleep) then, I suggest, there will also be objective values, even without consciousness."

9   The case for "altruism" in the animal world is widely debated but by no means settled. I rest my own reflections on this on the view that whatever version of "altruism" may be accepted, in the last analysis it is individual living beings that would benefit from it, aside from their species. For more on this, see James G. Lennox, "Philosophy of Biology," in Members of the Department of History and Philosophy of Science, University of Pittsburgh, *Introduction to the Philosophy of Science* (Englewood Cliffs, NJ: Prentice Hall, 1992), 295.

10 Tibor R. Machan, *Human Rights and Human Liberties* (Chicago, IL: Nelson-Hall Co., 1975) and *Individuals and Their Rights*. See, also, Machan, "A Reconsideration of Natural Rights Theory," *American Philosophical Quarterly*, Vol. 17 (1982): 61-72, and "Towards a Theory of Natural Individual Human Rights," *New Scholasticism*, Vol. 61 (Winter 1987): 33-78, "Are Human Rights Real?" *Review Journal of Philosophy and Social Science*, Vol. 13 (1988): 1-22, and "Natural Rights Liberalism," *Philosophy & Theology*, Vol. 4 (Spring 1990): 253-65.

11 See, for more, Garrett Hardin, "Tragedy of the Commons," *Science*, Vol. 162 (December 13, 1968): 1243-48. Hardin's point had been advanced, much earlier, by Aristotle, with more explicit normative, albeit utilitarian, punch.

The point is that unless some sphere of personal jurisdiction is identified, individual and thus effective responsibility—in the case of Aristotle and Hardin, vis-à-vis the consumption of and care for resources—will be obscured, leading to confusion and indeterminacy.

12 John Locke, *Two Treatises on Civil Government*.

13 A good example of the view on plants is Christopher Stone's *Should Trees Have Standing* (Palo Alto, CA: William Kaufmann, 1975). The animal rights case is presented most thoroughly by Tom Regan, *The Case for Animal Rights* (Berkeley, CA: University of California Press, 1984). Not all anti-anthropocentricists are animal rights advocates but most probably because they eschew the concept of rights altogether, not because they would draw a fundamental (morally and politically significant) distinction between other animals and human beings. Some of the points discussed in the next several paragraphs form portions of previously published essays in *Public Affairs Quarterly* and *Journal des Economists et des Etudes Humaines* concerned with whether animal rights exists and the handling of pollution under capitalism, respectively.

14 Bernard E. Rollin, *Animal Rights and Human Morality* (Buffalo, NY: Prometheus Books, 1981), 14.

15 For more on this, see Mortimer Adler, *The Differences of Man and the Difference it Makes* (New York: World Publishing Co., 1968), and, Machan, *Individuals and Their Rights*. The former work concerns the issue of whether the human species is fundamentally distinct, the latter whether talk about "the nature of X" can have an objective foundation or must be nominal. For more on this, see Joel Wallman, *Aping Language* (New York: Cambridge University Press, 1992). Wallman argues that language is a uniquely human attribute and that these attempts establish nothing to contradict that fact. Cf., Donald R. Griffin, *Animal Minds* (Chicago: University of Chicago Press, 1992). Griffin, on the other hand, argues that higher mentality is not unique to human beings, although he does not establish that any other animal aside from human beings is *uniquely dependent* on higher mental functions for the sustenance and flourishing of its life.

16 Aristotle, *Politics*, Bk. II, Ch. 3; 1262a30-40.

17 Ludwig von Mises, *Socialism*, 2nd ed. (New Haven: Yale University Press, 1951).

18 Hardin, "The Tragedy of the Commons."

19 I should note here that some of these are still in dispute and it would be rash to treat them as proven. Nevertheless, it is also fair to say that arguments made against the possibility of rational allocation of economic resources, the prudent use of the commons, etc., are widely admitted to be telling. This is certainly not the place where we could decide the matter once and for all. I will assume, however, that enough trouble faces collectivist political systems, at least as far as fostering human productivity while avoiding having to conscript labor power are concerned, that drastic revisions would need to be made in order for them to become feasible. For example, the recent effort to develop what is called a market socialism has run into serious theoretical difficulties. See, e.g., David Schweickard, *Capitalism or Worker Control* (New York: Praeger, 1980), Julian Le Grand and Saul Estrin, eds., *Market Socialism* (New York: Clarendon Press, 1989); Ian Forbes, *Market Socialism* (London: Fabian Society, 1986); David Miller, *Market, State, and Community: Theoretical Foundations of Market Socialism* (New York: Oxford University Press, 1989); James A. Yunker, *Socialism Revised and Modernized: The Case for Pragmatic Market Socialism* (New York: Praeger, 1992); Anders Aslund, *Market Socialism or the Restoration of Capitalism?* (New York: Cambridge University Press, 1992). See, however, Anthony De Jasay, *Market Socialism: A Scru-*

tiny—"This Square Circle" (London: Institute of Economic Affairs, 1990), N. Scott Arnold, *The Political Philosophy of Market Socialism* (London: Oxford University Press, 1994).

20 Robert Heilbroner, "After Communism," *The New Yorker*, September 10, 1990, 92.

21 Ibid., 99.

22 Ibid., 100.

23 In other words, a feasible political system must focus on prohibitions, enforced by officers of the law, rather than on outcomes. For a good discussion of this point—contrasting end-state and procedural features of a political order—see Robert Nozick, *Anarchy, State, and Utopia* (New York: Basic Books, 1974).

24 For a more detailed discussion of the natural rights libertarian approach to environmental problems, see Tibor R. Machan, "Pollution and Political Theory," in T. Regan, ed., *Earthbound* (New York: Random House, 1984). A more developed version of the argument showing that the dumping of externalities is to be treated as a crime (assault, trespassing, etc.) may be found in Tibor R. Machan, *Private Rights, Public Illusions* (New Brunswick, NJ: Transaction Books, 1993).

The essence of this approach is that if one is unable to conduct one's activities—productive, recreational, etc.—in a fashion that does not impose uninvited burdens on third parties—i.e., to use the economist's jargon, if one is unable to internalize one's negative externalities—one simply may not carry forth with them. Full cost of such production must lie with the agent and no unwelcome "free" rides may be taken. In contrast to standard approaches to solving environmental problems caused by human beings, namely, via the establishment of government regulatory agencies (which are beset with all the "public choice" and "tragedy of the commons" problems, especially in democratic welfare states), here the issue of one of criminal law and dumpers, just as trespassers, assaulters, rapists, arsonists, and the like, would be prosecuted. If someone with AIDS negligently or intentionally infects another who has not had the chance to exercise free choice in the matter, the perpetrator is prosecuted under the criminal law. Anyone with a serious contagious disease exposing others to his or her illness would suffer the same fate. There is no government regulation—rationing involved here, only prohibition and the conviction of violators. No doubt, complexities attend all of this, yet there seems to be nothing extraordinarily difficult about determination of threshold levels and prosecution of those who dump once the threshold has been reached. The individual rights approach is simply stricter than the utilitarian, social (risk) cost-benefit approach, yet the same science and technology can be employed in administering both systems.

25 See Machan, *Individuals and Their Rights*. See, also, Tibor Machan, *Private Rights and Public Illusions* (New Brunswick, NJ: Transaction Books, 1995).

26 See, Stephen Jay Gould, *Wonderful Life* (New York: W.W. Norton, 1989).

CASE STUDY 1

ACTIONS SPEAK LOUDER THAN WORDS: REBUILDING MALDEN MILLS

DAVID MEELER AND SRIVATSA SESHADRI

Founded in 1906, Malden Mills is a privately held textile mill located in Massachusetts. Like many other textile mills in the US, late in the twentieth century Malden Mills faced financial difficulty and eventually declared bankruptcy. If this were an average story of a bankrupt textile manufacturer in New England, Malden Mills would have folded long ago. But the owner, Aaron Feuerstein, spent millions of research dollars to develop entirely new fabrics, and re-opened the old mill right there in Massachusetts. By world-salary standards, this was an expensive move. The revolutionary new fabrics were Polartec® and Polarfleece®.

Polartec® and Polarfleece® are highly versatile and technical fabrics that hold little moisture, provide excellent insulation, offer low weight, etc. These fabrics are currently used by outdoor enthusiasts, extreme athletes, and various US Special Forces teams. Developing such a high-tech fabric might make you think that Malden Mills heavily emphasizes advanced research and development in their profit-making strategy. When speaking at MIT's Industrial Development lecture series in 1997, Feuerstein said "You can have the best engineers, the best R&D guy, the best technical expert, figure out how to get better quality. But in the last analysis, it's the man on the floor who is going to get that quality for you. If he feels he's part of the enterprise and he feels he is treated the way he should be treated, he will go the extra mile to provide that quality."

In short, Aaron Feuerstein is committed to the idea that Malden's workers—white collar and blue collar alike—are the strongest asset the mill can have. A quick survey of any Fortune 500 company will reveal a publicly stated commitment to the value of their workers. For example, General Motors (whose devastating plant closing in Flint, MI was the subject of the film *Roger & Me*) states "We are committed to developing and deploying employee skills, talent and potential effectively, improving the diversity of our workforce, influencing and shaping our performance to drive business outcomes and giving employees unmatched career opportunities. We see a clear link between our investment in human performance and our market performance and financial results." While many companies develop grandiose statements expressing a commitment to their employees, the fundamental difference between Malden Mills and other corporations, according to Feuerstein, "is that I consider our workers an asset, not an expense." Malden Mills demonstrates its appreciation of workers with actions, not mere words.

Developing new materials and re-opening the mill in an area requiring some of the highest wages in the world is not the only commitment Malden Mills made to its employees and communities. In 1995, a fire broke out at Malden Mills. The largest fire in Massachusetts for over 100 years destroyed three of Malden's 10 large buildings, ruining Polartec's® dyeing and finishing operations. A perfect opportunity, many would say, to relocate operations overseas and take advantage of lower wages and more liberal environmental regulations. Not so for Aaron Feuerstein. By the day after the fire, Feuerstein had announced that he would immediately rebuild the plant in Massachusetts, and keep employees on full salary for three months.

Employees at Malden Mills repay this loyalty by going those extra miles. One building crucial to Polartec® was saved from the fire in part due to the efforts of 36 employees who helped fight the fire into the night. Afterwards, make-shift operations were put in place to compensate for the production capacity lost in the fire. Feuerstein was focused not only on his employees' welfare; he was also concerned with the communities where his facilities are located, and the environmental impact his company has on the world. The new Polartec® plant was the first textile mill built in Massachusetts in over a century. In rebuilding, Feuerstein constructed the plant as a high-tech and environmentally conscious facility complete with heat-recovery generators. These ultra-low-NOx systems decreased the facility's emissions by 40%—a savings equivalent to the annual emissions of 4,300 vehicles. During the rebuilding phase, Malden Mills set up an employee retraining center that included GED courses, English as a second language, and basic computer courses to prepare employees to work at the new state-of-the-art facility. When *60 Minutes* asked Feuerstein about his business choices after the fire, his reply was simple: "I think it was a wise business decision, but that isn't why I did it. I did it because it was the right thing to do."

Analysis

One of the most important aspects we should note about the Malden Mill case is that at the time of the fire, it was privately owned. Without stock-holders scrutinizing his business decisions, Feuerstein could do just about anything without fear of being sued. This is in sharp contrast to Henry Ford, whose stockholders sued him for continually reducing the sales-price of his Model T automobile. The Ford stockholders contended that the price could remain stable, and that by reducing the price Ford was giving away their profits. Feuerstein's decisions were obviously expensive. Construction costs, wages, and benefits are all higher in America, as is the expense of building environmentally friendly industrial facilities. But it was Feuerstein's money. He could do with it as he pleased.

In the months after the fire, Feuerstein was lauded as a model of executive heart. He was hailed for his courage and his honorable code of ethics. But the tale of Malden Mills is not a complete triumph. As a result of the fire, Malden Mills lost a great deal of international business supplying upholstery fabric, and eventually had to shut down its upholstery division. Try as he might, Feuerstein could not prevent a plant-shutdown or the layoffs of approximately 400 workers. Rebuilding after the fire also left the company with an enormous debt, and Malden Mills filed for Chapter 11 bankruptcy protection. Since large creditors then held a significant stake in Malden Mills, their voice would guide future business decisions. By the end of 2003, Malden Mills emerged from bankruptcy, and within six months Feuerstein was out and a new CEO took the reigns. Within one year Michael Spillane, President and CEO of Malden Mills, had put together a new senior management team and dedicated his tenure to increasing profitability, in part, through cost controls. By mid 2005, GE Commercial Finance, owner of Malden Mills, was looking for a buyer.

Questions

1. Consider the actions of Feuerstein and his statement: "I think it was a wise business decision, but that isn't why I did it. I did it because it was the right thing to do." In hindsight, given that a small-town lost a major employer when the upholstery division was shut down, employees lost jobs, the mill went into bankruptcy, the creditors got the raw end of the deal—in other words everyone suffered in the long-term—how could you argue that the decisions of Feuerstein were ethical and wise? Were the decisions socially responsible? Why or Why not?

2. Suppose that Malden Mills had been a publicly traded company in which you held stock. Upon hearing news of the fire and CEO's decisions, how would you react? How would your reactions change if you were an employee? A customer? Was Feuerstein favoring the interests of some stakeholders over those of others?

3. If, through the good luck of substantial market demand, the mill had survived, would you view the ethicality of the decisions differently?

a. What if the good luck turned out to be an enormous contract to provide uniform clothing for military, police, or fire and rescue forces?

b. What if the good luck turned out to be extremely high demand for the products from gang members? (Note: It is legal to be a gang member.)

CHARITY BEGINS AT HOME: NEPOTISM
DAVID MEELER AND SRIVATSA SESHADRI

Sultan Haseem operates three "mom and pop" retail stores in Karachi, Pakistan. His ten-employee operation consists of himself, and, being childless, his two nephews and seven others, mostly relatives. Tariq Mohammed, the older nephew, and Shaheed Hussain, the younger of the two nephews, were recruited in their teens and now, after 10 years, have been placed in charge of finance and purchasing respectively.

Wong Su Hong is the CEO of a not-for-profit organization in Kuala Lumpur, Malaysia. The 25-employee organization was created by leading business people to serve the under-privileged in the country. The organization, through a team of 100 volunteer-workers, collects left-over foods from restaurants and delivers them to the homeless the same day. Of the 25 employees, four are at management level, each responsible for fund-raising, accounting, public relations, and liaison with the Malaysian government. All four managers were recruited by Hong himself and are his brothers or brothers-in-law.

Camund Ltd. is a publicly traded, company based in Mumbai, India, with over 100,000 shareholders and yearly revenues of Rs. 2.5 billion (US: $50 million). The majority of the shares are owned by two families—the Bahais and the Sheths. The men at the helm of the company are from these families. These families control 11.3% of the equity and all the directors and senior managers are family members. Recruitment is decentralized and each manager is free to recruit whoever they like. They tend to recruit friends, and kith and kin.

Ronald Whitefoot is the CEO of a large software company in San Jose, CA. The firm launched a successful IPO (initial public offering) two years ago increasing the firm's equity base to $50 million. Whitefoot still holds a 55% stake in the company and twelve of the fifteen Directors on the Board are his close relatives.

Analysis

Nepotism is generally considered undesirable in the United States. It is defined by the Society for Human Resource Management as "Favoritism shown to relatives by individuals in a position of authority, such as managers or supervisors." Its most explicit nature is revealed in the recruiting of close friends or family members by managers. While it is not illegal in the United States it is generally frowned upon by US investors, since there is strong evidence that it leads to inefficiency and poor performance of the company.

In Asia however, nepotism is viewed quite differently. In Japan nepotism can almost be seen as the traditional model for business enterprises. For example, the keiretsu system establishes a mock "family" of companies intimately linked with one another. One's ethical obligations are thought to be stronger to those who are closest to you. So members of a keiretsu family will do business primarily with one another. Family members are the closest, and those who are most different from you (i.e., foreigners) are the farthest away. This is why Western businesses often criticize the keiretsu system for being unfair. By its very nature, the keiretsu system requires favoritism to other Japanese companies and reduced ethical obligations to foreign companies. For example, if a supplier in your keiretsu cannot provide the quality needed for your products, rather than switch suppliers, your company will work with your keiretsu-"sibling" to refine the production techniques until your quality standards have been met. Similar to this is the concept of Guanxi in China. Guanxi is loosely seen by Western businesses as "relationship circles" but it connotes more than that. Guanxi is also an obligation to return favors at some future time rather like blank IOUs. Thus this breeds nepotism. Asian countries see nepotism, not as an ethical issue, but good business sense. As one Asian businessman once said, "Who better to trust than your own friends and family?" Asians tend to believe in "Better the devil you know than an unknown god." Additionally, a fatalistic attitude towards life in general allows them to attribute the negative consequences of nepotism to "acts of God" rather than questioning the tradition of nepotism.

Questions

1. Do you think nepotism is unethical? Why? When you graduate and apply for jobs, do you hope a family member or close friend will be able to hire you?

2. In which of the above four examples would you say the nepotism is a non-issue? In which of the examples is it ethically significant? Why or why not?

3. How would the financial performance (positive or negative) of a company where rampant nepotism exists affect your answers?

4. Suppose you are considering investing in a company, and as you read the annual report, you notice that several of the top executives are related. How does this affect your decision to invest? Would you invest in Whitefoot's software company?

5. Suppose you are a new employee in a company. During your first week on the job there is an office-party to celebrate the promotion of one of your supervisors. At the party you learn that the person receiving the promotion is related to the company president. Do you worry that favoritism might limit your chances for advancement in the company?

6. What do you think is the role of culture in influencing the perception that nepotism is unethical behavior? Are there universal moral norms that should be followed by all multi-nationals, whether "in Rome" or not?

Rights and Obligations of Employees and Employers

ANAND VAIDYA

Rights and Obligations of Employees and Employers

One of the most basic relations in the business world is the relationship between an employer and an employee. Regarding this basic relationship, a pair of related ethical questions arises. What are the rights and obligations of employers with respect to their employees? And, correspondingly: What are the rights and obligations of employees with respect to their employer? There are many issues that surround this relationship. In this unit we focus on: employment at will, whistleblowing, drug testing, and safety in the workplace. These issues are but a subset of the total set of issues that one could consider. In fact there are issues, such as genetic testing (which is closely related to drug testing) that could be a concern in the future, as technology advances. As the editors of this volume conceive it, the ethical questions that are considered in this unit are, in some sense, more particular to the business setting than any other setting in which similar questions may arise, and provide a foundation for exploring issues that could arise in the future.

Employment at will is the doctrine that employment is voluntary and indefinite for both employers and employees. With regard to the employer, it means that the employer may release or fire an employee at any time for no reason whatsoever. What employment at will fundamentally means from the perspective of the employer is that an employer voluntarily offers work to an employee and, because the employer voluntarily offers work, the employer may take it away at any time without having to offer a reason. Given that employment is a social good, the employment at will doctrine is ethically controversial. As a consequence of job insecurity, there is a potential for exploitation. In a situation in which there is a surplus of people to work, the fact that an employer can simply discharge an employee for no reason may allow the employer to extract additional work from the employee lest the employee be replaced by someone else who will bear these greater burdens.

With regard to the employee, the doctrine of employment at will means that the employee may leave work at any time. From the perspective of the employee, what is offered to the employer is the employee's labor. Since the labor was voluntarily given, it may voluntarily be taken away. Although it is less common to talk of potentials for abuse by the employee, it is clearly possible. Consider a company that is working on a project which is due in two weeks. Suppose that one employee of the company has specialized skills which are had by no other employee within the company and cannot be readily replaced from elsewhere. Further suppose that, without this employee, the project cannot continue. If this employee decides to suddenly leave the corporation during this crucial period, then the company would suffer a serious loss.

Another central topic is whistleblowing. Whistleblowing is simply the practice of outing a corporation for illegal or suspect practices of which the general public should have knowledge. One could, for example, blow the whistle on a car company for not meeting the safety standards required for motor vehicles. On the other hand, one could blow the whistle on a company for filing false reports on their earnings, as occurred in the Enron scandal. The main ethical issues that surround whistleblowing have to do with what kinds of things one should blow the whistle on, and what steps should be taken *prior* to going public with information that could potentially discredit the company.

In general, most ethicists agree that if one suspects or has evidence that a company is acting irresponsibly or illegally, then one should first attempt to solve the problem through some internal channel, since this is both less destructive and, potentially, more efficacious. An employee not only has an obligation to the public to inform them of any irresponsible or intentional wrong doing on the part of the company, but also an obligation to not cause undue harm to the welfare of the company and its employees. In addition, employees have an obligation not to blow the whistle on a company unless the evidence they have reasonably shows that specific members are violating explicit policies of the corporation, are in violation of specific external ethical codes that regulate the corporation, or else are working against the welfare of the community at large. There is a potential in whistleblowing for unfounded (or, even worse, malicious) whistleblowing, and as such a person considering blowing the whistle on an organization must take certain steps.

Drug testing in business is a good instance of a more general ethical issue that is exemplified in a specific way in the business context. It is an issue that arises in the military, education, and athletics. The background question that leads to the specific issue of drug testing is the following: What information about an employee or potential employee is an employer entitled access to? In choosing to hire an employee, is an employer entitled to know a candidate's political beliefs, sexual practices, personal habits, or religious beliefs? In choosing to promote, retain, and evaluate an employee, is an employer allowed to do so on the basis of information about the client's voting practices, eating habits, and extracurricular activities? The central issue is over what kind of information is job-relevant. Many ethicists agree over the following principle. If a piece of information is not job-relevant, then an employer may not use it in choosing to hire, retain, promote, or evaluate an employee. The substantive question is whether a specific piece of information, such as drug use, is job-relevant.

In the case of drug use, one could argue that, for certain kinds of jobs, whether an employee uses drugs is simply job-irrelevant due to the nature of the job. For example, on the one hand one could argue that commercial airplane pilots must undergo drug testing, since drugs affect pilot performance, and could put passengers at risk. And on the other hand, one could argue that mail clerks need not undergo drug testing, since drug use does not affect job-performance. Alternatively, one might think that an employer has a *right* (as owner, for example) to know whatever they would like to know, regardless of the grounds. In addition, one might worry that the use of "job relevance" as a criterion in the argument may be too vague, insofar as it might allow for the possible justification of acquiring information about too many aspects of an employee's life (i.e., sleeping and eating habits).

Historically, one issue that has been of central importance for workers has been safety in the workplace. This issue becomes even more salient in a situation where there is a surplus of labor. When such a surplus exists, an employer could simply choose not to provide high enough safety standards in order to attract and retain employees simply *because* there is a surplus. So, there is both a question of what are the minimal safety standards to which an employee is entitled, and a question as to what is the ground of this. It is sometimes claimed in the debate on sweatshops, for example, that sweatshop workers could simply choose not to work at the sweatshop if they believe that the hours are too long and the safety standards and pay are too low. However, this claim fails to take into consideration the circumstances that bring about the possibility of sweatshop labor in the first place.

EMPLOYMENT AT WILL

PATRICIA H. WERHANE AND TARA J. RADIN

Employment at Will and Due Process

The principle of Employment at Will (EAW) is a common-law doctrine that states that, in the absence of law or contract, employers have the right to hire, promote, demote, and fire whomever and whenever they please. In 1887, the principle was stated explicitly in a document by H.G. Wood entitled *Master and Servant*. According to Wood, "A general or indefinite hiring is prima facie a hiring at will."[1] Although the term "master-servant," a medieval expression, was once used to characterize employment relationships, it has been dropped from most of the recent literature on employment.

In the United States, EAW has been interpreted as the rule that, when employees are not specifically covered by union agreement, legal statute, public policy, or contract, employers "may dismiss their employees at will ... for good cause, for no cause, *or even for causes morally wrong*, without being thereby guilty of legal wrong."[2] At the same time "at will" employees enjoy rights parallel to employer prerogatives, because employees may quit their jobs for any reason whatsoever (or no reason) without having to give any notice to their employers. "At will" employees range from part-time contract workers to CEOs, including all those workers and managers in the private sector of the economy not covered by agreements, statutes, or contracts. Today at least 60% of all employees in the private sector in the United States are "at will" employees. These employees have no rights to due process or to appeal employment decisions, and the employer does not have any obligation to give reasons for demotions, transfers, or dismissals. Interestingly, while employees in the *private* sector of the economy tend to be regarded as "at will" employees, *public* sector employees have guaranteed rights, including due process, and are protected from demotion, transfer, or firing without cause.

Due process is a means by which a person can appeal a decision in order to get an explanation of that action and an opportunity to argue against it. Procedural due process is the right to a hearing, trial, grievance procedure, or appeal when a decision is made concerning oneself. Due process is also substantive. It is the demand for rationality and fairness: for good reasons for decisions. EAW has been widely interpreted as allowing employees to be demoted, transferred or dismissed without due process, that is, without having a hearing and without requirement of good reasons or "cause" for the employment decision. This is not to say that employers do not have reasons, usually good reasons, for their decisions. But there is no moral or legal obligation to state or defend them. EAW thus sidesteps the requirement of procedural and substantive due process in the workplace, but it does not preclude the institution of such procedures or the existence of good reasons for employment decisions.

EAW is still upheld in the state and federal courts of this country, although exceptions are made when violations of public policy and law are at issue. According to the *Wall Street Journal*, the court has decided in favor of the employees in 67% of the wrongful discharge suits that have taken place during the past three years. These suits were won not on the basis of a rejection of the principle of EAW but, rather, on the basis of breach of contract, lack of just cause for dismissal when company policy was in place, or violations of public policy. The court has carved out the "public policy" exception so as not to encourage fraudulent or wrongful behavior on the part of employers, such as in cases where employees are asked to break a law or to violate state public policies, and in cases where employees are not allowed to exercise their fundamental rights, such as the rights to vote, to serve on a jury, and to collect worker compensation. For example, in one case, the court reinstated an employee who was fired for reporting theft at his plant on the grounds that criminal conduct requires such.[3] In another case, the court reinstated a physician who was fired from the Ortho Pharmaceutical Corporation for refusing to seek approval to test a certain drug on human subjects. The court held that safety clearly lies in the interest of public welfare, and employees are not to be fired for refusing to jeopardize public safety.[4]

During the last ten years, a number of positive trends have become apparent in employment practices and in state and federal court adjudications of employment disputes. Shortages of skilled managers, fear of legal repercussions, and a more genuine interest in employee rights claims and reciprocal obligations have resulted in a more careful spelling out of employment contracts, the development of elaborate grievance procedures, and in general less arbitrariness in employee treatment. While there has not been a universal revolution in thinking about employee rights, an increasing number of companies have qualified their EAW prerogatives with restrictions in firing without cause. Many companies have developed grievance procedures and other means for employee complaint and redress.

Interestingly, substantive due process, the notion that employers should give good reasons for their employment actions, previously dismissed as legal and philosophical nonsense, has also recently developed positive advocates. Some courts have found that it is a breach of contract to fire a long-term employee when there is not sufficient cause—under normal economic conditions even when the implied contract is only a verbal one. In California, for ex-

ample, 50% of the implied contract cases (and there have been over 200) during the last five years have been decided in favor of the employee, again, without challenging EAW. In light of this recognition of implicit contractual obligations between employees and employers, in some unprecedented court cases *employees* have been held liable for good faith breaches of contract, particularly in cases of quitting without notice in the middle of a project and/or taking technology or other ideas to another job.

These are all positive developments. At the same time, there has been neither an across-the-board institution of due process procedures in all corporations nor any direct challenges to the *principle* (although there have been challenges to the practice) of EAW as a justifiable and legitimate approach to employment practices. Moreover, as a result of mergers, downsizing, and restructuring, hundreds of thousands of employees have been laid off summarily without being able to appeal those decisions.

"At will" employees, then, have no rights to demand an appeal to such employment decisions except through the court system. In addition, no form of due process is a requirement preceding any of these actions. Moreover, unless public policy is violated, the law has traditionally protected employers from employee retaliation in such actions. It is true that the scope of what is defined as "public policy" has been enlarged so that "at will" dismissals without good reason are greatly reduced. It is also true that many companies have grievance procedures in place for "at will" employees. But such procedures are voluntary, procedural due process is not *required*, and companies need not give any reasons for their employment decisions.

In what follows we shall present a series of arguments defending the claim that the right to procedural and substantive due process should be extended to all employees in the private sector of the economy.

EAW is often justified for one or more of the following reasons:

1. The proprietary rights of employers guarantee that they may employ or dismiss whomever and whenever they wish.

2. EAW defends employee and employer rights equally, in particular the right to freedom of contract, because an employee voluntarily contracts to be hired and can quit at any time.

3. In choosing to take a job, an employee voluntarily commits herself to certain responsibilities and company loyalty, including the knowledge that she is an "at will" employee.

4. Extending due process rights in the workplace often interferes with the efficiency and productivity of the business organization.

5. Legislation and/or regulation of employment relationships further undermine an already overregulated economy.

Let us examine each of these arguments in more detail. The principle of EAW is sometimes maintained purely on the basis of proprietary rights of employers and corporations. In dismissing or demoting employees, the employer is not denying rights to *persons*. Rather, the employer is simply excluding that person's *labor* from the organization.

This is not a bad argument. Nevertheless, accepting it necessitates consideration of the proprietary rights of employees as well. To understand what is meant by "proprietary rights of employees" it is useful to consider first what is meant by the term "labor." "Labor" is sometimes used collectively to refer to the workforce as a whole. It also refers to the activity of working. Other times it refers to the productivity or "fruits" of that activity. Productivity, labor in the third sense, might be thought of as a form of property or at least as something convertible into property, because the productivity of working is what is graded for remuneration in employee-employer work agreements. For example, suppose an advertising agency hires an expert known for her creativity in developing new commercials. This person trades her ideas, the product of her work (thinking), for

pay. The ideas are not literally property, but they are tradable items because, when presented on paper or on television, they are sellable by their creator and generate income. But the activity of working (thinking in this case) cannot be sold or transferred.

Caution is necessary, though, in relating productivity to tangible property, because there is an obvious difference between productivity and material property. Productivity requires the past or present activity of working, and thus the presence of the person performing this activity. Person, property, labor, and productivity are all different in this important sense. A person can be distinguished from his possessions, a distinction that allows for the creation of legally fictional persons such as corporations or trusts that can "own" property. Persons cannot, however, be distinguished from their working, and this activity is necessary for creating productivity, a tradable product of one's working.

In dismissing an employee, a well-intentioned employer aims to rid the corporation of the costs of generating that employee's work products. In ordinary employment situations, however, terminating that cost entails terminating that employee. In those cases the justification for the "at will" firing is presumably proprietary. But treating an employee "at will" is analogous to considering her a piece of property at the disposal of the employer or corporation. Arbitrary firings treat people as things. When I "fire" a robot, I do not have to give reasons, because a robot is not a rational being. It has no use for reasons. On the other hand, if I fire a person arbitrarily, I am making the assumption that she does not need reasons either. If I have hired people, then, in firing them, I should treat them as such, with respect, throughout the termination process. This does not preclude firing. It merely asks employers to give reasons for their actions, because reasons are appropriate when people are dealing with other people.

This reasoning leads to a second defense and critique of EAW. It is contended that EAW defends employee and employer rights equally. An employer's right to hire and fire "at will" is balanced by a worker's right to accept or reject employment. The institution of any employee right that restricts "at will" hiring and firing would be unfair unless this restriction were balanced by a similar restriction controlling employee job choice in the workplace. Either program would do irreparable damage by preventing both employees and employers from continuing in voluntary employment arrangements. These arrangements are guaranteed by "freedom of contract," the right of persons or organizations to enter into any voluntary agreement with which all parties of the agreement are in accord. Limiting EAW practices or requiring due process would negatively affect freedom of contract. Both are thus clearly coercive, because in either case persons and organizations are forced to accept behavioral restraints that place unnecessary constraints on voluntary employment agreements.

This second line of reasoning defending EAW, like the first, presents some solid arguments. A basic presupposition upon which EAW is grounded is that of protecting equal freedoms of both employees and employers. The purpose of EAW is to provide a guaranteed balance of these freedoms. But arbitrary treatment of employees extends prerogatives to managers that are not equally available to employees, and such treatment may unduly interfere with a fired employee's prospects for future employment if that employee has no avenue for defense or appeal. This is also sometimes true when an employee quits without notice or good reason. Arbitrary treatment of employees or employers therefore violates the spirit of EAW—that of protecting the freedoms of both the employees and employers.

The third justification of EAW defends the voluntariness of employment contracts. If these are agreements between moral agents, however, such agreements imply reciprocal obligations between the parties in question for which both are accountable. It is obvious that, in an employment contract, people are rewarded for their performance. What is seldom noticed is that, if part of the employment contract

is an expectation of loyalty, trust, and respect on the part of an employee, the employer must, in return, treat the employee with respect as well. The obligations required by employment agreements, if these are free and noncoercive agreements, must be equally obligatory and mutually restrictive on both parties. Otherwise one party cannot expect—morally expect—loyalty, trust, or respect from the other.

EAW is most often defended on practical grounds. From a utilitarian perspective, hiring and firing "at will" is deemed necessary in productive organizations to ensure maximum efficiency and productivity, the goals of such organizations. In the absence of EAW unproductive employees, workers who are no longer needed, and even troublemakers, would be able to keep their jobs. Even if a business could rid itself of undesirable employees, the lengthy procedure of due process required by an extension of employee rights would be costly and time-consuming, and would likely prove distracting to other employees. This would likely slow production and, more likely than not, prove harmful to the morale of other employees.

This argument is defended by Ian Maitland, who contends,

> [I]f employers were generally to heed business ethicists and institute workplace due process in cases of dismissals and take the increased costs or reduced efficiency out of workers' paychecks—then they would expose themselves to the pirating of their workers by other employers who would give workers what they wanted instead of respecting their rights in the workplace.... In short, there is good reason for concluding that the prevalence of EAW does accurately reflect workers' preferences for wages over contractually guaranteed protections against unfair dismissal.[5]

Such an argument assumes (a) that due process increases costs and reduces efficiency, a contention that is not documented by the many corporations that have grievance procedures, and (b) that workers will generally give up some basic rights for other benefits, such as money. The latter is certainly sometimes true, but not always so, particularly when there are questions of unfair dismissals or job security. Maitland also assumes that an employee is on the same level and possesses the same power as her manager, so that an employee can choose her benefit package in which grievance procedures, whistleblowing protections, or other rights are included. Maitland implies that employers might include in that package of benefits their rights to practice the policy of unfair dismissals in return for increased pay. He also at least implicitly suggests that due process precludes dismissals and layoffs. But this is not true. Procedural due process demands a means of appeal, and substantive due process demands good reasons, both of which are requirements for other managerial decisions and judgments. Neither demands benevolence, lifetime employment, or prevents dismissals. In fact, having good reasons gives an employer a justification for getting rid of poor employees.

In summary, arbitrariness, although not prohibited by EAW, violates the managerial ideal of rationality and consistency. These are independent grounds for not abusing EAW. Even if EAW itself is justifiable, the practice of EAW, when interpreted as condoning arbitrary employment decisions, is not justifiable. Both procedural and substantive due process are consistent with, and a moral requirement of, EAW. The former is part of recognizing obligations implied by freedom of contract, and the latter, substantive due process, conforms with the ideal of managerial rationality that is implied by a consistent application of this common law principle.

NOTES

1 H.G. Wood, *A Treatise on the Law of Master and Servant* (Albany, NY: John D. Parsons, Jr., 1877), 134.

2 Lawrence E. Blades, "Employment at Will versus Individual Freedom: on Limiting the Abusive Exercise of Employer Power," *Colombia Law Review* 67 (1967), 1405, quoted from *Payne v. Western*, 81 Tenn. 507 (1384), and *Hutton v. Watters*, 132 Tenn. 527, S.W. 134 (1915).

3 *Palmateer v. International Harvester Corporation*, 85 Ill. App. 2d 124 (1981).

4 Pierce v. Ortho Pharmaceutical Corporation, 845 N.J. 58, 417 A.2d 505 (1980). See also Brian Hershizer, "The New Common Law of Employment: Changes in the Concept of Employment at Will," *Labor Law Journal*, 36 (1985), 95-107.

5 Ian Maitland, "Rights in the Workplace: A Nozickian Argument," in Lisa Newton and Maureen Ford, eds., *Taking Sides* (Guilford, CT: Dushkin Publishing Group), 1990, 34-35.

◆ ◆ ◆ ◆ ◆

RICHARD A. EPSTEIN

In Defense of the Contract at Will

The persistent tension between private ordering and government regulation exists in virtually every area known to the law, and in none has that tension been more pronounced than in the law of employer and employee relations. During the last fifty years, the balance of power has shifted heavily in favor of direct public regulation, which has been thought strictly necessary to redress the perceived imbalance between the individual and the firm. In particular the employment relationship has been the subject of at least two major statutory revolutions. The first, which culminated in the passage of the National Labor Relations Act in 1935, set the basic structure for collective bargaining that persists to the current time. The second, which is embodied in Title VII of the Civil Rights

Act of 1964, offers extensive protection to all individuals against discrimination on the basis of race, sex, religion, or national origin. The effect of these two statutes is so pervasive that it is easy to forget that, even after their passage, large portions of the employment relation remain subject to the traditional common law rules, which when all was said and done set their face in support of freedom of contract and the system of voluntary exchange. One manifestation of that position was the prominent place that the common law, especially as it developed in the nineteenth century, gave to the contract at will. The basic position was set out in an oft-quoted passage from *Payne v. Western & Atlantic Railroad*:

> [M]en must be left, without interference to buy and sell where they please, and to discharge or retain employees at will for good cause or for no cause, or even for bad cause without thereby being guilty of an unlawful act per se. It is a right which an employee may exercise in the same way, to the same extent, for the same cause or want of cause as the employer.[1]

* * *

In the remainder of this paper, I examine the arguments that can be made for and against the contract at will. I hope to show that it is adopted not because it allows the employer to exploit the employee, but rather because over a very broad range of circumstances it works to the mutual benefit of both parties, where the benefits are measured, as ever, at the time of the contracts formation and not at the time of dispute. To justify this result, I examine the contract in light of the three dominant standards that have emerged as the test of the soundness of any legal doctrine: intrinsic fairness, effects upon utility or wealth, and distributional consequences. I conclude that the first two tests point strongly to the maintenance of the at-will rule, while the third, if it offers any guidance at all, points in the same direction.

I. The Fairness of the Contract At Will

The first way to argue for the contract at will is to insist upon the importance of freedom of contract as an end in itself. Freedom of contract is an aspect of individual liberty, every bit as much as freedom of speech, or freedom in the selection of marriage partners or in the adoption of religious beliefs or affiliations. Just as it is regarded as prima facie unjust to abridge these liberties, so too is it presumptively unjust to abridge the economic liberties of individuals. The desire to make one's own choices about employment may be as strong as it is with respect to marriage or participation in religious activities, and it is doubtless more pervasive than the desire to participate in political activity. Indeed for most people, their own health and comfort, and that of their families, depend critically upon their ability to earn a living by entering the employment market. If government regulation is inappropriate for personal, religious, or political activities, then what makes it intrinsically desirable for employment relations?

It is one thing to set aside the occasional transaction that reflects only the momentary aberrations of particular parties who are overwhelmed by major personal and social dislocations. It is quite another to announce that a rule to which vast numbers of individuals adhere is so fundamentally corrupt that it does not deserve the minimum respect of the law. With employment contracts we are not dealing with the widow who has sold her inheritance for a song to a man with a thin mustache. Instead we are dealing with the routine stuff of ordinary life; people who are competent enough to marry, vote, and pray are not unable to protect themselves in their day-to-day business transactions.

Courts and legislatures have intervened so often in private contractual relations that it may seem almost quixotic to insist that they bear a heavy burden of justification every time they wish to substitute their own judgment for that of the immediate parties to the transactions. Yet it is hardly likely that remote public bodies have better information about individual preferences than the parties who hold them. This basic principle of autonomy, moreover, is not limited to some areas of individual conduct and wholly inapplicable to others. It covers all these activities as a piece and admits no ad hoc exceptions.

This general proposition applies to the particular contract term in question. Any attack on the contract at will in the name of individual freedom is fundamentally misguided. As the Tennessee Supreme Court rightly stressed in *Payne*, the contract at will is sought by both persons.[2] Any limitation upon the freedom to enter into such contracts limits the power of workers as well as employers and must therefore be justified before it can be accepted. In this context the appeal is often to an image of employer coercion. To be sure, freedom of contract is not an absolute in the employment context, any more than it is elsewhere. Thus the principle must be understood against a backdrop that prohibits the use of private contracts to trench upon third-party rights, including uses that interfere with some clear mandate of public policy, as in cases of contracts to commit murder or perjury.

In addition, the principle of freedom of contract also rules out the use of force or fraud in obtaining advantages during contractual negotiations, and it limits taking advantage of the young, the feebleminded, and the insane. But the recent wrongful discharge cases do not purport to deal with the delicate situations where contracts have been formed by improper means or where individual defects of capacity or will are involved. Fraud is not a frequent occurrence in employment contracts, especially where workers and employers engage in repeat transactions. Nor is there any reason to believe that such contracts are marred by misapprehensions, since employers and employees know the footing on which they have contracted: the phrase "at will" is two words long and has the convenient virtue of meaning just what it says, no more and no less.

An employee who knows that he can quit at will understands what it means to be fired at will, even though he may not like it after the fact. So long as it is accepted that the employer is the full owner of his capital and the employee is the full owner of his labor, the two are free to exchange on whatever terms and conditions they see fit, within the limited constraints just noted. If the arrangement turns out to be disastrous to one side, that is his problem, and once cautioned, he probably will not make the same mistake a second time. More to the point, employers and employees are unlikely to make the same mistake once. It is hardly plausible that contracts at will could be so pervasive in all businesses and at all levels if they did not serve the interests of employees as well as employers. The argument from fairness then is very simple, but not for that reason unpersuasive.

II. The Utility of the Contract at Will

The strong fairness argument in favor of freedom of contract makes short work of the various for-cause and good-faith restrictions upon private contracts. Yet the argument is incomplete in several respects. In particular, it does not explain why the presumption in the case of silence should be in favor of the contract at will. Nor does it give a descriptive account of *why* the contract at will is so commonly found in all trades and professions. Nor does the argument meet on their own terms the concerns voiced most frequently by the critics of the contract at will. Thus, the commonplace belief today (at least outside the actual world of business) is that the contract at will is so unfair and one-sided that it cannot be the outcome of a rational set of bargaining processes any more than, to take the extreme case, a contract for total slavery. While we may not, the criticism continues, be able to observe them, defects in capacity contract formation nonetheless must be present: the ban upon the contract at will is an effective way to reach abuses that are pervasive but difficult to detect, so that modest government interference only strengthens the operation of market forces.

In order to rebut this charge, it is necessary to do more than insist that individuals as a general matter know how to govern their own lives. It is also necessary to display the structural strengths of the contract at will that explain why rational people would enter into such a contract, if not all the time, then at least most of it. The implicit assumption in this argument is that contracts are typically for the mutual benefit of both parties. Yet it is hard to see what other assumption makes any sense in analyzing institutional arrangements (arguably in contradistinction to idiosyncratic, nonrepetitive transactions). To be sure, there are occasional cases of regret after the fact, especially after an infrequent but costly, contingency comes to pass. There will be cases in which parties are naive, befuddled, or worse, Yet in framing either a rule of policy or a rule of construction, the focus cannot be on that biased set of cases in which the contract aborts and litigation ensues. Instead, attention must be directed to standard repetitive transactions, where the centralizing tendency powerfully promotes expected mutual gain. It is simply incredible to postulate that either employers or employees, motivated as they are by self-interest, would enter routinely into a transaction that leaves them worse off than they were before, or even worse off than their next best alternative.

From this perspective, then, the task is to explain how and why the at-will contracting arrangement (in sharp contrast to slavery) typically works to the mutual advantage of the parties. Here, as is common in economic matters, it does not matter that the parties themselves often cannot articulate the reasons that render their judgment sound and breathe life into legal arrangements that are fragile in form but durable in practice. The inquiry into mutual benefit in turn requires an examination of the full range of costs and benefits that arise from collaborative ventures. It is just at this point that the nineteenth-century view is superior to the emerging

modern conception. The modern view tends to lay heavy emphasis on the need to control employer abuse. Yet, as the passage from *Payne* indicates, the rights under the contract at will are fully bilateral, so that the employee can use the contract as a means to control the firm, just as the firm uses it to control the worker.

The issue for the parties, properly framed, is not how to minimize employer abuse, but rather how to maximize the gain from the relationship, which in part depends upon minimizing the sum of employer and employee abuse. Viewed in this way the private contracting problem is far more complicated. How does each party create incentives for the proper behavior of the other? How does each side insure against certain risks? How do both sides minimize the administrative costs of their contracting practices? ...

1. *Monitoring Behavior.* The shift in the internal structure of the firm from a partnership to an employment relation eliminates neither bilateral opportunism nor the conflicts of interest between employer and employee. Begin for the moment with the fears of the firm, for it is the firm's right to maintain at-will power that is now being called into question. In all too many cases, the firm must contend with the recurrent problem of employee theft and with the related problems of unauthorized use of firm equipment and employee kickback arrangements.... [The] proper concerns of the firm are not limited to obvious forms of criminal misconduct. The employee on a fixed wage can, at the margin, capture only a portion of the gain from his labor, and therefore has a tendency to reduce output. The employee who receives a commission equal to half the firm's profit attributable to his labor may work hard, but probably not quite as hard as he would if he received the entire profit from the completed sale, an arrangement that would solve the agency-cost problem only by undoing the firm....

The problem of management then is to identify the forms of social control that are best able to minimize these agency costs.... One obvious form of control is the force of law. The state can be brought in to punish cases of embezzlement or fraud. But this mode of control requires extensive cooperation with public officials and may well be frustrated by the need to prove the criminal offense (including mens rea) beyond a reasonable doubt, so that vast amounts of abuse will go unchecked. Private litigation instituted by the firm may well be used in cases of major grievances, either to recover the property that has been misappropriated or to prevent the individual employee from further diverting firm business to his own account. But private litigation, like public prosecution, is too blunt an instrument to counter employee shirking or the minor but persistent use of firm assets for private business....

Internal auditors may help control some forms of abuse, and simple observation by coworkers may well monitor employee activities. (There are some very subtle tradeoffs to be considered when the firm decides whether to use partitions or separate offices for its employees.) Promotions, bonuses, and wages are to also critical in shaping the level of employee performance. But the carrot cannot be used to the exclusion of the stick. In order to maintain internal discipline, the firm may have to resort to sanctions against individual employees. It is far easier to use those powers that can be unilaterally exercised: to fire, to demote, to withhold wages, or to reprimand. These devices can visit very powerful losses upon individual employees without the need to resort to legal action, and they permit the firm to monitor employee performance continually in order to identify both strong and weak workers and to compensate them accordingly. The principles here are constant, whether we speak of senior officials or lowly subordinates, and it is for just this reason that the contract at will is found at all levels in private markets....

In addition, within the employment context firing does not require a disruption of firm operations, much less an expensive division of its assets. It is instead a clean break with consequences that are immediately clear to both sides. The lower cost of both firing and quitting, therefore, helps account for the very widespread popularity of employment-at-will contracts. There is no need to resort to any theory of economic domination or inequality of bargaining power to explain at-will contracting, which appears with the same tenacity in relations between economic equals and subordinates and is found in many complex commercial arrangements, including franchise agreements, except where limited by statutes.

Thus far, the analysis generally has focused on the position of the employer. Yet for the contract at will to be adopted ex ante, it must work for the benefit of workers as well. And indeed it does, for the contract at will also contains powerful limitations on employers' abuses of power. To see the importance of the contract at will to the employee, it is useful to distinguish between two cases. In the first, the employer pays a fixed sum of money to the worker and is then free to demand of the employee whatever services he wants for some fixed period of time. In the second case, there is no fixed period of employment. The employer is free to demand whatever he wants of the employee, who in turn is free to withdraw for good reason, bad reason, or no reason at all.

The first arrangement invites abuse by the employer, who can now make enormous demands upon the worker without having to take into account either the worker's disutility during the period of service or the value of the worker's labor at contract termination. A fixed-period contract that leaves the worker's obligations unspecified thereby creates a sharp tension between the parties, since the employer receives all the marginal benefits and the employee bears all the marginal costs.

Matters are very different where the employer makes increased demands under a contract at will. Now the worker can quit whenever the net value of the employment contract turns negative. As with the employer's power to fire or demote, the threat to quit (or at a lower level to come late or leave early) is one that can be exercised without resort to litigation. Furthermore, that threat turns out to be most effective when the employer's opportunistic behavior is the greatest because the situation is one in which the worker has least to lose. To be sure, the worker will not necessarily make a threat whenever the employer insists that the worker accept a less favorable set of contractual terms, for sometimes the changes may be accepted as an uneventful adjustment in the total compensation level attributable to a change in the market price of labor. This point counts, however, only as an additional strength of the contract at will, which allows for small adjustments in both directions in ongoing contractual arrangements with a minimum of bother and confusion....

2. *Reputational Losses*. Another reason why employees are often willing to enter into at will employment contracts stems from the asymmetry of reputational losses. Any party who cheats may well obtain a bad reputation that will induce others to avoid dealing with him. The size of these losses tends to differ systematically between employers and employees—to the advantage of the employee. Thus in the usual situation there are many workers and a single employer. The disparity in number is apt to be greatest in large industrial concerns; where the at-will contract is commonly, if mistakenly, thought to be most unsatisfactory because of the supposed inequality of bargaining power. The employer who decides to act for bad reason or no reason at all may not face any legal liability under the classical common law rule. But he faces very powerful adverse economic consequences. If coworkers perceive the dismissal as arbitrary, they will take fresh stock of their own prospects, for they can no longer be certain that their faithful performance will ensure their security and advancement. The uncertain prospects created by arbitrary employer behavior is functionally indistinguishable from a reduction in wages unilaterally imposed by the employer. At the margin some workers will look elsewhere, and typically the best workers will have the greatest opportunities. By

the same token the large employer has more to gain if he dismisses undesirable employees, for this ordinarily acts as an implicit increase in wages to the other employees, who are no longer burdened with uncooperative or obtuse coworkers.

The existence of both positive and negative reputational effects is thus brought back to bear on the employer. The law may tolerate arbitrary behavior, but private pressures effectively limit its scope. Inferior employers will be at a perpetual competitive disadvantage with enlightened ones and will continue to lose in market share and hence in relative social importance. The lack of legal protection to the employees is therefore in part explained by the increased informal protections that they obtain by working in large concerns.

3. *Risk Diversification and Imperfect Information*. The contract at will also helps workers deal with the problem of risk diversification.... Ordinarily, employees cannot work more than one, or perhaps two, jobs at the same time. Thereafter the level of performance falls dramatically, so that diversification brings in its wake a low return on labor. The contract at will is designed in part to offset the concentration of individual investment in a single job by allowing diversification among employers *over time*. The employee is not locked into an unfortunate contract if he finds better opportunities elsewhere or if he detects some weakness in the internal structure of the firm. A similar analysis applies on the employer's side where he is a sole proprietor, though ordinary diversification is possible when ownership of the firm is widely held in publicly traded shares.

The contract at will is also a sensible private adaptation to the problem of imperfect information over time. In sharp contrast to the purchase of standard goods, an inspection of the job before acceptance is far less likely to guarantee its quality thereafter. The future is not clearly known. More important, employees, like employers, *know what they do not know*. They are not faced with a bolt from the blue, with an "unknown unknown." Rather they face a known unknown for which they can plan. The at-will contract is an essential part of that planning because it allows both sides to take a wait-and-see attitude to their relationship so that new and more accurate choices can be made on the strength of improved information. ("You can start Tuesday and we'll see how the job works out" is a highly intelligent response to uncertainty.) To be sure, employment relationships are more personal and hence often stormier than those that exist in financial markets, but that is no warrant for replacing the contract at will with a for-cause contract provision. The proper question is: will the shift in methods of control work a change for the benefit of both parties, or will it only make a difficult situation worse?

4. *Administrative Costs.* There is one last way in which the contract at will has an enormous advantage over its rivals. It is very cheap to administer. Any effort to use a for-cause rule will in principle allow all, or at least a substantial fraction of, dismissals to generate litigation. Because motive will be a critical element in these cases, the chances of either side obtaining summary judgment will be negligible. Similarly, the broad modern rules of discovery will allow exploration into every aspect of the employment relation. Indeed, a little imagination will allow the plaintiff's lawyer to delve into the general employment policies of the firm, the treatment of similar cases, and a review of the individual file. The employer for his part will be able to examine every aspect of the employee's performance and personal life in order to bolster the case for dismissal....

III. Distributional Concerns

Enough has been said to show that there is no principled reason of fairness or utility to disturb the common law's longstanding presumption in favor of the contract at will. It remains to be asked whether there are some hitherto unmentioned distributional consequences sufficient to throw that conclusion into doubt....

The proposed reforms in the at-will doctrine cannot hope to transfer wealth systematically from rich to poor on the model of comprehensive systems of taxation or welfare benefits. Indeed it is very difficult to identify in advance any deserving group of recipients that stands to gain unambiguously from the universal abrogation of the at-will contract. The proposed rules cover the whole range from senior executives to manual labor. At every wage level, there is presumably some differential in workers' output. Those who tend to slack off seem on balance to be most vulnerable to dismissal under the at-will rule; yet it is very hard to imagine why some special concession should be made in their favor at the expense of their more diligent fellow workers.

The distributional issues, moreover, become further clouded once it is recognized that any individual employee will have interests on both sides of the employment relation. Individual workers participate heavily in pension plans, where the value of the holdings depends in part upon the efficiency of the legal rules that govern the companies in which they own shares. If the regulation of the contract at will diminishes the overall level of wealth, the losses are apt to be spread far and wide, which makes it doubtful that there are any gains to the worst off in society that justify somewhat greater losses to those who are better off. The usual concern with maldistribution gives us situations in which one person has one hundred while each of one hundred has one and asks us to compare that distribution with an even distribution of, say, two per person. But the stark form of the numerical example does not explain how the skewed distribution is tied to the concrete choice between different rules governing employment relations. Set in this concrete context, the choices about the proposed new regulation of the employment contract do not set the one against the many but set the many against each other, all in the context of a shrinking overall pie. The possible gains from redistribution, even on the most favorable of assumptions about the diminishing marginal utility of money, are simply not present.

If this is the case, one puzzle still remains: who should be in favor of the proposed legislation? One possibility is that support for the change in common law rules rests largely on ideological and political grounds, so that the legislation has the public support of persons who may well be hurt by it in their private capacities. Another possible explanation could identify the hand of interest group politics in some subtle form. For example, the lawyers and government officials called upon to administer the new legislation may expect to obtain increased income and power, although this explanation seems insufficient to account for the current pressure. A more uncertain line of inquiry could ask whether labor unions stand to benefit from the creation of a cause of action for wrongful discharge. Unions, after all, have some skill in working with for-cause contracts under the labor statutes that prohibit firing for union activities, and they might be able to promote their own growth by selling their services to the presently nonunionized sector. In addition, the for-cause rule might give employers one less reason to resist unionization, since they would be unable to retain the absolute power to hire and fire in any event. Yet, by the same token, it is possible that workers would be less inclined to pay the costs of union membership if they received some purported benefit by the force of law without unionization. The ultimate weight of these considerations is an empirical question to which no easy answers appear. What is clear, however, is that even if one could show that the shift in the rule either benefits or hurts unions and their members, the answer would not justify the rule, for it would not explain why the legal system should try to skew the balance one way or the other. The bottom line therefore remains unchanged. The case for a legal requirement that renders employment contracts terminable only for cause is as weak after distributional considerations are taken into account as before....

Conclusion

The recent trend toward expanding the legal remedies for wrongful discharge has been greeted with wide approval in judicial, academic, and popular circles. In this paper, I have argued that the modern trend rests in large measure upon a misunderstanding of the contractual processes and the ends served by the contract at will. No system of regulation can hope to match the benefits that the contract at will affords in employment relations. The flexibility afforded by the contract at will permits the ceaseless marginal adjustments that are necessary in any ongoing productive activity conducted, as all activities are, in conditions of technological and business change. The strength of the contract at will should not be judged by the occasional cases in which it is said to produce unfortunate results, but rather by the vast run of cases where it provides a sensible private response to the many and varied problems in labor contracting. All too often the case for a wrongful discharge doctrine rests upon the identification of possible employer abuses, as if they were all that mattered. But the proper goal is to find the set of comprehensive arrangements that will minimize the frequency and severity of abuses by employers and employees alike. Any effort to drive employer abuses to zero can only increase the difficulties inherent in the employment relation. Here, a full analysis of the relevant costs and benefits shows why the constant minor imperfections of the market, far from being a reason to oust private agreements, offer the most powerful reason for respecting them. The doctrine of wrongful discharge is the problem and not the solution. This is one of the many situations in which courts and legislatures should leave well enough alone.

NOTES

1 *Payne v. Western Atl. RR*, 81 Tenn. 507, 518-19 (1884), overruled on other grounds, *Hutton v. Watters*, 132 Tenn. 527, 544, 179 S.W. 134, 138 (1915)....

2 Ibid.

WHISTLEBLOWING

RICHARD T. DE GEORGE

Whistleblowing

We shall restrict our discussion to a specific sort of whistleblowing, namely, *nongovernmental, impersonal, external whistleblowing*. We shall be concerned with (1) employees of profit-making firms, who, for moral reasons, in the hope and expectation that a product will be made safe, or a practice changed, (2) make public information about a product or practice of the firm that due to faulty design, the use of inferior materials, or the failure to follow safety or other regular procedures or state of the art standards (3) threatens to produce serious harm to the public in general or to individual users of a product. We shall restrict our analysis to this type of whistleblowing because, in the first place, the conditions that justify whistleblowing vary according to the type of case at issue. Second, financial harm can be considerably different from bodily harm. An immoral practice that increases the cost of a product by a slight margin may do serious harm to no individual, even if the total amount when summed adds up to a large amount, or profit. (Such cases can be handled differently from cases that threaten bodily harm.) Third, both internal and personal whistleblowing cause problems for a firm, which are for the most part restricted to those within the firm. External, impersonal whistleblowing is of concern to the general public, because it is the general public rather than the firm that is threatened with harm.

As a paradigm, we shall take a set of fairly clear-cut cases, namely, those in which serious bodily harm—including possible death—threatens either the users of a product or innocent bystanders because of a firm's practice, the design of its product, or the action of some person or persons within the firm. (Many of the famous whistleblowing cases are instances of such situations.) We shall assume clear cases where serious, preventable harm will result unless a company makes changes in its product or practice.

Cases that are less clear are probably more numerous, and pose problems that are difficult to solve, for example, how serious is *serious* and how does one tell whether a given situation is serious? We choose not to resolve such issues, but rather to construct a model embodying a number of distinctions that will enable us to clarify the moral status of whistleblowing, which may, in turn, provide a basis for working out guidelines for more complex cases.

Finally, the only motivation for whistleblowing we shall consider here is moral motivation. Those who blow the whistle for revenge, and so on, are not our concern in this discussion.

Corporations are complex entities. Sometimes those at the top do not want to know in detail the difficulties encountered by those below them. They wish lower-management to handle these difficulties as best they can. On the other hand, those in lower management frequently present only good news to those above them, even if those at the top do want to be told about difficulties. Sometimes, lower-management hopes that things will be straightened out without letting their superiors know that anything has gone wrong. For instance, sometimes a production schedule is drawn up, which many employees along the line know cannot be achieved. Each level has cut off a few days of the production time actually needed, to make his projection look good to those above. Because this happens at each level, the final projection is weeks, if not months, off the mark. When difficulties develop in actual production, each level is further squeezed and is tempted to cut corners in order not to fall too far behind the overall schedule. The cuts may be that of not correcting defects in a design, or of allowing a defective part to go through, even though a department head and the workers in that department know that this will cause trouble for the consumer. Sometimes a defective part will be annoying; sometimes it will be dangerous. If dangerous, external whistleblowing may be morally mandatory.

The whistleblower usually fares very poorly at the hands of his company. Most are fired. In some instances, they have been blackballed in the whole industry. If they are not fired, they are frequently shunted aside at promotion time, and treated as pariahs. Those who consider making a firm's wrongdoings public must therefore be aware that they may be fired, ostracized, and condemned by others. They may ruin their chances of future promotion and security; and they also may make themselves a target for revenge. Only rarely have companies praised and promoted such people. This is not surprising, because the whistleblower forces the company to do what it did not want to do, even if, morally, it was the right action. This is scandalous. And it is ironic that those guilty of endangering the lives of others— even of indirectly killing them—frequently get promoted by their companies for increasing profits.

Because the consequences for the whistleblower are often so disastrous, such action is not to be undertaken lightly. Moreover, whistleblowing may, in some cases, be morally justifiable without being morally mandatory. The position we shall develop is a moderate one, and falls between two extreme positions: that defended by those who claim that whistleblowing is always morally justifiable, and that defended by those who say it is never morally justifiable.

Whistleblowing as Morally Permitted

The kind of whistleblowing we are considering involves an employee somehow going public, revealing information or concerns about his or her firm in the hope that the firm will change its product, action, or policy, or whatever it is that the whistleblower feels will harm, or has harmed others, and needs to be rectified. We can assume that when one blows the whistle, it is not with the consent of the firm, but against its wishes. It is thus a form of disloyalty and of disobedience to the corporation. Whistleblowing of this type, we can further assume, does injury to a firm. It results in either adverse publicity or in an investigation of some sort, or both. If we adopt the principle that one ought not to do harm without sufficient reason, then, if the act of whistleblowing is to be morally permissible, some good must be achieved that outweighs the harm that will be done.

There are five conditions, which, if satisfied, change the moral status of whistleblowing. If the first three are satisfied, the act of whistleblowing will be morally justifiable and permissible. If the additional two are satisfied, the act of whistleblowing will be morally obligatory.

Whistleblowing is morally permissible if—

1. The firm, through its product or policy, will do serious and considerable harm to the public, whether in the person of the user of its product, an innocent bystander, or the general public.

Because whistleblowing causes harm to the firm, this harm must be offset by at least an equal amount of good, if the act is to be permissible. We have specified that the potential or actual harm to others must be serious and considerable. That requirement may be considered by some to be both too strong and too vague. Why specify "serious and considerable" instead of saying, "involve more harm than the harm that the whistleblowing will produce for the firm?" Moreover, how serious is "serious?" And how considerable is "considerable?"

There are several reasons for stating that the potential harm must be serious and considerable. First, if the harm is not serious and considerable, if it will do only slight harm to the public, or to the user of a product, the justification for whistleblowing will be at least problematic. We will not have a clear case. To assess the harm done to the firm is difficult; but though the harm may be rather vague, it is also rather sure. If the harm threatened by a product is slight or not certain, it might not be greater than the harm done to the firm. After all, a great many products involve some risk. Even with a well-constructed hammer, one can smash one's finger. There is some risk in operating any automobile, because no automobile is completely safe. There is always a trade-off between safety and cost. It is not immoral not to make the safest automobile possible, for instance, and a great many factors enter into deciding just how safe a car should be. An employee might see that a car can be made slightly safer by modifying a part, and might suggest that modification; but not making the modification is not usually grounds for blowing the whistle. If serious harm is not threatened, then the slight harm that is done say by the use of a product, can be corrected after the product is marketed (e.g., as a result of customer complaint). Our society has a great many ways of handling minor defects, and these are at least arguably better than resorting to whistleblowing.

To this consideration should be added a second. Whistleblowing is frequently, and appropriately, considered an unusual occurrence, a heroic act. If the practice of blowing the whistle for relatively minor harm were to become a common occurrence, its effectiveness would be diminished. When serious harm is threatened, whistleblowers are listened to by the news media, for instance, because it is news. But relatively minor harm to the public is not news. If many minor charges or concerns were voiced to the media, the public would soon not react as it is now expected to react to such disclosures. This would also be the case if complaints about all sorts of perceived or anticipated minor harm were reported to government agencies, although most people would expect that government agencies would act first on the serious cases, and only later on claims of relatively minor harm.

There is a third consideration. Every time an employee has a concern about possible harm to the public from a product or practice we cannot assume that he or she makes a correct assessment. Nor can we assume that every claim of harm is morally motivated. To sift out the claims and concerns of the disaffected worker from the genuine claims and concerns of the morally motivated employee is a practical problem. It may be claimed that this problem has nothing to do with the moral permissibility of the act of whistleblowing; but whistleblowing is a practical matter. If viewed as a technique for changing policy or actions, it will be justified only if effective. It can be trivialized. If it is, then one might plausibly claim that little harm is done to the firm, and hence the act is permitted. But if trivialized, it loses its point. If whistleblowing is to be considered a serious act with serious consequences, it should be reserved for disclosing potentially serious harm, and will be morally justifiable in those cases.

Serious is admittedly a vague term. Is an increase in probable automobile deaths, from 2 in 100,000 to 15 in 100,000 over a one-year period, serious? Although there may be legitimate debate on this issue, it is clear that matters that threaten death are prima facie serious. If the threatened harm is that a product may cost a few pennies more than otherwise, or if the threatened harm is that a part or product may cause minor inconvenience, the harm—even if multiplied by thousands or millions of instances—does not match the seriousness of death to the user or the innocent bystander.

The harm threatened by unsafe tires, which are sold as premium quality but that blow out at 60 or 70 mph, is serious, for such tires can easily lead to death. The dumping of metal drums of toxic waste into a river, where the drums will rust, leak, and cause cancer or other serious ills to those who drink the river water or otherwise use it, threatens serious harm. The use of substandard concrete in a building, such that it is likely to collapse and kill people, poses a serious threat to people. Failure to x-ray pipe fittings, as required in building a nuclear plant, is a failure that might lead to nuclear leaks; this involves potential serious harm, for it endangers the health and lives of many.

The notion of serious harm might be expanded to include serious financial harm, and kinds of harm other than death and serious threats to health and body. But as we noted earlier, we shall restrict ourselves here to products and practices that produce or threaten serious harm or danger to life and health. The difference between producing harm and threatening serious danger is not significant for the kinds of cases we are considering.

2.   Once an employee identifies a serious threat to the user of a product or to the general public, he or she should report it to his or her immediate superior and make his or her moral concern known. Unless he or she does so, the act of whistleblowing is not clearly justifiable.

Why not? Why is not the weighing of harm sufficient? The answer has already been given in part. Whistleblowing is a practice that, to be effective, cannot be routinely used. There are other reasons as well. First, reporting one's concerns is the most direct, and usually the quickest, way of producing the change the whistleblower desires. The normal assumption is that most firms do not want to cause death or injury, and do not willingly and knowingly set out to harm the users of their products in this way. If there are life-threatening defects, the normal assumption is, and should be, that the firm will be interested in correcting them—if not for moral reasons, at least for prudential reasons, viz., to avoid suits, bad publicity, and adverse consumer reaction. The argument from loyalty also supports the requirement that the firm be given the chance to rectify its action or procedure or policy before it is charged in public. Additionally, because whistleblowing does harm to the firm, harm in general is minimized if the firm is informed of the problem and allowed to correct it. Less harm is done to the firm in this way, and if the harm to the public

or the users is also averted, this procedure produces the least harm, on the whole.

The condition that one report one's concern to one's immediate superior presupposes a hierarchical structure. Although firms are usually so structured, they need not be. In a company of equals, one would report one's concerns internally, as appropriate.

Several objections may be raised to this condition. Suppose one knows that one's immediate superior already knows the defect and the danger. In this case reporting it to him or her would be redundant, and condition two would be satisfied. But one should not presume without good reason that one's superior does know. What may be clear to one individual may not be clear to another. Moreover, the assessment of risk is often a complicated matter. To a person on one level what appears as unacceptable risk may be defensible as legitimate to a person on a higher level, who may see a larger picture, and knows of offsetting compensations, and the like.

However, would not reporting one's concern effectively preclude the possibility of anonymous whistleblowing, and so put one in jeopardy? This might of course be the case; and this is one of the considerations one should weigh before blowing the whistle. We will discuss this matter later on. If the reporting is done tactfully,. moreover, the voicing of one's concerns might, if the problem is apparent to others, indicate a desire to operate within the firm, and so make one less likely to be the one assumed to have blown the whistle anonymously.

By reporting one's concern to one's immediate superior or other appropriate person, one preserves and observes the regular practices of firms, which on the whole promote their order and efficiency; this fulfills one's obligation of minimizing harm, and it precludes precipitous whistleblowing.

3.   If one's immediate superior does nothing effective about the concern or complaint, the employee should exhaust the internal procedures and possibilities within the firm. This usually

will involve taking the matter up the managerial ladder, and, if necessary—and possible—to the board of directors.

To exhaust the internal procedures and possibilities is the key requirement here. In a hierarchically structured firm, this means going up the chain of command. But one may do so either with or without the permission of those at each level of the hierarchy. What constitutes exhausting the internal procedures? This is often a matter of judgment. But because going public with one's concern is more serious for both oneself and for the firm, going up the chain of command is the preferable route to take in most circumstances. This third condition is satisfied of course if, for some reason, it is truly impossible to go beyond any particular level.

Several objections may once again be raised. There may not be time enough to follow the bureaucratic procedures of a given firm; the threatened harm may have been done before the procedures are exhausted. If, moreover, one goes up the chain to the top and nothing is done by anyone, then a great deal of time will have been wasted. Once again, prudence and judgment should be used. The internal possibilities may sometimes be exhausted quickly, by a few phone calls or visits. But one should not simply assume that no one at any level within the firm will do anything. If there are truly no possibilities of internal remedy, then the third condition is satisfied.

As we mentioned, the point of the three conditions is essentially that whistleblowing is morally permissible if the harm threatened is serious, and if internal remedies have been attempted in good faith but without a satisfactory result. In these circumstances, one is morally justified in attempting to avert what one sees as serious harm, by means that may be effective, including blowing the whistle.

We can pass over as not immediately germane the questions of whether in nonserious matters one has an obligation to report one's moral concerns to one's superiors, and whether one fulfills one's obligation once one has reported them to the appropriate party.

Whistleblowing as Morally Required

To say that whistleblowing is morally permitted does not impose any obligation on an employee. Unless two other conditions are met, the employee does not have a moral obligation to blow the whistle. To blow the whistle when one is not morally required to do so, and if done from moral motives (i.e., concern for one's fellow man) and at risk to oneself, is to commit a supererogatory act. It is an act that deserves moral praise. But failure to so act deserves no moral blame. In such a case, the whistleblower might be considered a moral hero. Sometimes he or she is so considered, sometimes not. If one's claim or concern turns out to be ill-founded, one's subjective moral state may be as praiseworthy as if the claim were well-founded, but one will rarely receive much praise for one's action.

For there to be an obligation to blow the whistle, two conditions must be met, in addition to the foregoing three.

4. The whistleblower must have, or have accessible, documented evidence that would convince a reasonable, impartial observer that one's view of the situation is correct, and that the company's product or practice poses a serious and likely danger to the public or to the use of the product.

One does not have an obligation to put oneself at serious risk without some compensating advantage to be gained. Unless one has documented evidence that would convince a reasonable, impartial observer, one's charges or claims, if made public, would be based essentially on one's word. Such grounds may be sufficient for a subjective feeling of certitude about one's charges, but they are not usually sufficient for others to act on one's claims. For instance, a newspaper is unlikely to print a story based simply on someone's undocumented assertion.

Several difficulties emerge. Should it not be the responsibility of the media or the appropriate regulatory agency or government bureau to carry out an investigation based on someone's complaint? It is reasonable for them to do so, providing they have some evidence in support of the complaint or claim. The damage has not yet been done, and the harm will not, in all likelihood, be done to the complaining party. If the action is criminal, then an investigation by a law-enforcing agency is appropriate. But the charges made by whistleblowers are often not criminal charges. And we do not expect newspapers or government agencies to carry out investigations whenever anyone claims that possible harm will be done by a product or practice. Unless harm is imminent, and very serious (e.g., a bomb threat), it is appropriate to act on evidence that substantiates a claim. The usual procedure, once an investigation is started or a complaint followed up, is to contact the party charged.

One does not have a moral obligation to blow the whistle simply because of one's hunch, guess, or personal assessment of possible danger, if supporting evidence and documentation are not available. One may, of course, have the obligation to attempt to get evidence if the harm is serious. But if it is unavailable—or unavailable without using illegal or immoral means—then one does not have the obligation to blow the whistle.

5. The employee must have good reason to believe that by going public the necessary changes will be brought about. The chance of being successful must be worth the risk one takes and the danger to which one is exposed.

Even with some documentation and evidence, a potential whistleblower may not be taken seriously, or may not be able to get the media or government agency to take any action. How far should one go, and how much must one try? The more serious the situation, the greater the effort required. But unless one has a reasonable expectation of success, one is not obliged to put oneself at great risk. Before going public, the potential whistleblower should know who (e.g., government agency, newspaper, columnist, TV reporter) will make use of his or her evidence, and how it will be handled. He or she should have good reason to expect that the action taken will result in the kind of change or result that he or she believes is morally appropriate.

The foregoing fourth and fifth conditions may seem too permissive to some and too stringent to others. They are too permissive for those who wish everyone to be ready and willing to blow the whistle whenever there is a chance that the public will be harmed. After all, harm to the public is more serious than harm to the whistleblower, and, in the long run, if everyone saw whistleblowing as obligatory, without satisfying the last two conditions, we would all be better off. If the fourth and fifth conditions must be satisfied, then people will only rarely have the moral obligation to blow the whistle.

If, however, whistleblowing were mandatory whenever the first three conditions were satisfied, and if one had the moral obligation to blow the whistle whenever one had a moral doubt or fear about safety, or whenever one disagreed with one's superiors or colleagues, one would be obliged to go public whenever one did not get one's way on such issues within a firm. But these conditions are much too weak, for the reasons already given. Other, stronger conditions, but weaker than those proposed, might be suggested. But any condition that makes whistleblowing mandatory in large numbers of cases, may possibly reduce the effectiveness of whistleblowing. If this were the result, and the practice were to become widespread, then it is doubtful that we would all be better off.

Finally, the claim that many people very often have the obligation to blow the whistle goes against the common view of the whistleblower as a moral hero, and against the commonly held feeling that whistleblowing is only rarely morally mandatory.

This feeling may be misplaced. But a very strong argument is necessary to show that although the general public is morally mistaken in its view, the moral theoretician is correct in his or her assertion.

A consequence of accepting the fourth and fifth conditions stated is that the stringency of the moral obligation of whistleblowing corresponds with the common feeling of most people on this issue. Those in higher positions and those in professional positions in a firm are more likely to have the obligation to change a firm's policy or product—even by whistleblowing, if necessary—than are lower-placed employees. Engineers, for instance, are more likely to have access to data and designs than are assembly-line workers. Managers generally have a broader picture, and more access to evidence, than do non-managerial employees. Management has the moral responsibility both to see that the expressed moral concerns of those below them have been adequately considered and that the firm does not knowingly inflict harm on others.

The fourth and fifth conditions will appear too stringent to those who believe that whistleblowing is always a supererogatory act, that is always moral heroism, and that it is never morally obligatory. They might argue that, although we are not permitted to do what is immoral, we have no general moral obligation to prevent all others from acting immorally. This is what the whistleblower attempts to do. The counter to that, however, is to point out that whistleblowing is an act in which one attempts to prevent harm to a third party. It is not implausible to claim both that we are morally obliged to prevent harm to others at relatively little expense to ourselves, and that we are morally obliged to prevent great harm to a great many others, even at considerable expense to ourselves.

The five conditions outlined can be used by an individual to help decide whether he or she is morally permitted or required to blow the whistle. Third parties can also use these conditions when attempting to evaluate acts of whistleblowing by others, even though third parties may have difficulty determining whether the whistleblowing is morally motivated. It might be possible successfully to blow the whistle anonymously. But anonymous tips or stories seldom get much attention. One can confide in a government agent, or in a reporter, on condition that one's name not be disclosed. But this approach, too, is frequently ineffective in achieving the results required. To be effective, one must usually be willing to be identified, to testify publicly, to produce verifiable evidence, and to put oneself at risk. As with civil disobedience, what captures the conscience of others is the willingness of the whistleblower to suffer harm for the benefit of others, and for what he or she thinks is right.

Precluding the Need for Whistleblowing

The need for moral heroes shows a defective society and defective corporations. It is more important to change the legal and corporate structures that make whistleblowing necessary than to convince people to be moral heroes.

Because it is easier to change the law than to change the practices of all corporations, it should be illegal for any employer to fire an employee, or to take any punitive measures, at the time or later, against an employee who satisfies the first three aforementioned conditions and blows the whistle on the company. Because satisfying those conditions makes the action morally justifiable, the law should protect the employee in acting in accordance with what his or her conscience demands. If the whistle is falsely blown, the company will have suffered no great harm. If it is appropriately blown, the company should suffer the consequences of its actions being made public. But to protect a whistleblower by passing such a law is no easy matter. Employers can make life difficult for whistleblowers without firing them. There are many ways of passing over an employee. One can be relegated to the back room of the firm, or be given unpleasant jobs. Employers can find reasons not to promote one or to give one raises. Not all of this can be prevented by law, but some of the more blatant practices can be prohibited.

Second, the law can mandate that the individuals responsible for the decision to proceed with a faulty product or to engage in a harmful practice be penalized. The law has been reluctant to interfere with the operations of companies. As a result, those in the firm who have been guilty of immoral and illegal practices have gone untouched even though the corporation was fined for its activity.

A third possibility is that every company of a certain size be required, by law, to have an inspector general or an internal operational auditor, whose job it is to uncover immoral and illegal practices. This person's job would be to listen to the moral concerns of employees, at every level, about the firm's practices. He or she should be independent of management, and report to the audit committee of the board, which, ideally, should be a committee made up entirely of outside board members. The inspector or auditor should be charged with making public those complaints that should be made public if not changed from within. Failure on the inspector's part to take proper action with respect to a worker's complaint, such that the worker is forced to go public, should be prima facie evidence of an attempt to cover up a dangerous practice or product, and the inspector should be subject to criminal charges.

In addition, a company that wishes to be moral, that does not wish to engage in harmful practices or to produce harmful products, can take other steps to preclude the necessity of whistleblowing. The company can establish channels whereby those employees who have moral concerns can get a fair hearing without danger to their position or standing in the company. Expressing such concerns, moreover, should be considered a demonstration of company loyalty and should be rewarded appropriately. The company might establish the position of ombudsman, to hear such complaints or moral concerns. Or an independent committee of the board might be established to hear such complaints and concerns. Someone might even be paid by the company to present the position of the would-be whistleblower, who would argue for what the company should do, from a moral point of view, rather than what those interested in meeting a schedule or making a profit would like to do. Such a person's success within the company could depend on his success in precluding whistleblowing, as well as the conditions that lead to it.

◆ ◆ ◆ ◆ ◆

ROBERT A. LARMER

Whistleblowing and Employee Loyalty

Whistleblowing by an employee is the act of complaining, either within the corporation or publicly, about a corporation's unethical practices. Such an act raises important questions concerning the loyalties and duties of employees. Traditionally, the employee has been viewed as an agent who acts on behalf of a principal, i.e., the employer, and as possessing duties of loyalty and confidentiality. Whistleblowing, at least at first blush, seems a violation of these duties and it is scarcely surprising that in many instances employers and fellow employees argue that it is an act of disloyalty and hence morally wrong.[1]

It is this issue of the relation between whistleblowing and employee loyalty that I want to address. What I will call the standard view is that employees possess *prima facie* duties of loyalty and confidentiality to their employers and that whistleblowing cannot be justified except on the basis of a higher duty to the public good. Against this standard view, Ronald Duska has recently argued that employees do not have even a *prima facie* duty of loyalty to their employers and that whistleblowing needs, therefore, no moral justification.[2] I am going to criticize both views. My suggestion is that both misunderstand the relation between loyalty and whistleblowing. In their place I will propose a third more adequate view.

Duska's view is more radical in that it suggests that there can be no issue of whistleblowing and employee loyalty, since the employee has no duty to be loyal to his employer. His reason for suggesting that the employee owes the employer, at least the corporate employer, no loyalty is that companies are not the kinds of things which are proper objects of loyalty. His argument in support of this rests upon two key claims. The first is that loyalty, properly understood, implies a reciprocal relationship and is only appropriate in the context of a mutual surrendering of self-interest. He writes,

> It is important to recognize that in any relationship which demands loyalty the relationship works both ways and involves mutual enrichment. Loyalty is incompatible with self-interest, because it is something that necessarily requires we go beyond self-interest. My loyalty to my friend, for example, requires I put aside my interests some of the time.... Loyalty depends on ties that demand self-sacrifice with no expectation of reward, e.g., the ties of loyalty that bind a family together.[3]

The second is that the relation between a company and an employee does not involve any surrender of self-interest on the part of the company, since its primary goal is to maximize profit. Indeed, although it is convenient, it is misleading to talk of a company having interests. As Duska comments,

> A company is not a person. A company is an instrument, and an instrument with a specific purpose, the making of profit. To treat an instrument as an end in itself, like a person, may not be as bad as treating an end as an instrument, but it does given the instrument a moral status it does not deserve....[4]

Since, then, the relation between a company and an employee does not fulfill the minimal requirement of being a relation between two individuals, much less two reciprocally self-sacrificing individuals, Duska feels it is a mistake to suggest the employee has any duties of loyalty to the company.

This view does not seem adequate, however. First, it is not true that loyalty must be quite so reciprocal as Duska demands. Ideally, of course, one expects that if one is loyal to another person that person will reciprocate in kind. There are, however, many cases where loyalty is not entirely reciprocated, but where we do not feel that it is misplaced. A parent, for example, may remain loyal to an erring teenager, even though the teenager demonstrates no loyalty to the parent. Indeed, part of being a proper parent is to demonstrate loyalty to your children whether or not that loyalty is reciprocated. This is not to suggest any kind of analogy between parents and employees, but rather that it is not nonsense to suppose that loyalty may be appropriate even though it is not reciprocated. Inasmuch as he ignores this possibility, Duska's account of loyalty is flawed.

Second, even if Duska is correct in holding that loyalty is only appropriate between moral agents and that a company is not genuinely a moral agent, the question may still be raised whether an employee owes loyalty to fellow employees or the shareholders of the company. Granted that reference to a company as an individual involves reification and should not be taken too literally, it may nevertheless constitute a legitimate shorthand way of describing relations between genuine moral agents.

Third, it seems wrong to suggest that simply because the primary motive of the employer is economic, considerations of loyalty are irrelevant. An employee's primary motive in working for an employer is generally economic, but no one on that account would argue that it is impossible for her to demonstrate loyalty to the employer, even if it turns out to be misplaced. All that is required is that her primary economic motive be in some degree qualified by considerations of the employer's welfare. Similarly, the fact that an employer's primary motive is economic does not imply that it is not qualified by considerations of the employee's welfare. Given the possibility of mutual qualification of admittedly primary economic motives, it is fallacious to argue that employee loyalty is never appropriate.

In contrast to Duska, the standard view is that loyalty to one's employer is appropriate. According to it, one has an obligation to be loyal to one's employer and, consequently, a *prima facie* duty to protect the employer's interests. Whistleblowing constitutes, therefore, a violation of duty to one's employer and needs strong justification if it is to be appropriate. Sissela Bok summarizes this view very well when she writes

> the whistleblower hopes to stop the game; but since he is neither referee nor coach, and since he blows the whistle on his own team, his act is seen as a violation of loyalty. In holding his position, he has assumed certain obligations to his colleagues and clients. He may even have subscribed to a loyalty oath or a promise of confidentiality. Loyalty to colleagues and to clients comes to be pitted against loyalty to the public interest, to those who may be injured unless the revelation is made.[5]

The strength of this view is that it recognizes that loyalty is due one's employer. Its weakness is that it tends to conceive of whistleblowing as involving a tragic moral choice, since blowing the whistle is seen not so much as a positive action, but rather the lesser of two evils. Bok again puts the essence of this view very clearly when she writes that "a would-be whistleblower must weigh his responsibility to serve the public interest *against* the responsibility he owes to his colleagues and the institution in which he works" and "that [when] their duty [to whistleblow] ... *so overrides loyalties to colleagues and institutions*, they [whistleblowers] often have reason to fear the results of carrying out such a duty."[6] The employee, according to this understanding of whistleblowing, must choose between two acts of betrayal, either her employer or the public interest, each in itself reprehensible.

Behind this view lies the assumption that to be loyal to someone is to act in a way that accords with what that person believes to be in her best interests. To be loyal to an employer, therefore, is to act in a way which the employer deems to be in his or her best interests. Since employers very rarely approve of whistleblowing and generally feel that it is not in their best interests, it follows that whistleblowing is an act of betrayal on the part of the employee, albeit a betrayal made in the interests of the public good.

Plausible though it initially seems, I think this view of whistleblowing is mistaken and that it embodies a mistaken conception of what constitutes employee loyalty. It ignores the fact that

> the great majority of corporate whistleblowers ... [consider] themselves to be very loyal employees who ... [try] to use "direct voice" (internal whistleblowing), ... [are] rebuffed and punished for this, and then ... [use] "indirect voice" (external whistleblowing). They ... [believe] initially that they ... [are] behaving in a loyal manner, helping their employers by calling top management's attention to practices that could eventually get the firm in trouble.[7]

By ignoring the possibility that blowing the whistle may demonstrate greater loyalty than not blowing the whistle, it fails to do justice to the many instances where loyalty to someone constrains us to act in defiance of what that person believes to be in her best interests. I am not, for example, being disloyal to a friend if I refuse to loan her money for an investment I am sure will bring her financial ruin; even if she bitterly reproaches me for denying her what is so obviously a golden opportunity to make a fortune.

A more adequate definition of being loyal to someone is that loyalty involves acting in accordance with what one has good reason to believe to be in that person's best interests. A key question, of course, is what constitutes a good reason to think that something is in a person's best interests. Very often, but by no means invariably, we accept that a person thinking that something is in her best interests is a sufficiently good reason to think that it actually is. Other times, especially when we feel that she is being rash, foolish, or misinformed we are prepared, precisely by virtue of being loyal, to act contrary to the person's wishes. It is beyond the scope of this paper to investigate such cases in detail, but three general points can be made.

First, to the degree that an action is genuinely immoral, it is impossible that it is in the agent's best interests. We would not, for example, say that someone who sells child pornography was acting in his own best interests, even if he vigorously protested that there was nothing wrong with such activity. Loyalty does not imply that we have a duty to refrain from reporting the immoral actions of those to whom we are loyal. An employer who is acting immorally is not acting in her own best interests and an employee is not acting disloyally in blowing the whistle.[8] Indeed, the argument can be made that the employee who blows the whistle may be demonstrating greater loyalty than the employee who simply ignores the immoral conduct, inasmuch as she is attempting to prevent her employer from engaging in self-destructive behaviour.

Second, loyalty requires that, whenever possible, in trying to resolve a problem we deal directly with the person to whom we are loyal. If, for example, I am loyal to a friend I do not immediately involve a third party when I try to dissuade my friend from involvement in immoral actions. Rather, I approach my friend directly, listen to his perspective on the events in question, and provide an opportunity for him to address the problem in a morally satisfactory way. This implies that, whenever possible, a loyal employee blows the whistle internally. This provides the employer with the opportunity to either demon-

strate to the employee that, contrary to first appearances, no genuine wrongdoing had occurred, or, if there is a genuine moral problem, the opportunity to resolve it.

This principle of dealing directly with the person to whom loyalty is due needs to be qualified, however. Loyalty to a person requires that one acts in that person's best interests. Generally, this cannot be done without directly involving the person to whom one is loyal in the decision-making process, but there may arise cases where acting in a person's best interests requires that one act independently and perhaps even against the wishes of the person to whom one is loyal. Such cases will be especially apt to arise when the person to whom one is loyal is either immoral or ignoring the moral consequences of his actions. Thus, for example, loyalty to a friend who deals in hard narcotics would not imply that I speak first to my friend about my decision to inform the police of his activities, if the only effect of my doing so would be to make him more careful in his criminal dealings. Similarly, a loyal employee is under no obligation to speak first to an employer about the employer's immoral actions, if the only response of the employer will be to take care to cover up wrongdoing.

Neither is a loyal employee under obligation to speak first to an employer if it is clear that by doing so she placed herself in jeopardy from an employer who will retaliate if given the opportunity. Loyalty amounts to acting in another's best interests and that may mean qualifying what seems to be in one's own interests, but it cannot imply that one take no steps to protect oneself from the immorality of those to whom one is loyal. The reason it cannot is that, as has already been argued, acting immorally can never really be in a person's best interests. It follows, therefore, that one is not acting in a person's best interests if one allows oneself to be treated immorally by that person. Thus, for example, a father might be loyal to a child even though the child is guilty of stealing from him, but this would not mean that the father should let the child continue to steal. Similarly, an employee may be loyal to an employer even though she takes steps to protect herself against unfair retaliation by the employer, e.g., by blowing the whistle externally.

Third, loyalty requires that one is concerned with more than considerations of justice. I have been arguing that loyalty cannot require one to ignore immoral or unjust behaviour on the part of those to whom one is loyal, since loyalty amounts to acting in a person's best interests and it can never be in a person's best interests to be allowed to act immorally. Loyalty, however, goes beyond considerations of justice in that, while it is possible to be disinterested and just, it is not possible to be disinterested and loyal. Loyalty implies a desire that the person to whom one is loyal take no moral stumbles, but that if moral stumbles have occurred that the person be restored and not simply punished. A loyal friend is not only someone who sticks by you in times of trouble, but someone who tries to help you avoid trouble. This suggests that a loyal employee will have a desire to point out problems and potential problems long before the drastic measures associated with whistleblowing become necessary, but that if whistleblowing does become necessary there remains a desire to help the employer.

In conclusion, although much more could be said on the subject of loyalty, our brief discussion has enabled us to clarify considerably the relation between whistleblowing and employee loyalty. It permits us to steer a course between the Scylla of Duska's view that, since the primary link between employer and employee is economic, the ideal of employee loyalty is an oxymoron and the Charybdis of the standard view that, since it forces an employee to weigh conflicting duties, whistleblowing inevitably involves some degree of moral tragedy. The solution lies in realizing that to whistleblow for reasons of morality is to act in one's employer's best interests and involves, therefore, no disloyalty.

NOTES

1 The definition I have proposed applies most directly to the relation between privately owned companies aiming to realize a profit and their employees. Obviously, issues of whistleblowing arise in other contexts, e.g., governmental organizations or charitable agencies, and deserve careful thought. I do not propose, in this paper, to discuss whistleblowing in these other contexts, but I think my development of the concept of whistleblowing as positive demonstration of loyalty can easily be applied and will prove useful.

2 Duska, R. 1985, "Whistleblowing and Employee Loyalty," in J.R. Desjardins and J.J. McCall, eds., *Contemporary Issues in Business Ethics* (Belmont, CA: Wadsworth), 295-300.

3 Duska, 297.

4 Duska, 298.

5 Bok, S. 1983, "Whistleblowing and Professional Responsibility," in T.L. Beauchamp and N.E. Bowie, eds., *Ethical Theory and Business*, 2nd ed. (Englewood Cliffs, NJ: Prentice-Hall Inc.), 261-69, 263.

6 Bok, 261-62, emphasis added.

7 Near, J.P. and P. Miceli. 1985, "Organizational Dissidence: The Case of Whistle-Blowing," *Journal of Business Ethics* 4, 1-16, 10.

8 As Near and Miceli note "The whistle-blower may provide valuable information helpful in improving organizational effectiveness ... the prevalence of illegal activity in organizations is associated with declining organizational performance" (1).

The general point is that the structure of the world is such that it is not in a company's long-term interests to act immorally. Sooner or later a company which flouts morality and legality will suffer.

DRUG TESTING

JOSEPH DESJARDINS AND RONALD DUSKA

Drug Testing in Employment

According to one survey, nearly one-half of all Fortune 500 companies were planning to administer drug tests to employees and prospective employees by the end of 1987.[1] Counter to what seems to be the current trend in favor of drug testing, we will argue that it is rarely legitimate to override an employee's or applicant's right to privacy by using such tests or procedures.[2]

Opening Stipulations

We take privacy to be an "employee right" by which we mean a presumptive moral entitlement to receive certain goods or be protected from certain harms in the workplace.[3] Such a right creates a *prima facie* obligation on the part of the employer to provide the relevant goods or, as in this case, refrain from the relevant harmful treatment. These rights prevent employees from being placed in the fundamentally coercive position where they must choose between their job and other basic human goods.

Further, we view the employer-employee relationship as essentially contractual. The employer-employee relationship is an economic one and, unlike relationships such as those between a government and its citizens or a parent and a child, exists primarily as a means for satisfying the economic interests of the contracting parties. The obligations that each party incurs are only those that it voluntarily takes on. Given such a contractual relationship, certain areas of the employee's life remain their own private concern and no employer has a right to invade them. On these presumptions we maintain that certain information about an employee is rightfully private, i.e., the employee has a right to privacy.

The Right to Privacy

According to George Brenkert, a right to privacy involves a three-place relation between a person A, some information X, and another person B. The right to privacy is violated only when B deliberately comes to possess information X about A, and no relationship between A and B exists which could justify B's coming to know X about A.[4] Thus, for example, the relationship one has with a mortgage company would justify that company's coming to know about one's salary, but the relationship one has with a neighbor does not justify the neighbor's coming to know that information. Hence, an employee's right to privacy is violated whenever personal information is requested, collected and/or used by an employer in a way or for any purpose that is *irrelevant to* or in *violation of* the contractual relationship that exists between employer and employee.

Since drug testing is a means for obtaining information, the information sought must be relevant to the contract in order for the drug testing not to violate privacy. Hence, we must first decide if knowledge of drug use obtained by drug testing is job-relevant. In cases where the knowledge of drug use is not relevant, there appears to be no justification for subjecting employees to drug tests. In cases where information of drug use is job-relevant, we need to consider if, when, and under what conditions using a means such as drug testing to obtain that knowledge is justified.

Is Knowledge of Drug Use Job-Relevant Information?

There seem to be two arguments used to establish that knowledge of drug use is job-relevant information. The first argument claims that drug use adversely affects job performance thereby leading to lower productivity, higher costs, and consequently lower profits. Drug testing is seen as a way of avoiding these adverse effects. According to some estimates twenty-five billion dollars ($25,000,000,000) are lost each year in the United States because of drug use.[5] This occurs because of loss in productivity, increase in costs due to theft, increased rates in health and liability insurance, and such. Since employers are contracting with an employee for the performance of specific tasks, employers seem to have a legitimate claim upon whatever personal information is relevant to an employee's ability to do the job.

The second argument claims that drug use has been and can be responsible for considerable harm to the employee him/herself, fellow employees, the employer, and/or third parties, including consumers. In this case drug testing is defended because it is seen as a way of preventing possibly harm. Further, since employers can be held liable for harms done both to third parties, e.g., customers, and to the employee or his/her fellow employees, knowledge of employee drug use will allow employers to gain information that can protect themselves from risks such as liability. But how good are these arguments? We turn to examine the arguments more closely.

The First Argument: Job Performance and Knowledge of Drug Use

The first argument holds that drug use leads to lower productivity and consequently implies that knowledge of drug use obtained through drug testing will allow an employer to increase productivity. It is generally assumed that people using certain drugs have their performances affected by such use. Since enhancing productivity is something any employer desires, any use of drugs that reduces productivity affects the employer in an undesirable way, and that use is, then, job-relevant. If such production losses can be eliminated by knowledge of the drug use, then knowledge of that drug use is job-relevant information. On the surface this argument seems reasonable. Obviously some drug use in lowering the level of performance can decrease productivity. Since the employer is entitled to a certain level of performance and drug use adversely affects performance, knowledge of that use seems job-relevant.

But this formulation of the argument leaves an important question unanswered. To what level of performance are employers entitled? Optimal performance, or some lower level? If some lower level, what? Employers have a valid claim upon some *certain level* of performance, such that a failure to get form up to this level would give the employer a justification for disciplining, firing or at least finding fault with the employee. But that does not necessarily mean that the employer has a right to a maximum or optimal level of performance, a level above and beyond a certain level of acceptability. It might be nice if the employee gives an employer a maximum effort or optimal performance, but that is above and beyond the call of the employee's duty and the employer can hardly claim a right at all times to the highest level of performance of which an employee is capable.

That there are limits on required levels of performance and productivity becomes clear if we recognize that job performance is person-related. It is person-related because one person's best efforts at a particular task might produce results well below the norm, while another person's minimal efforts might produce results abnormally high when compared to the norm. For example a professional baseball player's performance on a ball field will be much higher than the average person's since the average person is unskilled in baseball. We have all encountered people who work hard with little or no results, as well as people who work little with phenomenal results. Drug use in very talented people might diminish their performance or productivity, but that performance would still be better than the performance of the average person or someone totally lacking in the skills required. That being said, the important question now is whether the employer is entitled to an employee's maximum effort and best results, or merely to an effort sufficient to perform the task expected.

If the relevant consideration is whether the employee is producing as expected (according to the normal demands of the position and contract), not whether he/she is producing as much as possible, then knowledge of drug use is irrelevant or unnecessary. Let's see why.

If the person is producing what is expected, knowledge of drug use on the grounds of production is irrelevant since, *ex hypothesi* the production is satisfactory. If, on the other hand, the performance suffers, then, to the extent that it slips below the level justifiably expected, the employer has *prima facie* grounds for warning, disciplining or releasing the employee. But the justification for this is the person's unsatisfactory performance, not the person's use of drugs. Accordingly, drug use information is either unnecessary or irrelevant and consequently there are not sufficient grounds to override the right of privacy. Thus, unless we can argue that an employer is entitled to optimal performance, the argument fails.

This counter-argument should make it clear that the information which is sub-relevant, and consequently which is not rightfully private, is information about an employee's level of performance and not information about the underlying causes of that level. The fallacy of the argument which promotes drug testing in the name of increased productivity is the assumption that each employee is obliged to perform at an optimal, or at least quite high, level. But this is required under few, if any, contracts. What is required contractually is meeting the normally expected levels of production or performing the tasks in the job-description adequately (not optimally). If one can do that under the influence of drugs, then on the grounds of job-performance at least, drug use is rightfully private. If one cannot perform the task adequately, then the employee is not fulfilling the contract, and knowledge of the cause of the failure to perform is irrelevant on the contractual model.

Of course, if the employer suspects drug use or abuse as the cause of the unsatisfactory performance, then she might choose to help the person with counseling or rehabilitation. However, this does not seem to be something morally required of the employer. Rather, in the case of unsatisfactory performance, the employer has a *prima facie* justification for dismissing or disciplining the employee.

Before turning to the second argument which attempts to justify drug testing, we should mention a factor about drug use that is usually ignored in talk of productivity. The entire productivity argument is irrelevant for those cases in which employees use performance enhancing drugs. Amphetamines and steroids, for example, can actually enhance some performances. This points to the need for care when tying drug testing to job-performance. In the case of some drugs used by athletes, for example, drug testing is done because the drug-influenced performance is too good and therefore unfair, not because it leads to inadequate job-performance. In such a case, where the testing is done to ensure fair competition, the testing may be justified. But drug testing in sports is an entirely different matter than drug-testing in business.

To summarize our argument so far: Drug use may affect performance, but as long as the performance is at an acceptable level, the knowledge of drug use is irrelevant. If the performance is unacceptable, then that is sufficient cause for action to be taken. In this case an employee's failure to fulfill his/her end of a contract makes knowledge of the drug use unnecessary.

The Second Argument: Harm and the Knowledge of Drug Use to Prevent Harm

Even though the performance argument is inadequate, there is an argument that seems somewhat stronger. This is an argument based on the potential for drug use to cause harm. Using a type of Millian argument, one could argue that drug testing might be justified if such testing led to knowledge that would enable an employer to prevent harm. Drug use certainly can lead to harming others. Consequently, if knowledge of such drug use can prevent harm, then, knowing whether or not one's employee uses drugs might be a legitimate concern of an employer in certain circumstances. This second argument claims that knowledge of the employee's drug use is job-relevant because employees who are under the influence of drugs can pose a threat to the health and safety of themselves and others, and an employer who knows of that drug use and the harm it can cause has a responsibility to prevent it. Employers have both a general duty to prevent harm and the specific responsibility for harms done by their employees. Such responsibilities are sufficient reason for an employer to claim that information about an employee's drug use is relevant if that knowledge can prevent harm by giving the employer grounds for dismissing the employee or not allowing him/her to perform potentially harmful tasks. Employers might even claim a right to reduce unreasonable risks, in this case the risks involving legal and economic liability for harms caused by employees under the influence of drugs, as further justification for knowing about employee drug use.

This second argument differs from the first in which only a lowered job performance was relevant information. In this case, even to allow the performance is problematic, for the performance itself, more than being inadequate, can hurt people. We cannot be as sanguine about the prevention of harm as we can about inadequate production. Where drug use can cause serious harms, knowledge of that use becomes relevant if the knowledge of such use can lead to the prevention of harm and drug testing becomes justified as a means for obtaining that knowledge.

As we noted, we will begin initially by accepting this argument on roughly Millian grounds where restrictions on liberty are allowed in order to prevent harm to others. (The fact that one is harming oneself, if that does not harm others is not sufficient grounds for interference in another's behavior according to Mill.) In such a case an employer's obligation to prevent harm may override the obligation to respect an employee's privacy.

But let us examine this more closely. Upon examination, certain problems arise, so that even if there is a possibility of justifying drug testing to prevent harm, some caveats have to be observed and some limits set out.

Jobs with Potential to Cause Harm

To say that employers can use drug testing where that can prevent harm is not to say that every employer has the right to know about the drug use of every employee. Not every job poses a serious enough threat to justify an employer coming to know this information.

In deciding which jobs pose serious enough threats certain guidelines should be followed. First the potential for harm should be *clear* and *present*. Perhaps all jobs in some extended way pose potential threats to human well-being. We suppose an accountant's error could pose a threat of harm to someone somewhere. But some jobs like those of airline pilots, school bus drivers, public transit drivers and surgeons, are jobs in which unsatisfactory performance poses a clear and present danger to others. It would be much harder to make an argument that job performances by auditors, secretaries, executive vice-presidents for public relations, college teachers, professional athletes, and the like, could cause harm if those performances were carried on under the influence of drugs. They would cause harm only in exceptional cases.[6]

Not Every Person Is to Be Tested

But, even if we can make a case that a particular job involves a clear and present danger for causing harm if performed under the influence of drugs, it is not appropriate to treat everyone holding such a job the same. Not every job-holder is equally threatening. There is less reason to investigate an airline pilot for drug use if that pilot has a twenty-year record of exceptional service than there is to investigate a pilot whose behavior has become erratic and unreliable recently, or than one who reports to work smelling of alcohol and slurring his words. Presuming that every airline pilot is equally threatening is to deny individuals the respect that they deserve as autonomous, rational agents. It is to ignore previous history and significant differences. It is also probably inefficient and leads to the lowering of morale. It is the likelihood of causing harm, and not the fact of being an airline pilot *per se*, that is relevant in deciding which employees in critical jobs to test.

So, even if knowledge of drug use is justifiable to prevent harm, we must be careful to limit this justification to a range of jobs and people where the potential for harm is clear and present. The jobs must be jobs that clearly can cause harm, and the specific employee should not be someone who is reliable with a history of such reliability. Finally, the drugs being tested should be those drugs, the use of which in those jobs is really potentially harmful.

Limitations on Drug Testing Policies

Even when we identify those jobs and individuals where knowledge of drug use would be job-relevant information, we still need to examine whether some procedural limitations should not be placed upon the employer's testing for drugs. We have said that in cases where a real threat of harm exists and where

evidence exists suggesting that a particular employee poses such a threat, an employer could be justified in knowing about drug use in order to prevent the potential harm. But we need to recognize that as long as the employer has the discretion for deciding when the potential for harm is clear and present, and for deciding which employees pose the threat of harm, the possibility of abuse is great. Thus, some policy limiting the employer's power is called for.

Just as criminal law places numerous restrictions protecting individual dignity and liberty on the state's pursuit of its goals, so we should expect that some restrictions be placed on an employer in order to protect innocent employees from harm (including loss of job and damage to one's personal and professional reputation). Thus, some system of checks upon an employer's discretion in these matters seems advisable. Workers covered by collective bargaining agreements or individual contracts might be protected by clauses on those agreements that specify which jobs pose a real threat of harm (e.g., pilots but not cabin attendants) and what constitutes a just cause for investigating drug use. Local, state, and federal legislatures might do the same for workers not covered by employment contracts. What needs to be set up is a just employment relationship—one in which an employee's expectations and responsibilities are specified in advance and in which an employer's discretionary authority to discipline or dismiss an employee is limited.

Beyond that, any policy should accord with the nature of the employment relationship. Since that relationship is a contractual one, it should meet the condition of a morally valid contract, which is informed consent. Thus, in general, we would argue that only methods that have received the informed consent of employees can be used in acquiring information about drug use.[7]

A drug testing policy that requires all employees to submit to a drug test or to jeopardize their job would seem coercive and therefore unacceptable. Being placed in such a fundamentally coercive position of having to choose between one's job and one's privacy does not provide the conditions for truly free consent. Policies that are unilaterally established by employers would likewise be unacceptable. Working with employees to develop company policy seems the only way to ensure that the policy will be fair to both parties. Prior notice of testing would also be required in order to give employees the option of freely refraining from drug use. It is morally preferable to prevent drug use than to punish users after the fact, since this approach treats employees as capable of making rational and informed decisions.

Further procedural limitations seem advisable as well. Employees should be notified of the results of the test, they should be entitled to appeal the results (perhaps through further tests by an independent laboratory) and the information obtained through tests ought to be kept confidential. In summary, limitations upon employer discretion for administering drug tests can be derived from the nature of the employment contract and from the recognition that drug testing is justified by the desire to prevent harm, not the desire to punish wrongdoing.

Effectiveness of Drug Testing

Having declared that the employer might have a right to test for drug use in order to prevent harm, we still need to examine the second argument a little more closely. One must keep in mind that the justification of drug testing is the justification of a means to an end, the end of preventing harm, and that the means are a means which intrude into one's privacy. In this case, before one allows drug testing as a means, one should be clear that there are not more effective means available.

If the employer has a legitimate right, perhaps duty, to ascertain knowledge of drug use to prevent harm, it is important to examine exactly how effectively, and in what situations, the *knowledge* of the drug use will prevent the harm. So far we have just assumed that they will prevent the harm. But how?

Let us take an example to pinpoint the difficulty. Suppose a transit driver, shortly before work, took some cocaine which, in giving him a feeling of invulnerability, leads him to take undue risks in his driving. How exactly is drug testing going to contribute to the knowledge which will prevent the potential accident?

It is important to keep in mind that: (1) if the knowledge doesn't help prevent the harm, the testing is not justified on prevention grounds; (2) if the testing doesn't provide the relevant knowledge, it is not justified either; and finally, (3) even if it was justified, it would be undesirable if a more effective means for preventing harm were discovered.

Upon examination, the links between drug testing, knowledge of drug use, and prevention of harm are not as clear as they are presumed to be. As we investigate, it begins to seem that the knowledge of the drug use even though relevant in some instances, is not the most effective means to prevent harm.

Let us turn to this last consideration first. Is drug testing the most effective means for preventing harm caused by drug use?

Consider. If someone exhibits obviously drugged or drunken behavior, then this behavior itself is grounds for preventing the person from continuing on the job. Administering urine and blood tests, sending the specimens out for testing and waiting for a response, will not prevent harm in this instance. Much drug testing, because of the time lapse involved, is equally superfluous in those cases where an employee is in fact under the influence of drugs, but exhibits no or only subtly impaired behavior.

Thus, even if one grants that drug testing somehow prevents harm an argument can be made that there might be much more effective methods of preventing potential harm such as administering dexterity tests of the type employed by police in possible drunk-driving cases, or requiring suspect pilots to pass flight simulator tests.[8] Eye-hand coordination, balance, reflexes, and reasoning ability can all be tested with less intrusive, more easily administered, reliable technologies which give instant results. Certainly if an employer has just cause for believing that a specific employee presently poses a real threat of causing harm, such methods are just more effective in all ways than are urinalysis and blood testing.

Even were it possible to refine drug tests so that accurate results were immediately available, that knowledge would only be job-relevant if the drug use was clearly the cause of impaired job performance that could harm people. Hence, testing behavior still seems more direct and effective in preventing harm than testing for the presence of drugs *per se*.

In some cases, drug use might be connected with potential harms not by being causally connected to motor-function impairment, but by causing personality disorders (e.g., paranoia, delusions, etc.) that affect judgmental ability. Even though in such cases a *prima facie* justification for urinalysis or blood testing might exist, the same problems of effectiveness persist. How is the knowledge of the drug use attained by urinalysis and/or blood testing supposed to prevent the harm? Only if there is a causal link between the use and the potentially harmful behavior, would such knowledge be relevant. Even if we get the results of the test immediately, there is the necessity to have an established causal link between specific drug use and anticipated harmful personality disorders in specific people.

But it cannot be the task of an employer to determine that a specific drug is causally related to harm-causing personality disorders. Not every controlled substance is equally likely to cause personality changes in every person in every case. The establishment of the causal link between the use of certain drugs and harm-causing personality disorders is not the province of the employer, but the province of experts studying the effects of drugs. The burden of proof is on the employer to establish that the substance being investigated has been independently connected with the relevant psychological impairment and then, predict on that basis that the specific employee's psychological judgment has been or will soon be impaired in such a way as to cause harm.

But even when this link is established, it would seem that less intrusive means could be used to detect the potential problems, rather than relying upon the assumption of a causal link. Psychological tests of judgment, perception and memory, for example, would be a less intrusive and more direct means for acquiring the relevant information which is, after all, the likelihood of causing harm and not the presence of drugs *per se*. In short, drug testing even in these cases doesn't seem to be very effective in preventing harm on the spot.

Still, this does not mean it is not effective at all. Where it is most effective in preventing harm is in its getting people to stop using drugs or in identifying serious drug addiction. Or to put it another way, urinalysis and blood tests for drug use are most effective in preventing potential harm when they serve as a deterrent to drug use *before* it occurs, since it is very difficult to prevent harm by diagnosing drug use *after* it has occurred but before the potentially harmful behavior takes place.

Drug testing can be an effective deterrent when there is regular or random testing of all employees. This will prevent harm by inhibiting (because of the fear of detection) drug use by those who are occasional users and those who do not wish to be detected.

It will probably not inhibit or stop the use by the chronic addicted user, but it will allow an employer to discover the chronic user or addict, assuming that the tests are accurately administered and reliably evaluated. If the chronic user's addiction would probably lead to harmful behavior of others, the harm is prevented by taking that user off the job. Thus regular or random testing will prevent harms done by deterring the occasional user and by detecting the chronic user.

There are six possibilities for such testing:

1. regularly scheduled testing of all employees;
2. regularly scheduled testing of randomly selected employees;
3. randomly scheduled testing of all employees;
4. randomly scheduled testing of randomly selected employees;
5. regularly scheduled testing of employees selected for probable cause; or finally,
6. randomly scheduled testing of employees selected for probable cause.

Only the last two seem morally acceptable as well as effective.

Obviously randomly scheduled testing will be more effective than regularly scheduled testing in detecting the occasional user, because the occasional users can control their use to pass the tests, unless of course tests were given so often (a practice economically unfeasible) that they needed to stop together. Regular scheduling probably will detect the habitual or addicted user. Randomly selecting people to test is probably cheaper, as is random scheduling, but it is not nearly as effective as testing all. Besides, the random might miss some of the addicted altogether, and will not deter the risk takers as much as the risk aversive persons. It is, ironically, the former who are probably potentially more harmful.

But these are merely considerations of efficiency. We have said that testing without probable cause is unacceptable. Any type of regular testing of all employees is unacceptable. We have argued that testing employees without first establishing probable cause is an unjustifiable violation of employee privacy. Given this, and given the expense of general and regular testing of all employees (especially if this is done by responsible laboratories), it is more likely that random testing will be employed as the means of deterrence. But surely testing of randomly selected innocent employees is as intrusive to those tested as is regular testing. The argument that there will be fewer tests is correct on quantitative grounds, but qualitatively the intrusion and unacceptability are the same. The claim that employers should be allowed to sacrifice the well-being of (some few) innocent employees to deter (some equally few) potentially harmful employees seems, on the face of it, unfair. Just as we do not allow the state randomly to tap the telephones of just any citizen in order to prevent crime, so we ought not allow employers to drug test all employees randomly to prevent harm. To do so is again to treat innocent employees solely as a means to the end of preventing potential harm.

This leaves only the use of regular or random drug testing as a deterrent in those cases where probable cause exists for believing that a particular employee poses a threat of harm. It would seem that in this case, the drug testing is acceptable. In such cases only the question of effectiveness remains: Are the standard techniques of urinalysis and blood testing more effective means for preventing harms than alternatives such as dexterity tests? It seems they are effective in different ways. The dexterity tests show immediately if someone is incapable of performing a task, or will perform one in such a way as to cause harm to others. The urinalysis and blood testing will prevent harm indirectly by getting the occasional user to curtail their use, and by detecting the habitual or addictive user, which will allow the employer to either give treatment to the addictive personality or remove them from the job. Thus we can conclude that drug testing is effective in a limited way, but aside from inhibiting occasional users because of fear of detection and discovering habitual users, it seems problematic that it does much to prevent harm that couldn't be achieved by other means.

Consider one final issue in the case of the occasional user. They are the drug users who do weigh the risks and benefits and who are physically and psychologically free to decide. The question in their case is not simply "will the likelihood of getting caught by urinalysis or blood testing deter this individual from using drugs?" Given the benefits of psychological tests and dexterity tests described above, the question is "will the rational user be more deterred by urinalysis or blood testing than by random psycho-logical or dexterity tests?" And, if this is so, is this increase in the effectiveness of a deterrent sufficient to offset the increased expense and time required by drug tests?[9] We see no reason to believe that behav-ioral or judgment tests are not, or cannot be made to be, as effective in determining what an employer needs to know (i.e., that a particular employee may presently be a potential cause of harm). If the be-havioral, dexterity and judgment tests can be as ef-fective in determining a potential for harm, we see no reason to believe that they cannot be as effective a deterrent as drug tests. Finally, even if a case can be made for an increase in deterrent effect of drug test-ing, we are skeptical that this increased effectiveness will outweigh the increased inefficiencies.

In summary, we have seen that deterrence is ef-fective at times and under certain conditions allows the sacrificing of the privacy rights of innocent em-ployees to the future and speculative good of pre-venting harms to others. However, there are many ways to deter drug use when that deterrence is legit-imate and desirable to prevent harm. But random testing, which seems the only practicable means which has an impact in preventing harm, is the one which most offends workers' rights to privacy and which is most intrusive of the rights of the innocent. Even when effective, drug testing as a deterrent must be checked by the rights of employees.

Illegality Contention

At this point critics might note that the behavior which testing would try to deter is, after all, illegal. Surely this excuses any responsible employer from being overly protective of an employee's rights. The fact that an employee is doing something illegal should give the employer a right to that informa-tion about his private life. Thus, it is not simply that drug use might pose a threat of harm to others, but that it is an illegal activity that threatens others. But again, we would argue that illegal activity itself is ir-relevant to job performance. At best conviction rec-ords might be relevant, but, of course, since drug tests are administered by private employers we are not only exploring the question of conviction, we are also ignoring the fact that the employee has not even been arrested for the alleged illegal activity.

Further, even if the due process protections and the establishment of guilt is acknowledged, it still does not follow that employers have a claim to know about all illegal activity on the part of their employees.

Consider the following example: Suppose you were hiring an auditor whose job required certifying the integrity of your firm's tax and financial records. Certainly, the personal integrity of this employee is vital to the adequate job performance. Would we al-low the employer to conduct, with or without the employee's consent, an audit of the employee's own personal tax return? Certainly if we discover that this person has cheated on his/her own tax return we will have evidence of illegal activity that is relevant to this person's ability to do the job. Given one's own legal liability for filing falsified statements, the em-ployee's illegal activity also poses a threat to others. But surely, allowing private individuals to audit an employee's tax returns is too intrusive a means for discovering information about that employee's in-tegrity. The government certainly would never allow this violation of an employee's privacy. It ought not to allow drug testing on the same grounds. Why tax returns should be protected in ways that urine, for example, is not, raises interesting questions of fair-ness. Unfortunately, this question would take us be-yond the scope of this paper.

Voluntariness

A final problem that we also leave undeveloped con-cerns the voluntariness of employee consent. For most employees, being given the choice between submitting to a drug test and risking one's job by refusing an employer's request is not much of a decision at all. We believe that such decisions are less than voluntary and thereby would hold that employers cannot escape our criticisms simply by including within the employment contract a drug testing clause.[10] Furthermore, there is reason to believe that those most in need of job security will be those most likely to be subjected to drug testing. Highly skilled, professional employees with high job mobility and security will be in a stronger position to resist such intrusions than will less skilled, easily replaced workers. This is why we should not anticipate surgeons and airline pilots being tested, and should not be surprised when public transit and factory workers are. A serious question of fairness arises here as well.

Drug use and drug testing seem to be our most recent social "crises." Politicians, the media, and employers expend a great deal of time and effort addressing this crisis. Yet, unquestionably, more lives, health, and money are lost each year to alcohol abuse than to marijuana, cocaine and other controlled substances. We are well-advised to be careful in considering issues that arise due to such selective social concern. We will let other social commentators speculate on the reasons why drug use has received scrutiny while other white-collar crimes and alcohol abuse are ignored. Our only concern at this point is that such selective prosecution suggests an arbitrariness that should alert us to questions of fairness and justice.

In summary, then, we have seen that drug use is not always job-relevant, and if drug use is not job-relevant, information about it is certainly not job-relevant. In the case of performance it may be a cause of some decreased performance, but it is the performance itself that is relevant to an employee's position, not what prohibits or enables him to do the job. In the case of potential harm being done by an employee under the influence of drugs, the drug use seems job-relevant, and in this case drug testing to prevent harm might be legitimate. But how this is practicable is another question. It would seem that standard motor dexterity or mental dexterity tests, immediately prior to job performance, are more efficacious ways of preventing harm, unless one concludes that drug use invariably and necessarily leads to harm. One must trust the individuals in any system in order for that system to work. One cannot police everything. It might work to randomly test people, to find drug users, and to weed out the few to forestall possible future harm, but are the harms prevented sufficient to override the rights of privacy of the people who are innocent and to overcome the possible abuses we have mentioned? It seems not.

Clearly, a better method is to develop safety checks immediately prior to the performance of a job. Have a surgeon or a pilot or a bus driver pass a few reasoning and motor-skill tests before work. The cause of the lack of a skill, which lack might lead to harm, is really a secondary issue.

Drug Testing for Prospective Employees

Let's turn finally to drug testing during a pre-employment interview. Assuming the job description and responsibilities have been made clear, we can say that an employer is entitled to expect from prospective employee whatever performance is agreed to in the employment contract. Of course, this will always involve risks, since the employer must make a judgment about future performances. To lower this risk, employers have a legitimate claim to some information about the employee. Previous work experience, training, education, and the like are obvious candidates since they indicate the person's ability to do the job. Except in rare circumstances drug use itself is irrelevant for determining an employee's ability to perform. (Besides, most people who are interviewing know enough to get their systems clean if the prospective employer is going to test them.)

We suggest that an employer can claim to have an interest in knowing (a) whether or not the prospective employee *can* do the job and (b) whether there is reason to believe that once hired the employee *will* do the job. The first can be determined in fairly straightforward ways: past work experience, training, education, etc. Presumably past drug use is thought more relevant to the second question. But there are straightforward and less intrusive means than drug testing for resolving this issue. Asking the employee "Is there anything that might prevent you from doing this job?" comes first to mind. Hiring the employee on a probationary period is another way. But to inquire about drug use here is to claim a right to know too much. It is to claim a right to know not only information about what an employee can do, but also a right to inquire into whatever background information *might* be (but not necessarily is) causally related to what an employee *will* do. But the range of factors that could be relevant here, from medical history to psychological dispositions to family plans, is surely too open-ended for an employer to claim as a *right* to know.

It might be responded that what an employee is entitled to expect is not a certain level of output, but a certain level of effort. The claim here would be that while drug use is only contingently related to what an employee can do, it is directly related to an employee's motivation to do the job. Drug use then is *de facto* relevant to the personal information that an employer is entitled to know.

But this involves an assumption mentioned above. The discussion so far has assumed that drugs will adversely affect job performance. However, some drugs are performance enhancing whether they are concerned with actual output or effort. The widespread use of steroids, painkillers, and dexadrine among professional athletes are perhaps only the most publicized instances of performance enhancing drugs. (A teacher's use of caffeine before an early-morning class is perhaps a more common example.) More to the point, knowledge of drug use tells little about motivation. There are too many other variables to be considered. Some users are motivated and some are not. Thus the motivational argument is faulty.

We can conclude, then, that whether the relevant consideration for prospective employees is output or effort, knowledge of drug use will be largely irrelevant for predicting. Employers ought to be positivistic in their approach. They should restrict their information gathering to measurable behavior and valid predictions (What has the prospect done? What can the prospect do? What has the prospect promised to do?), and not speculate about the underlying causes of this behavior. With a probationary work period always an option, there are sufficient non-intrusive means for limiting risks available to employers without having to rely on investigations into drug use.

In summary, we believe that drug use is information that is rightfully private and that only in exceptional cases can an employer claim a right to know about such use. Typically, these are cases in which knowledge of drug use could be used to prevent harm. However, even in those cases we believe that there are less intrusive and more effective means available than drug testing for gaining the information that would be necessary to prevent the harm. Thus, we conclude that drug testing of employees is rarely justified, and mostly inefficacious.

NOTES

Versions of this paper were read to the Department of Philosophy at Southern Connecticut State University and to the Society of Business Ethics. The authors would like to thank those people, as well as Robert Baum and Norman Bowie, the editors of *Business and Professional Ethics Journal*, for their many helpful comments. Professor Duska wishes to thank the Pew Memorial Trust for a grant providing released time to work on this paper.

1 *The New Republic*, March 31, 1986.
2 This trend primarily involves screening employees for such drugs as marijuana, cocaine, amphetamines, barbiturates, and opiates (e.g., heroin, methadone and morphine). While alcohol is also a drug that can be abused in the

workplace, it seldom is among the drugs mentioned in conjunction with employee testing. We believe that testing which proves justified for controlled substances will, *a fortiori*, be justified for alcohol as well.

3 "A Defense of Employee Rights," Joseph DesJardins and John McCall, *Journal of Business Ethics*, Vol. 4 (1985). We should emphasize that our concern is with the moral rights of privacy for employees and not with any specific or prospective legal rights. Readers interested in pursuing the legal aspects of employee drug testing should consult: "Workplace Privacy Issues and Employee Screening Policies" by Richard Lehe and David Middlebrooks in *Employee Relations Law Journal* (Vol. 11, no. 3) 407-21; and "Screening Workers for Drugs: A Legal and Ethical Framework" by Mark Rothstein, in *Employee Relations Law Journal* (Vol. 11, no. 3) 422-36.

4 "Privacy, Polygraphs, and Work," George Brenkert, *Business and Professional Ethics Journal*, Vol. 1, no. I (Fall 1981). For a more general discussion of privacy in the workplace see "Privacy in Employment" by Joseph DesJardins, in *Moral Rights in the Workplace*, edited by Gertrude Ezorsky (SUNY Press, 1987). A good resource for philosophical work on privacy can be found in "Recent Work on the Concept of Privacy" by W.A. Parent, in *American Philosophical Quarterly* (Vol. 20, Oct. 1983) 341-56.

5 *US News and World Report*, Aug. 1983; *Newsweek*, May 1983.

6 Obviously we are speaking here of harms that go beyond the simple economic harm which results from unsatisfactory job performance. These economic harms were discussed in the first argument above. Further, we ignore such "harms" as providing bad role-models for adolescents, harms often used to justify drug tests for professional athletes. We think it unreason-

able to hold an individual responsible for the image he/she provides to others.

7 The philosophical literature on informed consent is often concerned with "informed consent" in a medical context. For an interesting discussion of informed consent in the workplace, see Mary Gibson, *Workers Rights* (Rowman and Allanheld, 1983) especially 13-14 and 74-75.

8 For a reiteration of this point and a concise argument against drug testing see Lewis L. Maltby, "Why Drug Testing is a Bad Idea," *Inc.* June, 1987, 152-53. "But the fundamental flaw with drug testing is that it tests for the wrong thing. A realistic program to detect workers whose condition puts the company or other people at risk would test for the condition that actually creates the danger. The reason drunk or stoned airline pilots and truck drivers are dangerous is their reflexes, coordination, and timing are deficient. This impairment could come from many situations—drugs, alcohol, emotional problems—the list is almost endless. A serious program would recognize that the real problem is workers' impairment, and test for that. Pilots can be tested in flight simulators. People in other jobs can be tested by a trained technician in about 20 minutes—at the job site" (152).

9 This argument is structurally similar to the argument against the effectiveness of capital punishment as a deterrent offered by Justice Brennen in the Supreme Court's decision in *Furman v. Georgia*.

10 It might be argued that since we base our critique upon the contractual relationship between employers and employees, our entire position can be undermined by a clever employer who places within the contract a privacy waiver for drug tests. A full answer to this would require an account of the free and rational subject that the contract model presupposes. While

acknowledging that we need such an account to prevent just any contract from being morally legitimate, we will have to leave this debate to another time. Interested readers might find "The Moral Contract between Employers and Employees" by Norman Bowie, in *The Work Ethic in Business*, edited by Hoffman and Wyly (Oelgeschlager and Gunn, 1981) 195-202, helpful here.

◆ ◆ ◆ ◆ ◆

MICHAEL CRANFORD

Drug Testing and the Right to Privacy: Arguing the Ethics of Workplace Drug Testing

Drug testing is becoming an increasingly accepted method for controlling the effects of substance abuse in the workplace. Since drug abuse has been correlated with a decline in corporate profitability and an increase in the occurrence of work-related accidents, employers are justifying drug testing on both legal and ethical grounds. Recent estimates indicate that the costs to employers of employee drug abuse can run as high as $60 billion per year.[1] Motorola, before implementing its drug testing program in 1991, determined that the cost of drug abuse to the company—in lost time, impaired productivity, and health care and workers compensation claims—amounted to $190 million in 1988, or approximately 40% of the company's net profit for that year.[2] As these effects on the workplace are viewed in light of a much larger social problem—one which impacts health care and the criminal justice system, and incites drug-related acts of violence—advocates of drug testing argue that the workplace is an effective arena for engaging these broader concerns. The drug-free workplace is viewed as causally antecedent and even sufficient to the development of drug-free communities.

The possibility of using workplace drug interventions to effect social change may obscure the more fundamental question of whether or not drug testing is an ethical means of determining employee drug abuse. While admitting that drug testing could mitigate potential harms, some CEOs have elected not to follow the trend set by Motorola and an estimated 67% of large companies,[3] and instead argue that drug testing surpasses the employer's legitimate sphere of control by dictating the behavior of employees on their own time and in the privacy of their own homes.[4] Recent arguments in favor of a more psychologically-sensitive definition of employee privacy place employer intrusions into this intimate sphere of self-disclosure on even less certain ethical grounds.[5] The ethical status of workplace drug testing can be expressed as a question of competing interests, between the employer's right to use testing to reduce drug-related harms and maximize profits, over against the employee's right to privacy, particularly with regard to drug use which occurs outside the workplace.

In this paper I will attempt to bring clarity to this debate and set the practice of workplace drug testing on more certain ethical grounds by advancing an argument which justifies workplace drug testing. I will begin by showing that an employee's right to privacy is violated when personal information is collected or used by the employer in a way which is irrelevant to the contractual relationship which exists between employer and employee. I will then demonstrate that drug testing is justified within the terms of the employment contract, and therefore does not amount to a violation of an employee's right to privacy. After responding to a battery of arguments to the contrary, I will propose that while drug testing can be ethically justified under the terms of an employment contract, it still amounts to treating employees as a means to an economic end, and is therefore fundamentally inconsistent with a substantive valuation of human worth and dignity.

Privacy and Performance of Contract

Legal definitions of privacy inevitably rely on the 1890 *Harvard Law Review* article "The Right to Privacy" by Samuel Warren and Louis Brandeis. This article offered an understanding of privacy for which a constitutional basis was not recognized until the 1965 case *Griswold v. Connecticut* (381 U.S. 479). In both instances, privacy was understood as an individual's right "to be let alone," with the Griswold decision according citizens a "zone of privacy" around their persons which cannot be violated by governmental intrusion. This definition, utilized by the Court in numerous decisions since the 1965 ruling, will not be adequate for describing the employee's claim to privacy in an essentially social and cooperative setting like the workplace. In such a condition an absolute right "to be let alone" cannot be sustained, and it may well prove impossible for an employee to maintain a "zone of privacy" when the terms of employment entail certain physical demands. This is not to argue that a right to privacy does not exist in this setting; rather, we must conclude that the aforementioned conditions are not necessary components in such a right.[6]

A more useful definition begins with the idea of a person's right to control information about herself and the situations over which such a right may be legitimately extended. For example, information to the effect that an individual possesses a rare and debilitating disease is generally considered private, but a physician's coming to know that a patient has such a disease is not an invasion of privacy. One might also note that while eavesdropping on a conversation would normally constitute an invasion of privacy, coming to know the same information because the individual inadvertently let it slip in a casual conversation would not. These and other examples demonstrate that the right to privacy is not violated by the mere act of coming to know something private, but is instead contingent on the relationship between the knower and the person about whom the information is known.

George Brenkert formulates this understanding as follows: Privacy involves a relationship between a person A, some information X, and another individual Z. A's right of privacy is violated only when Z comes to possess information X and no relationship exists between A and Z that would justify Z's coming to know X.[7] Brenkert notes that what would justify Z coming to know X is a condition in which knowing X and having a certain access to A will enable Z to execute its role in the particular relationship with A. In such a case, Z is entitled to information X, and A's privacy is in no way violated by the fact that Z knows. Thus, a physician is justified in coming to know of a patient's disease (say, by running certain diagnostic tests), since knowing of the disease will enable her to give the patient medical treatment. One cannot be a physician to another unless one is entitled to certain information and access to that person. Conversely, one can yield one's right to privacy by disclosing information to another that the relationship would not normally mandate. To maintain a right to privacy in a situation where another would normally be entitled to the information to enable them to fulfill the terms of the relationship is, quite simply, to violate the terms of the relationship and make fulfillment of such terms impossible. In the case of our earlier example, to refuse a physician access to the relevant points of one's health status is to make a physician-patient relationship impossible. Similarly, to refuse an employer access to information regarding one's capability of fulfilling the terms of an employment contract is to violate an employer-employee relationship.

The argument advanced at this point is that drug testing involves access to and information about an employee that are justified under the terms of the implicit contractual agreement between employer and employee. An employer is therefore entitled to test employees for drug use. This statement relies on at least two important assumptions. First, a contractual model of employer-employee relations is assumed over against a common law, agent-principal model. It is not the case that employees relinquish all privacy rights in return for employment, as the common law relationship may imply, but rather that the terms of the contract, if it is valid, set reasonable boundaries for employee privacy rights consistent with the terms and expectations of employment. The argument offered here is that drug testing does not violate those boundaries. I am also assuming that drug abuse has a measurable and significant impact on an employee's ability to honor the terms of the employment contract. Employers are entitled to know about employee drug abuse on the grounds that such knowledge is relevant to assessing an employee's capability to perform according to the terms of the agreement. Without arguing for the connection between drug abuse and employee performance at length, the reader's attention is directed to studies which, if not absolutely incontestable in their methodology, are nonetheless reasonably set forth.[8]

In support of this argument, I would first direct attention to other types of information about an employee that an employer is entitled to know, and in coming to know such information does not violate the employee's privacy. Employers are entitled to information about a current or prospective employee's work experience, education, and job skills—in short, information relevant for determining whether or not the employee is capable of fulfilling her part of the contract. More critically, the employer is not only entitled to such information, but is entitled to obtain such information through an investigatory process, both to confirm information the employee has voluntarily yielded about her qualifications, as well as to obtain such relevant information as may be lacking (i.e., inadvertently omitted or, perhaps, intentionally withheld).

Brenkert further adds that an employer is entitled to information which relates to elements of one's social and moral character:

> A person must be able not simply to perform a certain activity, or provide a service, but he must also be able to do it in an acceptable manner—i.e., in a manner which is approximately as efficient as others, in an honest manner, and in a manner compatible with others who seek to provide the services for which they were hired.[9]

Again, the employer is entitled to know, in the case of potential employees, if they are capable of fulfilling their part of the contract, and, in the case of existing employees, if they are adhering to the terms and expectations implicit in the contract. While this latter case can often be confirmed by direct observation of the employee's actions at the work site, on occasion the employer is entitled to information regarding behavior which can be observed at the workplace but originates from outside of it (such as arriving at work late, or consuming large quantities of alcohol prior to arriving). As all of these actions may be in violation of the term of employment, the employer is entitled to know of them, and in coming to know of them does not violate the employee's privacy.

My point in offering these examples is to suggest that drug testing is a method of coming to know about an employee's ability to fulfill the terms of contract which is analogous to those listed. An exploratory process, in seeking to verify an employee's ability to do a certain job in connection with reasonable expectations for what that job entails, may also validly discover characteristics or tendencies that would keep the employee from performing to reasonable expectations. Drug testing is precisely this sort of process. As a part of the process of reviewing employee performance to determine whether or not they are fulfilling the terms and expectations of employment satisfactorily, drug testing may be validly included among other types of investigatory methods, including interviews with coworkers, skills and proficiency testing, and (in some professions) medical examinations. The fact that an employee may not want to submit to a drug test is entirely beside the point; the employee may just as likely prefer not to include a complete list of personal references, or prefer that the employer not review her relations with other employees. In all these cases, the employer is entitled to know the relevant information, and in coming to know these things does not violate the employee's privacy. The employee may withhold this information from the employer, but this action is tantamount to ending the employer-employee relationship. Such a relationship, under the terms of employment, includes not only each party's commitment to benefit the other in the specific way indicated, but also entitles each to determine if the other is capable of performance according to the terms of contract. In this way, each retains the free ability to terminate the relationship on the grounds of the other's nonperformance.

Of course, not just any purpose of obtaining information relevant to evaluating performance under the terms of contract can automatically be considered reasonable. For instance, an employer cannot spy on a prospective employee in her own home to determine if she will be a capable employee. I offer the following criteria as setting reasonable and ethical limits on obtaining relevant information (though note that the requirement of relevancy is in each case already assumed).

1. The process whereby an employer comes to know something about an employee (existing or prospective) must not be unnecessarily harmful or intrusive

The information may not result from investigatory processes which are themselves degrading or humiliating by virtue of their intrusiveness (e.g., strip searches, spying on an employee while they use the bathroom, interviewing a divorced spouse, or searching an employee's locker) or which may prove

unhealthy (e.g., excessive use of x-rays, or torture). (Note: Degrading processes of securing information must be distinguished from processes of securing information which is itself degrading. The latter is not necessarily in violation of this or successive criteria.)

2. The process whereby an employer comes to know something about an employee must be efficient and specific

The information must result from an efficient and specific process—i.e., a process which is the most direct of competing methods (though without compromising point 1 above), and should result in information which corresponds to questions of performance under the terms of the employment contract, and should not result in information that does not so correspond. For example, detailed credit checks may help a bank decide whether a prospective employee is a capable manager of finances, but not directly (only inferentially), and it would also provide a great deal of information that the employer is not entitled to see. Consulting the employee's previous employer, on the other hand, may provide the relevant information directly and specifically.

3. The process whereby an employer comes to know something about an employee must be accurate, or if not itself precise, then capable of confirmation through further investigation

The information must result from a dependable source; if a source is not dependable and is incapable of being verified for accuracy, the employer is not justified in pursuing this avenue of discovery. Thus, the polygraph must be excluded, since it is occasionally inaccurate and may in such cases result in information that cannot be verified. In addition, disreputable sources of information, or sources that may have an interest in misrepresenting the information being sought, should not be used.

Having outlined these, I offer my argument in full: Drug testing is not only a method of coming to know about an employee's ability to fulfill the terms of contract which is analogous to those listed earlier, but which also is reasonable under the criteria listed above.

1.   Drug testing is not harmful or intrusive

In the Supreme Court case *Samuel K. Skinner v. Railway Labor Executives' Association* (489 U.S. 602), the Court determined that both blood and urine tests were minimally intrusive.[10] While the Court acknowledged that the act of passing urine was itself intensely personal (Ibid., 617), obtaining a urine sample in a medical environment and without the use of direct observation amounted to no more than a minimal intrusion (Ibid., 626). The Court justified not only testing of urine but also testing of blood by focusing on the procedure of testing (i.e., "experience ... teaches that the quantity of blood extracted is minimal," Ibid., 625) and pointing out that since such tests are "commonplace and routine in everyday life," the tests posed "virtually no risk, trauma, or pain" (Ibid., 625). The Court's findings on this case are compelling, and are consistent with my contention that drug testing is not unnecessarily harmful or intrusive. While such testing does amount to an imposition upon an employee (i.e., by requiring her to report to a physician and provide a urine sample) in a way that may not be commonplace for many employees, the Court ruled that since this takes place within an employment context (where limitations of movement are assumed), this interference is justifiable and does not unnecessarily infringe on privacy interests (Ibid., 624-25).

2.   Drug testing is both efficient and specific

In fact, drug testing is the most efficient means of discovering employee drug abuse. In addition to providing direct access to the information in question, the results of drug testing do not include information that is irrelevant. The test targets a specific set of illegal substances. It can be argued (and has been) that drug testing is not efficient because it does not test for impairment—only for drug use. But this point ignores the fact that the test is justified on a correlation between drug abuse and employee productivity more generally; impairment is itself difficult or impossible to measure, since the effects of a given quantity of substance vary from individual to individual and from one incidence of use to another. The fact that impairment is an elusive quantity cannot diminish the validity of testing for drug abuse. This criticism also ignores the fact that the test is an effective means of deterring impairment, providing habitual users a certain expectation that their drug use will be discovered if it is not controlled.

3.   Drug testing can be conducted in a way which guarantees a high degree of precision

It is well known that the standard (and relatively inexpensive) EMIT test has a measurable chance of falsely indicating drug use, and is also susceptible to cross-reactivity with other legal substances. But confirmatory testing, such as that performed using gas chromatography/mass spectrometry, can provide results at a high level of accuracy. This confirmatory testing, as well as a host of other stringent safeguards, is required of all laboratories certified by the National Institute on Drug Abuse.[11]

In summary, my contention is that an employer is entitled to drug test on the grounds that the information derived is relevant to confirm the employee's capacity to perform according to the terms of employment, and that such testing is a reasonable means of coming to know such information. Other points in favor of drug testing, which are not essential to my preceding argument but congruent with it, include the following two items.

First, drug testing is an opportunity for employer beneficence. Testing permits the employer to diagnose poor employee performance and require such individuals to participate in employer-sponsored counseling and rehabilitative measures. Employers are permitted to recognize that drug abuse is a disease with a broad social impact that is not addressed if employees who perform poorly as a result of drug abuse are merely terminated.[12] Second, a specific diagnosis of drug abuse in the case of poor employee performance might protect the employer from wrongful termination litigation, in the event that an employee refuses to seek help regarding their abuse. The results of drug testing might confirm to the court that the termination was effected on substantive and not arbitrary grounds.

Drug Testing and Questions of Justification

A number of arguments have been offered which suggest that drug testing is not justified under terms of contract, or is not a reasonable method by which an employer may come to know of employee drug abuse, and therefore amounts to a violation of employee privacy. These arguments include a rejection of productivity as a justification for testing, charges that testing is coercive, and that it amounts to an abuse of employee privacy by controlling behavior conducted outside the workplace. I will respond to each of these in turn.

First, some have charged that arguing from an employer's right to maximize productivity to a justification for drug testing is problematic. DesJardins and Duska point out that employers have a valid claim on some level of employee performance, such that a failure to perform to this level would give the employer a justification for firing or finding fault with the employee. But it is not clear that an employer has a valid claim on an optimal level of employee performance, and that is what drug testing is directed at achieving. As long as drug abuse does not reduce an employee's performance beyond a reasonable level, an employer cannot claim a right to the highest level of performance of which an employee is capable.[13]

DesJardins and Duska further point out the elusiveness of an optimal level of performance. Some employees perform below the norm in an unimpaired state, and other employees might conceivably perform above the norm in an impaired state. "If the relevant consideration is whether the employee is producing as expected (according to the normal demands of the position and contract) not whether he/she is producing as much as possible, then knowledge of drug use is irrelevant or unnecessary."[14] This is because the issue in question is not drug use *per se*, but employee productivity. Since drug use need not correlate to expectations for a given employee's productivity, testing for drug use is irrelevant. And since it is irrelevant to fulfillment of the employment contract, testing for drugs is unjustified and therefore stands in violation of an employee's privacy.

While I agree that it is problematic to state that an employer has a right to expect an optimal level of performance from an employee, I would argue that the employer does have a right to a workplace free from the deleterious effects of employee drug abuse.[15] Drug testing, properly understood, is not directed at effecting optimal performance, but rather performance which is free from the effects of drug abuse. Since the assessment which justifies drug testing is not based on the impact of drug abuse on a given employee's performance, but is correlated on the effects of drug abuse on workplace productivity more generally, drug testing does measure a relevant quantity.

It is also overly simplistic to state that employers need not test for drugs when they can terminate employees on the mere basis of a failure to perform. Employers are willing to tolerate temporary factors which may detract from employee performance; e.g., a death in the family, sickness, or occasional loss of sleep. But employers have a right to distinguish these self-correcting factors from factors which may be habitual, ongoing, and increasingly detrimental to productivity, such as drug abuse. Such insight might dramatically impact their course of action with regard to how they address the employee's failure to perform. It is therefore not the case, as DesJardins and Duska suggest, that "knowledge of the cause of the failure to perform is irrelevant."[16]

A more critical series of arguments against basing drug testing on an employer's right to maximize productivity has been leveled by Nicholas Caste. First, Caste attacks what he identifies as "the productivity argument":

> The productivity argument essentially states that since the employer has purchased the employee's time, the employer has a proprietary right to ensure that the time purchased is used as efficiently as possible.... the employer must be concerned with "contract enforcement" and must attempt somehow to motivate the employee to attain maximal production capacity. In the case of drug testing, the abuse of drugs by employees is seen as diminishing their productive capacity and is thus subject to the control of the employer.[17]

From this argument, Caste states, one can infer that any manipulation is acceptable as long as it is maximizing productivity, and he defines manipulation as an attempt to produce a response without regard for that individual's good, as he or she perceives it.[18] Caste goes on to give two examples of hypothetical drugs which, assuming the productivity argument, an employer would be justified in requiring employees to take. The first drug increases employee productivity while also increasing pleasure and job satisfaction. The second drug increases productivity while inflicting painful side-effects on the employee. The fact that the productivity argument appears to sanction the use of both drugs, and in fact cannot morally distinguish between them, seems to argue for its invalidity. Since the productivity argument cannot distinguish between causing an employee pleasure or pain, by adopting its logic one would be forced to the morally unacceptable conclusion that an employee's best interests are irrelevant.

Caste points out that what is wrong with the second drug is not that it causes pain "but that it is manipulatively intrusive. It establishes areas of control to which the employer has no right."[19] He concludes that what is wrong with the productivity argument is that it is manipulative. And what is wrong with manipulation is not the effects it produces (which may, coincidentally, be in the subject's best interests) but rather that it undermines the subject's autonomy by not allowing their desires to be factored into the decision making process.[20] Since drug testing is justified by appeal to productivity arguments, it also is fundamentally manipulative and results in a morally unacceptable degree of employee control. Drug testing is therefore unethical, and should be rejected.

One could point out that our system of modern law regulates behavior in a way that would also have to be considered manipulative, according to Caste's definition, but he avoids this counterexample by stating that in a democratic system, citizens have a chance to participate in the legislative process. Since their desires participate through the election of representatives who make the laws, Caste argues that our legal system does not destroy autonomy the way mandatory drug testing does, by dictating behavior without any room for autonomy.[21] Before I address the critical oversight here, I should point out that one might rescue drug testing from the charge of being manipulative by using the same argument that Caste did to rescue our legal system. One can exercise the same degree of autonomy with respect to drug testing legislation as one currently does with legislation generally by participating in our electoral system. Since employees have an ability to elect representatives who can limit the use of drug testing, one could argue that drug testing also "does not destroy the individual's autonomy in that he or she retains the capability of input into the governing process."[22] In point of fact, individual autonomy is limited in both cases, as it must necessarily be in any contractual obligation, making any expressed distinction here trivial.

The failure of Caste's argument becomes clear when we realize that, if he is correct, virtually every action required of an employee at a work site would qualify as manipulative—whether the action in question was in her best interests or not, and whether or not she desired to comply, since Caste defines manipulation as a function of restricting autonomy. Dress codes, starting times, and basic performance expectations all may be similarly justified by appeal to the productivity argument—but most of us are not prepared to count these things as manipulative or unjustified. Requirements of this sort are not instances of manipulation, but are justified expectations which honor a contractual agreement. Similarly, an employee who demands a paycheck of her employer is engaging in manipulation, according to Caste's definition—but this cannot be correct. In the contract, each party is apprised that the other has a right to benefit from the arrangement, and each has a commensurate responsibility to uphold their part. Accountability to the terms of the contract does not amount to manipulation when the accountability in question is reasonable. In agreement with Caste's original criticism, it is not true that an employer has a right to ensure maximal productivity. But an employer does have the right to hold an employee accountable to the terms of the contract, which express reasonable expectations of productivity. From this it cannot be inferred, however, that just any activity to maximize (or even minimally ensure) productivity is justifiable, since the contractual model expressly allows that the employee has certain morally justified claims that cannot be bargained away in return for employment. Since the productivity argument, as Caste depicts it, is in fact not a justification for drug testing under a contractual model, it is not the case that drug testing must be rejected.

In a similar vein, some argue that any testing which involves coercion is inherently an invasion of employee privacy. Placing employees in a position where they must choose between maintaining their privacy or losing their jobs is fundamentally coercive. "For most employees, being given the choice between submitting to a drug test and risking one's job by refusing an employer's request is not much

of a decision at all."[23] While Brenkert's arguments against the use of the polygraph are directed at that device's inability to distinguish the reason behind a positive reading (which may not, in many instances, indicate an intentional lie), his argument that the polygraph is coercive is pertinent to the question of drug testing as well.

Brenkert notes that if an employee

> ... did not take the test and cooperate during the test, his application for employment would either not be considered at all or would be considered to have a significant negative aspect to it. This is surely a more subtle form of coercion. And if this be the case, then one cannot say that the person has willingly allowed his reactions to the questions to be monitored. He has consented to do so, but he has consented under coercion. Had he a truly free choice, he would not have done so.[24]

Brenkert's point is surprising, in that his own understanding is that A's privacy is limited by what Z is entitled to know in order to execute its role with respect to A. If Z (here, the corporation) is entitled to know X (whether or not the employee abuses drugs) in order to determine if A (the employee) is capable of performing according to the terms of employment, then the employee has no right to privacy with respect to the information in question. While this does not authorize the corporation to obtain the information in just any manner, the mere fact that the employee would *prefer* that the employer not know cannot be sufficient to constitute a right to privacy in the face of the employer's legitimate entitlement. The employee can freely choose to withhold the information, but this is not so much invoking a right to privacy as it is rejecting the terms of contract.

If Brenkert's criticism of employer testing were valid, then potentially all demands made by the employer on the employee—from providing background information to arriving at work on time—

would count as coercive, since in every case where the employee consents to the demand there is a strong possibility that she would not have consented if she was offered a truly free choice. But these demands are reasonable, and the employer is entitled to demand them under the terms of employment, just as the employee is entitled to profit by acceding to such demands.

The final argument considered here is the charge that drug testing is an attempt to "control the employee's actions in a time that has not actually been purchased."[25] Even if we assume that an employer has the right to maximize profitability by controlling the employee's behavior during normal work hours, the employer has no right to control what an employee does in her free time. To attempt to do so is a violation of employee rights. This argument also falls flat, however, when we realize that the demands of a standard employment contract inherently place limitations on an employee's free time. In a sense, the employment contract demands priority, requiring the employee to organize her free time around her employment schedule in a way that permits her to honor the contractual obligation. For instance, time traveling to and from work occurs during an employee's "free time," and is dependent on the employee's own personal resources, but is rightfully assumed within the terms of the contract. Time and money spent shopping for work attire also falls outside the normal time of employment, but is essential for honoring a mandatory dress code. These are not normally considered violations of an employee's private life, or unethical "controls" placed on an employee by an employer, but are justified, again, under the terms of contract. Drug testing is justified similarly.

Reservations and Policy Recommendations

At least one troubling aspect of drug testing remains to be considered prior to recommendations on policy, and that is the ethics of profit maximization as a justification for including employee testing under the terms of an employment agreement. As Caste correctly observed, the fact that drug testing may be in the best interests of employees is ancillary to the employer's productivity goals.[26] While drug testing may turn out to further the interests of employees by forcing them to confront self-destructive behavior, this correlation between employee's interests and the financial goals of the corporation is merely fortuitous. If drug testing were not perceived as being in the best interests of the company from a financial point of view, then drug testing would not be the issue it is today.

In counterpoint, one could argue that the financial status of the company is inherently intertwined with the good of employees; as the corporation becomes increasingly profitable, employees are increasingly benefited. One might even argue that, in light of such a framework, profit maximization is central to society and therefore inherently consistent with its values.[27] This model is overly simplified, however; we can easily envision a situation where a corporation, attempting to maximize its profits, does so in a way that is inconsistent with a substantive social ethic but is not otherwise limited by market values. Appealing to profit maximization as a social ethic does not alleviate these tensions.

It is the position adopted in this article that a corporation is entitled to drug test its employees to determine employee capacity to perform according to the terms of the employment contract. That drug testing is not, however, in the large majority of cases, directed at maximizing the employee's best interests, suggests that employers should avail themselves of their right to drug test within reasonable limits. In light of this conclusion, the following policy recommendations are directed at employers, with the goal of balancing the employer's right to drug test with a more substantive regard for the dignity and privacy of employees.

1. Testing should focus on a specifically targeted group of employees

In the case of employers who are testing without regard for questions of safety, I would strongly urge that testing only be done when probable cause exists to suspect that an employee is using controlled substances. Probable cause might include uncharacteristic behavior, obvious symptoms of impairment, or a significantly diminished capacity to perform their duties. Utilizing probable cause minimizes the intrusive aspect of testing by yielding a higher percentage of test-positives (i.e., requiring probable cause before testing will inherently screen out the large majority of negatives). Even with this stipulation, a drug program may provide a reasonable deterrence factor at the workplace.

It should be noted that this qualification does not apply in cases of job applicants. Employers who insist on testing potential employees will typically do so under a general suspicion of drug use, and may in that case assume a condition of probable cause.

2.   When testing is indicated, it should not be announced ahead of time

Regularly scheduled testing runs the risk of losing its effectiveness by providing an employee sufficient time to contrive a method of falsifying the sample. Drug testing, if it is to be used at all, should be used in a way which maximizes its effectiveness and accuracy.

3.   Employees who test positive for drug abuse should be permitted the opportunity to resolve their abusive tendencies and return to work without penalty or stigma

Employees should only be terminated for an inability to resolve their abuse, once early detection and substantial warning have been made. Employers can mitigate the dehumanizing aspect of this technology by using it as an opportunity to assist abusive employees with their problems, and permitting them to return to their old positions if they can remedy their habitual tendencies. Toxicological testing should

therefore be accompanied by a full range of employee assistance interventions.

Acknowledgements

I would like to thank Prof. Bill May at the University of Southern California and the anonymous second reader for their suggestions and detailed criticism in regard to the points raised in this paper (without implicating either of them in the position adopted herein).

NOTES

1 According to SAMHSA (Substance Abuse and Mental Health Services Administration), cited in Ira A. Lipman, "Drug Testing is Vital in the Workplace," *USA Today Magazine* 123 (January 1995), 81.

2 Dawn Gunsch, "Training Prepares Workers for Drug Testing," *Personnel Journal* 72 (May 1993), 52.

3 According to the US Bureau of Labor Statistics, cited in Rob Brookler, "Industry Standards in Workplace Drug Testing," *Personnel Journal* 71 (April 1992), 128.

4 See Lewis L. Maltby, "Why Drug Testing is a Bad Idea," *Inc.* (June 1987), 152.

5 On this point see Michele Simms, "Defining Privacy in Employee Health Screening Cases: Ethical Ramifications Concerning the Employee/Employer Relationship," *Journal of Business Ethics* 13 (1994), 315-25.

6 DesJardins further argues that these conditions are not sufficient to constitute a right to privacy. In the example of subliminal advertising, if it was effective, one's right "to be let alone" would be violated, but without any clear violation of one's privacy (Joseph R. DesJardins, "An Employee's Right to Privacy," in J.R. DesJardins and J.J. McCall [eds.], *Contemporary Issues in Business Ethics* [Belmont, CA: Wadsworth, 1985], 222).

7 George G. Brenkert, "Privacy, Polygraphs, and Work," *Business and Professional Ethics Journal* 1 (1981), 23. In agreement see DesJardins, "An Employee's Right to Privacy," 222; Joseph Des-Jardins and Ronald Duska, "Drug Testing in Employment," *Business and Professional Ethics Journal* 6 (1987), 3-4 (above).

8 See for example US Department of Health and Human Services, *Drugs in the Workplace: Research and Evaluation Data*, ed. S.W. Gust and J.M. Walsh (National Institute on Drug Abuse Monograph 91, 1989), and National Research Council/Institute of Medicine, *Under the Influence? Drugs and the American Work Force*, ed. J. Normand, R.O. Lempert and C.P. O'Brien (Committee on Drug Use in the Workplace, 1994). For example, a prospective study of preemployment drug testing in the US Postal Service showed after 1.3 years of employment that employees who had tested positive for illicit drug use at the time they were hired were 60% more likely to be absent from work than employees who tested negative (*Drugs in the Workplace*, 128-32; Under the Influence, 134).

9 Brenkert, "Privacy, Polygraphs, and Work," 25.

10 While the legal opinion itself only summarizes and does not in and of itself justify a moral argument, it does in this case demonstrate a broad consensus and both rational and intuitive appeals to the matter at hand.

11 See Brookler, "Industry Standards in Workplace Drug Testing," 129.

12 *Contra* DesJardins and Duska, who state, "Of course, if the employer suspects drug use or abuse as the cause of the unsatisfactory performance, then she might choose to help the person with counseling or rehabilitation. However, this does not seem to be something morally required of the employer. Rather, in the case of unsatisfactory performance, the employer has a prima facie justification for dismissing or disciplining the employee" ("Drug Testing in Employment," 6-7).

13 DesJardins and Duska, "Drug Testing in Employment," 5.

14 Ibid., 6.

15 Implicit in this statement is the assumption that employees do not have an absolute right to abuse drugs. This is a point I am neither able (for lack of space) nor interested in taking up at this point, but would instead appeal to a broad societal consensus on drug abuse, legislation against the use of illicit substances (and abuse of legal substances), and various negative social correlates to drug use. Thus, I am convinced that drug abuse can be distinguished from other legitimate (but potentially deleterious) behaviors, such as poor dietary habits.

16 Ibid.

17 Nicholas J. Caste, "Drug Testing and Productivity," *Journal of Business Ethics* 11 (1992), 301.

18 Ibid., 302.

19 Ibid., 303.

20 As a side note, I should point out that Caste has gone wrong in assessing his own definition of manipulation (understood as an attempt to produce a response without regard for that individual's good, as they perceived it). What is wrong with manipulation is *not* that it undermines autonomy, since undermining autonomy is neither a necessary nor a sufficient component in manipulation as he defines it (i.e., I can undermine your autonomy in a way which is in complete accord with your good as you perceive it, and this would not qualify as manipulation). If the subject willingly embraces the act in question, and is in complete agreement with a policy mandating the action, it would still be manipulative under Caste's definition, since manipulation turns not on the effect, nor on the victim's will, but on the motivation of the agent behind the act.

21 Ibid., 302.

22 Ibid.

23 DesJardins and Duska, "Drug Testing in Employment," 16-17. This is also implied in DesJardins, "An Employee's Right to Privacy," 226, but in neither case is the argument fully developed.

24 Brenkert, "Privacy, Polygraphs, and Work," 28-29.

25 Caste, "Drug Testing and Productivity," 303. See also Maltby, "Why Drug Testing is a Bad Idea," 152.

26 Caste, "Drug Testing and Productivity," 302. Caste goes too far when he attributes to corporations following the productivity argument an "absence of concern for the individual employee" (303), but I am in agreement that employer beneficence is, in the case of drug testing, at best an afterthought.

27 See Patrick Primeaux and John Stieber, "Profit Maximization: The Ethical Mandate of Business," *Journal of Business Ethics* 13 (1994), 287-94.

SAFETY IN THE WORKPLACE

ANITA M. SUPERSON

The Employer-Employee Relationship and the Right to Know

I

Dangers lurk in the workplace. It has been reported that more than 2,200,000 workers are disabled, and more than 14,000 are killed annually as a result of accidents on the job.[1] The causes include safety hazards such as fires, explosions, electrocution, dangerous machinery, as well as health hazards such as loud noise, harmful dusts, asbestos particles, toxic gases, carcinogens, and radiation.[2] The fact that these and other dangers exist is problem enough; but even more problematic is that an employee's awareness of such dangers, prior to being exposed to them, is often minimal, at best. If an employee is to have any say in what happens to his person, what needs to be established—at least more firmly than it is current-

ly—is an employee's[3] right to know about the presence of health and safety hazards in the workplace.

In what follows, I shall first examine the current status of an employee's right to know. I shall argue that it is the very nature of the employer-employee relationship that gives rise to an employee's limited awareness of on-the-job hazards. Next, I shall offer what I think are the philosophical justifications for an employee's right to know. Finally, in light of these justifications, I shall argue that establishing an employee's right to know will, in fact, benefit both the employee and the employer, and be one step toward achieving a fiduciary relationship.

Throughout this essay, I compare the employer-employee relationship to that of the physician and patient. Although there are some disparities between the two, the comparison is helpful in that it points out that the moral basis for establishing a right to know for a patient is the same as for an employee, yet the two are not accorded the same recognition by the law. To show that the right to know for patients is not recognized as being the same for employees, yet that it is based on the same philosophical foundation for the same reasons, only strengthens the argument for establishing a right to know in the workplace.

II

In the medical setting a person's right to know about risks involved in different kinds of treatment has been recognized under the guise of informed consent. Recently, there have been many attempts in the law and in various health codes to ensure that patients have given informed consent to medical treatments or experimentation. In *Canterbury v. Spence*, 1972, Circuit Court Judge Spotswood W. Robinson III rules that since "every human being of adult years and sound mind has a right to determine what shall be done with his own body," a physician has a "duty of reasonable disclosure of the choices with respect to proposed therapy and the dangers inherently and potentially involved."[4] Similarly, the American Hospital Association's *Patient's Bill of Rights* (1973) states that "The patient has the right to receive from his physician information necessary to give informed consent prior to the start of any procedure and/or treatment."[5] Again, the Nuremberg Code, which focuses on guidelines used in human experimentation carried out in Nazi Germany, specifies that the human subject "should have sufficient knowledge and comprehension of the elements of the subject matter involved as to enable him to make an understanding and enlightened decision."[6] These and other such examples show that through informed consent, a patient's or research subject's right to know about the risks and hazards involved in medical procedures is firmly entrenched. We shall see later that this right is protected by the law. Though the amount of information given to patients may vary among physicians, consent forms must be signed by the patient or by his next of kin. This is true for all patients undergoing most invasive forms of treatment (e.g., surgery).

But the headway that has been made in the medical setting is, unfortunately, unparalleled in the workplace. It was not until 1980 that the Occupa-

tional Safety and Health Administration (OSHA) of the United States Department of Labor established the legal right of an employee to "access to employer maintained exposure and medical records relevant to employees exposed to toxic substances and harmful physical agents."[7] In 1983, OSHA issued a final rule requiring

> chemical manufacturers and importers to assess the hazards of chemicals which they produce and import, and all employers having workplaces in the manufacturing division ... to provide information to their employees concerning hazardous chemicals by means of hazard communication programs including labels, material safety data sheets, training, and access to written records. In addition, distributors of hazardous chemicals are required to ensure that containers they distribute are properly labeled, and that a material safety data sheet is provided to their customers ...[8]

On the same note, the National Institute for Occupational Safety and Health (NIOSH) reported that workers had the right to know whether or not they were exposed to hazardous chemical and physical agents regulated by the Federal Government.[9] Finally, the National Labor Relations Act (NLRA) recognizes a labor union's right to information that is relevant to a collective bargaining issue, including safety rules and practices.[10] Although these regulations are a step in the direction of securing a worker's right to know, they are insufficient.

First, though the OSHA rulings recently have been expanded from simply permitting access to an employer's exposure and medical records to requiring assessment of the hazards of chemicals and providing information about such chemicals to an employee by means of labels and material safety data sheets, they fail to extend protection through information to many workers. The 1983 regulation applies only to employees in the manufacturing division, yet does not apply to employees in other divisions such as mining, construction, trade, etc. The reasoning underlying OSHA's restriction to manufacturing is that it has determined that the employees in this division "are at the greatest risk of experiencing health effects from exposure to hazardous chemicals."[11] The agency thus hoped to regulate that sector in which it could be most effective for the greatest number of employees. So, although warning labels and safety data sheets, as well as the assessment of hazards which they necessitate, certainly are positive steps toward securing a worker's right to know, they apply to about only fifty per cent of all workers.[12]

Second, the OSHA rulings apply only to employees which the agency defines as "a current employee, a former employee, or an employee being assigned or transferred to work where there will be exposure to toxic substances or harmful physical agents."[13] The rulings exclude provision of information regarding hazards to the *prospective* employee. This is problematic because the prospective employee is faced with a similar choice, that is, the choice of whether or not to take on a job which entails working in hazardous conditions. Yet providing this information to prospective employees may raise problems in itself. Employers may find this too time-consuming a task to perform for *each* person contending for a position; or, they may feel an obligation to provide this information only to employees since it is this group of persons which has pledged some degree of loyalty to the company. These problems, though, should be worked around for the sake of the prospective employee who will avoid the trouble of committing himself to a job if he knows in advance that the hazardous working conditions outweigh the benefits of taking on the job.

Third, the OSHA rulings do not apply to all safety and health hazards. The 1980 ruling regulates "toxic substances and harmful physical agents," and the 1983 ruling regulates "hazardous chemicals." Clearly, these rulings do not account for a whole spectrum of on-the-job hazards, some of which were mentioned at the outset of this essay. A worker's right to know of these hazards has yet to be firmly established.

This is not to imply that an employer has no responsibility to keep his workplace safe. In fact, in 1970, the Occupational Safety and Health Act (OSHAct) was passed, establishing safety and health standards for all workers other than those employed by federal, state, and local governments. The Act requires an employer to ensure that his workplace is "free from recognized hazards that are causing or likely to cause death or serious physical harm."[14] But this Act, too, is insufficient. It has been reported[15] that the Act protects against only "recognized hazards," defined as those which "can be detected by the common human senses, unaided by testing devices, and which are generally known in the industry to be hazards." Indeed, this leaves many hazards unaccounted for. It is those hazards not prohibited by law about which the employee may not be informed.

The NIOSH report is inadequate in similar ways. The Institute recognizes a worker's right to know only whether or not they were exposed to hazardous chemical and physical agents regulated by the Federal Government. Its inadequacies are that it does not recognize a right to know of hazards prior to exposure to them, and that like the OSHA rulings, it applies only to chemical and physical agents, rather than all on-the-job hazards.

Finally, the National Labor Relations Act accords some protection to employees who belong to labor unions but is also limited. It established that labor unions had a right to "information that is in the hands of the employer and is relevant to bargainable issues."[16] An employee's right to know about hazardous working conditions is usually recognized as being "relevant to bargainable issues." But what sometimes occurs is a conflict between the employee's right to know and the company's right to keep trade secrets. A trade secret has been defined under the *Restatement of Torts* as "any formula, device, or information, used in a business which gives its holder a competitive advantage over those without the secret."[17] Now if a labor union requests information about job hazards, but this information will expose an employer's trade secrets, thereby jeopardizing his competitive advantage, the employer need not necessarily release this information. And in different cases, the law has favored both sides.

In *Borden Chemical*, an administrative law judge of the National Labor Relations Board determined that Borden had refused to bargain in good faith when it failed to release information to the labor union. It was then ordered to supply the information to the union. The reason behind the ruling was that Borden failed to show that disclosure of the information would damage its competitive position.[18] Essentially, Borden failed to show how its trade secrets would reach its competitors.[19] In *Colgate-Palmolive*, however, an administrative law judge ruled that the employer was obliged to reveal a list of chemicals in the workplace *except* those constituting trade secrets.[20] Colgate-Palmolive apparently showed how it would be disadvantaged were its trade secrets to be revealed. We can surmise from these two cases and from the OSHA and NIOSH rulings that an employee's right to know is not accorded full protection by the law, and, in fact, may be denied by the law.

III

Why is the right to know in the workplace not firmly grounded? It is the argument of this section that protection of such a right is limited because of the very nature of the employer-employee relationship.

This relationship can be best defined as a nonfiduciary one, meaning that there is little or no trust on behalf of each party in the actions of the other party. This lack of trust stems from the expectations each party has for forming a personal relationship. In most cases, the expectations dictate a non-personal interaction. The employee often feels the same; he views himself as a person for hire, whose function is to perform a certain job for the company or institution in exchange for wages and perhaps a few fringe benefits. If the employee does not like his job for whatever reason, he is free to leave. The employer is also free (for the most part) to fire any employee who is not performing his job in what the employer judges to be a favorable way. As a result, many employees remain with a certain company for only a short period of time, thus making it difficult to come to know their employer personally, if this be at all possible.

Both the employer and employee normally do not enter into their relation thinking that they can trust each other to look out for the other's interests. Probably the only form of trust existent between the two parties is that the employer will pay the employee a wage that at least matches the work he puts out, and that the employee will perform the job he is asked to do in a way that is normally expected. These are the roles both the employer and employee expect each other to take on. It would be difficult to establish a fiduciary relationship under such expectations. What adds to the difficulty is that often the employer and employee do not even know each other at any kind of personal level. I ask rhetorically: How can a fiduciary relationship be established if no relationship has been established?

Another feature of the employer-employee relationship which adds to its nonfiduciary nature is the reasons both the employee and the employer have for entering into their relationship. The employee enters a relationship with his employer primarily for monetary reasons; he seeks employment in order to earn wages with which he can secure the goods he needs to live. The employer, on the other hand, enters a relationship primarily for the sake of profit-making. His position in respect to that of the employee is one of power. It derives its power from the fact that the employer offers the employee a benefit—wages—if he accepts and performs a job. The employer stands to benefit directly from his employee. He needs a certain job to be done; the company's profits depend upon whether the task is accomplished. And the financial success of the company is directly related to the employer.

Both the expectations of the employee and employer, as well as the reasons for each entering into the relationship, make it likely that an employer would use his employee merely as a means to his own end, to borrow a notion from Kant. That is, the employer, seeking to augment his profits (the end), may use the employee merely as a means to achieve that end. One way in which he could do this is to fail to inform an employee about hazardous work conditions. Failure to inform an employee about these hazards is to deny him information that may affect his decision to stay on the job. And by remaining on the job, the employee works in part for the employer's benefit, that is, to increase the company's profits. In this way, the employee is used as a means to the employer's end.

More specifically, if the expectations of both the employer and employee of each other are as I have described, it is easy for the former to use the latter as a means to an end because being so far removed on a personal level from the employee, he does not feel a sense of obligation towards the employee's welfare. All he has invested in the relationship is that the job gets done. And since the employee does not view the relationship as a fiduciary one, he has no basis for trusting the employer to ensure that the workplace is free from hazards, or at least to inform him of the hazards that do exist. Indeed it would be nice for the employer to do either; yet the employee probably does not expect it, and certainly cannot trust his employer to do so.

And, if the reasons the employer and employee have for entering their relationship are as I have described, this is another reason why an employer may use his employee merely as a means to his own end. If the employer is aware of the power he holds over his employee, that is, that he to a large extent controls the employee's means of livelihood, he may feel no obligation to inform the employee about on-the-job hazards. In fact, somewhat ironically, the employer may even go so far as to view the employee as using *him*, the *employer*, as a means to an end. This belief is based upon the fact that the employee may take on a job solely for the purpose of obtaining money, perhaps with minimum effort put forth, and that the employee is free to leave when he so desires. If the employer has this attitude toward his employee, it becomes easier for him not to inform the employee of hazards in the workplace.

The nature of the employer-employee relationship differs from that of the physician-patient in these two respects. Specifically, the expectations of the physician and patient are of a much more trusting nature. Oftentimes, the physician and patient have established a personal relationship; they, for example, know somewhat about each other's lifestyles, values, etc. Patients generally expect and trust their physician to act in their best interests. They expect that physicians will inform them of the hazards and risks involved in various medical treatments, and that together they will arrive at a decision about what is the best course of action to take. And if the physician fails to inform his patient about these hazards and risks, the patient usually assumes that the information was withheld for his, the patient's, own benefit.

Furthermore, the reasons for the patient and physician entering a relationship are different from that of the employer and employee. Patients seek the advice of a physician because, simply put, they want to be treated for an illness. They expect that the physician will do this, and will give the patient information on forms of treatment. This is what the patient pays for, and thus expects to receive. The physician, in turn, should feel that he has an obligation to provide this information to the patient, unless he can justify withholding it.

The physician's reasons for entering the relationship are different from the employer's. Rather than being solely, or at least primarily, profit-motivated, physicians often view their role as one of benefitting the sick. Certainly there are many physicians who enter the profession for monetary reasons: I do not wish to deny this. Yet, as any physician would admit, there are easier ways to make money. Still, the physician, like the employer, is in a power position. But the source of the physician's power is different. He does not stand to benefit from performing a certain therapy on any *particular* patient (unless, of course, the patient is indeed unique), for it is likely that another patient will choose to undergo that treatment. And, more importantly, physicians will always have patients seeking their services because persons will always get sick. Unless a physician is so inadequate, he can rest assured that he will be in business for a long time. This gives him less reason to deny patients information they need concerning the hazards of treatment. Thus, a physician's power position is not as threatened by loss of profit as is an employer's. He therefore has less reason than an employer to use a person merely as a means to his own end.

Moreover, an employer's reasons for withholding information are often different from those of the physician. While the physician may feel he is acting in the patient's best interests (whether or not he is certainly is open to debate) when he withholds information concerning the risks of treatment, this is not often the case with the employer. The employer withholds information about on-the-job hazards not because he wishes to protect the employee, or to act in the employee's best interests, but because he wants to protect his own interests. He wants the company to profit, and this may be possible only if certain hazardous assignments are made. The employer may feel that he is justified in withholding information about risks from the employee. After all, the employee does not have to stay on *this* job; he is free to leave. The employer's reasons for withholding information are thus, unlike those of most physicians, self-interested. It is these features of the employer-employee relationship, namely, the expectations of both parties, their reasons for entering into the rela-

tionship, and the employer's reasons for withholding information, which all contribute to the nonfiduciary nature of this relationship. These features may, of course, all be a result of the capitalist system. If this be so, some persons may argue that the very nature of the employer-employee relationship can be changed only by changing the socio-economic system. I believe this is false, and in Section V I will argue that establishing an employee's right to know will, in fact, make headway in changing the relationship into one that is fiduciary in nature.

IV

We have seen that the nature of the employer-employee relationship is such that it is difficult to establish an employee's right to know. Employers, on the one hand, find little or no reason to give their employees information about hazards in the workplace. In turn, employees find little or no reason to expect to receive this information. The differences in the nature of the relationship are, in all probability, responsible for the dissimilarities in the establishment of the right to know. But should this difference exist? Is there a difference in the choices faced by a person as patient versus a person as employee that will justify the difference in the recognition of the right to know?

I suggest that there is not. Although many disparities exist between the relationships, an important similarity grounds the right to know. It is this: in both cases, the person wants to know the dangers involved for the *same* reasons. He wants to know the risks that may be incurred to his body so that he can decide whether or not to expose himself to those risks. The information is needed for him to make a reasonable choice.

In both situations, the moral basis of the right to know lies in the principle of autonomy. Much talk has been generated about this principle since Mill and Kant recognized its importance. Although the literature offers a variety of definitions, this principle is usually defined in such a way as to include the notion of making one's own decisions affecting one's own life without coercion from others. In order for one to make a responsible decision, he must be informed about the choices with which he is faced. Just as a patient must be informed about the risks involved in a certain treatment in order for him to decide if he wants that treatment, an employee, too, must be informed about the hazards involved in working under certain conditions if he is to make a responsible, autonomous choice about whether or not to subject his person to such risks. In either case, if such information is not disclosed, the person's autonomy has been placed in jeopardy.

The choice faced by both the patient and the employee is one of whether or not to subject one's person to risk of harm. It may be objected that the harms which may be incurred in the workplace are less serious than those which may be incurred in the medical setting. But this is simply not true. The harms incurred in the workplace may be just as serious, and may not be as immediate as those incurred in the medical setting. For example, side-effects from an operation or from taking certain drugs are often known by the patient and/or his physician soon after they are incurred. Harms resulting from on-the-job hazards, however, often take considerable time to manifest themselves, and often require long-term exposure to take effect. For example, chronic berylliosis, constituted by coughing, dyspnea, and anorexia, may appear years after exposure to beryllium.[21] And cancer may take years to manifest itself after exposure to coal tar, paraffin, asbestos, vinyl chloride, and benzene. Other toxic materials do not produce side-effects in the exposed person, but instead in his or her children. These are either mutagenic in nature, in which case they change the genetic makeup of the offspring, or teratogenic, in which case they are capable of causing birth defects in the offspring.[22] This is not to imply that all harms incurred in the medical setting are immediate, and those incurred on the job are made manifest years after exposure; instead the point is that many do follow this pattern.

Because the harms incurred in the workplace often are made manifest years later, it is more difficult for an employer to face liability charges. In the medical realm, patients can be awarded damages either in battery or in negligence. Traditionally, patients can sue physicians for damages in battery if they are touched, treated, or researched upon without consent.[23] In a British Columbia case, it was reported[24] that a patient who suffered loss of smell and partial loss of taste after surgery was awarded damages in battery because she was unaware of these risks at the time of her consent. In America, failure to disclose risks to patients "is considered a breach of the physician's general duty to care to give reasonable information and advice to his patient."[25] To be awarded damages in battery, the patient need only establish that "what was done differed substantially from that to which he assented."[26]

Patients can sue also for damages in negligence. In Canada, it is reported that the physician should inform the patient of the nature and seriousness of treatment lest he be held negligent. The duty in negligence "is based on the nature of the physician-patient relationship as a trust," thus imposing a "basic requirement of honesty upon the physician."[27] In order for a physician to be found negligent, the patient must show that there was a breach of the duty of disclosure and that he, the patient, would not have consented had the required disclosure been given, and that he suffered a loss as a result.[28]

Although a patient can sue for damages in either battery or negligence, an employee has no such privilege. Establishment of workmen's compensation has prevented the right to sue in tort.[29] Prior to the establishment of workmen's compensation, employees could settle under tort law and receive payments for both loss of income as well as for "pain and suffering." Workmen's compensation statutes, however, include payment for loss of income, but only limited payment for "pain and suffering."[30] One source reports that no payment for pain and suffering is included.[31] Thus, employers do not have to pay for the full consequences of their negligence. Employees themselves must shoulder most of the burden of costs for employer negligence. This seems especially unjust when we are reminded of the fact that an employee's right to know is not firmly established.

One basis, then, for establishing a right to know in the workplace is that it ensures that an employee is given information necessary for him to be able to make a choice which may significantly affect his life. Informing an employee of workplace hazards puts him in the position of deciding whether or not he wants to be exposed to hazards, and thereby is one step in the direction of promoting his autonomy. Establishment of a right to know is especially important for the worker since he does not have much recourse against his employer if damages ensue.

Another basis for establishing this right lies in the notion of fairness of contract. When a person is hired for a job, there is an implicit contract made between the employer and employee, the terms of which spell out that person X will do job A and will be paid by person Y. This contract requires, like any fair contract, that both parties know what they are contracting to. It is insufficient that an employee know he is consenting to do a certain job in a certain way at a certain pace, and so on. If hazards which may produce harm to his person are involved, he should be made aware of them before he enters the contract. If he is not made aware of the hazards, and enters the contract with the employer, he is not giving fully informed consent to the relevant terms of the contract. The contract is thus unfair.

A third basis for establishing an employee's right to know is partly economic, partly moral. It lies in Milton Friedman's notion of business' social responsibility, namely "to use its resources and engage in activities designed to increase its profits so long as it stays within the rules of the game, which is to say, engages in open and free competition, without deception or fraud."[32] The moral justification for the right to know, using Friedman's terms of business' social responsibility, lies in his normative judgment

that business should not engage in deceptive practices. Though Friedman does not spell out what this entails, surely withholding information from the prospective employee—information which is likely to influence his decision—is a deceptive practice, prohibited even on Friedman's libertarian analysis of business in the free market system.

An economic justification for the right to know also can be found in Friedman and other free market advocates. It is this: in order to ensure that the free market really is free, persons should be able to enter the occupation of their choosing (at least insofar as they meet the qualifications). This choice must be informed. If information about job hazards is withheld, the choice will not be fully informed. And if the choice is not fully informed, it is not truly free. Thus, ignoring the right to know, besides violating moral principles such as autonomy and fairness of contract, violates one of the fundamental economic bases of the free market system.

V

If an employee's right to know becomes firmly established, certain implications are likely to follow. On the negative side, the employer will be faced with the difficult task of determining how much and what kind of information ought to be given to the employee. The employer will have to devote time and effort to find out just what hazards exist, and to convey the results of his findings to the employee. And if the risks involved in taking on a certain job are very high, or very serious, the employer may have difficulty in hiring someone for the job. Also, the company's trade secrets undoubtedly will sometimes be revealed.

While I do not wish to diminish the inconvenience these implications bring to the employer, none is too important to override the employee's right to know. Indeed, there certainly are ways to lessen the inconvenience while still bringing about the desired effects.

More importantly though, it is reasonable to assume that both parties are likely to benefit by establishing an employee's right to know.

It benefits the employee in several ways. First, since the employer will have to ascertain what are hazards in the workplace, he may eliminate at least some of them for the sake of attracting employees. Thus, the environment may be safer for the employee. Second, if the employee is presented with the relevant information about on-the-job hazards, it places into the hands of the employee the informed decision of whether or not to accept a position. The employee can then make his own choice of whether or not to expose himself to those hazards. Moreover, informing the employee of hazards in the workplace ensures him that the contract made with his employer is fair and not based upon deception. In these ways, it establishes trust in the employer.

The employer, too, benefits. Once he has given such information to his employee, if the employee willingly accepts the job knowing that to which he has consented, and is in some way harmed, the employer would decrease his liability in many cases. After all, it was the employee's decision to expose himself to the hazards. He knew what to expect, and is responsible for his decision. The employer, in many cases, will avoid paying compensation.

Most important is that the right to know may go so far as to establish a fiduciary relationship between employer and employee, much the same as that existent between many patients and their physicians. Part of what is involved in such a relationship is that both parties trust each other to look after each other's best interests. The employer can accomplish this by improving his work environment, by informing his employee of existent hazards, and the like.

The employee, also, can look out for his employer's best interests by unifying his goals with the goals of his employer. If the employee is made aware of risks involved in taking on a certain job, and yet he consents to taking on that job (assuming, of course, that he understands the risks and is not coerced into the job perhaps by another person or because he is unable to find an alternative), he has invested a part of himself into that relationship. He admits his willingness to work for an employer to achieve his employer's goals. The goals of the employer are then shared with the employee. And since the employee knows he is not being deceived about the conditions under which he works, he may have more incentive to do his job well. This, too, is likely to benefit the employer.

It is interesting to note, in conclusion, that the very nature of the employer-employee relationship which makes it difficult to secure an employee's right to know can, in fact, be changed into one of a fiduciary nature through the establishment of a right to know. We have seen that though the philosophical basis for securing a right to know in the workplace is the same as in the medical setting and that the harms which may possibly be incurred are similar, this right is more firmly grounded in the medical setting than in the workplace. What needs to be firmly established for the benefit of both the employer and employee in order to make headway in achieving a fiduciary relationship is an employee's right to know.

NOTES

1 Manuel G. Velasquez, *Business Ethics: Concepts and Cases* (Englewood Cliffs, NJ: Prentice-Hall, Inc., 1982), 311.

2 See Nicholas A. Ashford, *Crisis in the Workplace: Occupational Disease and Injury* (Cambridge, MA: The MIT Press, 1976), 68-83, for a thorough and interesting description of these hazards.

3 Although I shall use the term "employee" throughout this essay, my arguments shall apply also to the prospective employee since he is faced with a similar choice, that is, whether or not to accept a job in a hazardous work environment.

4 *Canterbury v. Spence*, US Court of Appeals, District of Columbia Circuit, May 19, 1972, 464 Federal Reporter, 2nd Series, 772.

5 "A Patient's Bill of Rights," American Hospital Association, reprinted in Mappes and Zembaty (eds.), *Biomedical Ethics* (New York: McGraw-Hill, Inc., 1981), 87-89.

6 "Declaration of Helsinki," World Medical Association, reprinted in Mappes and Zembaty, *op. cit.*, 145-47.

7 *Federal Register*, Vol. 45 no. 102, Friday, May 23, 1980, Rules and Regulations, Dept. of Labor, Occupational Safety and Health Administration, 23CFR Part 1910, 35212.

8 *Federal Register*, Vol. 48 no. 228, Friday, November 25, 1983, Rules and Regulations, Dept. of Labor, Occupational Safety and Health Administration, 29CFR Part 1910, 53280.

9 Ruth R. Faden and Tom L. Beauchamp, "The Right to Risk Information and the Right to Refuse Health Hazards in the Workplace," in *Ethical Theory of Business* (2nd ed.), Tom L. Beauchamp and Norman E. Bowie, eds. (Englewood Cliffs, NJ: Prentice-Hall, Inc., 1983), 196-206.

10 Tim D. Wermager, "Union's Right to Information vs. Confidentiality of Employer Trade Secrets: Accommodating the Interests Through Procedural Burdens and Restricted Disclosure," 66 *Iowa Law Review*, 1333-51, July, 1981.

11 *Federal Register*, Vol. 48 no. 228, Friday, November 25, 1983, Rules and Regulations, Dept. of Labor, Occupational Safety and Health Administration, 29CFR Part 1910 53284.

12 Ibid., Table 1, 53285.

13 Ibid., Vol. 45, 35215.

14 The Occupational Safety and Health Act of 1970 (Public Law 91-596), Section 5(a)(1), reprinted in Ashford, 545-75.

15 Robert Stewart Smith, *The Occupational Safety and Health Act: Its Goals and Its Achievements* (Washington, DC: American Enterprise Institute for Public Policy Research, 1976), 9.

16 Wermager, *op. cit.*, 1333.

17 David Carey Fraser, "Trade Secrets and the NLRA: Employee's Right to Health and Safety Information," 14 *University of San Francisco Law Review*, 495-524, Spring, 1980.

18 Wermager, *op. cit.*, 1335-36.

19 Wermager, *op. cit.*, 1343.

20 Wermager, *op. cit.*, 1345.

21 Ashford, *op. cit.*, 76.

22 Ashford, *op. cit.*, 78.

23 Karen Lebacqz and Robert J. Levine, "Informed Consent in Human Research: Ethical and Legal Aspects," in *Encyclopedia of Bioethics*, Vol. 2, Warren T. Reich, editor-in-chief (New York: The Free Press, 1978), 755-62.

24 Gilbert Sharpe, LLM, "Recent Canadian Court Decisions on Consent," *Bioethics Quarterly*, Vol. 2 No. 1 (Spring, 1980), 56-63.

25 Sharpe, ibid., 58.

26 Sharpe, ibid., 61.

27 Janice R. Dillon, "Informed Consent and the Disclosure of Risks of Treatment: The Supreme Court of Canada decides," *Bioethics Quarterly*, Vol. 3 No. 3 and 4, (Fall/Winter, 1981), 156-62.

28 Dillon, ibid., 160.

29 Ashford, *op. cit.*, 350.

30 Ashford, *op. cit.*, 392.

31 "Occupational Health Risks and the Worker's Right to Know," 90 *Yale Law Journal*, 1792-1810, July, 1981.

32 Milton Friedman, *Capitalism and Freedom* (Chicago: The University of Chicago Press, 1962), 13.

◆ ◆ ◆ ◆ ◆

TIBOR R. MACHAN

Human Rights, Workers' Rights, and the "Right" to Occupational Safety

Introduction

I take the position of the nonbeliever.[1] I do not believe in special workers' rights. I do believe that workers possess rights as human beings, as do publishers, philosophers, disc jockeys, students, and priests. Once fully interpreted, these rights may impose special standards at the workplace, as they may in hospitals, on athletics fields, or in the marketplace.

Human Rights

Our general rights, those we are morally justified to secure by organized force (e.g., government), are those initially identified by John Locke: life, liberty, and property. That is, we need ask no one's permission to live, to take actions, and to acquire, hold, or use peacefully the productive or creative results of our actions. We may, morally, resist (without undue force) efforts to violate or infringe upon our rights. Our rights are (1) absolute, (2) unalienable, and (3) universal: (1) in social relations no excuse legitimatizes their violation; (2) no one can lose these rights, though their exercise may be restricted (e.g., to jail) by what one chooses to do; and (3) everyone has these rights, whether acknowledged or respected by others or governments or under different descriptions (within less developed conceptual schemes).[2]

I defend this general rights theory elsewhere.[3] Essentially, since adults are rational beings with the moral responsibility to excel as such, a good or suitable community requires these rights as standards. Since this commits one to a virtuously self-governed life, others should respect this as equal members of the community. Willful invasion of these rights—the destruction of (negative) liberty—must be prohibited in human community life.

So-called positive freedom—that is, the enablement co do well in life—presupposes the prior importance of negative freedom. As, what we might call, self-starters, human beings will generally be best off if they are left uninterfered with to take the initiative in their lives.

Workers' Rights

What about special workers' rights? There are none. As individuals who intend to hire out their skills for what they will fetch in the marketplace, however, workers have the right to offer these in return for what others, (e.g., employers) will offer in acceptable compensation. This implies free trade in the labor market.

Any interference with such trade workers (alone or in voluntary cooperation) might want to engage in, with consent by fellow traders, would violate both the workers' and their traders' human rights. Freedom of association would thereby be abridged. (This includes freedom to organize into trade associations, unions, cartels, and so forth.)

Workers' rights advocates view this differently. They hold that the employee-employer relationship involves special duties owed by employers to employees, creating (corollary) rights that governments, given their purpose, should protect aside from negative rights, workers are owed respect of their positive rights to be treated with care and consideration.

This, however, is a bad idea. Not to be treated with care and consideration can be open to moral criticism. And lack of safety and health provisions may mean the neglect of crucial values to employees. In many circumstances employers should, morally, provide them.

This is categorically different from the idea of enforceable positive rights. (Later I will touch on unfulfilled reasonable expectations of safety and health provisions on the job!) Adults aren't due such service from free agents whose conduct should be guided by their own judgments and not some alien authority. This kind of moral servitude (abolished after slavery and serfdom) of some by others has been discredited.

Respect for human rights is necessary in a moral society—one needn't thank a person for not murdering, assaulting, or robbing one—whereas being provided with benefits, however crucial to one's well being, is more an act of generosity than a right.

Of course moral responsibilities toward others, even strangers, can arise. When those with plenty know of those with little, help would ordinarily be morally commendable. This can also extend to the employment relationship. Interestingly, however, government "regulation may impede risk-reducing change, freezing us into a hazardous present when a safer future beckons."[4]

My view credits all but the severely incapacitated with the fortitude to be productive and wise when ordering their affairs, workers included. The form of liberation that is then viral to workers is precisely the bourgeois kind: being set free from subjugation to others, including governments. Antibourgeois "liberation" is insultingly paternalistic.[5]

Alleging Special Workers' Rights

Is this all gross distortion? Professor Braybrooke tells us, "Most people in our society ... must look for employment and most (raking them one by one) have no alternative to accepting the working conditions offered by a small set of employers—perhaps one employer in the vicinity."[6] Workers need jobs and cannot afford to quibble. Employers can wait for the most accommodating job prospects.

This in part gives rise to special workers' rights doctrines, to be implemented by government occupational safety, health and labor-relations regulators, which then "makes it easier for competing firms to heed an important moral obligation and to be, if they wish, humane."[7]

Suppose a disadvantaged worker, seeking a job in a coal mine, asks about safety provision in the mine. Her doing so presupposes that (1) she has other alternatives, and (2) it's morally and legally optional to care about safety at the mine, not due to workers by right. Prior to government's energetic prolabor interventions, safety, health, and related provisions for workers had been lacking. Only legally mandated workers' rights freed workers from their oppressive lot. Thus, workers must by law be provided with safety, health care, job security, retirement, and other viral benefits.

Workers' rights advocates deny that employers have the basic (natural or human) private property rights to give them full authority to set terms of employment. They are seen as nonexclusive stewards of the workplace property, property obtained by way of historical accident, morally indifferent historical necessity, default, or theft. There is no genuine free labor market. There are no jobs to offer since they are not anyone's to give. The picture we should have of the situation is that society should be regarded as a kind of large team or family; the rights of its respective parts (individuals) flow not from their free and independent moral nature, but from the relationship of the needs and usefulness of individuals as regards the purposes of the collective.

By this account, everyone lacks the full authority to enter into exclusive or unilaterally determined and mutual agreements on his or her terms. Such terms—of production, employment, promotion, termination, and so on—would be established, in line with moral propriety, only by the agency (society, God, the party, the democratic assembly) that possesses the full moral authority to set them.

Let us see why the view just stated is ultimately unconvincing. To begin with, the language of rights does not belong within the above framework. That language acknowledges the reality of morally free and independent human beings and includes among them workers, as well as all other adults. Individual human rights assume that within the limits of nature, human beings are all efficacious to varying degrees, frequently depending upon their own choices. Once this individualist viewpoint is rejected, the very foundation for rights language disappears (notwithstanding some contrary contentions).[8]

Some admit that employers are full owners of their property, yet hold that workers, because they are disadvantaged, are owed special duties of care and considerateness, duties which in turn create rights the government should protect. But even if this were right, it is not possible from this position to establish enforceable *public* policy. From the mere existence of *moral* duties employers may have to employees, no enforceable public policy can follow; moral responsibilities require freely chosen fulfillment, not enforced compliance.

Many workers' rights advocates claim that a free labor market will lead to such atrocities as child labor, hazardous and health-impairing working conditions, and so forth. Of course, even if this were true, there is reason to think that OSHA-type regulatory remedies are illusionary. As Peter Huber argues, "regulation of health and safety is not only a major obstacle to technological transformation and innovation but also often aggravates the hazards it is supposed to avoid."[9]

However, it is not certain that a free labor market would lead to child labor and rampant neglect of safety and health at the workplace. Children are, after all, dependents and therefore have rights owed them by their parents. To subject children to hazardous, exploitative work, to deprive them of normal education and health care, could be construed as a violation of their individual rights as young, dependent human beings. Similarly, knowingly or negligently subjecting workers to hazards at the workplace (of which they were not made aware and could not anticipate from reasonable familiarity with the job) constitutes a form of actionable fraud. It comes under the prohibition of the violation of the right to liberty, at times even the right to life. Such conduct is actionable in a court of law and work-

ers, individually or organized into unions, would be morally justified, indeed advised, to challenge it.

A consistent and strict interpretation of the moral (not economic) individualist framework of rights yields results that some advocates of workers' rights are aiming for. The moral force of most attacks on the free labor market framework tends to arise from the fact that some so-called free labor market instances are probably violations of the detailed implications of that approach itself. Why would one be morally concerned with working conditions that are fully agreed to by workers? Such a concern reflects either the belief that there hadn't been any free agreement in the first place, and thus workers are being defrauded, or it reflects a paternalism that, when construed as paternalism proper instead of compassion, no longer carries moral force.

Whatever its motives, paternalism is also insulting and demeaning in its effect. Once it is clear that workers can generate their own (individual and/or collective) response to employers' bargaining power—via labor organizations, insurance, craft associations, and so on—the favorable air of the paternalistic stance diminishes considerably. Instead, workers are seen to be regarded as helpless, inefficacious, inept persons.

The "Right" to Occupational Safety

Consider an employer who owns and operates a coal mine. (We could have chosen any firm, privately or "publicly" owned, managed by hired executives with the full consent of the owners, including interested stockholders who have encrusted, by their purchase of stocks, others with the goal of obtaining economic benefits for them.) The firm posts a call for jobs. The mine is in competition with some of the major coal mines in the country and the world. But it is much less prosperous than its competitors. The employer is at present not equipped to run a highly-polished, well-outfitted (e.g., very safe) operation. That may lie in the future, provided the cost of production will not be so high as to make this impossible.

Some of the risks will be higher for workers in this mine than in others. Some of the mineshafts will have badly illuminated stairways, some of the noise will be higher than the levels deemed acceptable by experts, and some of the ventilation equipment will be primitive. The wages, too, will be relatively low in hopes of making the mine eventually more prosperous.

When prospective employees appear and are made aware of the type of job being offered, and its hazards they are at liberty to (a) accept or reject, (b) organize into a group and insist on various terms not in the offing, (c) bargain alone or together with others and set terms that include improvements, or (d) pool workers' resources, borrow, and purchase the firm.

To deny that workers could achieve such things is not yet to deny that they are (negatively) free to do so. But to hold that this would be extraordinary for workers (and thus irrelevant in this sort of case) is to (1) assume a historical situation not in force and certainly not necessary, (2) deny workers the capacity for finding a solution to their problems, or (3) deny that workers are capable of initiative.

Now suppose that employers are compelled by law to spend the firm's funds to meet safety requirements deemed desirable by the government regulators. This increased cost of production reduces available funds for additional wages for present and future employees, not to mention available funds for future prospect sites. This is what has happened: The employee-employer relationship has been unjustly intruded upon, to the detriment not only of the mine owners, but also of those who might be employed and of future consumers of energy. The myth of workers' rights is mostly to blame.

Conclusion

I have argued that the doctrine of special workers' rights is unsupported and workers, accordingly, possess those rights that all other humans possess, the right to life, liberty, and property. Workers are not a special species of persons to be treated in a paternalistic fashion and, given just treatment in the community, they can achieve their goals as efficiently as any other group of human beings.[10]

NOTES

1 I also wish to thank Bill Puka and Gertrude Ezorsky for their very valuable criticism of an earlier draft of this essay, despite their very likely disapproval of my views.

2 This observation rests, in part, on epistemological insights available, for example, in Hanna F. Pitkin, *Wittgenstein and Justice* (Berkeley, CA: University of California Press, 1972).

3 Tibor R. Machan, "A Reconsideration of Natural Rights Theory," *American Philosophical Quarterly* 19 (January 1980): 61-72.

4 Peter Huber, "Exorcists vs. Gatekeepers in Risk Regulation," *Regulation* (November/December 1983), 23.

5 But see Steven Kelman, "Regulation and Paternalism," *Rights and Regulation*, ed. T.R. Machan and M.B. Johnson (Cambridge, MA: Ballinger Publ. Co., 1983), 217-48.

6 David Braybrooke, *Ethics in the World of Business* (Totowa, NJ: Rowman and Allanheld, 1983), 223.

7 Ibid., 224.

8 For an attempt to forge a collectivist theory of rights, see Tom Campbell, *The Left and Rights* (London and Boston: Routledge and Kegan Paul, 1983).

9 Huber, "Exorcists vs. Gatekeepers," 23.

10 Ibid. Huber observes that "Every insurance company knows that life is growing safer, but the public is firmly convinced that living is becoming ever more hazardous" (23). In general, capitalism's benefits to workers have simply been acknowledged, especially by moral and political philosophers! It is impossible to avoid the simple fact that the workers of the world believe differs judging by what system they prefer to emigrate to whenever possible.

LIFESTYLES AND YOUR LIVELIHOOD: GETTING FIRED IN AMERICA

DAVID MEELER AND SRIVATSA SESHADRI

Deborah Hobbs, who lived with her boyfriend, was given three options by her boss: Get married, move out, or be fired. Lynne Gobbell put a John Kerry campaign sticker on her car and was given two options: Remove it or be fired. Boeing CEO Harry Stonecipher was fired for having consensual sex with another company executive. Employees at Weyco, Inc. lost their jobs when they refused to quit smoking after work. Michael Hanscom was fired from Microsoft and Ellen Simonetti was fired from Delta Airlines for pictures they posted on their personal websites. Perhaps the most notorious blogger who lost her job is Jessica Cutler, the US Senate staffer who chronicled her off-hour sexcapades. In today's digital and confessional age, the message is clear: companies feel free to dictate and scrutinize appropriate personal behavior for their employees.

Before we get too outraged, we should note that many of these firings were probably legitimate. After several earlier scandals, Boeing's new CEO, Harry Stonecipher, hyped the company's new company policies as evidence of the kinds of progress Boeing had made to clean up its operations. Those same policies explicitly forbade intimate relationships between workers and superiors. Since Stonecipher's affair was with a woman over whom he had no direct supervision, the board concluded that he had not violated the letter of the code. However, given recent scandals, they felt many of the details and circumstances surrounding Stonecipher's affair indicated poor judgment, which impaired his ability to retain confidence and lead the company forward. Michael Hanson worked for Xerox under a contract with Microsoft, and was bound by nondis-

closure agreements when he posted a photograph of Apple computers being offloaded at his Microsoft jobsite. Although he found it humorous, the photographs clearly violated the explicit policies governing his employment. Ellen Simonetti was happy to be a stewardess, and in her personal blog-gallery she posted some photographs of herself in uniform and on a plane, in pin-up style poses. Although Ellen was fully clothed and Delta was never able to specify exactly which company policy she violated, the pictures can be seen to reflect poorly on Delta. Ellen represented Delta airline when she wore company attire in a public forum.

Like many other companies in America, Weyco was ostensibly concerned about its growing healthcare costs. But things are not always as they appear. As a former football coach, Howard Weyers, president of Weyco, brings his in-control, non-nonsense judgment to his management decisions. He was quoted in a New York Times article saying "I spent all my life working with young men, honing them mentally and physically to a high performance. And I think that's what we need to do in the workplace ... You work for me, this is what I expect. You don't like it? Go someplace else." It seems that whatever activities Howard doesn't approve of, his employees had better not engage in—even in the privacy of their own homes. At least Weyco can claim that firing employees who fail their random nicotine tests helps the company reduce healthcare costs.

Still, other of these cases are harder to justify. Lynne Gobbell's boss exercised his right to political speech by having pro-Bush flyers inserted into each employee's paycheck; but Lynne has no legal recourse after losing her job. Deborah Hobbs was faced with the consequences of a law initially passed in 1805, and the ACLU is confident the law will be ruled unconstitutional. While Washington insiders expended great effort to deduce the identities of Jessica's lovers from clues in her blog, Ms. Cutler has kept the names of her lovers secret to this day. Little could be more personal than intimate sexual encounters, and being fired for chronicling your exploits seems intuitively unfair.

Perhaps it is most important to note that corporate intrusion into our off-the-clock lives is not a new phenomenon. By all accounts, Henry Ford was an innovative industrialist who brought prosperity and opportunity to hundreds of thousands of people. He is well known for implementing modern machine techniques in automobile production, but less well known for his social ideals. Henry Ford had no qualms about hiring immigrants and offered English classes to immigrant workers, and even started a nationwide phenomenon when he began hiring ex-convicts. Henry Ford was committed to bringing the benefits of an industrial society to everyone. The price of his cars actually went down year in and year out. Between 1910 and 1915, the price of Ford's *Model T* was reduced by more than half. At the same time, Ford paid his workers $5 a day—twice the average wage for an auto-worker. But Ford's benefits came with a price. The "Five Dollar Day" was split between wages and profit-sharing; and employees would get profits only after they were approved by Ford's "sociology department." One of the first requirements for the five dollar wage was fluency in English, combined with abandoning the customs of your native country and mandatory attendance at "community values" classes. Investigators from the sociology department checked on how clean the worker's home was, how personal finances were spent, whether alcohol or tobacco were being used (both of which were forbidden), church attendance, and even sexual habits. Ford didn't want anything to diminish his worker's capacity to be as efficient as possible.

Analysis

The United Nations Declaration of Human Rights includes a right to privacy. While governments might not intrude into our private lives, employers are using their economic power to control our personal lives. So, for those of us reared in UN member-nations, the idea that our employers could dictate our off-the-clock behavior, and then police our putatively private lives for evidence of non-compliance strikes us as absurd. How is it that companies can demand so much from their employees in the 9-5 world, and then dictate their personal behavior outside of work? The answer is quite simple: the vast majority of employees in the US are "at will." In brief, being employed "at will" means that you can quit your job at any time, for any reason. But it also means that you can be fired at any time, for almost any reason, including good reasons, bad reasons, or no reason at all. Unless you have an individual work contract or are governed by a collective bargaining agreement, you are an at-will employee. At-will employees can be hired, fired, demoted, promoted, transferred, etc., at any time so long as it is consistent with statutory law. Federally, there are a few grounds on which you cannot be fired. If you are fired on the basis of sex, religion, age, race, etc., then you have some legal recourse. But if you are fired because your cologne offends the boss, there is little you can do. Some states add other protections. For instance, five states have laws that forbid firing someone based on her political view or affiliations.

This trend is identified more broadly as "Lifestyle Discrimination." Most aspects of lifestyle discrimination are putatively tied to economics. Like Weyco, many companies look down on risky activities that are linked with increase costs. As early as 1988 an Administrative Management Society survey revealed that approximately 6000 companies in the US were discriminating against off-duty smokers. The ACLU suggests that discrimination against overweight employees is comparable.

Questions

1. In your opinion, are any of the above firings ethical? Why or why not? Of those firings you think are unethical, what is unethical about them?

2. What recourse can an employee who was a victim of unethical (not illegal) conduct of the employer take against the ex-employer?

3. Would Michael Cranford support Weyco's use of employee nicotine tests? Why or why not?

4. Suppose these employees had been asked by their employers to stop those behaviors, and given an opportunity to change. How do the arguments you put forth for question 1 above change? In a case like Weyco's, would it make a difference if the employers offered financial assistance with a smoking-abatement program?

5. What have you learned about the challenges of ethical decision making?

CASE STUDY 4

E-MAIL AND PRIVACY: A NOVEL APPROACH
MIKE BOWERN

Case Description[1]

Software Improvements Pty Ltd. is a small company located in Canberra, Australia. The company has a number of lines of business, which include selling software tools for modelling and development support; developing their own project support products; consulting; and developing and supporting an advanced electronic voting and vote counting system (eVACS®). The total number of people in the company varies between six and ten, including the Managing Director, depending on the work in hand.

Each member of the company has a specific area of responsibility, and while there is very little overlap of these areas, it is usual for another person to have a working knowledge of an associated field of the business. The company has adopted some of the ideas of Ricardo Semler,[2] including corporate planning, selection of new people, and setting salaries.

As with any organization, communication within the company is very important. A small office makes face-to-face meetings easy, and there are regular, formal company meetings over lunch. E-mail is the primary medium for communication with outside organizations, including customers, prospects, business partners and contacts, and people working away from the office.

Since the mid-1990s the company has had an open e-mail policy, whereby everyone receives all incoming e-mail messages, regardless of the addressee. Sent messages are regularly copied to others in the company, for example on matters on which the Managing Director needs to be kept informed. All messages are also copied to the Office Manager, who archives these together with all incoming e-mail. There has never been any objection from the people in the company to this practice.

Software Improvements believes they gain great benefit from this approach. It provides to each person a daily snapshot of what is happening in the company and its business areas. Regularly, a person not specifically part of an exchange of e-mails has been able to offer some advice or a useful comment on the particular matter being discussed. This is a good example of practical knowledge management.

If an urgent message arrives for a person who may not be available at the time, the office manager forwards the message to the addressee; and replies to the sender saying the person is currently unavailable but knows of the message, and will respond in due course. This is a good example of practical customer service.

Outgoing messages are not monitored or available to all people in the company. A person may send a private message, in the knowledge that any reply may be seen by all. In practice this tends to limit the types of message sent. For example, one would not usually send e-mails about personal finance or health matters. However one may send messages about activities with a professional society, in the knowledge that the replies could be read and could advertise the professional activities.

The people in the company decided to implement this practice in a democratic way at one of the regular staff meetings. There were no arguments against the proposal. If a person does not want messages from particular people to be read by others, he or she asks these people to send their messages to a private e-mail address. People joining the company are told of this policy, and usually accept this method of working. To date, no one has objected to this practice, but if they did object, the e-mail system could be configured to filter their messages to the one recipient.

While some customers and others outside the company are aware of this e-mail practice, there is no conscious effort made to inform all customers and others that their e-mails may be read by all people in the company.

Ethical Analysis

This is a simple case about the matter of privacy of e-mail messages. Some people have argued that e-mail messages should be regarded as postal mail and treated with the same level of privacy. Postal mail is treated as private between the sender and recipient, and generally it is against the law for mail in the postal system to be tampered with in any way.

Company e-mails are, or should be, written for business purposes, in the company's time, using equipment and software provided by the company. So managers could argue that the company has the right to monitor and access e-mail messages sent and received on its facilities. However, if a company has this right it also has an obligation to inform its employees that it monitors and accesses the e-mail messages they send and receive. The employees can then accept this situation, perhaps negotiate different arrangements, or leave the company; but these choices may not be as simple as this, and the result may be a matter of coerced consent rather than fully informed consent. For example, leaving the company may not really be an option in times when, or places where, there are few employment opportunities. Also negotiating different arrangements may not be easy if only one or a few employees are involved.

Wherever there is a policy of e-mail monitoring in the workplace, there should also be a policy of informed consent, whereby employees may give their consent to e-mail monitoring after they have been provided with the policy and all other relevant information about the monitoring process. James H. Moor[3] has proposed a number of principles to guide the setting of policies for privacy and the use of cyber-technology. These are:

- *The Publicity Principle*—where the rules and conditions (i.e., policies) governing privacy aspects should be clearly defined and known to those people affected by them, thus enabling informed consent.

- *The Justification of Exceptions Principle*—which allows for the privacy policy to be breached under certain circumstances, when the harm done by the breach of privacy is less than that if the policy were followed.
- *The Adjustment Principle*—which allows for changes to the policy to be made and publicized.

The e-mail monitoring policy in Software Improvements has generally followed these principles. The policy, as such, is not written down, but the decisions relating to e-mail access are documented in the notes of the regular staff meetings. The Publicity Principle was well and truly followed, since all of the staff were parties to making the decision.

Since this is an open policy, an exception would be for someone *not* to be able to see all incoming e-mail messages. If a person decided they did not want to see all messages, for example a part-time contractor who did not need this facility, then the e-mail system can be configured to enable this. Therefore the requirements of the Justification of Exceptions Principle can be met.

A point for debate in this case could be the matter of e-mail senders not knowing that their messages can be read by all of the people in the company. Often, when you make a telephone call to the Help Desk of a service provider, you hear a message to the effect that "your call may be monitored for training and quality purposes," and you have the option for this not to happen. This is a simple example of informed consent. If Software Improvements decides to inform their business contacts and others about their open e-mail policy then the Adjustment Principle could be followed to make and publicize the changes to their policy.

Study Questions

This case is different from the usual ones about e-mail monitoring by employers in companies. By being open about the policy and ensuring everyone is aware and accepts the approach, the usual problems of e-mail monitoring do not arise. However, there may be other issues. These questions are designed to help you think about these issues.

1. Do you accept the reasons that Software Improvements gives for adopting this practice of e-mail management? Could you work in such an environment? What objections might you have to this approach? Does the overall company benefit override the privacy of the individual?

2. Software Improvements is a small company, with about 10 people. The obvious response is that any more people would make this approach unworkable; but would it? Could other technology help to make this work in an organization of any size? For example could it be arranged for each project team to work in this way?

3. Do managers have a valid argument that the company has the right to monitor and access e-mail messages sent and received on its hardware and software facilities? Would the same argument apply to monitoring telephone usage for private calls, or private use of a car or a cell phone provided by the company?

4. Do you think that anybody sending a message to Software Improvements should be aware that it may be read by everyone in the company? How could they be made aware of this practice?

NOTES

1   This case has been published with the permission of Software Improvements Pty. Ltd.
2   Ricardo Semler, *Maverick* (New York: Warner Books Inc., 1993)
3   "Towards a Theory of Privacy in the Information Age," *Computers and Society* Vol. 27 (September 1997), 27-32.

UNIT 3

Justice and Fair Practice

ANAND VAIDYA

Justice and Fair Practice

In this unit, our attention will turn away from ethical issues that only arise in the business context. We will instead focus on some general ethical issues that occur also in the business context. We will be concerned with how they arise in the business context, and what the ethical issues surrounding them in that context are.

Affirmative action and sexual harassment are good examples of general ethical issues that arise in broader contexts, and not just in employment; for example, they both arise in educational contexts as well. One of the first projects in discussing these topics is getting clear about what is at issue and, in particular, defining what these concepts are. Once we have some understanding of the conceptual issues, then we can explore some of the normative dimensions.

Affirmative action is the practice of hiring or promoting a person in part on the basis of race or gender. Affirmative action has, and continues to be, a controversial practice. On the one hand, some people think that it either remedies past injustices or else promotes other important social goals, such as workplace diversity. On the other hand, critics see affirmative action as a sort of reverse discrimination that runs contrary to important meritocratic principles and sets up unqualified job candidates for failure and stigma.

Sexual harassment is the practice of harassing a person in a sexual manner. Sexual harassment from a moral point of view is less controversial than affirmative action. The main reason is that most contemporary theorists agree that it is morally impermissible to sexually harass a co-worker, and interfere with their right to perform their job by infringing upon their personal well-being. Even though there is a consensus about the moral impermissibility of sexual harassment, there are still important conceptual issues regarding the definition of sexual harassment that must be addressed. The definition must not be too narrow so as to exclude activity that is problematic. For example, sexual harassment cannot be limited to physical contact, since verbal comments are equally harmful. The definition must also not be so broad as to preclude a friendly advance between workers. In addition, although the moral focus in sexual harassment has been predominately on the rights of the accuser, it is also important to explore the rights of the accused.

Bluffing is yet another practice in business that is ethically important. On the face of it, bluffing appears to be an immoral practice, given that it seems to be a form of lying: when two negotiators bluff, they each make false claims about something (e.g., their "reserve prices," or the price at which they would consent to a transaction). However, several philosophers have argued that bluffing is actually morally permissible in the business context. Here the central move has been to identify features of business negotiation that somehow dissolve the putative relationship between bluffing and lying. For example, Albert Carr argues that one can bluff in a business negotiation because, in a business context, the norms differ from those of other situations wherein lying might be a fair ascription. In particular, Carr conceives of business negotiation through an analogy with poker; Carr thinks that, as bluffing is permissible in poker, so it is in business. The appropriateness of this analogy has been discussed by others, such as Thomas Carson and Fritz Allhoff, both of whom present alternative arguments for the moral legitimacy of bluffing.

In broad terms, bribery is understood as the transfer of a gift, often money, in return for a favor that often involves breaking a law or policy or which puts other competitors at an unfair disadvantage. We commonly associate "bribery" with paying someone for something we are not entitled to. However, given that a lot of business today is done globally, one has to take into consideration the perspective of other

324 JUSTICE AND FAIR PRACTICE

cultures and countries on the moral permissibility of bribery. In a great many places, offering a gift as part of a transaction is not considered bribery; it is simply understood as doing what it takes to get something done.

For example, suppose that getting a building permit in India takes four months and that applications are processed in the order in which they are received. But suppose that an American company building a hotel in India wants to have its permit filled in two months so that the project can get started. If members of the American firm were to pay government employees to process their paperwork sooner, then they would, under a classical Western analysis, be bribing government officials. However, from the context of what goes on in India, is this transaction of money for the processing of paperwork morally impermissible? In addition, in discussing bribery in the global context, one may want to discuss what kinds of gifts or payments are legitimate, and which ones are illegitimate.

Perhaps it is legitimate in the case above to offer funds to the government in order to process the paperwork because there is no competitive advantage gained by doing so. It is not as if another company is losing out by the bribe being made. One could also argue that using gifts in foreign countries in order to acquire contracts simply is part of making a bid. When an American company bids for a contract in a foreign country, part of the bid may result in gifts to various members of the party to which the bids are being submitted. In the articles in this section, issues surrounding the definition of bribery and its permissibility in foreign countries are considered.

In this unit we have aimed at issues that strike us as important and pervasive in the business context.

AFFIRMATIVE ACTION

METRO BROADCASTING, INC. v. FCC, 497 U.S. 547 (1990)

METRO BROADCASTING, INC. v. FCC, 497 U.S. 547 (1990): This decision upheld two "minority preference policies" of the FCC—the first, a program "awarding an enhancement for minority ownership in comparative proceedings" for new broadcast licenses; the second, a "minority 'distress sale' program," permitting "a limited category of existing radio and television broadcast stations to be transferred only to minority-controlled firms." Justice BRENNAN's majority opinion applied intermediate scrutiny and held that these policies did not violate equal protection principles. He emphasized that the policies were mandated by Congress, and

that Fullilove and, in his view, Croson supported his views. He stated: "It is of overriding significance [that] the FCC's minority ownership programs have been specifically approved—indeed, mandated—by Congress. In [Fullilove], Chief Justice Burger [observed that] when a program employing a benign racial classification is adopted by an administrative agency at the explicit direction of Congress, we are 'bound to approach our task with appropriate deference to the [Congress].' [A] majority of the Court in Fullilove did not apply strict scrutiny to the race-based classification at issue. [Three] Members would have upheld benign racial classifications that 'serve important governmental objectives and are substantially related to achievement of those objectives.' [Opinion of Marshall, J.] We apply that standard today. We hold that benign race-conscious measures mandated by Congress—even if those measures are not 'remedial' in the sense of being designed to compensate victims of past governmental or societal discrimination—are constitutionally permissible to the extent that they serve important governmental objectives within the power of Congress and are substantially related to achievement of those objectives. [Our] decision in [Croson] does not prescribe the level of scrutiny to be applied to a benign racial classification employed by Congress. [The] question of congressional action was not before the Court, and so Croson cannot be read to undermine our decision in Fullilove. In fact, much of the language and reasoning in Croson reaffirmed the lesson of Fullilove that race-conscious classifications adopted by Congress to address racial and ethnic discrimination are subject to a different standard than such classifications prescribed by state and local governments. [We] hold that the FCC minority ownership policies pass muster under the test we announce today. First, we find that they serve the important governmental objective of broadcast diversity. Second, we conclude that they are substantially related to the achievement of that objective. [The] interest in enhancing broadcast diversity is, at the very least, an important governmental objective and is therefore a sufficient basis for the Commission's minority ownership policies. Just as a 'diverse student body' contributing to a "'robust exchange of ideas'" is a 'constitutionally permissible goal' on which a race-conscious university admissions program may be predicated, the diversity of views and information on the airwaves serves important First Amendment values."

Justice Brennan also found that the minority ownership policies were substantially related to the achievement of the government's interest in broadcast diversity. He stated that "we must pay close attention to the expertise of the [FCC] and the factfinding of Congress when analyzing the nexus between minority ownership and programming diversity." He added: "The judgment that there is [such a nexus] does not rest on impermissible stereotyping. [While] we are under no illusion that members

of a particular minority group share some cohesive, collective viewpoint, we believe it a legitimate inference for Congress and the Commission to draw that as more minorities gain ownership and policy-making roles in the media, varying perspectives will be more fairly represented on the airwaves. The policies are thus a product of "'analysis'" rather than a "'stereotyped reaction'"; [based on 'habit']." He continued: "Finally, we do not believe that the minority ownership policies at issue impose impermissible burdens on nonminorities. Applicants [for licenses] have no settled expectation that their applications will be granted without consideration of public interest factors such as minority ownership." Justice STEVENS concurred, stating: "Today the Court squarely rejects the proposition that a governmental decision that rests on a racial classification is never permissible except as a remedy for a past wrong. I endorse this focus on the future benefit, rather than the remedial justification, of such decisions. [The] Court demonstrates that this case falls within the extremely narrow category of governmental decisions for which racial or ethnic heritage may provide a rational basis for differential treatment. The public interest in broadcast diversity—like the interest in an integrated police force, diversity in the composition of a public school faculty or diversity in the student body of a professional school—is in my view unquestionably legitimate."

Justice O'CONNOR, joined by Chief Justice Rehnquist and Justices Scalia and Kennedy, dissented, insisting on an across-the-board strict scrutiny standard, for federal as well as state actions. She elaborated: "Congress has considerable latitude [when] it exercises its 'unique remedial powers [under] § 5 of the Fourteenth Amendment' [Croson], but this case does not implicate those powers. [The] Court asserts that Fullilove supports its novel application of intermediate scrutiny to 'benign' race conscious measures adopted by Congress. [Several] reasons defeat this claim. First, Fullilove concerned an exercise of Congress' powers under § 5 of the Fourteenth

Amendment. [Second,] Fullilove applies at most only to congressional measures that seek to remedy identified past discrimination. [Finally,] even if Fullilove applied outside a remedial exercise of Congress' § 5 power, it would not support today's adoption of the intermediate standard of review proffered by Justice Marshall but rejected in Fullilove. [Six] Members of the Court rejected intermediate scrutiny in favor of some more stringent form of review. [And,] of course, Fullilove preceded our determination in Croson that strict scrutiny applies to preferences that favor members of minority groups, including challenges considered under the [Fourteenth Amendment]." "[Under] the appropriate standard, strict scrutiny, only a compelling interest may support the Government's use of racial classifications. Modern equal protection doctrine has recognized only one such interest: remedying the effects of racial discrimination. The interest in increasing the diversity of broadcast viewpoints is clearly not a compelling interest. It is simply too amorphous, too insubstantial, and too unrelated to any legitimate basis for employing racial classifications. [Our] traditional equal protection doctrine requires, in addition to a compelling state interest, that the Government's chosen means be necessary to accomplish and narrowly tailored to further the asserted interest. [The] chosen means, resting as they do on stereotyping and so indirectly furthering the asserted end, could not plausibly be deemed narrowly tailored. The Court instead finds the racial classifications to be 'substantially related' to achieving the Government's interest, a far less rigorous fit requirement. The FCC's policies fail even this requirement." She concluded: "In sum, the Government has not met its burden even under the Court's test that approves of racial classifications that are substantially related to an important governmental objective. Of course, the programs even more clearly fail the strict scrutiny that should be applied. The Court has determined, in essence, that Congress and all federal agencies are exempted, to some ill-defined but significant degree, from the Constitution's equal protection re-

quirements. This break with our precedents greatly undermines equal protection guarantees, and permits distinctions among citizens based on race and ethnicity which the Constitution clearly forbids." Justice KENNEDY, joined by Justice Scalia, also submitted a separate dissent. He ended with the statement: "I regret that after a century of judicial opinions we interpret the Constitution to do no more than move us from 'separate but equal' to 'unequal but benign.'"

◆ ◆ ◆ ◆ ◆

EDWIN C. HETTINGER

What Is Wrong with Reverse Discrimination?

Many people think it obvious that reverse discrimination is unjust. Calling affirmative action reverse discrimination itself suggests this. This discussion evaluates numerous reasons given for this alleged injustice. Most of these accounts of what is wrong with reverse discrimination are found to be deficient. The explanations for why reverse discrimination is morally troubling show only that it is unjust in a relatively weak sense. This result has an important consequence for the wider issue of the moral justifiability of affirmative action. If social policies which involve minor injustice are permissible (and perhaps required) when they are required in order to overcome much greater injustice, then the mild injustice of reverse discrimination is easily overridden by its contribution to the important social goal of dismantling our sexual and racial caste system.[1]

By "reverse discrimination" or "affirmative action" I shall mean hiring or admitting a slightly less well qualified woman or black, rather than a slightly more qualified white male,[2] for the purpose of helping to eradicate sexual and/or racial inequality, or for the purpose of compensating women and blacks for the burdens and injustices they have suffered due to past and ongoing sexism and racism.[3] There are weaker forms of affirmative action, such as giving preference to minority candidates only when qualifications are equal, or providing special educational opportunities for youths in disadvantaged groups. This paper seeks to defend the more controversial sort of reverse discrimination defined above. I begin by considering several spurious objections to reverse discrimination. In the second part, I identify the ways in which this policy is morally troubling and then assess the significance of these negative features.

Spurious Objections

1. Reverse Discrimination as Equivalent to Racism and Sexism

In a discussion on national television, George Will, the conservative news analyst and political philosopher, articulated the most common objection to reverse discrimination. It is unjust, he said, because it is discrimination on the basis of race or sex. Reverse discrimination against white males is the same evil as traditional discrimination against women and blacks. The only difference is that in this case it is the white male who is being discriminated against. Thus if traditional racism and sexism are wrong and unjust, so is reverse discrimination, and for the very same reasons.

But reverse discrimination is not at all like traditional sexism and racism. The motives and intentions behind it are completely different, as are its consequences. Consider some of the motives underlying traditional racial discrimination.[4] Blacks were not hired or allowed into schools because it was felt that contact with them was degrading, and sullied whites. These policies were based on contempt and loathing for blacks, on a feeling that blacks were suitable only for subservient positions and that they should never have positions of authority over whites. Slightly better qualified white males are not being turned down under affirmative action for any of these reasons. No

defenders or practitioners of affirmative action (and no significant segment of the general public) think that contact with white males is degrading or sullying, that white males are contemptible and loathsome, or that white males—by their nature—should be subservient to blacks or women.

The consequences of these two policies differ radically as well. Affirmative action does not stigmatize white males; it does not perpetuate unfortunate stereotypes about white males; it is not part of a pattern of discrimination that makes being a white male incredibly burdensome.[5] Nor does it add to a particular group's "already overabundant supply" of power, authority, wealth, and opportunity, as does traditional racial and sexual discrimination.[6] On the contrary, it results in a more egalitarian distribution of these social and economic benefits. If the motives and consequences of reverse discrimination and of traditional racism and sexism are completely different, in what sense could they be morally equivalent acts? If acts are to be individuated (for moral purposes) by including the motives, intentions, and consequences in their description, then clearly these two acts are not identical.

It might be argued that although the motives and consequences are different, the act itself is the same: reverse discrimination is discrimination on the basis of race and sex, and this is wrong in itself independently of its motives or consequences. But discriminating (i.e., making distinctions in how one treats people) on the basis of race or sex is not always wrong, nor is it necessarily unjust. It is not wrong, for example, to discriminate against one's own sex when choosing a spouse. Nor is racial or sexual discrimination in hiring necessarily wrong. This is shown by Peter Singer's example in which a director of a play about ghetto conditions in New York City refuses to consider any white applicants for the actors because she wants the play to be authentic.[7] If I am looking for a representative of the black community, or doing a study about blacks and disease, it is perfectly legitimate to discriminate against all whites. Their whiteness makes them unsuitable for my (legitimate) purposes. Similarly, if I am hiring a wet-nurse, or a person to patrol the women's change rooms in my department store, discriminating against males is perfectly legitimate.

These examples show that racial and sexual discrimination are not wrong in themselves. This is not to say that they are never wrong; most often they clearly are. Whether or not they are wrong, however, depends on the purposes, consequences, and context of such discrimination.

2. Race and Sex as Morally Arbitrary and Irrelevant Characteristics

A typical reason given for the alleged injustice of all racial and sexual discrimination (including affirmative action) is that it is morally arbitrary to consider race or sex when hiring, since these characteristics are not relevant to the decision. But the above examples show that not all uses of race or sex as a criterion in hiring decisions are morally arbitrary or irrelevant. Similarly, when an affirmative action officer takes into account race and sex, use of these characteristics is not morally irrelevant or arbitrary. Since affirmative action aims to help end racial and sexual inequality by providing black and female role models for minorities (and non-minorities), the race and sex of the job candidates are clearly relevant to the decision. There is nothing arbitrary about the affirmative action officer focusing on race and sex. Hence, if reverse discrimination is wrong, it is not wrong for the reason that it uses morally irrelevant and arbitrary characteristics to distinguish between applicants.

3. Reverse Discrimination as Unjustified Stereotyping

It might be argued that reverse discrimination involves judging people by alleged average characteristics of a class to which they belong instead of judging them on the basis of their individual characteristics, and that such judging on the basis of stereotypes is unjust. But the defense of affirmative action suggested in this paper does not rely on stereotyping. When an employer hires a slightly less well qualified woman or black over a slightly more qualified white male for the purpose of helping to overcome sexual and racial inequality, she judges the applicants on the basis of their individual characteristics. She uses this person's sex or skin color as a mechanism to help achieve the goals of affirmative action. Individual characteristics of the white male (his skin color and sex) prevent him from serving one of the legitimate goals of employment policies, and he is turned down on this basis.

Notice that the objection does have some force against those who defend reverse discrimination on the grounds of compensatory justice. An affirmative action policy whose purpose is to compensate women and blacks for past and current injustices judges that women and blacks on the average are owed greater compensation than are white males. Although this is true, opponents of affirmative action argue that some white males have been more severely and unfairly disadvantaged than some women and blacks.[8] A poor white male from Appalachia may have suffered greater undeserved disadvantages than the upper-middle class women or blacks with whom he competes. Although there is a high correlation between being female (or being black) and being especially owed compensation for unfair disadvantages suffered, the correlation is not universal.

Thus defending affirmative action on the grounds of compensatory justice may lead to unjust treatment of white males in individual cases. Despite the fact that certain white males are owed greater compensation than are some women or blacks, it is the latter that receive compensation. This is the result of judging candidates for jobs on the basis of the average characteristics of their class, rather than on the basis of their individual characteristics. Thus compensatory justice defenses of reverse discrimination may involve potentially problematic stereotyping.[9] But this is not the defense of affirmative action considered here.

4. Failing to Hire the Most Qualified Person is Unjust

One of the major reasons people think that reverse discrimination is unjust is because they think the most qualified person should get the job. But why should the most qualified person be hired?

a. *Efficiency*. One obvious answer to this question is that one should hire the most qualified person because doing so promotes efficiency. If job qualifications are positively correlated with job performance, then the more qualified person will tend to do a better job. Although it is not always true that there is such a correlation, in general there is, and hence this point is well taken. There are short term efficiency costs of reverse discrimination as defined here.[10]

Note that a weaker version of affirmative action has no such efficiency costs. If one hires a black or woman over a white male only in cases where qualifications are roughly equal, job performance will not be affected. Furthermore, efficiency costs will be a function of the qualifications gap between the black or woman hired, and the white male rejected: the larger the gap, the greater the efficiency costs.[11] The existence of efficiency costs is also a function of the type of work performed. Many of the jobs in our society are ones which any normal person can do (e.g., assembly line worker, janitor, truck driver, etc.). Affirmative action hiring for these positions is unlikely to have significant efficiency costs (assuming whoever is hired is willing to work hard). In general, professional positions are the ones in which people's performance levels will vary significantly, and hence these are the jobs in which reverse discrimination could have significant efficiency costs.

While concern for efficiency gives us a reason for hiring the most qualified person, it in no way explains the alleged injustice suffered by the white male who is passed over due to reverse discrimina-

tion. If the affirmative action employer is treating the white male unjustly, it is not because the hiring policy is inefficient. Failing to maximize efficiency does not generally involve acting unjustly. For instance, a person who carries one bag of groceries at a time, rather than two, is acting inefficiently, though not unjustly.

It is arguable that the manager of a business who fails to hire the most qualified person (and thereby sacrifices some efficiency) treats the owners of the company unjustly, for their profits may suffer, and this violates one conception of the manager's fiduciary responsibility to the shareholders. Perhaps the administrator of a hospital who hires a slightly less well qualified black doctor (for the purposes of affirmative action) treats the future patients at that hospital unjustly, for doing so may reduce the level of health care they receive (and it is arguable that they have a legitimate expectation to receive the best health care possible for the money they spend). But neither of these examples of inefficiency leading to injustice concern the white "male victim" of affirmative action, and it is precisely this person who the opponents of reverse discrimination claim is being unfairly treated.

To many people, that a policy is inefficient is a sufficient reason for condemning it. This is especially true in the competitive and profit oriented world of business. However, profit maximization is not the only legitimate goal of business hiring policies (or other business decisions). Businesses have responsibilities to help heal society's ills, especially those (like racism and sexism) which they in large part helped to create and perpetuate. Unless one takes the implausible position that business' only legitimate goal is profit maximization, the efficiency costs of affirmative action are not an automatic reason for rejecting it. And as we have noted, affirmative action's efficiency costs are of no help in substantiating and explaining its alleged injustice to white males.

b. *The Most Qualified Person Has a Right to the Job*. One could argue that the most qualified person for the job has a right to be hired in virtue of superior qualifications. On this view, reverse discrimination violates the better qualified white male's right to be hired for the job. But the most qualified applicant holds no such right. If you are the best painter in town, and a person hires her brother to paint her house, instead of you, your rights have not been violated. People do not have rights to be hired for particular jobs (though I think a plausible case can be made for the claim that there is a fundamental human right to employment). If anyone has a right in this matter, it is the employer. This is not to say, of course, that the employer cannot do wrong in her hiring decision; she obviously can. If she hires a white because she loathes blacks, she does wrong. The point is that her wrong does not consist in violating the right some candidate has to her job (though this would violate other rights of the candidate).

c. *The Most Qualified Person Deserves the Job.* It could be argued that the most qualified person should get the job because she deserves it in virtue of her superior qualifications. But the assumption that the person most qualified for a job is the one who most deserves it is problematic. Very often people do not deserve their qualifications, and hence they do not deserve anything on the basis of those qualifications.[12] A person's qualifications are a function of at least the following factors:

A. innate abilities,
B. home environment,
C. socioeconomic class of parents,
D. quality of the schools attended,
E. luck, and
F. effort or perseverance.

A person is only responsible for the last factor on this list, and hence one only deserves one's qualifications to the extent that they are a function of effort.[13]

It is undoubtedly often the case that a person who is less well qualified for a job is more deserving of the job (because she worked harder to achieve those lower qualifications) than is someone with superior qualifications. This is frequently true of women and blacks in the job market: they worked harder to overcome disadvantages most (or all) white males never faced. Hence, affirmative action policies which permit the hiring of slightly less well qualified candidates may often be more in line with considerations of desert than are the standard meritocratic procedures.

The point is not that affirmative action is defensible because it helps ensure that more deserving candidates get jobs. Nor is it that desert should be the only or even the most important consideration in hiring decisions. The claim is simply that hiring the most qualified person for a job need not (and quite often does not) involve hiring the most deserving candidate. Hence the intuition that morality requires one to hire the most qualified people cannot be justified on the grounds that these people deserve to be hired.[14]

d. *The Most Qualified Person Is Entitled to the Job.* One might think that although the most qualified person neither deserves the job nor has a right to the job, still this person is entitled to the job. By "entitlement" in this context, I mean a natural and legitimate expectation based on a type of social promise. Society has implicitly encouraged the belief that the most qualified candidate will get the job. Society has set up a competition and the prize is a job which is awarded to those applying with the best qualifications. Society thus reneges on an implicit promise it has made to its members when it allows reverse discrimination to occur. It is dashing legitimate expectations it has encouraged. It is violating the very rules of a game it created.

Furthermore, the argument goes, by allowing reverse discrimination, society is breaking an explicit promise (contained in the Civil Rights Act of 1964) that it will not allow race or sex to be used against one of its citizens. Title VII of that Act prohibits discrimination in employment on the basis of race or sex (as well as color, religion, or national origin).

In response to this argument, it should first be noted that the above interpretation of the Civil Rights Act is misleading. In fact, the Supreme Court has interpreted the Act as allowing race and sex to be considered in hiring or admission decisions.[15] More importantly, since affirmative action has been an explicit national policy for the last twenty years (and has been supported in numerous court cases), it is implausible to argue that society has promised its members that it will not allow race or sex to outweigh superior qualifications in hiring decisions. In addition, the objection takes a naive and utopian view of actual hiring decisions. It presents a picture of our society as a pure meritocracy in which hiring decisions are based solely on qualifications. The only exception it sees to these meritocratic procedures is the unfortunate policy of affirmative action. But this picture is dramatically distorted. Elected government officials, political appointees, business managers, and many others clearly do not have their positions solely or even mostly because of their qualifications.[16] Given the widespread acceptance in our society of procedures which are far from meritocratic, claiming that the most qualified person has a socially endorsed entitlement to the job is not believable.

5. Undermining Equal Opportunity for White Males

It has been claimed that the right of white males to an equal chance of employment is violated by affirmative action.[17] Reverse discrimination, it is said, undermines equality of opportunity for white males.

If equality of opportunity requires a social environment in which everyone at birth has roughly the same chance of succeeding through the use of his or her natural talents, then it could well be argued that given the social, cultural, and educational disadvantages placed on women and blacks, preferential treatment of these groups brings us closer to equality of opportunity. White males are full members of the community in a way in which women and blacks are not, and this advantage is diminished by affirmative action. Affirmative action takes away the greater than equal opportunity white males generally have, and thus it brings us closer to a situation in which all members of society have an equal chance of succeeding through the use of their talents.

It should be noted that the goal of affirmative action is to bring about a society in which there is equality of opportunity for women and blacks without preferential treatment of these groups. It is not the purpose of the sort of affirmative action defended here to disadvantage white males in order to take away the advantage a sexist and racist society gives to them. But noticing that this occurs is sufficient to dispel the illusion that affirmative action undermines the equality of opportunity for white males.[18]

Legitimate Objections

The following two considerations explain what is morally troubling about reverse discrimination.

1. Judging on the Basis of Involuntary Characteristics

In cases of reverse discrimination, white males are passed over on the basis of membership in a group they were born into. When an affirmative action employer hires a slightly less well qualified black (or woman), rather than a more highly qualified white male, skin color (or sex) is being used as one criterion for determining who gets a very important benefit. Making distinctions in how one treats people on the basis of characteristics they cannot help having (such as skin color or sex) is morally problematic because it reduces individual autonomy. Discriminating between people on the basis of features they can do something about is preferable, since it gives them some control over how others act towards them. They can develop the characteristics others use to give them favorable treatment and avoid those characteristics others use as grounds for unfavorable treatment.[19]

For example, if employers refuse to hire you because you are a member of the American Nazi party, and if you do not like the fact that you are having a hard time finding a job, you can choose to leave the party. However, if a white male is having trouble finding employment because slightly less well qualified women and blacks are being given jobs to meet affirmative action requirements, there is nothing he can do about this disadvantage, and his autonomy is curtailed.[20]

Discriminating between people on the basis of their involuntary characteristics is morally undesirable, and thus reverse discrimination is also morally undesirable. Of course, that something is morally undesirable does not show that it is unjust, nor that it is morally unjustifiable.

How morally troubling is it to judge people on the basis of involuntary characteristics? Notice that our society frequently uses these sorts of features to distinguish between people. Height and good looks are characteristics one cannot do much about, and yet basketball players and models are ordinarily chosen and rejected on the basis of precisely these features. To a large extent our intelligence is also a feature beyond our control, and yet intelligence is clearly one of the major characteristics our society uses to determine what happens to people.

Of course there are good reasons why we distinguish between people on the basis of these sorts of involuntary characteristics. Given the goals of basketball teams, model agencies, and employers in general, hiring the taller, better looking, or more intelligent person (respectively) makes good sense. It promotes efficiency, since all these people are likely to do a better job. Hiring policies based on these involuntary characteristics serve the legitimate purposes of these businesses (e.g., profit and serving the public), and hence they may be morally justified despite their tendency to reduce the control people have over their own lives.

This argument applies to reverse discrimination as well. The purpose of affirmative action is to help eradicate racial and sexual injustice. If affirmative action policies help bring about this goal, then they can be morally justified despite their tendency to reduce the control white males have over their lives.

In one respect this sort of consequentialist argument is more forceful in the case of affirmative action. Rather than merely promoting the goal of efficiency (which is the justification for businesses hiring naturally brighter, taller, or more attractive individuals), affirmative action promotes the non-utilitarian goal of an egalitarian society. In general, promoting a consideration of justice (such as equality) is more important than is promoting efficiency or utility.[21] Thus in terms of the importance of the objective, this consequentialist argument is stronger in the case of affirmative action. If one can justify reducing individual autonomy on the grounds that it promotes efficiency, one can certainly do so on the grounds that it reduces the injustice of racial and sexual inequality.

2. Burdening White Males without Compensation

Perhaps the strongest moral intuition concerning the wrongness of reverse discrimination is that it is unfair to job-seeking white males. It is unfair because they have been given an undeserved disadvantage in the competition for employment; they have been handicapped because of something that is not their fault. Why should white males be made to pay for the sins of others?

It would be a mistake to argue for reverse discrimination on the grounds that white males deserve to be burdened and that therefore we should hire women and blacks even when white males are better qualified.[22] Young white males who are now entering the job market are not more responsible for the evils of racial and sexual inequality than are other members of society. Thus reverse discrimination is not properly viewed as punishment administered to white males.

The justification for affirmative action supported here claims that bringing about sexual and racial equality necessitates sacrifice on the part of white males who seek employment. An important step in bringing about the desired egalitarian society involves speeding up the process by which women and blacks get into positions of power and authority. This requires that white males find it harder to achieve these same positions. But this is not punishment for deeds done.

Thomas Nagel's helpful analogy is state condemnation of property under the right of eminent domain for the purpose of building a highway.[23] Forcing some in the community to move in order that the community as a whole may benefit is unfair. Why should these individuals suffer rather than others? The answer is: Because they happen to live in a place where it is important to build a road. A similar response should be given to the white male who objects to reverse discrimination with the same "Why me?" question. The answer is: Because job-seeking white males happen to be in the way of an important road leading to the desired egalitarian society. Job-seeking white males are being made to bear the brunt of the burden of affirmative action because of accidental considerations, just as are homeowners whose property is condemned in order to build a highway.

This analogy is extremely illuminating and helpful in explaining the nature of reverse discrimination. There is, however, an important dissimilarity that Nagel does not mention. In cases of property condemnation, compensation is paid to the owner. Affirmative action policies, however, do not compensate white males for shouldering this burden of moving toward the desired egalitarian society. So affirmative action is unfair to job-seeking white males because they are forced to bear an unduly large share of the burden of achieving racial and sexual equality without being compensated for this sacrifice. Since we have singled out job-seeking white males from the larger pool of white males who should also help achieve this goal, it seems that some compensation from the latter to the former is appropriate.[24]

This is a serious objection to affirmative action policies only if the uncompensated burden is substantial. Usually it is not. Most white male "victims" of affirmative action easily find employment. It is highly unlikely that the same white male will repeatedly fail to get hired because of affirmative action.[25] The burdens of affirmative action should be spread as evenly as possible among all the job-seeking white males. Furthermore, the burden job-seeking white males face—of finding it somewhat more difficult to get employment—is inconsequential when compared to the burdens ongoing discrimination places on women and blacks.[26] Forcing job-seeking white males to bear an extra burden is acceptable because this is a necessary step toward achieving a much greater reduction in the unfair burdens our society places on women and blacks. If affirmative action is a necessary mechanism for a timely dismantlement of our racial and sexual caste system, the extra burdens it places on job-seeking white males are justified.

Still the question remains: Why isn't compensation paid? When members of society who do not deserve extra burdens are singled out to sacrifice for an important community goal, society owes them compensation. This objection loses some of its force when one realizes that society continually places undeserved burdens on its members without compensating them. For instance, the burden of seeking efficiency is placed on the shoulders of the least naturally talented and intelligent. That one is born less intelligent (or otherwise less talented) does not mean that one deserves to have reduced employment opportunities, and yet our society's meritocratic hiring procedures make it much harder for less naturally talented members to find meaningful employment. These people are not compensated for their sacrifices either.

Of course, pointing out that there are other examples of an allegedly problematic social policy does not justify that policy. Nonetheless, if this analogy is sound, failing to compensate job-seeking white males for the sacrifices placed on them by reverse discrimination is not without precedent. Furthermore, it is no more morally troublesome than is failing to compensate less talented members of society for their undeserved sacrifice of employment opportunities for the sake of efficiency.

Conclusion

This article has shown the difficulties in pinpointing what is morally troubling about reverse discrimination. The most commonly heard objections to reverse discrimination fail to make their case. Reverse discrimination is not morally equivalent to traditional racism and sexism since its goals and consequences are entirely different, and the act of treating people differently on the basis of race or sex is not necessarily morally wrong. The race and sex of the candidates are not morally irrelevant in all hiring decisions, and affirmative action hiring is an example where discriminating on the basis of race or sex is not morally arbitrary. Furthermore, affirmative action can be defended on grounds that do not involve stereotyping. Though affirmative action hiring of less well qualified applicants can lead to short run inefficiency, failing to hire the most qualified applicant does not violate this person's rights, entitlements, or deserts. Additionally, affirmative action hiring does not generally undermine equal opportunity for white males.

Reverse discrimination is morally troublesome in that it judges people on the basis of involuntary characteristics and thus reduces the control they have over their lives. It also places a larger than fair share of the burden of achieving an egalitarian society on the shoulders of job-seeking white males without compensating them for this sacrifice. But these problems are relatively minor when compared to the grave injustice of racial and sexual inequality, and they are easily outweighed if affirmative action helps alleviate this far greater injustice.[27]

NOTES

1 Thomas Nagel uses the phrase "racial caste system" in his illuminating testimony before the Subcommittee on the Constitution of the Senate Judiciary Committee, on June 18, 1981. This testimony is reprinted as "A Defense of Affirmative Action" in *Ethical Theory and Business*, 2nd edition, ed. Tom Beauchamp and Norman Bowie (Englewood Cliffs, NJ: Prentice-Hall, 1983), 483-87.

2 What should count as qualifications is controversial. By "qualifications" I refer to such things as grades, test scores, prior experience, and letters of recommendation. I will not include black skin or female sex in my use of "qualification," though there are strong arguments for counting these as legitimate qualifications (in the sense of characteristics which would help the candidate achieve the legitimate goals of the hiring or admitting institution). For these arguments see Ronald Dworkin, "Why Bakke Has No Case," *The New York Review of Books*, November 10th, 1977.

3 This paper assumes the controversial premise that we live in a racist and sexist society. Statistics provide immediate and powerful support for this claim. The fact that blacks comprise 12% of the US population, while comprising a minuscule percentage of those in positions of power and authority, is sufficient evidence that our society continues to be significantly racist in results, if not in intent. Unless one assumes that blacks are innately less able to attain, or less desirous of attaining, these positions to a degree that would account for this huge underrepresentation, one must conclude that our social organizations significantly disadvantage blacks. This is (in part) the injustice that I call racism. The argument for the charge of sexism is analogous (and perhaps even more persuasive given that women comprise over 50% of the population). For more supporting evidence,

see Tom Beauchamp's article "The Justification of Reverse Discrimination in Hiring" in *Ethical Theory and Business*, 495-506.

4 Although the examples in this paper focus more on racism than on sexism, it is not clear that the former is a worse problem than is the latter. In many ways, sexism is a more subtle and pervasive form of discrimination. It is also less likely to be acknowledged.

5 This is Paul Woodruff's helpful definition of unjust discrimination. See Paul Woodruff, "What's Wrong with Discrimination," *Analysis*, Vol. 36, No. 3 (1976), 158-60.

6 This point is made by Richard Wasserstrom in his excellent article "A Defense of Programs of Preferential Treatment," *National Forum* (The Phi Kappa Phi Journal), Vol. viii, No. 1 (Winter 1978), 15-18. The article is reprinted in *Social Ethics*, 2nd edition, ed. Thomas Mappes and Jane Zembaty (New York: McGraw-Hill, 1982), 187-91. The quoted phrase is Wasserstrom's.

7 Peter Singer, "Is Racial Discrimination Arbitrary?" *Philosophia*, Vol. 8 (November 1978), 185-203.

8 See, for example, Robert Simon, "Preferential Hiring: A Reply to Judith Jarvis Thomson," *Philosophy and Public Affairs*, Vol. 3, No. 3 (Spring 1974).

9 If it is true (and it is certainly plausible) that every black or woman, no matter how fortunate, has suffered from racism and sexism in a way in which no white male has suffered from racism and sexism, then compensation for this injustice would be owed to all and only blacks and women. Given this, arguing for affirmative action on the grounds of compensatory justice would not involve judging individuals by average features of classes of which they are members. Still it might be argued that for certain blacks and women such injustices are not nearly as severe as the different type of injustice suffered by some white males. Thus one would have to provide a reason for why we should compensate (with affirmative action) any black or woman before any white male. Perhaps administrative convenience is such a reason. Being black or female (rather than white and male) correlates nicely with the property of being more greatly and unfairly disadvantaged, and thus race and sex are useful rough guidelines for determining who most needs compensation. This does, however, involve stereotyping.

10 In the long run, however, reverse discrimination may actually promote overall societal efficiency by breaking down the barriers to a vast reservoir of untapped potential in women and blacks.

11 See Thomas Nagel, "A Defense of Affirmative Action," 484.

12 This is Wasserstrom's point. See "A Defense of Programs of Preferential Treatment," in *Social Ethics*, 190.

13 By "effort" I intend to include (1) how hard a person tries to achieve certain goals, (2) the amount of risk voluntarily incurred in seeking these goals, and (3) the degree to which moral considerations play a role in choosing these goals. The harder one tries, the more one is willing to sacrifice, and the worthier the goal, the greater are one's deserts. For support of the claim that voluntary past action is the only valid basis for desert, see James Rachels, "What People Deserve," in *Justice and Economic Distribution*, ed. John Arthur and William Shaw (Englewood Cliffs, NJ: Prentice-Hall, 1978), 150-63.

14 It would be useful to know if there is a correlation between the candidate who is most deserving (because she worked the hardest) and the one with the best qualifications. In other words, are better qualified candidates in general those who worked harder to achieve their qualifications? Perhaps people who have the

greatest natural abilities and the most fortunate social circumstances will be the ones who work the hardest to develop their talents. This raises the possibility, suggested by John Rawls, that the ability to put forward effort is itself a function of factors outside a person's control. See his *A Theory of Justice* (Cambridge, MA: Harvard University Press, 1971), 103-04. But if anything is under a person's control, and hence is something a person is responsible for, it is how hard she tries. Thus if there is an appropriate criterion for desert, it will include how much effort a person exerts.

15 See Justice William Brennan's majority opinion in United Steel Workers and Kaiser Aluminum v. Weber, United States Supreme Court, 443 U.S. 193 (1979). See also Justice Lewis Powell's majority opinion in the University of California v. Bakke, United States Supreme Court, 483 U.S. 265 (1978).

16 This is Wasserstrom's point. See "A Defense of Programs of Preferential Treatment," 189.

17 This is Judith Thomson's way of characterizing the alleged injustice. See "Preferential Hiring," *Philosophy and Public Affairs*, Vol. 2, No. 4 (Summer 1973).

18 If it is true that some white males are more severely disadvantaged in our society than are some women and blacks, affirmative action would increase the inequality of opportunity for these white males. But since these individuals are a small minority of white males, the overall result of affirmative action would be to move us closer toward equality of opportunity.

19 James Rachels makes this point in "What People Deserve," 159. Joel Feinberg has also discussed related points. See his *Social Philosophy* (Englewood Cliffs, NJ: Prentice-Hall, 1973), 108.

20 He could work harder to get better qualifications and hope that the qualifications gap between him and the best woman or black would become so great that the efficiency cost of pur-

suing affirmative action would be prohibitive. Still he can do nothing to get rid of the disadvantage (in affirmative action contexts) of being a white male.

21 For a discussion of how considerations of justice typically outweigh considerations of utility, see Manuel Velasquez, *Business Ethics* (Englewood Cliffs, NJ: Prentice-Hall, 1982), Chapter Two.

22 On the average, however, white males have unfairly benefited from the holding back of blacks and women, and hence it is not altogether inappropriate that this unfair benefit be removed.

23 Nagel, "A Defense of Affirmative Action," 484.

24 It would be inappropriate to extract compensation from women or blacks since they are the ones who suffer the injustice affirmative action attempts to alleviate.

25 This is a potential worry, however, and so it is important to ensure that the same white male does not repeatedly sacrifice for the goals of affirmative action.

26 Cheshire Calhoun reminded me of this point.

27 Of course one must argue that reverse discrimination is effective in bringing about an egalitarian society. There are complicated consequentialist arguments both for and against this claim, and I have not discussed them here. Some of the questions to be addressed are (1) How damaging is reverse discrimination to the self-esteem of blacks and women? (2) Does reverse discrimination promote racial and sexual strife more than it helps to alleviate them? (3) Does it perpetuate unfortunate stereotypes about blacks and women? (4) How long are we justified in waiting to pull blacks and women into the mainstream of our social life? (5) What sorts of alternative mechanisms are possible and politically practical for achieving affirmative action goals (for instance, massive early educa-

tional funding for children from impoverished backgrounds)?

◆ ◆ ◆ ◆ ◆

LOUIS P. POJMAN

The Moral Status of Affirmative Action

"A ruler who appoints any man to an office, when there is in his dominion another man better qualified for it, sins against God and against the State." (The Koran)

"[Affirmative Action] is the meagerest recompense for centuries of unrelieved oppression." (quoted by Shelby Steele as the justification for Affirmative Action)

Hardly a week goes by ... that the subject of Affirmative Action does not come up. Whether in the guise of reverse discrimination, preferential hiring, non-traditional casting, quotas, goals and time tables, minority scholarships, or race-norming, the issue confronts us as a terribly perplexing problem. During the last general election (November 7, 1996) California voters by a 55% to 45% vote approved Proposition 209 (called the "California Civil Rights Initiative") which would have made it illegal to discriminate on the basis of race or gender, hence ending affirmative action in California. A federal judge subsequently prohibited the bill from going into effect, arguing that it may violate the equal protection clause of the fourteenth amendment. Both sides have reorganized for a renewed battle. The Supreme Court is likely to decide the issue in the near future. Affirmative action was one of the issues that divided the Democratic and Republican parties during the 1996 election, the Democrats supporting it ("Mend it don't end it") and the Republicans opposing it ("affirmative action is reverse racism"). Other illus-

trations of the debate are Chicago's Mayor Daley's decision (in May 1995) to bypass the results of a Chicago police exam in order to promote minority officers, Administration Assistant Secretary of Education Michael Williams' judgment that Minority Scholarships are unconstitutional (which was overruled); the demand that Harvard Law School hire a black female professor; the revelations of race-norming in state employment agencies; as well as debates over quotas, underutilization guidelines, and diversity in employment; all testify to the importance of this subject for contemporary society.

There is something salutory as well as terribly tragic inherent in this problem. The salutory aspect is the fact that our society has shown itself committed to eliminating unjust discrimination. Even in the heart of Dixie there is a recognition of the injustice of racial discrimination. Both sides of the affirmative action debate have good will and appeal to moral principles. Both sides are attempting to bring about a better society, one which is color blind, but they differ profoundly on the morally proper means to accomplish that goal.

And this is just the tragedy of the situation: good people on both sides of the issue are ready to tear each other to pieces over a problem that has no easy or obvious solution. And so the voices become shrill and the rhetoric hyperbolic. The same spirit which divides the pro-choice movement from the right-to-life movement on abortion divides liberal pro-Affirmative Action advocates from liberal anti-Affirmative Action advocates. This problem, more than any other, threatens to destroy the traditional liberal consensus in our society. I have seen family members and close friends who until recently fought on the same side of the barricades against racial injustice divide in enmity over this issue. The anti-affirmative liberals ("liberals who've been mugged") have tended toward a form of neo-conservatism, and the pro-affirmative liberals have tended to side with the radical left to form the "politically correct ideology" movement.

In this paper I will confine myself primarily to Affirmative Action policies with regard to race, but much of what I say can be applied to the areas of gender and ethnic minorities.

I. Definitions

First let me define my terms:

Discrimination is simply judging one thing to differ from another on the basis of some criterion. "Discrimination" is a good quality, having reference to our ability to make distinctions. As rational and moral agents we need to make proper distinctions. To be rational is to discriminate between good and bad arguments, and to think morally is to discriminate between reasons based on valid principles and those based on invalid ones. What needs to be distinguished is the difference between rational and moral discrimination, on the one hand, and irrational and immoral discrimination, on the other hand.

Prejudice is a discrimination based on irrelevant grounds. It may simply be an attitude which never surfaces in action, or it may cause prejudicial actions. A prejudicial discrimination in action is immoral if it denies someone a fair deal. So discrimination on the basis of race or sex where these are not relevant for job performance is unfair. Likewise, one may act prejudicially in applying a relevant criterion on insufficient grounds, as in the case where I apply the criterion of being a hard worker but then assume, on insufficient evidence, that the black man who applies for the job is not a hard worker.

There is a difference between prejudice and bias. *Bias* signifies a tendency toward one thing rather than another where the evidence is incomplete or is based on non-moral factors. For example, you may have a bias toward blondes and I toward redheads. But prejudice is an attitude (or action) where unfairness is present—where one *should* know or do better—as in the case where I give people jobs simply because they are redheads. Bias implies ignorance or incomplete knowledge, whereas prejudice is

deeper, involving a moral failure—usually a failure to pay attention to the evidence. But note that calling people racist or sexist without good evidence is also an act of prejudice.

Equal opportunity exists when everyone has a fair chance at the best positions that society has at its disposal. Only native aptitude and effort should be decisive in the outcome, not factors of race, sex, or special favors.

Affirmative Action is the effort to rectify the injustice of the past as well as to produce a situation closer to the ideal of equal opportunity by special policies. Put this way, it is Janus-faced or ambiguous, having both a backward-looking and a forward-looking feature. The backward-looking feature is its attempt to correct and compensate for past injustice. This aspect of Affirmative Action is strictly deontological. The forward-looking feature is its implicit ideal of a society free from prejudice, where one's race or gender is irrelevant to basic opportunities. This is both deontological and utilitarian: deontological in that it aims at treating people according to their merits or needs, utilitarian in that a society perceived as fair will be a happier society.

When we look at a social problem from a backward-looking perspective, we need to determine who has committed or benefited from a wrongful or prejudicial act and to determine who deserves compensation for that act.

When we look at a social problem from a forward-looking perspective, we need to determine what a just society (one free from prejudice) would look like and how to obtain that kind of society. The forward-looking aspect of Affirmative Action is paradoxically race-conscious, because it uses race to bring about a society that is not race-conscious—that is color blind (in the morally relevant sense of this term).

It is also useful to distinguish two versions of Affirmative Action. *Weak Affirmative Action* involves such measures as the elimination of segregation (namely the idea of "separate but equal"), widespread advertisement of job opportunities to groups not previously represented in certain privileged positions, special scholarships for the disadvantaged classes (such as the poor), using under-representation or a history of past discrimination as a tie breaker when candidates are relatively equal, and the like.

Strong Affirmative Action involves more positive steps to eliminate past injustice, such as reverse discrimination, hiring candidates on the basis of race and gender in order to reach equal or nearly equal results, and proportionate representation in each area of society.

II. A Brief History of Affirmative Action

1. After a long legacy of egregious racial discrimination the forces of civil justice came to a head during the decade of 1954-1964. In the 1954 US Supreme Court decision, *Brown v. Board of Education*, racial segregation was declared inherently and unjustly discriminatory, a violation of the constitutional right to equal protection, and in 1964 Congress passed the Civil Rights Act which banned all forms of racial discrimination.

During this time the goal of the Civil Rights Movement was Equal Opportunity. The thinking was that if only we could remove the hindrances to progress, invidious segregation, discriminatory laws, and irrational prejudice against blacks, we could free our country from the evils of past injustice and usher in a just society in which the grandchildren of the slave could play together and compete with the grandchildren of the slave owner. We were after a color-blind society in which every child had an equal chance to attain the highest positions based not on his skin color but on the quality of his credentials. In the early 1960s when the idea of reverse discrimination was mentioned in Civil Rights groups, it was usually rejected as a new racism. The Executive Director of the NAACP, Roy Wilkins, stated this position unequivocally during congressional consideration of the 1964 civil rights law. "Our association has never been in favor of a quota system. We believe the quota system is unfair whether it is used for [blacks] or against [blacks].... [We] feel people ought to be hired because of their ability, irrespective of their color.... We want equality, equality of opportunity and employment on the basis of ability."[1]

So the Civil Rights Act of 1964 was passed outlawing discrimination on the basis of race or sex.

> Title VII, Section 703(a) Civil Rights Act of 1964: It shall be unlawful practice for an employer—(1) to fail or refuse to hire or to discharge any individual or otherwise to discriminate against any individual with respect to his compensation, terms, conditions, or privileges of employment, because of such individual's race, color, sex, or national origin; or
>
> (2) to limit, segregate, or classify his employees or applicants for employment opportunities or otherwise adversely affect his status as an employee because of such individual's race, color, religion, sex, or national origin. [42 U.S.C. 2000e-2(a).]
>
> ... Nothing contained in this title shall be interpreted to require any employer ... to grant preferential treatment to any individual or to any group ... on account of an imbalance which may exist with respect to the total numbers or percentage of persons of such race ... in any community, State, section, or other areas, or in the available work force in any community, State, section, or other area. [42 U.S.C. 2000e-2(j)]

The Civil Rights Act of 1964 espouses a meritocratic philosophy, calling for equal opportunity and prohibiting reverse discrimination as just another form of prejudice. The Voting Rights Act (1965) was passed and Jim Crow laws throughout the South were overturned. Schools were integrated and public accommodations opened to all. Brach Rickey's promotion of Jackie Robinson from the minor leagues in 1947 to play for the Brooklyn Dodgers was seen as the paradigm case of this kind of equal opportunity—the successful recruiting of a deserving person.

2. But it was soon noticed that the elimination of discriminatory laws was not producing the fully integrated society that leaders of the civil rights movement had envisioned. Eager to improve the situation, in 1965 President Johnson went beyond equal opportunity to Affirmative Action. He issued the famous Executive Order 11246 in which the Department of Labor was enjoined to issue government contracts with construction companies on the basis of race. That is, it would engage in reverse discrimination in order to make up for the evils of the past. He explained the act in terms of the shackled runner analogy.

> Imagine a hundred yard dash in which one of the two runners has his legs shackled together. He has progressed 10 yds., while the unshackled runner has gone 50 yds. How do they rectify the situation? Do they merely remove the shackles and allow the race to proceed? Then they could say that "equal opportunity" now prevailed. But one of the runners would still be forty yards ahead of the other. Would it not be the better part of justice to allow the previously shackled runner to make-up the forty yard gap; or to start the race all over again? That would be affirmative action towards equality. (President Lyndon Johnson 1965 inaugurating the Affirmative Action Policy of Executive Order 11246)

In 1967 President Johnson issued Executive Order 11375 extending Affirmative Action (henceforth "AA") to women. Note here that AA originates in the executive branch of government. Until the Kennedy-Hawkins Civil Rights Act of 1990, AA policy was never put to a vote or passed by Congress.

Gradually, the benefits of AA were extended to Hispanics, native Americans, Asians, and handicapped people.[2]

The phrase "An Equal Opportunity/Affirmative Action Employer" ("AA/EO") began to appear as official public policy. But few noticed an ambiguity in the notion of "AA" which could lead to a contradiction in juxtaposing it with "EO," for there are two types of AA. At first AA was interpreted as what I have called "Weak Affirmative Action," in line with equal opportunity, signifying wider advertisement of positions, announcements that applications from blacks would be welcomed, active recruitment and hiring blacks (and women) over *equally* qualified men. While few liberals objected to these measures, some expressed fears of an impending slippery slope towards reverse discrimination.

However, except in professional sports—including those sponsored by universities—Weak Affirmative Action was not working, so in the late 1960s and early 1970s a stronger version of Affirmative Action was embarked upon—one aimed at equal results, quotas (or "goals"—a euphemism for "quotas"). In *Swann v. Charlotte-Mecklenburg* (1971), regarding the busing of children out of their neighborhood in order to promote integration, the Court, led by Justice Brennan, held that Affirmative Action was implied in *Brown* and was consistent with the Civil Right Act of 1964. The NAACP now began to support reverse discrimination.

Thus began the search for minimally qualified blacks in college recruitment, hiring, and the like. Competence and excellence began to recede into second place as the quest for racial, ethnic, and gender diversity became the dominant goals. The slogan "We have to become race conscious in order to eliminate race consciousness" became the paradoxical justification for reverse discrimination.

3. In 1968 the Department of labor ordered employers to engage in utilization studies as part of its policy of eliminating discrimination in the work place. The office of Federal Contract Compli-

ance of the US Department of labor (Executive Order 11246) stated that employers with a history of *underutilization* of minorities and women were required to institute programs that went beyond passive nondiscrimination through deliberate efforts to identify people of "affected classes" for the purpose of advancing their employment. Many employers found it wise to adopt policies of preferential hiring in order to preempt expensive government suits.

Employers were to engage in "utilization analysis" of their present work force in order to develop "specific and result-oriented procedures" to which the employer commits "*every good-faith effort*" in order to provide "relief for members of an '*affected class*,' who by virtue of *past discrimination* continue to suffer the present effects of that discrimination." This self-analysis is supposed to discover areas in which such affected classes are underused, considering their availability and skills. "*Goals and timetables* are to be developed to guide efforts to correct deficiencies in the employment of affected classes people in each level and segment of the work force." Affirmative Action also calls for "rigorous examination" of standards and criteria for job performance, not so as to "dilute necessary standards" but in order to ensure that "arbitrary and discriminatory employment practices are eliminated" and to eliminate unnecessary criteria which "have had the effect of eliminating women and minorities" either from selection or promotion.[3]

4. In 1969 two important events occurred. (a) The Philadelphia Plan—The Department of labor called for "goals and time tables" for recruiting minority workers. In Philadelphia area construction industries, where these companies were all white, family run, businesses, the contractor's union took the case to court on the grounds that Title VII of the Civil Rights Act prohibits quotas. The Third Circuit Court of Appeals upheld the labor Department, and the Supreme Court refused to hear it. This case became the basis of the EEOC's aggressive pursuit of "goals and time tables" in other business situations.

(b) In the Spring of 1969 James Forman disrupted the service of Riverside Church in New York City and issued the Black Manifesto to the American Churches, demanding that they pay blacks $500,000,000 in reparations. The argument of the Black Manifesto was that for three and a half centuries blacks in America have been "exploited and degraded, brutalized, killed and persecuted" by whites; that this was part of the persistent institutional patterns of first, legal slavery and then, legal discrimination and forced segregation; and that through slavery and discrimination whites had procured enormous wealth from black labor with little return to blacks. These facts were said to constitute grounds for reparations on a massive scale. The American churches were but the first institutions to be asked for reparations.[4]

5. The Department of labor issued guidelines in 1970 calling for hiring representatives of *underutilized* groups. "*Nondiscrimination* requires the elimination of all existing discriminatory conditions, whether purposeful or inadvertent ... *Affirmative action* requires ... the employer to make additional efforts to recruit, employ and promote qualified members of groups formerly excluded" (HEW Executive Order 22346, 1972). In December of 1971 Guidelines were issued to eliminate underutilization of minorities, aiming at realignment of job force at every level of society.

6. In *Griggs v. Duke Power Company* (1971) the Supreme Court interpreted Title VII of the Civil Rights Act as forbidding use of aptitude tests and high school diplomas in hiring personnel. These tests were deemed presumptively discriminatory, employers having the burden of proving such tests relevant to performance. The notion of *sufficiency* replaced that of excellence or best qualified, as it was realized (though not explicitly stated) that the social goal of racial diversity required compromising the standards of competence.

7. In 1977, the EEOC called for and *expected* proportional representation of minorities in every area of work (including universities).

8. In 1978 the Supreme Court addressed the Bakke case. Alan Bakke had been denied admission to the University of California at Davis Medical School even though his test scores were higher than the 16 blacks who were admitted under the Affirmative Action quota program. He sued the University of California and the US Supreme Court ruled (*University of California v. Bakke*, July 28, 1978) in a 5 to 4 vote that reverse discrimination and quotas are illegal except (as Justice Powell put it) when engaged in for purposes of promoting diversity (interpreted as a means to extend free speech under the First Amendment) and restoring a situation where an institution has had a history of prejudicial discrimination. The decision was greeted with applause from anti-AA quarters and dismay from pro-AA quarters. Ken Tollett lamented, "The affirmance of Bakke would mean the reversal of affirmative action; it would be an officially sanctioned signal to turn against blacks in this country.... Opposition to special minority admissions programs and affirmative action is anti-black."[5]

But Tollett was wrong. The Bakke case only shifted the rhetoric from "quota" language to "goals and time tables" and "diversity" language. In the 1980s affirmative action was alive and well, with preferential hiring, minority scholarships, and "race norming" prevailing in all walks of life. No other white who has been excluded from admission to college because of his race has even won his case. In fact only a year later, Justice Brennan was to write in *US Steel v. Weber* that prohibition of racial discrimination against "any individual" in Title VII of the Civil Rights Act did not apply to discrimination against whites.[6]

9. Perhaps the last step in the drive towards equal results took place in the institutionalization of grading applicants by group related standards, race norming. Race norming is widely practiced but most of the public is unaware of it, so let me explain it.

Imagine that four men come into a state employment office in order to apply for a job. One is black, one Hispanic, one Asian and one white. They take the standard test (a version of the General Aptitude Test Battery or VG-GATB). All get a composite score of 300. None of them will ever see that score. Instead the numbers will be fed into a computer and the applicants' percentile ranking emerges. The scores are group-weighted. Blacks are measured against blacks, whites against whites, Hispanics against Hispanics. Since blacks characteristically do less well than other groups, the effect is to favor blacks. For example, a score of 300 as an accountant will give the black a percentile score of 87, an Hispanic a percentile score of 74 and a white or oriental a score of 47. The black will get the job as the accountant.

This is known as race norming. Until an anonymous governmental employee recently blew the whistle, this practice was kept a secret in several state employment services. Prof. Linda Gottfredson of the University of Delaware, one of the social scientists to expose this practice, has since had her funding cut off. In a recent letter published in the New York Times she writes:

> One of America's best-kept open secrets is that the Employment Service of the Department of labor has unabashedly promulgated quotas. In 1981 the service recommended that state employment agencies adopt a race-conscious battery to avoid adverse impact when referring job applicants to employers.... The score adjustments are not trivial. An unadjusted score that places a job applicant at the fifteenth percentile among whites would, after race-norming, typically place a black near the white fiftieth percentile. Likewise, unadjusted scores at the white fiftieth percentile would, after race-norming, typically place a black near the eighty-fifth percentile for white job applicants.... [I]ts use by 40 states in the last decade belies the claim that *Griggs* did not lead to quotas.[7]

10. In the *Ward Cove*, *Richmond*, and *Martin* decisions of the mid-1980s the Supreme Court limited preferential hiring practices, placing a greater burden of proof on the plaintiff, now required to prove that employers have discriminated. The Kennedy-Hawkins Civil Rights Act of 1990, which was passed by Congress last year, sought to reverse these decisions by requiring employers to justify statistical imbalances not only in the employment of racial minorities but also that of ethnic and religious minorities. Wherever under-representation of an "identified" group exists, the employer bears the burden of proving he is innocent of prejudicial behavior. In other words, the bill would make it easier for minorities to sue employers. President Bush vetoed the bill, deeming it a subterfuge for quotas. A revised bill is now in Congressional committee.

Affirmative Action in the guise of underutilized or "affected groups" now extends to American Indians, Hispanics-Spaniards (including Spanish nobles) but not Portuguese, Asians, the handicapped, and in some places Irish and Italians. Estimates are that 75% of Americans may obtain AA status as minorities: everyone except the white non-handicapped male. It is a strange policy that affords special treatment to the children of Spanish nobles and illegal immigrants but not the children of the survivors of Russian pogroms or Nazi concentration camps.

Of course, there is nothing new about the notions of racial discrimination and preferential treatment. The first case of racial discrimination is the fall of man, as standardly interpreted, in which the whole race is held accountable and guilty of Adam's sin. The notion of collective responsibility also goes way back in our history. The first case of preferential treatment is God's choosing Abel's sacrifice of meat and rejecting Cain's vegetarian sacrifice—which should give all Jewish-Christian vegetarians something to think about! The first case of preferential treatment in Greek mythology is that of the Achaian horse race narrated in the twenty-third book of the Iliad. Achilles had two prizes to give

out. First prize went to the actual winner. Antilochus, son of Nestor, came in second, but Achilles decided to give second prize to Eumelius because he was of a nobler rank, even though he had come in last. Antilochus complained, saying in effect, "If it is preordained that some other criterion than merit is to count for the award, why should we have a race at all?" Achilles was moved by this logic and gave the prize to Antilochus, offering Eumelius a treasure of his own.

Neither is Affirmative Action primarily an American problem. Thomas Sowell has recently written a book on the international uses of preferential treatment, *Preferential Policies: An International Perspective* in which he analyzes government mandated preferential policies in India, Nigeria, Malaysia, Sri Lanka, and the United States.[8] We will consider Sowell's study towards the end of this paper.

III. Arguments for Affirmative Action

Let us now survey the main arguments typically cited in the debate over Affirmative Action. I will briefly discuss seven arguments on each side of the issue.

1. Need for Role Models

This argument is straightforward. We all have need of role models, and it helps to know that others like us can be successful. We learn and are encouraged to strive for excellence by emulating our heroes and role models.

However, it is doubtful whether role models of one's own racial or sexual type are necessary for success. One of my heroes was Gandhi, an Indian Hindu, another was my grade school science teacher, one Miss DeVoe, and another was Martin Luther King. More important than having role models of one's own type is having genuinely good people, of whatever race or gender, to emulate. Furthermore, even if it is of some help to people with low self-esteem to gain encouragement from seeing others of their particular kind in leadership roles, it is doubtful whether this need is a sufficient condition to justify preferential hiring or reverse discrimination. What good is a role model who is inferior to other professors or business personnel? Excellence will rise to the top in a system of fair opportunity. Natural development of role models will come more slowly and more surely. Proponents of preferential policies simply lack the patience to let history take its own course.

2. The Need of Breaking the Stereotypes

Society may simply need to know that there are talented blacks and women, so that it does not automatically assign them lesser respect or status. We need to have unjustified stereotype beliefs replaced with more accurate ones about the talents of blacks and women. So we need to engage in preferential hiring of qualified minorities even when they are not the most qualified.

Again, the response is that hiring the less qualified is neither fair to those better qualified who are passed over nor an effective way of removing inaccurate stereotypes. If competence is accepted as the criterion for hiring, then it is unjust to override it for purposes of social engineering. Furthermore, if blacks or women are known to hold high positions simply because of reverse discrimination, then they will still lack the respect due to those of their rank. In New York City there is a saying among doctors, "Never go to a black physician under 40," referring to the fact that AA has affected the medical system during the past fifteen years. The police use "Quota Cops" and "Welfare Sergeants" to refer to those hired without passing the standardized tests. (In 1985, 180 black and hispanic policemen, who had failed a promotion test, were promoted anyway to the rank of sergeant.) The destruction of false stereotypes will come naturally as qualified blacks rise naturally in fair competition (or if it does not—then the stereotypes may be justified). Reverse discrimination

sends the message home that the stereotypes are deserved—otherwise, why do these minorities need so much extra help?

3. Equal Results Argument

Some philosophers and social scientists hold that human nature is roughly identical, so that on a fair playing field the same proportion from every race and gender and ethnic group would attain to the highest positions in every area of endeavor. It would follow that any inequality of results itself is evidence for inequality of opportunity. John Arthur, in discussing an intelligence test, Test 21, puts the case this way.

> History is important when considering governmental rules like Test 21 because low scores by blacks can be traced in large measure to the legacy of slavery and racism: segregation, poor schooling, exclusion from trade unions, malnutrition, and poverty have all played their roles. Unless one assumes that blacks are naturally less able to pass the test, the conclusion must be that the results are themselves socially and legally constructed, not a mere given for which law and society can claim no responsibility.
>
> The conclusion seems to be that genuine equality eventually requires equal results. Obviously blacks have been treated unequally throughout US history, and just as obviously the economic and psychological effects of that inequality linger to this day, showing up in lower income and poorer performance in school and on tests than whites achieve. Since we have no reason to believe that difference in performance can be explained by factors other than history, equal results are a good benchmark by which to measure progress made toward genuine equality.[9]

The result of a just society should be equal numbers in proportion to each group in the work force.

However, Arthur fails even to consider studies that suggest that there are innate differences between races, sexes, and groups. If there are genetic differences in intelligence and temperament within families, why should we not expect such differences between racial groups and the two genders? Why should the evidence for this be completely discounted?

Perhaps some race or one gender is more intelligent in one way than another. At present we have only limited knowledge about genetic differences, but what we do have suggests some difference besides the obvious physiological traits.[10] The proper use of this evidence is not to promote discriminatory policies but to be *open* to the possibility that innate differences may have led to an over-representation of certain groups in certain areas of endeavor. It seems that on average blacks have genetic endowments favoring them in the development of skills necessary for excellence in basketball.

Furthermore, on Arthur's logic, we should take aggressive AA against Asians and Jews since they are over-represented in science, technology, and medicine. So that each group receives its fair share, we should ensure that 12% of the philosophers in the United States are black, reduce the percentage of Jews from an estimated 15% to 2%—firing about 1,300 Jewish philosophers. The fact that Asians are producing 50% of PhDs in science and math and blacks less than 1% clearly shows, on this reasoning, that we are providing special secret advantages to Asians.

But why does society have to enter into this results game in the first place? Why do we have to decide whether all difference is environmental or genetic? Perhaps we should simply admit that we lack sufficient evidence to pronounce on these issues with any certainty—but if so, should we not be more modest in insisting on equal results? Here is a thought experiment. Take two families of different racial groups, Green and Blue. The Greens decide to have only two children, to spend all their resources on them, to give them the best education. The two Green kids respond well and end up with achievement test scores in the 99th percentile. The Blues fail to practice family planning. They have 15 children. They can only afford two children, but lack of ability or whatever prevents them from keeping their family down. Now they need help for their large family. Why does society have to step in and help them? Society did not force them to have 15 children. Suppose that the achievement test scores of the 15 children fall below the twenty-fifth percentile. They cannot compete with the Greens. But now enters AA. It says that it is society's fault that the Blue children are not as able as the Greens and that the Greens must pay extra taxes to enable the Blues to compete. No restraints are put on the Blues regarding family size. This seems unfair to the Greens. Should the Green children be made to bear responsibility for the consequences of the Blues' voluntary behavior?

My point is simply that Arthur needs to cast his net wider and recognize that demographics and childbearing and -rearing practices are crucial factors in achievement. People have to take some responsibility for their actions. The equal results argument (or axiom) misses a greater part of the picture.

4. The Compensation Argument

The argument goes like this: blacks have been wronged and severely harmed by whites. Therefore white society should compensate blacks for the injury caused them. Reverse discrimination in terms of preferential hiring, contracts, and scholarships is a fitting way to compensate for the past wrongs.

This argument actually involves a distorted notion of compensation. Normally, we think of compensation as owed by a specific person A to another person B whom A has wronged in a specific way C. For example, if I have stolen your car and used it for a period of time to make business profits that would have gone to you, it is not enough that I return your car. I must pay you an amount reflecting your loss and my ability to pay. If I have only made $5,000 and only have $10,000 in assets, it would not be possible for you to collect $20,000 in damages—even though that is the amount of loss you have incurred.

Sometimes compensation is extended to groups of people who have been unjustly harmed by the greater society. For example, the United States government has compensated the Japanese-Americans who were interred during the Second World War, and the West German government has paid reparations to the survivors of Nazi concentration camps. But here a specific people have been identified who were wronged in an identifiable way by the government of the nation in question.

On the face of it the demand by blacks for compensation does not fit the usual pattern. Perhaps Southern States with Jim Crow laws could be accused of unjustly harming blacks, but it is hard to see that the United States government was involved in doing so. Furthermore, it is not clear that all blacks were harmed in the same way or whether some were *unjustly* harmed or harmed more than poor whites and others (e.g., short people). Finally, even if identifiable blacks were harmed by identifiable social practices, it is not clear that most forms of Affirmative Action are appropriate to restore the situation. The usual practice of a financial payment seems more appropriate than giving a high level job to someone unqualified or only minimally qualified, who, speculatively, might have been better qualified had he not been subject to racial discrimination. If John is the star tailback of our college team with a promising professional future, and I accidentally (but culpably) drive my pick-up truck over his legs, and so cripple him, John may be due compensation, but he is not due the tailback spot on the football team.

Still, there may be something intuitively compelling about compensating members of an oppressed group who are minimally qualified. Suppose that the Hatfields and the McCoys are enemy clans and some youths from the Hatfields go over and steal diamonds and gold from the McCoys, distributing it within the Hatfield economy. Even though we do not know which Hatfield youths did the stealing, we would want to restore the wealth, as far as possible, to the McCoys. One way might be to tax the Hatfields, but another might be to give preferential treatment in terms of scholarships and training programs and hiring to the McCoys.[11]

This is perhaps the strongest argument for Affirmative Action, and it may well justify some weak versions of AA, but it is doubtful whether it is sufficient to justify strong versions with quotas and goals and time tables in skilled positions. There are at least two reasons for this. First, we have no way of knowing how many people of group G would have been at competence level L had the world been different. Secondly, the normal criterion of competence is a strong prima facie consideration when the most important positions are at stake. There are two reasons for this: (1) society has given people expectations that if they attain certain levels of excellence they will be awarded appropriately and (2) filling the most important positions with the best qualified is the best way to insure efficiency in job-related areas and in society in general. These reasons are not absolutes. They can be overridden. But there is a strong presumption in their favor so that a burden of proof rests with those who would override them.

At this point we get into the problem of whether innocent non-blacks should have to pay a penalty in terms of preferential hiring of blacks. We turn to that argument.

5. Compensation from Those Who Innocently Benefited from Past Injustice

White males as innocent beneficiaries of unjust discrimination of blacks and women have no grounds for complaint when society seeks to rectify the tilted field. White males may be innocent of oppressing blacks and minorities (and women), but they have unjustly benefited from that oppression or discrimination. So it is perfectly proper that less qualified women and blacks be hired before them.

The operative principle is: He who knowingly and willingly benefits from a wrong must help pay for the wrong. Judith Jarvis Thomson puts it this way. "Many [white males] have been direct beneficiaries of policies which have down-graded blacks and women ... and even those who did not directly benefit ... had, at any rate, the advantage in the competition which comes of the confidence in one's full membership [in the community], and of one's right being recognized as a matter of course."[12] That is, white males obtain advantages in self respect and self-confidence deriving from a racist system which denies these to blacks and women.

Objection. As I noted in the previous section, compensation is normally individual and specific. If *A* harms *B* regarding *x*, *B* has a right to compensation from *A* in regards to *x*. If *A* steals *B*'s car and wrecks it, *A* has an obligation to compensate *B* for the stolen car, but *A*'s son has no obligation to compensate *B*. Furthermore, if *A* dies or disappears, *B* has no moral right to claim that society compensate him for the stolen car—though if he has insurance, he can make such a claim to the insurance company. Sometimes a wrong cannot be compensated, and we just have to make the best of an imperfect world.

Suppose my parents, divining that I would grow up to have an unsurpassable desire to be a basketball player, bought an expensive growth hormone for me. Unfortunately, a neighbor stole it and gave it to little Lew Alcindor, who gained the extra 18 inches—my 18 inches—and shot up to an enviable 7 feet 2 inches. Alias Kareem Abdul Jabbar, he excelled in basketball, as I would have done had I had my proper dose.

Do I have a right to the millions of dollars that Jabbar made as a professional basketball player—the unjustly innocent beneficiary of my growth hormone? I have a right to something from the neighbor who stole the hormone, and it might be kind of Jabbar to give me free tickets to the Laker basketball games, and perhaps I should be remembered in his will. As far as I can see, however, he does not *owe* me anything, either legally or morally.

Suppose further that Lew Alcindor and I are in high school together and we are both qualified to play basketball, only he is far better than I. Do I deserve to start in his position because I would have been as good as he is had someone not cheated me as a child? Again, I think not. But if being the lucky beneficiary of wrong-doing does not entail that Alcindor (or the coach) owes me anything in regards to basketball, why should it be a reason to engage in preferential hiring in academic positions or highly coveted jobs? If minimal qualifications are not adequate to override excellence in basketball, even when the minimality is a consequence of wrong-doing, why should they be adequate in other areas?

6. The Diversity Argument

It is important that we learn to live in a pluralistic world, learning to get along with those of other races and cultures, so we should have fully integrated schools and employment situations. Diversity is an important symbol and educative device. Thus preferential treatment is warranted to perform this role in society.

But, again, while we can admit the value of diversity, it hardly seems adequate to override considerations of merit and efficiency. Diversity for diversity's sake is moral promiscuity, since it obfuscates rational distinctions, and unless those hired are highly qualified the diversity factor threatens to become a fetish. At least at the higher levels of business and the professions, competence far outweighs considerations of diversity. I do not care whether the group of surgeons operating on me reflect racial or gender balance, but I do care that they are highly qualified. And likewise with airplane pilots, military leaders, business executives, and, may I say it, teachers and professors. Moreover, there are other ways of learning about other cultures besides engaging in reverse discrimination.

7. Anti-Meritocratic (Desert) Argument to Justify Reverse Discrimination: "No One Deserves His Talents"

According to this argument, the competent do not deserve their intelligence, their superior character, their industriousness, or their discipline; therefore they have no right to the best positions in society; therefore society is not unjust in giving these positions to less (but still minimally) qualified blacks and women. In one form this argument holds that since no one deserves anything, society may use any criteria it pleases to distribute goods. The criterion most often designated is social utility. Versions of this argument are found in the writings of John Arthur, John Rawls, Bernard Boxill, Michael Kinsley, Ronald Dworkin, and Richard Wasserstrom. Rawls writes, "No one deserves his place in the distribution of native endowments, any more than one deserves one's initial starting place in society. The assertion that a man deserves the superior character that enables him to make the effort to cultivate his abilities is equally problematic; for his character depends in large part upon fortunate family and social circumstances for which he can claim no credit. The notion of desert seems not to apply to these cases."[13] Michael Kinsley is even more adamant:

> Opponents of affirmative action are hung up on a distinction that seems more profoundly irrelevant: treating individuals versus treating groups. What is the moral difference between dispensing favors to people on their "merits" as individuals and passing out society's benefits on the basis of group identification?
>
> Group identifications like race and sex are, of course, immutable. They have nothing to do with a person's moral worth. But

the same is true of most of what comes under the label "merit." The tools you need for getting ahead in a meritocratic society—not all of them but most: talent, education, instilled cultural values such as ambition—are distributed just as arbitrarily as skin color. They are fate. The notion that people somehow "deserve" the advantages of those characteristics in a way they don't "deserve" the advantage of their race is powerful, but illogical.[14]

It will help to put the argument in outline form.

1. Society may award jobs and positions as it sees fit as long as individuals have no claim to these positions.
2. To have a claim to something means that one has earned it or deserves it.
3. But no one has earned or deserves his intelligence, talent, education or cultural values which produce superior qualifications.
4. If a person does not deserve what produces something, he does not deserve its products.
5. Therefore better qualified people do not deserve their qualifications.
6. Therefore, society may override their qualifications in awarding jobs and positions as it sees fit (for social utility or to compensate for previous wrongs).
7. So it is permissible if a minimally qualified black or woman is admitted to law or medical school ahead of a white male with excellent credentials or if a less qualified person from an "underutilized" group gets a professorship ahead of a far better qualified white male. Sufficiency and underutilization together outweigh excellence.

Objection. Premise 4 is false. To see this, reflect that just because I do not deserve the money that I have been given as a gift (for instance) does not mean that I am not entitled to what I get with that money. If you and I both get a gift of $100 and I bury mine in the sand for 5 years while you invest yours wisely and double its value at the end of five years, I cannot complain that you should split the increase 50/50 since neither of us deserved the original gift. If we accept the notion of responsibility at all, we must hold that persons deserve the fruits of their labor and conscious choices. Of course, we might want to distinguish moral from legal desert and argue that, morally speaking, effort is more important than outcome, whereas, legally speaking, outcome may be more important. Nevertheless, there are good reasons in terms of efficiency, motivation, and rough justice for holding a strong prima facie principle of giving scarce high positions to those most competent.

The attack on moral desert is perhaps the most radical move that egalitarians like Rawls and company have made against meritocracy, but the ramifications of their attack are far reaching. The following are some of its implications. Since I do not deserve my two good eyes or two good kidneys, the social engineers may take one of each from me to give to those needing an eye or a kidney—even if they have damaged their organs by their own voluntary actions. Since no one deserves anything, we do not deserve pay for our labors or praise for a job well done or first prize in the race we win. The notion of moral responsibility vanishes in a system of levelling.

But there is no good reason to accept the argument against desert. We do act freely and, as such, we are responsible for our actions. We deserve the fruits of our labor, reward for our noble feats and punishment for our misbehavior.

We have considered seven arguments for Affirmative Action and have found no compelling case for Strong AA and only one plausible argument (a version of the compensation argument) for Weak AA. We must now turn to the arguments against Affirmative Action to see whether they fare any better.[15]

IV. Arguments against Affirmative Action

1. Affirmative Action Requires Discrimination against a Different Group

Weak Affirmative Action weakly discriminates against new minorities, mostly innocent young white males, and Strong Affirmative Action strongly discriminates against these new minorities. As I argued in III.5, this discrimination is unwarranted, since, even if some compensation to blacks were indicated, it would be unfair to make innocent white males bear the whole brunt of the payments. In fact, it is poor white youth who become the new pariahs on the job market. The children of the wealthy have no trouble getting into the best private grammar schools and, on the basis of superior early education, into the best universities, graduate schools, managerial and professional positions. Affirmative Action simply shifts injustice, setting blacks and women against young white males, especially ethnic and poor white males. It does little to rectify the goal of providing equal opportunity to all. If the goal is a society where everyone has a fair chance, then it would be better to concentrate on support for families and early education and decide the matter of university admissions and job hiring on the basis of traditional standards of competence.

2. Affirmative Action Perpetuates the Victimization Syndrome

Shelby Steele admits that Affirmative Action may seem "the meagerest recompense for centuries of unrelieved oppression" and that it helps promote diversity. At the same time, though, notes Steele, Affirmative Action reinforces the spirit of victimization by telling blacks that they can gain more by emphasizing their suffering, degradation and helplessness than by discipline and work. This message holds the danger of blacks becoming permanently handicapped by a need for special treatment. It also sends to society at large the message that blacks cannot make it on their own.

Leon Wieseltier sums up the problem this way.

> The memory of oppression is a pillar and a strut of the identity of every people oppressed. It is no ordinary marker of difference. It is unusually stiffening. It instructs the individual and the group about what to expect of the world, imparts an isolating sense of aptness.... Don't be fooled, it teaches, there is only repetition. For that reason, the collective memory of an oppressed people is not only a treasure but a trap.
>
> In the memory of oppression, oppression outlives itself. The scar does the work of the wound. That is the real tragedy: that injustice retains the power to distort long after it has ceased to be real. It is a posthumous victory for the oppressors, when pain becomes a tradition. And yet the atrocities of the past must never be forgotten. This is the unfairly difficult dilemma of the newly emancipated and the newly enfranchised: an honorable life is not possible if they remember too little and a normal life is not possible if they remember too much.[16]

With the eye of recollection, which does not "remember too much," Steele recommends a policy which offers "educational and economic development of disadvantaged people regardless of race and the eradication from our society—through close monitoring and severe sanctions—of racial and gender discrimination."[17]

3. Affirmative Action Encourages Mediocrity and Incompetence

Last spring Jesse Jackson joined protesters at Harvard law School in demanding that the law School faculty hire black women. Jackson dismissed Dean of the Law School, Robert C. Clark's standard of choosing the best qualified person for the job as "Cultural anemia." "We cannot just define who is qualified in the most narrow vertical academic terms," he said. "Most people in the world are yellow, brown, black, poor, non-Christian and don't speak English, and they can't wait for some White males with archaic rules to appraise them."[18] It might be noted that if Jackson is correct about the depth of cultural decadence at Harvard, blacks might be well advised to form and support their own more vital law schools and leave places like Harvard to their archaism.

At several universities, the administration has forced departments to hire members of minorities even when far superior candidates were available. Shortly after obtaining my PhD in the late 1970s I was mistakenly identified as a black philosopher (I had a civil rights record and was once a black studies major) and was flown to a major university, only to be rejected for a more qualified candidate when it discovered that I was white.

Stories of the bad effects of Affirmative Action abound. The philosopher Sidney Hook writes that "At one Ivy League university, representatives of the Regional HEW demanded an explanation of why there were no women or minority students in the Graduate Department of Religious Studies. They were told that a reading knowledge of Hebrew and Greek was presupposed. Whereupon the representatives of HEW advised orally: 'Then end those old fashioned programs that require irrelevant languages. And start up programs on relevant things which minority group students can study without learning languages.'"[19]

Nicholas Capaldi notes that the staff of HEW itself was one-half women, three-fifths members of minorities, and one-half black—a clear case of racial over-representation.

In 1972 officials at Stanford University discovered a proposal for the government to monitor curriculum in higher education: the "Summary Statement ... Sex Discrimination Proposed HEW

Regulation to Effectuate Title IX of the Education Amendment of 1972" to "establish and use internal procedure for reviewing curricula, designed both to ensure that they do not reflect discrimination on the basis of sex and to resolve complaints concerning allegations of such discrimination, pursuant to procedural standards to be prescribed by the Director of the office of Civil Rights." Fortunately, Secretary of HEW Caspar Weinberger when alerted to the intrusion, assured Stanford University that he would never approve of it.[20]

Government programs of enforced preferential treatment tend to appeal to the lowest possible common denominator. Witness the 1974 HEW Revised Order No. 14 on Affirmative Action expectations for preferential hiring: "Neither minorities nor female employees should be required to possess higher qualifications than those of the lowest qualified incumbents."

Furthermore, no tests may be given to candidates unless it is *proved* to be relevant to the job.

> No standard or criteria which have, by intent or effect, worked to exclude women or minorities as a class can be utilized, unless the institution can demonstrate the necessity of such standard to the performance of the job in question.
>
> Whenever a validity study is called for ... the user should include ... an investigation of suitable alternative selection procedures and suitable alternative methods of using the selection procedure which have as little adverse impact as possible.... Whenever the user is shown an alternative selection procedure with evidence of less adverse impact and substantial evidence of validity for the same job in similar circumstances, the user should investigate it to determine the appropriateness of using or validating it in accord with these guidelines.[21]

At the same time Americans are wondering why standards in our country are falling and the Japanese are getting ahead. Affirmative Action with its twin idols, Sufficiency and Diversity, is the enemy of excellence. I will develop this thought below (IV.6).

4. Affirmative Action Policies Unjustly Shift the Burden of Proof

Affirmative Action legislation tends to place the burden of proof on the employer who does not have an "adequate" representation of "underutilized" groups in his work force. He is guilty until proven innocent. I have already recounted how in the mid-eighties the Supreme Court shifted the burden of proof back onto the plaintiff, while Congress is now attempting to shift the burden back to the employer. Those in favor of deeming disproportional representation "guilty until proven innocent" argue that it is easy for employers to discriminate against minorities by various subterfuges, and I agree that steps should be taken to monitor against prejudicial treatment. But being prejudiced against employers is not the way to attain a just solution to discrimination. The principle: innocent until proven guilty, applies to employers as well as criminals. Indeed, it is clearly special pleading to reject this basic principle of Anglo-American law in this case of discrimination while adhering to it everywhere else.

5. An Argument from Merit

Traditionally, we have believed that the highest positions in society should be awarded to those who are best qualified—as the Koran states in the quotation at the beginning of this paper. Rewarding excellence both seems just to the individuals in the competition and makes for efficiency. Note that one of the most successful acts of integration, the recruitment of Jackie Robinson in the late 1940s, was done in just this way, according to merit. If Robinson had been brought into the major league as a mediocre player or had batted .200 he would have been scorned and sent back to the minors where he belonged.

Merit is not an absolute value. There are times when it may be overridden for social goals, but there is a strong prima facie reason for awarding positions on its basis, and it should enjoy a weighty presumption in our social practices.

In a celebrated article Ronald Dworkin says that "Bakke had no case" because society did not owe Bakke anything. That may be, but then why does it owe anyone anything? Dworkin puts the matter in Utility terms, but if that is the case, society may owe Bakke a place at the University of California/Davis, for it seems a reasonable rule-utilitarian principle that achievement should be rewarded in society. We generally want the best to have the best positions, the best qualified candidate to win the political office, the most brilliant and competent scientist to be chosen for the most challenging research project, the best qualified pilots to become commercial pilots, only the best soldiers to become generals. Only when little is at stake do we weaken the standards and content ourselves with sufficiency (rather than excellence)—there are plenty of jobs where "sufficiency" rather than excellence is required. Perhaps we now feel that medicine or law or university professorships are so routine that they can be performed by minimally qualified people—in which case AA has a place.

But note, no one is calling for quotas or proportional representation of *underutilized* groups in the National Basketball Association where blacks make up 80% of the players. But if merit and merit alone reigns in sports, should it not be valued at least as much in education and industry?

6. The Slippery Slope

Even if Strong AA or Reverse Discrimination could meet the other objections, it would face a tough ques-

tion: once you embark on this project, how do you limit it? Who should be excluded from reverse discrimination? Asians and Jews are over-represented, so if we give blacks positive quotas, should we place negative quotas to these other groups? Since white males, "WMs," are a minority which is suffering from reverse discrimination, will we need a New Affirmative Action policy in the twenty-first century to compensate for the discrimination against WMs in the late twentieth century?

Furthermore, Affirmative Action has stigmatized the *young* white male. Assuming that we accept reverse discrimination, the fair way to make sacrifices would be to retire *older* white males who are more likely to have benefited from a favored status. Probably the least guilty of any harm to minority groups is the young white male—usually a liberal who has been required to bear the brunt of ages of past injustice. Justice Brennan's announcement that the Civil Rights Act did not apply to discrimination against whites shows how the clearest language can be bent to serve the ideology of the moment.[22]

7. The Mounting Evidence against the Success of Affirmative Action

Thomas Sowell of the Hoover Institute has shown in his book *Preferential Policies: An International Perspective* that preferential hiring almost never solves social problems. It generally builds in mediocrity or incompetence and causes deep resentment. It is a short term solution which lacks serious grounding in social realities.

For instance, Sowell cites some disturbing statistics on education. Although twice as many blacks as Asians students took the nationwide Scholastic Aptitude Test in 1983, approximately fifteen times as many Asian students scored above 700 (out of a possible 800) on the mathematics half of the SAT. The percentage of Asians who scored above 700 in math was also more than six times higher than the percentage of American Indians and more than ten times higher than that of Mexican Americans—as well as more than double the percentage of whites. As Sowell points out, in all countries studied, "intergroup performance disparities are huge" (108).

> There are dozens of American colleges and universities where the median combined verbal SAT score and mathematics SAT score total 1200 or above. As of 1983 there were less than 600 black students in the entire US with combined SAT scores of 1200. This meant that, despite widespread attempts to get a black student "representation" comparable to the black percentage of the population (about 11%), there were not enough black students in the entire country for the Ivy League alone to have such a "representation" without going beyond this pool—even if the entire pool went to the eight Ivy League Colleges.[23]

Often it is claimed that a cultural bias is the cause of the poor performance of blacks on SAT (or IQ tests), but Sowell shows that these test scores are actually a better predictor of college performance for blacks than for Asians and whites. He also shows the harmfulness of the effect on blacks of preferential acceptance. At the University of California, Berkeley, where the freshman class closely reflects the actual ethnic distribution of California high school students, more than 70% of blacks fail to graduate. All 312 black students entering Berkeley in 1987 were admitted under "Affirmative Action" criteria rather than by meeting standard academic criteria. So were 480 out of 507 Hispanic students. In 1986 the median SAT score for blacks at Berkeley was 952, for Mexican Americans 1014, for American Indians 1082 and for Asian Americans 1254. (The average SAT for all students was 1181.)

The result of this mismatching is that blacks who might do well if they went to a second tier or third tier school where their test scores would indicate they belong, actually are harmed by preferential treatment. They cannot compete in the institutions where high abilities are necessary.

Sowell also points out that Affirmative Action policies have mainly assisted the middle class black, those who have suffered least from discrimination. "Black couples in which both husband and wife are college-educated overtook white couples of the same description back in the early 1970s and continued to at least hold their own in the 1980s" (115).

Sowell's conclusion is that similar patterns of results obtained from India to the USA wherever preferential policies exist. "In education, preferential admissions policies have led to high attrition rates and substandard performances for those preferred students ... who survived to graduate." In all countries the preferred tended to concentrate in less difficult subjects which lead to less remunerative careers. "In the employment market, both blacks and untouchables at the higher levels have advanced substantially while those at the lower levels show no such advancement and even some signs of retrogression. These patterns are also broadly consistent with patterns found in countries in which majorities have created preferences for themselves...." (116).

The tendency has been to focus at the high level end of education and employment rather than on the lower level of family structure and early education. But if we really want to help the worst off improve, we need to concentrate on the family and early education. It is foolish to expect equal results when we begin with grossly unequal starting points—and discriminating against young white males is no more just than discriminating against women, blacks or anyone else.

Conclusion

Let me sum up. The goal of the Civil Rights movement and of moral people everywhere has been equal opportunity. The question is: how best to get there. Civil Rights legislation removed the legal barriers to equal opportunity, but did not tackle the deeper causes that produced differential results. Weak Affirmative Action aims at encouraging minorities in striving for the highest positions without unduly jeopardizing the rights of majorities, but the problem of Weak Affirmative Action is that it easily slides into Strong Affirmative Action where quotas, "goals," and equal results are forced into groups, thus promoting mediocrity, inefficiency, and resentment. Furthermore, Affirmative Action aims at the higher levels of society—universities and skilled jobs—yet if we want to improve our society, the best way to do it is to concentrate on families, children, early education, and the like. Affirmative Action is, on the one hand, too much, too soon and on the other hand, too little, too late.

Martin Luther said that humanity is like a man mounting a horse who always tends to fall off on the other side of the horse. This seems to be the case with Affirmative Action. Attempting to redress the discriminatory iniquities of our history, our well-intentioned social engineers engage in new forms of discriminatory iniquity and thereby think that they have successfully mounted the horse of racial harmony. They have only fallen off on the other side of the issue.[24]

NOTES

1 Quoted in William Bradford Reynolds, "Affirmative Action is Unjust," in D. Bender and B. Leone (eds.), *Social Justice* (St. Paul, MN, 1984), 23.

2 Some of the material in this section is based on Nicholas Capaldi's *Out of Order: Affirmative Action and the Crisis of Doctrinaire Liberalism* (Buffalo, NY, 1985), chapters 1 and 2. Capaldi, using the shackled runner analogy, divides the history into three stages: a *platitude stage* "in which it is reaffirmed that the race is to be fair, and a fair race is one in which no one has either special disadvantages or special advantages (equal opportunity)"; a *remedial stage* in which victims of past discrimination

are to be given special help overcoming their disadvantages; and a *realignment stage* "in which all runners will be reassigned to those positions on the course that they would have had if the race had been fair from the beginning" (181).

3 Wanda Warren Berry, "Affirmative Action is Just," in D. Bender and B. Leone, op. cit., 18.

4 Robert Fullinwider, *The Reverse Discrimination Controversy* (Totowa, NJ, 1970), 25.

5 Quoted in Fullinwider, op. cit., 4f.

6 See Lino A. Graglia, "Affirmative Action: The Constitution, and the 1964 Civil Rights Act," *Measure*, No. 92 (1991).

7 Linda Gottfredson, "Letters to the Editor," *New York Times*, Aug. 1, 1990 issue. Gender-norming is also a feature of the proponents of Affirmative Action. Michael Levin begins his book *Feminism and Freedom* (New Brunswick, 1987) with federal court case *Beckman v. NYFD* in which 88 women who failed the New York City Fire Department's entrance exam in 1977 filed a class-action sex discrimination suit. The court found that the physical strength component of the test was not job-related, and thus a violation of Title VII of the Civil Rights Act, and ordered the city to hire 49 of the women. It further ordered the fire department to devise a special, less-demanding physical strength exam for women. Following EEOC guidelines if the passing rate for women is less than 80% that of the passing rate of men, the test is presumed invalid.

8 Thomas Sowell, *Preferential Policies: An International Perspective* (New York, 1990).

9 John Arthur, *The Unfinished Constitution* (Belmont, CA, 1990), 238.

10 See Phillip E. Vernon's excellent summary of the literature in *Intelligence: Heredity and Environment* (New York, 1979) and Yves Christen "Sex Differences in the Human Brain," in Nicholas Davidson (ed.) *Gender Sanity* (Lan-

ham, 1989) and T. Bouchard, *et al.*, "Sources of Human Psychological Differences: The Minnesota Study of Twins Reared Apart," *Science*, Vol. 250 (1990).

11 See Michael Levin, "Is Racial Discrimination Special?" *Policy Review*, Fall issue (1982).

12 Judith Jarvis Thomson, "Preferential Hiring," in Marshall Cohen, Thomas Nagel and Thomas Scanlon (eds.), *Equality and Preferential Treatment* (Princeton, 1977).

13 John Rawls, *A Theory of Justice* (Cambridge, 1971), 104; See Richard Wasserstrom "A Defense of Programs of Preferential Treatment," *National Forum* (Phi Kappa Phi Journal), Vol. 58 (1978). See also Bernard Boxill, "The Morality of Preferential Hiring," *Philosophy and Public Affairs*, Vol. 7 (1978).

14 Michael Kinsley, "Equal Lack of Opportunity," *Harper's*, June issue (1983).

15 There is one other argument which I have omitted. It is one from precedence and has been stated by Judith Jarvis Thomson in the article cited earlier:

> Suppose two candidates for a civil service job have equally good test scores, but there is only one job available. We could decide between them by coin-tossing. But in fact we do allow for declaring for *A* straightaway, where *A* is a veteran, and *B* is not. It may be that *B* is a nonveteran through no fault of his own....Yet the fact is that *B* is not a veteran and *A* is. On the assumption that the veteran has served his country, the country owes him something. And it is plain that giving him preference is not an unjust way in which part of that debt of gratitude can be paid. (379f)

The two forms of preferential hiring are analogous. Veteran's preference is justified as a way of paying a debt of gratitude; preferential hiring is a way of paying a debt of compensation. In both cases innocent parties bear the burden of the community's debt, but it is justified.

My response to this argument is that veterans should not be hired in place of better qualified candidates, but that benefits like the GI scholarships are part of the contract with veterans who serve their country in the armed services. The notion of compensation only applies to individuals who have been injured by identifiable entities. So the analogy between veterans and minority groups seems weak.

16 Quoted in Jim Sleeper, *The Closest of Strangers* (New York, 1990), 209.

17 Shelby Steele, "A Negative Vote on Affirmative Action," *New York Times*, May 13, 1990 issue.

18 *New York Times*, May 10, 1990 issue.

19 Nicholas Capaldi, op. cit., 85.

20 Cited in Capaldi, op. cit., 95.

21 *Ibid.*

22 The extreme form of this New Speak is incarnate in the Politically Correct Movement ("PC" ideology) where a new orthodoxy has emerged, condemning white, European culture and seeing African culture as the new savior of us all. Perhaps the clearest example of this is Paula Rothenberg's book *Racism and Sexism* (New York, 1987) which asserts that there is no such thing as black racism; only whites are capable of racism (6). Ms. Rothenberg's book has been scheduled as required reading for all freshmen at the University of Texas. See Joseph Salemi, "Lone Star Academic Politics," No. 87 (1990).

23 Thomas Sowell, op. cit., 108.

24 I am indebted to Jim Landesman, Michael Levin, and Abigail Rosenthal for comments on a previous draft of this paper. I am also indebted to Nicholas Capaldi's *Out of Order* for first making me aware of the extent of the problem of Affirmative Action.

SEXUAL HARASSMENT

EDMUND WALL

The Definition of Sexual Harassment

As important as current managerial, legal and philosophical definitions of sexual harassment are, many of them omit the interpersonal features which define the concept. Indeed, the mental states of the perpetrator and the victim are the essential defining elements. In this essay arguments are presented against mere behavior descriptions of sexual harassment, definitions formulated in terms of the alleged discriminatory and coercive effects of a sexual advance, and the federal legal definition which omits reference to relevant mental states. It is argued that sexual harassment is essentially a form of invasive communication that violates a victim's privacy rights. A set of jointly necessary and sufficient conditions of sexual harassment are defended which purport to capture the more subtle instances of sexual harassment while circumventing those sexual advances that are not sexually harassive. [If X is a *necessary condition* of Y then the absence of X guarantees the absence of Y. Note, however, that the presence of X does not guarantee the presence of Y. For example, in humans a necessary condition of being a mother is being female, but being female does not guarantee that one is a mother. If X is a sufficient condition of Y then the presence of X guarantees the presence of Y. Note, however, that the absence of X does not guarantee the absence of Y. For example, in humans a sufficient condition of being male is being a father, but not being a father does not guarantee that one is not male.]

There are many types of behavior that may be classified as instances of sexual harassment, and some people, such as Kenneth Cooper, have proposed that managers explain the concept to their employees primarily through descriptions of various behavior patterns. Cooper addresses the sexual harassment of female employees by male managers in an essay which describes what he terms "six levels of sexual harassment." He seems to order these levels according to what he assumes to be two complementary considerations: a third party's ability to identify the perpetrator's behavior as sexually harassive and the severity of the infraction. The categories are presented in ascending order with the first category ostensibly representing the least flagrant type of behavior, the sixth category representing the most flagrant type of behavior. He writes that "obvious and blatant harassment may be decreasing, but borderline harassment behavior has never let up."[1] He takes the first four categories to be accounts of "borderline" cases.

He refers to the first type of behavior as "aesthetic appreciation." This refers to comments which "express a non-aggressive appreciation of physical or sexual features." For example, an alleged perpetrator says to a coworker: "Gee ... sigh ... you're looking better every day!"[2] Cooper refers to such examples as the most "innocent" type of sexual harassment, but believes that these examples, nevertheless, constitute sexual harassment. In such cases the harassment is concealed.

Does managerial behavior which falls under "aesthetic appreciation" necessarily constitute sexual harassment? Cooper argues that "regardless of how harmless these appreciative comments may seem, they are put-downs which lower the group stature of the target." The offender, he tells us, is in a "superior position" from which to judge the employee's physical attributes.[3]

Comments of "aesthetic appreciation" made by male managers to female employees may not be appropriate, but all such comments are not, as Cooper suggests, necessarily instances of sexual harassment. Cooper argues that managerial comments of "aesthetic appreciation" made to employees are sexually harassive because they are "put-downs which lower the group stature of the target." There is a problem here. Such comments are not necessarily a reflection of any group differential.4 Of course, the manager is in a "superior position" in relation to his employee, but only with respect to her corporate duties—not with respect to her physical attributes. The manager may try to use his corporate authority in order to force his employee to listen to his assessment of her physical attributes. Furthermore, the employee may feel as though she must submit to the manager's remarks, even if he does not openly attempt to coerce her. However, his sexually harassive behavior need not inherently be an exercise of corporate authority. It could simply be misguided human behavior which utilizes his corporate authority.

The second type of behavior which, according to Cooper, constitutes sexual harassment is "active mental groping." Under this heading Cooper places "direct verbal harassment," which evidently includes sexual jokes about the employee, and also the type of staring that may leave an employee feeling as though managers are "undressing them with their eyes."5 This is followed by "social touching." Cooper maintains that, along with the first two categories of behavior, this type of behavior is "borderline," since the offender remains "within normal social touching conventions." In other words this behavior misleadingly appears "totally innocent" to a "third party."6

As far as "social touching" is concerned, he distinguishes an innocent "friendly touch" from a "sensual touch." He does not provide an example of a "friendly touch," but an example of a "sensual touch" would be "a caressing hand laid gently on the [employee]," or the movement of the manager's hand up and down his employee's back.7 Unfortunately, Cooper offers no defense of his distinction between two types of touching. Neither does he clearly re-

late this distinction to his account of sexual harassment, although he seems to assume that a manager's "friendly touch" does not constitute sexual harassment, whereas his "sensual touch" would. He merely warns managers against any "social touching."

The reason why the distinction between an innocent "friendly touch" and a "sensual touch" makes sense is also the reason why behavior descriptions are not central to the definition of sexual harassment. The basis for the distinction lies in the manager's mental state. A sincerely "friendly touch" would depend, among other things, upon the manager's motive for touching his employee. Sexual harassment refers to a defect in interpersonal relations. Depending upon the manager's and employee's mental states, it is possible that some examples of managerial behavior which satisfy Cooper's first, most "innocent" category (i.e., "aesthetic appreciation"), would actually be more objectionable than his second and third categories (i.e., "active mental groping" and "social touching," respectively). Indeed, depending upon the manager's and employee's mental states, cases which fall under any of Cooper's first three categories of sexual harassment could be characterized as "innocent."

Consider the case in which a manager finds that one of his employees strikingly resembles his mother. He has managed this employee for three years without incident, and one day in the corporate dining room they begin to discuss their parents. He may tell her of the resemblance between her and his mother. He may stare at her for a long while (this would constitute "active mental groping" on Cooper's view). He may tell her that her cheek bones are as pretty as those of his mother (an example of "aesthetic appreciation" according to Cooper). Finally, he may put his hand on her shoulder (i.e., an example of friendly "social touching" on Cooper's view) and say "Oh well, I must be getting back to my desk." Given this scenario, it is obvious that at least some employees would take no offense at the manager's behavior. Such a case need not involve sexual harassment, even though mere behavior descriptions would lead up to the opposite conclusion.

Cooper refers to his fourth and final "borderline" category as "foreplay harassment." Unlike "social touching," the touching here is not "innocent in nature and location," although its inappropriateness is still concealed.[8] Examples of "foreplay harassment" include a manager noticing that a button on an employee's blouse is undone. Instead of telling her about it, he buttons it. Another example would be brushing up against her "as if by accident."[9]

Cooper suggests that the "scope, frequency, and feel" of the touching "shows an obvious intent on the part of the offender to push the limits of decency...."[10] In this description of sexual harassment Cooper alludes to the importance of the manager's motive, but does not make its importance explicit. He does not express it as one of the essential descriptions of sexual harassment. Accidental physical contact between a manager and his employee is not, of course, sexual harassment. When the manager deliberately makes contact with his employee from a certain motive or due to his negligence, then he becomes an offender. Whether or not he makes physical contact, he may still be an offender. Indeed, as Cooper recognizes, an employee could be sexually harassed without any physical contact between her and her manager.

Cooper overlooks the possibility that what appears to be "foreplay harassment" of an employee may not be. Even when a manager is sexually "petting" an employee in his office, as inappropriate as this behavior could be, he is not necessarily sexually harassing her. Consider the case in which a manager and an employee form an uncoerced agreement to engage in such inappropriate office behavior.[11] This is not sexual harassment. The general problem with behavior descriptions of sexual harassment can be seen when we attempt to construct examples of sexual harassment. The application of any of Cooper's four "borderline" categories to our examples may yield false determinations, depending upon the mental states involved.

Cooper's fifth and sixth categories are not "borderline," but involve flagrant sexual advances. They are "sexual abuse" and "ultimate threat," respectively. The latter which refers to a manager's coercive threats for sexual favors will be discussed later.[12] The former obviously involves sexual harassment.

Probably any behavior which constitutes sexual harassment (i.e., which satisfies certain descriptions of the manager's and employee's mental states) would probably constitute sexual abuse—whether physical or verbal. When an individual is maliciously or negligently responsible for unjustified harm to someone, it would seem that he has abused that person. Abuse can be subtle. It may include various ways of inflicting psychological harm. In fact, there is a more subtle form of sexual harassment accomplished through stares, gestures, innuendo, etc. For example, a manager may sexually harass his employee by staring at her and "undressing her with his eyes." *In light of this and the other limitations of behavior descriptions we need a set of jointly necessary and sufficient conditions of sexual harassment capable of capturing all subtle instances of sexual harassment while filtering out (even overt) sexual behavior which is not harassive.*

Wherein X is the sexual harasser and Y the victim, the following are offered as jointly necessary and sufficient conditions of sexual harassment:

1. X does not attempt to obtain Y's consent to communicate to Y, X's or someone else's purported sexual interest in Y.
2. X communicates to Y, X's or someone else's purported sexual interest in Y, X's motive for communicating this is some perceived benefit that he expects to obtain through the communication.
3. Y does not consent to discuss with X, X's or someone else's purported sexual interest in Y.
4. Y feels emotionally distressed because X did not attempt to obtain Y's consent to this discussion and/or because Y objects to the content of X's sexual comments.

The first condition refers to X's failure to attempt to obtain Y's consent to discuss someone's sexual interest in Y. X's involvement in the sexual harassment is not defined by the sexual proposition that X may make to Y. If the first condition was formulated in terms of the content of X's sexual proposition, then the proposed definition would circumvent some of the more subtle cases of sexual harassment. After all, Y may actually agree to a sexual proposition made to her by X and still be sexually harassed by X's attempting to discuss it with her. In some cases Y might not feel that it is the proper time or place to discuss such matters. In any event *sexual harassment primarily involves wrongful communication*. Whether or not X attempts to obtain Y's consent to a certain type of communication is crucial. What is inherently repulsive about sexual harassment is not the possible vulgarity of X's sexual comment or proposal, but his failure to show respect for Y's rights. It is the obligation that stems from privacy rights that is ignored. Y's personal behavior and aspirations are protected by Y's privacy rights. The intrusion by X into this moral sphere is what is so objectionable about sexual harassment. If X does not attempt to obtain Y's approval to discuss such private matters, then he has not shown Y adequate respect.

X's lack of respect for Y's rights is not a sufficient condition of sexual harassment. X's conduct must constitute a rights violation. Essentially, the second condition refers to the fact that X has acted without concern for Y's right to consent to the communication of sexual matters involving her. Here X "communicates" to Y that X or someone else is sexually interested in Y. This term includes not only verbal remarks made by X, but any purposeful conveyance such as gestures, noises, stares, etc. that violate its recipient's privacy rights. Such behavior can be every bit as intrusive as verbal remarks.

We need to acknowledge that X can refer to some third party's purported sexual interest in Y and still sexually harass Y. When he tells her, without her consent, that some third party believes she is physic-

ally desirable, this may be a form of sexual harassment. Y may not approve of X telling her this—even if Y and the third party happen to share a mutual sexual interest in each other. This is because X's impropriety lies in his invasive approach to Y. It does not hinge upon the content of what he says to Y. X may, for example, have absolutely no sexual interest in Y. but believes that such remarks would upset Y; thereby affording him perverse enjoyment. Likewise his report that some third party is sexually interested in Y may be inaccurate but this does not absolve him from his duty to respect Y's privacy.

X's specific motive for communicating what he does to Y may vary, but it always includes some benefit X may obtain from this illegitimate communication. X might or might not plan to have sexual relations with Y. Indeed, as we have seen, he might not have a sexual interest in Y at all and still obtain what he perceives to be beneficial to himself, perhaps the satisfaction of disturbing Y.[13] Perhaps, as some contemporary psychologists suggest, X's ultimate motive is to mollify his feelings of inferiority by controlling Y's feelings, actions, environment, etc. Yet another possibility is that X wants to conform to what he believes to be parental and/or peer standards for males. The proposed first and second conditions can account for these various motives. The point is that, whatever the perceived benefit, it is the utility of the approach as perceived by X, and not necessarily the content of his message, that is important to the harasser. Furthermore, the "benefit" that moves him to action might not be obtainable or might not be a genuine benefit, but, nevertheless, in his attempt to obtain it, he violates his victim's rights.

The third condition refers to Y's not consenting to discuss with X, X's or someone else's purported sexual interest in Y. Someone might argue that the first condition is now unnecessary, that X's failure to obtain Y's consent to the type of discussion outlined in the third condition will suffice; the provision concerning X's failure to *attempt* to obtain Y's consent is, therefore, unnecessary. This objection would be misguided, however. The first condition ensures that some sexual comments will not be unjustly labelled as "harassive." Consider the possibility that the second and third conditions are satisfied. For example, X makes a sexual remark about Y without her consent. Now suppose that the first condition is not satisfied, that is, suppose that X *did attempt* to obtain Y's consent to make such remarks. Furthermore, suppose that somewhere the communication between X and Y breaks down and X honestly believes he has obtained Y's consent to this discussion when, in fact, he has not. In this case, X's intentions being what they are, he does not sexually harass Y. X has shown respect for Y's privacy. Y may certainly feel harassed in this case, but there is no offender here. However, after X sees Y's displeasure at his remarks, it is now his duty to refrain from such remarks, unless, of course, Y later consents to such a discussion.

The case of the ignorant but well-intentioned X demonstrates the importance of distinguishing between accidents (and merely unfortunate circumstances) and sexual harassment. The remedy for avoiding the former is the encouragement of clear communication between people. Emphasis on clear communication would also facilitate the identification of some offenders, for some offenders would not refrain from making sexual remarks after their targets clearly expressed their objections to those remarks. The above case also reveals that the alleged victim needs to clearly express her wishes to others. For example, when she wishes not to discuss an individual's sexual interest in her, it would be foolish for her to make flirting glances at this individual. Such gestures may mislead him to conclude that she consents to this communication.

The first three conditions are not jointly sufficient descriptions of sexual harassment. What is missing is a description of Y's mental state. In sexual harassment cases the maligned communication must distress Y for a certain reason. Let us say that X has expressed sexual interest in Y without any attempt to obtain her consent. She, in fact, does not

consent to it. However, perhaps she has decided against the discussion because she finds X too refined and anticipates that his sexual advances will not interest her. Perhaps she welcomes crass discussions about sexual matters. In this case she might not be sexually harassed by X's remarks. As the fourth condition indicates, Y must be distressed because X did not attempt to ensure that it was permissible to make sexual comments to Y which involve her, or because the content of X's sexual comments are objectionable to Y. Yet another possibility is that both the invasiveness of X's approach and the content of what X says cause Y emotional distress. In this case, however, it would appear that Y would neither object to the content of X's sexual remarks nor to the fact that X did not attempt to obtain Y's consent to make these remarks to her. Due to Y's views concerning sexual privacy this case is similar to one in which X does not attempt to obtain Y's consent to discuss with how well she plays tennis, or some other mundane discussion about Y.

You may recall that we postponed a discussion of the relation of sexual harassment to coercion and discrimination against women. Let us now explore this relation.

The fact that male employers and managers represent the bulk of the reported offenders has caused some legal theorists and philosophers to conclude that sexual harassment necessarily involves discrimination against women as a class. This approach is unacceptable. The proposed description of sexual harassment in terms of interpersonal relations is incompatible with this account, and, it seems that sexual harassment is not necessarily tied to discrimination or to coercion.

In an essay entitled "Is Sexual Harassment Coercive?" Larry May and John C. Hughes argue that sexual harassment against women workers is "inherently coercive"—whether the harassment takes the form of a threat or an offer. They also maintain that the harm of sexual harassment against women "contributes to a pervasive pattern of discrimination and exploitation based upon sex."[14] They begin by defining sexual harassment as "the intimidation of persons in subordinate positions by those holding power and authority over them in order to exact sexual favors that would ordinarily not have been granted."[15]

May and Hughes recognize that male employees may be sexually harassed, but choose to limit their discussion to the typical case in which a male employer or manager sexually harasses a female employee. They choose this paradigm because it represents the "dominant pattern" in society and because they believe that, as a class, women have been conditioned by society to acquiesce "to male initiative."[16] According to May and Hughes women represent an injured class. The fact that men dominate positions of authority and status in our society renders women vulnerable to sexual harassment. Furthermore, the sexual harassment of female employees by male employers and managers sparks a general increase in the frequency of the crime, since such behavior reinforces male stereotypes of women as sexual objects.[17]

Even if May's and Hughes' social assumptions are accepted, that would not entail that their definition of sexual harassment is adequate. Their definition includes a power differential between the offender and the victim. Unhappily, this circumvents the sexual harassment between employees of equal rank, capabilities and recognition. Suppose that X and Y are co-workers for some company; X makes frequent comments concerning Y's sexual appeal and repeatedly propositions Y despite Y's refusals. Authority and rank are superfluous here. Y may be sexually harassed regardless of X's or Y's corporate status. As argued above in the critique of Cooper's article, the harassment at issue is not an extension of X's corporate authority, nor is the harassment essentially explained by the exercise of his authority. Rather, it is essentially explained by X's lack of respect for Y's right to refuse to discuss sexual matters pertaining to Y. If Y chooses not to enter Y's discussion or is upset by X's refusal to recognize Y's privacy rights, then sexual harassment has occurred. X's and Y's mental

states are essential, not some power differential between them.

Although the law vaguely recognizes the significance of Y's mental state in its sexual harassment definitions, the same is not true of X's mental state. For example, the California Department of Fair Employment and Housing (DFEH) completely omits the alleged perpetrator's mental state in their brief definition. Acknowledging that sexual harassment can occur between co-workers, they define it as "unwanted sexual advances, or visual, verbal or physical conduct of a sexual nature."[18] The difficulty with the DFEH's omission can be seen in the following counter-example. Y may be a paranoid individual who believes that any social advance by a member of the opposite sex somehow harms her. Perhaps X asks for a date and Y feels sexually harassed. Let us say that X is not yet planning to discuss with Y anyone's sexual interest in Y and that X terminates the discussion as soon as he notices Y's displeasure. On their definition the DFEH would be forced to consider this sexual harassment when clearly it is not. Although it involves an "unwanted sexual advance," X's mental state points to the innocence of his proposal.

Many of the examples that the DFEH use to illustrate their definition are also ambiguous. Unwanted "touching" is one example. In this case the commission might be referring to unwanted "sensual touching," but they offer no way of distinguishing a sensual from a merely friendly touch. Suppose that Y works in the sales office of some company and X works in the maintenance department. Y may object to X's touching her, but only because she does not want to stain her clothing. She knows that her friend, X, is not sexually interested in her and, if his hands were clean, she would have no objections to his occasional "friendly touch." This is not a case of sexual harassment, although it may, if it persists, show a lack of consideration on X's part. By ignoring the importance of mental states, the DFEH not only fails to identify the perpetrator's lack of respect for Y

in genuine sexual harassment cases, but also fails to acknowledge the importance of *Y*'s concerns. In this example *Y* did not feel sexually harassed, although she may have been upset because of her friend's inconsideration. In this subtle way California law does not do justice to the concerns of this alleged victim.

May's and Hughes' inaccurate definition of sexual harassment skews their inquiry. Their main objective is to illustrate the coercive nature of sexual harassment; more specifically, the coercive nature of sexual threats and offers made to women employees by male corporate authorities. They focus on the type of sexual advances that are tied to hiring, promotions or raises.[19] They briefly refer to a third type of sexual advance, one which is "merely annoying" and one which is "without demonstrable sanction or reward."[20] However, after introducing this third category the authors circumvent it. This oversight is a serious one. The essence of sexual harassment lies not in the content of the offender's proposal, but in the inappropriateness of his approach to the victim. It lies in the way he violates the victim's privacy. This is the "annoying" aspect of his approach which needs elucidating. May and Hughes could not pursue this third type of sexual advance because they had defined sexual harassment in terms of someone in authority acquiring some sexual favor from his employee. They set themselves the task of proving that sexual harassment is necessarily coercive. Their definition thereby hinged on the alleged coercive effects of the harasser's proposal, rather than on his mental state.

We still need to examine May's and Hughes' position that all sexual threats and offers made by male employers or managers to female employees are sexually harassive as well as coercive. They describe a conditional sexual threat from the employer's position: "If you don't provide a sexual benefit, I will punish you by withholding a promotion or raise that would otherwise be due, or ultimately fire you."[21] According to their "baseline" approach "sexual threats are coercive because they worsen the object-

ive situation the employee finds herself in." Before the threat the retention of her job only depended upon "standards of efficiency," whereas, after the threat, the performance of sexual favors becomes a condition of employment.[22] Presumably, these same "baseline" considerations also render the threat sexually harassive.

May and Hughes acknowledge that their "baseline account" of coercive threats is essentially Nozickian. Elsewhere, I have defended an interpersonal description of coercive threats against "baseline accounts."[23] According to my description *X* issues *Y* a coercive threat (in his attempt to get *Y* to do action "*A*") when *X* intentionally attempts to create the belief in *Y* that *X* will be responsible for harm coming to *Y* should *Y* fail to do *A*. *X*'s coercive threat is described primarily in terms of his intentions. His motive for attempting to create this belief in *Y* is his desire to bring about a state of affairs in which *Y*'s recognition of this possible harm to himself influences *Y* to do *A*. May and Hughes are correct that every conditional sexual threat issued by a male superior to a female subordinate is a coercive threat. (Indeed, a conditional sexual threat issued against anyone is a coercive threat.) The male employer would be trying to create the belief in the female employee that he will be responsible for harm coming to her (i.e., her termination, demotion, etc.) should she fail to comply with his sexual request. He would do this because he wants the prospect of this harm to motivate her to comply. Nevertheless, it is not true that every conditional sexual threat *as May and Hughes describe these threats* would be coercive. If, for example, the employer and the employee are playfully engaging in "banter" when he tells her that without her compliance he will fire her, then she is not being threatened. He does not intend to create the belief in her that harm will come to her. In this scenario she would not be sexually harassed either because the employer has a good faith belief that she consents to this "banter." Therefore, May and Hughes need a more rigorous description of coercive threats which includes the intentions of the person making the threat.

May and Hughes argue that if the employee wants to provide sexual favors to her employer regardless of the employer's demand, she is still coerced. They maintain that her objective baseline situation is still made worse, for now it would be very difficult for her to cease a sexual relationship with her employer should she choose to do so.[24] May and Hughes do not tell us who or what would specifically be making the coercive proposal if the *employee* propositioned the employer. After all, on their view, her offer would worsen her objective situation for the same reason his threat would. Perhaps they would refer to this as a coercive situation, or would find the employer's consent to the sexual relationship to include some sort of a coercive stance, but, nevertheless, their external analysis overlooks the mental state of the individual who is supposedly victimized. Depending upon her values and personal outlook she may, without reservation, accept her employer's demand as a "career opportunity." By excluding the employee's mental state in their "baseline analysis" they overlook the fact that her situation may improve after the demand and that, to her, the prospect of a permanent sexual relationship with her employer is no problem. According to this "baseline account" she would not be coerced or harassed. Unlike May's and Hughes' account, the proposed interpersonal account of sexual harassment maintains that an employee who receives a sexual threat from her employer is not necessarily sexually harassed. Let us say that he told her she must have sex with him or else be demoted. Still, she may welcome his demand as a "career opportunity." If she is not offended by his demand, then she is not sexually harassed by the threat.

As we have seen May and Hughes maintain that the sexual harassment of a female employee by a male corporate authority is coercive because it worsens the employee's employment situation. They say that sexual harassment by an employer erects an unfair employment condition against women as a class. May and Hughes therefore believe that the discriminatory nature of sexual harassment against female employees is tied to these "coercive" dimensions. They argue that, in general, men do not have to endure the maligned "job requirement" generally foisted upon women and that when men make sexual threats to their female subordinates they "establish a precedent for employment decisions based upon the stereotype that values women for their sexuality ..."[25] Because the sexual harassment of female employees by male employers worsens the employment situation of women by stereotyping them, we supposedly have a necessary relation between ("coercive") sexual harassment and discrimination.

May and Hughes are not alone in their belief that sexual harassment and discrimination are necessarily related. When they describe their arguments for the coercive-discriminatory effects of a male employer's sexual threat on a female employee, they refer to such a threat as an "instance of discrimination in the workplace."[26] Here they follow federal law by claiming that sexual threats in the workplace fall under the rubric of Title VII of the Civil Rights Act of 1964. They are relying on the fact that in 1980 the Equal Employment Opportunity Commission (EEOC) set a precedent by finding that sexual harassment is a form of sex discrimination.[27]

The prevailing belief that the sexual harassment of women is a form of sex discrimination is ill-founded. Even if we follow May and Hughes and limit our discussion to the sexual harassment of female employees by male employers, something that the EEOC cannot do, a male employer's sexual threat is not necessarily an "instance" of sex discrimination. For a given sexual harassment case, gender may not be a consideration at all. Picture the bisexual employer who is not in control of his sexual desires. He might indiscriminately threaten or proposition his employees without giving consideration to the gender of his victims. The additional "job requirement" referred to by May and Hughes would, in this case, apply to all employees male and female.

Indeed, since, as argued above, sexual harassment is primarily a matter of communication which infringes on basic privacy rights, there is no presumption of gender. Now, the EEOC does make reference to a candidate losing a job because another candidate who is less qualified has acquiesced to an employer's sexual threat, but this is not necessarily a case of sex discrimination as May and Hughes contend. Gender need not be the motive behind the employer's sexual threat. If the qualified candidate has been discriminated against, this may occur for a variety of reasons. Although the proposed interpersonal account is compatible with the assumptions that sexual harassment against women generally contributes to discrimination against women and that prejudice against women may be the motive of most male employers when they sexually harass female employees, we should avoid defining sexual harassment in terms of these assumptions.

Of course, the possibility that federal authority was misdirected when the EEOC set policy for sexual harassment in the workplace, does not entail that the EEOC's definition is incorrect. They maintain that unwelcome sexual advances, requests for sexual favors, and other verbal or physical conduct of a sexual nature constitute sexual harassment when

1. submission to such conduct is made either explicitly or implicitly a term or condition of an individual's employment,
2. submission to or rejection of such conduct by an individual is used as the basis for employment decisions affecting such an individual, or
3. such conduct has the purpose or effect of unreasonably interfering with an individual's work performance or creating an intimidating, hostile, or offensive working environment.

The EEOC'S conditions of sexual harassment not only appear to capture sexual threats and offers, but, also, "annoyances" and other more subtle violations. The EEOC's definition thereby avoids May's and Hughes' mistake. Their third condition also allows for sexual harassment between employees, something also lacking in May's and Hughes' account. Unfortunately, the EEOC's first two conditions seem to suggest that all sexual threats and offers made by employers to employees are sexually harassive. As argued above, not all sexual threats made by employers to employees must be sexually harassive, their inappropriateness notwithstanding. The EEOC's definition of sexual harassment is too inclusive because it fails to capture precisely the victim's mental state and the way that she reacts to the threat. In omitting a description of her mental state the EEOC's definition encourages the DFEH's oversight in allowing a paranoid "victim" to claim sexual harassment against a well-intentioned employer. Moreover, the EEOC makes no provision for the intentions of the employer.

Some states such as California maintain that sexually explicit materials which disturb employees are sexually harassive. This stance seems to be in line with the EEOC's definition. According to the EEOC the employer or employee who, for example, displays a sexually explicit poster may exhibit "physical conduct of a sexual nature" which creates an "offensive working environment." This is a difficult example, but it seems that an employee's mere disapproval of such materials does not entail that she is sexually harassed. Even if the disgruntled employee disapproves of the poster's explicit sexual representations, this does not mean that the person displaying the poster is intending to communicate anything to her and about her. Of course, in many cases he may be making a subtle statement to her about her sexual appeal. For example he may be using the poster in order to communicate his or someone else's sexual interest in her. According to the interpersonal account these cases would involve sexual harassment. If he is merely displaying the poster for his own benefit, however, then his behavior is rude, but not sexually harassive. There is a difference between the disrespect involved in rudeness, which indicates poor taste or a breach of etiquette, and the disrespect involved in sexual harassment. In the latter case the privacy of some specific individual has not been respected.

If May's and Hughes' position that all conditional sexual threats by male employers to female employees are sexually harassive and discriminatory in nature has successfully been overturned, their contention that the same considerations also apply to sexual offers collapses. They describe a sexual offer from the male employer's position: "If you provide a sexual benefit, I will reward you with a promotion or a raise that would otherwise not be due."[28] Since the benefit would ostensibly improve the employee's baseline situation, she is made an offer by her employer. Without the offer, she would not get the promotion or raise. Interestingly, May and Hughes argue that such offers actually worsen the employee's baseline situation and are, therefore, coercive offers. They do not explain how the employee's situation is simultaneously improved and worsened, but perhaps they have the following in mind: the employer's proposal is an offer because it may improve the employee's strategic status, whereas his offer is coercive because of certain social considerations. May and Hughes tell us that the employer's sexual offer changes the work environment so that the employee "is viewed by others, and may come to view herself, less in terms of her work productivity and more in terms of her sexual allure." Moreover, they say that, since women are more "economically vulnerable and socially passive than men," they are inclined to "offset [their] diminished status and to protect against later retaliation" by acquiescing to employer demands. Thus, according to May and Hughes, they are necessarily coerced by a male employer's sexual offer.[29]

May and Hughes argue that there is usually an implicit threat concealed in an employer's sexual offer and that this makes the offer coercive. Of course, here it may be the threat that is coercive and not the offer. What we are interested in is their argument that the employer's sexual offer itself is coercive because it reduces the female employee's self-esteem,

and also raises the spectre of some future threat (should the employee fail to comply or otherwise fall victim to the employer's "bruised" ego). Even if May and Hughes are correct and these are the general social effects of these sexual offers, this does not entail that a sexual offer made by a male employer to a female employee is coercive in nature. It would be unreasonable to suggest that every female employee would experience these hardships following a male employer's sexual offer. As mentioned in the discussion of sexual threats, the employee's values and personality contribute to the effects of an employer's presumably coercive proposal. Moreover, May's and Hughes' claim about the coercive effects of these sexual offers hinges upon their "baseline account" of coercion (which has been criticized above).

There is a more plausible alternative to a "baseline account" of coercive offers. An interpersonal account is possible. X makes Y a coercive offer when X intends to create the belief in Y that he will not prevent harm from coming to Y unless Y complies with his request. A genuine offer, on the other hand, would be limited to a mutual exchange of perceived benefits, or it may be a gift. This offer could become coercive if X attempts to cause Y to believe that her rejection of his request will result in some harm to her. Essentially, the coercive element is that X makes his proposed assistance in preventing this harm conditional upon Y's agreement to his request. He tries to use her belief that harm will occur as a way of controlling her. Not all offers by male employers to female employees are like this. Thus, on this interpersonal account, a male employer's offer is not coercive by nature.

We still need to address May's and Hughes' account of the implications of an employer's sexual offer to an employee. We are told that a non-compliant employee may worry that a disgruntled employer may threaten or harm her at some future date. This is certainly possible. However, such proposals are not coercive unless they involve the relevant intentions. The proposed account does acknowledge that an employer's non-coercive sexual offer might be sexually harassive. As argued above this depends upon the legitimacy of his approach to the employee and upon the employee's wishes. Moreover, the fact that, according to the proposed view, some of these sexual offers are non-coercive or sexually harassive does not alter the fact that an employer who is both considerate and prudent would avoid any behavior that could be construed as sexually harassive.[30]

NOTES

1 Kenneth C. Cooper, "The Six Levels of Sexual Harassment," *Contemporary Moral Controversies in Business*, ed. A. Pablo Iannone (New York: Oxford University Press, 1989), 190.

2 Ibid.

3 Ibid.

4 See especially 381ff. for a detailed discussion of sexual harassment and discrimination.

5 Cooper, *op. cit.*, 191.

6 Ibid.

7 Ibid.

8 Ibid.

9 Cooper, *op. cit.*, 191-92.

10 Cooper, *op. cit.*, 192.

11 See 377ff. for a discussion of coercion and sexual harassment.

12 Cooper, *op. cit.*, 192; see 379-81.

13 Some sociologists would disagree with me. They believe that the offender must have set himself a "sexual goal" in order for sexual harassment to occur. See K. Wilson and L. Kraus, "Sexual Harassment in the University." This paper was presented at the annual meetings of the American Sociological Association (Toronto, 1981).

14 Larry May and John C. Hughes, "Is Sexual Harassment Coercive?" *Moral Rights in the Workplace*, ed. Gertrude Ezorsky (Albany, NY: State University of New York, 1987), 115-22.

15 May and Hughes, *op. cit.*, 115.

16 Ibid.

17 May and Hughes, *op. cit.*, 118.

18 Pamphlet entitled "Sexual Harassment" (1990), distributed by the California Department of Fair Employment and Housing.

19 May and Hughes, *op. cit.*, 116-17.

20 May and Hughes, *op. cit.*, 117.

21 May and Hughes, *op. cit.*, 116-17.

22 May and Hughes, *op. cit.*, 117-18.

23 "Intention and Coercion," *Journal of Applied Philosophy*, Vol. 5 (1988), 75-85.

24 May and Hughes, *op. cit.*, 118.

25 May and Hughes, *op. cit.*, 118-19.

26 May and Hughes. *op. cit.*, 118.

27 Equal Employment Opportunity Commission, *Federal Register*, Vol. 45, No. 219 (10 November, 1980), Rules and Regulations, 74676-7.

28 May and Hughes, *op. cit.*, 117.

29 May and Hughes. *op. cit.*, 120.

30 I am grateful to Burleigh Wilkins for helpful comments on this paper.

◆ ◆ ◆ ◆ ◆

ANITA M. SUPERSON

A Feminist Definition of Sexual Harassment

1. Introduction

By far the most pervasive form of discrimination against women is sexual harassment (SH). Women in every walk of life are subject to it, and I would venture to say, on a daily basis.[1] Even though the law is changing to the benefit of victims of SH, the fact that SH is still so pervasive shows that there is too much tolerance of it, and that victims do not have sufficient legal recourse to be protected.

The main source for this problem is that the way SH is defined by various Titles and other sources does not adequately reflect the social nature of SH, or the harm it causes all women. As a result, SH comes to be defined in subjective ways. One upshot is that when subjective definitions infuse the case law on SH, the more subtle but equally harmful forms of SH do not get counted as SH and thus not afforded legal protection.

My primary aim in this paper is to offer an objective definition of SH that accounts for the group harm all forms of SH have in common. Though my aim is to offer a moral definition of SH, I offer it in hopes that it will effect changes in the law. It is only by defining SH in a way that covers all of its forms and gets at the heart of the problem that legal protection can be given to all victims in all circumstances.

I take this paper to be programmatic. Obviously problems may exist in applying the definition to cases that arise for litigation. In a larger project a lot more could be said to meet those objections. My goal in this paper is merely to defend my definition against the definitions currently appealed to by the courts in order to show how it is more promising for victims of SH. I define SH in the following way:

> Any behavior (verbal or physical) caused by a person, A, in the dominant class directed at another, B, in the subjugated class, that expresses and perpetuates the attitude that B or members of B's sex is/are inferior because of their sex, thereby causing harm to either B and/or members of B's sex.

II. Current Law on Sexual Harassment

Currently, victims of SH have legal recourse under Title VII of the Civil Rights Act of 1964, Title IX of the 1972 Education Amendments, and tort law.

The Civil Rights Act of 1964 states:

a) It shall be an unlawful employment practice for an employer—

  (1) to fail or refuse to hire or to discharge any individual; or otherwise to discriminate against any individual with respect to his compensation, terms, conditions, or privileges of employment because of such individual's race, color, religion, sex, or national origin....[2]

Over time the courts came to view SH as a form of sex discrimination. The main advocate for this was Catharine MacKinnon, whose book, *Sexual Harassment of Working Women*,[3] greatly influenced court decisions on the issue. Before it was federally legislated, some courts appealed to the Equal Employment Opportunity Commission (EEOC) *Guidelines on Discrimination Because of Sex* to establish that SH was a form of sex discrimination. The *Guidelines* (amended in 1980 to include SH) state that

> Harassment on the basis of sex is a violation of Sec. 703 of Title VII. Unwelcome sexual advances, requests for sexual favors, and other verbal or physical conduct of a sexual nature constitute sexual harassment when (1) submission to such conduct is made either explicitly or implicitly a term or condition of an individual's employment, (2) submission to or rejection of such conduct by an individual is used as the basis for employment decisions affecting such individual, or (3) such conduct has the purpose or effect of unreasonably interfering with an individual's work performance or creating an intimidating, hostile, or offensive working environment.[4]

In a landmark case,[5] *Meritor Savings Bank, FSB v. Vinson* (1986),[6] the Supreme Court, relying on the EEOC *Guidelines*, established that SH was a form of sex discrimination prohibited under Title VII. The case involved Mechelle Vinson, a teller-trainee, who was propositioned by Sidney Taylor, vice president and branch manager of the bank. After initially refusing, she agreed out of fear of losing her job. She allegedly had sexual relations with Taylor 40 or 50 times over a period of four years, and he even forcibly raped her several times, exposed himself to her in a restroom, and fondled her in public.[7]

Sexual harassment extends beyond the workplace. To protect students who are not employees of their learning institution, Congress enacted Title IX of the Education Amendments of 1972, which states:

> No person in the United States shall, on the basis of sex, be excluded from participation in, be denied the benefits of, or be subjected to discrimination under any educational program or activity receiving federal financial assistance.[8]

Cases of litigation under Title IX have been influenced by Meritor so that SH in educational institutions is construed as a form of sex discrimination.[9]

The principles that came about under Title VII apply equally to Title IX. Under either Title, a person can file two different kinds of harassment charges: *quid pro quo*, or hostile environment. *Quid pro quo* means "something for something."[10] *Quid pro quo* harassment occurs when "an employer or his agent explicitly ties the terms, conditions, and privileges of the victim's employment to factors which are arbitrary and unrelated to job performance."[11] Plaintiffs must show they "suffered a tangible economic detriment as a result of the harassment."[12] In contrast, hostile environment harassment occurs when the behavior of supervisors or co-workers has the effect of "unreasonably interfering with an individual's work performance or creates an intimidating, hostile, or offensive environment."[13] Hostile environment harassment established that Title VII (and presumably Title IX) were not limited to economic discrimination, but applied to emotional harm, as well. The EEOC *Guidelines* initiated the principle of hostile environment harassment which was used by the courts in many cases, including *Meritor*.

For each kind of SH (*quid pro quo* or hostile environment), courts can use one of two approaches: disparate treatment, or disparate impact.

Black's Law Dictionary defines disparate treatment as "[d]ifferential treatment of employees or applicants on the basis of their race, color, religion, sex, national origin, handicap, or veteran's status."[14] The key is to establish that the person was harassed because of her sex, and not because of other features (e.g., hair color). Disparate impact, in contrast, "involves facially neutral practices that are not intended to be discriminatory, but are discriminatory in effect."[15] Disparate *impact* came about because the facts did not always show that an employer blatantly discriminated on the basis of sex,[16] but the employer's practices still worked to the disadvantage of certain groups. Allegedly, "[f]or both *quid pro quo* and hostile environment sexual harassment, courts use disparate treatment theory."[17]

For women who are harassed other than in an employment or an educational setting, tort law [A *tort* is a private or civil, as opposed to public, wrong. We thus speak of civil as opposed to criminal offenses in the law.] can offer legal remedy. Also, torts can accompany a claim invoking Title VII (and presumably, Title IX).[18] Criminal suits apply only if the victim of harassment "is a victim of rape, indecent assault, common assault, assault causing bodily harm, threats, intimidation, or solicitation,"[19] and in these cases the suit will usually be for one of these charges, not harassment. To be taken seriously, the action requires police charges, a difficulty in SH cases.

Civil torts are a more promising way to go for victims of SH, though with limitations. The battery tort prohibits battery which is defined as "an intentional and unpermitted contact, other than that permitted by social usage."[20] The intent refers to intent to contact, not intent to cause the harm that may result from the contact. The assault tort prohibits assault, which is defined as "an intentional act, short of contact, which produces *apprehension* of battery."[21] The defendant must have intended to arouse psychic apprehension in his victim.[22] Victims can also appeal to the tort of intentional infliction of emotional distress. According to Section 46 of the *Restatement of Torts*,

Liability has been found only where the conduct has been so outrageous in character, and so extreme in degree, as to go beyond all possible bounds of decency, and to be regarded as atrocious, and utterly intolerable in a civilized community. Generally, the case is one in which the recitation of the facts to an average member of the community would arouse his resentment against the actor, and lead him to exclaim, "Outrageous."[23]

"[M]ere insults, indignities, threats, annoyances, petty oppression, or other trivialities" will not result in tort action because a person must be "hardened to a certain amount of rough language."[24] *The Restatement of Torts* invokes the reasonable man standard, claiming that the emotional distress must be "so severe that no reasonable man could be expected to endure it."[25] Moreover, the conduct must be done intentionally or recklessly.

Despite major advances made in the last few decades in the law on SH, I believe the law is still inadequate. The main problem in my view is that the law, reflecting the view held by the general public, fails to see SH for what it is: an attack on the group of *all* women, not just the immediate victim. Because of this, there is a failure to recognize the group harm that all instances of SH, not just the more blatant ones, cause all women. As a result, the law construes SH as a subjective issue, that is, one that is determined by what the victim feels and (sometimes) what the perpetrator intends. As a result, the burden of proof is wrongly shifted to the victim and off the perpetrator with the result that many victims are not legally protected.

For instance, victims filing complaints under Title VII (and presumably Title IX) are not protected unless they have a fairly serious case. They have to show under hostile environment harassment that the behavior unreasonably interfered with their work performance, and that there was a pattern of behavior on the defendant's behalf. Regarding the latter point, the EEOC *Guidelines* say that:

In determining whether alleged conduct constitutes sexual harassment, the Commission will look at the record as a whole and at the totality of the circumstances, such as the nature of the sexual advances and the context in which the alleged incidents occurred.[26]

It seems unlikely that the victim of isolated incidents of SH could have her complaint taken seriously under this assessment. Under *quid pro quo* harassment, the victim must show she suffered a tangible economic detriment. Disparate treatment cases might be difficult to show because not *all* members of the victim's class (e.g., the group of all females) are likely to be harassed by the defendant. This makes it unlikely that the victim will be able to show she was harassed because of her sex, and not because of some personal feature she has that others lack. Victims who are harassed outside of the workplace and educational institutions have to rely on tort law to make their case, but under it, defendants have a way out by claiming innocence of intention. Under the tort of intentional infliction of emotional distress, victims must have an extreme case in order to get protection.

Victims not protected include the worker who is harassed by a number of different people, the worker who suffers harassment but in small doses, the person who is subjected to a slew of catcalls on her two mile walk to work, the female professor who is subjected to leering from one of her male students, and the woman who does not complain out of fear. The number of cases is huge, and many of them are quite common.

To protect all victims in all circumstances, the law ought to treat SH as it is beginning to treat racial discrimination. In her very interesting paper, Mari Matsuda has traced the history of the law regarding racist speech.[27] Article 4 of the International Convention on the Elimination of All Forms of Racial

Discrimination which was unanimously adopted by the General Assembly December 21, 1965, prohibits not only acts of violence, but also the "mere dissemination of racist ideas, without requiring proof of incitement."[28] Apparently many states have signed and ratified the signing of the Convention, though the United States has not yet done so because of worries about freedom of speech protected by the first Amendment.[29] Aside from the Convention, the United Nations Charter, the Universal Declaration of Human Rights, the European Convention for the Protection of Human Rights and Fundamental Freedoms, the American Declaration of the Rights and Duties of Man, as well as the domestic law of several nations, have all recognized the right to equality and freedom from racism. In these and other codes, racist ideas are banned if they are discriminatory, related to violence, or express inferiority, hatred, or persecution.[30] On my view, some forms of SH are related to violence, and they *all* express inferiority whether or not they express hatred. At the root of the standard on racism that is gaining world-wide recognition is the view that racist speech "interferes with the rights of subordinated-group members to participate equally in society, maintaining their basic sense of security and worth as human beings."[31] Sexual harassment has the same effect, so it, too, should be prohibited. But I think SH can be afforded the best legal protection under antidiscrimination law instead of tort law, as this misses the social nature of SH. The world-wide standard against racist speech recognizes the group harm of racism by realizing that racist speech expresses inferiority; a similar standard against SH should be adopted.

III. The Social Nature of Sexual Harassment

Sexual harassment, a form of sexism is about domination, in articular, the domination of the group of men over the group of women.[32] Domination involves control or power which can be seen in the economic, political, and social spheres of society. Sexual harassment is not simply an assertion of power, for power can be used in beneficial ways. The power men have over women has been wielded in ways that oppress women. The power expressed in SH is oppression, power used wrongly.

Sexual harassment is integrally related to sex roles. It reveals the belief that a person is to be relegated to certain roles on the basis of her sex including not only women's being sex objects, but also their being caretakers, motherers, nurturers, sympathizers, etc. In general, the sex roles women are relegated to are associated with the body (v. mind) and emotions (v. reason).

When A sexually harasses B, the comment or behavior is really directed at the group of all women, not just a particular woman, a point often missed by the courts. After all, many derogatory behaviors are issued at women the harasser does not even know (e.g., scanning a stranger's body). Even when the harasser knows his victim, the behavior is directed at the particular woman because she happens to be "available" at the time, though its message is for all women. For instance, a catcall says not (merely) that the perpetrator likes a woman's body but that he thinks women are at least primarily sex objects and he—because of the power he holds by being in the dominant group—gets to rate them according to how much pleasure they give him. The professor who refers to his female students as "chicks" makes a statement that women are intellectually inferior to men as they can be likened to non-rational animals, perhaps even soft, cuddly ones that are to serve as the objects of (men's) pleasure. Physicians' using Playboy centerfolds in medical schools to "spice up their lectures" sends the message that women lack the competence to make it in a "man's world" and should perform the "softer tasks" associated with bearing and raising children.[33]

These and other examples make it clear that SH is not about dislike for a certain person; instead, it expresses a person's beliefs about women as a group on the basis of their sex, namely, that they are primarily emotional and bodily beings. Some theorists—Catharine MacKinnon, John Hughes and Larry May—have recognized the social nature of SH. Hughes and May claim that women are a disadvantaged group because

1. they are a social group having a distinct identity and existence apart from their individual identities,
2. they occupy a subordinate position in American society, and
3. their political power is severely circumscribed.[34]

They continue:

> Once it is established that women qualify for special disadvantaged group status, all practices tending to stigmatize women as a group, or which contribute to the maintenance of their subordinate social status, would become legally suspect.[35]

This last point, I believe, should be central to the definition of SH.

Because SH has as its target the group of all women, this *group* suffers harm as a result of the behavior. Indeed, when any one woman is in any way sexually harassed, all women are harmed. The group harm SH causes is different from the harm suffered by particular women as individuals: it is often more vague in nature as it is not easily causally tied to any particular incident of harassment. The group harm has to do primarily with the fact that the behavior reflects and reinforces sexist attitudes that women are inferior to men and that they do and ought to occupy certain sex roles. For example, comments and behavior that relegate women to the role of sex objects reinforce the belief that women *are* sex objects and that they *ought to* occupy this sex role. Similarly, when a female professor's cogent comments at department colloquia are met with frowns and rolled eyes from her colleagues, this behavior reflects and reinforces the view that women are not fit to occupy positions men arrogate to themselves.

The harm women suffer as a group from any single instance of SH is significant. It takes many forms. A Kantian analysis would show what is wrong with being solely a sex object. Though there is nothing wrong with being a caretaker or nurturer, etc., *per se*, it is sexist—and so wrong—to assign such roles to women. In addition, it is wrong to assign a person to a role she may not want to occupy. Basically women are not allowed to decide for themselves which roles they are to occupy, but this gets decided for them, no matter what they do. Even if some women occupy important positions in society that men traditionally occupy, they are still viewed as being sex objects, caretakers, etc., since all women are thought to be more "bodily" and emotional than men. This is a denial of women's autonomy, and degrading to them. It also contributes to women's oppression. The belief that women must occupy certain sex roles is both a cause and an effect of their oppression. It is a cause because women are believed to be more suited for certain roles given their association with body and emotions. It is an effect because once they occupy these roles and are victims of oppression, the belief that they must occupy these sex roles is reinforced.

Women are harmed by SH in yet another way. The belief that they are sex objects, caretakers, etc., gets reflected in social and political practices in ways that are unfair to women. It has undoubtedly meant many lost opportunities that are readily available to men. Women are not likely to be hired for jobs that require them to act in ways other than the ways the sex roles dictate, and if they are, what is expected of them is different from what is expected of men. Mothers are not paid for their work, and caretakers are not paid well in comparison to jobs traditionally held by men. Lack of economic reward is paralleled by lack of respect and appreciation for those occupying such roles. Certain rights granted men are likely not to be granted women (e.g., the right to bodily self-determination, and marriage rights).

Another harm SH causes all women is that the particular form sex stereotyping takes promotes two myths: (1) that male behavior is normally and naturally predatory, and (2) that females naturally (because they are taken to be primarily bodily and emotional) and even willingly acquiesce despite the appearance of protest.[36] Because the behavior perpetuated by these myths is taken to be normal, it is not seen as sexist, and in turn is not counted as SH.

The first myth is that men have stronger sexual desires than women, and harassment is just a natural venting of these desires which men are unable to control. The truth is, first, that women are socialized *not* to vent their sexual desires in the way men do, but this does not mean these desires are weaker or less prevalent. Masters and Johnson have "decisively established that women's sexual requirements are no less potent or urgent than those of men."[37] But second, SH has nothing to do with men's sexual desires, nor is it about seduction; instead, it is about oppression of women. Indeed, harassment generally does not lead to sexual satisfaction, but it often gives the harasser a sense of power.

The second myth is that women either welcome, ask for, or deserve the harassing treatment. Case law reveals this mistaken belief. In *Lipsett v. Rive-Mora*[38] (1987), the plaintiff was discharged from a medical residency program because she "did not react favorably to her professor's requests to go out for drinks, his compliments about her hair and legs, or to questions about her personal and romantic life."[39] The court exonerated the defendant because the plaintiff initially reacted favorably by smiling when shown lewd drawings of herself and when called sexual nicknames as she thought she had to appease the physician. The court said that "given the plaintiff's admittedly favorable responses to these flattering comments, there was no way anyone could consider them as 'unwelcome.'"[40] The court in *Swentek v. US Air*[41] (1987) reacted similarly when a flight attendant who was harassed with obscene remarks and gestures was denied legal recourse because previously she used vulgar language and openly discussed her sexual encounters. The court concluded that "she was the kind of person who could not be offended by such comments and therefore welcomed them generally."[42]

The idea that women welcome "advances" from men is seen in men's view of the way women dress. If a woman dresses "provocatively" by men's standards, she is said to welcome or even deserve the treatment she gets. One explanation harassing professors give for their behavior is that they are bombarded daily with the temptation of physically desirable young women who dress in what they take to be revealing ways.[43] When the case becomes public, numerous questions arise about the attractiveness of the victim, as if she were to blame for being attractive and the consequences thereof. Catcallers often try to justify their behavior by claiming that the victim should expect such behavior, given her tight-fitting dress or shorts, low-cut top, high heels, etc. This way of thinking infests discussions of rape in attempts to establish that women want to be raped, and it is mistaken in that context, too. The myth that women welcome or encourage harassment is designed "to keep women in their place" as men see it. The truth of the matter is that the perpetrator alone is at fault.

Both myths harm all women as they sanction SH by shifting the burden on the victim and all members of her sex: women must either go out of their way to avoid "natural" male behavior, or establish conclusively that they did not in any way want the behavior. Instead of the behavior being seen as sexist, it is seen as women's problem to rectify.

Last, but certainly not least, women suffer group harm from SH because they come to be stereotyped as victims.[44] Many men see SH as something they can do to women, and in many cases, get away with. Women come to see themselves as victims, and come to believe that the roles they can occupy are only the sex roles men have designated for them. Obviously these harms are quite serious for women, so the elimination of all forms of SH is warranted.

I have spoken so far as if it is only men who can sexually harass women, and I am now in a position to defend this controversial view. When a woman engages in the very same behavior harassing men engage in, the underlying message implicit in male-to-female harassment is missing. For example, when a woman scans a man's body, she might be considering him to be a sex object, but all the views about domination and being relegated to certain sex roles are absent. She cannot remind the man that he is inferior because of his sex, since given the way things are in society, he is not. In general, women cannot harm or degrade or dominate men as group, for it is impossible to send the message that one dominates (and so cause group harm) if one does not dominate. Of course, if the sexist roles predominant in our society were reversed, women could sexually harass men. The way things are, any bothersome behavior a woman engages in, even though it may be of a sexual nature, does not constitute SH because it lacks the social impact present in male-to-female harassment. Tort law would be sufficient to protect against this behavior, since it is unproblematic in these cases that tort law fails to recognize group harm.

IV. Subjective v. Objective Definitions of Sexual Harassment

Most definitions of "sexual harassment" make reference to the behavior's being "unwelcome" or "annoying" to the victim. *Black's Law Dictionary* defines "harassment" as a term used "to describe words, gestures and actions which tend to annoy, alarm and abuse (verbally) another person."[45] The *American Heritage Dictionary* defines "harass" as "to disturb or irritate persistently," and states further that "[h]arass implies systematic persecution by besetting with annoyances, threats, or demands."[46] The EEOC *Guidelines* state that behavior constituting SH is identified as "unwelcome sexual advances, requests for sexual favors, and other verbal or physical conduct of a sexual nature."[47] In their philosophical account of SH,

Hughes and May define "harassment" as "a class of annoying or unwelcome acts undertaken by one person (or group of persons) against another person (or group of persons)."[48] And Rosemarie Tong takes the feminists' definition of noncoercive SH to be that which "denotes sexual misconduct that merely annoys or offends the person to whom it is directed."[49]

The criterion of "unwelcomeness" or "annoyance" is reflected in the way the courts have handled cases of SH, as in *Lipsett*, *Swentek*, and *Meritor*, though in the latter case the court said that the voluntariness of the victim's submission to the defendant's sexual conduct did not mean that she welcomed the conduct.[50] The criterion of unwelcomeness or annoyance present in these subjective accounts of harassment puts the burden on the victim to establish that she was sexually harassed. There is no doubt that many women *are* bothered by this behavior, often with serious side-effects including anything from anger, fear, and guilt,[51] to lowered self-esteem and decreased feelings of competence and confidence,[52] to anxiety disorders, alcohol and drug abuse, coronary disturbances, and gastro-intestinal disorders.[53]

Though it is true that many women are bothered by the behavior at issue, I think it is seriously mistaken to say that whether the victim is bothered determines whether the behavior constitutes SH. This is so for several reasons.

First, we would have to establish that the victim was bothered by it, either by the victim's complaints, or by examining the victim's response to the behavior. The fact of the matter is that many women are quite hesitant to report being harassed, for a number of reasons. Primary among them is that they fear negative consequences from reporting the conduct. As is often the case, harassment comes from a person in a position of institutional power, whether he be a supervisor, a company-president, a member of a dissertation committee, the chair of the department, and so on. Unfortunately for many women, as a review of the case law reveals, their fears are warranted.[54] Women have been fired, their jobs have been made miserable forcing them to quit, professors have handed out unfair low grades, and so on. Worries about such consequences means that complaints are not filed, or are filed years after the incident, as in the Anita Hill v. Thomas Clarence case. But this should not be taken to imply that the victim was not harassed.

Moreover, women are hesitant to report harassment because they do not want anything to happen to the perpetrator, but just want the behavior to stop.[55] Women do not complain because they do not want to deal with the perpetrator's reaction when faced with the charge. He might claim that he was "only trying to be friendly." Women are fully aware that perpetrators can often clear themselves quite easily, especially in tort law cases where the perpetrator's intentions are directly relevant to whether he is guilty. And most incidents of SH occur without any witnesses—many perpetrators plan it this way. It then becomes the harasser's word against the victim's. To complicate matters, many women are insecure and doubt themselves. Women's insecurity is capitalized upon by harassers whose behavior is in the least bit ambiguous. Clever harassers who fear they might get caught or be reported often attempt to get on the good side of their victim in order to confuse her about the behavior, as well as to have a defense ready in case a charge is made. Harassers might offer special teaching assignments to their graduate students, special help with exams and publications, promotions, generous raises, and the like. Of course, this is all irrelevant to whether he harasses, but the point is that it makes the victim less likely to complain. On top of all this, women's credibility is very often questioned (unfairly) when they bring forth a charge. They are taken to be "hypersensitive." There is an attitude among judges and others that women must "develop a thick skin."[56] Thus, the blame is shifted off the perpetrator and onto the victim. Given this, if a woman thinks she will get no positive response—or, indeed, will get a negative one—from complaining, she is unlikely to do so.

Further, some women do not recognize harassment for what it is, and so will not complain. Sometimes this is because they are not aware of their own oppression, or actually seem to endorse sexist stereotypes. I recall a young woman who received many catcalls on the streets of Daytona Beach, Florida during spring break, and who was quite proud that her body could draw such attention. Given that women are socialized into believing their bodies are the most important feature of themselves, it is no surprise that a fair number of them are complacent about harassing behavior directed at them. Sandra Bartky provides an interesting analysis of why every woman is not a feminist, and I think it holds even for women who understand the issue.[57] Since for many women having a body felt to be "feminine" is crucial to their identity and to their sense of self "as a sexually desiring and desirable subject," feminism "may well be apprehended by a woman as something that threatens her with desexualization, if not outright annihilation."[58] The many women who resist becoming feminists are not likely to perceive harassing behavior as bothersome. It would be incorrect to conclude that the behavior is not harassment on the grounds that such victims are not bothered. What we have is a no win situation for victims: if the behavior bothers a woman she often has good reason not to complain; and if it does not bother her, she will not complain. Either way, the perpetrator wins. So we cannot judge whether women are bothered by the behavior on the basis of whether they say they are bothered.

Moreover, women's *behavior* is not an accurate indicator of whether they are bothered. More often than not, women try to ignore the perpetrator's behavior in an attempt not to give the impression they are encouraging it. They often cover up their true feelings so that the perpetrator does not have the satisfaction that his harassing worked. Since women are taught to smile and put up with this behavior, they might actually appear to enjoy it to some extent. Often they have no choice but to continue interacting with the perpetrator, making it very difficult to assert themselves. Women often make up excuses for not "giving in" instead of telling the perpetrator to stop. The fact that their behavior does not indicate they are bothered should not be used to show they were not bothered. In reality, women are fearful of defending themselves in the face of men's power and physical strength. Given the fact that the courts have decided that a lot of this behavior should just be tolerated, it is no wonder that women try to make the best of their situation.

It would be wrong to take a woman's behavior to be a sign that she is bothered also because doing so implies the behavior is permissible if she does not seem to care. This allows the *perpetrator* to be the judge of whether a woman is harassed, which is unjustifiable given the confusion among men about whether their behavior is bothersome or flattering. Sexual harassment should be treated no differently than crimes where harm to the victim is assessed in some objective way, independent of the perpetrator's beliefs. To give men this power in the case of harassment is to perpetuate sexism from all angles.

An *objective* view of SH avoids the problems inherent in a subjective view. According to the objective view defended here, what is decisive in determining whether behavior constitutes SH is not whether the victim is bothered, but whether the behavior is an instance of a practice that expresses and perpetuates the attitude that the victim and members of her sex are inferior because of their sex. Thus the Daytona Beach case counts as a case of SH because the behavior is an instance of a practice that reflects men's domination of women in that it relegates women to the role of sex objects.[59]

The courts have to some extent tried to incorporate an objective notion of SH by invoking the "reasonable person" standard. The EEOC *Guidelines*, as shown earlier, define SH partly as behavior that "has the purpose or effect of unreasonably interfering with an individual's work performance...."[60] The *Restatement of Torts*, referring to the tort of intentional infliction of emotional distress, states that the emotional distress must be "so severe that no *reasonable* man could be expected to endure it."[61]

In various cases the courts have invoked a reasonable man (or person) standard, but *not* to show that women who are not bothered still suffer harassment. Instead, they used the standard to show that even though a particular woman *was* bothered, she would have to tolerate such behavior because it was behavior a reasonable person would not have been affected by. In *Rabidue v. Osceola Refining Co.*[62] (1986), a woman complained that a coworker made obscene comments about women in general and her in particular. The court ruled that "a reasonable person would not have been significantly affected be the same or similar circumstances,"[63] and that "women must expect a certain amount of demeaning conduct in certain work environments."[64]

But the reasonable man standard will not work, since men and women perceive situations involving SH quite differently. The reasonable person standard fares no better as it becomes the reasonable man standard when it is applied by male judges seeing things through male eyes. Studies have shown that sexual overtures that men find flattering are found by women to be insulting. And even when men recognize behavior as harassment, they think women will be flattered by it.[65] The differences in perception only strengthen my point about the group harm that SH causes all women: unlike women, men can take sexual overtures directed at them to be complimentary because the overtures do not signify the stereotyping that underlies SH of women. A reasonable man standard would not succeed as a basis upon which to determine SH, as its objectivity is outweighed by the disparity found in the way the sexes assess what is "reasonable."

Related to this last topic is the issue of the harasser's intentions. In subjective definitions this is the counterpart to the victim's being bothered. Tort law makes reference to the injurer's intentions: in battery tort, the harasser's intent to contact, in assault tort, the harasser's intent to arouse psychic apprehension in the victim, and in the tort of intentional emotional distress, the harasser's intent or recklessness, must be established in order for the victim to win her case.

But like the victim's feelings, the harasser's intentions are irrelevant to whether his behavior is harassment. As I just pointed out, many men do not take their behavior to be bothersome, and sometimes even mistakenly believe that women enjoy crude compliments about their bodies, ogling, pinching, etc. From perusing cases brought before the courts, I have come to believe that many men have psychological feelings of power over women, feelings of being in control of their world, and the like, when they harass. These feelings might be subconscious, but this should not be admitted as a defense of the harasser. Also, as I have said, many men believe women encourage SH either by their dress or language, or simply by the fact that they tolerate the abuse without protest (usually out of fear of repercussion). In light of these facts, it would be wrongheaded to allow the harasser's intentions to count in assessing harassment, though they might become relevant in determining punishment. I am arguing for an objective definition of SH: it is the attitudes embedded and reflected *in the practice* the behavior is an instance of, not the attitudes or intentions of *the perpetrator*, that makes the behavior SH.

Yet the idea that the behavior must be directed at a certain person in order for it to count as harassment, seems to suggest that intentions do count in assessing harassment. This feature is evident both in my definition, as well as in that found in *Black's Law Dictionary* which takes harassment to be conduct directed against a specific person causing substantial emotional distress. If conduct is directed at a particular individual, it seems that the person expressing himself must be intentionally singling out that individual, wanting to cause her harm.

I think this is mistaken. Since the harasser can subconsciously enjoy the feeling of power harassing

gives him, or might even consider his behavior to be flattering, his behavior can be directed at a specific person (or group of persons) without implying any ill intention on his part. By "directed at a particular individual," I mean that the behavior is in some way observed by a particular person (or persons). This includes, for example, sexist comments a student hears her professor say, pornographic pictures a worker sees, etc. I interpret it loosely enough to include a person's overhearing sexist comments even though the speaker has no idea the person is within earshot (sometimes referred to as "nondirected behavior"). But I interpret it to exclude the bare knowledge that sexist behavior is going on (e.g., female employees knowing that there are pornographic pictures hidden in their boss's office). If it did not exclude such behavior it would have to include knowledge of *any* sexist behavior, even if no person who can be harmed by it ever observes it (e.g., pornographic magazines strewn on a desert island). Though such behavior is sexist, it fails to constitute SH.

V. Implications of the Objective Definition

One implication of my objective definition is that it reflects the correct way power comes into play in SH. Traditionally, SH has been taken to exist only between persons of unequal power, usually in the workplace or an educational institution. It is believed that SH in universities occurs only when a professor harasses a student, but not *vice versa*. It is said that students can cause "sexual hassle," because they cannot "destroy [the professor's] self-esteem or endanger his intellectual self-confidence," and professors "seldom suffer the complex psychological effects of sexual harassment victims."[66] MacKinnon, in her earlier book, defines SH as "the unwanted imposition of sexual requirements in the context of a relationship of unequal power."[67]

Though it is true that a lot of harassment occurs between unequals, it is false that harassment occurs *only* between unequals: equals and subordinates can harass. Indeed, power is irrelevant to tort law, and the courts now recognize harassment among coworkers under Title VII.

The one sense in which it is true that the harasser must have power over his victim is that men have power—social, political, and economic—over women as a group. This cannot be understood by singling out individual men and showing that they have power over women or any particular woman for that matter. It is power that all men have, in virtue of being men. Defining SH in the objective way I do allows us to see that this is the sense in which power exists in SH in all of its forms. The benefit of not restricting SH to cases of unequal institutional power is that all victims are afforded protection.

A second implication of my definition is that it gives the courts a way of distinguishing SH from sexual attraction. It can be difficult to make this distinction, since "traditional courtship activities" are often quite sexist and frequently involve behavior that is harassment. The key is to examine the practice the behavior is an instance of. If the behavior reflects the attitude that the victim is inferior because of her sex, then it is SH. Sexual harassment is not about a man's attempting to date a woman who is not interested, as the courts have tended to believe; it is about domination, which might be reflected, of course, in the way a man goes about trying to get a date. My definition allows us to separate cases of SH from genuine sexual attraction by forcing the courts to focus on the social nature of SH.

Moreover, defining SH in the objective way I do shifts the burden and the blame off the victim. On the subjective view, the burden is on the victim to prove that she is bothered significantly enough to win a tort case, or under Title VII, to show that the behavior unreasonably interfered with her work. In tort law, where the perpetrator's intentions are allowed to figure in, the blame could easily shift to the victim by showing that she in some way welcomed or even encouraged the behavior thereby relinquishing the perpetrator from responsibility. By focusing on the practice the behavior is an instance of, my definition has nothing to do with proving that the victim responds a certain way to the behavior, nor does it in any way blame the victim for the behavior.

Finally, defining SH in a subjective way means that the victim herself must come forward and complain, as it is her response that must be assessed. But given that most judges, law enforcement officers, and even superiors are men, it is difficult for women to do so. They are embarrassed, afraid to confront someone of the same sex as the harasser who is likely not to see the problem. They do not feel their voices will be heard. Working with my definition will I hope assuage this. Recognizing SH as a group harm will allow women to come to each other's aid as co-complainers, thereby alleviating the problem of reticence. Even if the person the behavior is directed at does not feel bothered, other women can complain, as they suffer the group harm associated with SH.

VI. Conclusion

The definition of SH I have defended in this paper has as its main benefit that it acknowledges the group harm SH causes all women, thereby getting to the heart of what is wrong with SH. By doing so, it protects all victims in all cases from even the most subtle kinds of SH, since all cases of SH have in common group harm.

Of course, as with any definition, problems exist. Though space does not allow that I deal with them, a few are worth mentioning. One is that many behaviors will count as SH, leading perhaps to an unmanageable number of claims. Another is that it will still be a matter of interpretation whether a given behavior meets the criteria for SH. Perhaps the most crucial objection is that since so many kinds of behavior count as SH, the right to free speech will be curtailed in unacceptable ways.[68]

I believe there are at least partial solutions to these problems. My proposal is only programmatic, and a thorough defense of it would include working through these and other problems. Such a defense will have to wait.

NOTES

1 Rosemarie Tong, "Sexual Harassment," in *Women and Values*, Marilyn Pearsall, ed., (Belmont, CA: Wadsworth Publishing Company, 1986), 148-66. Tong cites a *Redbook* study that reported 88 per cent of 9,000 readers sampled experienced some sort of sexual harassment (149).

2 Civil Rights Act of 1964, 42 U.S.C. Sec. 2000e-2(a) (1982).

3 Catharine A. MacKinnon, *Sexual Harassment of Working Women: A Case of Sex Discrimination* (New Haven: Yale University Press, 1979).

4 EEOC *Guidelines on Discrimination Because of Sex*, 29 C.F.R Sec. 1604.11(a) (1980).

5 The case was a landmark case because it established (1) federal legislation that SH is a form of sex discrimination, (2) that just because the victim "voluntarily" submitted to advances from her employer, it did not mean she welcomed the conduct, (3) that victims could appeal on grounds of emotional harm, not merely economic harm. For an excellent discussion of the history of the case as it went through the courts, see Joel T. Andreesen, "Employment Discrimination—The Expansion in Scope of Title VII to Include Sexual Harassment as a Form of Sex Discrimination," *Meritor Savings Bank, FSB v. Vinson, The Journal of Corporation Law*, Vol. 12, No. 3 (Spring, 1987), 619-38.

6 *Meritor Savings Bank, FSB v. Vinson*, 477 U.S. 57 (1986).

7 Joyce L. Richard, "Sexual Harassment and Employer Liability," *Southern University Law Review*, Vol. 12 (1986), 251-79. See 272-75 for an excellent discussion of the case.

8 Title IX of the Education Amendments of 1972, 20 USC. Sec. 1681 (1982).

9 For a very good discussion of the case law regarding Title IX, see Walter B. Connolly, Jr., and Alison B. Marshall, "Sexual Harassment of University or College Students by Faculty Members," *The Journal of College and University Law*, Vol. 15 (Spring, 1989), 381-403.

10 *Black's Law Dictionary*, 6th ed. (St. Paul, MN: West Publishing Co., 1990), 1248.

11 Michael D. Vhay, "The Harms of Asking: Towards a Comprehensive Treatment of Sexual Harassment," *The University of Chicago Law Review*, Vol. 55 (Winter, 1988), 334.

In the case of students, *quid pro quo* harassment can take the form of a professor threatening the student with a lower grade if she does not comply with his demands.

12 Ellen Frankel Paul, "Sexual Harassment as Sex Discrimination: A Defective Paradigm," *Yale Law & Policy Review*, Vol. 8, No. 2 (1990), 341.

13 EEOC *Guidelines, op. cit.*, at Sec. 1604.11(a).

14 *Black's Law Dictionary, op. cit.*, 470. It cites *Rich v. Martin Manetta Corp.*; D.C.Colo., 467 F.Supp. 587, 608.

15 *Topical Law Reports* (New York: Commerce Clearing House, Inc., 1988), 3030.

16 John C. Hughes and Larry May, "Sexual Harassment," *Social Theory and Practice*, Vol. 6, No. 3 (Fall, 1980), 260.

17 Frankel Paul, *op. cit.*, 337.

18 See Frankel Paul, Ibid., 359-60, for a list of cases invoking torts along with Title VII claims.

19 Rosemarie Tong, *Women, Sex, and the Law* (Savage, MD: Rowman and Littlefield Publishers, Inc., 1984), 71.

20 Frank J. Till, *Sexual Harassment: A Report on the Sexual Harassment of Students* (Washington, DC: National Advisory Council on Women's Educational Programs, 1980), pt. II, 13.

21 Ibid., 14.

22 Tong, *Women, Sex, and the Law, op. cit.*, 73.

23 *Restatement (Second) of Torts* Sec.46 (1965) comment a.

24 Ibid.

25 Ibid., comment j.

26 EEOC *Guidelines*, 29 C.F.R, Sec. 1604.11(b) (1985).

27 Mari J. Matsuda, "Public Response to Racist Speech: Considering the Victim's Story," *Michigan Law Review*, Vol. 87, No. 8 (August, 1989), 2345-2381.

28 Ibid., 2345, 2344.

29 Ibid., 2345.

30 Ibid., 2346.

31 Ibid., 2348.

32 This suggests that only men can sexually harass women. I will defend this view later in the paper.

33 Frances Conley, a 50-year-old distinguished neurophysician at Stanford University, recently came forward with this story. Conley resigned after years of putting up with sexual harassment from her colleagues. Not only did they use Playboy spreads during their lectures, but they routinely called her "hon," invited her to bed, and fondled her legs under the operating table. *Chicago Tribune*, Sunday, June 9, 1991. Section 1, 22.

34 Hughes and May, *op. cit.*, 264-65.

35 Ibid., 265.

36 These same myths surround the issue of rape. This is discussed fruitfully by Lois Pineau in "Date Rape: A Feminist Analysis," *Law and Philosophy* Vol. 8 (1989), 217-43.

37 MacKinnon, *op. cit.*, 152, is where she cites the study.

38 *Lipsett v. Rive-Mora*, 669 F.Supp. 1188 (D. Puerto Rico 1987).

39 Dawn D. Bennett-Alexander, "Hostile Environment Sexual Harassment: A Clearer View," *Labor Law Journal*, Vol. 42, No. 3 (March, 1991), 135.

40 Lipsett, *op. cit.*, Sec. 15.

41 *Swentek v. US Air*, 830 F.2d 552 (4th Cir. 1987).

42 *Swentek v. US Air*, Ibid., 44 Epd at 552.

43 Billie Wright Dziech and Linda Weiner, *The Lecherous Professor: Sexual Harassment on Campus* (Boston: Beacon Press, 1984), 63.

44 This harm is similar to the harm Ann Cudd finds with rape. Since women are the victims of rape, "they come to be seen as in need of protection, as weak and passive, and available to all men." See Ann E. Cudd, "Enforced Pregnancy, Rape, and the Image of Woman," *Philosophical Studies*, Vol. 60 (1990), 47-59.

45 *Black's Law Dictionary, op. cit.*, 717.

46 *American Heritage Dictionary of the English Language* (New York: American Heritage Publishing Co., Inc., 1973), 600.

47 EEOC *Guidelines, op. cit.*, Sec. 1604.11(a).

48 Hughes and May, *op. cit.*, 250.

49 Tong, *Women, Sex, and the Law, op. cit.*, 67.

50 *Meritor, op. cit.*, at 1113-16.

51 MacKinnon, *op. cit.*, 83.

52 Stephanie Riger, "Gender Dilemmas in Sexual Harassment Policies and Procedures," *American Psychologist*, Vol. 46 (1991), 497-505.

53 Martha Sperry, "Hostile Environment Sexual Harassment and the Imposition of Liability Without Notice: A Progressive Approach to Traditional Gender Roles and Power Based Relationships," *New England Law Review*, Vol. 24 (1980), 942, fns. 174 and 175.

54 See Catharine MacKinnon, *Feminism Unmodified: Discourses on Life and Law* (Cambridge: Harvard University Press, 1987), Chapter Nine, for a nice discussion of the challenges women face in deciding whether to report harassment. See also Ellen Frankel Paul, *op. cit.*, for an excellent summary of the case law on sexual harassment.

55 MacKinnon, *Sexual Harassment of Working Women, op. cit.*, 83.

56 See Frankel Paul, *op. cit.*, 333-65. Frankel Paul wants to get away from the "helpless victim syndrome," making women responsible for re-

porting harassment, and placing the burden on them to develop a tough skin so as to avoid being seen as helpless victims (362-63). On the contrary, what Frankel Paul fails to understand is that placing these additional burdens on women detracts from the truth that they are victims, and implies that they deserve the treatment if they do not develop a "tough attitude."

57 Sandra Bartky, "Foucault, Femininity and the Modernization of Patriarchal Power," in Sandra Bartky, *Femininity and Domination: Studies in the Phenomenology of Oppression* (New York: Routledge, Chapman, and Hall, Inc., 1990), 63-82. See especially 77-78.

58 Ibid., 77.

59 This case exemplifies my point that the behavior need not be persistent in order to construct harassment, despite the view of many courts. One catcall, for example, will constitute SH if catcalling is shown to be a practice reflecting domination.

60 EEOC *Guidelines, op. cit.*, Sec. 1604.11(a), my emphasis.

61 *Restatement (Second) of Torts*, Sec. 146, (1965), comment j, my emphasis.

62 *Rabidue v. Osceola Refining Co.*, 805 F2d (1986), Sixth Circuit Court.

63 Ibid., at 622.

64 Ibid., at 620-22.

65 Stephanie Riger, "Gender Dilemmas in Sexual Harassment Policies and Procedures," *American Psychologist*, Vol. 46. No. 5 (May 1991), 499 is where she cites the relevant studies.

66 Wright Dziech and Weiner, *op. cit.*, 24.

67 MacKinnon, *Sexual Harassment of Working Women, op. cit.*, 1. It is actually not clear that MacKinnon endorses this definition throughout this book, as what she says seems to suggest that harassment can occur at least between equals. In her most recent book, she recognizes that harassment "also happens among coworkers, from third parties, even by subordinates in

the workplace, men who are women's hierarchical inferiors or peers." Catharine A. MacKinnon, *Feminism Unmodified: Discourses on Life and Law* (Cambridge: Harvard University Press, 1987), 107.

68 For an excellent analysis on sexist speech and the limits of free speech as guaranteed by the Constitution, see Marcy Strauss, "Sexist Speech in the Workplace," *Harvard Civil Rights and Civil Liberties Law Review*, Vol. 25 (1990), 1-51. She cites the relevant case law concerning sexist speech that is not protected by First Amendment rights. She defends the view that the Constitution can prohibit speech demanding or requesting sexual relationships, sexually explicit speech directed at the woman, and degrading speech directed at the woman, but not sexually explicit or degrading speech that the woman employee knows exists in the workplace, even though it is not directed at her (43). She employs an interesting and useful distinction between speech that discriminates, and speech that merely advocates discrimination, recognizing that the state has an interest in regulating the former, given the harm it can cause.

◆ ◆ ◆ ◆ ◆

STEPHEN GRIFFITH

Sexual Harassment and the Rights of the Accused

Much of America sat transfixed before their television sets during the Supreme Court confirmation hearings for Judge Clarence Thomas while Anita Hill accused him of sexual harassment. The main topic of debate for most people following the hearings was whether it was Anita Hill or Clarence Thomas that was telling the truth, since their testimony was directly contradictory and there was essentially no independent evidence on either side. From a philosophical point of view, however, the most important issue illustrated by this whole affair concerns the nature of sexual harassment in itself. What is sexual harassment anyway, and why is it wrong, if it is? Even if Clarence Thomas did everything Anita Hill says he did, was his behavior seriously immoral, so much so as to justify denying him a seat on the Supreme Court? Opinions on this subject seem to range from saying that behavior of the sort alleged is the moral equivalent of rape to saying that it is simply a bit rude and inappropriate in the context within which it supposedly occurred. More recently, the President of the United States himself has been accused of sexual harassment. Although many people have reacted differently to this case than to that involving Justice Thomas, the wide variety of reactions to both of these cases and the vehemence of many of those reactions suggest that there is considerable confusion concerning the broad issue of sexual harassment which a careful philosophical analysis might help to alleviate.

Sexual misconduct of various sorts has become an increasingly serious problem in our society and must be dealt with both carefully and effectively whenever and wherever it occurs. All too frequently, individuals are sexually abused or assaulted by spouses, lovers, or total strangers, coerced into unwanted sexual activity by superiors, or subjected to unwanted sexual attention or embarrassment.[1] In response to these problems, a just society must have just and effective legislation: public and private institutions and corporations must have effective and fair policies and procedures; both this legislation and these policies and procedures must be consistent with the basic principles of justice, morality and fairness. The case for developing and implementing such legislation and policies has been made often and well, much progress along these lines has been made, and much more still needs to be done. Unfortunately, however, as is often the case in situations involving deeply felt causes, the understandable zeal for dealing with these problems has produced definitions of sexual harassment and attendant legislation and policies which contain the potential for serious abuse of human rights, especially the rights of the accused, and judging from various reports appearing in the media, the implementation of such policies and procedures has actually resulted in such abuse in some cases, especially in the groves of academe. The problem has been well expressed by a character in *Disclosure*, Michael Crichton's novel about sexual harassment:

> "the problem is that there's that third category, somewhere in the middle, between the two extremes," Fernandez said. "Where the behavior is gray. It's not clear who did what to whom. That's the largest category of complaints we see. So far, society's tended to focus on the problems of the victim, not the problems of the accused. But the accused has problems, too. A harassment claim is a weapon, Bob, and there are no good defenses against it. Anybody can use the weapon—and lots of people have."[2]

With regard to the problems of the accused, Maatman says the following:

> Many times the accused harasser must prove a negative: that harassment never took place. Putting aside legal liability, the mere charge of unwelcome sexual conduct itself can oftentimes destroy a career or stamp the accused as being of suspect morals and deficient judgment. Not surprisingly, sexual harassment complaints have the potential for malicious use, whereby an employee falsely asserts the charge as a weapon of retaliation, extortion, or to prevent or insulate a critical review of their own job performance.[3]

Although abuses of this sort may happen and continue to happen in only a small percentage of cases, the fact that any one instance of such abuse can deprive an innocent person of a livelihood, a career, or a good name suggests that we should be mindful of such possible abuses and take steps to minimize this possibility. My purpose in this paper is to suggest the adoption of a more precise definition of sexual harassment than those usually given and to illustrate how some of the abuses which are possible in the implementation of typical existing policies and procedures might thereby be avoided without significantly weakening the legitimate protections afforded by such policies.

The definition of sexual harassment given by the Equal Employment Opportunity Commission illustrates many of the problems referred to above. According to the EEOC,

> Unwelcome sexual advances, requests for sexual favors, and other verbal or physical conduct of a sexual nature constitute sexual harassment when
> (1) submission to such conduct is made either explicitly or implicitly a term or condition of an individual's employment;
> (2) submission to, or rejection of, such conduct by an individual is used as the basis for employment decisions affecting such, individual; or
> (3) such conduct has the purpose or effect of substantially interfering with an individual's work performance or creating an intimidating, hostile, or offensive working environment.[4]

The forms of conduct referred to in (1) and (2) fall under the rubric of what will be referred to in this paper as sexual coercion, a serious sexual offense which must be dealt with firmly and effectively whenever and wherever it occurs. Clause (3), on the other hand, taken at face value, could in principle be interpreted so as to apply to a wide variety of behaviors, some of which might not even be offensive to most normal people. This definition thus illustrates a regrettable tendency on the part of those most concerned with the issue of "sexual harassment" to define it much too broadly, so that all sorts of behavior, ranging from such serious sexual misconduct as rape to such relatively inconsequential behavior as the use of "inappropriate innuendo," are placed on a continuum and regarded as different forms of sexual harassment.[5] Thus, for example, gender harassment, seductive behavior, sexual bribery, sexual coercion, and sexual assault are all regarded by some writers as forms of sexual harassment.[6] Defining sexual harassment this broadly not only confuses the issue, but also has the unfortunate consequence that persons who have been accused of relatively minor offenses, often involving behavior which is not even morally blameworthy, are painted with the same accusatory brush as those accused of relatively serious crimes.[7] This has the doubly unfortunate effect of not only making relatively trivial offenses seem more serious than they are but also of trivializing more serious offenses.

There are several other problems with the EEOC definition of sexual harassment. In the first place, the crucial term "sexual" is left undefined, which leaves the entire scope of this definition unacceptably vague, as does the use of the term "substantially" in clause (3). In addition, its use of such subjective terms as "intimidating," "hostile," and "offensive" allows the accuser to define the offense, and the use of the expression "or effect" encourages us to ignore the intentions of the accused. Neither of these tendencies seems consistent with sound jurisprudence.

All of the above-mentioned defects in the EEOC definition of sexual harassment can be (and to a certain extent have been) substantially mitigated in courts of law. Some of the vagueness has been removed by precedent, and much potential abuse of the EEOC guidelines has doubtless been avoided by fair and experienced judges, impartial juries, rules of evidence, and all the other protections afforded the accused in our legal system. Unfortunately, however, the EEOC definition has also been used as a guideline for many corporate and institutional policies which are implemented in the absence of any of these protections, and it is here that most abuses have occurred.

I. Narrowing the Scope

The use which the term "sexual harassment" has come to have in both legal contexts and in scholarly work on this topic has probably become too entrenched to permit any hope that a narrower meaning can be given to the term at this time, but we can at least hope to distinguish more clearly among the wide variety of behaviors which are currently listed together under this heading. In particular, we can distinguish between those forms of behavior which ought reasonably to have been regarded as sexual harassment *per se* and other forms of sexual misconduct which have inappropriately come to be regarded as such.

A. Discrimination Based on Gender

As a first step, we can distinguish sexual misconduct in general from those offenses which involve unjustifiable discrimination on the basis of gender. Although most discrimination based on gender cannot be justified and should be eliminated whenever and wherever possible, a person's gender and sexual orientation must obviously play a differentiating role in that person's social interaction with other persons. Even if we find it prudent or necessary to limit the types of interaction which are permitted or encouraged in academic or workplace settings, it is not reasonable to stigmatize someone by accusing that person of sexual harassment simply in virtue of the fact that that person treats men and women differently in some respects in situations where this could reasonably be expected. Chivalry, for example, may be dead, and it is certainly "sexist." but its vestigial remnants are not offensive to reasonable people and can hardly be regarded as immoral.

What is more important, however, is that even unjustifiable discrimination on the basis of gender should not be regarded as an instance of "sexual" misconduct. It is simply an accident of the English language that the word "sex" and its cognates can refer either to sexual activity or to gender. It is perniciously discriminatory, for example, to prohibit women from pursuing certain careers on morally irrelevant grounds, but a person who does this is not thereby guilty of immoral sexual activity, and might in fact lead a morally exemplary life in that respect, despite having "sexist" views. It could be argued, of course, that there are in many cases important sociological and psychological links between discrimination on the basis of gender and what is here being referred to as sexual misconduct, and this is surely why they are so often regarded as different forms of the same thing (i.e., sexual harassment), but a similar point could be made concerning alcohol abuse. There are strong links of an even more obvious sort between alcohol abuse and sexual abuse, but that is no reason to regard alcohol abuse as a form of sexual misconduct or harassment. For most people, the term "sexual misconduct" and the term "discrimination" both have negative connotations, and appropriately so, but the former has a sort of "sleaziness" to it that the latter lacks. They imply completely different sorts of character flaws on the part of those to whom they can truthfully be applied, and this alone is reason enough to regard them as significantly different sorts of offenses. "Sexual" misconduct, including sexual harassment, ought to be defined as involving, either directly or indirectly, sexual activity of some sort, and discrimination on the basis of gender is not necessarily sexual in this sense.

B. Other Forms of Sexual Misconduct

Having distinguished discrimination based on gender from sexual misconduct, we must now distinguish various forms of sexual misconduct from each other. It will be useful to comment briefly upon those forms of sexual misconduct which have inappropriately become regarded as forms of sexual harassment before attempting to define sexual harassment *per se* more precisely.

1. Sexual Assault

The most serious and most obviously immoral type of sexual offense is sexual assault. This would apply not only to forcible rape as traditionally understood, but also to any form of clearly sexual behavior involving the use of physical force against a person without that person's consent. This is sometimes called "sexual imposition," especially in connection with less physically invasive forms of assault. Forcible rape, the most serious type of sexual assault, has long been regarded as a serious crime, and rightly so. It is clear that we must continue to develop and improve laws and institutional policies which deal effectively not only with forcible rape but also with other forms of sexual assault Although the EEOC definition does not regard sexual assault as a form of sexual harassment, there is a tendency among writers on this topic to list it as such, which may be motivated by an understandable desire on the part of those enraged by sexual harassment to taint it with the opprobrium commonly occasioned by instances of rape. Unfortunately, this runs the risk of having the Opposite effect of making sexual assault seem less serious than it is, especially since the vast majority of behaviors commonly regarded as sexually harassing are clearly less serious than sexual assault.

2. Sexual Coercion

The most serious type of sexual misconduct encompassed (inappropriately, according to our present argument) by the EEOC definition of sexual harassment is sexual coercion. It would be beyond the scope of this paper to attempt to define coercion *per se* in any detail. It will be sufficient for our present purposes simply to say that we are being coerced to do something if and only if (1) we are doing something which we would prefer not to do, and (2) we

are doing that thing primarily or entirely because someone else has unjustifiably threatened to harm us in some way if we do not. One is then guilty of sexual coercion if and only if one has coerced someone into engaging in sexual activity. In other words, sexual coercion is coercive for the same reasons that other forms of coercion are coercive, and its coercive nature is sufficient in itself to make it wrong, whether or not there are additional reasons for so regarding it.

To the extent that coercion in general involves the threat of harm, the threatened harm may be either physical or nonphysical in nature. Sexual coercion involving the threat of physical harm thus differs from sexual assault as defined above in that the victim of sexual coercion has a "choice," in an admittedly perverse sense, whether to accede to the offender's demands or run the risk of suffering the threatened harm, whereas a victim of sexual assault has no choice in any sense of the term.

It is important to note that successful sexual coercion involving the threat of physical harm can often be more harmful to the victim than the corresponding form of sexual assault, since the victim must suffer not only the indignity of compliance with the offender's demands but also the psychological trauma of feeling partially responsible for the outcome, which trauma often occurs despite assurances to the victim that resistance should not have been expected given the nature of the threats involved and the unlikelihood that the resistance would have been successful. This may help to explain why coercing persons to engage in sexual intercourse by threatening them with physical harm has traditionally been regarded as a form of rape, even if no overpowering force is used and no physical harm of the sort threatened ensues.

Whether the threatened harm is physical or nonphysical, it is important to note that coercion takes place only when it is both reasonable for the purported victim to believe that a threat has been made and unreasonable for the purported offender to deny that a threat has been made. The mere fact that a potential offender is in a position to inflict harm upon a potential victim clearly does not imply that the potential victim has been threatened with this harm. Moreover, the mere fact that a potential victim *feels* threatened, and thus fears that harm will occur unless sexual favors are granted, does not imply that a threat has occurred, even if the potential victim subsequently engages in unwanted sexual activity solely as a result of this fear.

It is important to point out that this can be true even in some cases where the fear in question is perfectly reasonable. If Smith knows or reasonably believes that persons answering some particular description often inflict harm upon persons like him in certain sorts of circumstances, and if he encounters Jones, a person of this description, in these circumstances, it is perfectly reasonable for Smith to fear Jones. Unless, however, Jones or these circumstances are described in such a way as to be inherently threatening (e.g., "a man brandishing a knife" or "during an armed robbery"), Jones cannot be accused of coercing Smith simply because Jones makes a request of Smith that Smith grants only or primarily because of this reasonable fear. In other words, Jones cannot be held responsible for the fact that persons like Jones sometimes or even often harm others in similar circumstances. This is a perfectly general point that applies to any situation involving encounters between persons of different general descriptions who have been stereotyped in some way.[8]

The point here is not that threats must be explicitly stated in order to be coercive. Brandishing a weapon is clearly a threat of physical harm, and threats can often be subtle and covert but nonetheless conveyed and received. The point here, once again, is that a person is not guilty of sexual coercion unless that person's behavior is truly threatening, which implies not only that the purported victim can reasonably regard the purported offender's behavior as threatening, but also that the purported offender realizes (or is at least in such a position that

he or she can reasonably be faulted for not realizing) that this behavior is likely to be regarded as threatening. Thus, engaging in sexual activity with someone who is in a position to inflict some sort of harm, even if one does so solely because one is fearful that this harm will otherwise ensue, does not by itself entail that one is a victim of sexual coercion. One is coerced only when one is actually threatened with harm.

Unlike sexual assault, which has always been regarded as a serious offense, sexual coercion has traditionally been recognized as such only when the victim has been threatened with bodily harm. One positive development in recent years has been that legal and institutional protection, largely under the rubric of the first two clauses in the EEOC definition of sexual harassment, has been extended to potential victims of sexual coercion involving threats of other types of harm, such as harm to their educational or professional careers. Sexual coercion of this sort is the most serious offense typically regarded as a form of sexual harassment. As is true, albeit to a lesser extent, in the case of sexual assault, there are both conceptual and practical difficulties involved in trying to decide how to handle sexual coercion. Suppose, for example, that a spouse or lover threatens to break off a relationship unless sexual favors are granted, as often happens. Breaking off a relationship could often be regarded as Potentially harmful to the threatened person, and threatening to do so for this reason might be morally opprobrious but it is nevertheless difficult to see how we could justify making such behavior illegal. Laws and policies concerning sexual coercion are most easily justified in cases where there is an institutional or corporate "power differential" between potential offenders and victims, and there would now be at least a rough consensus that this form of behavior is morally unacceptable and should be dealt with effectively when it occurs within this sort of context. It would also appear that there would be no insuperable difficulties involved in reaching a consensus as to how these offenses should be defined.⁹ The seriousness of this offense, and the relative ease with which a consensus could be reached concerning not only how to define it but also that it is morally unacceptable, provide ample justification for regarding sexual coercion as a specific type of sexual offense, differing both from the equally serious offense of sexual assault and from less serious forms of sexual misconduct, including sexual harassment *per se*.

3. Sexual Offers

Another sort of behavior sometimes regarded as a form of sexual harassment might be called a "sexual offer." Sexual offers are of two sorts. The first sort of sexual offer is one in which a person offers to confer an otherwise undeserved benefit in exchange for sexual favors. The second sort of sexual offer is one in which a person offers to confer sexual favors in exchange for an otherwise undeserved benefit. Since the refusal to confer sexual favors or undeserved benefits cannot be regarded as "harmful" in the relevant sense, sexual offers do not constitute coercive threats and cannot be regarded as a special case of sexual coercion. There is a clear moral difference between using or threatening to use one's power to harm someone, which is *prima facie* immoral, and using or offering to use one's power to benefit someone, which is not. Moreover, the so-called power differential which looms so large in most cases of sexual coercion is not so clearly relevant here. Any situation in which a person who has the "power" to confer an undeserved benefit in exchange for sexual favors is likely to make such an offer is also a situation in which the person to whom such an offer is made has the "power" to offer sexual favors in exchange for these benefits. It cannot be assumed that the lure of undeserved benefits to someone in a position to confer sexual favors is any more "powerful" than the lure of sexual favors to someone in a position to confer undeserved benefits, so the "power" in such cases is reciprocal. Finally, if *making* a sexual offer is to

be regarded as an offense, it is presumably because the relationship that would ensue if the offer were accepted would be in some way illicit or inappropriate. It therefore follows that if making such an offer is to be regarded as an offense, accepting one should also be so regarded, and for the same reason. Thus, other things being equal, making or accepting either sort of sexual offer must be equally offensive, and any policy which mandates sanctions for making one sort of offer must mandate similar sanctions for making the other and for accepting either sort of offer as well.

Sexual offers as here defined are commonly referred to in sexual harassment literature as "sexual bribery." Referring to them in this way is problematic for several reasons, some of which are inherent in the concept of bribery itself. In general, bribery is regarded as an offense primarily in a political context. It occurs when a public official who is in a position to confer benefits as a result of holding the position that she holds confers unmerited benefits on someone in exchange for personal gain. It is regarded as an offense partly because it is unjust to those who actually deserve but do not receive the benefits thus conferred and also because it contradicts the purpose for which the official has been given the authority to bestow the benefits in question. Suppose, however, that an elected public official exercises her legitimate authority in such a way that it happens to benefit certain constituents more than others, and suppose that those particular constituents contribute heavily, but in accordance with (admittedly nonexistent) campaign financing laws generally regarded as fair, to the reelection campaign of that official. This would not constitute bribery unless there was an explicit or tacit understanding between the official and her constituents that the benefits in question were to be conferred in exchange for the contributions. The mere fact that benefits have been conferred and contributions made does not imply that bribery occurred or was even attempted. Finally, it could be argued that any law which flatly prohibits public officials from benefiting their constituents or flatly prohibits those constituents from contributing to the campaigns of the elected officials of their choice is at least an infringement, if not a violation, of their rights.[10]

Similar considerations apply in the case of so-called sexual bribery. Offering sexual favors, even to someone in a position to confer undeserved benefits, may be immoral for some reason, but does not necessarily constitute attempted bribery. Neither does requesting such favors from persons one is in a position to benefit constitute soliciting a bribe, even if it is immoral for some other reason. It is only when granting the benefit or favor is made conditional on granting the other that something resembling bribery has occurred or been attempted. Unless this condition is stated explicitly, which is not often the case, any allegation of bribery would have to be based on the contention that the condition was somehow implicit in the context in which the behavior took place. In cases of this sort, the motives and intentions of the parties involved are of paramount importance, and these are often not entirely clear, even to the persons themselves. A person may convince himself that he is acquiescing to a request for sexual favors from his superior because he is in love with her when he really just wants a promotion, and a person may convince herself that an underling who has acquiesced to her request for sexual favors really deserves a promotion, when she is really just in love with him. Great care must therefore be taken in attempting to adjudicate a situation in which someone is accused of sexual bribery. Sexual offers of either sort may be immoral for a variety of reasons, and it may be prudent for institutions to develop policies which attempt to regulate and monitor such behavior, but it could be argued that any policy which flatly prohibits competent adults from making or accepting unconditional sexual offers or requests is an infringement if not a violation of their rights, even if making or accepting such offers or requests is often morally opprobrious in many cases.

4. Sexual Boorishness

Sexual boorishness is nonthreatening, expressive behavior of a sexual nature which is patently offensive to a morally decent and psychologically normal adult of either gender. Obscene gestures, the public display of obscene or pornographic photographs or drawings, the use of obscene language, and otherwise rude sexual comments can all be examples of sexual boorishness in a wide variety of circumstances. Sexual boorishness is most appropriately regarded as sexual misconduct under two circumstances. The first is when it is directed against a particular person and constitutes an instance of sexual harassment *per se*, as will be explained later. The second is when it creates what is sometimes misleadingly referred to as a "hostile environment."[11] This typically refers to a situation in which a person cannot participate in some particular educational experience or engage in some particular mode of employment without being subjected to what has been defined above as sexually boorish behavior. The point of referring to an "environment" here is to emphasize the fact that the behavior in question need not be directed at any one individual in particular. If it seems to be directed toward or primarily offensive to persons of some particular sexual orientation or gender, it can be regarded as a form of discrimination and treated as such. The term "hostile," however, is misleading in this context, because it can refer either to the motives of those responsible for the environment or to those aspects of the environment which render it harmful independently of their source. It is appropriate to hold someone morally responsible for a hostile environment only if they themselves have hostile motives or are indifferent to various consequences of their behavior which they know to be harmful to others. Human beings often express hostility toward one another in a wide variety of ways and for a wide variety of reasons, having to do with race, religion, politics, and moral beliefs, as well as sex and gender, and those who do so can be held morally responsible for the consequences of their actions, but we are understandably reluctant to impose sanctions on persons who engage in such behavior except in highly specific circumstances. For one thing, various persons might unknowingly contribute to a "hostile" environment by unintentionally bringing about certain physically or psychologically harmful aspects of that environment. There is no evidence, other than pseudo-Freudian generalizations of various sorts, that persons who indulge in sexual innuendo or humor, for example, are necessarily expressing hostility toward members of the opposite sex, or realize that their behavior is offensive or harmful in any way, even if, as a matter of fact, it is. The remedy in this case is communication, not punishment, and not "counseling" of a sort which implies that the accused person is somehow mentally ill. Some people are brought up using ethnic slurs without even realizing that they are doing so.[12] The same is true of at least some sexual boorishness. In both cases, the persons in question are often unaware that their behavior is even offensive.

Although sexual boorishness can be morally opprobrious even when it does not constitute a sanctionable offense, any attempt to legislate it, either legally or through corporate or institutional policy, must take both cultural differences and the right to freedom of expression into account. Respect for cultural and personal differences is especially important in connection with comments concerning a person's sexual attractiveness, since comments of this sort which are enthusiastically welcomed by some persons may be offensive to others. It is a plain and simple fact, for example, that some persons are pleased and flattered when someone describes them as "sexy," whereas others are embarrassed or even deeply offended. This does not imply that we must tolerate behavior of the extreme sort common in the most sexist societies, but it does imply that we must avoid adopting sexually repressive codes of behavior favored only by those at the Opposite end of the spectrum, who have no more right to impose their values on others than anyone else does.

II. *Sexual Harassment* Per se

Sexual coercion and sexual assault are clearly unacceptable and ought to be dealt with effectively and fairly whenever and wherever they occur. Sexual boorishness and sexual offers are more problematic. It would be beyond the scope of this paper to attempt the difficult task of deciding exactly when such forms of behavior are justifiably sanctionable and when they are not, but with appropriate and important qualifications, we might be able to justify laws and policies which regulate or prohibit these sorts of behavior in certain circumstances. With regard to sexual harassment *per se*, the challenge is to define it in such a way as not only to distinguish it from unjustifiable discrimination based on gender and the various sorts of sexual misconduct discussed above, but also in such a way as to enable us to determine, at least in principle, whether someone is or is not guilty of this offense. Unless we are able to do this, it is difficult to justify either legal or institutional sanctions concerning sexual harassment.

It would seem that the proper place to begin in an attempt to define sexual harassment would be to say that it must be both clearly sexual in nature and clearly a form of harassment.[13] It would thus be useful at this point to discuss both what it means to say that a form of behavior is sexual in nature and what it means to say that it is a form of harassment.

A. Sexual Behavior

With regard to the term "sexual," there is both a broad and a narrow use of the term. In the broad sense of the term, psychologists and others constantly remind us that almost any form of behavior can be regarded as sexual in some context or other. Since in cases of alleged sexual harassment, the question as to whether a particular bit or pattern of behavior constitutes an offense so often hinges on whether that behavior is or is not "sexual" in nature, it is especially important for the purpose of crafting a policy statement concerning sexual harassment to adopt, at least at the outset, a more narrow definition. Otherwise, we run the risk of being forced to regard far too many different sorts of behavior as instances of sexual harassment, especially if we give the term "harassment" an equally broad or vague definition. Any law or policy which is sufficiently vague so as to enable us to regard almost anything as an offense is obviously both unwise and unjustifiable. (Cf. the charges brought against Socrates in Athens.)

It will thus be useful at this point to distinguish among (1) behavior which is *prima facie* sexual in nature, (2) behavior which is *prima facie* nonsexual, and (3) behavior which is neither. To say that a bit of behavior is *prima facie* sexual is simply to say that, due to some. inherent features of the behavior in itself, it is sexual *unless* there are contextual circumstances which render it nonsexual. Thus, for example, behavior involving physical contact with genitalia is ordinarily sexual in nature, but would not ordinarily be considered sexual in those cases in which it occurred in connection with some justifiable medical procedure. Similarly, behavior is *prima facie* nonsexual if there is nothing inherent in that behavior which renders it sexual. It can therefore be presumed to be nonsexual in nature *unless* there is something extraordinary about the circumstances in which it occurs which renders it sexual. Such things as playing chess or reading a novel, for example, could be regarded as sexual activities only in highly extraordinary circumstances. Finally, and most importantly within the present context, there are bits of behavior which cannot be *presumed* to be either sexual or nonsexual independently of the context in which they occur. On being told, for example, that X kissed Y, we are not justified in presuming either that X's behavior was sexual or that it was nonsexual unless we know something about the context. Kissing is often a sexual activity, but parents kissing their children on the forehead are seldom if ever engaged in sexual activity, unless we define the term "sexual" much too broadly to be useful in the present context.

The foregoing distinctions are applicable to all forms of sexual misconduct, but will be seen to be especially important in the context of sexual harassment.

B. Harassment

With regard to harassment, *Black's Law Dictionary* defines it as a "petty misdemeanor" which involves the use of "words, gestures, and actions which tend to annoy, alarm, and abuse (verbally) another person."[14] It does not ordinarily refer to any form of coercion or assault. If I attempt to coerce someone or strike them in such a way as to physically harm them, I am guilty of something significantly more serious than harassment. Moreover, offering to reward someone for doing something they would not otherwise do, or to do something of this sort in exchange for a reward, even in cases where it is morally unacceptable to do so, would not ordinarily be considered a form of harassment. In general terms, harassment refers only to behavior which is annoying or offensive, not to behavior which is seriously harmful, threatening, or tempting in a morally pernicious manner. It also seems clear that typically A is harassing B only if A is engaged in behavior toward B which is unwanted by B, is known by A to be unwanted by B, and which is nevertheless repeated by A. Thus, for example, if I tap someone on the shoulder and ask a reasonable question, this would not ordinarily be regarded as harassment. If, however, I continue to do so even after the person in question has made it clear that he would prefer that I not do so, this might constitute harassment, even though my behavior in this instance is not inherently immoral. We might add that a bit of behavior would not ordinarily be regarded as a form of harassment unless it is of a sort which a reasonable person might find objectionable or annoying. If I regularly say "good morning" to my neighbor as I drive off to work in the morning and he is offended by this, I can hardly be accused of harassment, especially if he does not indicate that he is offended by it. Moreover, if I regularly wear a blue shirt and he is offended by this, I cannot be accused of harassing him even if he *does* tell me it offends him. In fact, any attempt on his part to discourage or prevent me from wearing blue shirts might constitute harassment on *his* part, or even worse.

C. Sexual Harassment

It would seem that similar considerations should apply to sexual harassment. Roughly speaking, sexual harassment is simply harassment in which the offending behavior is sexual in nature. In other words, to parallel what was said above about harassment in general, the term "sexual harassment" should not be applied to sexual coercion or sexual assault, nor should it be applied to situations in which persons are tempted to voluntarily engage in sexual behavior for morally inappropriate reasons. It should be applied only to sexual behavior which is merely annoying or offensive, not to behavior which is seriously harmful, threatening, or tempting in a morally pernicious manner. A person (A) should be said to be sexually harassing another person (B) only if A is engaged in sexual behavior toward B which is unwanted by B, is known by A to be unwanted by B, and which is nevertheless repeated by A. Finally, a bit of behavior would not ordinarily be regarded as a form of sexual harassment unless it is of a sort which a reasonable person might find objectionable or annoying.

Since the more intimate forms of sexual activity are those in which consent is clearly called for, it would be inappropriate to refer to any such behavior as sexual harassment. If consent is not given, a person who initiates such activity is guilty of sexual assault. If consent *is* given, initiating such behavior might be immoral for a variety of reasons, but it cannot be a clearly sanctionable offense unless it involves a morally unjustifiable sexual offer or is coercive. Since none of these three types of offenses are properly regarded as types of sexual harassment, it follows that sexual harassment cannot involve intim-

ate sexual activity, but must involve sexual activity of a less intimate sort. It must, in other words, involve behavior which is clearly sexual in nature, but not especially intimate.

We are now in a position to see why sexual harassment is so difficult to define, much less adjudicate. Most behavior which is *prima facie* sexual in nature is fairly intimate. Although, as mentioned above, intimate sexual behavior might sometimes involve morally unjustifiable sexual offers or constitute a form of sexual coercion or assault, it seldom if ever constitutes sexual harassment. Typical cases of sexual harassment involve behavior which is *not prima facie* sexual in nature, but is sexual due to its context, if at all. Most often, behavior which is not *prima facie* sexual in nature is clearly sexual only when it constitutes a sexual advance, but behavior of this sort which constitutes a sexual advance in one set of circumstances might not do so in another. Moreover, in many cases of purported sexual harassment, both parties will agree that certain behavior has occurred, but will strongly disagree as to how that behavior should be interpreted or described. For example, a purported victim of sexual harassment (A) may claim that a purported offender (B) has persisted in making "unwanted sexual advances" toward A by engaging in behavior toward A which A, but not B, regards as sexual in nature. If the behavior of B is *prima facie* sexual as defined above, the burden of proof will be on B to show that it was not sexual, and if this behavior is *prima facie* nonsexual, the burden of proof will be on A to show that it is sexual. But what if, as is often if not usually the case, it is neither? Since many types of sexual advance involve behavior which is not *prima facie* sexual in nature, there is often considerable disagreement between purported victims and purported offenders in such cases concerning whether the behavior of the purported offender was in fact a sexual advance. It thus becomes problematic whether any such bit of behavior satisfies one of the necessary conditions which such a bit must satisfy in order to be an instance of sexual harassment.

There are several logically possible ways of resolving this difficulty. One way would be to allow the precise nature of the purported offender's behavior to be subjectively determined by the purported victim. In other words, we might simply say that if the purported victim regards the purported offender's behavior as a sexual advance, then that settles the matter. The problem with this procedure, of course, is that there does not seem to be any *a priori* reason to prefer the subjective opinions of the purported victim to those of the purported offender. For one thing, the latter is surely in a better position to know the inherent nature of his or her motives or intentions.[15] In addition, since the guilt or innocence of the purported offender might well hinge on our determination of whether his or her behavior is sexual in nature, the principle that an accused person is innocent until proven guilty clearly implies that we should give the benefit of the doubt to the accused. But to accept the subjectively determined opinions of accused persons concerning their own behavior as definitive in such cases is to leave potential victims essentially unprotected, since accused persons will almost always describe their own motivations in such a way as to support a claim of innocence.

What is clearly called for here is some objective basis for determining whether a person's behavior is sexual in the relevant sense. Since we are now discussing behavior which is not *prima facie* sexual in nature, any determination must be based on contextual considerations. Among things to be considered will be the intentions and other psychological states of the accused and various social conventions pertaining to interpersonal relationships. In an increasingly multi-cultural world, however, there must be a wide variety of interpretations of what is to constitute a sexual advance, and a correspondingly wide variety of socially acceptable behaviors. Judas, for example, was not making or even pretending to make a homosexual advance when he betrayed Jesus with a kiss, and even today, Arab men often kiss and hold hands with no implication of homosexuality.

Similarly, in most cultures and subcultures, including those of the United States, there are many social contexts in which heterosexual embracing, kissing, and other forms of physical affection are not ordinarily considered to be sexual advances, even though there are some persons who seem to regard almost any sort of physical contact whatsoever as a sexual advance. As mentioned previously, we need not tolerate the sorts of behavior which would be regarded as acceptable in the most extremely sexist societies, but we also need not adopt a code of behavior so sexually repressive that we are required to regard all forms of unconsented-to physical contact or affection as sexual advances. No one narrow segment of society should be permitted to impose its interpretation of what constitutes a sexual advance or its views concerning what is socially acceptable on the rest of society. For all these reasons, great care must be taken in formulating legislation or institutional policies according to which a sexual advance can sometimes be a sanctionable offense. In particular, the term "sexual advance" cannot be defined in such a way as to automatically apply to bits of behavior which are often nonsexual in nature. Moreover, persons chosen to exercise judgment concerning whether a given bit of behavior constitutes a sexual advance in some particular context must be sufficiently broad-minded so as to instill confidence in all parties that such judgments will reflect an understanding of all the considerations referred to above.

D. Defining the Term

We are now in a position to attempt a more precise definition of sexual harassment. As a first approximation, consider the following:

(1) Person A is guilty of sexually harassing person B iff:

   (a) A's behavior toward B is clearly sexual in nature, but does not involve a morally unjustifiable sexual offer or constitute either sexual coercion or sexual assault.

(b)   A's behavior toward B is clearly unwanted by B.

The difficulty with this definition is that, depending on what we mean by "clearly" in (b), a person might be guilty of sexual harassment without having any way of being aware of that fact. It might be clear to any number of people that A's behavior is unwanted by B, but unless it is (or at least should be) clear to A, it is difficult to see how A's behavior can be morally sanctionable, unless, of course, it is inherently so for some reason.

Consider now the following substitute for (1), which is derived by substituting (b*) for (b) in (1):

(1*) Person A is guilty of sexually harassing person B iff:

(a)   A's behavior toward B is clearly sexual in nature, but does not involve a morally unjustifiable sexual offer or constitute either sexual coercion or sexual assault.

(b*)   A's behavior toward B is known by A to be unwanted by B.

A good case can be made for the view that if A's behavior satisfies both of these conditions, A's behavior is morally objectionable. It is perfectly reasonable to claim that there is something morally objectionable about engaging in sexual behavior toward a person when we know that that person does not want us to do so. The difficulty with this definition is that it excludes too much. Suppose, for example, A does not *know* that the behavior in question is unwanted by B, but has good reason to *believe* that it is. A's lack of *knowledge* of B's feelings would certainly no excuse A's behavior in this instance.

Perhaps, then, we can revise our definition again, by substituting (b**) for (b*):

(1**) Person A is guilty of sexually harassing person B iff:

(a)   A's behavior toward B is clearly sexual in nature, but does not involve a morally un-justifiable sexual offer or constitute either sexual coercion or sexual assault.

(b**)   A has good reason to believe that A's behavior toward B is unwanted by B.

Condition (b**), however, is still too strong. Suppose that A and B are total strangers, that they meet in circumstances in which it would ordinarily be thought inappropriate to make sexual advances, (e.g., in a supermarket) and that A makes a sexual advance toward B which is *prima facie* sexual in nature. Unless it is argued (implausibly) that no one ever wants to be propositioned by a total stranger, A might truthfully claim that although she has no good reason to believe that her behavior is wanted by B, she also has no good reason to believe that her behavior toward B is unwanted. We might nevertheless argue that A's behavior in this case might constitute at least a mild form of sexual misconduct. One way of doing so is to point out that such behavior is offensive to most people, whether or not it is offensive to everyone, and that it is morally unacceptable to behave in a way which is offensive to most people in this respect, even if there may be some people who do not find this behavior offensive.

This suggests a further modification in our proposed definition, as follows:

(1***) Person A is guilty of sexually harassing person B iff:

(a)   A's behavior toward B is clearly sexual in nature, but does not involve a morally unjustifiable sexual offer or constitute either sexual coercion or sexual assault.

(b***)   A has no reason to believe that A's behavior toward B might be wanted by B.

This definition clearly applies to behavior of the sort described above, but instead of excluding too much, it suffers from the opposite defect. Social conventions being what they are, there are many situations in which behavior satisfying both of these conditions would be perfectly acceptable. In the first place, if A and B know each other well enough, a sexual advance which is *prima facie* sexual in nature might be perfectly appropriate. In the second place, if A and B do not know each other well, sometimes the most appropriate way to determine whether a sexual advance is or is not wanted is simply to make one, especially if it is one which is *not prima facie* sexual in nature. There is clearly something amiss in our attempt to define sexual harassment so far.

Sexual relationships cannot exist unless they are initiated by someone. If doing something to initiate a sexual relationship is regarded as "making a sexual advance," it follows that sexual relationships cannot exist unless someone makes a sexual advance. Moreover, the first person to make such an advance in a sexual relationship must do so without knowing whether such an advance is wanted by the other person. The reason for this is that anything the other person did which would suffice to indicate that a sexual advance *was* wanted (or was even not unwanted) could be regarded as a sexual advance on the part of the other person, in which case, contrary to hypothesis, the person in question could not be the first person to make such an advance. Moreover, given this understanding of what constitutes a sexual advance, asking permission to make one is also tantamount to making one. Thus, sexual relationships cannot exist unless someone makes a sexual advance without knowing whether it is wanted.

What follows from this is that making sexual advances, even when it is not known whether they are or are not wanted, cannot be *prima facie* morally unacceptable, so that sexual harassment, if it is to be regarded as morally unacceptable, cannot be defined simply in terms of unwanted sexual advances. Many sexual advances which seem to be morally unacceptable, such as the example given above involving total strangers in the supermarket, are best regarded as instances of mere sexual boorishness, and not as forms of sexual harassment. In order to define sexual harassment correctly we must once again attend to the meaning of the term "harassment."

As we have seen, to harass someone is to *repeatedly* engage in behavior toward that person despite our knowledge or belief that the behavior is unwanted. The fact that the behavior is repeated is especially important in the case of sexual harassment. In the first place, since the only reasonable way to ascertain that a sexual advance is unwanted is often to make it, there are many cases in which one cannot be blamed for making one unless one has already made one and been rebuffed. In the second place, sexual harassment occurs most often among people who know each other but are not involved in a serious romantic or sexual relationship. Since it is considered excessively crude to attempt to initiate such a relationship by making sexual advances which are *prima facie* sexual in nature, people typically do so by making sexual advances which are *not prima facie* sexual in nature. This enables those who wish to reject such an advance to do so by simply responding to it as if it were not such an advance, and it enables those whose advances have been rebuffed to save face by pretending that they were not really making such an advance. The intent in these cases is not to deceive, but simply to minimize hurt feelings and embarrassment. Since, however, sexual advances of this kind are by hypothesis patterns of behavior that need not be regarded as sexual advances at all, it follows that people must often engage in the same patterns of behavior without intending to make any sexual advances. For this reason, it often happens that one person will interpret another person's behavior as a sexual advance when no such advance was intended. This alone is sufficient reason for not defining sexual harassment in terms of such ambiguous behavior.

It also explains, however, why it is so important that the behavior be repeated. Suppose that person A engages in behavior toward person B which A does not regard as sexual in nature but B does. As previously implied, the burden of proof will be on A if the behavior in question is *prima facie* sexual and on B if it is *prima facie* nonsexual. Moreover, even when it is neither, and regardless of what A or B claim to believe about the behavior in question, the context can sometimes make it clear whether this behavior is or is not sexual in nature. The problem is that, even when the context is completely specified, there are many cases in which there may be no clear consensus as to whether the behavior should be regarded as sexual or not. In a single instance of this sort, the benefit of the doubt must be given to the accused. Since, however, by hypothesis, the behavior in question is not *prima facie* nonsexual it could under some conceivable circumstances be regarded as sexual. Thus, if A knows that B regards it as sexual, whether or not A also so regards it, A cannot continue to engage in this behavior toward B without Presupposing that B will interpret A's behavior as sexual. Thus, unless A has sufficient reason to believe that B desires or at least has no objection to A's engaging in sexual behavior toward B, A's continuing to engage in the behavior in question shows disrespect toward B of a very serious sort.

We are now in a position to try once again to define sexual harassment. Consider the following:

(2) Person A is guilty of sexually harassing person B iff:

    (a) A has engaged in behavior toward B which is either *prima facie* sexual in nature or is such that B could reasonably regard it as such, but which does not constitute either sexual coercion, sexual assault, or a morally unjustifiable sexual offer.

    (b) A knows or has adequate reason to believe that B reasonably regards A's behavior as sexual in nature.

    (c) A knows or has adequate reason to believe that B does not want A to continue behaving in this manner toward B.

    (d) A continues to behave in the same manner toward B.

There are several noteworthy aspects of this definition. The first is that condition (a) is necessary but not sufficient. A single, isolated instance of sexual coercion, sexual assault, or a morally unjustifiable sexual offer constitutes a sexual offense, but no isolated bit of behavior can constitute an instance of sexual harassment. Sexual harassment does not involve behavior which is inherently immoral. It occurs only when persons engage in sexual behavior or behavior which could reasonably be interpreted as such toward persons whom they know or have reason to believe may not want them to engage in such behavior. No one can reasonably be expected to continually provide each person they encounter in their daily lives with a detailed description of all those forms of behavior which they regard as sexual, nor can they provide each person with a list of those forms of behavior which they would prefer the person in question not exhibit toward them. For this reason, it often happens that persons engage in such behavior without realizing that it is offensive to others. If those others never indicate in any way that they are offended, or if the behavior in question is such that no reasonable person would be offended by it, the person engaging in it cannot be regarded as having committed an offense.

E. Applications, Problems, and Remedies

Those who justifiably feel that they have been sexually harassed are often reluctant to complain or express their displeasure. Sometimes they are simply too polite and do not want to upset those that are offending them, and sometimes they are simply afraid to complain for fear of reprisal. These fears are sometimes justified, which is precisely why we need sexual harassment policies, but these policies must be such that those who have offended cannot be justifiably accused of an offense unless they have explicitly been made aware that their behavior has been offensive and they have nevertheless continued to engage in it.

Special problems obtain in cases in which the accuser and the accused have previously been involved in an admittedly consensual relationship. Sexual ad-

vances made within such relationships are often rebuffed, with no implication that future advances will
also be unwanted. For this reason, all the conditions
of our definition might be satisfied in such cases
even when it is obvious that no sanctionable offense
has occurred. For cases of this sort, some further
condition would have to be developed which would
enable us to determine when one party has made
it sufficiently clear to the other party that a sexual
relationship no longer exists, so that the conditions
spelled out in our definition would once again apply.
The point here is not that "anything goes" within a
relationship; the point is rather that the remedy for
intolerable behavior which occurs within a relationship is to end (or attempt to end) the relationship.

It is sometimes argued that sexual harassment
typically involves a "power differential" between
perpetrator and victim, in the sense that those who
are guilty of it typically occupy Positions which
give them some sort of authority over their victims.
There is an element of truth in this, but it must
be stated very carefully. In cases of sexual assault,
of course, the perpetrator typically overpowers or
threatens to overpower the victim, but it is possible
for a less powerful person to sexually assault a more
powerful one, especially if the more powerful person does not resist the assault. Differences in power
and authority are most prevalent in cases of sexual
coercion, especially those in which the threatened
harm is nonphysical in nature, since the ability of
the perpetrator to issue meaningful threats in these
cases depends on the power invested in the perpetrator by his or her position. It is important to point
out, however, that in cases of sexual coercion, it is
the illegitimate use or threatened use of this power
and not its mere possession that is relevant, and the
same is true in cases of sexual harassment. Suppose,
for example, that Abercrombie occupies a position
of power or authority with respect to Fitch, but that
Smith does not occupy a corresponding position
with respect to Wesson. It is nevertheless the case
that if the behavior of Abercrombie toward Fitch is

exactly the same as the behavior of Smith toward
Wesson and does not involve any threats or offers
to use this power or authority, Abercrombie cannot
be guilty of sexually harassing Fitch unless Smith is
guilty of sexually harassing Wesson. More specifically, suppose that Abercrombie and Smith both
request or accept offers of identical sexual favors
from Fitch and Wesson respectively, and there is no
difference in the observable behavior of Fitch and
Wesson. It may be, of course, that Fitch and Wesson have different motives for making these offers or
responding as they do to these requests. Fitch may
be attempting to curry favor with Abercrombie in
the hope that Abercrombie's power will be used to
Fitch's benefit, or Fitch may fear that Abercrombie's
power will be used against Fitch, whereas Wesson
cannot reasonably have either of these motivations
with respect to Smith. Since, however Abercrombie
has not, by hypothesis, given Fitch any reason to
think that this power and authority will be used in
either of these ways, Abercrombie is not responsible
for Fitch's hopes and fears, nor for the behavior that
flows from them. The most that one can say about
Abercrombie in this case is that Abercrombie ought
to be sensitive to the possibility that Fitch has these
motivations, and should take this possibility into account, whereas Smith has no such obligation with
respect to Wesson.

Suppose, however, that Abercrombie has taken
this possibility into account, and has, with adequate
reason, rejected it. Suppose that, as a matter of fact,
Fitch has no such motivations but responds enthusiastically, for morally appropriate reasons, to Abercrombie's request. Further suppose that, at some
later date, Fitch becomes angry with Abercrombie,
for some reason having nothing to do with Abercrombie's request, and decides to accuse Abercrombie of sexual harassment. Should we countenance
a policy which would support such an accusation
simply on the grounds that Abercrombie occupies
a position of power or authority over Fitch? Having power or authority over others sometimes puts

persons in a position which enables them to commit offenses which they would otherwise be unable to commit, but engaging in sexual behavior with someone over whom one has such power and authority does not necessarily constitute an abuse of one's position. The abuse of such power or authority cannot be tolerated, but neither can a policy which permits sanctions against individuals for engaging in otherwise acceptable behavior simply because they engage in this behavior with those with respect to whom they have this power or authority.

The above considerations are not intended to obviate the principles of professional ethics. When the position of power or authority entails professional responsibilities, as opposed to mere supervisory authority, for example, one must obviously carry out these responsibilities in an ethical manner. One reason for this is that professionals often-have even more actual power over those whom they serve than that which attaches to their office *per se*. Students, for example, are usually younger than their mentors and often overly impressionable if not awestruck by them, which makes them especially vulnerable to exploitation, and similar considerations apply to those who seek the advice and assistance of physicians, psychologists, attorneys, and other professionals. Institutions and professional organizations therefore have a right if not an obligation to establish and enforce appropriate standards of professional behavior on the part of their employees or members. Policies concerning sexual misconduct of various kinds, including sexual harassment as properly defined, can play an important role in publicizing and enforcing these standards, but must also be designed and implemented in such a way as to respect the rights of the professionals involved. As long as special consideration is given for those who are especially vulnerable to exploitation, any policy which prohibits affectionate or intimate relationships between truly consenting adults is reminiscent of laws against miscegenation.

One seldom noticed effect of sexual harassment policies on many college campuses is that the so-called power differential is actually reversed on these campuses. College professors do seem to have considerable power over their students. They have considerable if not total control, especially in those disciplines where most of the grading is necessarily discretionary, over the assignment of grades to students who might sometimes be academically required to successfully complete courses taught only by some particular member of a faculty. Students also depend on their professors for letters of recommendation both for employment and for future study, as well as for advice and assistance in other matters of some import, and most of these factors are amplified in graduate or professional school. On the other hand, undergraduates are seldom required to complete more than one course with any particular professor, and it is even less likely that a student is significantly dependent on any one professor for a letter of recommendation. In addition, even though most academic deans and department chairs are extremely reluctant to overrule an individual faculty member in the assignment of a student's grades, students who receive uncharacteristically low grades from professors and credibly complain to an appropriate college official that their professor attempted to coerce them into engaging in sexual activity usually receive a fair hearing, even in the absence of a sexual harassment policy.

With the advent of sexual harassment policies, however, students have acquired a great deal of essentially unchecked power over their professors. Any student who is ever alone with a professor, for example, can easily accuse that professor of making unwanted sexual advances or of attempted sexual coercion, whether or not any such accusation is true, and the accusation is likely to be taken seriously, if only because we have now collectively become sensitive to the fact that even true allegations of this sort were not always taken seriously in the past. We are especially likely to take such accusations seriously if there is more than one accuser bringing charges against the same faculty member, which is taken to imply that there has been an offensive "pattern of behavior" on the part of the accused. What we might fail to take into account in such cases is the Possibility that the same sort of "herd mentality" that sometimes inclines students to give false testimony in defense of a friend who has been accused of violating some sort of campus policy might also incline some students to give false testimony to "support" a friend who has convinced them of the accused's guilt. There is even some anecdotal evidence that students have sometimes been encouraged to bring such charges by politically motivated faculty members who disapprove of a specific colleague's behavior and wish to engage in a sort of "ethnic cleansing" of the faculty. The aforementioned "power differential," after all, gives politically motivated faculty members just as much power and influence over budding radical feminists as sexual harassers have over theirs, if not more, and due to their strong feelings on this issue, they may be just as likely to abuse this power. Although examples like this are surely atypical, it would be exceedingly naive to think they do not, much less cannot, occur, especially given the politically supercharged atmosphere afflicting many college campuses.

Situations like that described above are neither typical nor common, but many harassment policies are designed (inadvertently, we can hope) in such a way as to make them more likely.[16] In many cases, for example, students are permitted or even encouraged to make anonymous accusations, on the grounds that requiring them to identify themselves would make them vulnerable to reprisal or embarrassment. In some cases, secret files detailing such allegations are maintained without the knowledge of the accused until such time as sufficient "evidence" has been accumulated to bring charges. When charges are brought, they are sometimes deliberately vague, in order to conceal the identities of the accusers, and are sometimes not given in writing, and accusers are usually not required to face the accused. The accused seldom has the right to cross-examine either the accuser or witnesses that appear on the accuser's behalf, and is often not entitled to counsel that could perform this service on behalf of the accused. Few if any institutions, of course, attempt to dismiss tenured faculty on the basis of such a process alone. There is usually an additional step in the official dismissal process which does afford the accused with due process, but before this stage is reached, there is often an attempt on the part of the administration to intimidate the accused into resigning in order to avoid a spectacle which would be embarrassing both to the accused and to the institution. This is often effective, since accusations of this kind, even if proven false, do considerable harm to a faculty member, especially if they become publicly known, so that some persons would rather resign than suffer such harm. As Plato perspicuously points out in the *Apology*, people generally think that anyone accused of something vaguely nasty must have done *something* wrong in order to even be accused of such a thing. There is always the suspicion, gladly nourished by most accusers, as well as by administrators in cases where there has been a determination, justified or unjustified, of guilt, that there is more to the story than has been publicly revealed, and even the friends of the accused begin to question his or her character.

Another problem with many sexual harassment policies is that, based loosely on the EEOC statement (especially clause [3]), but without the refining process of the courts, offenses are ill-defined. It is seldom clear what constitutes an "unwanted sexual advance," and it is even less clear what contributes to the creation of an allegedly "hostile environment." This has a "chilling effect" on academic freedom, since faculty members never know when the positions that they take on controversial issues, the examples that they use as illustrations in class, the reading materials that they assign, or even some of the words that they use may prove to be offensive to someone and cost them their career. In some cases, action has been taken against a faculty member even when a clear majority of those students who should presumably be offended are not, and are even willing to testify that they are not, and this action has been taken on the grounds that even if these students are not offended, they should be. What this amounts to is that a small, nonrepresentative but vocal minority is being permitted to establish a strict code of conduct for everyone else.

Other problems are more subtle and thus more difficult to substantiate. There is a tendency, for example, to regard the accused as guilty until proven innocent. The reasonable position that accusations of this nature ought to be given a fair hearing is taken to mean that unless the accused can prove that the accuser is lying, the accusations must be believed. The burden of proof is on the accused, and any attempt to discredit the accuser or the accuser's witnesses is taken to be additional harassment or a form of reprisal. The entire process is all too often reminiscent of the Salem witch trials.

What needs to be done to enable sexual harassment policies to do their job without violating the rights of innocent people is implicit in what has already been said. Policies must be widely publicized and must clearly state what constitutes an offense. No action or mode of behavior should be regarded as a sanctionable offense unless there is a fairly wide consensus within the community that it ought to be so regarded. Accused persons must be told exactly what they have been accused of and who has accused them. They must have the right to cross-examine their accusers, or must at least have the right to have their accusers cross-examined by someone whom they have chosen to represent them. They must also be given the opportunity to determine such things as whether their accusers have any ulterior motives in accusing them, such as disappointment with a grade, feelings of rejection, strong ideological disapproval of the accused's position on controversial issues, desire to impress or please a deeply admired mentor who strongly disapproves of the accused, etc. Accused persons must also be given the opportunity to attempt to determine whether their accusers have previously been harassed or abused by someone with respect to whom they have no possibility of redress, whether they are emotionally disturbed, or whether they have been persuaded to bring charges by someone else who may or may not have a legitimate grievance against the accused.

It is not reasonable to expect sexual harassment policies to incorporate all the rights that would be afforded to the accused in a court of law. For one thing, sexual harassment policies should be primarily designed not to investigate, prosecute, and punish offenders, but to educate people and to work out differences between them in a mutually satisfactory manner. To the extent, however, that sexual harassment policies can have such dire consequences as dismissal and the termination of a career, accused persons should be afforded many of the same rights and privileges afforded them in a court of law, and for the same reasons. To do otherwise is a serious miscarriage of justice.[17]

NOTES

1 Although it seems obvious that the vast majority of victims of these offenses are women, the moral dimensions of the problem are gender-neutral and will be treated as such wherever possible in this paper.

2 Michael Crichton, *Disclosure* (Knopf, 1994), 397. For a realistic fictional account of the abuse of sexual harassment policies in academe, see *Oleanna*, a play by David Mamet (New York: Pantheon, 1992).

3 Gerald R. Maatman, Jr., "Primer on the Law of Sexual Harassment," *Federation of Insurance & Corporate Counsel Quarterly* 42, No. 3 (1992), 320.

4 Michele A. Paludi and Richard B. Barickman, *Academic and Workplace Sexual Harassment: A Resource Manual* (Albany: SUNY Press, 1991), 3.

5 Cf. F.M. Christensen, "'Sexual Harassment' Must Be Eliminated," *Public Affairs Quarterly* 8, No. 1 (1994).

6 Cf., e.g., Fitzgerald et al., *Journal of Vocational Behavior* 32, 152-75.

7 Behavior which is not morally blameworthy may sometimes be justifiably prohibited and thus regarded as an "offense" in appropriate institutional or corporate settings. In particular, it may be prohibited when it seriously detracts from institutional or corporate goals and when this prohibition is not itself a violation of the rights of those engaging in the behavior in question. The point here is thus not that only morally blameworthy behavior may be prohibited, but rather that those who engage in behavior which is not morally blameworthy, even when it is contrary to some morally justifiable policy, ought to be treated differently than those whose behavior is clearly and seriously immoral or illegal.

8 I have a gainfully employed, law-abiding, African-American male friend who once walked into a convenience market on a very cold day wearing a ski mask. The female clerk, who was alone in the store at the time, saw him and immediately started to hand him the contents of the cash register. Given her own past experience and her knowledge of crime statistics in that neighborhood, it could be argued that her fear of my friend was quite reasonable, and she certainly acted as she did because of this reasonable fear. My friend, however, could certainly not have been accused of coercion. He would not, of course, have been justified in keeping the contents of the cash register in these circumstances, and would probably have been prosecuted for doing so, since it was obvious that the clerk acted out of fear in this case. Suppose, however, that he had simply approached a stranger on the street and asked for a simple favor. If the stranger, without showing any fear, nevertheless granted the favor for this reason, could my friend have been accused of coercion?

9 The interpretation of the first two clauses of the EEOC statement is continually being refined in the courts, and even though there is no comparable refining process in academe, reasonable people could probably reach a consensus as to how such cases could be resolved there as well.

10 The problem here has been expressed fairly well in a form letter written by US Representative Barney Frank to his contributors, which I will quote at length. "Writing a thank-you note to campaign contributors in today's climate forces me to emulate Rube Goldberg without pictures. That is, I have to write something that reflects (1) my deep genuine gratitude on a personal level for your sending me a contribution to help me stay in Congress, counterbalanced by (2) my concern that someone reading this might infer something disparaging about your motives in engaging in the sinister process of 'campaign finance,' itself counterbalanced by (3) my interest in keeping you sufficiently happy with me—or insufficiently unhappy— so that you will continue to contribute, in turn counterbalanced by (4) my fear that the media will denounce me for accepting campaign contributions and thereby subjecting myself to improper influence, albeit from proper people." Reprinted in *Harper's*, August 1994, 17.

11 Cf. clause (3) of the EEOC statement.

12 My first landlord, an immigrant from Greece, informed me that the term "Greek" is an ethnic slur (the proper term is "Grecian"), but that it did not offend him, since the people that use this term are all "barbarians" anyway.

13 One virtue of the EEOC definition is that it does at least make it clear that only behavior which is sexual in nature can be regarded as a form of sexual harassment, although it unfortunately leaves the term "sexual" undefined.

14 *Black's Law Dictionary*, 5th edition, West, St. Paul, 645.

15 Many chronic sex offenders, of course, are subject to various types of self-deception concerning their own motives and behavior, but to the extent that this is true, it would seem to render them less responsible for their behavior and to make it more difficult to justify using sanctions against them.

16 It is beyond the scope of this paper to present an exhaustive survey of sexual harassment cases and policies. The following examples are all based on the author's personal knowledge of actual cases and policies.

17 I am deeply indebted to David Lyons, whose strong disagreement with the overall tone of this paper have helped to make his comments and criticisms of several earlier versions of it extremely valuable to me.

BLUFFING IN BUSINESS

ALBERT Z. CARR

Is Business Bluffing Ethical?

A respected businessman with whom I discussed the theme of this article remarked with some heat, "You mean to say you're going to encourage men to bluff? Why, bluffing is nothing more than a form of lying! You're advising them to lie!"

I agreed that the basis of private morality is a respect for truth and that the closer a businessman comes to the truth, the more he deserves respect. At the same time, I suggested that most bluffing in business might be regarded simply as game strategy—much like bluffing in poker, which does not reflect on the morality of the bluffer.

I quoted Henry Taylor, the British statesman who pointed out that "falsehood ceases to be falsehood when it is understood on all sides that the truth is not expected to be spoken"—an exact description of bluffing in poker, diplomacy, and business. I cited the analogy of the criminal court, where the criminal is not expected to tell the truth when he pleads "not guilty." Everyone from the judge down takes it for granted that the job of the defendant's attorney is to get his client off, not to reveal the truth; and this is considered ethical practice. I mentioned Representative Omar Burleson, the Democrat from Texas, who was quoted as saying, in regard to the ethics of Congress, "Ethics is a barrel of worms"[1]—a pungent summing up of the problem of deciding who is ethical in politics.

I reminded my friend that millions of businessmen feel constrained every day to say *yes* to their bosses when they secretly believe *no* and that this is generally accepted as permissible strategy when the alternative might be the loss of a job. The essential point, I said, is that the ethics of business are game ethics, different from the ethics of religion.

He remained unconvinced. Referring to the company of which he is president, he declared: "Maybe that's good enough for some businessmen, but I can tell you that we pride ourselves on our ethics. In 30 years not one customer has ever questioned my word or asked to check our figures. We're loyal to our customers and fair to our suppliers. I regard my handshake on a deal as a contract. I've never entered into price fixing schemes with my competitors. I've never allowed my salesmen to spread injurious rumors about other companies. Our union contract is the best in our industry. And, if I do say so myself, our ethical standards are of the highest!"

He really was saying, without realizing it, that he was living up to the ethical standards of the business game—which are a far cry from those of private life. Like a gentlemanly poker player, he did not play in cahoots with others at the table, try to smear their reputations, or hold back chips he owed them.

But this same fine man, at that very time, was allowing one of his products to be advertised in a way that made it sound a great deal better than it actually was. Another item in his product line was notorious among dealers for its "built-in obsolescence." He was holding back from the market a much-improved product because he did not want it to interfere with sales of the inferior item it would have replaced. He had joined with certain of his competitors in hiring a lobbyist to push a state legislature, by methods that he preferred not to know too much about, into amending a bill then being enacted.

In his view these things had nothing to do with ethics; they were merely normal business practice. He himself undoubtedly avoided outright falsehoods—never lied in so many words. But the entire organization that he ruled was deeply involved in numerous strategies of deception.

Pressure to Deceive

Most executives from time to time are almost compelled, in the interests of their companies or themselves, to practice some form of deception when negotiating with customers, dealers, labor unions, government officials, or even other departments of their companies. By conscious misstatements, concealment of pertinent facts, or exaggeration—in short, by bluffing—they seek to persuade others to agree with them. I think it is fair to say that if the individual executive refuses to bluff from time to time—if he feels obligated to tell the truth, the whole truth, and nothing but the truth—he is ignoring opportunities permitted under the rules and is at a heavy disadvantage in his business dealings.

But here and there a businessman is unable to reconcile himself to the bluff in which he plays a part. His conscience, perhaps spurred by religious idealism, troubles him. He feels guilty; he may develop an ulcer or a nervous tic. Before any executive can make profitable use of the strategy of the bluff, he needs to make sure that in bluffing he will not lose self-respect or become emotionally disturbed. If he is to reconcile personal integrity and high standards of honesty with the practical requirements of business, he must feel that his bluffs are ethically justified. The justification rests on the fact that business, as practiced by individuals as well as by corporations, has the impersonal character of a game—a game that demands both special strategy and an understanding of its special ethics.

The game is played at all levels of corporate life, from the highest to the lowest. At the very instant that a man decides to enter business, he may be forced into a game situation, as is shown by the recent experience of a Cornell honor graduate who applied for a job with a large company:

> This applicant was given a psychological test which included the statement, "Of the following magazines, check any that you have read either regularly or from time to time, and double-check those which interest you most: *Reader's Digest, Time, Fortune, Saturday Evening Post, The New Republic, Life, Look, Ramparts, Newsweek, Business Week, US News & World Report, The Nation, Playboy, Esquire, Harper's, Sports Illustrated*."
>
> His tastes in reading were broad, and at one time or another he had read almost all of these magazines. He was a subscriber to *The New Republic*, an enthusiast for *Ramparts*, and an avid student of the pictures in *Playboy*. He was not sure whether his

interest in *Playboy* would be held against him, but he had a shrewd suspicion that if he confessed to an interest in *Ramparts* and *The New Republic,* he would be thought a liberal, a radical, or at least an intellectual, and his chances of getting the job, which he needed, would greatly diminish. He therefore checked five of the more conservative magazines. Apparently it was a sound decision, for he got the job.

He had made a game player's decision, consistent with business ethics.

A similar case is that of a magazine space salesman who, owing to a merger, suddenly found himself out of a job:

> This man was 58, and, in spite of a good record, his chance of getting a job elsewhere in a business where youth is favored in hiring practice was not good. He was a vigorous, healthy man, and only a considerable amount of gray in his hair suggested his age. Before beginning his job search he touched up his hair with a black dye to confine the gray to his temples. He knew that the truth about his age might well come out in time, but he calculated that he could deal with that situation when it arose. He and his wife decided that he could easily pass for 45, and he so stated his age on his resume.
>
> This was a lie; yet within the accepted rules of the business game, no moral culpability attaches to it.

The Poker Analogy

We can learn a good deal about the nature of business by comparing it with poker. While both have a large element of chance, in the long run the winner is the man who plays with steady skill. In both games ultimate victory requires intimate knowledge of the rules, insight into the psychology of the other players, a bold front, a considerable amount of self-discipline, and the ability to respond swiftly and effectively to opportunities provided by chance.

No one expects poker to be played on the ethical principles preached in churches. In poker it is right and proper to bluff a friend out of the rewards of being dealt a good hand. A player feels no more than a slight twinge of sympathy, if that, when—with nothing better than a single ace in his hand—he strips a heavy loser, who holds a pair, of the rest of his chips. It was up to the other fellow to protect himself. In the words of an excellent poker player, former President Harry Truman, "If you can't stand the heat, stay out of the kitchen." If one shows mercy to a loser in poker, it is a personal gesture, divorced from the rules of the game.

Poker has its special ethics, and here I am not referring to rules against cheating. The man who keeps an ace up his sleeve or who marks the cards is more than unethical; he is a crook, and can be punished as such—kicked out of the game or,—in the Old West, shot.

In contrast to the cheat, the unethical poker player is one who, while abiding by the letter of the rules, finds ways to put the other players at an unfair disadvantage. Perhaps he unnerves them with loud talk. Or he tries to get them drunk. Or he plays in cahoots with someone else at the table. Ethical poker players frown on such tactics.

Poker's own brand of ethics is different from the ethical ideals of civilized human relationships. The game calls for distrust of the other fellow. It ignores the claim of friendship. Cunning deception and concealment of one's strength and intentions, not kindness and openheartedness, are vital in poker. No one thinks any the worse of poker on that account. And no one should think any the worse of the game of business because its standards of right and wrong differ from the prevailing traditions of morality in our society.

Discard the Golden Rule

This view of business is especially worrisome to people without much business experience. A minister of my acquaintance once protested that business cannot possibly function in our society unless it is based on the Judeo-Christian system of ethics. He told me:

> I know some businessmen have supplied call girls to customers, but there are always a few rotten apples in every barrel. That doesn't mean the rest of the fruit isn't sound. Surely the vast majority of businessmen are ethical. I myself am acquainted with many who adhere to strict codes of ethics based fundamentally on religious teachings. They contribute to good causes. They participate in community activities. They cooperate with other companies to improve working conditions in their industries. Certainly they are not indifferent to ethics.

That most businessmen are not indifferent to ethics in their private lives, everyone will agree. My point is that in their office lives they cease to be private citizens; they become game players who must be guided by a somewhat different set of ethical standards.

The point was forcefully made to me by a Midwestern executive who has given a good deal of thought to the question:

> So long as a businessman complies with the laws of the land and avoids telling malicious lies, he's ethical. If the law as written gives a man a wide-open chance to make a killing, he'd be a fool not to take advantage of it. If he doesn't, somebody else will. There's no obligation on him to stop and consider who is going to get hurt. If the law says he can do it, that's all the justification he needs. There's nothing unethical about that. It's just plain business sense.

This executive (call him Robbins) took the stand that even industrial espionage, which is frowned on by some businessmen, ought not to be considered unethical. He recalled a recent meeting of the National Industrial Conference Board where an authority on marketing made a speech in which he deplored the employment of spies by business organizations. More and more companies, he pointed out, find it cheaper to penetrate the secrets of competitors with concealed cameras and microphones or by bribing employees than to set up costly research and design departments of their own. A whole branch of the electronics industry has grown up with this trend, he continued, providing equipment to make industrial espionage easier.

Disturbing? The marketing expert found it so. But when it came to a remedy, he could only appeal to "respect for the golden rule." Robbins thought this a confession of defeat, believing that the golden rule, for all its value as an ideal for society, is simply not feasible as a guide for business. A good part of the time the businessman is trying to do unto others as he hopes others will not do unto him.[2] Robbins continued:

> Espionage of one kind or another has become so common in business that it's like taking a drink during Prohibition—it's not considered sinful. And we don't even have Prohibition where espionage is concerned; the law is very tolerant in this area. There's no more shame for a business that uses secret agents than there is for a nation. Bear in mind that there already is at least one large corporation—you can buy its stock over the counter—that makes millions by providing counterespionage service to industrial firms. Espionage in business is not an ethical problem; it's an established technique of business competition.

"We Don't Make the Laws"

Wherever we turn in business, we can perceive the sharp distinction between its ethical standards and those of the churches. Newspapers abound with sensational stories growing out of this distinction:

- We read one day that Senator Philip A. Hart of Michigan has attacked food processors for deceptive packaging of numerous products.[3]
- The next day there is a Congressional to-do over Ralph Nader's book, *Unsafe At Any Speed*, which demonstrates that automobile companies for years have neglected the safety of car-owning families.[4]
- Then another Senator, Lee Metcalf of Montana, and journalist Vic Reinemer show in their book, *Overcharge*, the methods by which utility companies elude regulating government bodies to extract unduly large payments from users of electricity.[5]

These are merely dramatic instances of a prevailing condition; there is hardly a major industry at which a similar attack could not be aimed. Critics of business regard such behavior as unethical, but the companies concerned know that they are merely playing the business game.

Among the most respected of our business institutions are the insurance companies. A group of insurance executives meeting recently in New England was startled when their guest speaker, social critic Daniel Patrick Moynihan, roundly berated them for "unethical" practices. They had been guilty, Moynihan alleged, of using outdated actuarial tables to obtain unfairly high premiums. They habitually delayed the hearings of lawsuits against them in order to tire out the plaintiffs and win cheap settlements. In their employment policies they used ingenious devices to discriminate against certain minority groups.[6]

It was difficult for the audience to deny the validity of these charges. But these men were business game players. Their reaction to Moynihan's attack was much the same as that of the automobile manufacturers to Nader, of the utilities to Senator Metcalf, and of the food processors to Senator Hart. If the laws governing their businesses change, or if public opinion becomes clamorous, they will make the necessary adjustments. But morally they have in their view done nothing wrong. As long as they comply with the letter of the law, they are within their rights to operate their businesses as they see fit.

The small business is in the same position as the great corporation in this respect. For example:

> In 1967 a key manufacturer was accused of providing master keys for automobiles to mail-order customers, although it was obvious that some of the purchasers might be automobile thieves. His defense was plain and straightforward. If there was nothing in the law to prevent him from selling his keys to anyone who ordered them, it was not up to him to inquire as to his customers' motives. Why was it any worse, he insisted, for him to sell car keys by mail, than for mail-order houses to sell guns that might be used for murder? Until the law was changed, the key manufacturer could regard himself as being just as ethical as any other businessman by the rules of the business game.[7]

Violations of the ethical ideals of society are common in business, but they are not necessarily violations of business principles. Each year the Federal Trade Commission orders hundreds of companies, many of them of the first magnitude, to "cease and desist" from practices which, judged by ordinary standards, are of questionable morality but which are stoutly defended by the companies concerned.

In one case, a firm manufacturing a well-known mouthwash was accused of using a cheap form of alcohol possibly deleterious to health. The company's chief executive, after testifying in Washington, made this comment privately:

We broke no law. We're in a highly competitive industry. If we're going to stay in business, we have to look for profit wherever the law permits. We don't make the laws. We obey them. Then why do we have to put up with this 'holier than thou' talk about ethics? It's sheer hypocrisy. We're not in business to promote ethics. Look at the cigarette companies, for God's sake! If the ethics aren't embodied in the laws by the men who made them, you can't expect businessmen to fill the lack. Why, a sudden submission to Christian ethics by businessmen would bring about the greatest economic upheaval in history!

It may be noted that the government failed to prove its case against him.

Cast Illusions Aside

Talk about ethics by businessmen is often a thin decorative coating over the hard realities of the game:

Once I listened to a speech by a young executive who pointed to a new industry code as proof that his company and its competitors were deeply aware of their responsibilities to society. It was a code of ethics, he said. The industry was going to police itself, to dissuade constituent companies from wrongdoing. His eyes shone with conviction and enthusiasm.

The same day there was a meeting in a hotel room where the industry's top executives met with the "czar" who was to administer the new code, a man of high repute. No one who was present could doubt their common attitude. In their eyes the code was designed primarily to forestall a move by the federal government to impose stern restrictions on the industry. They felt that the code would hamper them a good deal less than new federal laws would. It was, in other words, conceived as a protection for the industry, not for the public.

The young executive accepted the surface explanation of the code; these leaders, all experienced game players, did not deceive themselves for a moment about its purpose.

The illusion that business can afford to be guided by ethics as conceived in private life is often fostered by speeches and articles containing such phrases as, "It pays to be ethical," or, "Sound ethics is good business." Actually this is not an ethical position at all; it is a self-serving calculation in disguise. The speaker is really saying that in the long run a company can make more money if it does not antagonize competitors, suppliers, employees, and customers by squeezing them too hard. He is saying that oversharp policies reduce ultimate gains. That is true, but it has nothing to do with ethics. The underlying attitude is much like that in the familiar story of the shopkeeper who finds an extra $20 bill in the cash register, debates with himself the ethical problem—should he tell his partner?—and finally decides to share the money because the gesture will give him an edge over the s.o.b. the next time they quarrel.

I think it is fair to sum up the prevailing attitude of businessmen on ethics as follows:

We live in what is probably the most competitive of the world's civilized societies. Our customs encourage a high degree of aggression in the individual's striving for success. Business is our main area of competition, and it has been ritualized into a game of strategy. The basic rules of the game have been set by the government, which attempts to detect and punish business frauds. But as long as a company does not transgress the rules of the game set by law, it has the legal right to shape its strategy without reference to anything but its profits. If it takes a long-term view of its profits, it will preserve amicable relations, so far as possible, with those with whom it deals. A wise businessman will not seek advantage to the point where he generates dangerous hostility among employees, competitors, customers, government, or the public at large. But decisions in this area are, in the final test, decisions of strategy, not of ethics.

The Individual and the Game

An individual within a company often finds it difficult to adjust to the requirements of the business game. He tries to preserve his private ethical standards in situations that call for game strategy. When he is obliged to carry out company policies that challenge his conception of himself as an ethical man, he suffers.

It disturbs him when he is ordered, for instance, to deny a raise to a man who deserves it, to fire an employee of long standing, to prepare advertising that he believes to be misleading, to conceal facts that he feels customers are entitled to know, to cheapen the quality of materials used in the manufacture of an established product, to sell as new a product that he knows to be rebuilt, to exaggerate the curative powers of a medicinal preparation, or to coerce dealers.

There are some fortunate executives who, by the nature of their work and circumstances, never have to face problems of this kind. But in one form or another the ethical dilemma is felt sooner or later by most businessmen. Possibly the dilemma is most painful not when the company forces the action on the executive but when he originates it himself—that is, when he has taken or is contemplating a step which is in his own interest but which runs counter to his early moral conditioning. To illustrate:

- The manager of an export department, eager to show rising sales, is pressed by a big customer to provide invoices which, while containing no overt falsehood that would violate a US law, are so worded that the customer may be able to evade certain taxes in his homeland.

- A company president finds that an aging executive, within a few years of retirement and his pension, is not as productive as formerly. Should he be kept on?

- The produce manager of a supermarket debates with himself whether to get rid of a lot of half-rotten tomatoes by including one, with its good side exposed, in every tomato six-pack.

- An accountant discovers that he has taken an improper deduction on his company's tax return and fears the consequences if he calls the matter to the president's attention, though he himself has done nothing illegal. Perhaps if he says nothing, no one will notice the error.

- A chief executive officer is asked by his directors to comment on a rumor that he owns stock in another company with which he has placed large orders. He could deny it, for the stock is in the name of his son-in-law and he has earlier formally instructed his son-in-law to sell the holding.

Temptations of this kind constantly arise in business. If an executive allows himself to be torn between a decision based on business considerations and one based on his private ethical code, he exposes himself to a grave psychological strain.

This is not to say that sound business strategy necessarily runs counter to ethical ideals. They may frequently coincide; and when they do, everyone is gratified. But the major tests of every move in business, as in all games of strategy, are legality and profit. A man who intends to be a winner in the business game must have a game player's attitude.

The business strategist's decisions must be as impersonal as those of a surgeon performing an operation—concentrating on objective and technique, and subordinating personal feelings. If the chief executive admits that his son-in-law owns the stock, it is because he stands to lose more if the fact comes out later than if he states it boldly and at once. If the supermarket manager orders the rotten tomatoes to be discarded, he does so to avoid an increase in consumer complaints and a loss of goodwill. The company president decides not to fire the elderly executive in the belief that the negative reaction of other employees would in the long run cost the company more than it would lose in keeping him and paying his pension.

All sensible businessmen prefer to be truthful, but they seldom feel inclined to tell the *whole* truth. In the business game truth-telling usually has to be kept within narrow limits if trouble is to be avoided. The point was neatly made a long time ago (in 1888) by one of John D. Rockefeller's associates, Paul Babcock, to Standard Oil Company executives who were about to testify before a government investigating committee: "Parry every question with answers which, while perfectly truthful, are evasive of *bottom* facts."[8] This was, is, and probably always will be regarded as wise and permissible business strategy.

For Office Use Only

An executive's family life can easily be dislocated if he fails to make a sharp distinction between the ethical systems of the home and the office—or if his wife does not grasp that distinction. Many a businessman who has remarked to his wife, "I had to let Jones go today" or "I had to admit to the boss that Jim has been goofing off lately," has been met with an indignant protest. "How could you do a thing like that? You know Jones is over 50 and will have a lot of trouble getting another job." Or, "You did that to Jim? With his wife ill and all the worry she's been having with the kids?"

If the executive insists that he had no choice because the profits of the company and his own security were involved, he may see a certain cool and ominous reappraisal in his wife's eyes. Many wives are not prepared to accept the fact that business operates with a special code of ethics. An illuminating illustration of this comes from a Southern sales executive who related a conversation he had had with his wife at a time when a hotly contested political campaign was being waged in their state:

> I made the mistake of telling her that I had had lunch with Colby, who gives me about half my business. Colby mentioned that his company had a stake in the election. Then he said, "By the way, I'm treasurer of the citizens' committee for Lang. I'm collecting contributions. Can I count on you for a hundred dollars?"
>
> Well, there I was. I was opposed to Lang, but I knew Colby. If he withdrew his business I could be in a bad spot. So I just smiled and wrote out a check then and there. He thanked me, and we started to talk about his next order. Maybe he thought I shared his political views. If so, I wasn't going to lose any sleep over it.
>
> I should have had sense enough not to tell Mary about it. She hit the ceiling. She said she was disappointed in me. She said I hadn't acted like a man, that I should have stood up to Colby.
>
> I said, "Look, it was an either-or situation. I had to do it or risk losing the business."
>
> She came back at me with, "I don't believe it. You could have been honest with him. You could have said that you didn't feel you ought to contribute to a campaign for a man you weren't going to vote for. I'm sure he would have understood."
>
> I said, "Mary, you're a wonderful woman, but you're way off the track. Do you know what would have happened if I had said that? Colby would have smiled and said, 'Oh, I didn't realize. Forget it.' But in his

eyes from that moment I would be an odd-ball, maybe a bit of a radical. He would have listened to me talk about his order and would have promised to give it consideration. After that I wouldn't hear from him for a week. Then I would telephone and learn from his secretary that he wasn't yet ready to place the order. And in about a month I would hear through the grapevine that he was giving his business to another company. A month after that I'd be out of a job."

She was silent for a while. Then she said, "Tom, something is wrong with business when a man is forced to choose between his family's security and his moral obligation to himself. It's easy for me to say you should have stood up to him—but if you had, you might have felt you were betraying me and the kids. I'm sorry that you did it, Tom, but I can't blame you. Something is wrong with business!"

This wife saw the problem in terms of moral obligation as conceived in private life; her husband saw it as a matter of game strategy. As a player in a weak position, he felt that he could not afford to indulge an ethical sentiment that might have cost him his seat at the table.

Playing to Win

Some men might challenge the Colbys of business—might accept serious setbacks to their business careers rather than risk a feeling of moral cowardice. They merit our respect—but as private individuals, not businessmen. When the skillful player of the business game is compelled to submit to unfair pressure, he does not castigate himself for moral weakness. Instead, he strives to put himself into a strong position where he can defend himself against such pressures in the future without loss.

If a man plans to take a seat in the business game, he owes it to himself to master the principles by which the game is played, including its special ethical outlook. He can then hardly fail to recognize that an occasional bluff may well be justified in terms of the game's ethics and warranted in terms of economic necessity. Once he clears his mind on this point, he is in a good position to match his strategy against that of the other players. He can then determine objectively whether a bluff in a given situation has a good chance of succeeding and can decide when and how to bluff, without a feeling of ethical transgression.

To be a winner, a man must play to win. This does not mean that he must be ruthless, cruel, harsh, or treacherous. On the contrary, the better his reputation for integrity, honesty, and decency, the better his chances of victory will be in the long run. But from time to time every businessman, like every poker player, is offered a choice between certain loss or bluffing within the legal rules of the game. If he is not resigned to losing, if he wants to rise in his company and industry, then in such a crisis he will bluff—and bluff hard.

Every now and then one meets a successful businessman who has conveniently forgotten the small or large deceptions that he practiced on his way to fortune. "God gave me my money," old John D. Rockefeller once piously told a Sunday school class. It would be a rare tycoon in our time who would risk the horse laugh with which such a remark would be greeted.

In the last third of the twentieth century even children are aware that if a man has become prosperous in business, he has sometimes departed from the strict truth in order to overcome obstacles or has practiced the more subtle deceptions of the half-truth or the misleading omission. Whatever the form of the bluff, it is an integral part of the game, and the executive who does not master its techniques is not likely to accumulate much money or power.

NOTES

1 *The New York Times*, March 9, 1967.

2 See Bruce D. Henderson, "Brinkmanship in Business," *Harvard Business Review* March-April 1967, 49.

3 *The New York Times*, November 21, 1966.

4 New York: Grossman Publishers, Inc., 1965.

5 New York: David McKay Company, Inc., 1967.

6 *The New York Times*, January 17, 1967.

7 Cited by Ralph Nader in "Business Crime," *The New Republic*, July 1, 1967, 7.

8 Babcock in a memorandum to Rockefeller (Rockefeller Archives).

♦ ♦ ♦ ♦ ♦

THOMAS CARSON

Second Thoughts about Bluffing

I. Introduction

In the United States it is common, perhaps even a matter of course, for people to misstate their bargaining positions during business negotiations. I have in mind the following kinds of cases, all of which involve deliberate false statements about one's bargaining position, intentions, or preferences in a negotiation: 1. I am selling a house and tell a prospective buyer that $90,000 is absolutely the lowest price that I will accept, when I know that I would be willing to accept as little as $80,000 for the house. 2. A union negotiator says that $13.00 an hour is the very lowest wage that his union is willing to consider when, in fact, he has been authorized by the union to accept a wage as low as $12.00 an hour. 3. I tell a prospective buyer that I am in no hurry to sell my house when, in fact, I am desperate to sell it within a few days.[1] Such statements would seem to constitute

lies—they are deliberate false statements made with the intent to deceive others about the nature of one's own bargaining position. 1) and 2) clearly constitute lies according to standard dictionary definitions of lying. The *Oxford English Dictionary* defines the word "lie" as follows: "a false statement made with the intent to deceive." Also see *Webster's International Dictionary of the English Language*, (1929) "to utter a falsehood with the intent to deceive."

The cases described above should be contrasted with instances of bluffing which do not involve making false statements. An example of the latter case would be saying "I want more" in response to an offer which I am willing to accept rather than not reach an agreement at all. This paper will focus on cases of bluffing which involve deliberate false statements about one's bargaining position or one's "settlement preferences."

I will defend the following two theses:

a. Appearances to the contrary, this kind of bluffing typically does not constitute lying. (I will argue that standard dictionary definitions of lying are untenable and defend an alternative definition hinted at, but never clearly formulated, by W.D. Ross. On my definition, deliberate false statements about one's negotiating position usually do not constitute lies *in this society*.)

b. It is usually permissible to misstate one's bargaining position or settlement preferences when one has good reason to think that one's negotiating partner is doing the same and it is usually impermissible to misstate one's negotiating position if one does not have good reason to think that the other party is misstating her position (preferences).

There are significant puzzles and uncertainties involved in applying my definition of lying to cases of misstating one's bargaining position. Because of this, I intend to make an argument for b) independent of my argument for a). My arguments for b) are compatible with (but do not presuppose) the view that misstating one's position is lying and that lying is *prima facie* wrong. I will conclude the paper with a brief examination of other related deceptive stratagems in negotiations.[2]

II. The Economic Significance of Bluffing

In a business negotiation there is typically a range of possible agreements that each party would be willing to accept rather than reach no agreement at all. For instance, I might be willing to sell my home for as little as $80,000. (I would prefer to sell the house for $80,000 *today*, rather than continue to try to sell the house.)[3] My range of acceptable agreements extends upward without limit—I would be willing to accept any price in excess of $80,000 rather than fail to make the sale today. Suppose that a prospective buyer is willing to spend as much as $85,000 for the house. (She prefers to buy the house for $85,000 today rather than not buy it at all today.) The buyer's range of acceptable agreements presumably extends downward without limit—she would be willing to purchase the house for any price below $85,000. In this case the two bargaining positions overlap and an agreement is possible (today). Unless there is some overlap between the minimum bargaining positions of the two parties, no agreement is possible. For example, if the seller's lowest acceptable price is $80,000 and the buyer's highest acceptable price is $70,000 no sale will be possible unless at least one of the parties alters her position.

If there is an overlap between the bargaining positions of the negotiators, then the actual outcome will depend on the negotiations. Consider again our example of the negotiation over the sale of the house. The owner is willing to sell the house for as little as $80,000 and the prospective buyer is willing to pay as much as $85,000. Whether the house sells for $80,000, $85,000, somewhere between $80,000 and $85,000, or even whether it sells at all will be determined by the negotiations. In this case, it would

be very advantageous for either party to know the other person's minimum acceptable position and disadvantageous for either to reveal her position to the other.[4] For example, if the buyer knows that the lowest price that the seller is willing to accept is $80,000, she can drive him towards the limit of his range of acceptable offers. She knows that he will accept an offer of $80,000 rather than have her break off the negotiations. In negotiations both buyer and seller will ordinarily have reason to keep their own bargaining positions and intentions secret.

It can sometimes be to one's advantage to mislead others about one's own minimum bargaining position. In the present case, it would be to the seller's advantage to cause the buyer to think that $85,000 is the lowest price that he (the seller) will accept. For in this case the buyer would offer $85,000 for the house—the best possible agreement from the seller's point of view. (It would also be easy to imagine cases in which it would be to the buyer's advantage to mislead the seller about her bargaining position.) There are various ways in which the seller might attempt to bluff the buyer in order to mislead her about his position. 1. He might set a very high "asking price," for example, $100,000. 2. He might initially refuse an offer and threaten to cut off the negotiations unless a higher offer is made while at the same time being prepared to accept the offer before the other person breaks off the negotiations. (I have in mind something like the following. The prospective buyer offers $80,000 and the seller replies: "I want more than that; I'm not happy with $80,000 why don't you think about it and give me a call tomorrow.") 3. He might misrepresent his own bargaining position.

The kind of deception involved in 1) and 2) does not (or need not) involve lying or making false statements. 3) involves a deliberate false statement intended to deceive the other party and thus constitutes lying according to the standard definition of lying.

Attempting to mislead the other person about one's bargaining position can backfire and prevent a negotiation from reaching a mutually acceptable settlement which both parties would have preferred to no agreement at all. For example, suppose that the seller tells the buyer that he won't accept anything less than $95,000 for the house. If the buyer believes him she will break off the negotiations, since, by hypothesis, she is not willing to pay $95,000 for the house. Unless he knows the other person's bargaining position, a person who misrepresents his own position risks losing the opportunity to reach an acceptable agreement. By misstating one's position one also risks angering the other party and thereby causing him to modify his position or even break off the negotiations. (Truthful statements about one's own position might be perceived as lies and thus also risk alienating one's counterpart.)

III. The Concept of Lying

1. *The Standard Definition.* Standard dictionary definitions of lying are correct in holding that a lie must be a false statement. Showing that a statement is true is always sufficient to rebut the charge that one has told a lie. However, the two dictionary definitions cited earlier leave out an essential feature of lying. If a person's making a statement constitutes a lie, then it cannot be the case that she believes that it is true. Showing that one believed what one said is always sufficient to rebut a charge of lying.[5]

According to most standard definitions of lying, telling a lie necessarily involves the intention to deceive others. See for example, the definitions from the *OED* and *Webster's* presented at the beginning of the paper. These definitions and other definitions which imply that the intent to deceive is a necessary condition of lying prove inadequate for dealing with certain kinds of cases in which one is compelled or enticed to make false statements. Suppose that I witness a crime and clearly see that a particular individual committed the crime. Later, the same person is accused of the crime and, as a witness in court, I am asked whether or not I saw the defend-

ant commit the crime. I make the false statement that I did not see the defendant commit the crime, for fear of being harmed or killed by him. It does not follow that I hope or intend that my false statements deceive anyone. (I may hope that he is convicted in spite of my testimony.) Deceiving the jury is not a means to securing my goal of preserving my life. Giving false testimony is a necessary means to achieving this goal, but deceiving others is not, it is merely an unintended "side effect." Clearly, in both the ordinary language sense of "intentional act" and in the standard philosophical sense of the term my deceiving the jury in such a case would not be intentional.[6] But it seems clear that my false testimony would constitute a lie.[7] This objection can be put more generally as follows. It is (or rather can be) a lie if I say x (where x is something that I know is false) in order to achieve objective (o), even if others coming to believe x is a foreseeable side effect of the action and neither a part of (o) nor or a means to achieving (o).

2. *A New Definition of Lying.* I have defended an alternative analysis of the concept of lying in a paper written several years after the original paper on bluffing.[8] I still agree with much of this. I shall explain my definition here, repeating some of what I said in the paper on lying. I refer the reader to the paper on lying for a defense of my definition. (Also see the second paragraph of fn. 9 of and the first paragraph of III.1 for arguments not included in the earlier paper.) My definition of lying is inspired by Ross's claim that the duty not to lie is a special case of the duty to keep promises. Ross holds that (at least in ordinary contexts) we make an implicit promise to be truthful when we use language to communicate with others. To lie is to break an implicit promise to be truthful.[9]

Ross's view that making a statement (ordinarily) involves making an implicit promise that what one says is true suggests the following provisional definition of "lying" (Ross himself never attempts to define "lying"):

Y. A lie is a false statement which the "speaker" does not believe to be true made in a context in which the speaker warrants the truth of what he says.[10]

This definition handles the earlier counter-example. Not only is the implicit warranty of truthfulness in force in the case of the witness's testimony in court, the witness explicitly warrants the truth of what he says by swearing an oath. Another virtue of the present analysis is that it makes sense of the common view that lying involves a violation of trust. To lie, in my view, is to invite trust and encourage others to believe what one says by warranting the truth of what one says and at the same time to betray that trust by making false statements which one does not believe to be true.

3. *A Complication.* Problems are created by cases in which statements are made to groups of individuals who have differing levels of knowledge and sophistication, so that the truth of a given statement on a given occasion is warranted to some (but not all) of the people to whom the statement is made. Consider, for example, a greatly exaggerated account of a past event told to a mixed group containing both sophisticated adults and young children—"The dog who was chasing me was huge; he was at least ten feet tall." (Note, I am supposing that the context of this is not just "a story" but an account of something which was alleged to have actually happened.) In such a case one warrants the truth of what one says to the children but not to the adults. The very content of the narrative makes it clear to the adults that its truth is not being warranted to them. But there is nothing one does and nothing about the context or content of what one says which removes the default warranty of truth to the children. We need to relativize our concept of lying and allow for the possibility that in making a given statement or utterance on a particular occasion one might be lying to some members of one's audience, but not to others. I propose the following:

Z. *S lies to x* if, and only if, S makes a false statement which he does not believe to be true and in so doing warrants the truth of the statement to x.[11]

4. *The Concept of Warranting.* What does it mean to warrant the truth of what one says? I will not attempt to offer a definition with necessary and sufficient conditions. But I will try to sketch the outlines of an analysis. A warranty is a kind of promise. Following Austin and Searle, contemporary philosophers generally take promising to be a kind of performative act. To make a promise is to place oneself under an obligation to do something. This kind of analysis is claimed to be necessary in order to explain the difference between promising to do x and stating an intention to do x.[12] But special problems arise if we attempt to extend this account of promising as an analysis of warranting the truth of a statement. If one promises to do x it is very clear *which action* one is placing oneself under an obligation to perform (one is placing oneself under an obligation to do x). But often when one warrants the truth of a statement it is unclear whether one is placing oneself under an obligation to perform any *particular action*. To warrant the truth of a statement x is not necessarily to place oneself under an obligation to make it true that x. For one is usually not in a position to affect the truth of the statements one makes. If I warrant the truth of my statement that the moon is 250,000 miles from the earth I am not placing myself under an obligation to make it the case that the moon is 250,000 miles from earth. Nor will it do to say that to warrant the truth of x is to place oneself under an obligation to perform acts of compensation in case x turns out not to be true and others are harmed as a result of believing our statements. There simply is no general understanding about what (if anything) we owe others when they suffer harms or losses as a result of accepting false claims that we make. How can we characterize warranting the truth of a state-

ment? To warrant a statement as true is to invite others to rely on it and assure them that it can be relied upon. When warranting a statement one is granting others permission to complain if the statement does not turn out to be true.

In our linguistic community and all others of which I am aware there is a presumption for thinking that the warranty of truth is in force in any situation. *Convention* dictates that one warrants the truth of one's statements, in the absence of special contexts, special signals, or cues to the contrary. In the context of a work of fiction, in games such as "Risk," or when saying something in jest, one is not guaranteeing the truth of what one says. So, for example, one is not implicitly guaranteeing that what one says is true if in the course of a game of "Risk" one makes the false statement that one will not attack one's opponent, or when one says something manifestly false to a friend in a joking tone of voice. In many cases it is unclear whether those who speak or communicate can be said to be warranting the truth of what they say. For example, suppose that I deliberately make a false statement to a person whom I know to be very gullible but give a very subtle indication that I might be joking (I might, for example, raise an eyebrow). In such a case it is unclear whether I am warranting the truth of what I say and, therefore, unclear whether or not this should be considered a lie. Such cases should be considered borderline cases for the concept of lying. It is a virtue of the present analysis that they count as such.[13]

5. *Lying and Bluffing.* What are the implications of my analysis of lying for the issue of bluffing? Negotiations between experienced and "hardened" negotiators in our society (e.g., horse traders and realtors) are akin to a game of "Risk." It is understood that any statements one makes about one's role or intentions as a player during a game of "Risk" are not warranted to be true.[14] In negotiations between hardened and cynical negotiators statements about one's intentions or settlement preferences are not warranted to be true.[15] But it would be too strong to hold that nothing that one says in negotiations is warranted to be true. Convention dictates that other kinds of statements concerning the transaction being contemplated, e.g., statements to the effect that one has another offer, are warranted as true. So, for example, in my view, it would be a lie if I (the seller) were to falsely claim that someone else has offered me $85,000 for my house.[16]

I am strongly inclined to believe that statements about one's minimum negotiating position are not warranted to be true in negotiations between "hardened negotiators" who recognize each other as such. I cannot here propose general criteria for determining when one may be said to warrant the truth of what one says. Therefore, what follows is somewhat conjectural. A cynical negotiator typically does not expect (predict) that her counterpart will speak truthfully about his minimum negotiating position. This alone is not enough to remove the implicit warranty of truth. A pathological liar who denies his every misdeed warrants the truth of what he says, even if those he addresses do not *expect* (predict) that what he says is true. The crucial feature of a negotiation which distinguishes it from the foregoing case is that in ordinary negotiations each party *consents* to renouncing the ordinary warranty of truth. There are various ways in which people consent to removing the default warranty of truth. Business negotiations are ritualized activities to which certain unstated rules and expectations (both in the sense of predictions and demands) apply. It is not expected that one will speak truthfully about one's negotiating position. Those who understand this and who enter into negotiations with other parties who are known to share this understanding implicitly consent to the rules and expectations of the negotiating ritual. In so doing, they consent to remove the warranty of truth for statements about one's minimum negotiating position.

Here one might raise the following objection: "Of course I recognize that misstating one's position is *thought to be permissible*, but I strongly disapprove of that practice. I don't consent to being deceived when I enter into a negotiation simply because I know that others are likely to try to deceive me. In the old south it was an 'accepted' practice for blacks to be very deferential to whites in social interactions. But we cannot say that blacks who entered into social interactions with whites thereby gave their consent to abiding by the unwritten rules requiring deference."

Reply. There are relevant differences between the social code of the old south and our society's present rules and conventions for negotiations. Most people do not object to standard negotiating practices and those who enter into negotiations are justified in presuming acceptance of those practices by their counterparts. Further, those who do object to these practices can air their objections openly without fear of dire consequences. Most blacks objected very much to the social mores of the old south but were justifiably afraid of publicly airing their objections. Many whites deluded themselves into thinking that blacks did not object to their status, but few, if any, had adequate evidence for this view. My underlying principle here can be stated roughly as follows:

> Y implicitly consents to X's doing (act) *a* to him (Y) provided that: 1) X knows that: i) Y expects X to do *a* to him, ii) Y doesn't object to X's doing *a* to him, and iii) Y can, without fear of harm, object to X's doing *a* to him, and 2) Y knows that X knows that i)-iii).

Before moving on to other issues, I would again like to stress the following two points: 1. my application of my definition of lying to this case is tentative and conjectural, and 2. my arguments concerning the moral status of bluffing do not depend on the assumption that misstating one's bargaining position or intentions is (typically) not a case of lying (my arguments are compatible with the view that misstating one's position or intentions is lying).

IV. The Moral Status of Bluffing (Preliminary Considerations)

1. *General Strategy.* A fully adequate discussion of the morality of bluffing would require a definitive treatment of foundational questions in normative ethics. No account of the rightness or wrongness of bluffing can be considered final or definitive apart from our having found and justified a full-blown theory of right and wrong action or a definitive test for the truth or correctness of moral judgments.[17] I cannot undertake an examination of foundational questions in the present paper. I will have to make use of assumptions which cannot be fully defended here. My strategy is to rely on weak and relatively noncontroversial assumptions. I will assume that there is a substantial moral presumption against misstating one's negotiating position and ask whether there are countervailing moral considerations of sufficient weight to overcome this presumption. This strategy is compatible with most, but not all, plausible theories of right and wrong. My strategy is probably most congenial to an account of right and wrong similar to Ross's. Ross holds that there are a number of ultimate moral obligations: the duty to keep promises, the duty not to lie, duties of gratitude, and the duty not to harm others, etc. According to Ross, these are only *prima facie* moral duties and can be overridden if they conflict with weightier moral duties. Misstating one's bargaining position would seem to be *prima facie* wrong, not only on account of the economic harm it causes others, but also on account of the harm it causes the agent's character. It is also *prima facie* wrong on account of the fact that it undermines trust between human beings.[18] A Rossian moral theory would also be compatible with saying that misstating one's position is 1. *prima facie* wrong in virtue of being a case of intending to deceive others and 2. *prima facie* wrong in virtue of being a case of lying. [Ross himself does not hold #1]. He does not say that attempting to deceive others is *prima facie* wrong, but such a view is a plausible ex-

tension of his theory.] #2) assumes (contrary to my arguments of III.5) that misstating one's negotiating position typically constitutes lying. A utilitarian or consequentialist could also grant that there is a substantial moral presumption against deliberately misstating one's negotiating position. This presumption derives, in part, from the economic harm which the other party is likely to suffer. The harm to the agent's character which results from deception and/or lying and the indirect bad consequences of deception and/or lying (distrust) also create a moral presumption against misstating one's position.

My assumption that there is a substantial (but possibly overridable) moral presumption against misstating one's position is not compatible with an absolutist view according to which lying or attempting to deceive others is always wrong. If a certain act is always wrong no matter what, then it makes no sense to ask whether there are any moral considerations which might serve to justify it.[19]

I will begin by considering and then rejecting Albert Carr's very well-known and influential defense of bluffing. Then I will argue that my position about the moral status of bluffing [that it is usually morally permissible to misstate one's position if the other party has first misstated her position and usually impermissible to misstate one's position if the other party has not first misstated her position] is defensible on either a Rossian or utilitarian theory of right and wrong.

2. *Carr's Defense of Bluffing.* In a well-known paper Albert Carr argues that misstating one's negotiating position is morally permissible.[20] Business, he argues, is a game like poker—a game in which special norms apply. The moral norms appropriate to the game of business or a game of poker are different from those appropriate to ordinary contexts.

> No one expects poker to be played on the ethical principles preached in churches. In poker it is right and proper to bluff a friend out of the rewards of being dealt a good hand.... Poker's own brand of ethics is different from the ethical ideals of civilized human relationships. The game calls for distrust of the other fellow. It ignores the claim of friendship. Cunning, deception, and concealment of one's strength and intentions, not kindness and openheartedness, are vital in poker. No one thinks any the worse of poker on that account. And no one should think any the worse of business because its standards of right and wrong differ from the prevailing traditions of morality in our society....[21]

Carr claims that just as bluffing is permissible according to the special rules of poker, so it is permissible according to the rules of business.[22]

What are the rules of the business game? How can we determine whether or not a particular rule or practice is part of the business game? Carr's position is confused on this point. At a number of points he suggests that the "rules of the business game" are simply our society's conventional moral standards for business, i.e., those standards which are thought by most people to govern the conduct of businesspeople. Carr defends a number of questionable business practices and argues that they are all morally justifiable, *because* they are standard practice and are regarded as permissible by conventional morality.

> In his view these things had nothing to do with ethics; they were merely normal business practice.[23]

> This was a lie; yet within the accepted rules of the business game, no moral culpability attaches to it.[24]

In other passages Carr seems to assume that the appropriate rules for business are those set by the law.

> If the laws governing their business change, or if public opinion becomes clamorous, they will make the necessary adjustments.

But morally they have in their view done nothing wrong. As long as they comply with the letter of the law, they are within their rights to operate their businesses as they see fit.[25]

There are three possible ways to interpret the principle to which Carr appeals in trying to justify bluffing and other questionable business practices:

a. Any action or practice engaged in by businesspeople in a given society is morally permissible provided that it is consistent with the ethical rules or principles which are generally accepted in that society.

b. Any action or practice engaged in by businesspeople in a given society is morally permissible provided that it is consistent with the laws of that society.

c. Any action or practice engaged in by businesspeople in a given society is morally permissible provided that it is consistent with *both* i) the society's conventional ethical rules or principles governing those actions and practices, *and* ii) the laws of that society.

On any of these readings, Carr's argument is most implausible. One can't justify an act or practice *simply because* it is consistent with conventional morality. Similarly, the fact that an action or practice is permitted by the law does not suffice to establish its moral permissibility. Conventional morality and the law are not infallible moral guidelines. In the past, many immoral practices, most notably slavery, were condoned by the conventional morality and legal codes of our own and many other societies.

V. The Morality Bluffing on a Rossian Theory of Right and Wrong

1. *A Principle of Self-Defense.* Suppose that I am involved in a business negotiation and the other party makes a deliberate false statement about her negotiating position. Even though I'm fairly sure that she is not telling me the truth, she is likely to gain an advantage over me in the negotiations. Let us grant that her misstatement is a lie and that it is *prima facie* wrong to lie or intentionally deceive others.[26] Does the moral presumption against lying and deception require me to refrain from misstating my own position? Intuitively, I want to say "no." It seems to me that I would be justified in doing the same to her in order to protect my financial interests. In some extended use of the term, misstating my position to her would be a case of "self-defense."

Common sense would surely want to distinguish between "defensive" and "offensive" violations of *prima facie* moral rules. One violates rules against deception in a defensive manner if one deceives someone who is himself violating a *prima facie* rule in order to avoid or mitigate the harm that one will otherwise suffer as a result of the other person's violation of moral rules. One violates *prima facie* moral rules against deception in an offensive manner if one deceives people who are not deceiving one or violating any other moral rules in their treatment of one.[27] Common sense holds that there is a morally significant difference between defensive and offensive violations of *prima facie* moral rules. It also holds that defensive violations are justified within certain limits. Common sense would surely agree with Hobbes that we are not obligated to refrain from defending ourselves by doing x (when x is something that harms others), unless others are also refraining from xing. "For that" [to refrain from xing when others don't] "were to expose himself to prey (which no man is bound to do)."[28]

How can we best formulate a general principle of self-defense from within a Rossian theory of multiple *prima facie* duties? I suggest that circumstances which create a ground for claims of self-defense should be regarded as circumstances which nullify (or reduce the stringency of) the *prima facie* duties of the person being attacked (her duties to the person attacking her). A theory of self-defense provides (some of the) defeasibility conditions for *prima facie* duties.[29] Acts which are ordinarily *prima facie* wrong are not *prima facie* wrong (or at least less *prima facie* wrong) if they are necessary in order to protect oneself against harm caused by other people's offensive violations of *prima facie* moral rules. I suggest the following:

> SD. For any act *a* such that doing *a* to someone is ordinarily *prima facie* wrong qua act of a*ing someone, X's doing *a* to Y is *not prima facie* wrong qua act of *a*ing someone (or at least substantially *less prima facie* wrong qua act of *a*ing than it would otherwise be) provided that: 1. Y is doing or trying to do *a* (or something which is ordinarily equally *prima facie* wrong) to x, 2. X is likely to be harmed as a result, and 3. X can't prevent or mitigate this harm unless he does *a*.[30]

SD does not justify retaliation or the policy of "an eye for an eye and a tooth for a tooth." It does not imply that I am justified in hitting you in retaliation for your having hit me. SD only implies that the moral presumption against my hitting you is weakened or eliminated if my hitting you is *necessary* in order *to prevent you* from hitting me *and* thereby injuring me.

SD points to a large class of cases in which the presumption against violating moral rules is weakened or eliminated by conditions of self-defense. SD does not constitute a full theory of self-defense. It does not give either necessary or sufficient conditions for one's being justified (on balance) in violating *prima facie* duties. The reader might complain that I haven't given a complete theory of self-defense

with necessary and sufficient conditions for being justified in acting in self-defense.[31] But, given a Rossian theory of right and wrong which posits many different ultimate obligations which need to be "weighed" against each other in case of conflict, it is impossible to formulate (plausible) concise algorithmic principles for resolving all conflicts of duties, or even all conflicts of duty of a given type. The complexity of moral issues and relevant moral considerations is such as to render futile any such attempts to formulate simple necessary and sufficient conditions for right action. Any *plausible* general principles for resolving conflicts of duties would have to be extremely complex.[32] SD (or something like it) is at least *part of a* plausible Rossian theory of self-defense. It is a sufficiently strong principle that when taken in conjunction with other *prima facie* moral principles, it has clear implications for the issue of bluffing (see below [V.2]). It also helps to explain and support many of our common-sense convictions about the morality of self-defense.

2. *Application of SD to the issue of bluffing.* How can we apply SD to the issue of misstating one's position in a negotiation? SD is not an independent moral principle and by itself can neither permit or forbid any actions. SD implies that the moral presumption against lying to others (or deceiving others) about one's intentions in a negotiation is eliminated or greatly reduced provided: 1. the other person with whom one is negotiating is misstating her position (or doing something against which there is an equally strong moral presumption), and 2. she will thereby harm me unless I deceive her about my intentions (or do some other act against which there is an equally strong moral presumption). Given the prevalence of false claims about one's bargaining position in our society, a member of our society would be justified in assuming that statements about one's "final" position are false in the absence of special reasons for thinking to the contrary. (Such reasons might include knowing or having reason to believe that the other person is unusually scrupulous, honest, or naive.)[33]

It is more difficult to determine whether or not the second condition is satisfied. Those who misstate their positions often obtain a more favorable agreement than they would have been able to obtain otherwise. This benefit is almost always the other person's loss. If deception benefits me by enabling me to obtain a higher price for something that I am selling, it thereby harms the buyer by causing her to pay a higher price than she would have paid otherwise. It is possible for a negotiator to benefit from false statements about his position, even if the other party does not believe those statements. All that is necessary is that the other party revise her estimates about his position and intentions in a way that benefits him (the person who makes the misstatements). Suppose, for example, that I am selling my house and claim that $90,000 is the lowest price that I will accept, when, in fact, I would be willing to sell it for as little as $80,000. The potential buyer does not believe me, but she revises her best estimate of my intentions in light of this statement. Before, she thought that I would probably be willing to accept as little as $80,000 for the house. Now she thinks that I am unwilling to sell it for anything less than $85,000. ($85,000 is the most that she is willing to pay for the house.) As a result she will pay more for the house than she would have otherwise.[34]

It might be argued that other people's lies and/or misrepresentations in negotiations can only hurt one if one chooses to remain in the negotiations. They can't hurt one if one refuses to deal with the other person. Therefore, there can't be cases in which misstating one's own negotiating position or intentions (or doing something equally wrong) is the *only way* one can avoid being harmed by the other person's misrepresentations of her position; breaking off the negotiations and dealing with someone else is always an option. If successful, the foregoing argument shows that the appeal to "self-defense" will rarely, if ever, justify a person in misrepresenting her own bargaining position. I will now offer several reasons why we should reject this argument.

a) Sometimes people in a negotiation have no acceptable alternative to negotiating with a particular party. This is often the case in labor negotiations. An employer or labor union which has entered into collective bargaining agreements is required by law to negotiate with a particular union or employer and cannot decide that it will only talk with parties who scrupulously avoid deceptive practices in the negotiations. For either party to refuse to negotiate would be viewed as an "unfair labor practice" by the law; it would constitute a failure to "negotiate in good faith."[35]

b) There are cases in which one can refuse to negotiate with a given party, but only at considerable cost to oneself. Suppose that I am trying to buy a house in a tight real-estate market. S owns the only house that I can afford within a reasonable commuting distance to my job. In such cases it is implausible to maintain that one is obligated to bear the (high) costs of refusing to deal with the other person simply in order to avoid deceiving him (or lying to him) in response to *his* deception (or lies). It would be even less plausible to demand that an employee seek other employment rather than negotiate with a dishonest employer.

c) There are no doubt many cases in which it would be relatively easy for an individual involved in a negotiation to find someone else to deal with. But, given the pervasiveness of the practice of misstating one's settlement preferences, it might still be very difficult for that person to find someone else who would not also misstate her own preferences.

d) The appropriate benchmark for determining whether or not one is harmed by another person's misstatements in a negotiation is not the situation in which one (or both) of the parties break(s) off the negotiations, but rather what would have happened if the negotiations had taken place and the other person had not misstated her negotiating position. By breaking off the negotiations one would be worse off relative to this benchmark. Breaking off the negotiations does not usually enable one to avoid being harmed.

Summary

There is a substantial presumption against misrepresenting one's position when doing so does not fulfill the conditions of SD—see IV.1 and fn. 33. There are many ordinary cases in which misstating one's negotiating position constitutes "self-defense" in the sense elaborated in SD. In these cases the moral presumption against misstating one's position is greatly weakened, if not altogether eliminated. In those cases, considerations of self-interest and the interests of those who depend on one create a presumption for thinking it permissible to mislead others about one's bargaining preferences. I believe that cases in which it is permissible (on balance) to misstate one's position are quite frequent and more the rule than the exception. A presumption for thinking an act permissible or impermissible can be overturned by countervailing reasons or conflicting duties. There is no limit to the exceptions I could list but the following two things (while obvious) bear brief mention.

First, misstating one's negotiating position (intentions) can be morally permissible, even if it is not a case of self-defense. For example, suppose that I badly need to sell something for a very good price. I need the money for eye surgery without which I will be unable to work and support my children. Given this and given that the other party has no comparable needs, I might be justified in misstating my position to her, even if she is not doing the same to me. Similarly, misstating one's position might be wrong, all things considered, even if it is a genuine case of self-defense which satisfies the conditions of SD. For example, it might be wrong for an affluent person to drive a hard bargain (or use any kind of deception to do so) with someone whose financial situation is much worse than her own, even if the other person first misstates his position. To make this more persuasive, suppose that (innocent) dependents of a financially strapped deceiver will suffer greatly if one drives a hard bargain.[36]

VI. The Implications of Utilitarianism for the Moral Status of Misstating One's Position

In the preceding section of the paper I assumed the truth of a Rossian theory of right and wrong according to which there are a number of ultimate *prima facie* moral obligations and that these include the duty not to lie and the duty not to intentionally deceive others. Here, I will argue that utilitarianism leads to roughly the same conclusions concerning the morality of misstating one's position.

1. *Rule or Indirect Utilitarianism.* I cannot even begin to list all of the versions and formulations of indirect utilitarianism. I will restrict myself to considering Brandt's version of indirect utilitarianism ("ideal [acceptance] rule utilitarianism" [IARU]).[37] This is the most influential and widely discussed version of indirect utilitarianism. It also seems to me to be the most plausible. IARU can be formulated roughly as follows:

> IARU. An act is morally right provided that it is consistent with the set of moral rules whose acceptance by the members of the agent's society would maximize utility.

The ideal moral rules for our society and most other societies would include some kind of generalized principle of self-defense analogous to SD. Consider the following:

> SDU. It is permissible to harm another person by means of doing an act of type x, provided that 1. doing x (or some other act against which there is an equally strong moral presumption) is necessary in order to prevent that person from harming one by means of performing an act of type x (or is necessary in order to substantially mitigate the harm that the other person will (otherwise) inflict on one by doing (or trying to do) an act of type x), and 2. the harm one

inflicts on (innocent) third parties by xing does not outweigh the harm one prevents by doing x.

There are a number of reasons for thinking it desirable that people accept a principle such as this. A utilitarian would not want people to make it a policy to offer no resistance to those who harm them. If widely adopted, such a policy would invite and encourage predatory behavior. The general adoption of policies permitting "self-defense" would significantly deter and reduce predatory behavior. Apart from these indirect consequences, it is usually preferable that individuals defend themselves against harm (in accordance with SDU) rather than passively submit to being harmed. In most cases it is preferable that harm (whether death, personal injury, or loss of economic or political power) befall the attacker rather than the person acting in self-defense. For example, other things equal, the death of someone intent on murder is usually preferable to the death of his intended victim. Here, I am not supposing that the happiness or welfare of the virtuous is intrinsically preferable to that of the wicked or non-virtuous. It is quite enough to suppose that the lives, health, and economic power of non-predators generally have greater *extrinsic* value than those of predators.

It is important that predatory behavior be deterred, and, if not deterred, thwarted. These aims cannot be adequately served unless individuals are permitted to act in self-defense and harm others in ways that would otherwise be impermissible. However, very significant problems attach to principles of self-defense. The following list does not purport to be complete. i) The application or misapplication of principles permitting self-defense can result in excessive or disproportionate harm to the attacker or suspected attacker. For example, a shop keeper might shoot someone for shoplifting in his store. ii) Those who accept principles of self-defense might preemptively attack those they mistakenly believe to be attacking them or planning to attack them. iii) Prac-

ticing self-defense can break down one's inhibition and compunction against doing things which are impermissible in ordinary contexts. iv) The reliance on self-defense might lead to private enforcement of the law and privately exacted punishments or vendettas. v) Acts of self-defense can cause disproportionate harm to innocent third parties. SDU minimizes these problems as well as any adequate comprehensive principle of self-defense.

SDU deals well with problems i, iv, and v. No adequate principle of self-defense can fully avoid problems ii and iii. SDU has a simplicity and intuitive plausibility which minimize misapplication of the principle. The notion of reciprocity implicit in SDU is deeply felt by many people. This simplicity and intuitive plausibility also minimize the chance that defending oneself in accordance with SDU would weaken one's general inhibitions against acts which would otherwise be impermissible. SDU is a rather narrow principle and needs to be supplemented by other moral principles concerning self-defense. It does not speak to cases in which defending oneself requires that one perform harmful acts of a different sort than those being inflicted on one. (For example, defending oneself against attempted rape would involve doing something other than raping one's attacker.)[38] I only claim that something like SDU would be included in (or entailed by) the set of moral principles whose general acceptance by the members of most societies would maximize utility. It is possible to rely on a narrow principle such as SDU for the case of bluffing because in cases of bluffing one's own acts of self-defense are acts of the same sort that one is defending oneself against.

2. *Act-Utilitarianism.* Let us now consider the implications of act-utilitarianism (AU) for the issue of the permissibility of misstating one's negotiating position. Suppose that the other person has not (first) misstated her negotiating position. In ordinary cases of this sort AU implies that it would be wrong for one to misstate one's own position. In ordinary cases, the expected financial harm to the

other person will counter-balance the expected financial benefit to oneself. (If we take into account the fact that one's misstatements might pressure or panic the other person into an imprudent decision, the expected harm to the other person probably outweighs the expected benefit to oneself.) The indirect bad consequences of misstating one's position will outweigh competing considerations in most cases. Making deliberate false statements to further one's own financial interests in this case has a significant chance of contributing (marginally) to the deterioration of one's character by increasing one's propensity to lie or deceive others to advance one's own interests. Another typical indirect consequence of lying and deception is the distrust that it arouses in others if they come to know or suspect that one has tried to deceive them. Although this is usually a very important consideration, it carries little weight in this sort of case. People expect that others will misrepresent their positions during negotiations, unless they are negotiating with friends or relatives. One may confirm another person's distrust by misstating one's own position, but doing so cannot be said to *cause* distrust. In ordinary cases AU implies that concern about harm to the agent's character creates some presumption against misstating one's position to someone who doesn't do it first. It is a somewhat weaker presumption than exists on a Rossian view.[39] As we saw in part V, this presumption can be overridden by countervailing considerations including extreme financial distress or need.

Now let us consider the implications of AU for cases in which the other person misstates his negotiating position first. In ordinary cases the expected financial benefit to the person acting in self-defense is at least as great as the expected financial loss to the other party. The expected indirect consequences of misstating one's position in self-defence do not (on balance) create a presumption against misstating one's position. Making false statements in accordance with a plausible principle of self-defense such as SDU is unlikely to contribute to the harmful

propensity to lie or resort to deception in a broader range of cases. Because of the intuitive force of the ideas of reciprocity and self-defense one can make a clear distinction between this sort of case and cases of impermissible (offensive) lying or deception. Deceiving others or lying to them in self-defense may contribute to one's propensity to lie or deceive others in similar cases of self-defense. On balance, this is a good thing. Lying and/or deceiving others in self-defense may have the desirable consequence of disabusing them of the impression that they stand to gain an advantage over others by initiating lying and/or deception. In ordinary cases AU will justify misstating one's position in response to the misstatements of others. Doing so typically has roughly the same (or slightly better) consequences as not misstating one's position.

VII. *Variations on the Example*

1. Is *Lying Worse than Mere Deception*? Consider the following case. Suppose that I want the other party to hold false beliefs about my minimum bargaining position. I want him to think that $90,000 is the lowest price that I'm willing to accept for my house when, in fact, I'm willing to sell it for as little as $80,000. However, I am very much averse to lying about this and I believe that misstating my own position would be a lie. I am willing to try to deceive or mislead him about my intentions, but I am not willing to lie about them. Here, as in many cases, it is possible to think of true but equally misleading things to say so as to avoid lying. Suppose that our lowest acceptable selling price is $80,000, but I want you to think that it is actually around $85,000. Instead of lying, I could say "my wife told me to tell you that $85,000 is absolutely the lowest price that we are willing to accept." The trick here would be to have my wife utter the words "tell the buyer that $85,000 is absolutely the lowest price that we will accept." In saying this she would not be stating our minimum position, but rather help-

ing to create the ruse to fool the buyer. It is very doubtful that this is morally preferable to lying. Intuitively, it strikes me as worse. Many people (perhaps most) seem to believe that making true but deceptive statements is preferable to lying. This is demonstrated by the fact that many (most?) of us will, on occasion, go through verbal contortions or give very careful thought to exactly what we say in order to mislead others without lying. In this kind of case lying does not seem to be morally preferable to "mere deception."

Consider another example in which the difference between lying and mere deception does not seem to be morally significant. Suppose that two parents go out of town for the weekend leaving their two adolescent children home alone. The parents give their son strict orders that under no circumstances is he permitted to entertain his girlfriend in the house while they are away. The parents call during the weekend to "check up" on the children. They speak with their daughter. "What's going on there? What is your brother up to? He doesn't have Nora [his girlfriend] there does he?" The son is entertaining Nora in the house at the time that they call. The daughter does not want to get her brother in trouble, but, on the other hand, she doesn't want to lie. She does not answer the last question directly, but replies with the following true, but misleading, statement. "He's fine; he's watching the ball game with Bob." (Bob is a male friend who *is* there but is about to leave.)

2. *Claiming to have another offer*. In my view, the fact that misstating one's position is a very common practice can often help justify misstating one's own position. Because misstating one's bargaining position is such a widespread practice in our society, one is often justified in assuming that one's negotiating partner is misrepresenting her position. If the other person states a minimum bargaining position, then one is justified in thinking that she is misrepresenting that position, in the absence of reasons for thinking that she is not.

There are other ways of deceiving others about one's bargaining position which are not common practice. The following two cases are among the kinds that I have in mind here:

Case #1. I (the seller) say to a prospective buyer "I have another offer for $80,000, but I'll let you have it if you can beat the offer" when, in fact, I don't have another offer.

Case #2. I (the seller) want you to think that I have another offer. I have my brother come over and in your presence pretend to offer me $80,000 for the condo. (You don't know that he is my brother.) I say to my brother "the other person was here first. I'll have to let him/her see if he/she wants to meet the offer." I turn to the seller and say "It's yours for $80,000."[40]

What I say in the first case is clearly a lie. It is a deliberate false statement which is warranted to be true and is intended to deceive others. My action in this case is *prima facie* very wrong. I am putting extreme pressure on the other person and may panic her into a rash decision. Falsely claiming to have another offer could, in principle, be justified by appeal to SD. If the buyer was falsely representing the possibility of another comparable deal, then a Rossian theory might conceivably justify me in doing the same. This is very unlikely in the ordinary course of things. This means that it is unlikely that one could defend lying in such a case by appeal to the need to defend one's own interests. My actions in case #2 seem intuitively even worse than those in #1. Case #2 does not involve lying but it does involve an elaborate scheme of deception and is potentially very harmful to the buyer. The same general things that I said about case #1 apply here. My actions in this case are *prima facie* very wrong. In principle, a Rossian theory could justify those actions, but that is very unlikely. I will not undertake a detailed examination of the implications of utilitarianism for these two cases. I would refer the reader to the arguments of section VI.2 which purport to show that AU implies that it would (usually) be wrong to misstate one's position to someone who has not first misstated her own position. A parallel, but much stronger, argument could be given for thinking that AU implies that the kind of lying or deception involved in these two cases would usually be wrong.[41]

NOTES

I would like to thank Loyola University for a summer research grant in 1989 which enabled me to write the initial draft of this paper. An anonymous referee from this journal made many extremely helpful criticisms and suggestions. I am also indebted to Mark Johnson.

1 This example is taken from "Shrewd Bargaining on the Moral Frontier: Towards a Theory of Morality in Practice," J. Gregory Dees and Peter C. Crampton, *Business Ethics Quarterly*, Vol. 1, No. 2, April 1991, 143.

2 An earlier paper, "Bluffing in Labor Negotiations: Legal and Ethical Issues," (which I co-authored with Richard Wokutch and Kent Murrmann) *Journal of Business Ethics*, Volume 1, Number 1, 1982, 13-22, also discusses the issues addressed in the present paper. The earlier paper has been reprinted in the following anthologies: *Ethical Theory and Business*, second edition, Tom Beauchamp and Norman Bowie, eds. (Prentice Hall, 1983), *Business Ethics in Canada*, Deborah Poff and Wilfred Waluchow, eds. (Prentice Hall, 1987), *The Structure of the Legal Environment*, Bill Shaw and Art Wolfe, eds. (PWS Kent, 1987), *Contemporary Moral Controversies in Business*, A. Pablo Iannone ed. (Oxford, 1989). A shorter version of the earlier paper (co-authored with Wokutch alone) was reprinted in the following books: *Business Ethics*, Michael Hoffman, and Jennifer Mills Moore, eds. (McGraw Hill, 1984) and *Ethical Issues in Business*, third edition, Tom Donaldson, and Patricia Werhane, eds. (Prentice Hall, 1988). The present paper represents my own rethinking of these issues over the past ten years. The earlier paper defends a modified version of the standard definition of lying and argues that deliberately misstating one's negotiating position constitutes lying. Here, I argue that such misstatements are not lies. I still think that misstating one's position is (usually) morally permissible when the other party is misstating her position and (usually) impermissible when the other party is not misstating her position. However, the arguments of the earlier paper now seem to me to be weak and inconclusive. I will offer new (and hopefully stronger) arguments here. I have not consulted with either Wokutch or Murrmann in the writing of this paper.

3 I make this qualification because a person's bargaining position often changes over time. For example, if I have tried without success to sell my house for a long period of time, then I will probably be willing to accept a lower offer than I was willing to accept earlier. My example is also over-simplified in that I assume that the price of the house is the only thing being negotiated and that the price at which either party is willing to buy or sell the house is independent of any other factors which might be negotiated. In the case of the sale of a house such factors as the date of closing and whether or not the buyer needs to obtain a mortgage are also subject to negotiation and can affect the price of the house.

4 Successful bargainers must withhold or conceal their bargaining position (intentions) from others. I know of no serious argument for thinking it wrong to withhold (or fail to reveal) such information. The present paper is concerned with the morality of actively deceiving others (or lying to others) about one's intentions or settlement preferences.

5   Here one might argue for a stronger condition. Consider the following:

> In order to tell a lie it is necessary that one make a false statement that one believes is false (or believes is probably false).

I'm not sure whether we should opt for the stronger condition. The strong and weak conditions yield different results in the following sort of case. I make a statement when I don't have the slightest idea of whether or not it is true. Such statements are characteristic of bullshit. According to the strong condition (above) this statement cannot possibly be a lie (no matter what other conditions it satisfies), because I lack the belief that the statement is false or probably false. The weaker condition allows for the possibility that statements of this sort are lies.

6   As the words "intentional" and "intended" are used in ordinary language and by philosophers in discussions of questions of ethics and action-theory, the intended consequences of an action are those which the agent either i) aims at for their own sake, or ii) foresees and regards as necessary links in a causal chain leading to consequences which she aims at as ends. Cf. Alvin Goldman, *A Theory of Human Action* (Prentice-Hall, 1970), Chapter 3 and Michael Walzer, *Just and Unjust Wars* (Harper and Row, 1977), 153-56. Traditional "just war theory" makes much of the distinction between what is intended and what is merely foreseen. This distinction also has a very important place in scholastic ethics and is central to the "doctrine of the double effect."

7   The foregoing objection to the standard definition was proposed in my original paper on bluffing (co-authored with Wokutch and Murrmann), "Bluffing in Labor Negotiations: Moral and Legal Issues." In that paper Wokutch, Murrmann and I also proposed a slightly modified version of the standard definition:

> A lie is a deliberate false statement which is either intended to deceive others or foreseen to be likely to deceive others. (17)

Gary Jones claims that, with slight modification, our counter-example can be made to apply to the modified definition presented above ("Lying and Intentions," *Journal of Business Ethics* 1986, 247-49). Jones' criticisms are well-founded. This can be seen by considering the following variation on my earlier counter-example. I make false statements under oath in court but do not intend to deceive anyone by them. I *foresee* that no one will be deceived by my statements, because I know that the crime and my presence at the scene of the crime were recorded on a video camera so that there is almost no chance that the jury will be deceived by my false testimony. In that case, I neither intend nor foresee that my false statements will deceive others. Surely my false statements in court are lies, but they do not count as such on the revised version of the standard definition. (This example is taken from my paper "On the Definition of Lying: A Reply to Jones and Revisions," *Journal of Business Ethics*, 7, 509-14.) One might attempt to add further conditions to the standard definition so as to avoid this counter-example. But such moves seem to me to be *ad hoc*. The standard definition is, I believe, fundamentally flawed.

8   "On the Definition of Lying: A Reply to Jones and Revisions," *op. cit.*

9   W.D. Ross, *The Right and the Good* (Oxford, 1930), 21. Cf. Nicolai Hartman, *Ethics*, trans. Stanton Coit, (Humanities, 1975), 286.

It might seem implausible to claim that we are constantly making implicit promises (to be truthful) whenever we communicate with others. However, the following reflection persuades me otherwise. The expression "it's true that" is redundant in the context of ordinary statements and adds nothing to their meaning. Consider the following:

    i) The sky is blue.

    ii) It's true that the sky is blue.

i) and ii) mean exactly the same. In ordinary contexts, the expression "it's true that" adds nothing to the meaning of a statement. This is so because, in ordinary contexts, when one makes a statement one is understood to be guaranteeing its truth.

The view that I am defending here is what philosophers of language call the "transparency thesis." The classic statements of the transparency thesis are found in Frege, "My Basic Logical Insights," in *Posthumous Writings*, P. Long and R. White, trans. (Blackwell, 1959), 151, and Frank P. Ramsey, "Facts and Propositions," *The Foundations of Mathematics* (Routledge and Kegan Paul, 1931), 142-43. Ramsey writes:

> "It is true that Caesar was murdered" means no more than that Caesar was murdered, and "It is false that Caesar was murdered" means no more than that Caesar was not murdered. (142)

Strawson offers a noteworthy criticism of the transparency thesis in "Truth," *Analysis*, 1949. Strawson argues that we are not (and should not) always be willing to allow "x" and "it's true that x" to be used interchangeably. "It's true that x" can sometimes be used for purposes for which "x" is unsuitable. For example, suppose that I say that Ingrid is having an extra-marital affair and you deny it. My responding with "But it's *true* that she is having an affair," can constitute a stronger more emphatic response than simply repeating "she is having an affair." It would be foolish for me to try to resolve this exceedingly deep and difficult controversy in the present paper. I will take a safer course. I will try to show how my view (that in ordinary contexts asserting a statement involves war-

ranting its truth) can accommodate Strawson's criticisms of the transparency thesis. My view about the default warranty of truth is compatible with Strawson's view that "x" and "it's true that x" cannot always be used interchangeably. My view is consistent with the following two possibilities. 1) In some situations, asserting that x differs from asserting that x is true because the latter involves making a *stronger* warranty of truth than the former. 2) In some borderline cases, it is unclear whether or not making a statement involves warranting its truth. In such cases, saying that x is true warrants the truth of x, but merely saying that x does not. For example, suppose that I know of a humorous and improbable truth about Judy. I wish to assert this fact and warrant its truth in the context of a humorous "bull-session." Simply stating the fact in this situation may not (probably does not) constitute warranting its truth. In order to accomplish this it may be necessary for me to say something like "It's *true* that _____; I'm not kidding."

10 This represents a modification of the definition which I defended in "On the Definition of Lying ..." There I defended the following definition:

> A lie is a deliberate false statement made in a context in which the speaker warrants the truth of what he says.

11 For a further defense of Z and arguments against other alternative solutions to the present problem see "On the Definition of Lying ...," 512-13.

12 See John Searle, "How to Derive 'Ought' From 'Is,'" in *Theories of Ethics*, Philippa Foot, ed. (Oxford, 1968), 103-04.

13 It might be suggested that the notion of warranting makes implicit appeal to the notion of intention. It has been suggested to me that "to warrant the truth of a statement is to make an utterance under conditions where *normally*

the speaker intends that others believe him." This suggests that I have removed the notion of intention or the intent to deceive from the concept of lying only to smuggle it back in under the rubric of the concept of warranting. Normally we do intend that others believe our statements. It is difficult to imagine how it could be the case that the use of language involves the default warranty of truth if this were not the case. There would be no *point* in warranting the truth of what we say unless we sometimes intended that others believe what we say. There would be no point in having a *default* presumption that any given statement is warranted to be true unless we usually intended that others believe what we say. (The purpose of having such a warranty is to make it more likely that what we say will be believed.) I accept all of this, but it leaves untouched my earlier objection to the standard dictionary definition of lying. According to the OED, a *particular statement on a particular occasion* cannot constitute a lie unless the person who makes it intends that others believe *that particular statement*. I believe that I have shown this to be untenable. But my own definition of lying leaves open the question of what background conditions are necessary for it to be the case that using language to make statements carries a default warranty of truth.

14   To say that deliberate false statements about one's intentions as a player in a game of "Risk" are not lies might strike some people as counter-intuitive. Most people, however, do not have strong preanalytic intuitions as to whether or not such statements should count as lies. (I didn't have strong intuitions about this when I began to play "Risk." I played "Risk" before I began to work on the concept of lying.) This kind of case should not be considered a test for the adequacy of definitions of lying. It is not clear prior to philosophical reflection whether such statements should be considered lies. We should test definitions of lying by reference to cases in which our intuitions are clear and (nearly) unanimous and then use the most plausible definitions which meet those tests to settle the difficult cases.

15   Dees and Crampton distinguish between 1) deceiving another person about one's settlement preferences, e.g., misstating the lowest price one is willing to sell something for or misstating the strength of one's desire to reach a settlement quickly, and 2) deception about matters of empirical fact, e.g., lying about the condition of things for sale, or lying about the extent of one's injuries in a negotiation to determine damages to be paid in an accident case. Dees and Crampton marshall considerable evidence (including the American Bar Association's "Model Rules for Professional Conduct") to show that deception of type 1 is generally approved of or condoned and that deception of type 2 is not generally approved of. Their work provides support for my claim that misstatements of type 1 are not warranted to be true.

16   Dees and Crampton do not consider this kind of case, but it seems to be a case of deceiving others about material facts rather than deceiving them about one's state of mind.

17   R.M. Hare is very critical of those who make frequent appeal to moral intuitions in applied ethics. See "Comments on Critics," in *Hare and Critics*, D. Seanor and N. Fotion, eds. (Oxford, 1988), 206-07. *If* we had the kind of well-grounded decision procedure or test for moral judgments that Hare claims to give us, then it would be a mistake to do applied ethics by direct appeal to moral intuitions. It seems to be an implication of Hare's view that those of us who have not defended full-blown theories of right and wrong or full-blown tests for the correctness of moral judgments should not do applied ethics. (It would follow that the great

majority of those who write on issues of applied ethics should not do so.) This is a serious possibility and should not be lightly dismissed. In response to Hare, I would argue that issues of applied ethics are of practical urgency and should be addressed by moral philosophers *whether or not* they can defend any full blown ethical theories of the sort that Hare proposes. For my own part, I don't think that Hare's theory or any other theory has been adequately grounded. The fairly weak intuitions to which I appeal seem to me to be at least as well grounded as Hare's methodological principles. It is also worth noting that, even if I had done the kind of theoretical work which Hare would demand of me, I could not presuppose, as Hare can, familiarity with my theory or the reader's willingness to concede it sufficient importance or plausibility to merit paying attention to its detailed application to concrete issues.

18   For an excellent discussion of the importance of trust between individuals and the indirect bad consequences of lying see Sissela Bok, *Lying* (Vintage, 1978), 28-29.

19   Late in life Kant came to hold the view that lying is *always wrong*. See "On the Supposed Right to Tell Lies from Benevolent Motives," in *Moral Rules and Particular Circumstances*, B. Brody ed. (Prentice Hall, 1970), 32-33. (This essay was written in 1797.) In this work he defines a lie as an intentional false statement and claims that any deliberate false statement is morally wrong. In his earlier *Lectures on Ethics* (Harper and Row, 1963, Louis Infield, trans.) Kant takes a very different view. (The *Lectures on Ethics* are based on lectures delivered by Kant during the period 1775-81.) In the *Lectures on Ethics* he claims that a false statement is not a lie unless the speaker explicitly gives others to think that he intends to tell the truth. He also says that there is one (and only one) situation in which lying can be justified:

The forcing of a statement from me under conditions which convince me that improper use would be made of it is the only case in which I can be justified in telling a white lie. (228)

It seriously understates the extent to which Kant changed his views if we say that when Kant presented his *Lectures on Ethics* he thought that lying was *wrong in all but one kind of case* and then he later came to hold that lying was *always wrong*. This way of characterizing the changes in Kant's views overlooks the fact that Kant also changed his definition of lying. He moved from a narrow definition ("a lie is a deliberate false statement made in a context in which one has explicitly given others to think that one will speak the truth") to a much broader definition ("a lie is any deliberate false statement"). Many (most?) deliberate false statements are not made in contexts in which one explicitly gives others to think that one will tell the truth. In the *Lectures on Ethics* Kant gives no indication that he thinks that there is anything wrong with deliberate false statements made in contexts in which one has not explicitly given others to think that one intends to tell the truth. Many (most?) of the statements which Kant calls lies and claims to be wrong in "On the Supposed Right ..." are not claimed to be wrong in the *Lectures on Ethics*.

I think it quite implausible to hold that lying is always wrong. (It is curious that views expressed by Kant in his dotage should have so much influence.) Further, the categorical imperative does not commit one to an absolute prohibition against lying. I can only sketch the argument for this contention. Kant proposes the "categorical imperative" (CI) as a criterion or test for the rightness or wrongness of actions. He states the CI as follows:

Act only according to that maxim through which you can at the same time will that it should become a universal law. (*Groundwork for the Metaphysics of Morals*, [Harper and Row, 1964], Paton Trans., 88)

Kant gives two other formulations of the CI: i) "always treat humanity, whether in your own person or in the person of any other, never simply as a means, but at the same time as an end" (96), and "A rational being must always regard himself as making laws in a kingdom of ends" (101). For the purposes of my argument, I will use the "universal law" formulation of the CI. Kant claims that the three formulations of the CI are "merely so many formulations of the same law ..." (103). Note the following passage:

> It is, however, better if in moral *judgment* we proceed always in accordance with the strict method and take as our basis the universal formula of the categorical imperative: "*Act on the maxim which at the same time can be made a universal law.*" (104)

In the next paragraph on page 105 Kant restates the CI as follows:

> *Act on that maxim which can at the same time have for its object itself as a universal law of nature.*

The universal law formulation of the CI is equivalent to the following:

> An act is morally right if, and only if, the person who performed it would be willing to have everyone else follow the same principles which he employed in performing the act.

Kant argues that it is always wrong to make a promise in bad faith. His argument for this is his most well-known illustration of the notion of a "perfect duty." I will argue that this argument cannot be modified to show that the CI commits us to the view that lying is always wrong. [With modifications, my arguments can also be used to counter Kant's arguments about making promises in bad faith, but that is not my concern here.]

According to Kant, the CI commits us to an absolute prohibition against making promises in bad faith. The duty not to make promises in bad faith is a perfect duty. Not only are we *unwilling* to have everyone else follow maxims which permit making promises in bad faith, but such a state of affairs [everyone's following maxims which permit them to make promises in bad faith] is *impossible*. For universal adherence to such maxims would destroy the background of honesty and trust necessary for the existence of the institution of promise-keeping. An analogous argument to show that lying is always wrong would go something like the following:

> Not only are we *unwilling* to have everyone else follow maxims which permit lying, but such a state of affairs is impossible. For universal adherence to such maxims would destroy the background of honesty and trust necessary for the institution of language, and without language lying itself would be impossible.

Universal adherence to maxims such as "let me tell a lie whenever doing so would be to my advantage" *might* destroy the background of trust necessary for the institution of language to be viable. But this doesn't show that the CI commits us to an absolute prohibition against lying. Many cases of lying can be described by maxims universal adherence to which would not so greatly undermine trust between individuals as threaten the institution of language. Consider the following maxim:

> M. Let me lie when (and only when) lying is necessary in order to save the life of an innocent person.

Universal adherence to M. would not threaten the institution of language. At the present time lying is far more prevalent than it would be if M were universally adopted and adhered to. But the institution of language is not threatened. Further, it is clear that most of us would be *willing* to have everyone else follow the policy of lying when it is necessary in order to save lives.

20 Albert Carr, "Is Business Bluffing Ethical?" in *Ethical Issues in Business*, third edition, Thomas Donaldson and Patricia Werhane, eds. (Prentice Hall, 1988).

21 Carr, 72-73; see also 69 and 70.

22 Carr's analogy is misleading in that the kind of bluffing common in poker is non-verbal or non-linguistic. It involves such things as raising the pot in spite of having a weak hand, displaying calm and confidence, and feigning pleasure when drawing a bad card. Bluffing of this sort clearly does not involve lying. Bluffing in business, on the other hand, usually involves the use of language and often involves making deliberate false statements.

23 Carr, 70.

24 Carr, 72.

25 Carr, 73; also see 75.

26 I don't think that this statement is a lie. However, as I indicated earlier, my definition of lying might be taken to imply that it is a lie. It all turns on the question of whether she can be plausibly said to have warranted the truth of this statement.

27 I take this distinction from Greg Kavka's paper "When Two 'Wrongs' Make a Right: An Essay in Business Ethics," *Journal of Business Ethics*, 2, 1983, 61-66.

28 Kavka cites this passage from Hobbes in "When Two 'Wrongs' Make a Right..."

29 Ross at least implicitly recognizes defeasibility conditions for some *prima facie* duties. He recognizes conditions which are necessary in order for a promise to be morally binding, e.g., that it was not made on the basis of false testimony

on the part of the promisee, *The Foundations of Ethics* (Oxford, 1939), 94-98. Ross never discusses self-defense.

30 I am not endorsing SD per se. I am simply saying that it is a plausible principle to account for our convictions about "self-defense" *given* a Rossian ethical theory with i) multiple *prima facie* duties, ii) a commitment to common-sense as the ultimate ground or justification for moral judgments.

31 For something more nearly approximating necessary and sufficient conditions for being justified in acting in self-defense see Kavka and Dees and Crampton, *op. cit.*

32 Cf. Richard Brandt, *Ethical Theory* (Prentice Hall, 1959), 394. Ross never attempts to formulate necessary and sufficient conditions for right action or general criteria for resolving conflicts of duties. He apparently thinks that this cannot be done. I will now point to two considerations which strongly support (but do not prove) my claim that any plausible principles for resolving conflicts of duties would have to be so complex as to be impossible to formulate. First, it seems impossible to rank generic obligations in order of importance or weight. To take just one example, the duty not to lie cannot be ranked as always more (or less) important than the duty to keep promises. Even if we could formulate a plausible rank ordering of the generic duties, such an order would not be capable of resolving all conflicts of duties. Sometimes conflicts of duties involve conflicts between duties of a single general sort, e.g., a case in which one must choose between breaking a promise to one person and breaking a promise to another person. Further, conflicts of duties often involve conflicts between different *sets* of generic duties, e.g., a person might have to choose between a) performing an act which involves telling a lie, breaking a promise, and fulfilling an obligation of gratitude, and b)

an act which involves helping two people and harming one person.

33 My concern in this paper is with the morality of *individual* conduct (individual acts of bluffing or deception) rather than the morality or desirability of the practice itself. The pervasiveness of the practice of misstating one's settlement preferences is relevant to the application of SD. In negotiations one is justified in assuming that the other party's statements *about her negotiating position or intentions* are false or deceptive in the absence of special evidence to the contrary. (Note that one cannot make this assumption if the other person does not make any claims about her negotiating position.) The Rossian theory as I have elaborated and extended it implies that there is a moral presumption against deceiving those whom one knows are not deceiving one. This result is consistent with the spirit of Ross's theory. Deceiving others about one's negotiating position violates a number of Ross's *prima facie* duties. In this sort of case, no considerations (such as self-defense) nullify or greatly reduce this presumption. We can also view the case from the perspective or Ross's commitment to common-sense. The common-sense views of most people would hold that it is wrong to "take advantage of" an unusually honest or naive negotiating partner. I believe that his conclusion is defensible in its own right apart from any appeal to Ross. There *is* a strong moral presumption against deceiving others. The presumption remains in force in the absence of defeasibility conditions such as those spelled out in SD. See the section on utilitarianism where the same conclusion is defended.

34 The line of thought just presented is important for another reason. It enables one to avoid the following *apparent* dilemma:

> If I believe another person's claims about his negotiating position I can't say that he is misrepresenting his position, and if

I don't believe his claims about his position, then he cannot profit from them. It follows that I could never have reason to believe both that someone is misrepresenting his position to me *and* that he is profiting from those misrepresentations. Therefore, it would be impossible for me to be in a position in which I could give a presumptive justification for misstating my own negotiating position by appeal to SD.

The line of argument in the paragraph which precedes this footnote shows that we must reject the second horn of the dilemma; it is possible for someone to benefit from false representations of his negotiating position, even if the other person does not believe what he says. There are other ways in which one could benefit from such false statements even if they are not believed by others. Some people are likely to be initially very trusting of what other people say (I am such a person). One might give false reports about the other person's position considerable credence for a few minutes. This might cause one to panic and make an imprudent offer. Even if one is not caused to panic and make an imprudent offer in light of these reports, one might in one's initial response to such statements give the other party valuable information about one's own position, one's financial constraints and the strength of one's desire or desperation to reach a settlement.

35 In the case of The National Labor Relations Board vs. Truitt Manufacturing Company (1956) the US Supreme Court established what is known as the "honest claims doctrine." This doctrine requires that all parties to labor negotiations be honest in all claims and representations relevant to the negotiations, e.g., the company's profitability and ability to pay higher wages. However, the doctrine only applies to "objectively verifiable" statements. Statements

about one's intentions or negotiating position are specifically exempted by the "honest claims doctrine." The distinction drawn by the court in this case is very similar to the distinction which Dees and Crampton draw between deceiving others about one's "settlement preferences" and deceiving them about matters of empirical fact.

36 I am a bit hesitant about this point. It is plausible to hold that we should adopt the following policy: discharge all of our duties of financial beneficence by making contributions to charities and then act in a self-interested manner in the marketplace, making no further financial sacrifices and no attempt to determine which businesses most need our patronage.

37 See "Some Merits of One Form of Rule-Utilitarianism," in *Readings in Contemporary Ethical Theory*, K. Pahel and Marvin Schiller eds. (Prentice Hall, 1970), 282-307 and *A Theory of the Good and the Right* (Oxford, 1979), Chapter 15.

38 Is it permissible for a woman to kill a man, if that is the only way in which she can prevent him from raping her? SDU says nothing about this question. Note that SDU gives *sufficient* conditions for being justified in harming someone else, but it does not purport to give *necessary* conditions. SDU needs to be supplemented by other principles. What those principles are and how they would answer questions like the one which I raised above are matters of considerable controversy. But that something like SDU is part of (or entailed by) optimal moral principles for "self-defense" is reasonably clear.

39 Here I am assuming that AU means roughly "act-welfarist-consequentialism," or the view that the rightness or wrongness of an individual act is determined solely by the goodness or badness of the states of affairs which result from it and that the only intrinsically good or bad states of affairs are those which are constitutive of the welfare (or illfare) of human beings (and/or other sentient creatures). Versions of act-consequentialism which attach intrinsic value or disvalue to actions in virtue of their being of certain types, e.g., being an instance of lying or being an instance of breaking or fulfilling a promise, might be extentionally equivalent to Rossian theories. For a defense of such a version of consequentialism and defense of the claim that it is extentionally equivalent to a Rossian theory see A.C. Ewing, *The Definition of Good* (New York: Macmillan, 1947), Chapter 6.

40 Something like this once happened to me in a used car lot. My wife and I needed to purchase a used car within a week and the urgency of our situation was evident to the salesmen with whom we dealt. We were very interested in a particular car on the lot and made a low bid on the car. The salesman was haggling with us over the price in a very large and nearly empty showroom. He went across the room to talk with another salesman. The other salesman picked up a telephone and dialed a number. The phone at our salesman's desk rang immediately. Our salesman picked up his phone and we heard him say something like "Mr. Smith! Hello. You are still interested in the green Mercury. It's a very good car, best deal on the lot. Are you willing to make an offer? [pause] $3500! It just happens that I'm talking to a couple here who are also interested in the car...."

41 Dees and Crampton do not consider cases like #1 or #2. On their view, the deception involved in #1 and #2 counts as deception about matters of material fact rather than deception about one's preferences or intentions. Thus, the actions described in cases #1 and #2 would not be permitted by "the mutual trust perspective."

◆ ◆ ◆ ◆ ◆

FRITZ ALLHOFF

Business Bluffing Reconsidered

1. Introduction

Imagine that I walk into a car dealership and tell the salesperson that I absolutely cannot pay more than $10,000 for the car that I want. And imagine further she tells me that she absolutely cannot sell the car for less than $12,000. Assuming that neither one of us is telling the truth, we are bluffing about our reservation prices, the price above or below which we will no longer be willing to make the transaction. This is certainly a common practice and, moreover, is most likely minimally prudent—whether our negotiating adversary is bluffing or not, it will always be in our interest to bluff. Discussions of bluffing in business commonly invoke reservation prices, but need not; one could misrepresent his position in any number of areas including the financial health of a company poised for merger, the authority that has been granted to him by the parties that he represents, or even one's enthusiasm about a project. The goal of bluffing is quite simple: to enhance the strength of one's position during negotiations.

Bluffing has long been a topic of considerable interest to business ethicists.[1] On the one hand, bluffing seems to bear a strong resemblance to lying, and therefore might be thought to be *prima facie* impermissible. On the other, many people have the intuition that bluffing is an appropriate and morally permissible negotiating tactic. Given this tension, what is the moral standing of bluffing in business? The dominant position has been that it is permissible and work has therefore been done to show why the apparent impermissibility is either mismotivated or illusory. Two highly influential papers have taken different approaches to securing the moral legitimacy of bluffing. The first, by Albert Carr, argued that bluffing in business is analogous to bluffing in poker and therefore should not be thought to be impermissible insofar as it is part of the way that the game is played. The second, by Thomas Carson, presented a more subtle argument wherein the author reconstrued the concept of lying to require an implied warrantability of truth and, since business negotiations instantiate a context wherein claims are not warranted to be true, bluffing is not lying.

I think that both papers are on the right track to the solution to the problem, but that both authors' positions are problematic. In this paper, I will consider the arguments of both Carr and Carson, and I will present my criticisms of their ideas. Drawing off of their accounts, I will then develop my own argument as to why bluffing in business is morally permissible, which will be that bluffing is a practice that should be endorsed by all rational negotiators.

2. Albert Carr

Carr's article is somewhat informal and therefore lacks clear and rigorous argumentation. His thesis, however, is that business is a game, just like poker, and that bluffing is permitted under the rules of the game. To strengthen the analogy between business and poker, he points out that both business and poker have large elements of chance, that the winner is the one who plays with steady skill, and that ultimate victory in both requires knowledge of the rules, insight into the psychology of the other players, a bold front, self-discipline, and the ability to respond quickly and effectively to opportunities presented by chance.[2]

Even if we grant Carr that there are no morally relevant disanalogies between poker and business, which seems dubious, he still has a problem by trying to legitimize bluffing on the grounds that it is permitted by the rules of the game.[3] As Carson has pointed out, Carr seems somewhat confused as to how we determine the rules of the game.[4] In some passages, Carr seems to think that convention determines the rules, whereas in others he seems to think that the law delineates boundaries and all acts within those boundaries are permissible. Regardless, neither of these standards can help to establish the moral legitimacy of bluffing.

The reason is that either one of these moves would violate a long standing principle in moral philosophy, dating back to David Hume, that one cannot reason from what is the case to what ought to be the case.[5] There have been numerous conventions, such as discrimination, that have nevertheless been immoral. And there have also been numerous practices, such as slavery, that have been legally sanctioned but that are also immoral. Facts about the way that the society operates or about the way that the law is, can not be used to derive values. The two supports that Carr gives for the moral permissibility of bluffing are precisely the sorts of considerations that are patently disallowed in moral philosophy.

Carr hints at, but does not discuss, a potentially more promising notion, that of consent. Certainly bluffing in poker, and most likely bluffing in business, is a practice to which all involved parties consent, which is more than can be said for other conventions. But since the fact-value divide makes convention wholly irrelevant, consent would have to do the entirety of the work, and not merely be used to identify a special kind of convention. This is clearly not what Carr has in mind, and I do not propose to read it into his argument. Furthermore, I still do not think that consent alone establishes permissibility. Just as I may consensually enter a poker game knowing full well that bluffing might happen, I may consensually travel to a dangerous neighborhood knowing full well that a crime against me might happen. Since my consent in the latter case does not provide moral license for the act against me, consent can similarly not be used to legitimize bluffing in the former.

3. Thomas Carson

Carson approaches the problem from a different direction, though he arrives at more or less the same conclusion. His strategy is to deny that bluffing is a form of lying and, in order to make this argument, he takes issue with the conventional idea that lying is a false statement made with the intent to deceive and proposes instead that "a lie is a false statement which the 'speaker' does not believe to be true made in a context in which the speaker warrants the truth or what he says."[6] Bluffing is certainly lying in the traditional definition; the bluffer's statement is false and it is intended to deceive. But Carson thinks that his definition of lying excludes bluffing. Why? He argues that the second requirement, the warrantability of truth, is largely absent in negotiations. There are some claims made during negotiations that convention dictates to be warranted as true, such as claims to have another offer on the table. If I were to claim that I had another offer while I did not, this would be a lie because it would satisfy both parts of Carson's requirements. Claims about reservation prices, however, do not carry implied warrantability of truth—as a matter of fact, nobody *ever* takes such claims to be literally true. Carson therefore thinks that bluffing is not lying and should therefore not hold the moral disapprobations that we confer on lying.

There are, I think, two problems with Carson's defense of bluffing. The most obvious one is that, even if bluffing is not lying, it does not follow that it is morally permissible. It might be wrong for some other reason. For example, we might want to distinguish between lying and other kinds of deception which are still morally objectionable. Imagine that I leave my children home for the weekend and tell my oldest son that his girlfriend is not allowed in the house. If I call home to ask my younger son what my older son is doing and am told "he is talking to his friend Robert," this might be strictly and literally true only because his girlfriend is in the kitchen getting something to drink and is currently unavailable for conversation. The answer, though true and not a lie, is deceptive insofar as it masks a fact that my younger son knows to be salient. Or I might ask my older son directly whether his girlfriend is in the

434 BLUFFING IN BUSINESS

house and he truthfully answers no because she is still in transit to the house. Again, this answer is not a lie, but is deceptive. If we find such behavior morally objectionable, which many of us would, then the absence of lying alone does not secure moral license. And if it is not morally objectionable, some argument has to be given as to why; it certainly is not intuitively obvious that all non-lying deceptions are morally permissible. Therefore, the most that Carson's argument can establish is that bluffing does not carry the same *prima facie* wrongness that lying does, not that it is morally permissible, which is his desired conclusion.

The second problem is that Carson's account still requires the same dependence convention that caused trouble for Carr. Carson admits that he will not pursue specific guidelines to determine whether a context involves implied warrantability of truth, but the examples that he gestures at are suggestive of conventionality playing a strong role.[7] For instance, he says that statements made in negotiations between experienced negotiators are understood to be not warranted as true. But this is only the case because it is a matter of convention; we could easily imagine another society wherein negotiators do not bluff, but are honest about their reservation prices. We have already seen why convention alone cannot provide any reason to think that a practice is morally permissible.[8] To say it another way, we can meaningfully ask whether a practice is morally permissible *despite* its being conventional. A defense of bluffing must extend beyond mere conventionality and into the realm of moral philosophy, else it is doomed to violate the fact-value divide.

4. Bluffing, Role-differentiated Morality, and Endorsement

I will now develop what I think is the correct solution to the problem of bluffing in business. As I said earlier, I think that both Carr and Carson start off on the right track, but then go wrong for the reasons that I have presented.[9] In particular, both authors appeal to games in order to argue for the permissibility of bluffing in business; Carr uses a poker analogy and Carson argues that claims made during bluffing are similar to claims made during the game of Risk. But the problem that both authors have is that they infer moral legitimacy from the rules of their games, and this inference cannot be made. What we need is not an appeal to convention, but rather a moral argument that legitimizes bluffing within those games and that can be extended to bluffing in business.

One way that we could get this is to invoke what has become known as role-differentiated morality. Conventional wisdom within ethics has held that ethical rules are universal, and that everyone should be bound by the exact same moral laws. But work in professional ethics has recently come to challenge this idea.[10] These applications have come most auspiciously in legal ethics, where legal ethicists have often sought to defend ethically objectionable practices of lawyers (such as discrediting known truthful witnesses and/or enabling perjurious testimonies) on the grounds that the lawyer's role, that of zealous advocate, carries different moral rules than nonlawyer roles.[11] Though the applications have certainly been controversial, the underlying idea, role-differentiated morality, has garnered wide support.

Put simply, role-differentiated morality suggests the following three claims:

1. Certain roles make acts permissible that would otherwise be impermissible.
2. Certain roles make acts impermissible that would otherwise be permissible.
3. Certain roles make acts obligatory that would otherwise not be obligatory.

In this paper, I do not wish to provide an extended defense of the plausibility of role-differentiated morality; this has been done by other authors (including the two I cited above), and I do not feel that I have anything of value to add. What I will say in defense of the idea here is that it has tremendous intuitive resonance, as I think can be clearly shown through examples. In support of the first claim, we might say that soldiers fighting a just war are morally permitted to kill, whereas ordinary civilians are not. In support of the second claim, we could suggest that college professors should not have sexual relationships with their students (nor bosses with their subordinates), regardless of the act being consensual. In support of the third claim, we might claim that parents have special obligations to their children, such as providing for them and caring for them, that non-parents would not have towards the same child. I think the self-evidence of these examples gives strong support for the notion of role-differentiated morality.

Now, we can return to bluffing and ask whether some roles should allow for its moral permissibility.[12] I think that it is pretty clear that yes, some roles do allow for bluffing, while others definitely do not (though it remains, for now, an open question under which one bluffing in business falls). Some roles clearly do not morally permit bluffing. For example, consider a relationship between a husband and a wife. They have duties to each other to be honest and not to manipulate each other to secure advantages in negotiation. We might even want to say that negotiating, which is a necessary precondition for bluffing, is not the sort of activity in which husbands and wives should partake. Negotiating assumes conflicting aims of the negotiators and pits them against each other as adversaries, whereas husbands and wives should, ideally, share the same goals and cooperate. When disagreements do occur (such as on how much to pay for a new house), they should not negotiate against each other to determine their collective reservation price but rather should debate the issue and build a consensus as a unified front. I think that husband or wife is a role in which bluffing is not morally permissible,[13] but there are others, such as any fiduciary role wherein one is morally bound to be fully open with another.

There are, on the other hand, roles under which bluffing is morally permitted. Both Carr and Carson suggested that bluffing is permitted in games, and I think that they are exactly right. But they got the reason wrong, convention alone cannot deliver moral permissibility. Whatever justifies bluffing in these cases needs to have moral, rather than merely descriptive, force. I think that the key to these cases is that the players involved in the game actually *endorse* the practice of bluffing; people play these games for fun, and bluffing makes the games much more fun. If bluffing did not exist in poker, and everyone's bet merely reflected the strength of their hands, there would be no game at all since the final results would all be made apparent. Thus, insofar as anyone even wants to play poker in a meaningful way, he is committed to endorsing the practice of bluffing. Bluffing in Risk is similarly explained; bluffing adds an exciting (though in this case non-essential) element to the game to which players are attracted. If this were not the case, we would certainly expect a proliferation in strategy games in which there were no bluffing via diplomacy, and this is certainly not what we see. Bluffing, in some games, is a welcome feature in which participants actually want to be involved.

Is endorsement a moral feature? Absolutely. Imagine that my son takes $20 out of my wallet. There could be two scenarios leading up to this act. In one, he asks me for the money and I endorse his taking it (to pay the delivery person for pizza, let's say) and, in the other, he does not ask and instead takes it without my permission. Obviously he acted permissibly in the first scenario and impermissibly in the second, and it was my approval, or endorsement, of his actions that is the *only* morally relevant difference. Therefore, endorsement carries with it the moral force to legitimize certain acts (or practices), and I think that it is precisely what is necessary to legitimize bluffing in games.[14]

I hope to have established both the plausibility of role-differentiated morality and that bluffing is permitted in some roles, but not in others. I can now return to my central aim and ask under which category bluffing in business falls. I think that bluffing in business is permissible for the same reason that it is permissible in games, namely that the participants endorse the practice. To explain why, let us return to the example with which I started. When I go to the car dealer with a reservation price of $12,000, what that means is that, all factors considered, that car has to me a utility marginally greater than the $12,000 does. *Ex hypothesi*, I am already willing to spend the $12,000; if that were the best that I could do, I would accept the offer. Any price that I can achieve below $12,000 would obviously be an improvement on the situation. Bluffing and negotiating are the mechanisms wherein I can achieve a final sale at a price beneath my reservation price and, insofar as any rational agent would welcome that end, he should also endorse its means.

Furthermore, other than bluffing, I cannot think of another reasonable procedure for the buyer to lower the sale price below my reservation price (or for the seller to raise the sale price above his reservation price). I might, for example, try to do so by force or threats, but these are obviously immoral. I might also make outright lies, such as to assert that the dealer across town has already guaranteed me a lower price. As Carson has already argued, this seems seriously immoral. So I think it is quite reasonable to suppose not only that the prospective buyer would endorse bluffing, but that there are no other reasonable alternatives.

One response to my position might be that bluffing does help the individual but that in negotiations there is not one, but two bluffers, and that the addition of the second cancels out all advantage to the first. Therefore, bluffing would should not actually be endorsed, since it yields no expected improvement, and maybe even eschewed on the grounds that it takes time and energy. However, I do not see how the addition of another bluffer really changes anything. If the car dealer will go as low as $10,000 and I will pay as high as $12,000, then we would

both agree to (and, *ex hypothesi*, be happy with) any transaction at any price between and including $10,000 and $12,000. Assuming that the reservation price of the buyer is higher than the reservation price of the seller, the issue is not whether the two parties will come to mutually agreeable terms, the question is just what those terms will be. Ideally, each party would like to be able to bluff while having his opponent's position be transparent, but since that is obviously not a possibility, both should welcome bluffing as an opportunity to improve their positions.

It is also interesting to note that, without bluffing, the idea of negotiations itself almost (though not quite) becomes incoherent. Suppose that bluffing were not practiced, but that parties merely met and announced their respective reservation prices. I tell the car dealer that I will give him $12,000 for the car and she tells me that he will take as little as $10,000 for the car. Now what? I do not even know how to settle on a transaction price other than to do something arbitrary such as splitting the reservation window in half and settling at $11,000. This seems like the wrong answer for a number of reasons. Such resolutions could be inefficient (i.e., not Pareto optimal), not utilitarian, unfair to those who negotiate well, etc.[15] Negotiating is, I think, an essential part of business. To reach a transaction price, it makes the most sense for the buyer to start low and the seller high, and to reach some agreement in the middle. By announcing reservation prices, we would be creating a system that I find less attractive and, furthermore, would give the participants every reason to transgress and to bluff.

Finally, I think that there really is a lot of merit in the analogies between business negotiating and games (despite the criticisms by Koehn and others). But I would go further than claiming that it is *like* a game, it seems to me that it is a game. Perhaps this is not true in the sense that negotiators are drawn to their work because they find it amusing, this is false in a wide number of cases and I certainly do not mean to trivialize many serious negotiations. But if two parties come to the negotiating table and the reservation price of the buyer is higher than the reservation price of the seller, then we already know that, *ceteris paribus*, the transaction will occur and, furthermore, it will occur at a price to which both parties are amenable. It seems to me that the occurrence of the transaction and the satisfaction of the parties is what is really important, where the price falls within the reservation window just determines what each party gains (in terms of money not spent or extra money earned) *in addition* to a mutually beneficial transaction. Whether the stakes are millions of dollars or not, the parties are still merely trying to secure money that they would otherwise be satisfied without.

NOTES

1　The first important paper was Albert Carr's "Is Business Bluffing Ethical?" *Harvard Business Review* January/February 1968, 143-53. John Beach later reflects upon the treatment that the topic received in the years since Carr's publication (though Beach is somewhat critical of this response). See his "Bluffing: Its Demise as a Subject unto Itself," *Journal of Business Ethics* Vol. 4 (1985), 191-96. Then, Thomas Carson reconsiders Carr's classic treatment of the subject and proposes an alternative conception of business bluffing; see "Second Thoughts about Bluffing," *Business Ethics Quarterly* Vol. 3(4) (1993), 317-41. There are also numerous other examples within the literature, though I take these to be the most important.

2　Carr (1968), 72.

3　Daryl Koehn has, for example, argued that the analogy between business and poker is quite weak; he takes nine features that exist in games and argues that few, if any, of these exist in business. For the sake of argument, I am willing to grant Carr's analogy; I think that, even with this analogy, he is unable to secure the conclu-

sion that he desires. See Koehn's "Business and Game-Playing: The False Analogy," *Journal of Business Ethics* Vol. 16 (1997), 1447-52. Norman Bowie also argued against the legitimacy of adversarial models (such as poker) as proper characterizations of bargaining and negotiating. See his "Should Collective Bargaining and Labor Relations Be Less Adversarial?" *Journal of Business Ethics* Vol. 4 (1985) 283-91. Robert S. Adler and William J. Bigoness also challenge adversarial models in their work and find Carr's poker analogy to be flawed. See "Contemporary Ethical Issues in Labor-Management Issues in Labor-Management Relations," *Journal of Business Ethics* Vol. 11 (1992), 351-60.

4　Carson (1993), 324-25.

5　*A Treatise of Human Nature*, ed. P.H. Nidditch, 2nd ed. (Oxford: Oxford University Press, 1978), III.I.i.

6　Carson (1993), 320. I assume that speaker is placed in scare quotes in order to allow for the possibility of non-verbal lying, such as when someone gives false directions by pointing in the wrong direction without saying anything. This definition results partly from earlier work by Carson and a criticism that he consequently received from Gary Jones. To trace through this, start with Thomas Carson, Richard Wokutch, and James Cox's "An Ethical Analysis of Deception in Advertising," *Journal of Business Ethics* Vol. 4 (1985), 93-104. Jones's criticism can be found in "Lying and Intentions," *Journal of Business Ethics* Vol. 5 (1986), 347-49. And, finally, Carson's response is in "On the Definition of Lying: A Reply to Jones and Revisions," *Journal of Business Ethics* Vol. 7 (1988), 509-14.

7　Carson (1993), 321-22.

8　And, in an interesting recent article, Chris Provis argues that bluffing (or, more precisely, deception) is not as ubiquitous in business as everyone often assumes; he thinks that the appearance of bluffing can often be accounted for by genuine concessions. If Provis is correct, then Carson's reliance on conventionality is empirically flawed. Or, as I argue, the reliance on convention is conceptually flawed (in order to secure moral permissibility). So, either way, the approach will not work. See Provis's "Ethics, Deception, and Labor Negotiation," *Journal of Business Ethics* Vol. 28(2) (2000), 145-58.

9 As I have indicated, other authors have also criticized the two approaches. What I have tried to do however, is be as charitable as possible: to grant all of their assumptions (the analogies, the adversarial nature of negotiating, Carson's definition of lying, etc.) and then aspired to show that they still cannot, even on their own terms, secure their desired conclusions.

10 An especially good and influential article is Richard Wasserstrom's "Lawyer's as Professionals: Some Moral Issues," *Human Rights Quarterly* Vol. 5(1) (1975).

11 Monroe H. Freedman, "Professional Responsibility of the Criminal Defense Lawyer: The Three Hardest Questions," *Michigan Law Review* Vol. 27 (1966).

12 This step of my argument might be overly pedantic, and I might fare just as well if I skipped it and went directly to arguing for bluffing in business contexts specifically. However, I do think that it is an important part of the conceptual framework that I want to establish.

13 This is obviously not to say that husbands or wives cannot bluff in business situations, just that a husband cannot bluff *qua* husband nor a wife *qua* wife. The husband or wife who bluffs in business is not bluffing *qua* husband or *qua* wife, but rather *qua* businessperson.

14 John Rawls has argued that it is not morally permissible sell oneself into slavery (i.e., *even if* I endorsed the sale, it is still immoral). See his *Theory of Justice* (Cambridge: Harvard University Press, 1971). This poses an interesting objection to my idea that endorsement alone suggests *prima facie* permissibility. There are two ways that I could respond. First, I could disagree with Rawls and argue that any decision made by free and rational agents should be honored (so long as it did not harm others), that to do otherwise would show lack of respect for the being's rational nature. I am personally inclined towards this view, though I know that many are not. The other way that I could go would be to argue that Rawls' point merely indicates that people cannot voluntarily give up their rights and that consenting to being bluffed is not problematic since we do not have the moral right to be told the truth. I think that either of these responses could be profitably developed, though I will not do so here.

15 The "Split-the-Difference" theory of negotiating is discussed by Roger Bowlby and William Schriver in their "Bluffing and the 'Split-the-Difference' Theory of Wage Bargaining," *Industrial and Labor Relations Review* Vol. 31(2) (January 1978), 161-71. Their discussion, however, is quite empirical and numerical rather than normative.

REFERENCES

Adler, R.S. and W.J. Bigoness. 1992, "Contemporary Ethical Issues in Labor-Management Relations," *Journal of Business Ethics* 11.

Beach, J. 1985, "'Bluffing' its Demise as a Subject unto Itself," *Journal of Business Ethics* 4.

Bowie, N.E. 1985, "Should Collective Bargaining and Labor Relations Be Less Adversarial?" *Journal of Business Ethics* 4.

Bowlby, R.L. and W.R. Schriver. 1978, "Bluffing and the 'Split-the-Difference' Theory of Wage Bargaining," *Industrial and Labor Relations Review* 31(2).

Carr, A. 1968, "Is Business Bluffing Ethical?" *Harvard Business Review* (January/February).

Carson, T.L. 1993, "Second Thoughts about Bluffing," *Journal of Business Ethics* 3(4).

Carson, T.L. 1988, "On the Definitions of Lying: A Reply to Jones and Revisions," *Journal of Business Ethics* 7.

Carson, T.L., R.E. Wokutch and J.E. Cox, Jr. 1985, "An Ethical Analysis of Deception in Advertising," *Journal of Business Ethics* 4.

Freedman, M. 1966, "Professional Responsibility of the Criminal Defense Lawyer: The Three Hardest Questions," *Michigan Law Review* 27.

Hume, D. 1978, *A Treatise of Human Nature* (2nd ed.). P.H. Nidditch (ed.). (Oxford: Oxford University Press).

Jones, G.E. 1986, "Lying and Intentions," *Journal of Business Ethics* 5.

Koehn, D. 1997, "Business and Game-Playing: The False Analogy," *Journal of Business Ethics* 16.

Post, F.R. 1990, "Collaborative Collective Bargaining: Toward an Ethically Defensible Approach to Labor Negotiations," *Journal of Business Ethics* 9.

Provis, C. 2000, "Ethics, Deception, and Labor Negotiation," *Journal of Business Ethics* 28.

Rawls, J. 1971, *A Theory of Justice* (Cambridge: Harvard University Press).

Wasserstrom, R. 1975, "Lawyer's as Professionals: Some Moral Issues," *Human Rights Quarterly* 5(1).

BRIBERY AND EXPLOITATION

BILL SHAW

Foreign Corrupt Practices Act: A Legal and Moral Analysis

1. Introduction

Bribery of foreign public officials is common throughout the world today. Since the passage of the Foreign Corrupt Practices Act in 1977,[1] American businesses operating abroad are well advised to behave ethically and avoid the practice of bribing foreign public officials.

Even though many American businessmen claim that this law is harming our country's interests abroad,[2] the United States is not the only country to have passed such a law. Sweden has also enacted criminal legislation dealing specifically with the bribery of foreign officials.[3]

In light of this act, it is extremely important for managers to develop a system that will communicate to their employees the fact that a company will not tolerate bribery of foreign officials. Penalties for single violation include the possibility of a $1,000,000 fine for business firms and a $10,000 fine coupled with five years imprisonment for individuals (officers, directors, employees of the firm).[4] In addition, individuals who are fined cannot be reimbursed by the business that they work for.[5]

SEC v. Ashland Oil

A recent example will show how serious a violation of the Foreign Corrupt Practices Act of 1977 can be and the type of situation that is likely to produce a violation of this act. One such case is *SEC v. Ashland Oil, Inc.*, which was filed in the United States District Court for the District of Columbia in 1986.[6]

According to the SEC complaint, Ashland Oil and its then CEO Orin Atkins agreed to pay an entity controlled by an Omani government official approximately $29 million for a majority interest in Midlands Chrome, Inc., a price which was far more than it was worth, allegedly for the purpose of obtaining crude oil at a highly favorable price.[7] When Atkins proposed the acquisition of Midlands Chrome to the Ashland board of directors, he allegedly told the board that while the acquisition was a high risk project, it "had the potential for being more than offset by a potential crude oil contract."[8]

Even though the mining claims owned by Midlands Chrome did not prove profitable, Ashland was awarded a crude oil contract by the Omani government for 20000 barrels of oil a day for one year at a $3 per barrel discount from the regular selling price.[9] Ashland claimed that the discount was in consideration of technical services rendered by it to Oman.[10] Solely through this contract Ashland could have profited by more than $40 million over the life of the contract simply by taking the oil it received at a discount and immediately selling it on the spot market.[11] The case was settled with Ashland Oil, Inc. and Atkins agreeing to an injunction against future violations.[12]

The SEC action against Ashland is only the third such suit to be brought under the Foreign Corrupt Practices Act of 1977 and the first against a major corporation.[13] The Ashland case was also the first to involve an ostensibly legitimate business transaction.[14] It gives evidence that the SEC is willing to look at the substance of the transaction even if the transaction is done in a proper form. While the SEC has not brought a large number of actions under the Foreign Corrupt Practices Act of 1977, this does not mean that it is totally apathetic. As the Ashland case vividly shows, managers cannot afford to ignore this act and do so only at great peril.

The next section of this paper will examine the conduct that the Foreign Corrupt Practices Act prohibits. In addition, the reach and types of prohibited acts will be examined in light of the ethical constructs of utility, justice and rights. It is hoped that by performing this analysis, we can determine whether or not the Foreign Corrupt Practices Act promotes ethical business conduct. If it does in fact promote ethical conduct, or if in some ways it falls short of that objective, we will be better able to judge whether it needs fine tuning, a major overhaul, or no modification at all.

2. Foreign Corrupt Practices Act: Prohibited Conduct in Light of Ethical Considerations

The Foreign Corrupt Practices Act attempts to eliminate bribery of foreign officials by US corporate officials and their agents through both an antibribery and an accounting provision. The antibribery provision prohibits certain issuers, domestic concerns, or their agents from being involved directly or indirectly in making specified payments to foreign officials, officials of foreign political parties, or candidates for foreign political office for the purpose of obtaining or retaining business.[15] The accounting provision requires each reporting entity to keep books and records that accurately reflect the entity's transactions and to devise and maintain an adequate system of internal controls to assure that the entity's assets are used for proper corporate purposes.[16]

In order to determine whether the Foreign Corrupt Practices Act goes as far as ethical standards would demand, we will first examine the types or categories of bribes. Then we must determine whether or not the Foreign Corrupt Practices Act prohibits the classes of bribes we conclude are unethical.

W. Michael Reisman has broken bribes into three different classes based upon the purpose and effect of the transaction.[17] Reisman's categories are as follows: transaction bribes, variance bribes, and outright purchases.[18] A transaction bribe, more commonly identified as a grease payment, is a payment that is routinely and impersonally made to a public official to secure or accelerate the performance of his official function.[19] A variance bribe occurs where the briber pays an official to secure the suspension or non-application of a legal norm in an instance where its application would be appropriate.[20] The third of Reisman's groups, outright purchase, is where payment is made in order to secure the favor of a foreign employee who remains in place in an organization to which he appears to pay full loyalty while actually favoring the briber's conflicting interest.[21]

A determination of whether each of these types of payments are ethical or not can be made by examining them under a utilitarian, moral rights, and social justice framework. The answer to this inquiry will assist us in deciding whether the Foreign Corrupt Practices Act and its costs of administration are a sufficient means of inducing, or compelling, ethical behavior from US business firms.

A. Utility

The utilitarian framework holds that ethical conduct is that which produces the greatest net benefits for society as a whole, i.e., the greatest good for the greatest number.[22] This principle assumes that all benefits and costs of an action can be measured on a common scale and then added to or subtracted from one another.[23]

In examining whether transaction bribes, variance bribes, and outright purchases are ethical, the utilitarian framework is not a great deal of help. This is because the utilitarian system of analysis is case specific with each instance being judged on its own unique facts.[24] Therefore, a bribe will be ethical or not in a particular situation based on the societal benefits and costs of making the bribe. In looking at the benefits of the bribe, one would have to include the increase in business that would not have resulted but for the bribe of a foreign official. Some of the costs of bribery include the actual monetary payment, and damage to the reputation of the company and to American business in the eyes of foreign nationals. Therefore, because utilitarianism is situation specific and the fact that quantification of the

benefits and costs may be difficult if not impossible, one cannot say that foreign bribery is unethical in all instances.

B. Moral Rights

A right is an individual's entitlement to something.[25] It is a morally justifiable claim to some good or to protection from harm.[26] A person has a right when that person is entitled to act in a certain way or is entitled to have others act in a certain way toward him or her.[27]

It will be helpful to look at each type of bribe under the rights analysis to determine whether there are any grounds upon which they may be supported. Basically, conduct that does not interfere with another's rights, and does not coerce another party is judged to be moral under a rights analysis.[28]

The first type of bribe, the transaction bribe, speeds action by foreign officials that they would otherwise take. This type of bribe clearly does not coerce an official to take action he would not otherwise take but it may interfere with other rights. By getting a foreign official to expedite your request, you are causing other people's interests to be put on the back burner. Every party has the right to equal treatment. By bribing a foreign official to get speedier service, you are violating the rights of other people to equal treatment.

On the other hand, such a system can be justified where such payments are above-board and each party has the ability to get speedier treatment. As long as this type of system is the regular method of doing business and all parties know about it, all competitors are on an equal footing. The crux of the matter here is whether the payments are in fact bribes and therefore unethical because all parties do not have equal rights, or whether the payments are governmentally "approved" and made in the normal course of business.

The variance bribe on the other hand is unethical because it violates competitors' rights to equal treatment. Beyond that it is a contract for the performance of an illegal act. In a like manner, the outright purchase or the procurement of a company man is unethical because it binds the employee to perform illegal and disloyal acts, i.e., acting against the interests of his employer to further the ends of some other party. Such an arrangement is often maintained by coercion or duress and thus violates the rights of the employee as well. This coercion or duress is the result of the ability of the briber to threaten to reveal the relationship between the briber and the employee if the employee does not continue to cooperate.

C. Social Justice

The last ethical framework for examining these three types of bribes is justice or fairness. It is the nature of these concepts to demand that comparative, balanced, and even-handed treatment be given to the members of a group when benefits and burdens are distributed, when rules and laws are administered, when members of a group cooperate or compete with each other, and when people are punished for the wrongs they have done or compensated for the wrongs they have suffered.[29]

The transaction bribe under the fairness criteria will be unethical if companies that are similar in all respects relevant to the kind of treatment in question are not given similar benefits, even if they are dissimilar in other irrelevant respects.[30] The question then becomes whether companies that do not bribe receive the same treatment as those that do bribe. With a transaction bribe all companies get the same service but the company that pays a bribe gets it faster. One could conclude that slower service is not the same service at all and thus the companies are not treated equally because one company paid a bribe. The two companies are not treated equally, thus the bribe is unethical. The decision whether this treatment is ethical or not turns on the conclusion whether the services each receives is the same or different, and if different, on whether unequal

treatment that has been induced by the bribe can be justified.

The variance bribe is unethical based on fairness principles because some companies can avoid the imposition of a law by the payment of a bribe. Such payment should not have any influence on whether or not a law is enforced in a particular instance. Thus one company is receiving favored treatment based on something that should not affect the enforcement of a law.

Outright purchases are unethical under a fairness analysis. The employee is not giving his benefits to the employer as he should be, but is instead giving his benefits to someone else because of the payment of bribes. The payment of bribes should not be made to affect an employee's loyalty; he should render all the benefits to the entity that is employing him, not to the one bribing him.

The above ethical analysis shows us that under a rights and fairness analysis, transaction bribes may or may not be ethical while variance and outright purchase bribes are unethical. Utilitarian analysis cannot be used effectively to decide which of these three types of bribes is unethical.

The Foreign Corrupt Practices Act outlaws variance and outright purchase bribes, but allows transaction or grease bribes.[31] By contrast, each of these types of bribes are expressly prohibited in domestic US situations;[32] transaction bribes are outlawed in many countries.[33] This would seem to support the analysis that the above transaction bribes are in fact unethical.

On the basis of this inquiry, one must conclude that the Foreign Corrupt Practices Act does not cover as much ground as ethical behavior would demand. Thus if a company behaves ethically, it will not only satisfy the minimum standard of the Foreign Corrupt Practices Act but also go beyond that which is legally required.

In the next section of this paper, the focus will be on two of the major problem areas of the Act. Businessmen claim that it is these ambiguities that are effectively hampering their operations overseas.

3. Problems with Foreign Corrupt Practices Act

The Senate Report on S.708 asserts that "as a result of unnecessary interpretive problems, US business has lost legitimate export opportunities and has incurred unreasonable costs in attempts to comply with the Foreign Corrupt Practices Act provisions."[34] Senator Dixon claims that the Act in its "present form acts as an export disincentive."[35]

There are two ambiguities in particular that are considered by the business community to be major stumbling blocks. These two problems are questions about the "reason to know" language[36] of the Act and its accounting provisions.[37]

A. "Reason to Know"

Under the Foreign Corrupt Practices Act, the individuals that can be held liable for bribery are not only those who directly or indirectly bribe a foreign official but, also those who *know or have reason to know* that a bribe is being given.[38] The reason to know standard has been criticized because it is vague and ambiguous.[39]

While it is relatively certain that this language covers payments made to agents for the purpose of being passed along as bribes to foreign officials, it is uncertain what other areas are covered.[40] Adding to the question of the coverage of this statute is the fact that the Act itself gives no guidelines explaining the meaning of the reason to know standard and there have not been enough cases under the Foreign Corrupt Practices Act to flesh out the full extent of its meaning.

Without effective court pronouncements on what constitutes a reason to know, it is difficult to assess whether this standard mandates (1) a regular system of procedures designed to detect corruption, (2) due diligence type reviews of company records, (3) board of director liability for the behavior of employees solely because the board has managerial review power. The best we can do is examine what commentators and governmental bodies have said.

It has been asserted that "the effect of the reason to know language is to create a standard of negligence that imposes a duty on corporate management to inquire about possible improper or illegal payments."[41] It is thus hoped that the anti-bribery provision would produce accountability, and that to avoid criminal accountability, "self-enforcing, preventive mechanisms" would be introduced at the corporate level.[42]

Two recent SEC suits, both of which were settled by consent decrees, make the SEC opinion about the reach of the reason to know language clear. Based on the SEC's complaints in *SEC v. Katy Industries*[43] and *SEC v. Oil Refining Corp.*[44] it is obvious that the SEC believes that if a party has *any reason to suspect* that a payment will be used to influence public officials, then that party could be liable under the Foreign Corrupt Practices Act.[45]

If the Act needs to be amended to eliminate ambiguities because it is acting as an "export inhibitor," presumably due to the uncertainty of how to comply with its provisions,[46] such amendment should wait the day that a decline in exports can be persuasively, if not conclusively, attributed to the Act rather than to interest rates, strength of the dollar, price, quality and the like. A number of times in the recent past bills have been proposed in Congress to eliminate this language, but as of this writing all have failed because the equation, "F.C.P.A. causes a decline in exports," is too simplistic to carry the day.

Even though the "reason to know" language has drawn fire and may at some stage be due for revision, it is not the only controversial provision of the Foreign Corrupt Practices Act. This act also contains accounting provisions that have caused a certain amount of trouble for American businesses.

B. Accounting Provisions

The Foreign Corrupt Practices Act accounting provisions, set forth in 15 U.S.C. sec. 78m, require that every issuer, "make and keep books, records, and accounts, which in reasonable detail, accurately and fairly reflect the transactions and dispositions of the assets of the issuer." In addition, this section requires issuers to "devise and maintain a system of internal accounting controls sufficient to provide reasonable assurances that transactions are executed in accordance with management's authorization;" recorded in a way that will "permit the preparation of financial statements in conformity with generally accepted accounting principles;" and permit the disbursement of assets "only in accordance with management's general or specific authorization."[47] Finally, the recorded assets should be "compared with existing assets at reasonable intervals" with "appropriate action" being taken when differences are found.[48]

It is important to note that the accounting restrictions do not apply just to illegal foreign payments but to the everyday operations of the business as well. By requiring more in-depth accounting disclosure, it will be much more difficult, if not impossible, for businesses to hide foreign bribes in their accounting records and financial statements.

While it is a good idea for Congress to make it more difficult to cover up illegal bribes through stricter accounting rules, it is not clear that the Foreign Corrupt Practices Act has succeeded in this regard. The reason for this is that many businessmen and accountants feel that the accounting requirements are not giving them sufficient guidance and are leading them into a no-win situation.[49]

These companies fear that failing to live up to uncertain standards will expose companies to criminal penalties,[50] therefore businesses are keeping more and better records than is necessary under the Act or good business practice.[51] The end result is that the cost of complying with the act has greatly increased the costs of doing business.[52] It is therefore not surprising that in a recent Harris Poll, 68% of businessmen favored a reduction in the amount of required record keeping under the Foreign Corrupt Practices Act.[53]

Further, and most significantly, no concrete standard has been set forth to determine what information must be reported in accounting records. Two differing possibilities exist, *reasonableness* and *materiality*. The SEC claims that only reasonable detail of transactions must be recorded.[54] The American Bar Association, on the other hand, claims that only material information need be disclosed.[55]

In order to help businesses get a firm handle on what is required of them, one of these two standards, or some other, needs to be chosen. While reasonableness is a commonly used legal standard, materiality is the preferable standard because it is one that accountants and businessmen are most familiar with and one that will effectively advance the purpose of the Act.

In accounting, materiality has been defined as "the magnitude of an omission or misstatement of accounting information that, *in the light of surrounding circumstances*, makes it probable that the judgement of a reasonable person relying on the information would have been changed or influenced by the omission or misstatement."[56] This means that if the omission or inclusion of an amount would not change or influence the decision of a rational decision maker, it is immaterial.[57]

Under this standard, information about all foreign bribes would have to be reported. This is the type of information that would influence the judgement of a rational decision maker since it reflects on the legal and moral tone of a company. At the same time, business would not have to keep track of trivial expenses that would not influence the decision of a rational decision maker. Therefore, all foreign bribes would be reported because they are material. Expenses that are not material would only be reported if the benefit of recording them outweighed the cost of collecting and recording them.[58]

Thus the materiality standard will reduce management uncertainty about what items need to be reported and reduce some of the burdensome expenses businesses are now incurring by going too far in their reporting efforts. Since managers and accountants have a firm grasp of the concept, it can produce the desired results in accounting records in minimum time. Such a system taken as a whole would reasonably meet the statute's specified objectives and would satisfy its requirements.

4. *Conclusion*

The Foreign Corrupt Practices Act of 1977, while scarcely litigated, has had a significant impact on operations of US business firms at home and abroad. In fact, it demands no more than that companies and their employees behave ethically.

Despite this goal, ambiguities in the statute have reduced its effectiveness. A genuine export crisis—one that is distinctly tied to the operation of the Act—may bring about some future adjustment to the reason to know standard. For the time being, however, clarity in the accounting requirement, which can be easily introduced, is the more pressing issue. With a vigorous enforcement effort, the Act can restore the reputation for fair and honest dealings that has long characterized US business firms in the international marketplace.

NOTES

1 The Foreign Corrupt Practices Act of 1977, 15 U.S.C. 78a, 78tn. 78dd-1,-2. 78ff.

2 *Business Accounting and Foreign Trade Simplification Act: Hearings on S.708 Before the Subcommittee on Securities and the Subcommittee on International Finance and Monetary Policy of the Senate Committee on Banking, Housing and Urban Affairs*, 97 Cong., first session 1-2 (1981) (statement of Senator D'Amato).

3 Swedish Penal Code, SFS 1977: 103 (Jan 1, 1978).

4 The Foreign Corrupt Practices Act of 1977, 15 U.S.C 78dd-2.

5 *Ibid.*

6 *Oil Company, Former CEO Settle Foreign Corrupt Payment Charges*, 18 Sec. Reg. & L Rep. (BNA) 1006 (July 11, 1986).

7 *Ibid.*

8 *Ibid.*

9 *Ibid.*

10 *Ibid.*

11 *Ibid.*

12 *The Wall Street Journal*, July 10, 1986, 54.

13 *Oil Company, Former CEO Settle Foreign Corrupt Payment Charges*, 18 Sec. Reg. & L Rep. (BNA) 1006 (July 11, 1986).

14 *Ibid.*

15 Porrata-Doria, *Amending the Foreign Corrupt Practices Act of 1977: Repeating the Mistakes of the Past*, 38 Rutgers LR 29, 30 (1985).

16 *Ibid.*, 31.

17 W. Michael Reisman, *Folded Lies* (1979).

18 *Ibid.*, 69.

19 *Ibid.*

20 *Ibid.*, 75.

21 *Ibid.*, 88-89.

22 M. Velasquez, *Business Ethics: Concepts and Cases*, 46 (1982).

23 *Ibid.*, 47.

24 *Ibid.*, 36. The case-specific utilitarianism discussed in the text is known as *act utilitarianism*. A variation of this, known as *rule utilitarianism*, focuses not on the specific, unique facts of a case, but on the long-term and seeks to determine which rule of conduct, bribery or non-bribery, will produce the most consistent long-term guidance with the least loss of utility. In other words, rule utilitarianism will not quite maximize utility on a case-by-case basis, but it will, on the positive side, make up for that by providing stability and consistency. However, both versions of utilitarianism demand too much in terms of seeing into the fu-

ture and quantifying the results to be of value to this analysis.

25 *Ibid.*, 59.

26 DesJardins, "An Employee's Right to Privacy," in *Contemporary Issues in Business Ethics* 223 (J. DesJardins and J. McCall, eds.) 1985.

27 M. Velasquez, *Business Ethics: Concepts and Cases*, 59 (1982).

28 *Ibid.*, 65.

29 *Ibid.*, 75.

30 *Ibid.*, 77.

31 Porrata-Doria, *supra* Note 15, 36.

32 18 U.S.C. sec. 201 (g) (1982).

33 See Note, *The Foreign Corrupt Practices Act of 1977: A Solution or a Problem* 11 *Cal. W.* Int'l L. J. 111. 128-134 (1981).

34 Bader and Shaw, *Amendment of the Foreign Corrupt Practices Act* 15 N.Y.U.J. INT'L L & Pol.627. 634 (1983).

35 127 Cong. Rec. S. 13975 (daily ed. Nov. 23, 1981).

36 15 U.S.C. 78dd-l. dd-2 (1977).

37 15 U.S.C. 78m (1977).

38 15 U.S.C. 78dd-1. dd-2 (1977).

39 Porrata-Doria, *supra* Note 15, 37.

40 *Ibid.*

41 Bader and Shaw. *supra* Note 34, 631.

42 S. Rep. No. 114, 95th Cong., 1st Session 4 at 10 (1977).

43 [July-Dec] Sec. Reg. & L Rep. (BNA) No. 469 at A-1 (N.D.Ill. Aug 30, 1978) (settled by consent decree).

44 [July-Dec] Sec. Reg. & L Rep. (BNA) No. 513 at A-23 (D.D.C. July 19. 1979) (settled by consent decree).

45 Porrata-Doria, *supra* Note 15, 42.

46 *Business Accounting and Foreign Trade Simplification Act: Joint Hearing on S.414 Before the Subcommittees on International Finance and Monetary Policy and Securities of the Senate Committee on Banking, Housing, and Urban Affairs, 98th Congress.* 1st Session 25 (1983)

(statement of William E. Brock, United States Trade Representative) at 50.

47 15 U.S.C. sec. 78m (1977).

48 *Ibid.*

49 Statement of William E. Brock, United States Trade Representative, *supra* Note 46.

50 *Ibid.*, 26.

51 Porrata-Doria, *supra* Note 15, 45.

52 Statement of William E. Brock. United States Trade Representative, *supra* Note 46, 26.

53 Business Week. *The Antibribery Act Splits Executives*, Sept. 19, 1983, 15.

54 S.E.C. Release No. 34-17, 500, 3 Fed. Sec. L Rep. (CCH) paragraph 23, 632H at 17, 233-5 (Jan 29, 1981).

55 ABA Committee on Corporate Law and Accounting, *A Guide to the New Section 13(b)(2) Accounting Requirements of the Securities Exchange Act of 1934*, 33 Bus. Law 307, 315 (1978).

56 Financial Accounting Standards Board, *FASB Concepts Statement 2*, May 1980 (emphasis supplied).

57 Welsch, Newman and Zlatkovich. *Intermediate Accounting 7th ed.* (1986), 22.

58 Financial Accounting Standards Board, *supra* Note 56.

◆ ◆ ◆ ◆ ◆

JEFFREY A. FADIMAN

A Traveler's Guide to Gifts and Bribes

"What do I say if he asks for a bribe?" I asked myself while enduring the all-night flight to Asia. Uncertain, I shared my concern with the man sitting beside me, a CEO en route to Singapore. Intrigued, he passed it on to his partners next to him. No one seemed sure.

Among American executives doing business overseas, this uncertainty is widespread. Consider, for example, each of the following situations:

- You are invited to the home of your foreign colleague. You learn he lives in a palatial villa. What gift might both please your host and ease business relations? What if he considers it to be a bribe? What if he *expects* it to be a bribe? Why do you feel uneasy?
- Your company's product lies on the dock of a foreign port. To avoid spoilage, you must swiftly transport it inland. What "gift," if any, would both please authorities and facilitate your business? What if they ask for "gifts" of $50? $50,000? $500,000? When does a gift become a bribe? When do you stop feeling comfortable?
- Negotiations are complete. The agreement is signed. One week later, a minister asks your company for $1 million—"for a hospital"—simultaneously suggesting that "other valuable considerations" might come your way as the result of future favors on both sides. What response, if any, would please him, satisfy you, and help execute the signed agreement?
- You have been asked to testify before the Securities and Exchange Commission regarding alleged violations of the Foreign Corrupt Practices Act. How would you explain the way you handled the examples above? Would your ex-

planations both satisfy those in authority and ensure the continued overseas operation of your company?

Much of the discomfort Americans feel when faced with problems of this nature is due to US law. Since 1977, congressional passage of the Foreign Corrupt Practices Act has transformed hypothetical problems into practical dilemmas and has created considerable anxiety among Americans who deal with foreign governments and companies. The problem is particularly difficult for those conducting business in the developing nations, where the rules that govern payoffs may differ sharply from our own. In such instances, US executives may face not only legal but also ethical and cultural dilemmas: How do businesspeople comply with customs that conflict with both their sense of ethics and this nation's law?

One way to approach the problem is to devise appropriate corporate responses to payoff requests. The suggestions that follow apply to those developing Asian, African, and Middle Eastern nations, still in transition toward industrial societies, that have retained aspects of their communal traditions. These approaches do not assume that those who adhere to these ideals exist in selfless bliss, requesting private payments only for communal ends, with little thought of self-enrichment. Nor do these suggestions apply to situations of overt extortion, where US companies are forced to provide funds. Instead they explore a middle way in which non-Western colleagues may have several motives when requesting a payoff, thereby providing US managers with several options.

Decisions and Dilemmas

My own first experience with Third World bribery may illustrate the inner conflict Americans can feel when asked to break the rules. It occurred in East Africa and began with this request: "Oh, and Bwana,

I would like 1,000 shillings as Zawadi, my gift. And, as we are now friends, for Chai, my tea, an eight-band radio, to bring to my home when you visit."

Both *Chai* and *Zawadi* can be Swahili terms for "bribe." He delivered these requests in respectful tones. They came almost as an afterthought, at the conclusion of negotiations in which we had settled the details of a projected business venture. I had looked forward to buying my counterpart a final drink to complete the deal symbolically in the American fashion. Instead, after we had settled every contractual aspect, he expected money.

The amount he suggested, although insignificant by modern standards, seemed large at the time. Nonetheless, it was the radio that got to me. Somehow it added insult to injury. Outwardly, I kept smiling. Inside, my stomach boiled. My own world view equates bribery with sin. I expect monetary issues to be settled before contracts are signed. Instead, although the negotiations were complete, he expected me to pay out once more. Once? How often? Where would it stop? My reaction took only moments to formulate. "I'm American," I declared. "I don't pay bribes." Then I walked away. That walk was not the longest in my life. It was, however, one of the least commercially productive.

As it turned out, I had misunderstood him—in more ways than one. By misinterpreting both his language and his culture, I lost an opportunity for a business deal and a personal relationship that would have paid enormous dividends without violating either the law or my own sense of ethics.

Go back through the episode—but view it this time with an East African perspective. First, my colleague's language should have given me an important clue as to how he saw our transaction. Although his limited command of English caused him to frame his request as a command—a phrasing I instinctively found offensive—his tone was courteous. Moreover, if I had listened more carefully, I would have noted that he had addressed me as a superior: he used the honorific *Bwana*, meaning "sir," rather than *Rafiki*

(or friend), used between equals. From his perspective, the language was appropriate; it reflected the differences in our personal wealth and in the power of the institutions we each represented.

Having assigned me the role of the superior figure in the economic transaction, he then suggested how I should use my position in accord with his culture's traditions—logically assuming that I would benefit by his prompting. In this case, he suggested that money and a radio would be appropriate gifts. What he did not tell me was that his culture's traditions required him to use the money to provide a feast—in my honor—to which he would invite everyone in his social and commercial circle whom he felt I should meet. The radio would simply create a festive atmosphere at the party. This was to mark the beginning of an ongoing relationship with reciprocal benefits.

He told me none of this. Since I was willing to do business in local fashion, I was supposed to know. In fact, I had not merely been invited to a dwelling but through a gateway into the maze of gifts and formal visiting that linked him to his kin. He hoped that I would respond in local fashion. Instead, I responded according to my cultural norms and walked out both on the chance to do business and on the opportunity to make friends.

The legal side. Perhaps from a strictly legal perspective my American reaction was warranted. In the late 1970s, as part of the national reaction to Watergate, the SEC sued several large US companies for alleged instances of bribery overseas. One company reportedly authorized $59 million in contributions to political parties in Italy, including the Communist party. A second allegedly paid $4 million to a political party in South Korea. A third reportedly provided $450,000 in "gifts" to Saudi generals. A fourth may have diverted $377,000 to fly plane-loads of voters to the Cook Islands to rig elections there.

The sheer size of the payments and the ways they had been used staggered the public. A US senate committee reported "corrupt" foreign payments involving hundreds of millions of dollars by more than 400 US corporations, including 117 of the *Fortune* "500." The SEC described the problem as a national crisis.

In response, Congress passed the Foreign Corrupt Practices Act in 1977. The law prohibits US corporations from providing or even offering payments to foreign political parties, candidates, or officials with discretionary authority under circumstances that might induce recipients to misuse their positions to assist the company to obtain, maintain, or retain business.

The FCPA does not forbid payments to lesser figures, however. On the contrary, it explicitly allows facilitating payments ("grease") to persuade foreign officials to perform their normal duties, at both the clerical and ministerial levels. The law establishes no monetary guidelines but requires companies to keep reasonably detailed records that accurately and fairly reflect the transactions.

The act also prohibits indirect forms of payment. Companies cannot make payments of this nature while "knowing or having reason to know" that any portion of the funds will be transferred to a forbidden recipient to be used for corrupt purposes as previously defined. Corporations face fines of up to $1 million. Individuals can be fined $10,000—which the corporation is forbidden to indemnify—and sentenced to a maximum of five years in prison. In short, private payments by Americans abroad can mean violation of US law, a consideration that deeply influences US corporate thinking.

The ethical side. For most US executives, however, the problem goes beyond the law. Most Americans share an aversion to payoffs. In parts of Asia, Africa, and the Middle East, however, certain types of bribery form an accepted element of their commercial traditions. Of course, nepotism, shakedown, and similar practices do occur in US business; these practices, however, are both forbidden by law and universally disapproved.

Americans abroad reflect these sentiments. Most see themselves as personally honest and profession-ally ethical. More important, they see themselves as preferring to conduct business according to the law, both American and foreign. They also know that virtually all foreign governments—including those notorious for corruption—have rigorously enforced statutes against most forms of private payoff. In general, there is popular support for these anticorruption measures. In Malaysia, bribery is publicly frowned on and punishable by long imprisonment. In the Soviet Union, Soviet officials who solicit bribes can be executed.

Reflecting this awareness, most US businesspeople prefer to play by local rules, competing in the open market according to the quality, price, and services provided by their product. Few, if any, want to make illegal payments of any kind to anybody. Most prefer to obey both local laws and their own ethical convictions while remaining able to do business.

The cultural side. Yet, as my African experience suggests, indigenous traditions often override the law. In some developing nations, payoffs have become a norm. The problem is compounded when local payoff practices are rooted in a "communal heritage," ideals inherited from a preindustrial past where a community leader's wealth—however acquired—was shared throughout the community. Those who hoarded were scorned as antisocial. Those who shared won status and authority. Contact with Western commerce has blurred the ideal, but even the most individualistic businesspeople remember their communal obligations.

Contemporary business practices in those regions often reflect these earlier ideals. Certain forms of private payoff have endured for centuries. The Nigerian practice of *dash* (private payments for private services), for example, goes back to fifteenth century contacts with the Portuguese, in which Africans solicited "gifts" (trade goods) in exchange for labor. Such solicitation can pose a cultural dilemma to Americans who may be unfamiliar with the communal nuances of non-Western commercial conduct. To cope, they may denigrate these traditions, perceiving colleagues who solicit payments as unethical and their culture as corrupt.

Or they may respond to communal business methods by ignoring them, choosing instead to deal with foreign counterparts purely in Western fashion. This approach will usually work—up to a point. Non-Western businesspeople who deal with US executives, for example, are often graduates of Western universities. Their language skills, commercial training, and professional demeanor, so similar to ours, make it comfortable to conduct business. But when these same colleagues shift to non-Western behavior, discussing gifts or bribes, Americans are often shocked.

Obviously, such reactions ignore the fact that foreign businesspeople have more than one cultural dimension. Managers from developing countries may hold conflicting values: one instilled by exposure to the West, the other imposed by local tradition. Non-Western businesspeople may see no conflict in negotiating contracts along Western lines, then reverting to indigenous traditions when discussing private payments. For Americans, however, this transition may be hard to make.

My experience suggests that most non-Westerners are neither excessively corrupt nor completely communal. Rather, they are simultaneously drawn to both indigenous and Western ideals. Many have internalized the Western norms of personal enrichment along with those of modern commerce, while simultaneously adhering to indigenous traditions by fulfilling communal obligations. Requests for payoffs may spring from both these ideals. Corporate responses must therefore be designed to satisfy them both.

Background for Payoffs

Throughout non-Western cultures, three traditions form the background for discussing payoffs: the inner circle, future favors, and the gift exchange. Though centuries old, each has evolved into a modern business concept. Americans who work in the Third World need to learn about them so they can work within them.

The inner circle. Most individuals in developing nations classify others into some form of "ins" and "outs." Members of more communal societies, influenced by the need to strive for group prosperity, divide humanity into those with whom they have relationships and those with whom they have none. Many Africans, for instance, view people as either "brothers" or "strangers." Relationships with brothers may be real—kin, however distant—or fictional, extending to comrades or "mates." Comrades, however, may both speak and act like kin, address one another as family, and assume obligations of protection and assistance that Americans reserve for nuclear families.

Together, kin and comrades form an inner circle, a fictional "family," devoted to mutual protection and prosperity. Like the "old boy networks" that operate in the United States, no single rule defines membership in the inner circle. East Africans may include "age mates," individuals of similar age; West Africans, "homeboys," all men of similar region; Chinese, members of a dialect group; Indians, members of a caste. In most instances, the "ins" include extended families and their friends.

Beyond this magic circle live the "outs": strangers, aliens, individuals with no relationship to those within. Communal societies in Southern Africa, for example, describe these people in all their millions as "predators," implying savage creatures with whom the "ins" lack any common ground. The motives of outsiders inspire fear, not because there is danger but simply because they are unknown. Although conditioned to display courtesy, insiders prefer to restrict both social and commercial dealings to those with whom they have dependable relationships. The ancient principle can still be found in modern commerce; non-Western businesspeople often prefer to restrict commercial relationships to those they know and trust.

Not every US manager is aware of this division. Those who investigate often assume that their nationality, ethnic background, and alien culture automatically classify them as "outs." Non-Western colleagues, however, may regard specific Westerners as useful contacts, particularly if they seem willing to do business in local fashion. They may, therefore, consider bringing certain individuals into their inner circles in such a manner as to benefit both sides.

Overseas executives, if asked to work within such circles, should find their business prospects much enhanced. These understandings often lead to implicit quid pro quos. For example, one side might agree to hire workers from only one clan; in return the other side would guarantee devoted labor. As social and commercial trust grows, the Westerners may be regarded less and less as aliens or predators and more and more as comrades or kin. Obviously, this is a desirable transition, and executives assigned to work within this type of culture may wish to consider whether these inner circles exist, and if so, whether working within them will enhance business prospects.

The future favor. A second non-Western concept that relates to payoffs is a system of future favors. Relationships within the inner circles of non-Western nations function through such favors. In Japan, the corresponding system is known as "inner duty" or *giri*. On Mt. Kenya, it is "inner relationship," *uthoni*. Filipinos describe it as "inner debt," *utani na loob*. All systems of this type assume that any individual under obligation to another has entered a relationship in which the first favor must be repaid in the future, when convenient to all sides.

Neither side defines the manner of repayment. Rather, both understand that some form of gift or service will repay the earlier debt with interest. This repayment places the originator under obligation. The process then begins again, creating a lifelong cycle. The relationship that springs from meeting lifelong obligations builds the trust that forms a basis for conducting business.

My own introduction to the future favors system may illustrate the process. While conducting business on Mt. Kenya in the 1970s, I visited a notable local dignitary. On completing our agenda, he stopped my rush to leave by presenting me a live and angry hen. Surprised, I stammered shaky "thank-yous," then walked down the mountain with my kicking, struggling bird. Having discharged my obligation—at least in Western terms—by thanking him, I cooked the hen, completed my business, eventually left Kenya, and forgot the incident.

Years later, I returned on different business. It was a revelation. People up and down the mountain called out to one another that I had come back to "return the dignitary's hen." To them, the relationship that had sprung up between us had remained unchanged throughout the years. Having received a favor, I had now come back to renew the relationship by returning it.

I had, of course, no such intention. Having forgotten the hen incident, I was also unaware of its importance to others. Embarrassed, I slipped into a market and bought a larger hen, then climbed to his homestead to present it. Again I erred, deciding to apologize in Western fashion for delaying my return. "How can a hen be late?" he replied. "Due to the bird, we have *uthoni* [obligations, thus a relationship]. That is what sweetens life. What else was the hen for but to bring you here again?"

These sentiments can also operate within non-Western commercial circles, where business favors can replace hens, but *uthoni* are what sweetens corporate life. Western interest lies in doing business; non-Western, in forming bonds so that business can begin. Westerners seek to discharge obligations; non-Westerners, to create them. Our focus is on producing short-term profit; theirs, on generating future favors. The success of an overseas venture may depend on an executive's awareness of these differences.

The gift exchange. One final non-Western concept that can relate to payoffs is a continuous exchange of gifts. In some developing nations, gifts form the catalysts that trigger future favors. US executives often wish to present gifts appropriate to cultures where they are assigned, to the point where at least one corporation has commissioned a special study of the subject. They may be less aware, however, of the long-range implications of gift giving within these cultures. Two of these may be particularly relevant to CEOs concerned with payoffs.

In many non-Western commercial circles, the tradition of gift giving has evolved into a modern business tool intended to create obligation as well as affection. Recipients may be gratified by what they receive, but they also incur an obligation that they must some day repay. Gift giving in these cultures may therefore operate in two dimensions: one meant to provide short-term pleasure; the other, long-range bonds.

This strategy is common in Moslem areas of Africa and Asia. Within these cultures, I have watched export merchants change Western clientele from browsers to buyers by inviting them to tea. Seated, the customers sip at leisure, while merchandise is brought before them piece by piece. The seller thus achieves three goals. His clients have been honored, immobilized, and placed under obligation.

In consequence, the customers often feel the need to repay in kind. Lacking suitable material gifts, they frequently respond as the merchant intends: with decisions to buy—not because they need the merchandise but to return the seller's gift of hospitality. The buyers, considering their obligation discharged, leave the premises believing relations have ended. The sellers, however, hope they have just begun. Their intent is to create relationships that will cause clients to return. A second visit would mean presentation of another gift, perhaps of greater value. That, in turn, might mean a second purchase, leading to further visits, continued gifts, and a gradual deepening of personal and commercial relations intended to enrich both sides.

The point of the process, obviously, is not the exchanges themselves but the relationships they en-gender. The gifts are simply catalysts. Under ideal circumstances the process should be unending, with visits, gifts, gestures, and services flowing back and forth among participants throughout their lives. The universally understood purpose is to create reciprocal good feelings and commercial prosperity among all concerned.

Gift giving has also evolved as a commercial "signal." In America, gifts exchanged by business colleagues may signal gratitude, camaraderie, or perhaps the discharge of minor obligations. Among non-Westerners, gifts may signal the desire to begin both social and commercial relationships with members of an inner circle. That signal may also apply to gifts exchanged with Westerners. If frequently repeated, such exchanges may be signals of intent. For Americans, the signal may suggest a willingness to work within a circle of local business colleagues, to assume appropriate obligations, and to conduct business in local ways. For non-Western colleagues, gifts may imply a wish to invite selected individuals into their commercial interactions.

Approaches to Payoffs

While US corporations may benefit from adapting to local business concepts, many indigenous business traditions, especially in developing regions, are alien to the American experience and therefore difficult to implement by US field personnel—as every executive who has tried to sit cross-legged for several hours with Third World counterparts will attest.

Conversely, many non-Western administrators are particularly well informed about US business practices, thus permitting US field representatives to function on familiar ground. Nonetheless, those willing to adapt indigenous commercial concepts to US corporate needs may find that their companies can benefit in several ways. Through working with a circle of non-Western business colleagues, and participating fully in the traditional exchange of gifts and favors, US executives may find that their companies increase the chance of preferential treatment; use local methods and local contacts to gain market share; develop trust to reinforce contractual obligations; and minimize current risk, while maximizing future opportunities by developing local expertise.

Corporations that adapt to local business concepts may also develop methods to cope with local forms of payoff. Current approaches vary from culture to culture, yet patterns do appear. Three frequently recur in dealings between Americans and non-Westerners: gifts, bribes, and other considerations.

Gifts: the direct request. This form of payoff may occur when key foreign businesspeople approach their US colleagues to solicit "gifts." Solicitations of this type have no place in US business circles where they could be construed as exploitation. Obviously, the same may hold true overseas, particularly in areas where shakedown, bribery, and extortion may be prevalent. There is, however, an alternative to consider. To non-Western colleagues, such requests may simply be a normal business strategy, designed to build long-term relationships.

To US businesspeople, every venture is based on the bottom line. To non-Western colleagues, a venture is based on the human relationships that form around it. Yet, when dealing with us they often grow uncertain as to how to form these relationships. How can social ties be created with Americans who speak only of business, even when at leisure? How can traditions of gift giving be initiated with people unaware of the traditions? Without the exchange of gifts, how can obligations be created? Without obligations, how can there be trust?

Faced with such questions, non-Western business colleagues may understandably decide to initiate gift-giving relationships on their own. If powerful, prominent, or wealthy, they may simply begin by taking on the role of giver. If less powerful or affluent, some may begin by suggesting they become recipients. There need be no dishonor in such action, since petitioners know they will repay with future favors whatever inner debt they incur.

The hosts may also realize that, as strangers, Americans may be unaware of local forms of gift giving as well as their relationship to business norms. Or they may be cognizant of such relationships but may have no idea of how to enter into them. In such instances, simple courtesy may cause the hosts to indicate—perhaps obliquely—how proper entry into the local system should be made. Such was the unfortunate case with my East African colleague's request for the eight-band radio.

Cultural barriers can be difficult to cross. Most Americans give generously, but rarely on request. When solicited, we feel exploited. Solicitations may seem more relevant, however, if examined from the perspective of the non-Western peoples with whom we are concerned.

Often, in societies marked by enormous gaps between the rich and the poor, acts of generosity display high status. To withhold gifts is to deny the affluence one has achieved. Non-Western counterparts often use lavish hospitality both to reflect and to display their wealth and status within local society. When Americans within these regions both represent great wealth through association with their corporations and seek high status as a tool to conduct business, it may prove more profitable for the corporation to give than to receive.

In short, when asked for "gifts" by foreign personnel, managers may consider two options. The first option is to regard each query as extortion and every petitioner as a potential thief. The second is to consider the request within its local context. In nations where gifts generate a sense of obligation, it may prove best to give them, thereby creating inner debts among key foreign colleagues in the belief that they will repay them over time. If such requests indeed reflect a local way of doing business, they may be gateways into the workings of its commercial world. One US option, therefore, is to consider the effect of providing "gifts"—even on direct request— in terms of the relationships required to implement the corporation's long-range plans.

Bribes: the indirect request. A second approach to payoffs, recurrent in non-Western business circles, is the indirect request. Most Third World people prefer the carrot to the stick. To avoid unpleasant confrontation, they designate third parties to suggest that "gifts" of specified amounts be made to those in local power circles. In explanation they cite the probability of future favors in return. No line exists, of course, dividing gifts from bribes. It seems that direct solicitation involves smaller amounts, while larger ones require go-betweens. On occasion, however, the sums requested can be staggering: in 1976, for example, US executives in Qatar were asked for a $1.5 million "gift" for that nation's minister of oil.

US responses to such queries must preserve both corporate funds and executive relationships with those in power. While smaller gifts may signal a desire to work with the local business circles, a company that supplies larger sums could violate both local antipayoff statutes and the FCPA. Conversely, outright rejection of such requests may cause both the go-betweens and those they represent to lose prestige and thus possibly prompt retaliation.

In such instances, the FCPA may actually provide beleaguered corporate executives with a highly convenient excuse. Since direct compliance with requests for private funds exposes every US company to threats of negative publicity, blackmail, legal action, financial loss, and damage to corporate image, it may prove easy for Americans to say no—while at the same time offering nonmonetary benefits to satisfy both sides.

US competitors may, in fact, be in a better situation than those companies from Europe and Japan that play by different rules. Since the principle of payoffs is either accepted or encouraged by many of their governments, the companies must find it difficult to refuse payment of whatever sums are asked.

Nor should the "right to bribe" be automatically considered an advantage. Ignoring every other factor, this argument assumes contracts are awarded solely on the basis of the largest private payoff. At the most

obvious level, it ignores the possibility that products also compete on the basis of quality, price, promotion, and service—factors often crucial to American success abroad. US field representatives are often first to recognize that payoffs may be only one of many factors in awarding contracts. In analyzing US competition in the Middle East, for instance, one executive of an American aircraft company noted: "The French have savoir faire in giving bribes discreetly and well, but they're still not ... backing up their sales with technical expertise." The overseas executive should consider to what degree the right to bribe may be offset by turning the attention of the payoff seekers to other valuable considerations.

Other considerations: the suggested service. A third approach, often used by members of a non-Western elite, is to request that US companies contribute cash to public service projects, often administered by the petitioners themselves. Most proposals of this type require money. Yet if American executives focus too sharply on the financial aspects, they may neglect the chance to work other nonmonetary considerations into their response. In many developing nations, nonmonetary considerations may weigh heavily on foreign colleagues.

Many elite non-Westerners, for example, are intensely nationalistic. They love their country keenly, deplore its relative poverty, and yearn to help it rise. They may, therefore, phrase their requests for payoffs in terms of a suggested service to the nation. In Kenya, for example, ministerial requests to US companies during the 1970s suggested a contribution toward the construction of a hospital. In Indonesia, in the mid-1970s, a top executive of Pertamina, that nation's government-sponsored oil company, requested contributions to an Indonesian restaurant in New York City as a service to the homeland. In his solicitation letter, the executive wrote that the restaurant was in fact intended to "enhance the Indonesian image in the USA, ... promote tourism, ... and attract the interest of the US businessmen to investments in Indonesia."

Westerners may regard such claims with cynicism. Non-Westerners may not. They recognize that, even if the notables involved become wealthy, some portion of the wealth, which only they can attract from abroad, will still be shared by other members of their homeland.

That belief is worth consideration, for many elite non-Westerners share a second concern: the desire to meet communal obligations by sharing wealth with members of their inner circle. Modern business leaders in communal cultures rarely simply hoard their wealth. To do so would invite social condemnation. Rather, they provide gifts, funds, and favors to those in their communal settings, receiving deference, authority, and prestige in return.

This does not mean that funds transferred by Western corporations to a single foreign colleague will be parceled out among a circle of cronies. Rather, money passes through one pair of hands over time, flowing slowly in the form of gifts and favors to friends and kin. The funds may even flow beyond this inner circle to their children, most often to ensure their continued education. Such generosity, of course, places both adult recipients and children under a long-term obligation, thereby providing donors both with current status and with assurance of obtaining future favors.

In short, non-Western colleagues who seek payoffs may have concerns beyond their personal enrichment. If motivated by both national and communal idealism, they may feel that these requests are not only for themselves but also a means to aid much larger groups and ultimately their nation.

A Donation Strategy

Requests for payoffs give executives little choice. Rejection generates resentment, while agreement may lead to prosecution. Perhaps appeals to both communal and national idealism can open up a third alternative. Consider, for example, the possibility of deflecting such requests by transforming private payoffs into public services. One approach would be to respond to requests for private payment with well-publicized, carefully tailored "donations"—an approach that offers both idealistic and practical appeal.

This type of donation could take several forms. The most obvious, a monetary contribution, could be roughly identical to the amount requested in private funds. Donating it publicly, however, would pay off important foreign colleagues in nonmonetary ways.

At the national level, for instance, the most appropriate and satisfying corporate response to ministerial requests for "contributions" toward the construction of a hospital, such as occurred in Kenya, might be actually to provide one, down to the final door and stethoscope, while simultaneously insisting that monetary payments of any kind are proscribed by US law.

The same principle can apply at local levels. Top executives of smaller companies, faced with requests for funds by influential foreign counterparts, might respond by donating to medical, educational, or agricultural projects at the provincial, district, or even village level, focusing consistently on the geographic areas from which those associates come. The donation strategy can even operate at interpersonal levels. How, for example, would my African colleague have reacted had I responded to his request by offering to "donate" whatever would be needed for a special feast—including a radio?

US executives could also weave "other considerations" into the donation, encouraging foreign colleagues to continue business interaction. Many US companies now simply donate funds. Those in Bali, Indonesia, contribute large sums to local temples. Those in Senegal donate to irrigation projects. Companies in South Africa support 150 Bantu schools for black Africans.

Yet donations alone seem insufficient. To serve as an alternative to payoffs, the concept should have practical appeal. Consider, for example, the story of a Western company in Zaire. During the 1970s, Zaire's economy decayed so badly that even ranking civil servants went unpaid. As a result, key Zairian district officials approached officers of the Western company, requesting private funds for future favors. Instead, the company responded with expressions of deference and "donations" of surplus supplies, including goods that could be sold on the black market. The resulting cash flow enabled the officials to continue in their posts. This in turn allowed them to render reciprocal services, both to their district and to the company. By tailoring their contribution to local conditions, the company avoided draining its funds, while providing benefits to both sides.

There are many ways to tailor donations. At the most obvious level, funds can support social projects in the home areas of important local colleagues. Funds or even whole facilities can be given in their names. Production centers can be staffed by members of their ethnic group. Educational, medical, and other social services can be made available to key segments of a target population based on the advice of influential foreign counterparts. Given the opportunity, many non-Westerners would direct the contributions toward members of their inner circles profiting from local forms of recognition and prestige. These practices, often used in one form or another in the United States, can provide non-Western counterparts with local recognition and authority and supply a legal, ethical, and culturally acceptable alternative to a payoff.

Donating services. US companies may also deflect payoff proposals by donating services, gratifying important foreign colleagues in nonmonetary fashion, and thus facilitating the flow of future business. In 1983, for example, a British military unit, part of the Royal Electrical and Mechanical Engineers, planned an African overland vehicle expedition across the Sahara to Tanzania. On arrival, they were "expected" to make a sizable cash donation to that nation to be used in support of its wildlife.

Usually this meant meeting a minister, handing over a check, and taking a picture of the transfer. Instead, the British assembled thousands of dollars worth of tools and vehicle parts, all needed in Tanzanian wildlife areas for trucks on antipoaching patrols. Tanzania's weakened economy no longer permitted the import of enough good tools or parts, which left the wildlife authorities with few working vehicles. As a result, wild-game management had nearly halted. By transporting the vital parts across half of Africa, then working alongside local mechanics until every vehicle was on the road, the British reaped far more goodwill than private payments or even cash donations would have gained. More important, they paved the way for future transactions by providing services meant to benefit both sides.

Donating jobs. A third alternative to private payoffs may be to donate jobs, particularly on projects meant to build goodwill among a host nation's elite. In the 1970s, for example, Coca-Cola was the object of a Middle Eastern boycott by members of the Arab League. Conceivably, Coca-Cola could have sought to win favor with important individuals through gifts or bribes. Instead, the company hired hundreds of Egyptians to plant thousands of acres of orange trees. Eventually the company carpeted a considerable stretch of desert and thereby created both employment and goodwill.

More recently, Mexico refused to let IBM become the first wholly owned foreign company to make personal computers within its borders. Like Coca-Cola in Egypt, IBM employed a strategy of national development: it offered a revised proposal, creating both direct and indirect employment for Mexican nationals, in numbers high enough to satisfy that nation's elite. Such projects do more than generate goodwill. Those able to involve key foreign colleagues in ways that lend prestige on local terms may find they serve as viable alternatives to bribery.

Good Ethics, Good Business

Three strategies do not exhaust the list. US executives in foreign countries should be able to devise their own variants based on local conditions. Each approach should further social progress while offering local status instead of US funds. Americans may find their non-Western colleagues more inclined to do business with corporations that lend prestige than with those whose representatives evade, refuse, or simply walk away. It should not harm a company to gain a reputation for providing social services instead of bribes. A corporation that relies too much on payoffs will be no more respected within non-Western business circles than developing nations that rely too much on payoffs are now respected in US business circles.

Similarly, since the legal dilemma would be resolved, home offices might respond more favorably to overseas requests for funds. Whereas funding for private payments remains illegal, proposals to "donate" the same amounts toward host-nation development could be perceived as public relations and cause-related marketing. Home offices should not fear legal action. While the FCPA prohibits payments to foreign political parties, candidates, or officials with discretionary authority, nowhere does it prohibit the use of funds to aid developing societies, and it requires only that companies keep detailed records that accurately and fairly reflect the transactions.

Businesspeople can also resolve the ethical dilemma. Turning private payoffs into public services should meet both US and corporate moral standards. While one measure of corporate responsibility is to generate the highest possible returns for investors, this can usually be best achieved within a climate of goodwill. In contemporary Third World cultures, this climate can more often be created by public services than by private payoffs. To sell cola, Coke did not bribe ministers, it planted trees. Certainly, host governments will look most favorably on companies that seek to serve as well as to profit, especially through "gifts" that show concern for local ways.

Finally, the cultural dilemmas can also be resolved. Non-Western business practices may be difficult to comprehend, especially when they involve violations of US legal, commercial, or social norms. Nonetheless, US business options are limited only by our business attitudes. If these can be expanded through selective research into those local concepts that relate to payoffs, responses may emerge to satisfy both congressional and indigenous demands. What may initially appear as begging, bribery, or blackmail may be revealed as local tradition, cross-cultural courtesy, or attempts to make friends. More important, when examined from a non-American perspective, mention of "gifts," "bribes," and "other valuable considerations" may signal a wish to do business.

CASE STUDY 5

SEXUAL HARASSMENT IN THE WORKPLACE
DARCI DOLL

Case Description

Kevin had been employed as a research assistant at a biotechnology firm. Over the course of several years, Kevin received regular advancements in recognition of the positive contributions he had made for the company. Most recently, he was promoted as the Vice President of Research and Development. Shortly after this promotion, his associate Bridget began seeking him out more often than usual. She would initiate small talk or compliment him in passing. Believing that Bridget was innocently trying to initiate a friendly work relationship, Kevin thanked her for her compliments and would engage in conversation with her when work permitted. Over time, Bridget's compliments began to occur more frequently and became less innocent in nature. Bridget would make sexual innuendos toward Kevin and would openly express her sexual attraction to him. While the nature of these comments made Kevin uncomfortable, he believed that if he ignored them and let time take its course, Bridget would omit the sexual content from their conversations. After enduring these comments for several weeks, Kevin took Bridget aside and requested that she refrain from making sexual references toward him. He explained to her that in addition to making him uncomfortable, the comments were inappropriate for the work environment.

Initially, Kevin's intervention seemed to have had the desired results. Kevin's encounters with Bridget returned to their original nature and he began to feel comfortable at work again. However, a week later Bridget's sexual comments began to resurface. She repeatedly suggested they have an affair

and that he leave his wife for her. Kevin would respond that he was happily married and that he was not interested in having an affair. In addition, he would remind Bridget that he was not comfortable engaging in dialogue containing sexual content. Despite his protests and requests that Bridget refrain from making suggestive comments, the intensity continued to increase. Her comments became more obscene and she started leaving notes for him at work. When it became apparent that Bridget was not going to respect his requests, Kevin began to consider taking action. While the content was of a sexual nature, Kevin was uncertain whether or not Bridget's behavior could be labeled as sexual harassment. First, Kevin was concerned that since Bridget did not hold a position of authority over him, his complaints would not be valid. Second, Kevin worried that gender standards would be detrimental to his position. Specifically, Kevin felt that the fact that the majority of sexual harassment cases are filed against men by women would weaken his case. In addition, the majority of his encounters with Bridget had gone unwitnessed. He feared that the situation would turn into a case of his word against hers and that no one would give him the benefit of the doubt. With all of the uncertainty, Kevin was hesitant to take action. While he was unbearably uncomfortable at work, Kevin did not want to risk his job over filing a sexual harassment claim, nor did he want to cause tension at work. On the other hand, his work was suffering because of Bridget's remarks. Fearing that he could lose his job if he did not remedy the problem, Kevin began to research sexual harassment. Upon weighing the consequences, Kevin decided to go forward with filing a sexual harassment complaint against Bridget.

Ethical Analysis

Is Kevin's claim against Bridget justified? It is clear that the sexual nature of Bridget's comments were making Kevin uncomfortable at work. But is his discomfort sufficient grounds for filing a sexual harassment complaint? The following guidelines for sexual harassment are offered under Title VII of the 1964 Civil Rights Act:

> Unwelcome sexual advances, requests for sexual favors, and other verbal or physical conduct of a sexual nature constitute sexual harassment when (1) submission to such conduct is made either explicitly or implicitly a term or condition of an individual's employment, (2) submission to or rejection of such conduct by an individual is used as the basis for employment decisions affecting such individual, or (3) such conduct has the purpose or effect of unreasonably interfering with an individual's work performance or creating an intimidating, hostile, or offensive working environment.[1]

From this, two types of sexual harassment have been established. The first part of the guidelines depict quid pro quo cases while the last part refers to a hostile work environment. Kevin's case clearly does not meet the criteria of being quid pro quo; his refusal or acceptance of Bridget's advances does not have a direct effect on his position at work, nor do her suggestions constitute a term of his employment. Further, while Bridget's comments made Kevin uncomfortable, there is no evidence that his response to her advances would have a direct impact on his job in either a negative or positive way.

The second form of sexual harassment is less direct and seems more applicable to Kevin's situation. In Kevin's case, Bridget's suggestive comments resulted in an uncomfortable work setting. This discomfort caused Kevin's work to suffer which could have negative consequences on his employment status. Thus, it is arguable that Kevin's work performance suffered due to frequent harassment from Bridget. Bridget, however, argues that she was engaging in harmless flirting. In support of her position, she refers to the fact that in sexual harassment cases against men appeals are often made to the fact that men are by nature less sensitive about sexual dialogue. Bridget had assumed that Kevin would be able to handle her flirtation without being offended. In addition, Kevin's rejection of her attention was delayed; she was operating under the impression that they had an established friendship wherein this sort of banter would be appropriate. While this is a seemingly viable defense, its validity is called into question when compared with the fact that Kevin had repeatedly requested that Bridget omit sexual topics from their conversations. When the positions of the two involved parties are involved, the lines seem less clear. On the one hand, Kevin is clearly distressed about his relationship with Bridget and feels he is being harassed. On the other hand, Bridget is adamant that she was not intending to cause Kevin such discomfort. Instead, she maintains that she had been initiating harmless flirtation and her comments were not intended to be taken seriously. While fairness dictates that both positions be taken into consideration, it makes certainty difficult to attain. Ironically, it is this appeal to fairness that complicates the identification of sexual harassment.

Study Questions

1. If you were on the committee that handled Kevin and Bridget's case, how would you rule? Upon your ruling, what methodology would you initiate to remedy the conflict? If you side with Kevin, what action would you take against Bridget? If, however, you feel Bridget has been

unfairly accused, how would you handle the strife between the two coworkers?

2. If Kevin's accusations are correct and Bridget was behaving inappropriately, it is not certain that she intended to cause Kevin strife. To what extent should she be punished?

3. Sexual harassment is labeled as an infringement on a person's basic rights to freedom. What rights and freedoms are specifically compromised? Which ethical theories are most relevant to the issue of sexual harassment and why?

4. In your judgment, does sexual harassment qualify as a form of discrimination?

5. Do you feel that the current guidelines for sexual harassment are sufficient? If you were chosen to provide a more precise account of sexual harassment, what would it be?

6. Does one's right to free speech have priority over a person's right to be free from harassment? Explain your position.

NOTE

1   *Guidelines on Discrimination on the Basis of Sex* (Washington, DC: Equal Opportunity Commission, November 10, 1980).

CASE STUDY 6

THE ETHICS OF BLUFFING: ORACLE'S TAKEOVER OF PEOPLESOFT
PATRICK LIN

Case Description

On June 6, 2003, Oracle ambushed PeopleSoft with an unsolicited $5.1 billion cash offer to buy the rival technology company. This set the stage for the two Silicon Valley giants—both led by egos that were just as large—to play out a tale about power, drama, and deceit.

First, to introduce the players: Larry Ellison is Oracle's chairman, a swash-buckling personality known for his extravagance, such as financing the boat racing team that won in the America's Cup later in 2003. Equally aggressive, Craig Conway was PeopleSoft's CEO at the time and had once described Oracle, his former employer, as a "sociopathic company."

Just days before Oracle's hostile takeover bid, PeopleSoft had announced its agreement to buy another rival, J.D. Edwards, for $1.7 billion in stock—a deal which would make it the world's second-largest business software company behind SAP. PeopleSoft rejected Oracle's $16-per-share offer as too low a price to be taken seriously and therefore simply a marketing ploy or distraction.

For more than a year, Oracle and PeopleSoft fought in the courtroom and the boardroom. Oracle successfully fended off an antitrust trial that examined whether the proposed takeover would be anti-competitive and harm the industry as well as customers. This was followed by PeopleSoft's surprise vote of no-confidence in Conway by the board of directors, resulting in his firing in October 2004.

During the same period, Oracle had raised, re-raised, and even lowered its acquisition price, eventually tendering its "best and final" offer of $24 per share. PeopleSoft again rejected this offer, calling Oracle on its bluff. After more than twelve offers, Oracle's last bid of $26.50 per share was accepted by PeopleSoft in December 2004, and the merger was completed in 2005.

But Oracle was not the only one apparently bluffing in this bitter battle. Back in June 2003, PeopleSoft implemented a "poison pill" plan that, should the company be taken over, its customers would be entitled to a refund of up to five times the licensing fees they have paid to the company. This tactic would commit the company to costly future obligations, with the intention to dissuade Oracle from its takeover ambitions. PeopleSoft eventually let this policy expire less than a year later.

In another high-profile deal, a different kind of bluff was played out in the AOL-Time Warner merger, announced on January 10, 2000. The financial community was puzzled and shocked at how a scrappy New Economy start-up such as America Online could ever make a bid for Time Warner, a decades-old media empire, in a deal originally worth $165 billion. Many considered AOL's stock to be severely overvalued, but AOL had convinced Time Warner otherwise.

The AOL-Time Warner merger was cleared by regulators in early 2001, but the impending stock market crash, led by overvalued dot-com and technology companies, forced AOL-Time Warner to write off $99 billion in losses in 2002—causing some to observe that AOL had successfully "bluffed" that its 30 million dial-up Internet subscribers were worth Time Warner's much larger, established and iconic global business.

Ethical Analysis

In the Oracle-PeopleSoft case, it is easy to see why bluffing would occur. The two parties were fierce ad-versaries, and there was personal animosity between the two company chiefs. As a result, the usual niceties in negotiation—such as trust and honesty—were replaced by a no-holds-barred fight. If all is fair in love and war, and business is war (at least in this case), then bluffing seems to be rather innocuous, compared to other tactics employed and that were possible.

Likewise, workforce negotiations also offer key opportunities for bluffing, since these relationships can be acrimonious. Some employee unions are quick to threaten a strike (or suggest that a strike is strongly possible) if their demands are not met. On the other side, the company may be bluffing when it refuses to negotiate further, insisting that its last offer was the best it could do or that it would be forced into bankruptcy or layoffs without more employee concessions. If one side has been bluffing, we would expect that a strike can be averted in last-minute negotiations—hiding the bluff by finding some token area of agreement or another face-saving reason.

But as the AOL-Time Warner deal shows, a negotiation need not involve adversaries. If "hype" or exaggeration counts as bluffing, then untold numbers of dot-com companies may have bluffed their way into key relationships and millions of dollars in private funding, ultimately unable to deliver on their sales and revenue forecasts. However, in order for this to count as a bluff, it seems that one must knowingly exaggerate, rather than really believing one's own hype.

It is not just soul-less corporations that bluff; we do it too. Any situation where one can state "This is my final offer" or "Do this, or else" is a potential opportunity to bluff. From negotiating salaries to buying a car, many of us might have bluffed our way into a better deal by suggesting that we might be unable to accept such a low offer (or to afford such a high price), when that amount really is acceptable.

But we should be careful not to completely confuse bluffing with lying, since not all cases of bluffing involve the making of false statements. Bluffing in poker does not, for example; it simply involves misdirection by taking an action that conceals the strength of one's cards, such as betting a lot of money when one has a weak hand. Depending on how AOL made its case to Time Warner, they might not have made a false statement—perhaps only overly-optimistic forecasts. PeopleSoft implemented a poison-pill policy that could be renewed after a given date, but it didn't seem to make any (false) warranty that it would renew it. On the other hand, Oracle's "best and final" offer appears to be a false statement, since they subsequently raised that offer. Or maybe they just simply changed their mind. This highlights the difficulty of identifying even a failed bluff, much less discerning true intentions to determine whether a bluff is in progress.

Study Questions

1. What exactly is bluffing—how should we define it? Where bluffing involves making false statements, where is the line between bluffing and lying, if one exists at all?

2. How else might one bluff in business without making a claim or threat that one has no intention of carrying out? Does creating doubt in the other party's mind, when a decision has already been made in one's own mind, count as a bluff?

3. Since the two are often compared, what are the relevant similarities as well as differences between poker and business? If bluffing (and even lying) might be permitted under the rules of a game, is business a game in which bluffing is permitted or even necessary?

4. We usually think of bluffing in the context of negotiations, but should intentional "hype" or exaggeration be thought of as bluffing too? Why doesn't story-telling count as bluffing?

5. If bluffing is so pervasive and conducted by otherwise ethical people such as ourselves, does that suggest that it is morally permissible?

6. Could we argue that bluffing (at least in the form that involves making false statements) is simply lying under mitigating circumstances—such as if the other party bluffs first, or if we believe the car dealer is making an unfairly-high profit? Or are we simply rationalizing unethical behavior?

7. When we bluff by making a false statement, are our intentions different than if we were merely lying? If so, are these intentions morally relevant? If not, does that help make the case that there is no difference between the two?

UNIT 4

Distributive Justice

FRITZ ALLHOFF

Distributive Justice

Distributive justice, most fundamentally, is about how to distribute the *social product*, by which I mean all of the things that society produces. Most generally, the social product consists in *goods and services*; more specifically, we might talk about material goods, social goods (e.g., health care), financial goods (e.g., money), and services (e.g., the police force). No matter which facet of the social product we are talking about, it is going to be *finite*, which is to say that each member of society cannot have an infinite amount of it and, in many cases, the amount that any individual member could have would be far lower than that which she or he would ideally prefer. Because of the finitude of the social product, society has to make decisions about how to *allocate* its constituent parts, and such allocations might be judged to be of various moral status. In this unit on distributive justice, we will try to get clear on some of the options that are available, as well as some of the moral arguments for each approach.

Since the above discussion might sound abstract, let us consider a more concrete example: salaries and wages. Generally, we take the social product to be an aggregation of all sorts of features (enumerated above), but one of the simplest ways to get clear about what is at stake is to consider just one of those features. Take all of the salaries and wages that everyone in society earns, and then add them up. Now, we can try to figure out what to do with that money. One obvious idea is that we should return the salaries and wages to the people who earn them: if you make $40,000 a year, then we would give you back $40,000. Or, more to the point, there might not be any *distribution* at all since you would just keep what you made.

But there is a problem with such an approach, namely that no public goods (e.g., roads) would ever be funded since all of the money was returned to whomever earned it. This then suggests a refinement on the above practice, namely the institution of *taxes*. Through taxation, some centralized authority will retain some of the earnings of the citizenry, and those tax revenues will be spent on projects to serve that citizenry. This now leads to two important questions: what is the appropriate level of taxation? And who should bear that burden?

In regards to the first question, there is widespread disagreement. One approach would be to favor a *minimal* level of taxation in which few goods and services would be provided by the government; this is often called a *libertarian* approach, and is advocated in this volume by John Locke and Robert Nozick. The libertarian might think that the government should retain money for some things (e.g., roads), but not for others (e.g., the National Endowment of the Arts). The argument against retention of more money by the government is that certain elements of the citizenry might not *endorse* less essential programs, and therefore we might think that such retentions are morally problematic since they would be *forced* to pay for them. (Note this is not to say that libertarians would not support, for example, the arts, just that they would oppose the *government* intervening in ways that such support was compulsory.)

While this might sound like a good argument for libertarianism, things get a little more tricky when we consider some of the programs that would probably *not* be part of the minimal state, such as an extensive welfare system. Here, the problem might be that tax revenues to support welfare would be taken from parts of the citizenry who would not be *benefiting* from the system; one class of society (*viz.* the working class) would be subsidizing another (*viz.* the non-working class), perhaps against the will of the former. But, consider the alternative: that there is no welfare system and that the most vulnerable members of society are not provided for.[1] This, we might think, is morally problematic insofar as society has an obligation to provide for all of its members and, therefore, the government should be allowed to redistribute some of the social produce from the working class to provide for those in need.

The notion of the modern welfare state, for example, is defended by John Rawls, who argues that the well-off should only be able to benefit insofar as the least well-off are also improved. Less abstractly, this would mean that the wealthy could only be entitled to more money so long as they made some provisions to help the non-wealthy; usually this would be effected by some sort of progressive tax rate wherein the increasingly wealthy pay an increasingly high tax rate, perhaps up to some limit. Rawls' position could be made even more extreme such as, for example, we see in Karl Marx (or, more contemporarily, in Kai Nielsen): while Rawls wants to favor a moderate redistribution through the welfare state, Marx envisions a far more extensive redistribution along the lines of his famous "from each according to his ability, to each according to his need."

On a Marxian system, the government might retain *all* of the social product, and then distribute it according to some particular principles. Imagine, for example, that your medical bills are high, $50,000 per year. And further imagine that your income is low, $25,000 per year. Then imagine that my medical bills are non-existent and that my income is high, $75,000 per year. It is possible, on the Rawlsian system, that the redistribution would not be *enough* to help you meet your needs: even if $10,000 of my earnings go into a health care fund from which you might benefit, you might still face a shortfall. One option would be an extreme redistribution: the government takes your $25,000 and my $75,000, pays your $50,000 in medical bills, and then splits the remaining $50,000 amongst us, giving us $25,000 each. Note that, in this scenario, your health needs were provided for in a way that a Rawlsian system might not have supported (and that a libertarian system almost certainly would not). But also note that I only end up with $25,000 of the $75,000 that I earned; two-thirds of my income went to paying for your medical bills and income. Is this a *fair* system? Is it more important to provide for the needs of everyone in society or else to respect the autonomy of its members, even if such respect leads to the failure to meet the needs of the most vulnerable?

These are some of the questions that arise in discussions of distributive justice and which will be addressed by the selections in this section. While most of the discussion above pertains to money in particular (as a simple element of the social product), there are other features on which we might focus; *private property* is one of these. Money, of course, is one instance of private property, though there are others, such as land. Or *ideas*, which gives rise to debates about *intellectual* property in particular. Regarding property in general, we offer selections by Locke (mentioned above), as well as by Gerald A. Cohen, who advocates a Marxian approach to property. We also offer two selections on intellectual property; these are written by Edwin C. Hettinger and Lynn Sharp Paine.

NOTE

1 Note that I wish to consider an idealized welfare state and not one in which we might object to the recipients not really being in need.

CLASSICAL THEORIES OF CONTRACTS, PROPERTY, AND CAPITALISM

THOMAS HOBBES

Excerpts from *Leviathan*

Chapter XIII: Of the Natural Condition of Mankind as Concerning their Felicity and Misery

NATURE hath made men so equal in the faculties of body and mind as that, though there be found one man sometimes manifestly stronger in body or of quicker mind than another, yet when all is reckoned together the difference between man and man is not so considerable as that one man can thereupon claim to himself any benefit to which another may not pretend as well as he. For as to the strength of body, the weakest has strength enough to kill the strongest, either by secret machination or by confederacy with others that are in the same danger with himself.

And as to the faculties of the mind, setting aside the arts grounded upon words, and especially that skill of proceeding upon general and infallible rules, called science, which very few have and but in few things, as being not a native faculty born with us, nor attained, as prudence, while we look after somewhat else, I find yet a greater equality amongst men than that of strength. For prudence is but experience, which equal time equally bestows on all men in those things they equally apply themselves unto. That which may perhaps make such equality incredible is but a vain conceit of one's own wisdom, which almost all men think they have in a greater degree than the vulgar; that is, than all men but themselves, and a few others, whom by fame, or for concurring with themselves, they approve. For such is the nature of men that howsoever they may acknowledge many others to be more witty, or more eloquent or more learned, yet they will hardly believe there be many so wise as themselves; for they see their own wit at hand, and other men's at a distance. But this proveth rather that men are in that point equal, than unequal. For there is not ordinarily a greater sign of the equal distribution of anything than that every man is contented with his share.

From this equality of ability ariseth equality of hope in the attaining of our ends. And therefore if any two men desire the same thing, which nevertheless they cannot both enjoy, they become enemies; and in the way to their end (which is principally their own conservation, and sometimes their delectation only) endeavour to destroy or subdue one another. And from hence it comes to pass that where an invader hath no more to fear than another man's single power, if one plant, sow, build, or possess a convenient seat, others may probably be expected to come prepared with forces united to dispossess and deprive him, not only of the fruit of his labour, but also of his life or liberty. And the invader again is in the like danger of another.

And from this diffidence of one another, there is no way for any man to secure himself so reasonable as anticipation; that is, by force, or wiles, to master the persons of all men he can so long till he see no other power great enough to endanger him: and this is no more than his own conservation requireth, and is generally allowed. Also, because there be some that, taking pleasure in contemplating their own power in the acts of conquest, which they pursue farther than their security requires, if others, that otherwise would be glad to be at ease within modest bounds, should not by invasion increase their power, they would not be able, long time, by standing only on their defence, to subsist. And by consequence, such augmentation of dominion over men being necessary to a man's conservation, it ought to be allowed him.

Again, men have no pleasure (but on the contrary a great deal of grief) in keeping company where there is no power able to overawe them all. For every man looketh that his companion should value him at the same rate he sets upon himself, and upon all signs of contempt or undervaluing naturally endeavours, as far as he dares (which amongst them that have no common power to keep them in quiet is far enough to make them destroy each other), to extort a greater value from his contemners, by damage; and from others, by the example.

So that in the nature of man, we find three principal causes of quarrel. First, competition; secondly, diffidence; thirdly, glory.

The first maketh men invade for gain; the second, for safety; and the third, for reputation. The first use violence, to make themselves masters of other men's persons, wives, children, and cattle; the second, to defend them; the third, for trifles, as a word, a smile, a different opinion, and any other sign of undervalue, either direct in their persons or by reflection in their kindred, their friends, their nation, their profession, or their name.

Hereby it is manifest that during the time men live without a common power to keep them all in awe, they are in that condition which is called war; and such a war as is of every man against every man. For war consisteth not in battle only, or the act of fighting, but in a tract of time, wherein the will to contend by battle is sufficiently known: and therefore the notion of time is to be considered in the nature of war, as it is in the nature of weather. For as the nature of foul weather lieth not in a shower or two of rain, but in an inclination thereto of many days together: so the nature of war consisteth not in actual fighting, but in the known disposition thereto during all the time there is no assurance to the contrary. All other time is peace.

Whatsoever therefore is consequent to a time of war, where every man is enemy to every man, the same consequent to the time wherein men live without other security than what their own strength and their own invention shall furnish them withal. In such condition there is no place for industry, because the fruit thereof is uncertain: and consequently no culture of the earth; no navigation, nor use of the commodities that may be imported by sea; no commodious building; no instruments of moving and removing such things as require much force; no knowledge of the face of the earth; no account of time; no arts; no letters; no society; and which is worst of all, continual fear, and danger of violent death; and the life of man, solitary, poor, nasty, brutish, and short.

It may seem strange to some man that has not well weighed these things that Nature should thus dissociate and render men apt to invade and destroy one another: and he may therefore, not trusting to this inference, made from the passions, desire perhaps to have the same confirmed by experience. Let him therefore consider with himself: when taking a journey, he arms himself and seeks to go well accompanied; when going to sleep, he locks his doors; when even in his house he locks his chests; and this when he knows there be laws and public officers, armed, to revenge all injuries shall be done him; what opinion he has of his fellow subjects, when he rides armed; of his fellow citizens, when he locks his doors; and of his children, and servants, when he locks his chests. Does he not there as much accuse mankind by his actions as I do by my words? But neither of us accuse man's nature in it. The desires, and other passions of man, are in themselves no sin. No more are the actions that proceed from those passions till they know a law that forbids them; which till laws be made they cannot know, nor can any law be made till they have agreed upon the person that shall make it.

It may peradventure be thought there was never such a time nor condition of war as this; and I believe it was never generally so, over all the world: but there are many places where they live so now. For the savage people in many places of America, except the government of small families, the concord whereof dependeth on natural lust, have no government at all, and live at this day in that brutish manner, as I said before. Howsoever, it may be perceived what manner of life there would be, where there were no common power to fear, by the manner of life which men that have formerly lived under a peaceful government use to degenerate into a civil war.

But though there had never been any time wherein particular men were in a condition of war one against another, yet in all times kings and persons of sovereign authority, because of their independency, are in continual jealousies, and in the state and posture of gladiators, having their weapons pointing, and their eyes fixed on one another; that is, their forts, garrisons, and guns upon the frontiers of their kingdoms, and continual spies upon their neighbours, which is a posture of war. But because they uphold thereby the industry of their subjects, there does not follow from it that misery which accompanies the liberty of particular men.

To this war of every man against every man, this also is consequent; that nothing can be unjust. The notions of right and wrong, justice and injustice, have there no place. Where there is no common power, there is no law; where no law, no injustice. Force and fraud are in war the two cardinal virtues. Justice and injustice are none of the faculties neither of the body nor mind. If they were, they might be in a man that were alone in the world, as well as his senses and passions. They are qualities that relate to men in society, not in solitude. It is consequent also to the same condition that there be no propriety, no dominion, no mine and thine distinct; but only that to be every man's that he can get, and for so long as he can keep it. And thus much for the ill condition which man by mere nature is actually placed in; though with a possibility to come out of it, consisting partly in the passions, partly in his reason.

The passions that incline men to peace are: fear of death; desire of such things as are necessary to commodious living; and a hope by their industry to obtain them. And reason suggesteth convenient articles of peace upon which men may be drawn to agreement. These articles are they which otherwise are called the laws of nature, whereof I shall speak more particularly in the two following chapters.

Chapter XIV: Of the First and Second Natural Laws, and of Contracts

THE right of nature, which writers commonly call jus naturale, is the liberty each man hath to use his own power as he will himself for the preservation of his own nature; that is to say, of his own life; and consequently, of doing anything which, in his own judgement and reason, he shall conceive to be the aptest means thereunto.

By liberty is understood, according to the proper signification of the word, the absence of external impediments; which impediments may oft take away part of a man's power to do what he would, but cannot hinder him from using the power left him according as his judgement and reason shall dictate to him.

A law of nature, lex naturalis, is a precept, or general rule, found out by reason, by which a man is forbidden to do that which is destructive of his life, or taketh away the means of preserving the same, and to omit that by which he thinketh it may be best preserved. For though they that speak of this subject use to confound jus and lex, right and law, yet they ought to be distinguished, because right consisteth in liberty to do, or to forbear; whereas law determineth and bindeth to one of them: so that law and right differ as much as obligation and liberty, which in one and the same matter are inconsistent.

And because the condition of man (as hath been declared in the precedent chapter) is a condition of war of every one against every one, in which case every one is governed by his own reason, and there is nothing he can make use of that may not be a help unto him in preserving his life against his enemies; it followeth that in such a condition every man has a right to every thing, even to one another's body. And therefore, as long as this natural right of every man to every thing endureth, there can be no security to any man, how strong or wise soever he be, of living out the time which nature ordinarily alloweth men to live. And consequently it is a precept, or general rule of reason: that every man ought to endeavour peace, as far as he has hope of obtaining it; and when he cannot obtain it, that he may seek and use all helps and advantages of war. The first branch of which rule containeth the first and fundamental law of nature, which is: to seek peace and follow it. The second, the sum of the right of nature, which is: by all means we can to defend ourselves.

From this fundamental law of nature, by which men are commanded to endeavour peace, is derived this second law: that a man be willing, when others are so too, as far forth as for peace and defence of himself he shall think it necessary, to lay down this right to all things; and be contented with so much liberty against other men as he would allow other men against himself. For as long as every man holdeth this right, of doing anything he liketh; so long are all men in the condition of war. But if other men will not lay down their right, as well as he, then there is no reason for anyone to divest himself of his: for that were to expose himself to prey, which no man is bound to, rather than to dispose himself to peace. This is that law of the gospel: Whatsoever you require that others should do to you, that do ye to them. And that law of all men, quod tibi fieri non vis, alteri ne feceris.

To lay down a man's right to anything is to divest himself of the liberty of hindering another of the benefit of his own right to the same. For he that renounceth or passeth away his right giveth not to any other man a right which he had not before, because there is nothing to which every man had not right by nature, but only standeth out of his way that he may enjoy his own original right without hindrance from him, not without hindrance from another. So that the effect which redoundeth to one man by another man's defect of right is but so much diminution of impediments to the use of his own right original.

Right is laid aside, either by simply renouncing it, or by transferring it to another. By simply renouncing, when he cares not to whom the benefit thereof redoundeth. By transferring, when he intendeth the benefit thereof to some certain person or persons. And when a man hath in either manner abandoned or granted away his right, then is he said to be obliged, or bound, not to hinder those to whom such right is granted, or abandoned, from the benefit of it: and that he ought, and it is duty, not to make void that voluntary act of his own: and that such hindrance is injustice, and injury, as being sine jure; the right being before renounced or transferred. So that injury or injustice, in the controversies of the world, is somewhat like to that which in the disputations of scholars is called absurdity. For as it is there called an absurdity to contradict what one maintained in the beginning; so in the world it is called injustice, and injury voluntarily to undo that which from the beginning he had voluntarily done. The way by which a man either simply renounceth or transferreth his right is a declaration, or signification, by some voluntary and sufficient sign, or signs, that he doth so renounce or transfer, or hath so renounced or transferred the same, to him that accepteth it. And these signs are either words only, or actions only; or, as it happeneth most often, both words and actions. And the same are the bonds, by which men are bound and obliged: bonds that have their strength, not from their own nature (for nothing is more easily broken than a man's word), but from fear of some evil consequence upon the rupture.

Whensoever a man transferreth his right, or renounceth it, it is either in consideration of some right reciprocally transferred to himself, or for some other good he hopeth for thereby. For it is a voluntary act: and of the voluntary acts of every man, the object is some good to himself. And therefore there be some rights which no man can be understood by any words, or other signs, to have abandoned or transferred. As first a man cannot lay down the right of resisting them that assault him by force to take away his life, because he cannot be understood to aim thereby at any good to himself. The same may be said of wounds, and chains, and imprisonment, both because there is no benefit consequent to such patience, as there is to the patience of suffering another to be wounded or imprisoned, as also because a man cannot tell when he seeth men proceed against him by violence whether they intend his death or not. And lastly the motive and end for which this renouncing and transferring of right is introduced is nothing else but the security of a man's person, in his life, and in the means of so preserving life as not to be weary of it. And therefore if a man by words, or other signs, seem to despoil himself of the end for which those signs were intended, he is not to be understood as if he meant it, or that it was his will, but that he was ignorant of how such words and actions were to be interpreted.

The mutual transferring of right is that which men call contract.

There is difference between transferring of right to the thing, the thing, and transferring or tradition, that is, delivery of the thing itself. For the thing may be delivered together with the translation of the right, as in buying and selling with ready money, or exchange of goods or lands, and it may be delivered some time after.

Again, one of the contractors may deliver the thing contracted for on his part, and leave the other to perform his part at some determinate time after, and in the meantime be trusted; and then the contract on his part is called pact, or covenant: or both parts may contract now to perform hereafter, in which cases he that is to perform in time to come, being trusted, his performance is called keeping of promise, or faith, and the failing of performance, if it be voluntary, violation of faith.

When the transferring of right is not mutual, but one of the parties transferreth in hope to gain thereby friendship or service from another, or from his friends; or in hope to gain the reputation of charity, or magnanimity; or to deliver his mind from the pain of compassion; or in hope of reward in heaven; this is not contract, but gift, free gift, grace: which words signify one and the same thing.

Signs of contract are either express or by inference. Express are words spoken with understanding of what they signify: and such words are either of the time present or past; as, I give, I grant, I have given, I have granted, I will that this be yours: or of the future; as, I will give, I will grant, which words of the future are called promise.

Signs by inference are sometimes the consequence of words; sometimes the consequence of silence; sometimes the consequence of actions; sometimes the consequence of forbearing an action: and generally a sign by inference, of any contract, is whatsoever sufficiently argues the will of the contractor.

Words alone, if they be of the time to come, and contain a bare promise, are an insufficient sign of a free gift and therefore not obligatory. For if they be of the time to come, as, tomorrow I will give, they are a sign I have not given yet, and consequently that my right is not transferred, but remaineth till I transfer it by some other act. But if the words be of the time present, or past, as, I have given, or do give to be delivered tomorrow, then is my tomorrow's right given away today; and that by the virtue of the words, though there were no other argument of my will. And there is a great difference in the signification of these words, volo hoc tuum esse cras, and cras dabo; that is, between I will that this be thine tomorrow, and, I will give it thee tomorrow: for the word I will, in the former manner of speech, signifies an act of the will present; but in the latter, it signifies a promise of an act of the will to come: and therefore the former words, being of the present, transfer a future right; the latter, that be of the future, transfer nothing. But if there be other signs of the will to transfer a right besides words; then, though the gift be free, yet may the right be understood to pass by words of the future: as if a man propound a prize to him that comes first to the end of a race, the gift is free; and though the words be of the future, yet the right passeth: for if he would not have his words so be understood, he should not have let them run.

In contracts the right passeth, not only where the words are of the time present or past, but also where they are of the future, because all contract is mutual translation, or change of right; and therefore he that promiseth only, because he hath already received the benefit for which he promiseth, is to be understood as if he intended the right should pass: for unless he had been content to have his words so understood, the other would not have performed his part first. And for that cause, in buying, and selling, and other acts of contract, a promise is equivalent to a covenant, and therefore obligatory.

He that performeth first in the case of a contract is said to merit that which he is to receive by the performance of the other, and he hath it as due. Also when a prize is propounded to many, which is to be given to him only that winneth, or money is thrown amongst many to be enjoyed by them that catch it; though this be a free gift, yet so to win, or so to catch, is to merit, and to have it as due. For the right is transferred in the propounding of the prize, and in throwing down the money, though it be not determined to whom, but by the event of the contention. But there is between these two sorts of merit this difference, that in contract I merit by virtue of my own power and the contractor's need, but in this case of free gift I am enabled to merit only by the benignity of the giver: in contract I merit at the contractor's hand that he should depart with his right; in this case of gift, I merit not that the giver should part with his right, but that when he has parted with it, it should be mine rather than another's. And this I think to be the meaning of that distinction of the Schools between meritum congrui and meritum condigni. For God Almighty, having promised para-

dise to those men, hoodwinked with carnal desires, that can walk through this world according to the precepts and limits prescribed by him, they say he that shall so walk shall merit paradise ex congruo. But because no man can demand a right to it by his own righteousness, or any other power in himself, but by the free grace of God only, they say no man can merit paradise ex condigno. This, I say, I think is the meaning of that distinction; but because disputers do not agree upon the signification of their own terms of art longer than it serves their turn, I will not affirm anything of their meaning: only this I say; when a gift is given indefinitely, as a prize to be contended for, he that winneth meriteth, and may claim the prize as due.

If a covenant be made wherein neither of the parties perform presently, but trust one another, in the condition of mere nature (which is a condition of war of every man against every man) upon any reasonable suspicion, it is void: but if there be a common power set over them both, with right and force sufficient to compel performance, it is not void. For he that performeth first has no assurance the other will perform after, because the bonds of words are too weak to bridle men's ambition, avarice, anger, and other passions, without the fear of some coercive power; which in the condition of mere nature, where all men are equal, and judges of the justness of their own fears, cannot possibly be supposed. And therefore he which performeth first does but betray himself to his enemy, contrary to the right he can never abandon of defending his life and means of living.

But in a civil estate, where there a power set up to constrain those that would otherwise violate their faith, that fear is no more reasonable; and for that cause, he which by the covenant is to perform first is obliged so to do.

The cause of fear, which maketh such a covenant invalid, must be always something arising after the covenant made, as some new fact or other sign of the will not to perform, else it cannot make the covenant void. For that which could not hinder a man from promising ought not to be admitted as a hindrance of performing.

He that transferreth any right transferreth the means of enjoying it, as far as lieth in his power. As he that selleth land is understood to transfer the herbage and whatsoever grows upon it; nor can he that sells a mill turn away the stream that drives it. And they that give to a man the right of government in sovereignty are understood to give him the right of levying money to maintain soldiers, and of appointing magistrates for the administration of justice.

To make covenants with brute beasts is impossible, because not understanding our speech, they understand not, nor accept of any translation of right, nor can translate any right to another: and without mutual acceptation, there is no covenant.

To make covenant with God is impossible but by mediation of such as God speaketh to, either by revelation supernatural or by His lieutenants that govern under Him and in His name: for otherwise we know not whether our covenants be accepted or not. And therefore they that vow anything contrary to any law of nature, vow in vain, as being a thing unjust to pay such vow. And if it be a thing commanded by the law of nature, it is not the vow, but the law that binds them.

The matter or subject of a covenant is always something that falleth under deliberation, for to covenant is an act of the will; that is to say, an act, and the last act, of deliberation; and is therefore always understood to be something to come, and which judged possible for him that covenanteth to perform.

And therefore, to promise that which is known to be impossible is no covenant. But if that prove impossible afterwards, which before was thought possible, the covenant is valid and bindeth, though not to the thing itself, yet to the value; or, if that also be impossible, to the unfeigned endeavour of performing as much as is possible, for to more no man can be obliged.

Men are freed of their covenants two ways; by performing, or by being forgiven. For performance is the natural end of obligation, and forgiveness the restitution of liberty, as being a retransferring of that right in which the obligation consisted.

Covenants entered into by fear, in the condition of mere nature, are obligatory. For example, if I covenant to pay a ransom, or service for my life, to an enemy, I am bound by it. For it is a contract, wherein one receiveth the benefit of life; the other is to receive money, or service for it, and consequently, where no other law (as in the condition of mere nature) forbiddeth the performance, the covenant is valid. Therefore prisoners of war, if trusted with the payment of their ransom, are obliged to pay it: and if a weaker prince make a disadvantageous peace with a stronger, for fear, he is bound to keep it; unless (as hath been said before) there ariseth some new and just cause of fear to renew the war. And even in Commonwealths, if I be forced to redeem myself from a thief by promising him money, I am bound to pay it, till the civil law discharge me. For whatsoever I may lawfully do without obligation, the same I may lawfully covenant to do through fear: and what I lawfully covenant, I cannot lawfully break.

A former covenant makes void a later. For a man that hath passed away his right to one man today hath it not to pass tomorrow to another: and therefore the later promise passeth no right, but is null.

A covenant not to defend myself from force, by force, is always void. For (as I have shown before) no man can transfer or lay down his right to save himself from death, wounds, and imprisonment, the avoiding whereof is the only end of laying down any right; and therefore the promise of not resisting force, in no covenant transferreth any right, nor is obliging. For though a man may covenant thus, unless I do so, or so, kill me; he cannot covenant thus, unless I do so, or so, I will not resist you when you come to kill me. For man by nature chooseth the lesser evil, which is danger of death in resisting, rather than the greater, which is certain and present death in not resisting. And this is granted to be true by all men, in that they lead criminals to execution, and prison, with armed men, notwithstanding that such criminals have consented to the law by which they are condemned.

A covenant to accuse oneself, without assurance of pardon, is likewise invalid. For in the condition of nature where every man is judge, there is no place for accusation: and in the civil state the accusation is followed with punishment, which, being force, a man is not obliged not to resist. The same is also true of the accusation of those by whose condemnation a man falls into misery; as of a father, wife, or bene-factor. For the testimony of such an accuser, if it be not willingly given, is presumed to be corrupted by nature, and therefore not to be received: and where a man's testimony is not to be credited, he is not bound to give it. Also accusations upon torture are not to be reputed as testimonies. For torture is to be used but as means of conjecture, and light, in the further examination and search of truth: and what is in that case confessed tendeth to the ease of him that is tortured, not to the informing of the tortur-ers, and therefore ought not to have the credit of a sufficient testimony: for whether he deliver himself by true or false accusation, he does it by the right of preserving his own life.

The force of words being (as I have formerly noted) too weak to hold men to the performance of their covenants, there are in man's nature but two imaginable helps to strengthen it. And those are either a fear of the consequence of breaking their word, or a glory or pride in appearing not to need to break it. This latter is a generosity too rarely found to be presumed on, especially in the pursuers of wealth, command, or sensual pleasure, which are the greatest part of mankind. The passion to be reckoned upon is fear; whereof there be two very general objects: one, the power of spirits invisible; the other, the power of those men they shall therein offend. Of these two, though the former be the greater power, yet the fear of the latter is commonly the greater fear. The fear of the former is in every man his own religion, which hath place in the nature of man before civil society. The latter hath not so; at least not place enough to keep men to their promises, because in the condition of mere nature, the inequality of power is not dis-cerned, but by the event of battle. So that before the time of civil society, or in the interruption thereof by war, there is nothing can strengthen a covenant of peace agreed on against the temptations of avarice, ambition, lust, or other strong desire, but the fear of that invisible power which they every one wor-ship as God, and fear as a revenger of their perfidy. All therefore that can be done between two men not subject to civil power is to put one another to swear by the God he feareth: which swearing, or oath, is a form of speech, added to a promise, by which he that promiseth signifieth that unless he perform he renounceth the mercy of his God, or calleth to him for vengeance on himself. Such was the heathen form, Let Jupiter kill me else, as I kill this beast. So is our form, I shall do thus, and thus, so help me God. And this, with the rites and ceremonies which every one useth in his own religion, that the fear of breaking faith might be the greater.

By this it appears that an oath taken according to any other form, or rite, than his that sweareth is in vain and no oath, and that there is no swear-ing by anything which the swearer thinks not God. For though men have sometimes used to swear by their kings, for fear, or flattery; yet they would have it thereby understood they attributed to them div-ine honour. And that swearing unnecessarily by God is but profaning of his name: and swearing by other things, as men do in common discourse, is not swearing, but an impious custom, gotten by too much vehemence of talking.

It appears also that the oath adds nothing to the obligation. For a covenant, if lawful, binds in the sight of God, without the oath, as much as with it; if unlawful, bindeth not at all, though it be confirmed with an oath.

◆ ◆ ◆ ◆ ◆

JOHN LOCKE

Excerpts from *The Second Treatise of Human Government*

Chapter V: Of Property

Sec. 25. Whether we consider natural reason, which tells us, that men, being once born, have a right to their preservation, and consequently to meat and drink, and such other things as nature affords for their subsistence: or revelation, which gives us an account of those grants God made of the world to Adam, and to Noah, and his sons, it is very clear, that God, as king David says, Psal. cxv. 16. has given the earth to the children of men; given it to mankind in common. But this being supposed, it seems to some a very great difficulty, how any one should ever come to have a property in any thing: I will not content myself to answer, that if it be difficult to make out property, upon a supposition that God gave the world to Adam, and his posterity in common, it is impossible that any man, but one universal monarch, should have any property upon a supposition, that God gave the world to Adam, and his heirs in succession, exclusive of all the rest of his posterity. But I shall endeavour to shew, how men might come to have a property in several parts of that which God gave to mankind in common, and that without any express compact of all the commoners.

Sec. 26. God, who hath given the world to men in common, hath also given them reason to make use of it to the best advantage of life, and convenience. The earth, and all that is therein, is given to men for the support and comfort of their being. And tho' all the fruits it naturally produces, and beasts it feeds, belong to mankind in common, as they are produced by the spontaneous hand of nature; and no body has originally a private dominion, exclusive of the rest of mankind, in any of them, as they are thus in their natural state: yet being given for the use of men, there must of necessity be a means to appropriate them some way or other, before they can be of any use, or at all beneficial to any particular man. The fruit, or venison, which nourishes the wild Indian, who knows no enclosure, and is still a tenant in common, must be his, and so his, i.e., a part of him, that another can no longer have any right to it, before it can do him any good for the support of his life.

Sec. 27. Though the earth, and all inferior creatures, be common to all men, yet every man has a property in his own person: this no body has any right to but himself. The labour of his body, and the work of his hands, we may say, are properly his. Whatsoever then he removes out of the state that nature hath provided, and left it in, he hath mixed his labour with, and joined to it something that is his own, and thereby makes it his property. It being by him removed from the common state nature hath placed it in, it hath by this labour something annexed to it, that excludes the common right of other men: for this labour being the unquestionable property of the labourer, no man but he can have a right to what that is once joined to, at least where there is enough, and as good, left in common for others.

Sec. 28. He that is nourished by the acorns he picked up under an oak, or the apples he gathered from the trees in the wood, has certainly appropriated them to himself. No body can deny but the nourishment is his. I ask then, when did they begin to be his? when he digested? or when he eat? or when he boiled? or when he brought them home? or when he picked them up? and it is plain, if the first gathering made them not his, nothing else could. That labour put a distinction between them and common: that added something to them more than nature, the common mother of all, had done; and so they became his private right. And will any one say, he had no right to those acorns or apples, he thus appropriated, because he had not the consent of all mankind to make them his? Was it a robbery thus to assume to himself what belonged to all in common? If such a consent as that was necessary, man had starved, notwithstanding the plenty God had given him. We see in commons, which remain so by compact, that it is the taking any part of what is common, and removing it out of the state nature leaves it in, which begins the property; without which the common is of no use. And the taking of this or that part, does not depend on the express consent of all the commoners. Thus the grass my horse has bit; the turfs my servant has cut; and the ore I have digged in any place, where I have a right to them in common with others, become my property, without the assignation or consent of any body. The labour that was mine, removing them out of that common state they were in, hath fixed my property in them.

Sec. 29. By making an explicit consent of every commoner, necessary to any one's appropriating to himself any part of what is given in common, children or servants could not cut the meat, which their father or master had provided for them in common, without assigning to every one his peculiar part. Though the water running in the fountain be every one's, yet who can doubt, but that in the pitcher is his only who drew it out? His labour hath taken it out of the hands of nature, where it was common, and belonged equally to all her children, and hath thereby appropriated it to himself.

Sec. 30. Thus this law of reason makes the deer that Indian's who hath killed it; it is allowed to be his goods, who hath bestowed his labour upon it, though before it was the common right of every one. And amongst those who are counted the civilized part of mankind, who have made and multiplied positive laws to determine property, this original law of nature, for the beginning of property, in what was before common, still takes place; and by virtue

thereof, what fish any one catches in the ocean, that great and still remaining common of mankind; or what ambergrise any one takes up here, is by the labour that removes it out of that common state nature left it in, made his property, who takes that pains about it. And even amongst us, the hare that any one is hunting, is thought his who pursues her during the chase: for being a beast that is still looked upon as common, and no man's private possession; whoever has employed so much labour about any of that kind, as to find and pursue her, has thereby removed her from the state of nature, wherein she was common, and hath begun a property.

Sec. 31. It will perhaps be objected to this, that if gathering the acorns, or other fruits of the earth, &c. makes a right to them, then any one may ingross as much as he will. To which I answer, Not so. The same law of nature, that does by this means give us property, does also bound that property too. God has given us all things richly, 1 Tim. vi. 12. is the voice of reason confirmed by inspiration. But how far has he given it us? To enjoy. As much as any one can make use of to any advantage of life before it spoils, so much he may by his Tabour fix a property in: whatever is beyond this, is more than his share, and belongs to others. Nothing was made by God for man to spoil or destroy. And thus, considering the plenty of natural provisions there was a long time in the world, and the few spenders; and to how small a part of that provision the industry of one man could extend itself, and ingross it to the prejudice of others; especially keeping within the bounds, set by reason, of what might serve for his use; there could be then little room for quarrels or contentions about property so established.

Sec. 32. But the chief matter of property being now not the fruits of the earth, and the beasts that subsist on it, but the earth itself; as that which takes in and carries with it all the rest; I think it is plain, that property in that too is acquired as the former.

As much land as a man tills, plants, improves, cultivates, and can use the product of, so much is his property. He by his labour does, as it were, inclose it from the common. Nor will it invalidate his right, to say every body else has an equal title to it; and therefore he cannot appropriate, he cannot inclose, without the consent of all his fellow-commoners, all mankind. God, when he gave the world in common to all mankind, commanded man also to labour, and the penury of his condition required it of him. God and his reason commanded him to subdue the earth, i.e., improve it for the benefit of life, and therein lay out something upon it that was his own, his labour. He that in obedience to this command of God, subdued, tilled and sowed any part of it, thereby annexed to it something that was his property, which another had no title to, nor could without injury take from him.

Sec. 33. Nor was this appropriation of any parcel of land, by improving it, any prejudice to any other man, since there was still enough, and as good left; and more than the yet unprovided could use. So that, in effect, there was never the less left for others because of his enclosure for himself: for he that leaves as much as another can make use of, does as good as take nothing at all. No body could think himself injured by the drinking of another man, though he took a good draught, who had a whole river of the same water left him to quench his thirst: and the case of land and water, where there is enough of both, is perfectly the same.

Sec. 34. God gave the world to men in common; but since he gave it them for their benefit, and the greatest conveniencies of life they were capable to draw from it, it cannot be supposed he meant it should always remain common and uncultivated. He gave it to the use of the industrious and rational, (and labour was to be his title to it) not to the fancy or covetousness of the quarrelsome and contentious. He that had as good left for his improvement, as

was already taken up, needed not complain, ought not to meddle with what was already improved by another's labour: if he did, it is plain he desired the benefit of another's pains, which he had no right to, and not the ground which God had given him in common with others to labour on, and whereof there was as good left, as that already possessed, and more than he knew what to do with, or his industry could reach to.

Sec. 35. It is true, in land that is common in England, or any other country, where there is plenty of people under government, who have money and commerce, no one can inclose or appropriate any part, without the consent of all his fellowcommoners; because this is left common by compact, i.e., by the law of the land, which is not to be violated. And though it be common, in respect of some men, it is not so to all mankind; but is the joint property of this country, or this parish. Besides, the remainder, after such enclosure, would not be as good to the rest of the commoners, as the whole was when they could all make use of the whole; whereas in the beginning and first peopling of the great common of the world, it was quite otherwise. The law man was under, was rather for appropriating. God commanded, and his wants forced him to labour. That was his property which could not be taken from him where-ever he had fixed it. And hence subduing or cultivating the earth, and having dominion, we see are joined together. The one gave title to the other. So that God, by commanding to subdue, gave authority so far to appropriate: and the condition of human life, which requires labour and materials to work on, necessarily introduces private possessions.

Sec. 36. The measure of property nature has well set by the extent of men's labour and the conveniencies of life: no man's labour could subdue, or appropriate all; nor could his enjoyment consume more than a small part; so that it was impossible for any man, this way, to intrench upon the right of another, or acquire to himself a property, to the prejudice of his neighbour, who would still have room for as good, and as large a possession (after the other had taken out his) as before it was appropriated. This measure did confine every man's possession to a very moderate proportion, and such as he might appropriate to himself, without injury to any body, in the first ages of the world, when men were more in danger to be lost, by wandering from their company, in the then vast wilderness of the earth, than to be straitened for want of room to plant in. And the same measure may be allowed still without prejudice to any body, as full as the world seems: for supposing a man, or family, in the state they were at first peopling of the world by the children of Adam, or Noah; let him plant in some inland, vacant places of America, we shall find that the possessions he could make himself, upon the measures we have given, would not be very large, nor, even to this day, prejudice the rest of mankind, or give them reason to complain, or think themselves injured by this man's incroachment, though the race of men have now spread themselves to all the corners of the world, and do infinitely exceed the small number was at the beginning. Nay, the extent of ground is of so little value, without labour, that I have heard it affirmed, that in Spain itself a man may be permitted to plough, sow and reap, without being disturbed, upon land he has no other title to, but only his making use of it. But, on the contrary, the inhabitants think themselves beholden to him, who, by his industry on neglected, and consequently waste land, has increased the stock of corn, which they wanted. But be this as it will, which I lay no stress on; this I dare boldly affirm, that the same rule of propriety, (viz.) that every man should have as much as he could make use of, would hold still in the world, without straitening any body; since there is land enough in the world to suffice double the inhabitants, had not the invention of money, and the tacit agreement of men to put a value on it, introduced (by consent) larger possessions, and a right to them; which, how it has done, I shall by and by shew more at large.

Sec. 37. This is certain, that in the beginning, before the desire of having more than man needed had altered the intrinsic value of things, which depends only on their usefulness to the life of man; or had agreed, that a little piece of yellow metal, which would keep without wasting or decay, should be worth a great piece of flesh, or a whole heap of corn; though men had a right to appropriate, by their labour, each one of himself, as much of the things of nature, as he could use: yet this could not be much, nor to the prejudice of others, where the same plenty was still left to those who would use the same industry. To which let me add, that he who appropriates land to himself by his labour, does not lessen, but increase the common stock of mankind: for the provisions serving to the support of human life, produced by one acre of inclosed and cultivated land, are (to speak much within compass) ten times more than those which are yielded by an acre of land of an equal richness lying waste in common. And therefore he that incloses land, and has a greater plenty of the conveniencies of life from ten acres, than he could have from an hundred left to nature, may truly be said to give ninety acres to mankind: for his labour now supplies him with provisions out of ten acres, which were but the product of an hundred lying in common. I have here rated the improved land very low, in making its product but as ten to one, when it is much nearer an hundred to one: for I ask, whether in the wild woods and uncultivated waste of America, left to nature, without any improvement, tillage or husbandry, a thousand acres yield the needy and wretched inhabitants as many conveniencies of life, as ten acres of equally fertile land do in Devonshire, where they are well cultivated?

Before the appropriation of land, he who gathered as much of the wild fruit, killed, caught, or tamed, as many of the beasts, as he could; he that so imployed his pains about any of the spontaneous products of nature, as any way to alter them from the state which nature put them in, by placing any of his labour on them, did thereby acquire a propriety in them: but if they perished, in his possession, without their due use; if the fruits rotted, or the venison putrified, before he could spend it, he offended against the common law of nature, and was liable to be punished; he invaded his neighbour's share, for he had no right, farther than his use called for any of them, and they might serve to afford him conveniencies of life.

Sec. 38. The same measures governed the possession of land too: whatsoever he tilled and reaped, laid up and made use of, before it spoiled, that was his peculiar right; whatsoever he enclosed, and could feed, and make use of, the cattle and product was also his. But if either the grass of his enclosure rotted on the ground, or the fruit of his planting perished without gathering, and laying up, this part of the earth, notwithstanding his enclosure, was still to be looked on as waste, and might be the possession of any other. Thus, at the beginning, Cain might take as much ground as he could till, and make it his own land, and yet leave enough to Abel's sheep to feed on; a few acres would serve for both their possessions. But as families increased, and industry inlarged their stocks, their possessions inlarged with the need of them; but yet it was commonly without any fixed property in the ground they made use of, till they incorporated, settled themselves together, and built cities; and then, by consent, they came in time, to set out the bounds of their distinct territories, and agree on limits between them and their neighbours; and by laws within themselves, settled the properties of those of the same society: for we see, that in that part of the world which was first inhabited, and therefore like to be best peopled, even as low down as Abraham's time, they wandered with their flocks, and their herds, which was their substance, freely up and down; and this Abraham did, in a country where he was a stranger. Whence it is plain, that at least a great part of the land lay in common; that the inhabitants valued it not, nor claimed property in any more than they made use of. But when there was not room enough in the same place, for their herds to feed together, they by consent, as Abraham and Lot did, Gen. xiii. 5. separated and inlarged their pasture, where it best liked them. And for the same reason Esau went from his father, and his brother, and planted in mount Seir, Gen. xxxvi. 6.

Sec. 39. And thus, without supposing any private dominion, and property in Adam, over all the world, exclusive of all other men, which can no way be proved, nor any one's property be made out from it; but supposing the world given, as it was, to the children of men in common, we see how labour could make men distinct titles to several parcels of it, for their private uses; wherein there could be no doubt of right, no room for quarrel.

Sec. 40. Nor is it so strange, as perhaps before consideration it may appear, that the property of labour should be able to over-balance the community of land: for it is labour indeed that puts the difference of value on every thing; and let any one consider what the difference is between an acre of land planted with tobacco or sugar, sown with wheat or barley, and an acre of the same land lying in common, without any husbandry upon it, and he will find, that the improvement of labour makes the far greater part of the value. I think it will be but a very modest computation to say, that of the products of the earth useful to the life of man nine tenths are the effects of labour: nay, if we will rightly estimate things as they come to our use, and cast up the several expences about them, what in them is purely owing to nature, and what to labour, we shall find, that in most of them ninety-nine hundredths are wholly to be put on the account of labour.

Sec. 41. There cannot be a clearer demonstration of any thing, than several nations of the Americans are of this, who are rich in land, and poor in all the comforts of life; whom nature having furnished as liberally as any other people, with the materials of plenty, i.e., a fruitful soil, apt to produce in abundance, what might serve for food, raiment, and delight; yet for want of improving it by labour, have not one hundredth part of the conveniencies we enjoy: and a king of a large and fruitful territory there, feeds, lodges, and is clad worse than a day-labourer in England.

Sec. 42. To make this a little clearer, let us but trace some of the ordinary provisions of life, through their several progresses, before they come to our use, and see how much they receive of their value from human industry. Bread, wine and cloth, are things of daily use, and great plenty; yet notwithstanding, acorns, water and leaves, or skins, must be our bread, drink and cloathing, did not labour furnish us with these more useful commodities: for whatever bread is more worth than acorns, wine than water, and cloth or silk, than leaves, skins or moss, that is wholly owing to labour and industry; the one of these being the food and raiment which unassisted nature furnishes us with; the other, provisions which our industry and pains prepare for us, which how much they exceed the other in value, when any one hath computed, he will then see how much labour makes the far greatest part of the value of things we enjoy in this world: and the ground which produces the materials, is scarce to be reckoned in, as any, or at most, but a very small part of it; so little, that even amongst us, land that is left wholly to nature, that hath no improvement of pasturage, tillage, or planting, is called, as indeed it is, waste; and we shall find the benefit of it amount to little more than nothing.

This shews how much numbers of men are to be preferred to largeness of dominions; and that the increase of lands, and the right employing of them, is the great art of government: and that prince, who shall be so wise and godlike, as by established laws of liberty to secure protection and encouragement to the honest industry of mankind, against the oppression of power and narrowness of party, will quickly be too hard for his neighbours: but this by the by. To return to the argument in hand,

Sec. 43. An acre of land, that bears here twenty bushels of wheat, and another in America, which, with the same husbandry, would do the like, are, without doubt, of the same natural intrinsic value: but yet the benefit mankind receives from the one in a year, is worth 5l. and from the other possibly not worth a penny, if all the profit an Indian received from it were to be valued, and sold here; at least, I may truly say, not one thousandth. It is labour then which puts the greatest part of value upon land, without which it would scarcely be worth any thing: it is to that we owe the greatest part of all its useful products; for all that the straw, bran, bread, of that acre of wheat, is more worth than the product of an acre of as good land, which lies waste, is all the effect of labour: for it is not barely the plough-man's pains, the reaper's and thresher's toil, and the baker's sweat, is to be counted into the bread we eat; the labour of those who broke the oxen, who digged and wrought the iron and stones, who felled and framed the timber employed about the plough, mill, oven, or any other utensils, which are a vast number, requisite to this corn, from its being feed to be sown to its being made bread, must all be charged on the account of labour, and received as an effect of that: nature and the earth furnished only the almost worthless materials, as in themselves. It would be a strange catalogue of things, that industry provided and made use of, about every loaf of bread, before it came to our use, if we could trace them; iron, wood, leather, bark, timber, stone, bricks, coals, lime, cloth, dying drugs, pitch, tar, masts, ropes, and all the materials made use of in the ship, that brought any of the commodities made use of by any of the workmen, to any part of the work; all which it would be almost impossible, at least too long, to reckon up.

Sec. 44. From all which it is evident, that though the things of nature are given in common, yet man, by being master of himself, and proprietor of his own person, and the actions or labour of it, had still in himself the great foundation of property; and that, which made up the great part of what he applied to the support or comfort of his being, when invention and arts had improved the conveniencies of life, was perfectly his own, and did not belong in common to others.

Sec. 45. Thus labour, in the beginning, gave a right of property, wherever any one was pleased to employ it upon what was common, which remained a long while the far greater part, and is yet more than mankind makes use of. Men, at first, for the most part, contented themselves with what unassisted nature offered to their necessities: and though afterwards, in some parts of the world, (where the increase of people and stock, with the use of money, had made land scarce, and so of some value) the several communities settled the bounds of their distinct territories, and by laws within themselves regulated the properties of the private men of their society, and so, by compact and agreement, settled the property which labour and industry began; and the leagues that have been made between several states and kingdoms, either expresly or tacitly disowning all claim and right to the land in the others possession, have, by common consent, given up their pretences to their natural common right, which originally they had to those countries, and so have, by positive agreement, settled a property amongst themselves, in distinct parts and parcels of the earth; yet there are still great tracts of ground to be found, which (the inhabitants thereof not having joined with the rest of mankind, in the consent of the use of their common money) lie waste, and are more than the people who dwell on it do, or can make use of, and so still lie in common; tho' this can scarce happen amongst that part of mankind that have consented to the use of money.

Sec. 46. The greatest part of things really useful to the life of man, and such as the necessity of subsist-

ing made the first commoners of the world look after, as it doth the Americans now, are generally things of short duration; such as, if they are not consumed by use, will decay and perish of themselves: gold, silver and diamonds, are things that fancy or agreement hath put the value on, more than real use, and the necessary support of life. Now of those good things which nature hath provided in common, every one had a right (as hath been said) to as much as he could use, and property in all that he could effect with his labour; all that his industry could extend to, to alter from the state nature had put it in, was his. He that gathered a hundred bushels of acorns or apples, had thereby a property in them, they were his goods as soon as gathered. He was only to look, that he used them before they spoiled, else he took more than his share, and robbed others. And indeed it was a foolish thing, as well as dishonest, to hoard up more than he could make use of. If he gave away a part to any body else, so that it perished not uselesly in his possession, these he also made use of. And if he also bartered away plums, that would have rotted in a week, for nuts that would last good for his eating a whole year, he did no injury; he wasted not the common stock; destroyed no part of the portion of goods that belonged to others, so long as nothing perished uselesly in his hands. Again, if he would give his nuts for a piece of metal, pleased with its colour; or exchange his sheep for shells, or wool for a sparkling pebble or a diamond, and keep those by him all his life he invaded not the right of others, he might heap up as much of these durable things as he pleased; the exceeding of the bounds of his just property not lying in the largeness of his possession, but the perishing of any thing uselesly in it.

Sec. 47. And thus came in the use of money, some lasting thing that men might keep without spoiling, and that by mutual consent men would take in exchange for the truly useful, but perishable supports of life.

Sec. 48. And as different degrees of industry were apt to give men possessions in different proportions, so this invention of money gave them the opportunity to continue and enlarge them: for supposing an island, separate from all possible commerce with the rest of the world, wherein there were but an hundred families, but there were sheep, horses and cows, with other useful animals, wholsome fruits, and land enough for corn for a hundred thousand times as many, but nothing in the island, either because of its commonness, or perishableness, fit to supply the place of money; what reason could any one have there to enlarge his possessions beyond the use of his family, and a plentiful supply to its consumption, either in what their own industry produced, or they could barter for like perishable, useful commodities, with others? Where there is not some thing, both lasting and scarce, and so valuable to be hoarded up, there men will not be apt to enlarge their possessions of land, were it never so rich, never so free for them to take: for I ask, what would a man value ten thousand, or an hundred thousand acres of excellent land, ready cultivated, and well stocked too with cattle, in the middle of the inland parts of America, where he had no hopes of commerce with other parts of the world, to draw money to him by the sale of the product? It would not be worth the enclosing, and we should see him give up again to the wild common of nature, whatever was more than would supply the conveniencies of life to be had there for him and his family.

Sec. 49. Thus in the beginning all the world was America, and more so than that is now; for no such thing as money was any where known. Find out something that hath the use and value of money amongst his neighbours, you shall see the same man will begin presently to enlarge his possessions.

Sec. 50. But since gold and silver, being little useful to the life of man in proportion to food, raiment, and carriage, has its value only from the consent of men, whereof labour yet makes, in great part, the measure, it is plain, that men have agreed to a disproportionate and unequal possession of the earth, they having, by a tacit and voluntary consent, found out, a way how a man may fairly possess more land than he himself can use the product of, by receiving in exchange for the overplus gold and silver, which may be hoarded up without injury to any one; these metals not spoiling or decaying in the hands of the possessor. This partage of things in an inequality of private possessions, men have made practicable out of the bounds of society, and without compact, only by putting a value on gold and silver, and tacitly agreeing in the use of money: for in governments, the laws regulate the right of property, and the possession of land is determined by positive constitutions.

Sec. 51. And thus, I think, it is very easy to conceive, without any difficulty, how labour could at first begin a title of property in the common things of nature, and how the spending it upon our uses bounded it. So that there could then be no reason of quarrelling about title, nor any doubt about the largeness of possession it gave. Right and conveniency went together; for as a man had a right to all he could employ his labour upon, so he had no temptation to labour for more than he could make use of. This left no room for controversy about the title, nor for encroachment on the right of others; what portion a man carved to himself, was easily seen; and it was useless, as well as dishonest, to carve himself too much, or take more than he needed.

◆ ◆ ◆ ◆ ◆

ADAM SMITH

Excerpts from *An Inquiry into the Nature and Causes of the Wealth of Nations*

Book I, Chapter I: Of the Division of Labour

The greatest improvement in the productive powers of labour, and the greater part of the skill, dexterity, and judgment with which it is any where directed, or applied, seem to have been the effects of the division of labour.

The effects of the division of labour, in the general business of society, will be more easily understood, by considering in what manner it operates in some particular manufactures. It is commonly supposed to be carried furthest in some very trifling ones; not perhaps that it really is carried further in them than in others of more importance: but in those trifling manufactures which are destined to supply the small wants of but a small number of people, the whole number of workmen must necessarily be small; and those employed in every different branch of the work can often be collected into the same workhouse, and placed at once under the view of the spectator. In those great manufactures, on the contrary, which are destined to supply the great wants of the great body of the people, every different branch of the work employs so great a number of workmen, that it is impossible to collect them all into the same workhouse. We can seldom see more, at one time, than those employed in one single branch. Though in such manufactures, therefore, the work may really be divided into a much greater number of parts, than in those of a more trifling nature, the division is not near so obvious, and has accordingly been much less observed.

To take an example, therefore, from a very trifling manufacture; but one in which the division of labour has been very often taken notice of, the trade of the pin-maker; a workman not educated to this business (which the division of labour has rendered a distinct trade), nor acquainted with the use of the machinery employed in it (to the invention of which the same division of labour has probably given occasion), could scarce, perhaps, with his utmost industry, make one pin in a day, and certainly could not make twenty. But in the way in which this business is now carried on, not only the whole work is a peculiar trade, but it is divided into a number of branches, of which the greater part are likewise peculiar trades. One man draws out the wire, another straights it, a third cuts it, a fourth points it, a fifth grinds it at the top for receiving the head; to make the head requires two or three distinct operations; to put it on, is a peculiar business, to whiten the pins is another; it is even a trade by itself to put them into the paper; and the important business of making a pin is, in this manner, divided into about eighteen distinct operations, which, in some manufactories, are all performed by distinct hands, though in others the same man will sometimes perform two or three of them. I have seen a small manufactory of this kind where ten men only were employed, and where some of them consequently performed two or three distinct operations. But though they were very poor, and therefore but indifferently accommodated with the necessary machinery, they could, when they exerted themselves, make among them about twelve pounds of pins in a day. There are in a pound upwards of four thousand pins of a middling size. Those ten persons, therefore, could make among them upwards of forty-eight thousand pins in a day. Each person, therefore, making a tenth part of forty-eight thousand pins, might be considered as making four thousand eight hundred pins in a day. But if they had all wrought separately and independently, and without any of them having been educated to this peculiar business, they certainly could not each of them have made twenty, perhaps not one pin in a day; that is, certainly, not the two hundred and fortieth, perhaps not the four thousand eight hundredth part of what they are at present capable of performing, in consequence of a proper division and combination of their different operations.

In every other art and manufacture, the effects of the division of labour are similar to what they are in this very trifling one; though, in many of them, the labour can neither be so much subdivided, nor reduced to so great a simplicity of operation. The division of labour, however, so far as it can be introduced, occasions, in every art, a proportionable increase of the productive powers of labour. The separation of different trades and employments from one another, seems to have taken place, in consequence of this advantage. This separation too is generally carried furthest in those countries which enjoy the highest degree of industry and improvement; what is the work of one man in a rude state of society, being generally that of several in an improved one. In every improved society, the farmer is generally nothing but a farmer; the manufacturer, nothing but a manufacturer. The labour too which is necessary to produce any one complete manufacture, is almost always divided among a great number of hands. How many different trades are employed in each branch of the linen and woollen manufactures, from the growers of the flax and the wool, to the bleachers and smoothers of the linen, or to the dyers and dressers of the cloth! The nature of agriculture, indeed, does not admit of so many subdivisions of labour, nor of so complete a separation of one business from another, as manufactures. It is impossible to separate so entirely, the business of the grazier from that of the corn-farmer, as the trade of the carpenter is commonly separated from that of the smith. The spinner is almost always a distinct person from the weaver; but the ploughman, the harrower, the sower of the seed, and the reaper of the corn, are often the same. The occasions for those different sorts of labour returning with the different seasons of the year, it is impossible that one man should be constantly employed in any one of them.

This impossibility of making so complete and entire a separation of all the different branches of labour employed in agriculture, is perhaps the reason why the improvement of the productive powers of labour in this art, does not always keep pace with their improvement in manufactures. The most opulent nations, indeed, generally excel all their neighbours in agriculture as well as in manufactures; but they are commonly more distinguished by their superiority in the latter than in the former. Their lands are in general better cultivated, and having more labour and expence bestowed upon them, produce more in proportion to the extent and natural fertility of the ground. But this superiority of produce is seldom much more than in proportion to the superiority of labour and expence. In agriculture, the labour of the rich country is not always much more productive than that of the poor; or, at least, it is never so much more productive, as it commonly is in manufactures. The corn of the rich country, therefore, will not always, in the same degree of goodness, come cheaper to market than that of the poor. The corn of Poland, in the same degree of goodness, is as cheap as that of France, notwithstanding the superior opulence and improvement of the latter country. The corn of France is, in the corn provinces, fully as good, and in most years nearly about the same price with the corn of England, though, in opulence and improvement, France is perhaps inferior to England. The corn-lands of England, however, are better cultivated than those of France, and the corn-lands of France are said to be much better cultivated than those of Poland. But though the poor country, notwithstanding the inferiority of its cultivation, can, in some measure, rival the rich in the cheapness and goodness of its corn, it can pretend to no such competition in its manufactures; at least if those manufactures suit the soil, climate, and situation of the rich country. The silks of France are better and cheaper than those of England, because the silk manufacture, at least under the present high duties upon the importation of raw silk, does not so well suit the climate of England as that of France. But the hard-ware and the coarse wool-lens of England are beyond all comparison superi-or to those of France, and much cheaper too in the same degree of goodness. In Poland there are said to be scarce any manufactures of any kind, a few of those coarser household manufactures excepted, without which no country can well subsist.

This great increase of the quantity of work which, in consequence of the division of labour, the same number of people are capable of performing, is owing to three different circumstances; first to the increase of dexterity in every particular workman; secondly, to the saving of the time which is com-monly lost in passing from one species of work to another; and lastly, to the invention of a great num-ber of machines which facilitate and abridge labour, and enable one man to do the work of many.

First, the improvement of the dexterity of the workman necessarily increases the quantity of the work he can perform; and the division of labour, by reducing every man's business to some one simple operation, and by making this operation the sole em-ployment of his life, necessarily increases very much the dexterity of the workman. A common smith, who, though accustomed to handle the hammer, has never been used to make nails, if upon some particu-lar occasion he is obliged to attempt it, will scarce, I am assured, be able to make above two or three hun-dred nails in a day, and those too very bad ones. A smith who has been accustomed to make nails, but whose sole or principal business has not been that of a nailer, can seldom with his utmost diligence make more than eight hundred or a thousand nails in a day. I have seen several boys under twenty years of age who had never exercised any other trade but that of making nails, and who, when they exerted them-selves, could make, each of them, upwards of two thousand three hundred nails in a day. The making of a nail, however, is by no means one of the sim-plest operations. The same person blows the bellows, stirs or mends the fire as there is occasion, heats the iron, and forges every part of the nail: In forging the

head too he is obliged to change his tools. The dif-ferent operations into which the making of a pin, or of a metal button, is subdivided, are all of them much more simple, and the dexterity of the person, of whose life it has been the sole business to perform them, is usually much greater. The rapidity with which some of the operations of those manufactures are performed, exceeds what the human hand could, by those who had never seen them, be supposed ca-pable of acquiring.

Secondly, the advantage which is gained by saving the time commonly lost in passing from one sort of work to another, is much greater than we should at first view be apt to imagine it. It is impossible to pass very quickly from one kind of work to another; that is carried on in a different place, and with quite dif-ferent tools. A country weaver, who cultivates a small farm, must lose a good deal of time in passing from his loom to the field, and from the field to his loom. When the two trades can be carried on in the same workhouse, the loss of time is no doubt much less. It is even in this case, however, very considerable. A man commonly saunters a little in turning his hand from one sort of employment to another. When he first begins the new work he is seldom very keen and hearty; his mind, as they say, does not go to it, and for some time he rather trifles than applies to good pur-pose. The habit of sauntering and of indolent careless application, which is naturally, or rather necessarily acquired by every country workman who is obliged to change his work and his tools every half hour, and to apply his hand in twenty different ways almost every day of his life; renders him almost always slothful and lazy, and incapable of any vigorous application even on the most pressing occasions. Independent, there-fore, of his deficiency in point of dexterity, this cause alone must always reduce considerably the quantity of work which he is capable of performing.

Thirdly, and lastly, every body must be sensible how much labour is facilitated and abridged by the application of proper machinery. It is unnecessary to give any example. I shall only observe, therefore, that the invention of all those machines by which labour is so much facilitated and abridged, seems to have been originally owing to the division of labour. Men are much more likely to discover easier and readier methods of attaining any object, when the whole attention of their minds is directed towards that single object, than when it is dissipated among a great variety of things. But in consequence of the division of labour, the whole of every man's attention comes naturally to be directed towards some one very simple object. It is naturally to be expected, therefore, that some one or other of those who are employed in each particular branch of labour should soon find out easier and readier methods of performing their own particular work, wherever the nature of it admits of such improvement. A great part of the machines made use of in those manufactures in which labour is most subdivided, were originally the inventions of common workmen, who, being each of them employed in some very simple operation, naturally turned their thoughts towards finding out easier and readier methods of performing it. Whoever has been much accustomed to visit such manufactures, must frequently have been shewn very pretty machines, which were the inventions of such workmen, in order to facilitate and quicken their own particular part of the work. In the first fire-engines, a boy was constantly employed to open and shut alternately the communication between the boiler and the cylinder, according as the piston either ascended or descended. One of those boys, who loved to play with his companions, observed that, by tying a string from the handle of the valve which opened this communication, to another part of the machine, the valve would open and shut without his assistance, and leave him at liberty to divert himself with his play-fellows. One of the greatest improvements that has been made upon this machine, since it was first invented, was in this manner the discovery of a boy who wanted to save his own labour.

All the improvements in machinery, however, have by no means been the inventions of those who had occasion to use the machines. Many improvements have been made by the ingenuity of the makers of the machines, when to make them became the business of a peculiar trade; and some by that of those who are called philosophers or men of speculation, whose trade it is not to do any thing, but to observe every thing; and who, upon that account, are often capable of combining together the powers of the most distant and dissimilar objects. In the progress of society, philosophy or speculation becomes, like every other employment, the principal or sole trade and occupation of a particular class of citizens. Like every other employment too, it is subdivided into a great number of different branches, each of which affords occupation to a peculiar tribe or class of philosophers; and this subdivision of employment in philosophy, as well as in every other business, improves dexterity, and saves time. Each individual becomes more expert in his own peculiar branch, more work is done upon the whole, and the quantity of science is considerably increased by it.

It is the great multiplication of the productions of all the different arts, in consequence of the division of labour, which occasions, in a well-governed society, that universal opulence which extends itself to the lowest ranks of the people. Every workman has a great quantity of his own work to dispose of beyond what he himself has occasion for; and every other workman being exactly in the same situation, he is enabled to exchange a great quantity of his own goods for a great quantity, or, what comes to the same thing, for the price of a great quantity of theirs. He supplies them abundantly with what they have occasion for, and they accommodate him as amply with what he has occasion for, and a general plenty diffuses itself through all the different ranks of the society.

Observe the accommodation of the most common artificer or day-labourer in a civilized and thriving country, and you will perceive that the number of people of whose industry a part, though but a small part, has been employed in procuring him this accommodation, exceeds all computation. The woollen coat, for example, which covers the day-labourer, as coarse and rough as it may appear, is the produce of the joint labour of a great multitude of workmen. The shepherd, the sorter of the wool, the wool-comber or carder, the dyer, the scribbler, the spinner, the weaver, the fuller, the dresser, with many others, must all join their different arts in order to complete even this homely production. How many merchants and carriers, besides, must have been employed in transporting the materials from some of those workmen to others who often live in a very distant part of the country! how much commerce and navigation in particular, how many ship-builders, sailors, sail-makers, rope-makers, must have been employed in order to bring together the different drugs made use of by the dyer, which often come from the remotest corners of the world! What a variety of labour too is necessary in order to produce the tools of the meanest of those workmen! To say nothing of such complicated machines as the ship of the sailor, the mill of the fuller, or even the loom of the weaver, let us consider only what a variety of labour is requisite in order to form that very simple machine, the shears with which the shepherd clips the wool. The miner, the builder of the furnace for smelting the ore, the feller of the timber, the burner of the charcoal to be made use of in the smelting-house, the brick-maker, the brick-layer, the workmen who attend the furnace, the mill-wright, the forger, the smith, must all of them join their different arts in order to produce them. Were we to examine, in the same manner, all the different parts of his dress and household furniture, the coarse linen shirt which he wears next his skin, the shoes which cover his feet, the bed which he lies on, and all the different parts which compose it, the kitchen-grate at which he prepares his victuals, the coals which he makes use of for that purpose, dug from the bowels of the earth, and brought to him perhaps by a long sea and a long land carriage, all the other utensils of his kitchen, all the furniture of his table, the knives and forks, the earthen or pewter plates upon which he serves up and divides his victuals, the different hands employed in preparing his bread and his beer, the glass window which lets in the heat and the light, and keeps out the wind and the rain, with all the knowledge and art requisite for preparing that beautiful and happy invention, without which these northern parts of the world could scarce have afforded a very comfortable habitation, together with the tools of all the different workmen employed in producing those different conveniencies; if we examine, I say, all these things, and consider what a variety of labour is employed about each of them, we shall be sensible that without the assistance and co-operation of many thousands, the very meanest person in a civilized country could not be provided, even according to what we very falsely imagine, the easy and simple manner in which he is commonly accommodated. Compared, indeed, with the more extravagant luxury of the great, his accommodation must no doubt appear extremely simple and easy; and yet it may be true, perhaps, that the accommodation of an European prince does not always so much exceed that of an industrious and frugal peasant, as the accommodation of the latter exceeds that of many an African king, the absolute master of the lives and liberties of ten thousand naked savages.

Book I, Chapter II: Of the Principle which Gives Occasion to the Division of Labour

This division of labour, from which so many advantages are derived, is not originally the effect of any human wisdom, which foresees and intends that general opulence to which it gives occasion. It is the necessary, though very slow and gradual, consequence of a certain propensity in human nature which has in view no such extensive utility; the propensity to truck, barter, and exchange one thing for another.

Whether this propensity be one of those original principles in human nature, of which no further account can be given; or whether, as seems more probable, it be the necessary consequence of the faculties of reason and speech, it belongs not to our present subject to enquire. It is common to all men, and to be found in no other race of animals, which seem to know neither this nor any other species of contracts. Two greyhounds, in running down the same hare, have sometimes the appearance of acting in some sort of concert. Each turns her towards his companion, or endeavours to intercept her when his companion turns her towards himself. This, however, is not the effect of any contract, but of the accidental concurrence of their passions in the same object at that particular time. Nobody ever saw a dog make a fair and deliberate exchange of one bone for another with another dog. Nobody ever saw one animal by its gestures and natural cries signify to another, this is mine, that yours; I am willing to give this for that. When an animal wants to obtain something either of a man or of another animal, it has no other means of persuasion but to gain the favour of those whose service it requires. A puppy fawns upon its dam, and a spaniel endeavours by a thousand attractions to engage the attention of its master who is at dinner, when it wants to be fed by him. Man sometimes uses the same arts with his brethren, and when he has no other means of engaging them to act according to his inclinations, endeavours by every servile and fawning attention to obtain their good will. He has not time, however, to do this upon every occasion. In civilized society he stands at all times in need of the cooperation and assistance of great multitudes, while his whole life is scarce sufficient to gain the friendship of a few persons. In almost every other race of animals each individual, when it is grown up to maturity, is entirely independent, and in its natural state has occasion for the assistance of no other living creature. But man has almost constant occasion for the help of his brethren, and it is in vain for him to expect it from their benevolence only.

He will be more likely to prevail if he can interest their self-love in his favour, and show them that it is for their own advantage to do for him what he requires of them. Whoever offers to another a bargain of any kind, proposes to do this. Give me that which I want, and you shall have this which you want, is the meaning of every such offer; and it is in this manner that we obtain from one another the far greater part of those good offices which we stand in need of. It is not from the benevolence of the butcher, the brewer, or the baker, that we expect our dinner, but from their regard to their own interest. We address ourselves, not to their humanity but to their self-love, and never talk to them of our own necessities but of their advantages. Nobody but a beggar chuses to depend chiefly upon the benevolence of his fellow-citizens. Even a beggar does not depend upon it entirely. The charity of well-disposed people, indeed, supplies him with the whole fund of his subsistence. But though this principle ultimately provides him with all the necessaries of life which he has occasion for, it neither does nor can provide him with them as he has occasion for them. The greater part of his occasional wants are supplied in the same manner as those of other people, by treaty, by barter, and by purchase. With the money which one man gives him he purchases food. The old cloaths which another bestows upon him he exchanges for other old cloaths which suit him better, or for lodging, or for food, or for money, with which he can buy either food, cloaths, or lodging, as he has occasion.

As it is by treaty, by barter, and by purchase, that we obtain from one another the greater part of those mutual good offices which we stand in need of, so it is this same trucking disposition which originally gives occasion to the division of labour. In a tribe of hunters or shepherds a particular person makes bows and arrows, for example, with more readiness and dexterity than any other. He frequently exchanges them for cattle or for venison with his companions; and he finds at last that he can in this manner get more cattle and venison, than if he himself went to the field to catch them. From a regard to his own interest, therefore, the making of bows and arrows grows to be his chief business, and he becomes a sort of armourer. Another excels in making the frames and covers of their little huts or moveable houses. He is accustomed to be of use in this way to his neighbours, who reward him in the same manner with cattle and with venison, till at last he finds it his interest to dedicate himself entirely to this employment, and to become a sort of house-carpenter. In the same manner a third becomes a smith or a brazier; a fourth a tanner or dresser of hides or skins, the principal part of the clothing of savages. And thus the certainty of being able to exchange all that surplus part of the produce of his own labour, which is over and above his own consumption, for such parts of the produce of other men's labour as he may have occasion for, encourages every man to apply himself to a particular occupation, and to cultivate and bring to perfection whatever talent or genius he may possess for that particular species of business.

The difference of natural talents in different men is, in reality, much less than we are aware of; and the very different genius which appears to distinguish men of different professions, when grown up to maturity, is not upon many occasions so much the cause, as the effect of the division of labour. The difference between the most dissimilar characters, between a philosopher and a common street porter, for example, seems to arise not so much from nature, as from habit, custom, and education. When they came into the world, and for the first six or eight years of their existence, they were perhaps, very much alike, and neither their parents nor playfellows could perceive any remarkable difference. About that age, or soon after, they come to be employed in very different occupations. The difference of talents comes then to be taken notice of, and widens by degrees, till at last the vanity of the philosopher is willing to acknowledge scarce

any resemblance. But without the disposition to truck, barter, and exchange, every man must have procured to himself every necessary and conveniency of life which he wanted. All must have had the same duties to perform, and the same work to do, and there could have been no such difference of employment as could alone give occasion to any great difference of talents.

As it is this disposition which forms that difference of talents, so remarkable among men of different professions, so it is this same disposition which renders that difference useful. Many tribes of animals acknowledged to be all of the same species, derive from nature a much more remarkable distinction of genius, than what, antecedent to custom and education, appears to take place among men. By nature a philosopher is not in genius and disposition half so different from a street porter, as a mastiff is from a greyhound, or a greyhound from a spaniel, or this last from a shepherd's dog. Those different tribes of animals, however, though all of the same species, are of scarce any use to one another. The strength of the mastiff is not in the least supported either by the swiftness of the greyhound, or by the sagacity of the spaniel, or by the docility of the shepherd's dog. The effects of those different geniuses and talents, for want of the power or disposition to barter and exchange, cannot be brought into a common stock, and do not in the least contribute to the better accommodation and conveniency of the species. Each animal is still obliged to support and defend itself, separately and independently, and derives no sort of advantage from that variety of talents with which nature has distinguished its fellows. Among men, on the contrary, the most dissimilar geniuses are of use to one another; the different produces of their respective talents, by the general disposition to truck, barter, and exchange, being brought, as it were, into a common stock, where every man may purchase whatever part of the produce of other men's talents he has occasion for.

Book IV, Chapter II: Of Restraints upon the Importation from Foreign Countries of Such Goods as Can Be Produced at Home

... Every individual is continually exerting himself to find out the most advantageous employment for whatever capital he can command. It is his own advantage, indeed, and not that of the society, which he has in view. But the study of his own advantage naturally, or rather necessarily, leads him to prefer that employment which is most advantageous to the society ...

As every individual, therefore, endeavours as much as he can both to employ his capital in the support of domestic industry, and so to direct that industry that its produce may be of the greatest value; every individual necessarily labours to render the annual revenue of the society as great as he can. He generally, indeed, neither intends to promote the public interest, nor knows how much he is promoting it. By preferring the support of domestic to that of foreign industry, he intends only his own security; and by directing that industry in such a manner as its produce may be of the greatest value, he intends only his own gain, and he is in this, as in many other cases, led by an invisible hand to promote an end which was no part of his intention. Nor is it always the worse for the society that it was no part of it. By pursuing his own interest he frequently promotes that of the society more effectually than when he really intends to promote it. I have never known much good done by those who affected to trade for the public good. It is an affectation, indeed, not very common among merchants, and very few words need be employed in dissuading them from it.

◆ ◆ ◆ ◆ ◆

KARL MARX

Estranged Labor

We have started out from the premises of political economy. We have accepted its language and its laws. We presupposed private property; the separation of labor, capital, and land, and likewise of wages, profit, and capital; the division of labor; competition; the conception of exchange value, etc. From political economy itself, using its own words, we have shown that the worker sinks to the level of a commodity, and moreover the most wretched commodity of all; that the misery of the worker is in inverse proportion to the power and volume of his production; that the necessary consequence of competition is the accumulation of capital in a few hands and hence the restoration of monopoly in a more terrible form; and that, finally, the distinction between capitalist and landlord, between agricultural worker and industrial worker, disappears and the whole of society must split into the two classes of *property owners* and propertyless *workers*.

Political economy proceeds from the fact of private property. It does not explain it. It grasps the *material* process of private property, the process through which it actually passes, in general and abstract formulae which it then takes as *laws*. It does not *Comprehend* these laws—*i.e.*, it does not show how they arise from the nature of private property. Political economy fails to explain the reason for the division between labor and capital. For example, when it defines the relation of wages to profit, it takes the interests of the capitalists as the basis of its analysis—*i.e.*, it assumes what it is supposed to explain. Similarly, competition is frequently brought into the argument and explained in terms of external circumstances. Political economy teaches us nothing about the extent to which these external and apparently accidental circumstances are only the expression of a necessary development. We have seen how exchange itself appears to political economy as an accidental fact. The only wheels which political economy sets in motion are *greed*, and the *war of the avaricious—Competition*.

Precisely because political economy fails to grasp the interconnections within the movement, it was possible to oppose, for example, the doctrine of competition to the doctrine of monopoly, the doctrine of craft freedom to the doctrine of the guild, and the doctrine of the division of landed property to the doctrine of the great estate; for competition, craft freedom, and division of landed property were developed and conceived only as accidental, deliberate, violent consequences of monopoly, of the guilds, and of feudal property, and not as their necessary, inevitable, and natural consequences.

We now have to grasp the essential connection between private property, greed, the separation of labor, capital and landed property, exchange and competition, value and the devaluation [*Entwertung*] of man, monopoly, and competition, etc.—the connection between this entire system of estrangement [*Entfremdung*] and the *money* system.

We must avoid repeating the mistake of the political economist, who bases his explanations on some imaginary primordial condition. Such a primordial condition explains nothing. It simply pushes the question into the grey and nebulous distance. It assumes as facts and events what it is supposed to deduce—namely, the necessary relationships between two things, between, for example, the division of labor and exchange. Similarly, theology explains the origin of evil by the fall of Man—*i.e.*, it assumes as a fact in the form of history what it should explain.

We shall start out from a *present-day* economic fact.

The worker becomes poorer the more wealth he produces, the more his production increases in power and extent. The worker becomes an ever cheaper commodity the more commodities he produces. The *devaluation* of the human world grows in direct proportion to the *increase in value* of the world

of things. Labor not only produces commodities; it also produces itself and the workers as a *commodity* and it does so in the same proportion in which it produces commodities in general.

This fact simply means that the object that labor produces, it product, stands opposed to it as *something alien*, as a power independent of the producer. The product of labor is labor embodied and made material in an object, it is the *objectification* of labor. The realization of labor is its objectification. In the sphere of political economy, this realization of labor appears as a *loss of reality* for the worker, objectification as loss of and bondage to the object, and appropriation as estrangement, as *alienation* [*Entausserung*].

So much does the realization of labor appear as loss of reality that the worker loses his reality to the point of dying of starvation. So much does objectification appear as loss of the object that the worker is robbed of the objects he needs most not only for life but also for work. Work itself becomes an object which he can only obtain through an enormous effort and with spasmodic interruptions. So much does the appropriation of the object appear as estrangement that the more objects the worker produces the fewer can he possess and the more he falls under the domination of his product, of capital.

All these consequences are contained in this characteristic, that the worker is related to the product of labor as to an *alien* object. For it is clear that, according to this premise, the more the worker exerts himself in his work, the more powerful the alien, objective world becomes which he brings into being over against himself, the poorer he and his inner world become, and the less they belong to him. It is the same in religion. The more man puts into God, the less he retains within himself. The worker places his life in the object; but now it no longer belongs to him, but to the object. The greater his activity, therefore, the fewer objects the worker possesses. What the product of his labor is, he is not. Therefore, the greater this product, the less is he himself. The externalization [*Entausserung*] of the worker in his product means not only that his labor becomes an object, an external existence, but that it exists *outside* him, independently of him and alien to him, and beings to confront him as an autonomous power; that the life which he has bestowed on the object confronts him as hostile and alien.

Let us not take a closer look at objectification, at the production of the worker, and the estrangement, the loss of the object, of his product, that this entails.

The workers can create nothing without nature, without the sensuous external world. It is the material in which his labor realizes itself, in which it is active and from which, and by means of which, it produces.

But just as nature provides labor with the means of life, in the sense of labor cannot live without objects on which to exercise itself, so also it provides the means of life in the narrower sense, namely the means of physical subsistence of the worker.

The more the worker appropriates the external world, sensuous nature, through his labor, the more he deprives himself of the means of life in two respects: firstly, the sensuous external world becomes less and less an object belonging to his labor, a means of life of his labor; and, secondly, it becomes less and less a means of life in the immediate sense, a means for the physical subsistence of the worker.

In these two respects, then, the worker becomes a slave of his object; firstly, in that he receives an object of labor, *i.e.*, he receives work, and, secondly, in that he receives means of subsistence. Firstly, then, so that he can exists as a worker, and secondly as a physical subject. The culmination of this slavery is that it is only as a worker that he can maintain himself as a physical subject and only as a physical subject that he is a worker.

(The estrangement of the worker in his object is expressed according to the laws of political economy in the following way:

the more the worker produces, the less he has to consume;

the more value he creates, the more worthless he becomes;

the more his product is shaped, the more misshapen the worker;

the more civilized his object, the more barbarous the worker;

the more powerful the work, the more powerless the worker;

the more intelligent the work, the duller the worker and the more he becomes a slave of nature.)

Political economy conceals the estrangement in the nature of labor by ignoring the direct relationship between the worker (labor) and production. It is true that labor produces marvels for the rich, but it produces privation for the worker. It produces palaces, but hovels for the worker. It produces beauty, but deformity for the worker. It replaces labor by machines, but it casts some of the workers back into barbarous forms of labor and turns others into machines. It produces intelligence, but it produces idiocy and cretinism for the worker.

The direct relationship of labor to its products is the relationship of the worker to the objects of his production. The relationship of the rich man to the objects of production and to production itself is only a *consequence* of this first relationship, and confirms it. Later, we shall consider this second aspect. Therefore, when we ask what is the essential relationship of labor, we are asking about the relationship of the worker to production.

Up to now, we have considered the estrangement, the alienation of the worker, only from one aspect— *i.e.*, his relationship to the products of his labor. But estrangement manifests itself not only in the result, but also in the act of production, within the activity of production itself. How could the product of the worker's activity confront him as something alien if it were not for the fact that in the act of production he was estranging himself from himself? After all, the product is simply the resume of the activity, of the production. So if the product of labor is aliena-tion, production itself must be active alienation, the alienation of activity, the activity of alienation. The estrangement of the object of labor merely summar-izes the estrangement, the alienation in the activity of labor itself.

What constitutes the alienation of labor?

Firstly, the fact that labor is external to the worker—*i.e.*, does not belong to his essential being; that he, therefore, does not confirm himself in his work, but denies himself, feels miserable and not happy, does not develop free mental and physical energy, but mortifies his flesh and ruins his mind. Hence, the worker feels himself only when he is not working; when he is working, he does not feel him-self. He is at home when he is not working, and not at home when he is working. His labor is, there-fore, not voluntary but forced, it is *forced labor*. It is, therefore, not the satisfaction of a need but a mere *means* to satisfy needs outside itself. Its alien character is clearly demonstrated by the fact that as soon as no physical or other compulsion exists, it is shunned like the plague. External labor, labor in which man alienates himself, is a labor of self-sac-rifice, of mortification. Finally, the external charac-ter of labor for the worker is demonstrated by the fact that it belongs not to him but to another, and that in it he belongs not to himself but to another. Just as in religion the spontaneous activity of the human imagination, the human brain, and the hu-man heart, detaches itself from the individual and reappears as the alien activity of a god or of a devil, so the activity of the worker is not his own spon-taneous activity. It belongs to another, it is a loss of his self.

The result is that man (the worker) feels that he is acting freely only in his animal functions—eating, drinking, and procreating, or at most in his dwelling and adornment—while in his human functions, he is nothing more than animal.

It is true that eating, drinking, and procreating, etc., are also genuine human functions. However, when abstracted from other aspects of human activ-ity, and turned into final and exclusive ends, they are animal.

We have considered the act of estrangement of practical human activity, of labor, from two aspects: (1) the relationship of the worker to the product of labor as an alien object that has power over him. The relationship is, at the same time, the relationship to the sensuous external world, to natural objects, as an alien world confronting him, in hostile opposition. (2) The relationship of labor to the *act of production* within labor. This relationship is the relationship of the worker to his own activity as something which is alien and does not belong to him, activity as pas-sivity [*Leiden*], power as impotence, procreation as emasculation, the worker's own physical and mental energy, his personal life—for what is life but activ-ity?—as an activity directed against himself, which is independent of him and does not belong to him. Self-estrangement, as compared with the estrange-ment of the object [*Sache*] mentioned above.

We now have to derive a third feature of estranged labor from the two we have already examined.

Man is a species-being, not only because he prac-tically and theoretically makes the species—both his own and those of other things—his object, but also—and this is simply another way of saying the same thing—because he looks upon himself as the present, living species, because he looks upon him-self as a universal and therefore free being.

Species-life, both for man and for animals, con-sists physically in the fact that man, like animals, lives from inorganic nature; and because man is more universal than animals, so too is the area of inorganic nature from which he lives more universal. Just as plants, animals, stones, air, light, etc., theor-etically form a part of human consciousness, partly as objects of science and partly as objects of art—his spiritual inorganic nature, his spiritual means of life, which he must first prepare before he can enjoy and digest them—so, too, in practice they form a part of human life and human activity. In a physical sense, man lives only from these natural products, whether in the form of nourishment, heating, clothing, shelter, etc. The universality of man manifests itself in practice in that universality which makes the whole of nature his inorganic body, (1) as a direct means of life and (2) as the matter, the object, and the tool of his life activity. Nature is man's inorganic body—that is to say, nature insofar as it is not the human body. Man lives from nature—i.e., nature is his body—and he must maintain a continuing dialogue with it is he is not to die. To say that man's physical and mental life is linked to nature simply means that nature is linked to itself, for man is a part of nature.

Estranged labor not only (1) estranges nature from man and (2) estranges man from himself, from his own function, from his vital activity; because of this, it also estranges man from his species. It turns his species-life into a means for his individual life. Firstly, it estranges species-life and individual life, and, secondly, it turns the latter, in its abstract form, into the purpose of the former, also in its abstract and estranged form.

For in the first place labor, life activity, productive life itself, appears to man only as a means for the satisfaction of a need, the need to preserve physical existence. But productive life is species-life. It is life-producing life. The whole character of a species, its species-character, resides in the nature of its life activity, and free conscious activity constitutes the species-character of man. Life appears only as a means of life.

The animal is immediately one with its life activity. It is not distinct from that activity; it is that activity. Man makes his life activity itself an object of his will and consciousness. He has conscious life activity. It is not a determination with which he directly merges. Conscious life activity directly distinguishes man from animal life activity. Only because of that is he a species-being. Or, rather, he is a conscious being—i.e., his own life is an object for him, only because he is a species-being. Only because of

that is his activity free activity. Estranged labor reverses the relationship so that man, just because he is a conscious being, makes his life activity, his being [Wesen], a mere means for his existence.

The practical creation of an objective world, the fashioning of inorganic nature, is proof that man is a conscious species-being—i.e., a being which treats the species as its own essential being or itself as a species-being. It is true that animals also produce. They build nests and dwelling, like the bee, the beaver, the ant, etc. But they produce only their own immediate needs or those of their young; they produce only when immediate physical need compels them to do so, while man produces even when he is free from physical need and truly produces only in freedom from such need; they produce only themselves, while man reproduces the whole of nature; their products belong immediately to their physical bodies, while man freely confronts his own product. Animals produce only according to the standards and needs of the species to which they belong, while man is capable of producing according to the standards of every species and of applying to each object its inherent standard; hence, man also produces in accordance with the laws of beauty.

It is, therefore, in his fashioning of the objective that man really proves himself to be a species-being. Such production is his active species-life. Through it, nature appears as his work and his reality. The object of labor is, therefore, the objectification of the species-life of man: for man produces himself not only intellectually, in his consciousness, but actively and actually, and he can therefore contemplate himself in a world he himself has created. In tearing away the object of his production from man, estranged labor therefore tears away from him his species-life, his true species-objectivity, and transforms his advantage over animals into the disadvantage that his inorganic body, nature, is taken from him.

In the same way as estranged labor reduces spontaneous and free activity to a means, it makes man's species-life a means of his physical existence.

Consciousness, which man has from his species, is transformed through estrangement so that species-life becomes a means for him.

(3) Estranged labor, therefore, turns man's species-being—both nature and his intellectual species-power—into a being alien to him and a means of his individual existence. It estranges man from his own body, from nature as it exists outside him, from his spiritual essence [*Wesen*], his human existence.

(4) An immediate consequence of man's estrangement from the product of his labor, his life activity, his species-being, is the estrangement of man from man. When man confronts himself, he also confronts other men. What is true of man's relationship to his labor, to the product of his labor, and to himself, is also true of his relationship to other men, and to the labor and the object of the labor of other men.

In general, the proposition that man is estranged from his species-being means that each man is estranged from the others and that all are estranged from man's essence.

Man's estrangement, like all relationships of man to himself, is realized and expressed only in man's relationship to other men.

In the relationship of estranged labor, each man therefore regards the other in accordance with the standard and the situation in which he as a worker finds himself.

We started out from an economic fact, the estrangement of the worker and of his production. We gave this fact conceptual form: estranged, alienated labor. We have analyzed this concept, and in so doing merely analyzed an economic fact.

Let us now go on to see how the concept of estranged, alienated labor must express and present itself in reality.

If the product of labor is alien to me, and confronts me as an alien power, to whom does it then belong?

To a being *other* than me.

Who is this being?

The gods? It is true that in early times most production—*e.g.*, temple building, etc., in Egypt, India, and Mexico—was in the service of the gods, just as the product belonged to the gods. But the gods alone were never the masters of labor. The same is true of nature. And what a paradox it would be if the more man subjugates nature through his labor and the more divine miracles are made superfluous by the miracles of industry, the more he is forced to forgo the joy or production and the enjoyment of the product out of deference to these powers.

The alien being to whom labor and the product of labor belong, in whose service labor is performed, and for whose enjoyment the product of labor is created, can be none other than man himself.

If the product of labor does not belong to the worker, and if it confronts him as an alien power, this is only possible because it belongs to a man other than the worker. If his activity is a torment for him, it must provide pleasure and enjoyment for someone else. Not the gods, not nature, but only man himself can be this alien power over men.

Consider the above proposition that the relationship of man to himself becomes objective and real for him only through his relationship to other men. If, therefore, he regards the product of his labor, his objectified labor, as an alien, hostile, and powerful object which is independent of him, then his relationship to that object is such that another man—alien, hostile, powerful, and independent of him—is its master. If he relates to his own activity as unfree activity, then he relates to it as activity in the service, under the rule, coercion, and yoke of another man.

Every self-estrangement of man from himself and nature is manifested in the relationship he sets up between other men and himself and nature. Thus, religious self-estrangement is necessarily manifested in the relationship between layman and priest, or, since we are dealing here with the spiritual world, between layman and mediator, etc. In the practical, real world, self-estrangement can manifest itself only in the practical, real relationship to other men. The medium through which estrangement progresses is itself a practical one. So through estranged labor man not only produces his relationship to the object and to the act of production as to alien and hostile powers; he also produces the relationship in which other men stand to his production and product, and the relationship in which he stands to these other men. Just as he creates his own production as a loss of reality, a punishment, and his own product as a loss, a product which does not belong to him, so he creates the domination of the non-producer over production and its product. Just as he estranges from himself his own activity, so he confers upon the stranger and activity which does not belong to him.

Up to now, we have considered the relationship only from the side of the worker. Later on, we shall consider it from the side of the non-worker.

Thus, through estranged, alienated labor, the worker creates the relationship of another man, who is alien to labor and stands outside it, to that labor. The relation of the worker to labor creates the relation of the capitalist—or whatever other word one chooses for the master of labor—to that labor. Private property is therefore the product, result, and necessary consequence of alienated labor, of the external relation of the worker to nature and to himself.

Private property thus derives from an analysis of the concept of alienated labor—*i.e.*, alienated man, estranged labor, estranged life, estranged man.

It is true that we took the concept of alienated labor (alienated life) from political economy as a result of the movement of private property. But it is clear from an analysis of this concept that, although private property appears as the basis and cause of alienated labor, it is in fact its consequence, just as the gods were originally not the cause but the effect of the confusion in men's minds. Later, however, this relationship becomes reciprocal.

It is only when the development of private property reaches its ultimate point of culmination that this, its secret, re-emerges; namely, that is (a) the product of alienated labor, and (b) the means through which labor is alienated, the realization of this alienation.

This development throws light upon a number of hitherto unresolved controversies.

(1) Political economy starts out from labor as the real soul of production and yet gives nothing to labor and everything to private property. Proudhon has dealt with this contradiction by deciding for labor and against private property [see his 1840 pamphlet, *Qu'est-ce que la propriété?*]. But we have seen that this apparent contradiction is the contradiction of estranged labor with itself and that political economy has merely formulated laws of estranged labor.

It, therefore, follows for us that wages and private property are identical: for there the product, the object of labor, pays for the labor itself, wages are only a necessary consequence of the estrangement of labor; similarly, where wages are concerned, labor appears not as an end in itself but as the servant of wages. We intend to deal with this point in more detail later on: for the present we shall merely draw a few conclusions.

An enforced rise in wages (disregarding all other difficulties, including the fact that such an anomalous situation could only be prolonged by force) would therefore be nothing more than better pay for slaves and would not mean an increase in human significance or dignity for either the worker or the labor.

Even the equality of wages, which Proudhon demands, would merely transform the relation of the present-day worker to his work into the relation of all men to work. Society would then be conceived as an abstract capitalist.

Wages are an immediate consequence of estranged labor, and estranged labor is the immediate cause of private property. If the one falls, then the other must fall too.

(2) It further follows from the relation of estranged labor to private property that the emancipation of society from private property, etc., from

servitude, is expressed in the political form of the emancipation of the workers. This is not because it is only a question of their emancipation, but because in their emancipation is contained universal human emancipation. The reason for this universality is that the whole of human servitude is involved in the relation of the worker to production, and all relations of servitude are nothing but modifications and consequences of this relation.

Just as we have arrived at the concept of private property through an analysis of the concept of estranged, alienated labor, so with the help of these two factors it is possible to evolve all economic categories, and in each of these categories—*e.g.*, trade, competition, capital, money—we shall identify only a particular and developed expression of these basic constituents.

But, before we go on to consider this configuration, let us try to solve two further problems.

(1) We have to determine the general nature of private property, as it has arisen out of estranged labor, in its relation to truly human and social property.

(2) We have taken the estrangement of labor, its alienation, as a fact and we have analyzed that fact. How, we now ask, does man come to alienate his labor, to estrange it? How it this estrangement founded in the nature of human development? We have already gone a long way towards solving this problem by transforming the question of the origin of private property into the question of the relationship of alienated labor to the course of human development. For, in speaking of private property, one imagines that one is dealing with something external to man. In speaking of labor, one is dealing immediately with man himself. This new way of formulating the problem already contains its solution.

As to (1): The general nature of private property and its relationship to truly human property.

Alienated labor has resolved itself for us into two component parts, which mutually condition one another, or which are merely different expressions of one and the same relationship. Appropriation appears as estrangement, as alienation; and alienation appears as appropriation, estrangement as true admission to citizenship.

We have considered the one aspect, alienated labor in relation to the worker himself—*i.e.*, the relation of alienated labor to itself. And as product, as necessary consequence of this relationship, we have found the property relation of the non-worker to the worker and to labor. Private property as the material, summarized expression of alienated labor embraces both relations—the relation of the worker to labor and to the product of his labor and the non-workers, and the relation of the non-worker to the worker and to the product of his labor.

We have already seen that, in relation to the worker who appropriates nature through his labor, appropriation appears as estrangement, self-activity as activity for another and of another, vitality as a sacrifice of life, production of an object as loss of that object to an alien power, to an *alien* man. Let us now consider the relation between this man, who is *alien* to labor and to the worker, and the worker, labor, and the object of labor.

The first thing to point out is that everything which appears for the worker as an activity of alienation, of estrangement, appears for the non-worker as a situation of alienation, of estrangement.

Secondly, the real, practical attitude of the worker in production and to the product (as a state of mind) appears for the non-worker who confronts him as a theoretical attitude.

Thirdly, the non-worker does everything against the worker which the worker does against himself, but he does not do against himself what he does against the worker.

Let us take a closer look at these three relationships.

CONTEMPORARY THEORIES OF DISTRIBUTION AND PROPERTY

JOHN RAWLS

Excerpts from
A Theory of Justice

3. The Main Idea of the Theory of Justice

My aim is to present a conception of justice which generalizes and carries to a higher level of abstraction the familiar theory of the social contract as found, say, in Locke, Rousseau, and Kant.[1] In order to do this we are not to think of the original contract as one to enter a particular society or to set up a particular form of government. Rather, the guiding idea is that the principles of justice for the basic structure of society are the object of the original agreement. They are the principles that free and rational persons concerned to further their own interests would accept in an initial position of equality as defining the fundamental terms of their association. These principles are to regulate all further agreements; they specify the kinds of social cooperation that can be entered into and the forms of government that can be established. This way of regarding the principles of justice I shall call justice as fairness.

Thus we are to imagine that those who engage in social cooperation choose together, in one joint act, the principles which are to assign basic rights and duties and to determine the division of social benefits. Men are to decide in advance how they are to regulate their claims against one another and what is to be the foundation charter of their society. Just as each person must decide by rational reflection what constitutes his good, that is, the system of ends which it is rational for him to pursue, so a group of persons must decide once and for all what is to

count among them as just and unjust. The choice which rational men would make in this hypothetical situation of equal liberty, assuming for the present that this choice problem has a solution, determines the principles of justice.

In justice as fairness the original position of equality corresponds to the state of nature in the traditional theory of the social contract. This original position is not, of course, thought of as an actual historical state of affairs, much less as a primitive condition of culture. It is understood as a purely hypothetical situation characterized so as to lead to a certain conception of justice.[2] Among the essential features of this situation is that no one knows his place in society, his class position or social status, nor does any one know his fortune in the distribution of natural assets and abilities, his intelligence, strength, and the like. I shall even assume that the parties do not know their conceptions of the good or their special psychological propensities. The principles of justice are chosen behind a veil of ignorance. This ensures that no one is advantaged or disadvantaged in the choice of principles by the outcome of natural chance or the contingency of social circumstances. Since all are similarly situated and no one is able to design principles to favor his particular condition, the principles of justice are the result of a fair agreement or bargain. For given the circumstances of the original position, the symmetry of everyone's relations to each other, this initial situation is fair between individuals as moral persons, that is, as rational beings with their own ends and capable, I shall assume, of a sense of justice. The original position is, one might say, the appropriate initial status quo, and thus the fundamental agreements reached in it are fair. This explains the propriety of the name "justice as fairness": it conveys the idea that the principles of justice are agreed to in an initial situation that is fair. The name does not mean that the concepts of justice and fairness are the same, any more than the phrase "poetry as metaphor" means that the concepts of poetry and metaphor are the same.

Justice as fairness begins, as I have said, with one of the most general of all choices which persons might make together, namely, with the choice of the first principles of a conception of justice which is to regulate all subsequent criticism and reform of institutions. Then, having chosen a conception of justice, we can suppose that they are to choose a constitution and a legislature to enact laws, and so on, all in accordance with the principles of justice initially agreed upon. Our social situation is just if it is such that by this sequence of hypothetical agreements we would have contracted into the general system of rules which defines it. Moreover, assuming that the original position does determine a set of principles (that is, that a particular conception of justice would be chosen) it will then be true that whenever social institutions satisfy these principles those engaged in them can say to one another that they are cooperating on terms to which they would agree if they were free and equal persons whose relations with respect to one another were fair. They could all view their arrangements as meeting the stipulations which they would acknowledge in an initial situation that embodies widely accepted and reasonable constraints on the choice of principles. The general recognition of this fact would provide the basis for a public acceptance of the corresponding principles of justice. No society can, of course, be a scheme of cooperation which men enter voluntarily in a literal sense; each person finds himself placed at birth in some particular position in some particular society, and the nature of this position materially affects his life prospects. Yet a society satisfying the principles of justice as fairness comes as close as a society can to being a voluntary scheme, for it meets the principles which free and equal persons would assent to under circumstances that are fair. In this sense its members are autonomous and the obligations they recognize self-imposed.

One feature of justice as fairness is to think of the parties in the initial situation as rational and mutually disinterested. This does not mean that the parties are egoists, that is, individuals with only certain kinds of interests, say in wealth, prestige, and domination. But they are conceived as not taking an interest in one another's interests. They are to presume that even their spiritual aims may be opposed, in the way that the aims of those of different religions may be opposed. Moreover, the concept of rationality must be interpreted as far as possible in the narrow sense, standard in economic theory, of taking the most effective means to given ends. I shall modify this concept to some extent, as explained later (§25), but one must try to avoid introducing into it any controversial ethical elements. The initial situation must be characterized by stipulations that are widely accepted.

In working out the conception of justice as fairness one main task clearly is to determine which principles of justice would be chosen in the original position. To do this we must describe this situation in some detail and formulate with care the problem of choice which it presents. These matters I shall take up in the immediately succeeding chapters. It may be observed, however, that once the principles of justice are thought of as arising from an original agreement in a situation of equality, it is an open question whether the principle of utility would be acknowledged. Offhand it hardly seems likely that persons who view themselves as equals, entitled to press their claims upon one another, would agree to a principle which may require lesser life prospects for some simply for the sake of a greater sum of advantages enjoyed by others. Since each desires to protect his interests, his capacity to advance his conception of the good, no one has a reason to acquiesce in an enduring loss for himself in order to bring about a greater net balance of satisfaction. In the absence of strong and lasting benevolent impulses, a rational man would not accept a basic structure merely because it maximized the algebraic sum of advantages irrespective of its permanent effects on his own basic rights and interests. Thus it seems that the principle of utility is incompatible with the conception of social cooperation among equals for mutual advantage. It appears to be inconsistent with the idea of reciprocity implicit in the notion of a well-ordered society. Or, at any rate, so I shall argue.

I shall maintain instead that the persons in the initial situation would choose two rather different principles: the first requires equality in the assignment of basic rights and duties, while the second holds that social and economic inequalities, for example inequalities of wealth and authority, are just only if they result in compensating benefits for everyone, and in particular for the least advantaged members of society. These principles rule out justifying institutions on the grounds that the hardships of some are offset by a greater good in the aggregate. It may be expedient but it is not just that some should have less in order that others may prosper. But there is no injustice in the greater benefits earned by a few provided that the situation of persons not so fortunate is thereby improved. The intuitive idea is that since everyone's well-being depends upon a scheme of cooperation without which no one could have a satisfactory life, the division of advantages should be such as to draw forth the willing cooperation of everyone taking part in it, including those less well situated. The two principles mentioned seem to be a fair basis on which those better endowed, or more fortunate in their social position, neither of which we can be said to deserve, could expect the willing cooperation of others when some workable scheme is a necessary condition of the welfare of all.[3] Once we decide to look for a conception of justice that prevents the use of the accidents of natural endowment and the contingencies of social circumstance as counters in a quest for political and economic advantage, we are led to these principles. They express the result of leaving aside those aspects of the social world that seem arbitrary from a moral point of view.

The problem of the choice of principles, however, is extremely difficult. I do not expect the answer I shall suggest to be convincing to everyone. It is, therefore, worth noting from the outset that justice as fairness, like other contract views, consists of two parts: (1) an interpretation of the initial situation and of the problem of choice posed there, and (2) a set of principles which, it is argued, would be agreed to. One may accept the first part of the theory (or some variant thereof), but not the other, and conversely. The concept of the initial contractual situation may seem reasonable although the particular principles proposed are rejected. To be sure, I want to maintain that the most appropriate conception of this situation does lead to principles of justice contrary to utilitarianism and perfectionism, and therefore that the contract doctrine provides an alternative to these views. Still, one may dispute this contention even though one grants that the contractarian method is a useful way of studying ethical theories and of setting forth their underlying assumptions.

Justice as fairness is an example of what I have called a contract theory. Now there may be an objection to the term "contract" and related expressions, but I think it will serve reasonably well. Many words have misleading connotations which at first are likely to confuse. The terms "utility" and "utilitarianism" are surely no exception. They too have unfortunate suggestions which hostile critics have been willing to exploit; yet they are clear enough for those prepared to study utilitarian doctrine. The same should be true of the term "contract" applied to moral theories. As I have mentioned, to understand it one has to keep in mind that it implies a certain level of abstraction. In particular, the content of the relevant agreement is not to enter a given society or to adopt a given form of government, but to accept certain moral principles. Moreover, the undertakings referred to are purely hypothetical: a contract view holds that certain principles would be accepted in a well-defined initial situation.

The merit of the contract terminology is that it conveys the idea that principles of justice may be conceived as principles that would be chosen by rational persons, and that in this way conceptions of justice may be explained and justified. The theory of justice is a part, perhaps the most significant part, of the theory of rational choice. Furthermore, principles of justice deal with conflicting claims upon the advantages won by social cooperation; they apply to the relations among several persons or groups. The word "contract" suggests this plurality as well as the condition that the appropriate division of advantages must be in accordance with principles acceptable to all parties. The condition of publicity for principles of justice is also connoted by the contract phraseology. Thus, if these principles are the outcome of an agreement, citizens have a knowledge of the principles that others follow. It is characteristic of contract theories to stress the public nature of political principles. Finally there is the long tradition of the contract doctrine. Expressing the tie with this line of thought helps to define ideas and accords with natural piety. There are then several advantages in the use of the term "contract." With due precautions taken, it should not be misleading.

A final remark. Justice as fairness is not a complete contract theory. For it is clear that the contractarian idea can be extended to the choice of more or less an entire ethical system, that is, to a system including principles for all the virtues and not only for justice. Now for the most part I shall consider only principles of justice and others closely related to them; I make no attempt to discuss the virtues in a systematic way. Obviously if justice as fairness succeeds reasonably well, a next step would be to study the more general view suggested by the name "rightness as fairness." But even this wider theory fails to embrace all moral relationships, since it would seem to include only our relations with other persons and to leave out of account how we are to conduct ourselves toward animals and the rest of nature. I do not contend that the contract notion offers a way to approach these questions which are certainly of the first importance; and I shall have to put them aside. We must recognize the limited scope of justice as fairness and of the general type of view that it exemplifies. How far its conclusions must be revised once these other matters are understood cannot be decided in advance.

4. The Original Position and Justification

I have said that the original position is the appropriate initial status quo which insures that the fundamental agreements reached in it are fair. This fact yields the name "justice as fairness." It is clear, then, that I want to say that one conception of justice is more reasonable than another, or justifiable with respect to it, if rational persons in the initial situation would choose its principles over those of the other for the role of justice. Conceptions of justice are to be ranked by their acceptability to persons so circumstanced. Understood in this way the question of justification is settled by working out a problem of deliberation: we have to ascertain which principles it would be rational to adopt given the contractual situation. This connects the theory of justice with the theory of rational choice.

If this view of the problem of justification is to succeed, we must, of course, describe in some detail the nature of this choice problem. A problem of rational decision has a definite answer only if we know the beliefs and interests of the parties, their relations with respect to one another, the alternatives between which they are to choose, the procedure whereby they make up their minds, and so on. As the circumstances are presented in different ways, correspondingly different principles are accepted. The concept of the original position, as I shall refer to it, is that of the most philosophically favored interpretation of this initial choice situation for the purposes of a theory of justice.

But how are we to decide what is the most favored interpretation? I assume, for one thing, that there is a broad measure of agreement that principles of justice should be chosen under certain conditions. To justify a particular description of the initial situation one shows that it incorporates these commonly shared presumptions. One argues from widely accepted but weak premises to more specific conclusions. Each of the presumptions should by itself be natural and plausible; some of them may seem innocuous or even trivial. The aim of the contract approach is to establish that taken together they impose significant bounds on acceptable principles of justice. The ideal outcome would be that these conditions determine a unique set of principles; but I shall be satisfied if they suffice to rank the main traditional conceptions of social justice.

One should not be misled, then, by the somewhat unusual conditions which characterize the original position. The idea here is simply to make vivid to ourselves the restrictions that it seems reasonable to impose on arguments for principles of justice, and therefore on these principles themselves. Thus it seems reasonable and generally acceptable that no one should be advantaged or disadvantaged by natural fortune or social circumstances in the choice of principles. It also seems widely agreed that it should be impossible to tailor principles to the circumstances of one's own case. We should insure further that particular inclinations and aspirations, and persons' conceptions of their good do not affect the principles adopted. The aim is to rule out those principles that it would be rational to propose for acceptance, however little the chance of success, only if one knew certain things that are irrelevant from the standpoint of justice. For example, if a man knew that he was wealthy, he might find it rational to advance the principle that various taxes for welfare measures be counted unjust; if he knew that he was poor, he would most likely propose the contrary principle. To represent the desired restrictions one imagines a situation in which everyone is deprived of this sort of information. One excludes the knowledge of those contingencies which sets men at odds and allows them to be guided by their prejudices. In this manner the veil of ignorance is arrived at in a natural way. This concept should cause no difficulty if we keep in mind the constraints on arguments that it is meant to express. At any time we can enter the original position, so to speak, simply by following a certain procedure, namely, by arguing for principles of justice in accordance with these restrictions.

It seems reasonable to suppose that the parties in the original position are equal. That is, all have the same rights in the procedure for choosing principles; each can make proposals, submit reasons for their acceptance, and so on. Obviously the purpose of these conditions is to represent equality between human beings as moral persons, as creatures having a conception of their good and capable of a sense of justice. The basis of equality is taken to be similarity in these two respects. Systems of ends are not ranked in value; and each man is presumed to have the requisite ability to understand and to act upon whatever principles are adopted. Together with the veil of ignorance, these conditions define the principles of justice as those which rational persons concerned to advance their interests would consent to as equals when none are known to be advantaged or disadvantaged by social and natural contingencies.

There is, however, another side to justifying a particular description of the original position. This is to see if the principles which would be chosen match our considered convictions of justice or extend them in an acceptable way. We can note whether applying these principles would lead us to make the same judgments about the basic structure of society which we now make intuitively and in which we have the greatest confidence; or whether, in cases where our present judgments are in doubt and given with hesitation, these principles offer a resolution which we can affirm on reflection. There are questions which we feel sure must be answered in a certain way. For example, we are confident that religious intolerance and racial discrimination are unjust. We think that we have examined these things with care and have reached what we believe is an impartial judgment not likely to be distorted by an excessive attention to our own interests. These convictions are provisional fixed points which we presume any conception of justice must fit. But we have much less assurance as to what is the correct distribution of wealth and authority. Here we may be looking for a way to remove our doubts. We can check an interpretation of the initial situation, then, by the capacity of its principles to accommodate our firmest convictions and to provide guidance where guidance is needed.

In searching for the most favored description of this situation we work from both ends. We begin by describing it so that it represents generally shared and preferably weak conditions. We then see if these conditions are strong enough to yield a significant set of principles. If not, we look for further premises equally reasonable. But if so, and these principles match our considered convictions of justice, then so far well and good. But presumably there will be discrepancies. In this case we have a choice. We can either modify the account of the initial situation or we can revise our existing judgments, for even the judgments we take provisionally as fixed points are liable to revision. By going back and forth, sometimes altering the conditions of the contractual circumstances, at others withdrawing our judgments and conforming them to principle, I assume that eventually we shall find a description of the initial situation that both expresses reasonable conditions and yields principles which match our considered judgments duly pruned and adjusted. This state of affairs I refer to as reflective equilibrium.4 It is an equilibrium because at last our principles and judgments coincide; and it is reflective since we know to what principles our judgments conform and the premises of their derivation. At the moment everything is in order. But this equilibrium is not necessarily stable. It is liable to be upset by further examination of the conditions which should be imposed on the contrac-

tual situation and by particular cases which may lead us to revise our judgments. Yet for the time being we have done what we can to render coherent and to justify our convictions of social justice. We have reached a conception of the original position.

I shall not, of course, actually work through this process. Still, we may think of the interpretation of the original position that I shall present as the result of such a hypothetical course of reflection. It represents the attempt to accommodate within one scheme both reasonable philosophical conditions on principles as well as our considered judgments of justice. In arriving at the favored interpretation of the initial situation there is no point at which an appeal is made to self-evidence in the traditional sense either of general conceptions or particular convictions. I do not claim for the principles of justice proposed that they are necessary truths or derivable from such truths. A conception of justice cannot be deduced from self-evident premises or conditions on principles; instead, its justification is a matter of the mutual support of many considerations, of everything fitting together into one coherent view.

A final comment. We shall want to say that certain principles of justice are justified because they would be agreed to in an initial situation of equality. I have emphasized that this original position is purely hypothetical. It is natural to ask why, if this agreement is never actually entered into, we should take any interest in these principles, moral or otherwise. The answer is that the conditions embodied in the description of the original position are ones that we do in fact accept. Or if we do not, then perhaps we can be persuaded to do so by philosophical reflection. Each aspect of the contractual situation can be given supporting grounds. Thus what we shall do is to collect together into one conception a number of conditions on principles that we are ready upon due consideration to recognize as reasonable. These constraints express what we are prepared to regard as limits on fair terms of social cooperation. One way to look at the idea of the original position, therefore, is to see it as an expository device which sums up the meaning of these conditions and helps us to extract their consequences. On the other hand, this conception is also an intuitive notion that suggests its own elaboration, so that led on by it we are drawn to define more clearly the standpoint from which we can best interpret moral relationships. We need a conception that enables us to envision our objective from afar: the intuitive notion of the original position is to do this for us.[5]

11. Two Principles of Justice

I shall now state in a provisional form the two principles of justice that I believe would be agreed to in the original position. The first formulation of these principles is tentative. As we go on I shall consider several formulations and approximate step by step the final statement to be given much later. I believe that doing this allows the exposition to proceed in a natural way.

The first statement of the two principles reads as follows.

> First: each person is to have an equal right to the most extensive scheme of equal basic liberties compatible with a similar scheme of liberties for others.

> Second: social and economic inequalities are to be arranged so that they are both (a) reasonably expected to be to everyone's advantage, and (b) attached to positions and offices open to all.

There are two ambiguous phrases in the second principle, namely "everyone's advantage" and "open to all." Determining their sense more exactly will lead to a second formulation of the principle in §13. The final version of the two principles is given in §46; §39 considers the rendering of the first principle.

These principles primarily apply, as I have said, to the basic structure of society and govern the as-

signment of rights and duties and regulate the distribution of social and economic advantages. Their formulation presupposes that, for the purposes of a theory of justice, the social structure may be viewed as having two more or less distinct parts, the first principle applying to the one, the second principle to the other. Thus we distinguish between the aspects of the social system that define and secure the equal basic liberties and the aspects that specify and establish social and economic inequalities. Now it is essential to observe that the basic liberties are given by a list of such liberties. Important among these are political liberty (the right to vote and to hold public office) and freedom of speech and assembly; liberty of conscience and freedom of thought; freedom of the person, which includes freedom from psychological oppression and physical assault and dismemberment (integrity of the person); the right to hold personal property and freedom from arbitrary arrest and seizure as defined by the concept of the rule of law. These liberties are to be equal by the first principle.

The second principle applies, in the first approximation, to the distribution of income and wealth and to the design of organizations that make use of differences in authority and responsibility. While the distribution of wealth and income need not be equal, it must be to everyone's advantage, and at the same time, positions of authority and responsibility must be accessible to all. One applies the second principle by holding positions open, and then, subject to this constraint, arranges social and economic inequalities so that everyone benefits.

These principles are to be arranged in a serial order with the first principle prior to the second. This ordering means that infringements of the basic equal liberties protected by the first principle cannot be justified, or compensated for, by greater social and economic advantages. These liberties have a central range of application within which they can be limited and compromised only when they conflict with other basic liberties. Since they may be limited when they clash with one another, none of these liberties is absolute; but however they are adjusted to form one system, this system is to be the same for all. It is difficult, and perhaps impossible, to give a complete specification of these liberties independently from the particular circumstances—social, economic and technological—of a given society. The hypothesis is that the general form of such a list could be devised with sufficient exactness to sustain this conception of justice. Of course, liberties not on the list, for example, the right to own certain kinds of property (e.g., means of production) and freedom of contract as understood by the doctrine of laissez-faire are not basic; and so they are not protected by the priority of the first principle. Finally, in regard to the second principle, the distribution of wealth and income, and positions of authority and responsibility, are to be consistent with both the basic liberties and equality of opportunity.

The two principles are rather specific in their content, and their acceptance rests on certain assumptions that I must eventually try to explain and justify. For the present, it should be observed that these principles are a special case of a more general conception of justice that can be expressed as follows.

> All social values—liberty and opportunity, income and wealth, and the social bases of self-respect—are to be distributed equally unless an unequal distribution of any, or all, of these values is to everyone's advantage.

Injustice, then, is simply inequalities that are not to the benefit of all. Of course, this conception is extremely vague and requires interpretation.

As a first step, suppose that the basic structure of society distributes certain primary goods, that is, things that every rational man is presumed to want. These goods normally have a use whatever a person's rational plan of life. For simplicity, assume that the chief primary goods at the disposition of society are rights, liberties, and opportunities, and income and wealth. (Later on in Part Three the primary good of self-respect has a central place.) These are the social primary goods. Other primary goods such as health and vigor, intelligence and imagination, are natural goods; although their possession is influenced by the basic structure, they are not so directly under its control. Imagine, then, a hypothetical initial arrangement in which all the social primary goods are equally distributed: everyone has similar rights and duties, and income and wealth are evenly shared. This state of affairs provides a benchmark for judging improvements. If certain inequalities of wealth and differences in authority would make everyone better off than in this hypothetical starting situation, then they accord with the general conception.

Now it is possible, at least theoretically, that by giving up some of their fundamental liberties men are sufficiently compensated by the resulting social and economic gains. The general conception of justice imposes no restrictions on what sort of inequalities are permissible; it only requires that everyone's position be improved. We need not suppose anything so drastic as consenting to a condition of slavery. Imagine instead that people seem willing to forego certain political rights when the economic returns are significant. It is this kind of exchange which the two principles rule out; being arranged in serial order they do not permit exchanges between basic liberties and economic and social gains except under extenuating circumstances (§§26, 39).

For the most part, I shall leave aside the general conception of justice and examine instead the two principles in serial order. The advantage of this procedure is that from the first the matter of priorities is recognized and an effort made to find principles to deal with it. One is led to attend throughout to the conditions under which the absolute weight of liberty with respect to social and economic advantages, as defined by the lexical order of the two principles, would be reasonable. Offhand, this ranking appears extreme and too special a case to be of much interest; but there is more justification for it than would appear at first sight. Or at any rate, so I shall maintain (§82). Furthermore, the distinction between fundamental rights and liberties and economic and social benefits marks a difference among primary social goods that suggests an important division in the social system. Of course, the distinctions drawn and the ordering proposed are at best only approximations. There are surely circumstances in which they fail. But it is essential to depict clearly the main lines of a reasonable conception of justice; and under many conditions anyway, the two principles in serial order may serve well enough.

The fact that the two principles apply to institutions has certain consequences. First of all, the rights and basic liberties referred to by these principles are those which are defined by the public rules of the basic structure. Whether men are free is determined by the rights and duties established by the major institutions of society. Liberty is a certain pattern of social forms. The first principle simply requires that certain sorts of rules, those defining basic liberties, apply to everyone equally and that they allow the most extensive liberty compatible with a like liberty for all. The only reason for circumscribing basic liberties and making them less extensive is that otherwise they would interfere with one another.

Further, when principles mention persons, or require that everyone gain from an inequality, the reference is to representative persons holding the various social positions, or offices established by the basic structure. Thus in applying the second principle I assume that it is possible to assign an expectation of well-being to representative individuals holding these positions. This expectation indicates their life prospects as viewed from their social station. In general, the expectations of representative persons depend upon the distribution of rights and duties throughout the basic structure. Expectations are connected: by raising the prospects of the representative man in one position we presumably increase or decrease the prospects of representative men in other positions. Since it applies to institu-

tional forms, the second principle (or rather the first part of it) refers to the expectations of representative individuals. As I shall discuss below (§14), neither principle applies to distributions of particular goods to particular individuals who may be identified by their proper names. The situation where someone is considering how to allocate certain commodities to needy persons who are known to him is not within the scope of the principles. They are meant to regulate basic institutional arrangements. We must not assume that there is much similarity from the standpoint of justice between an administrative allotment of goods to specific persons and the appropriate design of society. Our common sense intuitions for the former may be a poor guide to the latter.

Now the second principle insists that each person benefit from permissible inequalities in the basic structure. This means that it must be reasonable for each relevant representative man defined by this structure, when he views it as a going concern, to prefer his prospects with the inequality to his prospects without it. One is not allowed to justify differences in income or in positions of authority and responsibility on the ground that the disadvantages of those in one position are outweighed by the greater advantages of those in another. Much less can infringements of liberty be counterbalanced in this way. It is obvious, however, that there are indefinitely many ways in which all may be advantaged when the initial arrangement of equality is taken as a benchmark. How then are we to choose among these possibilities? The principles must be specified so that they yield a determinate conclusion. I now turn to this problem.

20. The Nature of the Argument for Conceptions of Justice

The intuitive idea of justice as fairness is to think of the first principles of justice as themselves the object of an original agreement in a suitably defined initial situation. These principles are those which rational persons concerned to advance their interests would accept in this position of equality to settle the basic terms of their association. It must be shown, then, that the two principles of justice are the solution for the problem of choice presented by the original position. In order to do this, one must establish that, given the circumstances of the parties, and their knowledge, beliefs, and interests, an agreement on these principles is the best way for each person to secure his ends in view of the alternatives available.

Now obviously no one can obtain everything he wants; the mere existence of other persons prevents this. The absolutely best for any man is that everyone else should join with him in furthering his conception of the good whatever it turns out to be. Or failing this, that all others are required to act justly but that he is authorized to exempt himself as he pleases. Since other persons will never agree to such terms of association these forms of egoism would be rejected. The two principles of justice, however, seem to be a reasonable proposal. In fact, I should like to show that these principles are everyone's best reply, so to speak, to the corresponding demands of the others. In this sense, the choice of this conception of justice is the unique solution to the problem set by the original position.

By arguing in this way one follows a procedure familiar in social theory. That is, a simplified situation is described in which rational individuals with certain ends and related to each other in certain ways are to choose among various courses of action in view of their knowledge of the circumstances. What these individuals will do is then derived by strictly deductive reasoning from these assumptions about their beliefs and interests, their situation and the options open to them. Their conduct is, in the phrase of Pareto, the resultant of tastes and obstacles.[6] In the theory of price, for example, the equilibrium of competitive markets is thought of as arising when many individuals each advancing his own interests give way to each other what they can best part with in return for what they most desire. Equilibrium is the result of agreements freely struck between willing traders. For each person it is the best situation that he can reach by free exchange consistent with the right and freedom of others to further their interests in the same way. It is for this reason that this state of affairs is an equilibrium, one that will persist in the absence of further changes in the circumstances. No one has any incentive to alter it. If a departure from this situation sets in motion tendencies which restore it, the equilibrium is stable.

Of course, the fact that a situation is one of equilibrium, even a stable one, does not entail that it is right or just. It only means that given men's estimate of their position, they act effectively to preserve it. Clearly a balance of hatred and hostility may be a stable equilibrium; each may think that any feasible change will be worse. The best that each can do for himself may be a condition of lesser injustice rather than of greater good. The moral assessment of equilibrium situations depends upon the background circumstances which determine them. It is at this point that the conception of the original position embodies features peculiar to moral theory. For while the theory of price, say, tries to account for the movements of the market by assumptions about the actual tendencies at work, the philosophically favored interpretation of the initial situation incorporates conditions which it is thought reasonable to impose on the choice of principles. By contrast with social theory, the aim is to characterize this situation so that the principles that would be chosen, whatever they turn out to be, are acceptable from a moral point of view. The original position is defined in such a way that it is a status quo in which any agreements reached are fair. It is a state of affairs in which the parties are equally represented as moral persons and the outcome is not conditioned by arbitrary contingencies or the relative balance of social forces. Thus justice as fairness is able to use the idea of pure procedural justice from the beginning.

It is clear, then, that the original position is a purely hypothetical situation. Nothing resembling it need ever take place, although we can by deliberately following the constraints it expresses simulate the reflections of the parties. The conception of the original position is not intended to explain human conduct except insofar as it tries to account for our moral judgments and helps to explain our having a sense of justice. Justice as fairness is a theory of our moral sentiments as manifested by our considered judgments in reflective equilibrium. These sentiments presumably affect our thought and action to some degree. So while the conception of the original position is part of the theory of conduct, it does not follow at all that there are actual situations that resemble it. What is necessary is that the principles that would be accepted play the requisite part in our moral reasoning and conduct.

One should note also that the acceptance of these principles is not conjectured as a psychological law or probability. Ideally anyway, I should like to show that their acknowledgment is the only choice consistent with the full description of the original position. The argument aims eventually to be strictly deductive. To be sure, the persons in the original position have a certain psychology, since various assumptions are made about their beliefs and interests. These assumptions appear along with other premises in the description of this initial situation. But clearly arguments from such premises can be fully deductive, as theories in politics and economics attest. We should strive for a kind of moral geometry with all the rigor which this name connotes. Unhappily the reasoning I shall give will fall far short of this, since it is highly intuitive throughout. Yet it is essential to have in mind the ideal one would like to achieve.

A final remark. There are, as I have said, many possible interpretations of the initial situation. This conception varies depending upon how the contracting parties are conceived, upon what their beliefs and interests are said to be, upon which alternatives are available to them, and so on. In this sense, there are many different contract theories. Justice as fairness is but one of these. But the question of justification is settled, as far as it can be, by showing that there is one interpretation of the initial situation which best expresses the conditions that are widely thought reasonable to impose on the choice of principles yet which, at the same time, leads to a conception that characterizes our considered judgments in reflective equilibrium. This most favored, or standard, interpretation I shall refer to as the original position. We may conjecture that for each traditional conception of justice there exists an interpretation of the initial situation in which its principles are the preferred solution. Thus, for example, there are interpretations that lead to the classical as well as the average principle of utility. These variations of the initial situation will be mentioned as we go along. The procedure of contract theories provides, then, a general analytic method for the comparative study of conceptions of justice. One tries to set out the different conditions embodied in the contractual situation in which their principles would be chosen. In this way one formulates the various underlying assumptions on which these conceptions seem to depend. But if one interpretation is philosophically most favored, and if its principles characterize our considered judgments, we have a procedure for justification as well. We cannot know at first whether such an interpretation exists, but at least we know what to look for.

24. The Veil of Ignorance

The idea of the original position is to set up a fair procedure so that any principles agreed to will be just. The aim is to use the notion of pure procedural justice as a basis of theory. Somehow we must nullify the effects of specific contingencies which put men at odds and tempt them to exploit social and natural circumstances to their own advantage. Now in order to do this I assume that the parties are situated behind a veil of ignorance. They do not know how the various alternatives will affect their own particular case and they are obliged to evaluate principles solely on the basis of general considerations.[7]

It is assumed, then, that the parties do not know certain kinds of particular facts. First of all, no one knows his place in society, his class position or social status; nor does he know his fortune in the distribution of natural assets and abilities, his intelligence and strength, and the like. Nor, again, does anyone know his conception of the good, the particulars of his rational plan of life, or even the special features of his psychology such as his aversion to risk or liability to optimism or pessimism. More than this, I assume that the parties do not know the particular circumstances of their own society. That is, they do not know its economic or political situation, or the level of civilization and culture it has been able to achieve. The persons in the original position have no information as to which generation they belong. These broader restrictions on knowledge are appropriate in part because questions of social justice arise between generations as well as within them, for example, the question of the appropriate rate of capital saving and of the conservation of natural resources and the environment of nature. There is also, theoretically anyway, the question of a reasonable genetic policy. In these cases too, in order to carry through the idea of the original position, the parties must not know the contingencies that set them in opposition. They must choose principles the consequences of which they are prepared to live with whatever generation they turn out to belong to.

As far as possible, then, the only particular facts which the parties know is that their society is subject to the circumstances of justice and whatever this implies. It is taken for granted, however, that they know the general facts about human society. They understand political affairs and the principles of economic theory; they know the basis of social organization and the laws of human psychology. Indeed, the parties are presumed to know whatever general facts affect the choice of the principles of justice. There are no limitations on general information, that is, on general laws and theories, since conceptions of justice must be adjusted to the characteristics of the systems of social cooperation which they are to regulate, and there is no reason to rule out these facts. It is, for example, a consideration against a conception of justice that, in view of the laws of moral psychology, men would not acquire a desire to act upon it even when the institutions of their society satisfied it. For in this case there would be difficulty in securing the stability of social cooperation. An important feature of a conception of justice is that it should generate its own support. Its principles should be such that when they are embodied in the basic structure of society men tend to acquire the corresponding sense of justice and develop a desire to act in accordance with its principles. In this case a conception of justice is stable. This kind of general information is admissible in the original position.

The notion of the veil of ignorance raises several difficulties. Some may object that the exclusion of nearly all particular information makes it difficult to grasp what is meant by the original position. Thus it may be helpful to observe that one or more persons can at any time enter this position, or perhaps better, simulate the deliberations of this hypothetical situation, simply by reasoning in accordance with the appropriate restrictions. In arguing for a conception of justice we must be sure that it is among the permitted alternatives and satisfies the stipulated formal constraints. No considerations can be advanced in its favor unless they would be rational ones for us to urge were we to lack the kind of knowledge that is excluded. The evaluation of principles must proceed in terms of the general consequences of their public recognition and universal application, it being assumed that they will be complied with by everyone. To say that a certain conception of justice would be chosen in the original position is equivalent to saying that rational deliberation satisfying certain conditions and restrictions would reach a certain conclusion. If necessary, the argument to this result could be set out more formally. I shall, however, speak throughout in terms of the notion of the original position. It is more economical and suggestive, and brings out certain essential features that otherwise one might easily overlook.

These remarks show that the original position is not to be thought of as a general assembly which includes at one moment everyone who will live at some time; or, much less, as an assembly of everyone who could live at some time. It is not a gathering of all actual or possible persons. If we conceived of the original position in either of these ways, the conception would cease to be a natural guide to intuition and would lack a clear sense. In any case, the original position must be interpreted so that one can at any time adopt its perspective. It must make no difference when one takes up this viewpoint, or who does so: the restrictions must be such that the same principles are always chosen. The veil of ignorance is a key condition in meeting this requirement. It insures not only that the information available is relevant, but that it is at all times the same.

It may be protested that the condition of the veil of ignorance is irrational. Surely, some may object, principles should be chosen in the light of all the knowledge available. There are various replies to this contention. Here I shall sketch those which emphasize the simplifications that need to be made if one is to have any theory at all. (Those based on the Kantian interpretation of the original position are given later, §40.) To begin with, it is clear that since the differences among the parties are unknown to them, and everyone is equally rational and similarly situated, each is convinced by the same arguments. Therefore, we can view the agreement in the original position from the standpoint of one person selected at random. If anyone after due reflection prefers a conception of justice to another, then they all do, and a unanimous agreement can be reached. We can, to make the circumstances more vivid, imagine that the parties are required to communicate with each other through a referee as intermediary, and that he is to announce which alternatives have been suggested and the reasons offered in their support. He forbids the attempt to form coalitions, and

he informs the parties when they have come to an understanding. But such a referee is actually superfluous, assuming that the deliberations of the parties must be similar.

Thus there follows the very important consequence that the parties have no basis for bargaining in the usual sense. No one knows his situation in society nor his natural assets, and therefore no one is in a position to tailor principles to his advantage. We might imagine that one of the contractees threatens to hold out unless the others agree to principles favorable to him. But how does he know which principles are especially in his interests? The same holds for the formation of coalitions: if a group were to decide to band together to the disadvantage of the others, they would not know how to favor themselves in the choice of principles. Even if they could get everyone to agree to their proposal, they would have no assurance that it was to their advantage, since they cannot identify themselves either by name or description. The one case where this conclusion fails is that of saving. Since the persons in the original position know that they are contemporaries (taking the present time of entry interpretation), they can favor their generation by refusing to make any sacrifices at all for their successors; they simply acknowledge the principle that no one has a duty to save for posterity. Previous generations have saved or they have not; there is nothing the parties can now do to affect that. So in this instance the veil of ignorance fails to secure the desired result. Therefore, to handle the question of justice between generations, I modify the motivation assumption and add a further constraint (§22). With these adjustments, no generation is able to formulate principles especially designed to advance its own cause and some significant limits on savings principles can be derived (§44). Whatever a person's temporal position, each is forced to choose for all.[8]

The restrictions on particular information in the original position are, then, of fundamental importance. Without them we would not be able to work out any definite theory of justice at all. We would have to be content with a vague formula stating that justice is what would be agreed to without being able to say much, if anything, about the substance of the agreement itself. The formal constraints of the concept of right, those applying to principles directly, are not sufficient for our purpose. The veil of ignorance makes possible a unanimous choice of a particular conception of justice. Without these limitations on knowledge the bargaining problem of the original position would be hopelessly complicated. Even if theoretically a solution were to exist, we would not, at present anyway, be able to determine it.

The notion of the veil of ignorance is implicit, I think, in Kant's ethics (§40). Nevertheless the problem of defining the knowledge of the parties and of characterizing the alternatives open to them has often been passed over, even by contract theories. Sometimes the situation definitive of moral deliberation is presented in such an indeterminate way that one cannot ascertain how it will turn out. Thus Perry's doctrine is essentially contractarian: he holds that social and personal integration must proceed by entirely different principles, the latter by rational prudence, the former by the concurrence of persons of good will. He would appear to reject utilitarianism on much the same grounds suggested earlier: namely, that it improperly extends the principle of choice for one person to choices facing society. The right course of action is characterized as that which best advances social aims as these would be formulated by reflective agreement, given that the parties have full knowledge of the circumstances and are moved by a benevolent concern for one another's interests. No effort is made, however, to specify in any precise way the possible outcomes of this sort of agreement. Indeed, without a far more elaborate account, no conclusions can be drawn.9 I do not wish here to criticize others; rather, I want to explain the necessity for what may seem at times like so many irrelevant details.

Now the reasons for the veil of ignorance go beyond mere simplicity. We want to define the original position so that we get the desired solution. If a knowledge of particulars is allowed, then the outcome is biased by arbitrary contingencies. As already observed, to each according to his threat advantage is not a principle of justice. If the original position is to yield agreements that are just, the parties must be fairly situated and treated equally as moral persons. The arbitrariness of the world must be corrected for by adjusting the circumstances of the initial contractual situation. Moreover, if in choosing principles we required unanimity even when there is full information, only a few rather obvious cases could be decided. A conception of justice based on unanimity in these circumstances would indeed be weak and trivial. But once knowledge is excluded, the requirement of unanimity is not out of place and the fact that it can be satisfied is of great importance. It enables us to say of the preferred conception of justice that it represents a genuine reconciliation of interests.

A final comment. For the most part I shall suppose that the parties possess all general information. No general facts are closed to them. I do this mainly to avoid complications. Nevertheless a conception of justice is to be the public basis of the terms of social cooperation. Since common understanding necessitates certain bounds on the complexity of principles, there may likewise be limits on the use of theoretical knowledge in the original position. Now clearly it would be very difficult to classify and to grade the complexity of the various sorts of general facts. I shall make no attempt to do this. We do however recognize an intricate theoretical construction when we meet one. Thus it seems reasonable to say that other things equal one conception of justice is to be preferred to another when it is founded upon markedly simpler general facts, and its choice does not depend upon elaborate calculations in the light of a vast array of theoretically defined possibilities. It is desirable that the grounds for a public conception of justice should be evident to everyone when circumstances permit. This consideration favors, I believe, the two principles of justice over the criterion of utility.

NOTES

1 As the text suggests, I shall regard Locke's *Second Treatise of Government*, Rousseau's *The Social Contract*, and Kant's ethical works beginning with *The Foundations of the Metaphysics of Morals* as definitive of the contract tradition. For all of its greatness, Hobbes's *Leviathan* raises special problems. A general historical survey is provided by J.W. Gough, *The Social Contract*, 2nd ed. (Oxford: The Clarendon Press, 1957), and Otto Gierke, *Natural Law and the Theory of Society*, trans. with an introduction by Ernest Barker (Cambridge: The University Press, 1934). A presentation of the contract view as primarily an ethical theory is to be found in G.R. Grice, *The Grounds of Moral Judgment* (Cambridge: The University Press, 1967). See also §19, note 30.

2 Kant is clear that the original agreement is hypothetical. See *The Metaphysics of Morals*, pt. I *(Rechtslehre)*, especially §§47, 52; and pt. II of the essay "Concerning the Common Saying: This May Be True in Theory but It Does Not Apply in Practice," in *Kant's Political Writings*, ed. Hans Reiss and trans. by H.B. Nisbet (Cambridge: The University Press, 1970), 73-87. See Georges Vlachos, *La Pensée politique de Kant* (Paris: Presses Universitaires de France, 1962), 326-35; and J.G. Murphy, *Kant: The Philosophy of Right* (London: Macmillan, 1970), 109-12, 133-36, for a further discussion.

3 For the formulation of this intuitive ideal I am indebted to Allan Gibbard.

4 The process of mutual adjustment of principles and considered judgments is not peculiar to moral philosophy. See Nelson Goodman, *Fact, Fiction, and Forecast* (Cambridge, MA: Harvard University Press, 1955), 65-68, for parallel remarks concerning the justification of the principles of deductive and inductive inference.

5 Henri Poincaré remarks: "Il nous faut une faculté qui nous fasse voir le but de loin, et, cette faculté, c'est l'intuition." *La Valeur de la science* (Paris: Flammarion, 1909), 27.

6 *Manuel d'économie politique* (Paris, 1909), Ch. III, §23. Pareto says: "L'équilibre résulte précisément de cette opposition des goûts et des obstacles."

7 The veil of ignorance is so natural a condition that something like it must have occurred to many. The formulation in the text is implicit, I believe, in Kant's doctrine of the categorical imperative, both in the way this procedural criterion is defined and the use Kant makes of it. Thus when Kant tells us to test our maxim by considering what would be the case were it a universal law of nature, he must suppose that we do not know our place within this imagined system of nature. See, for example, his discussion of the topic of practical judgment in *The Critique of Practical Reason*, Academy Edition, Vol. 5, 68-72. A similar restriction on information is found in J.C. Harsanyi, "Cardinal Utility in Welfare Economics and in the Theory of Risk-taking," *Journal of Political Economy*, Vol. 61 (1953). However, other aspects of Harsanyi's view are quite different, and he uses the restriction to develop a utilitarian theory. See the last paragraph of §27.

8 Rousseau, *The Social Contract*, Bk. II, Ch. IV, par. 5.

9 See R.B. Perry, *The General Theory of Value* (New York: Longmans, Green and Company, 1926), 674-82.

◆ ◆ ◆ ◆ ◆

ROBERT NOZICK

Excerpts from
Anarchy, State and Utopia

Distributive Justice

The minimal state is the most extensive state that can be justified. Any state more extensive violates people's rights. Yet many persons have put forth reasons purporting to justify a more extensive state. It is impossible within the compass of this book to examine all the reasons that have been put forth. Therefore, I shall focus upon those generally acknowledged to be most weighty and influential, to see precisely wherein they fail. In this chapter we consider the claim that a more extensive state is justified, because necessary (or the best instrument) to achieve distributive justice; in the next chapter we shall take up diverse other claims.

The term "distributive justice" is not a neutral one. Hearing the term "distribution," most people presume that some thing or mechanism uses some principle or criterion to give out a supply of things. Into this process of distributing shares some error may have crept. So it is an open question, at least, whether *re*distribution should take place; whether we should do again what has already been done once, though poorly. However, we are not in the position of children who have been given portions of pie by someone who now makes last minute adjustments to rectify careless cutting. There is no *central* distribution, no person or group entitled to control all the resources, jointly deciding how they are to be doled out. What each person gets, he gets from others who give to him in exchange for something, or as a gift. In a free society, diverse persons control different resources, and new holdings arise out of the voluntary exchanges and actions of persons. There is no more a distributing or distribution of shares than there is a distributing of mates in a society in which persons choose whom they shall marry. The total result is the product of many individual decisions which the different individuals involved are entitled to make. Some uses of the term "distribution," it is true, do not imply a previous distributing appropriately judged by some criterion (for example, "probability distribution"); nevertheless, despite the title of this chapter, it would be best to use a terminology that clearly is neutral. We shall speak of people's holdings; a principle of justice in holdings describes (part of) what justice tells us (requires) about holdings. I shall state first what I take to be the correct view about justice in holdings, and then turn to the discussion of alternate views.

Section I

The Entitlement Theory

The subject of justice in holdings consists of three major topics. The first is the *original acquisition of holdings*, the appropriation of unheld things. This includes the issues of how unheld things may come to be held, the process, or processes, by which unheld things may come to be held, the things that may come to be held by these processes, the extent of what comes to be held by a particular process, and so on. We shall refer to the complicated truth about this topic, which we shall not formulate here, as the principle of justice in acquisition. The second topic concerns the *transfer of holdings* from one person to another. By what processes may a person transfer holdings to another? How may a person acquire a holding from another who holds it? Under this topic come general descriptions of voluntary exchange, and gift and (on the other hand) fraud, as well as reference to particular conventional details fixed upon in a given society. The complicated truth about this subject (with placeholders for conventional details) we shall call the principle of justice in transfer. (And we shall suppose it also includes principles governing how a person may divest himself of a holding, passing it into an unheld state.)

If the world were wholly just, the following inductive definition would exhaustively cover the subject of justice in holdings.

1. A person who acquires a holding in accordance with the principle of justice in acquisition is entitled to that holding.
2. A person who acquires a holding in accordance with the principle of justice in transfer, from someone else entitled to the holding, is entitled to the holding.
3. No one is entitled to a holding except by (repeated) applications of 1 and 2.

The complete principle of distributive justice would say simply that a distribution is just if everyone is entitled to the holdings they possess under the distribution.

A distribution is just if it arises from another just distribution by legitimate means. The legitimate means of moving from one distribution to another are specified by the principle of justice in transfer. The legitimate first "moves" are specified by the principle of justice in acquisition.[1] Whatever arises from a just situation by just steps is itself just. The means of change specified by the principle of justice in transfer preserve justice. As correct rules of inference are truth-preserving, and any conclusion deduced via repeated application of such rules from only true premises is itself true, so the means of transition from one situation to another specified by the principle of justice in transfer are justice-preserving, and any situation actually arising from repeated transitions in accordance with the principle from a just situation is itself just. The parallel between justice-preserving transformations and truth-preserving transformations illuminates where it fails as well as where it holds. That a conclusion could have been deduced by truth-preserving means from premises that are true suffices to show its truth. That from a just situation a situation *could* have arisen via justice-preserving means does *not* suffice to show its justice. The fact that a thief's victims voluntarily *could* have

presented him with gifts does not entitle the thief to his ill-gotten gains. Justice in holdings is historical; it depends upon what actually has happened. We shall return to this point later.

Not all actual situations are generated in accordance with the two principles of justice in holdings: the principle of justice in acquisition and the principle of justice in transfer. Some people steal from others, or defraud them, or enslave them, seizing their product and preventing them from living as they choose, or forcibly exclude others from competing in exchanges. None of these are permissible modes of transition from one situation to another. And some persons acquire holdings by means not sanctioned by the principle of justice in acquisition. The existence of past injustice (previous violations of the first two principles of justice in holdings) raises the third major topic under justice in holdings: the rectification of injustice in holdings. If past injustice has shaped present holdings in various ways, some identifiable and some not, what now, if anything, ought to be done to rectify these injustices? What obligations do the performers of injustice have toward those whose position is worse than it would have been had the injustice not been done? Or, than it would have been had compensation been paid promptly? How, if at all, do things change if the beneficiaries and those made worse off are not the direct parties in the act of injustice, but, for example, their descendants? Is an injustice done to someone whose holding was itself based upon an unrectified injustice? How far back must one go in wiping clean the historical slate of injustices? What may victims of injustice permissibly do in order to rectify the injustices being done to them, including the many injustices done by persons acting through their government? I do not know of a thorough or theoretically sophisticated treatment of such issues. Idealizing greatly, let us suppose theoretical investigation will produce a principle of rectification. This principle uses historical information about previous situations and injustices done in them (as defined by the first two principles of justice and rights against interference), and information about the actual course of events that flowed from these injustices, until the present, and it yields a description (or descriptions) of holdings in the society. The principle of rectification presumably will make use of its best estimate of subjunctive information about what would have occurred (or a probability distribution over what might have occurred, using the expected value) if the injustice had not taken place. If the actual description of holdings turns out not to be one of the descriptions yielded by the principle, then one of the descriptions yielded must be realized.[2]

The general outlines of the theory of justice in holdings are that the holdings of a person are just if he is entitled to them by the principles of justice in acquisition and transfer, or by the principle of rectification of injustice (as specified by the first two principles). If each person's holdings are just, then the total set (distribution) of holdings is just. To turn these general outlines into a specific theory we would have to specify the details of each of the three principles of justice in holdings: the principle of acquisition of holdings, the principle of transfer of holdings, and the principle of rectification of violations of the first two principles. I shall not attempt that task here. (Locke's principle of justice in acquisition is discussed below.)

Historical Principles and End-Result Principles

The general outlines of the entitlement theory illuminate the nature and defects of other conceptions of distributive justice. The entitlement theory of justice in distribution is *historical*, whether a distribution is just depends upon how it came about. In contrast, *current time-slice principles* of justice hold that the justice of a distribution is determined by how things are distributed (who has what) as judged by some *structural* principle(s) of just distribution. A utilitarian who judges between any two distributions

by seeing which has the greater sum of utility and, if the sums tie, applies some fixed equality criterion to choose the more equal distribution, would hold a current time-slice principle of justice. As would someone who had a fixed schedule of trade-offs between the sum of happiness and equality. According to a current time-slice principle, all that needs to be looked at, in judging the justice of a distribution, is who ends up with what; in comparing any two distributions one need look only at the matrix presenting the distributions. No further information need be fed into a principle of justice. It is a consequence of such principles of justice that any two structurally identical distributions are equally just. (Two distributions are structurally identical if they present the same profile, but perhaps have different persons occupying the particular slots. My having ten and your having five, and my having five and your having ten are structurally identical distributions.) Welfare economics is the theory of current time-slice principles of justice. The subject is conceived as operating on matrices representing only current information about distribution. This, as well as some of the usual conditions (for example, the choice of distribution is invariant under relabeling of columns), guarantees that welfare economics will be a current time-slice theory, with all of its inadequacies.

Most persons do not accept current time-slice principles as constituting the whole story about distributive shares. They think it relevant in assessing the justice of a situation to consider not only the distribution it embodies, but also how that distribution came about. If some persons are in prison for murder or war crimes, we do not say that to assess the justice of the distribution in the society we must look only at what this person has, and that person has, and that person has, ... at the current time. We think it relevant to ask whether someone did something so that he *deserved* to be punished, deserved to have a lower share. Most will agree to the relevance of further information with regard to punishments and penalties. Consider also desired things. One

516 CONTEMPORARY THEORIES OF DISTRIBUTION AND PROPERTY

traditional socialist view is that workers are entitled to the product and full fruits of their labor; they have earned it; a distribution is unjust if it does not give the workers what they are entitled to. Such entitlements are based upon some past history. No socialist holding this view would find it comforting to be told that because the actual distribution A happens to coincide structurally with the one he desires D, A therefore is no less just than D; it differs only in that the "parasitic" owners of capital receive under A what the workers are entitled to under D, and the workers receive under A what the owners are entitled to under D, namely very little. This socialist rightly, in my view, holds onto the notions of earning, producing, entitlement, desert, and so forth, and he rejects current time-slice principles that look only to the structure of the resulting set of holdings. (The set of holdings resulting from what? Isn't it implausible that how holdings are produced and come to exist has no effect at all on who should hold what?) His mistake lies in his view of what entitlements arise out of what sorts of productive processes.

We construe the position we discuss too narrowly by speaking of *current* time-slice principles. Nothing is changed if structural principles operate upon a time sequence of current time-slice profiles and, for example, give someone more now to counterbalance the less he has had earlier. A utilitarian or an egalitarian or any mixture of the two over time will inherit the difficulties of his more myopic comrades. He is not helped by the fact that *some* of the information others consider relevant in assessing a distribution is reflected, unrecoverably, in past matrices. Henceforth, we shall refer to such unhistorical principles of distributive justice, including the current time-slice principles, as *end-result principles* or *end-state principles*.

In contrast to end-result principles of justice, *historical principles* of justice hold that past circumstances or actions of people can create differential entitlements or differential deserts to things. An injustice can be worked by moving from one dis-

tribution to another structurally identical one, for the second, in profile the same, may violate people's entitlements or deserts; it may not fit the actual history.

Patterning

The entitlement principles of justice in holdings that we have sketched are historical principles of justice. To better understand their precise character, we shall distinguish them from another subclass of the historical principles. Consider, as an example, the principle of distribution according to moral merit. This principle requires that total distributive shares vary directly with moral merit; no person should have a greater share than anyone whose moral merit is greater. (If moral merit could be not merely ordered but measured on an interval or ratio scale, stronger principles could be formulated.) Or consider the principle that results by substituting "usefulness to society" for "moral merit" in the previous principle. Or instead of "distribute according to moral merit," or "distribute according to usefulness to society," we might consider "distribute according to the weighted sum of moral merit, usefulness to society, and need," with the weights of the different dimensions equal. Let us call a principle of distribution *patterned* if it specifies that a distribution is to vary along with some natural dimension, weighted sum of natural dimensions, or lexicographic ordering of natural dimensions. And let us say a distribution is patterned if it accords with some patterned principle. (I speak of natural dimensions, admittedly without a general criterion for them, because for any set of holdings some artificial dimensions can be gimmicked up to vary along with the distribution of the set.) The principle of distribution in accordance with moral merit is a patterned historical principle, which specifies a patterned distribution. "Distribute according to I.Q." is a patterned principle that looks to information not contained in distributional matrices. It is not historical, however, in that it does not look to any past actions creating differential entitlements to evaluate a distribution; it requires only distributional matrices whose columns are labeled by I.Q. scores. The distribution in a society, however, may be composed of such simple patterned distributions, without itself being simply patterned. Different sectors may operate different patterns, or some combination of patterns may operate in different proportions across a society. A distribution composed in this manner, from a small number of patterned distributions, we also shall term "patterned." And we extend the use of "pattern" to include the overall designs put forth by combinations of end-state principles.

Almost every suggested principle of distributive justice is patterned: to each according to his moral merit, or needs, or marginal product, or how hard he tries, or the weighted sum of the foregoing, and so on. The principle of entitlement we have sketched is *not* patterned.[3] There is no one natural dimension or weighted sum or combination of a small number of natural dimensions that yields the distributions generated in accordance with the principle of entitlement. The set of holdings that results when some persons receive their marginal products, others win at gambling, others receive a share of their mate's income, others receive gifts from foundations, others receive interest on loans, others receive gifts from admirers, others receive returns on investment, others make for themselves much of what they have, others find things, and so on, will not be patterned. Heavy strands of patterns will run through it; significant portions of the variance in holdings will be accounted for by pattern-variables. If most people most of the time choose to transfer some of their entitlements to others only in exchange for something from them, then a large part of what many people hold will vary with what they held that others wanted. More details are provided by the theory of marginal productivity. But gifts to relatives, charitable donations, bequests to children, and the like, are not best conceived, in the first instance, in this manner. Ignoring the strands of pattern, let us suppose for

the moment that a distribution actually arrived at by the operation of the principle of entitlement is random with respect to any pattern. Though the resulting set of holdings will be unpatterned, it will not be incomprehensible, for it can be seen as arising from the operation of a small number of principles. These principles specify how an initial distribution may arise (the principle of acquisition of holdings) and how distributions may be transformed into others (the principle of transfer of holdings). The process whereby the set of holdings is generated will be intelligible, though the set of holdings itself that results from this process will be unpatterned.

The writings of F.A. Hayek focus less than is usually done upon what patterning distributive justice requires. Hayek argues that we cannot know enough about each person's situation to distribute to each according to his moral merit (but would justice demand we do so if we did have this knowledge?); and he goes on to say, "our objection is against all attempts to impress upon society a deliberately chosen pattern of distribution, whether it be an order of equality or of inequality." However, Hayek concludes that in a free society there will be distribution in accordance with value rather than moral merit; that is, in accordance with the perceived value of a person's actions and services to others. Despite his rejection of a patterned conception of distributive justice, Hayek himself suggests a pattern he thinks justifiable: distribution in accordance with the perceived benefits given to others, leaving room for the complaint that a free society does not realize exactly this pattern. Stating this patterned strand of a free capitalist society more precisely, we get "To each according to how much he benefits others who have the resources for benefiting those who benefit them." This will seem arbitrary unless some acceptable initial set of holdings is specified, or unless it is held that the operation of the system over time washes out any significant effects from the initial set of holdings. As an example of the latter, if almost anyone would have bought a car from Henry Ford, the supposition that it was an arbitrary matter who held the money then (and so bought) would not place Henry Ford's earnings under a cloud. In any event, *his* coming to hold it is not arbitrary. Distribution according to benefits to others *is* a major patterned strand in a free capitalist society, as Hayek correctly points out, but it is only a strand and does not constitute the whole pattern of a system of entitlements (namely, inheritance, gifts for arbitrary reasons, charity, and so on) or a standard that one should insist a society fit. Will people tolerate for long a system yielding distributions that they believe are unpatterned? No doubt people will not long accept a distribution they believe is *unjust*. People want their society to be and to look just. But must the look of justice reside in a resulting pattern rather than in the underlying generating principles? We are in no position to conclude that the inhabitants of a society embodying an entitlement conception of justice in holdings will find it unacceptable. Still, it must be granted that were people's reasons for transferring some of their holdings to others always irrational or arbitrary, we would find this disturbing. (Suppose people always determined what holdings they would transfer, and to whom, by using a random device.) We feel more comfortable upholding the justice of an entitlement system if most of the transfers under it are done for reasons. This does not mean necessarily that all deserve what holdings they receive. It means only that there is a purpose or point to someone's transferring a holding to one person rather than to another; that usually we can see what the transferrer thinks he's gaining, what cause he thinks he's serving, what goals he thinks he's helping to achieve, and so forth. Since in a capitalist society people often transfer holdings to others in accordance with how much they perceive these others benefiting them, the fabric constituted by the individual transactions and transfers is largely reasonable and intelligible.[4] (Gifts to loved ones, bequests to children, charity to the needy also are nonarbitrary components of the fabric.) In stressing the large strand of distribution in accordance with benefit to others, Hayek shows the point of many transfers, and so shows that the system of transfer of entitlements is not just spinning its gears aimlessly. The system of entitlements is defensible when constituted by the individual aims of individual transactions. No overarching aim is needed, no distributional pattern is required.

To think that the task of a theory of distributive justice is to fill in the blank in "to each according to his _____" is to be predisposed to search for a pattern, and the separate treatment of "from each according to his _____" treats production and distribution as two separate and independent issues. On an entitlement view these are *not* two separate questions. Whoever makes something, having bought or contracted for all other held resources used in the process (transferring some of his holdings for these cooperating factors), is entitled to it. The situation is *not* one of something's getting made, and there being an open question of who is to get it. Things come into the world already attached to people having entitlements over them. From the point of view of the historical entitlement conception of justice in holdings, those who start afresh to complete "to each according to his _____" treat objects as if they appeared from nowhere, out of nothing. A complete theory of justice might cover this limit case as well; perhaps here is a use for the usual conceptions of distributive justice.

So entrenched are maxims of the usual form that perhaps we should present the entitlement conception as a competitor. Ignoring acquisition and rectification, we might say:

> From each according to what he chooses to do, to each according to what he makes for himself (perhaps with the contracted aid of others) and what others choose to do for him and choose to give him of what they've been given previously (under this maxim) and haven't yet expended or transferred.

This, the discerning reader will have noticed, has its defects as a slogan. So as a summary and great simplification (and not as a maxim with any independent meaning) we have:

From each as they choose, to each as they are chosen.

How Liberty Upsets Patterns

It is not clear how those holding alternative conceptions of distributive justice can reject the entitlement conception of justice in holdings. For suppose a distribution favored by one of these non-entitlement conceptions is realized. Let us suppose it is your favorite one and let us call this distribution D_1; perhaps everyone has an equal share, perhaps shares vary in accordance with some dimension you treasure. Now suppose that Wilt Chamberlain is greatly in demand by basketball teams, being a great gate attraction. (Also suppose contracts run only for a year, with players being free agents.) He signs the following sort of contract with a team: In each home game, twenty-five cents from the price of each ticket of admission goes to him. (We ignore the question of whether he is "gouging" the owners, letting them look out for themselves.) The season starts, and people cheerfully attend his team's games; they buy their tickets, each time dropping a separate twenty-five cents of their admission price into a special box with Chamberlain's name on it. They are excited about seeing him play; it is worth the total admission price to them. Let us suppose that in one season one million persons attend his home games, and Wilt Chamberlain winds up with $250,000, a much larger sum than the average income and larger even than anyone else has. Is he entitled to this income? Is this new distribution D_2, unjust? If so, why? There is *no* question about whether each of the people was entitled to the control over the resources they held in D_1; because that was the distribution (your favorite) that (for the purposes of argument)

we assumed was acceptable. Each of these persons *chose* to give twenty-five cents of their money to Chamberlain. They could have spent it on going to the movies, or on candy bars, or on copies of *Dissent* magazine, or of *Monthly Review*. But they all, at least one million of them, converged on giving it to Wilt Chamberlain in exchange for watching him play basketball. If D_1 was a just distribution, and people voluntarily moved from it to D_2, transferring parts of their shares they were given under D_1 (what was it for if not to do something with?), isn't D_2 also just? If the people were entitled to dispose of the resources to which they were entitled (under D_1), didn't this include their being entitled to give it to, or exchange it with, Wilt Chamberlain? Can anyone else complain on grounds of justice? Each other person already has his legitimate share under D_1. Under D_1, there is nothing that anyone has that anyone else has a claim of justice against. After someone transfers something to Wilt Chamberlain, third parties *still* have their legitimate shares; *their* shares are not changed. By what process could such a transfer among two persons give rise to a legitimate claim of distributive justice on a portion of what was transferred, by a third party who had no claim of justice on any holding of the others *before* the transfer?[5] To cut off objections irrelevant here, we might imagine the exchanges occurring in a socialist society, after hours. After playing whatever basketball he does in his daily work, or doing whatever other daily work he does, Wilt Chamberlain decides to put in *overtime* to earn additional money. (First his work quota is set; he works time over that.) Or imagine it is a skilled juggler people like to see, who puts on shows after hours.

Why might someone work overtime in a society in which it is assumed their needs are satisfied? Perhaps because they care about things other than needs. I like to write in books that I read, and to have easy access to books for browsing at odd hours. It would be very pleasant and convenient to have the resources of Widener Library in my back yard. No society, I assume, will provide such resources close to each person who would like them as part of his regular allotment (under D_1). Thus, persons either must do without some extra things that they want, or be allowed to do something extra to get some of these things. On what basis could the inequalities that would eventuate be forbidden? Notice also that small factories would spring up in a socialist society, unless forbidden. I melt down some of my personal possessions (under D_1) and build a machine out of the material. I offer you, and others, a philosophy lecture once a week in exchange for your cranking the handle on my machine, whose products I exchange for yet other things, and so on. (The raw materials used by the machine are given to me by others who possess them under D_1, in exchange for hearing lectures.) Each person might participate to gain things over and above their allotment under D_1. Some persons even might want to leave their job in socialist industry and work full time in this private sector. I shall say something more about these issues in the next chapter. Here I wish merely to note how private property even in means of production would occur in a socialist society that did not forbid people to use as they wished some of the resources they are given under the socialist distribution D_1. The socialist society would have to forbid capitalist acts between consenting adults.

The general point illustrated by the Wilt Chamberlain example and the example of the entrepreneur in a socialist society is that no end-state principle or distributional patterned principle of justice can be continuously realized without continuous interference with people's lives. Any favored pattern would be transformed into one unfavored by the principle, by people choosing to act in various ways; for example, by people exchanging goods and services with other people, or giving things to other people, things the transferrers are entitled to under the favored distributional pattern. To maintain a pattern one must either continually interfere to stop people from transferring resources as they wish to, or continually (or periodically) interfere to take from some persons resources that others for some reason chose to transfer to them. (But if some time limit is to be set on how long people may keep resources others voluntarily transfer to them, why let them keep these resources for *any* period of time? Why not have immediate confiscation?) It might be objected that all persons voluntarily will choose to refrain from actions which would upset the pattern. This presupposes unrealistically (1) that all will most want to maintain the pattern (are those who don't, to be "re-educated" or forced to undergo "self-criticism"?), (2) that each can gather enough information about his own actions and the ongoing activities of others to discover which of his actions will upset the pattern, and (3) that diverse and far-flung persons can coordinate their actions to dovetail into the pattern. Compare the manner in which the market is neutral among persons' desires, as it reflects and transmits widely scattered information via prices, and coordinates persons' activities.

It puts things perhaps a bit too strongly to say that every patterned (or end-state) principle is liable to be thwarted by the voluntary actions of the individual parties transferring some of their shares they receive under the principle. For perhaps some *very* weak patterns are not so thwarted.[6] Any distributional pattern with any egalitarian component is overturnable by the voluntary actions of individual persons over time; as is every patterned condition with sufficient content so as actually to have been proposed as presenting the central core of distributive justice. Still, given the possibility that some weak conditions or patterns may not be unstable in this way, it would be better to formulate an explicit description of the kind of interesting and contentful patterns under discussion, and to prove a theorem about their instability. Since the weaker the patterning, the more likely it is that the entitlement system itself satisfies it, a plausible conjecture is that any patterning either is unstable or is satisfied by the entitlement system.

Sen's Argument

Our conclusions are reinforced by considering a recent general argument of Amartya K. Sen. Suppose individual rights are interpreted as the right to choose which of two alternatives is to be more highly ranked in a social ordering of the alternatives. Add the weak condition that if one alternative unanimously is preferred to another then it is ranked higher by the social ordering. If there are two different individuals each with individual rights, interpreted as above, over different pairs of alternatives (having no members in common), then for some possible preference rankings of the alternatives by the individuals, there is no linear social ordering. For suppose that person *A* has the right to decide among (*X, Y*) and person *B* has the right to decide among (*Z, W*); and suppose their individual preferences are as follows (and that there are no other individuals). Person *A* prefers *W* to *X* to *Y* to *Z*, and person *B* prefers *Y* to *Z* to *W* to *X*. By the unanimity condition, in the social ordering *W* is preferred to *X* (since each individual prefers it to *X*), and *Y* is preferred to *Z* (since each individual prefers it to *Z*). Also in the social ordering, *X* is preferred to *Y*, by person *A*'s right of choice among these two alternatives. Combining these three binary rankings, we get *W* preferred to *X* preferred to *Y* preferred to *Z*, in the social ordering. However, by person *B*'s right of choice, *Z* must be preferred to *W* in the social ordering. There is no transitive social ordering satisfying all these conditions, and the social ordering, therefore, is nonlinear. Thus far, Sen.

The trouble stems from treating an individual's right to choose among alternatives as the right to determine the relative ordering of these alternatives within a social ordering. The alternative which has individuals rank *pairs* of alternatives, and separately rank the individual alternatives is no better; their ranking of pairs feeds into some method of amalgamating preferences to yield a social ordering of pairs; and the choice among the alternatives in the highest ranked pair in the social ordering is made by the individual with the right to decide between this pair. This system also has the result that an alternative may be selected although *everyone* prefers some other alternative; for example, *A* selects *X* over *Y*, where (*X, Y*) somehow is the highest ranked *pair* in the social ordering of pairs, although everyone, including *A*, prefers *W* to *X*. (But the choice person *A* was given, however, was only between *X* and *Y*.)

A more appropriate view of individual rights is as follows. Individual rights are co-possible; each person may exercise his rights as he chooses. The exercise of these rights fixes some features of the world. Within the constraints of these fixed features, a choice may be made by a social choice mechanism based upon a social ordering; if there are any choices left to make! Rights do not determine a social ordering but instead set the constraints within which a social choice is to be made, by excluding certain alternatives, fixing others, and so on. (If I have a right to choose to live in New York or in Massachusetts, and I choose Massachusetts, then alternatives involving my living in New York are not appropriate objects to be entered in a social ordering.) Even if all possible alternatives are ordered first, apart from anyone's rights, the situation is not changed: for then the highest ranked alternative *that is not excluded by anyone's exercise of his rights* is instituted. Rights do not determine the position of an alternative or the relative position of two alternatives in a social ordering; they *operate upon* a social ordering to constrain the choice it can yield.

If entitlements to holdings are rights to dispose of them, then social choice must take place *within* the constraints of how people choose to exercise these rights. If any patterning is legitimate, it falls within the domain of social choice, and hence is constrained by people's rights. *How else can one cope with Sen's result?* The alternative of first having a social ranking with rights exercised within *its* constraints is no alternative at all. Why not just select the top-ranked alternative and forget about rights? If that top-ranked alternative itself leaves some room for individual choice (and here is where "rights" of choice is supposed to enter in) there must be something to stop these choices from transforming it into another alternative. Thus Sen's argument leads us again to the result that patterning requires continuous interference with individuals' actions and choices.

Redistribution and Property Rights

Apparently, patterned principles allow people to choose to expend upon themselves, but not upon others, those resources they are entitled to (or rather, receive) under some favored distributional pattern D_1. For if each of several persons chooses to expend some of his D_1 resources upon one other person, then that other person will receive more than his D_1 share, disturbing the favored distributional pattern. Maintaining a distributional pattern is individualism with a vengeance! Patterned distributional principles do not give people what entitlement principles do, only better distributed. For they do not give the right to choose what to do with what one has; they do not give the right to choose to pursue an end involving (intrinsically; or as a means) the enhancement of another's position. To such views, families are disturbing; for within a family occur transfers that upset the favored distributional pattern. Either families themselves become units to which distribution takes place, the column occupiers (on what rationale?), or loving behavior is forbidden. We should note in passing the ambivalent position of radicals toward the family. Its loving relationships are seen as a model to be emulated and extended across the whole society, at the same time that it is denounced as a suffocating institution to be broken and condemned as a focus of parochial concerns that interfere with achieving radical goals. Need we say that it is not appropriate to enforce across the wider society the relationships of love and care appropriate within a family, relationships which are voluntarily undertaken?[7] Incidentally, love is an interesting instance of another relationship that is historical, in that (like justice) it depends upon what actually occurred. An adult may come to love another because of the other's characteristics; but it is the other person, and not the characteristics, that is loved. The love is not transferrable to someone else with the same characteristics, even to one who "scores" higher for these characteristics. And the love endures through changes of the characteristics that gave rise to it. One loves the particular person one actually encountered. Why love is historical, attaching to persons in this way and not to characteristics, is an interesting and puzzling question.

Proponents of patterned principles of distributive justice focus upon criteria for determining who is to receive holdings; they consider the reasons for which someone should have something, and also the total picture of holdings. Whether or not it is better to give than to receive, proponents of patterned principles ignore giving altogether. In considering the distribution of goods, income, and so forth, their theories are theories of recipient justice; they completely ignore any right a person might have to give something to someone. Even in exchanges where each party is simultaneously giver and recipient, patterned principles of justice focus only upon the recipient role and its supposed rights. Thus discussions tend to focus on whether people (should) have a right to inherit, rather than on whether people (should) have a right to bequeath or on whether persons who have a right to hold also have a right to choose that others hold in their place. I lack a good explanation of why the usual theories of distributive justice are so recipient oriented; ignoring givers and transferrers and their rights is of a piece with ignoring producers and their entitlements. But why is it *all* ignored?

Patterned principles of distributive justice necessitate *re*distributive activities. The likelihood is small that any actual freely-arrived-at set of holdings fits a given pattern; and the likelihood is nil that it will continue to fit the pattern as people exchange and give. From the point of view of an entitlement theory, redistribution is a serious matter indeed, involving, as it does, the violation of people's rights. (An exception is those takings that fall under the principle of the rectification of injustices.) From other points of view, also, it is serious.

Taxation of earnings from labor is on a par with forced labor.[8] Some persons find this claim obviously true: taking the earnings of n hours labor is like taking n hours from the person; it is like forcing the person to work n hours for another's purpose. Others find the claim absurd. But even these, *if* they object to forced labor, would oppose forcing unemployed hippies to work for the benefit of the needy.[9] And they would also object to forcing each person to work five extra hours each week for the benefit of the needy. But a system that takes five hours' wages in taxes does not seem to them like one that forces someone to work five hours, since it offers the person forced a wider range of choice in activities than does taxation in kind with the particular labor specified. (But we can imagine a gradation of systems of forced labor, from one that specifies a particular activity, to one that gives a choice among two activities, to ...; and so on up.) Furthermore, people envisage a system with something like a proportional tax on everything above the amount necessary for basic needs. Some think this does not force someone to work extra hours, since there is no fixed number of extra hours he is forced to work, and since he can avoid the tax entirely by earning only enough to cover his basic needs. This is a very uncharacteristic view of forcing for those who *also* think people are forced to do something *whenever* the alternatives they face are considerably worse. However, *neither* view is correct. The fact, that others intentionally intervene, in violation of a side constraint against aggression, to threaten force to limit the alternatives, in this case to paying taxes or (presumably the worse alternative) bare subsistence, makes the taxation system one of forced labor and distinguishes it from other cases of limited choices which are not forcings.

The man who chooses to work longer to gain an income more than sufficient for his basic needs prefers some extra goods or services to the leisure and activities he could perform during the possible non-working hours; whereas the man who chooses not to work the extra time prefers the leisure activities to the extra goods or services he could acquire by working more. Given this, if it would be illegitimate for a tax system to seize some of a man's leisure (forced labor) for the purpose of serving the needy, how can it be legitimate for a tax system to seize some of a man's goods for that purpose? Why should we treat the man whose happiness requires certain material goods or services differently from the man whose preferences and desires make such goods unnecessary for his happiness? Why should the man who prefers seeing a movie (and who has to earn money for a ticket) be open to the required call to aid the needy, while the person who prefers looking at a sunset (and hence need earn no extra money) is not? Indeed, isn't it surprising that redistributionists choose to ignore the man whose pleasures are so easily attainable without extra labor, while adding yet another burden to the poor unfortunate who must work for his pleasures? If anything, one would have expected the reverse. Why is the person with the nonmaterial or nonconsumption desire allowed to proceed unimpeded to his most favored feasible alternative, whereas the man whose pleasures or desires involve material things and who must work for extra money (thereby serving whomever considers his activities valuable enough to pay him) is constrained in what he can realize? Perhaps there is no difference in principle. And perhaps some think the answer concerns merely administrative convenience. (These questions and issues will not disturb those who think that forced labor to serve the needy or to realize some favored end-state pattern is acceptable.) In a fuller discussion we would have (and want) to extend our argument to include interest, entrepreneurial profits, and so on. Those who doubt that this extension can be carried through, and who draw the line here at taxation of income from labor, will have to state rather complicated patterned *historical* principles of distributive justice, since end-state principles would not distinguish *sources* of income in any way. It is enough for now to get away from end-state principles and to make clear how various patterned principles are dependent upon particular views about the sources or the illegitimacy or the lesser legitimacy of profits, interest, and so on; which particular views may well be mistaken.

What sort of right over others does a legally institutionalized end-state pattern give one? The central core of the notion of a property right in X, relative to which other parts of the notion are to be explained, is the right to determine what shall be done with X; the right to choose which of the constrained set of options concerning X shall be realized or attempted. The constraints are set by other principles or laws operating in the society; in our theory, by the Lockean rights people possess (under the minimal state). My property rights in my knife allow me to leave it where I will, but not in your chest. I may choose which of the acceptable options involving the knife is to be realized. This notion of property helps us to understand why earlier theorists spoke of people as having property in themselves and their labor. They viewed each person as having a right to decide what would become of himself and what he would do, and as having a right to reap the benefits of what he did.

This right of selecting the alternative to be realized from the constrained set of alternatives may be held by an *individual* or by a *group* with some procedure for reaching a joint decision; or the right may be passed back and forth, so that one year I decide what's to become of X, and the next year you do (with the alternative of destruction, perhaps, being excluded). Or, during the same time period, some types of decisions about X may be made by me, and others by you. And so on. We lack an adequate, fruitful, analytical apparatus for classifying the *types* of constraints on the set of options among which choices are to be made, and the *types* of ways decision powers can be held, divided, and amalgamated. A *theory* of property would, among other things, contain such a classification of constraints and decision modes, and from a small number of principles would follow a host of interesting statements about the *consequences* and effects of certain combinations of constraints and modes of decision.

When end-result principles of distributive justice are built into the legal structure of a society, they (as do most patterned principles) give each citizen an enforceable claim to some portion of the total social product; that is, to some portion of the sum total of the individually and jointly made products. This total product is produced by individuals laboring, using means of production others have saved to bring into existence, by people organizing production or creating means to produce new things or things in a new way. It is on this batch of individual activities that patterned distributional principles give each individual an enforceable claim. Each person has a claim to the activities and the products of other persons, independently of whether the other persons enter into particular relationships that give rise to these claims, and independently of whether they voluntarily take these claims upon themselves, in charity or in exchange for something.

Whether it is done through taxation on wages or on wages over a certain amount, or through seizure of profits, or through there being a big *social pot* so that it's not clear what's coming from where and what's going where, patterned principles of distributive justice involve appropriating the actions of other persons. Seizing the results of someone's labor is equivalent to seizing hours from him and directing him to carry on various activities. If people force you to do certain work, or unrewarded work, for a certain period of time, they decide what you are to do and what purposes your work is to serve apart from your decisions. This process whereby they take this decision from you makes them a *part-owner* of you; it gives them a property right in you. Just as having such partial control and power of decision, by right, over an animal or inanimate object would be to have a property right in it.

End-state and most patterned principles of distributive justice institute (partial) ownership by others of people and their actions and labor. These principles involve a shift from the classical liberals' notion of self-ownership to a notion of (partial) property rights in *other* people.

Considerations such as these confront end-state and other patterned conceptions of justice with the question of whether the actions necessary to achieve the selected pattern don't themselves violate moral side constraints. Any view holding that there are moral side constraints on actions, that not all moral considerations can be built into end states that are to be achieved (see Chapter 3, 28-30), must face the possibility that some of its goals are not achievable by any morally permissible available means. An entitlement theorist will face such conflicts in a society that deviates from the principles of justice for the generation of holdings, if and only if the only actions available to realize the principles themselves violate some moral constraints. Since deviation from the first two principles of justice (in acquisition and transfer) will involve other persons' direct and aggressive intervention to violate rights, and since moral constraints will not exclude defensive or retributive action in such cases, the entitlement theorist's problem rarely will be pressing. And whatever difficulties he has in applying the principle of rectification to persons who did not themselves violate the first two principles are difficulties in balancing the conflicting considerations so as correctly to formulate the complex principle of rectification itself; he will not violate moral side constraints by applying the principle. Proponents of patterned conceptions of justice, however, often will face head-on clashes (and poignant ones if they cherish each party to the clash) between moral side constraints on how individuals may be treated and their patterned conception of justice that presents an end state or other pattern that *must* be realized.

May a person emigrate from a nation that has institutionalized some end-state or patterned distributional principle? For some principles (for example, Hayek's) emigration presents no theoretical problem. But for others it is a tricky matter. Consider a nation having a compulsory scheme of minimal social provision to aid the neediest (or one organized so as to maximize the position of the worst-off group); no one may opt out of participating in it. (None may say, "Don't compel me to contribute to others and don't provide for me via this compulsory mechanism if I am in need.") Everyone above a certain level is forced to contribute to aid the needy. But if emigration from the country were allowed, anyone could choose to move to another country that did not have compulsory social provision but otherwise was (as much as possible) identical. In such a case, the person's *only* motive for leaving would be to avoid participating in the compulsory scheme of social provision. And if he does leave, the needy in his initial country will receive no (compelled) help from him. What rationale yields the result that the person be permitted to emigrate, yet forbidden to stay and opt out of the compulsory scheme of social provision? If providing for the needy is of overriding importance, this does militate against allowing internal opting out; but it also speaks against allowing external emigration. (Would it also support, to some extent, the kidnapping of persons living in a place without compulsory social provision, who could be forced to make a contribution to the needy in your community?) Perhaps the crucial component of the position that allows emigration solely to avoid certain arrangements, while not allowing anyone internally to opt out of them, is a concern for fraternal feelings within the country. "We don't want anyone here who doesn't contribute, who doesn't care enough about the others to contribute." That concern, in this case, would have to be tied to the view that forced aiding tends to produce fraternal feelings between the aided and the aider (or perhaps merely to the view that the knowledge that someone or other voluntarily is not aiding produces unfraternal feelings).

Locke's Theory of Acquisition

Before we turn to consider other theories of justice in detail, we must introduce an additional bit of complexity into the structure of the entitlement theory. This is best approached by considering Locke's attempt to specify a principle of justice in acquisition. Locke views property rights in an unowned object as originating through someone's mixing his labor with it. This gives rise to many questions. What are the boundaries of what labor is mixed with? If a private astronaut clears a place on Mars, has he mixed his labor with (so that he comes to own) the whole planet, the whole uninhabited universe, or just a particular plot? Which plot does an act bring under ownership? The minimal (possibly disconnected) area such that an act decreases entropy in that area, and not elsewhere? Can virgin land (for the purposes of ecological investigation by high-flying airplane) come under ownership by a Lockean process? Building a fence around a territory presumably would make one the owner of only the fence (and the land immediately underneath it).

Why does mixing one's labor with something make one the owner of it? Perhaps because one owns one's labor, and so one comes to own a previously unowned thing that becomes permeated with what one owns. Ownership seeps over into the rest. But why isn't mixing what I own with what I don't own a way of losing what I own rather than a way of gaining what I don't? If I own a can of tomato juice and spill it in the sea so that its molecules (made radioactive, so I can check this) mingle evenly throughout the sea, do I thereby come to own the sea, or have I foolishly dissipated my tomato juice? Perhaps the idea, instead, is that laboring on something improves it and makes it more valuable; and anyone is entitled to own a thing whose value he has created. (Reinforcing this, perhaps, is the view that laboring

is unpleasant. If some people made things effortlessly, as the cartoon characters in *The Yellow Submarine* trail flowers in their wake, would they have lesser claim to their own products whose making didn't *cost* them anything?) Ignore the fact that laboring on something may make it less valuable (spraying pink enamel paint on a piece of driftwood that you have found). Why should one's entitlement extend to the whole object rather than just to the *added value* one's labor has produced? (Such reference to value might also serve to delimit the extent of ownership; for example, substitute "increases the value of" for "decreases entropy in" in the above entropy criterion.) No workable or coherent value-added property scheme has yet been devised, and any such scheme presumably would fall to objections (similar to those) that fell the theory of Henry George.

It will be implausible to view improving an object as giving full ownership to it, if the stock of unowned objects that might be improved is limited. For an object's coming under one person's ownership changes the situation of all others. Whereas previously they were at liberty (in Hohfeld's sense) to use the object, they now no longer are. This change in the situation of others (by removing their liberty to act on a previously unowned object) need not worsen their situation. If I appropriate a grain of sand from Coney Island, no one else may now do as they will with *that* grain of sand. But there are plenty of other grains of sand left for them to do the same with. Or if not grains of sand, then other things. Alternatively, the things I do with the grain of sand I appropriate might improve the position of others, counterbalancing their loss of the liberty to use that grain. The crucial point is whether appropriation of an unowned object worsens the situation of others.

Locke's proviso that there be "enough and as good left in common for others" (sect. 27) is meant to ensure that the situation of others is not worsened. (If this proviso is met is there any motivation for his further condition of nonwaste?) It is often said that this proviso once held but now no longer does.

But there appears to be an argument for the conclusion that if the proviso no longer holds, then it cannot ever have held so as to yield permanent and inheritable property rights. Consider the first person Z for whom there is not enough and as good left to appropriate. The last person Y to appropriate left Z without his previous liberty to act on an object, and so worsened Z's situation. So Y's appropriation is not allowed under Locke's proviso. Therefore the next to last person X to appropriate left Y in a worse position, for X's act ended permissible appropriation. Therefore X's appropriation wasn't permissible. But then the appropriator two from last, W, ended permissible appropriation and so, since it worsened X's position, W's appropriation wasn't permissible. And so on back to the first person A to appropriate a permanent property right.

This argument, however, proceeds too quickly. Someone may be made worse off by another's appropriation in two ways: first, by losing the opportunity to improve his situation by a particular appropriation or any one; and second, by no longer being able to use freely (without appropriation) what he previously could. A *stringent* requirement that another not be made worse off by an appropriation would exclude the first way if nothing else counterbalances the diminution in opportunity, as well as the second. A *weaker* requirement would exclude the second way, though not the first. With the weaker requirement, we cannot zip back so quickly from Z to A, as in the above argument; for though person Z can no longer *appropriate*, there may remain some for him to *use* as before. In this case Y's appropriation would not violate the weaker Lockean condition. (With less remaining that people are at liberty to use, users might face more inconvenience, crowding, and so on; in that way the situation of others might be worsened, unless appropriation stopped far short of such a point.) It is arguable that no one legitimately can complain if the weaker provision is satisfied. However, since this is less clear than in the case of the more stringent proviso, Locke may have

intended this stringent proviso by "enough and as good" remaining, and perhaps he meant the non-waste condition to delay the end point from which the argument zips back.

Is the situation of persons who are unable to appropriate (there being no more accessible and useful unowned objects) worsened by a system allowing appropriation and permanent property? Here enter the various familiar social considerations favoring private property: it increases the social product by putting means of production in the hands of those who can use them most efficiently (profitably); experimentation is encouraged, because with separate persons controlling resources, there is no one person or small group whom someone with a new idea must convince to try it out; private property enables people to decide on the pattern and types of risks they wish to bear, leading to specialized types of risk bearing; private property protects future persons by leading some to hold back resources from current consumption for future markets; it provides alternate sources of employment for unpopular persons who don't have to convince any one person or small group to hire them, and so on. These considerations enter a Lockean theory to support the claim that appropriation of private property satisfies the intent behind the "enough and as good left over" proviso, *not* as a utilitarian justification of property. They enter to rebut the claim that because the proviso is violated no natural right to private property can arise by a Lockean process. The difficulty in working such an argument to show that the proviso is satisfied is in fixing the appropriate baseline for comparison. Lockean appropriation makes people no worse off than they would be *how*? This question of fixing the baseline needs more detailed investigation than we are able to give it here. It would be desirable to have an estimate of the general economic importance of original appropriation in order to see how much leeway there is for differing theories of appropriation and of the location of the baseline. Perhaps this importance can be measured by the percentage of all income that is based upon untransformed raw materials and given resources (rather than upon human actions), mainly rental income representing the unimproved value of land, and the price of raw material *in situ*, and by the percentage of current wealth which represents such income in the past.[10]

We should note that it is not only persons favoring private property who need a theory of how property rights legitimately originate. Those believing in collective property, for example those believing that a group of persons living in an area jointly own the territory, or its mineral resources, also must provide a theory of how such property rights arise; they must show why the persons living there have rights to determine what is done with the land and resources there that persons living elsewhere don't have (with regard to the same land and resources).

The Proviso

Whether or not Locke's particular theory of appropriation can be spelled out so as to handle various difficulties, I assume that any adequate theory of justice in acquisition will contain a proviso similar to the weaker of the ones we have attributed to Locke. A process normally giving rise to a permanent bequeathable property right in a previously unowned thing will not do so if the position of others no longer at liberty to use the thing is thereby worsened. It is important to specify *this* particular mode of worsening the situation of others, for the proviso does not encompass other modes. It does not include the worsening due to more limited opportunities to appropriate (the first way above, corresponding to the more stringent condition), and it does not include how I "worsen" a seller's position if I appropriate materials to make some of what he is selling, and then enter into competition with him. Someone whose appropriation otherwise would violate the proviso still may appropriate provided he compensates the others so that their situation is not thereby worsened; unless he does compensate these

others, his appropriation will violate the proviso of the principle of justice in acquisition and will be an illegitimate one.[11] A theory of appropriation incorporating this Lockean proviso will handle correctly the cases (objections to the theory lacking the proviso) where someone appropriates the total supply of something necessary for life.[12]

A theory which includes this proviso in its principle of justice in acquisition must also contain a more complex principle of justice in transfer. Some reflection of the proviso about appropriation constrains later actions. If my appropriating all of a certain substance violates the Lockean proviso, then so does my appropriating some and purchasing all the rest from others who obtained it without otherwise violating the Lockean proviso. If the proviso excludes someone's appropriating all the drinkable water in the world, it also excludes his purchasing it all. (More weakly, and messily, it may exclude his charging certain prices for some of his supply.) This proviso (almost?) never will come into effect; the more someone acquires of a scarce substance which others want, the higher the price of the rest will go, and the more difficult it will become for him to acquire it all. But still, we can imagine, at least, that something like this occurs: someone makes simultaneous secret bids to the separate owners of a substance, each of whom sells assuming he can easily purchase more from the other owners; or some natural catastrophe destroys all of the supply of something except that in one person's possession. The total supply could not be permissibly appropriated by one person at the beginning. His later acquisition of it all does not show that the original appropriation violated the proviso (even by a reverse argument similar to the one above that tried to zip back from Z to A). Rather, it is the combination of the original appropriation *plus* all the later transfers and actions that violates the Lockean proviso.

Each owner's title to his holding includes the historical shadow of the Lockean proviso on appropriation. This excludes his transferring it into an agglomeration that does violate the Lockean proviso and excludes his using it in a way, in coordination with others or independently of them, so as to violate the proviso by making the situation of others worse than their baseline situation. Once it is known that someone's ownership runs afoul of the Lockean proviso, there are stringent limits on what he may do with (what it is difficult any longer unreservedly to call) "his property." Thus a person may not appropriate the only water hole in a desert and charge what he will. Nor may he charge what he will if he possesses one, and unfortunately it happens that all the water holes in the desert dry up, except for his. This unfortunate circumstance, admittedly no fault of his, brings into operation the Lockean proviso and limits his property rights.[13] Similarly, an owner's property right in the only island in an area does not allow him to order a castaway from a shipwreck off his island as a trespasser, for this would violate the Lockean proviso.

Notice that the theory does not say that owners do have these rights, but that the rights are overridden to avoid some catastrophe. (Overridden rights do not disappear; they leave a trace of a sort absent in the cases under discussion.) There is no such external (and *ad hoc*?) overriding. Considerations internal to the theory of property itself, to its theory of acquisition and appropriation, provide the means for handling such cases. The results, however, may be coextensive with some condition about catastrophe, since the baseline for comparison is so low as compared to the productiveness of a society with private appropriation that the question of the Lockean proviso being violated arises only in the case of catastrophe (or a desert-island situation).

The fact that someone owns the total supply of something necessary for others to stay alive does *not* entail that his (or anyone's) appropriation of anything left some people (immediately or later) in a situation worse than the baseline one. A medical researcher who synthesizes a new substance that effectively treats a certain disease and who refuses to sell except on his terms does not worsen the situation of others by depriving them of whatever he has appropriated. The others easily can possess the same materials he appropriated; the researcher's appropriation or purchase of chemicals didn't make those chemicals scarce in a way so as to violate the Lockean proviso. Nor would someone else's purchasing the total supply of the synthesized substance from the medical researcher. The fact that the medical researcher uses easily available chemicals to synthesize the drug no more violates the Lockean proviso than does the fact that the only surgeon able to perform a particular operation eats easily obtainable food in order to stay alive and to have the energy to work. This shows that the Lockean proviso is not an "end-state principle"; it focuses on a particular way that appropriative actions affect others, and not on the structure of the situation that results.

Intermediate between someone who takes all of the public supply and someone who makes the total supply out of easily obtainable substances is someone who appropriates the total supply of something in a way that does not deprive the others of it. For example, someone finds a new substance in an out-of-the-way place. He discovers that it effectively treats a certain disease and appropriates the total supply. He does not worsen the situation of others; if he did not stumble upon the substance no one else would have, and the others would remain without it. However, as time passes, the likelihood increases that others would have come across the substance; upon this fact might be based a limit to his property right in the substance so that others are not below their baseline position; for example, its bequest might be limited. The theme of someone worsening another's situation by depriving him of something he otherwise would possess may also illuminate the example of patents. An inventor's patent does not deprive others of an object which would not exist if not for the inventor. Yet patents would have this effect on others who independently invent the object. Therefore, these independent inventors, upon whom the burden of proving independent discovery may rest, should not be excluded from utilizing their own invention as they wish (including selling it to others). Furthermore, a known inventor drastically lessens the chances of actual independent invention. For persons who know of an invention usually will not try to reinvent it, and the notion of independent discovery here would be murky at best. Yet we may assume that in the absence of the original invention, sometime later someone else would have come up with it. This suggests placing a time limit on patents, as a rough rule of thumb to approximate how long it would have taken, in the absence of knowledge of the invention, for independent discovery.

I believe that the free operation of a market system will not actually run afoul of the Lockean proviso. (Recall that crucial to our story in Part I of how a protective agency becomes dominant and a *de facto* monopoly is the fact that it wields force in situations of conflict, and is not merely in competition, with other agencies. A similar tale cannot be told about other businesses.) If this is correct, the proviso will not play a very important role in the activities of protective agencies and will not provide a significant opportunity for future state action. Indeed, were it not for the effects of previous *illegitimate* state action, people would not think the possibility of the proviso's being violated as of more interest than any other logical possibility. (Here I make an empirical historical claim; as does someone who disagrees with this.) This completes our indication of the complication in the entitlement theory introduced by the Lockean proviso.

NOTES

1 Applications of the principle of justice in acquisition may also occur as part of the move from one distribution to another. You may find an unheld thing now and appropriate it. Acquisitions also are to be understood as included when, to simplify, I speak only of transitions by transfers.

2 If the principle of rectification of violations of the first two principles yields more than one description of holdings, then some choice must be made as to which of these is to be realized. Perhaps the sort of considerations about distributive justice and equality that I argue against play a legitimate role in *this* subsidiary choice. Similarly, there may be room for such considerations in deciding which otherwise arbitrary features a statute will embody, when such features are unavoidable because other considerations do not specify a precise line; yet a line must be drawn.

3 One might try to squeeze a patterned conception of distributive justice into the framework of the entitlement conception, by formulating a gimmicky obligatory "principle of transfer" that would lead to the pattern. For example, the principle that if one has more than the mean income one must transfer everything one holds above the mean to persons below the mean so as to bring them up to (but not over) the mean. We can formulate a criterion for a "principle of transfer" to rule out such obligatory transfers, or we can say that no correct principle of transfer, no principle of transfer in a free society will be like this. The former is probably the better course, though the latter also is true.

Alternatively, one might think to make the entitlement conception instantiate a pattern, by using matrix entries that express the relative strength of a person's entitlements as measured by some real-valued function. But even if the limitation to natural dimensions failed to exclude this function, the resulting edifice would *not* capture our system of entitlements to *particular* things.

4 We certainly benefit because great economic incentives operate to get others to spend much time and energy to figure out how to serve us by providing things we will want to pay for. It is not mere paradox mongering to wonder

whether capitalism should be criticized for most rewarding and hence encouraging, not individualists like Thoreau who go about their own lives, but people who are occupied with serving others and winning them as customers. But to defend capitalism one need not think businessmen are the finest human types. (I do not mean to join here the general maligning of businessmen, either.) Those who think the finest should acquire the most can try to convince their fellows to transfer resources in accordance with *that* principle.

5 Might not a transfer have instrumental effects on a third party, changing his feasible options? (But what if the two parties to the transfer independently had used their holdings in this fashion?) I discuss this question below, but note here that this question concedes the point for distributions of ultimate intrinsic noninstrumental goods (pure utility experiences, so to speak) that are transferrable. It also might be objected that the transfer might make a third party more envious because it worsens his position relative to someone else. I find it incomprehensible how this can be thought to involve a claim of justice. On envy, see Chapter 8.

Here and elsewhere in this chapter, a theory which incorporates elements of pure procedural justice might find what I say acceptable, *if* kept in its proper place; that is, if background institutions exist to ensure the satisfaction of certain conditions on distributive shares. But if these institutions are not themselves the sum or invisible-hand result of people's voluntary (nonaggressive) actions, the constraints they impose require justification. At no point does *our* argument assume any background institutions more extensive than those of the minimal night-watchman state, a state limited to protecting persons against murder, assault, theft, fraud, and so forth.

6 Is the patterned principle stable that requires merely that a distribution be Pareto-optimal? One person might give another a gift or bequest that the second could exchange with a third to their mutual benefit. Before the second makes this exchange, there is not Pareto-optimality. Is a stable pattern presented by a principle choosing that among the Pareto-optimal positions that satisfies some further condition *C*? It may seem that there cannot be a counterexample, for won't any voluntary exchange made away from a situation show that the first situation wasn't Pareto-optimal? (Ignore the implausibility of this last claim for the case of bequests.) But principles are to be satisfied over time, during which new possibilities arise. A distribution that at one time satisfies the criterion of Pareto-optimality might not do so when some new possibilities arise (Wilt Chamberlain grows up and starts playing basketball); and though people's activities will tend to move then to a new Pareto-optimal position, *this* new one need not satisfy the contentful condition *C*. Continual interference will be needed to insure the continual satisfaction of *C*. (The theoretical possibility of a pattern's being maintained by some invisible-hand process that brings it back to an equilibrium that fits the pattern when deviations occur should be investigated.)

7 One indication of the stringency of Rawls' difference principle, which we attend to in the second part of this chapter, is its inappropriateness as a governing principle even within a family of individuals who love one another. Should a family devote its resources to maximizing the position of its least well off and least talented child, holding back the other children or using resources for their education and development only if they will follow a policy through their lifetimes of maximizing the position of their least fortunate sibling? Surely not. How then can this even be considered as the appropriate

policy for enforcement in the wider society? (I discuss below what I think would be Rawls' reply: that some principles apply at the macro level which do not apply to micro-situations.)

8 I am unsure as to whether the arguments I present below show that such taxation merely *is* forced labor; so that "is on a par with" means "is one kind of." Or alternatively, whether the arguments emphasize the great similarities between such taxation and forced labor, to show it is plausible and illuminating to view such taxation in the light of forced labor. This latter approach would remind one of how John Wisdom conceives of the claims of metaphysicians.

9 Nothing hangs on the fact that here and elsewhere I speak loosely of *needs*, since I go on, each time, to reject the criterion of justice which includes it. If, however, something did depend upon the notion, one would want to examine it more carefully. For a skeptical view, see Kenneth Minogue, *The Liberal Mind* (New York: Random House, 1963), 103-12.

10 I have not seen a precise estimate. David Friedman, *The Machinery of Freedom* (New York: Harper and Row, 1973), xiv, xv, discusses this issue and suggests 5 per cent of US national income as an upper limit for the first two factors mentioned. However he does not attempt to estimate the percentage of current wealth which is based upon such income in the past. (The vague notion of "based upon" merely indicates a topic needing investigation.)

11 Fourier held that since the process of civilization had deprived the members of society of certain liberties (to gather, pasture, engage in the chase), a socially guaranteed minimum provision for persons was justified as compensation for the loss (Alexander Gray, *The Socialist Tradition* [New York: Harper and Row, 1968], 188). But this puts the point too strongly. This compensation would be due those persons, if any, for whom the process of civilization was

a *net loss*, for whom the benefits of civilization did not counterbalance being deprived of these particular liberties.

12 For example, Rashdall's case of someone who comes upon the only water in the desert several miles ahead of others who also will come to it and appropriates it all. Hastings Rashdall, "The Philosophical Theory of Property," in *Property, its Duties and Rights* (London: MacMillan, 1915).

We should note Ayn Rand's theory of property rights ("Man's Rights" in *The Virtue of Selfishness* [New York: New American Library, 1964], 94), wherein these follow from the right to life, since people need physical things to live. But a right to life is not a right to whatever one needs to live; other people may have rights over these other things (see Chapter 3 of this book). At most, a right to life would be a right to have or strive for whatever one needs to live, provided that having it does not violate anyone else's rights. With regard to material things, the question is whether having it does violate any right of others. (Would appropriation of all unowned things do so? Would appropriating the water hole in Rashdall's example?) Since special considerations (such as the Lockean proviso) may enter with regard to material property, one *first* needs a theory of property rights before one can apply any supposed right to life (as amended above). Therefore the right to life cannot provide the foundation for a theory of property rights.

13 The situation would be different if his water hole didn't dry up, due to special precautions he took to prevent this. Compare our discussion of the case in the text with Hayek, *The Constitution of Liberty*, 136; and also with Ronald Hamowy, "Hayek's Concept of Freedom; A Critique," *New Individualist Review*, April 1961, 28-31.

◆ ◆ ◆ ◆ ◆

KAI NIELSEN

A Moral Case for Socialism

I

In North America socialism gets a bad press. It is under criticism for its alleged economic inefficiency and for its moral and human inadequacy. I want here to address the latter issue. Looking at capitalism and socialism, I want to consider, against the grain of our culture, what kind of moral case can be made for socialism.

The first thing to do, given the extensive, and, I would add, inexcusably extensive, confusions about this, is to say what socialism and capitalism are. That done I will then, appealing to a cluster of values which are basic in our culture, concerning which there is a considerable and indeed a reflective consensus, examine how capitalism and socialism fare with respect to these values. Given that people generally, at least in Western societies, would want it to be the case that these values have a stable exemplification in our social lives, it is appropriate to ask the question: which of these social systems is more likely stably to exemplify them? I shall argue, facing the gamut of a careful comparison in the light of these values, that, everything considered, socialism comes out better than capitalism. And this, if right, would give us good reason for believing that socialism is preferable—indeed morally preferable—to capitalism if it also turns out to be a feasible socio-economic system.

What, then, are socialism and capitalism? Put most succinctly, capitalism requires the existence of private *productive* property (private ownership of the means of production) while socialism works toward its abolition. What is essential for socialism is public ownership and control of the means of production and public ownership means just what it says: *ownership by the public.* Under capitalism there is a domain of private property rights in the means of production which are not subject to political determination. That is, even where the political domain is a democratic one, they are not subject to determination by the public; only an individual or a set of individuals who own that property can make the final determination of what is to be done with that property. These individuals make the determination and not citizens at large, as under socialism. In fully developed socialism, by contrast, there is, with respect to productive property, no domain which is not subject to political determination by the public, namely by the citizenry at large. Thus, where this public ownership and control is genuine, and not a mask for control by an elite of state bureaucrats, it will mean genuine popular and democratic control over productive property. What socialism is *not* is *state* ownership in the absence of, at the very least, popular sovereignty, i.e., genuine popular control over the state apparatus including any economic functions it might have.

The property that is owned in common under socialism is the means of existence—the productive property in the society. Socialism does not proscribe the ownership of private personal property, such as houses, cars, television sets and the like. It only proscribes the private ownership of the means of production.

The above characterizations catch the minimal core of socialism and capitalism, what used to be called the essence of those concepts. But beyond these core features, it is well, in helping us to make our comparison, to see some other important features which characteristically go with capitalism and socialism. Minimally, capitalism is private ownership of the means of production but it is also, at least characteristically, a social system in which a class of capitalists owns and controls the means of production and hires workers who, owning little or no means of production, sell their labor-power to some capitalist or other for a wage. This means that a capitalist society will be a class society in which there will be two principal classes: capitalists and workers. Socialism by contrast is a social system in which every able-bodied person is, was or will be a worker. These workers commonly own and control the means of production (this is the characteristic form of public ownership). Thus in socialism we have, in a perfectly literal sense, a classless society for there is no division between human beings along class lines.

There are both pure and impure forms of capitalism and socialism. The pure form of capitalism is competitive capitalism, the capitalism that Milton Friedman would tell us is the real capitalism while, he would add, the impure form is monopoly or corporate capitalism. Similarly the pure form of socialism is democratic socialism, with firm workers' control of the means of production and an industrial as well as a political democracy, while the impure form is state bureaucratic socialism.

Now it is a noteworthy fact that, to understate it, actually existing capitalisms and actually existing socialisms tend to be the impure forms. Many partisans of capitalism lament the fact that the actually existing capitalisms overwhelmingly tend to be forms of corporate capitalism where the state massively intervenes in the running of the economy. It is unclear whether anything like a fully competitive capitalism actually exists—perhaps Hong Kong approximates it—and it is also unclear whether many of the actual players in the major capitalist societies (the existing capitalists and their managers) want or even expect that it is possible to have laissez-faire capitalism again (if indeed we ever had it). Some capitalist societies are further down the corporate road than other societies, but they are all forms of corporate, perhaps in some instances even monopoly, capitalism. Competitive capitalism seems to be more of a libertarian dream than a sociological reality or even something desired by many informed and tough-minded members of the capitalist class. Socialism has had a similar fate. Its historical exemplifications tend to be of the impure forms, namely the bureaucratic state socialisms. Yugoslavia is perhaps to socialism what Hong Kong is to capitalism. It is a candidate for what might count as an exemplification, or at least a near approximation, of the pure form.

This paucity of exemplifications of pure forms of either capitalism or socialism raises the question of whether the pure forms are at best unstable social systems and at worse merely utopian ideals. I shall not try directly to settle that issue here. What I shall do instead is to compare *models* with *models*. In asking about the moral case for socialism, I shall compare forms that a not inconsiderable number of the theoretical protagonists of each take to be pure forms but which are still, they believe, historically feasible. But I will also be concerned to ask whether these models—these pure forms—can reasonably be expected to come to have a home. If they are not historically feasible models, then, even if we can make a good theoretical moral case for them, we will have hardly provided a good moral case for socialism or capitalism. To avoid bad utopianism we must be talking about forms which could be on the historical agenda. (I plainly here do not take "bad utopianism" to be pleonastic.)

II

Setting aside for the time being the feasibility question, let us compare the pure forms of capitalism and socialism—that is to say, competitive capitalism and democratic socialism—as to how they stand with respect to sustaining and furthering the values of freedom and autonomy, equality, justice, rights and democracy. My argument shall be that socialism comes out better with respect to those values.

Let us first look at freedom and autonomy. An autonomous person is a person who sets ends for herself and, in optimal circumstances, is able to pursue those ends. But freedom does not only mean being autonomous; it also means the absence of unjustified political and social interference in the pursuit of one's ends. Some might even say that it is just the absence of interference with one's ends. Still it is self-direction—autonomy—not non-interference which is *intrinsically* desirable. Non-interference is only valuable where it is an aid to our being able to do what we want and where we are sufficiently autonomous to have some control over our wants.

How do capitalism and socialism fare in providing the social conditions which will help or impede the flourishing of autonomy? Which model society would make for the greater flourishing of autonomy? My argument is (a) that democratic socialism makes it possible for more people to be more fully autonomous than would be autonomous under capitalism; and (b) that democratic socialism also interferes less in people's exercise of their autonomy than any form of capitalism. All societies limit liberty by interfering with people doing what they want to do in some ways, but the restrictions are more extensive, deeper and more undermining of autonomy in capitalism than in democratic socialism. Where there is private ownership of productive property, which, remember, is private ownership of the means of life, it cannot help but be the case that a few (the owning and controlling capitalist class) will have, along with the managers beholden to them, except in periods of revolutionary turmoil, a firm control, indeed a domination, over the vast majority of people in the society. The capitalist class with the help of their managers determines whether workers (taken now as individuals) can work, how they work, on what they work, the conditions under which they work and what is done with what they produce (where they are producers) and what use is made of their skills and the like. As we move to welfare state capitalism—a compromise still favoring capital which emerged out of long and bitter class struggles—the state places some restrictions on some of these powers of capital. Hours, working conditions and the like are controlled in certain ways. Yet whether workers work and continue to work, how they work and on what, what is done with what they produce, and the

rationale for their work are not determined by the workers themselves but by the owners of capital and their managers; this means a very considerable limitation on the autonomy and freedom of workers. Since workers are the great majority, such socio-economic relations place a very considerable limitation on human freedom and indeed on the very most important freedom that people have, namely their being able to live in a self-directed manner, when compared with the industrial democracy of democratic socialism. Under capitalist arrangements it simply cannot fail to be the case that a very large number of people will lose control over a very central set of facets of their lives, namely central aspects of their work and indeed in many instances, over their very chance to be able to work.

Socialism would indeed prohibit capitalist acts between consenting adults; the capitalist class would lose its freedom to buy and sell and to control the labor market. There should be no blinking at the fact that socialist social relations would impose some limitations on freedom, for there is, and indeed can be, no society without norms and some sanctions. In any society you like there will be some things you are at liberty to do and some things that you may not do. However, democratic socialism must bring with it an industrial democracy where workers by various democratic procedures would determine how they are to work, on what they are to work, the hours of their work, under what conditions they are to work (insofar as this is alterable by human effort at all), what they will produce and how much, and what is to be done with what they produce. Since, instead of there being "private ownership of the means of production," there is in a genuinely socialist society "public ownership of the means of production," the means of life are owned by everyone and thus each person has a *right* to work: she has, that is, a right to the means of life. It is no longer the private preserve of an individual owner of capital but it is owned in common by us all. This means that each of us has an equal right to the means of life. Members of the capitalist class would have a few of their liberties restricted, but these are linked with owning and controlling capital and are not the important civil and political liberties that we all rightly cherish. Moreover, the limitation of the capitalist liberties to buy and sell and the like would make for a more extensive liberty for many, many more people.

One cannot respond to the above by saying that workers are free to leave the working class and become capitalists or at least petty bourgeoisie. They may indeed all in theory, taken *individually*, be free to leave the working class, but if many in fact try to leave the exits will very quickly become blocked. Individuals are only free on the condition that the great mass of people, taken collectively, are not. We could not have capitalism without a working class and the working class is not free within the capitalist system to cease being wage laborers. We cannot all be capitalists. A people's capitalism is nonsense. Though a petty commodity production system (the family farm writ large) is a logical possibility, it is hardly a stable empirical possibility, and, what is most important for the present discussion, such a system would not be a capitalist system. Under capitalism, most of us, if we are to find any work at all, will just have to sell (or *perhaps* "rent" is the better word) our labor-power as a commodity. Whether you sell or rent your labor power or, where it is provided, you go on welfare, you will not have much control over areas very crucial to your life. If these are the only feasible alternatives facing the working class, working class autonomy is very limited indeed. But these are the only alternatives under capitalism.

Capitalist acts between consenting adults, if they become sufficiently widespread, lead to severe imbalances in power. These imbalances in power tend to undermine autonomy by creating differentials in wealth and control between workers and capitalists. Such imbalances are the name of the game for capitalism. Even if we (perversely I believe) call a system of petty commodity production capitalism, we still must say that such a socio-economic system is inherently unstable. Certain individuals would win out in this exchanging of commodities and in fairly quick order it would lead to a class system and the imbalances of power—the domination of the many by the few—that I take to be definitive of capitalism. By abolishing capitalist acts between consenting adults, then (but leaving personal property and civil and political liberties untouched), socialism protects more extensive freedoms for more people and in far more important areas of their lives.

III

So democratic socialism does better regarding the value that epitomizes capitalist pride (*hubris*, would, I think, be a better term), namely autonomy. It also does better, I shall now argue, than capitalism with respect to another of our basic values, namely democracy. Since this is almost a corollary of what I have said about autonomy I can afford to be briefer. In capitalist societies, democracy must simply be *political* democracy. There can in the nature of the case be no genuine or thorough workplace democracy. When we enter the sphere of production, capitalists and not workers own, and therefore at least ultimately control, the means of production. While capitalism, as in some workplaces in West Germany and Sweden, sometimes can be pressured into allowing an ameliorative measure of worker control, once ownership rights are given up, we no longer have private productive property but public productive property (and in that way social ownership): capitalism is given up and we have socialism. However, where worker control is restricted to a few firms, we do not yet have socialism. What makes a system socialist or capitalist depends on what happens across the whole society, not just in isolated firms. Moreover, managers can become very important within capitalist firms, but as long as ownership, including the ability to close the place down and liquidate the business, rests in the hands of capitalists we can have no genuine workplace democracy. Socialism, in its pure form, carries with it, in a way capitalism in any form cannot, workplace democracy. (That some of the existing socialisms are anything but pure does not belie this.)

Similarly, whatever may be said of existing socialisms or at least of some existing socialisms, it is not the case that there is anything in the very idea of socialism that militates against political as well as industrial democracy. Socialists are indeed justly suspicious of some of the tricks played by parliamentary democracy in bourgeois countries, aware of its not infrequent hypocrisy and the limitations of its stress on purely legal and formal political rights and liberties. Socialists are also, without at all wishing to throw the baby out with the bath water, rightly suspicious of any simple reliance on majority role, unsupplemented by other democratic procedures and safeguards. But there is nothing in socialist theory that would set it against political democracy and the protection of political and civil rights; indeed there is much in socialism that favors them, namely its stress on both autonomy and equality.

The fact that political democracy came into being and achieved stability within capitalist societies may prove something about conditions necessary for its coming into being, but it says nothing about capitalism being necessary for sustaining it. In Chile, South Africa and Nazi Germany, indeed capitalism has flourished without the protection of civil and political rights or anything like a respect for the democratic tradition. There is nothing structural in socialism that would prevent it from continuing those democratic traditions or cherishing those political and civil rights. That something came about under certain conditions does not establish that these conditions are necessary for its continued existence. That men initially took an interest in chess does not establish that women cannot quite naturally take an interest in it as well. When capitalist societies with long-flourishing democratic traditions move to socialism there is no reason at all to believe that they will not continue to be democratic. (Where societies

previously had no democratic tradition or only a very weak one, matters are more problematic.)

IV

I now want to turn to a third basic value, equality. In societies across the political spectrum, *moral* equality (the belief that everyone's life matters equally) is an accepted value. Or, to be somewhat cynical about the matter, at least lip service is paid to it. But even this lip service is the compliment that vice pays to virtue. That is to say, such a belief is a deeply held considered conviction in modernized societies, though it has not been at all times and is not today a value held in all societies. This is most evident concerning moral equality.

While this value is genuinely held by the vast majority of people in capitalist societies, it can hardly be an effective or functional working norm where there is such a diminishment of autonomy as we have seen obtains unavoidably in such societies. Self-respect is deeply threatened where so many people lack effective control over their own lives, where there are structures of domination, where there is alienated labor, where great power differentials and differences in wealth make for very different (and often very bleak) life chances. For not inconsiderable numbers, in fact, it is difficult to maintain self-respect under such conditions unless they are actively struggling against the system. And, given present conditions, fighting the system, particularly in societies such as the United States, may well be felt to be a hopeless task. Under such conditions any real equality of opportunity is out of the question. And the circumstances are such, in spite of what is often said about these states, that equality of condition is an even more remote possibility. But without at least some of these things moral equality cannot even be approximated. Indeed, even to speak of it sounds like an obscene joke given the social realities of our lives.

Although under welfare-state capitalism some of the worst inequalities of capitalism are ameliorated, workers still lack effective control over their work, with repercussions in political and public life as well. Differentials of wealth cannot but give rise to differentials in power and control in politics, in the media, in education, in the direction of social life and in what options get seriously debated. The life chances of workers and those not even lucky enough to be workers (whose ranks are growing and will continue to grow under capitalism) are impoverished compared to the life chances of members of the capitalist class and its docile professional support stratum.

None of these equality-undermining features would obtain under democratic socialism. Such societies would for starters, be classless, eliminating the power and control differentials that go with the class system of capitalism. In addition to political democracy, industrial democracy and all the egalitarian and participatory control that goes with that would in turn, reinforce moral equality. Indeed it would make it possible where before it was impossible. There would be a commitment under democratic socialism to attaining or at least approximating, as far as it is feasible, equality of condition; and this, where approximated would help make for real equality of opportunity, making equal life chances something less utopian than it must be under capitalism.

In fine, the very things, as we have seen, that make for greater autonomy under socialism than under capitalism, would in being more equally distributed, make for greater equality of condition, greater equality of opportunity and greater moral equality in a democratic socialist society than in a capitalist one. These values are values commonly shared by both capitalistically inclined people and those who are socialistically inclined. What the former do not see is that in modern industrial societies, democratic socialism can better deliver these goods than even progressive capitalism.

There is, without doubt, legitimate worry about bureaucratic control under socialism. But that is a worry under any historically feasible capitalism as well, and it is anything but clear that state bureaucracies are worse than great corporate bureaucracies. Indeed, if socialist bureaucrats were, as the socialist system requires, really committed to production for needs and to achieving equality of condition, they might, bad as they are, be the lesser of two evils. But in any event democratic socialism is not bureaucratic state socialism, and there is no structural reason to believe that it must—if it arises in a society with skilled workers committed to democracy—give rise to bureaucratic state socialism. There will, inescapably, be some bureaucracy, but in a democratic socialist society it must and indeed will be controlled. This is not merely a matter of optimism about the will of socialists, for there are more mechanisms for democratic control of bureaucracy within a democratic socialism that is both a political and an industrial democracy, than there can be under even the most benign capitalist democracies—democracies which for structural reasons can never be industrial democracies. If, all that notwithstanding, bureaucratic creepage is inescapable in modern societies, then that is just as much a problem for capitalism as for socialism.

The underlying rationale for production under capitalism is profit and capital accumulation. Capitalism is indeed a marvelous engine for building up the productive forces (though clearly at the expense of considerations of equality and autonomy). We might look on it, going back to earlier historical times, as something like a forced march to develop the productive forces. But now that the productive forces in advanced capitalist societies are wondrously developed, we are in a position to direct them to far more humane and more equitable uses under a socio-economic system whose rationale for production is to meet human needs (the needs of everyone as far as this is possible). This egalitarian thrust, together with the socialists' commitment to attaining, as far as that is possible, equality of condition, makes it clear that socialism will produce more equality than capitalism.

V

In talking about autonomy, democracy and equality; we have, in effect, already been talking about justice. A society or set of institutions that does better in these respects than another society will be a more just society than the other society.

Fairness is a less fancy name for justice. If we compare two societies and the first is more democratic than the second; there is more autonomy in the first society than in the second; there are more nearly equal life chances in the first society than in the second and thus greater equality of opportunity; if, without sacrifice of autonomy, there is more equality of condition in the first society than in the second; and if there is more moral equality in the first society than in the second, then we cannot but conclude that the first society is a society with more fairness than the second and, thus, that it is the more just society. But this is exactly how socialism comes out vis-à-vis even the best form of capitalism.

A society which undermines autonomy, heels in democracy (where democracy is not violating rights), makes equality impossible to achieve and violates rights cannot be a just society. If, as I contend, that is what capitalism does, and cannot help doing, then a capitalist society cannot be a just society. Democratic socialism, by contrast, does not need to do any of those things, and we can predict that it would not, for there are no structural imperatives in democratic socialism to do so and there are deep sentiments in that tradition urging us not to do so. I do not for a moment deny that there are similar sentiments for autonomy and democracy in capitalist societies, but the logic of capitalism, the underlying structures of capitalist societies—even the best of capitalist societies—frustrate the realization of the states of affairs at which those sympathies aim. A radical democrat with a commitment to human rights, to human autonomy and moral equality and fair equality of opportunity ought to be a democratic socialist and a firm opponent of capitalism—even a capitalism with a human face.

◆ ◆ ◆ ◆ ◆

G.A. COHEN

Illusions About Private Property and Freedom

1. In capitalist societies everyone owns something, be it only his own labour power, and each is free to sell what he owns and to buy whatever the sale of it enables him to buy.[1] Many claims made on capitalism's behalf may reasonably be doubted, but here is a freedom which it certainly bestows.

It is clear that under capitalism everyone has this freedom, unless being free to sell something is incompatible with being forced to sell it: but I do not think it is. For one is in general free to do anything which one is forced to do.

There are several reasons for affirming this possibly surprising thesis. The most direct argument in favour of it is as follows: you cannot be forced to do what you are not able to do, and you are not able to do what you are not free to do. Hence you are free to do what you are forced to do.

I am not, in the foregoing argument, equating being free to do something with being able to do it.[2] Being free to do A is a necessary but not a sufficient condition of being able to do A. I may be unable to do something not because I am unfree to, but because I lack the relevant capacity. Thus I am no doubt free to swim across the English Channel, but I am nevertheless unable to. If I were a much better swimmer, but forbidden by well-enforced law to swim it, then, again, I would be unable to swim it. The argument of the last paragraph goes through on what is often called the "negative" or "social" conception of freedom, according to which I am free to do whatever nobody would prevent me from doing. I have no quarrel with that conception in this paper.

A second argument for the claim that I am free to do what I am forced to do is that one way of frustrating someone who would force me to do something is by rendering myself not free to do it: it follows, by contraposition, that if I am forced to do it, I am free to do it. To illustrate: I commit a crime, thereby causing myself to be gaoled, so that I cannot be forced by you to do something I abhor. If you still hope to force me to do it you will have to make me free to do it (by springing me from jail).

Look at it this way: before you are forced to do *A*, you are, at least in standard cases, free to do *A* and free not to do *A*. The force removes the second freedom, but why suppose that it removes the first? It puts no obstacle in the path of your doing *A*, and you therefore remain free to do it.

We may conclude, not only that being free to do *A* is compatible with being forced to do *A*, but that being forced to do *A entails* being free to do *A*. Resistance to this odd-sounding but demonstrable result reflects failure to distinguish the idea of *being free to do something* from other ideas, such as the idea of *doing something freely*. I am free to do what I am forced to do even if, as is usually true,[3] I do not do it freely, and even though, as is always true, I am not free with respect to whether or not I do it.

I labour this truth—that one is free to do what one is forced to do—because it, and failure to perceive it, help to explain the character and the persistence of a certain ideological disagreement. Marxists say that working class people are forced to sell their labour power. Bourgeois thinkers celebrate the freedom of contract manifest not only in the capitalist's purchase of labour power but also in the worker's sale of it. If Marxists are right[4] working class people are importantly unfree: they are not free not to sell their labour power. But it remains true that (unlike chattel slaves) they are free to sell their labour power. The unfreedom asserted by Marxists is compatible with the freedom asserted by bourgeois thinkers. Indeed: if the Marxists are right the bourgeois thinkers are right, unless they also think, as characteristically they do, that the truth they emphasise refutes the Marxist claim. The bourgeois thinkers go wrong

not when they say that the worker is free to sell his labour power, but when they infer that the Marxist cannot therefore be right in his claim that the worker is forced to. And Marxists[5] share the bourgeois thinkers' error when they think it necessary to deny what the bourgeois thinkers say. If the worker is not free to sell his labour power, of what freedom is a foreigner whose work permit is removed deprived?

2. Freedom to buy and sell is one freedom, of which in capitalism there is a great deal. It belongs to capitalism's essential nature. But many think that capitalism is, quite as essentially, a more comprehensively free society. Very many people, including philosophers, who try to speak carefully, use the phrase "free society" as an alternative name for societies which are capitalist.[6] And many contemporary English-speaking philosophers and economists call the doctrine which recommends a purely capitalist society "libertarianism," not, as might be thought more apt, "libertarianism with respect to buying and selling."

It is not only the libertarians themselves who think that is the right name for their party. Many who reject their aims concede the name to them: they agree that unmodified capitalism is comprehensively a realm of freedom. This applies to *some* of those who call themselves "liberals."

These liberals assert, plausibly, that liberty is a good thing, but they say that it is not the only good thing. So far, libertarians will agree. But liberals also believe that libertarians wrongly sacrifice other good things in too total defence of the one good of liberty. They agree with libertarians that pure capitalism is liberty pure and simple, or anyway *economic*[7] liberty pure and simple, but they think the various good things lost when liberty pure and simple is the rule justify restraints on liberty. They want a capitalism modified by welfare legislation and state intervention in the market. They advocate, they say, not unrestrained liberty, but liberty restrained by the demands of social and economic security. They think that what they call a free economy is too damaging to those, who, by nature or circumstance, are ill placed to achieve a minimally proper standard of life within it, so they favour, within limits, taxing the better off for the sake of the worse off, although they believe that such taxation reduces liberty. They also think that what they call a free economy is subject to fluctuations in productive activity and misallocations of resources which are potentially damaging to everyone, so they favour measures of interference in the market, although, again, they believe that such interventions diminish liberty. They do not question the libertarian's description of capitalism as the (economically) free society. But they believe that economic freedom may rightly and reasonably be abridged. They believe in a compromise between liberty and other values, and that what is known as the welfare state mixed economy achieves the right compromise.

I shall argue that libertarians, and liberals of the kind described, misuse the concept of freedom. This is not a comment on the attractiveness of the institutions they severally favour, but on the rhetoric they use to describe them. If, however, as I contend, they misdescribe those institutions, then that is surely because the correct description of them would make them less attractive, so my critique of the defensive rhetoric is indirectly a critique of the institutions the rhetoric defends.

My central contention is that liberals and libertarians see the freedom which is intrinsic to capitalism, but do not give proper notice to the unfreedom which necessarily accompanies it.

To expose this failure of perception, I shall criticise a description of the libertarian position provided by Antony Flew in his *Dictionary of Philosophy*. It is there said to be "whole-hearted political and economic liberalism, opposed to any social or legal constraints on individual freedom."[8] Liberals of the kind I described above would avow themselves unwhole-hearted in the terms of this definition. For they would say that they support certain (at any rate) legal constraints on individual freedom.

Now a society in which there are *no* "social and legal constraints on individual freedom" is perhaps imaginable, at any rate by people who have highly anarchic imaginations. But, be that as it may, the Flew definition misdescribes libertarians, since it does not apply to defenders of capitalism, which is what libertarians profess to be, and are.

For consider. If the state prevents me from doing something I want to do, it evidently places a constraint on my freedom. Suppose, then, that I want to perform an action which involves a legally prohibited use of your property. I want, let us say, to pitch a tent in your large back garden, because I have no home or land of my own, but I have got hold of a tent, legitimately or otherwise. If I now try to do what I want to do, the chances are that the state will intervene on your behalf. If it does, I shall suffer a constraint on my freedom. The same goes for all unpermitted uses of a piece of private property by those who do not own it, and there are always those who do not own it, since "private ownership by one person ... presupposes non-ownership on the part of other persons."[9] But the free enterprise economy advocated by libertarians rests upon private property: you can sell and buy only what you respectively own and come to own. It follows that the Flew definition is untrue to its *definiendum*, and that "libertarianism" is a questionable name for the position it now standardly denotes.

How could Flew publish the definition I have criticised? I do not think he was being dishonest. I would not accuse him of appreciating the truth of this particular matter and deliberately falsifying it. Why then is it that Flew, and libertarians like him,[10] see the unfreedom in prospective state interference with your use of your property, but do not see the unfreedom in the standing intervention against my use of it entailed by the fact that it *is* your private property? What explains their monocular vision?

One explanation is a tendency to take as part of the structure of human existence in general, and therefore as no "social or legal constraint" on freedom, any structure around which, *merely as things are*, much of our activity is organised. In capitalist society the institution of private property is such a structure. It is treated as so *given* that the obstacles it puts on freedom are not perceived, while any impingement on private property itself is immediately noticed. Yet private property pretty well *is* a distribution of freedom *and* unfreedom. It is necessarily associated with the liberty of private owners to do as they wish with what they own, but it no less necessarily withdraws liberty from those who do not own it. To think of capitalism as a realm of freedom is to overlook half of its nature. (I am aware that the tendency to this failure of perception is stronger, other things being equal, the more private property a person has. I do not think really poor people need to have their eyes opened to the simple conceptual truth I emphasise. I also do not claim that anyone of sound mind will for long deny that private property places restrictions on freedom, once the point has been made. What is striking is that the point so often needs to be made, against what should be *obvious* absurdities, such as Flew's definition of "libertarianism.")

I have supposed that to prevent someone from doing something he wants to do is to make him, in that respect, unfree: I am unfree whenever someone interferes, *justifiably or otherwise*, with my actions. But there is a definition of freedom which is implicit in much libertarian writing,[11] and which entails that interference is *not* a sufficient condition of unfreedom. On that definition, which I shall call the *moralised* definition, I am unfree only when someone does or would *unjustifiably* interfere with me. If one now combines this moralised definition of freedom with a moral endorsement of private property, one reaches the result that the protection of legitimate private property cannot restrict anyone's freedom. It will follow from the moral endorsement of private property that you and the police are justified in preventing me from pitching my tent on your land, and, because of the moralised definition of freedom, it will then further follow that you and the police do not thereby restrict my freedom. So here we have another explanation of how intelligent philosophers are able to say what they do about capitalism, private property and freedom. But the characterisation of freedom which figures in the explanation is unacceptable. For it entails that a properly convicted murderer is not rendered unfree when he is justifiably imprisoned.

Even justified interference reduces freedom. But suppose for a moment that, as libertarians say or imply, it does not. On that supposition one cannot readily argue that interference with private property is wrong *because* it reduces freedom. For one can no longer take for granted, what is evident on a morally neutral account of freedom, that interference with private property *does* reduce freedom. Under a moralised account of freedom one must abstain from that assertion until one has shown that private property is morally defensible. Yet libertarians tend *both* to use a moralised definition *and* to take it for granted that interference with private property diminishes the owner's freedom. Yet they can take that for granted only on an account of freedom in which it is equally obvious that the protection of private property diminishes the freedom of nonowners, to avoid which consequence they retreat to a moralised definition of the concept.

Still, libertarians who embrace the moralised definition of freedom need not occupy this inconsistent position. They can escape it by justifying private property on grounds other than considerations of freedom. They can contrive, for example, to represent interference with rightfully held private property as unjust, and *therefore*, by virtue of the moralised definition, invasive of freedom. This is a consistent position.[12] But it still incorporates an unacceptable definition of freedom, and the position is improved[13] if that is eliminated. We then have a defence of private property on grounds of justice. Freedom falls out of the picture.[14]

3. I now want to consider a possible response to what I said about pitching a tent on your land. It

might be granted that the prohibition on my doing so restricts my freedom, but not, so it might be said, my *economic* freedom. If the connection between capitalism and freedom is overstated by libertarians and others, the possibility that capitalism is *economic* freedom still requires consideration.

The resurrected identification will survive only if the unavailability to me of your garden is no restriction on my economic freedom. I can think of only one reason for saying so. It is that I am not here restricted with respect to whether I may sell something I own, or buy something in exchange for what I own. If that is economic freedom, then my lack of access to your garden does not limit my economic freedom.

A different definition of economic freedom would include in it freedom to use goods and services. It is hard to say whether such a definition is superior to the less inclusive one just considered, since "neither the tradition of political philosophy nor common understanding provides us with a ... set of categories of economic liberty" comparable to the acknowledged set of categories of political liberty,[15] perhaps because the boundary of the economic domain is unclear.[16] A reasoned attempt to construct a clear concept of economic freedom might be a valuable exercise, but it is not one which I can report having completed. I am accordingly unable to recommend any particular characterisation of economic freedom.

I can nevertheless reply to the present claim, as follows: either economic freedom includes the freedom to use goods and services, or it does not. If it does, then capitalism withholds economic freedom wherever it grants it, as the tent case shows. If, on the other hand, economic freedom relates only to buying and selling, then the case for identifying economic freedom and free enterprise looks better. But we have to define "economic freedom" narrowly to obtain this result. On a wide but eligible definition of economic freedom, capitalism offers a particular limited form of it. On a narrow definition, the lim-

itations recede, but we are now talking about a much narrower freedom.

To those who do not think this freedom is narrow, I offer three comments, which may move them a little:

(i) The freedom in question is, fully described, freedom to sell what I own and to buy whatever the sale of what I own enables me to buy. Importantly, that freedom is not identical with freedom to buy and sell just anything at all, which is much broader, and which is not granted by capitalism. For first, one is evidently not free to sell what belongs to somebody else. This is, to be sure, true by definition: there logically *could* not be that freedom, in any society. But this does not diminish the importance of noticing that capitalism does not offer it.[17] And secondly, one is free to buy, not anything at all, but only that which the sale of what one owns enables one to buy. A poor man is not free to buy a grand piano, even if one necessary condition of that freedom—he is not legally forbidden to do so—is satisfied.

(ii) It is an important fact about freedom in general, and hence about the freedom under discussion, that it comes in degrees. That I am free to do something does not say *how* free I am to do that thing, which might be more or less. To cite just one dimension in which freedom's degree varies, my freedom to do A is, other things equal, smaller, the greater is the cost to me of doing A. It might be true of both a poor man and a rich man that each is free to buy an £8 ticket to the opera, yet the rich man's freedom to do so is greater, since, unlike the poor man, he will not have to give up a few decent meals, for example, in order to buy the ticket. Since it is consistent with the capitalist character of a society that it should contain poor people, the buying and selling freedom which capitalism grants universally can be enjoyed in very limited degrees.

Now some will disagree with my claim that freedom varies in degree in the manner just described.

They will deny that some people have a higher degree of a certain freedom than others (who also have that freedom), and will say, instead, that for some people it is relatively easy to exercise a freedom which others, who also have it, find it difficult to exercise. But even if they are right, the substance of my case is unweakened. For it is scarcely intelligible that one should be interested in how much freedom people have in a certain form of society without being interested in how readily they are able to exercise it.

(iii) Finally, we should consider the *point* of the freedom to buy and sell, as far as the individual who has it is concerned. For most citizens, most of the time, that point is to obtain goods and services of various sorts. When, therefore, goods and services are available independently of the market, the individual might not feel that his lack of freedom to *buy* them is a particularly significant lack. A lack of freedom to buy medical services is no serious restriction on liberty in a society which makes them publicly available on a decent scale. In a socialist society certain things will be unbuyable, and, consequently, unsellable. But, as long as they are obtainable by other means, one should not exaggerate the gravity of the resulting restrictions on freedom.

Still, restrictions on freedom do result. I may not *want* to buy a medical or an educational service, but I am nevertheless unfree to, if the transaction is forbidden. Note that I would not be unfree to if a certain popular account of freedom were correct, according to which I am unfree only when what I *want* to do is something I shall or would be prevented from doing. But that account is false.[18] There are important connections between freedom and desire, but the straightforward one maintained in the popular account is not among them. Reference to a man's desires is irrelevant to the question "What is he free to do?" but it is, I believe, relevant to the question "How much freedom (comprehensively) does he have?" and consequently to the politically crucial question of comparing the amounts of freedom

enjoyed in different societies. As far as I know, the vast philosophical literature on freedom contains no sustained attempt to formulate criteria for answering questions about quantity of freedom. I attempted a discussion of such criteria in an earlier draft of this paper, but the response to it from many friends was so skeptical that I decided to abandon it I hope to return to it one day, and I hope that others will address it too.

4. I have wanted to show that private property, and therefore capitalist society, limit liberty, but I have not shown that they do so more than communal property and socialist society. Each *form* of society is by its nature congenial and hostile to various sorts of liberty, for variously placed people. And *concrete* societies exemplifying either form will offer and withhold additional liberties whose presence or absence may not be inferred from the nature of the form itself. Which form is better for freedom, all things considered, is a question which may have no answer in the abstract: it may be that which form is better for freedom depends entirely on the historical circumstances.

I am here separating two questions about capitalism, socialism, and freedom. The first, or *abstract* question, is which form of society is, just as such, better for freedom, not, and this is the second, and *concrete* question, which form is better for freedom in the conditions of a particular place and time.[19] The first question is interesting, but difficult and somewhat obscure. I shall try to clarify it presently. I shall then indicate that two distinct ranges of consideration bear on the second question, about freedom in a particular case, considerations which must be distinguished not only for theoretical but also for political reasons.

Though confident that the abstract interpretation of the question, which form, if any, offers more liberty, is meaningful, I am not at all sure what its meaning is. I do not think we get an answer to it favouring one form if and only if that form would in all circumstances provide more freedom than the other. For I can understand the claim that socialism is by nature a freer society than capitalism even though it would be a less free society under certain conditions.

Consider a possible analogy. It will be agreed that sports cars are faster than jeeps, even though jeeps are faster on certain kinds of terrain. Does the abstract comparison, in which sports cars outclass jeeps, mean, therefore, that sports cars are faster on *most* terrains? I think not. It seems sufficient for sports cars to be faster in the abstract that there is some unbizarre terrain on which their maximum speed exceeds the maximum speed of jeeps on any terrain. Applying the analogy, if socialism is said to be freer than capitalism in the abstract, this would mean that there are realistic concrete conditions under which a socialist society would be freer than *any* concrete capitalist society would be. This, perhaps, is what some socialists mean when they say that socialism is a freer society, for some who say that would acknowledge that in some conditions socialism, or what would pass for it,[20] would be less free than at any rate some varieties of capitalism.

There are no doubt other interesting abstract questions, which do not yield to the analysis just given. Perhaps, for example, the following intractably rough prescription could be made more useable: consider, with respect to each form of society, the sum of liberty which remains when the liberties it withholds by its very nature are subtracted from the liberties it guarantees by its very nature. The society which is freer in the abstract is the one where that sum is larger.

So much for the abstract issue. I said that two kinds of consideration bear on the answer to concrete questions, about which form of society would provide more freedom in a particular here and now. We may look upon each form of society as a set of rules which generates, in particular cases, particular enjoyments and deprivations of freedom. Now the effect of the rules in a particular case will depend, in the first place, on the resources and traditions which prevail in the society in question. But secondly, and distinctly, it will also depend on the ideological and political views of the people concerned. (This distinction is not always easy to make, but it is never impossible to make it.) To illustrate the distinction, it could be that in a given case collectivisation of agriculture would provide more freedom on the whole for rural producers, were it not for the fact that they do not *believe* it would, and would therefore resist collectivisation so strongly that it could be introduced only at the cost of enormous repression. It could be that though socialism might distribute more liberty in Britain now, capitalist ideology is now here so powerful, and the belief that socialism would reduce liberty is, accordingly, so strong, that conditions *otherwise* propitious for realising a socialism with a great deal of liberty are not favourable in the final reckoning, since the final reckoning must take account of the present views of people about how free a socialist society would be.

I think it is theoretically and politically important to attempt a reckoning independent of that final reckoning.

It is theoretically important because there exists a clear question about whether a socialist revolution would expand freedom whose answer is not determined by people's beliefs about what its answer is. *Its* answer might be "yes," even though most people think its answer is "no," and even though, as a result, "no" is the correct answer to the further, "final reckoning" question, for whose separateness I am arguing. Unless one separates the questions, one cannot coherently evaluate the ideological answers to the penultimate question which help to cause the ultimate question to have the answer it does.

It is also politically necessary to separate the questions, because it suits our rulers not to distinguish the two levels of assessment. The Right can often truly say that, all things considered, socialism would diminish liberty, where, however, the chief reason why this is so is that the Right, with its powerful ideological arsenal, have convinced enough people that it is so. Hence one needs to argue for an answer which does not take people's conviction into account, partly, of course, in order to combat and transform those convictions. If, on the other hand, you want to defend the status quo, then I recommend that you confuse the questions I have distinguished.

The distinction between concrete questions enables me to make a further point about the abstract question, which *form* of society provides more freedom. We saw above that a plausible strategy for answering it involves asking concrete questions about particular cases. We may now add that the concrete questions relevant to the abstract one are those which prescind from people's beliefs about their answers.

I should add, finally, that people's beliefs about socialism and freedom affect not only how free an achieved socialist society would be, but also how much restriction on freedom would attend the process of achieving it. (Note that there is a somewhat analogous distinction between how much freedom we have in virtue of the currently maintained capitalist arrangements, and how much we have, or lose, because of the increasingly repressive measures used to maintain them.) Refutation of bourgeois ideology is an imperative task for socialists, not as an alternative to the struggle for socialism, but as part of the struggle for a socialism which will justify the struggle which led to it.

5. I said above that capitalism and socialism offer different sets of freedoms, but I emphatically do not say that they provide freedom in two different senses of that term. To the claim that capitalism gives people freedom some socialists respond that what they get is *merely bourgeois* freedom. Good things can be meant by that response: that there are important particular liberties which capitalism does not confer; and/or that I do not have freedom, but only a necessary condition of it, when a course of action (for example, skiing) is, though not *itself* against the law, unavailable to me anyway, because other laws (for example, those

of private property, which prevent a poor man from using a rich man's unused skis) forbid me the means to perform it. But when socialists suggest that there is no "real" freedom under capitalism, at any rate for the workers, or that socialism promises freedom of a higher and as yet unrealised kind, then I think their line is theoretically incorrect and politically disastrous. For there is freedom under capitalism, in a plain, good sense, and if socialism will not give us more of it, we shall rightly be disappointed. If the socialist says he is offering a new variety of freedom, the advocate of capitalism will carry the day with his reply that he prefers freedom of the known variety to an unexplained and unexemplified rival. But if, as I would recommend, the socialist argues that capitalism is, all things considered, inimical to freedom *in the very sense* of "freedom" in which, as he should concede, a person's freedom is diminished when his private property is tampered with, then he presents a challenge which the advocate of capitalism, by virtue of his own commitment, cannot ignore.

For it is a contention of socialist thought that capitalism does not live up to its own professions. A fundamental socialist challenge to the libertarian is that pure capitalism does not protect liberty in general, but rather those liberties which are built into private property, an institution which also limits liberty. And a fundamental socialist challenge to the liberal is that the modifications of modified capitalism modify not liberty, but private property, often in the interest of liberty itself. Consequently, transformations far more revolutionary than a liberal would contemplate might be justified on the very same grounds as those which support liberal reform.

A homespun example shows how communal property offers a differently shaped liberty, in no different sense of that term, and, in certain circumstances, more liberty than the private property alternative. Neighbours *A* and *B* own sets of household tools. Each has some tools which the other lacks. If *A* needs tools of a kind which only *B* has, then, private property being what it is, he is not free to take

B's one for a while, even if B does not need it during that while. Now imagine that the following rule is imposed, bringing the tools into partly common ownership: each may take and use a tool belonging to the other without permission provided that the other is not using it and that he returns it when he no longer needs it, or when the other needs it, whichever comes first. *Things being what they are* (a substantive qualification: we are talking, as often we should, about the real world, not about remote possibilities) the communising rule would, I contend, increase tool-using freedom, on any reasonable view. To be sure, some freedoms are removed by the new rule. Neither neighbour is as assured of the same easy access as before to the tools that were wholly his. Sometimes he has to go next door to retrieve one of them. Nor can either now charge the other for use of a tool he himself does not then require. But these restrictions probably count for less than the increase in the range of tools available. No one is as sovereign as before over any tool, so the privateness of the property is reduced. But freedom is probably expanded.

It is true that each would have more freedom still if he were the sovereign owner of *all* the tools. But that is not the relevant comparison. I do not deny that full ownership of a thing gives greater freedom than shared ownership of that thing. But no one did own all the tools before the modest measure of communism was introduced. The kind of comparison we need to make is between, for example, sharing ownership with ninety-nine others in a hundred things and fully owning just one of them. I submit that which arrangement nets more freedom is a matter of cases. There is little sense in one hundred people sharing control over one hundred toothbrushes. There is an overwhelming case, from the point of view of freedom, in favour of our actual practice of public ownership of street pavements. Denationalising the pavements in favour of private ownership of each piece by the residents adjacent to it would be bad for freedom of movement.

But someone will say: ownership of private property is the only example of *full* freedom. Our practice with pavements may be a good one, but no one has full freedom with respect to any part of the pavement, since he cannot, for instance, break it up and put the result to a new use, and he cannot prevent others from using it (except, perhaps, by the costly means of indefinitely standing on it himself, and he cannot even do that when laws against obstruction are enforced). The same holds for all communal possessions. No one is fully free with respect to anything in which he enjoys a merely shared ownership. Hence even if private property entails unfreedom, and even if there is freedom without private property, *there is no case of full freedom which is not a case of private property.* The underlined thesis is unaffected by the arguments against libertarianism in sections 2 and 3 of this paper.

There are two things wrong with this fresh attempt to associate freedom and private property. First, even if it is true that every case of full freedom is a case of private property, a certain number of full freedoms need not add up to more freedom overall than a larger number of partial freedoms: so it is not clear that the underlined thesis supports any interesting conclusion.

The thesis is, moreover, questionable in itself. It is a piece of bourgeois ideology masquerading as a conceptual insight The argument for the thesis treats freedom fetishistically, as control over *material things*. But freedom, in the central sense of the term with which we have been occupied, is freedom to *act*, and if there is a concept of full freedom in that central sense, then it is inappropriate, if we want to identify it, to focus, from the start, on control over *things*. I can be fully free to walk to your home when and because the pavement is communally owned, even though I am not free to destroy or to sell a single square inch of that pavement. To be sure, action requires the use of matter, or at least space,[21] but it does not follow that to be fully free to perform an action with certain pieces of matter in a certain portion of space I need full control over the matter and the space, since some forms of control will be unnecessary to the action in question. The rights I need over things to perform a given action depend on the nature of that action.

The thesis under examination is, then, either false, or reducible to the truism that one has full freedom *with respect to a thing* only if one privately owns that thing. But why should we be especially interested in full freedom with respect to a *thing*, unless, of course, we are already ideologically committed to the overriding importance of private property?

6. Recall the example of the tools, described above. An opponent might say: the rules of private property allow neighbours to *contract* in favour of the stated arrangement. If both would gain from the change, and they are rational, they will agree to it. No communist property rule, laid down independently of contract, is needed.

This is a good reply with respect to the case at hand. For that case my only counter is the weakish one that life under capitalism tends to generate an irrationally strong attachment to purely private use of purely private property, which can lead to neglect of mutually gainful and freedom-expanding options.

That point aside, it must be granted that contracts often establish desirably communal structures, sometimes with transaction costs which communist rules would not impose, but also without the administrative costs which often attach to public regulation.

But the stated method of achieving communism cannot be generalised. We could not by contract bring into shared ownership those non-household tools and resources which Marxists call means of production. They will never be won for socialism by contract,[22] since they belong to a small minority, to whom the rest can offer no quid pro quo. Most of the rest must lease their labour power to members of that minority, in exchange for some of the proceeds of their labour on facilities in whose ownership they do not share.

So we reach, at length, a central charge with respect to freedom which Marxists lay against capitalism, and which is, in my view, well founded: that in capitalist society the great majority of people are forced, because of the character of the society, to sell their labour power to others. In properly refined form, this important claim about capitalism and liberty is, I am sure, correct. I have attempted to refine it elsewhere.[23]

NOTES

1 The present paper rewrites and extends arguments first presented on 9-17 of "Capitalism, Freedom and the Proletariat," which appeared in Alan Ryan (ed.), *The Idea of Freedom: Essays in Honour of Isaiah Berlin*, Oxford, 1979. The position of the proletariat with respect to freedom, discussed on 17-25 of that paper, is not treated here. I return to that issue in a forthcoming article on "The Structure of Proletarian Unfreedom."

2 I point this out because the argument was thus misinterpreted by Galen Strawson in a review of *The Idea of Freedom* which appeared in *Lycidas*, the journal of Wolfson College, Oxford. See *Lycidas*, 7, 1978-79, 35-36.

3 It is not true that whenever I am forced to do something I act unfreely, not, at any rate, if we accept Gerald Dworkin's well-defended claim that "*A* does *X* freely if ... *A* does *X* for reasons which he doesn't mind acting from" ("Acting Freely," *Nous*, 1970, 381). On this view some forced action is freely performed: if, for example, I am forced to do something which I had wanted to do and had fully intended to do, then, unless I resent the supervenient coercion, I do it freely.

4 I consider whether they are right in the latter half of "Capitalism, Freedom and the Proletariat," and in "The Structure of Proletarian Unfreedom."

5 Such as Ziyad Husami, if he is a Marxist, who says of the wage worker: "Deprived of the ownership of means of production and means of livelihood, he is forced (not free) to sell his labour power to the capitalist" ("Marx on Distributive Justice," *Philosophy and Public Affairs*, Fall, 1978, 51-52). I contend that the phrase in parentheses introduces a falsehood into Husami's sentence, a falsehood which Karl Marx avoided when he said of the worker that "the time for which he is free to sell his labour power is the time for which he is forced to sell it" (*Capital*, I, Moscow, 1961, 302).

6 See, for example, Jan Narveson, "A Puzzle about Economic Justice in Rawls' Theory," *Social Theory and Practice*, 1976, 3; James Rachels, "What People Deserve," in J. Arthur and W. Shaw (eds.), *Justice and Economic Distribution*, Englewood Cliffs, 1978, 151.

7 See 229 below on what might be meant by *economic* liberty.

8 *A Dictionary of Philosophy*, London, 1979, 188.

9 Karl Marx, *Capital*, III, Moscow, 1970, 812.

10 The question also applies to anti-libertarian liberals of the kind described on 225-26, such as Isaiah Berlin and H.L.A. Hart. See "Capitalism, Freedom and the Proletariat," 13, on Berlin, and my forthcoming essay "Respecting Private Property," on Hart.

11 And sometimes also explicit: see Robert Nozick, *Anarchy, State and Utopia*, New York, 1974, 262.

12 I argued elsewhere that, unlike libertarians, liberals of the kind described on 225-26 *necessarily* proceed inconsistently, that their idea of compromise between freedom and other values requires vacillation between neutral and moralised versions of freedom. But Bill Shaw and Tim Scanlon have convinced me that my argument is inconclusive. See "Capitalism, Freedom and the Proletariat," 13.

13 It is improved intellectually in that a certain objection to it no longer applies, but ideologically speaking it is weakened, since there is more ideological power in a recommendation of private property on grounds of justice *and* freedom—however confused the relationship between them may be—than in a recommendation of private property on grounds of justice alone.

14 The justice argument for private property is not examined in what follows. I deal with it at length in "Respecting Private Property."

15 Thomas Scanlon, "Liberty, Contract and Contribution," in G. Dworkin et al. (eds.), *Markets and Morals*, Washington, 1977, 54; and see also 57.

16 This suggestion is due to Chris Proviso.

17 Cheyney Ryan's discussion of "capacity rights" is relevant here. See his "The Normative Concept of Coercion," *Mind*, forthcoming.

18 See Isaiah Berlin, *Four Essays on Liberty*, Oxford, 1969, xxxviii ff., 139-40. The point was originally made by Richard Wollheim, in a review of Berlin's *Two Concepts of Liberty*. See too Hillel Steiner, "Individual Liberty," *Proceedings of the Aristotelian Society*, 1974-75, 34.

19 One may also distinguish not, as above, between the capitalist form of society and a particular capitalist society, but between the capitalist form in general and specific forms of capitalism, such as competitive capitalism, monopoly capitalism, and so on (I provide a systematic means of generating specific forms in *Karl Marx's Theory of History*, Oxford, 1978, Chapter III, sections [6] and [8]). This further distinction is *at* the abstract level, rather than between abstract and concrete. I prescind from it here to keep my discussion relatively uncomplicated. The distinction would have to be acknowledged, and employed, in any treatment which pretended to be definitive.

20 Which way they would put it depends on how they would define socialism. If it is defined as public ownership of the means of production, and this is taken in a narrowly juridical sense, then it is compatible with severe restrictions on freedom. But if, to go to other extreme, it is defined as a condition in which the free development of each promotes, and is promoted by, the free development of all, then only the attempt to institute socialism, not socialism, could have negative consequences for freedom.

21 This fact is emphasised by Hillel Steiner in section III of his "Individual Liberty," but he goes too far when he says: "My theorem is ... that *freedom is the personal possession of physical objects*" (48). I claim that the "theorem" is just bourgeois ideology. For further criticism of Steiner, see Onora O'Neill, "The Most Extensive Liberty," *Proceedings of the Aristotelian Society*, 1979-80, 48.

22 Unless the last act of this scenario qualifies as a contract: in the course of a general strike a united working class demands that private property in major means of production be socialised, as a condition of resumption of work, and a demoralised capitalist class meets the demand. (How, by the way, could "libertarians" object to such a revolution? For hints see Robert Nozick, "Coercion," in P. Laslett *et al.*, [eds.] *Philosophy, Politics and Society*, Fourth Series, Oxford, 1972.)

23 See note 1 above.

INTELLECTUAL PROPERTY

EDWIN C. HETTINGER

Justifying Intellectual Property

Property institutions fundamentally shape a society. These legal relationships between individuals, different sorts of objects, and the state are not easy to justify. This is especially true of intellectual property. It is difficult enough to determine the appropriate kinds of ownership of corporeal objects (consider water or mineral rights); it is even more difficult to determine what types of ownership we should allow for noncorporeal, intellectual objects, such as writings, inventions, and secret business information. The complexity of copyright, patent, and trade secret law reflects this problem.

According to one writer "patents are the heart and core of property rights, and once they are destroyed, the destruction of all other property rights will follow automatically, as a brief postscript."[1] Though extreme, this remark rightly stresses the importance of patents to private competitive enterprise. Intellectual property is an increasingly significant and widespread form of ownership. Many have noted the arrival of the "post-industrial society"[2] in which the manufacture and manipulation of physical goods is giving way to the production and use of information. The result is an ever-increasing strain on our laws and customs protecting intellectual property.[3] Now, more than ever, there is a need to carefully scrutinize these institutions.

As a result of both vastly improved information handling technologies and the larger role information is playing in our society, owners of intellectual property are more frequently faced with what they call "piracy" or information theft (that is, unauthorized access to their intellectual property). Most readers of this article have undoubtedly done something considered piracy by owners of intellectual property. Making a cassette tape of a friend's record, videotaping television broadcasts for a movie library, copying computer programs or using them on more than one machine, photocopying more than one chapter of a book, or two or more articles by the same author—all are examples of alleged infringing activities. Copyright, patent, and trade secret violation suits abound in industry, and in academia, the use of another person's ideas often goes unacknowledged. These phenomena indicate widespread public disagreement over the nature and legitimacy of our intellectual property institutions. This article examines the justifiability of those institutions.

Copyrights, Patents, and Trade Secrets

It is commonly said that one cannot patent or copyright ideas. One copyrights "original works of authorship," including writings, music, drawings, dances, computer programs, and movies; one may not copyright ideas, concepts, principles, facts, or knowledge. Expressions of ideas are copyrightable; ideas themselves are not.[4] While useful, this notion of separating the content of an idea from its style of presentation is not unproblematic.[5] Difficulty in distinguishing the two is most apparent in the more artistic forms of authorship (such as fiction or poetry), where style and content interpenetrate. In these mediums, more so than in others, *how* something is said is very much part of *what* is said (and vice versa).

A related distinction holds for patents. Laws of nature, mathematical formulas, and methods of doing business, for example, cannot be patented. What one patents are inventions—that is, processes, machines, manufacturers, or compositions of matter. These must be novel (not previously patented); they must constitute nonobvious improvements over past inventions; and they must be useful (inventions that do not work cannot be patented). Specifying what sorts of "technological recipes for production"[6] constitute patentable subject matter involves distinguishing specific applications and utilizations from the underlying unpatentable general principles.[7] One cannot patent the scientific principle that water boils at 212 degrees, but one can patent a machine (for example, a steam engine) which uses this principle in a specific way and for a specific purpose.[8]

Trade secrets include a variety of confidential and valuable business information, such as sales, marketing, pricing, and advertising data, lists of customers and suppliers, and such things as plant layout and manufacturing techniques. Trade secrets must not be generally known in the industry, their nondisclosure must give some advantage over competitors, and attempts to prevent leakage of the information must be made (such as pledges of secrecy in employment contracts or other company security policies). The formula for Coca-Cola and bids on government contracts are examples of trade secrets.

Trade secret subject matter includes that of copyrights and patents: anything which can be copyrighted or patented can be held as a trade secret, though the converse is not true. Typically a business must choose between patenting an invention and holding it as a trade secret. Some advantages of trade secrets are

1. they do not require disclosure (in fact they require secrecy), whereas a condition for granting patents (and copyrights) is public disclosure of the invention (or writing);
2. they are protected for as long as they are kept secret, while most patents lapse after seventeen years; and
3. they involve less cost than acquiring and defending a patent.

Advantages of patents include protection against reverse engineering (competitors figuring out the invention by examining the product which embodies it) and against independent invention. Patents give their owners the *exclusive* right to make, use, and sell the invention no matter how anyone else comes up with it, while trade secrets prevent only improper acquisition (breaches of security).

Copyrights give their owners the right to reproduce, to prepare derivative works from, to distribute copies of, and to publicly perform or display the "original work of authorship." Their duration is the author's life plus fifty years. These rights are not universally applicable, however. The most notable exception is the "fair use" clause of the copyright statute, which gives researchers, educators, and libraries special privileges to use copyrighted material.[9]

Intellectual Objects as Nonexclusive

Let us call the subject matter of copyrights, patents, and trade secrets "intellectual objects."[10] These objects are nonexclusive: they can be at many places at once and are not consumed by their use. The marginal cost of providing an intellectual object to an additional user is zero, and though there are communications costs, modern technologies can easily make an intellectual object unlimitedly available at a very low cost.

The possession or use of an intellectual object by one person does not preclude others from possessing or using it as well.[11] If someone borrows your lawn mower, you cannot use it, nor can anyone else. But if someone borrows your recipe for guacamole, that in no way precludes you, or anyone else, from using it. This feature is shared by all sorts of intellectual objects, including novels, computer programs, songs, machine designs, dances, recipes for Coca-Cola, lists of customers and suppliers, management techniques, and formulas for genetically engineered bacteria which digest crude oil. Of course, sharing intellectual objects does prevent the original possessor from selling the intellectual object to others, and so this sort of use is prevented. But sharing in no way hinders *personal* use.

This characteristic of intellectual objects grounds a strong *prima facie* case against the wisdom of private and exclusive intellectual property rights. Why should one person have the exclusive right to possess and use something which all people could possess and use concurrently? The burden of justification is very much on those who would restrict the maximal use of intellectual objects. A person's right to exclude others from possessing and using a physical object can be justified when such exclusion is necessary for this person's own possession and unhindered use. No such justification is available for exclusive possession and use of intellectual property.

One reason for the widespread piracy of intellectual property is that many people think it is unjustified to exclude others from intellectual objects.[12] Also, the unauthorized taking of an intellectual object does not feel like theft. Stealing a physical object involves depriving someone of the object taken, whereas taking an intellectual object deprives the owner of neither possession nor personal use of that object—though the owner is deprived of potential profit. This nonexclusive feature of intellectual objects should be kept firmly in mind when assessing the justifiability of intellectual property.

Owning Ideas and Restrictions on the Free Flow of Information

The fundamental value our society places on freedom of thought and expression creates another difficulty for the justification of intellectual property. Private property enhances one person's freedom at the expense of everyone else's. Private intellectual property restricts methods of acquiring ideas (as do trade secrets), it restricts the use of ideas (as do patents), and it restricts the expression of ideas (as do copyrights)—restrictions undesirable for a number of reasons. John Stuart Mill argued that free thought and speech are important for the acquisition of true beliefs and for individual growth and development.[13] Restrictions on the free flow and use of ideas not only stifle individual growth, but impede the advancement of technological innovation and human knowledge generally.[14] Insofar as copyrights, patents, and trade secrets have these negative effects, they are hard to justify. Since a condition for granting patents and copyrights is public disclosure of the writing or invention, these forms of intellectual ownership do not involve the exclusive right to possess the knowledge or ideas they protect. Our society gives its inventors and writers a legal right to exclude others from certain uses of their intellectual works in return for public disclosure of these works. Disclosure is necessary if people are to learn from and build on the ideas of others. When they bring about disclosure of ideas which would have otherwise remained secret, patents and copyrights enhance rather than restrict the free flow of ideas (though they still restrict the idea's widespread use and dissemination). Trade secrets do not have this virtue. Regrettably, the common law tradition which offers protection for trade secrets encourages secrecy. This makes trade secrets undesirable in a way in which copyrights or patents are not.[15]

Labor, Natural Intellectual Property Rights, and Market Value

Perhaps the most powerful intuition supporting property rights is that people are entitled to the fruits of their labor. What a person produces with her own intelligence, effort, and perseverance ought to belong to her and to no one else. "Why is it mine? Well, it's mine because I made it, that's why. It wouldn't have existed but for me."

John Locke's version of this labor justification for property derives property rights in the product of labor from prior property rights in one's body.[16] A person owns her body and hence she owns what it does, namely, its labor. A person's labor and its product are inseparable, and so ownership of one can be secured only by owning the other. Hence, if a person is to own her body and thus its labor, she must also own what she joins her labor with—namely, the product of her labor.

This formulation is not without problems. For example, Robert Nozick wonders why a person should gain what she mixes her labor with instead of losing her labor. (He imagines pouring a can of tomato juice into the ocean and asks whether he thereby ought to gain the ocean or lose his tomato juice.)[17] More importantly, assuming that labor's fruits are valuable, and that laboring gives the laborer a property right in this value, this would entitle the laborer only to the value she added, and not to the *total* value of the resulting product. Though exceedingly difficult to measure, these two components of value (that attributable to the object labored on and that attributable to the labor) need to be distinguished.

Locke thinks that until labored on, objects have little human value, at one point suggesting that labor creates 99 per cent of their value.[18] This is not plausible when labor is mixed with land and other natural resources. One does not create 99 per cent of the value of an apple by picking it off a tree, though some human effort is necessary for an object to have value for us.

What portion of the value of writings, inventions, and business information is attributable to the intellectual laborer? Clearly authorship, discovery, or development is necessary if intellectual products are to have value for us; we could not use or appreciate them without this labor. But it does not follow from this that all of their value is attributable to that labor. Consider, for example, the wheel, the entire human value of which is not appropriately attributable to its original inventor.[19]

The value added by the laborer and any value the object has on its own are by no means the only components of the value of an intellectual object. Invention, writing, and thought in general do not operate in a vacuum; intellectual activity is not creation *ex nihilo*. Given this vital dependence of a person's thoughts on the ideas of those who came before her, intellectual products are fundamentally social products. Thus even if one assumes that the value of these products is entirely the result of human labor, this value is not entirely attributable to *any particular laborer* (or small group of laborers).

Separating out the individual contribution of the inventor, writer, or manager from this historical/social component is no easy task. Simply identifying the value a laborer's labor adds to the world with the market value or the resulting product ignores the vast contributions of others. A person who relies on human intellectual history and makes a small modification to produce something of great value should no more receive what the market will bear than should the last person needed to lift a car receive full credit for lifting it. If laboring gives the laborer the right to receive the market value of the resulting product, this market value should be shared by all those whose ideas contributed to the origin of the product. The fact that most of these contributors are no longer present to receive their fair share is not a reason to give the entire market value to the last contributor.[20]

Thus an appeal to the market value of a laborer's product cannot help us here. Markets work only after property rights have been established and enforced, and our question is what sorts of property rights an inventor, writer, or manager should have, given that the result of her labor is a joint product of human intellectual history.

Even if one could separate out the laborer's own contribution and determine its market value, it is still not clear that the laborer's right to the fruits of her labor naturally entitles her to receive this. Market value is a socially created phenomenon, depending on the activity (or nonactivity) of other producers, the monetary demand of purchasers, and the kinds of property rights, contracts, and markets the state has established and enforced. The market value of the same fruits of labor will differ greatly with variations in these social factors.

Consider the market value of a new drug formula. This depends on the length and the extent of the patent monopoly the state grants and enforces, on the level of affluence of those who need the drug, and on the availability and price of substitutes. The laborer did not produce these. The intuitive appeal behind the labor argument—"I made it, hence it's mine"—loses its force when it is used to try to justify owning something others are responsible for (namely, the market value). The claim that a laborer, in virtue of her labor, has a "natural right" to this socially created phenomenon is problematic at best.

Thus, there are two different reasons why the market value of the product of labor is not what a laborer's labor naturally entitles her to. First, market value is not something that is produced by those who produce a product, and the labor argument entitles laborers only to the products of their labor. Second, even if we ignore this point and equate the fruits of labor with the market value of those fruits, intellectual products result from the labor of many people besides the latest contributor, and they have claims on the market value as well.

So even if the labor theory shows that the laborer has a natural right to the fruits of labor, this does not establish a natural right to receive the full market value of the resulting product. The notion that a laborer is naturally entitled as a matter of right to receive the market value of her product is a myth. To what extent individual laborers should be allowed to receive the market value of their products is a question of social policy; it is not solved by simply insisting on a moral right to the fruits of one's labor.[21]

Having a moral right to the fruits of one's labor might also mean having a right to possess and personally use what one develops. This version of the labor theory has some force. On this interpretation, creating something through labor gives the laborer a *prima facie* right to possess and personally use it for her own benefit. The value of protecting individual freedom guarantees this right as long as the creative labor, and the possession and use of its product, does not harm others.

But the freedom to exchange a product in a market and receive its full market value is again something quite different. To show that people have a right to this, one must argue about how best to balance the conflicts in freedoms which arise when people interact. One must determine what sorts of property rights and markets are morally legitimate. One must also decide when society should enforce the results of market interaction and when it should alter those results (for example, with tax policy). There is a gap—requiring extensive argumentative filler—between the claim that one has a natural right to possess and personally use the fruits of one's labor and the claim that one ought to receive for one's product whatever the market will bear.

Such a gap exists as well between the natural right to possess and personally use one's intellectual creations and the rights protected by copyrights, patents, and trade secrets. The natural right of an author to personally use her writings is distinct from the right, protected by copyright, to make her work public, sell it in a market, and then prevent others from making copies. An inventor's natural right to use the invention for her own benefits is not the same as the right, protected by patent, to sell this invention in a market and exclude others (including independent inventors) from using it. An entrepreneur's natural right to use valuable business information or techniques that she develops is not the same as the right, protected by trade secret, to prevent her employees from using these techniques in another job.

In short, a laborer has a *prima facie* natural right to possess and personally use the fruits of her labor. But a right to profit by selling a product in the market is something quite different. This liberty is largely a socially created phenomenon. The "right" to receive what the market will bear is a socially created privilege, and not a natural right at all. The natural right to possess and personally use what one has produced is relevant to the justifiability of such a privilege, but by itself it is hardly sufficient to justify that privilege.

Deserving Property Rights Because of Labor

The above argument that people are naturally entitled to the fruits of their labor is distinct from the argument that a person has a claim to labor's fruits based on desert. If a person has a natural right to something—say her athletic ability—and someone takes it from her, the return of it is something she is *owed* and can rightfully demand. Whether or not she deserves this athletic ability is a separate issue. Similarly, insofar as people have natural property rights in the fruits of their labor, these rights are something they are owed, and not something they necessarily deserve.[22]

The desert argument suggests that the laborer deserves to benefit from her labor, at least if it is an attempt to do something worthwhile. This proposal is convincing, but does not show that what the laborer deserves is property rights in the object labored on. The mistake is to conflate the created object which makes a person deserving of a reward with what that reward should be. Property rights in the created object are not the only possible reward. Alternatives include fees, awards, acknowledgment, gratitude, praise, security, power status, and public financial support.

Many considerations affect whether property rights in the created object are what the laborer deserves. This may depend, for example, on what is created by labor. If property rights in the very things created were always an appropriate reward for labor, then as Lawrence Becker notes, parents would deserve property rights in their children.[23] Many intellectual objects (scientific laws, religious and ethical insights, and so on) are also the sort of thing that should not be owned by anyone.

Furthermore, as Becker also correctly points out, we need to consider the purpose for which the laborer labored. Property rights in the object produced are not a fitting reward if the laborer does not want them. Many intellectual laborers produce beautiful things and discover truths as ends in themselves.[24] The appropriate reward in such cases is recognition, gratitude, and perhaps public financial support, not full-fledged property rights, for these laborers do not want to exclude others from their creations.

Property rights in the thing produced are also not a fitting reward if the value of these rights is disproportional to the effort expended by the laborer. "Effort" includes

1. how hard someone tries to achieve a result,
2. the amount of risk voluntarily incurred in seeking this result, and
3. the degree to which moral consideration played a role in choosing the result intended.

The harder one tries, the more one is willing to sacrifice, and the worthier the goal, the greater are one's deserts.

Becker's claim that the amount deserved is proportional to the value one's labor produces is mistaken.[25] The value of labor's results is often significantly affected by factors outside a person's control, and no one deserves to be rewarded for being lucky. Voluntary past action is the only valid basis for determining desert.[26] Here only a person's effort (in the sense defined) is relevant. Her knowledge, skills, and achievements insofar as they are based on natural talent and luck, rather than effort expended, are not. A person who is born with extraordinary natural talents, or who is extremely lucky, *deserves* nothing on the basis of these characteristics. If such a person puts forward no greater effort than another, she deserves no greater reward. Thus, two laborers who expend equal amounts of effort deserve the same reward, even when the value of the resulting products is vastly different.[27] Giving more to workers whose products have greater social value might be justified if it is needed as an incentive. But this has nothing to do with giving the laborer what she deserves.

John Rawls considers even the ability to expend effort to be determined by factors outside a person's control and hence a morally impermissible criterion for distribution.[28] How hard one tries, how willing one is to sacrifice and incur risk, and how much one cares about morality are to *some extent* affected by natural endowments and social circumstances. But if the ability to expend effort is taken to be entirely determined by factors outside a person's control, the result is a determinism which makes meaningful moral evaluation impossible. If people are responsible for anything, they are responsible for how hard they try, what sacrifices they make, and how moral they are. Because the effort a person expends is much more under her control than her innate intelligence, skills, and talents, effort is a far superior basis for determining desert. To the extent that a person's expenditure of effort is under her control, effort is the proper criterion for desert.[29]

Giving an inventor exclusive rights to make and sell her invention (for seventeen years) may provide either a greater or a lesser reward than she deserves. Some inventions of extraordinary market value result from flashes of genius, while others with little market value (and yet great social value) require significant effort.

The proportionality requirement may also be frequently violated by granting copyright. Consider a five-hundred-dollar computer program. Granted, its initial development costs (read "efforts") were high. But once it has been developed, the cost of each additional program is the cost of the disk it is on—approximately a dollar. After the program has been on the market several years and the price remains at three or four hundred dollars, one begins to suspect that the company is receiving far more than it deserves. Perhaps this is another reason so much illegal copying of software goes on: the proportionality requirement is not being met, and people sense the unfairness of the price. Frequently, trade secrets (which are held indefinitely) also provide their owners with benefits disproportional to the effort expended in developing them.

The Lockean Provisos

We have examined two versions of the labor argument for intellectual property, one based on desert, the other based on a natural entitlement to the fruits of one's labor. Locke himself put limits on the conditions under which labor can justify a property right in the thing produced. One is that after the appropriation there must be "enough and as good left in common for others."[30] This proviso is often reformulated as a "no loss to others" precondition for property acquisition.[31] As long as one does not worsen another's position by appropriating an object, no objection can be raised to owning that with which one mixes one's labor.

Under current law, patents clearly run afoul of this proviso by giving the original inventor an exclusive right to make, use, and sell the invention. Subsequent inventors who independently come up with an already patented invention cannot even personally use their invention, much less patent or sell it. They clearly suffer a great and unfair loss because of the original patent grant. Independent inventors should not be prohibited from using or selling their inventions. Proving independent discovery of a publicly available patented invention would be difficult, however. Nozick's suggestion that the length of patents be restricted to the time it would take for independent invention may be the most reasonable administrative solution.[32] In the modern world of highly competitive research and development, this time is often much shorter than the seventeen years for which most patents are currently granted.

Copyrights and trade secrets are not subject to the same objection (though they may constitute a loss to others in different ways). If someone independently comes up with a copyrighted expression or a competitor's business technique, she is not prohibited from using it. Copyrights and trade secrets prevent only mimicking of other people's expressions and ideas.

Locke's second condition on the legitimate acquisition of property rights prohibits spoilage. Not only must one leave enough and as good for others, but one must not take more than one can use.[33] So in addition to leaving enough apples in the orchard for others, one must not take home a truckload and let them spoil. Though Locke does not specifically mention prohibiting waste, it is the concern to avoid waste which underlies his proviso prohibiting spoilage. Taking more than one can use is wrong because it is wasteful. Thus Locke's concern here is with appropriations of property which are wasteful.

Since writings, inventions, and business techniques are nonexclusive, this requirement prohibiting waste can never be completely met by intellectual property. When owners of intellectual property charge fees for the use of their expressions or inventions, or conceal their business techniques from others, certain beneficial uses of these intellectual products are prevented. This is clearly wasteful, since everyone could use and benefit from intellectual objects concurrently. How wasteful private ownership of intellectual property is depends on how beneficial those products would be to those who are excluded from their use as a result.

Sovereignty, Security, and Privacy

Private property can be justified as a means to sovereignty. Dominion over certain objects is important for individual autonomy. Ronald Dworkin's liberal is right in saying that "some sovereignty over a range of personal possessions is essential to dignity."[34] Not having to share one's personal possessions or borrow them from others is essential to the kind of autonomy our society values. Using or consuming certain objects is also necessary for survival. Allowing ownership of these things places control of the means of survival in the hands of individuals, and this promotes independence and security (at least for those who own enough of them). Private ownership of life's necessities lessens dependence between individuals, and takes power from the group and gives it to the individual. Private property also promotes privacy. It constitutes a sphere of privacy within which the individual is sovereign and less accountable for her actions. Owning one's own home is an example of all of these: it provides privacy, security, and a limited range of autonomy.

But copyrights and patents are neither necessary nor important for achieving these goals. The right to exclude others from using one's invention or copying one's work of authorship is not essential to one's sovereignty. Preventing a person from personally using her own invention or writing, on the other hand, would seriously threaten her sovereignty. An author's or inventor's sense of worth and dignity requires public acknowledgment by those who use the writing or discovery, but here again, giving the author or inventor the exclusive right to copy or use her intellectual product is not necessary to protect this.

Though patents and copyrights are not directly necessary for survival (as are food and shelter), one could argue that they are indirectly necessary for an individual's security and survival when selling her inventions or writings is a person's sole means of income. In our society, however, most patents and copyrights are owned by institutions (businesses, universities, or governments). Except in unusual cases where individuals have extraordinary bargaining power, prospective employees are required to give the rights to their inventions and works of authorship to their employers as a condition of employment. Independent authors or inventors who earn their living by selling their writings or inventions to others are increasingly rare.[35] Thus arguing that intellectual property promotes individual security makes sense only in a minority of cases. Additionally, there are other ways to ensure the independent intellectual laborer's security and survival besides copyrights and patents (such as public funding of intellectual workers and public domain property status for the results).

Controlling who uses one's invention or writing is not important to one's privacy. As long as there is no requirement to divulge privately created intellectual products (and as long as laws exist to protect people from others taking information they choose not to divulge—as with trade secret laws), the creator's privacy will not be infringed. Trying to justify copyrights and patents on grounds of privacy is highly implausible given that these property rights give the author or inventor control over certain uses of writings and inventions only after they have been publicly disclosed.

Trade secrets are not defensible on grounds of privacy either. A corporation is not an individual and hence does not have the personal features privacy is intended to protect.[36] Concern for sovereignty counts against trade secrets, for they often directly limit individual autonomy by preventing employees from changing jobs. Through employment contracts, by means of gentlemen's agreements among firms to respect trade secrets by refusing to hire competitors' employees, or simply because of the threat of lawsuits, trade secrets often prevent employees from using their skills and knowledge with other companies in the industry.

Some trade secrets, however, are important to a company's security and survival. If competitors could legally obtain the secret formula for Coke, for example, the Coca-Cola Company would be severely threatened. Similar points hold for copyrights and patents. Without some copyright protection, companies in the publishing, record, and movie industries would be severely threatened by competitors who copy and sell their works at lower prices (which need not reflect development costs). Without patent protection, companies with high research and development costs could be underpriced and driven out of business by competitors who simply mimicked the already developed products. This unfair competition could significantly weaken incentives to invest in innovative techniques and to develop new products.

The next section considers this argument that intellectual property is a necessary incentive for innovation and a requirement for healthy and fair competition. Notice, however, that the concern here is with the security and survival of private companies, not of individuals. Thus one needs to determine whether, and to what extent, the security and survival of privately held companies is a goal worth promoting. That issue turns on the difficult question of what type of economy is most desirable. Given a commitment to capitalism, however, this argument does have some force.

The Utilitarian Justification

The strongest and most widely appealed to justification for intellectual property is a utilitarian argument based on providing incentives. The constitutional justification for patents and copyrights— "to promote the progress of science and the useful arts"[37]—is itself utilitarian. Given the shortcomings of the other arguments for intellectual property, the justifiability of copyrights, patents) and trade secrets depends, in the final analysis, on this utilitarian defense.

According to this argument, promoting the creation of valuable intellectual works requires that intellectual laborers be granted property rights in those works. Without the copyright, patent, and trade secret property protections, adequate incentives for the creation of a socially optimal output of intellectual products would not exist. If competitors could simply copy books, movies, and records, and take one another's inventions and business techniques, there would be no incentive to spend the vast amounts of time, energy, and money necessary to develop these products and techniques. It would be in each firm's self-interest to let others develop products, and then mimic the result. No one would engage in original development, and consequently no new writings, inventions, or business techniques would be developed. To avoid this disastrous result, the argument claims, we must continue to grant intellectual property rights.

Notice that this argument focuses on the users of intellectual products, rather than on the producers. Granting property rights to producers is here seen as necessary to ensure that enough intellectual products (and the countless other goods based on these products) are available to users. The grant of property rights to the producers is a mere means to this end.

This approach is paradoxical. It establishes a right to restrict the current availability and use of intellectual products for the purpose of increasing the production and thus future availability and use of new intellectual products. As economist Joan Robinson says of patents: "A patent is a device to prevent the diffusion of new methods before the original investor has recovered profit adequate to induce the requisite investment. The justification of the patent system is that by slowing down the diffusion of technical progress it ensures that there will be more progress to diffuse ... Since it is rooted in a contradiction, there can be no such thing as an ideally beneficial patent system, and it is bound to produce negative results in particular instances, impeding progress unnecessarily even if its general effect is favorable on balance."[38] Although this strategy may work, it is to a certain extent self-defeating. If the justification for intellectual property is utilitarian in this sense, then the search for alternative incentives for the production of intellectual products takes on a good deal of importance. It would be better to employ equally powerful ways to stimulate the production and thus use of intellectual products which did not also restrict their use and availability.

Government support of intellectual work and public ownership of the result may be one such alternative. Governments already fund a great deal of basic research and development, and the results of this research often become public property. Unlike private property rights in the results of intellectual labor, government funding of this labor and public ownership of the result stimulate new inventions and writings without restricting their dissemination and use. Increased government funding of intellectual labor should thus be seriously considered.

This proposal need not involve government control over which research projects are to be pursued. Government funding of intellectual labor can be divorced from government control over what is funded. University research is an example. Most of this is supported by public funds, but government control over its content is minor and indirect. Agencies at different governmental levels could distribute funding for intellectual labor with only the most general guidance over content, leaving businesses, universities, and private individuals to decide which projects to pursue.

If the goal of private intellectual property institutions is to maximize the dissemination and use of information, to the extent that they do not achieve this result, these institutions should be modified. The question is not whether copyrights, patents, and trade secrets provide incentives for the production of original works of authorship, inventions, and innovative business techniques. Of course they do. Rather, we should ask the following questions: Do copyrights, patents, and trade secrets increase the availability and use of intellectual products more than they restrict this availability and use? If they do, we must then ask whether they increase the availability and use of intellectual products more than any alternative mechanism would. For example, could better overall results be achieved by shortening the length of copyright and patent grants, or by putting a time limit on trade secrets (and on the restrictions on future employment employers are allowed to demand of employees)? Would eliminating most types of trade secrets entirely and letting patents carry a heavier load produce improved results? Additionally, we must determine whether and to what extent public funding and ownership of intellectual products might be a more efficient means to these results.[39]

We should not expect an across-the-board answer to these questions. For example, the production of movies is more dependent on copyright than is academic writing. Also, patent protection for individual inventors and small beginning firms makes more sense than patent protection for large corporations (which own the majority of patents). It has been argued that patents are not important incentives for the research and innovative activity of large corporations in competitive markets.[40] The short-term advantage a company gets from developing a new product and being the first to put it on the market may be incentive enough.

That patents are conducive to a strong competitive economy is also open to question. Our patent system, originally designed to reward the individual inventor and thereby stimulate invention, may today be used as a device to monopolize industries. It has been suggested that in some cases "the patent position of the big firms makes it almost impossible for new firms to enter the industry"[41] and that patents are frequently bought up in order to suppress competition.[42]

Trade secrets as well can stifle competition, rather than encourage it. If a company can rely on a secret advantage over a competitor, it has no need to develop new technologies to stay ahead. Greater disclosure of certain trade secrets—such as costs and profits of particular product lines would actually increase competition, rather than decrease it, since with this knowledge firms would then concentrate on one another's most profitable products.[43] Furthermore, as one critic notes, trade secret laws often prevent a former employee "from doing work in just that field for which his training and experience have best prepared him. Indeed, the mobility of engineers and scientists is often severely limited by the reluctance of new firms to hire them for fear of exposing themselves to a lawsuit."[44] Since the movement of skilled workers between companies is a vital mechanism in the growth and spread of technology, in this important respect trade secrets actually slow the dissemination and use of innovative techniques.

These remarks suggest that the justifiability of our intellectual property institutions is not settled by the facile assertion that our system of patents, copyrights, and trade secrets provides necessary incentives for innovation and ensures maximally healthy competitive enterprise. This argument is not as easy to construct as one might at first think; substantial empirical evidence is needed. The above considerations suggest that the evidence might not support this position.

Conclusion

Justifying intellectual property is a formidable task. The inadequacies of the traditional justifications for property become more severe when applied to intellectual property. Both the nonexclusive nature of intellectual objects and the presumption against allowing restrictions on the free flow of ideas create special burdens in justifying such property.

We have seen significant shortcomings in the justifications for intellectual property. Natural rights to the fruits of one's labor are not by themselves sufficient to justify copyrights, patents, and trade secrets, though they are relevant to the social decision to create and sustain intellectual property institutions. Although intellectual laborers often deserve rewards for their labor, copyrights, patents, and trade secrets may give the laborer much more or much less than is deserved. Where property rights are not what is desired, they may be wholly inappropriate. The Lockean labor arguments for intellectual property also run afoul of one of Locke's provisos—the prohibition against spoilage or waste. Considerations of sovereignty, security, and privacy are inconclusive justifications for intellectual property as well.

This analysis suggests that the issue turns on considerations of social utility. We must determine whether our current copyright, patent, and trade secret statutes provide the best possible mechanisms for ensuring the availability and widespread dissemination of intellectual works and their resulting products. Public financial support for intellec-tual laborers and public ownership of intellectual products is an alternative which demands serious consideration. More modest alternatives needing consideration include modifications in the length of intellectual property grants or in the strength and scope of the restrictive rights granted. What the most efficient mechanism for achieving these goals is remains an unresolved empirical question.

This discussion also suggests that copyrights are easier to justify than patents or trade secrets. Patents restrict the actual usage of an idea (in making a physical object), while copyrights restrict only copying an expression of an idea. One can freely use the ideas in a copyrighted book in one's own writing, provided one acknowledges their origin. One cannot freely use the ideas a patented invention represents when developing one's own product. Furthermore, since inventions and business techniques are instruments of production in a way in which expressions of ideas are not, socialist objections to private ownership of the means of production apply to patents and trade secrets far more readily than they do to copyrights. Trade secrets are suspect also because they do not involve the socially beneficial public disclosure which is part of the patent and copyright process. They are additionally problematic to the extent that they involve unacceptable restrictions on employee mobility and technology transfer.

Focusing on the problems of justifying intellectual property is important not because these institutions lack any sort of justification, but because they are not so obviously or easily justified as many people think. We must begin to think more openly and imaginatively about the alternative choices available to us for stimulating and rewarding intellectual labor.

NOTES

1 Ayn Rand, *Capitalism: The Unknown Ideal* (New York: New American Library, 1966), 128.

2 See, for example, John Naisbitt's *Megatrends* (New York: Warner Books, 1982), chap. 1.

3 See R. Salaman and E. Hettinger, *Policy Implications of Information Technology*. NTIA Report 84-144, US Department of Commerce, 1984, 28-29.

4 For an elaboration of this distinction see Michael Brittin, "Constitutional Fair Use," in *Copyright Law Symposium*, No. 28 (New York: Columbia University Press, 1982), 142ff.

5 For an illuminating discussion of the relationships between style and subject, see Nelson Goodman's *Ways of Worldmaking* (Indianapolis: Hackett, 1978), chap. II, esp. sec. 2.

6 This is Fritz Machlup's phrase. See his *Production and Distribution of Knowledge in the United States* (Princeton: Princeton University Press, 1962), 163.

7 For one discussion of this distinction, see Deborah Johnson, *Computer Ethics* (Englewood Cliffs, NJ: Prentice-Hall, 1985), 100-01.

8 What can be patented is highly controversial. Consider the recent furor over patenting genetically manipulated animals or patenting computer programs.

9 What constitutes fair use is notoriously bewildering. I doubt that many teachers who sign copyright waivers at local copy shops know whether the packets they make available for their students constitute fair use of copyrighted material.

10 "Intellectual objects," "information," and "ideas" are terms I use to characterize the "objects" of this kind of ownership. Institutions which protect such "objects" include copyright, patent, trade secret, and trademark laws, as well as socially enforced customs (such as sanctions against plagiarism) demanding acknowledgment of the use of another's ideas. What is owned here are objects only in a very abstract sense.

11 There are intellectual objects of which this is not true, namely, information whose usefulness depends precisely on its being known only to a limited group of people. Stock tips and insider trading information are examples.

12 Ease of access is another reason for the widespread piracy of intellectual property. Modern information technologies (such as audio and video recorders, satellite dishes, photocopiers, and computers) make unauthorized taking of intellectual objects far easier than ever before. But it is cynical to submit that this is the major (or the only) reason piracy of information is widespread. It suggests that if people could steal physical objects as easily as they can take intellectual ones, they would do so to the same extent. That seems incorrect.

13 For a useful interpretation of Mill's argument, see Robert Ladenson, "Free Expression in the Corporate Workplace," in *Ethical Theory and Business*, 2nd ed., eds. T. Beauchamp and N. Bowie (Englewood Cliffs, NJ: Prentice-Hall, 1983), 162-69.

14 This is one reason the recent dramatic increase in relationships between universities and businesses is so disturbing: it hampers the disclosure of research results.

15 John Snapper makes this point in "Ownership of Computer Programs," available from the Center for the Study of Ethics in the Professions at the Illinois Institute of Technology. See also Sissela Bok, "Trade and Corporate Secrecy," in *Ethical Theory and Business*, 176.

16 John Locke, *Second Treatise of Government*, chap. 5. There are several strands to the Lockean argument. See Lawrence Becker, *Property Rights* (London: Routledge and Kegan Paul, 1977), chap. 4, for a detailed analysis of these various versions.

17 Robert Nozick, *Anarchy, State, and Utopia* (New York: Basic Books, 1974), 175.

18 Locke, *Second Treatise*, chap. 5, sec. 40.

19 Whether ideas are discovered or created affects the plausibility of the labor argument for intellectual property. "I discovered it, hence it's

mine" is much less persuasive than "I made it, hence it's mine." This issue also affects the cogency of the notion that intellectual objects have a value of their own not attributable to intellectual labor. The notion of mixing one's labor with something and thereby adding value to it makes much more sense if the object preexists.

20 I thank the Editors of *Philosophy* & *Affairs* for this way of making the point.

21 A libertarian might respond that although a natural right to the fruits of labor will not by itself justify a right to receive the market value of the resulting product, that right plus the rights of free association and trade would justify it. But marketplace interaction presupposes a set of social relations, and parties to these relations must jointly agree on their nature. Additionally, market interaction is possible only when property rights have been specified and enforced, and there is no "natural way" to do this (that is, no way independent of complex social judgments concerning the rewards the laborer deserves and the social utilities that will result from granting property rights). The sorts of freedoms one may have in a marketplace are thus socially agreed-upon privileges rather than natural rights.

22 For a discussion of this point, see Joel Feinberg, *Social Philosophy* (Englewood Cliffs, NJ: Prentice-Hall, 1973), 116.

23 Becker, *Property Rights*, 46.

24 This is becoming less and less true as the results of intellectual labor are increasingly treated as commodities. University research in biological and computer technologies is an example of this trend.

25 Becker, *Property Rights*, 52. In practice it would be easier to reward laborers as Becker suggests, since the value of the results of labor is easier to determine than the degree of effort expended.

26 This point is made nicely by James Rachels in "What People Deserve," in *Justice and Economic Distribution*, eds. J. Arthur and W. Shaw (Englewood Cliffs, NJ: Prentice-Hall, 1978), 150-63.

27 Completely ineffectual efforts deserve a reward provided that there were good reasons beforehand for thinking the efforts would payoff. Those whose well-intentioned efforts are silly or stupid should be rewarded the first time only and then counseled to seek advice about the value of their efforts.

28 See John Rawls, *A Theory of Justice* (Cambridge: Harvard University Press, 1971), 104: "The assertion that a man deserves the superior character that enables him to make the effort to cultivate his abilities is equally problematic; for his character depends in large part upon fortunate family and social circumstances for which he can claim no credit." See also 312: "the effort a person is willing to make is influenced by his natural abilities and skills, and the alternatives open to him. The better endowed are more likely, other things equal, to strive conscientiously."

29 See Rachels, "What People Deserve," 157-58, for a similar resistance to Rawls's determinism.

30 Locke, *Second Treatise*, chap. 5, sec. 27.

31 See Nozick, *Anarchy*, 175-82, and Becker, *Property Rights*, 42-43.

32 Nozick, *Anarchy*, 182.

33 Locke, *Second Treatise*, chap. 5, sec. 31.

34 Ronald Dworkin, "Liberalism," in *Public and Private Morality*, ed. Stuart Hampshire (Cambridge: Cambridge University Press, 1978), 139.

35 "In the United States about 60 per cent of all patents are assigned to corporations" (Machlup, *Production*, 168). This was the case twenty-five years ago, and I assume the percentage is even higher today.

36 Very little (if any) of the sensitive information about individuals that corporations have is information held as a trade secret. For a critical

discussion of the attempt to defend corporate secrecy on the basis of privacy see Russell B. Stevenson, Jr., *Corporations and Information* (Baltimore: Johns Hopkins University Press, 1980), chap. 5.

37 US Constitution, sec. 8, para. 8.

38 Quoted in Dorothy Nelkin, *Science as Intellectual Property* (New York: Macmillan, 1984), 15.

39 Even supposing our current copyright, patent, and trade secret laws did maximize the availability and use of intellectual products, a thorough utilitarian evaluation would have to weigh all the consequences of these legal rights. For example, the decrease in employee freedom resulting from trade secrets would have to be considered, as would the inequalities in income, wealth, opportunity, and power which result from these socially established and enforced property rights.

40 Machlup, *Production*, 168-69.

41 Ibid., 170.

42 See David Noble, *America by Design* (New York: Knopf, 1982), chap. 6.

43 This is Stevenson's point in *Corporations*, 11.

44 Ibid., 23. More generally, see ibid., chap. 2, for a careful and skeptical treatment of the claim that trade secrets function as incentives.

◆ ◆ ◆ ◆ ◆

LYNN SHARP PAINE

Trade Secrets and the Justification of Intellectual Property: A Comment on Hettinger

In a recent article Edwin Hettinger considers various rationales for recognizing intellectual property.[1] According to Hettinger, traditional justifications for property are especially problematic when applied to intellectual property because of its nonexclusive nature.[2] Since possessing and using intellectual objects does not preclude their use and possession by others, there is, he says a "strong prima facie case against the wisdom of private and exclusive intellectual property rights." There is, moreover, a presumption against allowing restrictions on the free flow of ideas.

After rejecting several rationales for intellectual property, Hettinger finds its justification in an instrumental, or "utilitarian,"[3] argument based on incentives.[4] Respecting rights in ideas makes sense, he says, if we recognize that the purpose of our intellectual property institutions is to promote the dissemination and use of information. To the extent that existing institutions do not achieve this result, they should be modified.[5] Skeptical about the effectiveness of current legal arrangements, Hettinger concludes that we must think more imaginatively about structuring our intellectual property institutions—in particular, patent, copyright, and trade secret laws—so that they increase the availability and use of intellectual products. He ventures several possibilities for consideration: eliminating certain forms of trade secret protections, shortening the copyright and patent protection periods, and public funding and ownership of intellectual objects.

Hettinger's approach to justifying our intellectual property institutions rests on several problematic assumptions. It assumes that all of our intellectual property institutions rise or fall together—that the rationale for trade secret protection must be the same as that for patent and copyright protection.[6] This assumption, I will try to show, is unwarranted. While it may be true that these institutions all promote social utility or wellbeing, the web of rights and duties understood under the general heading of "intellectual property rights" reflects a variety of more specific rationales and objectives.[7]

Second, Hettinger assumes that the rights commonly referred to as "intellectual property rights" are best understood on the model of rights in tangible and real property. He accepts the idea, implicit in the terminology, that intellectual property is like tangible property, only less corporeal. This assumption leads him to focus his search for the justification of intellectual property on the traditional arguments for private property. I will try to show the merits of an alternative approach to thinking about rights in ideas—one that does not depend on the analogy with tangible property and that recognizes the role of ideas in defining personality and social relationships.

The combined effect of these assumptions is that trade secret law comes in for particular serious criticism. It restricts methods of acquiring ideas; it encourages secrecy; it places unacceptable restrictions on employee mobility and technology transfer; it can stifle competition; it is more vulnerable to socialist objections. In light of these deficiencies, Hettinger recommends that we consider the possibility of "eliminating most types of trade secrets entirely and letting patents carry a heavier load." He believes that trade secrets are undesirable in ways that copyrights and patents are not.

Without disagreeing with Hettinger's recommendation that we reevaluate and think more imaginatively about our intellectual property institutions, I believe we should have a clearer understanding of the various rationales for these institutions than is reflected in Hettinger's article. If we unbundle the notion of intellectual property into its constituent

rights,[8] we find that different justifications are appropriate for different clusters of rights.[9] In particular, we find that the rights recognized by trade secret law are better understood as rooted in respect for individual liberty, confidential relationships, common morality, and fair competition than in the promotion of innovation and the dissemination of ideas. While trade secret law may serve some of the same ends as patent and copyright law, it has other foundations which are quite distinctive.[10]

In this article, I am primarily concerned with the foundations of trade secret principles. However, my general approach differs from Hettinger's in two fundamental ways. First, it focuses on persons and their relationships rather than property concepts. Second, it reverses the burden of justification, placing it on those who would argue for treating ideas as public goods rather than those who seek to justify private rights in ideas. Within this alternative framework, the central questions are how ideas may be legitimately acquired from others, how disclosure obligations arise, and how ideas become part of the common pool of knowledge. Before turning to Hettinger's criticisms of trade secret principles, it will be useful to think more broadly about the rights of individuals over their undisclosed ideas. This inquiry will illustrate my approach to thinking about rights in ideas and point toward some of the issues at stake in the trade secret area.

The Right to Control Disclosure

If a person has any right with respect to her ideas, surely it is the right to control their initial disclosure.[11] A person may decide to keep her ideas to herself, to disclose them to a select few, or to publish them widely. Whether those ideas are best described as views and opinions, plans and intentions, facts and knowledge, or fantasies and inventions is immaterial. While it might in some cases be socially useful for a person to be generous with her ideas, and to share them with others without restraint, there is no general obligation to do so. The world at large has no right to the individual's ideas.[12]

Certainly, specific undertakings, relationships, and even the acquisition of specific information can give rise to disclosure obligations. Typically, these obligations relate to specific types of information pertinent to the relationship or the subject matter of the undertaking. A seller of goods must disclose to potential buyers latent defects and health and safety risks associated with the use of the goods. A person who undertakes to act as an agent for another is obliged to disclose to the principal information she acquires that relates to the subject matter of the agency. Disclosure obligations like these, however, are limited in scope and arise against a general background right to remain silent.

The right to control the initial disclosure of one's ideas is grounded in respect for the individual. Just as a person's sense of herself is intimately connected with the stream of ideas that constitutes consciousness, her public persona is determined in part by the ideas she expresses and the way she expresses them. To require public disclosure of one's ideas and thoughts whether about "personal" or other matters—would distort one's personality and, no doubt, alter the nature of one's thoughts.[13] It would seriously interfere with the liberty to live according to one's chosen life plans. This sort of thought control would be an invasion of privacy and personality of the most intrusive sort. If anything is private, one's undisclosed thoughts surely are.[14]

Respect for autonomy, respect for personality, and respect for privacy lie behind the right to control disclosure of one's ideas, but the right is also part of what we mean by freedom of thought and expression. Frequently equated with a right to speak, freedom of expression also implies a *prima facie* right not to express one's ideas or to share them only with those we love or trust or with whom we wish to share.[15] These observations explain the peculiarity of setting up the free flow of ideas and unrestricted access as an ideal. Rights in ideas are desirable inso-far as they strengthen our sense of individuality and undergird our social relationships. This suggests a framework quite different from Hettinger's, one that begins with a strong presumption against requiring disclosure and is in favor of protecting people against unconsented-to acquisitions of their ideas.[16] This is the moral backdrop against which trade secrecy law is best understood.

Consequences of Disclosure

Within this framework, a critical question is how people lose rights in their ideas. Are these rights forfeited when people express their ideas or communicate them to others? Surely this depends on the circumstances of disclosure. Writing down ideas in a daily journal to oneself or recording them on a cassette should not entail such a forfeiture. Considerations of individual autonomy, privacy, and personality require that such expressions not be deemed available for use by others who may gain access to them.[17]

Likewise, communicating an idea in confidence to another should not render it part of the common pool of knowledge. Respect for the individual's desire to limit the dissemination of the idea is at stake, but so is respect for the relationship of trust and confidence among the persons involved. If A confides in B under circumstances in which B gives A reason to believe she will respect the confidence, A should be able to trust that B will not reveal or misuse the confidence and that third parties who may intentionally or accidentally discover the confidence will respect it.[18]

The alternative possibility is that by revealing her ideas to B, A is deemed to forfeit any right to control their use or communication. This principle is objectionable for a couple of reasons. First, it would most certainly increase reluctance to share ideas since our disclosure decisions are strongly influenced by the audience we anticipate. If we could not select our audience, that is, if the choice were only between keeping ideas to ourselves and sharing them with the world at large, many ideas would remain un-expressed, to the detriment of individual health as well as the general good.

Second, the principle would pose an impedi-ment to the formation and sustenance of various types of cooperative relationships—relationships of love and friendship, as well as relationships forged for specific purposes such as education, medical care, or business. It might be thought that only ideas of an intimate or personal nature are important in this regard. But it is not only "personal" relationships, but cooperative relationships of all types, that are at stake. Shared knowledge and information of varying types are central to work relationships and commun-ities—academic departments and disciplines, firms, teams—as well as other organizations. The posses-sion of common ideas and information, to the ex-clusion of those outside the relationship or group, contributes to the group's self-definition and to the individual's sense of belonging. By permitting and protecting the sharing of confidences, trade secret principles, among other institutions, permit "spe-cial communities of knowledge" which nurture the social bonds and cooperative efforts through which we express our individuality and pursue common purposes.[19]

Of course, by disclosing her idea to B, A runs the risk that B or anyone else who learns about the idea may use it or share it further. But if B has agreed to respect the confidence, either explicitly or by partici-pating in a relationship in which confidence is nor-mally expected, she has a *prima facie* obligation not to disclose the information to which she is privy.[20] Institutions that give A a remedy against third parties who appropriate ideas shared in confidence reduce the risk that A's ideas will become public resources if she shares them with B. Such institutions thereby support confidential relationships and the coopera-tive undertakings that depend on them.

Yet another situation in which disclosure should not be regarded as a license for general use is the case of disclosures made as a result of deceit or insin-cere promises. Suppose A is an entrepreneur who has created an unusual software program with substan-tial sales potential. Another party, B, pretending to be a potential customer, questions A at great length about the code and other details of her program. A's disclosures are not intended to be, and should not be deemed, a contribution to the general pool of know-ledge, nor should B be permitted to use A's ideas.[21] Respect for A's right to disclose her ideas requires that involuntary disclosures—such as those based on deceit, coercion, and theft of documents contain-ing expressions of those ideas—not be regarded as forfeitures to the common pool of knowledge and information. In recognition of A's right to control disclosure of her ideas and to discourage appropria-tion of her ideas against her wishes, we might expect our institutions to provide A with a remedy against these sorts of appropriation. Trade secret law pro-vides such a remedy.

Competitive fairness is also at stake if B is in competition with A. Besides having violated stan-dards of common morality in using deceit to gain access to A's ideas, B is in a position to exploit those ideas in the marketplace without having contributed to the cost of their development. B can sell her ver-sion of the software more cheaply since she enjoys a substantial cost advantage compared to A, who may have invested a great deal of time and money in developing the software. Fairness in a competitive economy requires some limitations on the rights of firms to use ideas developed by others. In a system based on effort, it is both unfair and ultimately self-defeating to permit firms to have a free ride on the efforts of their competitors.[22]

Problematic Issues

Respect for personal control over the disclosure of ideas, respect for confidential relationships, common morality, and fair competition all point toward rec-ognizing certain rights in ideas. Difficult questions will arise within this system of rights. If *A* is not an individual but an organization or group, should *A* have the same rights and remedies against *B* or third parties who use or communicate information shared with *B* in confidence? For example, suppose *A* is a corporation that hires an employee, *B*, to develop a marketing plan. If other employees of *A* reveal in confidence to *B* information they have created or assembled, should *A* be able to restrain *B* from using this information to benefit herself (at *A*'s expense)? Does it matter if *A* is a two-person corporation or a corporation with 100,000 employees? What if *A* is a social club or a private school?

Hettinger seems to assume that corporate *A*'s should not have such rights—on the grounds that they might restrict *B*'s employment possibilities. It is certainly true that giving *A* a right against *B* if she reveals information communicated to her in confidence could rule out certain jobs for *B*. However, the alternative rule—that corporate *A*'s should have no rights in ideas they reveal in confidence to others—has problems as well.

One problem involves trust. If our institutions do not give corporate *A*'s certain rights in ideas they reveal in confidence to employees, *A*'s will seek other means of ensuring that competitively valuable ideas are protected. They may contract individually with employees for those rights, and if our legal institutions do not uphold those contracts, employers will seek to hire individuals in whom they have personal trust. Hiring would probably become more dependent on family and personal relationships and there would be fewer opportunities for the less well connected. Institutional rules giving corporate *A*'s rights against employees who reveal or use information given to them in confidence are a substitute for personal bonds of trust. While such rules are not cost-free and may have some morally undesirable consequences, they help sustain cooperative efforts and contribute to more open hiring practices.

Contrary to Hettinger's suggestion, giving corporate *A*'s rights in the ideas they reveal in confi-

dence to others does not always benefit the strong at the expense of the weak, or the large corporation at the expense of the individual, although this is surely sometimes the case.[23] Imagine three entrepreneurs who wish to expand their highly successful cookie business. A venture capitalist interested in financing the expansion naturally wishes to know the details of the operation—including the prized cookie recipe—before putting up capital. After examining the recipe, however, he decides that it would be more profitable for him to sell the recipe to CookieCo, a multinational food company, and to invest his capital elsewhere. Without money and rights to prevent others from using the recipe, the corporate entrepreneurs are very likely out of business. CookieCo, which can manufacture and sell the cookies much more cheaply, will undoubtedly find that most of the entrepreneurs' customers are quite happy to buy the same cookies for less at their local supermarket.

Non-Property Foundations of Trade Secret Law

To a large extent, the rights and remedies mentioned in the preceding discussion are those recognized by trade secret law. As this discussion showed, the concept of property is not necessary to justify these rights. Trade secret law protects against certain methods of appropriating the confidential and commercially valuable ideas of others. It affords a remedy to those whose commercially valuable secrets are acquired by misrepresentation, theft, bribery, breach or inducement of a breach of confidence, espionage or other improper means.[24] Although the roots of trade secret principles have been variously located, respect for voluntary disclosure decisions and respect for confidential relationships provide the best account of the pattern of permitted and prohibited appropriations and use of ideas.[25] As Justice Oliver Wendell Holmes noted in a 1917 trade secret case, "The property may be denied but the confidence cannot be."[26] Trade secret law can also be seen as enforcing ordinary standards of morality in commercial relationships, thus ensuring some consistency with general social morality.[27]

It may well be true, as Hettinger and others have claimed, that the availability of trade secret protection provides an incentive for intellectual labor and the development of ideas. The knowledge that they have legal rights against those who "misappropriate" their ideas may encourage people to invest large amounts of time and money in exploring and developing ideas. However, the claim that trade secret protection promotes invention is quite different from the claim that it is grounded in or justified by this tendency. Even if common law trade secret rights did not promote intellectual labor or increase the dissemination and use of information, there would still be reasons to recognize those rights. Respect for people's voluntary disclosure decisions, respect for confidential relationships, standards of common morality, and fair competition would still point in that direction.

Moreover, promoting the development of ideas cannot be the whole story behind trade secret principles, since protection is often accorded to information such as customer data or cost and pricing information kept in the ordinary course of doing business. While businesses may need incentives to engage in costly research and development, they would certainly keep track of their customers and costs in any event. The rationale for giving protection to such information must be other than promoting the invention, dissemination, and use of ideas. By the same token, trade secret principles do not prohibit the use of ideas acquired by studying products available in the marketplace. If the central policy behind trade secret protection were the promotion of invention, one might expect that trade secret law, like patent law, which was explicitly fashioned to encourage invention, would protect innovators from imitators.

The fact that Congress has enacted patent laws giving inventors a limited monopoly in exchange for disclosure of their ideas without at the same time eliminating state trade secret law may be a further indication that trade secret and patent protection rest on different grounds.[28] By offering a limited monopoly in exchange for disclosure, the patent laws implicitly recognize the more fundamental right not to disclose one's ideas at all or to disclose them in confidence to others.[29]

Reassessing Hettinger's Criticism of Trade Secret Law

If we see trade secret law as grounded in respect for voluntary disclosure, confidential relationships, common morality, and fair competition, the force of Hettinger's criticisms diminishes somewhat. The problems he cites appear not merely in their negative light as detracting from an ideal "free flow of ideas," but in their positive role as promoting other important values.

Restrictions on Acquiring Ideas

Hettinger is critical, for example, of the fact that trade secret law restricts methods of acquiring ideas. But the prohibited means of acquisition misrepresentation, theft, bribery, breach of confidence, and espionage—all reflect general social morality. Lifting these restrictions would undoubtedly contribute to the erosion of important values outside the commercial context.

How much trade secrecy laws inhibit the development and spread of ideas is also open to debate. Hettinger and others have claimed that trade secrecy is a serious impediment to innovation and dissemination because the period of permitted secrecy is unlimited. Yet, given the fact that trade secret law offers no protection for ideas acquired by examining or reverse-engineering products in the marketplace, it would appear rather difficult to maintain technical secrets embodied in those products while still exploiting their market potential. A standard example used to illustrate the problem of perpetual secrecy, the Coke formula, seems insufficient to establish that this is a serious problem. Despite the complexity of modern technology, successful reverse-engineering is common. Moreover, similar technical advances are frequently made by researchers working independently. Trade secret law poses no impediment: in either case independent discoverers are free to exploit their ideas even if they are similar to those of others.

As for nontechnical information such as marketing plans and business strategies, the period of secrecy is necessarily rather short since implementation entails disclosure. Competitor intelligence specialists claim that most of the information needed to understand what competitors are doing is publicly available.[30] All of these considerations suggest that trade secret principles are not such a serious impediment to the dissemination of information.

Competitive Effects

Hettinger complains that trade secret principles stifle competition. Assessing this claim is very difficult. On one hand, it may seem that prices would be lower if firms were permitted to obtain cost or other market advantages by using prohibited means to acquire protected ideas from others. Competitor access to the Coke formula would most likely put downward pressure on the price of "the real thing." Yet, it is also reasonable to assume that the law keeps prices down by reducing the costs of self-protection. By giving some assurance that commercially valuable secrets will be protected, the law shields firms from having to bear the full costs of protection. It is very hard to predict what would happen to prices if trade secret protection were eliminated. Self-protection would be more costly and would tend to drive prices up, while increased competition would work in the opposite direction. There would surely be important differences in morale and productivity. Moreover, as noted, any price reductions for consumers would

come at a cost to the basic moral standards of society if intelligence-gathering by bribery, misrepresentation, and espionage were permitted.

Restrictions on Employee Mobility

Among Hettinger's criticisms of trade secret law, the most serious relate to restrictions on employee mobility. In practice, employers often attempt to protect information by overrestricting the postemployment opportunities of employees. Three important factors contribute to this tendency: vagueness about which information is confidential; disagreement about the proper allocation of rights to ideas generated by employees using their employers' resources; and conceptual difficulties in distinguishing general knowledge and employers specific knowledge acquired on the job. Courts, however, are already doing what Hettinger recommends, namely, limiting the restrictions that employers can place on future employment in the name of protecting ideas.[31] Although the balance between employer and employee interests is a delicate one not always equitably struck, the solution of eliminating trade secret protection altogether is overbroad and undesirable, considering the other objectives at stake.

Hypothetical Alternatives

Hettinger's discussion of our intellectual property institutions reflects an assumption that greater openness and sharing would occur if we eliminated trade secret protection. He argues that trade secret principles encourage secrecy. He speaks of the "free flow of ideas" as the ideal that would obtain in the absence of our intellectual property institutions. This supposition strikes me as highly unlikely. People keep secrets and establish confidential relationships for a variety of reasons that are quite independent of any legal protection these secrets might have. The psychology and sociology of secrets have been explored by others. Although much economic theory is premised on complete information, secrecy and private information are at the heart of day-to-day competition in the marketplace.

In the absence of something like trade secret principles, I would expect not a free flow of ideas but greater efforts to protect information through contracts, management systems designed to limit information access, security equipment, and electronic counterintelligence devices. I would also expect stepped-up efforts to acquire intelligence from others through espionage, bribery, misrepresentation, and other unsavory means. By providing some assurance that information can be shared in confidence and by protecting against unethical methods of extracting information and undermining confidentiality, trade secret principles promote cooperation and security, two important conditions for intellectual endeavor. In this way, trade secret principles may ultimately promote intellectual effort by limiting information flow.

The Burden of Justification

We may begin thinking about information rights, as Hettinger does, by treating all ideas as part of a common pool and then deciding whether and how to allocate to individuals rights to items in the pool. Within this framework, ideas are conceived on the model of tangible property.[32] Just as, in the absence of social institutions, we enter the world with no particular relationship to its tangible *assets* or natural resources, we have no particular claim on the world's ideas. In this scheme, *as* Hettinger asserts, the "burden of justification is very much on those who would restrict the maximal use of intellectual objects."

Alternatively, we may begin, as I do, by thinking of ideas in relation to their originators, who may or may not share their ideas with specific others or contribute them to the common pool. This approach treats ideas as central to personality and the social world individuals construct for themselves. Ideas

are not, in the first instance, freely available natural resources. They originate with people, and it is the connections among people, their ideas, and their relationships with others that provides a baseline for discussing rights in ideas. Within this conception, the burden of justification is on those who would argue for disclosure obligations and general access to ideas.

The structure of specific rights that emerges from these different frameworks depends not only on where the burden of justification is located, but also on how easily it can be discharged.[33] It is unclear how compelling a case is required to overcome the burden Hettinger sets up and, consequently, difficult to gauge the depth of my disagreement with him.[34] Since Hettinger does not consider the rationales for trade secret principles discussed here, it is not clear whether he would dismiss them altogether, find them insufficiently weighty to override the presumption he sets up, or agree that they satisfy the burden of justification.

One might suspect, however, from the absence of discussion of the personal and social dimension of rights in ideas that Hettinger does not think them terribly important, and that his decision to put the burden of justification on those who argue for rights in ideas reflects a fairly strong commitment to openness. On the assumption that our alternative starting points reflect seriously held substantive views (they are not just procedural devices to get the argument started) and that both frameworks require strong reasons to overcome the initial presumption, the resulting rights and obligations are likely to be quite different in areas where neither confidentiality nor openness is critical to immediate human needs. Indeed, trade secrecy law is an area where these different starting points would be likely to surface.

The key question to ask about these competing frameworks is which is backed by stronger reasons. My opposition to Hettinger's allocation of the burden of justification rests on my rejection of his cor ception of ideas as natural resources and on different views of how the world would look in the absence of our intellectual property institutions. In contrast, my starting point acknowledges the importance of ideas to our sense of ourselves and the communities (inducting work communities) of which we are a part. It is also more compatible with the way we commonly talk about ideas. Our talk about disclosure obligations presupposes a general background right not to reveal ideas. If it were otherwise, we would speak of concealment rights. To use the logically interesting feature of non exclusiveness as a starting point for moral reasoning about rights in ideas seems wholly arbitrary.

Conclusion

Knives, forks, and spoons are all designed to help us eat. In a sense, however, the essential function of these tools is to help us cut, since without utensils, we could still consume most foods with our hands. One might be tempted to say that since cutting is the essential function of eating utensils, forks and spoons should be designed to facilitate cutting. One might even say that insofar as forks and spoons do not facilitate cutting, they should be redesigned. Such a modification, however, would rob us of valuable specialized eating instruments.

Hettinger's train of thought strikes me as very similar. He purports to examine the justification of our various intellectual property institutions. However, he settles on a justification that really only fits patent and, arguably, copyright institutions. He then suggests that other intellectual property rights be assessed against the justification he proposes and redesigned insofar as they are found wanting. In ~icular, he suggests that trade secret principles be ~d to look more like patent principles. Het- to appreciate the various rationales be- ~ and duties understood under the ~al property," especially those rec- ~ law.

I agree with Hettinger that our intellectual property institutions need a fresh look from a utilitarian perspective.[35] The seventeen-year monopoly granted through patents is anachronistic given the pace of technological development today. We need to think about the appropriate balance between employer and employee rights in ideas developed jointly. Solutions to the problem of the unauthorized copying of software may be found in alternative pricing structures rather than in fundamental modifications of our institutions. Public interest considerations could be advanced for opening access to privately held information in a variety of areas. As we consider these specific questions, however, I would urge that we keep firmly in mind the variety of objectives that intellectual property institutions have traditionally served.[36] If, following Hettinger's advice, we single-mindedly reshape these institutions to maximize the short-term dissemination and use of ideas, we run the risk of subverting the other ends these institutions serve.

NOTES

1 Edwin C. Hettinger, "Justifying Intellectual Property," *Philosophy* & *Public Affairs* 18, No. 1 (Winter 1989): 31-52.

2 Thomas Jefferson agrees. See Jefferson's letter to Isaac McPherson, 13 August 1813, in *The Founder's Constitution*, ed. Philip B. Kurland and Ralph Lerner (Chicago: University of Chicago Press, 1987), 3:42.

3 Hettinger uses the term *utilitarian* in a very narrow sense to refer to a justification in terms of maximizing the use and dissemination of information. Some utilitarians might see intellectual property institutions as promoting objectives other than information dissemination. My discussion of the roots of trade secret principles is perfectly consistent with a utilitarian justification of those principles. Indeed, a utilitarian could argue (as many economists do) that giving people certain rights in ideas they

generate through their own labor advances social well-being by promoting innovation. See, e.g., Robert U. Ayres, "Technological Protection and Piracy: Some Implications for Policy," *Technological Forecasting and Social Change* 30 (1986): 5-18.

4 In Hettinger's paper and in mine, the terms *justification*, *goal*, *purpose*, *rationale*, and *objective* are used loosely and somewhat interchangeably. But, of course, identifying the purpose or goal of our intellectual property institutions does not automatically justify them. Some further legitimating idea or ultimate good, such as the general welfare or individual liberty, must be invoked. A difficulty with Hettinger's argument is that he identifies an objective for our intellectual property institutions—promoting the use and dissemination of ideas—and concludes that he has justified them. However, unless maximizing the use and dissemination of ideas is an intrinsic good, we would expect a further step in the argument linking this objective to an ultimate good. Hettinger may think this step can be made or is self-evident from his terminology. However, it is not clear whether he calls his justification "utilitarian" because of its consequentialist form or because he means to appeal to social wellbeing or some particular good he associates with utilitarianism.

5 Hettinger seems to think that he has provided a clear-cut objective against which to measure the effectiveness of our intellectual property institutions. Yet, a set of institutions that maximized the "dissemination and use of information" would not necessarily be most effective at "promoting the creation of valuable intellectual works" or promoting "the progress of science and the useful arts." A society might be quite successful at disseminating information, but rather mediocre at creating valuable intellectual works.

There is an inevitable tension between the objectives of innovation and dissemination. The same tension is present in other areas of law concerned with rights in information—insider trading, for example. For discussion of this tension, see Frank H. Easterbrook, "Insider Trading, Secret Agents, Evidentiary Privileges, and the Production of Information," 1981 *Supreme Court Review*, 309. While we struggle to piece together a system of information rights that gives due consideration to both objectives, we must be wary of the notion that there is a single optimal allocation of rights.

Indeed, the very idea of a "socially optimal output of intellectual products" is embarrassingly imprecise. What is a socially optimal output of poems, novels, computer programs, movies, cassette recordings, production processes, formulations of matter, stock tips, business strategies, etc.? How we allocate rights in ideas may affect the quality and kinds of intellectual products that are produced as well as their quantity and dissemination. Hettinger seems concerned primarily with quantity. The use of general terms like *intellectual product* and *socially optimal output* obscures the complexity of the empirical assessment that Hettinger proposes.

6 Hettinger mentions trademark as another of our intellectual property institutions, along with our social sanction on plagiarism, but his central discussion focuses on copyright, patent, and trade secret concepts. Neither trademark principles nor the prohibition on plagiarism fits comfortably with his justification in terms of increasing the dissemination and use of ideas. Both are more closely related to giving recognition to the source or originator of ideas and products.

7 It may be helpful to think of two levels of justification: (1) an intermediate level consisting of objectives, purposes, reasons, and explanations

for an institution or practice; and (2) an ultimate level linking those objectives and purposes to our most basic legitimating ideas such as the general good or individual liberty. Philosophers generally tend to be concerned with the ultimate level of justification while policymakers and judges more frequently operate at the intermediate level. Hettinger has, I think, mistaken an intermediate-level justification of patents and copyrights (promoting the dissemination and use of ideas) for an ultimate justification of intellectual property institutions.

8   Hettinger, of course, recognizes that various rights are involved. He speaks of rights to possess, to personally use, to prevent others from using, to publish, and to receive the market value of one's ideas. And he notes that one might have a natural right to possess and personally use one's ideas even if one might not have a natural right to prevent others from copying them. But he does not consider the possibility that the different rights involved in our concept of intellectual property may rest on quite varied foundations, some firmer than others.

9   It is generally accepted that the concept of property is best understood as a "bundle of rights." Just as the bundle of rights involved in home ownership differs substantially from the bundle of rights associated with stock ownership, the bundle of rights involved in patent protection differs from the bundle of rights involved in trade secret protection.

10 Today we commonly speak of copyright protection as providing incentives for intellectual effort, while at the same time ensuring widespread dissemination of ideas. As Hettinger notes, the effectiveness of copyright protection in achieving these aims may depend partly on the period of the copyright grant. Historically, at least before the first English copyright act, the famous 1710 Act of Anne, it appears that the dissemination of ideas was not so central. The common law gave the author an exclusive first right of printing or publishing her manuscript on the grounds that she was entitled to the product of her labor. The common law's position on the author's right to prohibit subsequent publication was less clear. See generally Wheaton v. Peters, 8 Pet. 591 (1834), reprinted in *The Founders' Constitution* 3:44-60.

11 Hettinger recognizes a right not to divulge privately created intellectual products, but he does not fit this right into his discussion. If the right is taken seriously, however, it will, I believe, undermine Hettinger's own conclusions.

12 We would hope that the right to control disclosure would be exercised in a morally responsible way and that, for example, people with socially useful ideas would share them and that some types of harmful ideas would be withheld. But the potential social benefits of certain disclosures cannot justify a general requirement that ideas be disclosed.

13 Here, I am using the term *personal* to refer to ideas about intimate matters, such as sexual behavior.

14 The right to control disclosure of one's thoughts might be thought to be no more than a reflection of technical limitations. Enforcing a general disclosure requirement presupposes some way of identifying the undisclosed thoughts of others. Currently, we do not have the technology to do this. But even if we did—or especially if we did—respect for the individual would preclude any form of monitoring people's thoughts.

15 On the relation between privacy and intimate relationships, see Charles Fried, "Privacy," *Yale Law Journal* 77 (1968): 475-93. Below, I will argue that confidentiality is central to other types of cooperative relationships as well.

16 Whether the presumption is overcome will depend on the importance of the objectives served

by disclosure, and the degree of violence done to the individual or the relationship at stake.

17 Technically, of course, others have access to ideas that have been expressed whereas they do not have access to undisclosed thoughts. But ease of access is not the criterion for propriety of access.

18 This is the fundamental principle behind the prohibition on insider trading.

19 The phrase "special communities of knowledge" comes from Kim Lane Scheppele, *Legal Secrets* (Chicago: University of Chicago Press, 1988), 14.

20 In practice, this *prima facie* obligation may sometimes be overridden when it conflicts with other obligations, e.g., the obligation to prevent harm to a third party.

21 An actual case similar to this was litigated in Pennsylvania. See *Continental Data Systems, Inc. v. Eaton Corporation*, 638 F. Supp. 432 (D.C.E.D. Pa. 1986).

22 For the view that fair and honest business competition is the central policy underlying trade secret protection, see Ramon A. Klitzke, "Trade Secrets: Importing Quasi-Property Rights," *Business Lawyer* 41 (1986): 557-70.

23 It appears that Hettinger is using the term *private company* in contrast to individuals rather than to public companies—those whose shares are sold to the public on national stock exchanges. If one wishes to protect individuals, however, it might be more important to distinguish small, privately held companies from large, publicly held ones than to distinguish individuals from companies. Many individuals, however, are dependent on large, publicly held companies as their livelihood.

24 *Uniform Trade Secrets Act with 1985 Amendments*, sec. 1, in *Uniform Laws Annotated*, Vol. 14 (1980 with 1988 Pocket Part). The Uniform Trade Secrets Act seeks to codify and standardize the common law principles of trade

secret law as they have developed in different jurisdictions.

25 See Klitzke, "Trade Secrets." Different theories of justification are discussed in Ridsdale Ellis, *Trade Secrets* (New York: Baker, Voorhis, 1953). Kim Lane Scheppele is another commentator favoring the view that breach of confidence is what trade secret cases are all about. See *Legal Secrets*, 241. In their famous article on privacy, Warren and Brandeis find the roots of trade secret principles in the right to privacy. Samuel D. Warren and Louis D. Brandeis, *Harvard Law Review* 4 (1890): 212.

26 E.I. DuPont de Nemours Powder Co. v. Masland, 244 U.S. 100 (1917).

27 One commentator has said, "The desire to reinforce 'good faith and honest, fair dealing' in business is the mother of the law of trade secrets." Russell B. Stevenson, Jr., *Corporations and Information* (Baltimore: Johns Hopkins University Press, 1980), 19.

28 Support for this interpretation is found in Justice Thurgood Marshall's concurring opinion in *Kewanee Oil Co. v. Bicron Corp.*, 416 U.S. 470, 494 (1974). The court held that the federal patent laws do not preempt state trade secret laws.

29 Congress may have realized that trying to bring about more openness by eliminating trade secret protection, even with the added attraction of a limited monopoly for inventions that qualify for patent protection, would be inconsistent with fundamental moral notions such as respect for confidential relationships, and would probably not have worked anyway.

30 See, e.g., the statement of a *manager* of a competitor surveillance group quoted in Jerry L. Wall, "What the Competition Is Doing: Your Need to Know," *Harvard Business Review* 52 (November-December 1974): 34. See generally Leonard M. Fuld, *Competitor Intelligence:*

How to Get It—How to Use It (New York: John Wiley and Sons, 1985).

31 See e.g., John Burgess, "Unlocking Corporate Shackles," *Washington Business*, 11 December 1989, 1.

32 Hettinger speaks of ideas as objects, and of rights in ideas as comparable to water or mineral rights. Indeed, according to Hettinger, the difficulty in justifying intellectual property rights arises because ideas are not in all respects like tangible property, which he thinks is more easily justified.

33 The Editors of *Philosophy & Public Affairs* encouraged me to address this point.

34 His argument from maximizing the production and dissemination of ideas suggests that the presumption in favor of free ideas is not terribly strong: it can be overridden by identifying some reasonable objective likely to be served by assigning exclusive rights.

35 That is, we should look at the effects of these institutions on social well-being in general and select the institutions that are best on the whole.

36 A utilitarian assessment will also include consideration of the various interests that would be affected by alternative allocations of intellectual property rights. For example, denying authors copyright in their works may increase the power and profit of publishers and further impair the ability of lesser-known writers to find publication outlets. One scholar has concluded that America's failure to recognize the copyrights of aliens before 1891 stunted the development of native literature. For fifty years before the passage of the Platt-Simmonds Act, publishing interests vigorously and successfully opposed recognition of international copyright. This is understandable since the works of well-known British authors were available to publishers free of charge. Publishers were not terribly concerned with the artistic integrity of these works. They sometimes substituted alternative endings, mixed the works of different authors, and edited as economically necessary. There were few reasons to take the risks involved in publishing the works of unknown and untested American writers who might insist on artistic integrity. See generally Aubert J. Clark, *The Movement for International Copyright in Nineteenth Century America* (Westport, CT: Greenwood Press, 1973).

CASE STUDY 7

INTELLECTUAL PROPERTY ACROSS NATIONAL BORDERS

JOHN WECKERT AND MIKE BOWERN

Case Description

Because of the Internet, national borders are becoming transparent. This is creating some interesting, and urgent, ethical problems, given the often conflicting moral and legal customs and structures in different countries. This case covers two associated news items about intellectual property issues across national borders. This first news item, paraphrased from Cochrane,[1] is about proposed legislation which allows hacking to protect IP.

A bill before the US House of Representatives would "give American copyright holders freedom to hack PCs used to illicitly share files over peer-to-peer (P2P) networks, without fear of prosecution or litigation." "A copyright owner shall not be liable in any criminal or civil action for disabling, interfering with, blocking, diverting or otherwise impairing the unauthorized distribution, display, performance or reproduction of his or her copyrighted work on a publicly accessible peer-to-peer file-trading network," the bill says.

The global nature of file sharing means people in other countries otherwise outside the reach of US authorities will in effect be directly subject to US law. There is no provision in the bill to protect or isolate PCs in other countries.

The bill immunizes copyright holders from most claims by PC owners, provided the US Attorney-General is given seven days' notice of their interdiction. Copyright holders must say what methods they will use—such as a worm or denial of service—but that information would not be made public. They will not be permitted to disrupt the operation of the targeted PCs or networks generally, "except as may be reasonably necessary" to protect their copyrighted works. That loophole could foreseeably allow disabling of a PC's normal operations—its operating system, hardware such as the processor chip, attacking Internet routers or deleting the user's file-sharing software. The Attorney-General may veto copyright holders' hacking rights if they engage in a "pattern or practice of impairing ... computer files or data without a reasonable basis to believe that infringement of copyright has occurred."

Those whose PCs are disabled will be unable to claim damages if the total is less than $US50 for each "impairment" to an interdicted copyright work. For amounts greater than $US250 they must appeal to the US Attorney-General, who will have 120 days to determine if the complaint has merit, before they can file suit in a US court.

The second news item is paraphrased from Hamdan,[2] and describes how a Minister in the Malaysian government may encourage the use of pirated software in schools.

The Domestic Trade and Consumer Affairs Ministry of Malaysia may consider allowing schools and social organisations to use pirated computer software for educational purposes. Minister Tan Sri Muhyiddin Yassin said the exemption for such institutions and organisations was to encourage usage among Malaysians and speed up computer literacy among students.

However, he stressed that other sectors, especially the commercial sector like companies and factories, would be booked if they were found to be using pirated software. "We are concerned over the rampant sale and use of pirated computer software in the country and will continue to conduct raids to curb it. But for educational purposes and to encourage computer usage, we may consider allowing schools and social organisations to use pirated software," he said.

Muhyiddin said the ministry would launch another joint raid with the Business Software Alliance to check the illegal use of pirated computer software soon. He said it was not easy to curb such piracy and the computer software industry had noted that the problem was worse in the United States.

Ethical Analysis

Given that the two stories in this case involve legal systems in various countries, it might be argued that the important issues are legal and not moral. That they are legal is not in question, but it does not follow that they are not also moral. In an ideal situation the legal system codifies, to some extent, the moral mores of the society—the moral precedes the legal. The moral should also precede the legal in interactions between countries. The situation here is of course a little different, because there is often disagreement about what is moral in these cases, and when attempts are made to develop a legal framework, these differences will almost certainly come to the fore. It is important to examine the moral questions so that there is a firmer foundation on which to build the legal structure between nations. A variety of ethical issues are raised by the case, but here we will limit the analysis, and just consider in turn, intellectual property and cultural imperialism.

The case illustrates quite starkly a dramatic difference in attitudes to intellectual property in different countries. On the one hand there is a country considering using pirated software in its schools, and on the other, a country contemplating enforcing its copyright laws globally.

To justify this enforcement, unauthorized copying must really be quite wicked. But is it? Ownership of intellectual property is defended most strongly by those most wedded to capitalism, for the obvious reason that intellectual property is seen as a commodity with monitory value. Not all cultures, however, see things this way, and therefore, in some cultures, there is a much greater tendency for intellectual property to be in the public domain, so copying is not seen as a particular evil.

Consider the Malaysian example. Suppose that pirated software is used in schools. What is the problem? No other users are deprived of its use, and no-one is losing any sales because of it. The schools have no money to buy the software (or the Government does not have the money to give them), so either they use it without paying, or they do not use it at all. So by copying, they gain and nobody loses. It is not difficult to understand this point of view. It is however, very different from the view of the supporters of the proposed bill in the US, as outlined in the first report.

The second issue is cultural imperialism, which can be described as one society imposing its cultural values on another society. The case illustrates a situation that could be interpreted in this way. The original report about the new US law, which was in the Australian press, says: "File sharing's global nature means Australians otherwise outside the reach of US authorities will in effect be directly subject to US law. There are no provisions to protect or isolate PCs in other countries."

The proposed US copyright law would, it seems, make people worldwide subject to US law, regardless of intellectual property laws in their own countries. This does seem to be a clear case where one society is imposing its cultural values on another, but probably without realizing that this is what it is doing. It believes that it is upholding a value that is universal, or ought to be. There is no suggestion that the proposed US bill is directed at Malaysia. The two news reports coincidentally came out more or less at the same time.

What should be done about these, and similar global issues? Raising the problems is easy; knowing how to solve them justly is not. In the case described, all countries could be forced to abide by intellectual property laws as they operate in most Western countries. But it is not clear that this would be just. There is nothing sacred about the notion of intellectual property, and not all societies see it as important. If such laws are enforced this would need to be done in the light of individual societies' customs and their ability to pay.

This brief analysis indicates that solutions acceptable globally will be difficult, if not impossible, to find. But given that the Internet is global, more or less, these problems must be faced. There is no way of avoiding them.

Study Questions

1. In the case of the US copyright law, the available technology could allow the US view to be imposed on Malaysia, and schools could have their computers disabled, and so on, by the copyright owners. In the case of the Malaysian schools, should this be allowed to happen?

2. Should there be a law that allows any American copyright holder to hack into any computer, regardless of where in the world that computer is?

3. Would the use of open source or free software be a solution to part of this problem, for the computers' system software? How could this apply to music and video material?

4. Should the Malaysian government allow the use of pirated software in the country's schools?

NOTES

1 Cochrane, Nathan, 2002, "Hollywood Seeks the Right to Hack," *The Age*, 30 July. <http://www.theage.com.au/articles/2002/07/26/1027497416300.html>.

2 Hamdan Raja Abdullah, 2002, "Schools May Get to Use Pirated Software," 28 July. <http://pgoh.free.fr/pirated.html>.

CASE STUDY 8

COPY THAT, RED LEADER: IS FILE-SHARING PIRACY?

DAVID MEELER AND SRIVATSA SESHADRI

In 1999, an 18 year old college drop-out set a course of events in motion that shook the recording industry. Shawn Fanning had just penned the computer code for Napster®. According to *Time*, Fanning was nicknamed "Napster" because of his hairstyle. Shawn's idea was fairly simple: find a way to coordinate users so they could share computer files with one another. From 5¼″ floppies to flash-drives, computer users are always in search of ways to easily move files from one computer to another. Most of this is innocuous enough. You write a paper in your apartment, copy it to your flash-drive, and go to campus to print it. Sometimes, of course, we share files with friends or acquaintances. When we create these files, there is no problem. But when the file you share is the creative property of someone else, you may have infringed the author's copyright.

What made Napster® so effective is that it provided a platform upon which users could search and share the files of countless others. Napster's® initial plan was elegant. First, it created a catalog of each user's "shared" files, then allowed all users to search this "master-list" of files. In effect, Napster® operated like an introduction service. If you wanted a certain hit-song you "told" Napster® by entering a search string; Napster® would then find a user who had the file you wanted to download, and "introduce" the two of you: One user who has the file, and another user who wants the file.

The underlying problem is that music recordings—which the vast majority of Napster® users were interested in sharing with one another—are copyrighted material. Copyright is a difficult concept for some to grasp. Copyright is merely one form of intellectual property. In short, intellectual property allows people to own their creativity in the same way we can own physical property. Intellectual property gives to creators ownership of their intellectual and creative work. Copyright generally covers such things as music, films, sound recordings and broadcasts, literary and artistic works, and is sometimes thought to include software and multimedia. Any transaction requires that parties exchange goods of value. If I hand over my hard-earned cash to buy a music-recording, then it seems that I *own* the recording. If not, what have I bought? While it is true that I own the physical recording itself, it does not follow that I own the *content* recorded on the medium. It's the difference between owning this copy of the book you are reading and owning the picture on the cover. As it turns out, most musical artists don't own the copyrights to their songs. Rather, the labels who produce the recordings often own them. So Napster® facilitated the practice of illegally depriving recording labels of their rightful fees. Napster® lost its court battles and its servers were shut down. It is now owned by media behemoth Bertelsmann—who owns BMG and Sony—and offers a paid subscription service for sharing legally copyrighted files.

Analysis

Although Napster® lost its court cases, many of the important issues remain unsettled. Due to the simplicity of its set-up, Napster® was easily shut down. All of its files were on a single server. Current file-sharing networks, such as Fasttrack, operate on a decentral-ized network, so they are incredibly difficult to shut down. At the time of this printing, the US Supreme Court is deliberating a new case brought against these distributed file-sharing networks. A decision in *Metro-Goldwyn-Mayer Studios Inc. v. Grokster, Ltd.* is expected soon, and the winner is anyone's guess.

In 1984, Sony Corp. was exonerated when Universal Studios sued them for contributing to copyright infringements with their Betamax® technology. The Supreme Court's ruling then was based on the fact that most people used VCRs to record television broadcasts so they could watch them at a later time. This innocent practice is known as time-shifting. As the Supreme Court saw things, comparatively few VCR owners were pirating movies. This decision rested on the fact that VCRs had "substantial non-infringing uses." However, it is widely known that the vast majority of file-sharing involves copyright infringement, and is therefore plainly illegal. Although file-sharing software *has* legitimate uses, it is unclear what the Supreme Court might say about the technology since it is rarely used legitimately.

Study Questions

1. Does it seem natural to you to justify intellectual property with traditional arguments for private property? Why or why not?

2. Patents issued for new inventions last only a few years. When they expire, others may use the patent to make their own versions of the invention. Would similar time-limits on copyright be justifiable? Or should copyright protections continue to exist in perpetuity? Why or why not?

3. Suppose the copied music files are used by a teacher in a music class? Does the educational use change your moral assessment of the copyright violation?

4. How does your ethical assessment of copyright violation change if we consider copying a movie? A book? Computer code?

Advertising, Marketing, and the Consumer

ANAND VAIDYA

Advertising, Marketing, and the Consumer

A stakeholder is any group that has a vested interest in the activities of a corporation because they affect the welfare of the group. A stakeholder group is one that can be harmed by the activities of a corporation. Many corporations produce products for consumers to purchase. The goal of these corporations is to acquire consumers, so as to increase profit. As a consequence consumers are perhaps the most important stakeholder group since a corporation's fundamental source of profit stems from actual and potential consumers of their products and/or services. Because of the centrality of consumers, there are several ethical questions that surround the acquisition of such consumers. Some of these ethical questions pertain to and arise out of the prima facie obligation corporations have to disclose to potential consumers information about their products. Given that there are several different ways in which a corporation could advertise its product there is an open question over which ways are permissible.

With respect to advertising there are three central questions. First, one might legitimately ask how much information about a product is a corporation morally required to provide. Are they required to give all of the information or only some, and if only some, which information is morally required?

Second, given that corporations have to provide some information, what are the requirements on how that information is to be presented? Or, in other words, are there certain ways of presenting the information that are impermissible? Suppose that some information about some product is required—such as information pertaining to when it is harmful; yet, when that product is advertised, the information pertaining to when it is harmful is presented in a way in which a normal consumer would be unable to understand it. Question: Has the corporation satisfied its requirement to provide the information even though it is not comprehensible by the average consumer? So not only are there questions about what information a corporation is required to provide about its products, but also how this information should be presented.

Third, are corporations required to tell the truth about their products? And from where does the consumer's right to the truth and the accurate representation of the truth about a product derive? Quite often we see advertisements that use statistical claims (e.g., ninety per cent of doctors endorse some product). However, it is well-known that statistical information can be represented in various ways to make it look as if the claim being made is much stronger than the claim actually is. Insofar as advertisements use statistical information, there are open questions about when a certain use of statistical information constitutes a fallacy or a misrepresentation. In addition, we might ask: What are the boundaries on bending the claim that a group of "experts" supports a product?

Besides these questions about the representation of information, there are also deep philosophical questions about advertising. One of them—a question that steps outside of applied ethics and into broader issues about freewill and human motivation—has to do with the creation of desire. One might argue that various forms of advertising are immoral because they override an agent's autonomy; "autonomy" refers to our independence in thought and action. Autonomous agents that freely choose to buy a product on the basis of reliable information are responsible for the consequences the product brings upon them and others.

If I buy a product that I know may discolor my hair, but at the same time may greatly pollute the environment, then if both of these things happen, not only am I responsible for the damage it brings to my hair, but I am also responsible for the pollution it brings to the environment. However, if the process that brings about my acquisition of the object somehow overrides my autonomy, so that I am not really acting as myself, but am being manipulated, then it could be argued that I am not really responsible for the harm caused because I was not free in choosing to buy and use the product. Thus, if the process of advertising in some way overrides a consumers' autonomy such that they become compelled to purchase some item, then the form of advertising in question might be regarded as immoral. Humans have basic desires for food, shelter, and sex. Often things are advertised to us in ways that play to those desires.

The general question in this area is over whether our autonomy is overridden when advertising caters to our basic human desires. Are we, in a sense, *compelled* to buy things because of the nature of some advertisements? And if so, is it not the obligation of those that manufacture and market those products to not present them in a way that overrides a consumer's free choice.

Another important question concerning consumers is whether *targeting* a certain group of people for advertising is permissible. Targeting is the practice of intentionally aiming at a certain group of

consumers. Suppose commercials for a specific kind of medicine are always run at a certain time of night when older people who are more likely to have the associated condition are watching television. We would say in this case that targeting these individuals by running a commercial at a time when they are more likely to watch it is morally permissible, perhaps because we deem the product to be healthy. However, consider the tremendous amount of commercials about unhealthy snack foods that are played during children's programming. In this case, corporations are targeting children and creating in them the desire for certain unhealthy snack foods to which they subsequently become enamored. Many people hold that targeting children is impermissible. At times it appears that the judgment is related to the harmfulness of the product. The general question in this area is: When is targeting a specific group morally permissible?

In this unit, we have selected essays that explore both specific moral issues related to advertising and information, as well as articles that are concerned with more theoretical issues surrounding the creation of desire.

TRUTH AND DECEPTION IN ADVERTISING

TIBOR R. MACHAN

Advertising: The Whole or Only Some of the Truth?

When commercial advertising is criticized, often some assumption surfaces that should be explored more fully. I have in mind in particular the hidden premises that advertising is first and foremost a means for conveying information. Another assumption which lingers in the background of criticisms of advertising is that ethics requires that those

who sell goods and services should first of all help customers.

My aim here is to defend the approach to advertising that does not require of merchants that they tell all. So long as merchants are honest, do not mislead or deceive, they are acting in a morally satisfactory manner. It is not good for them—and there is nothing in morality that requires it of them—to take up the task of informing consumers of the conditions most favorable to them in the market place, to aid them in their efforts to find the best deal.

The following passage will help introduce us to the topic. It illustrates the kind of views that many philosophers who work in the field of business ethics seem to find convincing.

> Merchants and producers have many ways of concealing truth from the customers—not by lying to them, but simply by not telling them facts that are relevant to the question of whether they ought to purchase a particular product or whether they are receiving full value for their money.[1]

The author goes on to state that "it is certainly unethical for (salesmen and businessmen) to fail to tell their customers that they are not getting full value for their money."[2] He cites David Ogilvy, a successful advertiser, admitting that "he is 'continuously guilty' of *suppressio veri*, the suppression of the truth."[3] In other words, what advertisers do ethically or morally wrong is to fail to tell all, the whole truth, when they communicate to others about their wares, services, goods, products, or whatnot.

Yet there is something unrealistic, even farfetched, about this line of criticism. To begin with, even apart from advertising, people often enough advance a biased perspective on themselves, their skills, looks, and so on. When we go out on a first date, we tend to deck ourselves out in a way that certainly highlights what we consider our assets and diminishes our liabilities. When we send out our resumes in our job search efforts, we hardly tell all. When we just dress for the normal day, we tend to choose garb that enhances our looks and covers up what is not so attractive about our whole selves.

Burton Leiser, the critic we have been using to illustrate the prevailing view of advertising, is not wholly unaware of these points, since he continues with his quotation from Ogilvy, who says, "Surely it is asking too much to expect the advertiser to describe the shortcomings of his product. One must be forgiven for 'putting one's best foot forward.'" To this Leiser exclaims, "So the consumer is not to be told all the relevant information; he is not to be given all the facts that would be of assistance in making a rea-sonable decision about a given purchase ..."[4] Nevertheless, Leiser does not tell us what is ethically wrong in such instance, of *suppressio veri*. In fact, the claim that in all advertising one must present the whole truth, not just be truthful about one's subject matter, presupposes the very problematic ethical view that one ought to devote oneself *primarily* to bettering the lot of other people. What commerce rests on ethically, implicitly or explicitly, is the very different doctrine of *caveat emptor* (let him [the purchaser] beware), which assumes that prudence is a virtue and should be practiced by all, including one's customers. I will argue here that the merchant's ethical stance is more reasonable than that of the critics.

I. The Vice of Suppressio Veri

Leiser and many others critical of business and sales practices assume that in commercial transactions persons owe others the whole truth and nothing but the truth. This is why they believe that merchants act unethically in failing to tell their customers something that customers might ask about if they would only think of everything relevant to their purchasing activities. Leiser gives a good example:

> Probably the most common deception of this sort is price deception, the technique some high-pressure salesmen use to sell their goods by grossly inflating their prices to two, three, and even four times their real worth. Again, there may be no "untruth" in what they say; but they conceal the important fact that the same product, or one nearly identical to it, can be purchased for far less at a department or appliance store....

Before I discuss the ethical points in these remarks, a word, first, about the alleged simplicity of learning whether some item for sale by a merchant is in fact available for purchase "for far less" elsewhere. The idea is, we may take it, that the customer will indeed obtain what he or she wants by purchasing this item from some other seller. This ignores the fact that it may be quite important for customers to purchase some items in certain places, in certain kinds of environments, even from certain types of persons (e.g., ones with good manners). Sheer accessibility can be crucial, as well as atmosphere, the merchant's demeanor, and so on. If it is legitimate for customers to seek satisfaction from the market, it is also legitimate to seek various combinations of satisfaction, not simply product or price satisfaction.

Let us, however, assume that a customer could have obtained all that she wanted by going elsewhere to purchase the item at a price "far less" than what it costs at a given merchant's store. Is there a responsibility on the merchant's part (if she knows this) to make the information available to the customer? Or even more demandingly, is it ethically required that the merchant become informed about these matters and convey the information to potential customers?

The answer depends on a broader ethical point. What are the standards by which human beings should conduct themselves, including in their relationship to others? If something on the order of the altruist's answer is correct, then, in general, *suppressio veri* is wrongful. Telling the whole truth would help other people in living a good human life. Altruism here means not the ideal of equal respect for everyone as a human being, advocated by Thomas Nagel.[5] Rather it is the earlier sense of having one's primary duty to advance the interest of others.[6] A merchant need not be disrespectful toward his customers by not informing them of something that perhaps they ought to have learnt in the first place. By volunteering information that quite conceivably a customer should, as a matter of his personal moral responsibility (as a prudent individual), have obtained, a merchant might be meddling in matters not properly his own, which could be demeaning.

But an altruism in terms of which one is responsible to seek and obtain the well-being of his fellow human beings would render *suppressio veri* morally wrong. Such an altruism is certainly widely advocated, if not by philosophers then at least by political reformers. For example, Karl Marx states, in one of his earliest writings, that "The main principle ... which must guide us in the selection of a vocation is the welfare of humanity ..." and that "man's nature makes it possible for him to reach his fulfillment only by working for the perfection and welfare of his society."[7] Here he states precisely the morality of altruism initially espoused by August Comte, who coined the term itself and developed the secular "religion" by which to promote the doctrine.[8]

Now only by the ethics of altruism does it follow unambiguously that a merchant who does not tell all "is certainly unethical." Neither the more common varieties of utilitarianism, nor Kant's theory, as it is often understood, implies this. If we are to live solely to do good for others, then when we have reason to believe that telling the whole truth will promote others' well-being (without thwarting the well-being of yet some other person), we morally ought to tell the whole truth to this person. So when a merchant has reason to believe that telling his customer about lower prices elsewhere (for goods which he sells at higher price) will benefit his customer, he ought morally to do so.

But for it to be established that this is what a merchant ought morally to do for any customer, and that not doing so "is certainly unethical," the sort of altruism Marx and Comte defended would have to be true. No other ethical viewpoint seems to give solid support to the above claim about what "is certainly unethical."

Still, might one perhaps be able to show the whole truth thesis correct by other means than depending on a strong altruistic moral framework? Not very plausibly.

Intuitionism, as generally understood, would not override the well entrenched belief that when one embarks on earning a living and deals with perfect strangers, one should not promote one's weaknesses, one should *not* volunteer information detrimental to one's prospects. I doubt anyone would seriously advise job seeking philosophers to list on their CVs rejected articles and denied promotions—that would be counterintuitive.

It is also doubtful that most versions of utilitarianism would support a very strong general principle of self-sacrifice from which it can be shown that it "is certainly unethical" not to tell the whole truth. There could be many good utilitarian reasons to support at least a substantial degree of *caveat emptor* in the marketplace. For example, if the classical and neoclassical defenses—and the Marxian explanation of the temporary necessity—of the unregulated market of profit seeking individuals have any merit, it is for utilitarian reasons that the competitive, self-interested conduct of market agents should be encouraged. This would preclude giving away information free of charge, as a matter of what is right from a utilitarian perspective of maximizing the good of society, which in this case would be wealth.

Even a Kantian deontological ethics, as generally understood, advises against talking over what is very plausibly another person's moral responsibility, namely, seeking out the knowledge to act prudently and wisely. The Kantian idea of moral autonomy may not require seeking one's personal happiness in life, as the Aristotelian concept of the good moral life does, but it does require leaving matters of morality to the discretion of the agent. Meddling with the agent's moral welfare would conceivably be impermissibly intrusive. By reference to the categorical imperative it is difficult to imagine why one should invite commercial failure in one's market transactions, a failure that is surely possible if one is occupied not with promoting one's success but with the success of one's potential customers.

It seems then, that the altruist ethics, which makes it everyone's duty to further the interests of other people, is indeed the most plausible candidate for making it "certainly unethical" to suppress the truth in commercial transactions. Yet, of course, troubles abound with altruism proper.

When properly universalized, as all *bona fide* moralities must be, the doctrine in effect obligates everyone to refuse any help extended. Such a robust form of altruism creates a veritable daisy-chain of self-sacrifice. None is left to be the beneficiary of human action. Perhaps, therefore, what should be considered is a less extreme form of altruism, one which obligates everyone to be helpful whenever he or she has good reason to think that others would suffer without help.

Specifically, the altruism that might be the underpinning of the criticism of advertising ethics illustrated above should be thought of more along Rawlsian lines. According to this view we owe help to others only if they are found in special need, following the lead of Rawls's basic principle that "All social values—liberty and opportunity, income and wealth, and the bases of self-respect—are to be distributed equally unless an unequal distribution of any, or all, of these values is to everyone's advantage."[9]

But this form of moderate egalitarianism no longer supports the prevailing idea of proper business ethics.[10] In complying with this principle the merchant should, in the main—except when informed of special disadvantages of potential customers—put a price on his product that will sell the most of his wares at the margin. That is exactly what economists, who assume that merchants are profit maximizers, would claim merchants will do. And this is the kind of conduct that the merchant has reason to believe will ensure the equal distribution of values, as far as she can determine what that would be. The reason is that from the perspective of each merchant qua merchant it is reasonable in the course of commerce to consider potential customers as agents with equal status to merchants who are interested in advancing their economic interests. From this, with no additional information about some possible special disadvantage of the customer, merchants must see themselves as having equal standing to customers and as having legitimate motives for furthering their own interests.[11]

Thus, the Rawlsian egalitarian moral viewpoint will not help to support the doctrine that merchants owe a service to customers. Only the robust form of altruism we find in Marx and some others is a good candidate for the morality that, for example, Leiser assumes must guide our merchant. Ethical views other than altruism might support the view that the merchant ought to be extra helpful to special persons—family, friends, associates, even neighbors—but not to everyone. Even a narrow form of subjective "ethical" egoism can lead merchants to regard it as their responsibility to be helpful toward *some* other people. For instance, a merchant might consider most of his customers close enough friends that the morality of friendship, which need not be altruistic and may be egoist, would guide him to be helpful even to the point of risking the loss of business. Or, alternatively, were it the case that having the reputation of being helpful leads to increased patronage from members of one's community, then in just such a community such a subjective egoist would properly engage in helping behavior, including now and then informing his customers of more advantageous purchases in other establishments.

II. *The Morality of* Caveat Emptor

In contrast to the assumption of altruism as a guide to business conduct, I wish to suggest a form of egoism as the appropriate morality in terms of which to understand commerce. I have in mind a form of egoism best called "classical" because, as I have argued elsewhere,[12] it identifies standards of (egoistic) conduct by reference to the teleological conception of the human self spelled out in the works of classical philosophers, especially Aristotle, but modified in line with an individualism that arises from the ontology of human nature.[13] The idea, briefly put, is that each individual should seek to promote his interests as a human being and as the individual he is ... Classical egoism regards the individual person as the ultimate, though not sole, proper beneficiary of that individual's own moral conduct. The standards

of such conduct are grounded on the nature of the individual as a *human being*, as we as that particular person, thus in a moral universe which is coherent there need be no fundamental conflict between the egoistic conduct of one person and the egoistic conduct of another.

Accordingly, in the case of our merchant, he should abide by the basic moral principle of right reason, and the more particular implication of this namely the virtue of honesty, as he answers the questions his customer puts to him. He might, for example, even refuse to answer some question instead of either giving help or lying. It is a person's moral responsibility to promote his rational self-interest. And taking up the task of merchandising goods and services can qualify for various individuals with their particular talents and opportunities in life, as promoting one's rational self-interest. So a merchant could be acting with perfect moral propriety in not offering help to a customer with the task of information gathering (especially when it is clear that competing merchants are doing their very best to publicize such information as would be valuable to customers). The responsibility of merchants is to sell conscientiously their wares, not to engage in charitable work by carrying out tasks that other persons ought to carry out for themselves.

It might be objected that if someone asks an informed merchant, "Is the same product available for a lower price somewhere else?" no other alternative but letting the customer know the answer exists— it could be rather strained to refuse to answer. But there are many ways to deflect answering that do not mark someone as a deceiver. Smiling at the customer, the merchant might quietly put a question in response to the question: "Well, do you actually want me to help you to take your business elsewhere?" Should it be clear to the merchant that the customer isn't going to be satisfied with the wares available in his or her establishment, it would make perfectly good sense to offer help—and indeed countless merchants do frequently enough. Thus, when one looks for shoes, one frequently finds that one merchant will guide a customer to another where some particular style or size is likely to be available. Both good merchandising and ordinary courtesy would support such a practice, although it is doubtful that any feasible ethical system would make it obligatory!

In terms of the classical egoism that would seem to give support to these approaches to ethical issues in business, it does not follow that one would be acting properly by lying to avoid putting oneself at a competitive disadvantage. One's integrity, sanity, reputation, generosity and one's respect for others are more important to oneself than competitive advantage. Yet neither is prudence merely a convenience, and seeking a competitive advantage in the appropriate ways would indeed be prudent.[14]

Of course showing that this morality is sound would take us on a very long journey, although some work has already been done to that end.[15] As I have noted already, in numerous noncommercial situations human beings accept the form of conduct which characterizes ordinary but decent commercial transactions as perfectly proper. In introducing ourselves to people we have never met, for example, we do not advance information that would be damaging to the prospects of good relations. We do not say, "I am John Doe. When I am angry, I throw a fit, and when in a bad mood I am an insufferable boor." When we send an invitation to our forthcoming party, we do not say, "While this party may turn out to be pleasant, in the past we have had some very boring affairs that also set out to be fun." Innumerable noncommercial endeavors, including professional ones, are characterized by "putting our best foot forward," leaving to others the task of making sure whether they wish to relate to us. The fields of romance, ordinary conversation, political advocacy, and so forth all give ample evidence of the widespread practice of putting our best foot forward and letting others fend for themselves. We do not lie, mislead or deceive others by not mentioning to them, un-

solicited, our bad habits, our foibles. As suggested before, we are not lying or misleading others when in sending along our resumes or CVs we do not list projects that have been rejected.

The exceptions to this are those cases in which we have special obligations arising out of special moral relationships such as friendship, parenthood, collegialty, and so on. In these—as well as in contractual relationships where the obligations arise out of explicitly stated intent instead of implied commitments and promises—one can have obligated oneself to be of assistance even in competition or contest. Friends playing tennis could well expect one another to lend a hand when skills are quite uneven. Parents should not allow their children to fend for themselves, with limited information, as the children embark upon various tasks. And in emergency cases it is also reasonable to expect strangers to set aside personal goals that ordinarily would be morally legitimate.

Commercial relationships usually take place between strangers. The only purpose in seeking out other persons is for the sake of a good deal. Even here, sometimes further bonds emerge, but those are essentially beside the point of commerce. So the moral aspects of personal intimacy would not be the proper ethics for commercial relationships, anymore than they would be for sport or artistic competitions.

Some, of course, envision the good human community as a kind of large and happy family, the "brotherhood of man," as Marx did (not only early in his life but, insofar as his normative model of the ultimately good human society was concerned, for all of his career). For them the fact that some human beings interact with others solely for "narrow," "selfish" economic purposes will be a lamentable feature of society—to be overcome when humanity reaches maturity, perhaps, or to be tolerated only if out of such selfishness some public good can be achieved.[16]

But this alleged ideal of social life cannot be made to apply to human beings as they in fact are found among us. That vision, even in Marx, is appropriate only for a "new man," not the actual living persons we are (in our time). For us this picture of universal intimacy must be rejected in favor of one in which the multifaceted and multidimensional possibility of pursuit of personal happiness—albeit in the tradition of Aristotle, not Bentham and contemporary microeconomists—is legally protected (not guaranteed, for that is impossible). For them commercial interaction or trade does not place the fantastic burden on the parties involved that would be required of them if they needed to "be forgiven for putting one's best foot forward."

I have tried to offer some grounds for conceiving of trade in such a way that the unreasonable burden of having to tell others the whole truth, blemishes and all, need not be regarded as morally required. None of the above endorse cheating, deception, false advertising, and the like. It does recommend that you look at the practice of commercial advertising—as well as other practices involving the presentation of oneself or one's skills and wares in a favorable light—as morally legitimate, justified, even virtuous (insofar as it would be prudent).

III. Product Liability: Some Caution

One line of objection that has been suggested to the above approach is the failing to tell all about the features of a commercial transaction on the part of those embarking on it is like not telling someone about a defect in a product. When a merchant sells an automobile tire, if he is aware that this tire is defective, the mere fact that his customer does not explicitly inquire about defects does not appear to be, on its face, sufficient justification for suppression of the truth of the fact. But is this not just what my analysis above would permit on egoistic grounds? And would that not be sufficient ground, as James Rachels argues[17] in another context against egoism, for rejecting the argument?

Without embarking on a full discussion of the topic of product liability, let me point out some possible ways of approaching the issues that are consistent with the moral perspective I have taken on truth

telling. First, as in law, so in morality there is the "reasonable man" standard which can be appealed to considering personal responsibility. After all, a merchant is selling an automobile tire and it is implicit in that act that he is selling something that will, to the best of available knowledge, function in that capacity when utilized in normal circumstances.

One problem with this response is that it comes close to begging the question. Just what the reasonable expectation is in such cases of commercial transaction is precisely at issue. If it is true that *caveat emptor* is justified, then why not go the full distance and make the buyer beware of all possible hitches associated with the transaction?

The answer to that question introduces the second approach to handling the product liability issue…. I am thinking here of the need for a distinction between what is essential about some item and what is incidental or merely closely associated with it. And when we are concerned about truth telling—and I have not tried to reject the requirement of honesty, only that of telling everything that one knows *and* that may be of help to the buyer—it is more than likely that in the very identification of what one is trading, one commits oneself to having to give any information that is pertinent to the nature of the item or service at hand. Concerning automobile tires, their function as reliable equipment for transport on ordinary roads is a good candidate for an essential feature. So not telling of a defect in tires pertaining to this feature would amount to telling a falsehood, that is, saying one is trading *x* when in fact one is trading *not-x* (inasmuch as the absence of an essential feature of *x* would render whatever is identified as *x* a fake, something that would in the context of commercial transactions open the party perpetrating the misidentification to charges of fraud).

This is not to claim that what is essential about items must remain static over time. The context has a good deal to do with the determination of essential attributes of items and services, and convention and practice are not entirely inapplicable to that determination. Here is where a certain version of the theory of rational expectations would be useful and may indeed already function in some instances of tort law. As J. Roger Lee puts it,

> I have rights. They do not come out of agreements with others, being prior to and presupposed by such agreements. But standard relations with others, which I will call "rational expectations frameworks" fix the criteria of their application to situations in everyday life. And rational expectation frameworks are a guide to those criteria.
>
> ... For example, if I go into a bar and order a scotch on the rocks, then it is reasonable to expect that I'll get what I order and that neither it nor the place where I sit will be boobytrapped. There are countless examples of this.[18]

It is possible to show that from a robust or classical ethical egoist standpoint, *the truth about an item or service being traded should be told*. But this does not show that the whole truth should be told, including various matters associated with the buying and selling of the item or service in question—such as, its price elsewhere, its ultimate suitability to the needs of the buyer, its full value and so on. This perspective, in turn, does not imply that defective products or incompetent service are equally suitable objects of trade in honest transactions.[19,20]

NOTES

1 Burton Leiser, "Deceptive Practices in Advertising," in Tom L. Beauchamp and Norman Bowie (eds.), *Ethical Theory and Business* (Englewood Cliffs: Prentice-Hall, 1979), 479. Leiser's rendition of this view is perhaps the most extreme. Others have put the matter more guardedly, focusing more on the kind of suppression that conceals generally harmful aspects of products than on failure to inform the public of its comparative disadvantage vis-à-vis similar or even identical substitutes. Yet the general statements of the ethical point, in contrast to the examples cited, are very close to Leiser's own. See, e.g., Vincent Barry, *Moral Issues in Business* (Belmont: Wadsworth Publishing Company, 1983), Chapter 8. Barry chides advertisers "for concealing fact ... when its availability would probably make the desire, purchase, or use of a product less likely than in its absence" (278).

2 Leiser, *op. cit.*

3 Ibid., 484.

4 Ibid., 479.

5 Thomas Nagel, *The Possibility of Altruism* (Oxford: Clarendon Press, 1970).

6 This is the sense of the term as it occurs in the writings of August Comte who reportedly coined it. Thus the *Oxford English Dictionary* reports that the term was "introduced into English by the translators and expounders of Comte," e.g., Lewis' *Comte's Philosophy*, Sc. I. xxi. 224: "Dispositions influenced by the purely egoist impulses we call popularly 'bad,' and apply the term 'good' to those in which altruism predominates" (1853), *The Compact Edition*, 65.

7 Lloyd D. Easton and Kurt H. Guddat (eds.), *Writings of the Young Marx on Philosophy and Society* (Garden City: Anchor Books, 1967), 39. See, for a recent statement, W. Maclagan, "Self and Others: A Defense of Altruism," *The Philosophical Quarterly*, Vol. 4, No. 15 (1954), 109-27. As Maclagan states it, "I call my view 'altruism' assuming a duty to relieve the distress and promote the happiness of our fellows." He adds that such a virtue requires "that a man may and should discount altogether his own pleasure or happiness as such when he is deciding what course of action to pursue" (110).

8 Wilhelm Windelband, *A History of Philosophy*, Vol. II (New York: Harper Torchbooks, 1968), 650ff.

9 John Rawls, *A Theory of Justice* (Cambridge, MA: Harvard University Press 1971), 62.

10 Because of the intimate association of ethics and altruism (self-sacrifice), so defenders of the value of commerce or business have settled for a total disassociation of business and morality. See, e.g., Albert Carr, "Is Business Bluffing Ethical?" in Thomas Donaldson and Patricia H. Werhane (eds.), *Ethical Issues in Business* (Englewood Cliffs, NJ: Prentice-Hall, 1979), 46-52 (above pp. 400–08).

11 I believe that this point about the compatibility of Rawls' egalitarianism and the market economy has been argued in James Buchanan, "Hobbesian Interpretation of the Rawlsian Difference Principle," *Kyklos* Vol. 29 (1976), 5-25.

12 Tibor R. Machan, "Recent Work in Ethical Egoism," *American Philosophy Quarterly*, Vol. 16 (1979), 1-15. See also T.R. Machan, "Ethics and the Regulation of Professional Ethics," *Philosophia*, Vol. 8 (1983), 337-48.

13 *Nicomachean Ethics*, 119a 12. This point is stressed in W.F.R. Hardie, "The First Good in Aristotle's Ethics," *Philosophy*, Vol. 40 (1965), 277-95.

14 For more elaborate development of these points, see Tibor R. Machan, *Human Rights and Human Liberties* (Chicago: Nelson-Hall, 1975), Chapter 3.

15 See, e.g., Eric Mack, "How to Derive Ethical Egoism," *The Personalist*, Vol. 59 (1971), 735-43.

16 The entire tradition of classical economics embodies this point, made forcefully by Mandeville's *The Fable of the Bees* and Adam Smith's *The Wealth of Nations*.

17 James Rachels, "Two Arguments Against Ethical Egoism," *Philosophia*, Vol. 4 (1974), 297-314.

18 J. Roger Lee, "Choice and Harms," in T.R. Machan and M. Bruce Johnston (eds.), *Rights and Regulations: Ethical, Political, and Economic Issues* (Cambridge, MA: Ballinger, 1983), 168-69.

19 For more on product liability, see Richard A. Epstein, *A Theory of Strict Liability* (San Francisco: Cato Institute, 1980). See, also, Tibor R. Machan, "The Petty Tyranny of Government Regulations," in M.B. Johnson and T.R. Machan (eds.), *Rights and Regulations, op. cit.*

20 This paper was presented to the American Association for the Philosophic Study of Society, San Francisco, California, March 27, 1987. I wish to express my appreciation for the opportunity to give this paper to a very receptive and helpful audience at that meeting. I want also to thank the anonymous reviewer for the *Public Affairs Quarterly* for very helpful suggestions.

◆ ◆ ◆ ◆ ◆

JOHN WAIDE

The Making of Self and World in Advertising

In this paper I will criticize a common practice I call associative advertising. Briefly, associative advertising induces people to buy (or buy more of) a product by associating that market product with such deep-seated non-market goods as friendship, acceptance and esteem from others, excitement and power even though the market good seldom satisfies or has any connection with the non-market desire. The fault in associative advertising is not that it is deceptive or that it violates the autonomy of its audience—on this point I find Robert Arrington's arguments persuasive ("Advertising and Behavior Control," *Journal of Business Ethics* 1 (1982), 3-12). Instead, I will argue against associative advertising by examining the virtues and vices at stake. In so doing, I will offer an alternative to Arrington's exclusive concern with autonomy and behavior control.

My main criticism is two-fold: (a) Advertisers must surely desensitize themselves to the compassion, concern, and sympathy for others that are central emotions in a virtuous person, and (b) associative advertising influences its audience to neglect the non-market cultivation of our virtues and to substitute market goods instead, with the result that we become worse and, quite likely, less happy persons.

In this paper I will criticize a common practice I call associative advertising. The fault in associative advertising is not that it is deceptive or that it violates the autonomy of its audience—on this point I find Arrington's arguments persuasive.[1] Instead, I will argue against associative advertising by examining the virtues and vices at stake. In so doing, I will offer an alternative to Arrington's exclusive concern with autonomy and behavior control.

Associative advertising is a technique that involves all of the following:

1. The advertiser wants people[2] to buy (or buy more of) a product. This objective is largely independent of any sincere desire to improve or enrich the lives of the people in the target market.

2. In order to increase sales, the advertiser identifies some (usually) deep-seated non-market good for which the people in the target market feel a strong desire. By "non-market good" I mean something which cannot, strictly speaking, be bought or sold in a marketplace. Typical non-market goods are friendship, acceptance and esteem of others. In a more extended sense we may regard excitement (usually sexual) and power as non-market goods since advertising in the USA usually uses versions of these that cannot be bought and sold. For example, "sex appeal" as the theme of an advertising campaign is not the market-good of prostitution, but the non-market good of sexual attractiveness and acceptability.

3. In most cases, the marketed product bears only the most tenuous (if any) relation to the non-market good with which it is associated in the advertising campaign. For example, soft drinks cannot give one friends, sex, or excitement.

4. Through advertising, the marketed product is associated with the non-market desire it cannot possibly satisfy. If possible, the desire for the non-market good is intensified by calling into question one's acceptability. For example, mouthwash, toothpaste, deodorant, and feminine hygiene ads are concocted to make us worry that we stink.

5. Most of us have enough insight to see both (a) that no particular toothpaste can make us sexy and (b) that wanting to be considered sexy is at least part of our motive for buying that toothpaste. Since we can (though, admittedly, we often do not bother to) see clearly what the appeal of the ad is, we are usually not lacking in relevant information or deceived in any usual sense.

6. In some cases, the product actually gives at least partial satisfaction to the non-market desire—but only because of advertising.[3] For example, mouthwash has little prolonged effect on stinking breath, but it helps to reduce the intense anxieties reinforced by mouthwash commercials on television because we at least feel that we are doing the proper thing. In the most effective cases of associative advertising, people begin to talk like ad copy. We begin to sneer at those who own the wrong things. We all become enforcers for the advertisers. In general, if the advertising images are effective enough and reach enough people, even preposterous marketing claims can become at least partially self-fulfilling.

Most of us are easily able to recognize associative advertising as morally problematic when the consequences are clear, extreme, and our own desires and purchasing habits are not at stake. For example, the marketing methods Nestlé used in Africa involved associative advertising. Briefly, Nestlé identified a large market for its infant formula—without concern for the well-being of the prospective consumers. In order to induce poor women to buy formula rather than breastfeed, Nestlé selected non-market goods on which to base its campaigns—love for one's child and a desire to be acceptable by being modern. These appeals were effective (much as they are in advertising for children's clothing, toys, and computers in the USA). Through billboards and radio advertising, Nestlé identified parental love with formula feeding and suggested that formula is the modern way to feed a baby. Reports indicate that in some cases mothers of dead babies placed cans of formula on their graves to show that the parents cared enough to do the very best they could for their children, even though we know the formula may have been a contributing cause of death.[4]

One might be tempted to believe that associative advertising is an objectionable technique only when used on the very poorest, most powerless and ignorant people and that it is the poverty, powerlessness, and ignorance which are at fault. An extreme example like the Nestlé case, one might protest, surely doesn't tell us much about more ordinary associative advertising in the industrialized western nations. The issues will become clearer if we look at the conceptions of virtue and vice at stake.

Dewey says "the thing actually at stake in any serious deliberation is not a difference of quantity [as utilitarianism would have us believe], but what kind of person one is to become, what sort of self is in the making, what kind of a world is in the making."[5] Similarly, I would like to ask who we become as we use or are used by associative advertising. This will not be a decisive argument. I have not found clear, compelling, objective principles—only considerations I find persuasive and which I expect many others to find similarly persuasive. I will briefly examine how associative advertising affects (a) the people who plan and execute marketing strategies and (b) the people who are exposed to the campaign.

(a) Many advertisers[6] come to think clearly and skillfully about how to sell a marketable item by associating it with a non-market good which people in the target market desire. An important ingredient in this process is lack of concern for the well-being of the people who will be influenced by the campaign. Lloyd Slater, a consultant who discussed the infant formula controversy with people in both the research and development and marketing divisions of Nestlé, says that the R&D people had made sure that the formula was nutritionally sound but were troubled or even disgusted by what the marketing department was doing. In contrast, Slater reports that the marketing people simply did not care and that "those guys aren't even human" in their reactions.[7] This evidence is only anecdotal and it concerns an admittedly extreme case. Still, I believe that the effects of associative advertising[8] would most likely be the same but less pronounced in more ordinary cases. Furthermore, it is quite common for advertisers in the USA to concentrate their attention on selling something that is harmful to many people, e.g., candy that rots our teeth, and cigarettes. In general, influencing people without concern for their well-being is likely to reduce one's sensitivity to the moral motive of concern for the well-being of others. Compassion, concern, and sympathy for others, it seems to me, are clearly central to moral virtue.[9] Associative advertising must surely undermine this sensitivity in much of the advertising industry. It is, therefore, *prima facie* morally objectionable.

(b) Targets of associative advertising (which include people in the advertising industry) are also made worse by exposure to effective advertising of this kind. The harm done is of two kinds:

(1) We often find that we are buying more but enjoying it less. It isn't only that products fail to live up to specific claims about service-life or effectiveness. More often, the motives ("reasons" would perhaps not be the right word here) for our purchases consistently lead to disappointment. We buy all the right stuff and yet have no more friends, lovers, excitement or respect than before. Instead, we have full closets and empty pocket books. Associative ad-

vertising, though not the sole cause, contributes to these results.

(2) Associative advertising may be less effective as an advertising technique to sell particular products than it is as an ideology[10] in our culture. Within the advertising which washes over us daily we can see a number of common themes, but the most important may be "You are what you own."[11] The quibbles over which beer, soft drink, or auto to buy are less important than the over-all message. Each product contributes its few minutes each day, but we are bombarded for hours with the message that friends, lovers, acceptance, excitement, and power are to be gained by purchases in the market, not by developing personal relationships, virtues, and skills. Our energy is channeled into careers so that we will have enough money to be someone by buying the right stuff in a market. The not very surprising result is that we neglect non-market methods of satisfying our non-market desires. Those non-market methods call for wisdom, compassion, skill, and a variety of virtues which cannot be bought. It seems, therefore, that insofar as associative advertising encourages us to neglect the non-market cultivation of our virtues and to substitute market goods instead, we become worse and, quite likely, less happy persons.

To sum up the argument so far, associative advertising tends to desensitize its practitioners to the compassion, concern, and sympathy for others that are central to moral virtue and it encourages its audience to neglect the cultivation of non-market virtues. There are at least five important objections that might be offered against my thesis that associative advertising is morally objectionable.

First, one could argue that since each of us is (or can easily be if we want to be) aware of what is going on in associative advertising, we must want to participate and find it unobjectionable. Accordingly, the argument goes, associative advertising is not a violation of individual autonomy. In order to reply to this objection I must separate issues.

(a) Autonomy is not the main, and certainly not the only, issue here. It may be that I can, through diligent self-examination, neutralize much of the power of associative advertising. Since I can resist, one might argue that I am responsible for the results—*caveat emptor* with a new twist.[12] If one's methodology in ethics is concerned about people and not merely their autonomy, then the fact that most people are theoretically capable of resistance will be less important than the fact that most are presently unable to resist.

(b) What is more, the ideology of acquisitiveness which is cultivated by associative advertising probably undermines the intellectual and emotional virtues of reflectiveness and self-awareness which would better enable us to neutralize the harmful effects of associative advertising. I do not know of specific evidence to cite in support of this claim, but it seems to me to be confirmed in the ordinary experience of those who, despite associative advertising, manage to reflect on what they are exposed to.

(c) Finally, sneer group pressure often makes other people into enforcers so that there are penalties for not going along with the popular currents induced by advertising. We are often compelled even by our associates to be enthusiastic participants in the consumer culture. Arrington omits consideration of sneer group pressure as a form of compulsion which can be (though it is not always) induced by associative advertising.

So far my answer to the first objection is incomplete. I still owe some account of why more people do not complain about associative advertising. This will become clearer as I consider a second objection.

Second, one could insist that even if the non-market desires are not satisfied completely, they must be satisfied for the most part or we would stop falling for associative advertising. This objection seems to me to make three main errors:

(a) Although we have a kind of immediate access to our own motives and are generally able to see what motives an advertising campaign uses, most of us lack even the simple framework provided by my analysis of associative advertising. Even one who sees that a particular ad campaign is aimed at a particular non-market desire may not see how all the ads put together constitute a cultural bombardment with an ideology of acquisitiveness—you are what you own. Without some framework such as this, one has nothing to blame. It is not easy to gain self-reflective insight, much less cultural insight.

(b) Our attempts to gain insight are opposed by associative advertising which always has an answer for our dissatisfactions—buy more or newer or different things. If I find myself feeling let down after a purchase, many voices will tell me that the solution is to buy other things too (or that I have just bought the wrong thing). With all of this advertising proposing one kind of answer for our dissatisfactions, it is scarcely surprising that we do not usually become aware of alternatives.

(c) Finally, constant exposure to associative advertising changes[13] us so that we come to feel acceptable as persons when and only when we own the acceptable, fashionable things. By this point, our characters and conceptions of virtue already largely reflect the result of advertising and we are unlikely to complain or rebel.

Third, and perhaps most pungent of the objections, one might claim that by associating mundane marketable items with deeply rooted non-market desires, our everyday lives are invested with new and greater meaning. Charles Revson of Revlon once said that "In the factory we make cosmetics; in the store we sell hope."[14] Theodore Levitt, in his passionate defense of associative advertising, contends that[15]

> Everyone in the world is trying in his [or her] special personal fashion to solve a primal problem of life—the problem of rising above his [or her] own negligibility, of escaping from nature's confining, hostile and unpredictable reality, of finding significance, security, and comfort in the things he [or she] must do to survive.

Levitt adds: "Without distortion, embellishment, and elaboration, life would be drab, dull, anguished, and at its existential worst."[16] This objection is based on two assumptions so shocking that his conclusion almost seems sensible.

(a) Without associative advertising would our lives lack significance? Would we be miserable in our drab, dull, anguished lives? Of course not. People have always had ideals, fantasies, heroes, and dreams. We have always told stories that captured our aspirations and fears. The very suggestion that we require advertising to bring a magical aura to our shabby, humdrum lives is not only insulting but false.

(b) Associative advertising is crafted not in order to enrich our daily lives but in order to enrich the clients and does not have the interests of its audience at heart. Still, this issue of intent, though troubling, is only part of the problem. Neither is the main problem that associative advertising images somehow distort reality. Any work of art also is, in an important sense, a dissembling or distortion. The central question instead is whether the specific appeals and images, techniques and products, enhance people's lives.[17]

A theory of what enhances a life must be at least implicit in any discussion of the morality of associative advertising. Levitt appears to assume that in a satisfying life one has many satisfied desires—*which* desires is not important.[18] To propose and defend an alternative to his view is beyond the scope of this paper. My claim is more modest—that it is not enough to ask whether desires are satisfied. We should also ask what kinds of lives are sustained, made possible, or fostered by having the newly synthesized desires. What kind of self and world are in the making, Dewey would have us ask. This self and world are always in the making. I am not arguing that there is some natural, good self which advertising changes and contaminates. It may be that not only advertising, but also art, religion, and education in general, always synthesize new desires.[19] In each case, we should look at the lives. How to judge the value of these lives and the various conceptions of virtue they will embody is another question. It will be enough for now to see that it is an important question.

Now it may be possible to see why I began by saying that I would suggest an alternative to the usual focus on autonomy and behavior control.[20] Arrington's defense of advertising (including, as near as I can tell, what I call associative advertising) seems to assume that we have no standard to which we can appeal to judge whether a desire enhances a life and, consequently, that our only legitimate concerns are whether an advertisement violates the autonomy of its audience by deceiving them or controlling their behavior. I want to suggest that there is another legitimate concern—whether the advertising will tend to influence us to become worse persons.[21]

Fourth, even one who is sympathetic with much of the above might object that associative advertising is necessary to an industrial society such as ours. Economists since Galbraith[22] have argued about whether, without modern advertising of the sort I have described, there would be enough demand to sustain our present levels of production. I have no answer to this question. It seems unlikely that associative advertising will end suddenly, so I am confident that we will have the time and the imagination to adapt our economy to do without it.

Fifth, and last, one might ask what I am proposing. Here I am afraid I must draw up short of my mark. I have no practical political proposal. It seems obvious to me that no broad legislative prohibition would improve matters. Still, it may be possible to make small improvements like some that we have already seen. In the international arena, Nestlé was censured and boycotted, the World Health Organization drafted infant formula marketing guidelines, and finally Nestlé agreed to change its practices. In the USA, legislation prohibits cigarette advertising on television.[23] These are tiny steps, but an important journey may begin with them.

Even my personal solution is rather modest. *First*, if one accepts my thesis that associative advertising is harmful to its audience, then one ought to avoid doing it to others, especially if doing so would require that one dull one's compassion, concern, and sympathy for others. Such initiatives are not entirely without precedent. Soon after the surgeon general's report on cigarettes and cancer in 1964, David Ogilvy and William Bernbach announced that their agencies would no longer accept cigarette accounts and *New Yorker* magazine banned cigarette ads.[24] *Second*, if I am even partly right about the effect of associative advertising on our desires, then one ought to expose oneself as little as possible. The most practical and effective way to do this is probably to banish commercial television and radio from one's life. This measure, though rewarding,[25] is only moderately effective. Beyond these, I do not yet have any answers.

In conclusion, I have argued against the advertising practice I call associative advertising. My main criticism is two-fold: (a) Advertisers must surely desensitize themselves to the compassion, concern, and sympathy for others that are central emotions in a virtuous person, and (b) associative advertising influences its audience to neglect the non-market cultivation of our virtues and to substitute market goods instead, with the result that we become worse and, quite likely, less happy persons.

NOTES

1 Robert L. Arrington, "Advertising and Behavior Control," *Journal of Business Ethics* 1, 3-12.

2 I prefer not to use the term "consumers" since it identifies us with our role in a market, already conceding part of what I want to deny.

3 Arrington, 8.

4 James B. McGinnis, *Bread and Justice* (New York: Paulist Press, 1979), 224. McGinnis cites as his source INFACT Newsletter, September 1977, 3. Formula is often harmful because poor

families do not have the sanitary facilities to prepare the formula using clean water and utensils, do not have the money to be able to keep up formula feeding without diluting the formula to the point of starving the child, and formula does not contain the antibodies which a nursing mother can pass to her child to help immunize the child against common local bacteria. Good accounts of this problem are widely available.

5 John Dewey, *Human Nature and Conduct* (New York: Random House, 1930), 202.

6 This can be a diverse group including (depending upon the product) marketing specialists, sales representatives, or people in advertising agencies. Not everyone in one of these positions, however, is necessarily guilty of engaging in associative advertising.

7 This story was told by Lloyd E. Slater at a National Science Foundation Chatauqua entitled "Meeting World Food Needs" in 1980-81. It should not be taken as a condemnation of marketing professionals in other firms.

8 One could argue that the deficiency in compassion, concern, and sympathy on the part of advertisers might be a result of self-selection rather than of associative advertising. Perhaps people in whom these moral sentiments are strong do not commonly go into positions using associative advertising. I doubt, however, that such self-selection can account for all the disregard of the audience's best interests.

9 See Lawrence A. Blum, *Friendship, Altruism and Morality* (Boston: Routledge and Kegan Paul, 1980) for a defense of moral emotions against Kantian claims that emotions are unsuitable as a basis for moral judgment and that only a purely rational good will offers an adequate foundation for morality.

10 I use "ideology" here in a descriptive rather than a pejorative sense. To be more specific, associative advertising commonly advocates only a part of a more comprehensive ideology. See

Raymond Geuss, *The Idea of a Critical Theory* (Cambridge University Press, 1981), 5-6.

11 For an interesting discussion, see John Lachs, "To Have and To Be," *Personalist* 45 (Winter, 1964), 5-14; reprinted in John Lachs and Charles Scott, *The Human Search* (New York: Oxford University Press, 1981), 247-55.

12 This is, in fact, the thrust of Arrington's arguments in "Advertising and Behavior Control."

13 I do not mean to suggest that only associative advertising can have such ill effects. Neither am I assuming the existence of some natural, pristine self which is perverted by advertising.

14 Quoted without source in Theodore Levitt, "The Morality (?) of Advertising," *Harvard Business Review*, July-August 1970; reprinted in Vincent Barry, *Moral Issues in Business*, (Belmont, CA: Wadsworth Publishing Company, 1979), 256.

15 Levitt (in Barry), 252.

16 Levitt (in Barry), 256.

17 "Satisfying a desire would be valuable then if it sustained or made possible a valuable kind of life. To say this is to reject the argument that in creating the wants he [or she] can satisfy, the advertiser (or the manipulator of mass emotion in politics or religion) is necessarily acting in the best interests of his [or her] public." Stanley Benn, "Freedom and Persuasion," *Australasian Journal of Philosophy* 45 (1969); reprinted in Beauchamp and Bowie, *Ethical Theory and Business*, second edition (Englewood Cliffs, NJ: Prentice-Hall, 1983), 374.

18 Levitt's view is not new. "Continual success in obtaining those things which a man from time to time desires—that is to say, continual prospering—is what men call felicity." Hobbes, *Leviathan* (Indianapolis: Bobbs-Merrill, 1958), 61.

19 This, in fact, is the principal criticism von Hayek offered of Galbraith's argument against the "dependence effect." E.A. von Hayek, "The Non Sequitur of the 'Dependence Ef-

fect,'" *Southern Economic Journal*, April 1961; reprinted in Tom L. Beauchamp and Norman E. Bowie, *Ethical Theory and Business*, second edition (Englewood Cliffs, NJ: Prentice-Hall, 1983), 363-66.

20 Taylor R. Durham, "Information, Persuasion, and Control in Moral Appraisal of Advertising," *The Journal of Business Ethics* 3, 179. Durham also argues that an exclusive concern with issues of deception and control leads us into errors.

21 One might object that this requires a normative theory of human nature, but it seems to me that we can go fairly far by reflecting on our experience. If my approach is to be vindicated, however, I must eventually provide an account of how, in general, we are to make judgments about what is and is not good (or life-enhancing) for a human being. Clearly, there is a large theoretical gulf between me and Arrington, but I hope that my analysis of associative advertising shows that my ap-

proach is plausible enough to deserve further investigation.

22 The central text for this problem is *The Affluent Society* (Houghton Mifflin, 1958). The crucial passages are reprinted in many anthologies, e.g., John Kenneth Galbraith, "The Dependence Effect," in W. Michael Hoffman and Jennifer Mills Moore, *Business Ethics: Readings and Cases in Corporate Morality* (New York: McGraw-Hill, 1984), 398-433.

23 "In March 1970 Congress removed cigarette ads from TV and radio as of the following January. (The cigarette companies transferred their billings to print and outdoor advertising. Cigarette sales reached new records.)" Stephen Fox, *The Mirror Makers: A History of American Advertising and its Creators* (New York: William Morrow and Co., 1984), 305.

24 Stephen Fox, 303-04.

25 See, for example, Jerry Mander, *Four Arguments for the Elimination of Television* (New York: Morrow Quill Paperbacks, 1977).

CREATION OF DESIRE IN ADVERTISING

ROGER CRISP

Persuasive Advertising, Autonomy, and the Creation of Desire

In this paper, I shall argue that all forms of a certain common type of advertising are morally wrong, on the ground that they override the autonomy of consumers. One effect of an advertisement might be the creation of a desire for the advertised product. How such desires are caused is highly relevant as to

whether we would describe the case as one in which the autonomy of the subject has been overridden. If I read an advertisement for a sale of clothes, I may rush down to my local clothes store and purchase a jacket I like. Here, my desire for the jacket has arisen partly out of my reading the advertisement. Yet, in an ordinary sense, it is based on or answers to certain properties of the jacket—its colour, style, material. Although I could not explain to you why my tastes are as they are, we still describe such cases as examples of autonomous action, in that all the decisions are being made by me: What kind of jacket do I like? Can I afford one? And so on. In certain other cases, however, the causal history of a desire may be different. Desire can be caused, for instance, by subliminal suggestion. In New Jersey, a cinema flashed sub-threshold advertisements for ice cream onto the screen during movies, and reported a dramatic increase in sales during intermissions. In such cases, choice is being deliberately ruled out by the method of advertising in question. These customers for ice cream were acting "automatonously," rather than autonomously. They did not buy the ice cream because they happened to like it and decided they would buy some, but rather because they had been subjected to subliminal suggestion. Subliminal suggestion is the most extreme form of what I shall call, adhering to a popular dichotomy, persuasive, as opposed to informative, advertising. Other techniques include puffery, which involves the linking of the product through suggestive language and images, with the unconscious desire of consumers for power, wealth, status, sex, and so on; and repetition, which is self-explanatory, the name of the product being "drummed into" the mind of the consumer.

The obvious objection to persuasive advertising is that it somehow violates the autonomy of consumers. I believe that this objection is correct, and that, if one adopts certain common-sensical standards for autonomy, non-persuasive forms of advertising are not open to such an objection. Very high standards for autonomy are set by Kant, who requires that an agent be entirely external to the causal nexus found in the ordinary empirical world, if his or her actions are to be autonomous. These standards are too high, in that it is doubtful whether they allow *any* autonomous action. Standards for autonomy more congenial to common sense will allow that my buying the jacket is autonomous, although continuing to deny that the people in New Jersey were acting autonomously. In the former case, we have what has come to be known in recent discussions of freedom of the will as *both* free will and free action. I both decide what to do, and am not obstructed in carrying through my decision into action. In the latter

case, there is free action, but not free will. No one prevents the customers buying their ice cream, but they have not themselves made any genuine decision whether or not to do so. In a very real sense, decisions are made for consumers by persuasive advertisers, who occupy the motivational territory properly belonging to the agent. If what we mean by autonomy, in the ordinary sense, is to be present, the possibility of decision must exist alongside.

Arrington (1982) discusses, in a challenging paper, the techniques of persuasive advertising I have mentioned, and argues that such advertising does not override the autonomy of consumers. He examines four notions central to autonomous action, and claims that, on each count, persuasive advertising is exonerated on the charge we have made against it. I shall now follow in the footsteps of Arrington, but argue that he sets the standards for autonomy too low for them to be acceptable to common sense, and that the charge therefore still sticks.

(A) Autonomous Desire

Arrington argues that an autonomous desire is a first-order desire (a desire for some object, say, Pongo Peach cosmetics) accepted by the agent because it fulfils a second-order desire (a desire about a desire, say, a desire that my first-order desire for Pongo Peach be fulfilled), and that most of the first-order desires engendered in us by advertising are desires that we do accept. His example is an advertisement for Grecian Formula 16, which engenders in him a desire to be younger. He desires that both his desire to be younger and his desire for Grecian Formula 16 be fulfilled.

Unfortunately, this example is not obviously one of persuasive advertising. It may be the case that he just has this desire to look young again rather as I had certain sartorial tastes before I saw the ad about the clothes sale, and then decides to buy Grecian Formula 16 on the basis of these tastes. Imagine this form of advertisement: a person is depicted using

Grecian Formula 16, and is then shown in a position of authority, surrounded by admiring members of the opposite sex. This would be a case of puffery. The advertisement implies that having hair coloured by the product will lead to positions of power, and to one's becoming more attractive to the opposite sex. It links, by suggestion, the product with my unconscious desires for power and sex. I may still claim that I am buying the product because I want to look young again. But the reasons for my purchase are my unconscious desires for power and sex, and the link made between the product and the fulfilment of those desires by the advertisement. These reasons are not reasons I could avow to myself as good reasons for buying the product, and, again, the possibility of decision is absent.

Arrington's claim is that an autonomous desire is a first-order desire which we accept. Even if we allow that it is possible for the agent to consider whether to accept or to repudiate first-order desires induced purely by persuasive advertising, it seems that all first-order desires induced purely by persuasive advertising will be non-autonomous in Arrington's sense. Many of us have a strong second-order desire not to be manipulated by others without our knowledge, and for no good reason. Often, we are manipulated by others without our knowledge but for a good reason, and one that we can accept. Take an accomplished actor: much of the skill of an actor is to be found in unconscious body language. This manipulation we see as essential to our being entertained, and thus acquiesce in it. What is important about this case is that there seems to be no diminution of autonomy. We can still judge the quality of the acting, in that the manipulation is part of its quality. In other cases, however, manipulation ought not to be present, and these are cases where the ability to decide is importantly diminished by the manipulation. Decision is central to the theory of the market-process: I should be able to decide whether to buy product A or product B, by judging them on their merits. Any manipulation here I shall

repudiate as being for no good reason. This is not to say, incidentally, that once the fact that my desires are being manipulated by others has been made transparent to me, my desire will lapse. The people in New Jersey would have been unlikely to cease their craving for ice cream, if we had told them that their desire had been subliminally induced. But they would no longer have voice acceptance of this desire, and, one assumes, would have resented the manipulation of their desires by the management of the cinema.

It is no evidence for the claim that most of our desires are autonomous in this sense that we often return to purchase the same product over and over again. For this might well show that persuasive advertising has been supremely efficient in inducing non-autonomous desires in us, which we are unable even to attempt not to act on, being unaware of their origin. Nor is it an argument in Arrington's favour that certain members of our society will claim not to have the second-order desire we have postulated. For it may be that this is a desire which we can see one that human beings *ought* to have, a desire which would be in their interests to have, and the lack of which is itself evidence of profound manipulation.

(B) Rational Desire and Choice

One might argue that the desires induced by advertising are often irrational, in the sense that they are not present in an agent in full possession of the facts about the product. This argument fails, says Arrington, because if we require all the facts about a thing before we can desire that thing, then all our desires will be irrational; and if we require only the relevant information, then prior desires determine the relevance of information. Advertising may be said to enable us to fulfil these prior desires, through the transfer of information, and the supplying of means to ends is surely a paradigm example of rationality.

But, what about persuasive, as opposed to informative, advertising? Take puffery. Is it not true that a person may buy Pongo Peach cosmetics, hoping for an adventure in paradise, and that the product will not fulfil these hopes? Are they really in possession of even the relevant facts? Yes, says Arrington. We wish to purchase subjective effects, and these are genuine enough. When I use Pongo Peach, I will experience a genuine feeling of adventure.

Once again, however, our analysis can help us to see the strength of the objection. For a desire to be rational, in any plausible sense, that desire must at least not be induced by the interference of other persons with my system of tastes, against my will and without my knowledge. Can we imagine a person, asked for a reason justifying their purchase of Pongo Peach, replying: "I have an unconscious desire to experience adventure and the product has been linked with this desire through advertising"? If a desire is to be rational, it is not necessary that all the facts about the object be known to the agent, but one of the facts about that desire must be that it has not been induced in the agent through techniques which the agent cannot accept. Thus, applying the schema of Arrington's earlier argument, such a desire will be repudiated by the agent as non-autonomous and irrational.

Arrington's claim concerning the subjective effects of the products we purchase fails to deflect the charge of overriding autonomy we have made against persuasive advertising. Of course, very often the subjective effects will be lacking. If I use Grecian Formula 16, I am unlikely to find myself being promoted at work, or surrounded by admiring members of the opposite sex. This is just straight deception. But even when the effects do manifest themselves, such advertisements have still overridden my autonomy. They have activated desires which lie beyond my awareness, and over behaviour flowing from which I therefore have no control. If these claims appear doubtful, consider whether this advertisement is likely to be successful: "Do you have a feeling of adventure? Then use this brand of cosmetics." Such an advertisement will fail, in that it appeals to a *conscious* desire, either which we do not have, or which we realise will not be fulfilled by purchasing a certain brand of cosmetics. If the advertisement were for a course in mountain-climbing, it might meet with more success. Our conscious self is not so easily duped by advertising, and this is why advertisers make such frequent use of the techniques of persuasive advertising.

(C) Free Choice

One might object to persuasive advertising in that it creates desires so covert that an agent cannot resist them, and that acting on them is therefore neither free nor voluntary. Arrington claims that a person acts or chooses *freely* if they can adduce considerations which justify their act in their mind; and *voluntarily* if they been aware of a reason for acting otherwise, they could have done so. Only occasionally, he says, does advertising prevent us making free and voluntary choices.

Regarding free action, it is sufficient to note that, according to Arrington, if I were to be converted into a human robot, activated by an Evil Genius who has implanted electrodes in my brain, my actions would be free as long as I could cook up some justification for my behaviour. I want to dance this jig because I enjoy dancing. (Compare: I want to buy this ice cream because I like ice cream.) If my argument is right, we are placed in an analogous position by persuasive advertising. If we no longer mean by freedom of action the mere non-obstruction of behaviour, are we still ready to accept that we are engaging in free action? As for whether the actions of consumers subjected to persuasive advertising are voluntary in Arrington's sense, I am less optimistic than he is. It is likely, as we have suggested, that the purchasers of ice cream or Pongo Peach would have gone ahead with their purchase even if they had been made aware that their desires had been induced in them by persuasive advertising. But they would now claim that they themselves had not made the decision, that they were acting on a desire engendered in them which they did not accept, and that there was, therefore, a good reason for them not to make the purchase. The unconscious is not obedient to the commands of the conscious, although it may be forced to listen.

In fact, it is odd to suggest that persuasive advertising does give consumers a choice. A choice is usually taken to require the weighing-up of reasons. What persuasive advertising does is to remove the very conditions of choice.

(D) Control or Manipulation

Arrington offers the following criteria for control:

A person C controls the behaviour of another person P if
(1) C intends P to act in a certain way A
(2) C's intention is causally effective in bringing about A, and
(3) C intends to ensure that all of the necessary conditions of A are satisfied.

He argues that advertisements tend to induce a desire for X, given a more basic desire for Y. Given my desire for adventure, I desire Pongo Peach cosmetics. Thus, advertisers do not control consumers, since they do not intend to produce all of the necessary conditions for our purchases.

Arrington's analysis appears to lead to some highly counter-intuitive consequences. Consider again my position as human robot. Imagine that Evil Genius relies on the fact that I have certain basic unconscious desires in order to effect his plan. Thus, when he wants me to dance a jig, it is necessary that I have a more basic desire, say, ironically, for power. What the electrodes do is to jumble up my practical reasoning processes, so that I believe that I am dancing the jig because I like dancing, while, in reality, the desire to dance stems from a link between the dance and the fulfilment of my desire for power, forged by the electrodes. Are we still happy to say that I am not controlled? And does not persuasive advertising bring about a similar jumbling-up of the practical reasoning processes of consumers? When I buy Pongo Peach, I may be unable to offer a reason for my purchase, or I may claim that I want to look good. In reality, I buy it owing to the link made by persuasive advertising between my unconscious desire for adventure and the cosmetic in question.

A more convincing account of behaviour control would be to claim that it occurs when a person causes another person to act for reasons which the other person could not accept as good or justifiable reasons for the action. This is how brain-washing is to be distinguished from liberal education, rather than on Arrington's ground that the brain-washer arranges all the necessary conditions for belief. The student can both accept that she has the beliefs she has because of her education and continue to hold those beliefs as true, whereas the victim of brain-washing could not accept the explanation of the origin of her beliefs, while continuing to hold those beliefs. It is worth recalling the two cases we mentioned at the beginning of this paper. I can accept my tastes in dress, and do not think that the fact that their origin is unknown to me detracts from my autonomy, when I choose to buy the jacket. The desire for ice cream, however, will be repudiated, in that it is the result of manipulation by others, without good reason.

***

It seems, then, that persuasive advertising does override the autonomy of consumers, and that, if the overriding of autonomy, other things being equal, is immoral, then persuasive advertising is immoral.

An argument has recently surfaced which suggests that, in fact, other things are not equal, and that persuasive advertising, although it overrides autonomy, is morally acceptable. This argument was first developed by Nelson (1978), and claims that persuasive advertising is a form of informative advertising, albeit an indirect form. The argument runs at two levels: first, the consumer can judge from the mere fact that a product is heavily advertised, regardless of the form or content of the advertisements, that that product is likely to be a market-winner. The reason for this is that it would not pay to advertise market-losers. Second, even if the consumer is taken in by the content of the advertisement, and buys the product for that reason, he is not being irrational. For he would have bought the product anyway, since the very fact that it is advertised means that it is a good product. As Nelson says:

> It does not pay consumers to make very thoughtful decisions about advertising. They can respond to advertising for the most ridiculous, explicit reasons and still do what they would have done if they had made the most careful judgements about their behavior. "Irrationality" is rational if it is cost-free.

Our conclusions concerning the mode of operation of persuasive advertising, however, suggest that Nelson's argument cannot succeed. For the first level to work, it would have to be true that a purchaser of a product can evaluate that product on its own merits, and then decide whether to purchase it again. But as we have seen, consumers induced to purchase products by persuasive advertising are not buying those products on the basis of a decision founded upon any merit the products happen to have. Thus, if the product turns out to be less good than less heavily advertised alternatives, they will not be disappointed, and will continue to purchase, if subjected to the heavy advertising which induced them to buy in the first place. For this reason, heavy persuasive advertising is not a sign of quality, and the fact that a product is advertised does not suggest that it is good. In fact, if the advertising has little or no informative content, it might suggest just the opposite. If the product has genuine merits, it should be possible to mention them. Persuasive advertising as the execu-

tives on Madison Avenue know, can be used to sell anything regardless of its nature or quality.

For the second level of Nelson's argument to succeed, and for it to be in the consumer's interest to react even unthinkingly to persuasive advertising, it must be true that the first level is valid. As the first level fails, there is not even a *prima facie* reason for the belief that it is in the interest of the consumer to be subjected to persuasive advertising. In fact, there are two weighty reasons for doubting this belief. The first has already been hinted at: products promoted through persuasive advertising may well not be being sold on their merits, and may, therefore, be bad products, or products that the consumer would not desire on being confronted with unembellished facts about the product. The second is that this form of "rational irrationality" is anything but cost-free. We consider it a great cost to lose our autonomy. If I were to demonstrate to you conclusively that if I were to take over your life, and make your decisions for you, you would have a life containing far more of whatever you think makes life worth living, apart from autonomy, than if you were to retain control, you would not surrender your autonomy to me even for these great gains in other values. As we mentioned above in our discussion of autonomous desire, we have a strong second-order desire not to act on first-order desires induced in us unawares by others, for no good reason, and now we can see that that desire applies even to cases in which we would *appear* to be better off in acting on such first-order desires.

Thus, we may conclude that Nelson's argument in favour of persuasive advertising is not convincing. I should note, perhaps, that my conclusion concerning persuasive advertising echoes that of Santilli (1983). My argument differs from his, however, in centering upon the notions of autonomy and causes of desires acceptable to the agent, rather than upon the distinction between needs and desires. Santilli claims that the arousal of a desire is not a rational process, unless it is preceded by a knowledge of actual needs. This I believe, is too strong. I may well have no need of a new tennis-racket, but my desire for one, aroused by informative advertisements in the newspaper, seems rational enough. I should prefer to claim that a desire is autonomous and at least *prima facie* rational if it is not induced in the agent without his knowledge and for no good reason, and allows ordinary processes of decision-making to occur.

Finally, I should point out that, in arguing against all persuasive advertising, unlike Santilli, I am not to be interpreted as bestowing moral respectability upon all informative advertising. Advertisers of any variety ought to consider whether the ideological objections often made to their conduct have any weight. Are they, for instance, imposing a distorted system of values upon consumers, in which the goal of our lives is to consume, and in which success is measured by one's level of consumption? Or are they entrenching attitudes which prolong the position of certain groups subject to discrimination, such as women or homosexuals? Advertisers should also carefully consider whether their product will be of genuine value to any consumers, and, if so, attempt to restrict their campaigns to the groups in society which will benefit (see Durham, 1984). I would claim, for instance, that all advertising of tobacco-based products, even of the informative variety, is wrong, and that some advertisements for alcohol are wrong, in that they are directed at the wrong audience. Imagine, for instance, a liquor-store manager erecting an informative bill-board opposite an alcoholics' rehabilitation center. But these are secondary questions for prospective advertisers. The primary questions must be whether they are intending to employ the techniques of persuasive advertising, and, if so, how these techniques can be avoided.

REFERENCES

Arrington, R. 1982, "Advertising and Behaviour Control," *Journal of Business Ethics* I, 1.

Durham, T. 1984, "Information, Persuasion, and Control in Moral Appraisal of Advertising Strategy," *Journal of Business Ethics* III, 3.

Nelson, P. 1978, "Advertising and Ethics," in *Ethics, Free Enterprise, and Public Policy*, (eds.) R. De George and J. Pichler, New York: Oxford University Press.

Santilli, P. 1983, "The Informative and Persuasive Functions of Advertising. A Moral Appraisal," *Journal of Business Ethics* II, I.

◆ ◆ ◆ ◆ ◆

ROBERT L. ARRINGTON

Advertising and Behavior Control

Consider the following advertisements:

1. "A woman in *Distinction Foundations* is so beautiful that all other women want to kill her."

2. Pongo Peach color for Revlon comes "from east of the sun ... west of the moon where each tomorrow dawns." It is "succulent on your lips" and "sizzling on your finger tips (and on your toes goodness knows)." Let it be your "adventure in paradise."

3. "Musk by English Leather—The Civilized Way to Roar."

4. "Increase the value of your holdings. Old Charter Bourbon Whiskey—The Final Step Up."

5. Last Call Smirnoff Style: "They'd never really miss us, and it's kind of late already, and it's quite a long way, and I could build a fire, and you're looking very beautiful, and we could have another martini, and it's awfully nice just being home ... you think?"

6. A Christmas Prayer. "Let us pray that the blessing of peace be ours—the peace to build and grow, to live in harmony and sympathy with others, and to plan for the future with confidence." New York Life Insurance Company.

These are instances of what is called puffery—the practice by a seller of making exaggerated, highly fanciful or suggestive claims about a product or service. Puffery, within ill-defined limits, is legal. It is considered a legitimate, necessary, and very successful tool of the advertising industry. Puffery is not just bragging; it is bragging carefully designed to achieve a very definite effect. Using the techniques of so-called motivational research, advertising firms first identify our often hidden needs (for security, conformity, oral stimulation) and our desires (for power, sexual dominance and dalliance, adventure) and then they design ads which respond to these needs and desires. By associating a product, for which we may have little or no direct need or desire, with symbols reflecting the fulfillment of these other, often subterranean interests, the advertisement can quickly generate large numbers of consumers eager to purchase the product advertised. What woman in the sexual race of life could resist a foundation which would turn other women envious to the point of homicide? Who can turn down an adventure in paradise, east of the sun when tomorrow dawns? Who doesn't want to be civilized and thoroughly libidinous at the same time? Be at the pinnacle of success—drink Old Charter. Or stay at home and dally a bit—with Smirnoff. And let us pray for a secure and predictable future, provided for by New York Life, God willing. It doesn't take very much motivational research to see the point of these sales pitches. Others are perhaps a little less obvious. The need to feel secure in one's home at night can be used to sell window air conditioners, which drown out small noises and provide a friendly, dependable companion. The fact that baking a cake is symbolic of giving birth to a baby used to prompt advertisements for cake mixes which glamorized the "creative" housewife. And other strategies, for example involving cigar symbolism, are a bit too crude to mention, but are nevertheless very effective.

Don't such uses of puffery amount to manipulation, exploitation, and downright control? In his very popular book *The Hidden Persuaders*, Vance Packard points out that a number of people in the advertising world have frankly admitted as much:

> As early as 1941 Dr. Dichter (an influential advertising consultant) was exhorting ad agencies to recognize themselves for what they actually were—"one of the most advanced laboratories in psychology." He said the successful ad agency "manipulates human motivations and desires and develops a need for goods with which the public has at one time been unfamiliar—perhaps even undesirous of purchasing." The following year *Advertising Agency* carried an ad man's statement that psychology not only holds promise for understanding people but "ultimately for controlling their behavior."[1]

Such statements lead Packard to remark: "With all this interest in manipulating the customer's subconscious, the old slogan 'let the buyer beware' began taking on a new and more profound meaning."[2] B.F. Skinner, the high priest of behaviorism, has expressed a similar assessment of advertising and related marketing techniques. Why, he asks, do we buy a certain kind of car?

> Perhaps our favorite TV program is sponsored by the manufacturer of that car. Perhaps we have seen pictures of many beautiful or prestigeful persons driving it—in pleasant or glamorous places. Perhaps the car has been designed with respect to our motivational patterns: the device on the hood is a phallic symbol; or the horsepower has been stepped up to please our competitive spirit in enabling us to pass other cars swiftly (or, as the advertisements say, "safely"). The concept of freedom that has emerged as part of the cultural practice of our group makes little or no provision for recognizing or dealing with these kinds of control.[3]

In purchasing a car we may think we are free, Skinner is claiming, when in fact our act is completely controlled by factors in our environment and in our history of reinforcement. Advertising is one such factor.

A look at some other advertising techniques may reinforce the suspicion that Madison Avenue controls us like so many puppets. TV watchers surely have noticed that some of the more repugnant ads are shown over and over again, *ad nauseam*. My favorite, or most hated, is the one about A-1 Steak Sauce which goes something like this: Now, ladies and gentlemen, what is hamburger? It has succeeded in destroying my taste for hamburger, but it has surely drilled the name of A-1 Sauce into my head. And that is the point of it. Its very repetitiousness has generated what ad theorists call *information*. In this case it is indirect information, information derived not from the content of what is said but from the fact that it is said so often and so vividly that it sticks in one's mind—i.e., the information yield has increased. And not only do I always remember A-1 Sauce when I go to the grocers, I tend to assume that any product advertised so often has to be good—and so I usually buy a bottle of the stuff.

Still another technique. On a recent show of the television program "Hard Choices" it was demonstrated how subliminal suggestion can be used to control customers. In a New Orleans department store, messages to the effect that shoplifting is wrong, illegal, and subject to punishment were blended into the Muzak background music and masked so as not to be consciously audible. The store reported a dramatic drop in shoplifting. The program host conjectured whether a logical extension of this technique would be to broadcast subliminal advertising messages to the effect that the store's $15.99 sweater special is the "bargain of a lifetime." Actually, this application of subliminal suggestion to advertising has already taken place. Years ago in New Jersey a cinema was reported to have flashed subthreshold ice cream ads onto the screen during regular showings of the film—and, yes, the concession stand did a landslide business.[4]

Puffery, indirect information transfer, subliminal advertising—are these techniques of manipulation and control whose success shows that many of us have forfeited our autonomy and become a community, or herd, of packaged souls?[5] The business world and the advertising industry certainly reject his interpretation of their efforts. *Business Week*, for example, dismissed the charge that the science of behavior, as utilized by advertising, is engaged in human engineering and manipulation. It editorialized to the effect that "it is hard to find anything very sinister about a science whose principal conclusion is that you get along with people by giving them what they want."[6] The theme is familiar: businesses just give the consumer what he/she wants; if they didn't they wouldn't stay in business very long. Proof that the consumer wants the products advertised is given by the fact that he buys them, and indeed often returns to buy them again and again.

The techniques of advertising we are discussing have had their more intellectual defenders as well. For example, Theodore Levitt, Professor of Business Administration at the Harvard Business School, has defended the practice of puffery and the use of techniques depending on motivational research.[7] What would be the consequences, he asks us, of deleting all exaggerated claims and fanciful associations from advertisements? We would be left with literal descriptions of the empirical characteristics of products and their functions. Cosmetics would be presented as facial and bodily lotions—and powders which produce certain odor and color changes; they would no longer offer hope or adventure. In addition to the fact that these products would not then sell as well, they would not, according to Levitt, please us as much either. For it is hope and adventure we want when we buy them. We want automobiles not just for transportation, but the feelings of power and status they give us. Quoting T.S. Eliot to the effect that "Human kind cannot bear very much reality," Levitt argues that advertising is an effort to "transcend nature in the raw," to "augment what nature has so crudely fashioned." He maintains that "everybody everywhere wants to modify, transform, embellish, enrich and reconstruct the world around him." Commerce takes the same liberty with reality as the artist and the priest—in all three instances the purpose is "to influence the audience by creating illusions, symbols, and implications that promise more than pure functionality." For example, "to amplify the temple in men's eyes, (men of cloth) have, very realistically, systematically sanctioned the embellishment of the houses of the gods with the same kind of luxurious design and expensive decoration that Detroit puts into a Cadillac." A poem, a temple, a Cadillac—they all elevate our spirits, offering imaginative promise and symbolic interpretations of our mundane activities. Seen in this light, Levitt claims, "Embellishment and distortion are among advertising's legitimate and socially desirable purposes." To reject these techniques of advertising would be "to deny man's honest needs and values."

Phillip Nelson, a Professor of Economics at SUNY-Binghamton, has developed an interesting defense of indirect information advertising.[8] He argues that even when the message (the direct information) is not credible, the fact that the brand is advertised, and advertised frequently, is valuable indirect information for the consumer. The reason for this is that the brands advertised most are more likely to be better buys—losers won't be advertised a lot, for it simply wouldn't pay to do so. Thus even if the advertising claims made for a widely advertised product are empty, the consumer reaps the benefit of the indirect information which shows the product to be a good buy. Nelson goes so far as to say that advertising, seen as information and especially as indirect information, does not require an intelligent human response. If the indirect information has been received and has had its impact, the consumer will purchase the better buy even if his explicit reason for doing so is silly, e.g., he naively believes an endorsement of the product by a celebrity. Even though his behavior is overtly irrational, by acting on the indirect information he is

nevertheless doing what he ought to do, i.e., getting his money's worth. "'Irrationality' is rational," Nelson writes, "if it is cost-free."

I don't know of any attempt to defend the use of subliminal suggestion in advertising, but I can imagine one form such an attempt might take. Advertising information, even if perceived below the level of conscious awareness, must appeal to some desire on the part of the audience if it is to trigger a purchasing response. Just as the admonition not to shoplift speaks directly to the superego, the sexual virtues of TR-7's, Pongo Peach, and Betty Crocker cake mix present themselves directly to the id, bypassing the pesky reality principle of the ego. With a little help from our advertising friends, we may remove a few of the discontents of civilization and perhaps even enter into the paradise of polymorphous perversity.[9]

The defense of advertising which suggests that advertising simply is information which allows us to purchase what we want, has in turn been challenged. Does business, largely through its advertising efforts, really make available to the consumer what he/she desires and demands? John Kenneth Galbraith has denied that the matter is as straightforward as this.[10] In his opinion the desires to which business is supposed to respond, far from being original to the consumer, are often themselves created by business. The producers make both the product and the desire for it, and the "central function" of advertising is "to create desires." Galbraith coins the term "The Dependence Effect" to designate the way wants depend on the same process by which they are satisfied.

David Braybrooke has argued in similar and related ways.[11] Even though the consumer is in a sense, the final authority concerning what he wants, he may come to see, according to Braybrooke, that he was mistaken in wanting what he did. The statement "I want x," he tells us, is not incorrigible but is "ripe for revision." If the consumer had more objective information than he is provided by product puffing, if his values had not been mixed up by motivational research strategies (e.g., the confusion of sexual and automotive values), and if he had an expanded set of choices instead of the limited set offered by profit-hungry corporations, then he might want something quite different from what he presently wants. This shows, Braybrooke thinks, the extent to which the consumer's wants are a function of advertising and not necessarily representative of his real or true wants.

The central issue which emerges between the above critics and defenders of advertising is this: do the advertising techniques we have discussed involve a violation of human autonomy and a manipulation and control of consumer behavior, *or* do they simply provide an efficient and cost-effective means of giving the consumer information on the basis of which he or she makes a free choice. Is advertising information, or creation of desire?

To answer this question we need a better conceptual grasp of what is involved in the notion of autonomy. This is a complex, multifaceted concept, and we need to approach it through the more determinate notions of (a) autonomous desire, (b) rational desire and choice, (c) free choice, and (d) control or manipulation. In what follows I shall offer some tentative and very incomplete analyses of these concepts and apply the results to the case of advertising.

(a) Autonomous desire Imagine that I am watching TV and see an ad for Grecian Formula 16. The thought occurs to me that if I purchase some and apply it to my beard, I will soon look younger—in fact I might even be myself again. Suddenly want to be myself! I want to be young again! So I rush out and buy a bottle. This is our question: was the desire to be younger manufactured by the commercial, or was it "original to me" and truly mine? Was it autonomous or not?

F.A. von Hayek has argued plausibly that we should not equate nonautonomous desires, desires which are not original to me or truly mine, with those which are culturally induced.[12] If we did equate the two, he points out, then the desires for music, art, and knowledge could not properly be attributed to a person as original to him, for these are surely induced culturally. The only desires a person would really have as his own in this case would be the purely physical ones for food, shelter, sex, etc. But if we reject the equation of the nonautonomous and the culturally induced, as van Hayek would have us do, then the mere fact that my desire to be young again is caused by the TV commercial—surely an instrument of popular culture transmission—does not in and of itself show that this is not my own, autonomous desire. Moreover, even if I never before felt the need to look young, it doesn't follow that this new desire is any less mine. I haven't always liked 1969 Aloxe Corton Burgundy or the music of Satie, but when the desires for these things first hit me, they were truly mine.

This shows that there is something wrong in setting up the issue over advertising and behavior control as a question whether our desires are truly ours *or* are created in us by advertisements. Induced and autonomous desires do not separate into two mutually exclusive classes. To obtain a better understanding of autonomous and nonautonomous desires, let us consider some cases of a desire which a person does not *acknowledge* to be his own even though he *feels* it. The kleptomaniac has a desire to steal which in many instances he repudiates, seeking by treatment to rid himself of it. And if I were suddenly overtaken by a desire to attend an REO concert, I would immediately disown this desire, claiming possession or momentary madness. These are examples of desires which one might have but with which one would not identify. They are experienced as foreign to one's character or personality. Often a person will have what Harry Frankfurt calls a second-order desire, that is to say, a desire not to have another desire.[13] In such cases, the first-order desire is thought of as being nonautonomous, imposed on one. When on the contrary a person has a second-order desire to maintain and fulfill a first-order desire, then the first-order desire is truly his own, autonomous, original to him. So there is in fact a distinction between desires which are the agent's own and those which are not, but this is not the same as the distinction between desires which are innate to the agent and those which are externally induced.

If we apply the autonomous/nonautonomous distinction derived from Frankfurt to the desires brought about by advertising, does this show that advertising is responsible for creating desires which are not truly the agent's own? Not necessarily, and indeed not often. There may be some desires I feel which I have picked up from advertising and which I disown—for instance, my desire for A-1 Steak Sauce. If I act on these desires it can be said that I have been led by advertising to act in a way foreign to my nature. In these cases my autonomy has been violated. But most of the desires induced by advertising I fully accept, and hence most of these desires are autonomous. The most vivid demonstration of this is that I often return to purchase the same product over and over again, without regret or remorse. And when I don't, it is more likely that the desire has just faded than that I have repudiated it. Hence, while advertising may violate my autonomy by leading me to act on desires which are not truly mine, this seems to be the exceptional case.

Note that this conclusion applies equally well to the case of subliminal advertising. This may generate subconscious desires which lead to purchases, and the act of purchasing these goods may be inconsistent with other conscious desires I have, in which case I might repudiate my behavior and by implication the subconscious cause of it. But my subconscious desires may not be inconsistent in this way with my conscious ones; my id may be cooperative and benign rather than hostile and malign.[14] Here again, then, advertising may or may not produce desires which are "not truly mine."

What are we to say in response to Braybrooke's argument that insofar as we might choose differently if advertisers gave us better information and more options, it follows that the desires we have are to be attributed more to advertising than to our own real inclinations? This claim seems empty. It amounts to saying that if the world we lived in, and we ourselves, were different, then we would want different things. This is surely tame, but it is equally true of our desire for shelter as of our desire for Grecian Formula 16. If we lived in a tropical paradise we would not need or desire shelter. If we were immortal, we would not desire youth. What is true of all desires can hardly be used as a basis for criticizing some desires by claiming that they are nonautonomous.

(b) Rational desire and choice Braybrooke might be interpreted as claiming that the desires induced by advertising are often irrational ones in the sense that they are not expressed by an agent who is in full possession of the facts about the products advertised or about the alternative products which might be offered him. Following this line of thought, a possible criticism of advertising is that it leads us to act on irrational desires or to make irrational choices. It might be said that our autonomy has been violated by the fact that we are prevented from following our rational wills or that we have been denied the "positive freedom" to develop our true, rational selves. It might be claimed that the desires induced in us by advertising are false desires in that they do not reflect our essential, i.e., rational, essence.

The problem faced by this line of criticism is that of determining what is to count as rational desire or rational choice. If we require that the desire or choice be the product of an awareness of all the facts about the product, then surely every one of us is always moved by irrational desires and makes nothing but irrational choices. How could we know all the facts about a product? If it be required only that we possess all of the available knowledge about the product advertised, then we still have to face the problem that not all available knowledge is relevant to a rational choice. If I am purchasing a car, certain engineering features will be, and others won't be, relevant, *given what I want in a car*. My prior desires determine the relevance of information. Normally a rational desire or choice is thought to be one based upon relevant information, and information is relevant if it shows how other, prior desires may be satisfied. It can plausibly be claimed that it is such prior desires that advertising agencies acknowledge, and that the agencies often provide the type of information that is relevant in light of these desires. To the extent that this is true, advertising does not inhibit our rational wills or our autonomy as rational creatures.

It may be urged that much of the puffery engaged in by advertising does not provide relevant information at all but rather makes claims which are not factually true. If someone buys Pongo Peach in anticipation of an adventure paradise, or Old Charter in expectation of increasing the value of his holdings, then he/she is expecting purely imaginary benefits. In no literal sense will the one product provide adventure and the other increased capital. A purchasing decision based on anticipation of imaginary benefits is not, it might be said, a rational decision, and a desire for imaginary benefits is not a rational desire.

In rejoinder it needs to be pointed out that we often wish to purchase subjective effects which in being subjective are nevertheless real enough. The feeling of adventure or of enhanced social prestige and value are examples of subjective effects promised by advertising. Surely many (most?) advertisements directly promise subjective effects which their patrons actually desire (and obtain when they purchase the product), and thus the ads provide relevant information for rational choice. Moreover, advertisements often provide accurate indirect information on the basis of which a person who wants a certain subjective effect rationally chooses a product. The mechanism involved here is as follows.

To the extent that a consumer takes an advertised product to offer a subjective effect and the product does not, it is unlikely that it will be purchased again. If this happens in a number of cases, the product will be taken off the market. So here the market regulates itself, providing the mechanism whereby misleading advertisements are withdrawn and misled customers are no longer misled. At the same time, a successful

bit of puffery being one which leads to large and repeated sales, produces satisfied customers and more advertising of the product. The indirect information provided by such large-scale advertising efforts provides a measure of verification to the consumer who is looking for certain kinds of subjective effect. For example, if I want to feel well dressed and in fashion, and I consider buying an Izod Alligator shirt which is advertised in all of the magazines and newspapers, then the fact that other people buy it and that this leads to repeated advertisements shows me that the desired subjective effect is real enough and that I indeed will be well dressed and in fashion if I purchase the shirt. The indirect information may lead to a rational decision to purchase a product because the information testifies to the subjective effect that the product brings about.[15]

Some philosophers will be unhappy with the conclusion of this section largely because they have a concept of true, rational, or ideal desire which is not the same as the one used here. A Marxist, for instance, may urge that any desire felt by alienated man in a capitalistic society is foreign to his true nature. Or an existentialist may claim that the desires of inauthentic men are themselves inauthentic. Such concepts are based upon general theories of human nature which are unsubstantiated and perhaps incapable of substantiation. Moreover, each of these theories is committed to a concept of an ideal desire which is normatively debatable and which is distinct from the ordinary concept of a rational desire as one based upon relevant information. But it is in the terms of the ordinary concept that we express our concern that advertising may limit our autonomy in the sense of leading us to act on irrational desires, and if we operate with this concept we are driven again to the conclusion that advertising may lead, but probably most often does not lead, to an infringement of autonomy.

(c) **Free choice** It might be said that some desires are so strong or so covert that a person cannot resist them, and that when he acts on such desires he is not acting freely or voluntarily but is rather the victim of irresistible impulse or an unconscious drive. Perhaps those who condemn advertising feel that it produces this kind of desire in us and consequently reduces our autonomy.

This raises a very difficult issue. How do we distinguish between an impulse we *do* not resist and one we *could* not resist, between freely giving in to a desire and succumbing to one? I have argued elsewhere that the way to get at this issue is in terms of the notion of acting for a reason.[16] A person acts or chooses freely if he does so for a reason, that is, if he can adduce considerations which justify in his mind the act in question. Many of our actions are in fact free because this condition frequently holds. Often, however, a person will act from habit, or whim, or impulse, and on these occasions he does not have a reason in mind. Nevertheless he often acts voluntarily in these instances, i.e., he could have acted otherwise. And this is because if there *had been* a reason for acting otherwise of which he was aware, he would in fact have done so. Thus acting from habit or impulse is not necessarily to act in an involuntary manner. If, however, a person is aware of a good reason to do x and still follows his impulse to do y, then he can be said to be impelled by irresistible impulse and hence to act involuntarily. Many kleptomaniacs can be said to act involuntarily, for in spite of their knowledge that they likely will be caught and their awareness that the goods they steal have little utilitarian value to them, they nevertheless steal. Here their "out of character" desires have the upper hand, and we have a case of compulsive behavior.

Applying these notions of voluntary and compulsive behavior to the case of behavior prompted by advertising, can we say that consumers influenced by advertising act compulsively? The unexciting answer is: sometimes they do, sometimes not. I may have an overwhelming, TV induced urge to own a Mazda Rx-7 and all the while realize that I can't afford one without severely reducing my family's caloric intake to a dangerous level. If, aware of this good reason not to purchase the car, I nevertheless do so, this shows that I have been the victim of TV compulsion. But if I have the urge, as I assure you I do, and don't act on it, or if in some other possible world I could afford an Rx-7, then I have not been the subject of undue influence by Mazda advertising. Some Mazda Rx-7 purchasers act compulsively; others do not. The Mazda advertising effort in general cannot be condemned, then, for impairing its customers' autonomy in the sense of limiting free or voluntary choice. Of course the question remains what should be done about the fact that advertising may and does *occasionally* limit free choice. We shall return this question later.

In the case of subliminal advertising we may find an individual whose subconscious desires are activated by advertising into doing something his calculating, reasoning ego does not approve. This would be a case of compulsion. But most of us have a benevolent subconsciousness which does not overwhelm our ego and its reasons for action. And therefore most of us can respond to subliminal advertising without thereby risking our autonomy. To be sure, if some advertising firm developed a subliminal technique which drove all of us to purchase Lear jets, thereby reducing our caloric intake to the zero point, then we would have a case of advertising which could properly be censured for infringing our right to autonomy. We should acknowledge that this is possible, but at the same time we should recognize that it is not an inherent result of subliminal advertising.

(d) Control or manipulation Briefly let us consider the matter of control and manipulation. Under what conditions do these activities occur? In a recent paper on "Forms and Limits of Control" I suggested the following criteria.[17]

A person C controls the behavior of another person P *if*

1. *C* intends *P* to act in a certain way *A*;
2. *C*'s intention is causally effective in bringing about *A*; and

3. *C* intends to ensure that all of the necessary conditions of *A* are satisfied.

These criteria may be elaborated as follows. To control another person it is not enough that one's actions produce certain behavior on the part of that person; additionally one must intend that this happen. Hence control is the intentional production of behavior. Moreover, it is not enough just to have the intention; the intention must give rise to the conditions which bring about the intended effect. Finally, the controller must intend to establish by his actions any otherwise unsatisfied necessary conditions for the production of the intended effect. The controller is not just influencing the outcome, not just having input; he is as it were guaranteeing that the sufficient conditions for the intended effect are satisfied.

Let us apply these criteria of control to the case of advertising and see what happens. Conditions (1) and (3) are crucial. Does the Mazda manufacturing company or its advertising agency intend that I buy an Rx-7? Do they intend that a certain number of people buy the car? *Prima facie* it seems more appropriate to say that they hope a certain number of people will buy it, and hoping and intending are not the same. But the difficult term here is "intend." Some philosophers have argued that to intend *A* it is necessary only to desire that *A* happen and to believe that it will. If this is correct, and if marketing analysis gives the Mazda agency a reasonable belief that a certain segment of the population will buy its product, then, assuming on its part the desire that this happen, we have the conditions necessary for saying that the agency intends that a certain segment purchase the car. If I am a member of this segment of the population, would it then follow that the agency intends that I purchase an Rx-7? Or is control referentially opaque? Obviously we have some questions here which need further exploration.

Let us turn to the third condition of control, the requirement that the controller intend to activate or bring about any otherwise unsatisfied necessary conditions for the production of the intended effect. It is in terms of this condition that we are able to distinguish brainwashing from liberal education. The brainwasher arranges all of the necessary conditions for belief. On the other hand, teachers (at least those of liberal persuasion) seek only to influence their students—to provide them with information and enlightenment which they may absorb *if they wish*. We do not normally think of teachers as controlling their students, for the students' performances depend as well on their own interests and inclinations.

Now the advertiser—does he control, or merely influence, his audience? Does he intend to ensure that all of the necessary conditions for purchasing behavior are met, or does he offer information and symbols which are intended to have an effect only *if* the potential purchaser has certain desires? Undeniably advertising induces some desires, and it does this intentionally; but more often than not it intends to induce a desire for a particular object, given that the purchaser already has other desires. Given a desire for youth, or power, or adventure, or ravishing beauty, we are led to desire Grecian Formula 16, Mazda Rx-7's, Pongo Peach, and Distinctive Foundations. In this light, the advertiser is influencing us by appealing to independent desires we already have. He is not creating those basic desires. Hence it seems appropriate to deny that he intends to produce all of the necessary conditions for our purchases, and appropriate to deny that he controls us.[18]

Let me summarize my argument. The critics of advertising see it as having a pernicious effect on the autonomy of consumers, as controlling their lives and manufacturing their very souls. The defense claims that advertising only offers information and in effect allows industry to provide consumers with what they want. After developing some of the philosophical dimensions of this dispute, I have come down tentatively in favor of the advertisers. Advertising may, but certainly does not always or even frequently, control behavior, produce compulsive behavior, or create wants which are not rational or are not truly those of the consumer. Admittedly it may in individual cases do all of these things, but it is innocent of the charge of intrinsically or necessarily doing them or even, I think, of often doing so. This limited potentiality, to be sure, leads to the question whether advertising should be abolished or severely curtailed or regulated because of its potential to harm a few poor souls in the above ways. This is a very difficult question, and I do not pretend to have the answer. I only hope that the above discussion, in showing some of the kinds of harm that can be done by advertising and by indicating the likely limits of this harm, will put us in a better position to grapple with the question.

NOTES

1 Vance Packard, *The Hidden Persuaders* (New York: Pocket Books, 1958), 20-21.

2 Ibid., 21.

3 B.F. Skinner, "Some Issues Concerning the Control of Human Behavior: A Symposium," in Karlins and Andrews (eds.), *Man Controlled* (New York: The Free Press, 1972).

4 For provocative discussions of subliminal advertising, see W.B. Key, *Subliminal Seduction* (New York: The New American Library, 1973), and W.B. Key, *Media Sexploitation* (Englewood Cliffs, NJ: Prentice-Hall, Inc., 1976).

5 I would like to emphasize that in what follows I am discussing these techniques of advertising from the standpoint of the issue of control and not from that of deception. For a good and recent discussion of the many dimensions of possible deception in advertising, see Alex C. Michalos, "Advertising: Its Logic, Ethics, and Economics," in A. Blair and R.H. Johnson (eds.), *Informal Logic: The First International Symposium* (Pt. Reyes, CA: Edgepress, 1980).

6 Quoted by Packard, *op. cit.*, 220.

7 Theodore Levitt, "The Morality (?) of Advertising," *Harvard Business Review* 48 (1970), 84-92.

8 Phillip Nelson, "Advertising and Ethics," in Richard T. De George and Joseph A. Pichler (eds.), *Ethics, Free Enterprise, and Public Policy* (New York: Oxford University Press, 1978), 187-98.

9 For a discussion of polymorphous perversity see Norman O. Brown, *Life Against Death* (New York: Random House, 1969), chapter III.

10 John Kenneth Galbraith, *The Affluent Society*, reprinted in Tom L. Beauchamp and Norman E. Bowie (eds.), *Ethical Theory and Business* (Englewood Cliffs: Prentice-Hall, 1979), 496-501.

11 David Braybrooke, "Skepticism of Wants, and Certain Subversive Effects of Corporations on American Values," in Sidney Hook (ed.), *Human Values and Economic Policy* (New York: New York University Press, 1967); reprinted in Beauchamp and Bowie (eds.), *op. cit.*, 502-08.

12 F.A. von Hayek, "The *Non Sequitur* of the 'Dependence Effect,'" *Southern Economic Journal* (1961); reprinted in Beauchamp and Bowie (eds.), *op. cit.*, 508-12.

13 Harry Frankfurt, "Freedom of the Will and the Concept of a Person," *Journal of Philosophy* LXVIII (1971), 5-20.

14 For a discussion of the difference between a malign and a benign subconscious mind, see P.H. Nowell-Smith, "Psychoanalysis and Moral Language," *The Rationalist Annual* (1954); reprinted in P. Edwards and A. Pap (eds.), *A Modern Introduction to Philosophy*, Revised Edition (New York: The Free Press, 1965), 86-93.

15 Michalos argues that in emphasizing a brand name—such as Bayer Aspirin—advertisers are illogically attempting to distinguish the indistinguishable by casting a trivial feature of a product as a significant one which separates it from other brands of the same product. The brand name is said to be trivial or unimportant "from the point of view of the effectiveness of the product or that for the sake of which the product is purchased" (*op. cit.*, 107). This claim

ignores the role of indirect information in advertising. For example, consumers want an aspirin they can trust (trustworthiness being part of "that for the sake of which the product is purchased"), and the indirect information conveyed by the widespread advertising effort for Bayer Aspirin shows that this product is judged trustworthy by many other purchasers. Hence the emphasis on the name is not at all irrelevant but rather is a significant feature of the product from the consumer's standpoint, and attending to the name is not at all an illogical or irrational response on the part of the consumer.

16 Robert L. Arrington, "Practical Reason, Responsibility and the Psychopath," *Journal for the Theory of Social Behavior* 9 (1979), 71-89.

17 Robert L. Arrington, "Forms and Limits of Control," delivered at the annual meeting of the Southern Society for Philosophy and Psychology, Birmingham, Alabama, 1980.

18 Michalos distinguishes between appealing to people's tastes and molding those tastes (*op. cit.*, 104), and he seems to agree with my claim that it is morally permissible for advertisers to persuade us to consume some article *if* it suits our tastes (105). However, he also implies that advertisers mold tastes as well as appeal to them. It is unclear what evidence is given for this claim, and it is unclear what is meant by tastes. If the latter are thought of as basic desires and wants, then I would agree that advertisers are controlling their customers to the extent that they intentionally mold tastes. But if by molding tastes is meant generating a desire for the particular object they promote, advertisers in doing so may well be appealing to more basic desires, in which case they should not be thought of as controlling the consumer.

IS TARGETING ETHICAL?

LYNN SHARP PAINE

Children as Consumers: An Ethical Evaluation of Children's Television Advertising

Television sponsors and broadcasters began to identify children as a special target audience for commercial messages in the mid-1960s.[1] Within only a few years, children's television advertising emerged as a controversial issue. Concerned parents began to speak out and to urge the networks to adopt codes of ethics governing children's advertising. By 1970, the issue had attracted the attention of the Federal Trade Commission (FTC) and the Federal Communica-tions Commission (FCC). The FCC received some 80,000 letters in support of a proposed rule "looking toward the elimination of sponsorship and commercial content in children's programming."[2] Public attention to the controversy over children's television advertising peaked between 1978 and 1980, when the FTC, under its authority to regulate unfair and deceptive advertising, held public hearings on its proposal to ban televised advertising directed to or seen by large numbers of young children. More recently parents have complained to the FCC about so-called program-length commercials, children's programs designed around licensed characters.[3]

As this brief chronology indicates, children's television advertising has had a history of arousing people's ethical sensibilities. In this paper I want to propose some explanations for why this is so and to argue that there are good ethical reasons that advertisers should refrain from directing commercials to young children. However, because so much of the public debate over children's advertising has focused on the FTC's actions rather than explicitly on the ethical aspects of children's advertising, a few preliminary remarks are called for.

First, it is important to bear in mind that the ethical propriety of directing television advertising to young children is distinct from its legality. Even if advertisers have a constitutional right to advertise lawful products to young children in a nondeceptive way, it is not necessarily the right thing to do.[4] Our system of government guarantees us rights that it may be unethical to exercise on certain occasions. Terminology may make it easy to lose sight of the distinction between "having a right" and the "right thing to do," but the distinction is critical to constitutional governance.[5] In this paper I will take no position on the scope of advertisers' First Amendment rights to freedom of speech. I am primarily interested in the moral status of advertising to young children.

A second preliminary point worth noting is that evaluating the ethical status of a practice, such as advertising to young children, is a different exercise from evaluating the propriety of governmental regulation of that practice. Even if a practice is unethical, there may be legal, social, economic, political, or administrative reasons that the government cannot or should not forbid or even regulate the practice. The public policy issues faced by the FTC or any other branch of government involved in regulating children's advertising are distinct from the ethical issues facing advertisers. The fact that it may be impossible or unwise for the government to restrict children's advertising does not shield advertisers from ethical responsibility for the practice.

Finally, I want to point out that public opinion regarding children's advertising is a measure neither of its ethical value nor of the propriety of the FTC's actions. Two critics of the FTC declared that it had attempted to impose its conception of what is good on an unwilling American public.[6] There is reason to doubt the writers' assumption about the opinions of the American public regarding children's advertising,[7] but the more critical point is the implication of their argument: that the FTC's actions would have been appropriate had there been a social consensus opposing child-oriented advertising. Majority opinion, however, is neither the final arbiter of justified public policy, nor the standard for assaying the ethical value of a practice like children's advertising. As pointed out earlier, constitutional limits may override majority opinion in the public policy arena. And although publicly expressed opinion may signal ethical concerns (as I suggested in mentioning the letters opposing commercial sponsorship of children's television received by the FCC), social consensus is not the test of ethical quality. We cannot simply say that children's advertising is ethically all right because many people do not object to it or because people's objections to it are relatively weak. An ethical evaluation requires that we probe our ethical principles and test their relation to children's advertising. Publicly expressed opposition may signal that such probing is necessary, but it does not establish an ethical judgement one way or the other.

... For purposes of this discussion, I will set aside the legal and public policy questions involved in government restrictions on children's advertising. Instead, as promised, I will explore the ethical issues raised by the practice of directing television advertising to young children. In the process of this investigation, I will necessarily turn my attention to the role of consumers in a free market economy, to the capacities of children as they relate to consumer activities, and to the relationships between adults and children within the family.

By *young children* I mean children who lack the conceptual abilities required for making consumer decisions, certainly children under eight. Many researchers have investigated the age at which children can comprehend the persuasive intent of advertising.[8] Depending on the questions employed to test comprehension of persuasive intent, the critical age has been set as low as kindergarten age or as high as nine or ten.[9] Even if this research were conclusive, however, it would not identify the age at which children become capable of making consumer decisions. Comprehending persuasive intent is intellectually less complex than consumer decision-making. Even if children appreciate the selling intent behind advertising, they may lack other conceptual abilities necessary for responsible consumer decisions. Child psychologists could perhaps identify the age at which these additional abilities develop. For purposes of this discussion, however, the precise age is not crucial. When I use the term child or children I am referring to "young children"—those who lack the requisite abilities.

Children's advertising is advertising targeted or directed to young children.[10] Through children's advertising, advertisers attempt to persuade young children to want and, consequently, to request the advertised products. Although current voluntary guidelines for children's advertising prohibit advertisers from explicitly instructing children to request that their parents buy the advertised product, child-oriented advertising is designed to induce favorable attitudes that result in such requests.[11] Frequently child-oriented ads utilize themes and techniques that appeal particularly to children: animation, clowns, magic, fantasy effects, superheroes, and special musical themes.[12] They may involve simply the presentation of products, such as cereals, sweets, and toys that appeal to young children with announcements directed to them.[13] The critical point in understanding child-directed advertising, however, is not simply the product, the particular themes and techniques employed, or the composition of the audience viewing the ad, but whether the advertiser intends to sell to or through children. Advertisers routinely segment their markets and target their advertising.[14] The question at issue is whether children are appropriate targets.

Advertising directed to young children is a subcategory of advertising seen by them, since children who watch television obviously see a great deal of advertising that is not directed toward them—ads for adult consumer products, investment services, insurance, and so on. Occasionally children's products are advertised by means of commercials directed to adults. The toy manufacturer Fisher-Price, for example, at one time advertised its children's toys and games primarily by means of ads directed to mothers.[15] Some ads are designed to appeal to the whole family. Insofar as these ads address young children they fall within the scope of my attention.

My interest in television advertising directed to young children, as distinct from magazine or radio advertising directed to them, is dictated by the nature of the medium. Television ads portray vivid and lively images that engage young children as the printed words and pictures of magazines, or even the spoken words of radio, could never do. Because of their immediacy television ads can attract the attention of young children who have not yet learned to read. Research has shown that young children develop affection for and even personal relationships with heavily promoted product characters appearing on television.[16] At the same time, because of their immaturity, these children are unable to assess the status of these characters as fictional or real, let alone assess whatever minimal product information they may disclose.[17] Technical limitations make magazine advertising and radio advertising inherently less likely to attract young children's attention. Consequently, they are less susceptible to ethical criticisms of the sort generated by television advertising.

Children as Consumers

The introduction of the practice of targeting children for televised commercial messages challenged existing mores. At the obvious level, the practice was novel. But at a deeper level, it called into question traditional assumptions about children and their proper role in the marketplace. The argument advanced on behalf of advertising to children by the Association of National Advertisers (ANA), the American Association of Advertising Agencies (AAAA), and the American Advertising Federation (AAF) reflects the rejection of some of these traditional assumptions:

> Perhaps the single most important benefit of advertising to children is that it provides information to the child himself, information which advertisers try to gear to the child's interests and on an appropriate level of understanding. This allows the child to learn what products are available, to know their differences, and to begin to make decisions about them based on his own personal wants and preferences.... Product diversity responds to these product preferences and ensures that it is the consumer himself who dictates the ultimate success or failure of a given product offering.[18]

The most significant aspect of this argument supporting children's advertising is its vision of children as autonomous consumers. Children are represented as a class of consumers possessing the relevant decision-making capacities and differing from adult consumers primarily in their product preferences. Children are interested in toys and candy, while adults are interested in laundry detergent and investment services. That children may require messages tailored to their level of understanding is acknowledged, but children's conceptual abilities are not regarded as having any other special significance. Advocates of children's advertising argue that it gives children "the same access to the marketplace which adults have, but keyed to their specific areas of interest."[19] When children are viewed in this way—as miniature adults with a distinctive set of product preferences—the problematic nature of advertising to them is not apparent. Indeed, it appears almost unfair not to provide children with televised information about products available to satisfy their special interests. Why should they be treated differently from any other class of consumers?

There are, however, significant differences between adults and young children that make it inappropriate to regard children as autonomous consumers. These differences, which go far beyond different product preferences, affect children's capacities to function as responsible consumers and suggest several arguments for regarding advertising to them as unethical. For purposes of this discussion, the most critical differences reflect children's understanding of self, time, and money.

Child-development literature generally acknowledges that the emergence of a sense of one's self as an independent human being is a central experience of childhood and adolescence.[20] This vague notion, "having a sense of one's self as an independent human being" encompasses a broad range of capacities—from recognition of one's physical self as distinct from one's mother to acceptance of responsibility for one's actions and choices. Nor do children acquire these capacities gradually in the course of maturation. While this mastery manifests itself as self-confidence and self-control in an ever-widening range of activities and relationships, it depends more fundamentally upon the emergence of an ability to see oneself as oneself. The reflexive nature of consciousness—the peculiar ability to monitor, study, assess, and reflect upon oneself and even upon one's reflections—underlies the ability to make rational choices. It permits people to reflect upon their desires, to evaluate them, and to have desires about what they shall desire. It permits them to see themselves as one among others and as engaging in relationships with others. Young children lack—or have only in nascent form—this ability to take a higher-order perspective on themselves and to see themselves as having desires or preferences they may wish to cultivate, suppress, or modify. They also lack the self-control that would make it possible to act on these higher-order desires if they had them.

Closely related to the sense of self, if not implicit in self-reflection, is the sense of time. Children's understanding of time—both as it relates to their own existence and to the events around them—is another area where their perspectives are special. Preschoolers are intrigued with "time" questions: "When is an hour up?" "Will you be alive when I grow up?" "When did world begin and when will it end?" "Will I be alive for all the time after I die?" Young children's efforts to understand time are accompanied by a limited ability to project themselves into the future and to imagine themselves having different preferences in the future. It is generally true that children have extremely short time horizons. But children are also struggling with time in a more fundamental sense: they are testing conceptions of time as well as learning to gauge its passage by conventional markers.[21] Young children's developing sense of time goes hand in hand with their developing sense of self. Their capacity for self-reflection, for evaluating their desires, and for making rational choices is intimately related to their understanding of their own continuity in time.

Young children are in many ways philosophers: they are exploring and questioning the very fundamentals of existence.[22] Since they have not accepted many of the conventions and assumptions that guide ordinary commercial life, they frequently pose rather profound questions and make insightful observations. But although young children are very good at speculation, they are remarkably unskilled in the sorts of calculations required for making consumer judgements. In my experience, many young children are stymied by the fundamentals of arithmetic and do not understand ordinal relations among even relatively small amounts—let alone the more esoteric notions of selling in exchange for money. Research seems to support the observation that selling is a difficult concept for children. One study found that only 48 per cent of six-and-a-half- to seven-and-a-half-year-olds could develop an understanding of the exocentric (as distinct from egocentric) verb *to sell*.[23] A five-year-old may know from experience in making requests that a $5.00 trinket is too expensive, but when she concludes that $5.00 is also too

much to pay for a piano, it is obvious that she knows neither the exchange value of $5.00, the worth of a piano, nor the meaning of *too expensive*.[24]

What is the significance of the differences between adults and young children I have chosen to highlight—their differing conceptions of self, time, and money? In the argument for advertising quoted earlier, it was stated that advertising to children enables them "to learn what products are available, to know their differences, and to begin to make decisions about them based on [their] own personal wants and preferences." Ignore, for the moment, the fact that existing children's advertising, which concentrates so heavily on sugared foods and toys, does little either to let children know the range of products available or differences among them and assume that children's advertising could be more informative.[25] Apart from this fact, the critical difficulty with the argument is that because of children's, shall we say, "naive" or "unconventional" conceptions of self, time, and money, they know very little about their own personal wants and preferences—how they are related or how quickly they will change or about how their economic resources might be mobilized to satisfy those wants. They experience wants and preferences but do not seem to engage in critical reflection, which would lead them to assess, modify, or perhaps even curtail their felt desires for the sake of other more important or enduring desires they may have or may expect to have in the future. Young children also lack the conceptual wherewithal to engage in research or deliberative processes that would assist them in knowing which of the available consumer goods would most thoroughly satisfy their preferences, given their economic resources. The fact that children want so many of the products they see advertised is another indication that they do not evaluate advertised products on the basis of their preferences and economic resources.[26]

There is thus a serious question whether advertising really has or can have much at all to do with children's beginning "to make decisions about [prod-

ucts] based on [their] own personal wants and preferences" until they develop the conceptual maturity
to understand their own wants and preferences and
to assess the value of products available to satisfy
them.[27] If children's conceptions of self, time, and
money are not suited to making consumer decisions,
one must have reservations about ignoring this fact
and treating them as if they were capable of making
reasonable consumer judgements anyway ...

Children's Advertising and Basic Ethical Principles

My evaluation of children's advertising has proceed-
ed from the principle of consumer sovereignty, a
principle of rather narrow application. Unlike more
general ethical principles, like the principle of veracity, the principle of consumer sovereignty applies
in the specialized area of business. Addressing the
issue of children's advertising from the perspective
of special business norms rather than more general
ethical principles avoids the problem of deciding
whether the specialized or more general principles
should have priority in the moral reasoning of business people.[28] Nevertheless, children's advertising
could also be evaluated from the standpoint of the
more general ethical principles requiring veracity
and fairness and prohibiting harmful conduct.

Veracity

The principle of veracity, understood as devotion to
truth, is much broader than a principle prohibiting
deception. Deception, the primary basis of the FTC's
complaint against children's advertising, is only one
way of infringing the principle of veracity. Both critics and defenders of children's advertising agree that
advertisers should not intentionally deceive children
and that they should engage in research to determine
whether children are misled by their ads. The central issue regarding veracity and children's advertising, however, does not relate to deception so much

as to the strength of advertisers' devotion to truth.
Advertisers generally do not make false statements
intended to mislead children. Nevertheless, the particular nature of children's conceptual worlds makes
it exceedingly likely that child-oriented advertising
will generate false beliefs or highly improbable product expectations.

Research shows that young children have difficulty differentiating fantasy and reality[29] and frequently place indiscriminate trust in commercial
characters who present products to them.[30] They
also develop false beliefs about the selling characters
in ads[31] and in some cases have unreasonably optimistic beliefs about the satisfactions advertised products will bring them.[32]

This research indicates that concern about the
misleading nature of children's advertising is legitimate. Any parent knows—even one who has not
examined the research—that young children are easily persuaded of the existence of fantasy characters.
They develop (what seem to their parents) irrational
fears and hopes from stories they hear and experiences they misinterpret. The stories and fantasies children see enacted in television commercials receive the
same generous and idiosyncratic treatment as other
information. Children's interpretations of advertising claims are as resistant to parental correction as
their other fantasies are. One can only speculate on
the nature and validity of the beliefs children adopt
as a result of watching, for example, a cartoon de-
picting a pirate captain's magical discovery of break-
fast cereal. Certainly, many ads are designed to create
expectations that fun, friendship, and popularity will
accompany possession of the advertised product. The
likelihood that such expectations will be fulfilled is
something young children cannot assess.

To the extent that children develop false beliefs
and unreasonable expectations as a result of viewing
commercials, moral reservations about children's advertising are justified. To the extent advertisers know
that children develop false beliefs and unreasonable
expectations, advertisers' devotion to truth and to
responsible consumerism are suspect.

Fairness and Respect for Children

The fact that children's advertising benefits advertisers while at the same time nourishing false beliefs, unreasonable expectations, and irresponsible consumer desires among children calls into play principles of fairness and respect. Critics have said that child-oriented advertising takes advantage of children's limited capacities and their suggestibility for the benefit of the advertisers. As expressed by Michael Pertschuk, former chairman of the FTC, advertisers "seize on the child's trust and exploit it as weakness for their gain."[33] To employ as the unwitting means to the parent's pocketbook children who do not understand commercial exchange, who are unable to evaluate their own consumer preferences, and who consequently cannot make consumer decisions based on those preferences does indeed reflect a lack of respect for children. Such a practice fails to respect children's limitations as consumers, and instead capitalizes on them. In the language of Kant, advertisers are not treating children as "ends in themselves": they are treating children solely as instruments for their own gain.

In response to the charge of unfairness, supporters of children's advertising sometimes point out that the children are protected because their parents exercise control over the purse strings.[34] This response demonstrates failure to appreciate the basis of the unfairness charge. It is not potential economic harm that concerns critics: it is the attitude toward children reflected in the use of children's advertising that is central. As explained earlier, the attitude is inappropriate or unfitting.

Another frequent response to the charge of unfairness is that children actually do understand advertising.[35] A great deal of research has focused on whether children distinguish programs from commercials, whether they remember product identities, whether they distinguish program characters from commercial characters, and whether they recognize the persuasive intent of commercials.[36] But even showing that children "understand" advertising in all these ways would not demonstrate that children have the consumer capacities that would make it fair to advertise to them. The critical questions are not whether children can distinguish commercial characters from program characters,[37] or even whether they recognize persuasive intent, but whether they have the concepts of self, time, and money that would make it possible for them to make considered consumer decisions about the products they see advertised. Indeed, if children recognize that commercials are trying to sell things but lack the concepts to assess and deliberate about the products advertised, the charge that advertisers are "using" children or attempting to use them to sell their wares is strengthened. Intuitively, it seems that if children were sophisticated enough to realize that the goods advertised on television are for sale, they would be more likely than their younger counterparts to request the products.[38]

Harm to Children

Another principle to which appeal has been made by critics of television advertising is the principle against causing harm. The harmful effects of children's advertising are thought to include the parent-child conflict generated by parental refusals to buy requested products, the unhappiness and anger suffered by children whose parents deny their product requests, the unhappiness children suffer when advertising-induced expectations of product performance are disappointed, and unhappiness experienced by children exposed to commercials portraying lifestyles more affluent than their own.[39]

Replies to the charge that children's advertising is harmful to children has pinpointed weaknesses in the claim. One supporter of children's advertising says that the "harm" to children whose parents refuse their requests has not been adequately documented.[40] Another, claiming that some experts believe conflicts over purchases are instructive in educating children to make choices denies that parent-child conflict is harmful.[41] As these replies suggest, demonstrating that children's advertising is harmful to children, as distinct from being misleading or unfair to them, involves much more than showing that it has the effects enumerated. Agreement about the application of the principle against causing harm depends on conceptual as well as factual agreement. A conception of harm must first be elaborated, and it must be shown to include these or other effects of advertising. It is not obvious, for example, that unhappiness resulting from exposure to more different life-styles is in the long run harmful.

Research indicates that children's advertising does contribute to the outcomes noted.[42] Certainly, child-oriented television advertising is not the sole cause of these effects, but it does appear to increase their frequency and even perhaps their intensity.[43] I believe that a conception of harm including some of these effects could be developed, but I will not attempt to do so here. I mention this argument rather to illustrate another general ethical principle on which an argument against children's advertising might be based....

Conclusion

How might advertisers implement their responsibilities to promote consumer satisfaction and consumer responsibility and satisfy the principles of veracity, fairness, and nonmaleficence? There are degrees of compliance with these principles: some marketing strategies will do more than others to enhance consumer satisfaction, for example. One way compliance can be improved is by eliminating child-oriented television advertising for children's products and substituting advertising geared to mature consumers. Rather than employing the techniques found in advertising messages targeted to children under eleven,[44] advertisers could include product information that would interest adult viewers and devise ways to let child viewers know that consumer decisions require responsible decision-making skills. If much of the information presented is incomprehensible to the five-year-olds in the audience, so much the bet-

ter.[45] When they reach the age at which they begin to understand consumer decision-making, they will perhaps have greater respect for the actual complexity of their responsibilities as consumers.

The problems of child-oriented advertising can best be dealt with if advertisers themselves recognize the inappropriateness of targeting children for commercial messages. I have tried to show why, within the context of a free market economy, the responsibilities of advertisers to promote consumer satisfaction and not to discourage responsible consumer decisions should lead advertisers away from child-oriented advertising. The problem of what types of ads are appropriate given these constraints provides a challenging design problem for the many creative people in the advertising industry. With appropriate inspiration and incentives, I do not doubt that they can meet the challenge.

Whether appropriate inspiration and incentives will be forthcoming is more doubtful. Children's advertising seems well entrenched and is backed by powerful economic forces,[46] and it is clear that some advertisers do not recognize, or are unwilling to acknowledge, the ethical problems of child-focused advertising.[47] The trend toward programming designed around selling characters is especially discouraging.

Even advertisers who recognize that eliminating child-oriented advertising will promote consumer satisfaction and consumer responsibility may be reluctant to reorient their advertising campaigns because of the costs and risks of doing so. Theoretically, only advertisers whose products would not withstand the scrutiny of adult consumers should lose sales from such a reorientation. It is clear that in the short run a general retreat from children's advertising would result in some lost revenues for makers, advertisers, and retail sellers of products that do not sell as well when advertised to adults. It is also possible that television networks, stations, and entrenched producers of children's shows would lose revenues and that children's programming might be jeopardized by the lack of advertisers' interest in commercial time during children's programs.

On the other hand, a shift away from children's advertising to adult advertising could result in even more pressure on existing adult commercial time slots, driving up their prices to a level adequate to subsidize children's programming without loss to the networks. And there are alternative means of financing children's television that could be explored.[48] The extent to which lost revenues and diminished profits would result from recognizing the ethical ideals I have described is largely a question of the ability of all the beneficiaries of children's television advertising to respond creatively. The longer-term effect of relinquishing child-focused advertising would be to move manufacturers, advertisers, and retailers in the direction of products that would not depend for their success on the suggestibility and immaturity of children. In the long run, the result would be greater market efficiency.

NOTES

Some notes have been deleted and the remaining ones renumbered.

An earlier version of this paper was delivered at a workshop on advertising ethics at the University of Florida in April 1984. I want to thank Robert Baum for organizing the workshop and to express my appreciation to all the workshop participants who commented on my paper, but especially to Katherine Clancy, Susan Elliott, Kathleen Henderson, Betsy Hilbert, Craig Shulstad, and Rita Weisskoff. I also want to acknowledge the helpful criticisms of Eric Douglas, Paul Farris, and Anita Niemi.

1 Richard P. Adler, "Children's Television Advertising: History of the Issue," in *Children and the Faces of Television*, ed. Edward L. Palmer and Aimee Dorr (New York: Academic Press, 1980), 241; hereafter cited as Palmer and Dorr.

2 Adler, 243.

3 Daniel Seligman, "The Commercial Crisis," *Fortune* 108 (November 14, 1983): 39.

4 For discussion of the constitutionality of banning children's advertising, see C. Edwin Baker, "Commercial Speech: A Problem in the Theory of Freedom," *Iowa Law Review* 62 (October 1976): 1; Martin H. Redish, "The First Amendment in the Marketplace: Commercial Speech and the Values of Free Expression," *George Washington Law Review* 39 (1970-71): 429; Gerald J. Thain, "The 'Seven Dirty Words' Decision: A Potential Scrubbrush for Commercials on Children's Television?" *Kentucky Law Journal* 67 (1978-79): 947.

5 This point has been made by others. See, e.g., Ronald Dworkin, "Taking Rights Seriously," in *Taking Rights Seriously* (Cambridge, MA: Harvard University Press, 1977), 188ff.

6 Susan Bartlett Foote and Robert H. Mnookin, "The 'Kid Vid' Crusade," *Public Interest* 61 (Fall 1980): 91.

7 One survey of adults found the following attitudes to children's commercials: strongly negative (23%); negative (50%); neutral (23%); positive (4%). These negative attitudes are most pronounced among parents of kindergarten-age children. The survey is cited in Thomas S. Robertson, "Television Advertising and Parent-Child Relations," in *The Effects of Television Advertising on Children*, ed. Richard P. Adler, Gerald S. Lesser, Laurene Krasay Meringoff, et al. (Lexington, MA: Lexington Books, 1980), 197; hereafter cited as Adler et al.

8 E.g., M. Carole Macklin, "Do Children Understand TV Ads?" *Journal of Advertising Research* 23 (February-March 1983): 63-70; Thomas Robertson and John Rossiter, "Children and Commercial Persuasion: An Attribution Theory Analysis," *Journal of Consumer Research* 1 (June 1974): 13-20. See also summaries of research in David Pillemer and Scott Ward, "Investigating the Effects of Television Advertising on Children: An Evaluation of the Empirical Studies," Draft read to American Psychological Assn., Div. 23, San Francisco, California, August 1977; John R. Rossiter, "The Effects of Volume

and Repetition of Television Commercials," in Adler et al., 160-62; Ellen Wartella, "Individual Differences in Children's Responses to Television Advertising," in Palmer and Dorr, 312-14.

9   Wartella, 313.

10   Compare the definition of "child-oriented television advertising" adopted by the FTC in its Final Staff Report and Recommendation: "advertising which is in or adjacent to programs either directed to children or programs where children constitute a substantial portion of the audience." See "FTC Final Staff Report and Recommendation," *In the Matter of Children's Advertising*, 43 *Federal Register* 17967, March 31, 1981, 2.

11   *Self-Regulatory Guidelines for Children's Advertising*, by Children's Advertising Review Unit, Council of Better Business Bureau, Inc., 3rd ed. (New York, 1983), 6.

12   F. Earle Barcus, "The Nature of Television Advertising to Children," in Palmer and Dorr, 276-77.

13   Barcus, 275.

14   Research has been developed to support advertisers targeting child audiences. See, e.g., Gene Reilly Group, Inc., *The Child* (Darien, CT: The Child, Inc., 1973), cited in Robert B. Choate, "The Politics of Change," in Palmer and Dorr, 329.

15   Thomas Donaldson and Patricia H. Werhane, *Ethical Issues in Business* (Englewood Cliffs, NJ: Prentice-Hall, Inc., 1979), 294. In a telephone interview a representative of Fisher-Price's advertising agency told me that Fisher-Price continues to focus its advertising on parents because most Fisher-Price toys appeal to the very young.

16   See "FTC Final Staff Report and Recommendation," 21-22, n.51, for a description of studies by Atkin and White. Atkin found that 90% of the three-year-olds studied and 73% of the seven-year-olds thought that selling characters like them. White found that 82% of a group of four- to seven-year-olds thought that the selling figures ate the products they advertised and wanted the children to do likewise.

17   Studies indicate that there is very limited use of product information in children's television advertising. Predominant are "appeals to psychological states, associations with established values, and unsupported assertions about the qualities of the products." Barcus, 279.

18   Submission before the FTC, 1978, quoted in Emilie Griffin, "The Future is Inevitable: But Can it Be Shaped in the Interest of Children?" in Palmer and Dorr, 347.

19   Griffin, 344.

20   E.g., Frances L. Ilg, Louise Bates Ames, and Sidney M. Baker, *Child Behavior*, rev. ed. (New York: Harper & Row, 1981).

21   On the child's conception of time, see Jean Piaget, *The Child's Conception of Time* (New York: Basic Books, 1970).

22   Some intriguing illustrations of children's philosophical questions and observations are recounted in Gareth B. Matthews, *Philosophy and the Young Child* (Cambridge, MA: Harvard University Press, 1980).

23   "FTC Final Staff Report and Recommendation," 27-28, citing the work of Geis.

24   My five-year-old son reasoned thus to explain why a five-dollar piano would be too expensive.

25   Toys, cereals, and candies are the products most heavily promoted to children; Barcus, 275-76.

26   The FTC concluded on the basis of relevant literature that children tend to want whatever products are advertised on television; "FTC Final Staff Report and Recommendation," 8. For data on the extent to which children want what they see advertised on television, see Charles K. Atkin, "Effects of Television Advertising on Children," in Palmer and Dorr, 289-90.

27 The results of one study of children's understanding of television advertising messages suggested that although "parents cannot 'force' early sophistication in children's reactions to television advertising, their attention and instruction can enhance the process." Focusing on children's capacities to understand advertising rather than on their capacities to make decisions, the article supports the general proposition that the child's conceptual world differs in many ways from that of the adult. The critical question is, of course: even if we can promote earlier understanding of advertising and consumer decisions, should we do so? See John R. Rossiter and Thomas S. Robertson, "Canonical Analysis of Developmental, Social, and Experimental Factors in Children's Comprehension of Television Advertising," *Journal of Genetic Psychology* 129 (1976): 326.

28 For general discussion of this issue see Alan H. Goldman, *The Moral Foundations of Professional Ethics* (Totowa, NJ: Rowman and Littlefield, 1980), chap. 5.

29 See T.G. Bever, M.L. Smith, B. Bengen, and T.G. Johnson, "Young Viewers' Troubling Response to TV Ads," *Harvard Business Review*, November-December 1975, 109-20.

30 "FTC Final Staff Report and Recommendation" 21-22, n. 51, describes the work of Atkin supporting the conclusion that children trust selling characters. Atkin found in a group of three- to seven-year-olds that 70% of the three-year-olds and 60% of the seven-year-olds trusted the characters about as much as they trusted their mothers.

31 "FTC Final Staff Report and Recommendation," at 21-22, no. 51, describes the work of White, who found that many children in a group of four- to seven-year-olds she studied believe that the selling figures eat the advertised products and want the children to do likewise and that the selling figures want the children to eat things that are good for them.

32 Atkin, 300.

33 Quoted in Foote and Mnookin, 92.

34 June Esserman of Child Research Services, Inc. quoted in *Comments of M & M/Mars, Children's Television Advertising Trade Regulation Rule-Making Proceeding*, Federal Trade Commission (November 1978), 4.

35 *Comments of M & M/Mars*, 5. See also Macklin, n. 8, *supra*.

36 See n. 8, *supra*.

37 For a similar view of the relevance of children's ability to distinguish commercial characters from program characters, see Scott Ward, "Compromise in Commercials for Children," *Harvard Business Review*, November-December 1978, 133.

38 Recent research indicates that as children become more aware of advertising's persuasive intent, the frequency of their requests does not decline. This finding is contrary to earlier research purportedly showing that awareness of persuasive intent leads to a decline in the number of requests; Rossiter, 163-65.

39 Atkin, 295-301.

40 Foote and Mnookin, 95.

41 *Comments of M & M/Mars*, 64. Cf. n. 27, *supra*.

42 Atkin, 298-301. See also Scott Ward and Daniel B. Wackman, "Children's Purchase Influence Attempts and Parental Yielding," *Journal of Marketing Research*, August 1972, 318.

43 For example, one study found that heavy viewers of Saturday morning television got into more arguments with their parents over toy and cereal denials than did light viewers; Atkin 298-301. See also Ward and Wackman, 318.

44 The majority of advertising directed to children is targeted to children two-to-eleven or six-to-eleven years of age; "FTC Final Staff Report and Recommendation," 46.

45 For the view that children's special capacities and limitations should be respected but that children should not be "contained" in a special children's world isolated from that of adults, see Valerie Polakow Suransky, *The Erosion of Childhood* (Chicago: University of Chicago Press, 1982).

46 It was estimated that the coalition established to fight the FTC proceedings in 1978 put together a "war chest" of $15-30 million. According to news reports the coalition included several huge law firms, the national advertising association, broadcasters and their associations, the US Chamber of Commerce, the Grocery Manufacturers of America, the sugar association, the chocolate and candy manufacturers, cereal companies and their associations, and more; Choate, 334. It is interesting to note that supporters of children's advertising tend not to be people who spend a great deal of time with children.

47 "In the area of children's products, the US is an advertiser's paradise compared with many countries," Christopher Campbell, International Marketing Director at the Parker Brothers subsidiary of General Mills, quoted in Ronald Alsop, "Countries' Different Ad Rules Are Problem for Global Firms," *Wall Street Journal*, September 27, 1984, 33. According to Alsop, "The other countries' aim is to protect kids from exploitation."

48 It is interesting to note that in 1949 42% of the children's programs broadcast were presented without advertiser sponsorship; Melody, 36.

◆ ◆ ◆ ◆ ◆

GEORGE G. BRENKERT

Marketing To Inner-City Blacks: PowerMaster And Moral Responsibility

I. Introduction

The nature and extent of marketers' moral obligations is a matter of considerable debate. This is particularly the case when those who are targeted by marketers live in disadvantaged circumstances and suffer various problems disproportionately with other members of the same society. An interesting opportunity to explore this difficult area of marketing ethics is presented by Heileman Brewing Company's failed effort to market PowerMaster, a malt liquor, to inner-city blacks. The story of PowerMaster is relatively simple and short. Its ethical dimensions are much more complicated.[1]

In the following, I wish to consider the moral aspects of this case within the context of a market society such as the US which permits the forms of advertising it presently does.[2] To do so, I first briefly evaluate three kinds of objections made to the marketing of PowerMaster. I contend that none of these objections taken by itself clearly justifies the criticism leveled at Heileman. Heileman might reasonably claim that it was fulfilling its economic, social and moral responsibilities in the same manner as were other brewers and marketers.

Accordingly, I argue that only if we look to the collective effects of all marketers of malt liquor to the inner-city can we identify morally defensible grounds for the complaints against marketing campaigns such as that of PowerMaster. The upshot of this argument is that marketers must recognize not only their individual moral responsibilities to those they target, but also a collective responsibility of all marketers for those market segments they jointly target. It is on this basis that Heileman's marketing of PowerMaster may be faulted. This result is note-worthy in that it introduces a new kind of moral consideration which has rarely been considered in discussions of corporate moral responsibilities.

II. Heileman and PowerMaster

G. Heileman Brewing Co. is a Wisconsin brewer which produces a number of beers and malt liquors, including Colt Dry, Colt 45, and Mickey's. In the early 1990s, competition amongst such brewers was increasingly intense. In January 1991, Heileman was facing such economic difficulties that it filed for protection from creditors under Chapter 11 of the US Bankruptcy Code (Horovitz, 1991b: D1). To improve its financial situation, Heileman sought to market, beginning in June 1991, a new malt liquor called "PowerMaster." At that time there was considerable growth in the "up-strength malt liquor category." In fact, "this higher-alcohol segment of the business [had] been growing at an explosive 25% to 30% a year" (Freedman, 1991a: B1). To attempt to capitalize on this market segment, Heileman produced PowerMaster, a malt liquor that contained 5.9% alcohol, 31% more alcohol than Heileman's top-selling Colt 45 (4.5% alcohol). Reportedly, when introduced, only one other malt liquor (St. Ides) offered such a powerful malt as PowerMaster (Freedman, 1991a: B1).

Further, since malt liquor had become "the drink of choice among many in the inner city," Heileman focused a significant amount of its marketing efforts on inner-city blacks.[3] Heileman's ad campaign played to this group with posters and billboards using black male models. Advertisements assured consumers that PowerMaster was "Bold Not Harsh." Hugh Nelson, Heileman's marketing director, was reported to have claimed that "the company's research ... shows that consumers will opt for PowerMaster not on the basis of its alcohol content but because of its flavor. The higher alcohol content gives PowerMaster a 'bold not nasty' taste ..." (Freedman, 1991a: B4).

In response, a wide variety of individuals and groups protested against Heileman's actions. Critics claimed that both advertisements and the name "PowerMaster" suggested the alcoholic strength of the drink and the "buzz" that those who consumed it could get. Surgeon General Antonia Novello criticized the PowerMaster marketing scheme as "insensitive" (Milloy, 1991: B3). Reports in The Wall Street Journal spoke of community activists and alcohol critics branding Heileman's marketing campaign as "socially irresponsible" (Freedman, 1991b: B1). "Twenty-one consumer and health groups, including the Center for Science in the Public Interest, also publicly called for Heileman to halt the marketing of PowerMaster and for BATF to limit the alcohol content of malt liquor" (Colford and Teinowitz, 1991: 29). A reporter for the LA Times wrote that "at issue is growing resentment by blacks and other minorities who feel that they are being unfairly targeted—if not exploited—by marketers of beer, liquor and tobacco products" (Horovitz, 1991: D6). Another reporter for the same paper claimed that "[a]nti-alcohol activists contend that alcoholic beverage manufacturers are taking advantage of minority groups and exacerbating inner-city problems by targeting them with high-powered blends" (Lacey, 1992: A32). And Reverend Calvin Butts of the Abyssinian Baptist Church in New York's Harlem said that "this [Heileman] is obviously a company that has no sense of moral or social responsibility" (Freedman, 1991a: B1).

Though the Bureau of Alcohol, Tobacco and Firearms (BATF) initially approved the use of "PowerMaster" as the name for the new malt liquor, in light of the above protests it "reacted by enforcing a beer law that prohibits labels 'considered to be statements of alcoholic content'" (Milloy, 1991: B3). It insisted that the word "Power" be removed from the "PowerMaster" name (Freedman, 1991b: B1). As a consequence of the actions of the BATF and the preceding complaints, Heileman decided not to market PowerMaster.

III. The Objections

The PowerMaster marketing campaign evoked three distinct kinds of moral objections:[4]

First, because its advertisements drew upon images and themes related to power and boldness, they were criticized as promoting satisfactions only artificially and distortedly associated with the real needs of those targeted. As such, the PowerMaster marketing campaign was charged with fostering a form of moral illusion.[5]

Second, Heileman was said to lack concern for the harm likely to be caused by its product. Blacks suffer disproportionately from cirrhosis of the liver and other liver diseases brought on by alcohol. In addition, alcohol-related social problems such as violence and crime are also prominent in the inner-city. Accordingly, Heileman was attacked for its lack of moral sensitivity.

Third, Heileman was accused of taking unfair advantage of those in the inner-city whom they had targeted. Inner-city blacks were said to be especially vulnerable, due to their life circumstances, to advertisements and promotions formulated in terms of power, self-assertion and sexual success. Hence, to target them in the manner they did with a product such as PowerMaster was a form of exploitation. In short, questions of justice were raised.

It is important not only for corporations such as Heileman but also for others concerned with such marketing practices to determine whether these objections show that the PowerMaster marketing program was morally unjustified. The economic losses in failed marketing efforts such as PowerMaster are considerable. In addition, if the above objections are justified, the moral losses are also significant.

The first objection maintained that by emphasizing power Heileman was, in effect, offering a cruel substitute for a real lack in the lives of inner-city blacks. PowerMaster's slogan, "Bold not Harsh," was said to project an image of potency. "The brewers' shrewd marketing," one critic maintained, "has

turned malt liquor into an element of machismo" (Lacey, 1992: A1). George Hacker, Director of the National Coalition to Prevent Impaired Driving, commented that "the real irony of marketing Power-Master to inner-city blacks is that this population is among the most lacking in power in this society" (Freedman, 1991a: B1).

This kind of criticism has been made against many forms of advertising. The linking of one's product with power, fame, and success not to mention sex is nothing new in advertising.[6] Most all those targeted by marketers lack (or at least want) those goods or values associated with the products being promoted. Further, other malt liquor marketing campaigns had referred to power. For example, another malt liquor, Olde English "800," claimed that "It's the Power." The Schlitz Red Bull was associated with the phrase "The Real Power" (Colford and Tenowitz, 1991: 1). Nevertheless, they were not singled out for attack or boycott as PowerMaster was.

Accordingly, however objectionable it may be for marketers to link a product with something which its potential customers (significantly) lack and which the product can only symbolically or indirectly satisfy, this feature of the PowerMaster marketing campaign does not uniquely explain or justify the complaints that were raised against the marketing of PowerMaster. In short, this objection appears far too general in scope to justify the particular attention given PowerMaster. Heileman could not have reasonably concluded, on its basis, that it was being particularly morally irresponsible. It was simply doing what others had done and for which they had not been boycotted or against which such an outcry had not been raised. It is difficult to see how Heileman could have concluded that it was preparing a marketing program that would generate the social and moral protest it did, simply from an examination of its own plan or the similar individual marketing programs of other brewers.

The second objection was that the marketers of PowerMaster showed an especial lack of sensitivity in that a malt liquor with the potency of PowerMaster would likely cause additional harm to inner-city blacks. According to various reports, "alcoholism and other alcohol-related diseases extract a disproportionate toll on blacks. A 1978 study by the National Institute on Alcohol Abuse and Alcoholism found that black men between the ages of 25 and 44 are 10 times more likely than the general population to have cirrhosis of the liver" (*NY Times*, 1991). Fortune reported that "The Department of Health and Human Services last spring released figures showing a decline in life expectancy for blacks for the fourth straight year—down to 69.2 years, vs. 75.6 years for whites. Although much of the drop is attributable to homicide and AIDS, blacks also suffer higher instances of ... alcohol-related illnesses than whites" (*Fortune*, 1991: 100). Further, due to the combined use of alcohol and cigarettes, blacks suffer cancer of the esophagus at a disproportional rate than the rest of the population.[7] Similarly, assuming that black women would drink PowerMaster, it is relevant that the impact of alcohol use in the inner-city is also manifested in an increased infant mortality rate and by newborn children with fetal alcohol syndrome (*The Workbook*, 1991: 18). Finally, a malt liquor with a high percentage of alcohol was expected to have additional harmful effects on the levels of social ills, such as violence, crime, and spousal abuse. As such, PowerMaster would be further destructive of the social fabric of the inner-city.[8]

Under these circumstances, the second objection maintained, anyone who marketed a product which would further increase these harms was being morally obtuse to the problems inner-city blacks suffer. Accordingly, Heileman's PowerMaster marketing campaign was an instance of such moral insensitivity.

Nevertheless, this objection does not seem clearly applicable when pointed simply at PowerMaster. Surely inner-city blacks are adults and should be allowed, as such, to make their own choices, even if those choices harm themselves, so long as they are not deceived or coerced when making those choices and they do not harm others. Since neither deception nor coercion were involved in PowerMaster's marketing campaign, it is an unacceptable form of moral paternalism to deny them what they might otherwise wish to choose.

Further, those who raised the above complaints were not those who would have drunk PowerMaster, but leaders of various associations both within and outside the inner-city concerned with alcohol abuse and consumption.[9] This was not a consumer-led protest. Reports of the outcry over PowerMaster contain no objections from those whom Heileman had targeted. No evidence was presented that these individuals would have found PowerMaster unsatisfactory. Argument is needed, for example, that these individuals had (or should have had) overriding interests in healthy livers. Obviously there are many people (black as well as white) who claim that their interests are better fulfilled by drinking rather than abstinence.

Finally, argument is also needed to show that this increase in alcoholic content would have any significant effects on the targeted group. It might be that any noteworthy effects would be limited because the increased alcoholic content would prove undesirable to those targeted since they would become intoxicated too quickly. "Overly rapid intoxication undercuts sales volume and annoys consumers," The Wall Street Journal reported (Freedman, 1991a: B1). Supposedly this consequence led one malt brewer to lower the alcoholic content of its product (Freedman, 1991a: B1). Furthermore, malt liquor is hardly the strongest alcohol which blacks (or others) drink. Reportedly, "blacks buy more than half the cognac sold in the United States" (The Workbook, 1991: 18). Cheap forms of wine and hard liquor are readily available. Thus, it is far from obvious what significant effects PowerMaster alone would have in the inner-city.

One possible response to the preceding replies brings us to the third objection. This response is that, though inner-city blacks might not be deceived or coerced into drinking PowerMaster, they were particularly vulnerable to the marketing campaign which Heileman proposed. Because of this, Heileman's marketing campaign (wittingly or unwittingly) would take unfair advantage of inner-city blacks.

Little, if any attempt, has been made to defend or to explore this charge. I suggest that there are at least three ways in which inner-city blacks—or anyone else, for that matter—might be said to be specially vulnerable.

A person would be cognitively vulnerable if he or she lacked certain levels of ability to cognitively process information or to be aware that certain information was being withheld or manipulated in deceptive ways. Thus, if people were not able to process information about the effects of malt liquor on themselves or on their society in ways in which others could, they would be cognitively vulnerable.

A person would be motivationally vulnerable if he or she could not resist ordinary temptations and/or enticements due to his or her own individual characteristics. Thus, if people were unable, as normal individuals are, to resist various advertisements and marketing ploys, they would be motivationally vulnerable.

And people would be socially vulnerable when their social situation renders them significantly less able than others to resist various enticements. For example, due to the poverty within which they live, they might have developed various needs or attitudes which rendered them less able to resist various marketing programs.

Nevertheless, none of these forms of vulnerability was explored or defended as the basis of the unfair advantage which the PowerMaster marketers were said to seek.[10] And indeed it is difficult to see what account could be given which would explain how the use of the name "PowerMaster," and billboards with a black model, a bottle of PowerMaster and the slogan "Bold Not Harsh" would be enough to subvert the decision making or motivational capacities of inner-city blacks. To the extent that they are adults and not under the care or protection of other individuals or agencies due to the state of their cognitive or motivational abilities, there is a prima facie case that they are not so vulnerable. Accordingly, the vulnerability objection raises the legitimate concern that some form of unjustified moral paternalism lurks behind it.

In short, if we consider simply the individual marketing program of PowerMaster, it is difficult to see that the three preceding objections justified the outcry against Heileman. Heileman was seeking to satisfy its customers. As noted above, none of the reported complaints came from them. Heileman was also seeking to enhance its own bottom line. But in doing so it was not engaged in fraud, deception or coercion. The marketing of PowerMaster was not like other morally objectionable individual marketing programs which have used factually deceptive advertisements (e.g., some past shaving commercials), taken advantage of the target group's special vulnerabilities (e.g., certain television advertisements to children who are cognitively vulnerable), or led to unusual harm for the group targeted (e.g., Nestlé's infant formula promotions to Third World Mothers). Black inner-city residents are not obviously cognitively vulnerable and are not, in the use of malt liquor, uniformly faced with a single significant problem such as Third World Mothers are (viz., the care of their infants). As such, it is mistaken to think that PowerMaster's marketing campaign was morally offensive or objectionable in ways in which other such campaigns have been. From this perspective, then, it appears that Heileman could be said to be fulfilling its individual corporate responsibilities.

IV. Associated Groups and Collective Responsibility

So long as we remain simply at the level of the individual marketing campaign of PowerMaster, it is doubtful that we can grasp the basis upon which the complaints against PowerMaster might be justified. To do so, we must look to the social level and the collection of marketing programs of which PowerMaster was simply one part. By pushing on the bounds within which other marketers had remained,[11] Power-Master was merely the spark which ignited a great deal of resentment which stemmed more generally from the group of malt liquor marketers coming into the inner-city from outside, aggressively marketing products which disproportionately harmed those in the inner-city (both those who consume the product and others), and creating marketing campaigns that took advantage of their vulnerabilities.[12]

As such, this case might better be understood as one involving the collective responsibility of the group of marketers who target inner-city blacks rather than simply the individual responsibility of this or that marketer. By "collective responsibility" I refer to the responsibility which attaches to a group (or collective), rather than to the individual members of the group, even though it is only through the joint action (or inaction) of group members that a particular collective action or consequence results. The objections of the critics could then more plausibly be recast in the form that the collection of the marketers' campaigns was consuming or wasting public health or welfare understood in a two-fold sense: first, as the lack of illness, violence, and crime, and second, as the presence of a sense of individual self that is based on the genuine gratification of real needs. When the individual marketers of a group (e.g., of brewers) engage in their own individual marketing campaigns they may not necessarily cause significant harms—or if they do create harm, the customers may have willingly accepted certain levels of individual risk of harm. However, their efforts may collectively result in significant harms not consciously assumed by anyone.

Similarly, though the individual marketing efforts may not be significant enough to expose the vulnerabilities of individuals composing their market segment, their marketing efforts may collectively create a climate within which the vulnerabilities of those targeted may play a role in the collective effect

of those marketing campaigns. Thus, it is not the presence of this or that billboard from PowerMaster which may be objectionable so much as the large total number of billboards in the inner-city which advertise alcohol and to which PowerMaster contributed. For example, it has been reported that "in Baltimore, 76 per cent of the billboards located in low-income neighborhoods advertise alcohol and cigarettes; in middle and upper-income neighborhoods it is 20 per cent" (*The Workbook*, 1991: 18). This "saturation advertising" may have an effect different from the effect of any single advertisement. Similarly, it is not PowerMaster's presence on the market as such, which raises moral questions. Rather, it is that alcohol marketers particularly target a group which not only buys "... more than half the cognac sold in the United States and ... consume[s] more than one-third of all malt liquor ..." (*The Workbook*, 1991: 18), but also disproportionately suffers health problems associated with alcohol. The connection between the amount of alcohol consumed and the alcohol related health problems is hardly coincidental. Further, if the level of alcohol consumption is significantly related to conditions of poverty and racism, and the consequent vulnerabilities people living in these conditions may suffer, then targeting such individuals may also be an instance of attempting to take unfair advantage of them.[13]

Now to make this case, it must be allowed that individual persons are not the only ones capable of being responsible for the effects of their actions. A variety of arguments have been given, for example, that corporations can be morally responsible for their actions. These arguments need not be recited here since even if they were successful, as I think some of them are, the marketers who target inner-city blacks do not themselves constitute a corporation. Hence, a different kind of argument is needed.

Can there be subjects of responsibility other than individuals and corporations? Virginia Held has argued that under certain conditions random collections of individuals can be held morally responsible.

She has argued that when it would be obvious to the reasonable person what a random collection of individuals ought to do and when the expected outcome of such an action is clearly favorable, then that random collection can be held morally responsible (Held, 1970: 476).

However, again the marketers of malt liquor to inner city blacks do not seem to fit this argument since they are not simply a random collection of individuals. According to Held, a random collection of individuals "... is a set of persons distinguishable by some characteristics from the set of all persons, but lacking a decision method for taking action that is distinguishable from such decision methods, if there are any, as are possessed by all persons" (Held, 1970: 471). The examples she gives, "passengers on a train" and "pedestrians on a sidewalk," fit this definition but are also compatible with a stronger definition of a group of individuals than the one she offers. For example, her definition would include collections of individuals with no temporal, spatial or teleological connection. Clearly marketers of malt liquor to inner-city blacks constitute a group or collection of individuals in a stronger sense than Held's random collection of individuals.

Consequently, I shall speak of a group such as the marketers who target inner-city blacks as an associated group. Such groups are not corporations. Nor are they simply random collections of individuals (in Held's sense). They are groups in a weaker sense than corporations, but a stronger sense than a random collection of individuals. I shall argue that such groups may also be the subject of moral responsibility. This view is based upon the following characteristics of such groups.

First, an associated group is constituted by agents, whether they be corporate or personal, who share certain characteristics related to a common set of activities in which they engage. Thus, the marketers who target inner-city blacks share the characteristic that they (and no one else) target this particular market segment with malt liquor. They engage in competition with each other to sell their malt liquor according to the rules of the (relatively) free market. Though they themselves do not occupy some single spatial location, the focus of their activities, the ends they seek, and their temporal relatedness (i.e., marketing to the inner-city in the same time period) are clearly sufficient to constitute them as a group.

Second, though such associated groups do not have a formal decision-making structure which unites them, Stanley Bates has reminded us that "there are other group decision methods, [that] ... are not formal ..." (Bates, 1971: 345).[14] For example, the brewers presently at issue might engage in various forms of implicit bargaining. These informal and implicit group decision methods may involve unstructured discussions of topics of mutual interest, individual group member monitoring of the expectations and intuitions of other group members, and recognition of mutual understandings that may serve to coordinate the expectations of group members (cf. Schelling, 1963). Further, brewers in the United States have created The Beer Institute, which is their Washington-based trade group, one of whose main purposes is to protect "the market environment allowing for brewers to sell beer profitably, free from what the group views as unfair burdens imposed by government bodies."[15] The Beer Institute provides its members with a forum within which they may meet annually, engage in workshops, discuss issues of mutual concern, agree on which issues will be lobbied before Congress on their behalf and may voluntarily adopt an advertising code to guide their activities.[16] Such informal decision-making methods amongst these brewers and suppliers are means whereby group decisions can be made.

Third, members of associated groups can be said to have other morally relevant characteristics which foster a group "solidarity" and thereby also unify them as a group capable of moral responsibility (cf. Feinberg, 1974: 234). These characteristics take three different forms. a) Members of the group share a community of interests. For example, they all wish to sell their products to inner-city blacks.[17] They all seek to operate with minimal restrictions from the government on their marketing activities within the inner-city. They all are attempting to develop popular malt liquors. They all strive to keep the costs of their operations as low as possible. b) Further, they are joined by bonds of sentiment linked with their valuing of independent action and successfully selling their products. Though they may try to out-compete each other, they may also respect their competitors when they perform well in the marketplace. c) Finally, they can be said to share a common lot in that actions by one brewer that bring public condemnation upon that brewer may also extend public attention and condemnation to the other brewers as well as happened in the Power-Master case. Similarly, regulations imposed on one typically also affect the others. Thus, heavy regulation tends to reduce all their profits, whereas light regulation tends to have the opposite effect.

The unity or solidarity constituted by the preceding characteristics among the various marketers would be openly manifested, for example, if the government were to try to deny them all access to the inner-city market segment. In such a circumstance, they would openly resist, take the government to court, and protest with united voice against the injustice done to them, both individually and as a group. In this sense, there is (at the least) a latent sense of solidarity among such marketers (cf. May, 1987: 37). When they act, then each acts in solidarity with the others and each does those things which accord with the kinds of actions fellow group members are inclined to take. All this may occur without the need for votes being taken or explicit directions given among the various brewers (cf. May, 1987: 40).

Fourth, associated groups like inner-city marketers can investigate the harms or benefits that their products and marketing programs jointly do to those who are targeted. They can also study the overall effects of their own individual efforts. They could do so both as individual businesses and as a group. In

the latter case, The Beer Institute might undertake such studies. Similarly, these marketers might jointly commission some other organization to study these effects. In short, they are capable both as individual businesses and as a group, of receiving notice as to the effects of their individual and collective actions. In short, communication amongst the group members is possible.

Finally, associated groups can modify their activities. They are not simply inevitably or necessarily trapped into acting certain ways. For example, the inner-city malt liquor marketers might voluntarily reduce the number of billboards they use within the inner-city. They might not advertise in certain settings or in certain forms of media. They might not use certain appeals, e.g., touting the high alcoholic content of their products. As such, they could take actions to prevent the harms or injustices of which they are accused. At present brewers subscribe to an advertising code of ethics which The Beer Institute makes available and has recently updated. The Beer Institute might even lobby the government on behalf of this group for certain limitations on marketing programs so as to eliminate moral objections raised against such marketing programs.

The preceding indicates that this group can act: it has set up The Beer Institute; it may react with unanimity against new regulations; it may defend the actions of its members; it may investigate the effects its group members have on those market segments which they have targeted. It does not act as a group in marketing particular malt liquors. The law prevents such collective actions. However, marketing malt liquor to particular groups is an action which this group may approve or disapprove.[18] The group lobbies Congress on behalf of its members' interests. The group has organized itself such that through development and support of The Beer Institute its interests are protected. There is no reason, then, that such a group may not also be morally responsible for the overall consequences of its members' marketing.

Does the preceding argument suggest that the group of marketers would run afoul of concerns about restraint of trade? The above argument need not imply that inner-city marketers are always a group capable of moral action and responsibility—only that under certain circumstances it could be. Hence, the above argument does not suggest that this group constitutes anything like a cartel. In addition, the above argument does not suggest that marketers agree on pricing formulas, on reserving certain distributional areas for this or that marketer, or similar actions which would constitute classic forms of restraint of trade. Further, the preceding argument leaves open what mechanisms might be legally used whereby these moral responsibilities are discharged. It might be that individual marketers voluntarily agree to such actions as they presently do with their advertising code. On the other hand, they might collectively appeal to the government to approve certain general conditions such that the playing field within which they compete would be altered to alleviate moral objections to their marketing campaigns, but would remain relatively level in comparison with their situations prior to the imposition of such conditions.

If the preceding is correct, then given the assumption that basic items of public welfare (e.g., health, safety, decision-making abilities, etc.) ought not to be harmed, two important conclusions follow regarding the marketing of malt liquor to inner-city blacks.

First, malt liquor marketers have a collective responsibility to monitor the effects of their activities and to ensure that they jointly do not unnecessarily cause harm to those they target or trade on their vulnerabilities. Assuming that malt liquor does harm inner-city blacks and that the marketing programs through which malt liquor is sold to this market segment play some significant causal role in creating this harm, then they have an obligation to alter their marketing to inner-city blacks in such a way that the vulnerabilities of inner-city blacks are not exploited and that unnecessary harm does not come to them.

Second, where the collective consequences of individual marketing efforts create the harms claimed for alcohol among inner-city blacks, and marketers as a group do not discharge the preceding collective responsibility, then there is a need for some agency outside those individual marketers to oversee or regulate their actions. Obviously, one form this may take is that of an industry or professional oversight committee; another form might be that of government intervention.

Two objections might be noted. It might be objected that the preceding line of argument faces the difficulty of determining the extent of harm which each marketer of malt liquor causes to the market segment targeted. Since this will be hard to determine, marketers of malt liquor may seek to escape the responsibility attributed to them. This difficulty, however, is no different in kind from other instances in which the actions of individual persons or businesses jointly produce a common problem. If the heavy trucks of several businesses regularly ply the city's streets contributing to the creation of potholes and broken asphalt, it will be difficult to determine the causal responsibility of each business. In all such instances there are difficult empirical and conceptual issues involved in establishing that harm has occurred, the levels at which it has occurred and the attendant moral responsibility. However, this is not to deny that such determinations can be made. I assume that similar determinations can be made in the present case.

Further, though it may be difficult to determine the harm which the marketing of a particular product may cause, it is less difficult—though by no means unproblematic—to determine the harm caused by the collection of marketing programs aimed at a particular market segment. Thus, though particular marketers may seek to escape individual responsibility for their actions, it will be much harder for them to escape their collective responsibilities. Still, we may anticipate that, in some cases, the results will be that an individual marketer has met his or her individual *and* collective responsibilities.

It might also be objected that this group cannot be responsible since it lacks control of its members. However, various forms of moral control are available to this group. They may try to persuade each other to change their course of action. And indeed, this occurred in the PowerMaster case: "Patrick Stokes, president of Anheuser-Busch Cos.' Anheuser-Busch Inc. unit and chairman of The Beer Institute, asked ... Heileman's president, to reconsider the strategy for PowerMaster, which 'appears to be intentionally marketed to emphasize high alcohol content'" (Freedman, 1991b: B1). They might seek to expel a member from The Beer Institute and the benefits which such membership carries.[19] Conceivably, they could turn to the public media to expose unethical practices on the part of that member. They might even, as with other groups within a nation state, seek outside help from the government. More positively, they could praise and hold up as models of marketing responsibility the marketing programs of certain group members. Thus, this group can be said to be able to exercise moral influence and control over its members which is not dissimilar to that which is exercised by other similar groups and more generally within society as a whole.

V. Collective Responsibility and Shared Responsibility

The nature of the collective responsibility discussed in the preceding section deserves further elaboration. Why, for example, should we not consider the responsibility attributed above to all marketers who target inner-city blacks as a form of shared (rather than collective) responsibility? By shared responsibility I understand that the responsibility for a certain event (or series of events) is shared or divided among a number of agents (personal or corporate). Shared or divided responsibility does not require that we are able to identify any group which could be said to be itself responsible for that (or those) event(s). As

such, under shared responsibility each of those identified is, at least partially, responsible for the event(s). Shared responsibility, then, is a distributional concept. Each agent involved is assumed to have played some causal role in the occurrence of the event(s) in question. This does not mean that each agent had to have done exactly what the others did. One person might have knowingly and secretly loaded a truck with toxic chemicals, another might have driven the truck to an unauthorized and dangerous dump site, and a third pulled the lever to dump the chemicals. Each one did something different, yet they all played contributory causal roles in the immoral (and illegal) dumping of toxic chemicals. They share responsibility for this event and their responsibility exhausts the responsibility which may be attributed under these circumstances. Such shared responsibility differs from individual responsibility in that when a number of moral agents participate together in the production of some event (or series of events) it may not be possible to determine what the contribution of each agent was and hence to establish the nature or extent of their individual responsibility (cf. May, 1992: 39). Thus, if several corporations each make one of their marketing experts available to solve a problem confronting a regional council on tourism, it may not be possible to determine the exact contribution of each expert or each corporation to the resolution of this problem. Still, to the extent that each corporation (and each marketing expert) contributed and was a necessary part of the solution, they all share responsibility for the solution.[20]

With collective responsibility, on the other hand, we must be able to identify some collective or group which itself has responsibility for the event (or series of events). Collective responsibility may or may not be distributional. Thus, some members of a group might be individually responsible as well as collectively responsible for what happens. In other instances, they may not be individually responsible, but only the group of which they are members be collectively responsible. For example, the members of some group might agree, by a divided vote, to undertake some project. Later, those who voted for the project may have died or left the group, while the negative voters (and others who have replaced the former members) remain. Still, that group remains responsible for (the completion of) the project, even though its individual members do not themselves have individual responsibilities for that project.[21]

Now with regard to the group of marketers who target inner-city blacks, we have seen that we can refer to this as a group, which, though it does not have a formal decision-making structure, may still act. Its members have common interests; they communicate with each other regarding those interests; they share a solidarity which unites them in approving various things their fellow members do and defending those members when criticized. Further, within this group we may distinguish four situations concerning the marketing program of individual brewers: (1) It itself harms inner-city blacks; (2) It contributes to the harm of inner-city blacks; (3) It is indeterminate in its harm, or contributory harm, to inner-city blacks; and (4) It does not itself harm, or contribute to the harm of, inner-city blacks. In the first case, the marketer is individually responsible for such harm as is caused. In the second case, the marketer has a shared responsibility with other marketers of this group. However, in the last two cases, though we may not speak of the individual or shared responsibility of the marketer, we may still speak of the collective responsibility of the group of marketers of which the last two are a part. We may also bring those in the first two cases under the same collective responsibility. The reason (in each of these cases) is that the group or collective of which they are members—whether they are individually responsible, share responsibility, or are responsible in neither of these cases—can collectively act, and could reduce such harms or evils by taking a stance against marketing practices which produce or foster them. For example, if Heileman dramatically revised its marketing campaign to inner-city blacks, but

Pabst and Anheuser-Busch did not, then there might be little change in the results for inner-city blacks. Hence, it is only if the members of this group act in concert, as a group, that the objections raised against the marketing of malt liquors such as PowerMaster be responded to. This collective responsibility of the group of marketers will mean that individual marketers incur other individual responsibilities to act in certain ways as members of that group, e.g., to bring the harm created to the attention of other group members, to work within the group to develop ways to reduce or eliminate marketing practices which foster such harm, and to act in concert with other group members to reduce harm to targeted groups. Accordingly, it seems reasonable to attribute a collective responsibility to the group of these marketers, and not simply a shared responsibility.

It is also correct to say that the moral responsibility of the group of inner-city marketers does not replace or negate the individual responsibility of the members of this group. Still, the collective responsibility of this group does not simply reduce to the individual responsibility of its members in that, as argued above, an individual member of this group might fulfill his/her individual moral responsibilities and still the group might not fulfill its collective responsibilities. Accordingly, marketers of alcohol to inner-city blacks may have individual, shared and collective responsibilities to which they must attend.

VI. Implications and Conclusion

The implications of this social approach to the PowerMaster case are significant:

First, marketers cannot simply look at their own individual marketing campaigns to judge their moral level. Instead, they must also look at their campaign within the context of all the marketing campaigns which target the market segment at which they are aiming. This accords with Garrett Hardin's suggestion that "the morality of an act is a function of the state of the system at the time it is performed" (Hardin, 1968: 1245; emphasis omitted). It is possible that marketers could fulfill their individual responsibilities but not their collective responsibilities.

Second, when the products targeted at particular market segments cause consumers to suffer disproportionately in comparison with other comparable market segments, marketers must determine the role which their products and marketing programs play in this situation. If they play a contributory role, they should (both individually and as a group) consider measures to reduce the harm produced. One means of doing this is to voluntarily restrict or modify their appeals to that market segment. In the present case, industry organizations such as The Beer Institute might play a leading role in identifying problems and recommending counter measures. Otherwise when harm occurs disproportionately to a market segment, or members of that segment are especially vulnerable, outside oversight and regulation may be appropriate.

Third, marketers have a joint or collective responsibility to the entire market segment they target, not simply for the effects of their own products and marketing campaigns, but more generally for the effects of the combined marketing which is being done to that segment. The protests against PowerMaster are best understood against the background of this collective responsibility.

Thus, when we think of responsibility in the market we must look beyond simply the responsibility of individual agents (be they personal or corporate). We must look to the responsibility of groups of persons as well as groups of corporations. Such responsibility is not personal or individual, but collective. Examination of the case of PowerMaster helps us to see this.

Accordingly, the preceding analysis helps to explain both why PowerMaster was attacked as it was and also why it seemed simply to be doing what other marketers had previously done. Further, it helps us to understand the circumstances under which the above objections against marketing malt liquor to inner-city blacks might be justified. However, much more analysis of this form of collective harm and the vulnerability which is said to characterize inner-city blacks needs to be undertaken.

Finally, it should be emphasized that this paper advocates recognition of a new subject of moral responsibility in the market. Heretofore, moral responsibility has been attributed to individuals and corporations. Random collections of individuals have little applicability in business ethics. However the concept of associated groups and their collective responsibility has not been previously explored. It adds a new dimension to talk about responsibility within current discussions in business ethics.[22]

NOTES

1 Though the case of PowerMaster is admittedly several years old, its importance for this paper lies in gaining a better understanding of the moral responsibilities of marketers, rather than in the case itself.

2 As such, I do not attempt to raise far broader moral questions concerning the moral legitimacy of advertising itself. Instead, I wish to examine the marketing of PowerMaster as much as possible within the current, albeit vague, moral limits of advertising.

3 Marc Lacey, "Marketing of Malt Liquor Fuels Debate," *LA Times*, December 15, 1992, A31. Lacey also noted that "Blacks, who make up 12% of the US population, represent 10% of beer drinkers but 28% of malt liquor consumers, according to a study by Shanken Communications Inc. of New York City" (ibid.). It should be noted that Heileman was only one of a number of malt liquor manufacturers who directed marketing campaigns at this market segment.

4 This paper does not consider this legal aspect of the case. However, critics said that the reference to power in "PowerMaster" referred to the alcoholic strength of the drink. Such references were prohibited by a law passed in 1935. It was

on this basis that BATF required that Heileman drop the word "power" from the name "PowerMaster."

5 The phrase "moral illusion" is not intended to suggest that those targeted by PowerMaster would have affirmed, had they been asked, that they gained the power they lacked by purchasing this malt liquor. On the other hand, critics did contend that an illegitimate form of value displacement or substitution was encouraged by advertisements such as those of PowerMaster.

6 It might be noted that the name "Powermaster" has been used for other products. Kleer-Flo uses it for water-based cleaning stations and Runnerless Molding Technology uses it for a filtering system designed to reroute electrical and nonelectrical disturbances. Needless to say, neither of these companies has been the object of protests against the use of the name "Powermaster."

7 The Reverend Jesse W. Brown claims that "African-Americans are twice as likely to die from cirrhosis of the liver than whites, and the rate of cancer of the esophagus is ten times higher for African-American males than for white males" (Brown, 1992: 17). These figures differ from others reported in this paper. I can only assume that they are due to differing "populations" being surveyed and different times during which the surveys were conducted.

8 An additional aspect of the objections against PowerMaster which only came out indirectly was the implication that the firms doing the marketing were based outside the inner-cities and were (presumably) predominately white. Thus, the impression given was that of outside whites marketing a product which might further harm poor blacks within the inner-city.

9 "'This is an activist reaction' to the product," said Heileman President Thomas Rattigan.

   'I'm not sure anyone has a feel of the public reaction'" (Teinowitz and Colford, 1991, 35).

10 Among the questions we need to ask are: Is everyone in the inner-city vulnerable? Are they all vulnerable in the same way(s)? Are those who drink malt liquor specially vulnerable in a way relevant for the present case? Is their vulnerability the only relevant one for this case?

11 It did this by placing the word "power" within its name and not simply the various advertisements for its product. It also pushed the bounds by raising the alcohol content to the highest (or one of the highest) level(s) of malt liquors.

12 Suppose that malt liquors had harmed inner-city blacks *proportionately*—their rates of cirrhosis of the liver and other diseases were at the same levels of other people in society, whether whites, Hispanics or Asians and whether upper class, middle class or lower class. The upshot would be that one part of the present complex web of criticisms would have to be modified. It might still be, however, that the level of harm was unacceptably high in comparison with those who did not drink.

This modification, however, would not, in itself, affect the other two criticisms having to do with the artificial gratifications being offered by the advertisements and with the vulnerability of those targeted. In the end, it appears, the vulnerability criticism is the criticism basic to this dispute.

13 Stanley I. Benn also distinguishes between the effects of individual advertisements and "the cumulative influence of an environment filled with a variety of advertisements all with the same underlying message ..." Stanley I. Benn, "Freedom and Persuasion," *The Australasian Journal of Philosophy*, Vol. 45 (1967), 274. Benn maintains that the former might be resistible, whereas the latter might not be.

14 Bates refers to the work of Thomas Schelling, *The Strategy of Conflict* (New York: Oxford University Press, 1963), in making this point.

15 "The Beer Institute," *Encyclopedia of Associations*, Carolyn A. Fischer and Carol A. Schwartz (eds.), Vol. 1 (New York: Gale Research Inc., 1995), 27.

16 In 1995, The Beer Institute claimed to have 280 members (ibid.).

17 I leave vague here any more specific statement of this common interest: e.g., to make more profit, to fulfill the needs of their customers, to enlarge their market share, etc., etc. On the importance of a common interest or outlook to define a(n) (unorganized) group see May, 1987: 33.

18 When PowerMaster was under attack, the President of The Beer Institute defended Heileman's marketing of PowerMaster: "The strange inference drawn from these charges is that this product is somehow being marketed unfairly. That's not true. Everyone sells his product to the people who prefer them ... People can make up their own minds about what product they prefer" (Farhi, 1991: A4).

19 In fact, this has never happened. One reason is that The Beer Institute might be sued by the expelled member for attempting to restrain trade.

20 The example is inspired by Michael J. Zimmerman, "Sharing Responsibility," *American Philosophical Quarterly*, Vol. 22, No. 2 (April, 1985).

21 This example is influenced by one from Joel Feinberg, "Collective Responsibility," in *Doing & Deserving* (Princeton: Princeton University Press, 1974), 249.

22 I am indebted to the following individuals for their helpful comments: James Bennett, Kathy Bohstedt, John Hardwig, John McCall, Betsy Postow, Leonard J. Weber, Andy Wicks and an anonymous reviewer for *Business Ethics Quarterly*. Barry Danilowitz helped in the identification and collection of relevant materials concerning the PowerMaster case.

BIBLIOGRAPHY

Bates, Stanley (1971), "The Responsibility of 'Random Collections,'" *Ethics*, 81, 343-49.

Benn, Stanley I. (1967), "Freedom and Persuasion," *The Australasian Journal of Philosophy*, 45, 259-75.

Brown, Jesse W. (1992), "Marketing Exploitation," *Business and Society Review*, Issue 83 (Fall), 17.

Colford, Steven W. and Teinowitz, Ira (1991), "Malt Liquor 'Power' Failure," *Advertising Age*, July 1, 1, 29.

Farhi, Paul (1991), "Surgeon General Hits New Malt Liquor's Name, Ads," *Washington Post*, June 26, A1, A4.

Feinberg, Joel (1974), "Collective Responsibility," in *Doing & Deserving*. Princeton: Princeton University Press, 222-51.

Fortune (1991), "Selling Sin to Blacks," October 21, 100.

Freedman, Alix (1991a), "Potent, New Heileman Malt Is Brewing Fierce Industry and Social Criticism," *Wall Street Journal*, June 17, B1, B4.

—— (1991b), "Heileman, Under Pressure, Scuttles PowerMaster Malt," *Wall Street Journal*, July 5, B1, B3.

Hardin, Garrett (1968), "The Tragedy of the Commons," *Science*, 162, 1243-48.

Held, Virginia (1970), "Can a Random Collection of Individuals Be Morally Responsible?" *The Journal of Philosophy*, 67, 471-81.

Horovitz, Bruce (1991), "Brewer Faces Boycott Over Marketing of Potent Malt Liquor," *LA Times*, June 25, D1, D6.

Lacey, Marc (1992), "Marketing of Malt Liquor Fuels Debate," *LA Times*, December 15, A32, A34.

May, Larry (1987), *The Morality of Groups*. Notre Dame: University of Notre Dame Press.

—— (1992), *Sharing Responsibility*. Chicago: The University of Chicago Press.

Milloy, Courland (1991), "Race, Beer Don't Mix," *The Washington Post*, July 9, B3.

New York Times, The (1991), "The Threat of Power Master," July 1, A12.

Schelling, Thomas (1963), *The Strategy of Conflict.* New York: Oxford University Press.

Teinowitz, Ira and Colford, Steven W. (1991), "Targeting Woes in PowerMaster Wake," *Advertising Age*, July 8, 1991, 35.

"The Beer Institute," *Encyclopedia of Associations* (1995), Carolyn A. Fischer and Carol A. Schwartz (eds.), Vol. 1, New York: Gale Research Inc.

Workbook, The (1991), "Marketing Booze to Blacks," Spring, 16, 18-19.

Zimmerman, Michael J. (1985), "Sharing Responsibility," *American Philosophical* Quarterly, 22, 115-22.

CASE STUDY 9

NESTLÉ AND ADVERTISING: AN ETHICAL ANALYSIS

CHRIS RAGG

Case Description

Since the 1970s, the Nestlé corporation has been the subject of an international boycott resulting from their methods of advertising. Nestlé, which owns Carnation, boasts that it is the world's largest food and beverage company. The set of products that have been the source of public outcry are newer versions of a product that Nestlé has been making since its inception in 1866: Baby formula. Boycotters argue that the advertising campaigns promoting the formula in third world countries have been unethical, and have helped cause the death of millions of infants.

According to UNICEF and the World Health Organization, approximately 1.5 million infants die each year from bottle-feeding, many from what has been called "baby bottle disease." This disease is an effect of the combination of the diarrhea, dehydration and malnutrition which result from unsafe bottle feeding. A typical case of baby-bottle disease might arise as follows: A poor set of parents purchase baby formula for their infant. Since the local water supply is contaminated and unsafe, however, the baby's ingestion of the diluted formula can soon lead to diarrhea, a common indicator of gastrointestinal distress and a cause of dehydration. Furthermore, due to the cost of the baby formula, the parents will often over-dilute it or spend less on additional food supplies, which can lead to malnutrition.

When growing up in an area with contaminated water, a bottle-fed child is 25 times more likely to die from diarrhea than a breastfed child. Even in areas with cleaner water, such as the United Kingdom, a bottle-fed child is ten times more likely to suffer the same fate. In most cases, in fact, doctors highly recommend that a mother breastfeed her child. Breastfed babies need no other food or drink for about the first six months of life, and have reduced risk of diabetes, pneumonia, ear infections, and some cancers. Further studies have shown that women who breastfeed may have a lower risk of breast and ovarian cancers. This does not imply, though, that bottle-feeding is never the best option. There are some cases where baby formula can be beneficial and, with the right information, mothers can decide whether or not theirs is such a case.

This requisite information, however, was not made available to many women in these poorer nations. In the 1960s and 1970s, Nestlé had extensive advertisement campaigns for its baby formula worldwide. Pamphlets were distributed highlighting the potential benefits of baby formula while ignoring the drawbacks. Free samples were also dispersed among the public. Nestlé's profit-driven actions began to outrage the public. Although they were not illegal, many of the boycotters claimed that Nestlé's actions were immoral and socially irresponsible. While corporations can justifiably try to turn the largest profit available, the boycotters claim that an ethical corporation must avoid deliberate harm in its pursuit of success.

Ethical Analysis

Advertisements are all around us; it would be difficult to go even one day without coming into contact with at least one. In our capitalist society, a good marketing strategy can be the difference between a successful and failed business venture. In light of this, it is not all that surprising that in some countries Nestlé reportedly spends more money promoting their product than the government spends on health education. The information available to young mothers, then, can be biased. In the United States there are laws against false advertising, but these laws only protect consumers from lies and unsubstantiated claims. But these are not the only ways that companies can fool the public. Many companies choose to tell the truth, but not quite the whole truth. As was the case with Nestlé's pamphlets thirty-five years ago, an advertisement can explain all the potential benefits of the product while neglecting to mention its potential drawbacks.

In 1981 the policy-setting body of the World Health Organization adopted the International Code of Marketing of Breast-milk Substitutes. Those who agreed to the code swore that they would not provide free samples to hospitals or mothers, promote their product for use with children under six months of age, or promote their product to health workers. Nestlé has publicly agreed to abide by these

standards. Nevertheless, it is claimed by IBFAN (the International Baby Foods Action Network) that Nestlé has repeatedly violated the code. In particular, there is evidence that Nestlé has aspired to win the approval of health care and hospital workers by giving them gifts, so that they will personally recommend Nestlé products to young mothers. This is often cheaper and more effective than trying to influence mothers one-by-one. Another strategy used by Nestlé has been to provide free samples to hospitals and maternity wards. A mother will then begin using the formula at the hospital, and by the time she leaves it will have interfered with her lactation process. Once home, the formula is no longer free and the mother is left without much choice but to purchase the product.

It does seem, however, that too many restrictions on advertising may lead us down a slippery slope. Nestlé's chocolate products, for instance, can help cause obesity, which leads to a host of health issues. It might be argued that, if all these restrictions apply to the advertisement of baby formula, then similar restrictions should apply to other unhealthy products. But then where will this proliferation of warnings and restrictions end? Surely manufacturers cannot be held accountable for all misuses of their product.

Study Questions

1. Must a company be forthright with all of the potentially negative side effects of its products? If not all, which ones?
2. Although it is not clear that Nestlé has done anything illegal, have they done something unethical?
3. Are a corporation's only responsibilities to obey the law and attempt to make as much of a profit as possible? Do the basic tenets of capitalism require anything more?
4. Is there a difference in the cases of the baby formula and the chocolate? If so, what is it?

CHILDREN AND TARGETING: IS IT ETHICAL?

BRENNAN JACOBY

Case Description

On June 3, 2001, Jennifer Smith began work at a large advertising firm. The following fall she was assigned to help with an ad campaign for Puff Fluffs, a new sugar cereal. As she researched her new subject, Jennifer found that previous studies done by the makers of Puff Fluffs showed children ages 6 to 10 enjoying the taste of Puff Fluffs. Since Jennifer's job was to do whatever she could to sell Puff Fluffs, her task became trying to get American youth ages 6 to 10 to buy the cereal, or have it purchased for them.

Jennifer soon started work on devising a full line of television and magazine ads, promoting Puff Fluffs. Being highly skilled in her job Jennifer knew what American youth would be drawn to. Following this knowledge, her advertisements consisted of bright colors, quick transitions, and she even invented a singing mascot to represent the sugar cereal.

In the spring of 2002 when Jennifer's ad campaign was complete, it was broadcast and distributed all over America. Every Saturday morning her television commercials were shown between the most popular cartoons, and her magazine ads could be seen in some of the newest comic books. As a result of Jennifer's advertising, Puff Fluffs saw a year of record sales.

Puff Fluff cereal sales were not the only records made in 2002. The number of obese adolescents in America soared to an all time high. Soon the media began pointing fingers at Jennifer's advertising firm saying that they should be held at least partly responsible for the health issues facing American children. After all, they where the ones targeting children with the unhealthy junk food product: Puff Fluffs.

Perplexed, Jennifer thought to herself, "I was just doing what I was supposed to. I was just doing my job ... wasn't I? Those kids can decide what to eat, or at least their parents should be able to help them! And besides, this is a free country. I was just exercising my First Amendment rights when I advertised Puff Fluffs."

In the following days legislation was passed barring advertisers from targeting youth with products that may have negative effects on their health. Jennifer has since lost her job, and the world of advertising has had to rethink their practices.

While the story of Jennifer and Puff Fluffs is fictitious, the outcome is quite close to reality. The health of America's youth has been dropping, and some have argued that advertisers are to be held partly responsible since they target youth with unhealthy food products. In fact the number of overweight children in America aged 6 to 11 more than doubled in the past 20 years, going from 7% in 1980 to 18.8% in 2004.[1] In addition, in December of 2005, The National Academy of Science issued a report stating that the advertising of junk food poses a threat to the health of young children.[2]

Made up of respected nutritionists, educators, psychologists and lawyers, the authors of the NAS report urged congress to consider restrictions on the marketing of junk food to children. It was thought that the food industry could play a large role in turning around the eating habits of youth. One of the authors of the National Academy of Science study wrote regarding the food industry, "If voluntary efforts by industry fail to successfully shift the emphasis of television advertising during children's programming away from high-calorie, low-nutrient products to healthier fare, Congress should enact legislation to mandate this change on both broadcast and cable television."[3] As of yet, legislation barring the targeting of youth by advertisers has not been made.

Ethical Analysis

If it is agreed that the targeting of youth by advertisers of unhealthy products has negative consequences, one must next consider what action should be taken? It seems that there are three possible responses.

First, it may be argued that each individual is an autonomous being with the ability to make decisions for him or herself. If children are unable to navigate such grounds as to what food to eat, parents or closely related individuals may be there to give direction. In other words, health begins at home, advertisers should not be held responsible.

Second, as was suggested by the National Academy of Science, advertisers could be expected to create and monitor their own set of ethical guidelines. Advertisers as a whole might decide that marketing less healthy foods is acceptable but specifically targeting youth with such products is not.

Third, as has been the case in other arenas of advertising, government legislated limitations could be placed on ads targeting youth. Bans have already been enacted that bar the targeting of youth with cigarette advertisements. Such legislation was formed on the basis that cigarettes are poor for one's health. If foods offering virtually no nutrition are viewed in the same light as cigarettes, it would not be too much to respond in the same way.

In her book, *Diet for a Small Planet*, Francis Moore Lappe articulated that,

> There is virtually unanimous opinion that high sugar, low nutrition foods—those which monopolize TV advertising threaten our health. So why not ban advertising of candy, sugared cereals, soft drinks, and other sweets?[4]

How might advertisers respond to Lappe? From the advertisers' perspective, it may seem that they are only doing their job. Companies award advertising firms with large amounts of funding in return for selling their product. Indeed, it is assumed that advertisers will use all the tools they have at their disposal. Regardless of how much sugar is in a product, advertisers are trying to get the product into the world of the consumer the best that they can.

Do advertisers have a right to advertise how they want and target who they will? When advertisers target youth are they doing nothing more than exercising their First Amendment Rights? Again, Lappe asks "... should we include in the definition of 'free speech' the capacity to dominate national advertising? Isn't there something amiss in this definition of rights?"[5]

Certainly, there may be far reaching repercussions of a decision to ban the advertising of junk food to children. Optimistically, such a ban might raise societal awareness to the effect advertising has on individuals of all ages and spark a new breed of consumers who think for themselves.

Pessimistically, advertising that negatively targets youth might be hard to distinguish from a form of targeting that does not harm the consumer. While it may be a rather simple task to count the calories on the panel of a cereal box to see if it is healthy or not, it may not be as easy to discern which toys, or books will help or hurt the constituencies they are aimed at.

Study Questions

1. How far reaching should First Amendment rights be in cases such as advertising to youth?
2. What might be the strengths and weaknesses of government legislating boundaries on advertising to children?

3. What sort of ramifications might occur from a ban on advertising less healthy products to children?

4. Should advertisers be held responsible if children become unhealthy after consuming a product they advertised?

NOTES

1 Center for Desease Control and Prevention, "Healthy Youth!" (2006). <http://www.cdc.gov/healthyyouth/obesity> (Accessed 13 April, 2006).

2 The National Academies, "Food Marketing Aimed at Kids Influences Poor Nutritional Choices, IOM Study Finds; Broad Effort Needed to Promote Healthier Products and Diets." (2005). <http://www4.nas.edu/news.nsf/6a3520dc2dbfc2ad85256ca8005c1381/e16a92687989758385257ocf00535d29?Open Document> (Accessed 13 April, 2006).

3 The National Academies.

4 Francis Moore Lappe, *Diet for a Small Planet* (New York: Ballantine Books, 1975), 140-57.

5 Lappe (1975), 155.

Sources

ALLHOFF, Fritz. "Business Bluffing: Reconsidered." *Journal of Business Ethics* 45.4 (2003): 283-89. Reprinted with kind permission from Springer Science and Business Media.

ARRINGTON, Robert L. "Advertising and Behavior Control." *Journal of Business Ethics* 1.1 (1982): 3-12. Reprinted with kind permission from Springer Science and Business Media.

BRENKERT, George F. "Marketing to Inner-City Blacks: Power Master and Moral Responsibility." *Business Ethics Quarterly* 8.1 (January 1998): 1-18. Reprinted by permission of *Business Ethics Quarterly*; "Private Corporations and Public Welfare." *Public Affairs Quarterly* 6.2 (April 1992): 155-68. Reprinted by permission of *Public Affairs Quarterly*.

BROWN, Karin. "Buddhist Ethics," from *Encyclopedia of Business Ethics and Society*. Edited by Robert W. Kolb. Los Angeles: Sage Publications, 2007. Reprinted by permission of Sage Publications Inc.

CARR, Albert Z. "Is Business Bluffing Ethical?" Originally published in *Harvard Business Review* January/February 1968. Reprinted by permission of Harvard Business School Publishing.

CARSON, Thomas. "Second Thoughts About Bluffing." *Business Ethics Quarterly* 3.4 (October 1993): 317-41. Reprinted by permission of *Business Ethics Quarterly*.

COHEN, Gerald A. "Illusions About Private Property and Freedom," from *Issues in Marxist Philosophy, 4th Edition*. Edited by John Mepham and David-Hillel Rubin. Atlantic Highlands, NJ: Humanities Press, 1979. Reprinted by permission of Gerald A. Cohen.

CRANFORD, Michael. "Drug Testing and the Right to Privacy." *Journal of Business Ethics* 17.16 (1998): 1805-15. Reprinted with kind permission from Springer Science and Business Media.

CRISP, Roger. "Persuasive Advertising, Autonomy, and the Creation of Desire." *Journal of Business Ethics* 6.5 (1987): 413-18. Reprinted with kind permission from Springer Science and Business Media.

DE GEORGE, Richard T. Excerpt from "Chapter 10: Whistle Blowing," from *Business Ethics, 5th edition*. New Jersey: Pearson Education, 1999. Copyright © 1999. Reprinted by permission of Pearson Education, Inc. Upper Saddle River, NJ.

DESJARDINS, Joseph and Ronald Duska. "Drug Testing in Employment." *Business and Professional Ethics Journal* 6 (1987): 3-21. Reprinted by permission of Joseph Desjardins and Ronald Duska.

DONALDSON, Thomas J. "The Ethics of Risk in the Global Economy." *Business and Professional Ethics Journal* 5.3 (1989): 39-56. Reprinted by permission of Thomas J. Donaldson; "Values in Tension: Ethics Away from Home." Originally published in *Harvard Business Review* September/October 1996. Reprinted by permission of Harvard Business School Publishing.

EPSTEIN, Richard A. "In Defense of the Contract at Will." *University of Chicago Law Review* 51.4 (October 1984): 947-82. Reprinted by permission of the *University of Chicago Law Review*.

FADIMAN, Jeffery. "A Traveler's Guide to Gifts and Bribes." *Harvard Business Review* May/June

1986. Reprinted by permission of Harvard Business School Publishing.

FREEMAN, R. Edward. "A Stakeholder Theory of the Modern Corporation." Copyright © 1994 by R. Edward Freeman. Reprinted by permission of the author.

FRIEDMAN, Milton. "The Social Responsibility of Business Is to Increase Its Profits." Originally published in *New York Times Magazine* September 13, 1970. Copyright © 1970 Milton Friedman. Reprinted with permission.

GLATZ, Richard. "Aristotelian Virtue Ethics and the Recommendations of Morality." Copyright © 2006 by Richard Glatz. Reprinted by permission of the author.

GRIFFITH, Stephen. "Sexual Harassment and the Rights of the Accused." *Public Affairs Quarterly* 13.1 (1999). Reprinted by permission of *Public Affairs Quarterly*.

HASNAS, John. "The Normative Theories of Business Ethics: A Guide for the Perplexed." *Business Ethics Quarterly* 8.1 (January 1998): 19-42. Reprinted by permission of *Business Ethics Quarterly*.

HETTINGER, Edwin C. "Justifying Intellectual Property." *Philosophy and Public Affairs* 18.1 (Winter 1989): 31-32. Reprinted by permission of Blackwell Publishing Ltd.; "What Is Wrong with Reverse Discrimination." *Business and Professional Ethics Journal* 6.3 (1987): 39-55. Reprinted by permission of Edwin Hettinger.

LARMER, Robert. "Whistleblowing and Employee Loyalty." *Journal of Business Ethics* 11.2 (1992): 125-28. Reprinted with kind permission from Springer Science and Business Media.

MACHAN, Tibor R. "Advertising: The Whole Truth or Only Some of the Truth?" *Public Affairs Quarterly* 1.4 (1987); "Environmental-

ism Humanized." *Public Affairs Quarterly* 7.2 (1993): 131-47. Both articles reprinted by permission of *Public Affairs Quarterly*; "Human Rights, Worker's Rights and the 'Right' to Occupational Safety," from *Moral Rights in the Workplace*. Edited by Gertrude Ezorsky. Albany, NY: State University of New York Press, 1987. Copyright © 1987, State University of New York, All rights reserved. Reprinted by permission of SUNY Press.

MAITLAND, Ian. "The Great Non-Debate Over International Sweatshops." *The British Academy of Management Annual Conference Proceedings* (1997): 240-65. Reprinted by permission of the author.

MANNING, Rita. "Caring as an Ethical Perspective." Copyright © 2006 by Rita Manning. Reprinted by permission of the author.

MAYER, Don and Anita Cava. "Ethics and the Gender Equality Dilemma for US Multinationals." *Journal of Business Ethics* 12.9 (September 1993): 701-08. Reprinted with kind permission from Springer Science and Business Media.

MEELER, David. "Utilitarian Ethics." Copyright © 2006 by David Meeler. Reprinted by permission of the author.

NIELSEN, Kai. "A Moral Case for Socialism." *Critical Review* 3.3-4 (Summer/Fall 1989): 542-52. Reprinted by permission of Kai Nielsen.

NOZICK, Robert. "The Entitlement Theory," from *Anarchy, State, and Utopia*. New York: Basic Books, 1974. Copyright © 1974 by Basic Books. Reprinted by permission of Basic Books, a member of Perseus Books, L.L.C.

PAINE, Lynn Sharpe. "Children as Consumers: An Ethical Evaluation of Children's Television Advertising." *Business and Professional Ethics Journal* 3.3-4 (1984): 119-45; "Trade Secrets and the Justification of Intellectual Property: A Comment on Hettinger." *Philosophy and Public Affairs* 20 (1991): 247-63. Reprinted by permission of Blackwell Publishers Ltd.

POFF, Deborah. "Reconciling the Irreconcilable: The Global Economy and the Environment." *Journal of Business Ethics* 13.6 (1994): 439-45. Reprinted with kind permission from Springer Science and Business Media.

POJMAN, Louis P. "The Moral Status of Affirmative Action." *Public Affairs Quarterly* 6.2 (1992): 181-206. Reprinted by permission of *Public Affairs Quarterly*.

RAWLS, John. Excerpts from *A Theory of Justice*. Cambridge, MA: The Belknap Press of Harvard University Press, 1971. Copyright © 1971, 1999 by the President and Fellows of Harvard College. Reprinted by permission of Harvard University Press.

SAGOFF, Mark. "At the Monument to General Meade or On Difference Between Beliefs and Benefits." *Arizona Law Review* 42.2 (Summer 2000): 433-62. Reprinted by permission of Mark Sagoff.

SALAZAR, Heather. "Kantian Business Ethics." Copyright © 2006 by Heather Salazar. Reprinted by permission of the author.

SEN, Amartya. "Does Business Ethics Make Economic Sense?" *Business Ethics Quarterly* 3.1 (January 1993): 45-54. Reprinted by permission of *Business Ethics Quarterly*.

SHAW, Bill. "Foreign Corrupt Practices Act: A Legal and Moral Analysis." *Journal of Business Ethics* 7.10 (1988): 789-95. Reprinted with kind permission from Springer Science and Business Media.

SHRADER-FRECHETTE, Kristin. "A Defense of Risk-Cost-Benefit Analysis," from *Environmental Ethics: Readings in Theory and Application 3rd Edition*. Edited by Louis P. Pojman. Stamford, CT: Wadsworth, 2001. Copyright © 2001. Reprinted by permission of Kristin Shrader-Frechette.

SUPERSON, Anita M. "A Feminist Definition of Sexual Harassment." *Journal of Social Philosophy* 24.1 (1993): 46-64. Reprinted by permission of Blackwell Publishing Ltd.; "The Employer-Employee Relationship and the Right to Know." *Business and Professional Ethics Journal* 3.4 (Fall 1984): 45-58. Reprinted by permission of Anita M. Superson.

VAIDYA, Anand Jayprakash. "Ill-Founded Criticisms of Business Ethics." Copyright © 2006 by Anand Jayprakash Vaidya. Reprinted by permission of the author.

VELASQUEZ, Manuel. "International Business, Morality, and the Common Good." *Business Ethics Quarterly* 2.1 (January 1992): 27-40. Reprinted by permission of *Business Ethics Quarterly*.

WAIDE, John. "The Making of Self and World in Advertising." *Journal of Business Ethics* 6.2 (1987): 73-79. Reprinted with kind permission from Springer Science and Business Media.

WALL, Edmund. "The Definition of Sexual Harassment." *Public Affairs Quarterly* 5.4 (1991): 371-85. Reprinted by permission of *Public Affairs Quarterly*.

WERHANE, Patricia H. and Tara J. Radin. "Employment at Will and Due Process." *Ethical Issues in Business*. Edited by T. Donaldson and P. Werhane. Upper Saddle River, NJ: Prentice-Hall, 1999. Reprinted by permission of the authors.